THE YEAR'S WORK IN ENGLISH STUDIES 1991

The Year's Work in English Studies

Volume 72 • 1991

Edited by
STEPHEN REGAN
ELAINE TREHARNE

and
PAUL DEAN
LIONEL KELLY
PETER KITSON
MARGARET REYNOLDS
DAVID WILLIAMS
(associate editors)

Published for
THE ENGLISH ASSOCIATION

by
BLACKWELL REFERENCE
HUMANITIES PRESS, ATLANTIC HIGHLANDS N.J.

First published 1993
Blackwell Publishers
108 Cowley Road
Oxford OX4 1JF

British Library Cataloguing in Publication Data

A CIP catalogue record for this book is available from the British Library.

ISBN 0–631–18667–0

First published 1994 in the United States of America
by Humanities Press International, Inc.,
Atlantic Highlands, NJ 07716

The Library of Congress has cataloged
this serial title as follows:

The Year's work in English studies. v.[1] 1919/20–
London, Published for the English Association by
Basil Blackwell [etc]
v.23 cm
Annual
ISSN 0084–4144 = Year's work in English studies.
ISBN 0–391–03836–2
1. English philology—History. 2. English philology—Bibliography. 3. English literature—History and criticism. 4. English literature—Periodicals.
I. English Association.
PE58.E6 22–10024
Library of Congress [8503r80]rev4 MARC-S

Printed and Bound in Great Britain by
Hartnolls Limited, Bodmin, Cornwall.

Preface

The Year's Work in English Studies is a narrative bibliography that records and evaluates scholarly writing on English language and on literature written in English. It is published by Blackwell Publishers on behalf of the English Association.

The Editors and the English Association are pleased to announce that this year's Beatrice White Prize has been awarded to James W. Earl for his article on '*Beowulf* and the Origins of Civilization', in A. J. Frantzen (ed.), *Speaking Two Languages: Traditional Disciplines and Contemporary Theory in Medieval Studies.*

The authors of *YWES* attempt to cover all significant contributions to English studies. Writers of articles can assist this process by sending offprints to the journal, and editors of journals that are not readily available in the U.K. are urged to join the many who send us complete sets. These should be addressed to The Editor, *YWES*, The English Association, The University of Leicester, 128 Regent Road, Leicester LE1 7PA.

Our coverage of articles and books is greatly assisted by the Modern Language Association of America, who supply proofs of their annual *International Bibliography* in advance of publication. We should like to record our gratitude for their generous co-operation.

The Editors

The English Association

This bibliography is an English Association publication. It is available through membership of the Association; non-members can purchase it through any good bookshop.
The object of the English Association is to promote the knowledge and appreciation of English language and literature.
The Association pursues these aims by creating opportunities of co-operation among all those interested in English; by furthering the recognition of English as essential in education; by discussing methods of English teaching; by holding lectures, conferences, and other meetings; by publishing a journal, books, and leaflets; and by forming local branches overseas and at home.

Publications

The Year's Work in English Studies. An annual bibliography. Published by Blackwell Publishers, Oxford and Cambridge, MA. (U.S.A.: Humanities Press.)

The Year's Work in Critical and Cultural Theory. The first issue of this new critical theory volume will appear in 1994. Published by Blackwell Publishers, Oxford and Cambridge, MA. (U.S.A.: Humanities Press.)

Essays and Studies. An annual volume of essays by various scholars assembled by the collector covering usually a wide range of subjects and authors from the medieval to the modern. Published by Boydell and Brewer, Woodbridge, Suffolk. (U.S.A.: Humanities Press.)

English. The journal of the Association, *English*, is published three times a year by the English Association.

Use of English. This journal is published three times a year by the English Association.

Benefits of Membership

Institutional Membership

Full members receive copies of *The Year's Work in English Studies, Essays and Studies, English* (three issues), and three *News-Letters.*

Ordinary Membership covers *English* (three issues) and three *News-Letters.*

Schools Membership covers two copies of each issue of *English*, one copy of *Essays and Studies* (optional), three *News-Letters*, and preferential booking for Sixth Form Conference places.

Individual Membership

Individuals take out basic membership, which entitles them to buy all regular publications of the English Association at a discounted price.

For further details write to The Secretary, The English Association, The University of Leicester, 128 Regent Road, Leicester LE1 7PA.

Contents

Abbreviations: **Journals, Series, and Reference Works** xi
Publishers xl

I **Reference, Literary History, and Bibliography** 1
Paul Bennett Morgan, National Library of Wales

II **English Language** 16
Kenneth Turner, University of Brighton; Michael K. C. MacMahon, University of Glasgow; Nicola Woods, Linacre College, Oxford; Frederike van der Leek, University of Amsterdam; Christian Kay, University of Glasgow; Richard Coates, University of Sussex; Jean Jacques Weber, University Centre Luxembourg

III **Old English Literature** 70
Clare A. Lees, University of Pennsylvania

IV **Middle English: Excluding Chaucer** 97
David J. Williams, University of Reading; Julia Boffey, Queen Mary and Westfield College, London; S. Powell, University of Salford; A. J. Fletcher, University College, Dublin; Anthony S. G. Edwards, University of Victoria, Victoria, B.C.

V **Middle English: Chaucer** 123
Lucinda Rumsey, Keble College, Oxford

VI **The Sixteenth Century: Excluding Drama After 1550** 141
R. E. Pritchard, University of Keele

VII **Shakespeare** 154
R. J. C. Watt, University of Dundee; James Knowles, University of Dundee; Dermot Cavanagh, University of Exeter; Paul Dean, Portsmouth Grammar School

VIII **Renaissance Drama: Excluding Shakespeare** 182
Michael Jardine, King Alfred's College, Winchester; Carol Rutter, University of Warwick; Sandra Clark, Birkbeck College, London

IX **The Earlier Seventeenth Century: Excluding Drama** 209
Melanie Hansen, London

X **Milton** 221
Thomas N. Corns, University College of North Wales

XI **The Later Seventeenth Century** 231
Stuart Gillespie, University of Glasgow; Edward Burns, University of Liverpool; Roger Pooley, University of Keele; James Ogden, University College of Wales, Aberystwyth

XII **The Eighteenth Century** 246
Stephen Copley, University of Wales, Cardiff; Alan Bower, University of Hull

XIII **The Nineteenth Century: Romantic Period** 269
Peter J. Kitson, University College of North Wales; John C. Whale, University of Leeds

XIV **The Nineteenth Century: Victorian Period** 314
Linda Williams, University of Liverpool; Donald Hawes, London; Laurel Brake, Birkbeck College, London

XV **The Twentieth Century** 361
Adrian Page, Bedford College of Higher Education; Julian Cowley, Luton College of Higher Education; Sue Vice, University of Sheffield; Susan Watkins, Chester College; Macdonald Daly, University of Nottingham; Stuart Sillars, Cambridge; Jem Poster, University of Oxford; Trevor Griffiths, University of North London; Lynda Morgan,

Buckinghamshire College of Higher Education; Anna McMullan, University of Reading

XVI **American Literature to 1900** **422**
Henry Claridge, University of Kent; Janet Goodwyn, Roehampton Institute of Higher Education

XVII **American Literature: The Twentieth Century** **454**
Lionel Kelly, University of Reading; Pat Righelato, University of Reading; Deborah L. Madsen, University of Leicester

XVIII **New Literatures in English** **510**
Gay Raines, University of Kent; Coral Ann Howells, University of Reading; Phillip Langran, University of Humberside; Paula Burnett, West London Institute of Higher Education; Jean-Pierre Durix, University of Dijon; Carole Durix, University of Dijon

Books Received **593**

Indexes, by Ann Dean

I Critics **617**

II Authors and Subjects Treated **642**

Abbreviations

1. Journals, Series, and Reference Works

A&D	*Art and Design*
A&E	*Anglistik und Englishunterricht*
ABäG	*Amsterdamer Beiträge zur Älteren Germanistik*
ABC	*American Book Collector*
ABELL	*Annual Bibliography of English Language and Literature*
ABMR	*Antiquarian Book Monthly Review*
ABQ	*American Baptist Quarterly*
ABR	*American Benedictine Review*
AC	*Archeologia Classica*
ACar	Analecta Cartusiana
ACLALSB	*ACLALS Bulletin*
ACM	*The Aligarh Critical Miscellany*
ACS	*Australian-Canadian Studies: A Journal for the Humanities and Social Sciences*
Acta	Acta (Binghamton, N.Y.)
ADS	*Australasian Drama Studies*
AEB	*Analytical and Enumerative Bibliography*
AF	Anglistische Forschungen
AfricanA	*African Affairs*
AfrSR	*The African Studies Review*
AgeJ	*The Age of Johnson: A Scholarly Annual*
Agenda	*Agenda*
AH	*Art History*
AHR	*The American Historical Review*
AI	*American Imago*
AJ	*Art Journal*
AJES	*The Aligarh Journal of English Studies* (now *The Aligarh Critical Miscellany)*
AJS	*American Journal of Semiotics*
AKML	Abhandlungen zur Kunst-, Musik- and Literaturwissenschaft
AL	*American Literature*
ALA	African Literature Association Annuals
ALASH	*Acta Linguistica Academiae Scientiarum Hungaricae*
AlexS	Alexander Shakespeare
ALH	*Acta Linguistica Hafniensia: International Journal of Lingiustics*
ALitASH	*Acta Litteraria Academiae Scientiarum Hungaricae*
ALLCJ	*Association for Literary and Linguistic Computing Journal*

Allegorica	*Allegorica*
ALR	*American Literary Realism, 1870–1910*
ALS	*Australian Literary Studies*
ALT	*African Literature Today*
Alternatives	*Alternatives*
AmerP	*American Poetry*
AmerS	*American Studies*
AmLH	*American Literary History*
AmLS	*American Literary Scholarship: An Annual*
AMon	*The Atlantic Monthly*
AmRev	*The Americas Review: A Review of Hispanic Literature and Art of the USA*
Amst	*Amerikastudien/American Studies*
AN	*Acta Neophilologica*
AnBol	*Analecta Bollandiana*
ANF	*Arkiv för Nordisk Filologi*
Anglia	*Anglia: Zeitschrift für Englische Philologie*
Anglistica	Anglistica
AnH	Analecta Husserliana
AnL	*Anthropological Linguistics*
AnM	*Annuale Mediaevale*
ANQ	*ANQ: A Quarterly Journal of Short Articles, Notes, and Reviews* (formerly *American Notes and Queries*)
AntColl	*The Antique Collector*
AntigR	*Antigonish Review*
Antipodes	*Antipodes*
ANZSC	*Australian and New Zealand Studies in Canada*
APBR	*Atlantic Provinces Book Review*
AppLing	*Applied Linguistics*
APR	*The American Poetry Review*
AQ	*American Quarterly*
Aquarius	*Aquarius*
AR	*The Antioch Review*
ArAA	*Arbeiten aus Anglistik und Amerikanistik*
Arcadia	*Arcadia*
Archiv	*Archiv für das Studium der Neueren Sprachen und Literaturen*
ARCS	*The American Review of Canadian Studies*
ArdenS	Arden Shakespeare
ArielE	*Ariel: A Review of International English Literature*
ArQ	*Arizona Quarterly*
ARS	Augustan Reprint Society
ArtB	*Art Bulletin*
ArthI	*Arthurian Interpretations*
ArthL	*Arthurian Literature*
AS	*American Speech*
ASch	*The American Scholar*
ASE	*Anglo-Saxon England*
ASInt	*American Studies International*
ASoc	*Arts in Society*

Aspects	*Aspects: Journal of the Language Society of the University of Essex*
AspectsAF	*Aspects of Australian Fiction*
ASPR	*Anglo-Saxon Poetic Records*
Assaph	*Assaph: Studies in the Arts (Theatre Studies)*
Assays	*Assays: Critical Approaches to Medieval and Renaissance Texts*
ASUI	*Analele Stiintifice ale Universitatii 'Al.I. Cuza' din Iasi (Serie Noua), e. Lingvistica*
ATQ	*American Transcendental Quarterly: A Journal of New England Writers*
AuBR	*Australian Book Review*
AuFolk	*Australian Folklore*
AuFS	*Australian Feminist Studies*
AuJL	*Australian Journal of Linguistics*
AUMLA	*Journal of the Australasian Universities Language and Literature Association*
AuS	*Australian Studies* (BASA)
AuSA	*Australian Studies* (Australia)
AusCan	*Australian–Canadian Studies*
AusPl	Australian Playwrights
AuWBR	*Australian Women's Book Review*
AvC	*Avalon to Camelot*
AY	*Arthurian Yearbook*
BakhtinN	*Bakhtin Newsletter*
BALF	*Black American Literature Forum*
BASAM	*BASA Magazine*
BathH	*Bath History*
BB	*Bulletin of Bibliography*
BBCS	*The Bulletin of the Board of Celtic Studies*
BBCSh	BBC Shakespeare
BBN	*British Book News*
BBSIA	*Bulletin Bibliographique de la Société Internationale Arthurienne*
BC	*The Book Collector*
BCan	*Books in Canada*
BCS	*B. C. Sudies*
BDEC	*Bulletin of the Department of English* (Calcutta)
BDP	Beiträge zur Deutschen Philologie
Belfagor	*Belfagor: Rassegna di Varia Umanità*
BEPIF	*Bulletin des Etudes Portugaises et Brésiliennes*
BFLS	*Bulletin de la Faculté des Lettres de Strasbourg*
BGDSL	*Beiträge zur Geschichte der Deutschen Sprache und Literatur*
BHI	*British Humanities Index*
BHL	*Bibliotheca Hagiographica Latina Antiquae et Mediae Aetatis*
BHR	*Bibliothèque d'Humanisme et Renaissance*
BHS	*Bulletin of Hispanic Studies*
BI	*Books at Iowa*

Bibliotheck	*The Bibliotheck: A Scottish Journal of Bibliography and Allied Topics*
Biography	*Biography: An Interdisciplinary Quarterly*
BIS	*Browning Institute Studies: An Annual of Victorian Literary and Cultural History*
BJA	*British Journal of Aesthetics*
BJCS	*British Journal of Canadian Studies*
BJDC	*The British Journal of Disorders of Communication*
BJECS	*British Journal for Eighteenth-Century Studies*
BJHS	*The British Journal for the History of Science*
BJL	*Belgian Journal of Linguistics*
BJPS	*The British Journal for the Philosophy of Science*
BJRL	*Bulletin of the John Rylands University Library of Manchester*
BJS	*British Journal of Sociology*
Blake	*Blake: An Illustrated Quarterly*
BLE	*Bulletin de Littérature Ecclésiastique*
BLJ	*The British Library Journal*
BLR	*The Bodleian Library Record*
BN	*Beiträge zur Namenforschung*
BNB	*British National Bibliography*
Boundary	*Boundary 2: A Journal of Postmodern Literature and Culture*
BP	*Banasthali Patrika*
BPMA	*Bulletin* (Philadelphia Museum of Art)
BPN	*The Barbara Pym Newsletter*
BQ	*Baptish Quarterly*
BRH	*Bulletin of Research in the Humanities*
Brick	*Brick: A Journal of Reviews*
BRMMLA	*Bulletin of the Rocky Mountain Modern Language Association*
BSANZB	*The Bibliographical Society of Australia and New Zealand Bulletin*
BSE	*Brno Studies in English*
BSEAA	*Bulletin de la Société d'Etudes Anglo-Américaines des XVIIe et XVIIIe Siècles*
BSJ	*The Baker Street Journal: An Irregular Quarterly of Sherlockiana*
BSLP	*Bulletin de la Société de Linguistique de Paris*
BSNotes	*Browning Society Notes*
BSRS	*Bulletin of the Society for Renaissance Studies*
BSSA	*Bulletin de la Société de Stylistique Anglaise*
BST	*Brontë Society Transactions*
BSUF	*Ball State University Forum*
BTHGNewsl	*Book Trade History Group Newsletter*
BTLV	*Bijdragen tot de Taal-, Land- en Volkenkunde*
BunyanS	*Bunyan Studies*
BuR	*Bucknell Review*
BurlM	*The Burlington Magazine*
BurnsC	*Burns Chronicle*

BWPLL	*Belfast Working Papers in Language and Linguistics*
BWVACET	*The Bulletin of the West Virginia Association of College English Teachers*
ByronJ	*The Byron Journal*
CABS	Contemporary Authors Bibliographical Series
CahiersE	*Cahiers Élisabéthains*
CAIEF	*Cahiers de l'Association Internationale des Études Françaises*
Caliban	*Caliban* (Toulouse, France)
Callaloo	*Callaloo*
CalR	*Calcutta Review*
CamObsc	*Camera Obscura: A Journal of Feminism and Film Theory*
CamR	*The Cambridge Review*
CanD	*Canadian Drama/L'Art Dramatique Canadienne*
C&L	*Christianity and Literature*
C&Lang	*Communication and Languages*
C&M	*Classica et Medievalia*
CanL	*Canadian Literature*
CanPo	*Canadian Poetry*
CapR	*Capilano Review*
CARA	Centre Aixois de Recherches Anglaises
Carib	*Carib*
CarR	*Caribbean Review*
Carrell	*The Carrell: Journal of the Friends of the University of Miami Library*
CASE	Cambridge Studies in Anglo-Saxon England
CaudaP	*Cauda Pavonis*
CBAA	*Current Bibliography on African Affairs*
CBEL	*Cambridge Bibliography of English Literature*
CCRev	*Comparative Civilizations Review*
CCrit	*Comparative Criticism: An Annual Journal*
CCTEP	*Conference of College Teachers of English Studies*
CCV	*Centro de Cultura Valenciana*
CD	The Critics Debate
CDALB	Concise Dictionary of American Literary Biography
CDCP	Comparative Drama Conference Papers
CdL	*Cahiers de Lexicologie*
CE	*College English*
CEA	*CEA Critic*
CEAfr	*Cahiers d'Études Africaines*
CE&S	*Commonwealth Essays and Studies*
CentR	*The Centennial Review*
Cervantes	*Cervantes*
CFM	*Canadian Fiction Magazine*
CFS	*Cahiers Ferdinand de Saussure: Revue de Linguistique Générale*
Chapman	*Chapman*
ChauR	*The Chaucer Review*
ChH	*Church History*
ChildL	*Children's Literature*

ChiR	*Chicago Review*
ChLB	*Charles Lamb Bulletin*
CHLSSF	*Commentationes Humanarum Litterarum Societatis Scientiarum Fennicae*
CHR	*Camden History Review*
CHum	*Computers and the Humanities*
CI	Critical Idiom
CILT	Amsterdam Studies in the Theory and History of the Language Sciences IV: Current Issues in Linguistic Theory
CISh	Contemporary Interpretations of Shakespeare
Cithara	*Cithara: Essays in the Judaeo-Christian Tradition*
CJ	*Classical Journal*
CJE	*Cambridge Journal of Education*
CJH	*Canadian Journal of History*
CJIS	*Canadian Journal of Irish Studies*
CJL	*The Canadian Journal of Linguistics*
CJR	*Christian Jewish Relations*
CL	*Comparative Literature* (Eugene, Oreg.)
CLAJ	*CLA Journal*
CLAQ	*Children's Literature Association Quarterly*
ClarkN	*The Clark Newsletter: Bulletin of the UCLA Center for Seventeenth- and Eighteenth-Century Studies*
CLC	*Columbia Library Columns*
ClioI	*Clio: A Journal of Literature, History, and the Philosophy of History*
CLQ	*Colby Library Quarterly*
CLS	*Comparative Literature Studies*
Clues	*Clues: A Journal of Detection*
CMCS	*Cambridge Medieval Celtic Studies*
CML	*Classical and Modern Literature*
CN	*Chaucer Newsletter*
CNew	*The Carlyle Newsletter*
CNIE	*Commonwealth Novel in English*
ColF	*Columbia Forum*
Collections	*Collections*
CollG	*Colloquia Germanica*
CollL	*College Literature*
Comitatus	*Comitatus: A Journal of Medieval and Renaissance Studies*
Commentary	*Commentary*
Commonwealth	*Commonwealth*
CompD	*Comparative Drama*
ConL	*Contemporary Literature*
Connotations	*Connotations*
ConnR	*Connecticut Review*
Conradian	*The Conradian*
Conradiana	*Conradiana: A Journal of Joseph Conrad Studies*
ContempR	*Contemporary Review*
Cosmos	*Cosmos*
CP	*Concerning Poetry*

CQ	*The Cambridge Quarterly*
CR	*The Critical Review*
CRCL	*Canadian Review of Comparative Literature*
CRev	*The Chesterton Review*
CRevAS	*Canadian Review of American Studies*
Crit	*Critique: Studies in Modern Fiction*
CritI	*Critical Inquiry*
Criticism	*Criticism: A Quarterly for Literature and the Arts*
Critique	*Critique* (Paris)
CritQ	*Critical Quarterly*
CritT	*Critical Texts: A Review of Theory and Criticism*
CRNLE	*The CRNLE Reviews Journal*
CRUX	*CRUX: A Journal on the Teaching of English*
CS	*Critical Survey*
CSLBull	*Bulletin of the New York C. S. Lewis Society*
CSR	*Christian Scholar's Review*
CTR	*Canadian Theatre Review*
CulC	*Cultural Critique*
CulS	*Cultural Studies*
CUNY	*CUNY English Forum*
CV2	*Contemporary Verse 2*
CVE	*Cahiers Victoriens et Edouardiens*
CWAAS	*Transactions of the Cumberland and Westmorland Antiquarian and Archaeological Society*
CWS	*Canadian Woman Studies*
DA	*Dictionary of Americanisms*
DAE	*Dictionary of American English*
DAEM	*Deutsches Archiv für Eforschung des Mittelalters*
DAI	*Dissertation Abstracts International*
DAL	*Descriptive and Applied Linguistics*
D&S	*Discourse and Society*
Daphnis	*Daphnis: Zeitschrift für Mittlere Deutsche Literatur*
DC	The Dickens Companions
DerbyM	*Derbyshire Miscellany*
Descant	*Descant*
DHLR	*The D. H. Lawrence Review*
DHS	*Dix-Huitième Siècle*
Diac	*Diacritics*
Dialogue	*Dialogue: Canadian Philosophical Review*
Dickensian	*The Dickensian*
DicS	*Dickinson Studies*
Dictionaries	*Dictionaries: Journal of the Dictionary Society of North America*
DLB	Dictionary of Literary Biography
DLN	*Doris Lessing Newsletter*
DM	*The Dublin Magazine*
DMT	Durham Medieval Texts
DNB	*Dictionary of National Biography*
DOE	*Dictionary of Old English*
Dolphin	*The Dolphin: Publications of the English Department,*

	University of Aarhus
DOST	*Dictionary of the Older Scottish Tongue*
DownR	*The Downside Review*
DQ	*Denver Quarterly*
DQR	*Dutch Quarterly Review of Anglo-American Letters*
DQu	*Dickens Quarterly*
DR	*Dalhousie Review*
Drama	*Drama: The Quarterly Theatre Review*
DrS	*Dreiser Studies*
DSA	*Dickens Studies Annual*
DU	*Der Deutschunterricht: Beiträge zu Seiner Praxis und Wissenschaftlichen Grundlegung*
DUJ	*Durham University Journal*
DVLG	*Deutsche Vierteljahrsschrift für Literaturwissenschaft und Geistesgeschichte*
EA	*Études Anglaises*
EAL	*Early American Literature*
E&D	*Enlightenment and Dissent*
E&S	*Essays and Studies*
E&Soc	*Economy and Society*
EAS	*Essays in Arts and Sciences*
EASt	*Englisch Amerikanische Studien*
EC	*Études Celtiques*
ECan	*Etudes Canadiennes/Canadian Studies*
ECCB	*Eighteenth Century: A Current Bibliography*
ECent	*The Eighteenth Century: Theory and Interpretation*
ECF	*Eighteenth-Century Fiction*
ECI	*Eighteenth-Century Ireland*
ECLife	*Eighteenth Century Life*
ECon	*L'Epoque Conradienne*
ECr	*L'Esprit Créateur*
ECS	*Eighteenth-Century Studies*
ECW	*Essays on Canadian Writing*
EDAMN	*The EDAM Newsletter*
EDH	*Essays by Divers Hands*
EdL	*Études de Lettres*
EdN	*Editors' Notes: Bulletin of the Conference of Editors of Learned Journals*
EDSL	*Encyclopedic Dictionary of the Sciences of Language*
EEMF	Early English Manuscripts in Facsimile
EHR	*The English Historical Review*
EI	*Études Irlandaises* (Lille)
EIC	*Essays in Criticism*
EinA	*English in Africa*
EiP	*Essays in Poetics*
EIRC	*Explorations in Renaissance Culture*
Éire	*Éire-Ireland*
EiT	*Essays in Theatre*
EJ	*English Journal*
ELangT	*ELT Journal: An International Journal for Teachers of English to Speakers of Other Languages*

ELet	*Esperienze Letterarie: Rivista Trimestrale di Critica e Cultura*
ELH	*Journal of English Literary History*
ELN	*English Language Notes*
ELR	*English Literary Renaissance*
ELS	*English Literary Studies*
ELT	*English Literature in Transition*
ELWIU	*Essays in Literature* (Western Illinois Univ.)
EM	*English Miscellany*
Embl	*Emblematica: An Interdisciplinary Journal of English Studies*
EMS	*English Manuscript Studies, 1100–1700*
EMu	*Early Music*
Encyclia	*Encyclia*
English	*English: The Journal of the English Association*
EnT	*English Today: The International Review of the English Language*
EPD	*English Pronouncing Dictionary*
ERR	*European Romantic Review*
ES	*English Studies*
ESA	*English Studies in Africa*
ESC	*English Studies in Canada*
ESQ	*ESQ: A Journal of the American Renaissance*
ESRS	*Emporia State Research Studies*
ESTC	*Eighteenth Century Short Title Catalogue*
EWIP	*Edinburgh University, Department of Linguistics, Work in Progress*
EWN	*Evelyn Waugh Newsletter*
EWPAL	*Edinburgh Working Papers in Applied Linguistics*
EWW	*English World-Wide*
Exemplaria	*Exemplaria*
Expl	*The Explicator*
Extrapolation	*Extrapolation: A Journal of Science Fiction and Fantasy*
FCEMN	*Mystics Quarterly* (formerly *Fourteenth-Century English Mystics Newsletter*)
FCS	*Fifteenth-Century Studies*
FDT	Fountainwell Drama Texts
FemR	*Feminist Review*
FH	*Die Neue Gesellschaft/Frankfurter Hefte*
FJS	*Fu Jen Studies: Literature and Linguistics* (Taipei)
FLH	*Folia Linguistica Historica*
Florilegium	*Florilegium: Carleton University Annual Papers on Classical Antiquity and the Middle Ages*
FMLS	*Forum for Modern Language Studies*
Folklore	*Folklore*
FoLi	*Folia Linguistica*
Forum	*Forum*
FranS	*Franciscan Studies*
FreeA	*Free Associations*
Frontiers	*Frontiers: A Journal of Women Studies*

FS	*French Studies*
FSt	*Feminist Studies*
Futures	*Futures*
GAG	Göppinger Arbeiten zur Germanistik
GaR	*Georgia Review*
GEFR	*George Eliot Fellowship Review*
GEGHL	*George Eliot–George Henry Lewes Newsletter*
GeM	*Genealogists' Magazine*
Genders	*Genders*
Genre	*Genre*
Gestus	*Gestus: A Quarterly Journal of Brechtian Studies*
GHJ	*George Herbert Journal*
GissingJ	*The Gissing Journal*
GJ	*Gutenberg-Jahrbuch*
GL	*General Linguistics*
GL&L	*German Life and Letters*
Glossa	*Glossa: An International Journal of Linguistics*
GLS	*Grazer Linguistische Studien*
GR	*The Germanic Review*
GrandS	*Grand Street*
Granta	*Granta*
Greyfriar	*Greyfriar: Siena Studies in Literature*
GRM	*Germanisch-Romanische Monatsschrift*
GSE	Gothenberg Studies in English
GSJ	*The Gaskell Society Journal*
GURT	*Georgetown University Round Table on Language and Linguistics*
H&T	*History and Theory*
HatcherR	*Hatcher Review*
HBS	Henry Bradshaw Society
HC	*The Hollins Critic*
HE	*History of Education*
Hecate	*Hecate: An Interdisciplinary Journal of Women's Liberation*
HEdQ	*History of Education Quarterly*
HEI	*History Of European Ideas*
HeineJ	*Heine Jahrbuch*
HEL	*Histoire Épistémologie Langage*
Helios	*Helios*
Hermathena	*Hermathena: A Trinity College Dublin Review*
HeyJ	*The Heythrop Journal*
HistJ	*The Historical Journal*
HistR	*Historical Research*
History	*History: The Journal of the Historical Association*
HJR	*The Henry James Review* (Baton Rouge, La.)
HL	*Historiographia Linguistica*
HBL	*Harvard Library Bulletin*
HLQ	*The Huntington Library Quarterly*
HNCIS	Harvester New Critical Introductions to Shakespeare
HNR	Harvester New Readings

HOPE	*History of Political Economy*
HPT	*History of Political Thought*
HQ	*Hopkins Quarterly*
HRB	*Hopkins Research Bulletin*
HSci	*History of Science*
HSE	*Hungarian Studies in English*
HSELL	*Hiroshima Studies in English Language and Literature*
HSJ	*Housman Society Journal*
HSL	*University of Hartford Studies in Literature*
HSN	*Hawthorne Society Newsletter*
HSSh	*Hungarian Studies in Shakespeare*
HSSN	*The Henry Sweet Society Newsletter*
HSt	*Hamlet Studies*
HT	*History Today*
HTR	*Harvard Theological Review*
HudR	*Hudson Review*
HumeS	*Hume Studies*
HumLov	*Humanistica Lovaniensia: Journal of Neo-Latin Studies*
HUSL	*Hebrew University Studies in Literature and the Arts*
HWJ	*History Workshop*
HWS	History Workshop Series
IAN	*Izvestiia Akademii Nauk S.S.S.R.* (Moscow)
I&C	*Ideology and Consciousness*
I&P	*Ideas and Production*
ICS	*Illinois Classical Studies*
IF	*Indogermanische Forschungen*
IFR	*The International Fiction Review*
IGK	*Irland: Gesellschaft und Kultur*
IJECS	*Indian Journal for Eighteenth Century Studies*
IJES	*Indian Journal of English Studies*
IJPR	*International Journal for the Philosophy of Religion*
IJSL	*International Journal of the Sociology of Language*
IJSS	*Indian Journal of Shakespeare Studies*
IJWS	*International Journal of Women's Studies*
ILR	*The Indian Literary Review*
ILS	*Irish Literary Supplement*
IMB	*International Medieval Bibliography*
Indexer	*Indexer*
IndH	*Indian Horizons*
IndL	*Indian Literature*
InG	*In Geardagum: Essays on Old and Middle English Language and Literature*
Inklings	*Inklings: Jahrbuch für Literatur und Ästhetik*
Inquiry	*Inquiry: An Interdisciplinary Journal of Philosophy*
Interlink	*Interlink*
IowaR	*The Iowa Review*
IRAL	*IRAL: International Review of Applied Linguistics in Language Teaching*
IS	*Italian Studies*
ISh	*The Independent Shavian*

ISJR	*Iowa State Journal of Research*
Island	*Island Magazine*
Islands	*Islands*
IUR	*Irish University Review: A Journal of Irish Studies*
JAAC	*Journal of Aesthetics and Art Criticism*
JAAR	*Journal of the American Academy of Religion*
JAF	*The Journal of American Folklore*
JAfM	*Journal of African Marxists*
JAIS	*Journal of Anglo-Italian Studies*
JAL	*Journal of Australian Literature*
JAmC	*Journal of American Culture*
JAMS	*Journal of the American Musicological Society*
JAmS	*Journal of American Studies*
JArabL	*Journal of Arabic Literature*
JAS	*Journal of Australian Studies*
JBeckS	*Journal of Beckett Studies*
JBS	*Journal of British Studies*
JCAKSU	*Journal of the College of Arts, King Saud University*
JCanL	*Journal of Canadian Literature*
JCC	*Journal of Canadian Culture*
JCF	*Journal of Canadian Fiction*
JChL	*Journal of Child Language*
JCL	*The Journal of Commonwealth Literature*
JCP	*Journal of Canadian Poetry*
JCSJ	*The John Clare Society Journal*
JCSR	*Journal of Canadian Studies/Revue d'Etudes Canadiennes*
JCSt	*Journal of Caribbean Studies*
JDECU	*Journal of the Department of English (University of Calcutta)*
JDHLS	*D. H. Lawrence: The Journal of the D. H. Lawrence Society*
JDJ	*John Donne Journal*
JDTC	*Journal of Dramatic Theory and Criticism*
JEDRBU	*Journal of the English Department, Rabindra Bharati University*
JEGP	*Journal of English and Germanic Philology*
JEH	*The Journal of Ecclesiastical History*
JEn	*Journal of English* (Sana'a Univ.)
JEngL	*Journal of English Linguistics*
JENS	*Journal of the Eighteen Nineties Society*
JEP	*Journal of Evolutionary Psychology*
JEPNS	*Journal of the English Place-Name Society*
JES	*Journal of European Studies*
JETS	*Journal of the Evangelical Theological Society*
JFR	*Journal of Folklore Research*
JGE	*JGE: The Journal of General Education*
JGH	*Journal of Garden History*
JGN	*The John Gower Newsletter*
JHI	*Journal of the History of Ideas*
JHLP	*Journal of Historical Linguistics and Philology*

JHP	*Journal of the History of Philosophy*
JIES	*The Journal of Indo-European Studies*
JIL	*Journal of Irish Literature*
JIPA	*Journal of the International Phonetic Association*
JIWE	*Journal of Indian Writing in English*
JJ	*Jamaica Journal*
JJA	*James Joyce Annual*
JJB	*James Joyce Broadsheet*
JJLS	*James Joyce Literary Supplement*
JJQ	*James Joyce Quarterly*
JL	*Journal of Linguistics*
JLH	*The Journal of Library History, Philosophy and Comparative Librarianship*
JLP	*Journal of Linguistics and Politics*
JLS	*Journal of Literary Semantics*
JLVSG	*Journal of the Loughborough Victorian Studies Group*
JMemL	*Journal of Memory and Language*
JMH	*Journal of Medieval History*
JML	*Journal of Modern Literature*
JMMLA	*Journal of the Midwest Modern Language Association*
JModH	*Journal of Modern History*
JMRS	*Journal of Medieval and Renaissance Studies*
JNPH	*Journal of Newspaper and Periodical History*
JNT	*Journal of Narrative Technique*
JNZL	*Journal of New Zealand Literature*
JP	*The Journal of Philosophy*
JPC	*Journal of Popular Culture*
JPCL	*Journal of Pidgin and Creole Languages*
JPhon	*Journal of Phonetics*
JPJ	*Journal of Psychology and Judaism*
JPrag	*Journal of Pragmatics*
JPRAS	*Journal of Pre-Raphaelite and Aesthetic Studies*
JPsyR	*Journal of Psycholinguistic Research*
JQ	*Journalism Quarterly*
JR	*Journal of Religion*
JRH	*The Journal of Religious History*
JRMMRA	*Journal of the Rocky Mountain Medieval and Renaissance Association*
JRSA	*Journal of the Royal Society of Arts*
JRUL	*Journal of the Rutgers University Libraries*
JSA	*Journal of the Society of Archivists*
JSaga	*Journal of the Faculty of Liberal Arts and Science, Saga University*
JSAS	*Journal of Southern African Studies*
JSSE	*Journal of the Short Story in English*
JTheoS	*The Journal of Theological Studies*
JWCI	*Journal of the Warburg and Courtauld Institutes*
JWIL	*Journal of West Indian Literature*
JWMS	*The Journal of the William Morris Society*
JWSL	*Journal of Women's Studies in Literature*

KanQ	*Kansas Quarterly*
KB	*Kavya Bharati*
KCLMS	King's College London Medieval Series
KJ	*The Kipling Journal*
KN	*Kwartalnik Neofilologiczny* (Warsaw)
KompH	*Komparatistische Hefte*
KPAB	*Kentucky Philological Association Bulletin*
KR	*Kenyon Review*
KSJ	*Keats–Shelley Journal*
KSR	*Keats–Shelley Review*
Kuka	*Kuka: Journal of Creative and Critical Writing* (Zaria, Nigeria)
Kunapipi	*Kunapipi*
KWS	*Key-Word Studies in Chaucer*
L&C	*Language and Communication*
Landfall	*Landfall: A New Zealand Quarterly*
L&H	*Literature and History*
L&LC	*Literary and Linguistic Computing*
L&M	*Literature and Medicine*
L&P	*Literature and Psychology*
L&S	*Language and Speech*
Language	*Language: Journal of the Linguistic Society of America*
Lang&S	*Language and Style*
LangQ	*USF Language Quarterly*
LangR	*Language Research*
LangS	*Language Sciences*
LanM	*Les Langues Modernes*
LB	*Leuvense Bijdragen*
LBR	*Luso-Brazilian Review*
LCrit	*The Literary Criterion* (Mysore, India)
LCUT	*The Library Chronicle of the University of Texas at Austin*
LDOCE	Longman Dictionary of Contemporary English
LeedsSE	*Leeds Studies in English*
Legacy	*Legacy: A Journal of Nineteenth-Century American Women Writers*
LeS	*Lingua e Stile*
Lexicographica	*Lexicographica: International Annual for Lexicography*
Lexicography	*Lexicography*
LFQ	*Literature/Film Quarterly*
LH	*Library History*
LHY	*The Literary Half-Yearly*
Library	*The Library*
LibrQ	*The Library Quarterly*
LingA	*Linguistic Analysis*
Ling&P	*Linguistics and Philosophy*
Ling&Philol.	*Linguistics and Philology*
LingB	*Linguistische Berichte*
LingI	*Linguistic Inquiry*
LingInv	*Linvisticæ* Investigationes
Lingua	*Lingua: International Review of General Linguistics*

Linguistics	*Linguistics*
Linguistique	*La Linguistique*
LIT	*LIT: Literature, Interpretation, Theory*
LitH	*Literary Horizons*
LitR	*The Literary Review: An International Journal of Contemporary Writing*
LJGG	*Literaturwissenschaftliches Jahrbuch im Auftrage der Görres-Gesellschaft*
LJHum	*Lamar Journal of the Humanities*
LMag	*London Magazine*
LockeN	*The Locke Newsletter*
LongR	*Long Room: Bulletin of the Friends of the Library, Trinity College, Dublin*
Lore&L	*Lore and Language*
LP	*Lingua Posnaniensis*
LPLD	*Liverpool Papers in Language and Discourse*
LR	*Les Lettres Romanes*
LRB	*London Review of Books*
LSE	Lund Studies in English
LSoc	*Language in Society*
LST	Longman Study Texts
LTM	Leeds Texts and Monographs
LTP	*LTP: Journal of Literature Teaching Politics*
LTR	*London Theatre Record*
LuK	*Literatur und Kritik*
LVC	*Language Variation and Change*
LWU	*Literatur in Wissenschaft und Unterricht*
MÆ	*Medium* Ævum
MAEL	Macmillan Anthologies of English Literature
Mana	*Mana*
M&H	*Medievalia et Humanistica*
M&L	*Music and Letters*
M&N	*Man and Nature/L'Homme et la Nature: Proceedings of the Canadian Society for Eighteenth-Century Studies*
Manuscripta	*Manuscripta*
MAR	*Mid-American Review*
MarkhamR	*Markham Review*
Matrix	*Matrix*
MBL	*Modern British Literature*
MC&S	*Media, Culture and Society*
MCI	Modern Critical Interpretations
MCJNews	*Milton Centre of Japan News*
McNR	*McNeese Review*
MCRel	*Mythes, Croyances et Religions dans le Monde Anglo-Saxon*
MCV	Modern Critical Views
MD	*Modern Drama*
Meanjin	*Meanjin*
MED	*Middle English Dictionary*
Mediaevalia	*Mediaevalia: A Journal of Mediaeval Studies*

Melus	*MELUS: The Journal of the Society of Multi-Ethnic Literature of the United States*
Meridian	*Meridian*
MESN	*Mediaeval English Studies Newsletter*
MET	Middle English Texts
METh	*Medieval English Theatre*
MFN	*Medieval Feminist Newsletter*
MFS	*Modern Fiction Studies*
MHL	Macmillan History of Literature
MHLS	*Mid-Hudson Language Studies*
MHRev	*The Malahat Review*
MichA	*Michigan Academician*
MiltonQ	*Milton Quarterly*
MiltonS	*Milton Studies*
MinnR	*Minnesota Review*
MissQ	*Mississippi Quarterly*
MissR	*The Missouri Review*
MJLF	*Midwestern Journal of Language and Folklore*
MLAIB	*Modern Language Association International Bibliography*
MLJ	*The Modern Language Journal*
MLN	[*Modern Language Notes*]
MLNew	*Malcolm Lowry Review*
MLQ	*Modern Language Quarterly*
MLR	*The Modern Language Review*
MLS	*Modern Language Studies*
MMD	Macmillan Modern Dramatists
MMG	Macmillan Master Guides
MOCS	*Magazine of Cultural Studies*
ModA	*Modern Age: A Quarterly Review*
ModM	Modern Masters
MosSp	*Moderne Sprachen*
Monist	*The Monist*
MonSP	*Monash Swift Papers*
Month	*The Month: A Review Of Christian Thought and World Affairs*
MOR	*Mount Olive Review*
Moreana	*Moreana: Bulletin Thomas More* (Angers, France)
Mosaic	*Mosaic: A Journal for the Interdisciplinary Study of Literature*
MP	*Modern Philology*
MPHJ	*Middlesex Polytechnic History Journal*
MPR	*The Mervyn Peake Review*
MQ	*Midwest Quarterly*
MQR	*Michigan Quarterly Review*
MR	*Massachusetts Review*
MRDE	*Medieval and Renaissance Drama in England*
MRTS	Medieval and Renaissance Texts and Studies
MS	*Mediaeval Studies*
MSC	Malone Society Collections
MSE	*Massachusetts Studies in English*

MSex	*Melville Society Extracts*
MSh	Macmillan Shakespeare
MSNH	Mémoires de la Société Néophilologique de Helsinki
MSpr	*Moderna Språk*
MSR	*Malone Society Reprints*
MSSN	*Medieval Sermon Studies Newsletter*
MT	*The Musical Times*
MTJ	*Mark Twain Journal*
MusR	*Music Review*
MW	*The Muslim World* (Hartford, Conn.)
MysticsQ	*Mystics Quarterly*
NA	*Nuova Antologia*
Names	*Names: Journal of the American Name Society*
N&Q	*Notes and Queries*
Navasilu	*Navasilu*
NB	*Namn och Bygd*
NCaS	New Cambridge Shakespeare
NCBEL	*New Cambridge Bibliography of English Literature*
NCC	*Nineteenth-Century Contexts*
NCL	*Nineteenth-Century Literature*
NConL	*Notes on Contemporary Literature*
NCP	*Nineteenth Century Prose*
NCS	New Clarendon Shakespeare
NCT	*Nineteenth Century Theatre*
NDQ	*North Dakota Quarterly*
NegroD	*Negro Digest*
Neoh	*Neohelicon*
Neophil	*Neophilologus*
NEQ	*The New England Quarterly*
NewA	*New African*
NewBR	*New Beacon Review*
NewC	*The New Criterion*
NewComp	*New Comparison: A Journal of Comparative and General Literary Studies*
NewF	*New Formations*
NewR	*New Republic*
NewSt	*Newfoundland Studies*
NewV	*New Voices*
NF	*Neophilologica Fennica*
NfN	*News from Nowhere*
NGC	*New German Critique*
NGS	*New German Studies*
NH	*Northern History*
NHR	*The Nathaniel Hawthorne Review*
NJL	*Nordic Journal of Linguistics*
NL	*Nouvelles Littéraires*
NL<	*Natural Language and Linguistic Theory*
NLH	*New Literary History: A Journal of Theory and Interpretation*
NLitsR	*New Literatures Review*

NLR	*New Left Review*
NLWJ	*The National Library of Wales Journal*
NM	*Neuphilologische Mitteilungen*
NMAL	*NMAL: Notes on Modern American Literature*
NMer	New Mermaids
NMS	*Nottingham Medieval Studies*
NN	*Nordiska Namenstudier*
NNER	*Northern New England Review*
Nomina	*Nomina: A Journal of Name Studies Relating to Great Britain and Ireland*
NoP	*Northern Perspective*
NOR	*New Orleans Review*
NortonCE	A Norton Critical Edition
Novel	*Novel: A Forum on Fiction*
NOWELE	*North-Western European Language Evolution*
NPS	New Penguin Shakespeare
NR	*The Nassau Review*
NRF	*La Nouvelle Revue Française*
NS	*Die Neueren Sprachen*
NSS	New Swan Shakespeare
NTQ	*New Theatre Quarterly*
NVSAWC	*Newsletter of the Victorian Studies Association of Western Canada*
NwJ	*Northward Journal*
NWR	*Northwest Review*
NWRev	*The New Welsh Review*
NYH	*New York History*
NYLF	New York Literary Forum
NYRB	*The New York Review of Books*
NYT	*New York Times*
NYTBR	*The New York Times Book Review*
NZListener	*New Zealand Listener*
OA	Oxford Authors
OB	*Ord och Bild*
Obsidian	*Obsidian II: Black Literature in Review*
OBSP	Oxford Bibliographical Society Publications
OED	*Oxford English Dictionary*
OENews	*Old English Newsletter*
OET	Oxford English Texts
OH	*Over Here: An American Studies Journal*
OHEL	Oxford History of English Literature
OhR	*The Ohio Review*
OL	*Orbis Litterarum*
OLR	*Oxford Literary Review*
OPBS	Occasional Papers of the Bibliographical Society
OpenGL	Open Guides to Literature
OpL	*Open Letter*
OPLiLL	*Occasional Papers in Linguistics and Language Learning*
OPSL	*Occasional Papers in Systemic Linguistics*
Orbis	*Orbis*

OS	Oxford Shakespeare
OSS	Oxford Shakespeare Studies
OT	*Oral Tradition*
Outrider	*The Outrider: A Publication of the Wyoming State Library*
Overland	*Overland*
PA	*Présence Africaine*
PAAS	*Proceedings of the American Antiquarian Society*
PacStud	*Pacific Studies*
Paideuma	*Paideuma: A Journal Devoted to Ezra Pound Scholarship*
P&L	*Philosophy and Literature*
P&P	*Past and Present*
P&R	*Philosophy and Rhetoric*
P&SC	*Philosophy and Social Criticism*
PAPA	*Publications of the Arkansas Philological Association*
PAPS	*Proceedingsof the American Philosophical Society*
PAR	*Performing Arts Resources*
Parabola	*Parabola: The Magazine of Myth and Tradition*
Paragraph	*Paragraph: The Journal of the Modern Critical Theory Group*
Parergon	*Parergon: Bulletin of the Australian and New Zealand Association for Medieval and Renaissance Studies*
ParisR	*The Paris Review*
Parnassus	*Parnassus: Poetry in Review*
PastM	Past Masters
PaterN	*Pater Newsletter*
PAus	*Poetry Australia*
PBA	*Proceedings of the British Academy*
PBerLS	*Proceedings of the Berkeley Linguistics Society*
PBSA	*Papers of the Bibliographical Society of America*
PBSC	*Papers of the Biographical Society of Canada*
PCL	*Perspectives on Contemporary Literature*
PCLAC	*Proceedins of the California Linguistics Association Conference*
PCLS	Proceedings of the Comparative Literature Symposium (Lubbock, Tex.)
PCP	*Pacific Coast Philology*
PCS	Penguin Critical Studies
PEAN	*Proceedings of the English Association North*
PE&W	*Philosophy East and West: A Quarterly of Asian and Comparative Thought*
PELL	*Papers on English Language and Literature* (Japana)
Performance	*Performance*
Peritia	*Peritia: Journal of the Medieval Academy of Ireland*
Persuasions	*Persuasions: Journal of the Jane Austen Society of North America*
PHist	*Printing History*
Phonetica	*Phonetica: International Journal of Speech Science*
PHOS	Publishing History Occasional Series
PhRA	*Philosophical Research Archives*
PhT	*Philosophy Today*

PIL	*Papers in Linguistics*
PIMA	*Proceedings of the Illinois Medieval Association*
PJCL	*The Prairie Journal of Canadian Literature*
PLL	*Papers on Language and Literature*
PLPLS	*Proceedings of the Leeds Philosophical and Literary Society, Literary and Historical Section*
PM	Penguin Masterstudies
PMHB	*Pennsylvania Magazine of History and Biography*
PMLA	*Publications of the Modern Language Association of America*
PNotes	*Pynchon Notes*
PNR	*PN Review*
PoeS	*Poe Studies*
Poetica	*Poetica: Zeitschrift für Sprach- und Literaturwissenschaft* (Amsterdam)
PoeticaJ	*Poetica: An International Journal of Linguistic-Literary Studies* (Tokyo)
Poetics	*Poetics: International Review for the Theory of Literature*
Poétique	*Poétique: Revue de Théorie et d'Analyse Littéraires*
PoetryCR	*Poetry Canada Review*
PoetryR	*Poetry Review*
PoetryW	*Poetry Wales*
POMPA	*Publications of the Mississippi Philological Association*
PostS	*Post Script: Essays in Film and the Humanities*
PoT	*Poetics Today*
PP	Penguin Passnotes
PP	*Philologica Pragensia*
PPMRC	*Proceedings of the International Patristic, Mediaeval and Renaissance Conference*
PPR	*Philosophy and Phenomenological Research*
PQ	*Philological Quarterly*
PQM	*Pacific Quarterly* (Moana)
PR	*Partisan Review*
PrairieF	*Prairie Fire*
Praxis	*Praxis: A Journal of Cultural Criticism*
Prépub	*(Pré)publications*
PRev	*The Powys Review*
PRIA	*Proceedings of the Royal Irish Academy*
PRIAA	Publications of the Research Institute of the Åbo Akademi Foundation
PRMCLS	*Papers from the Regional Meetings of the Chicago Linguistics Society*
Prospects	*Prospects: An Annual Journal of American Cultural Studies*
Proteus	*Proteus: A Journal of Ideas*
Proverbium	*Proverbium*
PrS	*The Prairie Schooner*
PSt	*Prose Studies*
PTBI	Publications of the Sir Thomas Browne Institute
PubH	*Publishing History*

PULC	*Princeton Univeristy Library Chronicle*
PURBA	*Panjab University Research Bulletin (Arts)*
PVR	*Platte Valley Review*
PY	*Phonology Yearbook*
QI	*Quaderni d'Italianistica*
QJS	*Quarterly Journal of Speech*
QLing	*Quantitative Linguistics*
QQ	*Queen's Quarterly*
Quadrant	*Quadrant* (Sydney)
Quarendo	*Quarendo*
Quarry	*Quarry*
RadP	*Radical Philosophy*
RAL	*Research in African Literatures*
RALS	*Resources for American Literary Study*
Ramus	*Ramus: Critical Studies in Greek and Roman Literature*
R&L	*Religion and Literature*
Raritan	*Raritan: A Quarterly Review*
RB	*Revue Bénédictine*
RBPH	*Revue Belge de Philologie et d'Histoire*
RCEI	*Revista Canaria de Estudios Ingleses*
RCF	*Review of Contemporary Fiction*
RDN	*Renaissance Drama Newsletter*
RE	*Revue d'Esthétique*
ReAL	*Re: Artes Liberales*
REALB	*REAL: The Yearbook of Research in English and American Literature* (Berlin)
RECTR	*Restoration and Eighteenth-Century Theatre Research*
RedL	*Red Letters: A Journal of Cultural Politics*
REED	Records of Early English Drama
REEDN	*Records of Early English Drama Newsletter*
Reinardus	*Reinardus*
REL	*Review of English Literature* (Kyoto)
Ren&R	*Renaissance and Reformation*
Renascence	*Renascence: Essays on Value in Literature*
RenD	*Renaissance Drama*
RenP	*Renaissance Papers*
RenQ	*Renaissance Quarterly*
Rep	*Representations*
RES	*The Review of English Studies*
Restoration	*Restoration: Studies in English Literary Culture, 1660–1700*
Rev	*Review* (Blacksburg, Va.)
RevAli	*Revista Alicantina de Estudios Ingleses*
Revels	Revels Plays
RevelsCL	Revels Plays Companion Library
RFEA	*Revue Française d'Etudes Américaines*
RH	*Recusant History*
Rhetorica	*Rhetorica: A Journal of the History of Rhetoric*
Rhetorik	*Rhetorik: Ein Internationales Jahrbuch*
RHL	*Revue d'Histoire Littéraire de la France*

RHT	*Revue d'Histoire du Théâtre*
Ricardian	*The Ricardian: Journal of the Richard III Society*
RL	Rereading Literature
RLC	*Revue de Littérature Comparée*
RLM	*La Revue des Lettres Modernes: Histoire des Idées des Littératures*
RLMC	*Rivista di Letterature Moderne e Comparate*
RLT	*Russian Literature Triquarterly*
RM	*Rethinking Marxism*
RMR	*Rocky Mountain Review of Language and Literature*
RMS	*Renaissance and Modern Studies*
RMSt	*Reading Medieval Studies*
RomN	*Romance Notes*
RomS	*Romance Studies*
ROO	*Room of One's Own: A Feminist Journal of Literature and Criticism*
RORD	*Research Opportunities in Renaissance Drama*
RPT	Russian Poetics in Translation
RQ	*Riverside Quarterly*
RR	*Romanic Review*
RRDS	Regents Renaissance Drama Series
RRestDS	Regents Restoration Drama Series
RS	*Renaissance Studies*
RSQ	*Rhetoric Society Quarterly*
RUO	*Revue de l'Université d'Ottawa*
RuskN	*Ruskin Newsletter*
RUUL	*Reports from the Uppsala University Department of Linguistics*
SAC	*Studies in the Age of Chaucer*
SAD	*Studies in American Drama, 1945–Present*
SAF	*Studies in American Fiction*
Saga-Book	*Saga-Book (Viking Society for Northern Research)*
Sagetrieb	*Sagetrieb: A Journal Devoted to Poets in the Pound–H.D.–Williams Tradition*
SAJL	*Studies in American Jewish Literature*
Sal	*Salmagundi: A Quarterly of the Humanities and Social Sciences*
SAntS	*Studia Anthroponymica Scandinavica*
SAP	*Studia Anglica Posnaniensia*
SAQ	*South Atlantic Quarterly*
SAR	*Studies in the American Renaissance*
SARB	*South African Review of Books*
SatR	*Saturday Review*
SB	*Studies in Bibliography*
SBHC	*Studies in Browning and His Circle*
SC	*The Seventeenth Century*
Scan	*Scandinavica: An International Journal of Scandinavian Studies*
ScanS	*Scandinavian Studies*
SCER	*Society for Critical Exchange Report*

SCJ	*The Sixteenth Century Journal*
SCL	*Studies in Canadian Literature*
ScLJ	*Scottish Literary Journal: A Review of Studies in Scottish Language and Literature*
ScLJ(S)	*Scottish Literary Journal Supplement*
SCN	*Seventeenth-Century News*
ScottN	*Scott Newsletter*
SCR	*The South Carolina Review*
Screen	*Screen* (London)
SCRev	*South Central Review*
Scriblerian	*The Scriblerian and the Kit Cats: A Newsjournal Devoted to Pope, Swift, and Their Circle*
Scripsi	*Scripsi*
Scriptorium	*Scriptorium: International Review of Manuscript Studies*
SDR	*South Dakota Review*
SECC	*Studies in Eighteenth-Century Culture*
SED	*Survey of English Dialects*
SEL	Studies in English Literature
SEL	*Studies in English Literature 1500–1900* (Rice Univ.)
SELing	*Studies in English Linguistics* (Tokyo)
SELit	*Studies in English Literature* (Tokyo)
Sem	*Semiotica: Journal of the International Association for Semiotic Studies*
Semiosis	*Semiosis: Internationale Zeitschrift für Semiotik und Ästhetik*
SER	*Studien zur Englischen Romantik*
Seven	*Seven: An Anglo-American Literary Review*
SF&R	Scholars' Facsimiles and Reprints
SFic	*Science Fiction: A Review of Speculative Literature*
SFNL	*Shakespeare on Film Newsletter*
SFQ	*Southern Folklore Quarterly*
SFR	*Stanford French Review*
SFS	*Science-Fiction Studies*
SH	*Studia Hibernica* (Dublin)
ShakB	*Shakespeare Bulletin*
ShakS	*Shakespeare Studies* (New York)
Sh&Sch	*Shakespeare and Schools*
ShawR	*Shaw: The Annual of Bernard Shaw Studies*
Shenandoah	*Shenandoah*
ShJE	*Shakespeare Jahrbuch* (Weimar)
ShJW	*Deutsche Shakespeare-Gesellschaft West Jahrbuch* (Bochum)
ShLR	*Shoin Literary Review*
ShN	*The Shakespeare Newsletter*
SHR	*Southern Humanities Review*
ShS	*Shakespeare Survey*
ShSA	*Shakespeare in Southern Africa*
ShStud	*Shakespeare Studies* (Tokyo)
ShY	*Shakespeare Yearbook*
SIcon	*Studies in Iconography*

Signs *Signs: Journal of Women in Culture and Society*
SiHoLS Studies in the History of the Language Sciences
SIM *Studies in Music*
SiP Shakespeare in Performance
SIR *Studies in Romanticism*
SJS *San José Studies*
SL *Studia Linguistica*
SLang *Studies in Language*
SLCS Studies in Language Companion Series
SLitI *Studies in the Literary Imagination*
SLJ *Southern Literary Journal*
SLRev *Stanford Literature Review*
SLSc *Studies in the Linguistic Sciences*
SMC Studies in Medieval Culture
SMed *Studi Medievali*
SMELL *Studies in Medieval English Language and Literature*
SMLit *Studies in Mystical Literature* (Taiwan)
SMRH *Studies in Medieval and Renaissance History*
SMS *Studier i Modern Språkvetenskap*
SMy *Studia Mystica*
SN *Studia Neophilologica*
SNew *Sidney Newletter*
SNNTS *Studies in the Novel* (North Texas State Univ.)
SOÅ *Sydsvenska Ortnamnssällskapets Årsskrift*
SoAR *South Atlantic Review*
Sociocrit *Sociocriticism*
SocN *Sociolinguistics*
SocT *Social Text*
SohoB Soho Bibliographies
SoQ *The Southern Quarterly*
SoR *The Southern Review* (Baton Rouge, La.)
SoRA *Southern Review* (Adelaide)
SoSt *Southern Studies: An Interdisciplinary Journal of the South*
Soundings *Soundings: An Interdisciplinary Journal*
Southerly *Southerly: A Review of Australian Literature*
SovL *Soviet Literature*
SP *Studies in Philology*
SPAN *SPAN: Newsletter of the South Pacific Association for Commonwealth Literature and Language Studies*
SPAS *Studies in Puritan American Spirituality*
Spectrum *Spectrum*
Speculum *Speculum: A Journal of Medieval Studies*
SPELL Swiss Papers in English Language and Literature
SphereHL Sphere History of Literature
Sphinx *The Sphinx: A Magazine of Literature and Society*
SpM *Spicilegio Moderno*
SpNL *Spenser Newsletter*
Sprachwiss *Sprachwissenschaft*
SPub *Studies in Publishing*

SPWVSRA	*Selected Papers from the West Virginia Shakespeare and Renaissance Association*
SQ	*Shakespeare Quarterly*
SR	*The Sewanee Review*
SRen	*Studies in the Renaissance*
SRSR	*Status Report on Speech Research* (Haskins Laboratories)
SSEL	Stockholm Studies in English
SSELER	Salzburg Studies in English Literature: Elizabethan and Renaissance
SSELJDS	Salzburg Studies in English Literature: Jacobean Drama Studies
SSELPDPT	Salzburg Studies in English Literature: Poetic Drama and Poetic Theory
SSELRR	Salzburg Studies in English Literature: Romantic Reassessment
SSEng	*Sydney Studies in English*
SSF	*Studies in Short Fiction*
SSL	*Studies in Scottish Literature*
SSt	*Spenser Studies*
SStud	*Swift Studies: The Annual of the Ehrenpreis Center*
Staffrider	*Staffrider*
STAH	*Strange Things Are Happening*
STC	*Short-Title Catalogue*
STGM	Studien und Texte zur Geistegeschichte des Mittelalters
StHum	*Studies in the Humanities*
StIn	*Studi Inglesi*
StLF	*Studi di Letteratura Francese*
StQ	*Steinbeck Quarterly*
StrR	*Structuralist Review*
StTCL	*Studies in Twentieth Century Literature*
Style	*Style* (De Kalb, Ill.)
SUAS	Stratford-upon-Avon Studies
SubStance	*SubStance: A Review of Theory and Literary Criticism*
SUS	*Susquehanna University Studies*
SussexAC	*Sussex Archaeological Collections*
SVEC	*Studies on Voltaire and the Eighteenth Century*
SWPLL	*Sheffield Working Papers in Language and Linguistics*
SWR	*Southwest Review*
SwR	*The Swansea Review: A Journal of Criticism*
TA	*Theatre Annual*
T&C	*Text and Context*
T&P	Text and Performance
TAPS	*Transactions of the American Philosophical Society*
TCBS	*Transactions of the Cambridge Bibliographical Society*
TCE	*Texas College English*
TCL	*Twentieth Century Literature*
TCS	*Theory, Culture and Society: Explorations in Critical Social Science*
TD	*Themes in Drama*
TDR	*The Drama Review*

TEAS	Twayne's English Authors Series
TEBS	*Edinburgh Bibliographical Society Transactions*
Telos	*Telos: A Quarterly Journal of Post-Critical Thought*
TenEJ	*Tennessee English Journal*
Te Reo	*Te Reo: Journal of the Linguistic Society of New Zealand*
Text	*Text: Transactions of the Society for Textual Scholarship*
TH	*Texas Humanist*
THA	*Thomas Hardy Annual*
Thalia	*Thalia: Studies in Literary Humor*
ThC	*Theatre Crafts*
Theater	*Theater*
Theoria	*Theoria: A Journal of Studies in the Arts, Humanities and Social Sciences* (Natal)
THES	*The Times Higher Education Supplement*
Thesis	*Thesis Eleven*
THIC	*Theatre History in Canada*
THJ	*The Thomas Hardy Journal*
ThN	*Thackeray Newsletter*
ThoreauQ	*The Thoreau Quarterly: A Journal of Literary and Philosophical Studies*
Thought	*Thought: A Review of Culture and Ideas*
Thph	*Theatrephile*
ThR	*Theatre Research International*
ThreR	*The Threepenny Review*
ThS	*Theatre Survey: The American Journal of Theatre History*
THSLC	*Transactions of the Historic Society of Lancashire and Cheshire*
THStud	*Theatre History Studies*
THY	*The Thomas Hardy Yearbook*
TiLSM	Trends in Linguistics Studies and Monographs
TJ	*Theatre Journal*
TJS	*Transactions* (The Johnson Society)
TkR	*Tamkang Review*
TL	*Theoretical Linguistics*
TLS	*TLS: The Times Literary Supplement*
TMLT	Toronto Medieval Latin Texts
TN	*Theatre Notebook*
TP	*Terzo Programma*
TPLL	*Tilbury Papers in Language and Literature*
TPr	*Textual Practice*
TPS	*Transactions of the Philological Society*
Traditio	*Traditio: Studies in Ancient and Medieval History, Thought, and Religion*
Transition	*Transition*
TRB	*The Tennyson Research Bulletin*
TRHS	*Transactions of the Royal Historical Society*
TriQ	*TriQuarterly*
Trivium	*Trivium*
Tropismes	*Tropismes*
TSAR	*The Toronto South Asian Review*

TSB	*Thoreau Society Bulletin*
TSL	*Tennessee Studies in Literature*
TSLang	Typological Studies in Language
TSLL	*Texas Studies in Literature and Language*
TSWL	*Tulsa Studies in Women's Literature*
TTR	*Trinidad and Tobago Review*
TUSAS	Twayne's United States Authors Series
TWAS	Twayne's World Authors Series
TWBR	*Third World Book Review*
TWQ	*Third World Quarterly*
TWR	*The Thomas Wolfe Review*
TYDS	*Transactions of the Yorkshire Dialect Society*
UCrow	*The Upstart Crow*
UCTSE	*University of Cape Town Studies in English*
UDR	*University of Dayton Review*
UE	*The Use of English*
UEAPL	*UEA Papers in Linguistics*
UES	*Unisa English Studies*
ULR	*University of Leeds Review*
UMSE	*University of Mississippi Studies in English*
Untold	*Untold*
UOQ	*University of Ottawa Quarterly*
URM	*Ultimate Reality and Meaning: Interdisciplinary Studies in the Philosophy of Understanding*
USSE	*University of Saga Studies in English*
UTQ	*University of Toronton Quarterly*
UWR	*The University of Windsor Review*
VCT	Les Voies de la Création Théâtrale
VEAW	Varieties of English around the World
Verbatim	*Verbatim: The Language Quarterly*
VIA	*VIA: The Journal of the Graduate School of Fine Arts, University of Pennsylvania*
Viator	*Viator: Medieval and Renaissance Studies*
VIJ	*Victorians Institute Journal*
VN	*Victorian Newsletter*
Voices	*VOICES*
VP	*Victorian Poetry*
VPR	*Victorian Periodicals Review*
VQR	*The Virginia Quarterly Review*
VS	*Victorian Studies*
VSB	*Victorian Studies Bulletin*
VWM	*Virginia Woolf Miscellany*
WAJ	*Women's Art Journal*
WAL	*Western American Literature*
W&I	*Word and Image*
W&L	*Women and Literature*
Wasafiri	*Wasafiri*
WascanaR	*Wascana Review*
WBEP	Wiener Beiträge zur Englischen Philologie
WC	World's Classics

WC	*The Wordsworth Circle*
WCR	*West Coast Review*
WCSJ	*Wilkie Collins Society Journal*
WCWR	*The William Carlos Williams Review*
Wellsian	*The Wellsian: The Journal of the H. G. Wells Society*
WEn	*World Englishes*
Westerly	*Westerly: A Quarterly Review*
WestHR	*West Hills Review: A Walt Whitman Journal*
WF	*Western Folklore*
WHR	*Western Humanities Review*
WLT	*World Literature Today*
WLWE	*World Literature Written in English*
WMQ	*The William and Mary Quarterly*
WolfenbüttelerB	*Wolfenbüttele Beiträge: Aus den Schätzen der Herzog August Bibliothek*
Women	*Women: a cultural review*
Word	*WORD: Journal of the International Linguistic Association*
WQ	*The Wilson Quarterly*
WRB	*Women's Review of Books*
WS	*Women's Studies: An Interdisciplinary Journal*
WSIF	*Women's Studies International Forum*
WSJour	*The Wallace Stevens Journal*
WTJ	*The Westminster Theological Journal*
WTW	Writers and Their Work
WVUPP	*West Virginia University Philological Papers*
WWR	*Walt Whitman Quarterly Review*
XUS	*Xavier Review*
YCC	*Yearbook of Comparative Criticism*
YeA	*Yeats Annual*
YER	*Yeats Eliot Review*
YES	*The Yearbook of English Studies*
YFS	*Yale French Studies*
YJC	*The Yale Journal of Criticism: Interpretation in the Humanities*
YLS	*Yearbook of Langland Studies*
YNS	York Note Series
YPL	*York Papers in Linguistics*
YR	*The Yale Review*
YULG	*Yale University Library Gazette*
YWES	*The Year's Work in English Studies*
ZAA	*Zeitschrift für Anglistik und Amerikanistik*
ZCP	*Zeitschrift für Celtische Philologie*
ZDA	*Zeitschrift für Deutsches Altertum und Deutsche Literatur*
ZDL	*Zeitschrift für Dialektologie und Linguistik*
ZGKS	*Zeitschrift der Gesellschaft für Kanada-Studien*
ZGL	*Zeitschrift für Germanistische Linguistik*
ZPSK	*Zeitschrift für Phonetik, Sprachwissenschaft und Kommunikationsforschung*
ZSpr	*Zeitschrift für Sprachwissenschaft*

ZVS	*Zeitschrift für Vergleichende Sprachforschung*

Volume numbers are supplied in the text, as are individual issue numbers for journals that are not continuously paginated through the year.

2. Publishers

AAAH	Acta Academiae Åboensis Humaniora, Åbo, Finland
A&B	Allison & Busby, London
A&R	Angus & Robertson, North Ryde, N.S.W.
A&U	Allen & Unwin (now Unwin Hyman)
A&UA	Allen & Unwin, North Sydney, N.S.W.
A&W	Almqvist & Wiksell International, Stockholm
AarhusUP	Aarhus UP, Aarhus, Denmark
Abbeville	Abbeville Press, New York
ABDO	Association Bourguignonne de Dialectologie et d'Onomastique, Dijon
AberdeenUP	Aberdeen UP, Aberdeen
Abhinav	Abhinav Pubns, New Delhi
Abingdon	Abingdon Press, Nashville, Tenn.
ABL	Armstrong Browning Library, Waco, Texas
Ablex	Ablex Pub., Norwood, N.J.
Åbo	Åbo Akademi, Åbo, Finland
Abrams	Harry N. Abrams, New York
Academic	Academic Press, London and Orlando, Fla.
Academy	The Academy Press, Dublin
AcademyC	Academy Chicago Pubs., Chicago
AcademyE	Academy Editions, London
Acadiensis	Acadiensis Press, Fredericton, New Brunswick, Canada
ACarS	Association for Caribbean Studies, Coral Gables, Fla.
ACC	Antique Collectors' Club, Woodbridge, Suffolk
ACCO	ACCO, Leuven, Belgium
ACP	Another Chicago Press, Chicago
ACS	Association for Canadian Studies, Ottawa
Addison-Wesley	Addison-Wesley, Wokingham, Berks.
Adosa	Adosa, Clermont-Ferrand, France
AF	Akademisk Forlag, Copenhagen
Affiliated	Affiliated East-West Press, New Delhi
AFP	Associated Faculty Press, New York
Africana	Africana Pub., New York
A-H	Arnold-Heinemann, New Delhi
Ahriman	Ahriman-Verlag, Freiburg im Breisgau, Germany
AIAS	Australian Institute of Aboriginal Studies, Canberra
Ajanta	Ajanta Pubns, Delhi
AK	Akadémiai Kiadó, Budapest
Al&Ba	Allyn & Bacon, Boston, Mass.
Albion	Albion, Appalachian State Univ., Boone, N.C.
Alderman	Alderman Press, London
AligarhMU	Aligarh Muslim Univ., Uttar Pradesh, India
Alioth	Alioth Press, Beaverton, Oreg.
Allen	W. H. Allen, London
Almond	Almond Press, Sheffield
AM	Aubier Montaigne, Paris
AMAES	Association des Médiévistes Angliciste de l'Enseignement Supérieur, Paris

Amate	The Amate Press, Oxford
AmberL	Amber Lane, Oxford
AMS	AMS Press, New York
AMU	Adam Mickiewicz Univ., Posnan
Anansi	Anansi Press, Toronto
Anma Libri	Anma Libri, Saratoga, Calif.
Antipodes	Antipodes Press, Plimmerton, New Zealand
Anvil	Anvil Press Poetry, London
APA	APA, Maarssen, Netherlands
APH	Associated Pub. House, New Delhi
APL	American Poetry and Literature Press, Philadelphia
APP	Australian Professional Pubns, Mosman, N.S.W.
Appletree	Appletree Press, Belfast
APS	American Philosophical Society, Philadelphia
Aquarian	The Aquarian Press, Wellingborough, Northants.
ArborH	Arbor House Pub., New York
Archon	Archon Books, Hamden Conn.
ArchP	Architectural Press Books, Guildford, Surrey
Ardis	Ardis Pubs., Ann Arbor, Mich.
Ariel	Ariel Press, London
Ark	Ark Paperbacks, London
Arkona	Arkona Forlaget, Aarhus, Denmark
Arlington	Arlington Books, London
Arnold	Edward Arnold, London
ArnoldEJ	E. J. Arnold & Son, Leeds
ARP	Australian Reference Pubns, N. Balwyn, Vic.
Arrow	Arrow Books, London
ASB	Anglo-Saxon Books, Middlesex
ASECS	American Society for Eighteenth-Century Studies, c/o Ohio State Univ. Columbus
AshfieldP	Ashfield Press, London
Aslib	Aslib, London
ASLS	Association for Scottish Literary Studies, Aberdeen
ASU	Arizona State Univ., Tempe
Atheneum	Atheneum Pubs., New York
Athlone	Athlone Press, London
Atlas	Atlas Press, London
Attic	Attic Press, Dublin
AucklandUP	Auckland UP, Auckland
AUG	Acta Universitatis Gothoburgensis, Sweden
AUP	Associated Univ. Presses, London and Toronto
AUPG	Academic & Univ. Pubs. Group, London
Aurum	Aurum Press, London
AUU	Acta Universitatis Umensis, Umeå, Sweden
AUUp	Acta Universitatis Upsaliensis, Uppsala
Avebury	Avebury Pub., Aldershot, Hampshire
Avero	Avero Pubns, Newcastle upon Tyne
A-V Verlag	A-V Verlag, Franz Fischer, Augsburg, Germany
AWP	Africa World Press, Trenton, N.J.
BA	British Academy, London

BAAS	British Association for American Studies, c/o Univ. of Keele
Bagel	August Bagel Verlag, Düsseldorf
Bahri	Bahri Pubns, New Delhi
Bamberger	Bamberger Books, Flint, Mich.
B&B	Boydell & Brewer, Woodbridge, Suffolk
B&J	Barrie & Jenkins, London
B&N	Barnes & Noble, Totowa, N.J.
B&O	Burns & Oates, Tunbridge Wells, Kent
B&S	Michael Benskin and M. L. Samuels, Middle English Dialect Project, Univ. of Edinburgh
BAR	British Archaeological Reports, Oxford
Barn Owl	Barn Owl Books, Taunton, Somerset
Barnes	A. S. Barnes, San Diego, Calif.
BathUP	Bath UP, Bath
Batsford	B. T. Batsford, London
BBC	BBC Pubns, London
BClark	Bruccoli Clark Pubs., Columbia, S.C.
BCP	Bristol Classical Press, Bristol
Beacon	Beacon Press, Boston, Mass.
Beck	C. H. Beck'sche Verlagsbuchandlung, Munich
Becket	Becket Pubns, London
Belknap	Belknap Press, Cambridge, Mass.
Belles Lettres	Société d'Edition les Belles Lettres, Paris
Bellew	Bellew Pub., London
Bellflower	Bellflower Press, Case Univ., Cleveland, Ohio
Benjamins	John Benjamins, Amsterdam
BenjaminsNA	John Benjamins North America, Philadelphia
BennC	Bennington College, Bennington, Vt.
Berg	Berg Pubs., Oxford
BFI	British Film Institute, London
BGUP	Bowling Green Univ. Popular Press, Bowling Green, Ohio
BibS	Bibliographical Society, London
Bilingual	Bilingual Press, Arizona State Univ., Tempe
Bingley	Clive Bingley, London
Binnacle	Binnacle Press, London
Biografia	Biografia Pubs., London
Bishopsgate	Bishopsgate Press, Tonbridge, Kent
BL	British Library, London
Black	Adam & Charles Black, London
Black Cat	Black Cat Press, Blackrock, Eire
Blackie	Blackie & Son, Glasgow
Black Moss	Black Moss, Windsor, Ont.
Blackstaff	Blackstaff Press, Belfast
Blackwell	Basil Blackwell, Oxford
BlackwellR	Blackwell Reference, Oxford
Blackwood	Blackwood, Pillans & Wilson, Edinburgh
Bl&Br	Blond & Briggs, London
Blandford	Blandford Press, London
Blaue Eule	Verlag die Blaue Eule, Essen

Bloodaxe	Bloodaxe Books, Newcastle upon Tyne
Bloomsbury	Bloomsbury Pub., London
BM	Bobbs-Merrill, New York
BMP	British Museum Pubns, London
Bodleian	The Bodleian Library, Oxford
Bodley	The Bodley Head, London
Bogle	Bogle L'Ouverture Pubns, London
BoiseSUP	Boise State UP, Boise, Idaho
Book Guild	The Book Guild, Lewes, E.Sussex
Borealis	Borealis Press, Ottawa
Borgo	Borgo Press, San Bernardino, Calif.
BostonAL	Boston Athenaeum Library, Boston, Mass.
Bouma	Bouma's Boekhuis, Groningen, Netherlands
Bowker	R. R. Bowker, New Providence, N.J.
Boyars	Marion Boyars, London and Boston, Mass.
Boydell	The Boydell Press, Woodbridge, Suffolk
Boyes	Megan Boyes, Allestree, Derbyshire
Bran's Head	Bran's Head Books, Frome, Somerset
Braumüller	Wilhelm Braumüller, Vienna
Breakwater	Breakwater Books, St John's, Newfoundland
Brentham	Brentham Press, St Alban's, Herts.
Brewer	D. S. Brewer, Woodbridge, Suffolk
Brewin	Brewin Books, Studley, War.
Bridge	Bridge Pub., S. Plainfield, N.J.
Brill	E. J. Brill, Leiden
Brilliance	Brilliance Books, London
Broadview	Broadview, London, Ont. and Lewiston, N.Y.
Bookside	Brookside Press, London
Browne	Sinclair Browne, London
Brownstone	Brownstone Books, Madison, Ind.
BrownUP	Brown UP, Providence, R.I.
Brynmill	Brynmill Press, Harleston, Norfolk
BSB	Black Swan Books, Redding Ridge, Conn.
BSP	Black Sparrow Press, Santa Barbara, Calif.
BSU	Ball State Univ., Muncie, Ind.
BuckUP	Bucknell UP, Lewisburg, Pa.
Bulzoni	Bulzoni Editore, Rome
Burnett	Burnett Books, London
Buske	Helmut Buske, Hamburg
CA	Creative Arts Book Co., Berkeley, Calif.
CAAS	Connecticut Academy of Arts and Sciences, New Haven
Cadmus	Cadmus Editions, Tiburon, Calif.
Cairns	Francis Cairns, Univ. of Leeds
Calaloux	Calaloux Pubns, Ithaca, N.Y.
Calder	John Calder, London
Camden	Camden Press, London
C&G	Carroll & Graf, New York
C&W	Chatto & Windus, London
Canongate	Canongate Pub., Edinburgh
Cape	Jonathan Cape, London

Capra	Capra Press, Santa Barbara, Calif.
Carcanet	The Carcanet New Press, Manchester, Lancs.
Cardinal	Cardinal, London
CaribB	Caribbean Books, Parkersburg, Iowa
CarletonUP	Carleton UP, Ottawa
Carucci	Carucci, Rome
Cass	Frank Cass, London
Cassell	Cassell, London
Cavaliere Azzurro	Cavaliere Azzurro, Bologna
Cave	Godfrey Cave Associates, London
CBA	Council for British Archaeology, London
CBS	Cambridge Bibliographical Society, Cambridge
CCP	Canadian Children's Press, Guelph, Ont.
CCS	Centre for Canadian Studies, Mount Allison Univ., Sackville, N.B.
CDSH	Centre de Documentation Sciences Humaines, Paris
Century	Century Pub., London
Ceolfrith	Ceolfrith Press, Sunderland, Tyne and Wear
CESR	Société des Amis du Centre d'Etudes Superieures de la Renaissance, Tours
CFA	Canadian Federation for trhe Humanities, Ottawa
CH	Croom Helm, London
C-H	Chadwyck-Healey, Cambridge
Chambers	W. & R. Chambers, Edinburgh
Champaign	Champaign Public Library and Information Center, Champaign, Ill.
Champion	Librairie Honoré Champion, Paris
Chand	S. Chand, Madras
ChelseaH	Chelsea House Pubs., New York, New Haven, and Philadelphia
Christendom	Christendom Pubns, Front Royal, Va.
Chronicle	Chronicle Books, London
ChuoUL	Chuo Univ. Library, Tokyo
Churchman	Churchman Pub., Worthing, W. Sussex
Cistercian	Cistercian Pubns, Kalamazoo, Mich.
CL	City Lights Books, San Francisco
CLA	Canadian Library Association, Ottawa
Clarendon	Clarendon Press, Oxford
Claridge	Claridge, St Albans, Herts.
Clarion	Clarion State College, Clarion, Pa.
Clark	T. & T. Clark, Edinburgh
Clarke	James Clarke, Cambridge
Classical	Classical Pub., New Delhi
CLCS	Centre for Language and Communication Studies, Trinity College, Dublin
ClogherHS	Clogher Historical Society, Monaghan, Eire
Clunie	Clunie Press, Pitlochry, Tayside
CMERS	Center for Medieval and Early Renaissance Studies, Binghamton, N.Y.
CML	William Andrews Clark Memorial Library, Los Angeles

CMST	Centre for Medieval Studies, Univ. of Toronto
Coach House	Coach House Press, Toronto
Colleagues	Colleagues Press, East Lansing, Mich.
Collector	The Collector Ltd, London
College-Hill	College-Hill Press, San Diego, Calif.
Collins	William Collins Sons, London
CollinsA	William Collins (Australia), Sydney
ColUP	Columbia UP, New York
Comedia	Comedia Pub. Group, London
Comet	Comet Books, London
Compton	The Compton Press, Tisbury, Wilts.
Constable	Constable, London
Contemporary	Contemporary Books, Chicago
Continuum	Continuum Pub., New York
Copp	Copp Clark Pitman, Mississuaga, Ontario, Canada
Corgi	Corgi Books, London
CorkUP	Cork UP, Cork, Eire
Cormorant	Cormorant Press, Victoria, B.C.
CornUP	Cornell UP, Ithaca, N.Y.
Cornwallis	The Cornwallis Press, Hastings, E. Sussex
Coronado	Coronado Press, Lawrence, Kansas
Cosmo	Cosmo Pubns, New Delhi
Coteau	Coteau Books, Regina, Saskatchewan, Canada
Cowley	Cowley Pubns, Cambridge, Mass.
Cowper	Cowper House, Pacific Grove, Calif.
CPP	Canadian Poetry Press, London, Ont.
Cresset	Cresset Library, London
Crossing	The Crossing Press, Freedom Calif.
Crossroad	Crossroad Pub., New York
Crown	Crown Pubs., New York
Crowood	The Crowood Press, Marlborough, Wilts.
CSAL	Centre for Studies in Australian Literature, Univ. of Western Australia, Nedlands
CSLI	Center for the Study of Language and Information, Stanford Univ.
CSU	Cleveland State Univ., Cleveland, Ohio
CTHS	Editions du Comité des Travaux Historiques et Scientifiques, Paris
CUAP	Catholic Univ. of America Press, Washington, D.C.
Cuff	Harry Cuff Pubns, St John's, Newfoundland
CULouvain	Catholic Univ. of Louvain, Louvain, Belgium
CULublin	Catholic Univ. of Lublin, Poland
CUP	Cambridge UP, Cambridge, New York, and Melbourne
Currency	Currency Pres, Paddington, N.S.W.
Currey	James Currey, London
CV	Cherry Valley Editions, Rochester, N.Y.
CVK	Cornelson-Velhagen & Klasing, Berlin
CWU	Carl Winter Universitätsverlag, Heidelberg
Da Capo	Da Capo Press, New York
Dacorum	Dacorum College, Hemel Hempstead, Herts.

Daisy	Daisy Books, Peterborough, Northants.
Dalkey	Dalkey Archive Press, Elmwood Park, Ill.
D&C	David & Charles, Newton Abbot, Devon
D&M	Douglas & McIntyre, Vancouver, B.C.
Dangaroo	Dangaroo Press, Mundelstrup, Denmark
Dawson	Dawson Publishing, Folkestone, Kent
DBP	Drama Book Pubs., New York
De Boeck	De Boeck-Wesmael, Brussels
De Graaf	De Graaf, Nierwkoup, Netherlands
Denoël	Denoël S.A.R.L., Paris
Dent	J. M. Dent, London
DentA	Dent, Ferntree Gully, Vic., Australia
Depanee	Depanee Printers and Pubs., Nugegoda, Sri Lanka
Deutsch	André Deutsch, London
Didier	Didier Erudition, Paris
Diesterweg	Verlag Moritz Diesterweg, Frankfurt-on-Main
Doaba	Doaba House, Delhi
Dobson	Dobson Books, Durham
Dolmen	Dolmen Press, Portlaoise, Eire
Donald	John Donald, Edinburgh
Donker	Adriaan Donker, Johannesburg
Doubleday	Doubleday, London and New York
Dove	Dove, Sydney
Dover	Dover Pubns, New York
Drew	Richard Drew, Ediburgh
Droste	Droste Verlag, Düsseldorf
Droz	Librairie Droz S.A., Geneva
DublinUP	Dublin UP, Dublin
Duckworth	Gerald Duckworth, London
Duculot	J. Duculot, Gembloux, Belgium
DukeUP	Duke UP, Durham, N.C.
Dundurn	Dundurn Press, Toronto and London, Ont.
Duquesne	Duquesne UP, Pittsburgh
Dutton	E. P. Dutton, New York
DWT	Dr Williams's Trust, London
EA	The English Association, London
Eason	Eason & Son, Dublin
Ebony	Ebony Books, Melbourne
Ecco	Ecco Press, New York
ECNRS	Editions du Centre National de la Recherche Scientifique, Paris
ECW	ECW Press, Downsview, Ont.
Eden	Eden Press, Montreal and St Albans, Vt.
EdinUP	Edinburgh UP, Edinburgh
Eerdmans	William Eerdmans, Grand Rapids, Mich.
EETS	Early English Text Society, c/o Exeter College, Oxford
Elephas	Elephas Books, Kewdale, Australia
Elm Tree	Elm Tree Books, London
Ember	Ember Press, Brixham, South Devon
EMSH	Editions de la Maison des Sciences de l'Homme, Paris

Enitharmon	Enitharmon Press, London
Enzyklopädie	Enzyklopädie, Leipzig
EPNS	English Place-Name Society, Beeston, Notts.
Epworth	The Epworth Press, Manchester
Eriksson	Paul Eriksson, Middlebury, Vt.
Erskine	Erskine Press, Harleston, Norfolk
ESI	Edizioni Scientifiche Italiane, Naples
ESL	Edizioni di Storia e Letteratura, Rome
EUFS	Editions Universitaires Fribourg Suisse
EUL	Edinburgh Univ. Library, Edinburgh
Europa	Europa Pubns, London
Exile	Exile Editions, Toronto, Ont.
Eyre	Eyre Methuen, London
FAB	Free Association Books, London
Faber	Faber & Faber, London
FAC	Fédération d'Activités Culturelles, Paris
FACP	Fremantle Arts Centre Press, Fremantle, W. A.
FALS	Foundation for Australian Literary Studies, James Cook Univ. of North Queensland, Townsville
F&F	Fels & Firn Press, San Anselmo, Calif.
F&S	Feffer & Simons, Amsterdam
Farrand	Farrand Press, London
Fay	Barbara Fay, Stuttgart
F-B	Ford-Brown, Houston, Texas
FDUP	Fairleigh Dickinson UP, Madison, N.J.
FE	Fourth Estate, London
Feminist	Feminist Press, New York
FictionColl	Fiction Collective, Brooklyn College, Brooklyn, N.Y.
Field Day	Field Day, Derry
Fifth House	Fifth House Publications, Saskatoon, Saskatchewan, Canada
FILEF	FILEF Italo-Australian Pubns, Leichhardt, N.S.W.
Fine	Donald Fine, New York
Fink	Fink Verlag, Munich
Flammarion	Flammarion, Paris
FlindersU	Flinders Univ. of South Australia, Bedford Park
FlorSU	Florida State Univ., Tallahassee, Fla.
FOF	Facts on File, New York
Folger	The Folger Shakespeare Library, Washington, D.C.
Folio	Folio Press, London
Fontana	Fontana Press, London
Footprint	Footprint Press, Colchester, Essex
FordUP	Fordham UP, New York
Foris	Foris Pubns, Dordrecht
Forsten	Egbert Forsten Pub., Groningen, Netherlands
Fortress	Fortress Press, Philadelphia
Francke	Francke Verlag, Berne
Franklin	Burt Franklin, New York
FreeP	Free Press, New York
FreeUP	Free UP, Amsterdam

Freundlich	Freundlich Books, New York
Frommann-Holzboog	Frommann-Holzboog, Stuttgart
FSP	Five Seasons Press, Madley, Hereford
FW	Fragments West/Valentine Press, Long Beach, Calif.
FWA	Fiji Writers' Association, Suva
FWP	Falling Wall Press, Bristol
Gale	Gale Research, Detroit, Mich.
Galilée	Galilée, Paris
Gallimard	Gallimard, Paris
G&G	Grevatt & Grevatt, Newcastle upon Tyne
G&M	Gill & Macmillan, Dublin
Garland	Garland Pub., New York
Gasson	Roy Gasson Associates, Wimborne, Dorset
Gateway	Gateway Editions, Washington, D.C.
Girasole	Edizioni del Girasole, Ravenna
GL	Goose Lane Editions, Fredericton, N.B.
GlasgowDL	Glasgow District Libraries, Glasgow
Gleerup	Gleerupska, Lund
Gliddon	Gliddon Books Pubs., Norwich
GMP	GMP Pub., London
GMSmith	Gibbs M. Smith, Layton, Utah
Golden Dog	The Golden Dog, Ottawa
Gollancz	Victor Gollancz, London
Gomer	Gomer Press, Llandysul, Dyfed
GothU	Gothenburg Univ. Gothenburg
Gower	Gower Pub., Aldershot, Hants.
Grafton	Grafton Books, London
Granta	Granta Publications, London
Granville	Granville Pub., London
Grasset	Grasset & Fasquelle, Paris
Grassroots	Grassroots, London
Graywolf	Graywolf Press, St Paul, Minn.
Greenhalgh	M. J. Greenhalgh, London
Greenhill	Greenhill Books, London
Greenwood	Greenwood Press, Westport, Conn.
Gregg	Gregg Publishing, Surrey
Greymitre	Greymitre Books, London
Groos	Julius Groos Verlag, Heidelberg
Grove	Grove Press, New York
Grüner	B. R. Grüner, Amsterdam
Gruyter	Walter de Gruyter, Berlin
Guernica	Guernica Editions, Montreal, Canada
Gulmohar	Gulmohar Press, Islamabad, Pakistan
HakluytS	Hakluyt Society, c/o British Library, London
Hale	Robert Hale, London
Hall	G. K. Hall, Boston, Mass.
Hambledon	Hambledon Press, London
H&I	Hale & Iremonger, Sydney
H&M	Holmes & Meier, London and New York
H&S	Hodder & Stoughton, London

H&SNZ	Hodder & Stoughton, Auckland
H&W	Hill & Wang, New York
Hansib	Hansib Pub., London
Harbour	Harbour Pub., Madeira Park, B.C.
Harman	Harman Pub. House, New Delhi
Harper	Harper & Row, New York
Harrap	Harrap, Edinburgh
HarvardUP	Harvard UP, Cambridge, Mass.
HBJ	Harcourt Brace Jovanovich, New York and London
HC	HarperCollins, London
Headline	Headline Book Pub., London
Heath	D. C. Heath, Lexington, Mass.
Heinemann	William Heinemann, London
HeinemannA	William Heinemann, St Kilda, Vic.
HeinemannC	Heinemann Educational Books, Kingston, Jamaica
HeinemannNZ	Heinemann Pubs., Auckland (now Heinemann Reed)
HeinemannR	Heinemann Reed, Auckland
Helm	Christopher Helm, London
Herbert	Herbert Press, London
Hern	Nick Hern Books, London
Heyday	Heyday Books, Berkeley, Calif.
HH	Hamish Hamilton, London
Hilger	Adam Hilger, Bristol
HM	Harvey Miller, London
HMSO	HMSO, London
Hodge	A. Hodge, Penzance, Cornwall
Hogarth	Hogarth Press, London
Hong KongUP	Hong Kong UP, Hong Kong
Horwood	Ellis Horwood, Hemel Hempstead, Herts.
HoughtonM	Houghton Mifflin, Boston, Mass.
Howard	Howard UP, Washington, D.C.
HRW	Holt, Rinehart & Winston, New York
Hueber	Max Hueber, Ismaning, Germany
HUL	Hutchinson Univ. Library, London
HullUP	Hull UP, Univ. of Hull
Humanities	Humanities Press, Atlantic Highlands, N.J.
Huntington	Huntington Library, San Marino, Calif.
Hutchinson	Hutchinson Books, London
HW	Harvester Wheatsheaf, Hemel Hempstead, Herts.
HWWilson	H. W. Wilson, New York
Hyland House	Hyland House Publishing, Victoria, Australia
Ian Henry	Ian Henry Pubns, Hornchurch, Essex
IAP	Irish Academic Press, Dublin
IBK	Innsbrucker Beiträge zur Kulturwissenschaft, Univ. of Innsbruck
ICA	Institute of Contemporary Arts, London
IHA	International Hopkins Association, Waterloo, Ont.
IJamaica	Institute of Jamaica Pubns, Kingston
Imago	Imago Imprint, New York
IndUP	Indiana UP, Bloomington, Ind.

Inkblot	Inkblot Pubns, Berkeley, Calif.
IntUP	International Universities Press, New York
Inventions	Inventions Press, London
IonaC	Iona College,. New Rochelle, N.Y.
IowaSUP	Iowa State UP, Ames, Iowa
IOWP	Isle of Wight County Press, Newport, Isle of Wight
IP	In Parenthesis, London
Ipswich	Ipswich Press, Ipswich, Mass.
ISI	ISI Press, Philadelphia
Italica	Italica Press, New York
IULC	Indiana Univ. Linguistics Club, Bloomington, Ind.
IUP	Indiana Univ. of Pennsylvania Press, Indiana, Pa.
Ivon	Ivon Pub. House, Bombay
Jacaranda	Jacaranda Wiley, Milton, Queensland
JadavpurU	Jadavpur Univ., Calcutta
James CookU	James Cook Univ. of North Queensland, Townsville
Jarrow	Parish of Jarrow, Tyne and Wear
Jesperson	Jesperson Press, St John's, Newfoundland
JHall	James Hall, Leamington Spa, Warwickshire
JHUP	Johns Hopkins UP, Baltimore, Md.
JIWE	JIWE Pubns, Univ. of Gulbarga, India
JLRC	Jack London Research Center, Glen Ellen, Calif.
Jonas	Jonas Verlag, Marburg, Germany
Joseph	Michael Joseph, London
Journeyman	The Journeyman Press, London
JT	James Thin, Edinburgh
Junction	Junction Books, London
Junius-Vaughan	The Junius-Vaughan Press, Fairview, N.J.
Jupiter	Jupiter Press, Lake Bluff, Ill.
JyväskyläU	Jyväskylä Univ., Jyväskylä, Finland
Kaibunsha	Kaibunsha, Tokyo
K&N	Königshausen & Neumann, Würzburg, Germany
K&W	Kaye & Ward, London
Kansai	Kansai Univ. of Foreign Studies, Osaka
Kardo	Kardo, Coatbridge, Scotland
Karia	Karia Press, London
Karnak	Karnak House, London
Karoma	Karoma Pubs., Ann Arbor, Mich.
KCL	King's College London
Kegan Paul	Kegan Paul International, London
Kenkyu	Kenkyu-Sha, Tokyo
Kennikat	Kennikat Press, Port Washington, N.Y.
Kensal	Kensal Press, Oxford
KenyaLB	Kenya Literature Bureau, Nairobi
Kerosina	Kerosina Pubns, Worcester Park, Surrey
Kerr	Charles H. Kerr, Chicago
Kestrel	Viking Kestrel, London
K/H	Kendall/Hunt Pub., Dubuque, Iowa
Kingsley	J. Kingsley Publishers, London
Kingston	Kingston Pubs., Kingston, Jamaica

Kinseido	Kinseido, Tokyo
Klostermann	Vittorio Klostermann, Frankfurt-on-Main
Knopf	Alfred A. Knopf, New York
Knowledge	Knowledge Industry Pubns, White Plains, N.Y.
Kraus	Kraus International Pubns, White Plains, N.Y.
KSUP	Kent State UP, Kent, Ohio
LA	Library Association, London
Lake View	Lake View Press, Chicago
LAm	Library of America, New York
Lancelot	Lancelot Press, Hantsport, N.S.
Landesman	Jay Landesman, London
L&W	Lawrence & Wishart, London
Lane	Allen Lane, London
Lang	Peter D. Lang, Frankfurt-on-Main and Berne
LC	Library of Congress, Washington, D.C.
LCP	Loras College Press, Dubuque, Iowa
LeedsUP	Leeds UP, Leeds
LeicsCC	Leicestershire County Council, Libraries and Information Service, Leicester
LeicUP	Leicester UP, Leicester
LeidenUP	Leiden UP, Leiden
Leopard's Head	Leopard's Head Press, Oxford
LeuvenUP	Leuven UP, Leuven, Belgium
Lexik	Lexik House, Cold Spring, N.Y.
LF	LiberFörlag, Stockholm
LH	Lund Humphries Pubs., London
Liberty	Liberty Classics, Indianapolis, Ind.
Libris	Libris, London
Liguori	Liguori, Naples
Lime Tree	Lime Tree Press, Octopus Publishing Group, London
LittleH	Little Hills Press, Burwood, N.S.W.
Liveright	Liveright Pub., New York
LiverUP	Liverpool UP, Liverpool
Livre de Poche	Le Livre de Poche, Paris
Llanerch	Llanerch Enterprises, Lampeter, Dyfed
Locust Hill	Locust Hill Press, West Cornwall, Conn.
Loewenthal	Loewenthal Press, New York
Longman	Longman Group, Harlow, Essex
LongmanNZ	Longman, Auckland
Longspoon	Longspoon Press, Univ. of Alberta, Edmonton
Lovell	David Lovell Publishing, Brunswick, Australia
Lowell	Lowell Press, Kansas City, Mo.
Lowry	Lowry Pubs., Johannesburg
LSUP	Louisiana State UP, Baton Rouge, La.
LundU	Lund Univ., Lund, Sweden
LUP	Loyola UP, Chicago
Lymes	Lymes Press, Newcastle, Staffs.
MAA	Medieval Academy of America, Cambridge, Mass.
Macmillan	Macmillan Pubs., London
Madison	Madison Books, Lanham, Md.

Madurai	Madurai Univ., Madurai, India
Maecenas	Maecenas Press, Iowa City, Iowa
Magabala	Magabala Books, Broome, W.A.
Mainstream	Mainstream Pub., Edinburgh
Maisonneuve	Maisonneuve Press, Washington, D.C.
Malone	Malone Society, c/o King's College, London
Mambo	Mambo Press, Gweru, Zimbabwe
ManCASS	Manchester Centre for Anglo-Saxon Studies, Univ. of Manchester
M&E	Macdonald & Evans, Estover, Plymouth, Devon
M&S	McClelland & Stewart, Toronto
Maney	W. S. Maney & Sons, Leeds
Mansell	Mansell Pub., London
Manufacture	La Manufacture, Lyons
ManUP	Manchester UP, Manchester
MarquetteUP	Marquette UP, Milwaukee, Wisc.
Marvell	The Marvell Press, Calstock, Cornwall
MB	Mitchell Beazley, London
McFarland	McFarland, Jefferson, N.C.
McG-QUP	McGill-Queen's UP, Montreal
McGraw-Hill	McGraw-Hill, New York
McIndoe	John McIndoe, Dunedin, New Zealand
McPheeG	McPhee Gribble Pubs., Fitzroy, Vic.
McPherson	McPherson, Kingston, N.Y.
ME	M. Evans, New York
Meany	P. D. Meany Pubs., Port Credit, Ont.
Meckler	Meckler Pub., Westport, Conn.
MelbourneUP	Melbourne UP, Carlton South, Vic.
Mellen	Edwin Mellen Press, Lewiston, N.Y.
MercerUP	Mercer UP, Macon, Ga.
Merlin	The Merlin Press, London
Methuen	Methuen, London
MethuenA	Methuen Australia, North Ryde, N.S.W.
MethuenC	Methuen, Toronto
Metro	Metro Pub., Auckland
Metzler	Metzler, Stuttgart
MGruyter	Mouton de Gruyter, Berlin, New York, and Amsterdam
MH	Michael Haag, London
MHRA	Modern Humanities Research Association, London
MI	Microforms International, Pergamon Press, Oxford
Micah	Micah Pubns, Marblehead, Mass.
MichSUP	Michigan State UP, East Lansing, Mich.
MidNAG	Mid Northumberland Arts Group, Ashington, Northumbria
Milestone	Milestone Pubns, Horndean, Hampshire
Millenium	Millenium Books, E. J. Dwyer Pty Ltd, Newtown, Australia
Millstream	Millstream Books, Bath
Milner	Milner, London
Minuit	Editions de Minuit, Paris
MIP	Medieval Institute Pubns, Western Michigan Univ.,

	Kalamazoo
MITP	Massachusetts Institute of Technology Press, Cambridge, Mass.
MLA	Modern Language Association of America, New York
MlM	Multilingual Matters, Clevedon, Avon
MLP	Manchester Literary and Philosophical Society, Manchester
Moonraker	Moonraker Press, Bradford-on-Avon, Wilts.
Moorland	Moorland Pub., Ashbourne, Derbys.
Moreana	Moreana, Angers, France
MorganSU	Morgan State Univ., Baltimore, Md.
Morrow	William Morrow, New York
Mosaic	Mosaic Press, Oakville, Ont.
Motilal	Motilal Books, Oxford
Motley	Motley Press, Romsey, Hampshire
Mouton	Mouton Pubs, New York and Paris
Mowbray	A. R. Mowbray, Oxford
MR	Martin Robertson, Oxford
MRS	Medieval and Renaissance Society, North Texas State Univ., Denton
MRTS	MRTS, Binghamton, N.Y.
MSUP	Memphis State UP, Memphis, Tenn.
MtAllisonU	Mount Allison Univ., Sackville, N.B.
Muller	Frederick Muller, London
Murray	John Murray, London
Mursia	Ugo Mursia, Milan
NAL	New American Library, New York
Narr	Gunter Narr Verlag, Tübingen
Nathan	Fernand Nathan, Paris
NBB	New Beacon Books, London
NBCAus	National Book Council of Australia, Melbourne
NCP	New Century Press, Durham
ND	New Directions, New York
NDT	Nottingham Drama Texts, c/o Univ., of Nottingham
NEL	New English Library, London
NELM	National English Literary Museum, Grahamstown, S. Africa
Nelson	Nelson Pubs., Melbourne
NeWest	NeWest Press, Edmonton, Alberta
New Horn	New Horn Press, Ibadan, Nigeria
NewIssuesP	New Issues Press, Western Michigan University
NH	New Horizon Press, Far Hills, N.J.
N-H	Nelson-Hall, Chicago
NHPC	North-Holland Pub., Amsterdam and New York
NIE	La Nuova Italia Editrice, Florence
Niemeyer	Max Niemeyer, Tübingen, Germany
Nightwood	Nightwood Editions, Toronto
NIUP	Northern Illinois UP, De Kalb, Ill.
NLB	New Left Books, London
NLC	National Library of Canada, Ottawa
NLP	New London Press, Dallas, Texas

NLS	National Library of Scotland, Edinburgh
NLW	National Library of Wales, Aberystwyth, Dyfed
Northcote	Northcote House Pubs., Plymouth
NortheasternU	Northeastern Univ., Boston, Mass.
NorthwesternUP	Northwestern UP, Evanston, Ill.
Norton	W. W. Norton, New York and London
NorUP	Norwegian University Press, Oslo
NPF	National Poetry Foundation, Orono, Maine
NPG	National Portrait Gallery, London
NPP	North Point Press, Berkeley, Calif.
NSP	New Statesman Pub., New Delhi
NSWUP	New South Wales UP, Kensington, N.S.W.
NTC	National Textbook, Lincolnwood, Ill.
NUC	Nipissing Univ. College, North Bay, Ont.
NUP	National Univ. Pubns, Millwood, N.Y.
NUU	New Univ. of Ulster, Coleraine
NWAP	North Waterloo Academic Press, Waterloo, Ont.
NWP	New World Perspectives, Montreal
NYPL	New York Public Library, New York
NYUP	New York UP, New York
O&B	Oliver & Boyd, Harlow, Essex
Oasis	Oasis Books, London
OBAC	Organization of Black American Culture, Chicago
O'Brien	The O'Brien Press, Dublin
OBS	Oxford Bibliographical Society, Bodleian Library, Oxford
Octopus	Octopus Books, London
OdenseUP	Odense UP, Odense
OE	Officina Edizioni, Rome
OEColl	Old English Colloquium, Berkeley, Calif.
Offord	John Offord Pubns, Eastbourne, E. Sussex
OhioUP	Ohio UP, Athens, Ohio
Oldcastle	Oldcastle Books, Harpenden, Herts.
Olms	Georg Olms, Hildesheim, Germany
Olschki	Leo S. Olschki, Florence
O'Mara	Michael O'Mara Books, London
Omnigraphics	Omnigraphics, Detroit, Mich.
Open Books	Open Books Pub., Wells, Somerset
OpenUP	Open UP, Buckingham and Philadelphia
OPP	Oxford Polytechnic Press, Oxford
Orbis	Orbis Books, London
Oriel	Oriel Press, Stocksfield, Northumb.
OrientUP	Oriental UP, London
Orwell	Orwell Press, Southwold, Suffolk
Oryx	Oryx Press, Phoenix, Ariz.
OSUP	Ohio State UP, Columbus, Ohio
OTP	Oak Tree Press, London
OUP	Oxford UP, Oxford
OUPAm	Oxford UP Inc., New York
OUPAus	Oxford UP, Melbourne
OUPC	Oxford UP, Toronto

OUPI	Oxford UP, New Delhi
OUPNZ	Oxford UP, Auckland
OUPSA	Oxford UP Southern Africa, Cape Town
Outlet	Outlet Book Co., New York
Owen	Peter Owen, London
Pacifica	Press Pacifica, Kailua, Hawaii
Paget	Paget Press, Santa Barbara, Calif.
PAJ	PAJ Pubns, New York
Paladin	Paladin Books, London
Pan	Pan Books, London
PanAmU	Pan American Univ., Edinburgh, Texas
P&C	Pickering & Chatto, London
Pandora	Pandora Press, London
Pantheon	Pantheon Books, New York
ParagonH	Paragon House Pubs., New York
Parousia	Parousia Pubns, London
Paternoster	Paternoster Press, Carlisle, Cumbria
Paulist	Paulist Press, Ramsey, N.J.
Paupers	Paupers' Press, Nottingham
Pavilion	Pavilion Books, London
PBFA	Provincial Booksellers's Fairs Association, Cambridge
Peachtree	Peachtree Pubs., Atlanta, Ga.
Pearson	David Pearson, Huntingdon, Cambs.
Peepal Tree	Peepal Tree Books, Leeds
Pelham	Pelham Books, London
Pembridge	Pembridge Press, London
Pemmican	Pemmican Publications, Winnipeg, Canada
Penguin	Penguin Books, Harmondsworth, Middx.
PenguinA	Penguin Books, Ringwood, Vic.
PenguinNZ	Penguin Books, Auckland
Penkevill	The Penkevill Pub. Co., Greenwood, Fla.
Penumbra	Penumbra Press, Moonbeam, Ont.
People's	People's Pubns, London
Pergamon	Pergamon Press, Oxford
Permanent	Permanent Press, Sag Harbor, N.Y.
Perpetua	Perpetua Press, Oxford
Pevensey	Pevensey Press, Newton Abbott, Devon
PH	Prentice-Hall, Englewood Cliffs, N.J.
Phaidon	Phaidon Press, London
PHI	Prentice-Hall International, Hemel Hempstead, Herts.
PhilL	Philosophical Library, New York
Phillimore	Phillimore, Chichester
Piatkus	Piatkus Books, London
Pickwick	Pickwick Pubns, Allison Park, Pa.
Pilgrim	Pilgrim Books, Norman, Okla.
PIMS	Pontifical Institute of Mediaeval Studies, Toronto
Pinter	Frances Pinter Pubs., London
Plains	Plains Books, Carlisle
Plenum	Plenum Pub., London and New York
Plexus	Plexus Pub., London

Ploughshares	Ploughshares Books, Watertown, Mass.
Pluto	Pluto Press, London
PML	Pierpont Morgan Library, New York
Polity	Polity Press, Oxford
Polygon	Polygon, Edinburgh
Poolbeg	Poolbeg Press, Swords, Co. Dublin
Porcepic	Press Porcepic, Victoria, B.C.
Porcupine	Porcupine's Quill, Canada
PortN	Port Nicholson Press, Wellington, N.Z.
Potter	Clarkson N. Potter, New York
Power	Power Pubns, Univ. of Sydney
PPUBarcelona	Promociones y Publicaciones Universitarias, Barcelona
PrestigeB	Prestige Books, New Delhi
Primavera	Edizioni Primavera, Giunti Publishing Group, Florence, Italy
Primrose	Primrose Press, Alhambra, Calif.
PrincetonUL	Princeton Univ. Library, Princeton, N.J.
PrincetonUP	Princeton UP, Princeton, N.J.
Printwell	Printwell Pubs., Jaipur, India
Prism	Prism Press, Bridport, Dorset
PRO	Public Record Office, London
Profile	Profile Books, Ascot, Berks
ProgP	Progressive Pubs., Calcutta
PSUP	Pennsylvania State UP, University Park, Pa.
Pucker	Puckerbrush Press, Orono, Maine
PUF	Presses Universitaires de France, Paris
PurdueUP	Purdue UP, Lafayette, Ind.
Pushcart	Pushcart Press, Wainscott, N.Y.
Pustet	Friedrich Pustet, Regensburg
Putnam	Putnam Pub. Group, New York
PWP	Poetry Wales Press, Ogmore by Sea, Mid Glam.
QED	Q.E.D. Press of Ann Arbor, Mich.
Quartet	Quartet Books, London
RA	Royal Academy of Arts, London
Rampant Lions	Rampant Lions Press, Cambridge
R&B	Rosenkilde & Bagger, Copenhagen
R&L	Rowman & Littlefield, Totowa, N.J.
RandomH	Random House, London and New York
Ravan	Ravan Press, Johannesburg
Ravette	Ravette, London
Rebel	The Rebel Press, London
Red Kite	Red Kite Press, Guelph, Ont.
Reference	Reference Press, Toronto
Regents	Regents Press of Kansas, Lawrence, Kansas
Reichenberger	Roswitha Reichenberger, Kessel, Germany
Reinhardt	Max Reinhardt, London
Remak	Remak, Alblasserdam, Netherlands
RenI	Renaissance Institute, Sophia Univ., Tokyo
Research	Research Pubns, Reading
RETS	Renaissance English Text Society, Chicago

RH	Ramsay Head Press, Edinburgh
RHS	Royal Historical Society, London
RIA	Royal Irish Academy, Dublin
RiceUP	Rice UP, Houston, Texas
Richarz	Hans Richarz, St Augustin, Germany
RICL	Research Institute for Comparative Literature, Univ. of Alberta
Rizzoli	Rizzoli International Pubns., New Yorks
RobartsCCS	Robarts Centre for Canadian Studies, York Univ., North York, Ont.
Robinson	Robinson Pub., London
Robson	Robson Books, London
Rodopi	Rodopi, Amsterdam
Roebuck	Stuart Roebuck, Suffolk
RoehamptonI	Roehampton Institute of Higher Education, London
Routledge	Routledge, London and New York
Royce	Robert Royce, London
RS	The Royal Society, London
RSC	Royal Shakespeare Co., London
RSL	Royal Society of Literature, London
RSVP	Research Society for Victorian Periodicals, Univ. of Leicester
RT	R.T. Pubns, London
Running	Running Press, Philadelphia
Russell	Michael Russell, Norwich
RutgersUP	Rutgers UP, New Brunswick, N.J.
Ryan	Ryan Pub., London
SA	Sahitya Akademi, New Delhi
SAI	Sociological Abstracts, San Diego, Calif.
Sage	Sage Pubns, London
Salamander	Salamander Books, London
S&A	Shukayr and Akasheh, Amman, Jordan
S&D	Stein & Day, Briarcliff Manor, N.Y.
S&J	Sidgwick & Jackson, London
S&M	Sun & Moon Press, Los Angeles
S&P	Simon & Pierre, Toronto
S&S	Simon & Schuster, New York and London
S&W	Secker & Warburg, London
Sangam	Sangam Books, London
Sangsters	Sangsters Book Stores, Kingston, Jamaica
SAP	Scottish Academic Press, Edinbugh
Saur	Bowker-Saur, Sevenoaks, Kent
Savacou	Savacou Pubns, Kingston, Jamaica
S-B	Schwann-Bagel, Düsseldorf
Scarecrow	Scarecrow Press, Metuchen, N.J.
Schäuble	Schäuble Verlag, Rheinfelden, Germany
Schneider	Lambert Schneider, Heidelberg
Schocken	Schocken Books, New York
Scholarly	Scholarly Press, St Clair Shores, Mich.
ScholarsG	Scholars Press, Georgia

Schöningh	Ferdinand Schöningh, Paderborn, Germany
Schwinn	Michael Schwinn, Neustadt, Germany
Scolar	Scolar Press, Aldershot, Hampshire
SCP	Second Chance Press, Sag Harbor, N.Y.
Scribe	Scribe Publishing, Colchester
Scribner	Charles Scribner's Sons, New York
Seafarer	Seafarer Books, London
Seaver	Seaver Books, New York
Segue	Segue, New York
Semiotext(e)	Semiotext(e), Columbia Univ., New York
Seren Books	Seren Books, Bridgend, Mid Glamorgan
Serpent's Tail	Serpent's Tail Pub., London
Sessions	William Sessions, York
Seuil	Editions du Seuil, Paris
7:84 Pubns	7:84 Pubns, Glasgow
Severn	Severn House, Wallington, Surrey
SF&R	Scholars' Facsimiles and Reprints, Delmar, N.Y.
SH	Somerset House, Teaneck, N.J.
Shalabh	Shalabh Book House, Meerut, India
ShAP	Sheffield Academic Press
Shearwater	Shearwater Press, Lenah Valley, Tasmania
Sheba	Sheba Feminist Pubs., London
Sheed&Ward	Sheed & Ward, London
Sheldon	Sheldon Press, London
SHESL	Société d'Histoire et d'Épistemologie des Sciences du Langage, Paris
Shinozaki	Shinozaki Shorin, Tokyo
Shinshindo	Shinshindo Pub., Tokyo
Shire	Shire Pubns, Princes Risborough, Bucks.
Shoe String	Shoe String Press, Hamden Conn.
SIAS	Scandinavian Institute of African Studies, Uppsala
SIL	Summer Institute of Linguistics, Academic Pubns, Dallas, Texas
Simon King	Simon King Press, Milnthorpe, Cumbria
Sinclair-Stevenson	Sinclair-Stevenson, London
SingaporeUP	Singapore UP, Singapore
SIUP	Southern Illinois UP, Carbondale, Ill.
SJSU	San Jose State Univ., San Jose, Calif.
Skilton	Charles Skilton, London
Skoob	Skoob Books Pub., London
Slatkine	Editions Slatkine, Paris
Slavica	Slavica Pubs., Columbus, Ohio
Sleepy Hollow	Sleepy Hollow Press, Tarrytown, N.Y.
SLG	SLG Press, Oxford
SMUP	Southern Methodist UP, Dallas, Texas
Smythe	Colin Smythe, Gerrards Cross, Bucks.
SNH	Société Néophilologique de Helsinki
SNLS	Society for New Language Study, Denver, Colo.
SOA	Society of Authors, London
Soho	Soho Book Co., London

SohoP	Soho Press, New York
Solaris	Solaris Press, Rochester, Mich.
SonoNis	Sono Nis Press, Victoria, B.C.
Sorbonne	Pubns de la Sorbonne, Paris
SorbonneN	Pubns du Conseil Scientifique de la Sorbonne Nouvelle, Paris
Souvenir	Souvenir Press, London
SPACLALS	South Pacific Association for Commonwealth Literature and Language Studies, Wollongong, N.S.W.
SPCK	SPCK, London
Spectrum	Spectrum Books, Ibadan, Nigeria
Split Pea	Split Pea Press, Edinburgh
Spokesman	Spokesman Books, Nottingham
Spoon River	Spoon River Poetry Press, Granite Falls, Minn.
SRC	Steinbeck Research Center, San Jose State Univ., San Jose, Calif.
SRI	Steinbeck Research Institute, Ball State Univ., Muncie, Ind.
SriA	Sri Aurobindo, Pondicherry, India
Sri Satguru	Sri Satguru Pubns, Delhi
SSA	John Steinbeck Society of America, Muncie, Ind.
SSAB	Sprakförlaget Skriptor AB, Stockholm
StanfordUP	Stanford UP, Stanford, Calif.
Staple	Staple, Matlock, Derbyshire
Starmont	Starmont House, Mercer Island, Wash.
Starrhill	Starrhill Press, Washington, D.C.
Station Hill	Station Hill, Barrytown, N.Y.
Stauffenburg	Stauffenburg Verlag, Tübingen, Germany
StDL	St Deiniol's Library, Hawarden, Clwyd
Steel Rail	Steel Rail Pub., Ottawa
Steiner	Franz Steiner, Wiesbaden, Germany
Sterling	Sterling Pub., New York
SterlingND	Sterling Pubs., New Delhi
St James	St James Press, Andover, Hampshire
St Martin's	St Martin's Press, New York
Stockwell	Arthur H. Stockwell, Ilfracombe, Devon
Stoddart	Stoddart Pub., Don Mills, Ont.
StPB	St Paul's Bibliographies, Winchester, Hampshire
STR	Society for Theatre Research, London
Strauch	R. O. U. Strauch, Ludwigsburg
Studio	Studio Editions, London
Stump Cross	Stump Cross Books, Stump Cross, Essex
Sud	Sud, Marseilles
Suhrkamp	Suhrkamp Verlag, Frankfurt-on-Main
Summa	Summa Pubns, Birmingham, Ala.
SUNYP	State Univ. of New York Press, Albany, N.Y.
Surtees	R. S. Surtees Society, Frome, Somerset
SusquehannaUP	Susquehanna UP, Selinsgrove, Pa.
SussexUP	Sussex UP, Univ. of Sussex, Brighton
Sutton	Alan Sutton, Stroud, Gloucester

S-W	Shepheard-Walwyn Pubs., London
Swallow	Swallow Press, Athens, Ohio
SWG	Saskatchewan Writers Guild, Regina
SydneyUP	Sydney UP, Sydney
SyracuseUP	Syracuse UP, Syracuse, N.Y.
Tabb	Tabb House, Padstow, Cornwall
Taishukan	Taishukan Pub., Tokyo
Talonbooks	Talonbooks, Vancouver
TamilU	Tamil Univ., Thanjavur, India
T&H	Thames & Hudson, London
Tantivy	Tantivy Press, London
Tarcher	Jeremy P. Tarcher, Los Angeles
Tate	Tate Gallery Pubns, London
Tavistock	Tavistock Pubns, London
Taylor	Taylor Pub., Bellingham, Wash.
TaylorCo	Taylor Pub., Dallas, Texas
TCG	Theatre Communications Group, New York
TCP	Three Continents Press, Washington, D.C.
TCUP	Texas Christian UP, Fort Worth, Texas
TEC	Third Eye Centre, Glasgow
Tecumseh	Tecumseh Press, Ottawa
Telos	Telos Press, St Louis, Mo.
TempleUP	Temple UP, Philadelphia
TennS	Tennyson Society, Lincoln
TexA&MUP	Texas A & M UP, College Station, Texas
TextileB	Textile Bridge Press, Clarence Center, N.Y.
TexTULib	Friends of the Univ. Library, Texas Tech Univ., Lubbock
The Smith	The Smith, New York
Thimble	Thimble Press, Stroud, Glos.
Thornes	Stanley Thornes, Cheltenham
Thorpe	D. W. Thorpe, Australia
Thorsons	Thorsons Pubs., London
Times	Times of Gloucester Press, Gloucester, Ont.
TMP	Thunder's Mouth Press, New York
Tombouctou	Tombouctou Books, Bolinas, Calif.
TorSVP	Sister Vision Press, Toronto
Totem	Totem Books, Don Mills, Ont.
Toucan	Toucan Press, St Peter Port, Guernsey
Touzot	Jean Touzot, Paris
TPF	Trianon Press Facsimiles, London
Tragara	Tragara Press, Edinburgh
Transaction	Transaction Pubs., New Brunswick, N.J.
Transcendental	Transcendental Books, Hartford, Conn.
Transworld	Transworld, London
TrinityUP	Trinity UP, San Antonio, Texas
TTUP	Texas Technical University Press, Lubbock
Tuduv	Tuduv, Munich
TulaneUP	Tulane UP, New Orleans, La.
TurkuU	Turku Univ., Turky, Finland
Turtle Island	Turtle Island Foundation, Berkeley, Calif.

Twayne	Twayne Pubs., Boston, Mass.
UAB	Univ. of Aston, Birmingham
UAdelaide	Univ. of Adelaide, Adelaide
UAlaP	Univ. of Alabama Press, Tuscaloosa
UAlbertaP	Univ. of Alberta Press, Edmonton
UAntwerp	Univ. of Antwerp, Antwerp
UArizP	Univ. of Arizona Press, Tucson
UArkP	Univ. of Arkansas Press, Fayetteville
UAthens	Univ. of Athens, Athens, Greece
UBarcelona	Univ. of Barcelona, Barcelona
UBCP	Univ. of British Columbia Press, Vancouver
UBergen	Univ. of Bergen, Bergen
UBrno	J.E. Purkyne Univ. of Brno, Brno, Czechoslovakia
UBrussels	Univ. of Brussels, Brussels
UCalgaryP	Univ. of Calgary Press, Calgary
UCalP	Univ. of California Press, Berkeley
UCAP	Univ. of Central Arkansas Press, Conway
UChicP	Univ. of Chicago Press, Chicago
UCopenP	Univ. of Copenhagen Press, Copenhagen
UDelP	Univ. of Delaware Press, Newark
UDijon	Univ. of Dijon, Dijon
UDur	Univ. of Durham, Durham
UErlangen-N	Univ. of Erlangen-Nuremberg, Germany
UEssex	Univ. of Essex, Colchester
UExe	Univ. of Exeter, Exeter
UFlorence	Univ. of Florence, Florence
UFlorP	Univ. of Florida Press, Florida
UGal	Univ. College, Galway
UGeoP	Univ. of Georgia Press, Athens
UGhent	Univ. of Ghent, Ghent
UGlasP	Univ. of Glasgow Press, Glasgow
UHawaiiP	Univ. of Hawaii Press, Honolulu
UIfeP	Univ. of Ife Press, Ile-Ife, Nigeria
UIllP	Univ. of Illinois Press, Champaign
UInnsbruck	Univ. of Innsbruck, Innsbruck
UIowaP	Univ. of Iowa Press, Iowa City
UKanP	Univ. of Kansas Press, Lawrence
UKL	Univ. of Kentucky Libraries, Lexington
ULavalP	Les Presses de l'Université Laval, Quebec
ULiège	Univ. of Liège, Liège, Belgium
ULilleP	Presses Universitaires de Lille, Lille
ULondon	Univ. of London, London
Ulster	Univ. of Ulster, Coleraine
U/M	Underwood/Miller, Los Angeles
UMalta	Univ. of Malta, Msida
UManitobaP	Univ. of Manitoba Press, Winnipeg
UMassP	Univ. of Massachusetts Press, Amherst
Umeå	Umeå Universitetsbibliotek, Umeå
UMel	Melbourne University Press, Victoria, Australia
UMichP	Univ. of Michigan Press, Ann Arbor

UMinnP	Univ. of Minnesota Press, Minneapolis
UMIRes	UMI Research Press, Ann Arbor, Mich.
UMissP	Univ. Of Missouri Press, Columbia
UMP	Univ. of Mississippi Press, Lafayette Co, Mississippi
UMysore	Univ. of Mysore, Mysore, India
UNancyP	Presses Universitaires de Nancy, France
UNCP	Univ. of North Carolina Press, Chapel Hill
Undena	Undena Pubns, Malibu, Calif.
UNDP	Univ. of Notre Dame Press, Notre Dame, Ind.
UNebP	Univ. of Nebraska Press, Lincoln
UNevP	Univ. of Nevada Press, Reno
UNewE	Univ. of New England, Armidale, N.S.W.
Ungar	Frederick Ungar, New York
Unicopli	Edizioni Unicopli, Milan
Universa	Uitgeverij Universa, Wetteren, Belgium
UNMP	Univ. of New Mexico Press, Albuquerque
UNott	Univ. of Nottingham, Nottingham
Unwin	Unwin Paperbacks, London
Unwin Hyman	Unwin Hyman, London
UOklaP	Univ. of Oklahoma Press, Norman
UOslo	Univ. of Oslo, Oslo
UOtagoP	Univ. of Otago Press, Dunedin, New Zealand
UOttawaP	Univ. of Ottawa Press, Ottawa
UPA	UP of America, Lanham, Md.
UParis	Univ. of Paris, Paris
UPColorado	UP of Colorado, Niwot
UPennP	Univ. of Pennsylvania Press, Philadelphia
UPFlor	Univ. Presses of Florida, Gainesville
UPittP	Univ. of Pittsburgh Press, Pittsburgh
UPKen	Univ. Press of Kentucky, Lexington
UPMissip	UP of Mississippi, Jackson
UPN	Université de Paris Nord, Paris
UPNE	UP Of New England, Hanover, N.H.
Uppsala	Uppsala Univ., Uppsala
UProvence	Univ. of Provence, Aix-en-Provence
UPValery	Univ. Paul Valery, Montpellier
UPVirginia	UP of Virginia, Charlottesville
UQP	Univ. of Queensland Press, St Lucia
URouen	Univ. of Rouen, Mont St Aignan
USalz	Institut für Anglistik und Amerikanistik, Univ. of Salzburg
USCP	Univ. of South Carolina Press, Columbia
USFlorP	Univ. of South Florida Press, Florida
USheff	Univ. of Sheffield, Sheffield
Usher	La Casa Usher, Florence
USPacific	Univ. of the South Pacific, Institute of Pacific Studies, Suva, Fiji
USzeged	Univ. of Szeged, Hungary
UtahSUP	Utah State UP, Logan
UTas	Univ. of Tasmania, Hobart
UTennP	Univ. of Tennessee Press, Knoxville

UTexP	Univ. of Texas Press, Austin
UTorP	Univ. of Toronto Press, Toronto
UVerm	Univ. of Vermont, Burlington
UVict	Univ. of Victoria, Victoria, B.C.
UWalesP	Univ. of Wales Press, Cardiff
UWAP	Univ. of Western Australia Press, Nedlands
UWarwick	Univ. of Warwick, Coventry
UWashP	Univ. of Washington Press, Seattle
UWaterlooP	Univ. of Waterloo Press, Waterloo, Ont.
UWI	Univ. of the West Indies, St Augustine, Trinidad
UWiscM	Univ. of Wisconsin, Milwaukee
UWiscP	Univ. of Wisconsin Press, Madison
UYork	Univ. of York, York
Valentine	Valentine Pub. and Drama, Rhinebeck, N.Y.
V&A	Victoria and Albert Museum, London
VanderbiltUP	Vanderbilt UP, Nashville, Tenn.
V&R	Vandenhoeck & Ruprecht, Göttingen, Germany
Vantage	Vantage Press, New York
Véhicule	Véhicule Press, Montreal
Verso	Verso Editions, London
VictUP	Victoria UP, Victoria Univ. of Wellington, New Zealand
Vikas	Vikas Pub. House, New Delhi
Viking	Viking Press, New York
VikingNZ	Viking, Auckland
Virago	Virago Press, London
Vision	Vision Press, London
VLB	VLB Editeur, Montreal
VR	Variorum Reprints, London
Vrin	J. Vrin, Paris
W&N	Weidenfeld & Nicolson, London
Water Row	Water Row Press, Sudbury, Mass.
Watkins	Paul Watkins, Stamford, Lincs.
WB	Wissenschaftliche Buchgesellschaft, Darmstadt
W/B	Woomer/Brotherson, Revere, Pa.
Webb&Bower	Webb & Bower, Exeter
Wedgestone	Wedgestone Press, Winfield, Kansas
WesleyanUP	Wesleyan UP, Middletown, Conn.
West	West Pub., St Paul, Minn.
Wheatsheaf	Wheatsheaf Books, Brighton
Whiteknights	Whiteknights Press, Univ. of Reading, Reading
Whitston	Whitston Pub., Troy, N.Y.
Whittington	Whittington Press, Herefordshire
WHP	Warren House Press, Sale, Cheshire
Wiener	Wiener Pub., New York
Wildwood	Wildwood House, Aldershot, Hampshire
Wiley	John Wiley & Sons, Chichester, New York, and Brisbane
Wilson	Philip Wilson, London
Winter	Carl Winter Universitätsverlag, Heidelberg, Germany
Winthrop	Winthrop Pubs., Cambridge, Mass.
WIU	Western Illinois Univ., Macomb, Ill.

WL	Ward Lock, London
WLUP	Wilfrid Laurier UP, Waterloo, Ont.
WMP	World Microfilms Pubns, London
WMU	Western Michigan Univ., Kalamazoo, Mich.
Wo-No	Wolters-Noordhoff, Groningen, Netherlands
Wolfhound	Wolfhound Press, Dublin
Wombat	The Wombat Press, Wolfville, N.S.
Woodstock	Woodstock Books, Oxford
Woolf	Cecil Woolf, London
Words	Words, Framfield, E. Sussex
WP	The Women's Press, London
WPC	The Women's Press of Canada, Toronto
WSUP	Wayne State UP, Detroit, Mich.
WVUP	West Virginia UP, Morgantown
W-W	Williams-Wallace, Toronto
WWU	Western Washington Univ., Bellingham
Xanadu	Xanadu Pubns, London
YaleUL	Yale Univ. Library Pubns, New Haven, Conn.
YaleUP	Yale UP, New Haven, Conn. and London
Yamaguchi	Yamaguchi Shoten, Kyoto
YorkP	York Press, Fredericton, N.B.
Younsmere	Younsmere Press, Brighton
Zed	Zed Books, London
Zena	Zena Pubns, Penrhyndeudraeth, Gwynedd
Zephyr	Zephyr Press, Somerville, Mass.
Zomba	Zomba Books, London
Zwemmer	A. Zwemmer, London

I

Reference, Literary History and Bibliography

PAUL BENNETT MORGAN

This chapter has three sections: 1. Reference Works; 2. Literary Histories; 3. Bibliography.

1. Reference Works

Sheer physical size seems an increasingly important factor in the production and marketing of reference works. If lifting a new one risks spinal injury, then it must surely be more comprehensive than a rival publisher's (which weighs a little less) and be a better bargain. From St James comes a battery of reference works evocative in style as well as size of the undisputed heavyweight champions, Garland. Of these, two turn out to be, in fact, UK reprints of Garland American editions: Robert Ross's *International Literature in English* and Katharina Wilson's *Encyclopedia of Continental Women Writers*. Both are necessarily selective but they are creditable resources in their respective fields, especially the former. Ross is a respected authority on literature in English, especially Australian writing, and the sixty essays in his volume are all labours of love, admirably presented, with selected critical readings as well as bibliographies. This volume lends a useful coherence to the study of literature in English, and gives ample evidence of its variety and vitality. D. L. Kirkpatrick's *Reference Guide to English Literature* and Paul E. Schellinger's *St James Guide to Biography* are not so successful. The former is a revamping of *Great Writers in the English Language* (1980) with the addition of a title index, and the latter a grab-bag of names from Abigail Adams to Hulderich Zwingli. Editorial principle seems to have been 'a little of everything does no harm', so that the 600 entries contain a few each of writers, artists, musicians, politicians, and so forth. For everyone included, a score of equally significant figures is left out. Thus Nijinsky is in but not Nureyev; the Buddha but not Lao Tse; Georgia O'Keefe but not Frida Kahlo; Lennon but not McCartney, and so on! The arbitrariness of this work makes it of very limited use. The last of these works from St James is Lesley Henderson's *Twentieth-Century Crime and Mystery Writers*. Comprehensive, authoritative, and with locations of manuscripts as well as bibliographies and biographical notes, for those with an interest in the genre this is an invaluable reference source.

Boris Ford takes an important step towards completing the *Cambridge Guide to the Arts in Britain* with the publication of *The Augustan Age*. This fifth volume in the set is well up to the high standard established by those already published. As before, Ford manages a broad survey without generalization, by the choice of expert contributors: Sally Jeffrey on architecture and Pat Rogers on literature, for example; by a generous but wise use of illustration and by well-researched biographical and bibliographical appendices. Sections on the individual arts are complemented by three chapters focusing on archetypal foci of the eighteenth century: Augustan Bath, Holkham Hall, Norfolk, and Vauxhall Gardens. These chapters work well, and play a strong part in this volume's evocation of British cultural life of the period. In *Victorian Art Reproductions in Modern Sources*, Kristine Garrigan has indexed illustrations of nineteenth-century paintings from eighty-four modern printed sources. As she writes in her preface, 'over the last two decades, Victorian art has begun to achieve long-denied aesthetic and academic respectability,' and the demand for pictorial sources has grown accordingly. The several thousand reproductions are listed by artist and title, and selectively by subject. I do have reservations about the utility of this work. Printed books remain in print a relatively short time these days; the majority of Garrigan's sources were published before 1980, and researchers must be prepared for a further challenge in actually laying hands on a work they need. There is also no indication of the size or quality of reproductions; as we all know, original works are often strikingly different from even the best photographic reproduction. The majority of reproductions described are also in monochrome. The majority, too, are of paintings located in Britain – a fact which ultimately justifies this volume. For an English researcher, the need to see G. F. Watts's *The Sower of the Systems* is a pleasant excuse to visit the Watts Gallery in Compton; for those of us who live in other parts of the world, this is a useful tool for locating the next best thing. I particularly appreciated the subject index where one is immediately able to put a finger on Victorian representations of Christmas, prisons, theatre audiences or shopkeepers, for example.

As the editors of *Brewer's Twentieth-Century Phrase and Fable* note in their introduction, 'because the twentieth century is not especially known for its fables, it has been necessary to interpret this word in the broader sense of "myths"; these range from famous murders and military disasters to political scandals and legendary film stars.' Much of the material in this new work has been drawn from the fourteenth edition of the principal *Brewer*, and – considering the quantity of warfare, murder, and scandal with which we are daily acquainted – the decision to treat modern references in a distinct volume from now on is a sensible one. The volatility of contemporary allusion can thus be accommodated at a different rate to that in the more established volume. This year also sees the appearance of *Brewer's Concise Dictionary of Phrase and Fable*, edited by B. Kirkpatrick, although I would be wary of buying an abridged *Brewer*; the phrase one wanted would be inevitably one of those omitted.

Bill Bryson's *Penguin Dictionary for Writers and Editors* is a new work aimed squarely at the market of the successful *Oxford Writers' Dictionary*. Both are recommended. The Oxford volume is more comprehensive; the Penguin volume is sometimes more informative, and takes more account of non-British English usage. New editions of the excellent *Chambers Concise Dictionary* and *Chambers Thesaurus* are matched by two new publications from OUP, the *Oxford Encyclopedic Dictionary* and *Oxford Thesaurus*. The *Oxford Concise* has recently taken a leaf (almost literally) out of the *Collins Concise Plus* by including considerably more general reference information, and the 1991 edition makes this popular change explicit by the new title. The *Oxford Thesaurus*, compiled by Laurence Urdang, is hailed as 'the new thesaurus for the 1990s' and it is indeed superior to the *Chambers Thesaurus*, which seems a crude synonym-list beside it. Urdang distinguishes between synonyms for different meanings under each headword, clearly labels each term geographically and stylistically, provides illustrative sentences, cross references, and an index. None of these features is present in the Chambers work, whose only advantage is an appendix of classified word lists, including specialist vocabularies (of the law and architecture, for example) and collective nouns (including the bizarre 'tok of capercailzies').

A number of authoritative reference works make a welcome appearance in paperback this year: Grimal's *Dictionary of Classical Mythology*, the Fleming and Pevsner *Penguin Dictionary of Architecture*, Baldick's *Concise Oxford Dictionary of Literary Terms*, Janet Todd's *Dictionary of British Women Writers*, David Crystal's *Cambridge Encyclopedia of Language*, Martin Manser's *Bloomsbury Good Word Guide*, and the concise 'Partridge', Paul Beale's updated edition of *A Concise Dictionary of Slang and Unconventional English*.

2. Literary Histories

(a) General Works

Gillian Tindall's *Countries of the Mind* discusses the meaning of place to writers through examination of various versions of landscapes as exploited by writers, and a wider consideration of how and why these 'countries of the mind' come about. Discussion is thematic rather than topographical, dealing with 'Versions of Paradise' and 'The Dream of Town' among other topics, and including chapters on the effect of railways on the sense of place, and on the metaphorical use of the house in fiction. Tindall has a relaxed, almost conversational tone, but this does not vitiate the book's incisiveness, and she has made a worthwhile contribution to the study of place in literature, a field which too often falls into mere literary travelogue. *Potboilers* is a useful survey by Jerry Palmer of popular fiction as an area of enquiry. He divides his study in half: first reviewing methods and concepts in currency over the last twenty years, then examining generic conventions in a selection of case studies. Palmer sometimes labours over matters which could be explained more simply (*film noir* and the concept of a serial, for example), but on the whole does well in explaining the field, warning of pitfalls (such as the differing definitions of violence used in different surveys of popular fiction), emphasizing empirical research on reader response rather than a putative implied reader, and alerting us to the better writings in the field, such as Radway's *Reading the Romance* (1984). Political fiction from Disraeli to the present is the subject of Christopher Harvie's *The Centre of Things*, a dry and entertaining re-evaluation of the genre. A lot of ground is covered – from *Coningsby* to *Yes, Minister* – and the language occasionally descends into diatribe ('Thatcherland, the home counties on which the *Sun* never set'), but when he focuses on a particular writer or issue (the contrast of intra- and extra-parliamentary political novels, for instance), Harvie's comments are always clear-sighted and useful. The Catholic novel in British literature receives praiseworthy attention in Thomas Woodman's *Faithful Fictions*. Abjuring a straightforward chronological study, Woodman deals with the historical aspect in a preliminary section, noting Adrian Hastings's observation that 'the British seem to believe there is only one true religion, Roman Catholicism, and that is wrong!' He then goes on to analyse the Catholic 'difference', images of the Church and the world, and finally the issue which principally concerns his subjects, 'the drama of good and evil that other writers do not see'. There is also an ample bibliography and a glossary of Catholic and theological terminology. Woodman's book is also commendable for the attention given to Alice Thomas Ellis, whose novels have yet to receive the serious critical attention they deserve.

Two further volumes in the EdinUP *Early Black Writers* series have appeared. Christopher Fyfe has edited *Our Children Free and Happy*, a selection of letters from Black settlers in Africa in the 1790s. Incited to escape from their American 'owners' during the War of Independence, thousands of freed slaves were able to return to Africa; the documents in this volume trace the unhappy story of what happened next, with explanatory notes and a linguistic analysis by Charles Jones. Of broader interest is the second work, *Black Writers in Britain, 1760-1890*, edited by the two responsible for the entire series, Paul Edwards and David Dabydeen. This volume contains nineteen contributors, ranging from Briton Hamilton, author of the first published work by a black writer in English (1760), to J. J. Thomas, whose *Froudacity* of 1889 is a witty and learned polemic against J. A. Froude's inaccurate and prejudiced history of the West Indies. Other remarkable contributors include William Davidson, one of the Cato Street conspirators, and Ignatius Sancho, friend and correspondent of Sterne and father of William Sancho, Joseph Banks's librarian. This is an excellent collection which deserves widespread attention. The same can be said of the collection of extended essays which comprises *The Oxford History of New Zealand Literature in English*, edited by Terry Sturm. Tied together by a substantial index and thorough bibliography more than 100 pages long, this volume's nine essays on distinct literary forms make an appropriate and coherent history of English writing in the Land of the Long White Cloud. As well as covering the traditional forms, the *History* embraces other valid areas of enquiry. Jane McRae surveys oral and written Maori literature, Peter Gibbons examines travel, historical and biographical writings in a section on 'Non-fiction', Dennis McEldowney writes on the development of publishing in New Zealand, and Terry Sturm himself is responsible for the essay on 'Popular Fiction' which discusses Ngaio Marsh among others.

Like George Orwell (another member of the literary awkward squad), Salman Rushdie writes far better within the discipline of the essay than the novel. This is not faint praise. *Imaginary Homelands*, which collects Rushdie's journalism and reviews from 1981 to 1991, is a wide-ranging, substantial and insightful gathering of seventy-five pieces, concluding with a poignant explanation of the author's embrace of Islam. The best pieces are those which deal with specific writers, bringing Rushdie's sometimes undisciplined imagination into focus. I was delighted to find reprinted here his account of travelling the Northern Territory with Bruce Chatwin, in search of material for *The Songlines*. I had read this in *The Australian* years ago, and had long lost the reference. His attitude to Kipling (another Orwell favourite) is fair and appreciative, and a comment on Kurt Vonnegut's falling off as a novelist is peculiarly interesting:

> Many years ago, Kurt Vonnegut asked me if I was serious about writing. I said I was. He then said, if I remember correctly, that there was trouble ahead, that one day I would not have a book to write and I would still have to write a book.
>
> It was a sad, and saddening, remark, because I don't think, though I may be wrong, that it was really about me.

Francis Wyndham's collection, *The Theatre of Embarrassment*, takes its title from an essay on the importance of embarrassment to the spectacle of drama as a crucial tactic in manipulation of the audience. As well as pieces on the theatre and reviews of books, the volume contains some fascinating essays on popular culture and film, including the Hammer horror series and the *Carry On* ... comedies. Long before they became thesis-fodder, Wyndham was delighting in print at the exuberance and technical skill of these films of the 1960s. Other essays discuss with perspicacity the mythology of Marlon Brando; the corrupting effect of self-consciousness on film; Ada Leverson (Wyndham's grandmother, by the way); and the perverse pleasure of dining alone. *A View from the Diner's Club* is the title of Gore Vidal's latest collection of essays. Vidal writes as ever, with élan, confidence, and the occasional catty remark. The contents divide equally between his twin interests, 'Book Chat' and 'Political'. The latter observes with scorn the fading era of Reagan and Thatcher as the tattered stage set of 1980s politics began to wobble and collapse around its principals. The former draws deserved attention to neglected figures such as Dawn Powell and Ford Madox Ford, who do not fit the official story of 'what-really-happened-to-English-Literature-in-the-twentieth-century'.

Now available in paperback are a number of the more notable works which have appeared in the last few years: Peter Keating's *The Haunted Study*, Martin Bernac's controversial *Black Athena*, Edward Said's *The World, the Text, and the Critic*, Thomas Richards's *The Commodity Culture of Victorian England*, and Jane Robinson's *Wayward Women: A Guide to Women Travellers*. A paperback edition of Mary Cadogan's *William Companion* should also be mentioned for those with an interest in children's literature, and those who still enjoy the adventures of William Brown in that prelapsarian world of 1930s Surrey.

(b) Anthologies

The stable of Oxford verse anthologies is now almost completely renovated with the publication of Emrys Jones's *New Oxford Book of Sixteenth-Century Verse* and Alastair Fowler's *New Oxford Book of Seventeenth-Century Verse*. Both volumes are certainly justified. Their predecessors were, as Jones is at pains to emphasize, heavily influenced by the cultural preferences of almost a century ago. Edmund Chambers's original sixteenth-century selection was dominated by his late-Victorian taste for genteel, lyrical poems; Grierson and Bullough's 1934 selection from the seventeenth century was influenced by their desire to foreground the Metaphysical poets. With a period so rich in verse as the 1500s, there is a core of material so remarkable it could not justifiably be excluded. Jones writes that this rich lode, indeed, takes up almost half of his selection. For the rest, however, he has ranged wide and plumbed deep to ensure this volume represents the best of the whole century, not just the Elizabethan era or, for that matter, not the 1590s alone! Satire, epigram, political and religious verse and complete longer poems are present, then, as well as the briefer lyrics of the Golden Age. *Anon* is better represented too, as are previously unpublished manuscript anthologies and verse by female poets. Fowler's seventeenth-century volume is similarly catholic in selection, including a sample of American colonial verse, more popular verse and a greater proportion of women's writing; he also attempts to strike a balance between the Metaphysical and Jonsonian schools. These additions to the Oxford verse anthologies are not simply a response to changing taste or commercial pressure, then, but a genuinely well justified and produced renovation of the series.

John Gross's new *Oxford Book of Essays* contains 140 examples of the form, and he evidently wishes he could have included more, making half-humorous reference to Chalmers's forty-five volumes. Individually the selections are all excellent pieces of writing: P. J. Kavanagh on his father, for example, or Joan Didion on the Hoover Dam. As a collection, however, it lacks any clear form or guiding principle. Gross writes that he intended leaving out literary essays, but confesses to breaking this rule. He writes that no abridgements were to be included, but put them in anyway. What did he intend and do, then, in the matter of selection? To include, he tells us, essays which were the best of their kind, or which he personally enjoyed, or which were historically significant! There is no attempt to arrange the contents by these very broad criteria or even by subject. There are no biographical notes. It resembles, in fact, that piece of confectionery beloved of Australian children, *Rocky Road*, in which fragments of every possible type of sweet and chocolate, it seems, are compressed into a large, barely digestible lump. To see how this job should be done, there is no better example than the superb *Hutchinson Book of Essays*, edited with much wit and imagination by Frank Delaney in 1990. *The Oxford Book of Friendship* is edited by D. J. Enright and David Rawlinson. Extracts are grouped under headings such as 'Animals', 'Among Men', and 'Dos and Don'ts', as well as 'Fears, Failures, and False Friends'. Friendship is a curious and difficult subject to pin down, and many of the extracts chosen seem to reflect on other matters – on affection, on gratitude, on sentimentality or self-pity, on chaste love. Take away all of these and one would have a slim volume, mostly from the section 'Among Women', where true sisterly companionship is healthily represented, notably in a series of examples of, and tributes to, George Eliot's genius for friendship.

The Faber Book of Madness is a well-assembled and often moving collection put together by Roy Porter (author of the 1987 *Social History of Madness*). In the main, he abjures the literary treatment of mental illness, omitting even John Clare, and includes instead writings by those who have experienced or treated madness over the last 200 years. By his assiduity in searching out these accounts, Porter enables the mentally ill to articulate forcefully the suffering induced by their illness. One of the most striking testimonies is by John Perceval, son of a nineteenth-century Prime Minister, whose *Narrative of the Treatment Received by a Gentleman, During a State of Mental Derangement* (1838-40) reveals, as Porter comments, 'unrivalled insight into the mental processes and emotional turmoil of the insane'. The experience he describes demonstrates how the anguish of mental illness is so often compounded by the ineptness of our treatment. Porter documents many of the approaches taken, from Bedlam to deep sleep therapy, psychoanalysis, and the scandal of how deinstitutionalization has been mismanaged. We evidently have great difficulty in comprehending, let alone alleviating, malfunction in what is, after all, not only the most complex organ in our body, but probably the most sophisticated structure in the universe.

The success of John Coote's *Faber Book of the Sea* has led him to be commissioned for a second anthology, *The Faber Book of Tales of the Sea*. There is nothing especially narrative about the contents of this volume, nor, it must be said, is the selection as imaginative as the original work's. Apart from excerpts from a handful of literary authors (Melville, Conrad, Golding), it is dominated by *good bad* writers such as Alistair Maclean, Tom Clancy, Hammond Innes, and James Michener. Much of the collection, then, is heavy reading about heavy weather – deadly unimaginative prose evocative only of a yacht club bore. Simon Rae has compiled what is probably the most comprehensive anthology ever on his subject in *The Faber Book of Drink, Drinkers, and Drinking*. Arranged in twenty-one thematic sections, it covers every aspect of the collision between booze and humanity – 'Drinkers', 'Liquor and the Law', 'Ill effects', and so on. The range of sources is broad indeed, from Christ turning water to wine (in the 'Celebrations' section) to Jeffrey Bernard mocking Alcoholics Anonymous (under 'Philosophies'). It is noticeable that of almost three hundred contributors, less than five per cent are women, and these generally write of the darker side of drinking. (This absence is less a matter of editorial prejudice, I am sure, than a reflection of the fact that women do not need to drink in order to be convivial.) The 'Rock Bottom' pieces are suitably scary, including the horror of John Healy's account of the meths-drinking world. These are countered by evocative descriptions of English pubs, of which Orwell's 'The Moon under Water' is the most seductive I have read. From Faber also comes one of the most impressive new anthologies of the year, Christopher Frayling's *Vampyres: Lord Byron to Count Dracula*. There is no shortage of works on this subject. The whole genre is of interest, right up to Anne Rice's masterful *Vampire Chronicles* of the 1980s, and there are other anthologies which treat the whole range of vampirological writings. Frayling's highly selective volume is more a casebook on Bram Stoker's *Dracula*, with excerpts from significant precursors (including the contributions of Lord Byron and John Polidori to the famous ghost-story session at Lake Geneva in 1816), passages from Stoker's working papers and *Dracula* itself. Of special value, too, is Frayling's own eighty-four page contribution, an impressive and scholarly investigation of Stoker's text and the genre as a whole.

The fortieth birthday of Peter Owen as an imprint is celebrated by *The Peter Owen Anthology*. The list of 'Authors We Have Published' indicates how important this very independent publishing house has been in introducing foreign authors to the reading public, influencing many English writers in turn. Colette, Cocteau, Hesse, Yukio Mishima, and Octavio Paz are among the representative twenty-one included in this justifiably proud volume introduced by D. J. Enright. *Conscience Be My Guide* is an anthology of writings by prisoners of conscience, compiled by Geoffrey Bould. The contents are gathered under various headings such as 'Forgiveness', 'Facing Death', 'Torture', and 'Family' – enabling figures as different as Socrates, Michael Tippett, Sacco and Vanzetti, and the Vietnamese poet Nguyen Chithien to get into a huddle, as it were, and compare experiences. The pieces are most interesting when their authors realize that all their assumptions must be questioned when placed *in extremis* like this. Some of the experiences described one would think impossible to put into words, and they are certainly painful and moving to read: Lucia Morales, a Chilean socialist forced to witness her daughter being raped, or Saida Botan Elmi, regularly tortured with electricity by the Somali authorities for over a year. Here, indeed, is surely one of the borders of language. By their nature, the contents of *The Chatto Book of Dissent*, edited by Mike Rosen and David Widgery, do not sit comfortably in a literary anthology. With few exceptions the excerpts chosen are ephemeral, naive, or pretentious, and not infrequently a combination of all three. *That Kind of Woman*, edited by Bronte Adams and Trudi Tate, is a highly enjoyable collection of short fiction by women writers of the early twentieth century. Some fascinating stories by lesser-known writers such as Dorothy Edwards and Nella Larsen are deservedly included, as well as unfamiliar pieces by Jean Rhys ('Illusion') and H. D. ('Kora and Ke'). In addition to being an attractive collection of tales, this volume is also 'a part of the feminist project of re-reading Modernism', as the editors boldly state. By highlighting the energetic participation of women in the Modernist experiment, and the attention they paid to female issues, Adams and Tate make a worthwhile contribution to that project. Ronald Blythe again proves his skill and delicacy as an anthologist with *Private Words*, a compilation of letters and diaries from the Second World War. By eschewing public sentiments and presenting a broad selection of writings on the private experience of war, Blythe has put together a remarkable and touching volume – unsentimental, yet aching with the complex of emotions provoked by that conflict. Perhaps because of the uniquely moral nature of that war, and the truly global scale of the fighting (so that loved ones were often imprisoned on the other side of the planet), there is a poignant eloquence about these writings which makes them well worth study. Many are previously unpublished, and Blythe has done a good job in searching them out from the Imperial War Museum archives and dusty trunks in attics.

Blythe's *Penguin Book of Diaries* is among the better anthologies to appear in paperback form this year, as well as Philip Kerr's *Penguin Book of Lies*, Bel Mooney's *Penguin Book of Marriage* (previously entitled *From This Day Forward*), William Trevor's *Oxford Book of Irish Short Stories*, Angela Carter's excellent *Virago Book of Fairy Tales*, and *Wartime Women*, Dorothy Sheridan's fascinating anthology of women's writing for Mass Observation from 1937–45.

3. Bibliography

(a) Theory

Sidney Berger considers the theory and practice of bibliographies in a new work from Mansell, *Design of Bibliographies*, which contains much good advice for those coming to work in this area for the first time (or indeed, on any subsequent occasion). A fascinating insight into the preparation of a modern scholarly edition is given in Matthew J. Bruccoli's provocatively titled 'Getting It Right: the publishing process and the correction of factual errors' (*LCUT* 21.41–60). While dealing specifically with Bruccoli's editing of the 1991 Cambridge edition of *The Great Gatsby*, the essay involves a far wider discussion of editorial principle. 'Fidelity to errors because they have become part of the fabric of a classic work of fiction is simplistic', he comments of so-called 'authorial error'. Yet if these are part of the acknowledged 'fabric' of the work, which all previous audiences have reacted to, is the editor always justified in removing them? If not, then when? Can the editor always claim, with clairvoyant confidence, that the author would in fact have wanted the error removed? What if the effect of such tampering is to make the work more veridical at the expense of altering its metaphorical or rhetorical structure? These are dangerous waters, and some modern editors may need reminding that 'fiction' means exactly that. The 'Queensboro Bridge' in *The Great Gatsby* is not a thing of steel and stone in New York City, but a literary construction within the heterocosmic universe of the novel. It is surely irrelevant, then, that the Bridge does not lead to the Astoria, as Bruccoli complains. Fitzgerald's Bridge does not lead anywhere, but exists for a few seconds only, to carry Gatsby safely across the East River each time someone reads the novel!

'Production of Meaning in Periodical Studies' is examined by Laurel Brake in a consideration of the *English Review* (*VPR* 24.163–70). Beyond emphasizing that it is possible to study a periodical separately as a literary and a publishing phenomenon, however, Brake adds little to the debate. Two issues of *VPR* are devoted to 'Victorian Art and the Press'. The most interesting essays examine the mass reproduction and popularizing of certain paintings; the commercial and technical background to this vulgarization, or democratization, of fine art is outlined well by Julie Codell in 'The Aura of Mechanical Reproduction: Victorian Art and the Press' (*VPR* 24.4–10).

(b) Reference Works

The revised *STC* (Pollard and Redgrave) is now complete with the publication of volume three of *A Short-Title Catalogue of Books printed in England, Scotland, and Ireland, and of English Books printed Abroad, 1475–1640.* Volume three contains a wealth of indexes to make the material in the main corpus of the work more accessible and meaningful. In addition to the primary index which lists works chronologically by printer or publisher, others cover Places of Publication other than London (including a section on Fictitious Places, such as the delightful Albionopolis, Pomadie, and Œnozythopolis), Signs and Addresses (aided by a foldout map of London in 1666), and Anomalous Imprints. The Addenda and Corrigenda are augmented by Concordances linking *STC* numbers with those in earlier bibliographies by Bosanquet, Duff, and Greg, and Philip Rider is responsible for a Chronological Index listing every work's number and abbreviated title by year of publication, putative or actual. This really is a remarkable achievement, and its enabling function will make it the first of the three volumes we will learn to reach for.

Robin Alston will surely add to the workload of British Library staff with publication of his invaluable *Handlist of Unpublished Finding Aids to the London Collections of the British Library.* Many hundreds of internal British Library lists are recorded, making research on as many topics considerably easier. Tibetan blockprints? Ask for OC139 at the India Office Reading Room. Fore-edge paintings? PB100 at the Main Enquiry Desk. And PB160 is a treasure too: a catalogue of books in National Trust properties, with locations. This modest-looking volume is an extraordinarily valuable resource, and will do much to help the Library provide a more *transparent* service. 'Ironically, bibliography has not been well served by indexers', notes John Feather in his welcome *Index to Selected Bibliographical Journals 1971–1985.* This work, sponsored by the OBS, continues the Bibliographical Society's index which ceased in 1970, and maintains its format and structure. Fifteen years is an absurdly long time to wait for a basic reference source in any field, and the mere 134 pages also show how selective the compiler has had to be. (Is not this something BLISS, for example, could be doing on a regular basis?) Feather and the OBS are to be congratulated for doing what no one else evidently had the stomach for, and the project to bring up to date, automate, and publish electronically the Bodley's index of bibliographical journals is also to be wished well. Denis Keeling has edited the sixth in his series of bibliographies of *British Library History*, for the period 1985–1988. Notable in this volume are coverage of the quincentenary of the Bodley, and developments in the field of library automation. Musicological, as well as literary and bibliographical studies have been done a great service by Carole Rose Livingston with the appearance of her massive *British Broadside Ballads of the Sixteenth Century: A Catalogue of the Extant Sheets and an Essay.* In addition to her descriptive catalogue of 288 ballads with indexes, Livingston discusses at length the provenance, proofreading and popularity of the form, and five broadside controversies of the Tudor period. She also notes that this work will be followed by a companion volume giving the full texts of all the ballads listed, together with an essay proving the fraudulence of John Payne Collier's ballad scholarship (and by extension, that of his inked additions to the Perkins Shakespeare Folio). D. F. Carothers's *Radio Broadcasting from 1920 to 1990: An Annotated Bibliography* was, unfortunately, unseen.

(c) Printing and Publishing History

Patricia Anderson's *The Printed Image and the Transformation of Popular Culture*

1790–1860 is a good book hampered, but not spoiled, by a sometimes prolix style. Anderson argues that the explosion of popular printed material in the first half of the nineteenth century – engendered by a combination of the mechanization of paper-making and printing and a reduction in paper and newspaper duty – enabled the creation and circulation of a new common iconography, via the hugely popular *Penny Magazine* and its successors. Thus, the first truly mass medium had an inherently pictorial quality, playing an important part in the development of the twentieth-century mass media as dominantly visual. Anderson notes, in particular, the beginning in this period of the wide dissemination of certain idealized images of female beauty – unrealistic forms against which women began to be judged, and to judge themselves.

The purity and simple beauty of Doves Press books, all in the one size, format, and typeface, have not always appealed to collectors. Francis Meynell called them 'literary Tiller Girls'. They are bookmen's books, and all the more attractive for that. Marianne Tidcombe has completed a formidable labour of love in *The Doves Bindery* which details the output of the Press's bindery between 1893 and 1916. Cobden-Sanderson ceased to bind personally after the Press was established in 1900, but he always remained the man who could write with fervour, 'I must not forget, in taking to the handicraft of bookbinding, that there are higher things in the world, higher ambitions even for me than to produce well-bound, beautifully-bound books.'

GJ 66 contains papers from a European symposium held in Mainz in 1989 on the current proliferation of printed materials. Lotte Helinga contributes on 'The British Library's Policies on Legal Deposit' (*GJ* 66.33–7), noting the projected doubling of publishers' output between 1975 and 2000, and also the mixed blessing of amateur desktop publishing. The main principle adopted by the Library to cope with this tidal wave of material has been selectivity – abandoning the aim of comprehensiveness in favour of curatorial decision-making. This is a sensible option, but one that throws greater and greater responsibility onto the Library's staff. Elsewhere in the volume, Paul Needham writes 'Further Corrective Notes on the Date of the Catholicon Press' (*GJ* 66.101–26) in response to Helinga's essay in *GJ* 64, and Nils Enlund contributes an interesting piece putting 'Electronic Full-Page Make-Up of Newspapers in Perspective' (*GJ* 66.318–23), describing the surprisingly long time it took to develop satisfactory systems after the first moves over twenty years ago.

Quarendo 21 contains an essay by Judith Ecsedy on 'The Printer's Device of the Elzeviers in Hungary' (*Quarendo* 21.125–38) which answers the question of why the *Non Solus* device was taken up by Hungarian printers in the seventeenth century, arguing that they not only sought to emulate the classical standards of Elzevier editions, but were also expressing a covert sympathy with the principles of Dutch Puritanism at the same time. Frans Janssen also contributes a substantial essay on 'Author and Printer in the History of Typographical Design' (*Quarendo* 21.11–37). That remarkable phenomenon, the American academic press, is examined by Paul Korshin in 'The Idea of an Academic Press at the *fin de siècle*' (*SPub* 22.67–77), with a prediction that electronic publication on 3.5 inch disc may be the medium of the future – seemingly unaware of the existing boom of publishing in CD form and the detailed academic discourse and exchange of information already taking place world-wide via the Internet.

(d) *Institutional and Private Library History*

Three of our most venerable libraries receive special attention this year. *The Library of the British Museum* is an avowed eulogy to the old Department of Printed Books, deceased in name since the 1970s, and currently being reincarnated as the British Library on the Euston Road. P. R. Harris has gathered seven essays which will be of interest to any who cared for the old BM. By 1997 the move to St Pancras should be complete and, as Harris explains:

> Many practices which have evolved in response to the design of the British Museum building will soon become unexplained oddities. It therefore seems desirable to place on record some aspects of the history of the Library and its work as it has developed for more than a century and a half.

His own contribution is a study of the move from Montague House to the British Museum building in the 1830s and early 1840s. F. J. Hill and Alec Hyatt King explain the idiosyncratic classification of material, and genesis of the General Catalogue, and Paul Cross provides a history of the Private Case, the once-secret pornographic collection which, he proves, dates from as early as 1841. The volume closes with a collection of reminiscences by Alec Hyatt King who served at the BM for forty-two years until 1976. King's memoirs are valuable, especially for the War years, although he does seem to have regarded exhibitions and even readers as necessary evils. In *Rude Words: A Discursive History of the London Library*, John Wells is less concerned with cataloguing procedures, and rather more concerned with the social lives of its members and staff. He makes clear that it is thanks to their good-will and generosity that the London Library continues to exist, and not to the appalling management from which it has suffered most of its life. This is an agreeable, relaxed account of a very different sort of library. I particularly liked Wells's undeniable observation that 'there is, as in most libraries, a heavily charged erotic atmosphere in the Reading Room: a girl undoing a button of her cardigan lifts a head from every armchair.' One wonders for whom a work such as David Rogers's *The Bodleian Library and its Treasures* is intended. The answer can only be the cultured overseas visitor, aching to buy an expensive souvenir from the Bodleian Gift Shop, yet disdaining the Bodleian tablemat set or the Bodleian bone china mug. This is a popular history of the library and its collections, and essentially an illustrated one – the contents page describes all the coloured plates, and the text functions primarily as a commentary upon these. There are over a hundred plates, and they do indeed make a 'sumshious' book (as Daisy Ashford would have called it). They include a portrait of 'Good Duke Humfrey' (who has the brutal good looks of a star football player), reproductions from *The Romance of Alexander* and other notable manuscripts and printed items, and numerous illustrations of the building and environs. David Rogers also manages to cover the history of the Library from its beginnings at St Mary's 200 years before Thomas Bodley's involvement, to consolidation in the seventeenth century. This is not a scholarly resource on the Bodley, then, but certainly a superb evocation of its historical collections for visitors and exiles.

Little of note was published on the private library this year. From this modest crop, attention should be drawn to Arthur and Janet Ing Freeman's *Anatomy of an Auction*, which disinters and performs an autopsy on an auction of rare books at Ruxley Lodge in 1919, revealing a classic case in bibliographic shady dealing; and the latest in the Publishing Pathways series, *Property of a Gentleman*, edited by Myers and Harris, which concentrates on the formation, organization, and dispersal of significant private libraries between 1620 and 1920. Colin Tite's latest research into one of the most important of these is published as 'A Catalogue of Sir Robert Cotton's Printed

Books?' (*BLJ* 17.1–11). Tite has examined British Library Add. Ms. 352 13, and, after looking at all the possible problems raised by this assignation, concludes that the list is Cottonian, taken over by Sir Robert from a previous owner, fitfully amended, and continued by his son.

Books Reviewed

Adams, Bronte, and Trudi Tate, eds. *That Kind of Woman: Stories from the Left Bank and Beyond*. Virago. pp. 280. pb £6.99. ISBN 1 85381 196 3.
Alston, Robin C. *Handlist of Unpublished Finding Aids to the London Collections of the British Library*. BL. pp. 186. £15. ISBN 0 7123 0246 8.
Anderson, Patricia. *The Printed Image and the Transformation of Popular Culture 1790–1860*. OUP. pp. 211. £30. ISBN 0 19 811236 X.
Baldick, Chris. *The Concise Oxford Dictionary of Literary Terms*. OUP. pp. 246. pb £6.99. ISBN 0 19 282893 2.
Beale, Paul, ed. *A Concise Dictionary of Slang and Unconventional English*. Routledge. pp. 534. £17.99. ISBN 0 415 06352 3.
Berger, Sidney E. *Design of Bibliographies: Observations, References, and Examples*. Mansell. pp. 198. £45. ISBN 0 7201 2077 2.
Bernac, Martin. *Black Athena: The Afroasiatic Roots of Classical Civilisation*. Vintage. pp. 575. pb £8.99. ISBN 0 09 988780 0.
Blythe, Ronald, ed. *Private Words: Letters and Diaries from the Second World War*. Viking. pp. 310. ISBN 0 6708 3204 9.
———, ed. *The Penguin Book of Diaries*. Penguin. pp. 364. pb £6.99. ISBN 0 140 12231 1.
Bould, Geoffrey, ed. *Conscience Be My Guide: An Anthology of Prison Writings*. Zed. pp. 262. hb £29.95, pb £9.95. ISBN 1 85649 010 6, 1 85649 011 4.
Brewer's Twentieth Century Phrase and Fable. Cassell. pp. 662. £16.95. ISBN 0 304 34059 6.
Briggs, Katherine M. *A Dictionary of British Folk-Tales in the English Language, Incorporating the F. J. Norton Collection*. Routledge. 2 vols. £65. ISBN 0 415 06696 4.
Bryson, Bill. *Penguin Dictionary for Writers and Editors*. Viking. pp. 403. £12.99. ISBN 0 6708 3767 9.
Cadogan, Mary. *William Companion*. Macmillan. pp. 224. pb £11.99. ISBN 0 333 56524 X.
Carothers, D. F. *Radio Broadcasting from 1920 to 1990: An Annotated Bibliography*. Garland. pp. 564. $70. ISBN 0 8240 1209 7.
Carter, Angela, ed. *The Virago Book of Fairy Tales*. Virago. pp. 242. pb £6.99. ISBN 1 8538 1440 7,
Chambers Concise Dictionary. Chambers. pp. 1296. £11.99. ISBN 0 550 10570 0.
Chambers Thesaurus. Chambers. pp. 755. £11.99. ISBN 0 550 10572 7.
Coote, John, ed. *The Faber Book of Tales of the Sea*. Faber. pp. 332. £15.99. ISBN 0 57116 137 5.
Crystal, David. *The Cambridge Encyclopedia of Language*. CUP. pp. 472. pb £14.95. ISBN 0 521 42443 7.
Edwards, Paul, and David Dabydeen, eds. *Black Writers in Britain 1760–1890*. EdinUP. £30. ISBN 0 7486 0267 4.
Enright, D. J., and David Rawlinson, eds. *The Oxford Book of Friendship*. OUP. pp.

364. £19. ISBN 0 19 214190 2.

Feather, John. *An Index to Selected Bibliographical Journals 1971–1985*. OBS. pp. 134. £7.50. ISBN 0 901420 47 6.

Fleming, John, Hugh Honour, and Nikolaus Pevsner. *Penguin Dictionary of Architecture*. 4th ed. pp. 497. pb £5.99. ISBN 0 140 51241 1.

Ford, Boris, ed. *The Cambridge Guide to the Arts in Britain*. Vol. 5: *The Augustan Age*. CUP. pp. 353. £30. ISBN 0 5213 0978 6.

Fowler, Alastair, ed. *The New Oxford Book of Seventeenth-Century Verse*. OUP. pp. 831. £30. ISBN 0 19 214164 3.

Frayling, Christopher. *Vampyres: Lord Byron to Count Dracula*. Faber. pp. 429. £17.50. ISBN 0 5711 6311 4.

Freeman, Arthur, and Janet Ing Freeman. *Anatomy of an Auction: Rare Books at Ruxley Lodge 1919*. Collector. pp. 169. £15. ISBN 0 903482 01 0.

Fyfe, Christopher, ed. *Our Children Free and Happy: Letters from Black Settlers in Africa in the 1790s*. EdinUP. pp. 105. £15. ISBN 0 7486 0270 4.

Garrigan, Kristine O. *Victorian Art Reproductions in Modern Sources: A Bibliography*. Garland. pp. 575. $75. ISBN 0 8240 3335 3.

Grimal, Pierre. *Dictionary of Classical Mythology*. Penguin. pp. 466. pb £5.99. ISBN 0 140 51235 7.

Gross, John, ed. *The Oxford Book of Essays*. OUP. pp. 680. pb £17.95. ISBN 0 19 214185 6.

Harris, P. R., ed. *The Library of the British Museum: Retrospective Essays on the Department of Printed Books*. BL. pp. 320. £35. ISBN 0 7123 0240 5.

Harvie, Christopher. *The Centre of Things: Political Fiction from Disraeli to the Present*. Unwin. pp. 245. hb £28, pb £11.95. ISBN 0 04 445593 3, 0 04 445592 5.

Henderson, Lesley, ed. *Twentieth-Century Crime and Mystery Writers*. St James. 3rd ed. pp. 1294. £55. ISBN 1 55862 031 1.

Jones, Emrys, ed. *The New Oxford Book of Sixteenth-Century Verse*. OUP. pp. 769. £25. ISBN 0 19 214126 0.

Keating, Peter. *The Haunted Study: A Social History of the English Novel*. Fontana. pp. 533. pb £7.99. ISBN 0 00686 213 6.

Keeling, Denis F., ed. *British Library History: A Bibliography 1985–1988*. StPB. pp. 192, £25. ISBN 0 906795 95 8.

Kerr, Philip, ed. *The Penguin Book of Lies*. Penguin. pp. 560. pb £9.99. ISBN 0 014 011690 7.

Kirkpatrick, B., ed. *Brewer's Concise Dictionary of Phrase and Fable*. Cassell. pp. 1312. pb £7.95. ISBN 0 304 34079 0.

Kirkpatrick, D. L., ed. *Reference Guide to English Literature*. St James. 2nd ed. 3 vols. £175. ISBN 1 55862 078 8.

Livingston, Carole Rose. *British Broadside Ballads of the Sixteenth Century: A Catalogue of the Extant Sheets and an Essay*. Garland. pp. 911. $96. ISBN 0 8240 7226 X.

Manser, Martin H., ed. *Bloomsbury Good Word Guide*. Bloomsbury. pp. 317. pb £4.99. ISBN 0 7475 0875 5.

Mooney, Bel, ed. *The Penguin Book of Marriage*. Penguin. pp. 373. pb £6.99. ISBN 0 140 13904 4.

Myers, Robin, and Michael Harris, eds. *Property of a Gentleman: The Formation, Organisation and Dispersal of the Private Library 1620–1920*. StPB. pp. 192. £32.50. ISBN 0 9067 9599 0.

Owen, Peter, sel. *The Peter Owen Anthology: Forty Years of Independent Publishing*. Owen. pp. 231. £16.50. ISBN 0 7206 0810 4.

Oxford Encyclopedic Dictionary. OUP. pp. 1767. £16.95. ISBN 0 19 861248 6.

Palmer, Jerry. *Potboilers: Methods, Concepts and Case Studies in Popular Fiction*. Routledge. pp. 219. £10.99. ISBN 0 415 00 978 2.

Pollard, A. W., and G. R. Redgrave. *A Short-Title Catalogue of Books printed in England, Scotland, and Ireland, and of English Books printed Abroad 1475–1640*. Vol. 3: *A Printers' and Publishers' Index, Other Indexes, and Appendices, Cumulative Addenda and Corrigenda*, by Katharine Patzer, with a Chronological Index by Philip R. Rider. BibS. pp. 405. £125. ISBN 0 19 721791 5.

Porter, Roy. *The Faber Book of Madness*. Faber. pp. 572. £14.99. ISBN 0 571 4387 3.

Rae, Simon. *The Faber Book of Drink, Drinkers, and Drinking*. Faber. pp. 554. £15.99. ISBN 0 5711 6229 0.

Richards, Thomas. *The Commodity Culture of Victorian England: Advertising and Spectacle 1851–1914*. Verso. pp. 306. pb £11.95. ISBN 0 86091 570 0.

Robinson, Jane. *Wayward Women: A Guide to Women Travellers*. OUP. pp. 368. pb £6.99. ISBN 0 19 282822 3.

Rogers, David. *The Bodleian Library and its Treasures 1320–1700*. Aidan Ellis. pp. 176. £50. ISBN 0 85628 128 X.

Rosen, Mike, and David Widgery, eds. *The Chatto Book of Dissent*. C&W. pp. 400. £14.99. ISBN 0 7011 3754 1.

Ross, Robert L., ed. *International Literature in English: Essays on the Major Writers*. St James. pp. 762. £55. ISBN 0 55862 162 8.

Rushdie, Salman. *Imaginary Homelands: Essays and Criticism 1981–1991*. Granta. pp. 432. £17.99. ISBN 0 14 014224 X.

Said, Edward. *The World, the Text, and the Critic*. Vintage. pp. 327. pb £7.99. ISBN 0 09 991620 7.

Schellinger, Paul E. *St James Guide to Biography*. St James. pp. 870. £85. ISBN 1 55862 146 6.

Sheridan, Dorothy, ed. *Wartime Women: An Anthology of Women's Wartime Writing for Mass Observation 1937–45*. Mandarin. pp. 267. pb £6.99. ISBN 0 7493 0741 2.

Sturm, Terry, ed. *The Oxford History of New Zealand Literature in English*. OUP. pp. 748. £30. ISBN 0 19 558211 X.

Tidcombe, Marianne. *The Doves Bindery*. BL. pp. 490. £90. ISBN 0 7123 0238 7.

Tindall, Gillian. *Countries of the Mind: the Meaning of Place to Writers*. Hogarth. pp. 254. £18. ISBN 0 7012 0917 8.

Todd, Janet, ed. *A Dictionary of British Women Writers*. Routledge. pp. 762. pb £16.99. ISBN 0 415 07261 1.

Trevor, William, ed. *The Oxford Book of Irish Short Stories*. OUP. pp. 592. pb £5.99. ISBN 0 19 282845 2.

Urdang, Laurence. *The Oxford Thesaurus: An A–Z Dictionary of Synonyms*. OUP. pp. 1042. £14.95. ISBN 0 19 869151 3.

Vidal, Gore. *A View from the Diner's Club: Essays 1987–1991*. Deutsch. pp. 242. £13.99. ISBN 0 2339 8730 4.

Wells, John. *Rude Words: A Discursive History of the London Library*. Macmillan. pp. 256. £17.50. ISBN 0 333 47519 4.

Wilson, Katharina M. *An Encyclopedia of Continental Women Writers*. St James. 2 vols. £125. ISBN 1 55862 151 2.

Woodman, Thomas. *Faithful Fictions: The Catholic Novel in British Literature*. OpenUP. pp. 193. £35. ISBN 0 335 09638 7.

Wyndham, Francis. *The Theatre of Embarrassment*. C&W. pp. 205. £15. ISBN 0 7011 3726 6.

II

English Language

KENNETH TURNER, MICHAEL K. C. MACMAHON, NICOLA WOODS, FREDERIKE VAN DER LEEK, CHRISTIAN KAY, RICHARD COATES and JEAN JACQUES WEBER

This chapter has nine sections: 1. General; 2. History of English Linguistics; 3. Dialectology and Sociolinguistics (including Creolistics); 4. Phonetics, Phonology and Orthography; 5. Morphology; 6. Syntax; 7. Vocabulary and Semantics; 8. Onomastics; 9. Stylistics. Section 1 is by Kenneth Turner; sections 2 and 4 are by Michael MacMahon; section 3 is by Nicola Woods; sections 5 and 6 are by Frederike van der Leek; section 7 is by Christian Kay; section 8 is by Richard Coates and section 9 is by Jean Jacques Weber.

1. General

The year's work gets under way with two interesting, informative and affordable books on the ins and outs of using text corpora as the basis for linguistic analysis. The first is John Sinclair's *Corpus, Concordance, Collocation*, which is the initial title in OUP's new series *Describing English Language*. The second is *English Corpus Linguistics: Studies in Honour of Jan Svartvik,* edited by Karin Aijmer and Bengt Altenberg. The first is an elegant defence of and introduction to the computerized processing of large texts: linguistics no longer languishes in the poor guise of individual vacillating intuition but instead is directed by the more objective fact of carefully observed usage and systematically retrievable data. This is almost wholly for the good. Sinclair acknowledges that his book contains only a modest sample of the material produced in the last ten years, but it is an invaluable introduction to the issues and more so now that billion-word corpora are projected. The second book is a collection of studies that report on several aspects of corpus linguistics. Geoffrey Leech's 'The state of the art in corpus linguistics' is particularly useful as is a number of papers in the descriptive section: Graeme Kennedy's '*Between* and *though*: The company they keep and the functions they serve' and Charles Meyer's 'A corpus-based study of apposition in English' both excited the interest of this reviewer, although he would not want their mention to imply that the other contributions to this very satisfactory collection were in any way less worthy. These studies honour Jan Svartvik and we take this opportunity to correct a sin of omission from last year. *The London-Lund Corpus of Spoken English,* edited by Jan Svartvik, arrived just a little too late for inclusion last year. The collection contains an initial paper that describes the London-Lund Corpus and provides basic information on all the 100 spoken texts, together with a bibliography of publications using the material. This is accompanied by a suite of papers reporting on the Text Segmentation for Speech project which aims to describe the linguistic rules that govern the prosodic segmentation of natural English speech. *English Computer Corpora*, edited by Stig Johansson and Anna-Brita Stenström, is the third volume in Mouton's *Topics in English Linguistics* series. In addition to papers on probabilistic grammar, syntactic and lexical analysis, speech processing, and regional and social variation, there is a useful survey of English machine-readable corpora by Lita Taylor, Geoffrey Leech and Steven Fligelstone and an extensive bibliography of publications relating to English computer corpora composed by Bengt Altenberg. The more specialist matter of *Lexical Acquisition* is treated with much rigour in a collection edited by Uri Zernik. This is the published record of the First International Workshop on Lexical Acquisition that was held in Detroit in 1989 and the papers all address the thorny problem of how to create and maintain a lexicon shell that is able to acquire new data and to adapt itself to the specificity of the text being read. I note briefly that Brian MacWhinney has made available a manual for use with the Child Language Data Exchange System (CHILDES), in particular for the tools CHAT and CLAN, as well as having provided a guide to the database. Finally, I mention *Negation in English Speech and Writing*, by Gunnel Tottie. Tottie takes the London-Lund Corpus of Spoken English, the Survey of English Usage and the Lancaster-Oslo/Bergen Corpus of British English and she presents a pragmatic theory of negation which deals with the different uses, concerning both frequencies and types of constructions, of negation in spoken and written language. This is a meticulous study, thoroughly researched and carefully presented, and a testament to the advantages of using computational corpora.

Proper English? is the first volume in Routledge's new *The Politics of Language* series. Tony Crowley has collected nearly twenty texts, the earliest from the end of the seventeenth century, the latest from within the last ten years, which orbit around the general thesis that a definition of language is always also a definition of human beings in the world. Also noticed in section 3 below, this is an encouraging beginning to what we hope will be an excellent series. Less politically, arguably, John Lyons offers the first volume of his essays in *Natural Language and Universal Grammar*. Apart from the convenience of having the published papers of a renowned scholar and linguist collected in a pair of volumes, we should in addition welcome the publication of some hitherto unpublished work. The first volume contains 'In defence of (so-called) autonomous linguistics', 'Linguistic theory and theoretical linguistics' and 'Natural, non-natural and unnatural languages: English, Urdu and other abstractions', all of which appear for the first time. This is a most important volume and I impatiently look forward to its partner entitled *Semantics, Subjectivity and Localism* which Lyons promises will appear 'shortly'. Two other collections of essays are published this year, both by eminent phoneticians. David Abercrombie's too short *Fifty Years in Phonetics* is, by his own admission, a 'somewhat miscellaneous collection of papers' although this did not lessen at all my enjoyment in reading them. John Laver collects 20 of his papers in *The Gift of Speech*. Abercrombie's is one influence that is evident in this collection which demonstrates the extent to which the study of speech has necessarily become a multidisciplinary enterprise. Some readers will be familiar with the TOPIC ... COMMENT column in *NL<* and may even enjoy reading it. Geoffrey Pullum's contributions to that column have been collected in *The Great Eskimo Vocabulary Hoax and Other Irreverent Essays on the Study of Language* and they are in some elusive sense both eminently sensible and very silly. Readers not familiar with the genre are recommended to discover it, for the present reviewer finds it close to impossible to describe.

The tide of textbooks continues to rise, although perhaps not as vigorously as in recent years. An important one is Manfred Görlach's *Introduction to Early Modern English* which first appeared in German in 1978 and which is suitably augmented and up-dated for the present edition. Your reviewer is not primarily, nor even secondarily, a linguistic historian but he nevertheless responded favourably to Görlach's clear style and presentation and experienced a profound education in the process. This book is perhaps the ideal introduction. A new Red Cambridge Textbook, *Gender*, by Greville Corbett, is both a splendid introduction *and* an important theoretical contribution to the study of one of the most puzzling grammatical categories. The introduction is effected through an examination of gender systems in over 200 languages, some of which are very little known, e.g. Khinalug, a member of the Lezgian subgroup of Northeast Caucasian, which has about 1,000 speakers. The theoretical contribution answers the question of how the exact number of genders in a given language is established. Briefly, and doing enormous violence to a very subtle proposal, Corbett argues that a distinction must be drawn between the controller gender, or agreement class of a noun, and the target gender, or the class of the element that agrees with the noun. Corbett shows how this distinction leads to, among other things, a solution to the controversial problem of gender in Rumanian. This book is a major achievement in linguistic illustration and explanation and it will have undergraduates, and more seasoned readers, on the edge of their seats. Andrew Spencer's *Morphological Theory* makes reference to circa 130 languages in an introduction that authoritatively charts the debates that have shaped this inquiry and which includes sections on the interfaces with phonology and syntax. The exercises are extremely helpful. *Doing Grammar*, by Max Morenberg, is a no-nonsense introduction to the most basic notions and techniques of syntactic argumentation. This is extremely good first-year undergraduate fare. *Syntactic Theory: A Unified Approach,* by Robert Borsley, is well intentioned. Borsley attempts to present some of the major syntactic phenomena via a comparison of Government and Binding Theory and Generalized Phrase Structure Grammar and it is certainly the case that there is much to be learned from placing theories together in this fashion. But at several points in the book a crucial turn of the argument seems to rest upon an implicit and unexplained assumption and this leaves even the sophisticated novice rather perplexed. The book has not fared well at the hands of the printers and there are more typos than is acceptable. *Introduction to Government and Binding Theory* is Liliane Haegeman's huge intermediate coursebook on mainstream GB Theory. The student, and teacher, has more than ample material here to hone to perfection their mastery of this framework and the extensive bibliographic references point them to more if the appetite remains unsatiated. It is to be regretted that in the 618 pages of this book a little space was not made for one of the decade's flavours: the computational implementation of grammatical theories. There is one small attempt to address this issue. Colin Beardon, David Lumsden and Geoff Holmes are the co-authors of a modest but helpful introduction to natural language and computational linguistics which comfortably complements some of the larger introductions on related methods that have appeared in the last two or three years.

Linguistic Theory is at the same time an odd book and a very interesting one. Robert de Beaugrande subjects some of the major texts to a kind of discourse analysis and he focuses on linguistic theory not as an agenda of theses but as a way of speaking. He says that even though linguistics is *about* language, the major works in linguistic theory have not been analysed *as* language. So the work of de Saussure, Sapir, Bloomfield, Pike, Hjelmslev, Chomsky, Firth, Halliday, van Dijk, Kintsch and Hartmann all comes under the discourse microscope and de Beaugrande is able to make several plausible claims about the development of terminology and the evolution and change in some of the major lines of argument both between different theorists and within the work of an individual theorist. The fashion for student-friendly reference works is still pronounced, and is perhaps getting more so. George Campbell has produced a massive *Compendium of the World's Languages* in which English gets an informative and useful entry. Many readers will succumb to the temptation to read among the other entries of languages that they didn't realize existed. The second of this year's contestants is *The Linguistics Encyclopedia,* edited by Kirsten Malmkjaer, and some facts about this volume would do well to be mentioned. A respectable body of twenty-four contributors has been assembled for this one and there is a total of eighty-two entries. Many of the contributors make just the single contribution: four make two contributions, one makes three and two make four. The editor, on the other hand, makes *forty-four* contributions and these are on such varied topics as 'Artificial Languages', 'Augmented Transition Network (ATN) Grammar', 'Bilingualism and Multilingualism', 'Creoles and Pidgins', 'Semantics' and 'Kinesics'. The breadth is really breathtaking, although in one case at least the entry is flawed on every point (e.g. 'Pragmatics'). *Some* of the contributions are informative resumés of the field – I liked in particular 'Artificial Intelligence', 'Corpora', 'Morphology' and 'Transformational Generative Grammar'. Much of the rest is just an exercise in self-promotion and is much less reliable. *Linguistic Purism,* by George Thomas, is the latest addition to Longman's handy *Studies in Language and Linguistics*. Its content is a little outside of our orbit – the author is a Slavicist – but because there is so much that can be learnt from it, and because it is a natural partner both to Crowley's collection mentioned above and to the Milroys' new edition to be mentioned below, it merits a brief mention here.

There is a healthy crop of reissues and *déjà vus* this year. Jean Aitchison updates *Language Change: Progress or Decay?* and it appears as the first volume in the new *Cambridge Approaches to Linguistics* series, which she edits. *Variety in Contemporary English*, by W. R. O'Donnell and Loreto Todd, is reissued and Peter Matthews offers a second edition of his Red Textbook *Morphology* as does Peter Roach of his *English Phonetics and Phonology*, these last two both revised. David Crystal's *The Cambridge Encyclopedia of Language* at last makes it into an affordable paperback as does Douglas Biber's *Variation Across Speech and Writing.* The British Education Secretary would do well to note the second edition of James and Lesley Milroy's *Authority in Language* which reflects on some of the changes in the political mood since the book first appeared. Consider the following line of reasoning from a cabinet minister, *c.*1985: 'If you allow standards to slip to the stage where good English is no better than bad English, where people turn up filthy at school, all those things tend to cause people to have no standards at all, and once you lose standards then there's no imperative to stay out of crime.' Keith Brown and Jim Miller's *Syntax: A Linguistic Introduction to Sentence Structure,* which also achieves second editionhood this year, might help some to halt the inevitable decline from ungrammaticality to delinquency. The heavy influence of the Standard Theory which was much in evidence in the first edition has been moderated and there is now a little more in the new edition on X-bars and functional relations. *Chomsky*, by John Lyons, always was an elegant introduction to Chomsky, transformational generative grammar and linguistic theory and we are pleased to see that the third edition, with a large new final chapter entitled 'The Chomskyan Revolution: A Progress Report (1991)', is made available this year. Much has happened in syntactic and linguistic theory since the last edition of this book fourteen years ago and Lyons does a first-rate job of bringing the interest of it to the reader. This one is essential first-year undergraduate reading although other classes of persons should not feel excluded.

On pragmatics, we welcome the second volume of Daniel Vanderveken's *Meaning and Speech Acts* which appears this year. This is in many ways an heroic attempt to design a logic that will be capable of expressing the logical forms of the illocutionary forces in natural language. The argument is very elegant and, in charitable moments, one believes that one is learning something about the structure of one part of English, but in general the level of formal sophistication that is required to get through some of the second volume is just so high that one could be forgiven for being sceptical about the project. It is perhaps an ironic observation that those original Austinian pragmatic arguments against the then-prevailing semantics should themselves now have become semanticized. A high level of formal expertise is also a necessary prerequisite to reading Alan Ramsay's *The Logical Structure of English* which we missed last year. *Structures for Semantics*, by Fred Landman, is intended as a much welcomed advanced course in logical and mathematical techniques that are used in semantics and some, like the present reviewer, will find a certain degree of illumination within its covers. A paperback edition is badly needed if this is to have any impact as a coursebook: the casebound edition costs £67. In simple narrative mode Howard Wettstein asks *Has Semantics Rested on a Mistake?* The answer is that it has, and this is because semantics has been too much concerned with propositions and truth-conditions and too little concerned with the excavation of the social practices in which meanings are embedded. This book contains arguments which are almost wholly critical but a footnote informs us that a more positive case is on its way.

There is not, after the flurry of activity in recent years, much pragmatics around this year, although Steven Davis has edited *Pragmatics: A Reader*. It is the first collection of canonical pragmatic texts, even though some of them have previously appeared in semantics and philosophy of language anthologies. It is an extremely useful collection and would have been more so had the editor provided a more careful introduction and added comments to the sections. These editorial infelicities are nowhere apparent in Jenny Cheshire's *English Around the World* which contains a wealth of sociolinguistic information by a variety of authors. There are overview papers which survey the context in which English is spoken and case study papers in which empirical research is reported. This one is a strong candidate for the sociolinguistics book of the year award. A more detailed view on the linguistic situation in the antipodes can be found in *Language in Australia*, edited by Suzanne Romaine, which has contributions on, among other topics, Aboriginal English, pidgins and creoles and varieties of Australian English, and in Michael Clyne's *Community Languages: The Australian Experience.* There are more than 250 languages other than English in use in Australia today and these two books convey some of the nature of that dynamic and diversity. Another continent is more than adequately represented in *English in Africa: An Introduction*, by Josef Schmied. This is the latest volume in the Longman Linguistics Library and it draws on the author's personal fieldwork and consequently is imbued with an authority that is absent in more traditional introductions. Closer to home, *Language Contact in the British Isles* contains the proceedings of the Eighth International Symposium on Language Contact in Europe, which was held in Douglas on the Isle of Man in September 1988. The editors, P. Sture Ureland and George Broderick, have presided over an intellectually attractive collection with several contributions being of interest. For example, Martyn Wakelin discusses 'The Cornishness of Cornwall's English' and John Hines considers 'Scandinavian English: a creole in context'. Hiberno-English is well represented, especially by Terence Odlin in 'Syntactic variation in Hiberno-English' and by Markku Filppula in 'Subordinating *and* Hiberno-English syntax: Irish or English origin?', who demonstrates that the roots of this item lie in the Irish substratum. This is an interesting and important collection which deserves to be consulted with frequency.

2. History of English Linguistics

Firstly grammar. *English Traditional Grammars. An International Perspective*, edited by Gerhard Leitner, is an important set of articles. There are nineteen in all, excluding an introduction by Leitner, and, as the subtitle indicates, they cover more than British work. Space prevents each being discussed; instead, attention will be drawn to a representative sample. In his introduction, 'Why Can't Someone Write a Nice Simple Grammar?', Leitner sets the tone of the volume by emphasizing the importance of work done on English grammar in the nineteenth century – a topic largely overlooked until now. Ian Michael's 'More than Enough English Grammars' sums up some of the main motivations behind nineteenth-century grammar-book writing in England: the rise of a more literate public, the demand that English should be modelled analytically on Latin (or the opposite, for some writers), and the desire to reflect usage rather than dry, school-room prescriptions. What emerges over the period of the century, then, is a set of changing views as to what a readable, popular grammar of English should be about. The question of usage and how it is to be assessed is part of the argument in Robert Burchfield's 'The Fowler Brothers and the Tradition of Usage Handbooks'. He compares some of the contents of *The King's English* with *Modern English Usage*, looks at the reception (mainly hostile) to the revised edition of the latter, and compares it briefly with some other modern works.

Alan Walton's 'Modality and the Modals in Traditional Grammars of English' deals with the various interpretations of modal verbs (though not in great detail) in the grammars by Henry Sweet, Etsko Cruisinga and George Curme; some comparisons are drawn with the views of Randolph Quirk and his colleagues. This article should be read alongside one by Anat Biletzki ('Richard Johnson: A Case of 18th-Century Pragmatics' (*HL* 18.281–99)), which, on the one hand, provides a useful reading of a particular aspect of Richard Johnson's *Grammatical Commentaries* (1706), namely Johnson's unease about accepting the Latinate system of moods in a grammar of English, and, on the other, shows how certain features of speech-act theory were anticipated in Johnson's criticisms of Latin-based analyses of English (especially John Lily's). Although Johnson did not provide a full-scale pragmatic reinterpretation of mood, there is sufficient evidence to show that he was well aware of the role of context in language use.

Returning to *English Traditional Grammars*, Charlotte Downey's 'Factors in the Growth of the English Language in 18th and 19th Century Ireland' considers the reception and influence of works like those by Lindley Murray; she rehearses some well-known facts about eighteenth- and nineteenth-century grammar. The real spin-off in this article is in what she says about differences between the Irish English and the English English verb system. Further exploration of the point she makes about a Gaelic substratum affecting Irish English grammar could be beneficial.

A second article by her in the same volume, 'Trends that Shaped the Development of 19th Century American Grammar Writing', sets the scene for the consideration of further differences between British (more especially English) English grammar and that of the (ex)colonies. Two streams of thinking about grammar, exemplified by Lindley Murray and Goold Brown on the one hand, and Roswell Smith and Samuel Greene on the other, characterize the growth of the school grammar-book industry in the USA from the early nineteenth century onwards. One notable linguist of the period, William Whitney, also contributed to this industry. His work is discussed in some detail by Kurt Wächtler ('W. D. Whitney's Essentials of English Grammar. For the Use of Schools (1877)'). Uncharacteristically, and rather unexpectedly, Whitney emerges as basically a traditionalist grammarian (with some leanings towards descriptivism). Heinrich Ramisch looks for the evidence of a conscious awareness of specifically American grammatical forms in the works of various grammarians from Henry Sweet to the present-day ('The Role of American English in Traditional Grammars of English').

The only item to report this year from the medieval grammatical field is Cynthia Bland's *The Teaching of Grammar in Late Medieval England. An Edition, with Commentary, of Oxford, Lincoln College MS Lat. 130*. This is a revised version of her 1984 PhD thesis, and consists of the text in Middle English, with an apparatus and background cultural commentary on two works on Latin grammar: an *accedence* text, possibly by Thomas Schort, a schoolmaster from Robert Londe's school in Bristol in the first half of the fifteenth century, and, secondly, a work on government (*regemen*) by John Wakefield; he too may have had a connection with Bristol. The emphasis is largely on the connection with earlier and other contemporary grammars.

As ever, the nineteenth century (and slightly earlier) has proved a rich vein to tap. Hans Aarsleff's 'The Original Plan for the OED and Its Background' (*TPS* 88. 151–61), which was missed last year, goes over some well-worn ground, yet succeeds in emphasizing the wider, moral, arguments in Victorian society about the relation between language and life espoused by Richard Chenevix Trench; these are compared with the ideas of John Horne Tooke and Charles Richardson. Graham Shorrocks presents a convincing case for Ellis in his 'A. J. Ellis as Dialectologist: A Reassessment' (*HL* 18.321–34). Many people refer to Ellis but rarely use the information in his works, especially his massive study of English dialects. (Robert Sanders' equally massive 1977 PhD thesis on Ellis might, incidentally, be emphasized in passing as a valuable and mostly overlooked source about the man's life and work.) As a further contribution to her research programme to reinstate the intellectual contributions of earlier scholars in semantics, Brigitte Nerlich dissects the ideas about language by the English psychologist George Stout, ('The Place of G. F. Stout's "Thought and Language" (1891) in the History of English Semantics' (*HL* 18.335–47)); see also *YWES* 71.

Rasmus Rask and Jacob Grimm are well-known names from nineteenth-century linguistics; that of Þorleifur Repp undoubtedly is not. Particularly in the English-using world, little has appeared about him. Andrew Wawn's study, *The Anglo Man: Þorleifur Repp, Philology and Nineteenth-Century Britain*, fills a gap in our understanding of a notable (and notorious) anglophile. Repp, despite ten restless and difficult years working as an Assistant Librarian in the Advocates' Library in Edinburgh, retained to the end his affection for British literature and politics; his opinions on early nineteenth-century linguistic scholarship were less sanguine. This is a well researched study – it does not purport to be a full biography – which will inform as well as amuse.

Sweet's contribution to phonetics and applied phonetics, especially in Europe, is the subject of Michael MacMahon's 'Sweet, Europe and Phonetics' (*HSSN* 17.12–18). Something of the background to the formation and future development of the Henry Sweet Society for the History of Linguistic Ideas can be found in Vivian Salmon's 'The Henry Sweet Society: A Report on the First Seven Years' (*HSSN* 16.3–5).

For well over thirty years now, Garland Cannon has been a notable contributor to the scholarly literature on Sir William Jones. His *The Life and Mind of Oriental Jones: Sir William Jones, the Father of Modern Linguistics* (1990, but published 1991) provides us with a detailed biography of Jones set against the intellectual history of the second half of the eighteenth century. Those who know Cannon's earlier studies will recognize, inevitably, some repetitiveness; but there is enough new material, including some previously unpublished letters by Jones, to make this a fascinating biography. The sub-title is, perhaps, unfortunate. Jones was far more than a philologist attempting to establish connections between languages: he was a jurist, a politician, an historian, an amateur botanist and chemist, amongst other pursuits. Although one might have wished to read more in this book about the precise impact of his ideas, both on Sanskrit studies and on work to do with genetic connections amongst languages, particularly in the years following his early death, much of the vitality and integrity of Jones's professional and private life is captured by Cannon. This is certainly recommended reading.

In the United States, there is a lot of looking back and taking stock going on. In *First Person Singular II. Autobiographies by North American Scholars in the Language Sciences*, edited by Konrad Koerner, we find some honest and often candid accounts by fifteen linguists (including people like Dwight Bolinger, Joseph Greenberg and Eugene Nida) of how they came into linguistics, how they got on with colleagues, how they reacted to developments in their subjects, and so on. The tone of their reminiscences reveals a fondness for a type or types of linguistics of ultimately European or American descriptivist origin, which has little or no truck with some of the excesses of (Post-)Chomskyism. As Paul Garvin neatly puts it: 'I see the current cognitive bandwagon as just an attempt to broaden from this horrible generative straight jacket.' As a sourcebook on the myriad currents that have fed into American linguistics, it is of considerable use. In similar reminiscing mood is the collection of papers by David Abercrombie *Fifty Years in Phonetics*. All but four of the fourteen have appeared already, some in Departmental Working Papers form. It is the first one, in which Abercrombie looks back on his fifty years in phonetics, that should be obligatory reading: he comes across (as indeed he was) as a humane and erudite professional linguist.

Stephen Murray has already established a reputation as a historian of the sociology of linguistics in the USA, with his various studies of how and why linguistics developed or faded at different places and at different times. His 'The First Quarter Century of the Linguistic Society of America, 1924–1949' (*HL* 18.1–48) is a valuable survey, packed with detail. One wishes he had looked just a little further into the period after 1949 than he does and said more about the rise of the Chomskyan brand of linguist. Inevitably, during this latter period, Bloomfieldian linguistics is supposed to have gone into abeyance, at least amongst the theorizing neophytes. Two articles, however, paint a different picture. The first, by Archibald Hill ('The Linguistic Society of America and North American Linguistics 1950–1968' (*HL* 18.49–152)), despite its somewhat plodding style of exposition (year-by-year, meeting-by-meeting), reveals the continuation of various versions of linguistics during this period; not everything was Chomskyan. The other, again by Stephen Murray, 'How Dark was the

Eclipse of Bloomfield?' (*HL* 18.251–3), counters Robert Hall's view that between the 1960s and the 1980s Bloomfield's work was all but forgotten (or despised). Indeed, one might underline the fact that, as emerges from all of the articles referred to above, slick one-line obituaries of pre-Chomskyan linguistics seem not to have taken account of the wider range of opinions and interests beyond the confines of departmental backyards. Still on the subject of Bloomfield, there are useful, though not earth-shattering, pieces of information about Bloomfield's own proposed revisions to *Language* in Sidney Smith's 'Bloomfield's Revisions of Language (1933)' (*HL* 18.167–80).

The role of linguists and others in developing the Intensive Language Programs in the USA in the last two years of the Second World War is described by Robert Hall Jnr in his '165 Broadway – A Crucial Node in American Structural Linguistics' (*HL* 18.153–66). Particularly revealing is the information about the strained relations, both personal and professional, between the resident Americans and the various refugee-scholars (including Roman Jakobson) who worked for the École Libre des Hautes Études further down the road in New York. Additional, and more decidedly gossipy, information is to be found in Herbert Penzl's 'Reminiscences of 165 Broadway, 1943–1945' (*HL* 18.247–50).

Linguistic historiography is, of course, not free from disputatiousness. Michael Silverstein ('Problems of Sapir Historiography' (*HL* 18.181–204)) and Regna Darnell ('On the Occasion of Silversteinian Musings on the State of Sapiriana' (*HL* 18.419–44)) lock horns over the style and content of Darnell's biography of Sapir. I think she wins this one.

Finally, make a point of reading Tim Pulju's witty spoof 'A Short History of American Linguistics, as Seen by a Linguistics Student' (*HL* 18.221–46), and pray that your own undergraduates don't get their uncritical hands on it!

3. Dialectology and Sociolinguistics (including Creolistics)

English Around The World edited by Jenny Cheshire is of particular interest to sociolinguists since it not only challenges many of the traditional assumptions of the discipline, but also points to new ways forward for sociolinguistic investigation. The volume comprises a collection of forty-four papers organized into twelve sections, which deal with the varieties of English spoken in, for example, Canada, South Asia, East Africa and the Pacific. Each section is introduced by a researcher who is an expert in the field: Suzanne Romaine on the Pacific, Gregory Guy on Australia, J. K. Chambers on Canada. The volume largely excludes research into varieties used in the UK and USA on the grounds that research findings in these areas have already been widely disseminated.

As an example of the challenge to traditional sociolinguistic thought, Siachitema's paper on 'Language use and choice in a Zambian setting' shows that it is no longer necessarily the case that where English exists side-by-side with other languages of a speech community its use will be restricted to certain (high) domains. Rather, Siachitema reports that in Zambia both English and the indigenous variety – Nyanja – are used in the home environment and in informal speech encounters generally. Another popular assumption in sociolinguistics is dispelled by Faraht Khan's paper on final consonant cluster simplification in the English spoken in Aligarh, North India. Specifically, Khan finds that in contrast to many research findings based on Western culture and communities, in Indian English, female speakers do not use more prestigious linguistic forms than men. In fact, Khan's results highlight the opposing pattern: women use more stigmatized variants (deletion of final stops) than men.

The collection of papers edited by Suzanne Romaine on *Language in Australia* also casts doubt on some long-held beliefs in sociolinguistic study. This volume contains twenty-five articles organized into five parts: Aboriginal and Islander languages, Pidgin and Creole languages, transplanted languages other than English, varieties of Australian English, and public policy and social issues. In the section on Aboriginal languages, Peter Sutton highlights the limited nature of traditional sociolinguistic definitions of speech community. In fact, Sutton argues that one of the most significant differences between Aboriginal and Western linguistic culture is that, although there were a large number of aboriginal languages, these did not correlate with well-bounded aboriginal societies or groups. Horvath's article on migrant communities and language change in Australia also questions the traditional definition of speech community, and particularly the assumption that the limits of speech communities coincide with those of recognized geographical boundaries. Other articles on Aboriginal languages include Malcolm and Kaldor's study of the phonological, lexical and discourse features of Aboriginal English, and Diana Eades' paper on communicative strategies in Aboriginal English.

The overview of pidgin and creole languages is provided by Peter Muhlhausler, and this section also includes a paper by Muhlhausler on Queensland Kanaka English. Muhlhausler illustrates how Queensland Kanaka English, a little-studied variety spoken by Melanesians working on plantations in Queensland between 1864 and 1904, is an excellent example of Hall's (*Pidgin and Creole Languages*, 1966) definition of a pidgin as a variety which comes into existence for a specific reason and function, lasts as long as the situation, and then dies. Muhlhausler argues that Kanaka English died as a result of the 'White Australia' policy after 1900 and the consequent repatriation of the Melanesian workforce. Roger Keesing has also published a paper on Melanesian pidgin this year (*JPCL* 6.215–29). Keesing claims that analysis of a recent pidgin text recorded in the West Solomons provides evidence to suggest that (i) a single pidgin English was used in all plantation areas (Queensland, Fiji, Samoa, New Caledonia) and recruiting grounds (New Hebrides, Solomons, Bismarks) until the end of the 1880s; and (ii) that 'much of the syntactic elaboration found in contemporary dialects of Melanesian pidgin had taken place by a century ago.' We should also mention at this point that *JPCL* includes two articles on Tok Pisin this year: a paper by Sankoff and Mazzie on 'Determining noun phrases in Tok Pisin' (6.1–24) in which the authors discuss the grammaticalization of noun phrases in this pidgin variety; and a paper by John Verhaar discussing the function of *i* in Tok Pisin (6.231–66). Returning to Romaine's *Language in Australia*, we should briefly note that other varieties considered in the section on pidgin and creole languages include Kriol and Torres Strait Creole.

Articles on Australian English varieties in Romaine's volume include a contribution by Pauline Bryant discussing variation in the lexicon of Australian English, a paper by Anne Pauwels on gender differences (in which she considers the use of the high rise tone – a melodic pattern which seems to be of ever-increasing use in Australian English), and Barbara Horvath's study of the role played by migrant communities in the process of language change – see above. Finally, on the topic of Australian languages it is well worth mentioning Dixon's article 'A Changing Language Situation: the decline of Dyirbal, 1963–1989' (*LSoc* 20.183–200), in which Dixon reports on how and why Dyirbal has died 'faster than I could record it', and provides a perceptive and thought-provoking narrative on 25 years of research into the Dyirbal languages.

This year has also seen a significant number of papers on varieties of New Zealand English (NZE). Perhaps the main impact of these is that they highlight the inappropriateness of grouping together the English varieties of the antipodes: the use of English in New Zealand is distinct from English use in Australia, not least because of the contact with Maori. Tony Deverson reports on the influence of the Maori language, and particularly Maori vocabulary, on NZE in *EnT* (7.ii.18–25), and Donn Baynard examines both Maori varieties of English and other varieties of NZE in his paper 'A taste of Kiwi: attitudes to accent, speaker gender, and perceived ethnicity across the Tasman' (*AuJL* 11.1–37). Baynard investigates New Zealanders' attitudes to three types of NZE accent (broad, general and cultivated) as well as to RP, Australian, and North American varieties, and finds that although New Zealanders are rejecting 'cultivated' varieties in favour of more general accents, they nevertheless continue to value RP speech, and also show a tendency to prefer North American and Australian English above their own. Significantly, this is a result also found by Bell and Holmes in their overview of New Zealand varieties (in Cheshire's *English Around the World*): Bell and Holmes report that 'in contrast to findings in other countries, marked local accents in New Zealand are ranked low for personal attractiveness as well as social prestige.'

Baynard's attitudinal study indicates a strong relationship between perceived Maori/Polynesian ethnic origin and perceived lower socioeconomic class. More generally, Baynard found a widespread New Zealand stereotype of Maori and Polynesians as 'unemployed' and 'uneducated'. On this topic, it is certainly worth mentioning Richard Benton's article (also in *English Around the World*) in which he questions the assumption that there is a variety of Maori English which is distinguishable from other varieties of NZE. Benton argues that there is a lack of evidence for a distinct Maori accent, and that if there are differences between Maori and other New Zealand varieties, then they may be in areas difficult to quantify such as Semantics and Metaphor. Finally here, we should note, if only in passing, that Joshua Fishman's *Reversing Language Shift* gives a detailed account of Maori as part of his discussion of why most efforts to reverse language shift are, at best, only indifferently successful. Apart from Maori, Fishman provides case studies of numerous other languages including Irish and Basque.

This year has seen the publication of the first systematic sociolinguistic analysis of the use of English in the African continent. This is Josef Schmied's *English in Africa: An Introduction*. Schmied begins his work with an historical account of the arrival of English in Africa, and highlights how patterns of invasion, contact and settlement (traced through the historical periods of early trading connections, imperial rule and independence) have led to complex present-day sociopolitical and sociolinguistic situations. In his analysis of the sociolinguistic position of English in Africa, Schmied deals with the important issue of distinguishing between official and national languages, and reports that while some speakers believe that English fulfils both of these functions, others argue that the notion of nationhood is to do with solidarity and loyalty, both of which are expressed by the use of African languages. Schmied also comments on the difficulty of assessing how many speakers of English there are in Africa, and the underlying theoretical problem of deciding what level of competence is necessary before it is valid to say that a speaker-hearer 'knows' a language. One chapter of the volume concentrates on a detailed analysis of the forms of African English, and specifically patterns of variation (e.g. in pronunciation, grammar and discourse) between African varieties of English and Standard English. Schmied also discusses the role of English in education and assesses the arguments for and against using English as the medium of instruction in African schools. Other topics covered in this volume include the use of English in African literature, attitudes towards English and, in the final chapter, a discussion of the methodological issues involved in carrying out research in the third world, a section in which Schmied pays particular attention to the ethical problems involved in researching in Africa and other countries with a colonial history.

Kembo Sure's paper 'Language functions and language attitudes in Kenya' (*EWW* 12.245–60) examines the attitudes of primary and secondary school aged children in relation to the declared official functions of Kiswahili and English in Kenya. Opinions elicited from primary school children showed that although attitudes towards Kiswahili were favourable, nevertheless children were greatly aware of the utilitarian value of English. In the case of secondary school children, however, Sure found that students played down the utilitarian aspect of English 'in order not to compromise their loyalty to their country'. Sure concludes that the quest for English is motivated by socioeconomic gains which are associated with its possession, while Kiswahili is symbolic of nationhood and political independence.

Finally, on the topic of African languages, we should briefly mention a few papers which appear in *WEn* this year: Raphael Atoye's 'Word stress in Nigerian English' (10.1–6); Tatilayo Ufomata's 'Englishization of Yoruba Phonology' (10.33–52); Paul Mbangwana's 'Invigorative and hermetic innovations in English in Yaoundé' (10.53–63); and finally, Edmund Bamiro's two papers – 'Nigerian Englishes in Nigerian English Literature' (10.7–18) and 'The social and functional power of Nigerian English' (10.275–86).

Moving from Africa to the Americas, *LVC* (3.33–74) includes a paper by Labov, Karen, and Miller on 'Near-mergers and suspension of phonemic contrast', and looks specifically at the near-merger of /er/ and /ʌr/ in Philadelphia. The authors provide a detailed analysis which shows that although a 'small difference' is maintained in the production of /er/ and /ʌr/, nevertheless in the Philadelphian community there has been a general decrease in the 'semantic utility' of this contrast. Labov et al. take this as evidence to suggest the limitations of a categorical view of phonology, and as questioning the assumption of symmetry in speech production and perception. Speaking of phonology, this is perhaps also the place to mention, albeit briefly, Gregory Guy's 'Explanation in variable phonology: an exponential model of morphological constraints' (*LVC* 3.1–22) which aims to provide a detailed analysis and explanation of the morphological constraints which condition reduction of final consonant clusters (*-t, d* deletion) in English. Guy also has a paper in *LVC* (3.223–39) in which he extends his theory of variable lexical phonology.

Continuing on the theme of sociolinguistic work on American English varieties, we should note Bailey, Wikle and Sand's paper on 'The focus of linguistic change in Texas' (*EWW* 12.195–214), which reports on a new approach to identifying innovative speech areas. From the basis of a study of eleven phonological variables in Texas speech, Bailey et al. argue that in contrast to often-held assumptions, the emergence of focal areas is not primarily a consequence of city size. Indeed, the authors argue that it may not be cities themselves but rather their suburbs which take the lead in the spread of a linguistic innovation. Bailey et al. conclude that features such as the demographic make-up of cities, their location in particular dialect areas, and their proximity to innovations spreading from other regions are all important to their emergence (and that of their suburbs) as focal areas. Also on the topic of language change, Bailey, Wikle, Tillery and Sand's paper 'The apparent time construct' (*LVC* 3.241–64) aims to test the assumption made by apparent time studies that differences among generations of similar adults mirror diachronic developments in a language. From the basis of detailed consideration, the authors conclude that the apparent time construct is 'unquestionably a valid and useful analytic tool'.

Papers dealing with African American vernacular (AAV) varieties include Rickford et al.'s 'Rappin on the copula coffin', a study of copula deletion in AAV (*LVC* 3.103–32), which aims specifically to address the two questions of whether the contraction and deletion of 'is' should be considered separately from 'are', and whether the methods traditionally employed to compute contraction and deletion affect the results obtained. *LVC* (3.301–39) also includes a paper by Poplack and Tagliamonte giving 'the first systematic linguistic documentation of African Nova Scotian English'.

This year has seen a number of publications on American Indian varieties of English. In *EWW* (12.25–61), Beth Craig argues in favour of a continuity hypothesis (expansion, stabilization and decreolization) to explain the development of today's American Indian varieties from an original pidgin English. Eung-Do Cook's paper 'Linguistic divergence in Fort Chipewyan' (*LSoc* 20.423–40) provides a critical analysis of Scollon and Scollon's analysis of Chipewyan speech, and argues that there is no evidence for convergence but rather for intra-linguistic divergence in this Athapaskan language. And Guy Lanoue's article (*LSoc* 20.87–115) on the influence of English on Sekani (once spoken by 500–1000 people in north central British Columbia) reports that English has remained as the everyday language for Sekani speakers even though its influence has long since ceased. Lanoue concludes that English now functions as a language in which young speakers represent and express their ideas of pan-Indianism: that is, English has been adopted by young speakers to show unity and allegiance to a particular political aim.

From the basis of their investigation of language use in Canada, Morrison, Reimer, and Shaver report on the problems faced by English speakers in Quebec (*EWW* 12.63–74). Specifically, they highlight how after the 1980 referendum on Quebec's independence, Anglophones were forced to see themselves as a minority group and that as a consequence, there has been a mass exodus particularly of young Anglophones from the Eastern townships of Quebec. Richard Bailey also considers the use of English in Canada, and specifically variation across dialects of Canadian English in volume 7:iii of *EnT* (20–5). Finally, we should mention Lucas and Valli's paper 'ASL or contact signing: issues of judgement' (*LSoc* 20.201–16), in which the authors report both on the forms of signing which result from contact between American Sign Language and English, and also (and of equal interest) on how social information about a signer can influence interlocutors' judgements about the sign language being used.

Moving on to the islands around America, in a paper entitled 'Varilingual Competence' (*EWW* 12.87–102), Valerie Youssef discusses the interaction between exposure to different linguistic varieties and patterns of stylistic shifting in the speech of three young Trinidadian children. Youssef reports that the mixing and patterns of shifting shown by the children reflected mixing in the language input to them, and specifically that the children's linguistic choices functioned in a Trinidadian–Standard English complex which 'rendered their development varilingual'. Youssef also has a paper in *LVC* (3.75–101) in which she discusses the variable use of English and Trinidadian verb forms by a child exposed to both language varieties. Youssef finds that as early as 2·7 years, the child used the verb forms of each language variably according to such factors as addressee, discourse mode, semantic intent, and grammatical factors.

In his paper 'Creoles at the intersection of variable processes: *-t, d* deletion and past-marking in the Jamaican Mesolect' (*LVC* 3.171–89), Peter Patrick addresses the question of whether well-known patterns of deletion in numerous varieties of English (e.g. African, American Appalachian) also occur in Jamaican creole mesolectal speech. From detailed analysis, Patrick concludes that the difference in *-t, d* deletion between mesolectal Jamaican Creole and American dialects is a difference in past marking: a difference which he contends is both 'important' and has a 'definite creole flavour'.

Salikoko Mufwene's paper 'Some reasons why Gullah is not dying yet' (*EWW* 12.215–43), presents the argument that Gullah (a creole language spoken in the Georgia and South Carolina Sea Islands) has been mis-characterized as 'post-creole continua'. Mufwene's essential claim is that far from showing rapid change, Gullah has remained fairly stable over the past sixty years: for example, Mufwene reports that there have been no significant changes in Gullah's grammatical system. Mufwene proposes a convincing argument to suggest that the reason why Gullah has been classed as a dying language is that it is a highly stigmatized variety which is not used with outsiders and is thus not easy to elicit.

JPCL also includes a number of papers on pidgin and creole languages of islands around America. In volume six, Derek Bickerton gives a critical analysis of the recent 'gradualness' hypothesis of creole development, and argues in favour of his theory of the 'catastrophic' single-generational account of creole genesis (25–58). Moving from Hawaii to Haiti, we should mention John Lumsden's paper 'On the argument structure of certain Haitian predicates – *rete*, 'to remain', *possib* – 'possible'' (*JPCL* 6.59–72). And finally, we should briefly note Margaret Marshall's analysis of the verb and noun phrase constructions in the French creole spoken in Mon Louis Island, Alabama (*JPCL* 6.73–87).

Other island language studies include Watson-Gegeo and Gegeo's 'The impact of church affiliation on language use in Kwara'ae (Solomon Islands)' (*LSoc* 20.533–56). This paper reports that members of different religious affiliations signal their separate identities not only through the linguistic code, but also through the use of certain discourse patterns and strategies of nonverbal communication. We should also point out that volume 88 of *IJSL* this year is devoted to languages of the Philippines, and includes an article by Bautista who considers explicitly the relationship between English and Philippine varieties (19–32). In *EnT* (7:iv.17–21), Isagani R. Cruz also discusses the language situation in the Philippines and reports on the interplay between Filipino and English in contemporary usage.

Outside of the articles included in *English Around the World*, relatively little has been published on varieties of Indian English this year. As a qualification to this, we should mention Vinod Dubey's 'The lexical style of Indian newspapers' (*WEn* 10.19–32); Rajeshwari Pandharipande's paper on Sanskrit and its relationship to English in Indian communities (*EnT* 7:ii.7–10); Tariq Rahman's report on the lexicon of Pakistani English (*EnT* 7:ii.32–38); and Raj N. Bakshi's analysis of the 'idiosyncratic vocabulary items' of Indian English (*EnT* 7:iii.43–6).

We have come across only three papers on the relationship between English and Chinese, all of which appear in *WEn*: Scollon and Wong-Scollon's paper on 'Topic confusion in English-Asian discourse' (10.113–26), Jung-Ying Lu's analysis of 'code-switching between Mandarin and English' (10.127–38), and Kamwangamalu and Cher-Leng's analysis of Chinese-English code-mixing (10.247–61).

One of the most significant publications this year in English Dialectology is Trudgill and Chambers' (eds.) *Dialects of English: Studies in Grammatical Vari-*

ation. The volume includes a collection of papers from the 1970s and 1980s dealing with aspects of grammatical variation in British, American and Australian English dialects. Divided into five main parts – pronouns, verb systems, aspect, non-finite verbs and adverbials – the papers included deal mainly although not exclusively with 'traditional dialects' rather than with mainstream non-standard forms. For it is in such traditional varieties, Trudgill and Chambers argue, that grammatical variation is shown most clearly. Dialects commented on include those employed in Ireland, Scotland, South-West England, and American English varieties such as that of Newfoundland and the Appalachian Mountains. Exceptions to the emphasis on traditional dialects include Cheshire's paper on the use of *ain't* in Reading, and Eisikovits's analysis of grammatical variation in the variety of English spoken in Sydney. The collection also includes a paper by Labov on 'The boundaries of a grammar: inter-dialectal reactions to positive *any more*'. The main impact of the volume, and the reason for its significance, is that it establishes syntax as a level of linguistic structure open to variation analysis: an approach to linguistic study which has hitherto been mainly concerned with the phonological level. Indeed, in the volume, Trudgill and Chambers suggest that since grammatical variants 'evade the conscious awareness of listeners and speakers' then grammatical (syntactic as well as morphological) features may prove to be the most useful for variation analysis.

In speaking of research which extends the scope of (socio) linguistics, we should go no further before mentioning the work of Ronald Macaulay published this year – *Locating Dialect in Discourse: the Language of Honest Men and Bonnie Lasses in Ayr*. This research (first mentioned by Ken Turner in a review of Macaulay's pilot study paper – *YWES* 1989) provides an analysis not only of phonological, morphological, lexical and syntactic features, but also gives a description of variation in discourse features. More importantly, Macaulay points to the importance of bringing together the concerns of sociolinguistics and discourse analysis: specifically, he argues that to achieve a full account of language use, it is necessary to identify the relationship between both linguistic context (textual distribution of variables) and extra-linguistic context (speaker variables). Macaulay's work is thus a study in what he and others have termed micro-sociolinguistics. However, unlike many such studies, it does not simply deal with quantitative variation, but rather uses quantitative methods as a basis from which to provide more qualitative comment. Macaulay concludes his work with a call for a more honest approach in sociolinguistic methodology and particularly in interview techniques. Specifically, Macaulay rejects the notion of the 'sociolinguistic interview' in which various styles are elicited by artificial means, and argues that interviewers must instead obey the 'norms of polite conversation' and carry out detailed initial research in order to find out under what conditions informants are willing to talk. This call for honesty is not out of place in a work which itself provides detailed evidence for all arguments and hypotheses pursued. Macaulay is also able to present complex analysis and ideas in a clear and concise way which makes the volume understandable for those who do not have any formal linguistic training, and yet compelling for those who have.

Terence Odlin's paper 'Irish idioms and language transfer' (*EWW* 12.175–93) examines the transfer of Irish Gaelic idioms into Irish English speech. Odlin aims to identify the factors which encourage cross-linguistic influence in bilingual settings. He concludes that in the west of Ireland, three main factors have encouraged bilinguals to minimize the differences between Irish Gaelic and Irish English: (i) structural similarities between the two languages; (ii) the presence of a large number of bilinguals whose speech provided a model of the target language; and (iii) the unavoidability of schooling for most children during the decades in which bilingualism was especially common. Finally, in this review of British English dialects, we should briefly note Beat Glauser's paper 'Transition areas versus focal areas in English Dialectology' (*EWW* 12.1–24), in which he claims that although speaker-hearers are quite often willing to give opinions on dialect boundaries, nevertheless focal areas are in fact rather 'insignificant' and 'transition is the rule'. Glauser concludes that there is little overlap between 'boundaries of the mind' and those of linguistic surveys.

This year has also seen the publication of a number of works concerned with the use of minority languages in Britain and the relationship between these varieties and English. Of these works the most comprehensive and authoritative is Safder Alladina and Viv Edwards's collection *Multilingualism in the British Isles*. Arranged in two volumes, the collection is organized into seven geolinguistically-based parts: older mother tongues of Britain, languages of Eastern Europe, Mediterranean languages, Asian languages, the languages of West Africa and the Caribbean, and languages of the Middle East. Each article has a similar structure providing information on the sociolinguistic situation in the country of origin of the language, the history of the arrival and settlement of the different speech communities, and the results for the language and speech community of contact with English. Each paper remarks on the difficulties encountered by speakers of minority languages in gaining recognition and acceptance of the languages spoken. For example, in his paper on British Sign Language (BSL), Paddy Ladd notes that BSL has not only been a language struggling for its existence but 'has also had a struggle to be accepted as a *bona fide* language at all'. The result of contact between English and minority varieties is often shown to result in complex linguistic situations. Ali Haouas reports that many of the Moroccan community resident in Britain work in settings alongside other non-native speakers, and that, as a consequence, communication tends to take the form of a simplified 'survival' English. The result of this is that for many adult speakers in the Moroccan speech community Arabic is still the dominant language. However, although parents in Moroccan homes address their children in Arabic, because of the influence and teaching of the school, children respond in English.

The collection of papers edited by Colin Williams – *Linguistic Minorities, Society and Territory* – also concentrates on the problems faced by minority speakers and the relationship between English and minority languages. However, this is where the similarity with Alladina and Edwards's collection ends. For while Alladina and Edwards use geolinguistics simply as a practical method for grouping the languages under consideration, in Williams's collection, geolinguistics (and the role of this discipline in furthering our understanding of the 'plight of linguistic minorities') is a central theme. Indeed, as Williams states in his introduction, the volume is very much a companion to *Language in Geographic Context* (Williams, 1988). As a consequence of this theme, the articles included in the volume are written by experts in local authority planning as well as by (socio)linguists. Generally, this means that the papers tend to be more concerned with describing and detailing figures of population, policy, and the economic conditions affecting speakers of minority varieties, rather than, for instance, with attitudes towards minority languages. More specifically, there is considerable emphasis on maps, diagrams and graphic representation of minority language situations. Indeed, one complete chapter (Williams and Ambrose) is devoted to a consideration of the strengths and weaknesses of language-mapping techniques, and to discussing the way forward for illustrating and graphically depicting complex language situations.

On the topic of minority languages, we should mention, albeit briefly, Ben Rampton's paper 'Interracial Panjabi in a British Adolescent peer Group' (*LSoc* 20.iii.391–422), in which Rampton reports on a tendency for native English speakers as well as Panjabi adolescents to use Panjabi as a 'language of local association'; and Marilyn Martin-Jones's article on 'Linguistic minorities in three British cities' (*IJSL* 90.37–56). Also, although not dealing with the English language *per se*, we should nevertheless note the publication of James Tollefson's *Planning Language, Planning Inequality: Language Planning in the Community*. In this engaging volume Tollefson deals with the question of why millions of speakers fail to learn and speak the language varieties necessary for their survival in the modern world. Each chapter presents a detailed case study dealing with 'real-life' language problems facing people around the world. Chapters included cover such topics as the ideology of language planning theory, mother-tongue maintenance, and language policy and migration. Finally, we should mention Barbara Horvath and P. Vaughan's *Community languages: A handbook*, in which Horvath and Vaughan provide details on languages which, over the past hundred years or so, migrants have brought to countries which are primarily English-speaking. Each chapter deals with a different language (e.g. Arabic, Cantonese, Gujerati, Kurdish etc.) and provides information on such topics as the origin, the development, and the colloquial speech forms of each variety.

Moving away from regional varieties of English to publications dealing with forms used by particular social groups and in specific channels of communication, we should first review Alan Bell's *The Language of News Media*. In this volume, Bell gives a clear and comprehensive account of the language employed in what he terms 'the narratives of our time' – that is, communications from daily news stories in the press, television and radio. Bell identifies three significant themes: the process of production of media communication, the notion and structure of the news story, and last, but certainly not least, the role of media audiences. It is, of course, Bell's investigations of the influence and effects of audience that are best known, and his hypothesis that 'the essence of style is that speakers are responding to their audience' is the crucial theme of his latest work. Bell has the rare quality of being able to present factual information in a manner which is totally compelling: this is one of the books this year which once picked up is impossible to put down.

Coupland, Coupland and Giles's *Language, Society and the Elderly* extends sociolinguistic analysis to a community of speakers who have hitherto been largely ignored by (socio)linguists in a way which, the authors argue, has 'mirrored society's reticence to engage with older people'. The essential aim of the volume is to contribute to and develop the field of gerontological sociolinguistics, and specifically to dispel the decrement hypothesis of language in old age: the authors aim to show that decrement by no means necessarily relates to the aging process, and that it is important to see the elderly as a static (rather than only) transitional social unit. Added to their analysis of the elderly as a social group in their own right, the authors also examine the dynamics of intergenerational talk – an examination carried out using the concepts of speech accommodation theory developed in another volume edited by Giles, Coupland and Coupland this year: *Contexts of Accommodation*. Other works of interest published by Giles and Coupland during the past year are *Language: Contexts and Consequences*; and, in conjunction with Wieman, *Miscommunication and Problematic Talk*. In the former, Giles and Coupland provide a social psychological discussion of interpersonal and intergroup processes in a variety of language encounters. In the latter, Coupland, Giles and Wieman edit a collection of fifteen papers discussing the topics of misunderstanding, misattribution, social inequality, conflict and nonsuccess in linguistic encounters. The collection includes papers by Nancy Henley and Cheris Kramarae, Elinor Ochs, and Alan Bell.

Turning now finally to the always engrossing topic of linguistic prescriptivism, we should mention first Tony Crowley's *Proper English? Readings in Language, History and Cultural Identity*. In this volume, Crowley brings together a collection of texts spanning over three hundred years which, the editor argues, not only give insights into the question of what is proper English, but also provide some answers to the related but 'more significant' questions of 'who are the proper English?' and 'what are the criteria for proper Englishness in a number of different areas of social and cultural life?' The volume opens with John Locke's 'An essay concerning human understanding', and includes extracts from Thomas Sheridan's 'A course of lectures on elocution', Henry James's 'The speech of American women', and John Marenbon's 'English our English'. Another collection dealing with the issue of prescriptivism is Burke and Porter's *Language, Self and Society: A Social History of Language*. In this volume the editors bring together nine articles organized in three main parts: authoritative tongues, language and social authority, meaning and the self. There is also an afterword by Dell Hymes who concentrates on discussing the interplay between sociolinguistics and the historical study of languages. Other articles on prescriptivism include Robert Eagleson's paper on the Plain English lobby in Australia (in Romaine's *Language in Australia*), and a paper in *EnT* (7.40–3) by the Plain English campaigner Martin Cutts.

Finally on this issue, we should certainly mention the publication of the second edition of Milroy and Milroy's *Authority in Language* – an updated version of their comprehensive commentary on the causes and consequences of linguistic prescriptivism. The other second edition of relevance this year is O'Donnell and Todd's *Variety in Contemporary English* – a revised version of their introduction to language variation and diversity aimed at college and university students beginning the study of linguistics. And to close this section we should note with some cheer that Florian Coulmas's classic account of *The Writing Systems of the World* has been published in paperback this year, making it now a work which is not only authoritative but also affordable.

4. Phonetics, Phonology, and Orthography

Compared with earlier years, this one has been relatively quiet. The most conspicuous point to emerge from Peter Lucas's 'Some Aspects of the Historical Development of English Consonant Phonemes' (*TPS* 89.37–64) is that a solid, more-or-less Praguian, phonemic interpretation of the consonant system from Old English to Middle English (with the occasional foray into later centuries) is still justifiable; there isn't a phonological process rule in sight. Even so, some engagement with more recent, if trendier, theories would have been welcome – if only to counter them.

Donka Minkova promises us more than she actually gives in *The History of Final Vowels in English: The Sound of Muting*. This is description and explanation of the loss of schwa during the Middle English period, not a full-scale survey of final vowels throughout the last millennium. Her review of the literature from Morsbach (1896) onwards is refreshingly clear – and where there have been, and still are, controversies, she is quick to point them out. She argues that the explanation for schwa-loss (slower of course in Adjective endings) lies in a Hayesian, non-linear, account of the prosodic organization of the vocabulary in question. My objection to this is the assumption, made by the theory (not her), about the location of boundaries between items on the same hierarchical level. That being so, Minkova deserves credit for putting the question of [e]-loss firmly back on the historical agenda.

A further example of the continuing appeal of non-linear phonology as a theoretical model for elucidating problems in the history of English is Christopher McCully's 'Non-Linear Phonology and Elizabethan Prosody' (*TPS* 89.1–35). This is intriguing. He argues that a factor, hitherto overlooked, in explaining the development of the quantitative movement in verse composition during the second half of the sixteenth century (Campion, Sidney et al.) may have been the acceptability by then of word-stress templates imported into English over the previous few centuries from the Romance languages. This same argument has been heard informally before, of course. McCully's achievement is to tackle it in a detailed way and with due regard for the difficulties in establishing precisely how English of the later sixteenth century would have sounded, both in verse recitation and in normal, informal colloquial speech.

Charles Jones has done a service to students of eighteenth- and nineteenth-century phonology with his edition, from two surviving MS copies, of Sylvester Douglas (Lord Glenbervie's) *A Treatise on the Provincial Dialect of Scotland*, dating from about 1779. Douglas's aim was to detail, for the benefit of those Scots wishing to acquire a London-sounding pronunciation, the differences between the pronunciation of English in Scotland, which, though not 'rural' or 'vulgar', still contained certain residual Scottish features, and that of London English. Douglas's text is part pronouncing dictionary and part exposition of some of the phonetic/phonological features of the two Englishes. In his introduction, Jones treats in some detail various aspects of Douglas's statements, and relates them to what can reasonably be constructed from other sources about Scottish English of this period. Even so, there are some nagging questions. What sort of Scottish English was Douglas describing? What was Douglas's own accent like? (He was born in Aberdeen but moved about a lot within Britain.) Is it possible to reconstruct pronunciations by working solely in terms of phonetic symbols? Shouldn't vowel sounds in particular be located on a chart? Our thanks, nevertheless, to Jones for making available an important addition to the relatively small database on non-London English from this period.

Staying with London but slightly later in time, we note Lynda Mugglestone's 'The Fallacy of the Cockney Rhyme: From Keats and Earlier to Auden' (*RES* 42.57–66), a valuable study which adduces a good deal of useful information about variable rhoticity in English accents from the late eighteenth and nineteenth centuries. Keats could rhyme THOUGHTS and SORTS, but several of his contemporaries frowned on this as 'vulgar'. Mugglestone shows the extent to which Keats's Cockneyish phonology and that of pre-Jonesian RP were at variance, and how in later years they moved closer together. A puzzle from the end of the nineteenth century, namely the authorship of the 'Arthur the Rat' passage, sometimes used in English phonetic field-work, is solved by Michael MacMahon in his 'The Woman Behind Arthur' (*JIPA* 21.29–31).

Vowels have, as ever, attracted attention. Kenneth de Jong returns to an old problem in his 'An Articulatory Study of Consonant-Induced Vowel Duration Changes in English' (*Phonetica* 48.1–17), namely the precise reasons for differences of vowel length in words like SIT, SID, DISH. Is it voicing, or manner of articulation, or both, or what? A detailed study, using X-ray microbeams, of two speakers of American English leads to several conclusions, but still leaves puzzles. The approach he has adopted is, however, promising, and one looks for more extensive studies with larger numbers of speakers.

The source of the distinction in some forms of South African English between the stressed vowels of FINISH and FINNISH has been commented on before (influence from Afrikaans? Chain-shifting involving the front vowels? A Southern English source historically?). John Taylor, in his 'Remarks on the Kin-Pin Vowels in South African English' (*EWW* 12.75–85) suggests a different solution. Using the spectrographic evidence of a single speaker's vowel productions, he jumps to the conclusion that it may have been the 'exaggeration' of allophonic differences which led to the phonemicization of the different sounds. There are parallels for this sort of thing, as we know, in other areas of the history of English, but he fails to show convincingly why this should have come about in South African English and not in other accents.

Not separating allophones, but merging phonemes is the subject of Vivian Brown's 'Evolution of the Merger of /ɪ/ and /ɛ/ before Nasals in Tennessee' (*AS* 66.303–15). Using written documents from the nineteenth century as well as the USA dialect surveys, she speculates that the source of the homophony of words like PIN and PEN may be the original English dialect that gave rise to this particular form of American English in the first place.

On the decidedly more physiological and acoustic sides of the subject, we should note, first of all, John Laver's *The Gift of Speech. Papers in the Analysis of Speech and Voice* (titlepage 1991; published 1992). This is a gem of a book. Almost all of the twenty articles have appeared before (often in specialist publications), but having them here allows easy access to a body of significant ideas and conclusions in fields such as the neurolinguistics of speech and normal and pathological voice qualities; it also allows one a considered evaluation of Laver's contributions to phonetics over nearly thirty years. The research-based content of much of them will not make the book easy-going for first-year students; for more advanced students, though, it will be a boon. My only reservation is the price: a paperback edition should be considered, as the book deserves a wide circulation. One of Laver's mentors is Peter Ladefoged, to whom he pays eloquent thanks, both in the book and in 'A Tribute to Peter Ladefoged' (*JIPA* 21.1–3). Another of Laver's mentors was David Abercrombie, the author of *Fifty Years in Phonetics: Selected Papers*. Coming from an older generation, whose ideas about phonetics were largely formed before the experimental and computational era of the 1950s onwards, Abercrombie reflects a different style of preoccupation (accents of English, writing systems, suprasegmentals, etc.). Like Laver's, almost all of the articles have been published before, and they too are worth reading, for the elegance of their exposition and the independence from intellectual fashions that comes through strongly in their content.

Finally, anyone looking for an up-to-date and yet readable account of speech acoustics would be advised to turn to Stuart Rosen and Peter Howell's *Signals and Systems for Speech and Hearing*. It won't displace Dennis Fry's *Physics of Speech*; but it will certainly complement it, especially because of the clarity of its argument. Despite its rather opaque title, I have found that it has gained strong support amongst students: they commend it for its sensible and intelligible style. I agree.

5. Morphology

Productivity is a notion that is not only central to morphological theory but one that, as Harald Baayen and Rochelle Lieber observe in their breakthrough 'Productivity and English Derivation: a Corpus-based Study' (*Linguistics* 29.801–43), also continues to be problematical. In his well-known 1976 study *Word Formation in Generative*

Grammar, Mark Aronoff argues that, rather than seeing the productivity of word-formation rules (WFR) as directly quantifiable in terms of the number of word types occurring with the WFR's affix, the productivity index should be a ratio of actual word types with the relevant affix to those possible (given the constraints a WFR may be subject to, such as 'applies only to Latinate base'). Baayen and Lieber point out, however, that measured this way, productivity does not tally with our intuitions and that, in fact, the above is an index of 'unproductivity': only for unproductive WFRs can one estimate the number of 'possible' types. Inspired by Schultink's 1961 insight that true morphological productivity involves new formations which are coined *unintentionally* and whose number is in principle uncountable, Baayen and Lieber propose to measure a WFR's 'strict' productivity (i.e. productivity relative to a fixed corpus) in terms of the ratio in the corpus of the number of types occurring only once with the relevant affix (*hapax legomena*) to the overall number of tokens with the same affix. For a WFR to be highly productive in this sense, the number of tokens needn't be high, only the *hapax*-token ratio has to be high; moreover, even though the ratio is bound to go down as the corpus increases in size (more chance of repetition), the hallmark of true productivity (new formations) will continue to be reflected in even very large corpora. Descriptively, this study provides a whole new set of data in the form of a(n intuitively satisfactory) ranking of a large number of English affixal classes in terms of their degree of productivity. Apart from this, it opens our eyes to the fact that verbal base words are significantly less conducive to derivational processes than nominal ones, reveals that including tokens in the count produces theoretically more reliable results than basing the count on types alone and, lastly, makes it possible to 'make a principled distinction between truly productive 'vogue' morphemes such as *-ee* and unproductive affixes like *-esque* which are sporadically found in neologisms' (p. 839). Gregory Stump tackles another notorious stumbling block in morphological theory in terms of 'A paradigm-based theory of morpho-semantic mismatches' (*Language* 67.675–725). If, to concentrate on one English example, the comparative of *unhappy* is analysed as [$_A$ [$_A$ *un-* [$_A$ *happi*]]-*er*], the analysis is semantically adequate (the comparative morpheme modifies the unit 'unhappy') but morphologically implausible (by and large, the comparative suffix *-er* joins only with adjectives of at most two syllables); the reverse is the case for the alternative analysis [$_A$ *un-* [$_A$ [$_A$ *happi*] *-er*]]. Stump argues that such morphosemantic 'mismatches' can be smoothly dealt with if, (i) one's approach to inflectional semantics is paradigm-based (that is, the meaning of a word *w* is a function of its root *x* and of the slot *w* fills in *x*'s paradigm; thus, if *w* is *happier*, its meaning is a function of the root *happy* and of the comparative slot) and (ii) each morpholexical rule (MLR) is supplemented by a so-called 'paradigm function', i.e. a function from the root of a lexeme to one of the inflected words in that lexeme's paradigm, regardless of whether the inflected word is built up directly from its root or not. Thus *happy*, *bad* and *unhappy* involve three distinct comparative paradigm functions. *Happy* is the maximally default case: its value is straightforwardly the output of the comparative MLR applied to *happy*, i.e. [$_A$ [$_A$ *happi*] *-er*]; for *bad*, its value is simply listed as [$_A$ *worse*] and for *unhappy* its value is recursively defined, as the output of the WFR forming un-adjectives applied to the value of the above comparative paradigm function of *happy*. Thus morphological structure is regular and mismatches are resolved by paradigm functions. Taro Kageyama advocates a modular morphological approach to deal with the ModE problem that he tackles in 'Light Verb Constructions and the Syntax-Morphology Interface' (in Nakajima), i.e. the structural ambivalence of constructions like *they made an allusion to the secret* (the *to*-PP and the predicational NP *an allusion* behave as distinct complements despite the fact that the PP is dependent on *allusion* for θ-role assignment). Assuming that at D-structure the *to*-PP is a structural complement of *allusion*, he proposes to resolve the problem in terms of a word formation rule, 'abstract incorporation'; this rule makes, through co-indexing, one 'word' of the light verb *make* and the NP *an allusion*. The analysis thus provides support for the Modular Morphology theory, which allows for word formation operations in both the syntax and the lexicon.

In the historical field, Roger Lass launches a frontal attack against a 'neogrammarian' view of morphological change in 'Of data and "datives": Ruthwell Cross *rodi* Again' (*NM* 92.395–403). The question, as usually put, is: shouldn't eOE locative *rodi* have an *-e* rather than an *i-* ending (*rod* being an ō-stem), or is it perhaps a deliberate archaism (it being part of the Ruthwell Cross rune)? Lass sees the form as both genuine and unproblematic instead; the real problem is an untenable view of the evolution of Germanic morphology as always 'following the book' with regard to case endings and declension classes. Given the fact that the Germanic 'dative' collapsed a number of IE case categories into one while the morphological relics of the other categories were still around, eighth-century *rod* allowed, more likely than not, for both *-i* and *-e* 'datives', much in the same way that we can nowadays choose between *schemata* or *schemas* as plural for *schema*, the choice possibly depending on individual speakers, on educational or regional factors or whatever. Lass's message in short: 'Not all lineages are coherent, and not all populations are homogeneous' (p. 400). Karl Sandred is also concerned with 'anomolous' OE morphological forms in 'Nominal Inflection in the Old English of the Anglo-Saxon Land Charters' (*SN* 63:3–12). In these charters there occur a number of feminine nouns with masculine/neuter inflections, especially the genitive ending *-es*, cf. *burges* (< feminine *burg*) in *Sunnan burges bóc* 'the charter of Sunbury'. These genitive nouns appear to be used in a secondary 'habitation' sense rather than their primary 'nature' sense and Sandred suggests (giving Tengstrand credit for the idea) that this choice of gender was conceptually induced, the nouns with 'habitative' sense assuming the (masculine/neuter) gender of conceptually related words like *hām* and *land*. In 'The Germanic Seventh Class of Strong Verbs' (*NOWELE* 18.97–100) Frederik Kortlandt discusses the threefold reflex of the Proto-Germanic reduplicated preterite in OE and other Germanic languages, i.e. (1) reduplicated preterites, as in Gothic *haihait*, OE *heht* 'called', (2) *r*-preterites, as in OE *reord* 'advised' and (3) ē-preterites as in OE *fēong*. Kortlandt reviews previous accounts of the evolution of (2) and (3), providing supplementary arguments for the proposal that (3) is basically due to *e*-infixation (before the present tense root vowel) and rounding; thus OE *fēong* 'seized' is a straightforward example of *e*-infixation before root vowel *a* and subsequent rounding under the influence of nasal *ng* (the combination of root *a* and nasal *ng* is still evident in ModE *fang* 'tooth' and ModDutch *vangen* 'catch'). He further argues that the *r*-preterite in (2) is a case of reduplication plus metathesis; thus the reduplicated form **rerōd*, undergoing metathesis, yields OE *reord* 'advised' (cf. non-reduplicated OE infinitival *rǣdan* 'advise'). Hans Peters' 'Two Suffixes Reconsidered: Old English *-ild* and *-incel*' (*ES* 72.106–22) is also of a surveying and supplementary nature. He provides all occurrences of *-ild* and *-incel* words and reviews the various existing accounts of their origin and meaning (*-ild* produces ME feminine agentive nouns, *-incel* is an OE diminutive suffix) and concludes: (i) that the most feasible account of the origin of *-ild* is the one given by the EOD (< Germanic **-iþljâ*, which undergoes metathesis into *-ild*) though this means that the two extant OE *-eld/ild* words, not being feminine agentive nouns, must have another origin, and (ii) that there are two competing accounts for the evolution of *-incel*: either it is a conglomerate of Germanic suffixes (which means that the absence of *i*-umlaut is hard to explain, cf. *tūnincel* 'small farm', rather than **tȳincel*) or else the basis is **winkīld* 'child', but then the formation of non-personal compounds (e.g. *stānincel* 'little stone') is, OE *winceld* 'child' still being in existence, problematic.

Angus McIntosh conducts a subtle and, to me, fascinating investigation into 'Old English Adjectives with Derivative *-lic* Partners' (*NM* 92.297–310), distinguishing three adjectival classes, two of which I will explicate here. (i) The base form qualifies an animate substantive (usually a person), whereas the co-existing *-lic* form qualifies a substantive with 'secondarily animate reference' (p. 299); a substantive, in other words, that denotes what persons do, feel, experience etc. Thus McIntosh has found uses of *earm* and *wīs* referring to a person and of *earmlic* and *wīslic* referring to a deed and understanding respectively, and numerous other such pairs. (ii) OE also has base forms as well as their *-lic* partners qualifying an animate substantive; in that case the quality expressed by the *-lic* form is inferred (through observation) from the animate being's behaviour. Thus *mōdig* means 'intrepid', whereas *mōdiglic* means 'intrepid looking'/'having the appearance of being intrepid'. Morton Donner examines similar co-existing pairs for 'Adverb forms in Middle English' (*ES* 72.1–11) and also finds that the adverb with suffix (OE *-lice* > ME-*li*, later *-ly*) tends to have a secondary ('subjective') meaning, complementary to the primary ('objective') meaning of its 'flat' partner (OE *-e* ending, later zero); thus he finds eME *bright* used to indicate how the moon shines, and *brightly* to refer to how anchoresses should understand God's runes. Throughout ME, his data reveal, a systematic correlation between form and meaning prevailed, be it 'not with the force of linguistic rule but only as a freely disregarded convention' (p.7). In other words, the forms also get used interchangeably, the reason being that the *-li/y* suffix uniquely signals adverbial status once the OE adverbial *-e* is no longer pronounced and, subsequently, lost altogether.

Thomas Nunnally investigates 'grammatical efficiency' (his subtitle) in 'Morphology and Word Order within the Old English Noun Phrase' (*NM* 92.421–31), looking at OE genitive marking within genitive noun phrase modifiers (GNPM). These range from being marked highly ambiguously (e.g. *sæ grund* 'the depth of the sea', where *sæ* could signal many another than genitive case) through non-redundantly marked (*sceapa gegurlum* 'sheeps's clothing') to redundantly marked (*þæs cildes sawle* 'that child's soul'). Since Nunnally finds that about one in every ten GNPMs in the West Saxon Gospel of Matthew (a translation intended for unlearned people) was, case-wise, ambiguous, he concludes that, already in OE, it was not just morphology but also word order that played a non-negligible role in signalling syntactic function, each GNPM being adjacent to its head. Of literary interest, lastly, is 'The Creation and Use of Compound Words in Jacobean Tragedy', which shows, author Inna Koskenniemi argues (*NM* 92.63–73), that Renaissance writers favoured compounds for the sake of quick movement of dramatic dialogue (cf. belly-hour in 'What hour is't, Lollio? Towards belly-hour, sir' in Middleton and Rowley's *The Changeling*); that many of them were nonce formations thus follows from their being largely dependent on their particular context for interpretation.

6. Syntax

(a) Modern English

Ever since Peter Rosenbaum's seminal study on English complement constructions (dating back to 1967), linguists have been struggling with the question of how to account in a principled manner for the interpretation of the unexpressed subject ('PRO' in the current jargon) of infinitival complements. Rosenbaum's was a syntactic solution: the Minimal Distance Principle (MDP), which (in its updated version) says that the matrix NP argument that is *minimally distant* from it, controls ('provides the reference for') the PRO subject. This theory is not unproblematic (and that goes for its many syntactic successors as well): certain verbs, *promise* for one, misbehave, 'remote' control is by definition not covered and the theory sheds no light on the well-known asymmetry in passivization possibilities ('Visser's generalization') exhibited by different control verbs, cf. *Tracy was persuaded/*promised to leave by Sandy*. The alternative offered by Ivan Sag and Carl Pollard in 'An Integrated Theory of Complement Control' (*Language* 67.63–113) hinges on two assumptions: (i) controller assignment is semantically rather than syntactically based and (ii) control phenomena result from the interplay of controller assignment and (syntactic) Binding; together, these make a principled explanation of the grammar of English complement control possible, one that uniformly covers local as well as remote control phenomena in both verb and noun complements. There are, Sag and Pollard argue, (at least) three semantic classes of control predicates which each have their own designated controller role (the 'influence' role for 'influence' predicates such as *persuade/persuasion*, the 'committor' role for 'commitment' predicates such as *promise/attempt* and the 'experiencer' role for 'orientation' predicates such as *expect/expectation*) and control theory is semantic in that it involves coindexation of the semantic argument filling the (designated) controller role with the one filling the infinitival complement's subject role (where coindexation of two arguments means 'being anchored to the same referent'). As for (Sag and Pollard's version of) Binding, the unexpressed subject (not a structural one) has anaphoric status and is as such locally bound by a matrix object *or* subject (if such is available; if not, an antecedent is found at discourse level). What this means is that, as far as Binding is concerned, the unexpressed subject in *Sandy promised Tracy to leave* can pick its referent from either the subject or the object of *promise*, but in fact the choice is, control theory requiring that the 'committor' argument act as controller, limited down to the subject of *promise*; the reverse is the case in sentences with e.g. *persuade*. Though as yet unable to give an entirely satisfactory account of Visser's generalization, Sag and Pollard are, it seems to me, definitely on the right track, which cannot, in my opinion, be said for Richard Larson's highly artificial attempt, in '*Promise* and the Theory of Control' (*LingI* 22.103–39), to reinstate the MDP as the backbone of control theory. In his view, the difference between verbs like *promise* and *persuade* is that the former, but not the latter, is a 'dative' verb. Larson argues that in the case of dative verbs the *to*-infinitive is the notional 'direct object', the NP argument having only 'oblique' status and this means that at D-structure the former occupies the VP specifier slot, while the latter is in the (syntactically more deeply embedded) complement position; it is at this level that the MDP identifies the matrix subject as controller for the infinitival subject. Dative Shift, Larson holds, is responsible for the subsequent rearrangement of the two arguments (promotion of the NP, demotion of the *to*-infinitive) and therefore for the *apparent* violation of the MDP at S-level. With non-dative *persuade* type verbs, the *to*-infinitive has oblique status already at D-structure and the MDP straightforwardly assigns controller status to the NP that is – both at D- and at S-structure – 'direct object'. Passivization of this latter construction does not affect the D-structure position of the controller NP, but in the case of *promise* the controller NP is demoted to a position (in the *by*-phrase) where it no longer commands the infinitive phrase and can therefore no longer exercise control. In short, Visser's generalization has theorem status, as desired. The original motivation for Larson's double object analysis (cf. *YWES* 71) was to prevent the two objects from being sister nodes (their asymmetrical behaviour with regard to Binding is in conflict with their being sisters). However, as Satomi Honda notes in 'The Dative-Accusative Asymmetry in Double Object Constructions' (*Ling&Philol* 11.85–101), this analysis leaves unexplained why, contrary to what Chomsky's Empty Category Principle (ECP) predicts, *wh*-movement of the first object leads to unacceptability, cf. **Who did you give a book*. Honda therefore resorts to Kayne's analysis of the dative NP as governed by an empty preposition which transmits case from the matrix verb onto the dative NP; the second NP object is then assumed to have inherent case. *Wh*-extraction from an empty-headed PP inevitably leads to an ECP violation and the analysis also predicts a case conflict, hence ungrammaticality, for e.g. **The book was given Mary*, *the book* having both inherent and nominative case.

There is a variety of other studies that also deal with complementation one way or another. Masachiyo Amano, for one, writes 'On a Condition on the Distribution of Sentential Complements' (*Ling&Philol* 11.1–25), proposing certain conditions to account for the fact that English clausal arguments cannot occupy complement slots as freely as their NP variants. To give one example, the sentence **We talked about THAT YOU WERE COMING* is out because it violates the condition that any argument clause must be *directly* θ-marked at D-structure (this is not the case here, since prepositions only *transmit* θ-roles). Frits Stuurman, interested in '*If* and *whether*: Questions and Conditions' (*Lingua* 83:1–41), manages to account for both the standard and the non-standard uses of these two complementizers in a unified manner. Standardly, *whether* heads an interrogative complement, *if* a conditional adjunct; non-standardly, the two swop functions, cf. *Bill asked Mary IF SHE HAD BEEN SEEING JOHN/Bill wouldn't ask Mary out WHETHER SHE HAD BEEN SEEING JOHN OR NOT*. By identifying *whether* as [P,+WH] (*P* for 'preposition' and *+WH* for 'interrogative') and *if* as [P,0WH] (with [+WH] requiring, and [0WH] rejecting proper government), he neatly derives their standard functions (complements, as opposed to adjuncts, must be properly governed); neutralization of their syntactic features (from positive to neutral and vice versa) brings about the swap in usage, with *if*, now [P,+WH], heading an interrogative complement (provided it is governed by a 'strongly interrogative' verb), and *whether*, neutralized into [P,0WH], introducing a conditional adjunct (given a context with correlative *or*). Ever since the introduction of so-called 'small clause' (SC) complements into Government-Binding (GB) theory in the early eighties, there has been, Tomoyuki Tanaka notes, lack of agreement 'On the Categorial Status of Small Clauses' (*Ling&Philol* 11:61–83). Tanaka pleads for the view that SCs have a predicate-headed structure, bringing in as (new) argument that SCs cannot consist of two argument NPs hence must be assumed to lack an INFL node, witness the difference in grammaticality between **I proved [OUR PROFESSOR] [RIKI]* (SC complement) and *I proved [OUR PROFESSOR] [TO BE RIKI]* (INFL complement). The asymmetry between *John is eager/easy TO PLEASE* and *John's eagerness/*easiness TO PLEASE* constitutes another familiar complementation puzzle. Kunihiro Iwakura, identifying the problem as one 'On Government by Noun' (in Nakajima), argues that (i) adjectives (like verbs) can govern across categories but nouns cannot, not even across N' and that (ii) the complement of *eager/eagerness* is a sister of A/N (hence governed by default), whereas the complement of *easy/easiness* is a sister at A'/N' level; given (i), *easy* can, but *easiness* cannot govern its complement, hence lack of government by N accounts for the ungrammaticality of the *easiness* construction. A formally more explicit version of the above construction type *John is easy TO PLEASE* is, of course, *It is easy TO PLEASE JOHN* and the existence of such more as opposed to less explicit pairs is, Hajime Fukuchi argues in 'Syntactic Localization Phenomena in English' (in Nakajima), due to there being two opposing forces at work in language, the one demanding that syntactic forms express semantic content as explicitly as possible and the other working towards configurations becoming as tight as possible; the tightening is achieved by NP upgrading, a phenomenon that is, according to Fukuchi, also at work in many less obvious cases (e.g. in 'concealed propositions' such as *our advisor was pleased with THE HEADWAY WE MADE*, which 'really' means 'our advisor was pleased that we made headway') and awareness of the two forces at work is, in general, necessary for a proper understanding of language. English Nominal Gerund Phrases (NPGs), cf. the complement in *I don't remember YOUR HAVING BROKEN THE RECORD*, form a well-known embarassment for X-bar theory in that they (appear to) violate a cornerstone in its architecture, the endocentricity principle, which requires that every phrase have a unique head. Geoffrey Pullum provides a neat GPSG analysis of 'English Nominal Gerund Phrases as Noun Phrases with Verb-Phrase Heads' (*Linguistics* 29.63–99) which, while achieving factual coverage, also manages to (i) obey endocentricity, (ii) keep syntax morphology-free (so no Affix-hopping) and (iii) license only null-elements that are syntactically or semantically motivated. He proposes, that is, an analysis that sees the NPG as a single-headed construction with a hetero-categorial head, i.e. $[_{NP}$ NP's $[_{VP}\ V_{presprt} \ldots]]$, an analysis that is possible if one assumes that the Head Feature Condition (which passes on features from mother to daughter head nodes) applies by *default* rather than absolutely; in default cases the PS rule with double-bar N as input, while identifying the head, merely assigns it single-bar status, but in non-default cases it can also provide a special syntactic specification for the head instead (in this case: $V_{presprt}$), with a feature-co-occurrence restriction dictating that present participles are [-N,+V]. Juhani Rudanko, also concerned with gerunds, concentrates 'On Verbs Governing *in -ing* in Present-day English' (*ES* 72.55–72), as in *John delights IN FRUSTRATING HIS OPPONENTS*. The point of his paper seems to be that the four semantic classes that *in -ing* verbs divide into, reveal a certain internal as well as cross-class coherence; Rudanko's conclusion is, anyway, that the *in -ing* pattern 'has a fairly well-defined semantic function in present-day English' and won't be 'supplanted' (p. 72) by potentially rival constructions. Thomas Nunnally is, for didactic reasons, interested in 'The Possessive with Gerunds: What the Handbooks Say, and What They Should Say' (*AS* 66.359–70). Two types of gerunds must, he argues, be distinguished, the Nominal-Force Gerund (NFG, e.g. *THE HUNTING OF EAGLES is outlawed*) and the Verbal-Force Gerund (VFG, e.g. *HUNTING EAGLES is outlawed*), the most essential difference between the two being that NFGs can only take possessive subjects whereas VFGs can in principle choose between a possessive or a zero-suffix subject (depending, that is, on specific characteristics of the subject and on usage factors); handbooks, propagating by inbreeding (to use John Algeo's apt phrase) rather than keeping up with 'the field', all fail to give such much-looked-for information.

GB theory holds, as is pointed out by C. L. Baker in 'The Syntax of English *Not*: The Limits of Core Grammar' (*LingI* 22.387–429), that Universal Grammar (UG) is an invariant system of principles paired with a set of parameter specifications; the Core Grammar of any particular language is fully determined by UG and particular parameter settings, and even though resulting 'constructions' may appear to have been produced by 'rules', neither have more than epiphenomenal status. However, the notion Core Grammar is meaningless if it is not complemented by a peripheral component where rules, being outside the scope of UG, do have basic, irreducible status. How, then, does one decide whether a surface phenomenon reduces to general principles or exists in its own right? Linguists exhibit an overwhelmingly strong tendency to opt for reducibility, as is clear from the fact that there are currently three (competing) Core Grammar accounts of the syntax of English *not*. First there is Jean-Yves Pollock's proposal, in 'Verb Movement, Universal Grammar and the Structure of IP' (*LingI* 20.365–424), that (i) UG allows a verb to get its Tense and Agr(eement) features either by V-raising or by Affix-lowering (for English the latter is the unmarked option), that (ii) negative particles, such as English *not*, rather than having simple Adverb status, head a Neg(ative) P(hrase) of their own, and that (iii) there is a major parametric difference between English and French: Agr (which has its own projection, between Tense and V) is 'weak' (opaque for θ-role transmission) in English, 'strong' in French. Together, this enables Pollock to explain why, unlike French, English requires that a finite verb (Vf) precede the negative particle and why, in the absence of a modal, *have* or *be*, the Vf position is filled by *do* (rather than a main verb): NegPs are barriers for Affix-lowering and Agr, being weak, only allows for non-θ-marking verbs such as *have*, *be* and *do* to be V-raised into the Tense phrase. Satomi Niwa follows Pollock as to the weak status of Agr in English but argues, in 'NegP and V-movement' (*Ling&Philol* 11.103–17) that there is no need for a NegP; *not* fills the specifier position in AgrP and as such blocks strings like *John not laughs*, not at S-structure (Affix-lowering is not blocked, since there is no NegP), but at the level of Logical Form. Harumi Sawada proposes a yet different solution in 'The perfective *have* and the progressive *be* as Spec Verbs and the INFL system in English' (in Nakajima): there are 'spec verbs' (non-θ-marking verbs that are either base generated in, or 'shifted' into, VP specifier position) and 'head verbs' (θ-marking verbs that occupy zero-bar position in VP) but only 'spec verbs' allow for V-raising; with negation contexts ruling out Affix-lowering by requiring that Tense be lexically filled, it follows that only 'spec Vfs' and modals (base generated under Tense) can precede *not*. Baker (op. cit.) takes the trouble to work out what (in Pollock's case) opting for a Core analysis costs: (i) an extra parameter in UG; (ii) double base positions (modifying Tense or V) for English adverbs that can both precede and follow *not*; (iii) a special mechanism to undo the effect of possessive have being analysed as a non-θ-marking verb and (iv) no room for dialectal variation with respect to *do* support (in Niwa's and Sawada's case only (ii) can be left out). If UG is to be formulated in terms of a relatively simple set of principles and parameters that can be triggered by readily available data, the costs, Baker judges, are clearly too high and he proposes a simple rule which pivots around the English word *not*, appeals to particular features of verbs moving to its left (thus leaving room for dialectal variation), applies obligatorily and all in all represents the ideal format of a peripheral rule schema: English is an Affix-lowering language, pure and simple, all exceptions being just that, exceptions, irreducible.

At the heart of the Core-Periphery issue is of course the constant tug-of-war between accounting for the diversity of human languages and defining the notion 'possible grammar' as narrowly as possible, and in the familiar idealized view of language acquisition the latter notion is defined at the final stage of acquisition only. Masayuki Ike-uchi argues instead that, if the above two mutually conflicting goals are to be attained, one needs a 'dynamic' approach, one which recognizes the transitional, step-by-step nature of acquisition and views UG as constraining possible grammars at each stage in the process, with different grammars being possible at different stages.

He makes a case for this approach in 'An Analysis of English Descriptive Genitives in the Dynamic Theory of Syntax' (in Nakajima), which sets out to handle the dual syntactic status of the so-called descriptive genitive, adjectival on the one hand (witness its ability to conjoin with adjectives, as in *his pointed BOAR'S teeth*) and nominal on the other (it can, for instance, have its own determiner, as in *my THIS YEAR'S examination questions*). In the dynamic view, the English descriptive genitive is first acquired as a straightforward nominal construction, $[_{NP}[_{Det}\textit{his}]\ [_{NP}\textit{BOY'S}]\ [_{N'}\textit{cheeks}]]$; modelling itself on the almost synonymous construction of a NP containing a pre-nominal adjective, $[_{NP}[_{Det}\textit{his}][_{AP}\textit{boyish}][_{N'}\textit{cheeks}]]$, a tree-grafting rule superimposes an AP on the originally purely nominal descriptive genitive, thus achieving the required dual categorial status: $[_{NP}[_{Det}\textit{his}]\ [_{AP}[_{NP}\textit{BOY'S}]]\ [_{N'}\textit{cheeks}]]$. In the adult grammar the AP gets base generated by means of a context-sensitive phrase structure rule which makes itself available by modelling itself on the antecedent tree-grafting rule: in this way the adult grammar follows from, and is constrained by, its immediate predecessor in the acquisition process. A different move away from 'traditional' Core grammar theory is made by Teresa Espinal, who re-examines 'The Representation of Disjunct Constituents' (*Language* 67.726–62) in light of non-linear grammatical theory, proposing that sentences containing parenthetical constituents do not form two-dimensional structures with a singleton root node (as has been variously proposed in the literature), but constitute three-dimensional syntactic objects whose separate planes converge at the terminal string, with 'host' and 'disjunct(s)' each codifying autonomous syntactic information and having their own root nodes. Given this format, it follows that (conceptual as well as utterance level) comprehension and wellformedness judgements of host-disjunct structures are inevitably underdetermined by principles of (sentence) grammar and Espinal proposes a set of higher-level principles and conditions to control (i) syntactic wellformedness (e.g. a condition on interruption to prevent strings like **the, BETWEEN YOU AND ME, porter was drinking a brandy*), (ii) conceptual wellformedness (conditions on mapping and saturation to ensure that the host proposition in a string like *John has left, I THINK* is assigned the 'thinkee' role, a role it cannot get from *think* through government since there is no syntactic relation between this verb and the disjunct's host) and (iii) degree of relevance (e.g. a condition licensing speaker-attitude adverbials such as *confidentially* in *CONFIDENTIALLY, John left the family business*).

In earlier stages of generative theory, Binding was accounted for in terms of the Specified Subject Constraint (SSC) and the Nominative Island Constraint (NIC), but in GB theory the NIC is subsumed under the SSC. Yshihisa Kitagawa's 'Binding under the Internal Subject Hypothesis' (in Nakajima) challenges the validity of this move on empirical grounds and proposes instead that anaphors must be bound (and pronominals free) within a Lexical Case Island (LIC). If, as Kitagawa further argues, genitive case is the only non-lexical case in English, the LIC resolves both the ungrammaticality of e.g.**they think that EACH OTHER are geniuses* (the anaphor is bound outside its Nominative Island) as well as the traditional problem of the partial distributional overlap of anaphors and pronominals in English, cf. $\textit{they}_{i/j}$ *think that* $\textit{EACH OTHER}_i\textit{'S/THEIR}_j$ *pictures are on sale* (the genitive position is free of a Lexical Case Island). Eva Koktova, to move to another area of pronoun interpretation, draws attention to the possibility of 'Intrasentential Anaphora' (*ALH* 23.49–81), reopening the sixties' argumentation on forward and backward anaphora in complex sentences. While reinstalling Ronald Langacker's condition that a pronoun cannot both precede and command its antecedent, she points out that even if this condition is at work (as in *She likes the man who kissed Leslie*, where she both precedes and commands *Leslie*) coreference is possible through 'Renaming', i.e. if *she* picks up the identical referent from some NP in the preceding context.

GB accounts of English syntactic phenomena are particularly numerous this year and in what follows I will merely epitomize such papers (rather a medley of them) as are primarily concerned with (highly technical) theory-internal issues. Thus there are Miki Saito's 'DP and Wh-movement from a Noun Phrase' (*Ling&Philol* 11.119–33), which shows that certain *wh*-extractions from NP are best accounted for in an approach that introduces determiners as a separate functional maximal category (DP); Heizo Nakajima's 'Transportability, Scope Ambiguity of Adverbials and the Generalized Binding Theory' (*JL* 27.337–74), which works out an account of the movement and scope possibilities of English adverbials that is completely predictable from Generalized Binding theory, and six other Japanese contributions (the first five in Nakajima): by Naoki Fukui on 'Strong and Weak Barriers: Remarks on the Proper Characterization of Barriers', which gets rid of certain stipulative constraints in Chomsky's Barriers theory by allowing only *functional* categories a maximal projection; by Heizo Nakajima on 'Binding Path and Dependent Categories', which argues that any antecedent-dependent relation is fully accountable in terms of conditions on the initial, the middle and the final parts of the syntactic path connecting them; by Shigeo Tonoike on 'The Comparative Syntax of English and Japanese: Relating Unrelated Languages', which constitutes an ambitious attempt to show that English and Japanese, though historically unrelated, are structurally very close in that, from a syntactic viewpoint, they are each other's mirror images; by Masaru Nakumara 'On "Null Operator" Constructions', which argues for a differentiated treatment of empty elements: null anaphors in *tough*-movement constructions, PRO in purpose clauses and operators in parasitic gap cases; by Shuji Chiba on 'Non-localizable Contextual Features: Present Subjunctives in English', which accounts for the distribution of English subjunctive complements in terms of a [+ Subj(unctive)] feature carried by the governor (X) of the complement, the feature being either an inherent part of X's make-up or one that is inherited from another category (provided X itself is not negatively specified for the feature), cf. *The widow wrote in her will THAT BALL BE GIVEN PART OF HER PROPERTY*, where it is the presence of *in her will* (*write* obviously not being a [+Subj] verb) that licenses the subjunctive in the complement, and by Makoto Kondo, whose 'Notes on Parasitic Gap Constructions: Traces or Bound Pronominals' (*Ling&Philol* 11.27–42) defends Chomsky's current approach to parasitic gaps against competing accounts. Nakajima's volume also includes two articles aiming to expose the inadequacies of purely syntactic accounts. Thus Ken-ichi Takami argues for 'A Functional Approach to Preposition Stranding in English', essentially claiming that P-stranding occurs when the NP complement of a preposition is informationally of prime importance, and Susumo Kuno, making some 'Remarks on Quantifier Scope', shows that the ambiguity of certain multiple-quantifier constructions cannot be properly accounted for unless one takes a wide variety of (syntactic, semantic, discourse-based and pragmatic) factors into consideration. 'Middles in English and the Argument Structure' (in *Ling&Philol* 11) gives us, lastly, Hiroaki Tanaka's lexical account of middle constructions in English (*This book sells easily*): middle verbs (unlike ergative verbs) have a transitive base in the lexicon but, having assigned 'arbitrary' reference to their agent argument, they change their argument structure into one which is devoid of the agent argument and the next-most prominent thematic argument automatically becomes the syntactic subject.

For those interested in English language/grammar in general there is a number of books worth mentioning here. Of interest for language learners is Sydney Greenbaum's *An Introduction to English Grammar*, which, after a brief introduction to the notion 'Grammar' and its relation to language variety, divides into two main parts, the first descriptive: an outline of the grammar of English, and the second concerned with application: punctuation, usage problems, the effect of grammatical choices on writing style and the grammar of literary language, with the tail of the book offering a useful spelling appendix, a grammar glossary and a large number of exercises. In short, a highly practical and accessible guide to the study of English language and usage. R. M. W. Dixon's *A New Approach to English Grammar, on Semantic Principles* is quite different in nature; its overall aim, based on the intuition that the grammatical properties of words should be a function of their meanings, is to provide a semantically oriented framework for grammatical analysis, the essential methodological principle being that generalizations can be teased out of the data inductively by studying their syntax in close conjunction with their semantics. Starting from the tenet that 'the lexical words of a language can be grouped into a number of semantic types, each of which has a common component, and a typical set of grammatical properties' (p. 75), Dixon applies this idea (largely) to English verbs, dividing them into some thirty-odd semantic types (including the distinct set of semantic roles typical for each class), which he then projects onto their basic syntax. Having thus classified the most common English verbs (about 900 of them), Dixon discusses a number of syntactic phenomena (e.g. complementation, transitivity and causatives, the passive) and attempts to show how the semantic properties of individual verbs match their ability to fit into certain syntactic construction types. The net result is, sad to say, somewhat disappointing. Dixon's observations/descriptions come across as impressionistic and fail to provide really new insights or give a strong sense of 'system'. This is, I think, due to the fact that Dixon, ignoring the existence of numerous highly sophisticated semantico-syntactic analyses of English verbal constructions (I am thinking, for instance, of work by Steven Pinker, cf. *YWES* 70.105, by Len Talmy, and by Beth Levin, Malka Rappaport and others in the framework of the MIT Lexicon Project), largely approaches English as if it were newly discovered, as yet unexplored territory, and the effect is predictably primitive. Dixon's inductive stance classifies his work as 'old grammar' if looked at through the eyes of Frits Stuurman who (cf. also *YWES* 70.110) sees twentieth-century ModE grammar as dividing into two mainstreams, the one inductive and comprehensive (hence 'open'), the other deductive and exclusive (hence 'narrow'). The first, ranging from Sweet and Poutsma to Quirk et al., gets labelled 'Old Grammar' (OG), the second, covering Chomskyan generative grammar, is dubbed 'New Grammar' (NG). In his *Two Grammatical Models of Modern English. The Old and New from A to Z*, Stuurman introduces the reader briefly to his OG and NG representatives (part I), argues against an NG tendency to regard itself as building on rather than standing in juxtaposition with OG (part II) and, in the core of his study (part III), considers twenty-six problems (*A for ALL, B for BE, C for COMPLEMENTATION* etc.) from both the OG and the NG angle, his two-fold aim being to make students of English aware of the fundamental differences between the two approaches and to create 'grammatological tolerance' and 'understanding of the pluriformity in English grammar'. For readers interested in a functional analysis of (English) language, Anna Siewierska's *Functional Grammar* can be recommended, in that it not only provides a clear outline of (the central issues of) this approach but also brings out, through comparison with other current grammatical frameworks, its strong as well as its weak points. Stig Johansson and Anna-Brita Stenström are the editors of a collection of papers that give the reader insight into what use is currently being made of *English Computer Corpora* in the field of probabilistic grammatical analysis, syntax, lexis, speech, regional/social variation, and specialized language; there are also two contributions on specific software, a highly useful, detailed survey of English machine-readable texts and a bibliography of works drawing on computerized English language corpora. The two syntax papers are by Pieter de Haan and Christian Mair. The former is 'On the Exploration of Corpus Data by Means of Problem-Oriented Tagging: Postmodifying Clauses in the English Noun Phrase' and provides a statistical analysis of the patterns of postmodifying clauses, of the functions of the NPs they modify, of their positions and of relative pronouns in (non)restrictive clauses; the latter emphasizes, in 'Quantitative or Qualitative Corpus Analysis? Infinitival Complement Clauses in the Survey of English Usage Corpus', how a combination of statistical and textlinguistic analysis of computer corpus material can provide solid evidence for insights that otherwise have mere intuitive status; thus the correlation found between Extraposition of *to*-infinitival subject clauses and types of matrix predicate (the ratio of extraposed vs. non-extraposed cases is 14:1 if the matrix predicate is a one-place adjective but 2.5:1 if it is a verb) provides confirmation for the intuitive understanding of Extraposition as serving a particular discourse function ('end-focus'): verbs being informationally far richer than one-place adjectives form, for that very reason, an obstacle for Extraposition.

There are this year two quite exciting papers on syntactic change in progress, both concerning American English. Thus Michael Montgomery and Guy Bailey's study '*In which*: A New Form in Written English?' (*AS* 66.147–63) presents us with a variety of truly recent (mid-seventies) nonstandard uses of *in which* (they have collected a total of 408 examples, of which about 80% is from student papers, mainly freshman-level); by far the most common case (194 in number) is that of *in which* used as a generalized relative pronoun, as in *Please accept my apology IN WHICH my staff has caused* and if one subsumes cases of relative clauses beginning with *in which* and ending with a duplicate stranded preposition (*in* or otherwise, cf. ... *his car stopped in the house IN WHICH he was looking FOR*) under the same heading, the total of *in which* cases used as equivalent to *which* comes to 272. The new construction came to arise, Montgomery and Bailey assume (suggesting a variety of sources for the particular choice of *in which*), due to basic 'insecurity with the patterns of written English and a desire to write formally' (p. 152) and if it spreads into speech (there is some evidence already), this will be for the selfsame reason: the ambition to be formal. Suzanne Romaine and Deborah Lange discuss another case of ongoing syntactic innovation in 'The Use of + *like* as a Marker of Reported Speech and Thought: A Case of Grammaticalization in Progress' (*AS* 66.227–79); this concerns the pair *be* + *like* in its 'quotative function' (equivalent to 'say') that is employed, mainly by young women, in lively, 'to-and-fro' dialogue, as in *She said: 'What are you doing here?' And I'm LIKE, 'Nothing much' ... And she's LIKE 'Um ... well, that's cool'*. Romaine and Lange discuss, in detail, the historical grammaticalization process ultimately leading to the quotational discourse function of *like* exemplified above, which they see as motivated by its meaning of 'similar to' in that it is used to get across the expressive content of the speaker's internal thought rather than her precise words.

There are three contributions which I have left for the finale of this section because they are less concerned with syntax proper than with the semantic rationale for certain distributional facts. Connor Ferris, for instance, is interested in 'Time Reference in English Adjectives and Separative Qualification' (*Linguistics* 29.569–90), drawing attention to what he calls 'separative' adjectives of time such as *former* in *Susie's FORMER husband lives in Senegal*; such an adjective does not simply qualify the referent of its noun (as in *a BEAUTIFUL flower*) nor does it qualify its noun's content alone (as in *a TOTAL stranger*) but instead it relates, in time, the entity performing a particular role expressed by the sentence and a description of that entity (the *x* living in Senegal now was at an earlier time describable as 'Susie's husband'). It is for this reason, Ferris points out, that separative adjectives (and they do not only occur in time expressions, cf. *SO-CALLED humanitarians, APPARENT leader*) can only occur attributively: in predicative position, an adjective can only refer to the NP it qualifies *as a whole* (lexical description, entity described and the relation between them); notice how cases which allow for a standard and a separative meaning (e.g. *Eddy's OLD school*) disambiguate as soon as the adjective is given predicative position (*Eddy's school, which is OLD*). Verbal expressions of time, and the rationale for different formal choices in English and Dutch, are what Lia Korrel's monograph *Duration in English* is about. There are three major differences in the use of the present perfect in English and Dutch, two of which I will discuss here: (i) English uses the present perfect to express 'duration so far' (*HE HAS BEEN in hospital FOR THREE DAYS*), Dutch the simple present; (ii) in combination with time adverbials, English uses the simple past (*I RECEIVED his letter A WEEK AGO*), Dutch (often) the present perfect. Korrel, working within Gustave Guillaume's theory of 'Psychomechanics', describes the meanings of the simple present/present perfect forms and their past congeners in terms of Mood and Aspect, two separate systems representing time as containing an event and as contained in an event respectively. The indicative mood presents time as two stretches, divided by one's moment of consciousness into the past (time containing remembered events) and non-past. Aspect (in English and Dutch) is concerned with duration either within or after an event: the simple forms present it as unrolling and the perfective forms present the event in its aftermath, the effect of its unrolling. To be able to mentally represent (kinetic) time, Korrel argues further (following Guillaume), we have to project it onto (static) space, and for this reason we can never represent what is 'present' in our consciousness accurately: the 'now' is either seen as what is directly ahead of us (English; interception is 'too early') or as what is directly behind us (Dutch; interception is 'too late'). This explains the different uses described in (i): if the present, as in English, signals what directly follows one's consciousness, excluding all of the past, the present perfect can only be selected to express an event explicitly having duration in the past (*for three days*): the situation is presented as in the aftermath of the three-days-event; however, if the present includes what directly precedes one's consciousness, as in Dutch, then the simple present is not excluded and it signals that 'one sums up what has happened so far and goes on from there' (p. 124). The difference noted under (ii) follows in the same way. The mention of *yesterday* makes it impossible to use a form that includes what directly follows one's consciousness, hence the present perfect is out in English; in Dutch the aftermath of the event is presented as part of what immediately preceded consciousness and the past time adverbial can here be seen as signalling when the aftermath set in. Korrel thus ingeniously manages to reduce the problematic English–Dutch contrasts to a simple difference in parameter setting, the 'now' viewed as before or after one's consciousness, while keeping the underlying mood and aspect systems constant. Bernd Kortmann, lastly, conducts an interesting, corpus-based investigation of *Free Adjuncts and Absolutes in English*, FA and ABS for short. His central concern is to see what motivates the differences in use and interpretation between the FA (e.g. *INFLATING HER LUNGS, Mary screamed*) and the ABS (e.g. *THE COACH BEING CROWDED, Fred had to stand*) and how such differences connect with their syntax. The most obvious difference is the covert nature of the subject of the FA, as opposed to its being overt in the ABS, which means that the ABS, is by its very nature, semantically more informative than the FA. Kortmann further notices that, where it is typical for the subject of the unaugmented ABS to have a referential (part-whole) relationship with some NP in the main clause, this is only atypically the case with the *with*-augmented ABS. It follows that FA, *with*- augmented and unaugmented ABS forms range from less to more semantically informative. As for the link between adjunct and main clause, Kortmann further observes, neither the unaugmented FA nor the ABS (with or without *with*), wears its semantic relation with its main clause on its sleeve, so to speak; this raises the obvious question how the addressee can be plausibly argued to resolve such semantic indeterminacy. It is generally claimed that only a limited set of semantic relations is available to the FA/ABS and, furthermore, that only a subset of this set actually gets searched in any particular case. As a further constraint, Kortmann proposes that the members of the set of available relations are inherently ranked according to their degree of informativeness (the relation 'attendant circumstances' is, for instance, a very weak one, as opposed to e.g. 'concession/contrast', which is strongly informative). In his search for a plausible semantic relation, the addressee will, naturally, be guided by evidence from previous discourse and/or world knowledge; if this only substantiates a 'weak' relation, then such will be selected, but the evidence may, of course, also warrant a strongly informative relation. Interestingly, Kortmann finds, as a general tendency, that there is 'an increasing proportion of "more informative" interpretations from unaugmented absolutes, via augmented absolutes to free adjuncts'(p. 136). What this means is that the usage of a form that in its own right (cf. the discussion of FA/ABS subjects above) is semantically richest, correlates with the addressee's choices of the weakest semantic relation between adjunct and main clause, *and vice versa*. This, in fact, Kortmann points out, follows directly from the general pragmatic principle that semantically most reduced *forms* invite the most informative *interpretation* from the addressee, and vice versa. And these FA/ABS findings show, more generally, how pragmatic principles are co-responsible for determining propositional content which, in turn means further evidence that one cannot simply maintain that pragmatics starts where semantics stops.

(b) Early Syntax

Word order and typology are, as usual, favourite issues. With regard to OE formatives such as *fram*, *ongean*, *to*, many of them appear to be able to occupy both pre- and post-NP position. Fran Colman, wondering 'What Positions Fit In?' (in Kastovsky) looks into some thirty-odd putative postpositional cases to see whether there may be alternative analyses circumventing the need for a postpositional analysis, one argument against it being that it implies frequent 'tangling' (separation of the argument NP from 'its' preposition) and unrestricted tangling is unlikely given that case syncretism is already quite strong in OE. Rejecting the argument that many postpositions are due to clitic movement of a pronominal object out of the PP into pre-verbal position – it leaves unexplained why the putative postpositions so often go with a case that differs from the one to be expected from the prepositional mate (dative instead of accusative or genitive) – she considers the possibility that the isolated NP is an ungoverned 'ethic' dative, arguing that the lonely P-form could be an elliptical PP or, in other cases, could have prefixed itself to the verb. Typologically, then, OE may not be as postpositional as is often claimed. P-V compounding is also, for Michiko Ogura, the explanation why, of all the possible orderings of the elements in

'*Cweðan* + *to* + Dative of Person' (in *Neophil* 75.270–78) only *to* + *cwæð* + NP_{dative} does not occur: to-V-NP_{dative} strings are only acceptable in OE if *to*-V acts as a compound verb and with *cweðan* it is only *to*, and never the verb, that governs the dative. Ogura's interest in *cweðan* is not limited to possible word order. 'Is Indirect Discourse Following OE *cweðan* Always in the Subjunctive Mood?', she wonders in *ES* (72.393–9) and finds, after a thorough investigation of the OE data, that one cannot simply classify *cweðan* as a verb introducing indirect discourse in the subjunctive mood: though for eOE this seems to have been the rule, the ban on the use of the indicative mood in indirect speech seems to get lifted when *cweðan* gets regularly used in the present tense, witness this frequent combination in interlinear glosses.

Languages, it is generally claimed, move typologically from para- to hypotaxis but the evolution of the English connector *for* shows differently according to Andreas Jucker's 'Between Hypotaxis and Parataxis: Clauses of Reason in *Ancrene Wisse*' (in Kastovsky); whereas OE *for* exhibits more properties characteristic for subordination than for coordination in the beginning of its grammatical life, a comparison of *for* in *Ancrene Wisse* with *for* in ModE shows, contrary to typological wisdom, a movement in the direction of greater parataxis. In the same volume, Leiv Breivik derives convincing arguments 'On the Typological Status of Old English' from the development of existential sentences in English (sentences with existential *be* or a lexical variant, with or without *there*). In OE, dummy topics including *there*, are introduced to comply with the V2 constraint. However, OE *there* also occurs in embedded clauses as well as postverbally in main clauses, both positions that are independent of the V2 constraint. OE must, Breivik therefore concludes, have already reached the (typologically advanced) V2 stage which includes the optional introduction of dummy fillers. When, later, V2 makes way for SVO, *there* takes on dummy subject status and thus, automatically, becomes obligatory in all existentials. Why does English become SVO? Language-internal developments alone do not suffice for an explanation, is Andrei Danchev's claim in 'Language Typology and Some Aspects of the SVO development in English' (in Kastovsky); we should also view this change from an overall 'language change' typology. In line with an interactive, bi-directional model of language change (economy versus elaboration), it makes sense for ME to enter a period of simplification after the rich structural complexity of OE. The creolization resulting from intensive contact with French leads quite naturally to the ME loss of case and hence to the adoption of a fixed word order and SVO is the natural candidate for adoption, it being available from French as well as constituting an iconic hence unmarked order and therefore fitting in with the ME trend towards simplification or markedness breakdown. Thus, language contact rather than a local V2 constraint provides, according to Danchev, the major explanation for SVO arising in English. Robert Stockwell and Donka Minkova, focussing on language-internal explanation, challenge the widely accepted view of syntactic change as necessarily unidirectional (from main to embedded clause), building their case on 'Subordination and Word Order Change in the History of English' (in Kastovsky). The basic word order in OE, they argue, is V2 in main clauses and Vfinal in subclauses, with V3 order (ADV/COMP-S(ubject)-Vf...) creeping into the latter on analogy with a subset of main clauses, i.e. those exhibiting S-Vf ... order. By the thirteenth century this V3 order has become predominant in subclauses and it is, of course, standard in ModE. Since main clauses continue to exhibit V2 order long after the adoption of V3 in subclauses, subclausal V3 must, Stockwell and Minkova conclude, have been the model on which the change from V2 to V3 was based and the claim that subclauses are by definition more conservative to change than main clauses is untenable. Support for this conclusion can, according to Andreas Juckert in 'Word Order Changes in Early Middle English' (*SAP* 23.31–42), be found in eME *Ancrene Wisse*: the main clauses of this treatise all exhibit V2 order (part of which is SV), whereas in ninety percent of all its subclauses with a pronominal object, this object is extraposed so that the surface order fits the V2 (hence SV) pattern. Hard and fast evidence for Vfinal in subclauses is, in other words, rapidly disappearing, which is why they are ready to be reanalysed as having SVO order. David Lightfoot argues exactly the opposite in *How to Set Parameters*. Given a parameter-setting model of Universal Grammar, and given the essential (clausal) locality of grammatical processes, it makes sense, he argues, to assume that children need only have access to main clauses to acquire their language (degree-0 learning) and in his book he sets out to provide evidence for a number of diachronic changes (largely concerning English) to show that these changes not only *can* be traced to experience with main clauses only, but also *must* be so interpreted. With regard to the verb-order change in English (Ch. 3) his argument runs as follows. OE main clauses provide two signals for VO order, the first decreasing and the second increasing in frequency in the course of OE: verb-finality (in coordination structures) and particle-finality (the verb, fronted under V2, leaves 'its' particle behind). The word order parameter gets reset to VO once, by the end of the eleventh century, main clause Vfinal has disappeared, particles have started to wander to non-final positions and SVO (i.e. V2 order with topicalized subject) has become predominant in main clauses while SOV is still the norm in subclauses. This parametric change, though mainly visible in embedded clauses (there is plenty of evidence there of a cataclysmic change from (S)OV to (S)VO), *must* have, Lightfoot argues triumphantly, been triggered by main clause evidence: had the child relied on evidence from embedded clauses, it would have stuck to OV. That ME main clauses, unlike their embedded counterparts, continue to exhibit other than SVO order for centuries to come, is simply a sign of V2 (by definition excluded from subclauses) carrying over from OE into ME. Crucial in the matter is, of course, the interpretation of the data: is, at the turning point, subclausal SOV still 'the norm', as Lightfoot would have it, or is the evidence for this word order, as Juckert claims, 'rapidly disappearing'?

Lightfoot also reopens the debate regarding the nature and cause of a number of other widely discussed diachronic changes in English, such as the introduction of passive infinitives in certain contexts (ch. 4); the innovation of a number of passive constructions and, following it, both 'subject-to-subject' and 'subject-to-object' raising constructions (ch. 5); and the disappearance of impersonal constructions and the reanalysis of modals and the loss of V-to-INFL (ch. 6), showing how alternative solutions are required in light of the triggering experience that must be assumed to have given rise to the changes. The first of these changes provides, according to Lightfoot, further proof that only an 'unembedded binding Domain' (i.e. the main clause plus, if an infinitival complement follows, the latter's subject and INFL) is accessible to the language learner. Lightfoot builds on the findings of Olga Fischer, who observes that in most syntactic contexts where ModE employs a periphrastic passive infinitive, OE prefers to convey the same message by means of an active infinitive form and wonders why 'The Rise of the Passive Infinitives in English' occurred (in Kastovsky). Only after (pre)modals do OE and ModE both use the passive infinitive (cf. *and he mot na beon eft gefullod* 'he may never be baptised again'), but in other environments OE uses the active infinitive, usually with *to* but postverbally also in its bare form (cf. *Ic seah turf tredan* 'I saw the grass be trod'). A number of syntactic developments conspire to get the active infinitive replaced by its passive counterpart, the crucial factor being, as Fischer points out, the (ME) adoption of VO order: once that has settled, an NP preceding an active infinitive can no longer be analysed as the latter's D-structure object, so the passive infinitive is introduced in its stead, thus guaranteeing that the original meaning is be maintained. Technically this means, in Lightfoot's view, a change from *I saw* PRO_S *the* $grass_O$ *tread* to *I saw the* $grass_S$ *be trod* and the fact that the active infinitive gets replaced by its passive counterpart constitutes empirical proof, he argues, that the embedded infinitive is not part of the child's triggering experience, or else it would have maintained the same surface order (e.g. by treating the construction as 'middle'); the change in form from active to passive means that the child simply does not see the infinitive. In other words, the rise of the passive infinitive cannot be explained unless one assumes degree-0 learning.

George Jack sets himself the relatively more modest aim of describing 'The Infinitive in Early Middle English Prose' (*NM* 92.311–41) as far as inflection, *for to/to* versus zero marking and selection of syntactic functions is concerned; he argues that to some extent the choice between plain as opposed to *for to/to* infinitive can be ascribed to contextual utility (overt marker desirable or not) and syntactic function (the plain infinitive fitting into nominal slots, the marked one into PP slots) but that one can also see a change in the English infinitival system going on in that the *to* infinitive, in OE filling PP slots, also comes to occupy nominal slots in eME, with the *for to* infinitive taking over its prepositional function. An application of Jack's 'contextual utitility' criterion can be found in OE/ME strings of a modal governing two coordinated infinitives, the first plain and the second marked by *to*, and Teresa Fanego suggests, in her study 'On the Origin and History of the English Type (*and*) *none but he to marry with Nan Page*' (*ES* 72.512–8), that the ultimate source of infinitival constructions of this 'Nan Page' type lies in such OE/ME 'M-inf-conj-*to*-inf' strings; these occur especially frequently with *shall* in ME, whence the construction's meaning of 'future arrangement', a meaning that still survives in examples like *We shall assemble at ten forty-five, the … procession to start at precisely eleven*. Is, Bruce Mitchell asks himself, 'Ælfric's *Catholic Homilies* ii.440.20: an Example of *habban* with the Accusative and Infinitive?' (*N&Q* 236.17–18); his answer is that *bysegan* in the example (*seo swustor hi wolde habban to hire bysegan*) is more likely to be a nominal than an infinitive, suggesting as translation 'her sister wished to have her as her industrious one (i.e. fellow-worker)', construction-wise comparable to *We habbað us to fæder Abraham*.

Periphrastic *do* remains popular as ever: witness the following four contributions (all in Kastovsky). Terttu Nevalainen's 'Motivated Archaism: the Use of Affirmative Periphrastic *do* in Early Modern English Liturgical Prose' compares the usage of affirmative do in the 1552 edition of the Common Prayer Book and its 1662 revision and provides a convincing, well-documented (variationist) case for the hypothesis that the retainment/innovation of this affirmative *do* in the new edition was, in Labov's terms, a 'change from above', i.e. a conscious linguistic selection on the part of the revisers to maintain the religious flavour of the text. Matti Rissanen suggests that relating 'Spoken Language and the History of *do*-Periphrasis' may help explain the rise and development of periphrastic *do*. Also concerning himself with affirmative instances, Rissanen argues (i) that periphrastic *do* may well have been part and parcel of the spoken language from OE onwards and (ii) that the usage of its affirmative variant is not linguistically conditioned in spoken language the way it is in written language (witness the sixteenth century preference for *do* in syntactic contexts like the following: SU-*do*-ADV-V; SU-X-*do*-V; *do*-V#). If discoursal periphrastic *do* was already available in OE, new potential sources for its colleague in written language suggest themselves, he argues, e.g. reanalysis of *do* plus verbal noun (cf. OE *gefeoht don*) during the general ME collapse of (un)inflected infinitives, present participles and verbal nouns into infinitives. It would also explain why, as Rissanen finds from a text-based frequency count of affirmative *do* over three adjacent eModE periods, *do* first arose in speech-related texts to then enter the written language when and where it could help strengthen the dominant sixteenth-century prose style. Dieter Stein, also looking at affirmative periphrastic *do*'s fortunes in eModE, advocates an approach that takes the 'Semantic Aspects of Syntactic Change' as its starting point. The binding factor behind the syntactic structures favouring do (cf. Rissanen above) is, he argues, their intensity semantics, cf. e.g. *as this bloody tyrant did furiously fare with fair Philomela*. The Renaissance ideal of a euphuistic and emphatic mode of expression is, therefore, directly responsible for the sudden rise of *do* in the sixteenth century and the later fight against emotional expressive language components for its subsequent decline in declarative contexts. Susan Wright, discussing Malory's use of periphrastic *do* in 'On the Stylistic Basis of Syntactic Change' argues that 'Anaphoric *do* is one of the midwives in the emergence and spread of the auxiliary *do*' (p. 486). Characteristic for Malory's style is his use of loose, iconic parataxis and his focus on individuating characters and their responses. The natural structural function of anaphoric *do* to make loose syntax cohere and its rhetorical effect of linking the utterances of different characters inspired Malory, Wright argues, to put periphrastic *do* to similar uses: when employed in coordinated syntax it achieves an emphatic, foregrounding effect and it adds extra, lexical highlight to dialogue otherwise intensified by the use of adverbials and repetition. Malory's frontier use of periphrastic *do* thus exemplifies, Wright argues, how a change in syntax can be stylistically rather than syntactically induced.

Grammaticalization, as defined by Elizabeth Traugott and Ekkehard König in 'The Semantics-Pragmatics of Grammaticalization' (in Traugott and Heine, Vol. I), refers to the process 'whereby lexical items in the course of time acquire a new status as grammatical, morpho-syntactic forms, and in the process come to code relations that either were not coded before or were coded differently' (p. 189). The changes in function that a word goes through runs, roughly, from signalling (i) something in 'objective' reality through, (ii) coherence in text to, (iii) 'subjective' speaker attitude; thus OE *siþþan* starts out as a preposition meaning 'after' (first spatial, then also temporal), then develops the extra function of temporal connective to finally extend, functionally, to expressing causal relations as well. The effect in cases of this type is 'information strengthening', which is, and this is Traugott and König's main contention, a type of metonymy (semantic transfer through contiguity, here based in the discourse world). The process that ends in the evolution of a new grammatical function is, we may conclude from their paper, largely semantic-pragmatic in nature and the question arises how apt the term 'grammaticalization' really is. John Anderson is quite explicit on this point, arguing in 'Should' (in Kastovsky) that, in the absence of what he refers to as 'syntactic saliency', the term 'grammaticalization' has no meaning. To attribute grammaticalization to OE *sceolde*, and hence classify it as an auxiliary, on account of (i) desemanticization, (ii) morphological defectiveness, (iii) growing periphrasticity and (iv) selectional transparency, comes down to anachronistic thinking and labelling: the (sub)category 'auxiliary' was, by definition, nonexistent until a subgroup of ModE verbs, including *should*, developed so-called NICE-syntax. Clearly, factors (i)-(iv) helped pave the way for this syntactic innovation, but theirs cannot be more than a 'pre-grammaticalizing' function. Frequency of tokens in text is, in fact, as emphasized by Sandra Thompson and Anthony Mulac in 'A

Quantitative Perspective on the Grammaticization of Epistemic Parentheticals in English' (in Traugott and Heine, Vol. II), the bridging factor towards forms acquiring new grammatical status. Their paper is concerned with the interplay of so-called '*that*-deletion' and the grammaticalization of epistemic phrases (EP) and, ultimately, Epistemic Parentheticals (EPAR). *That*, they argue, gets deleted when the complement rather than the main clause subject functions as discourse topic, the 'author' endorsing the complement-assertion rather than attributing it to someone else; the 'main' clause subject and its epistemic verb behave, in fact, like unitary EPs (comparable to e.g. *maybe*). Thus, rather than taking the traditional view that '*that*-deletion' is an (optional) syntactic process, Thompson and Mulac see it as a grammaticalization process, leading from *I think that he isn't coming* to *I think he isn't coming* and ultimately to *He isn't coming I think*: *that*-less S-V strings are reanalysed as EPs which, for those S-V combinations which are frequent enough (*I*/*you* combined with *think*/*guess*) can float, i.e. acquire EPAR status. That frequency can also have a conservative effect is shown by Gunnel Tottie in 'Lexical Diffusion in Syntactic Change: Frequency as a Determinant of Linguistic Conservatism in the Development of Negation in English' (in Kastovsky). Tottie investigates the distribution of *not*- versus *no*-negation (*I did not see anyone* vs. *I saw no one*) in ModE and finds the former to be clearly predominant over the latter in written, but not in spoken language, a difference which is not just attributable to a difference in production constraints (such as fragmentation for spoken and integration for written language), since certain verbs (existential *be* and stative *have*) collocate with *no*-negation much more frequently than lexical verbs, with copular *be* coming somewhere in between; even amongst lexical verbs, certain specimens, e.g. *do*, *know*, *give* and *make*, show conservatism. There is diachronic evidence supporting the hypothesis that ModE witnesses a development from *no*- to *not*-negation and the question is why certain verbs lag behind; this, Tottie argues, must be due to the preservative strength of collocations: habitually co-occurring words remain longer in use than words that have no regular co-occurrence. The reason that the copula *be* is not nearly as conservative as existential *be* and stative *have* is, she argues, likely to be due to the fact that the latter two often go with indefinite NPs, so that there is a real choice available, whereas copulas show no preference for indefinite NPs.

Also concerned with negation is Daniel Noland, whose 'A Diachronic Survey of English Negative Concord' (*AS* 66.171–80) shows that Negative Concord (the spread of a negative element from a main to a subclause without this influencing the sentence's meaning), contrary to Labov's claim that it occurs only in Black English vernacular, has been a native construction since at least Alfred's time (cf. *Hi nyllaþ geswican þæt hi oðre men ne reafigen* 'They will not cease (not) to rob other men') and has only been lost from standard English due to eighteenth-century 'prescriptive pressures' (p.177). Adverbial shifting, another instance of grammaticalization, is the process whereby an adverb is raised from 'lowly intensifier' (p. 418) to Sentence Adverbial (SA), cf. *a surprisingly good vodka* and *Surprisingly, the vodka was very good*. Comparing 'Adverbial Shifts: Evidence from Norwegian and English' (in Kastovsky), Toril Swan finds that English is, quantitatively, ahead of other Germanic languages in its tendency to thus adverbialize speaker comments, arguing that this may well be due to the fact that English has no special morphological endings for SAs and can simply use the existing highly flexible *-ly* forms in initial (or final) position; in a language like Norwegian, special morphological endings develop (*rart nok* 'strangely enough'), the result being an SA that may have medial position and has therefore a less clearly disjunctive function.

Terttu Nevalainen's *BUT, ONLY, JUST. Focusing Adverbial Change in Modern English 1500–1900* traces the process of semantic change and adverbial redistribution of English exclusives from a grammaticalization as well as a variation point of view, finding that where in eModE the 'exclusive' category has a two-prototype core (*only* and *but*), this has become a single prototype (*only*) by the time of lModE, with *just* on its way (especially in oral language) to giving the category two-prototype status again. At the eModE stage *only* and *but* are, across registers, more or less complementary in distribution, with non-scalar *only* ('no other than') preferring referential focus and definite F(ocus) C(onstituent)s, whereas inherently scalar *but* ('no more than') favours non-referential focus and indefinite or quantified FCs, both preferences that make sense, grammaticalization-wise, in that they are clearly etymologically conditioned (*only* < OE ān 'one', *but* < OE *ne...butan* 'not outside'). However, from the early seventeenth century onwards, *only* seems to take over from *but*, adding scalar meaning, nonreferential focus and indefinite/quantified FC to its repertoire and thus following the general grammaticalization pattern of 'subjectification'. *But* becomes, in fact, a marked, literate form and Nevalainen attributes its retirement from the prototype scene to its inherently scalar (hence subjective) meaning: subjective expressions are, by their very nature, unstable, especially so in oral contexts. Thus a combined grammaticalization-variation approach leads, as Nevalainen points out, to optimal insights regarding patterns of both semantic and redistributional change. Mats Rydén, also concerned with redistribution, gives a brief sketch of 'The *be/have* Variation with Intransitives in its Crucial Phase' in the eighteenth and nineteenth centuries (in Kastovsky). The two verbs are in complementary variation, in terms of perfective marking, from lOE onwards, with *have* in the minority; around 1700 the ratio is about 1:3, and some hundred years later this ratio is the reverse, the chief reason for this change being the functional diversity of *be* (copula, passive and perfective marker). On the positive side, we can see *have* getting promoted in combination with verbs expressing action or duration, in iterative contexts and, grammatically, in combination with e.g. the past perfect, which is less obviously stative than its present-perfect counterpart.

Another variationist study by Helena Raumolin-Brunberg, based on the writings of Sir Thomas More, compares *The Noun Phrase in Early Sixteenth-Century English* with its counterpart in Present-day (standard) English (PE). By and large, she finds, the eModE speaker has the same inventory of expressive items and structures available as PE speakers, the differences lying more in a shift in their distribution (cf. the obsolescence as a type of e.g. *a goodly cry and ioyfull*, where PE speakers can only resort to using two pre-head modifiers), the most striking change (and one that can be only disclosed by statistical research) being, perhaps, a general shift towards greater compactness; this is, for instance, apparent from the relative PE increase in (i) NPs that combine both pre- and post-head modification at the expense of only post-head modification, (ii) compounding and (iii) prepositional, participial and nominal post-head modifiers at the expense of relative clause modifers.

There are a few more contributions to be mentioned here that do not readily fit in with any of the above topics (all except the last one occurring in Kastovsky). Veronica Kniesza is concerned with 'Prepositional Phrases Expressing Adverbs of Time from Late Old English to Early Middle English', discussing the relations between prepositions and the type of arguments they govern. Anatoli Muhkin and Natalya Yulikova's 'Locative Valency of the English Verb: a Historical Approach' emphasizes the relevance of the study of valency, seen as a syntactic property of verbal lexemes, for diachronic purposes. The potential problem of syntactic indeterminacy regarding

'Pronoun and Reference in Old English Poetry' is, according to Hans-Jürgen Diller, counterbalanced by what appears to be the OE poet's intuitive ability to anticipate the audience's need for information; a variety of rhetorical devices (topic continuity, framing, grounding), metre and familiarity with characters conspire to evoke a richly informative discourse model in the listener and thus to help him resolve referential vagueness. Also discourse-oriented is Udo Fries's attempt to apply, in the words of editor Dieter Kastovsky ('Introduction', p. 3), 'principles of transphrastic text-linguistics and discourse analysis' to 'Question-Answer Sequences in Old English'. And finally there is what authors Bertil Sundby, Anne Kari Bjørge and Kari Haugland abbreviate as BENG, *A Dictionary of English Normative Grammar 1700–1800*, which, on the basis of fourteen 'error typologies', inventorizes and classifies the forms that eighteenth-century grammarians found fault with for some reason or other, the idea being that there is a great deal to be learned from these grammarians's views regarding deviant grammar and their attitudes towards correctness.

7. Vocabulary and Semantics

(a) *Vocabulary*

Some useful articles occurred in recent festschrifts. In *Language Usage and Description: Studies presented to N. E. Osselton on the occasion of his retirement*, edited by Ingrid Tieken-Boon van Ostade and John Frankis, Joan Beal discusses the effects of alliteration and rhyme in newspaper usage in '*Toy Boys* and *Lager Louts*: Motivation by Linguistic Form?' John Frankis writes on phonaesthesia in 'Middle English Ideophones and the Evidence of Manuscript Variants: Explorations in the Lunatic Fringe of Language', while Bob Rigter casts some 'Light on the Dark Etymology of JAZZ in the *Oxford English Dictionary*'. Wim Tigges examines current usage in '*Positive* and *Negative* in Formal British English: A Point of Modern English Usage', and Herman Wekker deals with 'English Grammars and Dictionaries for Foreign Learners'. Sylviane Granger edited *Perspectives on the English Lexicon: A Tribute to Jacques van Roey*. Part I, *Aspects of lexicon organisation*, includes an article by Willy Martin 'On the dynamic organization of [computer] lexicons'; part II, *Descriptive lexicological studies*, has articles on lexical morphology, usage and loan-words; part III deals with *Lexicographic issues* and part IV with *Vocabulary learning and teaching*.

A complete issue of the *International Journal of Lexicography* (4.iii) was devoted to the topic of 'Building a Lexicon', with articles by B. T. S. Atkins on 'The Contribution of Lexicography' (167–204), Branimir K. Boguraev, the issue editor, on 'The Contribution of Computers' (227–60) and Beth Levin on 'The Contribution of Linguistics' (205–26). Harry M. Logan discusses 'Electronic Lexicography' in *CHum* (25.351–61). *EnT* continued to be a fruitful source of lexical insights and offbeat information, as in David Crystal's 'Having it up to here: the asymmetrical lexicon' (7.43–4), where he ponders on the unequal lexical representation of such related concepts as Friendship/Enmity or Red/Green, and Keith White's 'Aureate or inkpot?', which places the burgeoning technical terminology of literary theory in the context of the historical debate on ornate language in English (7.45–8).

It was a good year for bad language, producing Geoffrey Hughes's fascinating analysis of *Swearing: A Social History of Foul Language, Oaths and Profanity in English* and the equally intriguing *Euphemism and Dysphemism: Language Used as Shield and Weapon* by Keith Allan and Kate Burridge. A flourishing register of a more limited historical spread is dealt with in John A. Barry's *Technobabble*, which analyses, not entirely sympathetically, the linguistic characteristics of computerese and its encroachment on English generally. Those of us who have struggled with this form of 'English' may recognize the characteristics described in the publishers' blurb: '...logorrhea, excessive use of the passive voice, anthropomorphism, vague and abstract language, euphemism, obfuscation, solecism, synecdoche, and mangled metaphors'! A plea for further examination of a less controversial register is made by Graham Shorrocks in 'Towards a survey of angling terminology: an untapped source of traditional and dialectal usage' (*TPS* 89.123–9), where the author points out that fishing as a pastime or occupation is geographically, socially and diachronically widespread and therefore likely to yield a rich lexical harvest.

Diachronic lexicology provided a good spread of material, especially for earlier periods. The twentieth century is represented by John Algeo's article, 'Vogue words through five decades' (*EnT* 7.44–6), which looks at the period from 1940–90 and provides such splendid examples of elegant coinages from the 1970's as *Watergoof, Watergaffe* and *Waterbugger*. W. F. Bolton, in *Shakespeare's English: Language in the History Plays*, which makes extensive use of computer analysis, has chapters on the vocabulary of *King John* and on pragmatics in *Henry VIII*. William Caxton's habit of borrowing heavily from the source language in his translations (as distinct from his original prose) is discussed by Miguel Márquez in 'Aspects of Vocabulary Building in Caxton's *Recuyell of the Historyes of Troy*' (*ES* 72:328–49), and *OED* and *MED* antedatings are noted. W. Rothwell makes a plea for more work in a neglected field in 'The Missing Link in English Etymology: Anglo-French' (*MÆ* 60.173–96).

Among important contributions to Old English lexicology, and potentially to the broader field of the evolution of semantic universals, is Earl R. Anderson on 'The Uncarpentered World of Old English Poetry' (*ASE* 20.65–80), a world where, lexically at least, the circular predominates over the angular. Steven Fanning deals with terminology for Anglo-Saxon kings and rulers in 'Bede, Imperium, and the Bretwaldas' (*Speculum* 66.1–26), while Angus McIntosh casts new light on an Old English suffix in 'Old English Adjectives with Derivative *-lic* Partners: Some Semantic Problems' (*NM* 92.297–310). *N&Q* 38 contains several short articles on the meanings of individual words, such as those by Andrew Breeze on 'Old English *ealfara* 'pack-horse': a Spanish-Arabic Loanword' (15–17) and 'Old English *franca* 'spear': Welsh *ffranc*' (149–51), or Alex Nicholls' 'Bede "awe-inspiring" Not "monstrous": Some Problems with Old English *aglæca*' (147–8). A book I have not yet managed to see is Richard North's *Pagan Words and Christian Meanings* (Rodopi).

(b) Semantics

Much new work on lexis and semantics is now based on the analysis of computer corpora. *Using Corpora: Proceedings of the Seventh Annual Conference of the UW Centre for the New OED and Text Research* contains relevant articles, such as Marti Hearst on 'Toward Noun Homonym Disambiguation Using Local Context in Large Text Corpora' (1–22) and John Justeson and Slava Katz on 'Redefining Antonymy: The Textual Structure of a Semantic Relation' (138–53). An attempt to reveal the stylistic 'fingerprint' of an author through computer analysis of lexical density is described by David I. Holmes in 'Vocabulary Richness and the Prophetic Voice' (*L&LC* 6.259–68). General books on corpora which contain material of interest to the semanticist include *Corpus, Concordance, Collocation* by John Sinclair, *English Corpus Linguistics: Studies in Honour of Jan Svartvik*, edited by Karin Aijmer and

Bengt Altenberg, and *English Computer Corpora: Selected Papers and Research Guide*, edited by Stig Johansson and Anna-Brita Stenström. I have not yet seen Nelleke Oostdijk's *Corpus Linguistics and the Automatic Analysis of English* (Rodopi).

Other new books deal with a variety of approaches to the subject. *Semantic Universals and Universal Semantics*, edited by Dietmar Zaefferer, attempts to reconcile philosophical and linguistic approaches to semantics by bringing together ten papers representing the two points of view. *Semantics: an international handbook of contemporary research*, edited by A. von Stechow and D. Wunderlich, contains 41 articles in English or German, predominantly truth-conditional in orientation. Patrick Suppes, in *Language for Humans and Robots*, develops his own theory of congruence of meaning through a number of studies of child language and of linguistic interaction with robots. Beatriz Garza-Cuarón presents a historical and analytical study of connotation in *Connotation and Meaning*, which ranges over linguistics, semiotics and literary criticism. Barbara Abbott suggests a semantics based on mental models in 'Some arguments for a mental semantics without sentences' (*Word* 42.251–75). Henry G. Burger, of Word Tree fame, has a wide-ranging review article on 'Roget, Darwin and Bohr: Parallelizing Evolutionary Diversification with Conceptual Classification' in the *International Journal of Lexicography* (23–67).

One very welcome event was the reappearance of Brent Berlin and Paul Kay's classic, *Basic Color Terms: Their Universality and Evolution*, with a revised preface and updated bibliography. Despite the many modifications to the theory which have followed the original publication of this work, it is still essential reading. Equally welcome was the publication in paperback of John R. Taylor's excellent overview of prototype theory, *Linguistic Categorization*.

Here we begin to approach the fuzzy edges of semantics. Michael Hoey's *Patterns of Lexis in Text* should probably be classified as discourse analysis, yet contains much to interest the semanticist. Pragmatics likewise forms boundaries with many areas of linguistics, but the collection of papers edited by Steven Davis, *Pragmatics: A Reader*, is certainly worth mentioning here. I must also record four books which I have not yet been able to see: *Linguistic Semantics* by William Frawley (Lawrence Erlbaum Associates); *Current Advances in Semantic Theory* edited by M. Stamenov (John Benjamins); *Politeness in Language: Studies in its History, Theory, and Practice* edited by Richard J. Watts, Sachiko Ide and Konrad Ehlich (de Gruyter); and *Cross-Cultural Pragmatics: the Semantics of Human Interaction* by Anna Wierzbicka (de Gruyter).

(c) Lexicography

John D. Battenburg produced a useful user-oriented study entitled *English Monolingual Learners' Dictionaries*, and Gabriele Stein an equally useful updated edition of Starnes and Noyes' classic, *The English Dictionary from Cawdrey to Johnson*, with an introduction describing work since 1946. The third and last volume of *Wörterbücher/Dictionaries/Dictionnaires*, the international encyclopedia of lexicography edited by Franz Josef Hasmann, Oskar Reichmann, Herbert Ernst Wiegand and Ladislav Zgusta, appeared. The team working on *DOE* in Toronto published *Dictionary of Old English: B*, edited by Ashley Crandell Amos et al. A progress report appears in *OENews* (25.42–3).

There were many new dictionaries from commercial publishers. Oxford University Press made a particularly strong showing with, among other things, the new edition of the single volume *Compact Oxford English Dictionary*, *The Oxford Dictionary of New Words* and *The Oxford Thesaurus*. The influence of the *Australian National Dictionary* was seen in volumes such as Joan Hughes's *Australian Words and their Origins*, R. M. W. Dixon et al.'s *Australian Aboriginal Words in English*, and G. A. Wilkes's *A Dictionary of Australian Colloquialisms*. Tony Deverson wrote on 'New Zealand English Lexis: the Maori Dimension' in *EnT* (7.18–25). The trend, relatively new in Britain at least, towards encyclopedic dictionaries, was seen in *The Oxford Encyclopedic English Dictionary*. A useful book for learners was the *Collins-Cobuild English Guide* vol. 2: *Word Formation*, by Jane Bradbury.

8. Onomastics

Julia Cresswell's *Dictionary of First Names* is definitely a cut above the average what-to-call-your-baby book. It is short of philological detail, in the sense that it usually offers translations rather than forms of name-elements (*Ralph* is 'counsel' + 'wolf'). What it does have to say is on the whole refreshingly reliable in comparison with its competitors (which now include a set of commercially-available mugs bearing supposed name-histories which are so awful as to beggar description). That is not to say it is faultless; I would rather not have met *Caractacos* on p. 48, or been told that *Caius/Gaius* is from *gaudere* on p. 46. 'Old Germanic' stalks its pages as it does in other similar books such as Withycombe's *Oxford Dictionary of Christian Names* (*YWES* 58); it is rarely clear whether reference is being made to attested Frankish forms, to reconstructed etyma, or what. Par for the course. The author does not get involved in some of the controversies that beset the ultimate origin of certain names (e.g. *Catherine*, *Mary*), but offers quite reasonable accounts of the recent popularity of many.

The Old English tribal name *Gewissæ* is scrutinized by Richard Coates, and the Celtic origins ascribed to it by some scholars rejected ('On some Controversy Surrounding *Gewissæ/Gewissei*, *Cedric* and *Ceawlin* (*Nomina* 13.1–11)). He concludes that it derives by nominalization from *gewis* 'sure, reliable', and proceeds to discuss the implications in this context of the West-Saxon kings' names *Cerdic* and *Ceawlin*, at least the former of which is certainly of British origin. Some questions about the phonology and dating of these names are also raised.

A. D. Mills's *A Dictionary of English Place Names* is a most welcome addition to the bookshelf, being the first comprehensive new dictionary of the names of places in England since the fourth edition of Eilert Ekwall's book *The Concise Oxford Dictionary of English Place-Names* (*YWES* 48) in 1960. It presents the results of thirty years' additional scholarship in a sober and rather conservative way – no outrageous hypotheses are advanced, and care is taken to represent alternative respectable opinions about difficult names. The nature of the book means that there is little room for detailed phonological discussion or for the strings of dated spellings that scholars consider crucial, and users are directed to the appropriate EPNS county survey volumes, where they exist, and a small number of non-EPNS books. It is therefore primarily a synthesis and synopsis of current knowledge for general users, and it fulfils this brief very well. There is a judicious twenty-page introduction explaining the scope of the book and the habits and preferences of place-name scholars.

Special pleasure attends the publication of a new EPNS volume; this year appears the double volume constituting the second part of Kenneth Cameron's *The Place-Names of Lincolnshire*. It covers Yarborough wapentake in Lindsey. The usual platitudes about depth of coverage, responsiveness to recent historical work, and meticulousness will be repeated here not because the reviewer is too jaded for original thought, but because they are accurate. Occasionally an etymology fails to satisfy in every detail (*Goxhill*, *Barnetby*) and there are enough unresolved problems to whet future scholars' appetites (*Kirmington*, *Stallingborough*).

On the Old English, or supposedly Old English, front: Richard Coates examines the evidence for the origin of 'The Name of Lewes' (*JEPNS* 23.5–15), concluding that there is really about equal evidence to suspect British or English origin; the cultural probabilities somewhat favour the English and the linguistic ones somewhat favour British. Ann Cole contributes a fine piece to the same journal on '*Burna* and *Brōc*. Problems in Retrieving the Old English Usage of these Place-Name Elements' (26–48). It consists of minute geographical and ecological analysis demonstrating that the prototypical *brōc* was a rain-fed stream with a muddy bed and rank vegetation, flowing over relatively impermeable subsoil; whereas a prototypical *burna* was a gravel-bedded clear stream, flowing from a seasonally-varying spring. In '*Exodus*, *Elene* and *The Rune Poem*: *milpæþ* "Army Road, Highway" ', Andrew Breeze declares he has discovered a Welsh loanword *mil* 'army' (now obsolete) in an English topographical word (*N&Q* 38.436–8), and makes an acceptable case for this. Victor Watts returns to a matter raised in a previous issue of *Nomina* (*YWES* 71) namely the phonological variation in the descendants of OE *sceaga* 'strip of woodland' ('*Shaw/ Shay* Revisited', *Nomina* 13.109–14). He ascribes the variation to the second, late and well-known, monophthongization of ME [au] resulting in an unrounded vowel (as in *safe*). The frequent variant *shave* has not yet been elucidated, to the reviewer's knowledge: room for more work here).

Whilst he was not an anglicist, it is proper at this point to record the death in 1991 of Kenneth H. Jackson. He was a Celticist of towering stature – some would say the greatest ever – who provided critical specialist guidance to the mainly anglistic scholars who have conducted the Survey of English Place-Names, and brought their pronouncements on names of Celtic origin to new standards of respectability.

There are just a few pieces on later names this year. Richard Coates explains the curiosity *Worthing Island* in William Worcestre's *Itineraries* (1478) as a reference to the Isle of Sheppey in Kent, based on a misinterpretation of the local place-name *Warden* (*N&Q* 38.445–6); and has a small piece on 'The Lost Street-Name *Bukettwin*, Lewes' in *Sussex Archaeological Collections* (129.252–3). John Field writes on 'Creatures Great and Small: Excursions among English Field-Names' (*Nomina* 13.91–108), which deals with the significance of animal-names in field-names. Geoffrey Wilson examines 'Railways, Developers and Place-Names: the case of Raynes Park' (*JEPNS* 23.16–25), elucidating the history of a name that was obscure to the editors of *The Place-Names of Surrey*; it derives from a family whose doings Wilson catalogues in detail.

English names, among others, are dealt with by Graeme Whittington in 'Place-Names in Northern Fife' (*Nomina* 13.13–23); he examines their significance for geographical-historical concerns such as settlement and agricultural history. Brian K. Roberts, already well-known for his work on village-plans, explores 'Late *-bý* names in the Eden Valley, Cumberland' (*Nomina* 13.25–40), and detects signs of deliberate plantation, probably dating from after 1092, in the outline of villages so named. On the margins of interest to specialists in English is Richard Coates' book *The Ancient and Modern Names of the Channel Islands: A Linguistic History*. The author tries to establish the limits of what can be known about the Roman period and later names, and the likeliest interpretation of these very problematical linguistic objects. The same author rejects a spurious 'Roman' name-form in '*Anderida*: Not the Roman Name of Pevensey' (*Sussex Archaeological Collections* (129.250–1).

9. Stylistics

This year saw the publication of Roger Sell's *Literary Pragmatics*. Literary pragmaticists aim at an interactive or contextualized account of literature, using a top-down approach (i.e. from 'world' to text) in an attempt to bridge the crippling language/literature dichotomy. The papers divide into more theoretical and more practical ones. The former include Nils Erik Enkvist's general overview of discourse stylistics ('On the Interpretability of Texts in General and of Literary Texts in Particular'), in which he argues that pragmatic interpretability depends on each individual reader's ability to construct around the text a scenario or 'text world' in which that text makes sense. Richard Watts, in 'Cross-Cultural Problems in the Perception of Literature', discusses cultural misunderstandings arising for Swiss-German readers of English literature, and explains them by reference to the 'reality set' into which these readers have been socialized. Roger Sell ('The Politeness of Literary Texts'), Ernest Hess-Lüttich ('How does the Writer of a Dramatic Text Interact with his Audiences? On the Pragmatics of Literary Communication') and Willie van Peer ('But What Is Literature? Toward a Descriptive Definition of Literature') struggle with important theoretical concepts: politeness, literary communication and literature respectively. In 'Textualization', Balz Engler rejects the notion of contextualization, because it presupposes and hence reinforces the idea of the autonomous text, and calls for a study of the history of textualization of literary texts. Such a study is in fact adumbrated in Jerome McGann's 'What Difference do the Circumstances of Publication Make to the Interpretation of a Literary Work?', which offers two interesting case studies: the mutilation of plate 3 of Blake's *Jerusalem* and the reception history of Byron's poem 'Fare Thee Well!'

Other practically orientated papers include Claes Schaar's discussion of literary fragments ('On Free and Latent Semantic Energy'), as well as Meir Sternberg's more thorough exploration of the formal, representational and perspectival ambiguities and instabilities of reported speech ('How Indirect Discourse Means: Syntax, Semantics, Poetics, Pragmatics'). Peter Verdonk's 'Poems as Text and Discourse: The Poetics of Philip Larkin' sets up an interesting correlation between Larkin's poetic principles and the methodology of literary stylistics, which he illustrates in an extended analysis of Larkin's poem 'Talking in Bed'. Ziva Ben-Porat studies the changing representations of Jerusalem and of autumn in Hebrew poetry. She presents a fascinating view of literature as a cultural force both affecting, and being affected by, conceptualization (hence the title: 'Two-Way Pragmatics: From World to Text and Back'). Finally, there are two excellent papers on metaphor. First, Gerard Steen's 'Understanding Metaphor in Literature: Toward an Empirical Study' discusses the comprehension of metaphor within the constructivist framework of the Empirical Study of Literature. Adrian Pilkington's 'Poetic Effects: A Relevance Theory Perspective', on the other hand, offers a spirited defence of the (nowadays rather unfashionable) essentialist position. Interestingly, his theory, which is based upon Sperber and Wilson's relevance account of poetic effects, encompasses and even foregrounds not only questions of interpretation but also questions of evaluation.

Approaches to the Analysis of Literary Discourse, edited by Eija Ventola, brings together a number of papers on stylistics which were presented at International

Systemic Congresses. Roger Sell ('Literary Genre and History') explores convergences and divergences between a literary-pragmatic and a socio-semiotic approach to genre through a reading of Tennyson's 'The Charge of the Light Brigade' and Yeats's 'Easter 1916'. Two papers focus on the nature of fictional dialogue: Femi Akindele's 'Dialogue and Discourse in a Nigerian English Fiction', and Karen Malcolm's sophisticated 'Prose Dialogue and Discourse' (which, however, fails to note such obvious points as for example the female gender of Atwood's narrator in *Surfacing*). Julia Lavid's 'Semantic Options in the Transitivity System' is a useful transitivity analysis of a passage from Melville's *Billy Budd*. Martina Björklund and Tuija Virtanen ('Variation in Narrative Structure') compare a children's story with an artistic story, and Eija Ventola's 'Phonological Meanings in Literary Prose Texts and their Translations' looks at how phonological meanings are preserved (or not) in Finnish and Swedish translations of Australian fiction.

Two monographs were published in the area of critical linguistics. First David Birch's *The Language of Drama* is a logical sequel to his *Language, Literature and Critical Practice* (*YWES* 70) in the sense that it is an application of the theory set out in the earlier book to an extensive body of (drama) texts. Birch discusses the work of a large number of modern dramatists, ranging from Beckett and Pinter to Caryl Churchill and Steven Berkoff. Also, he does not limit himself to mainstream English writers, but includes many post-colonial writers such as Athol Fugard and Wole Soyinka. Birch is not concerned with drama as a textual but as a discoursal phenomenon: he analyses the multiplicity of meanings constructed by writer, reader, analyst-critic, producer and audience in constantly changing contexts of performance. He rejects any privileging of the written text and argues that other semiotic systems, especially the visual and auditory elements of the production, contribute equally to the audience's construction of meaning. Critical practice thus goes beyond the surface meanings of the words (*what* the text means), focusing instead on the underlying struggle for power, domination and control (*how* the text means). Such an approach can create an awareness of the ways in which our realities are sociolinguistically constructed, and of the possibility of constructing alternative – less oppressive – realities. In the final chapters of the book, Birch explores different strategies of (ideological rather than just aesthetic) defamiliarization, linguistic shock tactics and carnivalesque uses of language, which can lead to social and political change through a 'process of destabilisation'. And it is such change that a critical drama praxis is ultimately concerned to foster.

The other monograph written within the general framework of critical linguistics is concerned with the (non-literary) discourse of the press. Based on the Hallidayan model of language, Roger Fowler's *Language in the News: Discourse and Ideology in the Press* presents news as a social practice, at once constructing and being constructed by social processes and social realities. Fowler's point is that any distinction between biased and unbiased discourse is illusory, as well as the frequently added corollary that any instance of biased discourse that we happen to come across has to be mercilessly eradicated. On the contrary, language is never a transparent, value-free medium, and therefore reality as constructed by language is always and unavoidably enmeshed with ideology. The book aims to make this ubiquitous ideological structure 'tangible', and so trains readers to resist the more stereotyped subject positions constructed for them in and by texts.

Turning now to journals, we find a number of papers that deal with stylistic theory. In a brief article ('Postmodernist Chutneys' *TPr* 5.1–7), David Birch opposes critical theory and practice to postmodernist and deconstructionist criticism. The article is something of a *tour de force*, with critic (Birch) and fictional character (Saleem Sinai, the narrator of Rushdie's *Midnight's Children*) deconstructing each other. But Birch makes the salutary observation that such deconstruction is only valid if it leads to political action and change: 'A textualism is needed, therefore, which ... is prepared to engage critically and politically with the consequences of the free play of signification, and not just the freeplay itself.' Horst Ruthrof ('Language and the Dominance of Modality' *Lang&S* 21.315–26) takes the first steps towards a comprehensive theory of covert or inferential modality, where modality is understood in a wide sense as 'the structurable field of the manners of speaking underlying all utterances'. And in 'Perspective as a Source of Style' (*Lang&S* 21.53–71; 119–37), Pauli Saukkonen presents a painstakingly detailed exploration of the consequences of his view that style can be defined in terms of a wide, all-embracing concept of 'perspective meaning'.

In the area of phonological and graphological studies there are, first of all, two statistical investigations: John Lord's ('Shakespeare and the Elizabethan Poetic Voice' *Lang&S* 21.72–97) of the characteristically 'sweet' sound of Shakespeare's sonnets, and Lawrence Schourup's ('Mosaic Rhyme' *Lang&S* 21.333–47) of the structure, positioning and functions of mosaic rhyme, a type of obtrusive rhyme frequently found in humorous verse. Other papers include Reuven Tsur, J. Glicksohn and C. Goodblatt's 'Gestalt Qualities in Poetry and the Reader's Absorption Style' (*JPrag* 16.487–500), which is an empirical study of how the perceived poetic effects vary according to the reader's degree of receptivity (or 'absorption'), Malcolm Hayward's 'A Connectionist Model of Poetic Metre' (*Poetics* 20.303–17), which applies McClelland and Rumelhart's connectionist model to the analysis of English poetic metre, and Ogo Ofuani's 'The Stylistic Significance of the Graphological Structure of Taban Lo Liyong's *Another Nigger Dead*' (*Lang&S* 21.301–14), which shows how graphological deviations create phonological and semantic ambiguities.

Now to studies focusing on the levels of syntax and lexis. Josiane Paccaud's 'The Progressive Form in *Under Western Eyes*' (*Lang&S* 21.107–18) is a short piece on Conrad's use of the progressive form, distinguishing between the progressive as an index of character, as a pointer towards important events, and as a marker of subjectivity or perspectival change. Dibakar Barua ('Syntactic and Semantic Structures in Sylvia Plath's "The Moon and the Yew Tree" ' *Lang&S* 21.35–51) undertakes a detailed linguistic analysis of Plath's poem in the (illusory?) hope of 'making the full range of its meaning accessible to the reader'. Inna Koskenniemi ('The Creation and Use of Compound Words in Jacobean Tragedy' *NM* 92.63–73) examines the Jacobean dramatists' use of (mostly neologistic) compounds to highlight themes of satire, intrigue, invective, etc. In 'An Interpretation of Elizabeth Bishop's Key Vocabulary: Or, Facts do not Speak for Themselves' (*Lang&S* 21.3–15), Anne Greenhalgh analyses Elizabeth Bishop's vocabulary in an attempt to get an insight into the thematic backbone of her poetry, what Greenhalgh calls (following Kenneth Burke) the poet's 'representative anecdote'. Last, but certainly not least, Guy Cook ('Stylistics with a Dash of Advertising' *Lang&S* 21.151–61) subjects a number of poster advertisements to a thorough stylistic analysis. He argues that the proliferation of meanings caused by lexical polysemy gives the advertising texts their literary feel, but at the same time they must be distinguished from literary texts because their intention (to sell the product) is fixed and known in advance.

Two papers in the area of pragmatics and discourse analysis focus on presuppositional constructions. Helen Aristar Dry and Susan Kucinkas, in 'Ghostly Ambiguity: Presuppositional Constructions in *The Turn of the Screw*' (*Style* 25.71–88), show that new information about James's ghosts is consistently taken for granted, assumed to be part of the writer's and reader's background knowledge, while what is foregrounded is the governess's inner life. This strategy of reversal of foreground and background information both undermines the reliability of the narrator in the eyes of the reader, and also explains why the critical controversy over the ghosts has been raging at least since Edmund Wilson's Freudian reading of *The Turn of the Screw*. John Wilson's 'The Linguistic Pragmatics of Terrorist Acts' (*D&S* 2.29–45) is also concerned with presuppositional constructions, but in a non-literary discourse type, namely the political language of parliamentary debate. Efurosibina Adegbija ('Towards a Speech-Act Approach to Nigerian Literature in English' *Lang&S* 21.259–69) ponders the advantages of a speech-act approach to Wole Soyinka's play *Madmen and Specialists*, though in terms made somewhat tentative by frequent use of the conditional: 'A speech-act approach to Nigerian literature in English would be both fruitful and intellectually productive in that it would fill a gap ... .' In 'Names and the Construction of Identity: Evidence from Toni Morrison's *Tar Baby*' (*Poetics* 20.173–92), Richard Gerrig and Mahzarin Banaji present a cognitive science view of how naming practices exploit mutual knowledge and contribute to social classification. A detailed study of the use of politeness strategies in a literary text is Donald E. Hardy's 'Strategic Politeness in Hemingway's "The Short Happy Life of Francis Macomber" ' (*Poetics* 20.343–62), which relies on Brown and Levinson's politeness model and in particular their notion of 'positive face'. Another more sociolinguistically oriented study is Vimala Herman's 'Dramatic Dialogue and the Systematics of Turn-Taking' (*Sem* 83.97–121), which applies insights derived from conversation analysis and ethnomethodology to an analysis of dramatic dialogue. In particular, she focuses on turn change and topic management strategies in a number of plays, showing how they can have thematic and/or ideological significance. Finally, two somewhat slight pieces: Yang Yonglin ('How to Talk to the Supernatural in Shakespeare' *LSoc* 20.247–61) looks at pronouns of address in Shakespearean drama and notes an almost universal use of *thou* to individual supernatural beings. And M. I. Osakwe ('The Styles of Abiku: Two Related Diatypes of English', *Lang&S* 21.98–103) compares J.P. Clark's 'Abiku' poem with Wole Soyinka's poem of the same name. He argues that differences between the two poems can be attributed to socio-situational factors and reaches the following momentous conclusion: 'The foregoing analysis has revealed among other things that the poems differ in style.'

Continued interest in the stylistic analysis of tropes is reflected in three papers on irony and four on metaphor. Sonia S'hiri, in 'Literary Discourse and Irony: Secret Communion and the Pact of Reciprocity' (*EWPAL* 2.126–42), combines a relevance theoretic approach to irony with Herbert Clark's notion of layers of discourse, reading the first sentence of Jane Austen's *Pride and Prejudice* as the narrator's echoic interpretation of the Bennets' state of mind, and a passage from Ambrose Bierce's 'Oil of Dog' as the author's ironic comment on his narrator's values. The general point is that the reader suspecting irony looks for an addresser in the higher discourse layer to whom the 'intention of irony' can be attributed. David Littman and Jacob Mey ('The Nature of Irony: Towards a Computational Model of Irony' *JPrag* 15.131–51) build up abstract representations of different types of ironic situations, distinguishing in particular between intentional and serendipitous goal/plan irony. 'Psychological Aspects of Irony Understanding' are discussed in Raymond Gibbs's and Jennifer O'Brien's article of that name (*JPrag* 16.523–30).

The outstanding contribution to 'metaphormania' is Yeshayahu Shen's 'Schemata, Categories and Metaphor Interpretation' (*PoT* 12.111–24), which sees metaphor as a mapping from a source domain onto a target domain and raises the further question of why certain properties of the source domain are more likely than others to get mapped onto the target domain. Shen proposes a solution within a hybrid model of metaphor comprehension which combines Dedre Gentner's structure-mapping theory with Tourangeau and Sternberg's theory of aptness in metaphor. Chanita Goodblatt's 'Semantic Fields and Metaphor: A Case Study' (*JLS* 20.173–87) is an attempt to unravel the semantic interlocking and perceptual conflicts of Dylan Thomas's metaphor chains. Finally, two papers in *Lang&S*: Gerald Doherty ('The Quest for the Proper Place: Plots and Counterplots in *Howards End*', *Lang&S* 21.271–83) highlights the dialectic interplay of metaphoric and metonymic plots in E. M. Forster's novel. Hamutal Bar-Yosef ('Speech in Metaphor', *Lang&S* 21.285–99) describes such stylistic phenomena as prosopopeia, dramatized personification, dramatized metonymy and substantivation of speech.

Focusing on narrative, we have Mounir Triki's 'The Representation of Self in Narrative' (*JLS* 20.78–96), which aims at setting up a typology of narrative voice, distinguishing in particular between the perceptual centre and the speaking voice. J. A. Alvarez Amorós' 'PossibleWorld Semantics, Frame Text, Insert Text, and Unreliable Narration: The Case of *The Turn of the Screw*' (*Style* 25.42–70) uses a complex text-linguistic framework, including a possible-world theory of fiction, to make a rather obvious distinction between 'frame text' (basically corresponding to what others call narrator discourse) and 'insert text' (or character discourse). J.-K. Adams ('Intention and Narrative' *JLS* 20.63–77) starts on a programme of rehabilitation of the concept of 'intention' in narrative analysis, which has been discredited ever since Wimsatt and Beardsley's 'intentional fallacy'. Both conversational and literary narratives are studied from the perspective of a combined discourse-analytic and narratological framework in Monika Fludernik's 'The Historical Present Tense Yet Again: Tense Switching and Narrative Dynamics in Oral and Quasi-Oral Storytelling' (*Text* 11.365–97). Joan Beal, in 'A Real Fright: Adolescents' Narratives of Vicarious Experience' (*Lang&S* 21.16–34), presents a Labovian analysis of oral narratives, but criticizes some of Labov's findings (especially the claimed correlation between use of evaluation and age). Brief mention also has to be made of Harold Mosher's investigation of 'descriptized narration', a mixed type of narration which combines narrative forms with descriptive functions ('Towards a Poetics of "Descriptized" Narration', *PoT* 12.425–45), and of Carol T. Torsello's highly interesting application of systemic-functional grammar to the study of point of view ('How Woolf Creates Point of View in *To the Lighthouse*' *OPSL* 5.159–74).

Lastly, a mixed bag of articles containing some quantitative and some rhetorical studies. Using a functional (Hallidayan) classification of adjectives, Michael Lucas ('Conrad's Adjectival Eccentricity', *Style* 25.123–50) compares Conrad and seven other nineteenth and twentieth century novelists in form and function of adjectives. Ruth Sabol's quantitative study ('Semantic Analysis and Fictive Worlds in Ford and Conrad', *L&LC* 6.97–103) contrasts the fictional worlds of *The Good Soldier* and *Lord Jim*, and Elena Semino's 'A Comparative Analysis of the Opening Passages of Two Short Stories on Quantitative Grounds' (*LeS* 26.449–63) looks at the perceptual experiences in Virginia Woolf's 'Solid Objects' and Dylan Thomas's 'The Visitor'. Laurel Brinton provides a useful survey of rhetorical schemes such as anaphora, asyndeton, hyperbaton, etc. in 'The Iconicity of Rhetorical Figures: "Schemes" as Devices for Textual Cohesion' (*Lang&S* 21.162–90). And Karen Newman ('The Inward Springs: Shakespeare's Rhetoric of Character', *Lang&S* 21.191–202) analyses a soliloquy from *Measure for Measure*, showing how the dialogic nature of the Shakespearean soliloquy creates 'the illusion of mental life'.

Books Reviewed

Abercrombie, David. *Fifty Years in Phonetics: Selected Papers*. Edinburgh University Press. pp. 127. £25.00. ISBN 0 7486 0196 1.

Aijmer, Karin, and Bengt Altenberg, eds. *English Corpus Linguistics: Studies in Honour of Jan Svartvik*. Longman. pp. 338. hb £28.00, pb £13.99. ISBN 0 582 05931 3, 0 582 05930 5.

Aitchison, Jean. *Language Change: Progress or Decay?* 2nd Edition. Cambridge University Press. pp. 256. hb £27.50, pb £7.95. ISBN 0 521 41101 7, 0 521 42283 3.

Alladina, S., and V. Edwards, eds. *Multilingualism in the British Isles. Longman Linguistics Library*. 2 vols. pp. Vol. 1: 287, Vol. 2: 278. pb £13.99 each. ISBN Vol.1, 0 582 01963 X, Vol 2, 0 582 06365 5.

Allan, Keith, and Kate Burridge. *Euphemism and Dysphemism*. Oxford University Press. pp. 263. £20. ISBN 0 19 5066227.

Amos, Ashley Crandell, et al. *Dictionary of Old English: B*. Pims. pp.7 + 9 fiches. Toronto.

Barry, John A. *Technobabble*. MITP. pp. 250. £19.95. ISBN 0 262 02333 4.

Battenburg, John D. *English Monolingual Learners' Dictionaries*. Niemeyer. pp. 170. DM 76. ISBN 3 48 30939 3.

Beardon, Colin, David Lumsden, and Geoff Holmes. *Natural Language and Computational Linguistics: An Introduction*. Ellis Horwood. pp. 232. pb £18.95. ISBN 0 13 612813 0.

Beaugrande, Robert de. *Linguistic Theory: The Discourse of Fundamental Works*. Longmans. pp. 403. hb £29.00, pb £15.99. ISBN 0 582 08210 2; 0 582 03725 5.

Bell, Alan. *The Language of News Media*. Blackwell Language in Society Series. pp. 277. hb £35.00, pb £11.95. ISBN 0 631 1642434 0, 0 631 16435 9.

Berlin, Brent, and Paul Kay. *Basic Colour Terms: Their Universality and Evolution*. 2nd edition. UCalP. pp. 189. pb. $16.20. ISBN 0 520 076354.

Biber, Douglas. *Variation Across Speech and Writing*. Cambridge University Press. pp. 290. pb £14.95. ISBN 0 521 42556 5.

Birch, David. *The Language of Drama*. Macmillan. pp.175. £30. ISBN 0 333 51637 0.

Bland, Cynthia Renée. *The Teaching of Grammar in Late Medieval England. An Edition, with Commentary, of Oxford, Lincoln College MS Lat. 130*. Colleagues Press. pp. 235. £19.95. ISBN 0 937191 16 7.

Bolton, W. F. *Shakespeare's English: Language in the History Plays*. Blackwell. pp. 256. £35.00. ISBN 0 631 16147 3.

Borsley, Robert D. *Syntactic Theory: A Unified Approach*. Edward Arnold. pp. 238. pb £12.99. ISBN 0 7131 6543 X.

Bradbury, Jane. *Word Formation*. Collins COBUILD English Guide vol. 2. Harper Collins. pp. 224. pb. £6.95. ISBN 0 00 370521 8.

Brown, Keith and Jim Miller. *Syntax: A Linguistic Introduction to Sentence Structure*. 2nd Edition. Harper Collins Academic. pp. 382. pb £14.95. ISBN 0 04 4455615.

Burke, P., and R. Porter, eds. *Language, Self and Society: A Social History of Language*. Polity Press. pp. 358. £45.00. ISBN 0 745 60765 9.

Cameron, Kenneth. *The Place Names of Lincolnshire, part two*. EPNS. pp. 326. £30. ISBN 0 904889 16 5.

Campbell, George L. *Compendium of the World's Languages*. Routledge. pp. 1574.

£150.00. ISBN 0 415 02937 6.

Cannon, Garland (titlepage 1990). *The Life and Mind of Oriental Jones. Sir William Jones, the Father of Modern Linguistics*. Cambridge University Press. pp. 409. £40.00. ISBN 0 521 39149 0.

Cheshire, Jenny, ed. *English Around the World: Sociolinguistic Perspectives*. Cambridge University Press. pp. 684. hb £60.00, pb £19.95. ISBN 0 521 33 080 7, 0 521 39565 8.

Clyne, Michael. *Community Languages: The Australian Experience*. Cambridge University Press. pp. 294. £35.00. ISBN 0 521 39330 2.

Coates, Richard. *The Ancient and Modern Names of the Channel Islands: A Linguistic History*. Paul Watkins. pp. 144. hb £16.95, pb £9.95. ISBN 1 871615 15 1, 1 871615 16 X.

Corbett, Greville. *Gender*. Cambridge University Press. pp. 363. hb £45.00, pb £14.95. ISBN 0 521 32939 6, 0 521 33845 X.

Coulmas, Florian. *The Writing Systems of the World*. Blackwell, The Language Library series. pp. 302. hb £42.50, pb £14.95. ISBN 0 631 16513 4, 0 631 18028 1.

Coupland, N., H. Giles, and J. Wieman. *Miscommunication and Problematic Talk*. Sage. pp. 374 . hb £41.00, pb £21.00. ISBN 0 8039 4032 7, 0 8039 4033 5.

———, J. Coupland and H. Giles, eds. *Language, Society and the Elderly: Discourse, Identity and Aging*. Blackwell, Language in Society Series. pp. 220. hb £35.00, pb £12.95. ISBN 0 631 18004 4, 0 631 18279 9.

Cresswell, Julia. *The Bloomsbury Dictionary of First Names*. Bloomsbury (1990). pp. 248. pb £7.99. ISBN 0 747509 70 0.

Crowley, T. *Proper English? Readings in Language, History and Cultural Identity*. Routledge, Politics of Language Series. pp. 268. hb £35.00, pb £10.99. ISBN 0 415 04678 5, 0 415 04679 3.

Crystal, David. *The Cambridge Encyclopedia of Language*. Cambridge University Press. pp. 470. pb £14.95. ISBN 0 521 42443 7.

Davis, Steven. ed. *Pragmatics: A Reader*. Oxford University Press. pp. 595. pb. £25.00. ISBN 0 19 505898 4.

Dixon, R. M. W. *A New Approach to English Grammar, on Semantic Principles*. OUP. pp. 398. $44. ISBN 0 198242 72 7.

———, W. S. Ramson, and Mandy Thomas. *Australian Aboriginal Words in English*. Oxford University Press. pp 266. £25.00. ISBN 0 19 553099 3.

Douglas, Sylvester (ed. Charles Jones). *A Treatise on the Provincial Dialect of Scotland*. Edinburgh UP. pp. 278. £37.50. ISBN 0 7486 0300 X .

Fishman, J. *Reversing Language Shift*. Multilingual Matters. pp. 448. hb £43.00, pb £18.95. ISBN 1 85359 122 X, 1 85359 121 1.

Fowler, Roger. *Language in the News: Discourse and Ideology in the Press*. Routledge. pp. 254. pb £10.99. ISBN 0 415 01419 0.

Garza-Cuarón, Beatriz. *Connotation and Meaning*. Approaches to Semiotics 99. Gruyter. pp. 286. DM 138. ISBN 3 11 012670 2.

Giles, H., and N. Coupland. *Language: Contexts and Consequences*. Open University Press. pp. 244. £10.99. ISBN 3 350 98738; 3 350 98872 X.

———, J. Coupland, and N. Coupland. *Contexts of Accommodation*. CUP. pp. 300. $42.50. ISBN 0 521 36151 6.

Görlach, Manfred. *Introduction to Early Modern English*. Cambridge University Press. pp. 456. hb £55.00, pb £19.50. ISBN 0 521 32529 3, 0 521 31046 6.

Granger, Sylviane, ed. *Perspectives on the English Lexicon: a Tribute to Jacques van*

Roey. Leuven: Peeters. pp. 303. pb. BF 1020. ISSN 0771 6524.

Greenbaum, Sydney. *An Introduction to English Grammar*. Longman. pp. 336. pb £12.50. ISBN 0 582039 57 6.

Haegeman, Liliane. *Introduction to Government and Binding Theory*. Blackwell. pp. 618. hb £50.00, pb £14.95. ISBN 0 631 16562 2, 0 63116563 0.

Hasmann, Franz Josef, Oskar Reichmann, Herbert Ernst Wiegand, and Ladislav Zgusta. eds. *Wörterbücher/Dictionaries/Dictionnaires: an International Encyclopedia of Lexicography*. Vol.3. Gruyter. pp. 1017. DM 780. ISBN 3 11 012421 1.

Hawkins, J. M. and R. E. Allen, eds. *The Oxford Encyclopedic English Dictionary*. Oxford University Press. pp. 1728. £16.95. ISBN 0 19 861248 6.

Hoey, Michael. *Patterns of Lexis in Text. Describing English Language*. Oxford University Press. pp. 276. pb. £12.95. ISBN 0 19 437142 5.

Horvath, Barbara, and P. Vaughan. *Community Languages: a Handbook*. Multilingual Matters. pp. 266. £39.00. ISBN 1 853 59091 6.

Hughes, Geoffrey. *Swearing: a Social History of Foul Language, Oaths and Profanity in English*. Blackwell. pp. 283. £16.95. ISBN 0 631 16593 2.

Hughes, Joan. *Australian Words and Their Origins*. Oxford University Press. pp. 678. £20.00. ISBN 0 19 553087 X.

Johansson, Stig and Anna-Brita Stenström, eds. *English Computer Corpora: Selected Papers and Research Guide*. Topics in English Linguistics 3. Gruyter. pp 402. hb. DM 158. ISBN 3 11 012395 9.

Kastovsky, Dieter, ed. *Historical English Syntax*. MGruyter. pp. 510. $134. ISBN 3 110124 31 9.

Koerner, Konrad, ed. *First Person Singular II. Autobiographies by North American Scholars in the Language Sciences*. Benjamins. pp. 303. £41.00. ISBN 90 272 4548 7.

Kortmann, B. *Free Adjuncts and Absolutes in English. Problems of Control and Interpretation*. Routledge. pp. 253. £40. ISBN 0 415063 91 4.

Landman, Fred. *Structures for Semantics*. Kluwer Academic Publishers. pp. 367. £67.00. ISBN 0 7923 1239 2.

Laver, John (1991; published March 1992). *The Gift of Speech. Papers in the Analysis of Speech and Voice*. Edinburgh University Press. pp. 400. £45.00. ISBN 0 7486 0313 1.

Leitner, Gerhard, ed. *English Traditional Grammars. An International Perspective*. Benjamins. pp. 392. £51.00. ISBN 90 272 4549 5.

Lightfoot, David. *How to Set Parameters: Arguments from Language Change*. MITP. pp. 214. $27.50. ISBN 0 2612121 53 0.

Lyons, John. *Chomsky*. 3rd Edition. Fontana Press. pp. 247. pb £5.99. ISBN 0 00 686229 2.

———. *Natural Language and Universal Grammar: Essays in Linguistic Theory*. Vol. 1. Cambridge University Press. pp. 290. £35.00. ISBN 0 521 24696 2.

Macaulay, Ronald. *Locating Dialect in Discourse*. OUP. pp. 293. hb £30.00. ISBN 0 19 506559 X.

MacWhinney, Brian. *The CHILDES Project: Tools for Analyzing Talk*. Lawrence Erlbaum Associates. pp. 360. hb £45.00, pb £18.95. ISBN 0 8058 1005 6, 0 8058 1006 4 .

Malmkjaer, Kirsten, ed. *The Linguistics Encyclopedia*. Routledge. pp. 575. £75.00. ISBN 0 415 02942 2.

Matthews, P. H. *Morphology*. Cambridge University Press. pp. 251. hb £35.00, pb £11.95. ISBN 0 521 41043 6, 0 521 42256 6.

Mills, A. D. *A Dictionary of English Place-Names*. OUP. pp. 388. £12.95. ISBN 0 198691 56 4.

Milroy, James and Lesley Milroy. *Authority in Language: Investigating Language Prescription and Standardisation*. 2nd Edition. Routledge. pp. 195. pb £11.99. ISBN 0 415 06575 5.

Minkova, Donka. *The History of Final Vowels in English: The Sound of Muting*. MGruyter. pp. 220. £36.95. ISBN 3 11 012763 6.

Morenberg, Max. *Doing Grammar*. Oxford University Press. pp. 176. pb £10.95. ISBN 0 19 506427 5.

Nakajima, Heizo, ed. *Current English Linguistics in Japan*. MGruyter. pp. 534. DM 256. ISBN 3 110117 81 9.

Nevalainen, Terttu. *BUT, ONLY, JUST. Focusing Adverbial Change in Modern English 1500–1900*. SNH. pp. 314. pb $30. ISBN 9 519603 05 0.

O'Donnell, W. R., and Loreto Todd. *Variety in Contemporary English*. (2nd Edition). Harper Collins Academic. pp. 165. pb £10.99. ISBN 0 415 08437 7.

Pullum, Geoffrey K. *The Great Eskimo Vocabulary Hoax and other Irreverent Essays on the Study of Language*. The University of Chicago Press. pp. 236. hb £34.25, pb £11.95. ISBN 0 226 68533 0, 0 226 68534 9.

Ramsay, Alan. *The Logical Structure of English: Computing Semantic Content*. Pitman Publishing. pp. 209. pb £19.99. ISBN 0 273 03287 9.

Raumolin-Brunberg, Helena. *The Noun Phrase in Early Sixteenth-Century English*. SNH. pp. 308. pb $30. ISBN 9 519416 29 3.

Roach, Peter. *English Phonetics and Phonology: A Practical Course*. 2nd Edition. Cambridge University Press. pp. 262. pb £7.50. ISBN 0 521 40718 4.

Romaine, Suzanne. *Language in Australia*. Cambridge University Press. pp. 415. £50.00. ISBN 0 521 32786 5.

Rosen, Stuart, and Peter Howell. *Signals and Systems for Speech and Hearing*. Academic. pp. 322. hb $83, pb $39.95. ISBN 0 12 597230 X, 0 12 597231 8.

Schmied, Josef. *English in Africa: An Introduction*. Longman. pp. 264. hb £25.00, pb £11.99. ISBN 0 582 07456 8, 0 582 07455 X.

Sell, Roger, ed. *Literary Pragmatics*. Routledge. pp. 264. £35.00. ISBN 0 415 05601 2 .

Seventh Annual Conference of the UW Centre for the New OED and Text Research. Waterloo, Ontario: UW Centre for the New OED. pp. 196. pb. $20.

Siewierska, Anna. *Functional Grammar*. Routledge. pp. 279. £40. ISBN 0 415026 44 X.

Sinclair, John. *Corpus, Concordance, Collocation. Describing English Language*. Oxford University Press. pp. 179. pb £11.95. ISBN 0 19 437144 1.

Spencer, Andrew. *Morphological Theory: An Introduction to Word Structure in Generative Grammar*. Blackwell. pp. 512. hb £50.00, pb £17.95. ISBN 0 631 16143 0, 0 631 16144 9.

Stein, Gabriele, W. T. de Starnes, and G. Noyes, eds. *The English Dictionary from Cawdrey to Johnson*. Benjamins. pp. 300. £51.90. ISBN 90 272454 44.

Stuurman, Frits. *Two Grammatical Models of Modern English. The Old and New From A to Z*. Routledge. pp. 301. ISBN 0 415047 43 9.

Sundby, Bertil, Anne Kari, and Kari Haugland. *A Dictionary of English Normative Grammar 1700–1800*. Benjamins. pp. 486. $95. ISBN 1 556193 58 9.

Suppes, Patrick. *Language for Humans and Robots*. Blackwell. pp. 384. £35.00. ISBN 0 631 18262 4.

Svartvik, Jan, ed. *The London-Lund Corpus of Spoken English: Description and*

Research. Lund University Press. pp. 350. pb $35.75. ISBN 91 7966 126 2

Taylor, John R. *Linguistic Categorization: Prototypes in Linguistic Theory*. Oxford University Press. pp. 288. pb. £10.95. ISBN 0 19 823918 1.

Thomas, George. *Linguistic Purism*. Longman. pp. 250. hb £24.00, pb £11.99. ISBN 0 582 03743 3, 0 582 03742 5.

Tieken-Boon van Ostade, Ingrid, and John Frankis, eds. *Language Use and Description: Studies presented to N. E. Osselton on the occasion of his retirement*. Rodopi. pp. 200. £25.00. ISBN 90 5183 312 1.

Tollefson, James. *Planning Language, Planning Inequality*. Longman, Language in Social Life Series. pp. 234. hb £22.00, pb £12.99. ISBN 0582 07454 1; 0582 04062 0.

Tottie, Gunnel. *Negation in English Speech and Writing: A Study in Variation*. Academic Press. pp. 353. £52.50. ISBN 0 12 696130 1.

Traugott, Elizabeth C., and Bernd Heine, eds. *Approaches to Grammaticalization*. 2 vols. Benjamins. pp. 360 (Vol. I); pp. 556 (Vol. II). pb $64.95. ISBN 1 556194 05 6.

Trudgill, P., and J. Chambers, eds. *Dialects of English: Studies in Grammatical Variation*. Longman Linguistics Library. pp. 306. pb £13.50. ISBN 0 582 02194 4.

Tulloch, Sara, ed. *The Oxford Dictionary of New Words*. Oxford University Press. pp. 320. £12.95. ISBN 0 19 869170 X.

Urdang, Laurence, ed. *The Oxford Thesaurus*. Oxford University Press. pp. 1024. £14.95. ISBN 0 19 869151 3.

Ureland, P. Sture, and George Broderick. eds. *Language Contact in the British Isles*. Tubingen, Max Niemeyer Verlag. (Linguistsche Arbeiten 238). pp. 717. pb DM 276. ISBN 3 484 30238 0.

Vanderveken, Daniel. *Meaning and Speech Acts: Volume 2 Formal Semantics of Success and Satisfaction*. Cambridge University Press. pp. 196. hb £30.00. ISBN 0 521 38216 5.

Ventola, Eija, ed. *Approaches to the Analysis of Literary Discourse*. Abo Academy Press. pp. 148. pb FIM105. ISBN 952 9616 00 7.

von Stechow, A., and D. Wunderlich, eds. *Semantics: an International Handbook of Contemporary Research*. Handbooks of Linguistics and Communication Science vol. 6. Gruyter. pp. 992. £243.25. ISBN 3 110 12696 6.

Wawn, Andrew. *The Anglo Man: Þorleifur Repp, Philology and Nineteenth-Century Britain*. Bókaútgáfa Mennigarsjóðs. pp. 270. ISBN 9979 822 08 2.

Weiner, E. S. C. and J. A. Simpson, eds. *The Compact Oxford English Dictionary*. New Edition. Oxford University Press. pp. 2416. £150. ISBN 0 19 861258 3.

Wettstein, Howard. *Has Semantics Rested on a Mistake? And Other Essays*. Stanford University Press. pp. 232. $29.50. ISBN 0 8047 1866 0.

Wilkes, G. A. *A Dictionary of Australian Colloquialisms*. OUP/SydneyUP. pp. 368. pb. £6.95. ISBN 0 424 00178 0.

Williams, Colin, ed. *Linguistic Minorities, Society and Territory*. Multilingual Matters. pp. 330. hb £59.00, pb £19.95. ISBN 1 85359 132 7; 1 85359 131 9.

Zaefferer, Dietmar, ed. *Semantic Universals and Universal Semantics*. Groningen-Amsterdam Studies in Semantics. pp. 242. £44.10. ISBN 3 11 013391 1.

Zernik, Uri. *Lexical Acquisition: Exploring On-Line Resources to Build a Lexicon*. Lawrence Erlbaum Associates. pp. 429. hb £52.95, pb £25.95. ISBN 0 8058 0829 9, 0 8058 1127 3.

III

Old English Literature

CLARE A. LEES

This chapter has the following sections: 1. Bibliography; 2. Social, Cultural, and Intellectual Background; 3. Literature: General; 4. Beowulf; 5. The Junius Manuscript; 6. The Poems of the Vercelli Book; 7. The Exeter Book; 8. Other Poems; 9. Prose.

1. Bibliography

The most comprehensive annual bibliographies for Old English scholars remain *ASE*, *OENews*, and *IMB*. As usual, *OENews* is packed with essential information for Anglo-Saxonists, including reports on research projects, conferences, publications, and other topics of related interest: the critical bibliography for 1989 appears in the winter issue (*OENews* 24:ii), and the bibliography for 1990 in the summer issue (24:iv). Among the brief notes this year is 'Some Modern Writers and Their *Fontes Anglo-Saxonici*' (*OENews* 24:iii.14–18) by Hugh Magennis, which assesses the extent to which OE literature is drawn on by modern writers. The article brings to view a considerable sampler of such writers – Gerard Manley Hopkins, Kingsley Amis, Seamus Heaney, Jorge Luis Borges, Louis MacNeice, Geoffrey Hill, and Ezra Pound, to name some of the most familiar – and reminds us that the reception of Old English goes well beyond its institutional academic domains. Magennis's discussion finds an interesting counter-part in Paul Acker's bibliographical note, 'The Arthur S. Napier Collection' (*OENews* 24:iii.19–20), which surveys the letters and papers of this distinguished Anglo-Saxonist now in the English Faculty Library, Oxford University. In the same issue, Thomas H. Ohlgren considers the representation of 'The Grumbling Monk in the Hereford Gospels' (*OENews* 24:iii.22–4). Ohlgren suggests that the monk in the canon tables of these Gospels is doubly chastized, both for breaking the vow of silence and for complaining about God's providence. The *Rule of St Benedict* provides Ohlgren with supporting textual evidence for his analysis.

Carol Neuman de Vegvar continues her iconographical series with 'Images of Women in Anglo-Saxon Art II: Midwifery in Harley 603' (*OENews* 25:i.54–6), which is a birth-scene illustrating Psalm 47.7. Vegvar points out that there were two traditions of iconography for birth-scenes in the early Medieval period: the one tactfully discrete, highly stylized, and reserved for scriptural birth-scenes; the other more 'realistic'. The Harley image offers an example of this latter tradition of relatively explicit labour that does not depict the birth of a particular scriptural figure, and derives, via the Utrecht Psalter, from late Antique representations. *Anglo-Saxon Art: Texts and Contexts* by Thomas H. Ohlgren continues the art-historical theme in *OENews* by offering the 17th volume in the *Subsidia* series. Ohlgren uses ten visual images to explore the relationships between images, texts, and Anglo-Saxon culture. The choice of image is lively and instructive: 'The *Hostis* Miniature and Grendel'; 'Jannes and Mambres in the *Marvels of the East*'; 'Ring-Giving in MS Harley 603'; 'The Monastic Warriors in MS Harley 603'; 'The Temptation of Adam and Eve in MS Junius 11'; 'Christ-Logos as Architect'; 'The Beasts of Battle in MS Reg. lat. 12'; 'The Crucifixion in Pierpoint Morgan Library M. 709'; 'The Gosforth Cross and Ragnarök'; and 'Odin and Christ on a Cross-Slab from Andreas, Isle of Man'. Each essay provides a commentary, which describes the image, reviews the scholarship, and offers a brief critical discussion.

2. Social, Cultural, and Intellectual Background

Steven Fanning's 'Bede, *Imperium*, and the Bretwaldas' (*Speculum* 66.1–26) reconsiders the institution of bretwaldaship in the polity of the early kingdoms. Fanning scrupulously examines Bede's use of 'imperial' vocabulary in the *Ecclesiastical History*, in the light of the long-lasting associations of the terms *imperium* and *regnum* in Latin writings from the late Antique to the early Medieval period, to question whether Bede actually demonstrates any coherent conception of the institution otherwise known as bretwaldaship. More questions follow. According to Fanning, Bede provides us with little evidence for our notion of Southumbrian hegemony, or even our sense of Bede's depiction of unified English people and Church. Early historians have been hinting in the direction of these conclusions for some time but few have gone so far as Fanning in this unsettling and revisionist argument.

Working from archaeological evidence, H. F. Hamerow also proposes a revision of current theoretical models, although in this case it is the explanation of perceived settlement patterns in the early and middle periods known as the Middle Saxon Shift that is under review. 'Settlement Mobility and the "Middle Saxon Shift": Rural Settlements and Settlement Patterns in Anglo-Saxon England' (*ASE* 20.1–17), does not find convincing evidence for the assumed widespread displacement of settlements in the late seventh and eighth centuries. Basing the discussion primarily on evidence from the Mucking site, Hamerow reopens the general question of the dating of settlement shift and its explanations. These issues cannot be satisfactorily resolved without further field-work which, as Hamerow notes, is unlikely to happen in the current economic climate. More precise evidence for settlement patterns in one region is offered by Della Hooke in *Worcestershire Anglo-Saxon Charter-Bounds* (1990). Hooke collects together all the topographical details in the relevant charters throughout the Anglo-Saxon period for Worcestershire–translating, identifying, and mapping the boundary clauses where possible. The result is a major scholarly resource, which pays eloquent testimony to the importance of the land in our understanding of Anglo-Saxon culture.

Another scholar alert to the sensitive interpretation of historical documents is R. H. C. Davis, whose essays are reprinted in *From Alfred the Great to Stephen*. The first four essays in the collection will be of greatest interest: 'Bede after Bede' (1989) addresses the reception of Bede's *History* and concentrates on its significance as a work of monastic history for those clerics working in reform periods in the late Anglo-

Saxon and post-Conquest periods; by contrast, 'East Anglia and the Danelaw' (1955), 'Alfred the Great: Propaganda and Truth' (1971), and 'Alfred and Guthrum's Frontier' (1982), present a specialized body of material carefully analysing the events and details of Alfred's reign and the nature of the Scandinavian settlement.

A further two essays in *ASE* 20 this year are concerned with the connections between the early English kingdoms and the continent. 'Adultery in Early Anglo-Saxon Society: Æthelberht 31 in Comparison with Continental Germanic Law', by Theodore John Rivers (19–25), takes a brief look at the provocatively ambiguous law addressing adultery in Æthelberht of Kent's early law code. This law appears to require the male adulterer to furnish the husband with another wife at his own expense, in addition to paying the husband's wergild. Surveying the evidence of the Germanic laws concerning adultery, many of which stress the payment of the wife's wergild or, in extreme cases, punishment by death, Rivers suggests that Æthelberht 31 contrasts with continental custom by providing for a different restitution. He notes, however, that there appears to have been no standardized law concerning adultery in the early period. Martin Werner, on the other hand, is not interested in Æthelberht but in Bertha, his wife, her bishop, Liudhard, and the early veneration of the Cross in 'The Liudhard Medalet' (27–41). Werner provides a detailed description of this rarely studied medalet, found among a group of objects in or near the churchyard of St Martin's, Canterbury, whose cross-design seems intended to recall the symbolic association of Bertha's kinswoman, Radegund, with the Cross – an association which is itself modelled on Helena and the finding of the True Cross. The design on Liudhard's medalet thus alludes to these three women, each of whom is represented as bringing the Cross to a non-Christian world.

A better-known early artifact is discussed by Marijane Osborn in 'The Seventy-Two Gentile Nations and the Theme of the Franks Casket' (*NM* 90.281–8). Osborn tackles the inter-related themes of the carvings and inscriptions on the casket with her hypothesis that the casket was an object used in missionary work. Accordingly, the artist turns the pagan allusions on the casket to Christian evangelical purposes by conflating Germanic material with Christian to create a theme that begins with the Fall and ends with salvation. Osborn points out that the number of runes plus dots on three of the sides of the casket is an allusion to the seventy-two disciples appointed by Christ, in addition to the original twelve: the parallel number of forty-two on the back panel is a number referred to in scriptural accounts of the Fall of Jerusalem and Leviathan in Apocr. 11.2 and 13.5.

Evidence for a different kind of connection between the continent and England is offered by James Graham-Campbell and Elisabeth Okasha's description of 'A Pair of Inscribed Anglo-Saxon Hooked Tags from the Rome (Forum) 1883 Hoard', with an introductory note by Michael Metcalf (*ASE* 20.221–9). Found with a major English coin hoard dating from the papacy of Marinus II (942–62), the hooked tags, possibly for a purse or money bag, share a unique divided inscription dedicated to the pope. The authors conclude that the hoard probably does not represent a treasure-hoard but early evidence for royal or ecclesiastical alms similar to that which later became known as 'Peter's Pence'.

B. C. Barker-Benfield's 'The Werden "Heptateuch" ' (*ASE* 20.43–64) complements Michelle P. Brown's study of a single-leaf from this manuscript (*YWES* 70.153) with a detailed study of its remaining 32 fragmentary leaves in Düsseldorf, Universitätsbibliothek, A. 19, which preserves text from each of the first seven books of the Old Testament. Barker-Benfield argues for a Werden provenance for this manuscript, which is probably early ninth century in date.

Phillip Pulsiano makes some important contributions to the study of psalter glosses this year with a series of articles refining our understanding of this textual practice. 'Old English Glossed Psalters: Editions versus Manuscripts' (*Manuscripta* 35.75–95) celebrates the increased vitality of psalter research but cautions us all against an unthinking reliance on printed editions. Pulsiano makes his point about the dangers of printed editions by assessing the accuracy of three recent editions in an article that is exemplary for its tactful discussion of the scholarship of others: James L. Rosier's 1962 edition of the Vitellius Psalter and A. P. Campbell's 1974 edition of the Tiberius Psalter are both found wanting – inconsistent either in accuracy of transcription, or in the preparation of textual notes. Andrew C. Kimmen's 1979 edition of the Stowe (or Spelman) Psalter, by contrast, is much more reliable. Pulsiano makes the most of these disappointing results by outlining his desiderata for future editions: accuracy of transcription, careful textual notes, and detailed introductions. A second article presents 'The Old English Introductions in the Vitellius Psalter' (*SN* 63.13–35), which prints these fragmentary introductions written in the margins in the hand of the main glossator for the first time. The similarities between these introductions and those in the Paris Psalter are made clear by the inclusion of the Paris Psalter texts for purposes of comparison. A different aspect of psalter-gloss analysis is provided in 'The Old English Gloss of the Lambeth Psalter and its Relations' (*NM* 92.195–210), which uses collations to reassess the relationship of this gloss with those of the A-type (Vespasian) and D-type (Regius) glosses. Pulsiano suggests that the Lambeth Psalter represents an independent tradition of glossing, which is interspersed with D-type glosses and also A-type glosses to a lesser extent. Further support for this independence is offered by comparison with the Stowe Psalter glosses, but Pulsiano is careful to point out that his suggestions require further research before they can be fully confirmed. This article finds its complement in 'Defining the A-Type (*Vespasian*) and D-Type (*Regius*) Psalter-Gloss Traditions' (*ES* 72.308–27), where Pulsiano offers a detailed collation of Psalms 1–30 in the Vespasian and Regius Psalters in order to get to grips with the relationship between these two glossing traditions. As a result, he distinguishes two markedly different sets of vocabularies over and above the expected degree of traditional uniformity in the two glosses. The implications of these important insights are developed with reference to the social and cultural milieu of the two manuscripts: the Regius glosses are probably closely related to the so-called 'Winchester' group of manuscripts and offer yet another piece of evidence for the linguistic practices of the 'Winchester' school.

A similar thought underpins Patrick P. O'Neill's 'Latin Learning at Winchester in the early Eleventh-Century: The Evidence of the Lambeth Psalter' (*ASE* 20.143–66), which restores the Lambeth Psalter to its place as an important, though possibly indirect, witness to psalter scholarship at Winchester. O'Neill's assessment of the manuscript suggests that it was probably not intended for liturgical use but for private prayer and study. The psalter, however, is unlikely to have been used for formal classroom study since it lacks key 'classbook' features.

Painstaking textual analysis combined with careful consideration of its cultural implications also characterizes Christine Franzen's *The Tremulous Hand of Worcester*. Franzen presents the first detailed overview of the work and career of the thirteenth-century scribe whose 'tremulous' (and probably congenital) glosses are so common a feature in the many OE manuscripts associated with Worcester. Although her analysis concentrates on the glosses in three homiliaries (Oxford, Bodley MSS Hatton 113, 114, and 115) and is described as 'preliminary', Franzen brings to bear on this material her extensive knowledge of those other manuscripts also glossed by this hand. The benefits of this approach to the 'Tremulous' hand, which has otherwise been examined only in relation to individual texts or manuscripts, are considerable. Indeed, Franzen is able to distinguish several 'layers' of glosses, some of which are previously unattributed to the 'Tremulous' hand and which appear to mark different stages in this scribe's learning of OE. The 'Tremulous' hand experiments first with revising the language of his old texts into Middle English but then abandons this practice as he becomes engaged on a more systematic study of OE. The scribe therefore switches to Latin glossing with the probable aid of an English-Latin word list (which appears to have been the earliest English glossary in first-letter alphabetical sequence). Franzen offers several plausible and interrelated explanations for the phenomenon of the 'Tremulous' hand's life-long project: the study of OE by this scribe, who may have been involved with the preparation of preaching materials, either for liturgical or pedagogic use, suggests that the knowledge of the language had otherwise died out in thirteenth-century Worcester. Whatever the case, there can be little doubt that the 'Tremulous' hand is an early example of a student obsessed by OE, and Franzen is to be congratulated on bringing to the fore the history of his scholarship.

Franzen's *The Tremulous Hand of Worcester* demonstrates the importance of a comprehensive but flexible approach to manuscript evidence. Similar issues are addressed by Michael Lapidge in his general argument about editorial principles. 'Textual Criticism and the Literature of Anglo-Saxon England' – the T. Northcote Toller Memorial Lecture for 1990 (*BJRL* 73.17–45) – begins by arguing that textual criticism is the process of 'reproducing what an author wrote'. This familiar formulation paradoxically draws attention to the practical difficulties of establishing just who was the author of a medieval text, let alone his or her authorial intentions. Lapidge complicates matters valuably by pointing out that the theory and practice of editing Anglo-Latin texts is rarely considered in relation to those of OE texts, which are often from the same period, and even, in some cases, from the same scriptorium or scribe. At first sight, the criteria for editing Anglo-Latin texts – the careful assessment of the manuscript evidence together with a knowledge of the Latinity and style of an individual author – appear remarkably similar to those for vernacular texts, but Lapidge notes that the former grow out of the history of editing classical Latin texts. This is an approach well known for its traditional contempt for the manuscript evidence as well as its daring and occasionally 'brilliant' emendations. And it is here that Lapidge takes editors of vernacular texts to task for their conservatism and for their apparent subservience to the manuscript rather than to the OE author or text. Offering one emendation to the 'corrupt' lines 182–84 of *The Battle of Maldon*, he suggests that vernacular editors could learn much from the editors of Anglo-Latin texts. Although it is certainly not impossible to emend *The Battle of Maldon* in fruitful ways, it is hard to imagine how a text known only from an eighteenth-century transcript is representative of the kinds of general difficulties faced by editors of OE manuscripts, but Lapidge's point is well taken. Equally, however, we need to consider the differences between Anglo-Latin and vernacular writings. Lapidge points out, rightly, that there has been no authorial edition of Cynewulf's poetry and this is certainly required: Cynewulf, however, remains the exception to the rule of the traditional anonymity of OE poetry. We need a better understanding of the concept of an OE vernacular author before we can edit on the criterion of the intended authorship of a particular writer.

Wulfstan of Winchester: The Life of St Æthelwold, by Lapidge and Michael Winterbottom, offers a good example of how Anglo-Latin texts are now edited.

Wulfstan's *Life of Æthelwold* survives only in late manuscripts (none are earlier than the twelfth century), so the editors reconstruct Wulfstan's orthographical practices on the evidence of two manuscripts known to have been written for his use at the Old Minster, Winchester. Their edition of the *Life* normalizes spelling so as to reflect as nearly as possible that assumed to be Wulfstan's in late-tenth-century Winchester. As important as the text and the translation is the inclusion of Ælfric's *Vita S. Æthelwoldi* and the lengthy introduction, which reconstructs the life and writing career both of Wulfstan and of Æthelwold. Wulfstan *Cantor* (the best-known Latin writer associated with Æthelwold's school) emerges as a major liturgical poet, scholar, and writer, who is in part responsible for promoting the cult of his teacher, Æthelwold. The perspective on Wulfstan is complemented by a general study of Æthelwold's cult and its later reception. Indeed, Lapidge and Winterbottom make a compelling case for the dependence of Ælfric's *Vita* on Wulfstan's, thus reversing the traditional argument that gives Ælfric's *Life* precedence. The book gathers together and reviews an impressive amount of evidence for Wulfstan, Æthelwold, Ælfric, and their scholarly work at Winchester in a study destined to be the *locus classicus* for our understanding of monastic life and culture in the reform period.

Several other works published this year also enhance our knowledge of monastic and liturgical practices. Students of the Benedictine Reform will welcome Joyce Hill's 'The "Regularis Concordia" and its Latin and Old English Reflexes' (*RB* 101.299–315). Hill provides a careful description of the Latin and OE witnesses to this important Latin consuetudinary that pays eloquent testimony to its limited though significant use in the heart of monastic Reform circles as well as to its adaptation for wider, secular use, especially by Wulfstan. Michael Lapidge's third offering this year is another important resource for liturgical scholars; an edition of the *Anglo-Saxon Litanies of the Saints*. As we have come to expect from Lapidge, the Introduction is as valuable as the texts: he provides accounts of the background of these litanies, reconsiders the case for their Insular origins and diffusion, and comments upon continental forms and the specific practices of the later Anglo-Saxon period before examining their subsequent influences. The texts themselves are prefaced by brief discussions of the relevant manuscripts and are followed by two useful indices – of saints and of liturgical forms. Phillip Pulsiano offers us the parallel texts of a Latin charm addressed to the Cross in 'British Library, Cotton Tiberius A. iii, fol. 59rv: An Unrecorded Charm in the Form of an Address to the Cross' (*ANQ* 4.3–5). In addition to publishing the Tiberius text, Pulsiano presents its variant from Cambridge, Corpus Christi College 391.

Lisa M. Bitel's *Isle of the Saints: Monastic Settlement and Christian Community in Early Ireland* (1990) provides an important study of Irish monasticism and its role in Christian communities, which is of interest to all scholars of hagiography and early monasticism. Bitel takes an interdisciplinary approach – drawing on archaeology, hagiography, and history – in order to examine the cultural phenomenon of the active integration of monastic and lay life in the early Irish period. The first part of the book considers monastic settlement and enclosure, while the second gradually broadens its focus from the *familia* to its clients and the division of labour, its relation to the social order, the *spirituales medici*, and the concepts and practice of hospitality, exile, and pilgrimage. The books offers a fine example of the kinds of cultural analyses afforded by a comparative study of even the most idealized hagiography.

We glimpse monastic practices of quite a different kind in *Monasteriales Indicia: The Anglo-Saxon Monastic Sign Language*, by Debby Banham, who edits and translates the only sign list extant from Anglo-Saxon England from London, B.L.,

Cotton Tiberius A. iii. As Banham notes in her introduction, this manuscript is certainly associated with the Reform movement (it also contains, for example, a copy of the Benedictine Rule and one of the copies of the *Regularis Concordia*). The sign list itself provides a fascinating example of Anglo-Saxon non-verbal communication and offers important insights into monastic life (I particularly like the sign for leeks). Moving to signs of a different kind, it is worth noting in a year in which studies of writing have proved popular (see section 3 below) that J. M. Kemble's *Anglo-Saxon Runes*, first printed in 1840, has been reissued by Bill Griffiths who includes additional notes and translations.

'St Joseph's Trade and Old English *Smiþ*' (*LeedsSE* 22.21–42), by James Bradley, addresses the widespread assumption that OE 'smiþ' refers both to metal-working and wood-working with a careful review of its semantic field. Since the OE uses for 'smiþ' do not appear to refer to wood-working in any way at all, Bradley rightly asks the question of how the Anglo-Saxons could have thought that Joseph's trade was a carpenter. As he goes on to show, however, Joseph's trade was in fact associated with metal-work. Bradley's compelling argument is based on the evidence from the Western exegetical tradition, which indicates that the early medieval references to Joseph the smith (and not carpenter) are firmly within the mainstream. OE 'smiþ', therefore, refers only to metal-work.

I conclude this section with two interesting papers on a slightly different aspect of Anglo-Saxon culture from a collection of essays, edited by Erik Kooper, called *This Noble Craft*. A thorough study of Anglo-Saxon attitudes toward sex is long overdue, but Anthony Davies provides us with a useful overview of the penitential, ecclesiastical, legal, and homiletic material in 'Sexual Behaviour in Later Anglo-Saxon England'. Davies is well aware of the dangers of accepting some of this evidence as proof of sexual behaviour (especially in the case of the penitentials), and balances this proscriptive material with references to recorded instances from, for example, the Charters or the *Anglo-Saxon Chronicle*, where possible. The vigour with which religious men such as Ælfric and Wulfstan sought to urge their congregation's conformation to the teachings of their faith makes absorbing reading, and the hostility of their Church to the pleasures of the flesh comes sharply into focus. Robin D. Smith's survey of 'Anglo-Saxon Maternal Ties' (in the same collection) makes less satisfactory reading, although it is clear that the paucity of the evidence is in part to blame. Smith starts with Tacitus' observations about maternal behaviour, drawing some familiar parallels between the female world of the home and the martial world of the warrior, and then continues with some brief remarks about the role of the mother in educating her children, the proscriptions against abortion, and the scant attention to gynaecology in the medical texts. Smith has identified an important area for study but this article remains largely suggestive and speculative rather than informative.

3. Literature: General

I start this section by welcoming the publication of *Old English Verse Texts From Many Sources: A Comprehensive Collection*, edited by Fred C. Robinson and E. G. Stanley for EEMF. Presenting facsimiles of OE verse texts from ninety-one manuscripts, this collection is indeed comprehensive and one of the most valuable scholarly works to appear in many years. Here we see OE verse in its most immediate context, to paraphrase Robinson – a context that includes transcripts, early printed books (where their texts provide primary witnesses to the relevant verses), and inscriptions.

One of the greatest values of the volume is the way it challenges the assumptions we make about OE verse and its relation to prose on the basis of printed editions. In addition to the facsimiles (which include the *Eadwine Psalter Verses* in full colour), the editors provide brief descriptions of individual texts, and relevant indices. It is impossible to do justice to this volume with such a short notice but its importance will be evident to all and its impact on scholarship in future years profound.

Anglo-Saxonists are now making increasingly vociferous contributions to the paradigm shifts now sweeping other areas of English studies, as is confirmed this year in several studies. Seth Lerer's *Literacy and Power in Anglo-Saxon Literature* is a useful place to start since it combines two popular aspects of these newer approaches: the avenues for study opened up by the conjunction of critical theory and Anglo-Saxon studies, and the relationship between literacy and orality in the period. Lerer's exploration of literacy takes a surprising direction, since he is concerned less with the material evidence for literacy than with its imaginative representation. Accordingly, Lerer analyses key scenes of literacy in Anglo-Latin and Anglo-Saxon texts to recover their use of what he calls a 'mythology of writing'. The book comprises a series of inter-related essays that range deliberately wide over the corpus so as to demonstrate the centrality of this mythology. In the first two chapters, Lerer explores the power of literacy to displace and reconceptualize earlier cultural forms. Thus Bede's account of Imma, for example, stresses how the symbolism of the eucharist relocates literate authority in the Christian sign rather than in the runic 'releasing letters', while his account of Cædmon redefines the origins of poetry and its associations with drinking in the Germanic world by using the specifically monastic concept of *ruminatio*. Similar patterns underpin the 'primal' scenes of literacy in Asser's *Life of Alfred*, which Lerer sees as enacting the replacement of English vernacular practices (as in the famous scene of Alfred competing with his siblings for the book of English poetry) by Latin models of authoritative learning (as in the scene of Alfred's miraculous acquisition of Latin skills). This process is, however, reversed by Alfred himself since the preface to the *Cura Pastoralis* illustrates the creation of an author. According to Lerer, Asser's own models of Latin authority and style are adopted by Alfred in his vernacular works. Subsequent chapters address the representation of vernacular literacy as a craft and skill, most often framed by discussion of the practices of Latin literacy. The Exeter Book Riddles, for example, offer a series of playfully intertextual explorations of poetics, which are analogous to the Anglo-Latin *enigmata* that provide texts for schoolroom study. Similarly, *Daniel*, with its mysterious and indecipherable writing and its prophetic scholarly interpreter, becomes a poem about writing situated at the intersection of the vernacular worlds of the riddles and the epic, the Latin world of schoolroom learning, and contemporary socio-political debates about lawmaking. Lerer concludes with a contrastive analysis of the two models of transmitting knowledge in *Beowulf* - the first exemplified in the public verbal world of Hrothgar's sermon, and the second in his private and literate reading of the runic inscription on the hilt of the sword, which Beowulf seizes in Grendel's mere. Throughout, Lerer stresses elite, hyper-literate, and largely Latinate models for interpreting Anglo-Saxon writing even as he explores the metaphors of craft which provide the vehicles for these moments. As a result, perhaps, Lerer appears to be less interested in the expressions of wonder, marvel, or miracle that dramatize these scenes.

In *Speaking Two Languages: Traditional Disciplines and Contemporary Theory in Medieval Studies*, edited by Allen J. Frantzen, each contributor identifies at least two theoretical 'languages' and examines the implications of their combination and articulation. This self-conscious examination of critical practices casts light on our relationship – our kinship – with our objects of study, opening up new areas of investigation and analysis. This point is made elegantly by Frantzen himself in his wide-ranging 'Prologue: Documents and Monuments: Difference and Interdisciplinarity in the Study of Medieval Culture', which deliberately defuses the oppositional nature of the old and the new by pointing to the cycles of innovation and obsolescence that characterize Medieval Studies. An increased self-consciousness on the part of the critic, Frantzen argues, demands a re-examination of the foundations of our disciplines as well as their current structures. Frantzen then uses the two 'languages' of literary study and archaeology (both in the Foucauldian and in traditional senses) to show how our much-vaunted interdisciplinarity sometimes amounts to little more than the repetition of sameness under the guise of difference. Both literary study and archaeology in fact neatly confirm each other's findings, as is demonstrated by the discussion of Sutton Hoo and *Beowulf*, where the aristocratic milieu of the poem is confirmed by and also confirms that of the archaeological evidence. In this example (as in many others), our critical delight in identification is achieved at the cost of suppressing other questions, other areas of study. Frantzen suggests that cultural studies offers a way of negotiating the impasse of traditional interdisciplinarity by emphasizing the materiality of the text as well as the textuality of the material. Our traditional emphasis on the aristocratic world, for example, would be enriched by an investigation of Anglo-Saxon labour, both in the analysis of texts (or documents) and in that of objects (monuments).

Martin Irvine's 'Medieval Textuality and the Archaeology of Textual Culture', in the same collection, begins with a similar premiss, namely that medieval textuality needs to be investigated in its material and discursive dimensions. Irvine uses a modified Foucauldian discourse analysis, incorporating an historical understanding of semiotics and reception theory (his first 'language'), in combination with traditional manuscript study and philology (his second 'language'). The article rightly goes beyond conventional genre theory and the habitual division of Anglo-Saxon writing into Latin and OE to explore the discursive relations that characterize Anglo-Saxon textuality. Three examples illustrate aspects of this system: Bede's narrative of Cædmon demonstrates the incorporation of orality into Latin textual practices – his miraculous poetry thus takes on the status of a gloss on sacred narrative; Alfred's *Prefaces* to Augustine's *Soliloquies* and Boethius's *De consolatione philosophiae* provide evidence for another macrogenre of the system – *compilatio*; and the poems compiled in the Anglo-Saxon Chronicle (*The Battle of Brunanburh* in particular), which offer images of continuity and power for the house of Wessex, provide the occasion for the description of the ideological functions of OE poetry within a specific textual environment.

While the essays by Earl, Lees, and Overing are reviewed in their relevant sections below (4, 5, 9), two other contributors to *Speaking Two Languages* address oral theory. John Miles Foley takes as his two 'languages' the oral traditional and written dynamics of OE poetry in 'Texts That Speak to Readers Who Hear: Old English Poetry and the Languages of Oral Tradition'. The article takes up an aspect of Foley's work well-rehearsed in recent years (see, for example, *YWES* 69.120) by arguing that the most fruitful means of understanding the orally-derived traditions immanent in OE verse is reception aesthetics. The article explores the aesthetic implications of the interplay between traditional associations and individual realizations of the phrase, theme, or type-scene. This approach usefully draws attention to the notions of voice and performance in OE poetry although the strategies for their recovery make practically no distinction between the textual and the oral. Adam Brooke Davis addresses this danger in his 'Epilogue: *De Scientia Interpretandi*: Oral Tradition and the Place of Other Theories in the Graduate Curriculum', which begins with a valuable reminder of the many competing 'languages' that our graduate students are required to speak. Davis then tackles the relation between the 'language' of oral-traditional scholarship and that of textual theories by underlining the different objects of study constructed by these approaches. The oral and the textual are brought into a dialectical relation, the analysis of which reveals the gains and limitations of each. Davis reminds us that one important dimension of our studies is the recovery of voices silenced by textual culture.

Allen J. Frantzen's new preface to the translation of *The Literature of Penance in Anglo-Saxon England* (*YWES* 64.94–5), *La Littérature de la pénitence dans l'Angleterre Anglo-Saxone* by Michel Lejeune shares some of Davis's concerns. This is no perfunctory preface to a revised edition: although Frantzen does revise his bibliography, he also rethinks some of his earlier conclusions about the importance of the penitentials in early medieval culture. The study of the penitentials, Frantzen suggests, can enhance our conception of early medieval piety, as well as contributing vital evidence for the nature of the medieval book in general and the construction of medieval administrative documents in particular. The importance of this material is indicated by their use of orality and textuality. The evidence of the penitentials, like that of the laws, has been sorely neglected in discussions of orality and literacy where the evidence of the poetry continues to occupy a much more prominent status. And yet, as Frantzen notes, the rituals for confession outlined by the manuscripts and the notions of voice and narrative that these texts draw upon in presenting a traditional body of material testify to their importance as communicative acts situated between oral and written production. In sum, the new preface maps out a new direction for research into the penitentials to put beside Frantzen's earlier work.

Even the collection of essays intended for beginning students entitled *The Cambridge Companion to Old English Literature*, edited by Malcolm Godden and Michael Lapidge, registers the changing critical face of Anglo-Saxon studies by offering a judicious mix of the more established critical views of OE literature with the occasionally brilliantly revisionist essay. The collection opens conventionally enough with essays on 'Anglo-Saxon Society and its Literature' by Patrick Wormald, 'The Old English Language' by Helmut Gneuss, and 'The Nature of Old English Verse' by Donald G. Scragg, each of which is a masterpiece of clarity and authoritative insights. It is as delightful to read Wormald's meditation on the relation between the use of the English vernacular and English statecraft, for example, as it is to hear Scragg explaining why the poetry cannot be dated with any confidence; and Gneuss's essay introduces concepts of, for example, language borrowing and contact, and register, in ways that go fruitfully beyond the more formally grammatical descriptions of the language that tend to characterize such introductory accounts. Janet Bately's 'The Nature of Old English Prose', as its title suggests, is the counterpart to Scragg's essay on the poetry but, while Scragg explicates verse-form, Bately is principally concerned with the range and contents of the prose. This essay provides a useful introduction to the prose corpus by summarizing its range, utility, as well as translation and prose styles.

Roberta Frank's brilliant 'Germanic Legend in Old English Literature', on the other hand, is the first of a group of essays whose intentions are more broadly thematic. Frank's own concern is to put into context, or rather cut down to size, the extravagant claims frequently made for the use of Germanic legend in OE poetry. Her incisive prose, dry wit, impressive command of the material, and critical generosity ('Our ignorance means that we may expect to make mistakes') combine to produce an essay of essential reading for all. Frank stresses the paucity of OE material on Germanic legend, and the narrowness of its concerns, yet she captures the peculiar excitement still generated by this slender corpus of *The Finnsburh Fragment*, *Waldere*, *Beowulf*, *Widsith*, and *Deor*. Frank's essay is followed by Katherine O'Brien O'Keeffe's 'Heroic Values and Christian Ethics', which offers a careful synthesis of established critical views of the ethical heroic world of the poetry and its problematic relationship with historical reality. The essay outlines the ideals of loyalty and vengeance in the poetry, with especial reference to *The Battle of Maldon*, but pays less attention to Christian ethics. These two essays find their complement in '*Beowulf*', by Fred C. Robinson, which is the only text given its own chapter in the collection. Robinson's sensitive and judicious account touches the familiar though necessary critical bases of narrative, style, heroism, and nostalgia, but also stresses our kinship with, and paradoxical distance from, this powerfully enigmatic poem.

Other essays in *The Cambridge Companion* also emphasize thematic issues, enabling contributors to range beyond the restrictions of individual texts or genres that can limit our more general perceptions of the corpus. 'Pagan Survivals and Popular Belief' by John D. Niles, for example, offers a wide survey of material – from Bede to *Beowulf* – in an essay that reworks the fundamental binarism of Christian/Germanic into pagan/popular in ways guaranteed to interest the beginning student, and Joseph B. Trahern Jnr provides valuable introductions to the concepts of fate and the 'Last Age' in 'Fatalism and the Millenium' – a study that, although brief, manages to cover the whole of the period and mixes the familiar (*Beowulf*) with the less so (*The Order of the World*). Two other essays examine the binarism of transience and transcendence in OE literature. 'Perceptions of Transience' by Christine Fell focuses on the so-called Elegies but includes discussion of Anglo-Latin, OE prose, and also Old Icelandic works; 'Perceptions of Eternity', by Milton McC. Gatch also goes well beyond the obvious poetic texts (*The Seafarer*, *The Dream of the Rood*, for example) to introduce the lesser known Judgement Day poems and homilies (for example, *Judgement Day II*, *Christ III*, and the prose *De die iudicii*) as well as the soul and body texts. A further pair of essays present introductions to OE scriptural writing: 'Biblical Literature: the Old Testament', by Malcolm Godden, skilfully covers not only the poetry – *Genesis A and B*, *Exodus*, *Daniel*, and even *Judith* but also the prose – Ælfric's biblical translations, and homilies by both Ælfric and Wulfstan; and 'Biblical Literature: the New Testament', by Barbara C. Raw provides a brief introduction to the key theological issues of salvation history and redemption and concentrates principally on the *Christ* poems.

Michael Lapidge's account of 'The Saintly Life in Anglo-Saxon England' presents a survey of hagiographical writing from a more traditional literary-historical perspective and, in consequence, stresses the separation of the spiritual and the literary. Lapidge outlines the prose traditions of, for example, Bede, the Old English martyrologist, and Ælfric, but provides only a minimal account of the verse. He underlines the importance of typology and theological conformity at the expense of the range of literary and spiritual responses that the worship of the saints clearly encourages in Anglo-Saxon prose writers and poets. Lapidge's essay with its concentration on textual traditions is clearly designed to accompany the final essay in the collection, Patrizia Lendinara's 'The World of Anglo-Saxon Learning', which outlines the nature of the Anglo-Saxon monastic school, the practice of glossing, and the the school curriculum, thus providing an important introduction to the scholars of the period.

Key texts crop up time and again in *The Cambridge Companion* – Bede's account of the sparrow and the hall, Cædmon, and *Beowulf* to mention only the most obvious – but in general the concentration on themes rather than genres works exceedingly well to introduce students to the range, power, and diversity of OE texts (the *Companion* also offers brief suggestions for further reading as additional encouragement). It is especially noteworthy that so many contributors integrate the non-canonical with the canonical, the prose with the poetry, the cultural (whether spiritual or political) with the literary.

Attentiveness to critical assumptions also characterizes Lois Bragg's *The Lyric Speakers of Old English Poetry*, which examines the limitations of our conventional generic classifications of the shorter OE poems. Taking as her point of departure the increasing critical interest in the role of the reader in co-creating meaning, Bragg suggests that the short poems conventionally classified as elegy, riddle, prayer, or charm, for example, could be usefully regrouped according to their use of the relationship between speaker and reader. The theoretical basis for such a reconceptualization of the short poems forms the first part of the book, where Bragg combines a relaxed survey of recent studies of the lyric with discussion of voice and subject from linguistics and explores both in relation to the manuscript culture of the poems. The second and longer part of *The Lyric Speakers* presents a taxonomy of speaker – inanimate, adoptable, nonpersonal, fictive, and personal – before concluding with more detailed readings of *The Wanderer* and *The Dream of the Rood*. Bragg's study brings together poetry more often kept apart – the charms with the Chronicle poems, for example – and thus provides food for future reflection. There are also some intriguing but undeveloped insights into concepts of subjectivity offered by the construction of the speaker in these poems, although Bragg's readings of individual texts are sometimes constrained by her larger project of classification. This is a short book and I look forward to Bragg's development of her insights in future studies.

Old English Poetry in Medieval Christian Perspective: A Doctrinal Approach by Judith N. Garde, on the other hand, takes what she calls a non-literary approach to the poetry. Informed by the thought that most of the poetry is didactic (in a general sense), Garde sets about redressing what she sees as the overly theological or overly literary emphases of most critical interpretation. Her studies of the Junius codex, *Christ I, II, and III*, *The Dream of the Rood*, the *Descent into Hell*, *Elene*, and the *Phoenix*, therefore examine the fundamental doctrinal issues of salvation history and redemption that she sees as animating the texts. Analysis of each poem is prefaced by (often idiosyncratic) summaries of its critical history, and discussion of medieval theology where relevant. This is a promising approach which tries to steer a course between the excesses of the exegetical and critical schools while in fact often relying on the contributions of both. It is refreshing to hear Garde assert, for example, that the OE poets were not interested in abstract theology; by failing to address the issue of aesthetics and didacticism (why these texts are poems and not, for example, homilies), however, Garde's argument is not as watertight as she thinks.

In *Pagan Words and Christian Meanings*, Richard North uses what is sometimes viewed as an outdated or unfashionable methodology – comparative philology – to revive an aspect of Anglo-Saxon studies often felt to be equally unfashionable – the search for Anglo-Saxon paganism in OE texts. As North demonstrates, however, neither the methodology nor the subject has been exhausted. North puts Old Icelandic and OE cultures side-by-side to offer a valuable corrective to the current critical taste for Christian (Mediterranean) meanings, sources, and analogues for OE literature. The comparative analysis of four key OE words for 'mind' ('myne', 'giedd', 'hyge', and '[mod]sefa') and their Old Icelandic cognates serve as points of entry into North's wide-ranging discussion of concepts for the mind in these two related cultures. This is not, however, an easy book to read: the vast amount of lexical and textual material occasionally obscures the larger picture; and the whole project is fraught with obvious methodological problems (issues of dating spring to mind). And yet there can be little doubt that *Pagan Words* offers us important insights into early medieval, largely non-Christian, concepts of the mind, which North classifies under the categories of psychic intervention, poetic soul, and physical mind. Anglo-Saxonists will be particularly interested in North's study of the 'anfloga' passage of *The Seafarer*, which may have associations with augury, otherwise known to us only from non-Christian Germanic contexts. Such material may indicate the poet's deliberate antiquarianism.

Moving from books to articles, we find Earl R. Anderson's 'The Uncarpentered World of Old English Poetry' (*ASE* 20.65–80) taking up the issue of the poetry's use of archaism. Noting the paucity of geometric terms in OE poetic vocabulary, Anderson considers how the poets promote an 'uncarpentered' perspective that praises, for example, the products of a technologically superior culture (those familiar references to Roman ruins), describes buildings as 'natural' structures and *vice versa*, and emphasizes internal, rather than external features of habitats. The poetic world of architecture is, in other words, more often curved – 'uncarpentered' – than straight. Notions of difference also underpin Ruth Waterhouse's 'Spatial Perception and Conceptions in the (Re-)Presenting and (Re-)Constructing of Old English Texts' (*Parergon* 9.87–102). Continuing her series of recent articles that challenge our habitual critical assumptions, Waterhouse here tackles the issue of how abstract concepts such as those of time and space are encoded within specific cultural frameworks. Working from manuscript illumination to written representation, she demonstrates how Anglo-Saxon notions of foreground and background, place and space, radically differ from our own. Waterhouse argues that modern readers and critics often infer markedly visual images from what is in fact very limited textual information. To show how the OE texts concentrate on action and its symbolism rather than on a coherent visual representation, Waterhouse analyses the accounts of the hall and mere in *Beowulf*, and the gates, walls, rooms, or floors in, for example, *Cynewulf and Cyneheard*, *Judith*, and the prose homily 'The Seven Sleepers'.

Finally, Daniel Donoghue presents a 'Postscript on *Style in Old English Poetry*' (*NM* 92.405–20), which supplements his 1987 book (*YWES* 69.121) with analysis of co-ordinate and subordinate clauses as well as tackling his category of auxiliaries. Donoghue stresses the importance of semantic weight in the scansion of auxiliaries, rather than the syntactical construction in which they are found or their metrical shape. B.R. Hutcheson re-examines the inconsistencies in A. J. Bliss's rules for the scansion of weak verbs, class I and II in 'The Scansion of Old English Weak Verbs in -ian' (*N&Q* 38.144–6), and proposes that all class II '-ian' verbs should be treated as disyllabic.

4. Beowulf

See also the essays by Lerer, Frantzen (in *Speaking Two Languages*), and Frank and Robinson in section 3. However much we enjoy arguing about the merit of individual essays in critical anthologies (who gets in; who stays out), anthologies of *Beowulf* criticism are always welcome and *Interpretations of 'Beowulf'*, edited by R. D. Fulk, is no exception. Arranged in chronological order and covering roughly 60 years of

Beowulf criticism (up to 1986), teachers and students are offered a healthy selection of essays (and occasionally self-contained extracts from longer works) on the style, themes, and structure of the poem. Studies of fate and Christianity are represented by 'Wyrd and Providence in Anglo-Saxon Thought' by Bertha S. Phillpotts (1928); '*Beowulf* – An Allegory of Salvation?' by M. B. McNamee, SJ (1960); Margaret E. Goldsmith's 'The Christian Perspective in *Beowulf*' (1962); and 'The Text of Fate' by Edward B. Irving Jnr (1968). The anthology also includes the justly celebrated '*Beowulf*: The Monsters and The Critics' by J. R. R. Tolkien (1936); 'Variation' by Arthur Gilchrist Brodeur (1959); Stanley B. Greenfield's 'Geatish History: Poetic Art and Epic Quality in *Beowulf*' (1963); 'The Interlace Structure of *Beowulf*' by John Leyerle (1967); and 'Frame Narratives and Fictionalization: Beowulf as Narrator' by Laurence N. de Looze (1984); T.A. Shippey's 'The Ironic Background' (1972); 'Tradition and Design in *Beowulf*' (1980) by Theodore M. Andersson, and Joseph Harris's '*Beowulf* in Literary History' (1982). Essays on style, on specific passages, or on individual figures include '*Him seo wen geleah*: The Design for Irony in Grendel's Last Visit to Heorot' by Richard N. Ringler (1966); 'Artful Avoidance of the Useful Phrase in *Beowulf*, *The Battle of Maldon*, and *Fates of the Apostles*' by Geoffrey F. Russom (1978); and John C. Pope's '*Beowulf* 505, "gehedde", and the Pretensions of Unferth' (1986). Francis P. Magoun Jr's early 'The Oral-Formulaic Character of Anglo-Saxon Narrative Poetry' (1953) is the only essay representing oral-formulaic approaches to the poem, while Jane Chance's 'Grendel's Mother as Epic Anti-Type of the Virgin and Queen' (1986) is the only feminist study. Among the more puzzling omissions is any discussion of the dating of the poem, but Fulk's introduction helpfully refers to other studies, while justifying his choice of essays. The introduction also claims to provide a brief overview of the relation of *Beowulf* criticism to the history of criticism more generally, although I am not convinced that all will agree with Fulk that, for example, T. A. Shippey's reading of *Beowulf* is reminiscent of reader-reception theory in general or the work of Stanley Fish in particular.

Interpretations of 'Beouwlf' contrasts usefully with the introduction to the poem offered by George Clark in *Beowulf* (1990), a contribution to the Twayne's English Author Series which loudly signals its intended appeal to students who are new to the poem. Clark offers useful and often judicious syntheses of New Critical readings on the poem's main thematic interests – its use of traditional materials, its depiction of the heroic age, the fights with the monsters, and its conception of the aristocracy (its 'royalist' nature, as Clark puts is) – prefaced by an analysis of J. R. R. Tolkien's inescapable impact on its critical interpretation, and appending a very brief bibliography. I confess to some surprise at discovering that Beowulf was born in 495 in the chronological list of the poem's legendary events, helpful though it may be to have some rough-and-ready guide to the dates of the Heroic Age. In fact for the most part, Clark avoids detailed summaries of the controversies that haunt the dating of the poem or its world.

Our knowledge of the nineteenth-century Dutch philologist, Pieter Cosijn's work on *Beowulf*, derives largely from references to his influential *Aanteekeningen op den Béowulf* (1892) in the better-known English language editions of, for example, Fr. Klaeber and E. K. Dobbie. This oversight is now rectifed by the translation, *Notes on 'Beowulf'*, by Rolf H. Bremmer, Jnr, Jan van den Berg, and David F. Johnson. Prefaced by a brief account of Cosijn's life and work by Bremmer, this book renders the Dutch scholar's work more accessible and thereby reinstates his important contribution to the scholarly study of *Beowulf* in the late nineteenth century.

Calvin B. Kendall's idea of the *Beowulf*-poet in *The Metrical Grammar of*

'Beowulf' will appease both the oral and literate schools of thought about the poem's genesis. Proceeding from the observation that the poet was literate and highly skilled in the oral-traditional arts of versification, Kendall sets out to describe the poet's use of traditional metrical grammar. The rules of syntax, metre, alliteration, and conventions that go into the make-up of the *Beowulf*-poet's line are not only different in certain respects from the grammatical rules of the language generally, but more importantly add up to a distinctive 'signature' of the *Beowulf*-poet that may then be usefully contrasted with the metrical grammars of other OE poets. Kendall's study begins with a general restatement of the rules assigning alliteration, developed largely from Hans Kuhn's work, and the key features of the principal kinds of half-lines, and then continues with descriptions of specific metrical effects: for example, displacement, stressed proclitic adjectives, the identification of clause-non-initial half-lines, half-lines with internal clause divisions, the relationship between alliteration and unstressed prefixes and copulative conjunctions, prepositions and proclitic adverbs, proclitic adjectives and pronouns, and the alliterative behaviour of compounds. Although this is a study for the specialist, Kendall's prose is admirably lucid throughout, and his brief concluding discussion about the possibility of assessing other metrical grammars promises much for future research.

Kevin S. Kiernan's work on the *Beowulf* manuscript has, at the very least, provoked an invaluable debate about the dating of the poem – itself a considerable achievement in *Beowulf* scholarship – yet I have been saddened to witness the downturn this debate has taken during my years as reviewer. This year Kiernan redresses Johan Gerritsen's recent studies of the manuscript (*YWES* 70.163) which, under the guise of scholarship, offer a barely concealed attack on Kiernan. In 'A Long Footnote for J. Gerritsen's "Supplementary" Description of B. L., Cotton MS Vitellius A. XV' (*ES* 72.489–96), Kiernan points out Gerritsen's unacknowledged debt to his own work – a debt that borders on plagiarism. Much to my surprise, it is only too clear from Gerritsen's 'A Reply to Dr Kiernan's "Footnote" ' that follows (*ES* 72.497–500) that he refuses to take Kiernan's work or his charges seriously. The story is not over. Gerritsen also publishes this year his 'The Thorkelin Transcripts of *Beowulf*: A Codicological Description, with Notes on their Genesis and History' (*Library* 13.1–22), which makes the astonishing claim that no 'adequate' description of the two transcripts has been published. He offers his own in recompense and relegates Kiernan's book on precisely this subject (*YWES* 67.124–5) to a dismissive footnote. Attentive readers of both scholars' work on the *Beowulf* manuscript and its transcripts will easily see the importance of Kiernan's scholarship.

Richard J. Schrader opens this year's crop of inevitable thematic studies of the poem with 'Succession and Glory in *Beowulf*' (*JEGP* 90.491–504). Schrader reads the Scyld Scefing prologue as a *translatio gloriae* and therefore argues that the celebration of glory (or what used to be called fame) is a key theme of the poem. He contrasts the poet's positioning of the selectively glorious line of the Danes that opens the poem – Danish kings with dubious reputations are excluded from this genealogy – with the largely inglorious Geatish line. The genealogy for the Geats, in fact, has to be reconstructed from its chaotic handling in the second part of the poem. How Beowulf himself is assimilated to the Danish line is thus set in relief (and, I might add, how Beowulf himself challenges the validity of genealogy altogether).

Allen J. Frantzen's 'Writing the Unreadable *Beowulf*: "Writan" and "Forwritan", the Pen and the Sword' (*Exemplaria* 3.327–57) meditates on two aspects of the poem's 'writing' and, along the way, offers Anglo-Saxonists a fine explanation of the concept of intertextuality itself. Frantzen demonstrates how *Beowulf* may be said to generate two different kinds of intertexts: those of its critical reconstruction or rewriting; and those of its text-internal representations of reading and writing. The distinction is crucial. Parts of the unreadable *Beowulf* have been rewritten by its editors and commentators, either because the manuscript is damaged or because the relevant lines do not conform to our notions of the poem's aesthetic or grammar; other sections are unreadable in quite a different sense – such as the story encoded on the magic sword found in the cave of Grendel's mother, which only Hrothgar reads. Drawing on the semantic fields of 'writan' ('to write, to carve') and 'forwritan' ('to write, to kill') to uncover the relationship between writing and death that lies quite literally at the heart of the poem, Frantzen connects the unreadable text on the sword hilt with other similar scenes in the poem – such as the Sigemund episode and the discussion of Wiglaf's sword – whose circumstances are deliberately left mysterious, their meaning unfixed. Ultimately, as Frantzen points out, even inscribed swords cannot put an end to monsters nor does writing stave off death.

Frantzen's and Lerer's (section 3 above) readings of *Beowulf* derive from a conviction of the poem's literate nature, from which both scholars theorize variously upon the responses of its readers. James W. Earl's '*Beowulf* and the Origins of Civilization' (in *Speaking Two Languages*, ed. Frantzen) goes the whole nine yards to explore the psychological responses that this original poem may be said to generate in its readers or listeners. Earl is – as ever – elegantly and deceptively straightforward. The process of reading, he argues, elicits some form of identification from the reader, which psychoanalysis is best equipped to explain. Our responses to *Beowulf* suggest that the poem may be said to sit in the place of the analyst – the screen for our projections – reading us as we read it. The ethical importance of silence in OE literature generally, the fact that *Beowulf* mourns the loss of Germanic origins, and the inexhaustable flow of *Beowulf* criticism, which cannot be fully explained only by its canonical status in the discipline, all lend plausible support to Earl's startling suggestion. The processes of identification are illustrated by Earl's interpretations of two of his dreams, which suggest to him how his own kinship with *Beowulf* is split between identifying with the author and the audience. (Not since Bede's account of Cædmon have dreams occupied such an important position in a narrative of origins!) A second illustration imagines how a hero and lord such as Byrhtnoth (of *The Battle of Maldon*) would read the hero and lord Beowulf – again, Earl argues, Byrhtnoth's reading would be split between identification with Beowulf and with his men. As a result, the poem's readers, like *Beowulf*'s warriors, are compelled into an identification with one another, and remain obedient to the authority of the idealized hero (or superego). This is a marvellous account of the bonding of the *comitatus* where, to paraphrase Tacitus, the lord has the freedom to fight for himself, for victory, and the warriors fight for their lord. In fact, Earl concludes that the mysterious figure of the hero intrigues us precisely because he has such freedom.

Paul Beekman Taylor is interested in origins of a more specific nature; namely, those of the hero's family. 'Beowulf's Family: Lexicography and Commodity' (*Archiv* 143.90–8) poses the question of the status of Beowulf's mother, given her description in lines 372–6 of the poem where Hrothgar acknowledges Hrethel's gift of his daughter to Ecgtheow. Taylor uses his lexicographical discussion of the phrase, 'to ham forgeaf', which refers to the marital gift of a daughter to ease political relations, in order to reconstruct Ecgtheow's career and relations with Hrethel. Noting that daughters are prominent in the poem only so far as they are instruments of alliances (which often fail), Taylor stresses that the importance of the gift of Beowulf's mother to Hrothgar (and hence to the poem) is that she provides a son, Beowulf. Defined in relation to her husband, son, and father, this mother, at least, has value only as a political commodity capable of child-bearing. This is an important counter-argument for those who regularly stress the political prominence of women in *Beowulf*.

Moving to discussion of individual lines and emendations, we find Daniel P. O'Donnell's 'The Collective Sense of Concrete Singular Nouns in *Beowulf*: Emendations of Sense' (*NM* 92.433–40). O'Donnell challenges the established view that singular concrete nouns in *Beowulf* have a collective sense by re-examining all the relevant examples and noting that, in each case, a singular meaning is equally possible. Andrew Breeze identifies connections between the poem's reference to Sigurd and the the twelfth- and thirteenth-century carvings on the south doorway of Santa María la Real, Sangüesa in '*Beowulf* 875–902 and the Sculptures at Sangüesa' (*N&Q* 38.2–13). Breeze provides a description of the sculptures, which include scenes from the well-known legend of Sigurd, and hypothesizes that this knowledge may have been brought to Spain via the town's connections with the Knights of St John. 'Perfecting the Old English Past: *Beowulf* 2 and Limits on the Equivalence of the Old English Simple Past and Present Perfect', by Mary Blockley, (*PQ* 70.123–39) ponders the fact that 'gefrunon' (line 2, for example) is regularly translated as a present perfect ('we have heard'), with the exception of lines 1966b–70a, by reviewing the use of past tense forms in the poem. The evidence strongly suggests that the indefinite past is represented by periphrastic forms in most cases, while simple past forms are used to imply shared contexts. The uneven overlap between the use of periphrastic forms to supplement the simple past in OE and Modern English can thus affect interpretation of the poem, especially in translation, and Blockley's article reminds us all that OE and Modern English use of these tenses are not necessarily equivalent.

Martin Puhvel is worried about 'The Meaning of "on frætewum", *Beowulf*, 962' (*NM* 92.441–3) as a description of Grendel, since the phrase usually refers either to ornaments or to weapons or war-gear, which Grendel is supposed to have scorned. He proposes instead the meaning 'covered with blood' or 'blood-stained' by noting that blood is often described in ornamental ways in the poetry. Deborah S. Frisby is also justifiably concerned about the meaning of 'dæda dollicra' to describe Beowulf in line 2646a. ' "Daring" and "Foolish" Renderings: On The Meaning of *Dollic* in *Beowulf* ' (*ANQ* 4.59–63) notes that, *Beowulf* apart, 'dollic' is most often used in a pejorative sense. Editors of *Beowulf*, however, preserve a more neutral, even honorific referent in the case of Beowulf himself, which is open to challenge. On the basis of this evidence, Frisby suggests that Wiglaf's description includes some criticism of our hero.

The final line of *Beowulf* is scrutinized by Dennis Cronan in ' "Lofgeorn": Generosity and Praise' (*NM* 92.187–94). Cronan makes the case that 'lofgeorn' must mean 'eager to deserve praise' in a positive sense by noting its otherwise pejorative uses in the prose tradition. The evidence for this paradox rests both on the use of 'lof' in the poetry, where praise is earned by generosity, and on the pejorative use of 'lofgeorn' to translate 'prodigus' in the OE *Benedictine Rule*. Cronan thus contrasts Christian and heroic meanings for the term, with prose and poetry providing the contextual boundaries.

5. The Junius Manuscript

See also the studies by Garde and Lerer in section 3. There is only one brief note on *Genesis A* this year. As its title suggests, 'OE Wrohtgeteme: "Crime Troop", Not

"Series of Crimes" ', by Karin Olsen (*N&Q* 38.438–42) reconsiders the meaning of this *hapax legomenon* in the light of examples such as 'heretema' ('leader of army'). The revised sense of 'crime troop' is also better supported by the text.

I begin the discussion of *Genesis B* by welcoming the new edition of *The Saxon Genesis: An Edition of the West Saxon "Genesis B" and the Old Saxon Vatican "Genesis"*, by A. N. Doane, which derives much of its importance from Doane's clear and comprehensive attempt to treat both poems as independent witnesses to a single *Heliand*-type Genesis cycle. The relationship between the two poems has been largely ignored by the separate legacies of Germanic and Anglo-Saxon criticism, and requires a double critical perspective for both poems in ways that occasionally exercise our critical imagination as well as our scholarly faculties. The book maintains such a perspective judiciously and will open many new avenues for thinking about these works. Doane offers us a brief introduction to the history of the search for the Saxon Genesis, in addition to studies of the manuscripts, language, style, and meter (supplying appendices on verse-forms and types), as well as commentaries on both editions, glossaries, and individual studies on specific aspects of the poem, including discussion of Satan, Adam and Eve, Cain and Enoch, Abraham and Sodom. The texts themselves are edited conservatively – a decision to which some may object (for example Michael Lapidge, section 3), although Doane's explanation for his practice is lucid and compelling.

'On Reading Eve: *Genesis B* and The Readers' Desire', by Gillian R. Overing (in *Speaking Two Languages*, ed. Frantzen) addresses the problems faced by the feminist critic as she speaks about patriarchal Anglo-Saxon poetry from both within and without the patriarchal domains of conventional criticism. Elizabeth Elstob's negotiations between the 'mother' tongue of Anglo-Saxon and the traditional authority of Latin in her preface to *The Rudiments of Grammar for the English-Saxon Tongue* (1715) provide Overing with the prelude to her own attempts to recover Eve and her meaning in *Genesis B*. Indeed, the interplay of these three female voices – Eve, Elstob, and Overing – is itself a powerful corrective to the traditional silencing of the feminine by patriarchal discourse. Overing's search for Eve begins with a survey of her representation in critical writing, where it is clear that critical desire is complicit with Eve's specific disappearance as a subject in the poem, whether viewed from a Christian or Germanic perspective. Eve is recoverable, however, via her symbolic associations with the body, food, sin, and language, which offer the feminist reader the possibility of a different reading of the Fall. Overing concentrates on the radical ambiguity of Eve's representation in the poem: at certain key points, the boundaries between the text's logical symbols collapse altogether, as is illustrated by the remarkable moment in lines 636–7 when Eve literally becomes the apple. At such moments, Overing argues, Eve's signification eludes meaning in conventional masculine terms and the possibility of her own subjectivity – however fleeting – is raised.

Eric Jager's reading of *Genesis B* covers much of the same ground as Overing but without considering the text's construction of gender. 'The Word in the "Breost"; Interiority and the Fall in *Genesis B*' (*Neophil* 75.279–90) takes 'breost' as the literal and psychological centre of the Fall, which links the inter-related themes of eating and knowing in the poem. Jager surveys the use of 'breost' and 'pectus' for intellectual and verbal processes in medieval literature and suggests that the OE poet uses these associations more thematically than the Old Saxon poet.

'*Exodus*, *Elene*, and *The Rune Poem*: *milpæþ* 'Army Road, Highway' by Andrew Breeze (*N&Q* 38.436–8) suggests that 'milpæþ' possibly derives from the Welsh 'mil', 'army'. Examining the recorded uses of the noun in OE poetry, it seems reasonable that it means 'army road, highway'.

It is a pleasure to note the revived interest in *Daniel* this year. Like Seth Lerer (section 3 above), Claire Fanger is concerned with the poet's exploration of the relation between teaching and prophecy. 'Miracle as Prophetic Gospel: Knowledge, Power and the Design of the Narrative in *Daniel*' (*ES* 72.123–35) also shares with Lerer a distaste for those critical readings that emphasize the problem of the poem's structure. Fanger goes further than Lerer, however, by attempting to put on one side *Daniel*'s evident didacticism to concentrate on the artistic treatment of its narrative. It is unclear to me how didacticism in a medieval text can be separated from that text's artistry, especially when that text is ostensibly concerned with teaching, although it is probably true that critical studies of didacticism are now as old-hat as those of unity. Yet Fanger makes a good case for the heightened linguistic artistry of those moments of the poem most concerned with prophecy, and thus focuses on the poet's exploitation of different perspectives on Daniel the prophet. For Fanger, the poem contrasts the unregenerative misreading of Daniel by the Chaldeans with that potent figure of mystery recuperated by its implied Christian readers. J. Anne George is also interested in the poem's representation of the prophet in '*Daniel* 416–29: an "identity crisis" resolved?' (*MÆ* 60.73–6). The 'identity crisis' turns out to be that of the unnamed 'ræswa' in lines 416–29 who counsels Nebuchadnezzar to release the three youths from the fiery furnace – thus solving one of the 'mysteries' of the text. Drawing on the similarities of the descriptions of the anonymous counsellor and the named prophet, George argues that this 'ræswa' is not an anonymous Babylonian, as has been previously assumed, but Daniel himself. In an intriguing twist to the argument, George points out that 'ræswa' can mean both 'ruler' and 'counsellor' and refers elsewhere in the poem both to Nebuchadnezzar and Daniel, thus inviting the reader to consider the similarities and differences between king and prophet-counsellor.

6. The Poems of the Vercelli Book

See also the studies by Bragg and Garde in section 3. Robert Boenig provides a service for students of the Andrew legend by translating its chief materials in Greek, Latin, and Old English in *The Acts of Andrew in the Country of the Cannibals*. Boenig's introduction offers a useful – though limited – orientation for the uninitiated, which concentrates unsurprisingly on the OE *Andreas* rather than the homiletic versions of the legend. The bibliography is similarly brief, and the translations are based on published editions without reference to their manuscripts (even in the case of the OE versions). Although this has the merit of bringing the Andrew materials to the attention of a much wider readership, it is a pity that Boenig provides so few pointers to more specialized reading. These defects are in part supplied by Boenig's second book on the poem, *Saint and Hero: "Andreas" and Medieval Doctrine*, also published this year. Here, Boenig offers his analysis of the poem as a contribution to current critical debates on authorial intentions and the social nature of the text. But what we get, in fact, is a conventional source-study contextualized by debates about penitential practice, the Sacrament, and the Atonement. Boenig notes the poet's use of penitential imagery at key moments in the poem, nor is there any doubt that the cannibalism so stressed by the poem (and its critics) may be related in broad terms to contemporary understanding of the Eucharist, yet Boenig's attempt to pin down these broad connections more specifically, however, is less successful. Few readers will see the parallels between text and context that he adduces, and many will wonder how the dynamics of Frederic Jameson's 'political unconscious' actually factor into Boenig's apparent New Historicist interpretation.

'Death Appropriated in *The Fates of Men*' (*SP* 88.123–39) by Karen Swenson re-examines the nature of the catalogues or lists in the poem, and finds that the first list (lines 10–57) reflects a non-Christian sensibility in its series of descriptions of ritual deaths. Since the second list is a catalogue of the gifts of men, Swenson argues that this latter, explicitly Christian, list is a later accretion that appropriates the themes of the earlier, and older list and thus recontextualizes its meaning.

Raymond J. S. Grant considers the problematic meaning of 'æt his lices heafdum' in ' "The Dream of the Rood", Line 63b: a Part-Time Idiom?' (*NM* 92.289–95). Grant argues that this is a conventional phrase used in the description of corpses at funerals by referring to fuller, parallel examples in the OE Bede and a marginal anonymous homily on the Virgin Mary, both of which are found in the same manuscript, Corpus Christi College, Cambridge 41.

7. The Exeter Book

See also the studies by Bragg, Lerer, and North in section 3. Bernard J. Muir has been 'Watching the Exeter Book Scribe Copy Old English and Latin Texts' (*Manuscripta* 35.3–22) as part of the preparation for his forthcoming new edition of the Exeter Book. That the scribe of the Exeter Book also copied the Lambeth Palace Library MS 149 and Oxford, Bodley MS 319 has long been known. Here, Muir compares the technique of the scribe in correcting both Latin and OE and discovers that, although the scribe was well aware of the principles of OE versification and a meticulous corrector of the vernacular material, he is less careful with the Latin. Muir, therefore, suggests that the scribe was less competent in this language.

Margaret Jennings has been re-examining the liturgical associations of *Christ III* in 'Structure in *Christ III*' (*NM* 92.445–55), in order to make sense of the immediacy with which the audience experiences the Last Judgement in the poem and its repetitive structure. Jennings argues that this experience parallels that in formal liturgical settings where the congregation actively participates in the reconstruction of scriptural history. She proposes that the readings for the Sunday Vigils for the Advent Night Office (probably the monastic office) offer analogues for the reduplicative pattern of the poem.

'Anonymous Polyphony and *The Wanderer*'s Textuality' by Carol Braun Pasternack (*ASE* 20.99–122) wishes to dissolve the boundaries between scribe and author, and sometimes even those between text and text. This kind of approach, which draws on contemporary theories of semiotics, textual production, and orality in order to question the status of a text *qua* text is becoming increasingly familiar (although it is possibly the first time that it has found favour with the editors of *ASE*). Pasternack's analysis of the structural 'movements' of *The Wanderer* is perhaps one of the more radical of this genre since she sees the text's highly conventional use of 'polyphony' as offering an indefinite series of intertexts (both Latin and OE texts) for the listener. In consequence, Pasternack suggests, the concepts of authorship, originality and influence can offer few critical insights into this boundless poetic world.

We are on more familiar territory with Colin A. Ireland's critical interpretation of *The Seafarer* in 'Some Analogues of the OE "Seafarer" from Hiberno-Latin Sources' (*NM* 92.1–14), which surveys Irish traditions for *peregrinatio*. Basing his study primarily, though not exclusively, on late seventh-century texts by Adonmnán,

Muirchú, and Tírechán (that is, on those texts most likely to have been known by English authors), Ireland assembles a considerable body of evidence for the function of pilgrimage, both penitential and sometimes punitive in intent. These two cultural similarities between English and Irish writing are enhanced by the stylistic parallels in their descriptions of nature poetry. Ireland concludes that the poem's depiction of seafaring pilgrimage transcends the allegorical. Peter Orton's longer study of the same poem takes a more New Critical approach. 'The Form and Structure of *The Seafarer*' (*SN* 63.37–55) opens by stressing the obscurity of the poem in spite of the wealth of critical work prompted by its interpretation. Orton overstates his case, but his points about the poem's lack of clear generic signals and the difficulty of assessing its use of stylistic disjointedness are well-taken. Orton's own reading concentrates on the character and emotions of the Seafarer as an outsider reconciling his situation with the claims of Christianity in his culture: he thereby downplays the allegorical suggestiveness of the text in favour of its more realistic associations. Is *The Partridge* really about a partridge and hence a remnant of an OE *Physiologus*? James W. Marchard grasps the problem in '*The Partridge*? An Old English Multiquote' (*Neophil* 75.603–11) by assessing the loopholes in the critical arguments about the nature of this text. In fact, the source for lines 4–11 appears to be a version of the Ezechiel Apocryphon, a composite work well used in the prose tradition, and the poem as a whole thus seems to have nothing at all to do with a partridge or indeed a *Physiologus*.

'Snake Rings in *Deor* and *Vǫlundarkviða*', by Robert Cox (*LeedsSE* 22.1–20) tackles the problem of the meaning of 'be wurman' in the Welund story by re-examining the evidence for its associations with serpent-patterned swords and/or arm and finger rings in the light of analogous references in *Vǫlundarkviða*. Noting the stylistic and cultural associations of snakes with arm and finger rings from the sixth to the eleventh centuries in England and Scandinavia, Cox plausibly suggests that the Welund example in *Deor* refers as much to such rings as it does to swords, thus neatly condensing Welund's own legendary characteristics as smith and hero.

Marie Nelson's 'Four Social Functions of the Exeter Book Riddles' (*Neophil* 75.445–50) begins the crop of notes on the ever-popular Riddles. The social functions that Nelson detects are verbal competitiveness, the opportunity to control and explore aggression both through role-playing and in response to a hostile natural world, and insights into the power to destroy. In addition, Nelson offers alternative solutions to two Riddles: Riddle 50, usually solved as 'fire' could also refer to 'anger'; and Riddle 33, 'ice' carries an alternative, 'hatred'. G. A. Lester reconsiders the meaning of '*Sindrum Begrunden* in Exeter Book Riddle No. 26' (*N&Q* 38.13–15). This is the well-known 'sacred codex' Riddle and Lester suggests that the process of 'pouncing' the parchment is alluded to in this phrase, which means 'ground away with cinders' rather than the previously thought 'with all impurities ground off'. A further two notes deal with Riddle 39. 'Stanley B. Greenfield's Solution of Riddle (ASPR) 39: "Dream" ' (*N&Q* 38.148–9), by E. G. Stanley, appears to confirm Greenfield's solution by identifying the motif of the mouthless dream that speaks in lines 10–13a, and therefore proposes one minor emendation to line 12b of 'ne' to 'se'. John Wilson's 'Old English Riddle No. 39: "Comet" ' (*N&Q* 38.442–3), which appears in the same journal, suggests that his solution of 'comet' is unambiguously announced in the first four lines of the poem, and fails to discuss alternative solutions. More ambitious is 'Signs and Solutions: A Semiotic Approach to the Exeter Book Riddles' by Wim Tigges (in *This Noble Craft*, ed. Kooper). Tigges notes the unsatisfactory nature of much critical writing on the OE Riddles, and suggests that a semiotic matrix, which analyses the transformations and shifts between various levels of phenomena used by the Riddle clues, may offer a useful model of how riddles work and how their solutions can be tested. This semiotic approach is based in part on the insight that our attention is directed away from the vital clues in most of the Riddles and, although Tigges is certainly correct to point out that we have still much to learn about the conventions of OE riddling (especially with respect to their classification of phenomena), the article makes some headway toward their analysis.

8. Other Poems

See also the article by Irvine in section 3. 'Poetic Language and the Paris Psalter: The Decay of the Old English Tradition', by M. S. Griffith (*ASE* 20.167–86), examines the use of poetic vocabulary in the verse of the Paris Psalter and finds it wanting. Although the Psalter does form part of the poetic tradition, its vocabulary suggests an extremely selective use of the traditional word-hoard (as is illustrated by the appendix). Griffith argues that this limited use of poetic language is related to the poet's general reluctance to use the heroic heritage. In consequence, the Psalter may be viewed as a recognition of the importance of traditional verse forms in sacred translation which, at the same time, demonstrates the limited value of a traditional heroic vocabulary in such translations. The poem may therefore be an important witness to the decline of OE poetry at the end of the period.

This year (1991) was the millenial celebration of the Battle of Maldon, which is commemorated by the publication of a collection of essays, *The Battle of Maldon AD 991*, edited by Donald Scragg. This collection offers multiple perspectives on the battle and on the poem, a structure which is, of course, suggested by the documentary evidence itself. It is only fitting, therefore, that this collection begins with editions, translations, and brief introductions to all the relevant contemporary evidence, preceded by a facsimile of David Casley's eighteenth-century transcript. The poem itself is presented by Donald Scragg; Janet M. Bately tackles 'The *Anglo-Saxon Chronicle*'; Michael Lapidge surveys 'The *Life of Oswald*'; and Alan Kennedy looks at 'Byrhtnoth's Obits and Twelfth-Century Accounts of the Battle of Maldon'. The second selection of essays considers the historical background: Simon Keynes provides a useful introduction to 'The Historical Context of the Battle of Maldon'; Niels Lund offers 'The Danish Perspective'; Richard Abels ponders 'English Tactics, Strategy and Military Organization in the Late Tenth Century'; Mark Blackburn examines 'Æthelred's Coinage and the Payment of Tribute'; and John McN. Dodgson surveys 'The Site of the Battle of Maldon'. Essays on the poem itself include the fascinating account of 'Byrhtnoth's Eighteenth-Century Context' by Kathryn Sutherland; Roberta Frank's witty and pugnacious '*The Battle of Maldon* and Heroic Literature'. Nicholas Brooks's discussion of 'Weapons and Armour' is complemented by Gale R. Crocker-Owen's 'Hawks and Horse-Trappings: the Insignia of Rank' and 'The Men Named in the Poem' by Margaret A. L. Locherbie-Cameron. The final group of essays considers the relationship between Byrhtnoth and Ely: Margaret A. L. Locherbie-Cameron's second contribution is 'Byrhtnoth and his Family', while Mildred Budny considers 'The Byrhtnoth Tapestry or Embroidery', Elizabeth Coatsworth looks at 'Byrhtnoth's Tomb', and Marilyn Deegan and Stanley Rubin measure 'Byrhtnoth's Remains: a Reassessment of his Stature'. The book, which also offers us a bibliography compiled by Wendy E. J. Collier, is lavishly presented, beautifully illustrated, and the contributions are full of insights into this most intriguing historical and literary event to which I can hardly do justice in so short a review.

We stay with *Maldon* to find Richard North worrying about the political aftermath of the battle and Byrhtnoth's dubious reputation in 'Getting To Know the General in *The Battle of Maldon*' (*MÆ* 60.1–15). North argues that the poem cannot have been composed in a political vacuum, and painstakingly reviews all the evidence – both literary and non-literary – for the poem's genesis. He hypothesizes that the climate of recrimination after the battle must have influenced the poet's version of events, and may account for Byrhtnoth's flawed representation in the text. This is the first time I have read an article on *Maldon* that suggests that the Vikings' taunts to Byrhtnoth are tinged with charges of effeminacy, although I remain uncertain how to relate this to North's overall thesis. Albert B. Lord, on the other hand, is concerned not with history but with the late survival of oral-traditional features in the poem in 'Ring Composition in *Maldon*; or, a Possible Case of Chiasmus in a Late Anglo-Saxon Poem' (in *The Ballad and Oral Literature*, ed. Harris). Lord detects a ring-composition in the poem's use of verbs to introduce speech, and thereby delineates a familiar envelope pattern. He suggests that the poet had an innate sense of this oral-traditional feature, which is also known as chiasmus in classical and medieval rhetorical texts.

Three articles continue the revival of interest in the *Solomon and Saturn* texts this year. Katherine O'Brien O'Keefe offers a source analysis of 'The Geographic List of *Solomon and Saturn II*' (*ASE* 20.123–41). O'Keeffe convincingly strips this text of its exotic orientalist associations with a study of the origins of the list (lines 176–92b), which in fact lie firmly within mainstream early medieval geographic texts. She points out that the list's closest analogues are Bede's *Nomina locorum*, the lesser known but influential *Cosmographia* of Aethicus Ister, and also, perhaps, Isidore's *Etymologiae*, but argues that the OE poem itself may be a largely original composition. Jonathan Wilcox finds further evidence for Saturn's intellectual inadequacy in a pun used in both poems in 'Eating Books: The Consumption of Learning in the Old English Poetic *Solomon and Saturn*' (*ANQ* 4.115–18). The reference to eating books is found in I, line 2a and II, line 234: in each case, the hint of consumption with benefit is confirmed by comparison with a positive scriptural example from Apocr. 10. 9–10. Wilcox concludes by noting the parallel use of this motif in the well-known 'Bookmoth' Riddle. Steven Davis challenges the accepted meaning of 'winrod' in 'Salomon (sic) and Saturn 235: *winrod*' (*N&Q* 38.443–4) by suggesting that a more acceptable meaning for this compound is 'joyous band or procession'.

William T. Whobrey's claim that 'King Alfred's Metrical Epilogue to the *Pastoral Care*' (*JEGP* 90.175–86) is a poem waiting to be taken seriously echoes that of James W. Earl's own study of Alfred's poetry (*YWES* 71). Whobrey's analysis of the Epilogue uses Alfred's description of the *Pastoral Care* as a 'wæterscipe' (line 1) as a point of entry into the Epilogue's complex web of associations delineating the Christian teacher. These associations are drawn not only from the Alfred's translation of the *Pastoral Care* but also from Scripture and Patristic commentary. As a result, Whobrey reads the Epilogue as a summary of Alfred's philosophy of teaching but, unlike Earl, barely looks at it as a poem.

9. Prose

See also the studies by Irvine and Lerer in section 3. 'Cornwall and the Authorship of the Old English *Orosius*' by Andrew Breeze (*N&Q* 38.152–4) tackles the spelling of OE 'Ercol' for Hercules in this text, which Breeze suggests is closely related to the Welsh, 'Erkwl', but appears to be Cornish. Noting Janet Bately's suggestion in her

1980 edition (*YWES* 61.32) that the aberrant spellings of foreign names might indicate a foreign translator, Breeze considers the possibility that the translator was Cornish or an Englishman taught by a Cornishman. William Schipper eliminates 'A Ghost Word in the Peterborough Chronicle (*ihyder*)' (*N&Q* 38.154) in the entry for 1094 by re-examining the evidence. He proposes 'thyder' as a more likely reading.

Homilies, related homiletic material, and sources again dominate this year. Thomas N. Hall continues his investigations into the apocryphal sources of OE writing this year with 'The Cross as Green Tree in the *Vindicta Salvatoris* and the Green Rod of Moses in *Exodus*' (*ES* 72.297–307). Hall examines a passage in both Latin and long OE versions of the *Vindicta Salvatoris* (one of the medieval appendices to the *Gospel of Nicodemus*) in which Christ is hanged on a green tree. Noting that this motif – otherwise unknown in written texts – is widely documented in visual representations of the Crucifixion in the period (which probably derive ultimately from Genesis 2.9 and its patristic exegesis), Hall suggests that the eighth/ninth century Latin *Vindicta* may provide evidence for its first recorded use in writing. In addition, the motif has implications for our interpretation of the 'grene tacen' of *Exodus* 281, lending support to those who favour a typological interpretation of that section of the poem.

Another Latin text, this time a composite ninth-century homily from Freising now in Munich, Bayerische Staatsbibliothek, Clm. 28135 provides Mary F. Wack and Charles D. Wright with 'A New Latin Source for the Old English "Three Utterances" Exemplum' (*ASE* 20.187–202), whose drastically abbreviated form is very close to one OE witness to the exemplum in Oxford, Bodley, Junius 85/86. The authors note the Insular features and associations of these texts, which suggest yet again that the sources for anonymous OE homilies include an Irish dimension. Staying with the anonymous homilies, we find Lewis E. Nicholson editing the fruits of a graduate seminar on the Vercelli Book in *The Vercelli Book Homilies: Translations from the Anglo-Saxon*. The translation of these twenty-three homilies will help, I hope, to broaden the audience for homiletic prose, although Francis M. Clough misses an opportunity to orient the new reader in the all too brief introduction. John F. Vickrey also turns his attention to the Vercelli homilies in 'A Source and an Allusion in Vercelli Homily XIV (Folio 77v, lines 1–17)' (*Neophil* 75.612–18). Vickrey finds further confirmation for this homilist's use of Caesarius of Arles's *Sermo 215*, in addition to passages from Gregory's *Dialogues*. He also detects allusions to Acts 14.21, Psalm 48 and Luke 16, and concludes by suggesting that this evidence is further support for the well-known idea that the Vercelli Book was intended for private, devotional reading.

Jonathan Wilcox offers a fascinating glimpse into the labyrinthine relationships between OE anonymous composite homilies in 'Napier's "Wulfstan" Homilies XL and XLII: Two Anonymous Works from Winchester?' (*JEGP* 90.1–19). Wilcox examines the similarities in content, style, and sources of these two homilies (whose shared material and relation to Vercelli II and Wulfstan's homilies have long invited speculation) in order to piece together their processes of composition. He argues that Napier XLII was composed at a centre – probably Winchester – which also had access to the earliest version of Napier XL as well as some of the Wulfstan homilies, thereby strengthening the case for their common authorship. It is rare to find a fruitful argument that identifies an anonymous author in the homiletic corpus, and Wilcox provides an important insight into the English practices associated with the school of Winchester.

Turning from the Winchester circle to Worcester and Wulfstan himself, J. E. Cross continues this year his important work redefining the evidence for his Latin compositions in 'Wulfstan's *De Antichristo* in a Twelfth-Century Worcester Manuscript' (*ASE* 20.203–20). Cross presents a description of the contents of Cambridge, St John's College 42 (B. 20), a late witness to the Pembroke-type sermonary, which includes not only a new variant text for the *De Antichristo* but also other related materials closely associated with Wulfstan. Cross concludes that the evidence of this manuscript demonstrates the continued use of pre-Conquest materials in post-Conquest environments. We stay with the Reform circle with Alex Nicholls's 'Bede "Awe-Inspiring" not "Monstrous": Some Problems with Old English *aglæca*' (*N&Q* 38.147–8), which notes that the only prose use of 'aglæca' occurs in a description of Bede as 'se æglæca lareow' in Byrhtferth's *Manual*. As a noun, this word carries the meaning of 'monstrous' or 'formidable' in the poetry (most notably in *Beowulf*), and Nicholls suggests that Byrhtferth uses it as a heroic adjective in this context, hence describing Bede as 'awe-inspiring'. Joyce Hill's identification of 'Missing Leaves from Worcester Cathedral Libary Maunscript F. 91' (*N&Q* 38.1–2) performs a useful service for all those interested in the sources of Ælfric's writings. She notes material missing between folios 205v and 206v of about two folios in length in this manuscript of Smaragdus of S. Mihiel's *Expositio libri comitis*, which dealt with the end of the exegesis for the Nineteenth Sunday after Pentecost, the exegesis for the Epistle for the feast of the Archangel Michael and part of the material for the gospel for the same day.

The translation skills of Ælfric come under review in two new studies. 'Ælfric as Translator: The Old English Prose *Genesis*' (*Anglia* 109.319–58) by Richard Marsden, which dismantles a critical commonplace about a much neglected text, namely Ælfric's so-called literal and sometimes even nonsensical translation of the first twenty-four chapters of the Vulgate Genesis. Marsden begins by reassessing the often misunderstood Hieronymian commonplace about scriptural translation (reiterated by Ælfric in the preface to the translation), in which fidelity to the Sacred text (word-for-word) is privileged but always balanced by a careful and pragmatic attention to its meaning in the host language (sense-for-sense). Ælfric's own Scriptural translation, as Marsden demonstrates by careful analysis of both source and text, is similarly opportunistic: far from being overly literal, Ælfric's *Genesis* often modifies, amplifies, or abbreviates the Vulgate in subtle ways that maintain fidelity while also conforming to Patristic interpretation and accommodating his audience's expectations. At stake here, of course, is the difference between Modern and early Medieval notions of fidelity to text in translating, as is also clear from 'Biblical Glosses in Ælfric's Translation of Genesis' (*N&Q* 38.286–92) by Frederick M. Biggs. Biggs in fact covers much the same ground as Marsden by examining examples of Ælfric's translation that indicate that he is not as faithful a translator as previously thought. He suggests that Ælfric may have incorporated well-known scriptural glosses into the translation and then goes on to consider his switch to rhythmical prose part-way through the text. Biggs suggests that this switch may have been a useful way for Ælfric to conceal the genuine difficulties of presenting a faithful version of Genesis to his particular audience, since the metrical demands of this style inevitably demand greater flexibility.

'Ælfric's "Life of St Vincent": The Question of Form and Function' by Alex Nicholls (*N&Q* 38.445–50) finds little plausibility in Susan Irvine's recent hypothesis that this *Life* was commissioned (*YWES* 71), and takes another look at its relation to the *Lives of Saints*. Noting that the text survives as a *passio*, as it indeed appears in the Latin source in the Corpus-Cotton Legendary, and that a reference to the *Life* in an exposition of John 12. 24–6 in Bodley 343 does not necessarily mean that the two ever formed a single composite text, Nicholls suggests that this *Life* was composed at roughly the same time as the other *Lives* in the *Lives of Saints* but omitted, perhaps due to the high number of texts for January. Another text often associated with the *Lives of Saints* is the *Legend of the Seven Sleepers*, whose relation to its sources is submitted to careful re-examination this year by Hugh Magennis in 'The Anonymous Old English *Legend of the Seven Sleepers* and its Latin Source' (*LeedsSE* 22.43–56). Magennis reviews the evidence for the knowledge of this legend in Anglo-Saxon England in both Latin and Old English, including sporadic OE references to the text, and then goes on to consider the full OE version (which is often highly imaginative in its treatment of the legend) and its Latin equivalents.

My own 'Working with Patristic Sources: Language and Context in Old English Homilies' (in *Speaking Two Languages*, ed. Frantzen) takes a broader and more theoretical overview of the homiletic genre and its relation to institutional and historical practices. I suggest that the complex apparatus of source-analysis carries with it certain disadvantages as well as its better-known merits, each of which needs further scrutiny. The traditional critical preference for the named highly scholarly author and works – Ælfric or Wulfstan – over anonymous works, for example, is not entirely supported by the manuscript evidence, while stylistic, aesthetic judgement tends to rest only on comparison of Latin source with vernacular text. Source-study, however, is an even more valuable resource if recent theoretical analyses of historicism, reception, and the contributions of historical sociolinguistics are taken into account. It is possible, for example, to redefine and explore the translation process from Latin to Old English by examining the vernacular authors use of, rather than dependence on, Latin materials. This emphasis on use helps us to rethink the reception of OE homilies in relation both to historical events such as the Benedictine Reform and in terms of their pragmatic importance as preaching texts.

Finally, Joseph McGowan reminds us of the existence of the much-neglected and fragmentary *Life of St Christopher* with a brief note offering a series of textual emendations in 'Notes on the OE Version of the *Vita Sancti Christophori*' (*Neophil* 75.451–5), while Raymond I. Page reconsiders the standard emendations of another neglected text in 'The Title of the Old English *Apollonius of Tyre*' (*ANQ* 4.171–2). Page scrutinizes the erasure in the text's rubric and points out that – though carefully executed – the rubricator has probably left the correction incomplete.

Books Reviewed

Banham, Debby, ed. *Monasteriales Indicia: The Anglo-Saxon Monastic Sign Language*. ASB. pp. 90. pb £8.95. ISBN 0 9516209 4 0.

Bitel, Lisa M. *Isles of the Saints: Monastic Settlement and Christian Community in Early Ireland*. CornUP (1990). pp. 268. $28.95. ISBN 0 8014 2471 2.

Boenig, Robert. *Saint and Hero: 'Andreas' and Medieval Doctrine*. BuckUP. pp. 133. £25. ISBN 0 8387 5187 3.

———, trans. *'The Acts of Andrew in the Country of the Cannibals': Translations from the Greek, Latin, and Old English*. Garland. pp. 121. $22.00. ISBN 0 8240 7088 7.

Bragg, Lois. *The Lyric Speakers of Old English Poetry*. FDUP. pp. 159. £24. ISBN 0 8386 3403 6.

Bremmer, Rolf H. Jr, Jan van den Berg, and David Johnson. eds. *Notes on Beowulf* Trans. from P. J. Cosijn. LTM 12. pp. 120. ISBN 0902296221.

Clark, George. *Beowulf*. Twayne. pp. 170. $25.95. ISBN 0 8057 6996 X.

Davis, R. H. C. *From Alfred the Great to Stephen*. Hambledon. pp. 318. £34.00. ISBN 1 85285 045 0.

Doane. A. N. *The Saxon Genesis: An Edition of the West Saxon 'Genesis B' and the Old Saxon Vatican 'Genesis'*. UWiscP. pp. 464. $45. ISBN 0 299 12800 8.

Franzen, Christine. *The Tremulous Hand of Worcester: A Study of Old English in the Thirteenth Century*. Clarendon. pp. 229. £40.00. ISBN 0 19 811742 6.

Frantzen, Allen J. *La littérature de la pénitence dans l'Angleterre Anglo-Saxone*. trans. Michel Lejeune. EUFS. pp. 217. ISBN 2 8271 0536 5.

———, ed. *Speaking Two Languages: Traditional Disciplines and Contemporary Theory in Medieval Studies*. SUNYP. pp. 297. pb $18.95. ISBN 0 7914 0506 0.

Fulk. R. D. ed. *Interpretations of 'Beowulf': A Critical Anthology*. IUP. pp. 282. hb $22.95, pb $10.95. ISBN 0 253 32437 8, 0 253 20639 1.

Garde, Judith N. *Old English Poetry in Medieval Christian Perspective: A Doctrinal Approach*. Brewer. pp. 232. £35.00. ISBN 0 85991 307 4.

Godden, Malcolm, and Michael Lapidge, eds. *The Cambridge Companion to Old English Literature*. CUP. pp. 298. hb £30.00, pb £10.95. ISBN 0 521 37438, 0521 377943.

Harris, Joseph, ed. *The Ballad and Oral Literature*. HarvardUP. pp. 317. hb £25.95, pb £11.95. ISBN 0 674 06045 8, 0 674 06046 6.

Hooke, Della. *Worcestershire Anglo-Saxon Charter-Bounds*. Boydell (1990). pp. 441. £45.00. ISBN 0950 3412.

Kemble, J. M., and Bill Griffiths. *Anglo-Saxon Runes*. ASB. pp. 75. pb £6.95. ISBN 0 9516209 0 8.

Kendall, Calvin B. *The Metrical Grammar of 'Beowulf'*. CASE 5. pp. 318. $59.50. ISBN 0 521 39325 6.

Kooper, Erik, ed. *This Noble Craft. Proceedings of the Xth Research Symposium of the Dutch and Belgian University Teachers of Old and Middle English and Historical Linguistics (1989)*. Rodopi. pp. 221. £20. ISBN 90 5183 299 0.

Lapidge, Michael, ed. *Anglo-Saxon Litanies of the Saints*. Henry Bradshaw Society 106. Boydell. pp. 328. £25.00. ISBN 1 870252 01 2.

———, and Michael Winterbottom, eds. *Wulfstan of Winchester: Life of St Æthelwold*. Clarendon. pp. 105. £42.50. ISBN 0 19 822266 1.

Lerer, Seth. *Literacy and Power in Anglo-Saxon Literature*. UNebP. pp. 268. $25.00. ISBN 0 8032 2895 3.

Nicholson, Lewis, ed. *The Vercelli Book Homilies: Translations from the Anglo-Saxon*. UPA. pp.170. $34.75. ISBN 0 8191 8116 1.

North, Richard. *Pagan Words and Christian Meanings*. Rodopi. pp. 198. pb £19. ISBN 90 5183 305 9.

Robinson, Fred C., and E. G. Stanley, eds. *Old English Verse Texts From Many Sources: A Comprehensive Collection*. EEMF 23. R&B. hb Dkr 12.475, pb Dkr. 10.975. ISBN 87 423 0536 5, 87 423 0538 1.

Scragg, D. G., ed. *The Battle of Maldon A. D. 991*. Blackwell. pp. 306. $52.95. ISBN 0 631 15987 8.

IV

Middle English: Excluding Chaucer

DAVID J. WILLIAMS, SUSAN POWELL, ALAN J. FLETCHER, A. S. G. EDWARDS and JULIA BOFFEY

This chapter has eleven sections: 1. General and Miscellaneous; 2. Alliterative Poetry; 3. The *Gawain*-Poet; 4. Piers Plowman; 5. Romances; 6. Gower, Lydgate, and Hoccleve; 7. Middle Scots Poetry; 8. Lyrics and Miscellaneous Verse; 9. Malory and Caxton; 10. Other Prose; 11. Drama. Sections 1 and 7 are by David J. Williams; sections 2, 4, 5, and 9 are by Susan Powell; sections 3, 10, and 11 are by Alan J. Fletcher; section 6 is by A. S. G. Edwards; section 8 is by Julia Boffey.

1. General and Miscellaneous

A collection of essays from the second York Manuscripts Conference must come first among this year's books: *Regionalism in Late Medieval Mss and Texts, Essays Celebrating the Publication of 'A Linguistic Atlas of Late Mediaeval English'*, edited by Felicity Riddy. After a brief foreword by Angus McIntosh, the first five papers 'provide models of different ways in which *LALME* can be applied to specific problems'. In 'Scribes and Manuscript Traditions', M. L. Samuels discusses texts 'translated' from one dialect to another. Scribal variation is seen as an important tool in the process of choosing the best way to edit a text. Michael Benskin explains 'The "Fit"-Technique', while Margaret Lasing discusses initial problems on the way towards a second *Atlas of Early Middle English* in 'Anchor Texts and Literary Manuscripts in Early Middle English'. Jeremy J. Smith writes on 'Tradition and Innovation in South West Midland Middle English', and Ronald Waldron on 'Dialect Aspects of Manuscripts of Trevisa's Translation of the *Polychronicon*', where he finds evidence pointing to some kind of control exercised over the practices of individual scribes copying Trevisa. Richard Beadle's 'Prolegomena to a Literary Geography of Later Medieval Norfolk' includes a list of manuscripts copied by Norfolk scribes. Peter Meredith looks at the N. Town plays manuscript, finding evidence that it repesents a process of compilation 'in which the parts are more important than the intended whole'. Colin Richmond, in 'What a Difference a Manuscript Makes: John Wyndham of Felbrigg, Norfolk (d.1475)', discusses a letter to John Paston that argues against awarding Wyndham the Norman Tebbit trophy for the nastiest self-made so-called gentleman. Julia Boffey and Carol M. Meale contribute 'Selecting the Text: Rawlinson C 86 and Some Other Books for London Readers', and John Scattergood 'The London Manuscripts of John Skelton's Poems'. Priscilla Bawcutt's paper on Dunbar manuscripts is reviewed in Section 7 below.

The papers collected in the Bennett Memorial Lectures volume, *Poetics: Theory and Practice in Medieval Literature*, (edited by Piero Boitani and Anna Torti) are mostly on Chaucer, but include Eugene Vance on '*Pearl*: Love and the Poetics of Participation', and Joerg O. Fichte on 'Grappling with Arthur or Is There an English Arthurian Verse Romance?', which pursues the definition of romance by examining transformations of the treatment of Arthur's court 'both as an actual place and as an abstract concept'. Helen Cooper's article on 'Generic Variations on the theme of Poetic and Civil Authority' has implications beyond her examples in Chaucer and Renaissance literature.

The essays in *Medieval Literature: Texts and Interpretation*, edited by Tim William Machan, are designed, as Machan says in his introduction, to 'explore the practical consequences of the relationships between textual criticism and literary interpretation'. The introduction is a valuable discussion of the theories involved in those relationships, using the contentious cases of *Piers Plowman* and the *Troilus* as his principal illustrations. Other essays are reviewed in the appropriate sections below.

The collaboratively developed volume *Speaking Two Languages: Traditional Disciplines and Contemporary Theory in Medieval Studies*, edited by Allen J. Frantzen, interprets 'critical methods as consciously chosen and spoken "languages" '. Each essay identifies distinct theoretical methodologies and explores the consequences of combining them and hence speaking two or more languages. The essays are focused on Old more often than Middle English examples, including Frantzen's introduction where the theoretical implications are nevertheless wider. In 'The Plot of *Piers Plowman* and the Contradictions of Feudalism', Britton J. Harwood aims to bring into relation with each other 'the history of texts and political and economic history', and begins by a critical examination of what he sees as the consequences of keeping the two separate, using as examples the work of Anna P. Baldwin and Myra Stokes. His own investigation begins from a search, in the manner of Macherey, for fissures, disparities in the text. Karma Lochrie's 'The Language of Transgression: Body, Flesh, and the Word in Mystical Discourse' argues that Kristeva's concept of abjection 'offers mystical scholarship a whole new area of study concerned with the practice of mystical discourse.'

Three books concerned with the theory of medieval literature have particular relevance to Middle English Studies. In *Truth and Convention in the Middle Ages: Rhetoric, Representation, and Reality*, Ruth Morse's specific concern is with medieval writers and readers of history, but the questions she asks of them have obvious wider application as an approach to medieval representation and intertextuality: 'What is it they mean when they appear not to mean what they say? Can we tell when that is? If representations are not literally true, how are they true?' She begins with an account of the tradition of rhetorical education and textual commentary, whence comes the 'familiar scheme of categories of style, method, and organization' which Morse argues is the basis of meaning in the period. Then comes a sceptical survey of the literary forms used by historians: what can look 'true' (or otherwise) is actually put there to make a point according to rhetorical rules. There are hints throughout of 'the conventional fallacy' as defined by John Burrow; it is not always clear why something should be considered false, even if analogues are to be found, why exactly we should doubt the linguistic ability of Charlemagne. Yet that chapter on biography is typically full of interest, with its reflections on the history of 'character'. Morse's disclaimers at the beginning and end show her awareness of the dangers of 'just another reconstruction of the past in our own image'. There are useful examples in each chapter, and the intention to add Latin and vernacular historians to the medieval authors normally studied by literary scholars must be applauded.

Rita Copeland's interests overlap with Morse's at many points in *Rhetoric, Hermeneutics and Translation in the Middle Ages*. Translation, in particular, the subject of one of Morse's chapters, is here the core of a study of the development of medieval vernacular writing out of an appropriation of the modes of academic discourse in the privileged sphere of Latin learning. Copeland sets out to describe the relationship between rhetoric and hermeneutics 'as critical practices'. She begins with the classical context, and the peculiar circumstances of the conflict between the claims of grammar and rhetoric in which the theory of translation was generated. Translation is seen, then and later, to be a manifestation as much of distance from, as of kinship with, the original, so that the book is a history of the increasing independence of translations and commentaries from their source texts as 'exegesis assumes the force of rhetorical performance'. Chapters on the *Ovide moralisé*, Martianus Capella, and the French and English traditions of translation and commentary on *The Consolation of Philosophy*, lead on to concluding examinations of the exegetical structures of *The Legend of Good Women* and the *Confessio Amantis*. It is a consistently rewarding book in detail, if the more general theoretical formulations are initially a little forbidding,

Robert S. Sturges's *Medieval Interpretation: Models of Reading in Literary Narrative 1100–1500* is concerned with French as well as English literature. It makes a cautious comparison of the medieval with the postmodern in studying two modes of thought in the Middle Ages about meaning and interpretation, which Sturges calls 'determinate and indeterminate' and sees as being in competition, especially in the fourteenth century. His English examples are in Chaucer and Malory.

A large proportion of the year's articles are manuscript studies in a variety of fields. Alan J. Fletcher gives us '*Magnus predicator et deuotus*: A Profile of the Life, Work, and Influence of the Fifteenth-Century Oxford Preacher, John Felton' (*MS* 53.125–75). Fletcher gives evidence to support the belief that the vicar of St Mary Magdalen, Oxford (1397–1434) was born in Northumberland, by investigating written dialects of the Middle English verses in his *Sermones dominicales*. Some show strong Northern characteristics, especially Oxford, Oriel College 10, which evidence suggests is the most faithful to the author's original. The article includes editions of two sermons; a portion of another together with an English reworking of it by the Gloucester redactor; the English verses from the *Sermones*.

Andrew Taylor's engaging search for 'The Myth of the Minstrel Manuscript' (*Speculum* 66.43–73) challenges the widespread assumption that there exists a body of manuscripts that once belonged to minstrels, starting with the example of the Oxford *Roland* manuscript, and continuing with texts (and claims) for Middle English romances and lyrics. Just about the only scrap to survive the interview is Bodley's Rawlinson D 913 which bears the contentious 'Maiden in the Moor'. Taylor argues that the codicological category 'minstrel text' grew from a stereotype, 'a romantic vision of the minstrel as penniless wanderer', whereas evidence shows that minstrels, far from living 'in a world of their own', were part of the community, leading 'stable, prosperous lives', and displaying 'pious and sophisticated' tastes. 'The hope for direct access to medieval oral narrative must be postponed.'

John B. Friedman, in '*Dies boni et mali, obitus, et contra hec remedium*: Remedies for Fortune in Some Late Medieval Manuscripts', (*JEGP* 90.311–26)

discusses a neglected genre that deals with fortunes, such matters as propitious and unpropitious days, and critical ages for death or sickness. The genre specifies counter measures against bad fortune in the form of magical texts, *nomina sacra*, and letters of the alphabet, and constitutes evidence of connexions between Late Antique syncretism, medieval charms, and the Humanistic interest in hieroglyphs.

George Jack examines 'The Language of the Early Middle English Texts in MS Royal 17. A. xxvii', which contains versions of *Juliene*, *Sawles Warde*, etc. (*SN* 63.128–42) and concludes that it 'seems likely to represent for the most part a single variety of ME'. John Thompson's case studies in 'Textual Instability and the Late Medieval Reputation of Some Middle English Religious Literature' (*Text* 5.175–94) attempt to understand the late medieval reader's experience in 'the complicated world in which religious literature was disseminated and read'.

Julia Crick follows her catalogue of the manuscripts of Geoffrey's *Historia* with a comprehensive and detailed study of the the development of the text, its circulation and reception, in *The Historia Regum Britannie of Geoffrey of Monmouth, IV: Dissemination and Reception in the Later Middle Ages*. Her evidence shows that 'despite its potential as an entertaining narrative, [the *Historia*] circulated, both in and outside Britain, by virtue of its functional value', and has much to tell us about the nature of history, and of other genres of writing, as understood by readers and authors in the MA.

Another approach to histories is 'The Presence of Rome in the Middle English Chronicles of the Fourteenth Century' (*JEGP* 90.187–207) by Caroline D. Eckhardt who considers the 'complex influence of Latinity' on those few chroniclers writing in English in the period, including their indebtedness to Geoffrey of Monmouth, and finds, as well as the evident strength of Rome in their works, a resistance to it in their structure, language, and style.

'Reinstating the female subject', Jocelyn Wogan-Browne, in 'Saints' Lives and the Female Reader' (*FMLS* 27.314–32), asks how the stories of persecution and torture were meant to affect the female audience, and discovers the unexpected presence of laughter among the appropriate responses. Her argument suggests a way to 'recover texts previously dismissed as too fantastical to be taken seriously'. She considers the degree of stylization in the violence, and finds a 'metonymic link between literary conventions and social conditions'. A reading of *Cligès* proposes a connexion between the genres of romance and hagiography, rather than the usual distinctions between them.

Although primarily concerned with Germany, Joachim Bumke's *Courtly Culture: Literature and Society in the High Middle Ages*, now translated by Thomas Dunlap, is an accessibly written book of much wider interest for students of medieval literature and history in general, as a critical exploration of courtly writing as a historical source.

France and the British Isles in the Middle Ages and the Renaissance, edited by Gillian Jondorf and D. N. Dumville, is a collection mainly on historical literature from the eighth to seventeenth century. The one item of interest to students of Middle English here is M. E. J. Hughes's survey of the variety of late fourteenth-century political poetry in 'Counselling the King: Perceptions of Court Politics in Poetry of the Reign of Richard II'.

A number of other books not directly relevant to Middle English studies may nevertheless be of interest: *Dante as Dramatist: The Myth of the Earthly Paradise and Tragic Vision in the Divine Comedy* by Franco Masciandaro; *Dante and Ovid: Essays in Intertextuality* by Madison U. Sowell; *Lorenzo de' Medici, Selected Poems and Prose*, edited in translation by Jon Thiem.

2. Alliterative Poetry

The culmination of Thomas Cable's work on the metre of alliterative poetry appears this year as a comprehensive and radical account of *The English Alliterative Tradition*. Rewriting the Old Philology of Oakden's *Alliterative Poetry in Middle English*, Cable's 'New Philology' most radically rejects the continuity of the alliterative tradition and reinstates the final *-e*. The bulk of the book deals with the medieval period (two chapters on Old and Early Middle English metre and two on fourteenth-century metre), but there is a fifth chapter on the modern period and a summary on the theoretical implications of Cable's thesis which provide controversial and demanding reading for anyone interested in metrics of whatever period.

Lesley Johnson's 'Tracking Layamon's *Brut*' (*LeedsSE* 22.139–65) is an assessment of past and present critical attention paid to Laȝamon's poem. Essentially a review of the recent edition by Barron and Weinberg (*YWES* 70.183) and the recent critique of Le Saux (*YWES* 70.183–4), and set in context by a lively and perceptive survey of Laȝamon scholarship, Johnson suggests the issue of national identity as one of contemporary relevance which might well be explored further in relation to Laȝamon's poem.

3. The *Gawain*-poet

1991 has been a productive year, with three books and several articles. Though marred by unfortunate misprints, *Text and Matter: New Critical Perspectives on the Pearl-Poet*, edited by Robert J. Blanch, Miriam Youngerman Miller and Julian N. Wasserman, contains some stimulating new contributions on the works of the *Gawain*-poet. 'The *Pearl* Dreamer and the Eleventh Hour', by Lynn Staley Johnson, is a sensitive, if somewhat diffuse, examination of the use of time in *Pearl*. Paul F. Reichardt writes on 'Animal Similes in *Pearl*', and on what he perceives their function and significance to be. Not everyone will find this article persuasive. Jane Chance investigates 'Allegory and Structure in *Pearl*: The Four Senses of the *Ars Praedicandi* and Fourteenth-Century Homiletic Poetry'. She emphasizes the tripartite divisions into which the poem has often been apportioned by critics, and seeks to offer a 'coherent and figurative justification' for them. She believes that the three levels of medieval exegesis above the *sensus litteralis* underlie and explain the three divisions. Britton J. Harwood makes an interesting case for 'The *Pearl* as Diptych'. He suggests that diptychs in the poet's material culture may have inspired a bipartite, chiastic structure in *Pearl*. Charlotte Gross argues well that 'Courtly Language in *Pearl*', as used by the dreamer, is deliberately inappropriate to the spiritual world that ought to be his concern, and that it registers his misapprehension of that world's values. In '*Cleanness* and the Terms of Terror', David Wallace suggests that the preoccupation of the *moderni* in the fourteenth century with the question of how personal salvation might be achieved has been reflected in strategies for striking terror in the reader adopted by the author of *Cleanness*. 'In God's Sight: Vision and Sacred History in *Purity*', by Sarah Stanbury, seeks to explore the thematic implications of the beatific vision and the relationship of this image to the poem's historical and narrative structures. Michael W. Twomey finds 'The Sin of *Untrawþe* in *Cleanness*' to reside in deviation from heterosexual norms and from loyalty to God. The poem's concern with *trawþe* is typical of other late-fourteenth century works. In 'The Impatient Reader of *Patience*', C. David Benson argues that the poet traps readers into experiencing that very impatience berated in the poem when they find themselves impatient with Jonah. 'The "Poynt" of *Patience*', by Lorraine Kochanske Stock, suggests how the characterization of Jonah in *Patience* may have been shaped as an example of the vice of *acedia* or sloth. '*þis Wrech Man in Warlowes Guttez*: Imagery and Unity of Frame and Tale in *Patience*', by George D. Schmidt, focuses on the poem's use of imagery to underline traditional meanings of the Jonah story, and on how the imagery also collaborates in the poem's themes of poverty and patience. John Plummer, in 'Signifying the Self: Language and Identity in *Sir Gawain and the Green Knight*', finds the subject of *Sir Gawain and the Green Knight* to be words themselves, the linguistic medium in which identities are created, modified or destroyed. This essay, unobtrusively informed by modern semiotic theory, makes compelling reading. Kathleen M. Ashley makes a case in 'Bonding and Signification in *Sir Gawain and the Green Knight*' that although *Sir Gawain and the Green Knight* problematizes acts of interpretation, it leads readers to acknowledge ambiguity, and ultimately to understand the need for active reinterpretation. Ross G. Arthur considers 'Gawain's Shield as *Signum*'. He argues for a dual significance, that it stands for the eternal truth of God and for the mutable faith of humans. Though overabundant in the range of meanings that it offers, the poem nevertheless does not offer readers *carte blanche*, but anticipates, indeed expects, a particular sort of structuring collaboration from them. Finally, Victoria L. Weiss compares '*Sir Gawain and the Green Knight* and the Fourteenth-Century Interlude'. She believes that like interludes, *Sir Gawain and the Green Knight* also trades upon the blurred distinction between the illusory play world and reality in the entry of the Green Knight into Camelot.

The second of the books this year is exclusively on *Sir Gawain and the Green Knight*. Gerald Morgan has gathered together much of his thinking on this poem in *Sir Gawain and the Green Knight and the Idea of Righteousness*. Some of its substance has appeared in print in articles before, and the book generally runs true to what we have come to expect of Morgan: the poem is viewed through the lens of scholasticism in order to uncover its shaping idea. Chapter one outlines the scholastic view of art, a view which recuperates that very notion of authorial intention that much postmodern theory has tried to kill off. It then proceeds to consider the hunting and bedroom scenes of the poem in some detail. Chapter two considers the reputation of Camelot, finding no criticism offered to the court, youthful and headstrong though it may be. Chapter three, countering much prevailing critical opinion, seeks to establish clarity, rather than ambiguity, in the Green Knight's portrait, and makes a sensible case for his handsomeness, as opposed to the (surely mistaken) grotesqueness that some critics have emphasized. The pentangle and its symbolic expression of the idea of the poem is treated in chapter four. Chapter five returns to the bedroom and hunting scenes, stressing the need to respect the primacy of action before character in any interpretation of these interrelated episodes which wishes to avoid anachronism. In chapter six Morgan turns to the definition of Gawain's fault. He presents a means of reconciling Gawain's failure to exchange the lady's girdle with Bertilak with the fact of his unblemished confession before leaving Hautdesert for the Green Chapel: quite simply, a penitent unaware of a moral lapse may still make a good confession if he is genuinely unaware of the lapse. Gawain's self-reproach for covetousness and cowardice is also explicated. The final chapter considers the judgement of Gawain's conduct. Even were we to haggle over points of detail in his interpretation, Morgan's work remains compelling, and a triumph of that common sense which, in some quarters at least, it has proved fashionable to theorize out of existence. Nowhere is this more evident than in the persuasive lucidity of Morgan's style and argument.

Sarah Stanbury's *Seeing the Gawain Poet* contains four central chapters, each on one of the four poems of Cotton Nero A. x, with an introduction and conclusion. Some of the matter has appeared in print before (see *YWES* 68.148), but this is substantially a new study, concerned chiefly with moments of perception and visual description in the four poems: her interest is in 'what is seen, how its properties are organized and placed spatially, who is seeing and from what precise visual vantage the viewer is positioned'. Moreover, the visual poetics of the poems are held to manifest a scepticism about knowing through the sense of sight. This scepticism is judged akin to epistemological questionings topical in the fourteenth century, about the limitations of sensory experience as a way of knowing. Though sometimes unnecessarily cumbersome both in expression and method, the book nevertheless holds tight to the text and has some interesting points to make.

We pass now to the sundry articles. In '*Sir Gawain and the Green Knight*: To Behead or Not to Behead – That *is* a Question' (*PQ* 70.1–12), Sheri Ann Strite points out that in contrast to the beheading analogues, nowhere in the exchange of blows agreement is it clearly stated that Gawain should necessarily behead the Green Knight. This reticence she proceeds to interpret in an interesting, if somewhat elaborate, way: Gawain's interpretation of the exchange agreement, his choice to turn it into a beheading on the chance that it might save his life, is itself available for interpretation as yet another example in the poem of the moral repercussions consequent on the making of choices. Geraldine Heng's 'Feminine Knots and the Other *Sir Gawain and the Green Knight*' (*PMLA* 106.500–14) seeks to retrieve a feminine text in *Sir Gawain and the Green Knight*, siting it at those moments where the poem's logic, the stage of the masculine actors in the text, falters and unravels. The intricate relationship between the four women of the poem cast the shadow of another 'endeles knot', this time a feminine one. The pentangle is presented as an oversimplification that must fail (curiously, Heng has failed to engage with any of Gerald Morgan's work in this area), while the girdle is an undersimplification, something approaching an allegory of language and an apt demonstration of the properties of the linguistic signifier, 'a signifier for the signifier, no less'. Gawain is marked and re-marked, first by the pentangle, and then by the girdle, the signature of the feminine text.

'*Pearl*'s Imperfection' (*SN* 63.57–67), by David Carson, provides three notes on the poem, yoked by a conclusion. First, he believes that the 'lost' line *472 of the poem was a strategic flaw; second, that the failure of the poem's stanzaic concatenation at line 721 is a deliberate expression of a thematically crucial point; and third, that none of the six stanzas of section 15, unusual in having six rather than five as have all other sections, can be regarded as otiose. His conclusion is that formal imperfections in the poem enact a humble awareness of the impossibility of humans ever to aspire to spiritual perfection unaided. Robert J. Blanch has produced a 'Supplement to the *Gawain*-Poet: An Annotated Bibliography, 1978–1985' (*ChauR* 25.363–86). Morton Donner's abstemiously grammatical study of 'The *Gawain*-Poet's Adverbs' (*ChauR* 26.65–82) is welcome for its critical objectivity, and justifies its claim that attention to 'matters of grammar can indeed be matters of poetry'.

In 'Interpretive Laughter in *Sir Gawain and the Green Knight*' (*PQ* 70:141–7), Robert Longsworth points out the pervasiveness of laughter in the poem, and sees it as frustrating the task of interpretation: is the laughter of approval or derision, for example? It is often hard to tell, and such ambiguities appropriately mock a reader's search for interpretive certitudes. In 'The Romance of Exchange: *Sir Gawain and the Green Knight*' (*Viator* 22.251–66), Stephanie Trigg treads wisely in her account of contemporary medievalists' negotiations with the past, and proceeds to argue for a particular form of exchange between the poem's narrative structure and the semiotic questions it raises. In addition, she investigates the exchanges made between the text and the contexts which produced it.

'Containment of Anger in the Medieval Poem, *Patience*' (*ELN* 29.1–14), by Carol V. Polhi, sees Jonah in *Patience* as 'a negative verbal sign, a figure whose angry flight from Jehovah points to the narrator's involvement in the emotion being disparaged', and in the poem generally an enclosure or containment of anger experienced alike by Jonah and the narrator. Adam Brooke Davis attempts to isolate 'What the Poet of *Patience* really did to the Book of Jonah' (*Viator* 22:267–78), and to illustrate in the process how *Patience* shows similar thematic concerns to *Pearl* and *Sir Gawain and the Green Knight.*

4. Piers Plowman

Two successive publications of *YLS* became available to me for review this year. Half of *YLS* 4 is taken up with a detailed analysis of 'The Illustrations of *Piers Plowman* in Bodleian Library MS Douce 104' by Kathleen L. Scott. This is the only manuscript with a cycle of illustrations, and thirty of the seventy-two miniatures are reproduced here, together with Scott's comprehensive description and discussion of all seventy-two of them. Two more articles complete the lengthier contributions to the volume. In 'The "Hungry Gap", Crop Failure, and Famine: The Fourteenth-Century Agricultural Crisis and *Piers Plowman*', Robert Worth Frank, Jr. interestingly investigates the effect of these three sources of fourteenth-century famine on social and moral issues raised by Langland in his poem (he and his contemporaries 'rarely managed to disentangle economics from morality'). In 'The Relationship of *Richard the Redeless* and *Mum and the Sothsegger*: Some New Evidence', Helen Barr uses computer technology to investigate the metre and language of the two poems and comes to the generally accepted conclusion that they are separate works. Amongst its notes, the volume includes 'A Simoniacal Moment in *Piers Plowman*', in which Alan J. Fletcher looks at the collusion of pardoner and priest in the Prologue to *Piers Plowman*; 'Reason's Horse', where J. A. Burrow provides an ingenious but dubious explanation of Reason's horse in Passus 4; '*Piers Plowman* A.5.155: "Pyenye" ', where Ralph Hanna III too stretches our credulity, here on the subject of Gluttony's eating habits; and 'Revisions in the Athlone Editions of the A and B Versions of *Piers Plowman*', where Kathleen M. Hewett-Smith provides a welcome but previously unavailable list of the revisions made in A and B when they were reissued in 1988. These turn out to be surprisingly minor – A's revisions largely involve lighter punctuation (but were accompanied by typographical errors which Hewett-Smith also lists), whereas B's revisions amounted to only one change. The volume also contains a review article, reviews, and the bibliography for 1989.

YLS 5 contains more articles than *YLS* 4, and they are in general not only shorter but also less rewarding. As a memorial volume, it begins with an appreciation of Robert E. Kaske by Fred C. Robinson, and several of the articles emphasize the contributors' appreciation of Kaske's personality and scholarship. They begin with 'Editing and the Limitations of the Durior Lectio', a well-substantiated warning by Robert Adams against the blanket application of the harder-reading theory. In ' "For God is After an Hand": *Piers Plowman* B.17.138–205', Frederick M. Biggs argues that Langland has altered the usual identification of the Holy Ghost from the finger to the palm of the hand in order to emphasize its centrality to the Samaritan's discussion. Helen Cooper argues in 'Gender and Personification in *Piers Plowman*' that Langland radically re-genders traditionally female personifications because he is culturally constrained to see his abstractions as projections of his male dreamer. Patrick J. Gallacher in 'Imagination, Prudence, and the *Sensus Communis*' emphasises Imaginatif's function as the sense experience which is directed by prudence. Thomas D. Hill discusses 'Universal Salvation and Its Literary Context in *Piers Plowman* B.18' and suggests that Langland's seemingly heterodox offer of mercy to all those in hell shows his 'deeply individual response to a difficult and perhaps unanswerable eschatological problem'. In ' "Persen with a Pater-Noster Paradys Oper Hevene": *Piers Plowman* C.11.296–98a', David F. Johnson relates Langland's alteration of the passage to a wish to tone down earlier radical theological statements. James H. Morey investigates 'The Fall in Particulate' in texts outside *Piers Plowman* and the precipitate fall in *Piers Plowman* itself. John Ruffing looks at 'The Crucifixion Drink in Piers Plowman B.18 and C.20' and sees the drink's death-retarding influence in the C-text as Satan's attempt to postpone his own downfall. Raymond St-Jacques provides a detailed discussion of 'Langland's *Christus Medicus* Image and the Structure of *Piers Plowman*'. Howard H. Schless investigates the respective allegorical methods of Langland and Dante in 'The Backgrounds of Allegory: Langland and Dante', and Lorraine Kochanske Stock, in 'Parable, Allegory, History, and *Piers Plowman*', argues for the centrality to the poem of the parable of the wheat and the tares. Michael W. Twomey traces the origins of 'Christ's Leap and Mary's Clean Catch in *Piers Plowman* B.12.136–44a and C.14.81–88a'. Míceál F. Vaughan in ' "Til I gan awake": The Conversion of Dreamer into Narrator in *Piers Plowman* B' argues that the first lines of the poem serve as the statement of contrition for previous sin which then leads into the confession which is the poem itself. The volume is also supplied with reviews and a bibliography for 1990.

In *The England of 'Piers Plowman'*, F. R. H. Du Boulay seeks to explain the England of the fourteenth century and Langland's role in it. Du Boulay is an historian, and his is an old-fashioned, sensible, and rather endearing account. The book demonstrates the approach whereby literature is scoured for what it is assumed to tell us of history, and du Boulay always takes the text at face value. His approach will do no harm and may introduce to the poem the layman or the young historian.

Steven F. Kruger's enigmatic title, 'Mirrors and the Trajectory of Vision in *Piers Plowman*' (*Speculum* 66.74–95), refers to the central thesis of his article, that dreams can act as mirrors with which medieval writers explore the trajectories of vision which lead either up to divine knowledge or down to the mundane. Kruger develops a complex pattern of trajectories which, he says, is part of a larger pattern of ambivalences in *Piers Plowman*, 'a pattern that repeatedly shows ideals corrupted by mundane reality and transcendent truths failing to meet the needs of humankind'. Ambivalence is also investigated by Britton J. Harwood in 'Dame Study and the Place of Orality in *Piers Plowman*' (*ELH* 57.1–17), though Harwood confines his range to the ambivalent attitude to literacy he finds Langland displaying in his representation of Dame Study's preoccupation with orality. In 'Piers or Will: Confusion of Identity in the Early Reception of *Piers Plowman*' (*MÆ* 60.273–84), J. R. Thorne argues that both early and late manuscript and printed book tradition privileges Piers over Will and confuses the two identities. Finally, Alan J. Fletcher writes interestingly on the significance of 'The hideous feet of Langland's peacock' (*NQ* 38.18–20) in the B-text of the poem.

Finally, in *This Noble Craft*, edited by Erik Kooper, Roger Eaton ('Langland's Malleable Lady Meed') argues that the ambiguity of Lady Meed, her seeming potential for good or ill, 'is resolved and the possiblity of a dual nature repudiated'.

Eaton also wants to define her 'not as wealth or material reward ... but as a false vision of reward'.

5. Romances

In his introduction to *Romance in Medieval England*, Maldwyn Mills, one of the book's three editors, rightly praises the liveliness of current romance research, which is clearly demonstrated by this collection of papers from the 1988 Gregynog conference. There are stimulating essays from the book's other two editors, Jennifer Fellows and Carol M. Meale. In 'Editing Middle English Romances', Fellows presents a rigorous analysis of the editorial methods available to romance editors and the reason why emendation might be necessary, and argues very sensibly and cogently against 'an excessively conservative scribolatry' – 'if we try to reduce every Middle English romance to a single "correct" version, we shall lose a great deal.' Meale provides a thorough description of the decorative scheme found in 'The Morgan Library copy of *Generides*' and discusses its history in East Anglia and the book-buying habits of East Anglian families. The standard set by the editors is maintained in the other contributions. In 'Collecting Middle English romances and some related book production activities in the later Middle Ages', John J. Thompson ranges widely in his discussion of the codicological factors affecting our understanding of three romance collections (the Thornton and Findern manuscripts, and Advocates MS 19.3.1) and concludes that their use as evidence of a collecting aim or even interest is fraught with problems. On the other hand, in her thorough investigation of just one manuscript ('The Percy Folio manuscript revisited'), Gillian Rogers does find herself able to come to some conclusions about the interests of the manuscript's antiquarian compiler. On similar lines, Lynne S. Blanchfield looks at the influence of Rate, the scribe of Ashmole 61, on the transmission of the manuscript's five romances and suggests that they show a greater coherence of purpose than has previously been assumed, having been reshaped by Rate in order to instruct the family unit in the devotional life. Blanchfield also suggests ('in a spirit of enquiry rather than of solution') an interesting connection between Rate and the Corpus Christi Guild in Leicester. In 'Northern *Octavian* and the question of class', John Simons argues that the text, whose archetype dates from just after the Black Death, reveals in the relationship of Florent and Clement the central elements of class-consciousness which that event generated. S. H .A. Shepherd in ' "This grete journee": *The Sege of Melayne*' argues strongly that the romance is better understood by comparison with medieval crusade propaganda than with other Charlemagne romances. Rosamund Allen provides 'Female perspectives in romance and history', suggesting that Laȝamon's women are more interesting than his men and better motivated than in Geoffrey and Wace, while Judith Weiss also highlights the dominant female when she looks at the recurrent figure of 'The wooing woman in Anglo-Norman romance'. In 'Romance as history, history as romance', Rosalind Field looks at the relationship between romance and history in the Matter of England romances of the thirteenth and fourteenth centuries and their Anglo-Norman predecessors. She rejects the romances as historical narratives, part of an assumed search for national identity, and instead argues energetically for their essentially literary qualities. Finally, the last two essays investigate conventional romance motifs – David Burnley the motif of 'Comforting the troops: an epic moment in popular romance' and Elizabeth Williams that of 'Hunting the deer: some uses of a motif-complex in Middle English romance and saint's life'.

Elizabeth Archibald's *Apollonius of Tyre* provides a definitive study of the Apollonius story, together with a text of the *Historia Apollonii*, with *en face* translation, and appendices of Latin and vernacular versions and medieval and Renaissance allusions. Archibald argues reasonably convincingly that, despite all appearance to the contrary, the *Historia* is a single narrative with some structural cohesiveness. Indeed, its extraordinarily long-lasting and far-ranging popularity may well be explained by its episodic and many-themed nature (though this is perhaps an over-positive interpretation of Archibald's comments on the story's success, which she explains by 'its indeterminate genre and lack of explicit motivation or moralization.').

A. C. Spearing writes interestingly and astutely on 'Marie de France and her Middle English Adapters' (*SAC* 12.117–56), comparing three Middle English romances (*Lai le Freine*, *Sir Landevale*, and Thomas Chestre's *Sir Launfal*) with the *lais* from which they derive.

Finally, L. O. Purdon looks at the two occurrences of ' "Ne yaf he nouth a stra" in *Havelok*' (*PQ* 69.377–83) and shows that they refer to the actual feudal act of renunciation (*exfestucatio*), which involved the throwing away of the straw or *festuca*. Though a metaphor in the poem, the image also 'serves to remind the audience of the feudal dimension of the earl's act of renunciation.'

6. Gower, Lydgate and Hoccleve

Gower studies continue their steady rate of growth, not least because of the tireless energy of R. F. Yeager, who has edited *Chaucer and Gower: Difference, Mutuality, Exchange*. This contains six essays examining different aspects of the relationship between the two poets. The most ambitious are the opening essays by Winthrop Wetherbee and A. J. Minnis. Wetherbee ('Latin Structure and Vernacular Space: Gower, Chaucer and the Boethian Tradition') sees in Boethius' *Consolation of Philosophy* a dialogic model represented in the *Confessio* in the relationship between Gower's English text and its Latin apparatus. Genius provides the link between these alternative linguistic worlds. Minnis ('*De Vulgari Auctoritate*: Chaucer, Gower and Men of Great Authority') offers a wide-ranging comparison of Chaucer's and Gower's conceptions of the role of the author, emphasizing Gower's use of the 'vocabulary and techniques of medieval commentary on Latin *auctores*' as well as his lengthy Prologue to 'authorize' his text. Several other essays examine more particular aspects of the relationship between Chaucer and Gower. Peter Nicholson examines Chaucer's and Gower's versions of the Tale of Constance ('Chaucer Borrows from Gower: The Sources of the *Man of Law's Tale*'), in which he speculates that Chaucer may have obtained his copy of Trivet from Gower. Nicholson explores other aspects of the same issue in an article on 'The Man of Law's Tale: What Chaucer Really Owed to Gower' (*ChauR* 23.163–81). The latter article argues that Gower's influence on Chaucer's Tale is much greater than has previously been acknowledged, and is much more significant that the few verbal borrowings previously noted. He suggests that 'Gower provided Chaucer's most significant model ... it was Gower's tale rather than Trevet's that Chaucer told to retell.' Chauncey Wood ('Chaucer's Most "Gowerian' Tale") urges the Parson's Tale as the one that comes closest to Gower's moral orientation. Peter G. Beidler ('Transformations in Gower's *Tale of Florent* and Chaucer's *Wife of Bath's Tale*') offers a detailed comparison of these two narratives. R. F. Yeager ('Learning to read in Tongues: Writing Poetry for a Trilingual Culture') examines some of the implications in the *Confessio* of the 'polylinguistic fluidity' of the late fourteenth century. Carolyn Dinshaw ('Rivalry, Rape and Manhood: Gower and Chaucer') yokes together rather unconvincingly the tradition of Chaucer's quarrel with Gower and Gower's *Tale of Philomela*.

Two other studies examine specific narratives in the *Confessio*. Craig Bertolet 'From Revenge to Reform: The Changing Face of 'Lucrece' and its Meaning in Gower's *Confessio Amantis*' (*PQ* 70.251–75) relates Gower's narrative to the larger preoccupations with kingship in Book VII. Elizabeth Archibald in *Apollonius of Tyre* has a brief discussion of Gower's narrative. Eichi Kobayashi's *The Story of Apollonius of Tyre in Old and Middle English* reprints Gower's narrative with a glossary. James Dean in 'Gower, Chaucer, and Rhyme Royal' (*SP* 88.251–75) finds a significant debt to Chaucer in Gower's use of rhyme royal in some of his French works, his 'Praise of Peace' and 'Amans' supplication in the *Confessio Amantis* (8:2217–2300). Nicolette Zeeman in 'The Verse of Courtly Love in the Framing Narrative of the *Confessio Amantis*' (*MÆ* 66.283–300) suggests that various traditions of such narratives are invoked in the *Confessio* to ultimately 'destabilize many assumptions encouraged in the preceding narrative' and to demonstrate the delusiveness of any courtly love narrative, including Gower's own. The final chapter of Rita Copeland's *Rhetoric, Hermeneutics and Translation in the Middle Ages* is concerned in part with the *Confessio* and examines the rhetorical functions of the text's *ordinatio*, its prologues and the figure of Genius, as well as the rhetorical principles of *compilatio* and *divisio*.

Lydgate studies are largely concerned with manuscript matters. George Keiser in '*Ordinatio* in the Manuscripts of John Lydgate's *Lyf of Our Lady*: Its Value for the Reader, Its Challenge for the Modern Editor' (in *Medieval Literature: Texts and Interpretation*) discusses the editorial implications of the *ordinatio* of some of the manuscripts of *The Life of Our Lady*. A. S. G. Edwards in 'Beinecke MS 661 and Early Fifteenth-Century English Manuscript Production' (*YULG* 66.181–96) discusses several manuscripts of *The Siege of Thebes*, written by Stephen Doddesham. The only extended critical article by Rosamund Allen is also on this poem (*Chaucer and Fifteenth-Century Poetry*), which she contextualizes primarily in terms of Chaucerian reception. Janet Cowen in 'Women as Exempla in Fifteenth-Century Verse of the Chaucerian tradition' comments briefly and perceptively on the treatment of the Jason and Medea story in Lydgate's *Troy Book* and *Fall of Princes* (*Chaucer and Fifteenth-Century Poetry*).

Interest in Hoccleve remains steady. James Simpson in 'Madness and Texts: Hoccleve's *Series*' (*Chaucer and Fifteenth-Century Poetry*) challenges conventional readings of Hoccleve's persona, one which he sees as constructed 'to create new models of personality, unauthorized by literary tradition.' Anna Torti has an extensive analysis of the *Regement of Princes* in *The Glass of Form* in which she suggests the interconnectedness of prologue and narrative in Hoccleve's poem through 'the fusion of his personal anxieties with the traditional presentation of *exempla*' to Prince Henry. D. R. Carlson, 'Thomas Hoccleve and the Chaucer Portrait,' (*HLQ* 54.283–300) argues for a relationship between early Chaucer portraits, particularly those in Hoccleve's *Regement*, and Hoccleve's attempts to establish his work in a relationship to that of his 'master' Chaucer. Janet Cowen in 'Women as Exempla in Fifteenth-Century Verse of the Chaucerian tradition' discusses Hoccleve's *Tale Jereslaus' Wife* in terms of the influence on it of Chaucer's *Legend of Good Women* (*Chaucer and Fifteenth-Century Poetry*).

7. Middle Scots Poetry

A number of illuminating articles appear in *Chaucer and Fifteenth-Century Poetry*, edited by Julia Boffey and Janet Cowen. Julia Boffey herself, in 'Chaucerian Prisoners: the Context of *The Kingis Quair*', conducts a fruitful exploration of the use made by a number of authors of the motif of imprisonment, 'a cluster of related structural, rhetorical and metaphorical possibilities' embodied for them partly in Chaucer's influential works. Reference to Charles d'Orléans, George Ashby, Thomas Usk, and of course Boethius, leads on to the *Quair*, where the Boethian parallels are modified 'by their incorporation into the model of an individual history'. The genre of prison complaint or consolation seems to have attracted poets concerned to connect 'texts with life and texts with other texts'.

Also reading James I, Robert Easting remarks on 'Another Borrowing from Chaucer's *Troilus* in *The Kingis Quair*'(*N&Q* 38.161). Not only does King James's stanza about Venus's little 'retrete' echo the temples of Venus in *The Knight's Tale* and the *Parliament of Fowls*, qualified as usual by James's softening of Chaucer's portrayal of the 'goddesse of delyte', but the qualification itself is an echo of the *Troilus* iii, 1361–3, allying this presentation of Venus with Troilus's experience of the supreme delights of love. It is symptomatic of James's imaginative debt to Chaucer that he amalgamates three separate Chaucerian moments in one stanza.

Henrietta Twycross-Martin, in 'Moral Pattern in *The Testament of Cresseid*', (*Chaucer and Fifteenth-Century Poetry*) studies the poem's relationship with Chaucer's *Troilus*, especially but not only Book V, a relationship that shows a great debt but also on examination differentiates the two poets' achievements. She argues that Henryson's moral about the necessity for fidelity in love, a narrower concern than that of Chaucer with the nature of love itself, is focused only on this world. She finds a 'pejorative' element in the portrayal of the narrator, and that, less detached than Chaucer's, this narrator and his subject matter, both 'inhabit the same imaginative universe, the one reacting upon the other'. The possibility is canvassed that 'Henryson is not merely imitating rhetorical patterns, but is using specific stylistic devices to recall precise moments in Book V' of the *Troilus*.

David J. Parkinson takes a different approach to 'Henryson's Scottish Tragedy' (*ChauR* 25.355–62), seeking to relate it to the nature of Middle Scots poetry in general, as he sees it, characterized by violent change, vigorous and disciplined verse, the narrative and imagery of exile. Parkinson finds that 'Cresseid's dying aspiration challenged the Middle Scots tradition to take the outcast seriously'.

Chaucer's *Knight's Tale*, noted as an influence by Twycross-Martin, appears again in Jane Roberts's reflections 'On Rereading Henryson's *Orpheus and Eurydice*' (*Chaucer and Fifteenth-Century Poetry*). 'Is it fanciful to suggest', she asks, 'that a deep knowledge of the implications of the Knight's Tale was a major shaping factor?' Roberts looks at other versions of the story (and the similar one of Perotheus and Theseus), in particular at what they may mean when they seem to end happily, and argues the importance of the dynamic relationship between tale and *moralitas*: 'Keeping the audience on its toes is part of the game'.

In 'Sir Gilbert Hay's *Alexander*: A Study in Transformations' (*MÆ* 60.61–72) John Cartwright studies Hay's changes to the Earthly Paradise episode in the Alexander story, from the moralizing *Iter*, and from the *Voyage* in the chivalric *Roman d'Alexandre*, to show Hay's interest not only in connecting the various episodes into a whole, but also in making this episode climactic, 'to make more interesting sense of the whole Alexander story than any other writer in Western Europe had managed to do'.

Priscilla Bawcutt (in Riddy, *Regionalism*) argues compellingly that among 'The Earliest Texts of Dunbar' more attention should be paid to other witnesses than Bannatyne, but also that in using Bannatyne account should be taken of recent discoveries about his scribal practices. The article is full of information about such suggestive discoveries and neglected areas. Attention is drawn, for example, to the evidence in Florentine Martin's inscription on the *Goldyn Targe* title-page that 'one of Dunbar's first readers was a literate layman, not a cleric, and not (as far as is known) a member of the royal household'.

8. Lyrics and Miscellaneous Verse

Martin Camargo's valuable study of *The Middle English Verse Love Epistle* considers a number of fourteenth- and fifteenth-century poems in relation to contemporary letters, to Latin and French literary antecedents, and to the influential epistolary models in Chaucer's *Troilus and Criseyde*. Formal and structural features are analysed in relation both to these models and to schemes used by teachers of *ars dictaminis*, and indications of 'genre awareness' are sought among comments left by scribes and readers of the poems. With extensive reference to the *Heroides*, epistolary forms of female complaint are traced through to the early sixteenth century, and an appendix provides the text of a *Letter of Dydo to Eneas* associated with the Chaucer apocrypha; another appendix lists all surviving English love epistles from *c*.1400 to 1568. Camargo traces convincing patterns in this large body of often neglected material, and makes discriminating use of modern critical theory to clarify issues of genre and of function. In the same series, Margit Sichert's *Die mittelenglische Pastourelle* confronts some related problems of taxonomy and with the aid of charts and diagrams attempts more rigid generic classification. Sichert aims to compare the conception of love in English and French *pastourelles* in an effort to determine the socio-psychological functions of the genre within the two cultures, and finds in the selected English poems a lack of frivolity and a marked tendency to moralize. One of the problems with such a comparison is the dearth of English material: *De clerico et puella*, 'In a fryht as y con fare fremede', 'As I stod on a day, me self under a tre', and 'Nou sprinkes the sprai' are strictly the only examples of the genre. Sichert widens the focus to include ballads of a *pastourelle* nature, but refrains from considering the possibility that English readers of this period probably read many of their *pastourelles* in French.

Women's voices in verse epistles and in *pastourelles* and related lyric genres, from *The Wife's Lament* onwards, are discussed in the wide-ranging and stimulating introduction to John Kerrigan's *Motives of Woe: Shakespeare and Female Complaint*, a critical anthology of English texts which in some way illuminate Shakespeare's *A Lover's Complaint*. Samples of fourteenth- and fifteenth-century lyrics which present female erotic or maternal experience are freshly edited and presented with brief textual notes and on-the-page glosses. Sarah McNamer writes about 'Female Authors, Provincial Settings: The Re-versing of Courtly Love in the Findern Manuscript' (*Viator* 22.279–310), offering palaeographical evidence and quotations from certain of the Paston letters to support her argument that several of the poems customarily ascribed to male authors in Cambridge University Library MS Ff. 1. 6 are in fact the work of women. She identifies these women writers, perhaps rather too readily, with certain of the individuals whose names have been copied into the collection, and sees reflected in their writings a sincerity rooted in their sober provincial concerns. A useful appendix supplies new editions of all the lyrics in the manuscript which appear to be spoken by women. A rather different aspect of the connection of women with lyrics is broached by Sarah Stanbury's article on 'The Virgin's Gaze: Spectacle and Transgression in Middle English Lyrics of the Passion' (*PMLA* 106.1083–93). Starting with Dante's seeming equivocation over the nature of Beatrice's gaze, as described in the *Purgatorio* and the *Vita Nuova*, Stanbury turns to Lacanian theory and to modern feminist film studies for terms which can elucidate the transgressive capacity of women's glances simultaneously to uplift and to seduce, and moves on to the 'visual transactions' inherent in lyrics of the passion (selected fairly randomly from Carleton Brown's anthologies of fourteenth- and fifteenth-century poems) which invite a reader-spectator to observe a suffering mother gazing at a suffering son. The discussion points to some inviting areas for future research, such as the implicit connections between lyrics of the passion and Holy Family romances. Certain religious lyrics also feature in Mark Allen's discussion of a teaching strategy which combines 'Middle English Drama and Middle English Lyrics', in *Approaches to Teaching Medieval English Drama*, edited by Richard K. Emmerson: lyrics of the passion are paired with the York play of the *Crucifixion*, nativity lyrics with the Wakefield *Second Shepherds' Play*, and lyrics about mortality and transience with *Everyman*.

Cameron Louis makes available 'Two Middle English Doomsday Poems' (*NM* 92.43–6) which have not previously been published. The first, from St John's College, Cambridge, MS 31, is an unusual dream vision, and the second, from the better-known Carthusian collection British Library, MS Additional 37049, complements a prose description of the Last Judgement. Louis also edits 'A Yorkist Genealogical Chronicle in Middle English Verse' (*Anglia* 109.87–93), hitherto unpublished and resembling John Lydgate's *Verses on the Kings of England*, from a roll among the papers of the Earl of Aylesford where it is accompanied by other genealogical texts in prose and verse and by a list of the mayors of Coventry. The political context of an earlier lyric, 'Syng y wold, butt, alas!', is interestingly reconstructed by Richard Firth Green, in 'Jack Philipot, John of Gaunt, and a Poem of 1380' (*Speculum* 66.330–41). Entitled *On the Times* by its early editor Thomas Wright, this macaronic piece has customarily been assigned to 1388, but Green is able to point to more specific evidence for dating in a nexus of puns on 'jakkes' – articles of clothing, coins, and perhaps also the London merchant Jack Philipot who contributed conspicuously to the war effort in 1380. Puns also concern Robert Easting, who indicates the range of 'Double-Meaning in *Atte ston castinges*' (*N&Q* 236.160) with reference to the equation made in this lyric, as in Chaucer's *Parliament of Fowls*, between wrestling and intercourse, and to the possible meaning of 'ston' as 'testicle'. Gwendolyn Morgan supplies a note on the interpretation of '*Erthe Toc of Erthe*' (*Expl* 49.199–200) with the suggestion that some occurrences of 'erthe' in this poem refer to Christ, the earthly form of God. Some of the more general interpretative problems which medieval lyrics pose for modern readers are highlighted in 'Middle English Lyrics: Texts and Interpretation' by Julia Boffey, in *Medieval Literature: Texts and Interpretation*, edited by Tim William Machan, which takes as its focus some lines in British Library MS Sloane 1212. These have been edited as two independent love lyrics in the style of Lydgate, but closer scrutiny undermines their status as independent, stable texts and highlights the perils attendant on interpretations conceived in a contextual void. Boffey also writes on 'Early Printers and English Lyrics: Sources, Selection, and Presentation of Texts' (*PBSA* 85.11–26), reviewing the role of lyrics in printed books prior to the important anthologies of the later sixteenth century.

In the field of miscellaneous verse are several new anthologies. John W. Conlee's critical anthology of *Middle English Debate Poetry* is constructed in sections which deal respectively with body and soul debates, alliterative debate poems, miscellaneous didactic and satiric debates, and *pastourelles*, and includes helpfully presented editions of otherwise often inaccessible material; it is good to see *The Debate of the Carpenters' Tools* and *The Parliament of Birds* here, for example, alongside the more familiar alliterative poems (*Winner and Waster*, *The Parliament of the Three Ages*, and *Death and Life*) and the currently much-discussed English *pastourelles*. A lengthy introduction illustrates the pervasiveness of the genre, summarizes some influential Latin debates, and reviews other important literary and pedagogical influences. Each text is accompanied by a headnote, a selective bibliography, and explicatory notes, and there is in conclusion a brief dedicated glossary. The *Six Ecclesiastical Satires* edited by James M. Dean seem to be similarly directed at specialist student readers, and come equipped with roughly the same kind of apparatus. Several of these texts are again alliterative (*Piers the Plowman's Crede* and the responses generated by the prose treatise *Jack Upland*), but the volume also includes the lollard *Plowman's Tale*, which was to become incorporated in the Chaucer apocrypha, and the intriguing discussion of the corruptions of convent life entitled *Why I Can't Be a Nun* (of which the editor here writes diplomatically 'It could be by a woman, I would think'). Like Conlee's collection, this book is attractively produced and offers stimulating teaching material for courses which venture beyond the conventional Middle English canon into the field of cultural studies.

Robert Easting's Early English Text Society anthology, *St Patrick's Purgatory*, contains as one would expect more scholarly apparatus, and a more detailed focus on the linguistic features and transmission of the works which it includes: a Latin prose *Tractarius de Purgatorio Sancti Patricii*, the earliest surviving account of God's revelation to St Patrick of an entrance to the other world; two versions of a fourteenth-century Middle English poem about a monk's visit to the purgatory, *Owayne Miles*, deriving (in the case of the first, through an Anglo-Norman reworking) from the Latin; and the related fifteenth-century prose *Vision of William of Stranton*. *Owayne Miles I* is edited from the unique surviving text in the Auchinleck Manuscript, National Library of Scotland 19. 2. 1, *Owayne Miles II* is offered in parallel texts based on the copies in British Library MS Cotton Caligula A. ii and the Brome Manuscript, Yale University Library 365; one of the notable features of these texts is their capacity to complement romances and works of diverse kinds in the manuscript anthologies in which they have survived. Easting's extensive and rewarding researches in this area are further documented in an article on 'Middle English Translations of the *Tractatus de Purgatorio Sancti Patricii*' in *The Medieval Translator II*, edited by Roger Ellis, where the different translations (which include a version in the *South English Legendary*) are compared.

Anne B. Thompson investigates 'Narrative Art in the *South English Legendary*' (*JEGP* 90.20–30) through a study of the legend of Mary Magdalen in relation to the Latin source in the *Legenda Aurea*. Concentrating on such matters as narrative voice and the use of dramatic dialogue she locates a search for a lively but essentially plain style common to some homiletic romances. In pursuit of 'The Sources of Lines 3562–3939 of the *Prick of Conscience*' (*Anglia* 109.87–93) Derek Britton solves an obscurity concerning an authority on purgatory named in British Library MS Cotton Galba E. ix, the basis of the standard edition, as 'Austyn': other manuscripts supply the reading 'Hostiene', probably Henricus Hostiensis, author of a *Summa Theologie* which may have been accessible to the author of the English poem through John of

Freiburg's *Summa Confessorum*. John Thompson considers 'Textual Interpolations in the Cotton Manuscript of the *Cursor Mundi*' (*NM* 92.15–27), where a fifteenth-century scribe has inserted material from the Southern Passion into the sections of the narrative dealing with the Crucifixion and Resurrection, and notes the susceptibility of texts like *Cursor Mundi* to development and change at the hands of readers and editors seeking ease of use and other perceived 'improvements'. *Cursor Mundi* is set alongside other such protean works, in verse and prose, in Thompson's more general treatment of 'Textual Instability and the Late Medieval Reputation of Some Middle English Religious Literature' (*Text* 5.175–94), where issues of textual integrity, and their reflection in features of medieval book production, are considered in the light of the particular requirements of certain medieval editors.

Problems of another order have confronted Bradford Y. Fletcher and A. Leslie Harris, who find 'Intentional Obscurity in a Fifteenth-Century Poem: The Case of *Piers of Fulham*' (*FCS* 18.93–107). Attempting to explicate the successfully concealed 'conceits' of love which are promised in a scribe's introduction to this work, they reach the conclusion that it is not a narrative poem but one depending on extended metaphors, mainly of fishing and fowling, 'placed in the mouth of a churlish speaker'. Francoise Le Saux writes 'Of Desire and Transgression: The Middle English *Vox and Wolf*' (*Reinardus* 3.69–79), reading the poem in conjunction with part of Branch IV of the French Roman de Renart to discover an English emphasis on the self-centred appetites of the fox which turns the work into a warning against desire, temptation, and the deceitfulness of language. In the avian world, E. G. Stanley offers a linguistic note to '*The Owl and the Nightingale* 1335: "þu liest iwis, þu fule þing!" ' (*N&Q* 236.152), confirming that the second person singular indicative of the Middle English verb *lien* is *liest* at both lines 367 and 1335, and W. A. Davenport, in *Chaucer and Fifteenth-Century Poetry*, edited by Julia Boffey and Janet Cowen, surveys 'Bird Poems from *The Parliament of Fowls* to *Philip Sparrow*', alluding to both neo-Chaucerian works and to lesser known pieces like the lyric 'Revertere' and the nightingale poems formerly attributed to Lydgate. In a carefully researched and engaging essay in the same volume Peter Brown writes on 'Journey's End: The Prologue to *The Tale of Beryn*', and makes a plausible case for the poem to be read as part of the publicity for the 1420 jubilee for the shrine of St Thomas at Canterbury, directed at audiences who would have known their Chaucer. While Frederick B. Jonassen, in 'Cathedral, Inn, and Pardoner in *The Prologue to the Tale of Beryn*' (*FCS* 18.109–32) invokes Bakhtin in reading the pardoner as a pivotal character in a series of contrasts in the poem between flesh and spirit, carnival and Lent. Brown argues that audiences would have perceived the point of the *Beryn*-author's subtle modifications to Chaucer's pardoner, and would have understood them as vilification of a representative of those practised competitors for the funds which the keepers of the shrine hoped to tap.

9. Malory and Caxton

The first volume of *AY* augurs well for the future of this new journal. There are three articles specific to this section, but, in addition, several which relate to French Arthurian material should be of interest to Malory scholars. Terence McCarthy's 'Reading the *Morte Darthur*' (*YWES* 69.164–5) would appear to have provoked some critical reaction. In 'The Weakening of the King: Arthur's Disintegration in *The Book of Sir Tristram*', Ginger Thornton rejects McCarthy's interpretation of Arthur's character in the book and argues instead for 'a new, weaker Arthur.' D. Thomas Hanks, Jnr, in 'Foil and Forecast: Dinadan in *The Book of Sir Tristram*' takes his starting-point from McCarthy's dismissal of the book. Hanks regrets the book's omission from teaching syllabuses – not reading *Tristram* means not reading Dinadan whom Malory has created to question the chivalric values of love and war. Hanks finds comedy in Dinadan, as does Dhira B. Mahoney elsewhere in Malory, in 'Malory's *Tale of Gareth* and the Comedy of Class'. The story of Gareth belongs to what Mahoney categorizes as Type 2 of the Fair Unknown story, where the Fair Unknown deliberately adopts obscurity. Malory's models were English metrical romances of this type, and particularly *Havelok*, where class conflict was emphasized as Malory emphasizes it in *Gareth*.

McCarthy and *Tristram* form the other two contributions to Malory in this section. McCarthy asks 'Did Morgan le Fay have a lover?' (*MÆ* 60.284–9), a reference to Vinaver's emendation of the Winchester manuscript at 78.28–79:3, and writes illuminatingly on the distinction between Caxton's *love* and Vinaver's emended *lover*. In 'Reconsidering Vinaver's Sources for Malory's *Tristram*' (*MP* 88.373–81), Michael N. Salda also calls Vinaver to account, this time for having disregarded his own injunction to read the sources. Salda argues for a re-evaluation of Vinaver's work on the French sources of the *Tristram* and suggests that there may be a composite 'source', the text of Paris, Bibliothèque Nationale, fonds français MS 103, and the structure of the 1489 first printing of the prose *Tristan*.

1991 also saw the publication of several works which, while not dealing specifically with Malory himself, are of interest to the Malory scholar. In a provoking and carefully argued study of *The Arthurian Romances of Chrétien de Troyes*, Donald Maddox investigates the 'textuality of crisis' in Chrétien's romances, each crisis generated by tension between Arthur as the upholder of the customs of the anterior order and his knights as representatives of the new chivalric dynamic. These successive crises combine to form an 'intertextuality of crisis' and the works demonstrate the failure of custom as an institution to maintain order. Elspeth Kennedy in 'Failure in Arthurian Romance' (*MÆ* 60.16–32), takes as her starting point the fact that in Arthurian romance the failure of others serves to highlight the success of the successful knight. She looks at patterns of success and failure in *Perlsevaus* and in the Vulgate cycle, and finds that, where *Perlsevaus* follows convention, this convention is challenged in the Vulgate cycle where there is no redemption of Lancelot's failure. Still on Chrétien, in *Arthurian Literature X*, Armel Diverres has produced a full and authoritative monograph on 'The Grail and the Third Crusade: Thoughts on *Le Conte del Graal* by Chrétien de Troyes'. A. H. W. Smith, in the same volume, takes up the question of 'Gildas the Poet' and suggests that Geoffrey of Monmouth's source for his *Historia Regum Britanniae* may used a Welsh or Breton poem, even if Geoffrey himself did not do so. Finally, *The Archaeology and History of Glastonbury Abbey*, edited by Lesley Abrams and James P. Carley, is a volume of essays dedicated to that most emotive of Arthurian sites, Glastonbury.

10. Other Prose

'On Reclaiming a Fragment of Prose from The Index of Middle English Verse: A Brief Lesson in Textual Criticism' (*NM* 92.29–30), by Larry E. Eldredge, demonstrates that a single line in English on f. 47 of Bodleian Library, MS Ashmole 1285, is not in fact a line of verse. He has found a fuller version in Trinity College Cambridge MS 323,

f. 28v, where it is clearly part of a prose penitential maxim. Irma Taavitsainenen edits 'Pater Noster: A Meditation connected with Richard Rolle in BL Royal MS. 17. C. XVII' (*NM* 92.31–41), and considers the evidence for its claim to inclusion in the Rolle canon.

Björn Waller has announced 'A Newly Discovered Guy de Chauliac Manuscript' (*N&Q* 38.159) in Cambridge, MS Jesus College Q. G. 23. This now brings to three the number of full versions of Chauliac in Middle English. William Schipper demonstrates the existence of 'A Ghost Word in the Peterborough Chronicle ("ihyder") (*N&Q* 38.154). Thorlac Turville-Petre has noticed an unusual fragment, 'A Middle English Life of St Zita' (*Nottingham Medieval Studies* 35.102–5) in Nottingham University Library MS Mi LM 37. He transcribes it and provides interesting notes on her cult.

R. N. Swanson has written a valuable note on 'The Origins of *The Lay Folk's Catechism*' (*MÆ* 60.92–100). He identifies and publishes from BL MS Cotton Galba E. x, fols. 73v–74r, a transcript of a letter from Archbishop Thoresby to John de Gaytryk requesting the translation into English of the pastoral material known today as *The Lay Folk's Catechism*. (A typographical error has converted Pecham on p. 94 to 'Pechman'.) In 'The Trope of the Scribe and the Question of Literary Authority in the Works of Julian of Norwich and Margery Kempe' (*Speculum* 66.820–38), Lynn Staley Johnson illustrates how Julian and Margery, in their different ways, seem aware of how to invoke the presence of the scribe, the mediator of their text, strategically. They turn him into a topos by means of which they can maintain control of their texts, even while ostensibly professing they have no control. The scribal topos allows the women to stake a claim to being considered authoritative in their own right. K. Lochrie, *Margery Kempe and translations of the Flesh* (UPennP), was not seen.

In 'Paul of Hungary's *Quoniam circa confessiones* (1219–21) and a Middle English Prose Tract on Confession' (in Kooper, *This Noble Craft*), F. N. M. Diekstra argues that what has previously been seen as two distinct treatises is in reality one single tract, and presents the Latin source of its opening section edited alongside the English. Susan Powell's 'John Mirk's *Festial* and the Pastoral Programme' (*LSE* 22.85–102) demonstrates the persistence of Mirk's original aim, to make the work part of a programme of pastoral publication, through its various metamorphoses from his own version to the print of 1532. Alan J. Fletcher's 'The Unity of the State Exists in the Agreement of its Minds: A Fifteenth-Century Sermon on the Three Estates' (*LSE* 22.103–37) is an edition preceded by a discussion of some of the 'compromises and adjustments' late fifteenth-century sermons might make in classical three-estates theory. Although constructed out of 'largely traditional parts', the particular example of the theory is unusual in being apparently adjusted to a contemporary clerical concern to affirm the institution of marriage, distinguishing 'the order of wedlock' from the spiritual. Leo M. Carruthers ('Richard Lavynham and the Seven Deadly Sins in *Jacob's Well*') examines the nature of the indebtedness of the author of *Jacob's Well* to his sources, in particular to Lavynham's *Litil Tretys*.

Finally, one essay in *Images of Sainthood in Medieval Europe* (edited by R. Blumenfeld-Kosinski and T. Szell) will be of concern to students of Middle English prose. Elizabeth Robertson considers 'The Corporeality of Female Sanctity in *The Life of Saint Margaret*', illustrating the English author's alterations to his Latin source work in the direction of highlighting Margaret's physical experiences. Her spirituality is conceived as finding its expression via the senses rather than the mind, and thus Robertson sees this saint's life as collaborating with a circumscribed medieval view of the way in which female spirituality operated.

11. Drama

This year has seen a flourish of collected papers and articles. *Drama in the Middle Ages: Comparative and Critical Essays*, edited by Clifford Davidson and John H. Stroupe, reprints a selection of articles from *CompD* since 1982. Some have been reviewed in previous *YWES* volumes, but a few have escaped notice and deserve mention here. ' "We happy herdsmen here": A Newly Discovered Shepherd's Carol possibly belonging to a Medieval Pageant', by John P. Cutts, transcribes the music and text of the said carol which is preserved in Bishop Smith's part-song manuscript in Carlisle Cathedral Library. Bruce Moore considers *Dame Sirith* and *The Harrowing of Hell*, two texts whose dramatic status has been questioned, in 'The Narrator within the Performance: Problems with Two Medieval "Plays" '. *Dame Sirith*, he believes, is better suited to performance by a small troupe than by a solo minstrel, as current thinking has it. He plausibly suggests that doubts about its dramatic status may derive from interventions in the text by a scribe who may not have understood the dramatic nature of what he was copying. Moreover, the presence of a narrator within both texts, which may account for the reluctance of some modern critics to own them as a drama, is entirely in keeping with other medieval plays whose dramatic status is not in doubt. In 'The Durham Play of Mary and the Poor Knight: Sources and Analogues of a Lost English Miracle Play', Stephen K. Wright demonstrates that the lost play that the *Durham Prologue* once prefaced must have been only distantly related to the two legends usually cited as being its source. Rather, it seems to have been akin to the Marian legend known as 'The Knight who denied Christ but not the Virgin', and which appears in the popular *Dialogues miraculorum* of Caesarius of Heisterbach. Lawrence M. Clopper rightly argues that '*Mankind* and its Audience' are more sophisticated and learned than has often been thought, though his identification of the character Mercy as a Dominican has little basis, and he stops short of the suggestion, one certainly worth airing, that *Mankind* may have been a University play. In '*Wisdom* Enthroned: Iconic Stage Portraits', Milla Riggio describes yet again her 1984 production of *Wisdom* and the semiotics of its performance. Ann Eljenholm Nichols writes briefly on 'Costume in the Moralities: The Evidence of East Anglian Art', and finds various points of comparison between drama and the depictions on East Anglian seven-sacrament fonts. Howard B. Norland shows how careful an adaptation of its French source to English cultural circumstances is *Johan Johan* in 'Formalizing English Farce: *Johan Johan* and its French Connection'. In 'Comedic and Liturgical Restoration in *Everyman*', John Cunningham proposes the term 'comedy' for describing the action of *Everyman* and points to the play's liturgical affinities, finding these to lie especially in the connection between its metaphors and those found in the accession prayer of the Mass.

The second collection, a selection of papers delivered at the Sixth Triennial Colloquium of the International Society for the Study of Medieval Drama, occupies the whole of *METh* 11 (1989), and is devoted to *Evil on the Medieval Stage*. André Lascombes treats 'De la fonction théâtrale des personnages du mal', in the N-Town Passion Play and the *Castle of Perserverance*, and focuses on the contest between the received theological stance against evil and evil's seductive aestheticization once presented on stage. John Brown gives a sensitive and absorbing account of how he conceived and justified his direction of 'The Devils in the York *Doomsday*' for a production mounted in 1988. Hans-Jürgen Diller investigates the correlation of speech and action of 'The Torturers in the English Mystery Plays', and concludes that, whatever their individual differences, the plays all keep spectators at a distance, refusing them participation in the action in a Bakhtinian sense. Cecilia Pietropoli's analysis of 'The Characterization of Evil in the Towneley Plays' finds that all the cycles, but especially Towneley, deal in a kind of poetic justice that ensures that the good are rewarded and the bad punished. Comedy, never simply gratuitous, exercises a punitive effect on sin, and in turn this is celebratory, because the chastisement of evil characters restores mankind's prospect of regaining salvation. Again on 'Evil in the Towneley Cycle', Alexandra F. Johnston offers a salutary alternative to Martin Stevens's view of the coherence of this cycle, arguing for its essential disparateness. However, if the cycle's anomalous pageants are removed, what remains is thematically united by an Augustinian view of good and evil, nowhere more evident than in the work of the Wakefield Master himself, where the City of Man is pitted against the City of God. In 'Action and Discourse in *The Harrowing of Hell*: The Defeat of Evil', Roberta Mullini gives a discursive account of the Harrowing plays, from which she distils a modest conclusion. Geoff Lester's 'Idle Words: Stereotyping by Language in the English Mystery Plays' is concerned to establish objectively that there is an evil 'style' or 'register' available to the authors of the mystery plays. Tabulation of selected linguistic features of the Cain and Abel plays helps him establish his point. ' "Farewell, Jentyll Jaffrey": Speech-Act Theory and *Mankind*', by Rosemary E. Caplan, employs speech-act theory in a searching way to classify the language of *Mankind* in terms of action and characterization. This play is well suited to such an approach. Garrett P. J. Epp's title mimics its subject. 'Passion, Pomp and Parody: Alliteration in the York Plays' investigates the uses of alliteration in the York cycle, finding in it subtle gradings which are indexed to character and situation. Lastly, Andrew Taylor, in his well argued and persuasive article ' "To Pley a Pagyn of Þe Devyl": *Turpiloquium* and the *Scurrae* in Early Drama', points out how the singing, dancing, tumbling and jesting vices in *Mankind*, and indeed in other early plays, associate them with secular entertainers. Such association, he concludes, vindicates religious plays and playing in the distinction it enforces between them and the base entertainment practices of low-life jongleurs and *scurrae*.

Evil is evidently the more arresting topic: another, rather smaller, collection of papers from the same Colloquium has been edited by Clifford Davidson and John H. Stroupe under the title *Iconographic and Comparative Studies in Medieval Drama*. Three of these will especially concern students of medieval drama in England, although all are of interest for comparative purposes. 'The Hierosphthitic Topos, or the Fate of Fergus: Notes on the N-Town *Assumption*', by Ann Eljenholm Nichols, illustrates how commonplace was the motif of physical incapacity sometimes inflicted as a result of coming into contact with saintly relics, whether the contact had occurred for malicious or innocent motives. She proceeds to treat of the topos in the N-Town *Assumption* play. Cherrell Guilfoyle ranges generally over 'The Staging of the First Murder in the Mystery Plays in England', and finds herself particularly fascinated by the murder weapon, the jawbone of the ass, its lineage, and the mechanics of the murder. Clifford Davidson rehearses an argument with which his work has become characteristically identified in recent years, that of the importance of trying to realize the visual dimension of early plays if they are to be approached at all adequately. Consequently, the ahistoricizing of critics like Gadamer is roundly rejected, and for some very sound reasons. (These three articles are also to be found in *CompD* 25.29–41, 42–51 and 66–76 respectively.)

Studies in Fifteenth-Century Stagecraft, by J. W. Robinson, though sounding broadly based, in fact concentrates on explicating the New Testament plays of the Wakefield Master and some of the corresponding plays of the York cycle, in particular plays by the York Realist. After an intriguing introduction on twentieth-century revivals of the York and Wakefield plays, Robinson launches into a general account of the Master and Realist, and the likely circumstances of performance of their work. Chapter two is an appreciation of the artistry of the York Nativity play, and an explication of its Brigittine associations. Chapter three sets the defective York Shepherd's play alongside the *Prima Pastorum* in comparison and contrast. The fourth chapter is on *Secunda Pastorum* exclusively. Chapter five compares and contrasts the York Slaughter of the Innocents with *Magnus Herodes*. The last chapter proceeds similarly with the York play of Christ before Annas and Caiaphas and the *Coliphizacio*. This book, if sometimes sloppy (for example, what the Lollards disputed was transubstantiation, not the doctrine of the Real Presence, and less a series of arguments than leisurely expositions, is a humane, sympathetic reading of the plays with which it is concerned.

It is always difficult to know quite how to pitch introductions to any subject. Should breadth of coverage be sacrificed to focus? Conversely, may not ignoring focus for the sake of breadth increase the likelihood of oversimplification? These unhappy irreconcilables, inevitable companions of anyone engaged in enterprises like this one, continue to haunt *Medieval Drama* by Christine Richardson and Jackie Johnston. Their book, in two parts, first surveys mystery plays and then moralities and interludes. Some plays receive comparatively extended treatment, while others are briefly alluded to, and the reason for this discrimination is declared to be the relative availability in print of the play in question. Of course, in the circumstances, such a pragmatic approach is understandable, but it is not a particularly imaginative way around the problem, and has resulted in a rather uneven book. Individual analyses are its most rewarding parts, and these sometimes engender stimulating generalizations. However, even here problems are occasionally encountered. The assumption, for example, that the play of *Mankind* was devised for a popular audience (p. 128), is debateable, while the syntactic investigation offered on p. 130 is not entirely plausible. Elsewhere, generalizations are in peril of being bland, or worse, reductive. Thus the account of staging reduces the actual richness of the evidence for staging practice, and a statement like the following: 'Costumes were contemporary ... distinctions ... were demonstrated by details of dress or uniform appropriate to contemporary local culture', while it may be a fair summary of current orthodox thinking about costuming in the mystery plays, would come to grief if close attention were paid to the very different evidence of the N. town stage directions. In sum, though locally admirable, as an introduction it still leaves something to be desired.

The Theatre of Medieval Europe, edited by Eckehard Simon, collects the deliberations of a 1986 conference convened at Harvard University on developments in research on early drama since the 1960s. The essays in part II, *English Drama*, are of nearest concern here. David Mills reports on 'Modern Editions of Medieval English Plays', and begins by emphasizing how any play edition should constantly challenge its users to construct the performance circumstances of its text, since any printed play is necessarily an anomaly, an inevitable compromise of the three-dimensional dramatic medium. He surveys the rationale behind antiquarian and subsequent scholarly editions, the latter published mainly by the EETS, facsimile editions and anthologies. Next, David Staines discusses the changing reception of 'The English Mystery Cycles', and notes especially two approaches currently in vogue: the thematic study of individual cycles and the comparative analysis of the same episode in various cycles. After subjecting both to a cogent critique, he moves on to an effective, if embryonic, characterization of the nature of the four chief mystery plays collections.

'*Castles* in the Air: The Morality Plays', by David Bevington, similarly traces the changing reception of the moralities, from their toleration as historical curiosities to their rescue as sophisticated dramatic forms. He also ponders their staging, and their relation to later Elizabethan drama (his review of secondary criticism here is particularly interesting) and to other contexts such as continental drama, anthropology and iconography. Alexandra F. Johnston describes the rise of the *Records of Early English Drama* enterprise and illustrates something of the spectacular transformation of our understanding of early drama that it is effecting in ' "All the World was a Stage": Records of Early English Drama'. Finally, Stanley J. Kahrl writes interestingly on the evolution of modern attempts to reconstruct 'The Staging of Medieval English Plays'.

To the question 'Is the Ashmole Fragment a Remnant of a Middle English Saint Play?' (*Neophil* 75.139–49), Stephen K. Wright answers it may well be, and judging by its parallels with the St Lawrence legend, its derivation from a play on the martyrdom of that saint would seem quite possible. Wright's analysis is careful and persuasive. Martin Stevens explains what he considers 'the Intertextuality of Late Medieval Art and Drama' (*NLH* 22.317–37), challenging in the process some current assumptions, largely those of Clifford Davidson, about their interplay. For Stevens, the posited symmetries between art and drama are insecure, and each is denigrated if it be merely regarded as a 'tool' by which the other may be explained. Focusing on a famous Passion panel by Hans Memling, he urges the semiotic intertextuality of the media rather than their causative interdependence. Finally, Albert H. Tricomi embarks eloquently on 'Reenvisioning England's Medieval Cycle Comedy' (*MRDE* 5.11–26). Essentially, he seeks to broaden our understanding of the comic in the plays by moving beyond the theological explanations of comedy which have held some sway in criticism since the 1960s.

The major edition this year is by Stephen Spector of *The N-Town Play*. Over the years, Spector has been putting out sound articles on N. town, especially on its prosody and codicology. This is probably why the sections of his introduction concerned with these matters are satisfyingly detailed. The inclusion of a thorough, traditional description of the language is equally as satisfying, as it stirs nostalgia for headier philological days of the EETS. Description of sources is sufficient, though here one suspects Spector to be not quite so readily at home: we can improve a little on the distant authority of Rabanus Maurus as sole source for Christ's commentary in the Last Supper play, for example: more likely Rabanus would have been mediated by an intervening source such as the *Glossa ordinairia*. A second companion volume contains a fuller commentary on each play, as well as three Appendixes (on the composition and development of the plays, their staging and their thematic concerns respectively). A conclusion and glossary complete the edition. In general we are well served here, and Spector has proved a worthy successor to Katharine Block, the first EETS editor of the plays by whose efforts so much was achieved.

J. J. Anderson compares 'The Towneley Shepherds and the York Primer' (*Neophil* 75.317–19), and concludes that the *Formulae Communes*, devotional commonplaces which prefaced the York Primer, may have provided the Wakefield Master with his source for some of the Latin used in the *Prima* and *Secunda Pastorum*. Thomas J. Jambeck teases out some of the rich exegesis on the day star of 2 Peter 1:16–19 to illuminate 'The "Day Star" Allusion in the *Secunda Pastorum*'(*MLQ* 50.297–308). He argues that in the allusion the Wakefield Master offers his audience a narrative signal as to how they should understand the action of the play. The epithet is seen as a metaphor of the timelessness of the mystery of the Incarnation. In 'The Limits of Typology and the Wakefield Master's *Processus Noe*' (*CompD* 25.168–87), Edgar

Schell argues that many modern readings of the Noah play fail because they confound *typological* understanding of the Flood narrative. A type has its own integrity and particularity at the same time as it may foreshadow its later fulfilment: appreciation of this dimension of type should not be lost, otherwise the type will merely collapse into identity with its fulfilment. This established, Schell considers the *Processus Noe* in its light. Martin Stevens applies the concepts of *compilatio* and *ordinatio*, as seminally expounded by Malcolm B. Parkes, to 'The Towneley Plays Manuscript (HM 1): *Compilatio* and *Ordinatio*' (*Text* 5.157–73). First, he considers other plays manuscripts, before proceeding to characterize the Towneley manuscript as a literary *compilatio* addressed to a reader. Thus, it may be useful in future to distinguish between actual play performance and the ends served by the manuscript in which the play texts are preserved.

Stephen K. Wright's explication of 'The York Creed Play in the Light of the Innsbruck Playbook of 1391' (*MRDE* 5.27–53) is an interesting and well argued attempt to reconstruct the content of the lost York play, by drawing attention to Continental plays which dramatize the Creed, especially those of the Innsbruck playbook.

Ron Tanner revisits 'Humor in *Everyman* and the Middle English Morality Play' (*PQ* 70.149–61), an unlikely prospect in *Everyman* at least, most would have thought, but not so for Tanner. He conceives 'medieval viewers clucking their tongues and nodding knowingly' at some of the scenes of the play, and goes on to try to rehabilitate our attitude to humour also in *Mankind* and *Youth*. Finally, Peter Happé has produced a most useful reference guide to *Song in Morality Plays and Interludes*. It comprises two main parts: first, an index of songs, burdens and titles arranged alphabetically, and second, an edition of the song texts and a checklist of song cues, arranged chronologically under play title. Two appendices are also included.

Books reviewed

Abrams, Lesley, and James. P. Carley, eds. *The Archaeology and History of Glastonbury Abbey: Essays in Honour of the Ninetieth Birthday of C. A. Ralegh Radford.* D. S. Brewer. pp. 351. £49.50. ISBN 0 85115 284 8.

Archibald, Elizabeth. *Apollonius of Tyre: Medieval and Renaissance Themes and Variations*. D. S. Brewer. pp. 250. £35.00. ISBN 0 85991 316 3.

Barber, Richard. *Arthurian Literature* X. D. S. Brewer (1990). pp. 160. £29.50. ISBN 0 85991 308 2.

Blanch, Robert J., Miriam Youngerman Miller, and Julian N. Wasserman, eds. *Text and Matter: New Critical Perspectives on the Pearl-Poet*. Whitson. pp. 273. $30. ISBN 0 878754 024.

Blumenfeld-Kosinski, Renate, and Timea Szell, eds. *Images of Sainthood in Medieval Europe*. CornUp. pp. 320. $37.50. ISBN 0 801 42507 7.

Boffey, Julia, and Janet Cowen, eds. *Chaucer and Fifteenth-Century Poetry*. King's College, London. pp. 174. pb £8.75. ISBN 0 953 217 X.

Boitani, Piero, and Anna Torti, eds. *Poetics, Theory and Practice in Medieval Literature*. The J. A. W. Bennett Memorial Lectures. 7th Series. Perugia. 1990. D. S. Brewer. pp. 207. £35.00. ISBN 0 85991 331 7.

Bumke, Joachim. *Courtly Culture: Literature and Society in the High Middle Ages*. Trans. Thomas Dunlap. UCalP. pp. 771. $49.95. ISBN 0 520 006634 0.

Cable, Thomas. *The English Alliterative Tradition*. UPennP. pp. 191. $29.95. ISBN 0 8122 3063 9.

Camargo, Martin. *The Middle English Verse Love Epistle*. Niemeyer. pp. 220. pb £30.15. ISBN 3 484 45028 2.

Conlee, John W., ed. *Middle English Debate Poetry: A Critical Anthology*. Colleagues. pp. 329. $38.00. ISBN 0 937191 18 3.

Copeland, Rita. *Rhetoric, Hermeneutics and Translation in the Middle Ages: Academic Traditions and Vernacular Texts*. Cambridge Studies in Medieval Literature 11. CUP. pp. 295. £35.00. ISBN 0521 38517 2.

Crick, Julia C. *The Historia Regum Britannie of Geoffrey of Monmouth, IV: Dissemination and Reception in the Later Middle Ages*. D. S. Brewer. pp. 352. £35.00. ISBN 085991 215 9.

Davidson, Clifford, and John H. Stroupe, eds. *Drama in the Middle Ages*. Second Series. AMS. pp. 400. $47.50. ISBN 0 404 61434 5.

———. *Illustrations of the Stage and Acting in England to 1580*. MIP. pb $19.95.

———, and John H. Stroupe, eds. *Iconographic and Comparative Studies in Medieval Drama*. MIP.

Dean, James M., ed. *Six Ecclesiastical Satires*. MIP. pp. 250. pb $8.95. ISBN 1 879288 05 2.

Diekstra, F. N. M., ed. *The Middle English 'Weye of Paradys' and the Middle French 'Voie de Paradis'*. Brill. pp. 544. 200 guilders. ISBN 9004091181

Du Boulay, F. R. H. *The England of Piers Plowman*. D. S. Brewer. pp. 147. £29.50. ISBN 0 85991 312 0.

Easting, Robert, ed. *St Patrick's Purgatory: Two Versions of 'Owayne Miles' and 'The Vision of William of Stranton' together with the long text of 'Tractatus de Purgatorio Sancti Patricii'*. EETS. pp. 337. £25. ISBN 0 19 722300 1.

Ellis, Roger. *The Medieval Translator II*. QMW. pp. 276. £27.50. ISBN 1 870 05904 2.

Emmerson, Richard K., ed. *Approaches to Teaching Medieval English Drama*. MLA (1990). pp. 182. $34. ISBN 0-87352-531-0.

Frantzen, Allen J., ed. *Speaking Two Languages: Traditional Disciplines and Contemporary Theory in Medieval Studies*. SUNYP. pp. 297. hb $54.50, pb $18.95. ISBN 07914 05052, 0 7914 0506 0.

Happé, Peter. *Song in Morality Plays and Interludes*. Medieval Theatre Monographs 1. The Short Run Press.

Jondorf, Gillian, and D. N. Dumville, eds. *France and the British Isles in the Middle Ages and the Renaissance. Essays by members of Girton College, Cambridge in Memory of Ruth Morgan*. Boydell. pp. 282. £35.00. ISBN 0 85115 487 5.

Kerrigan, John, ed. *Motives of Woe. Shakespeare and Female Complaint. A Critical Anthology*. Clarendon. pp. 310. £40.00. ISBN 0-19-811770-1.

Kobayashi, Eichi. *The Story of Apollonius of Tyre in Old and Middle English*. Sansyusya. pp. 158. ISBN 4 384 02183 6.

Kooper, Erik, ed. *This Noble Craft ... Proceedings of the Xth Research Symposium of the Dutch and Belgian University Teachers of Old and Middle English and Historical Linguistics*. Rodopi (1989). pp. 221. £20. ISBN 0 5183 299 0.

Machan, Tim William, ed. *Medieval Literature: Texts and Interpretation*. MRTS 79. SUNYP. pp. 198. $20.00. ISBN 0 86698 090 3.

Maddox, Donald. *The Arthurian Romances of Chrétien de Troyes: Once and Future Fictions*. CUP. pp. 180. pb £20. ISBN 0 521 39450 3.

Masciandaro, Franco. *Dante as Dramatist: the Myth of the Earthly Paradise and Tragic Vision in the Divine Comedy*. UPennP. pp. 241. £27.50. ISBN 0 8122 3069 8.

Mills, Maldwyn, Jennifer Fellows, and Carol M. Meale, eds. *Romance in Medieval England*. D. S. Brewer. pp. 228. £35.00. ISBN 0 85991 326 0.
Morgan, Gerald. *Sir Gawain and the Green Knight and the Idea of Righteousness*. Irish Academic Press. IR£27.50.
Morse, Ruth. *Truth and Convention in the Medieval Ages: Rhetoric, Representation and Reality*. CUP. pp. 295. £35.00. ISBN 0 521 30211 0.
Richardson, Christine, and Jackie Johnston. *Medieval Drama*. Macmillan. pp. 192. £9.99. ISBN 0333 454 766.
Riddy, Felicity, ed. *Regionalism in Late Medieval Mss and Texts. Essays Celebrating the Publication of 'A Linguistic Atlas of Late Mediaeval English'*. D. S. Brewer. pp. 214. £35.00. ISBN 0 85991 311 2.
Robinson, J. W. *Studies in Fifteenth-century Stagecraft*. MIP. pb $16.95.
Sichert, Margit. *Die Mittelenglische Pastourelle*. Niemeyer. pp. 213. DM 78. ISBN 3 484 45027 4.
Simon, Eckehard, ed. *The Theatre of Medieval Europe*. CUP. pp. 326. £35.00. ISBN 0521 385148.
Sowell, Madison U. *Dante and Ovid: Essays in Intertextuality*. MRTS 82. SUNYP. pp. 191.
Spector, S., ed. *The N-Town Plays*. EETS suppl. 11. OUP. pp. 413. £30. ISBN 0 197 22411 3.
Stanbury, Sarah. *Seeing the Gawain Poet*. UPennP. pp. 160. $22.95. ISBN 0 812231090.
Sturges, Robert S. *Medieval Interpretation: Models of Reading in Literary Narrative 1100–1500*. Southern Illinois UP. pp. 304. $39.95. ISBN 0 8093 1556 4.
Thiem, Jon, ed. *Lorenzo de' Medici, Selected Poems and Prose*. PennUP. pp. 192. £25.00. ISBN 0 271 007722 9.
Yeager, R. F., ed. *Chaucer and Gower. Difference, Mutuality, Exchange*. University of Victoria, BC. pp. 152. pb $8.50. ISBN 0 926 60454 4.

V

Middle English: Chaucer

LUCINDA RUMSEY

This chapter is divided into four sections: 1. General; 2. *Canterbury Tales*; 3. *Troilus and Criseyde*; 4. Other Works.

1. General

Lorrayne Y. Baird Lange, Bege K. Bowers and Bruce W. Hozeski, assisted by Hildegard Schnutten, have produced their annual bibliographical report, with 359 entries, for 'An Annotated Chaucer Bibliography 1989' (*SAC* 13.293–368). Bege K. Bowers has compiled 'Chaucer Research 1990: Report no. 51', which heralds the appearance of two major projects: the Chaucer Sources and Analogues and the Chaucer Studio (*ChauR* 26.184–204). The listings deal primarily with works by American scholars, 100 out of 431 entries dealing with the work of scholars in countries other than the United States.

Akio Oizumi has produced the computer-generated text of *A Complete Concordance to the Works of Geoffrey Chaucer* in ten volumes. This supersedes the John S. P. Tatlock and G. Kennedy edition of 1927. It is based upon the Riverside Chaucer and only the works in this edition have been concorded; i.e. the *Equatorie of the Planetis* is excluded but *Roman de la Rose* in its entirety and 'Poems not ascribed to Chaucer in the Manuscript' are included. In addition to an index of every occurrence of every word in Chaucer's works, Oizumi provides a ranking word-frequency list, an alphabetical list of hyphenated compounds, and an indication of the frequency with which individual words appear in rhyming position. Howell Chickering makes a convincing case for 'Unpunctuating Chaucer' (*ChauR* 25.96–109) . He argues that the punctuation added by modern editors pre-empts the range of possible interpretations of the text, and he demonstrates from his own experience of teaching Chaucer the value for students of working from an unpunctuated or facsimile text.

Derek Pearsall addresses 'The Problems of Writing a Life of Chaucer' (*SAC* 13.1–14) answering the sceptics who claim 'that it cannot be done, that it is not worth doing, or that it has been done'. He argues that an attempt to understand the association between life and works is a fruitful exercise, particularly since Chaucer cultivates in the reader an interest in himself as poet and individual. Pearsall offers a general caution, warning against the two extremes of reading relevance indiscriminately into all biographical and historical data and of limiting attention only to those events which find a neat match in the text. Chaucer's poetry may not seem to be noticeably influenced by major political events such as the Peasants' Revolt, but the changes which resulted from these circumstances are fully explored in his works. Finally, Pearsall hopes to find objectivity by taking a sceptical view of Chaucer's 'niceness', approaching Chaucer in some respects as a person he doesn't much like and whose views he disapproves of.

In 'Chaucer's Ancestry: Historical and Philological Re-assessments' (*ChauR* 25.171–89), Lister M. Matheson attempts a reinterpretation of documentary evidence dealing with Chaucer's direct paternal line. He suggests that the original surname of the family, Malyn, is a metronymic from Chaucer's grandmother Mary, and that Chaucer's grandfather took the name Le Chaucer from John Le Chaucer, to whom he was apprenticed, and who made him executor of his business affairs and bequeathed him money. A brief appendix to this article tentatively supports the view that Chaucer's birthplace was a tenement in Thomas Street, London. Rodney Delasanta reviews the historical evidence concerning 'Chaucer and Strode' (*ChauR* 26.205–18), and argues that if the Strode named in *Troilus and Criseyde* is the eminent pre-1373 Thomist philosopher, Chaucer would have been cognizant of the entire range of philosophical speculation of his day. This is a heady notion for scholars only too ready to credit Chaucer with specialist knowledge in numerous disciplines.

C. David Benson's edition of *Critical Essays on Chaucer's 'Troilus and Criseyde' and his Major Early Poems*, the companion volume to Malcolm Andrew's *Critical Essays on Chaucer's Canterbury Tales* (see below), contains twelve essays on *Troilus and Criseyde* and seven on the *House of Fame*, *Book of the Duchess* and *Parliament of Fowls*. Benson claims to make his selection based on the principles of quality and influence, and many of the best-known Chaucer critics are represented, ranging from G. L. Kittredge and C. S. Lewis to Jill Mann and Piero Boitani. The absence of a single essay on *Legend of Good Women* or the lyric poems is disappointing. The earlier collection edited by Schoeck and Taylor in 1961, which this volume aims to supplement, was entitled *'Troilus and Criseyde' and the Minor Poems*, a telling reflection of the change in critical perspective since the Sixties. That collection contained only four essays on the dream visions.

In 'The Premodern Text and the Postmodern Reader' (*Exemplaria* 2.1–21), Thomas Hahn provides an introduction to the debate undertaken by a conference entitled 'Reconceiving Chaucer: Literary Theory and Historical Interpretation', the papers for which comprise a special volume of *Exemplaria*. The ambitious aim of the debate is 'to refashion the terms of medieval criticism, and bring this endeavour into engagement with main currents of literary and cultural studies of the late twentieth century'. Most of the papers are arranged in the form of a debate, a pair of papers followed by a response which compares their approaches. In 'Fearing for Chaucer's Good Name' (*Exemplaria* 2.23–36), Elaine Tuttle Hansen divides the world of Chaucer criticism into three ages: the pre-feminist up to the 1970s, where issues of sexual politics were largely ignored; the feminist age from the 1970s, where Chaucer is viewed as a self-conscious social critic of the anti-feminist tradition; and the present post-feminist age which defends Chaucer's good name, while recognizing the gendered character of his imagination and his audience. Hansen fears that this last critical position might lead to a return 'to the pre-feminist status quo, where there is no actual or theoretical place for the woman reader and critic of Chaucer'.

John M. Fyler's paper, 'Man, Men and Women in Chaucer's Poetry', appears in abstract in *Exemplaria*, but is printed in full in Edwards and Spector, eds., *The Olde Daunce: Love, Friendship, Sex and Marriage in the Medieval World*. Fyler argues that

Chaucer shows in his poetry an awareness of the implications of the fact that the word 'man' may refer to the entire human race or to males alone. Drawing on the tradition of Genesis commentary, and upon plays on the relationship between meaning and sexual differentiation, he explores the issues of sexual politics as they are embedded in linguistic practice. Mary Nyquist continues the discussion in 'Ever (Wo)man's Friend: A Response to John Fyler and Elaine Tuttle Hansen' (*Exemplaria* 2.37–47). She concentrates primarily on the questions both papers raise about the problem of the adulation of the male canonical author: she suggests that the politics of adulation may be subverted by an ideologically informed reworking of the reception-history of an author's texts as well as the figure of the author; and by an investigation of the relations in a given historical period between literary and non-literary forms of debates concerning 'Woman'.

In 'Structure as Deconstruction: "Chaucer and Estates Satire in the General Prologue": or Reading Chaucer as A Prologue to the History of Disenchantment' (*Exemplaria* 2.241–61), H. Marshall Leicester propounds theories more fully treated in his book *The Disenchanted Self: Representing the Subject in the Canterbury Tales* (*YWES* 71). He defines 'disenchantment' as 'what had been thought to be other-originated, the product of transcendent forces not directly susceptible of human tampering and subversion, [which] is in fact humanly originated and the product of human creation'. Applying this element of modern theories of reading to the *Canterbury Tales*, he shows how the *General Prologue* challenges the traditional assumptions of Estates Satire, specifically by means of deconstruction.

In '*Troilus and Criseyde*: The Illusion of Allusion' (*Exemplaria* 2.263–77), A. C. Spearing uses recent work by John Fyler and Winthrop Wetherbee on classical and Dantean allusions in *Troilus and Criseyde* to ask, in a refreshingly direct manner, whether this text is as sophisticated in its allusions as these and other critics would have it. He fears not only that scholars expect Chaucer and his readers to have full recall of a vast range of texts, but also that making a reading of *Troilus and Criseyde* dependent upon the recognition of allusion renders the text inaccessible to any but the most highly qualified scholar. In 'Intention, Interpretation and the Limits of Meaning: A Response to A. C. Spearing and H. Marshall Leicester' (*Exemplaria* 2.279–85), Victoria Kahn sees the two papers as complementary in addressing the issue of authorial intention as a norm for literary interpretation, and in this respect Spearing's standpoint is more radical than Leicester's. 'Spearing thinks Chaucer couldn't have intended certain effects to be understood, though he did intend them, and thus shows how intention doesn't govern meaning; while Leicester uses the concept of intention in a totalising fashion to delimit the radical indeterminacy of meaning.'

In 'Your Praise is Performed by Men and Children: Language and Gender in the *Prioress's Prologue* and *Tale*' (*Exemplaria* 2.149–68), Judith Ferster begins by questioning the applicability of psychoanalysis to the study of Chaucer. She demonstrates how fruitful this application can be, not by providing a single coherent reading to the Tale but by showing how its meaning oscillates as we attribute it to different speakers, and as we attribute identity and intention to those speakers. In ' "Voice Memorial": Loss and Reparation in Chaucer's Poetry' (*Exemplaria* 2.169–202), Louise O. Fradenburg addresses the question of memory, and in particular the importance of loss, and why women do not appear as overmuch capable of consolation in Chaucer's poetry. R. Howard Bloch in 'Critical Communities and the Shape of the Medievalist's Desire: A Response to Judith Ferster and Louise Fradenburg' (*Exemplaria* 2.213–20), finds that the challenge of these two papers is the way that they 'problematize the critical act, to render it visible by reading our own desire into it', and he applauds Fradenburg's desire to 'construct a medievalism that is politically compassionate'. In 'Chaucer and the Noise of the People' (*Exemplaria* 2.71–88), John Ganim examines Chaucer's politics. Focusing on four passages which to some degree allude to the Peasants' Revolt, Ganim shows how these moments represent a pattern of constraint and release which illustrates Chaucer's ambivalent relations to the power of popular discourse.

In 'Textual Criticism and Literary Theory: Chaucer and His Readers' (*Exemplaria* 2.329–45), Seth Lerer looks at the interrelationship between textual and literary criticism in the work of Chaucer and his inheritors with a view to understanding 'how Chaucer's texts *invite* revision and request the reader to manipulate his source'. He examines the way that Chaucer's fifteenth-century readers, in particular John Shirley, acknowledge Chaucer's authority while recasting him according to their own tastes. In 'Postmodernism in Medieval England: Chaucer, Pynchon, Joyce and the Poetics of Fission' (*Exemplaria* 2.563–94), M. Keith Boocker finds that reading Chaucer through postmodernist authors shows parallels between Chaucer's attitude to literature and trends in modern literary theory. In the Biennial Chaucer Lecture, John Burrow examines various responses to Chaucer's 'Poems Without Endings' (*SAC* 13.17–37) namely the *House of Fame,* the *Legend of Good Women*, the *Cook's Tale* and the *Squire's Tale*. Until recent years, the assumption appears to have been that these poems are incomplete. Scribes left marginal notes to this effect or left spaces in the manuscripts in case a lost ending should be recovered, and poets from Caxton to Pope, apparently uncomfortable with the incomplete poems, provide endings of varying length and complexity. Modern critics often seek to justify the inconclusive narrative, and fragments stimulate the imagination of the contemporary critic suspicious of closure. Burrow fears that modern Chaucerians may be losing their capacity to deal with the accidental and the contingent. Velma Bourgeois Richmond compares Muriel Spark with her fellow-Catholic writer Chaucer in 'Chaucer's Religiosity and a Twentieth-Century Analogue, Muriel Spark' (*MLQ* 51.427–45). She argues that Spark creates, like him, 'a fictional world in which the grotesque, the comical, the aberrant are cast against belief in the Church'.

Chaucer and Gower: Difference, Mutuality, Exchange is a collection of essays edited by R. F. Yeager which aim to investigate the poetic interaction between Gower and Chaucer. (Individual essays are dealt with under the appropriate section.) In 'Latin Structure and Vernacular Space: Gower, Chaucer and the Boethian Tradition', Winthrop Wetherbee argues that the feature of Boethius' *Consolation* which appealed most to Chaucer as well as Gower was 'the consistency with which its philosphical affirmations are punctuated by existential doubt', a questioning of authority which Wetherbee finds strongly present in the works of both authors. In '*De Vulgari Auctoritate*: Chaucer, Gower and the Men of Great Authority', A. J. Minnis investigates the problem of vernacular poets in earning respect and authority as writers, since 'an *auctor amans* was a contradiction in terms', and suggests that Chaucer's strategy is to pursue the role of poet as *fictor*. In 'Learning to Speak in Tongues: Writing Poetry for a Trilingual Culture', R. F. Yeager argues that the access to, and familiarity with, the French, Latin and English languages which Chaucer and his contemporary readership was able to draw upon is a resource which the twentieth-century audience has difficulty appreciating. He uses the works of Gower as a sample of trilingual poetic vocabulary, which offers 'a window into the process of poetic choice and composition in late-medieval England'. Taking the pair of words 'nature' and 'kynde' and working from the assumption that the use of one synonym over another reveals attitudes towards the source or root language of the word, Yeager shows that for Gower the latinate 'nature' indicates the abstract quality possessed by rational humankind, whereas the native 'kynde' is used to mean the instinctual biological imperative. Chaucer, by comparison, appears to use the pair more randomly and even-handedly, as if he considered them truly synonymous.

In 'Legendary Women: Alceste and Criseyde Within "Boundes They Oghte Keepe" ' (*SCRev* 8.19–35), Fay Walker-Pelkey argues that Chaucer used the *Legend of Good Women* and in particular Alceste to provide a commentary on Criseyde in *Troilus and Criseyde*. In spite of the narrator's worship of the self-sacrificing Alceste, however, she is not set up as an ideal for wifehood to be preferred to the pragmatically surviving Criseyde. Chaucer's moral is that human beings are not acceptable as models or paradigms, and that marriage is not for keeping women constrained.

Turning to legendary men, Melvin Storm in 'From Knossos to *Knight's Tale*: The Changing Face of Chaucer's Theseus' (in Chance, ed., *The Mythographic Art*), traces the metamorphosis of the figure of Theseus as Chaucer uses him in different poems. Storm sees Theseus as 'growing up' from the simple villain of the *House of Fame*, to the more complex and sympathetic traitor of the legend of Ariadne in the *Legend of Good Women*. In the *Knight's Tale* he reaches maturity, as an example of morality and duty 'reflecting the conflicting claims of martial and courtly chivalry'.

2. Canterbury Tales

Malcolm Andrew's volume, *Critical Essays on Chaucer's Canterbury Tales*, provides a selection of essays and extracts from full-length works, beginning with a part of William Blake's *Descriptive Catalogue* (1809) describing his painting of the Canterbury Pilgrims. The majority of the essays in the collection were written within the last thirty years, concluding with a pair of articles by Peggy Knapp and Traugott Lawlor in 1987 on the advantages and disadvantages of a deconstructive reading of the *Tales*. Most articles deal with generally relevant issues rather than with interpretative readings of single tales, the aim being not only to show the range and variety of Chaucer criticism, but to represent significant trends and developments in the twentieth century.

In 'The Versification of *The Canterbury Tales*: A Computer-Based Statistical Study', Part I (*LSE* 21.81–103), Charles Barber and Nicholas Barber undertook a statistical analysis of a part of the Hengwrt MS of the *Canterbury Tales*, to investigate the pronunciation of unelided word-final unstressed *-e* .The analysis counted the syllables in the first thousand lines of the *Tales* in which word-final *-e* does not occur within the line, followed by a syllable count of the first thousand lines in which word-final *-e* occurs twice, and compared the syllable counts. The evidence adduced suggests that in about half the examples *-e* was pronounced. Part II of the study (*LSE* 22.57–83) attempts to isolate the words in which this occured, concluding with a summary of various words and word-categories in three groups; words in which unelided word-final unstressed *-e* was pronounced, words in which it was sometimes pronounced and words in which it was never pronounced.

'On Making an Edition of the *Canterbury Tales* in Modern Spelling' (*ChauR* 26.48–64) is Michael Murphy's proposal for a new-spell version of Chaucer which is 'not a translation, and not simply a normalised text, but an edition of the manuscript itself in modern spelling, line for line, an edited transliteration which just takes the normalisation process to its logical conclusion'. The other logical conclusion of this process, modern punctuation and the attendant consequences and problems for rhyme and rhythm, is briefly addressed but not resolved.

In his investigation of 'The Earliest Known Owners of *Canterbury Tales* Manuscripts and Chaucer's Secondary Audience' (*ChauR* 25.17–32), Malcolm Richardson concentrates on the lives and social milieu of Richard Southworth and John Stopyndon, two early owners of *Canterbury Tales* manuscripts. He offers some general comment on their roles and responsibilities as Chancery clerks, characterizing them as men of some intellectual merit, with commitment to reading, debate and the written word. Although he cannot positively state that Southworth and Stopyndon owned copies of the the *Canterbury Tales* for literary rather than mercenary interests, Richardson suggests that these men and others like them were the 'faint harbingers of a new London elite, secular and non-aristocratic, which would sustain vernacular literature over the next three centuries'.

Rebels and Rivals: The Contestive Spirit in the Canterbury Tales, a collection of papers edited by Susanna Fein, David Raybin and Peter Braeger, has a foreword by Derek Pearsall and concludes with 'A Memoir of Chaucer's Institute' by C. D. Benson, who describes the activities of the six-week Institute at the University of Connecticut in 1987, from which the papers in this volume were drawn. Individual essays are dealt with under their appropriate sections.

In 'The Inn, the Cathedral and the Pilgrimage of the *Canterbury Tales*' (*Rebels and Rivals*), Frederick B. Jonassen uses the socio-historicism of Mikhail Bakhtin and the social anthropology of Victor Turner to explore the significance of the symbolic *loci* of the Inn and the Cathedral. Standing at either end of the *Canterbury Tales*, they represent the opposition between the material and spiritual worlds, but they are reconciled by the pilgrimage and story-telling which forms a passage between them.

In an excellent and informative article 'Chaucer and Moral Philosophy: The Virtuous Women of the *Canterbury Tales*' (*MÆ* 60.241–56), Denise N. Baker demonstrates the influence of medieval ethics on Chaucer's characterization of the virtuous women in the tales ascribed to the Man of Law, the Clerk, the Physician, and the tale of Melibee. Medieval moralists drew on the writings of Cicero, Macrobius, Pseudo-Seneca and Martin of Broya, as is revealed in Peraldus's compendium of late medieval views about the four cardinal virtues, *Summa de Virtutibus*. Each heroine is identified with one of the cardinal virtues: Constance is a model of fortitude, the medieval definition of which emphasizes equanimity in the face of good or ill fortune; Griselda, although possessing qualities of fortitude and patience, is closest to an example of distributive justice in her voluntary rendering of duty to another; Virginia's character is elaborated, particularly with the introductory enconium, to emphasise her exemplification of temperance. However, the tale of Melibee needs little revision to present Prudence as a representation of the virtue after which she is named, with its connotations of intellectual discrimination.

In 'Aphrodite/Artemis// Emilia / Alison: The Semiotics of Perception' (*Exemplaria* 2.89–125), Hope Weissman takes as her theme masculine subjectivity as constituted in, and through, the male gaze, using the stories of Aphrodite in Homer's *Odyssey* and Artemis in Ovid's *Metamorphosis* to represent male mastery and disempowerment respectively, and in turn, using these figures to illustrate Emily's and Alison's responses to the male gaze. In 'Empowering New Discourse: Response to Eugene Vance and Hope Weissman' (*Exemplaria* 2.127–47), Stephen G. Nichols responds to a different version of Weissman's paper from that printed, which deals with Eglentyne rather than Emily, and considers this paper in tandem with Eugene Vance's article 'Chaucer's Pardoner: Relics, Discourse and Frames of Propriety' published in 1989 (*YWES* 70.224). In 'Chaucer's Body Politic: Social and Narrative Self-Regulation' (*Exemplaria* 2.221–40), David Wallace argues that an interchange of political and literary metaphors is essential for medieval texts and medieval societies to figure their own self-regulation, although those metaphors are finally found to be provisional and provisory. Using the latter part of fragment III of the *Canterbury Tales*, the Friar's and Summoner's exchange, Wallace offers an analysis of the *Canterbury Tales* as a self-regulating socio-literary system. In 'Moral and Aesthetic Falls on the Canterbury Way' (*SCRev* 8.36–49), Mark Allen focuses upon three falls or threatened falls in the links to the *Tales*; the Cook's fall from his horse in the Manciple's Prologue; the Host's threat to drop with boredom after the *Monk's Tale* and the Pardoner's warning in his *Prologue* of the danger of a riding accident. This imagery of falling reinforces the penitential motif of the pilgrimage, and aesthetic and moral concerns are combined in tales which become the confessions of their tellers.

In 'Chaucer's Zephirus: Dante's Zefiro, St. Dominic and the Idea of the *General Prologue*' (in Chance, ed., *The Mythographic Art*), Jane Chance suggests that the image of Zephirus, generally linked in Chaucer's works with the rebirth and renewal of Spring, has an additional association in the *Prologue* to the *Canterbury Tales* with the birth of St Dominic. Dante's *Paradiso* 12 describes the saint's birth as being influenced by Zephirus, and his founding of the Dominican order as causing spiritual renewal of the Church. This pagan image further highlights the dramatic tension between the desire for this world and for the next, demonstrated by the pilgrims in the *Canterbury Tales*. Taking 'A New Look At an Old Patient: Chaucer's Summoner and Medieval *Physiognomia*' (*ChauR* 25.266–75), Laura Braswell-Means diagnoses the Summoner as choleric and suggests that his humoral imbalances and his corrosive disease would be taken, in medieval physiognomial theory, to indicate moral corruption of his soul and the corrosion of his profession. In 'A Reconsideration of the Monk's Costume' (*ChauR* 26.133–46), Laura F. Hodges examines the Monk's costume details in historical context which reveals that he is neither excessively worldly nor particularly ascetic in his dress, and that his outfit is within the range of ordinary array worn by late fourteenth-century monks of his degree. On the way to this reasonable conclusion, we meet such extraordinary remarks as 'Similarly we need to re-evaluate the Monk's supple boots'.

In 'Up and Down, To and Fro: Spatial Relationships in the *Knight's Tale*' (*Rebels and Rivals*), William F. Woods looks at the ways in which spatial relationships 'contribute to the structural patterning of the *Knight's Tale*, thereby reflecting its social background and thematic content'. Three sorts of spatial movement are investigated: the vertical movement up and down of Fortune's wheel and life and death; the horizontal movement of the knights' restless wandering to and fro, which contrasts with the stability of Theseus; and the movement between the outer world and the inner landscape of the ideal. Palamon and Arcite are drawn to share the same narrative space as Emily, but in doing so they become increasingly separate from one another. In 'Medieval Visual Arts and the Barred Window in the *Knight's Tale*' (*ELN* 28.10–17), John Z. Zhang argues that the barred window through which the knights first see Emily signifies the carnal senses through which sin enters the soul. He concludes that Palamon's desire for, and marriage to, Emily is not a happy resolution but a defeat of the ideals of chivalry in favour of earthly love. Kolve's 'Imagery of Narrative' is the inspiration for Peter Brown in 'The Prison of Theseus and the Castle of Jalousie' (*ChauR* 26.147–62). He suggests that Palamon and Arcite's prison can be associated with the Castle of Jealousy in *Roman de la Rose*, an appropriate image in a text which stresses the imprisoning power of jealousy. Catherine Brown Tkacz investigates the links between 'Sampson and Arcite in the *Knight's Tale*' (*ChauR*

25.127–37). In the *Teseida*, Arcite's vow to cut his hair as a sign of his service to Mars associates him with Sampson, but Chaucer elaborates the parallel by Saturn's mention of Sampson's suicide, and by architectural details such as the shaking gates and pillars in Mars' temple. By these means Arcite is linked with Sampson in his traditional role as fool for love, with perhaps the added dimension, suggested by the convention of using Sampson and Delilah's relationship as a *psychomachia*, that Arcite fulfils the destructive role of Delilah towards himself by offering to cut off his own hair.

In ' "Alone Withouten Any Compaignye": The Mayings in Chaucer's *Knight's Tale*' (*ChauR* 25.284–301), Bruce Moore investigates the ambiguous significance of ritual and ceremony in the Tale, in particular Arcite's and Emily's celebrations of May. Such seasonal festivities are usually represented as communal activities; so the solitary nature of these observances in the *Knight's Tale* signifies for Moore a comment on Arcite's undesired isolation from the ritual bonds of the community, which ends in the solitude of the grave, and Emily's unachieved desire for freedom from those bonds, as expressed in her prayer to Diana for the preservation of her chastity. Howard Schless offers two notes: on '*Knight's Tale* 967–7, 1462–75 Theseus's Banner, Palamon's Mickey' (*ChauR* 25.80–3). Theseus's display of his banner after his promise to avenge the Theban women is shown, by reference to a history of martial law, to be a sign of the declaration of open war. Legal history may also explain, although not provide a source for, Chaucer's expansion upon the *Teseida* at ll. 1462–75, where Palamon drugs the jailor to effect an escape. Schless quotes an account of famous and sensational escapes from prison in the early fourteenth century which use this same ploy of slipping the guards a Mickey Finn. In a detailed and scholarly investigation of 'Romance and Epic in Chaucer's *Knight's Tale*' (*Exemplaria* 2.303–28), Winthrop Wetherbee looks at the representation of history in the *Knight's Tale* by examination of the classical epic which lies behind the chivalric romance. In coming to terms with epic history, the reality of the Knight's own world is incorporated into the tale, to make it a 'landmark in the history of realistic fiction'. In 'Surface and Secret in the *Knight's Tale*' (*ChauR* 26.1–16), Brooke Bergan makes the *Knight's Tale* the battlefield for oral epic narrative and written romance narrative. As one genre congeals into its opposite the secrets beneath the opaque surface of language can be revealed.

In 'Absolon's Musical Instruments' (*ELN* 28.7–15), Robert Boenig uses musical iconography to demonstrate how Absolon's two musical instruments, the rebec and the gittern, contribute to the musical irony of the *Miller's Tale*. The high-pitched rebec is traditionally likened to a screeching woman's voice, and the gittern is humorously represented in manuscript illuminations as a strung ass's jaw-bone. Boenig wonders whether Chaucer drew upon these conventions to hint at the poor quality of Absolon's music. Susanna Greer Fein asks 'Why Did Absolon Put a "Trewelove" Under His Tongue? Herb Paris as a Healing "Grace" in Middle English Literature' (*ChauR* 25.302–17), and looks at the Middle English popular and poetic tradition of the 'truelove' plant. She finds that it has a wide range of allusions, primarily as a talisman for earthly and divine love, appropriate for Absolon who rejects love of God in favour of fleshly desire. In 'Doubting Thomas and John the Carpenter's Oaths in the *Miller's Tale*' (*ELN* 29.15–17), Ed Malone notes that although the carpenter's oaths are generally held to refer to Thomas a' Beckett, he may be swearing by the disciple, 'doubting' Thomas. This Thomas was associated with builders and so is appropriate for a carpenter's oath, and swearing by the sceptical saint is doubly appropriate for the gullible John.

Three articles this year examine the theme of rivalry in the *Reeve's Tale*. Bruce

Kent Cowgill examines 'Clerkly Rivalry in the *Reeve's Tale*' (*Rebels and Rivals*) arguing that the clerks are engaged in competition with one another as well as revenging themselves upon the Miller. Cowgill points to the individualization of the clerks' characters, which is not found in sources and analogues of the *Tale*. He considers that John is the craftier of the two, but that Aleyn, although portrayed as dull-witted, shows more bravado in initiating the revenge by means of the Miller's daughter. Susanna Greer Fein in ' "Lat the Children Pleye": The Game Betwixt the Ages in the *Reeve's Tale*' (*Rebels and Rivals*), looks at the conflict between the clerks and the miller as a struggle between youth and age. The Reeve's *Prologue*, with its figure of the cask of life, is the first of a series of allusions to life as a cycle. The most explicit of these in the *Tale* itself is the mill-wheel, but the theme is picked up in such symbols as Symkyn's bald 'crown' and the baby's cradle. The conflicts and rivalries between the characters reflect the activities of life which distract young and old from the passage of time. In 'The Wife in Chaucer's *Reeve's Tale*: Siren of Sweet Vengance' (*ELN* 28.1–6), Gay L. Balliet asserts that the blow on the head that the Franklin receives from his wife is intentional rather than misdirected. In spite of evidence in the text to the contrary, Balliet finds that the wife's character and situation make her likely to wish to attack her husband. In 'The Failure of the Intellect in Chaucer's *Reeve's Tale*' (*ELN* 28.17–19), Jeffrey Baylor notes that Chaucer makes his clerks visit the miller with the intention of engaging in a battle of wits in order to emphasize the failure of university intellect in the face of brute violence and deceit. In 'The *Reeve's Tale*: About That Horse' (*ChauR* 26.99–106), Sandy Feinstein questions the likelihood that the clerks' horse would have been a stallion and considers what its symbolic role would have been if it were a gelding or mare. All horses are associated with lust and appetite, but as a gelding, Bayard might be an exemplum of frustrated impotence and thus represent the Reeve.

In 'The Man of Law's Tale: What Chaucer Really Owed to Gower' (*ChauR* 26.153–74), Peter Nicholson argues that Chaucer's debt to the *Man of Law's Tale* has never been adequately assessed, and by examination of parallels of detail and general narrative strategies, concludes that Gower provided Chaucer's most important model for the *Man of Law's Tale* and 'that it was Gower's tale rather than Trevet's that Chaucer chose to retell'. In 'Chaucer Borrows from Gower: The Sources of the *Man of Law's Tale*' (*Chaucer and Gower*), Peter Nicholson goes further in finding significant similarities between Chaucer's and Gower's versions of the tale of Constance which indicate that Chaucer was more indebted to Gower than to the *Chronicle* of Trevet. The evidence extrapolated from their texts suggests that both writers used a manuscript version of Trevet with very similar characteristics. This leads Nicholson to extend the notion of borrowing so far as to suggest that Gower not only provided a source for Chaucer in his version of the tale in the *Confessio Amantis* but also lent Chaucer the copy of Trevet's *Chronicle* which he had used. In 'Chaucer's MS of Nicholas Trevet's *Les Cronicles*' (*ChauR* 25.238–65), Robert M. Correale considers which of the extant manuscripts of the *Chronicle* is closest to the text Chaucer used when he wrote the *Man of Law's Tale*. The Paris Bibl. Nationale, francs 9687 MS appears to be the closest (although not the one that Chaucer consulted), and this manuscript will be used as the base text for the forthcoming Chaucer Library edition of *Les Cronicles*. Ann W. Astell finds that Chaucer's additions to his source are chiefly in the form of apostrophe, exclamatio and rhetorical questions interjected by the narrators, and prayers uttered by Constance. In 'Apostrophe, Prayer and the Structure of Satire in the *Man of Law's Tale*' (*SAC* 13.81–97), she shows how the *Tale* is turned into satire by the opposition of these two rhetorical figures, and the figures of the Man of Law and Constance who voice them. The Man of Law provides a commentary by his apostrophic speeches which stress the influence of Fortune in the *Tale*, in the alternation of joy and woe, whilst the more perspicuous Constance, directing prayers to God, asserts the power of Providence and sees her life, and thus the *Tale*, as 'a sequence of divine initiatives'. In ' "Unwemmed Custance": Circulation, Property and Incest in the *Man of Law's Tale*' (*Exemplaria* 2.287–302), R. A. Shoaf demonstrates, more by ingenious use of word-play than cogent argument, that Chaucer uses this tale to consider the circulation and corruption of the medium of poetry. 'Unwemmed Custance' is the ideal sign for the Man of Law to whom writing is a kind of hoarding, because she is constant and untarnished despite being circulated. The narrative, Shoaf argues, 'will be, finally, incestuous as well as (predictably) about incest, for in order to ensure the return of the same, it will be always and only about itself'. A. S. G. Edwards offers '*Man of Law's Tale* 517: A Conjectural Emendation' (*ChauR* 25.76–7). The line as it stands has Constance requesting the Constable 'The lyf out of hir body for to twynne', a plea for death which is at odds with her presentation elsewhere. Edwards conjectures that, although it has no support in the manuscripts, changing 'out' to 'not', to make the line refer instead to a plea for mercy, would be less problematic. In ' "I Speke In Prose": *Man of Law's Tale*, 96' (*NM* 92.469–70), A. S. G. Edwards notes that the term 'prose' is used in the Middle English *Stacions of Rome* to describe verse dealing with historical and religious history, and suggests that Chaucer may be using it in the same way to define his verse narrative in the *Man of Law's Tale* as religious and historical.

M. C. Seymour in 'Of This Cokes Tale' (*ChauR* 24.259–62), argues from bibliographical evidence that the *Cook's Tale* was originally complete, but that the final quire of the booklet which concluded with that tale was lost very early in the manuscript tradition.

Peter G. Beidler is tired of comparisons between Chaucer's and Gower's versions of the Loathly Lady story which simply evaluate Chaucer's version as 'better'. In 'Transformations in Gower's *Tale of Florent* and Chaucer's *Wife of Bath's Tale*' (*Chaucer and Gower*), he compares the details of the two tales to highlight the different purposes of the two authors. Gower uses the *Tale of Florent* to demonstrate to Amans how a courteous and near-perfect knight deals with a dangerous and hostile situation, and is rewarded for his obedience in matters of love. The *Wife of Bath's Tale* 'almost a feminist parody of the traditional romance' demonstrates to the pilgrims how an impulsive and imperfect knight can be tested and educated by women and transformed into a man worthy of love. Beidler's comparison is salutary but perhaps he overstates his case in his insistence that every detail of the two versions must serve his view of the author's very particular purpose.

For Susan K. Hagan, the Wife of Bath's potential as a feminist creation can only be judged within the limitations of the fourteenth-century privileged male perspective which created her. In 'The Wife Of Bath: Chaucer's Inchoate Experiment in Feminist Hermeneutics' (*Rebels and Rivals*), she argues that Chaucer's 'humanist' effort is ambitious and commendable, but the fairy's final submission to the knight's desire shows that the poet is incapable of formulating consistent and complete feminist hermeneutics. Richard Firth Green suggests as 'An Analogue to the "Marital Dilemma" in the *Wife of Bath's Tale*' (*ELN* 28.9–12) the French farce *Les deux maris et leurs deux femmes* (*c*.1500) in which two wives are compared, one a faithful termagent, the other amiable but unfaithful. Green suggests that this lesson in marital tolerance is closer in spirit to the end of the *Wife of Bath's Tale* than is the learned anti-feminist tradition. 'Mars in Taurus at the Nativity of the Wife of Bath' (*ELN*

28.16) indicates to Edgar S. Laird that the Wife was engaged in prostitution. His supposition is based upon the thirteenth-century *Compilatio de astrorum scientia.*

The *Summoner's Tale* has inspired some excellent articles this year. In ' "Ars-Metrik": Science, Satire and Chaucer's Summoner'(*Mosaic* 23.1–22), Timothy D. O'Brian explores with great ingenuity the cultural associations between the demonic and the mechanical as demonstrated in the *Summoner's Tale.* The tale provides ironic comment on the value of experimental science which aims to investigate God's 'privitee', but is reduced finally to 'ars-metrik'. In ' "New Science" from "Olde Bokes": A Bakhtinian Approach to the *Summoner's Tale*' (*ChauR* 25.138–51), James Andreas claims that the carnivalesque context of the *Summoner's Tale* has never been adequately assessed. He details the carnivalesque features which deflate Christian ritual and dogma: for example, the groping beneath Thomas's 'buttok', a parody of the sceptical disciple's search of Christ's wounds, and the Squire's mock allegorization and moralization of the division of the fart. In ' "My Spirit Hath his Fostryng in the Bible": The *Summoner's Tale* and the Holy Spirit' (*Rebels and Rivals*), Jay Ruud explores the numerous connotations of the term 'spirit', which include 'truth', 'wisdom' and even 'air' or 'wind' and shows how the Summoner with his mendacity, fleshly interests and wrath is seen to be inverting and perverting several Pauline and Franciscan injunctions appropriate for a Friar and inheritor of the Apostolic Spirit. The flesh/spirit distinction is given particularly graphic illustration in the image of friars gathering around the devil's arse, a parody, Ruud suggests, of the souls of the elect sheltering in Abraham's bosom. Linda Georgianna, in 'Lord's Churls and Friars: The Return to Social Order in the *Summoner's Tale*' (*Rebels and Rivals*), focuses on the social rather than religious dimension of the *Summoner's Tale*, in particular the significance of the court scene. Whereas the friar's dealings with Thomas are founded upon economy-based class relations by which Thomas pays for prayers with cash, the lord's treatment of the friar restores the hierarchical order and places him back within the feudal structure, by judging against him in favour of Thomas, and by mocking both the cash economy and the fraternal ideal of the friars.

In 'Irony in Boccaccio's *Decameron* and in Chaucer's *Clerk's Tale*' (*Forum* 27.1–22), Mark Pelan is not proposing that Chaucer knew the *Decameron*, but wishes rather to compare Chaucer's and Boccaccio's poetic procedures. Investigating the modes of poetic irony in the tenth day of the *Decameron* and in the *Clerk's Tale*, he suggests that Chaucer 'seeks in the unresolved inconsistencies of word and deed in his *Clerk's Tale* to draw our attention to better unformulated patterns of obedience in marriage'. In 'Mercury In the Garden: Mythographical Methods in the *Merchant's Tale* and *Decameron* 7.9' (in Chance, ed., *The Mythographic Spirit*), Janet Levarie Smarr argues that although *Decameron* 7.9 has fewer resemblances in plot to the *Merchant's Tale* than its other sources, Boccaccio's tale is closest to Chaucer's in its thematic development. The similar uses of mythographic and astrological associations, the symbolism of garden and pear-tree, and the figurative image of blindness show analogous treatments of the tale which go beyond simple borrowing of narrative detail. Far less coherent is 'Love in Hell: The Role of Pluto and Proserpine in Chaucer's *Merchant's Tale*' (*MLQ* 51.389–407) in which Elizabeth Simmons-O'Neill looks at the pear tree tale and the traditions and contexts upon which it draws, placing it in the broadest context of the international popular tale to give a sense of its history and audiences, a breadth of perspective which also makes the content unfocused and episodic. In 'Reading Chaucer's Earnest Games: Folk-mode or Literary Sophistication?' (*ELN* 29.16–20), Wolfgang E. H. Rudat argues that 'Chaucer is pitting his own *written/literary* "game" ... against the oral-folkloric tradition he is drawing upon.' As an example, he suggests an interaction between the impregnation of earth by April in the opening lines of the *General Prologue*, and the wedding night of January and May in the *Merchant's Tale,* whereby January's sexual prowess suffers by comparison with the cosmic ejaculation. A. S. G. Edwards argues in 'The *Merchant's Tale* and Moral Chaucer' (*MLQ* 51.409–26) that Chaucer avoids moral evaluation in the *Merchant's Tale*. By looking at the historical reception of the tale, from scribes who narrowed the age gap between May and January, and early editors who print an expurgated text, to Lydgate and Pope who rewrite the tale with a clear moral perspective, Edwards shows how readers have attempted to fill what they consider to be a moral vacuum in the narrative. In 'The Merchant's Wife's Tale: Language, Sex and Commerce in Margery Kempe and in Chaucer' (*Exemplaria* 2.595–626), Deborah S. Ellis looks at the implications for medieval women of language, sex and commerce as media of exchange, by offering an intertextual study of Margery Kempe and May from the *Merchant's Tale*.

In 'The Falcon's Complaint in the *Squire's Tale*' (*Rebels and Rivals*), Charles A. Owen Jnr gives a close textual analysis of the Falcon's complaint, comparing its poetics and structure with similar passages in *Anelida and Arcite* and the *Complaint of Mars*. He praises the sophistication and subtlety of the lament, evidence of Chaucer's increasing maturity in dealing with this conventional form.

In 'From Dorigen to the Vavasour: Reading Backwards' (in Edwards and Spector, eds., *The Olde Daunce*), Alan T. Gaylord writes about two distinct approaches to the *Franklin's Tale* and its portrayal of marital partnership. The reader is invited to compare 'reading forwards', largely ignoring the Franklin as an influence upon his tale and 'reading backwards', reading the tale entirely through the filter of the Franklin's character. He advises of the dangers of both approaches. James I. Wimsatt in 'Reason, Machaut and the Franklin' (*The Olde Daunce*) looks at the way the paradigm of consoler–consolation–consolee is developed through Boethius' *Consolatio*, the *Roman de La Rose,* Machaut's *Remede de Fortune* and Chaucer's *Troilus and Criseyde*, and stresses the centrality of the *Remede* in the development. He then uses the Franklin's contribution to the marriage debate, particularly his comments on friendship, to give a further example of how the *Remede* acts as an intermediary between the *Roman de La Rose* and the work of Chaucer.

Richard Firth Green's note on 'Chaucer's *Shipman's Tale,* lines 138–41' (*ChauR* 26.95–8) suggests repunctuating the wife's oath to end at l. 138 instead of l. 140, taking ll. 139–40 as the beginning of authorial commentary which makes for better sense and adds ironic effect.

Alan J. Fletcher offers convincing evidence of 'The Topical Hypocrisy of Chaucer's Pardoner' (*ChauR* 25.110–26). Although a conventional and familiar figure of religious hypocrisy, the Pardoner is used by Chaucer to 'introduce the resonance of the most urgent and topical theological argument of his day', the Lollard and anti-Lollard debate. This strategic choice enables Chaucer to condemn religious abuses without associating himself too obviously with either side, or with contentious current issues. William Kamowski's unsnappily titled ' "Coillons", Relics, Skepticism and Faith on Chaucer's Road to Canterbury: An Observation on the Pardoner's and the Host's Confrontation' (*ELN* 28.1–8), proposes that the host's angry reaction to the Pardoner's demand for veneration of his relics is an expression of the pilgrims' discomfort concerning the authenticity of relics in general. The Pardoner challenges his audience, who suspend their scepticism while on pilgrimage, to acknowledge that his fake relics are no more absurd than many that they will meet on the road to Canterbury. In 'The Pardoner's Self-reflexive *Peyne*: Textual Abuse of

The First Epistle to Timothy' (*SCRev* 8.6–16), Janet J. Montelaro reads the Pardoner's 'peyne' as more than his busy exertion to manipulate his audience. His deliberate corruption of biblical text reveals his own 'peyne', an anxiety concerning his sexual and spiritual deficencies. Charles Merrill and Mary Hamel print a version of the *Pardoner's Tale* from the Basakata people of Zaire in 'The Analogues to the *Pardoner's Tale* and A New African Version' (*ChauR* 26.175–83).

In 'Empathy and Enmity in the *Prioress's Tale*' (*The Olde Daunce*), Stephen Spector looks at the intersection of love and hate in the tale and the contradictions and conflicts in critical responses to the Prioress and her tale. Although he does not resolve the much-debated problem of Chaucer's anti-semitism, he questions the assumption of medieval hatred of the Jews in an appendix which gives an account of their position and treatment in medieval society. He addresses the artistic function of intolerance within the tale which seems at odds with the Prioress's sentimentality and sympathy, and demonstrates a detailed self-referentiality between teller and tale, by which the Prioress, in empathetic identification with the clergeon, feels intense enmity towards the Jews, who symbolise a threat to herself as innocent Christian. In 'Anti-Semitism in Chaucer's *Prioress's Tale*' (*ChauR* 25.277–84), Emily Stark Zitter argues that the tale is unquestionably anti-semitic and that the Prioress reveals, in the violent punishment of the Jews which concludes the tale, that she judges according to the Old Law rather than the New Law of repentance, forgiveness and grace. Zitter concludes with a serious caveat that the tale should be studied explicitly as anti-semitic, rather than that its falsehoods and misconceptions be excused and obscured.

In ' "Love's Hete" in the Prioress's *Prologue and Tale*' (*The Olde Daunce*), Marie Borroff asks whether the *Prioress's Tale* suggests that its teller has an inner spiritual life. She proposes that the Prioress identifies with the weakness and innocence of the infant in the Prologue, and with the clergeon in the *Tale*, thus figuring celestial love for herself as the 'thoughtless and instinctual bliss of the child surrounded by the loving care of its parents'. Recent criticism, such as the above articles, interprets the Prioress's character by emphasizing one particular trait, rather than 'Seeing the Prioress Whole' (*ChauR* 25.229–37), which for Hardy Long Frank means seeing her as a respected and professional official of the church. Her tale does not reveal her character as a 'thwarted mother', as many critics have suggested, but may be linked with the cult of Our Lady of the Puy, making it a tale calculated to appeal to the religious and social sensibilities of the burghers and courtiers of her audience.

In 'Romance and Parody' (in Aertsen and MacDonald, eds., *Companion to Middle English Romance*), Wim Tiggs looks at eleven romances which offer some degree of metatextual comment on the characteristics of the romance genre. Only the tale of Sir Thopas emerges clearly as a parody of a genre which is in itself so self-referential as to render the isolation of consciously and recognizably humorous elements problematic. The reason for Chaucer's unique achievement, Tiggs suggests, is that in his time good romances were still composed and enjoyed, and he was able to criticize a genre which offered little as a vehicle for his 'individual poetic spirit'.

Peter C. Braeger's abstract of an essay (not completed before his death in 1988) 'The Portrayals of Fortune in the Tales of the *Monk's Tale*' (appendix in *Rebels and Rivals)*, proposed to explore how descriptions of Fortune illuminate the tone, structure and character of the individual tales, and to assess what was distinctive in the connections which Chaucer made between the various aspects of Fortune and the stories of men and women who fall from greatness. In ' "And Pave it al of Silver and of Gold": The Humane Artistry of the *Canon's Yeoman's Tale*' (*Rebels and Rivals*), David Raybin counters the critical trend which dismisses this tale as the degraded inverse of the moral ideal offered by the *Second Nun's Tale*. The moral vision of the *Canon's Yeoman's Tale* may be earthbound but in the description of alchemical experiment it offers 'an exaltation of artistic strivin ... that is founded in Chaucer's intense interest in life in this world'. The divine perfection of the gold contrasts with the limitations of human accomplishment, but Chaucer celebrates rather than despises the earthly and earthy element of humankind.

In 'Treason in the *Manciple's Tale*' (*ChauR* 25.318–28), Peter C. Herman suggests that the crow's action in revealing Phoebus's wife's adultery must be reassessed in the light of the seriousness of Coronis's crime; cuckolding her husband with a man of lesser rank renders her guilty of treason as well as adultery. However the sneering tone of the crow's revelations makes its motivation questionable and the depravity of earthly politics is compounded by Phoebus's tyrannical reaction. In 'Chaucer's *Manciple's Tale* and the Poetics of Guile' (*ChauR* 25.329–42), Michaela Paasche Grudin is less pessimistic about the role of language and poetics in the *Manciple's Tale*. Despite Phoebus's silencing of the crow, Grudin claims that the tale illustrates how the poet survives by means of artfulness or guile. Also stressing the importance of language, Marc M. Pelan, in 'The Manciple's "Cosyn" to the "Dede" ' (*ChauR* 25.343–54), considers how Chaucer approaches the traditional legend dialectically, fragmenting it among conflicting voices. These contradictions are finally transcended in the 'sentence' of sacramental love.

In 'Chaucer's Parson and Other Priests' (*SAC* 13.41–80), Robert Swanson assesses the status of Chaucer's Parson, by testing his position against what is known of English clergy in the Middle Ages. As a secular cleric with a benefice which could be rented out, he belongs to an elite group of only six thousand rectors. To achieve this position he needed both patronage and education, but the rewards from tithes, offerings and farming would give him a comfortable living. This picture suggests to Swanson that Chaucer may not mean the Parson to be seen as an ideal paragon of poverty and virtue, and good example to the generally corrupt clergy, but rather as a successful and, perhaps typical, English clergyman.

Chauncey Wood argues that to find 'Chaucer's Most Gowerian Tale' (*Chaucer and Gower*) we need to go beyond the usual search for detailed correspondences between similar tales, to examine authorial characteristics of style and outlook, taking a more flexible approach to what a source is and how it influences an author. In pursuance of this thesis, he chooses the *Parson's Tale* as the most 'Gowerian' tale (or more accurately the *Canterbury Tales* as a whole when read in the light of the *Parson's Tale*), because it reveals Gower's and Chaucer's central concern with sin and its remedies. That the authors differ widely in their treatments of confession and penance does not discourage Wood. He recognizes that an attempt to calculate which is the most 'Gowerian' tale is of limited value, but is a useful strategy by which to approach a comparison and contrast of the two authors.

3. Troilus and Criseyde

C. David Benson and Barry Windeatt offer 'The Manuscript Glosses to Chaucer's *Troilus and Criseyde*' (*ChauR* 25.33–53), a list of every marginal notation in all the manuscripts of *Troilus and Criseyde*. Decorated oversized initials calling attention to particular passages, and word glosses, not marginal but over the text, are also included. Although some explanatory commentary to this list would have been helpful, it provides useful additional information about the editorial history of Chaucer's works, an area of scholarship much in favour in the 1990s.

The Chaucer Society printed seven transcriptions of the principal manuscripts of *Troilus and Criseyde* (1868–1902). Choosing the Corpus Christi College, Cambridge, (CP) MS, which is the basis for modern editions such as Robinson, Baugh, Donaldson and Barney (*The Riverside Chaucer*), Kathleen M. Hewitt-Smith investigates 'Transcript Error in the Text of Troilus' (*SAC* 13.99–119). She compares the manuscript with its transcription, finding 406 errors, and assesses the extent to which these errors have proliferated in the editions. Her findings suggest over-reliance upon the transcription by modern editors. She appends a list of the transcription errors, followed by line numbers indictating where these errors appear in the Robinson edition. The second printing of *The Riverside Chaucer* has taken Hewitt-Smith's findings into account.

In 'Shades of Incest and Cuckoldry: Pandarus and John of Gaunt' (*SAC* 13.121–40), H. Ansgar Kelly looks at the moral and legal implications of two speculations: Pandarus's sexual encounter with Criseyde after the consummation scene with Troilus in book III, and John of Gaunt's fathering of one or two children on Chaucer's wife, who may have been sister to Catherine Swynford. Past commentators have described the former as incestuous and the latter as cuckoldry, but Kelly would change the emphasis. In divine law, sexual intercourse creates a degree of affinity, so that Troilus and Criseyde, if not married, are united in such a way as to render Pandarus's intercourse with his friend's lover cuckoldry. If John of Gaunt had two sisters as mistresses the affinity created by intercourse with one of them would render the relationship with the other incestuous. Kelly is not convinced that either of these relationships ever took place, but uses the speculations to explore some alarming intricacies of medieval marriage law.

In 'Rivalry, Rape and Manhood: Gower and Chaucer' (*Chaucer and Gower*), Caroline Dinshaw takes the discredited notion of a quarrel between Chaucer and Gower as her starting point. She suggests that scholars have searched for a display of aggression between Chaucer and Gower as a means of consolidating their individual identities. This is achieved by eradicating any difference within the self, a difference which in male-dominated culture is gendered feminine. Linking aggression towards the feminine with rape, Dinshaw looks at Gower's version of the Philomela story, and by using this as a gloss upon *Troilus and Criseyde* posits that an interaction between these two texts reveals and resists the violent obliteration of the feminine, which suggests that male relations need not be based on the rivalry which critics have demanded of Chaucer and Gower, a rivalry formed at the expense of the Other. Gretchen Mieszkowski equates 'Chaucer's Much Loved Criseyde' (*ChauR* 26.109–32) with Simone de Beauvoir's quintessentially appealing woman of western culture and the ideal lady of romance, for whom absence of selfhood is essential for her extreme femininity. Chaucer's diminishment of Boccaccio's heroine creates a woman who is no more than a response to the men around her, and by making her less than human she is made incapable of sustaining love. In 'Declarations of "Entente" in *Troilus and Criseyde*' (*ChauR* 25.190–213), Elizabeth Archibald comments on the frequent use of 'entente' and 'entenciouns' in *Troilus and Criseyde* and shows how the words undergo a slippage of meaning which draws attention to the unreliability of stated intentions and the difficulty of interpreting them. The connotation of 'entente' especially when used of, or by, Pandarus, may indicate insincerity or sexual desire and intrigue.

A. C. Spearing, drawing on examples from a range of medieval texts, but primarily *Troilus and Criseyde,* considers 'The Medieval Poet as Voyeur' (*The Olde Daunce*), in particular the 'imaginative voyeurism' in which poet and audience are implicated in the writing and reading of love poetry. Pandarus's voyeuristic participation in the love scene between Troilus and Criseyde is analogous to the role of the narrator who is in a position to describe the scene, and the poem's audience who read and supplement the narrative with their imaginations. *Troilus and Criseyde* is successful in that the treatment of love transcends the degrading effects of voyeurism. In contrast, the *Manciple's Tale,* in which the crow metaphorically represents the poet in his witness and divulging of adultery, offers a more disillusioned perspective on the role and influence of the narrator.

Voyeurism gets another look-in in a paper by Sarah Stanbury, 'The Voyeur and the Private Life in *Troilus and Criseyde*' (*SAC* 13.141–58), which claims to be inspired by Spearing's paper but far outreaches it in subtlety. She explores the metonymy between the poem's construction of space and its representation of private power, 'the creation of private space and, the interior that is delineated by an entrance, a window, an external view, is one of the most remarkable and insistent features of the narration'. The view is as important as the space it scans for Stanbury, and she concentrates upon the ways in which gazes transect space, Pandarus's gaze in particular but Troilus's and Criseyde's as well.

Martin Camargo is more positive about Pandarus's role when he argues that although 'The Consolation of Pandarus' (*ChauR* 25.214–28) is finally flawed in comparison with that offered by Boethius' *Philosophy*, Chaucer is not presenting the analogy between Pandarus and Philosophy as merely ironic and parodic. Pandarus's response to Troilus as a fellow lover is sympathetic, guides him towards positive and optimistic action, and promotes a philosophy based on human experience which is opposite to that of the infallible and distant Philosophy, but nonetheless appealing.

Patricia R. Orr in 'Pallas Athena and the Threefold Choice in Chaucer's *Troilus and Criseyde*' (*The Mythographic Art*), finds fruitful resemblances between the allegorical treatments of the Judgement of Paris in the commentaries of Fulgentius and Bernardus Silvestris and the progress of Troilus through *Troilus and Criseyde*. The three goddesses represent the three lives given to all human beings and Troilus moves from service of Juno, representing riches and temporal power, to service of Venus, and finally after death and removal to the eighth sphere he attains wisdom, represented by Pallas Athene.

In 'Chaucer and Dictys' (*MÆ* 59.288–91), James Hoy wonders whether Chaucer had access to a copy of Dictys' *Ephemeris Belli Troiani* in view of the similarities between the Parliament scene in Book IV.176–82 of *Troilus and Criseyde*, and the council scene in *Ephemeris* II.25.

4. Other Works

In ' "Processe of Tyme": History, Consolation and the Apocalypse in the *Book of the Duchess*' (*Exemplaria* 2.659–83), Richard Rambuss investigates 'the complicated negotiations between the public world and the private, and between the historical world and the attempt to transcend it in the poem', finding the return to the castle an ambiguous conclusion which suggests apocalypse, but also the intrusion of history and temporality into the private imaginative realm.

In 'The *Parliament of Fowls* and Late Medieval Voluntarism' parts I (*ChauR* 25.1–16) and II (*ChauR* 25.85–95), Kathryn L. Lynch argues that this poem is a literary treatment of problems of the will. By drawing on medieval philosophical theory, Lynch shows how the formel's refusal to select a mate focuses the attention on the act of choice, and how the narrator's vacillation before the gates of the garden illustrates the conflict between determinism and free will. She concludes that the poem does not resolve the problem of free will, balancing optimism in the formel's decisive exercise of her right to postpone choice with pessimism at the narrator's confused indecision.

A. S. G. Edwards draws attention to '*House of Fame* 2018: An Unnecessary Emendation' (*ChauR* 25.78–9). The problematic line is printed by editors as 'Languisshe and eke in poynt to breste', following Caxton's and Thynne's editions, but Edwards suggests that the line makes more sense if 'languisshe' is replaced by 'laugh' as it is in the Fairfax 16 and Bodley 638 MSS.

In 'Faithful Translations: Love and the Question of Poetry in Chaucer' (*The Olde Daunce*), Robert Edwards finds that in the Prologue to the *Legend of Good Women*, the poet's crime is translation, not just in the narrow sense of turning from one language into another, but of transformation and adaptation. Edwards argues that Chaucer's translations are faithful to the complexity of an artistic vision, 'as Chaucer translates the authors who preserve a culture's memory, he also uncovers what the culture would supress'.

Three articles assess evidence concerning the authorship of the *Equatorie of the Planetis*. Pamela Robinson is convinced that the text is Chaucer's holograph, and in 'Geoffrey Chaucer and the *Equatorie of the Planetis*: The State of the Problem' (*ChauR* 26.17–30), affirms that this is proved by the note 'Radix Chaucer' which refers to calculations relevant only to that compiler and is further supported by the orthography of the manuscript which is similar to that in an Exchequer Record thought to be in Chaucer's hand. However, in 'Is the *Equatorie of the Planetis* a Chaucer Holograph?' (*ChauR* 26.31–42), A. S. G. Edwards and Linne R. Mooney assert that the text is a copy because of the presence of a copyist's error and erasures and deletions, and since the text's status as a holograph is the strongest evidence for Chaucer's authorship, it is unlikely to be his work. Jean E. Krochalis's 'Postscript: The *Equatorie of the Planetis* as a Translator's Manuscript' (*ChauR* 26.43–6) judges, on codicological grounds, that the text is neither holograph nor copy, but a translation from a Latin text, but Krochalis does not venture an opinion as to authorship.

In '*Anelida and Arcite*: Anti-feminist Allegory and Pro-feminist Complaint' (*ChauR* 26.83–94), Dale A. Favier stresses the tension existing between two impulses within the poem, 'in which men's betrayal of women represents poetic language's necessary betrayal of literal meaning'. A close reading of the poem which follows its three major divisions highlights Chaucer's shift of position from the invocation and the narrative, where the poet identifies with the betrayer in his break with the tradition of his source, to the complaint, where he assumes the voice of the betrayed Anelida who represents the stable, unchanging text.

In 'Chaucer's *Envoy to Bukton* and "Truth" in Biblical Interpretation: Some Medieval and Modern Contexts' (*NLH* 22.177–97), Lawrence Besserman examines the use of biblical allusion in *Envoy to Bukton*, showing how scriptural exegesis and the authority of experience combine to present a range of opinions on marriage. He offers detailed exposition of exegetical interpretation of John 18.38 'What is truth?'

Books Reviewed

Aertson, H., and A. A. MacDonald, eds. *Companion to Middle English Romance*. FreeUP. pp. 216. £14.50. ISBN 9062 56899 8.

Andrew, Malcolm, ed. *Critical Essays on Chaucer's 'Canterbury Tales'*. OUP. pp. 240. £32.50. ISBN 0335096018.

Benson, C. David, ed. *Critical Essays on Chaucer's 'Troilus and Criseyde' and his Major Early Poems.* OUP. pp. 246. £32.50. ISBN 0335094112.
Chance, Jane ed. *The Mythographic Art: Classical Fable and the Rise of the Vernacular in Early France and England.* UFlorP. pp. 322. pb $16.95. ISBN 0813009847.
Edwards Robert R., and Stephen Spector, eds. *The Olde Daunce: Love, Friendship, Sex, and Marriage in the Medieval World.* SUNYP. pp. 311. pb $17.95. ISBN 0791404404.
Fein, Susanna Greer, David Raybin, and Peter C. Braeger, eds. *Rebels and Rivals: The Contestive Spirit in the 'Canterbury Tales'.* MIP. ISBN 0918720419.
Oizumi, Akio, ed. *A Complete Concordance to the Works of Geoffrey Chaucer.* Olms. ISBN 34887094223.
Yeager, R. F., ed. *Chaucer and Gower: Difference, Mutuality, Exchange.* UVict. pp. 152. ISBN 0920604544.

VI

The Sixteenth Century: Excluding Drama after 1550

R. E. PRITCHARD

This chapter has three sections: 1. General; 2. The Earlier Sixteenth Century; 3. The Later Sixteenth Century.

1. General

We may begin appropriately with *The Yearbook of English Studies 21: Politics, Patronage and Literature in England 1558–1658*. Edited by Andrew Gurr, it is comprised of twenty essays covering poetry, prose and drama, grouped in three sections. The first nine essays deal with patronage, ranging from particular patrons or writers to consideration of a social system; the next eight consider texts with explicit or implicit political functions, and the remaining three provide various correctives, including a political reading of New Historicism itself, 'New Historicism for Old: New Conservatism for Old'. Here, M. D. Jardine develops the Left's political criticism of New Historicism as merely the 'old' historicism (Tillyard, Buxton) made chic, presenting a homogenized, consensual culture while denying the significance of ideological dissent and conflict. The volume begins with Arthur F. Marotti's 'Patronage, Poetry, and Print', reviewing the quest for (individual or bookstall) patronage by authors from Skelton to Jonson. Gascoigne deployed most of the available roles – unwilling victim of friends or printers, serious cultural contributor, servant of the great, provider of amorous entertainment, earnest defender of morality. Spenser's skilful manipulation of publishing conventions is noted: the publication of Sidney's writing legitimated gentlemanly printing; Jonson characteristically made the patron subject to the poet's standards and values, and early in the new century writers seemed securely established in their own new print culture. Mark Thornton Burnett concentrates on 'Apprentice Literature and the "Crisis" of the 1590s', suggesting how writers of material aimed at late-Elizabethan apprentices sought to defuse social and economic resentments by apparently contradictorily urging submissive industry and pursuit of individual success. Other essays (apart from those on drama, Donne, Jacobean women writers, and Milton) are noted later in this chapter.

Political readings continue. The Marxist terminology of Richard Halpern's introduction to his *Poetics of Primitive Accumulation* should not put off the uninitiated, for his relation of early modern texts to the progress of a protocapitalist system and culture is generally clear, illuminating and stimulating. After an impressive account of how Tudor educational theory and practice helped the development of a nascent bourgeois culture and movement towards capitalism, the attempt to relate Skelton to the rise of the capitalist state and reorganization of late feudal policy seems less successful, though the account of a proto-Veblenite *Utopia*, with its oppositions of Utopia and England, utility and excess, works quite well. J.-F. Lyotard's distinctions between the 'pragmatics' of narrative and scientific knowledge are applied to *The Shepheardes Calender* and E. K.'s glosses, bringing together contemporary political controversies and the volume's anxieties about interpretation. Most impressive is the account of *King Lear* – as Halpern says, '*Lear's* status as tragedy is not annulled but enhanced by its strategic response to the economic limits of aristocracy'.

Barry Taylor's *Vagrant Writing* 'pitches its enquiry', says the author, 'at the chiasmic intersection' where 'the semiotic force of social disorder' entangles with 'the social force of a disorderly semiotics': i.e. a Sussex-cultural-materialism-based account of the inter-relationship of late-Elizabethan socio-economic and stylistic practices. A declining system of (Neoplatonic or political) hierarchy, a feudal 'commonweal' where plain words manifest an unchanging Word, are set against developing cultural and linguistic change, individualism and relativism. The study ranges widely, with some interesting connections, from a paradigmatic analysis of Hooker's *Laws of Ecclesiastical Polity* through surveys of homilies, statutes and trading practices, to the effects of contradictory court values on Gascoigne and Puttenham, and courtiership and Neoplatonism in Castiglione and Jonson. The study's binary schematics provide a Procrustean double bed on which most subjects may lie; the verse quotations are laid out oddly, while the prose is occasionally a polysyllabic trudge.

Annabel Patterson's ambitious, historicist *Fables of Power* is concerned to emphasize the political uses of the Aesopian fable, which characteristically provides encoded commentaries on unequal power relationships. After a lively introduction to the theory and history of the fable, she discusses English Aesopian fable from Langland on, the chief examples being *The Shepheardes Calender* and *Mother Hubberds Tale*, the 'Old' *Arcadia* and Lyly's *Euphues and His England*. Spenser is relatively cautious, willing to wound but afraid to be struck; Sidney, more direct, provides a subtle analysis of current theories of monarchy, and Lyly celebrates the mystery of absolutism. There is also an interesting discussion of the Fable of the Belly in *Coriolanus*. Worth attention here is Timothy Hampton's study of other politically instructive writing, *Writing from History: the Rhetoric of Exemplarity in Renaissance Literature*, a survey of changing Renaissance depictions of exemplary figures from antiquity and their function as models for readers attuned to the heroic ethos central to Renaissance humanism. After reviewing Guillaume Budé, Erasmus and Machiavelli, Hampton discusses Tasso's *Gerusalemme Liberata*, Montaigne's *Essais*, Shakespeare's *Julius Caesar* and Cervantes' *Don Quixote*: the texts reflect the developing crisis of the aristocracy; as faith in humanist ideals weakens, the relation of the reader to both model and narrative becomes increasingly a matter of explicit scepticism.

The style of Lowell Gallagher's *Medusa's Gaze: Casuistry and Conscience in the Renaissance*, combining the jargons of Renaissance casuistry and modern deconstructionism (a topic and approach that the book seeks to correlate), together with contemporary American inkhorn, makes the reading unnecessarily hard going. If conscience made cowards of all Elizabethans, casuistry made survivors of many; Gallagher parallels orthodoxy and interpretation with *langue* and *parole*, deploying

Bakhtinian ideas of novelistic discourse. An extended and frequently acute discussion of Spenser's 'Legend of Justice' suggests the similarity of casuistry and equity; the book also includes accounts of the 'Siena Sieve' portrait of Elizabeth, her speeches to Parliament, and of Elizabethan casuistry.

Constance Jordan has read widely in Renaissance Italian, French and English writing on women; her *Renaissance Feminism: Literary Texts and Politicial Models* will be of considerable value in Renaissance feminist studies. An account of the English translation of Christine de Pisan's *Cité des Dames* precedes discussions of female rule – Vives (no), Elyot (possibly) and Agrippina of Nettesheim's *Of the Nobilitie and Excellencie of Womankynde* (guess). The theory of androgyny, with each sex possessing the other's qualities, with gender-roles and relationships consequently perceived as cultural and mutable, is seen to be of increasing importance in the period. Androgyny is linked with equity in Sidney's 1593 *Arcadia*, where the personal, sexual order and the public, political order are presented as essentially oxymoronic; the work as a whole is seen as feminist in so far as it values the feminine. The study also includes discussion of Continental and minor English seventeenth-century texts.

Jean R. Brink and others have edited seven essays, *Playing with Gender: A Renaissance Pursuit*. The first section discusses *Othello* and Middleton, and the third the Continental treatment of the idea of the hermaphrodite. In the second, Susanne Woods examines 'Amazonian Tyranny: Spenser's Radigund and Diachronic Mimesis', arguing for Spenser's sympathetic treatment of Radigund's behaviour being the consequence of her own mistreatment, and akin to the tactics enforced on him as a writer. Margaret M. Sullivan's interesting 'Amazons and Aristocrats: The Function of Pyrocles' Amazon Role in Sidney's Revised *Arcadia*' relates Sidney's anxieties about his own matrilineal access to the Dudley patrimonies to the *Arcadia's* concern with patriarchal control of marriage and property, and the conflicts of class and gender; the manuscript's interruption at the point of the women's claim for autonomy marks Sidney's own irresolution.

Howard V. Hendrix's *The Ecstasy of Catastrophe* is written in an earnest, religio-psychologistic style, with catalogues, pairings, paronomasias and chiasmic patternings, 'fissured and fishered ... a warp and woof of cross-woven threads: the subjective and the objective, the noetic and the noematic'. Chiefly, he examines Book One of Spenser's *Faerie Queene* and the *Mutabilitie Cantoes* and Milton's major epics, with subordinate discussions of Langland, the *Pearl* poet and Malory: the main ideas are that the normative (ideal) and the descriptive (actual) interact, and that the apocalyptic is not merely destructive but also fundamentally restorative. The opposite extreme of academic sobriety is manifested in Dilwyn Knox's *Ironia: Medieval and Renaissance Ideas on Irony*, a thematic study of classical and, more particularly, medieval and Renaissance discussions of irony, its theory and practice, whether as rhetorical trope or mode of thought. The writers discussed are almost entirely Continental (especially Italian) humanists, and there is no discussion of English theory or practice (four references to More); nevertheless, the study should provide useful material.

Three more general studies extend their survey far beyond the narrow bounds of this chapter. The most adventurous traveller is Reed Way Dasenbrock in his *Imitating the Italians: Wyatt, Spenser, Synge, Pound, Joyce*. He proposes two responses to Italy in English-language culture; one of sympathetic imitation, and one where writers (such as Nashe, Webster or, he suggests, E. M. Forster and D. H. Lawrence) find themselves fundamentally challenged, and define themselves against Italian culture. He indicates how Wyatt's adaptations of Petrarch depend on how far the model had to be redirected from praise to dispraise. Spenser's *Amoretti* involve a critique of Elizabethan Petrarchism, their married love paralleling death in the *Canzoniere* in providing sacred rest; *The Faerie Queene* as a whole (Books Three and Four receive extensive discussion) involves a critique of Petrarchist-Catholic values. By the end of the century, England sees itself less as an imitator of Renaissance Italy and more as an opponent of Catholic Italy. 'Renaissance, Mannerism, Baroque: will we ever find a way to use these terms securely and aptly in discussions of English poetry?' asks Louis L. Martz in the first of twelve essays written over the last thirty years and gathered into *From Renaissance to Baroque: Essays on Literature and Art*. Some essays suggest analogies between the literary and the visual arts; one argues – as have others – that Marlowe's *Hero and Leander* is complete, a tripartite design; another argues for the harmony and coherence of the *Amoretti*; another ranges from Virgil to *England's Helicon*, *The Winter's Tale*, *Hesperides* and *Paradise Lost* to present true pastoral as essentially healing. George Braden goes nearly as far with 'Unspeakable Love: Petrarch to Herbert' (in Harvey and Maus, eds, *Soliciting Interpretation*), tracing the motif of the tongue-tied lover, from sonnets by Petrarch to those of Sidney, Spenser and Shakespeare, analysing the struggles with the anxieties of influence and false motive in the progress towards self-knowledge (George Herbert providing a religious variant of the topic). John N. King soberly concludes this section with his bibliography of 'Recent Studies in Protestant Poetics' (*ELR* 21.283–307), covering the period from Bale to Bunyan, via Shepherd and Foxe.

2. The Earlier Sixteenth Century

In reviewing commentary directly related to earlier Tudor writing, we may begin with discussion of Skelton. David R. Carlson has edited and translated 'The Latin Writings of John Skelton' (*SP* 88:iv.1–125), relating his career to his contemporaries, considering his on-off relationship with early humanism, and his varying methods of circulating his writings. Appendices discuss the dating of *The Garland of Laurel*, and the occasions of such works as 'The Recule against Gaguyne'. Elsewhere, Carlson compares 'Skelton's *Garland of Laurel* and Robert Whittinton's "Lauri Apud Palladem Expostulatio" ' (*RES* 42.417–24), suggesting that the latter derives from Skelton's poem, which in turn encourages arguments for an early date for the *Garland*. Ilona M. McGuiness presents 'John Skelton's *Phyllyp Sparowe* as Satire' (*SCJ* 22:215–32), as part of the conservative Catholic response to humanist criticism of religious ritual: the interplay between the poem's liturgical framework and Jane's thoughts reveals the inadequacy of popular affective devotions and the Marian language of *fine amour* for achieving true spirituality.

Particularly welcome is Dominic Baker-Smith's judicious and informed *More's 'Utopia'*. His discussion sets the work in its immediate political and intellectual context – notably Erasmus and the *Encomium Moriae* – but is particularly helpful regarding Plato, Aristotle and Aquinas, as well as Lucian and Sallust. Narrative techniques and rhetorical subtleties, as well as the ideas and readers' conflicting responses, are reviewed, as the work is evaluated in its European cultural context. James Romm assesses 'More's Strategy of Naming in the *Utopia*' (*SCJ* 22.173–84), noting that, while many of More's ethnological names either ironically negate the people they describe (the Utopians) or identify some moral quality (the Macarians), many do neither. He argues that More has no single 'code' but intends only a teasing, undecidable ambiguity. Peter L. Rudnytsky's analysis of 'More's *History of King*

Richard III as an Uncanny Text' (in Logan and Rudnytsky, eds. *Contending Kingdoms*) deploys Freud's concept of the uncanny to examine motifs of doubling and repetition, expecially in the Hastings episode, both in More's text (presented as focusing sexual and Oedipal tensions in the material and the author) and in its relationship to its current political context, as the past was re-enacted in the present. David R. Carlson's exposure of 'Reputation and Duplicity: The Texts and Contexts of Thomas More's Epigram on Bernard André' (*ELH* 58.261–82) notes how More's epigram on André's *Hymni Christiani* seemed laudatory in that volume, but was revealed as denigratory in his own later *Epigrammata*.

From tacit competition to overt opposition: R. J. McCutcheon's account of 'The *Responsio ad Lutherum*: Thomas More's Inchoate Dialogue with Heresy' (*SCJ* 22.77–96), noting the fear that dialogue with heresy might seem to grant it intellectual standing, sees the *Responsio* as divided between straightforward diatribe and, through the use of interwoven quotation and commentary, the effect of dialogue. The tactic is to present Luther as literalistic and rigid by contrast with Morean probabilism and flexibility. *Moreana* has a special Tyndale number (28.106–7), though the first article, by Manfred Hoffman, is on 'Erasmus on Language and Intepretation', outlining Erasmus' views on the inter-relationship of styles of language and of living, of rhetoric and of theology: sacred rhetoric implies ethics, a harmonization of individuals with each other and with Christ. John A. R. Dick, in ' "To Dig Again the Wells of Abraham": Philology, Theology, and Scripture in Tyndale's *The Parable of Wicket Mammon*', demonstrates Tyndale's considerable doctrinal and stylistic indebtedness to Erasmus and Luther, while urging Tyndale's originality. Richard H. Graham also discusses 'Tyndale's Source and Tyndale's Originality: A Reading of *The Parable of Wicked Mammon*', noting Tyndale's use of Luther's sermon of the same title as well as his own elaborations and development of his own style. Dick then returns to the same text, in ' "To try his true frendes": Imagery as Argument', exploring Tyndale's comparison of his book, its author and its readers (all faulty, and likely to be consumed in flames), and incitement of the readers to antagonistic attitudes. Anne Richardson examines the use of 'Scripture as Evidence in Tyndale's *The Obedience of a Christian Man*', particularly his rejection of 'anarchistic' permissiveness in interpretation and allegorization in favour of fidelity to a literal sense, and James Andrew Clark relates 'The Bible, History and Authority in Tyndale's *The Practice of Prelates*', showing how Tyndale establishes himself as both auctor, dependent on scriptural material, and author, by individual election. Anne M. O'Donnell does a lot of adding up and listing in 'Scripture Versus Church in Tyndale's *Answer Unto Sir Thomas More's Dialogue*', to reveal Tyndale's most frequently-used biblical texts, his humanistic approach to language, his attitudes to the Fathers, Erasmus, More and his use of typology. John T. Day provides 'Proper Guidance in Reading the Bible: Tyndale's *A Pathway into the Holy Scripture*', comparing the 1525 and 1531 versions, and, in ' "Howe Diligently Wrote he to them": Tyndale's Own Letter, The Exposition of the First Epistle of St John', Donald J. Millus argues that Tyndale saw himself as a latter-day Paul, writing to the faithful overseas. Finally, Anne M. O'Donnell's 'Philology, Typology and Rhetoric in Tyndale's *Exposition upon the V, VI, VII, Chapters of Matthew*' discusses Tyndale's use of Luther, typology and sermon rhetoric, and projection of an individual, authoritative voice.

Anthony Miller compares 'Wyatt's "Myne Owne John Poyntz" and Juvenal' (*N&Q* 38.22) indicating how Wyatt draws on both Luigi Alamanni and Juvenal's third satire. Elaine V. Beilin analyses the technique of 'Anne Askew's Dialogue with Authority' (in *Contending Kingdoms*) showing how Askew manipulates dialogue, characterization and irony in her *Examinations* to discredit Catholic doctrinal authority and establish her own, while Janis Butler Holm, 'Struggling with the Letter: Vives's Preface to *The Instruction of a Christian Woman*' (ibid.), noting the contradiction between the *Instruction*'s professed *brevia* and apparent *copia*, relates instability of stylistic definition to instability of gender-role definition, exploring contradictions in the text, the possibilities of concordant and oppositional readings, and the varying pressures of changing cultural values.

Finally, following his earlier edition of Richard Whytford's *The Pype or Tonne of the Lyfe of Perfection*, James Hogg has brought out a facsimile of Whytford's *The boke of pacience*, while Veronica Lawrence has edited the seventeenth-century manuscript of *A looking glace for the religious*, attributed to Whytford.

3. The Later Sixteenth Century

(a) Sidney

Undoubtedly, this section must begin with Katherine Duncan-Jones's lucid and elegantly written biography, *Sir Philip Sidney: Courtier Poet*, setting his life and career in their social and cultural context. The main emphasis is less on the intellectual (one could have done with more on this) than on the personal, bringing out the contradictions in his character and particularly stressing the influence upon him of the women in his life, with accounts of his court career, and speculations on his sexual feelings and on the extent of his Catholic sympathies (greater, she suggests, than has usually been thought). There are clear and useful accounts of the writing, and the study is lively and attractive, with no trace of New Historicist or other recent theoretical approaches.

Alan Hager's *Dazzling Images: The Masks of Sir Philip Sidney* presents Sidney as master ironist or serious jester, tricking and entrapping his readers. 'Public affairs' writings, such as *The Lady of May* and the letters to the Queen and in defence of Leicester, work through deceptive masks and irony; two chapters on *Astrophel and Stella* analyse puns and word-play and distinguish author from absurd persona; the *Defence* is an Erasmian mock encomium, with a sophistic *rhetor* of many voices affirming almost nothing, but mocking and under-cutting Plato. Sidney's method here and in the *Arcadia* is a Fishy 'retroactive reading' or teaching by entangling, demanding continuous self-examination and correction by the reader. Åke Bergvall's *The 'Enabling of Judgement': Sir Philip Sidney and the Education of the Reader* has some similar points to make. Initially, he separates Sidney from Florentine Neoplatonism's dualistic privileging of spirit over body, and affiliation with Petrarchism, to align him with Augustinian Platonism's attempt at the ethical application of the divine Idea. Sidney's method requires an interactive reader, alert to the tactics and objectives of sophistic rhetoric. Bergvall chiefly analyses the use of the narrator in the 'old' *Arcadia* and the various techniques encouraging a sceptical response to the characters of the 'new' *Arcadia*, which he sees as less unproblematically heroic than has often been claimed. Joan Rees provides a more straightforward introduction to *Sir Philip Sidney and 'Arcadia'*. The approach is traditional, resistant to recent scepticisms about language, character, genre and meaning; instead, Rees discusses character, narrative method, morality, Sidney's humour, humanity and sympathetic treatment of women. Mary Ellen Lamb's account of *Gender and Authorship in the Sidney Circle*, an analysis of attitudes to women as writers and readers, focused on the Sidney circle, develops somewhat surprisingly.

The discussion of *Arcadia*, with the encouragement to readers to read 'as women', downplays the (masculine) element of state politics in favour of the (feminine) element of love and sexual politics; she then discusses attitudes to Mary suggested by various dedications (not surprisingly, writers seeking her patronage spoke more highly of that than of her own writing). Lamb makes much of Gordon Braden's view of Stoicism as the controlling of anger, which (otherwise not very apparent) she finds in Mary's writing; Mary Wroth's *Pamphilia to Amphilanthus* is also 'an angry text'. After discussing three poems attributed to an unknown female in the Sidney circle, the book concludes with renewed emphasis on women's anger, discussions of the pamphlets of 'Jane Anger' and others, and claims that attempts to suppress women's speech gave it 'enormous power'.

In 'Dialogues and Apologies: Sidney and Venice' (*SP* 88.236–49), David Rosand speculates about Sidney, Venice, Veronese and the possible influence on the *Apology* of Lodovico Dolce's defence of painting. David Farley-Hills argues, in 'Sidney and Poetic Madness' (*N&Q* 38.22), that Sidney's reference to Plato's 'rightly divine commendation unto Poetrie' suggests that he was less sceptical about the *furor poeticus* than has been claimed. Paul Allen Miller, in 'Sidney, Petrarch, and Ovid, or Imitation as Subversion' (*ELH* 58.499–522), observes an apparent contradiction between the values attributed to poetry in the *Defence* and the values expressed in *Astrophel and Stella*, where imitations of Petrarch and Ovid encourage the subversion of idealism, relating this to Sidney's own uncertainties (the conflicts of chivalry, humanism, status, Calvinism) to present the sequence as a profound effort at self-exploration. Joost Daalder says that the word-order in the line 'Do they call virtue there ungratefulness?', in 'Sidney's *Astrophel and Stella* 31' (*Expl* 49.135–6) is normal, so that the ladies accuse the lovers of ingratitude for not being content with the little they have been granted. The stories of Miso and Mopsa in Book Two of the 'new' *Arcadia* are, according to Clare Kinney's 'On the Margins of Romance, at the Heart of the Matter: Revisionary Fabulation in Sidney's *New Arcadia*' (*JNT* 21.143–52), more than comic relief: respectively, they reflect Pyrocles' own behaviour and desires, and the wilful wanderings of desire and narration.

Joan Rees puts together 'Sidney and *A Lover's Complaint*' (*RES* 42.157–67) suggesting that the Dido-Pamphilus episode in the revised *Arcadia* might have provided Shakespeare with some incentive and material for a treatment of exploitative sex. Jim Doelman has found 'A Seventeenth-Century Publication of Three of Sir Philip Sidney's Psalms' (*N&Q* 38.162–3), referred to by Drummond of Hawthornden. Anne Lake Prescott, in 'Evil Tongues at the Court of Saul: The Renaissance David as a Slandered Courtier' (*JMRS* 21.163–86), discusses the Renaissance reading of the Psalms as reflecting David's threatened position as a courtier, and how this provided a language for discussing the ambiguities of rebellion, authority and social mobility. Elsewhere, she discusses one of Sidney's models in 'Musical Strains: Marot's Double Role as Psalmist and Courtier' (in *Contending Kingdoms*).

(b) Spenser

The book of the year must be *The Spenser Encyclopaedia* (general editor, A. C. Hamilton), a huge, awe-inspiring volume, to tell you all you ever wanted to know about Spenser. Years in the composing, with more than 400 contributors, it covers a vast range of topics, from contemporaries and sources from Alabaster to Virgil, to discussions of the arts, biography, characters, the court, as well as myth, poetics, themes and women. The articles are compact and lucid, and up-to-date with recent scholarship and criticism. The implied reader is an intelligent senior undergraduate, but every tutor will be grateful for, and will learn from, this monumental work of scholarship.

Spenser Studies, edited by Patrick Cullen and Thomas P. Roche, Jnr, has reached its ninth volume. Here, Bruce Thornton presents a 'Rural Dialectic: Pastoral, Georgic and *The Shepeardes Calender*' (*SSt* 9.1–20), and Louis Waldman, noting the Renaissance tradition of onomastic riddles, offers 'Edmundus Kedemon' as the solution to 'Spenser's Pseudonym "E.K." and Humanistic Self-Naming' (*SSt* 9.21–32). Shohachi Fukuda extends analysis of 'The Numerological Patterning of *Amoretti* and *Epithalamion*' (*SSt* 9.33–48), with a pattern of 117 'cupids', with symmetries, pairings and significant numbers, while James H. Morey examines 'Spenser's Mythic Adaptations in *Muiopotmos*' (*SSt* 9.49–60), seeing that and *Daphnaida* as responses to Chaucer's Ovidian adaptation in *The Book of the Duchess*, relating Aragnoll and Clarion to Arachne and Astery, respectively. Margaret Christian's study of ' "The ground of Storie": Genealogy in *The Faerie Queene*' (*SSt* 9.61–80) relates Elizabethan genealogy, used for establishing a claim to a title, and for character-assessment, to the 'Briton moniments' and 'Antiquitie of Faerie Lond', and Donald V. Stump's account of 'The Two Deaths of Mary Stuart: Historical Allegory in Spenser's Book of Justice' (*SSt* 9.81–106) interprets the Radigund episode as deriving from the 1569–71 struggle between Elizabeth and Mary. Debra Belt's view of 'Hostile Audiences and the Courteous Reader in *The Faerie Queene*, Book VI' (*SSt* 9.107–36) relates the Blatant Beast to conventional references to malicious readers in contemporary prefaces': Spenser provides views of courteous and discourteous reader-response, and, in the Mount Acidale episode, a working model for poet-audience relationships. Similarly, Margaret P. Hannay, in ' "My Sheep are Thoughts": Self-Reflexive Pastoral in *The Faerie Queene*, Book VI, and the *New Arcadia*' (*SSt* 9.137–60), compares Sidney's and Spenser's attempts to guide the Queen's reading by means of stories of shepherd-knights' attempts to impress, and of envious misinterpretation. Stanley Stewart outlines the Ovidian tradition for 'Spenser and the Judgement of Paris' (*SSt* 9.161–208), reviewing Renaissance art from Cranach to Rubens, in relation to the August eclogue and the Paridell and Pastorella episodes. Anne Shaver, 'Rereading Mirabella' (*SSt* 9.209–25), interprets her story as evidence of Spenserian patriarchal unease at female independence of marriage, as Mirabella suffers for the real offence by the untouchable Queen. The volume concludes with A. Kent Hieatt's continuing speculations on 'Arthur's Deliverance of Rome? (Yet Again)' (*SSt* 9.243–8), and Ruth Samson Luborsky on the zodiacal figures in 'The Illustrations to *The Shepheardes Calender*: II' (*SSt* 9.249–53), while Willy Maley provides for 'Spenser and Ireland: A Select Bibliography' (*SSt* 9.227–42).

Two books on *The Faerie Queene* arrived. Russell J. Meyer's *'The Faerie Queene': Educating the Reader* provides a clear, brisk account of the main action, with little sense of the problematic, and with most complexities passed over. The main idea seems to be that Spenser's reader is to learn by experiencing the temptations faced by his heroes, while Spenser can still fashion 'a gentleman or noble person in vertuous and gentle discipline' as in days of yore. More thoughtfully, Kenneth Borris elucidates *Spenser's Poetics of Prophecy in 'The Faerie Queene V'*, to demonstrate the allegorizing of events in the Low Countries and Ireland in terms of Protestant apocalyptic; the Irena story contrasts Arthur's ideal establishment of peace through justice with the more limited successes of Artegall and the English. Borris usefully places Spenser's position, by echoing Joseph Wittreich's contrast of epic, which celebrates a culture's values, with prophecy, which criticizes and seeks to transform them.

S. K. Heninger Jnr and Lawrence Manley both have pieces linking Sidney and Spenser. Noting deconstruction's necessary incapacity for dealing with the logocentrism characteristic of the Renaissance, Heninger's 'Spenser, Sidney, and Poetic Form' (*SP* 88.141–52) explains the Platonic Idea and how it provides poetic form, as in the oracle of *Arcadia* and the temporal structure of Spenser's epic. In 'Fictions of Settlement: London 1590' (*SP* 88.201–24), Manley relates Sidney's and Spenser's epics to the complex cultural and political changes centred in London – the struggle between neo-feudalism and mercantilist individualism, where the absolutist state both protected the threatened nobility and encouraged commerce. Spenser provides various visions of the city, contrasting Troynovant and Cleopolis to establish London as the poem's symbol of historic achievement and cultural endurance. Manley provides a stimulating summary analysis of the contradictory politics of the 'new' *Arcadia*, which celebrates an obsolescent chivalric-feudal order while advancing humanist thinking, recognizing how the new order cannot be born without repudiating the past in which it is, nevertheless, rooted.

Harry Berger Jnr has a characteristically thoughtful and subtle consideration of 'Narrative as Rhetoric in *The Faerie Queene*' (*ELR* 21.3–48). Moving on from recent discussions of the (un)reliability of the narrator, he proposes the unreliability of the narration: the poem permits a 'reading-as-if-listening' passive acceptance of conventions and ideologies, while provoking a 'reading-as-if-reading' scepticism of them, in effect questioning the very narrative strategies, allegorical translations and episodic visualizations that put across its overt ideology, in a methodological-narrative irony that deconstructs the material and values it ostensibly celebrates. Richard Helgerson's 'Tasso on Spenser: The Politics of Chivalric Romance' (*YES* 21.153–67) argues that Spenser's Tasso-influenced, epic-minded modifications of his first 'hobgoblin' version of *The Faerie Queene* failed to conceal the original Ariostan-inspired pattern of chivalric romance, a mode that was associated with the attempted revival of neofeudal aristocratic autonomy and contrasted with the 'statist' principles of 'public service' and subordination to the controlling monarch, implicit in Tassoist epic. Peter De Sa Wiggins returns to the 'anxiety of influence' in considering 'Spenser's Use of Ariosto: Imitation and Allusion in Book One of *The Faerie Queene*' (*RQ* 44.257–79). Where Atlante's magic shield had been for Ariosto and his commentators an image of mundane illusion, for Spenser it symbolized the *Furioso* itself, that he, like Arthur, would surpass by revealing transcendent truth; the contest between Ruggiero and Mandricardo to carry the 'eagle' shield resembles that between Redcross and Sansjoy over Sansfoy's shield. Spenser's poem, suggests Wiggins, reveals the English Protestant's unease about his successful predecessor.

Richard A. Levin retells 'The Legende of the Redcrosse Knight and Una, or Of the Love of a Good Woman' (*SEL* 31.1–24) as a nice story of a serious, amorous young couple on their way to marriage. Robert J. Mueller, more earnestly, in ' "Infinite Desire": Spenser's Arthur and the Representation of Courtly Ambition' (*ELH* 58.7–72), links Guyon's comments on the picture of the Faerie Queene on his shield with the 1581 court pageant *The Four Foster Children of Desire* to show how Arthur's ambitious but unfulfilled quest images the real courtly pursuit of ultimately unpossessable status and power. J. A. Boss in turn compares 'Sidney's *Arcadia* and Spenser's "Sad Pourtraict" (*The Faerie Queene* II.1.39–40)' (*N&Q* 38.26–7), suggesting that the description of Spenser's dying Amavia derives from that of Sidney's fatally wounded Parthenia. Linda Gregerson invokes St Augustine and the venerable Lacan in her 'Protestant Erotics: Idolatry and Interpretation in Spenser's *Faerie Queene*' (*ELH* 58.1–34), analysing the stories of Malbecco and Britomart in order to consider questions of sexual and textual licentiousness and misinterpretation, the valuing of flesh and sign over spirit and truth. Dorothy Stevens moves 'Into Other Arms: Amoret's Evasion' (*ELH* 58.523–44), proposing that Amoret's behaviour with Aemylia in Lust's cave, and with Britomart ('the one happy bed scene in the whole poem'), suggests the poem's sympathies with women's preference for women and avoidance of men. Marion Glasser looks at 'Spenser as Mannerist Poet: The "Antique Image" in Book IV of *The Faerie Queene*' (*SEL* 31.25–50), comparing his method with that of artists such as Parmigianino and El Greco, as illustrating the stylizations of the Mannerist aesthetic. James Vink's provocative 'Spenser's Freudian *Mischpersonen*: Six types of Portmanteau Names in *The Faerie Queene*' (*P&R* 150.322–52) analyses how characters' qualities and connections are suggested through their names, by puns and other word-play, in a process comparable with Freud's theory of dreams' character-creation and condensation; the 'entrelaced' plots are merely *mischpersonen* seen diachronically, as characters and plot extend each other. Jacqueline T. Miller examines 'The Courtly Figure: Spenser's Anatomy of Allegory' (*SEL* 31.51–68), looking back via Louis Montrose to Puttenham's account of the courtier's characteristic mode of dissembling allegory, to see Calidore as a figure for allegory; the pastoral episodes set natural against artificial, the concealed against the open, as Spenser questions his own fashioning of a gentleman.

In 'The Poem as Sacrament: Spenser's *Epithalamion* and the Golden Section' (*JMRS* 21.251–68), David Chinitz observes a climax not only at the poem's mathematical centre, but also at its golden section, whereby the poem balances its action (wedding) against its function (eternizing). He then discusses the implications for considering intention, and the boundaries between fiction, metafiction and reality. Looking into 'Who Fashioned Edmund Spenser?: The Textual History of *Complaints*' (*SP* 88.153–68), Jean R. Brink argues that, far from Spenser planning the 1591 publication of *Complaints* to exploit the success of *The Faerie Queene* (the epic was no great publishing success), the *Complaints* would have threatened Spenser's position, and evidence suggests that the printer brought out the volume without regard to, or assistance from, the author.

(c) *Other Verse and Prose*

Steven W. May sets out to study *The Elizabethan Courtier Poets: The Poems and their Contexts* – who they actually were and what they actually wrote. He is fairly strict in his definition, admitting only thirty-two (including Elizabeth herself), suggesting that these constitute the tip, not of an iceberg, but of an ice-cube. An historical (non-historicist) survey reviews the earlier years' drab humanism and the 'golden' trinity of Dyer, Sidney and Fulke Greville, suggesting that Sidney's influence was largely confined to his own circle. A more utilitarian poetics dominates the work of Gorges, Ralegh and Essex, with writing closely related to career ends; Sir John Harington's court epigrams, and his entertaining Ariosto, contrast with the Sidney psalms and Greville's *Caelica*. The second part of the book provides brief accounts of the thirty-two, with some useful selections of previously unedited verse, notably by Essex and Oxford. Native English and Counter-Reformation devotional traditions are the contexts in which A. D. Cousins sets his *Catholic Religious Poets from Southwell to Crashaw*, beginning with accounts of Tudor plain style (Surrey, Vaux), Counter-Reformation poetic theory (Pontanus, Tasso, Gracian), emblem theory and practice (Hermann Hugo) and Ignatian meditation theory. The discussions of Southwell, Constable, Alabaster and seventeenth-century poets are sober and critically conservative, emphasizing devotional content and rhetorical organization; for some reason, there is an appendix on Ralegh's *Ocean to Cynthia*. George Klawitter has edited *Richard Barnfield: The Complete Poems*, including *Greenes Funeralls* and *The Encomion of Lady Pecunia*, as well as the better-known homo-erotic verse. The introduction provides accounts of the life and works, and explanation of the *roman-à-clef* aspects of the poems; there is also discussion of Greek and Renaissance homo-eroticism, and a complaint about hostility towards homo-erotic writing.

Arthur F. Marotti's discussion of 'The Transmission of Lyric Poetry and the Institutionalizing of Literature in the English Renaissance' (in *Contending Kingdoms*) overlaps slightly with his piece in *YES*. Here, he notes the variety of uses and social contexts for Renaissance lyric and the different ways of constructing manuscript anthologies, before considering how early printed anthologies echoed or modified those practices, both evoking a social context and recontextualizing lyrics as examples of fiction and genre as print enabled increasing authorial control.

Noting Renaissance hostility to publishing by women, Wendy Wall, in 'Isabella Whitney and the Female Legacy' (*ELH* 58.35–62), uses a discussion of printed moral texts by women apparently anticipating childbirth death, and 'bequeathed' to their unborn children, to introduce her analysis of Whitney's 'Last Will' as both ironic blazon of London as a heartless lover, and a paradoxical enablement of female will. M. L. Stapleton makes a case for 'Nashe and the Poetics of Obscenity: *The Choise of Valentines*' (*CML* 12.29–48): after outlining Ascham's theory of *imitatio*, Stapleton discusses Nashe's various kinds of imitation of Chaucer, Spenser and Ovid in his pornographic poem, the (in)action of which he outlines, as the poem 'has much to recommend it' and 'deserves some critical commentary'. Douglas and Mary Brooks-Davies proffer 'The Numbering of Sir Walter Ralegh's *Ocean to Cynthia*: A Problem Solved' (*N&Q* 38.31–4), claiming that Ralegh's manuscript used not arabic but roman numerals for a 'vi:th and last booke', suggesting a six-book mini-epic and revision of *Aeneid* VI. J. D. Alsop confirms 'Barnabe Googe's Birthdate' (*N&Q* 38.24) as 11 June 1540; A. A. MacDonald and A. M. Jansen discuss 'Dating *The Remedy of Love*: The Limitations of Lexicography' (*Neophil* 75.619–25), arguing against Skeat's 1530 date for the poem and proposing a late fifteenth-century origin.

Catherine Bates presents ' "A Large Occasion of Discourse": John Lyly and the Art of Civil Conversation' (*RES* 42.469–86), arguing for a courtly aesthetic and ethic in Lyly's narratives, where debate tends not towards virtuous action, such as marriage, but to open-ended, unresolved play of word and mind, with 'civil conversation' (as in Guazzo) and *'questione d'amore'* producing 'quandary' and 'muse'. William Keith Hall provides an effective Barthesian analysis of narrative technique in 'A Topography of Time: Historical Narration in John Stow's *Survey of London*' (*SP* 88.1–15), showing its complexity, beyond mere chronicle accumulation, with the interplay of topographical and chronological requirements, the assemblage of material, construction of a narrator and establishment of a past. Donald S. Lawless gives an account of 'Richard Crompton (*fl.* 1553–1599) Lawyer and Author' (*N&Q* 38.23–4), correcting some errors in *Aethenae Oxonienses* and the *DNB*.

Finally, we conclude as we begin, with politics, with David Womersley on 'Sir Henry Savile's Translation of Tacitus and the Political Interpretation of Elizabethan Texts' (*RES* 42.313–42): concentrating particularly on the essay on 'The Ende of Nero and Beginning of Galba', he presents the text as a cool, Machiavellian and heterodox judgement, relating it to contemporary figures, notably Essex. Womersley insists that in the closed Elizabethan society, politics were effectively the activities of an unusually concentrated oligarchy in an absolutist monarchy: recognizing that one is dealing with a relatively few individuals should discourage the anachronistic application of modern political theory and assumptions to Elizabethan political literature (but then, after this year's reading, one might wonder whether there was any other kind).

Books Reviewed

Baker-Smith, Dominic. *More's 'Utopia'*. HC. pp. 269. £40. ISBN 0 03 800078 7.

Bergvall, Åke. *The 'Enabling of Judgement': Sir Philip Sidney and the Education of the Reader*. Uppsala (1989). pp. 137. ISBN 91 554 2353 1, ISSN 0562 2719.

Borris, Kenneth. *Spenser's Poetics of Prophecy in 'The Faerie Queene V'*. VictUP. pp. 93. pb $8.50. ISBN 0 920604 56 0.

Brink, Jean R., Maryanne C. Horowitz, and Allison P. Coudert, eds. *Playing with Gender: A Renaissance Pursuit*. UIllP. pp. 142. $29.95. ISBN 0 252 01764 1.

Cousins, A. D. *The Catholic Religious Poets from Southwell to Crashaw*. Sheed&Ward. pp. 204. £19.95. ISBN 0 7220 1570 4.

Cullen, Patrick, and Thomas P. Roche, Jr, eds. *Spenser Studies: A Renaissance Poetry Annual, IX*. AMS. pp. 267. $45. ISBN 0 404 19209 2, ISSN 0195 9468.

Dasenbrock, Reed Way. *Imitating the Italians: Wyatt, Spenser, Synge, Pound, Joyce*. JHUP. pp. 282. £26. ISBN 0 8018 4147 X.

Duncan-Jones, Katherine. *Sir Philip Sidney: Courtier Poet*. HH. pp. 350. £20. ISBN 0 241 12650 9.

Gallagher, Lowell. *Medusa's Gaze: Casuistry and Conscience in the Renaissance*. StanfordUP. pp. 331. $29.50. ISBN 0 8047 1859 8.

Gurr, Andrew, ed. *The Yearbook of English Studies, 21. Politics, Patronage and Literature in England 1558–1658*. Special Number. MHRA. pp. 366. £30.50. ISBN 0 947623 38 8, ISSN 0306 2473.

Hager, Alan. *Dazzling Images: The Masks of Sir Philip Sidney*. UDelP, AUP. pp. 222. £29.95. ISBN 0 87413 390 4.

Halpern, Richard. *The Poetics of Primitive Accumulation: English Renaissance Culture and the Genealogy of Capital*. CornUP. pp. 321. hb $47.50, pb $17.55. ISBN 0 8014 2539 5, 0 8014 9772 8.

Hamilton, A. C., ed. *The Spenser Encyclopaedia*. UTorP, Routledge. pp. 858. £175. ISBN 0 8020 2676 1, 0 415 05637 3.

Hampton, Timothy. *Writing from History: The Rhetoric of Exemplarity in Renaissance Literature*. CornUP (1990). pp. 309. hb $47.25, pb $14.25. ISBN 0 8014 2460 7, 0 8014 9709 4.

Harvey, Elizabeth D., and Katharine Eisaman Maus, eds. *Soliciting Interpretation: Literary Theory and Seventeenth-Century English Poetry*. UChicP (1990). pp. 350. hb $47.50, pb $18.95. ISBN 0 226 31875 3, 0 226 31876 1.

Hendrix, Howard V. *The Ecstasy of Catastrophe: A Study of Apocalyptic Narrative from Langland to Milton*. Lang (1990). pp. 394. DM 39. ISBN 0 8204 0904 9.

Hogg, James, ed. *Richard Whytford, Volume 2. The boke of pacience*. USalz, Mellen. pp. 188. ISBN 3 7052 0600 1.

Jordan, Constance. *Renaissance Feminism: Literary Texts and Political Models*. CornUP (1990). pp. 319. hb $42.50, pb $12.95. ISBN 0 8014 2163 2, 0 8014 9732 9.

Klawitter, George, ed. *Richard Barnfield, The Complete Poems*. AUP, SusquehannaUP. pp. 249. £32. ISBN 0 945636 15 6.

Knox, Dilwyn. *Ironia: Medieval and Renaissance Ideas on Irony*. Brill (1989). pp.

237. Gld.86. ISBN 90 04 08965 9.

Lamb, Mary Ellen. *Gender and Authorship in the Sidney Circle.* UWiscP (1990). pp. 297. hb $37.50, pb $14.95. ISBN 0 299 12690 0, 0 299 12694 3.

Lawrence, Veronica, ed. *Richard Whytford, Volume I: A looking glace for the religious.* USalz, Mellen. pp. 96. ISBN 3 7052 0901 19.

Logan, Marie-Rose, and Peter L. Rudnytsky, eds. *Contending Kingdoms: Historical, Psychological, and Feminist Approaches to the Literature of Sixteenth-Century England and France.* WSUP. pp. 373. hb $44.95, pb $24.95. ISBN 0 8143 2149 6, 0 8143 2150 X.

Martz, Louis L. *From Renaissance to Baroque: Essays on Literature and Art.* UMissP. pp. 277. £39.95. ISBN 0 8262 0796 0.

May, Steven. *The Elizabethan Courtier Poets: The Poems and their Contexts.* UMissP. pp. 407. £31.50, $42. ISBN 08262 0749 9.

Meyer, Russel J. *'The Faerie Queene': Educating the Reader.* Twayne. pp. 146. pb £6.95. ISBN 0 8057 8122 6.

Patterson, Annabel. *Fables of Power: Aesopian Writing and Political History.* DukeUP. pp. 177. hb $29.95, pb $12.95. ISBN 0 8223 1106 2, 0 8223 1118 6.

Rees, Joan. *Sir Philip Sidney and 'Arcadia'.* FDUP, AUP. pp. 158. £22. ISBN 0 8386 3406 0.

Taylor, Barry. *Vagrant Writing: Social and Semiotic Disorders in the English Renaissance.* HW. pp.246. £35. ISBN 0 7450 0706 6.

VII

Shakespeare

R. J. C. WATT, JAMES KNOWLES, DERMOT CAVANAGH and PAUL DEAN

This chapter has the following sections: 1. Editions and Textual Matters; 2. Shakespeare in the Theatre; 3. Criticism. Section 1 is by R. J. C. Watt, section 2 is by Dermot Cavanagh, sections 3(a), 3(b) and 3(c) are by James Knowles and sections 3(d) and 3(e) are by Paul Dean.

1. Editions and Textual Matters

There are new editions of *Measure for Measure* from both Oxford and Cambridge. The OS is edited by N. W. Bawcutt, the NCaS by Brian Gibbons. Gibbons's introduction amounts to a short book in itself, and a good one, striking a balance between accessibility and detail, and illuminated throughout by extensive reference to other drama of the period. As usual in this series there is a lively and detailed account of the play as theatre; to this Gibbons adds a strong emphasis on its dramatic excitements. Extensive discussion of Shakespeare's sources is well related to the play. Gibbons is also good on contemporary London, on King James, and on the play's sceptical analysis of absolutism. Bawcutt's introduction is cautious, sceptical, and intelligent. Though more fully sourced, it is a little less spacious than that of Gibbons, and perhaps less accessible to non-specialists. Bawcutt plays down the King James connections, and says little on the play's general portrayal of rulers. He too devotes attention to the play's performance history. But where Gibbons finds dramatic excitement, Bawcutt detects artistic and moral problems, discussing them in terms which are by now very familiar.

In the editing itself these editions diverge notably. A few of Gibbons's explanatory notes are better than Bawcutt's, but in many cases Gibbons's annotation is diffuse and filled with matter of dubious relevance where Bawcutt is brief, intelligent, and to the point. Neither edition makes any great original contribution to the problems posed by the text, but whereas Bawcutt recognizes a textual problem when he sees one, Gibbons frequently displays the arch-conservatism which is merely an attempt to disguise helplessness in the face of difficulty. His reluctance to countenance departure from the Folio reading, even when F is near-nonsense, is not often convincingly argued. Some of his comments are merely fanciful: printing the famous (non-)word 'prenzie' (III.i.93, 96) he says that perhaps it is 'Shakespeare's coinage, fusing "princely" and "precise" '. This is hard to beat as an instance of confused and wishful thinking, wanting the fruits of emendation without daring to emend. In around twenty passages Gibbons sticks to F where Bawcutt adopts a preferable solution. There are another ten or so passages where both would have been better to depart from F. Each of these editions of *Measure for Measure* has strengths: Gibbons is the livelier critic, Bawcutt the better editor and all-rounder. But those interested in textual matters will not yet wholly abandon J. W. Lever's Arden edition, three decades old though it is.

Michael Hattaway's NCaS edition of *The Second Part of King Henry VI* follows his edition of the First Part noticed here last year. The old Arden edition by A. S. Cairncross is detailed though dated on textual problems, with much to say on revision and memorial reconstruction, but its literary introduction is woefully inadequate, a mere five pages. By contrast Hattaway's introduction, with its acute sensitivity to the play's achievement in the analysis of politics, may well be the best extended essay ever written on the play. Beginning with the claim that this is 'without doubt, a major play' Hattaway uses the word 'major' seven times in his first seventeen lines, but this is a rare infelicity. Rejecting the view that the plays endorse the Tudor myth, Hattaway stresses their anti-providential emphasis, seeing Shakespeare as sweeping away myth and miracle, replacing them with a radically secular view of history.

Since Hattaway is one of those who takes the Quartos to be memorial reconstructions rather than Shakespeare's revision of a play by others (he has no interest in theories of multiple authorship or revision), he pays attention to Quarto stage directions but is not greatly concerned to incorporate Q material in his text, which sticks closely to F. His annotation is a model, always cogent yet brief. And his text, though it follows F more conservatively than Cairncross, is that rarity these days, an enlightened conservatism (it is the enlightenment, of course, which is the rarity, not the other thing, which is the blight of the age). He often entertains intelligent argument about textual problems, rather than imposing a dogmatic view.

Those who like to think that there are three plays called *Hamlet* will welcome another fine compilation spawned by the revisionist fervour, *The Three-Text Hamlet*, edited by Paul Bertram and Bernice W. Kliman. The book is not facsimile but typeset, even unto turned letters; lineation is preserved even in prose. Such attempts to make the setting of type imitate facsimile always involve compromise, and can mislead. The introductory matter is minimal, and finding cross-references between corresponding passages in the different texts is not as convenient as it might be. But this handsome book is still a good way to read the play(s).

Grace Ioppolo claims that her book *Revising Shakespeare* is 'the first to establish in a materially concrete way that William Shakespeare was a deliberate, consistent, and persistent reviser' throughout his career. It starts well enough by showing that theories of revision flourished almost constantly for several centuries, with a rare exception being the period after E. K. Chambers made his attack on the disintegrationists. Four case studies then show how prevalent revision was in other dramatists of Shakespeare's period. Ioppolo ranges widely over Shakespeare discussing instances of putative revision, and the width is sometimes at the expense of depth. The section on *Hamlet* is a sketchy summary of the complex arguments which surround the early texts. On *Lear* she argues that Cordelia is at the heart of the revisions. But again and again the book fails to consider the other influences on the text besides revision. If the postulates of previous scholarship ('memorial reconstruction', 'foul papers') suit Ioppolo's purpose they are adopted without question: a more radical, sceptical, or thorough study would have acknowledged the problems they pose and considered how they affect her conclusions. Few would now want to maintain that Shakespeare never revised: the flaw in this book is its tendency to argue as if revision alone can account for every textual anomaly. Its pedestrian style does not altogether succeed in concealing the weaknesses of its absolutist argument.

More intellectually ambitious is Margreta de Grazia's *Shakespeare Verbatim: The Reproduction of Authenticity and the 1790 Apparatus*. The apparatus in question is not that at the foot of an editor's page but something more akin to ideological state apparatus: for de Grazia, Malone's edition is a work that shapes and positions subjects in Althusserean fashion. Dealing with biography and portraiture as well as texts, the book traces in great (and sometimes repetitive) detail Malone's efforts to 'authenticate' and 'historicise' the study of Shakespeare, and the way in which his Enlightenment project constructed a Shakespeare who was 'an exemplary instance of an autonomous self'. This venture into eighteenth-century cultural history quite deliberately does not examine a single passage of the plays, in Malone's or anyone else's editions; indeed, hardly a work by Shakespeare is ever even named. The author's interest is 'not in what Shakespeare wrote but in how what he wrote came to be reproduced in a form that continues to be accorded all the incontrovertibility of the obvious'. This is done with such intelligence and brio that one can just about accept the absence of Shakespeare from the book. But the partial absence of Malone is more serious: there is little which deals directly with what Malone actually wrote about Shakespeare (and no attempt at all to understand any of the 1,654 emendations he claimed to have made). The triumph of New Historicism sometimes appears to be in liberating itself from the historical reality which is its supposed material.

Colin Franklin's *Shakespeare Domesticated: The Eighteenth-Century Editions* is written from the point of view of a publisher and antiquarian bookseller. A pleasant survey of each of the major editions of the century, it has no pretensions to bibliographical expertise or scholarly knowledge. Robert F. Fleissner's book *Shakespeare and the Matter of the Crux* spends more time on puzzles of authorship, of the naming of characters, and of relations to topical events than it does on textual cruces. He adds a further instalment to the argument that *Love's Labour's Won* is really *Much Ado* in disguise: the only real evidence is from the order in which Francis Meres mentioned the plays. He considers the identity of Mr W. H. of the Sonnets, arguing that the most likely candidate is William Hall the stationer or printer. Fleissner has a penchant for these and other famous puzzles about which there will probably never be general agreement: hence he gives the impression of shoring up entrenched positions rather than breaking new ground. The chances are that he is on the right side of the argument about fifty per cent of the time, yet the evidence he adduces often relies on the most tenuous connections and on matter of very dubious relevance. A lover of conundrums, Fleissner is learned but often diffuse, ponderous, highly speculative and unconvincing. Pomposity is everywhere, with phrases such as 'the Stratford genius', 'the Danish Prince', 'the star-crossed tragedy', and 'the rotund rogue'. Talking of whom, he rejects Theobald's 'babld of green fields', calling Theobald 'a notorious emendator': his suggestion that there are echoes of heraldic images in the passage (*Henry V*, II.iii.16) is tenuous and quite unconvincing.

In *The Theory and Practice of Text-Editing*, edited by Ian Small and Marcus Walsh, are three essays of relevance. The late Philip Brockbank in 'Towards a Mobile text' looks back on recent editorial approaches to *Hamlet* and *Lear*, and then abruptly turns to a vision of the future where electronic variorum editions may offer infinite riches on a little screen. This vision has occurred to a number of people who have little practical idea of the labour which is needed to make it work. 'Rectifying Shakespeare's *Errors*: Romance and Farce in Bardeditry' is a pleasantly written essay in which Charles Whitworth muses on issues of editorial method raised in editing *The*

Comedy of Errors and then offers sensible though familiar accounts of several cruces in the play, together with remarks on performances. Russell Jackson in 'Victorian Editors of *As You Like It* and the Purposes of Editing' examines numerous Victorian school editions of the play and sheds much light on their moral and philological preoccupations and on reading habits in the period.

Turning to the periodicals, one is reminded that the human capacity to misconstrue Shakespeare in general, and Sonnet 51 in particular, seems endless. One might have supposed that MacDonald P. Jackson's eminently sane piece last year (*YWES* 71) would have finally put an end to nonsense about 'desire ... shall naigh no dull flesh' (10–11), but along comes Hans H. Meier with 'Shakespeare Restored: Sonnets 51.11 and 146.2' (*ES* 72.350–4), eschewing the compelling emendation *weigh* for *naigh* and proposing instead to read 'desire ... shall nay no dull flesh'. This gives the unfortunate sense 'my desire ... will not refuse the services of dull flesh': unfortunate in that the remaining three lines of the poem do indeed pointedly excuse the tired horse from further service. Let the neighing about this passage now cease. Meier is more cogent in his criticism of some customary assumptions made when emending the obviously corrupt opening of the second line of Sonnet 146 ('My sinful earth these rebel powers that thee array', where 'My sinful earth' is dittography from the previous line), but his suggestion, 'Amid these rebel powers ...' is an old one. A hundred other conjectures have been made: this is a passage where the original reading is irrecoverable.

Much more food for thought on the Sonnets comes from A. Kent Hieatt, Charles W. Hieatt and Anne Lake Prescott, who ask 'When Did Shakespeare Write *Sonnets 1609*?' (*SP* 88.69–109). Theirs is an ambitious stylometric study founded on the reasonable proposition that since we have a large body of relatively well-dated work by Shakespeare it may be possible to determine when the Sonnets were composed by examining similarities of vocabulary between the Sonnets and works of agreed date. Certain rare words are characteristic of Shakespeare's early career, others of his later. By looking at the proportions of early and late rare words in the Sonnets, they are able to suggest that most of the Sonnets were probably written in the period 1591–5, but that many of Sonnets 104 to 126 may belong to the years around the turn of the century. Further, since the first sixty sonnets show significant numbers of both early and late rare words, it is likely that they were written early but revised late, probably shortly before publication in 1609. The potential ability to reveal revision is a particularly interesting feature of their chosen method. Of course many other quantitative approaches to dating are possible, and it will be fascinating to see whether future studies using different techniques confirm these tentative conclusions.

Stanley Wells in '*A Midsummer Night's Dream* Revisited' (*CS* 3.14–29) reflects on changes in editorial approaches to the play since his NPS of 1967. His scepticism there about the play's having been written for a noble wedding has found support since. Nor does Wells find any new reason to abandon his scepticism about the related question of a supposed alternative ending for the play. The respect in which his views have changed is in now according the Folio text greater importance than he did previously, in that it is likely to represent a more theatrical version. The remainder of Wells's article goes well beyond textual matters with an authoritative account of selected scholarship and productions from recent years. In another retrospective piece, 'The Arden *Hamlet*: Some Reflections a Decade Later' (*SN* 63.47–8), Harold Jenkins concedes that if he were to edit the play again now, 'the question of some Shakespearean reworking ... would have to be confronted'. The other issue, of course, is that since the Arden which favoured Q2 we have had two Oxford editions which favour

F, seeing in it once again a more theatrical version of the play. Jenkins is unpersuaded: 'I should not accept F's theatrical cuts' and 'I should still regard Q2 as the more authoritative text', he says. He points out that there is a good deal of special pleading in the revision arguments, and that almost all the 'evidence' for revision is capable of alternative explanation. Whether right or wrong, Jenkins is at least one who would rather try to be right than be fashionable.

Ward Elliott and Robert Valenza's 'Was the Earl of Oxford the True Shakespeare? A Computer-Aided Analysis' (*N&Q* 38.501–6) is a report on a year's work by undergraduates in their 'Shakespeare Clinic', in which Shakespeare's poems were subjected to elaborate quantitative tests against twenty-seven other poets of the period. Their conclusion, that Shakespeare was not Bacon nor Marlowe nor the Earl of Oxford, is unexceptionable but sketchily argued. That article, though, is merely a puff for the real thing, and the same authors, now taking themselves more seriously as W. E. Y. Elliott and R. J. Valenza, offer their full account in 'A Touchstone for the Bard' (*CHum* 25.199–209). Their method, which they call modal analysis, is to count selected keywords and rank their modes in a way which, they claim, is less sensitive to subject-matter and genre than most studies of word frequencies. As well as ruling out all the Shakespeare claimants, their tests suggest that Shakespeare did not write 'Shall I Die', 'As This Is Endless', or 'Elegy by W. S.', but that the majority of poems in *The Passionate Pilgrim*, including some but not all of the unascribed poems, are highly Shakespearean.

Screeching owls, like neighing horses, are a recurring topic. In 'Illusions, Isaiah, and "Owles" in *The Comedy of Errors*' (*N&Q* 38.472–3), Terry Humby returns to a passage recently considered by others (*YWES* 68.221), offering further evidence that the apparently non-human form of the owl does not render it out of place in the line 'We talk with goblins, owls, and sprites' (II.ii.190). The case, such as it is, for retaining F *owles* has now been exhaustively made, but the argument is not closed since the line remains metrically defective. In 'An Emended *Much Ado About Nothing*, Act V, Scene iii' (*PBSA* 84.413–18), Jeffrey Rayner Myers tackles the problem of the missing or confused speech prefixes in the scene where Hero's presumed death is mourned. Hero's epitaph, apparently assigned to an extraneous 'Lord' in Q and F, is often given to Claudio; Myers proposes that it should be spoken by Leonato. This removes some difficulties while introducing others. Alan Dilnot, in 'Shakespeare, the Stanley Epitaphs, and Sir William Dugdale' (*N&Q* 38.499–501) tries to strengthen the case for regarding the epitaphs on the Stanley family in Tong Church, Shropshire, as being by Shakespeare. He suggests that Sir William Dugdale's ascription of the verses to Shakespeare may be the more reliable for his having had Lancashire connections, as did the Stanleys. This may be so, though there can be no certainty. In 'Pope's Influence on Shakespeare?' (*SQ* 42.57–9) Catherine Bates questions Rowe's emendation of *desire* to *defile* at *Henry V* III.iii.35. Merely because locks of hair are mentioned she thinks that the emendation must have been unconsciously influenced by Pope's *The Rape of the Lock*, and must therefore be wrong. This farrago of invention whips up a mystery where none exists.

Stephan Kukowski, in 'The Hand of John Fletcher in *Double Falsehood*' (*ShS* 43.81–9) argues that Fletcher's metrical habits, usage, and stylistic mannerisms are strongly evident in *The Double Falsehood*, the play published by Theobald in 1728. Since Shakespeare and Fletcher may well have collaborated on *Cardenio*, and since *The Double Falsehood* is a version of the Cardenio story, Kukowski thinks that Theobald's play may well preserve, as Theobald claimed, a few relics of a partly Shakespearean original, rather than being a Theobald forgery as some have sought to show. Joseph Candido considers 'The First Folio and Nicholas Rowe's 1714 *King John*' (*N&Q* 38.506–8). By tracing variants in a single play through the four Folios and Rowe's three editions, he clearly demonstrates that the person who prepared Rowe's third edition of 1714 (who may have been someone other than Rowe) took the trouble to consult early Folios, thereby removing a number of errors in Rowe's earlier editions which, as is well known, simply relied on F4. 'Fume/Fury in *2 Henry VI*', by N. F. Blake (*N&Q* 38.49–51) questions the frequently-adopted emendation *fury* at I.iii.150, arguing for the retention of the Folio's *fume* on the grounds that, together with 'tickled' in the same line, it refers to befuddlement as if through drink. The argument is somewhat strained; metre is also against it; and Hattaway in his edition rightly emends. Jonathan Bate's 'Shakespeare's Tragedies as Working Scripts' (*CS* 3.118–27) is derived from a lecture for schoolteachers on the ways in which Shakespeare the reviser can be presented in the classroom. This is a fine introduction to some of the issues which stand out if we refuse to conflate early texts of the tragedies: 'who rules Britain at the end of *Lear*, whether Hamlet delays, the representation of women in *Othello*, and the nature of the Weird Sisters in *Macbeth*.'

Eclectic as ever, *N&Q* prints two pieces by Eric Sams. In 'Assays of Bias' (*N&Q* 38.60–3) he returns to his attack on inconsistencies in theories about the textual origins of *Hamlet*. His main target here is the Wells–Taylor position that Q1 *Hamlet* was a memorial reconstruction. For Sams the 'house of cards' known as memorial reconstruction 'now lies in ruins'. This is, ahem, not obviously so. Sams's other contribution, 'The Painful Misadventures of *Pericles* Acts I–II' (*N&Q* 38.67–70), follows his familiar pattern, denying that Wilkins had any hand in the play. Sams is prolific in suggesting ways in which assumptions made by others can be challenged, but much less effective at persuading us of his own position, which is, as usual, that every version of every early printed text is Shakespeare's pure and simple. For him all agencies of transmission and corruption, and all possibility of adaptation by others, can be discounted: every variation can be ascribed to a revising Shakespeare. The sheer implausibility of this never strikes him. Sams is the amateur terrorist of contemporary Shakespearean textual criticism. Some of his bombs fail to explode; others make a nice bang but do rather little damage, since he still prefers assertion to careful demonstration supported by evidence.

Pace Sams, the flight from memorial reconstruction is by no means universal. Those this year who reject it in favour of revision do so largely by assertion, while Kathleen Irace, who believes in it, has something more solid to offer. In 'Reconstruction and Adaptation in Q *Henry V*' (*SB* 44.228–53), she analyses all corresponding lines in the Folio and Quarto texts of the play, assessing the degree of parallelism between each line in one text and its counterpart in the other, and ascribing them to their speakers. This reveals huge variation among the actors in the fidelity with which different parts were reproduced, and strongly suggests that three actors could have reconstructed the Quarto from 'a version similar to the Folio, which they apparently abridged as part of a single process of reconstruction and adaptation'. The passages not in Q tell a similar story. This careful and thorough argument, as well as giving memorial reconstruction a good run for its money, challenges Gary Taylor's conclusion that Q stems from a deliberate theatrical abridgement which was later reconstructed by reporter–actors.

'Statistical Inference in *A Textual Companion* to the Oxford Shakespeare' (*N&Q* 38.73–8) is another in M. W. A. Smith's long and valuable series of articles helping to put stylometry on proper statistical foundations. Smith has done a close examination of Gary Taylor's statistics, and reports 'fundamental flaws which seriously undermine the validity of Taylor's study'. He completely demolishes that section of *A Textual Companion* (*YWES* 68.216–7) which tries to make discriminations about authorship based on the analysis of function words. Even after correcting the mistaken assumptions in Taylor by providing revised figures, Smith concludes that Taylor's methods are unreliable. Of course the fact that *A Textual Companion* mishandled the issue does not mean that such methods in general have nothing to offer, and the value of Taylor's efforts may turn out to be that they stimulate others to do better. Indeed, not content with criticizing others, Smith also offers an original contribution of his own, 'The Authorship of *The Raigne of King Edward the Third*' (*L&LC* 6.166–74). Opinion is moving strongly in favour of this play being by Shakespeare, with Wells and Taylor expressing regret (see below) at not having included it in the Oxford *Complete Works*. Smith studies the play using a highly elaborate composite method based on the first words of speeches, all other words, and collocation pairs. His extensive comparisons with the work of eight other Elizabethan playwrights show that *Edward III* is even more likely to be by Shakespeare than *Richard II* (!), and that it dates from around 1590. Smith is now the leading figure in Shakespearean stylometric methodology. But matters have become so technical that very few Shakespeareans will be able to meet him on his own ground.

One of those few is MacD. P. Jackson, who returns to a familiar debate in 'George Wilkins and the First Two Acts of *Pericles*: New Evidence from Function Words' (*L&LC* 6.155–63). After summarizing the extensive evidence recently presented by M. W. A. Smith (*YWES* 68.114; 69.222; 70.255) which supports the view that the first two acts of the play are probably by Wilkins, Jackson presents his own complementary investigation based on the incidence of thirteen function words in 112 plays by twenty dramatists. Acts III to V of *Pericles* turn out to resemble *Cymbeline* more closely than they do any of the other 111 plays; Acts I and II resemble samples from Wilkins. 'Wilkins is more likely than Shakespeare to have been the main author of the first two acts', as Jackson cautiously puts it, and everyone except Eric Sams must surely agree. Jackson's evidence also gives no support to the view that the first two acts are a survival from an early Shakespeare play.

In '*Measure for Measure*, Middleton, and "brakes of ice" ' (*N&Q* 38.64–7), R. V. Holdsworth tackles the well-known crux at II.i.39, one of the play's most stubborn, 'Some run from brakes of ice and answer none'. He reads 'breaks of ice', meaning (literally) a breach in the ice on a frozen stream or pond, which makes the necessary pointed contrast with the minor 'fault' or crack of the following line; and (figuratively) a loss of virginity, a sense which he illustrates compellingly from Middleton. Holdsworth's interpretation, based on an emendation cautious enough to satisfy even the arch-conservatives, succeeds where so many have failed in relating this image convincingly to the play's central ethical issues: Angelo is the ice-breaker who would not answer for his sexual crimes. For good measure, Holdsworth throws in a budget of illumination on links between Middleton and Shakespeare.

J. Karl Franson, in 'Numbers in Shakespeare's Dedications to *Venus and Adonis* and *The Rape of Lucrece*' (*N&Q* 38.51–4), counts lines, words, and punctuation on the dedicatory pages of both poems, and suspects references to the fact that the Earl of Southampton was nineteen and twenty when the two poems were published. This piece will appeal to numerologists. Stephen Orgel in 'The Poetics of Incomprehensibility' (*SQ* 42.431–7) reproduces four of the most difficult passages in *The Winter's Tale*, claims that all attempts at both elucidation and emendation have been unsatisfactory, and suggests that they may well have struck a Renaissance audience as vague and confused. Orgel may be right to claim that the Renaissance was much more at ease with obscurity than we are, but if his views were taken as an editorial or readerly principle they would become an excuse for doing nothing by way of effort to understand. Had he considered David Ward's article (*YWES* 68.238) on one of the passages in question, he might not find it so incomprehensible.

'The Date of *The Merry Wives of Windsor*' by Elizabeth Schafer (*N&Q* 38.57–60) exposes weaknesses in the arguments for the widespread assumption that the play belongs to 1597. She notes that the passage about the Order of the Garter does not necessarily tie the play to the particular occasion of Lord Hunsdon's admission to the Order, offers alternative reasons why the play might have been set in Windsor, and shows that the verbal links between the play and *2 Henry IV* are a weak argument for dating since there are equally impressive links with *Henry V*. Two other essays on *Merry Wives* show how Shakespeare critics have realised that they can no longer leave textual problems to specialists. 'Levelling Shakespeare: Local Customs and Local Texts' (*SQ* 42.168–78) by Leah S. Marcus is an example of a growing tendency to blend theory, interpretation, and textual scholarship. This essay 'levels' the Quarto and Folio texts of *Merry Wives* in the sense that it takes them both equally seriously, and in doing so demonstrates the prevalence of references to Windsor and the Court in F which are lacking in Q, concluding that F was aimed at a Court audience, Q at a middle-class urban public. And even Elizabeth Pittenger's feminist account of *Merry Wives*, 'Dispatch Quickly: The Mechanical Reproduction of Pages' (*SQ* 42.389–408), glances at the doubleness of the early texts, rather imaginatively taking that doubleness as a figure of other kinds of duplicity in the play.

A whole issue of *AEB* (4, 1990, published 1991) is devoted to essays focused more or less closely on the Wells–Taylor Oxford *Complete Works*. S. P. Cerasano (21–34) explores the way in which editors from Malone to Wells–Taylor conceive of stage practice, and Patty S. Derrick (35–45) examines nineteenth-century prompt-books to suggest how the edition's stage directions might have benefited from them. Grace Ioppolo (46–58) reviews and praises Wells's and Taylor's theory and practice in dealing with revision in Shakespeare, though she would go further than they. Thomas A. Pendleton (59–71) joins the queue of those who want to smack the editors for calling Falstaff Oldcastle; he has done his homework, and his smack is more powerful than many of the earlier and more emotional reactions to the change of name. Ann Thompson (72–90) considers punctuation, particularly the absence of brackets in the edition – not, of course, the notorious 'broken' brackets of the stage directions (which Wells and Taylor now repent of) but the decision not to use round brackets in the main text; her topic proves to be far from mere pedantry. Stanley Wells and Gary Taylor themselves look back at their labours (6–20) and confess a few regrets, such as the broken brackets and the failure to record editorial decisions about stage directions. They now think they should have included *Edward III* and two versions of *Hamlet*. Nevertheless their article reminds us what a remarkable feat they pulled off in bringing the thing to a conclusion. Michael Dobson (91–7) looks at the knowledge which the edition assumes and does not assume in its readers, finds contradictions in assumptions about that mythical if necessary beast, the general reader, and situates the edition in its cultural context. Trevor H. Howard-Hill, who writes the preface to this collection, calls the Oxford *Complete Works* 'the greatest edition of this century'; Dobson wittily suggests ways in which it is a product of the Thatcher decade. Of an age, or for all time? Perhaps, as with Shakespeare, a bit of both.

I have saved up till last one of the most memorable pieces of the year, though one of the shortest. 'Reconstructing Shakespeare 1: The Roles that Shakespeare Performed' (*ShN* 63.16–17) is the first of a promised series of articles by Donald W.

Foster. He takes the method of studying vocabulary clusters, used in the past to help establish dating, and puts it to startling new use. His hypothesis is that since Shakespeare was likely to be acting in one play while writing another, and would have had to memorize the part of the character he played, the distinctive language of that character is likely to re-emerge diffused throughout the later play. By identifying vocabulary clusters which influence a subsequent play we are likely to be identifying the parts which Shakespeare himself performed. The claimed results are fascinating: Shakespeare seems often to have been on stage in the opening scene of a play, in a minor role, often that of an old man, perhaps lame, who carries a staff. If Foster's full evidence, yet to be presented, stands up to scrutiny, our view of Shakespeare, as actor and perhaps as writer, will be permanently altered. Shakespeare, it seems, may well have been John of Gaunt, Menenius, and Theseus, inserting their famous set-pieces for his own glee: once one has learned such things they are hard to forget, and not always comfortable to remember.

2. Shakespeare in the Theatre

The year's most striking account of contemporary Shakespearean performance emerges in Murray Cox's *Shakespeare Comes to Broadmoor*. Cox is a Consultant Psychotherapist at Broadmoor and has also maintained a long academic association with the Shakespeare Institute, which culminated in both professional and amateur stagings of *Hamlet*, *King Lear*, *Romeo and Juliet* and *Measure for Measure* within the hospital. The resulting book is awkwardly organized, but documents a courageous experiment. It primarily consists of a sequence of interviews with the actors and directors who took part, some fascinating material on the nature of the hospital itself (and the use of drama as therapy), and a collage of reactions from those involved. Many of these attest to the power of the experience and those involved in the production register how it reformed their conceptions of both the hospital and of the dramatic material they brought to it. Inevitably, the concern with madness and violence took on a new intensity and many of the performers speak of a heightened awareness of the reality of tragic experience. Tragedy's ability to shake assumptions took on a new force when, as one participant puts it, 'The thing that really struck me is how close we all are.'

Next to this, the 'wisdom and insight' claimed by the publisher for John Gielgud's *Shakespeare – Hit or Miss?* seems drastically misplaced. The book was produced through a series of interviews conducted by Gielgud's collaborator, John Miller, and is prone to chattiness and imprecision. Still, part of the interest of Gielgud's career remains in its being touched by so many of those who fashioned and re-fashioned Shakespearean production in the twentieth century – Granville-Barker, Olivier, Orson Welles, Peter Brook, Peter Hall – and he proves to be an actor winningly open to innovation. Appendices gather together critical reviews of his performances and some intriguing rehearsal notes he received from Granville-Barker when playing Lear in 1940.

There are two more additions to Macmillan's Text and Performance Series: Peter Holding's *Romeo and Juliet* is a pedestrian introduction that follows the format of isolating the text's central issues – here perceived as an exploration of conflicting registers of language, shaped by the play's ambivalent representation of Petrarchanism – and then surveys their treatment in contemporary performance. Holding examines the productions of Zeffirelli (1961), Terry Hands (1973 and 1989), Trevor

Nunn and Barry Kyle (1976), and Michael Bogdanov (1986), to discuss the tension between such a linguistically involved text and the demands of modern staging for clarifying visual images. Pamela Mason's *Much Ado About Nothing* is livelier and has a more comprehensive awareness of modern stage-history, analysing four key postwar performances and then offering a general survey of productions between 1981 and 1990. Mason usefully distinguishes the key areas a production must present – an artificial 'fashionable' society, the forms of independence represented by Beatrice and Benedick, the military ethic – in an economical manner. However, this series is being surpassed in quality by Manchester University Press's Shakespeare in Performance, which offers far more sophisticated and historically-informed critical responses.

Imaginative use is made of performance in two book-length critical studies. Thomas Cartelli's *Marlowe, Shakespeare and the Economy of Theatrical Experience* sees the two dramatists as participating in a provocative dramatic 'economy'. He attempts to demonstrate this by arguing for the degree of objectivity in evaluating authorial intention that is released by a performance-oriented methodology. Cartelli seeks to extend our sense of the range of reactions possible for an Elizabethan audience by recovering sociological evidence of their openness to irreverent and heterodox material. Through close readings of a number of plays, he argues that both dramatists encouraged an audience to engage with trangressive material (for example, the empathy created for rebels and regicides) and to think sceptically about established values. Some of Cartelli's readings are over-familiar and his sense of historical context – especially of 'establishment attitudes' – is often simplistic. This is, however, a carefully argued book with some stimulating reflection on how common elements of design in plays allow us to verify how audience response is being constituted in particular ways.

Kent Cartwright's *Shakespearean Tragedy and Its Double: The Rhythms of Audience Response* also concentrates on the effects of performance in trying to provide 'a spectatorial poetics of Shakespearean tragedy'. Cartwright is principally concerned with the ruling tension between the rhythms of engaged sympathetic response and the counter-rhythms of detached critical reflection created by the texts. Shakespearean tragedy engenders a paradoxical state of deepened responsiveness and heightened autonomy and Cartwright is resourceful in demonstrating how this is fashioned in detailed treatments of five plays, including *Hamlet*, *Othello* and *Antony and Cleopatra*. There is a particularly fine examination of how the carnivalesque undertone of *Romeo and Juliet* detaches an audience from the 'official' world of tragic necessity and a good account of how the secondary characters in *King Lear* act as elusive mediators of the audience's response. Cartwright is a valuable guide to the controlled degree of interpretative possibility that the tragedies generate – how they empower an audience to become 'performing playgoers'.

Lorne M. Buchman is also interested in the dynamic interplay between moments of identification and alienation in her excellent treatment of filmed Shakespeare: *Still in Movement: Shakespeare on Screen*. Buchman provides some sharp insights into individual directors by analysing how a given event in the text is experienced through contending perspectives. Her book is freshly organized to demonstrate how the plays are re-shaped by key cinematic techniques to activate a particular imaginative response. She provides detailed consideration of sequences from Brook, Kozintsev, Welles, and Olivier, and returns us to these classic adaptations with a new understanding of their shared cinematic nature. The book lucidly analyses the interaction of confined and expansive performing spaces, the importance of contextualization of action, filmic self-consciousness and manipulation of temporal structure. Overall, she makes a vigorous case for the importance of film as a medium both for releasing the potential of Shakespeare's drama and realizing new aspects of it.

Susan Willis's *The BBC Shakespeare Plays: Making the Televised Canon* offers the fullest critical account of this most ambitious of attempts to film Shakespeare. Willis is a thorough and intelligent guide through the manifold financial and political tensions that affected this project from its origins onwards and discriminates usefully between the style and aims of the three directorial regimes that successively controlled its production. She is equally alert to the different cultural contexts that made the broadcasting and reception of the series 'a different phenomenon in America than in Britain'. Her study continues to examine the demands of television as a medium for production, particularly as they were dealt with by Jonathan Miller, Elijah Moshinsky and Jane Howell, and concludes with eyewitness accounts of the making of *Troilus and Cressida*, *The Comedy of Errors*, and *Titus Andronicus*. Two lengthy appendices list the taping and transmission dates of all the plays and inventory BBC productions of Shakespeare prior to the series.

A number of useful studies of Renaissance performance conditions have appeared. John H. Astington has edited a collection of essays that help to explain the emergence and development of a 'theatrical culture' in Elizabethan London. In *The Development of Shakespeare's Theater*, Astington's nine contributors discuss a variety of crucial antecedents for the Renaissance theatre and revise views of its established nature. The topics examined include the growth of independent companies of actors, the factors that inhibited the utilization of boy players, hall-performance as providing a more flexible and diverse tradition for the use of theatrical space, the structure of the Globe and the performance features of the Rose, Swan and Phoenix. David Bradley addresses a neglected aspect of performance-history in *From Text to Performance in the Elizabethan Theatre: Preparing the Play for the Stage*. The unsung hero of Elizabethan play-houses emerges as the plotter who mapped out a skeleton ground-plan of the action to be performed. Of the seven extant theatre plots, only one has a play-text that survives to accompany it, Peele's *The Battle of Alcazar*, and the two are exhaustively compared. Bradley gleans some useful insights into the organization of the theatrical process from these little-regarded documents and he has fresh things to say on the size and composition of companies, how entrances were conventionally achieved and what happened when plays were adapted for changes in personnel or for other companies.

Some space should also be given to mention the revised edition of Peter Thomson's *Shakespeare's Theatre*, first published in 1983. This is a model introduction to the formation, structure and development of the Lord Chamberlain's Men which is utilized to provide instructive critical readings of *Twelfth Night*, *Macbeth* and *Hamlet*.

Three articles offer detailed treatments of particular productions. Michael A. Morrison reappraises 'John Barrymore's *Hamlet* at the Haymarket Theatre, 1925' (*NTQ* 7.246–60). Barrymore's performance had a sensational impact in London and Morrison argues that it also contributed importantly to a revaluation of the character of Hamlet, helping to dissolve Victorian conceptions of a genteel prince and encouraging the development of a harsher, more psychologically intense persona who spoke in a modern conversational style. In *THStud* (10.31–55), William P. Shaw's 'Text, Performance, and Perspective: Peter Brook's Landmark Production of *Titus Andronicus*' details the ingredients that went into the making of this legendary production. Brook substantially cut and rearranged the text to prune any overtly 'Elizabethan' elements of rhetoric or theatrical design that would impede an immediate apprehension of the play's primitive strength. Shaw describes the further expression of this directorial vision in set design, music, costuming, and acting, to provide a vivid account of a 'barbaric ritual'. Elizabeth Beroud's 'Scrutiny of a Mask' in *CahiersE* 49 is an exhaustive account and interpretation of Sam Mendes's 1990 RSC production of *Troilus and Cressida*.

Michael Mullin's 'Motley and *Romeo*: The Designers and the Text' (*TJ* 43.457–69) makes an elegant case for the importance of set and costume design in analysing the role of the mid-century 'Motley' design team in their work on five productions of *Romeo and Juliet*. Mullin emphasizes how important design is as a key ingredient in creating theatrical meaning, in helping isolate the essential pattern of a play – here, 'unbroken speed and interconnected enclosed spaces' – and in detecting changing directorial and cultural attitudes to dramatic texts. Geoffrey Bent's somewhat crudely written 'Chronicles of the Time: Acting as Applied Criticism in *Hamlet*' (*ThR* 16.17–29) examines the performances of Gielgud, Olivier and Burton as constituting modes of interpretation which are as diverse, subtle and as worthy of attention as any critical hypothesis. [D. C.]

Two books concentrate on *Lear* in performance: James P. Lusardi and June Schlueter's *Reading Shakespeare in Performance: 'King Lear'*, and Alexander Leggatt's *King Lear* in the SiP series. Lusardi and Schlueter focus on two television versions, Jonathan Miller's of 1982 with Michael Hordern, and Michael Elliott's of 1983 with Laurence Olivier. Both are discussed by Leggatt, who also takes in six others including Peter Brook's ground-breaking production of 1962 – the disturbing impact of which he conveys with the excitement of an eyewitness – and the controversial Gambon/Sher *Lear* of 1982. He is too polite about Sher's Fool, although he drops enough hints to show that he recognized what a vulgarly self-indulgent performance it was. The approaches of these two books are usefully complementary. Lusardi and Schlueter select six key episodes and provide in each case a discussion of the clues to staging contained in the text, followed by a detailed description of its televisual treatment. Their chapter on the Dover Cliff scene is a good illustration of their approach. They note the different possibilities – both countenanced by the text – for realistic or anti-illusionistic staging (actors labouring up an incline or simply wandering round a flat surface), the artifice which creates a sense of place through scenic description which a blind man cannot but accept, and the way in which Edgar's shock therapy turns on a purported miracle which is in fact a hoax, casting doubt on his spiritual moralizing about the kindly intervention of the gods – which is also undercut by his own subsequent experiences. They then show how Miller manipulates camera angles and distances so as to tantalize the audience about the spatiality of the scene, and how Elliott combines initial realism with anti-climax as Gloucester is found to have fallen only a short distance. Miller casts an ironic light on Edgar's achievement, Elliott creates an affecting tableau of parent/child reunion. Within its limits the book is successful. It is, however, both less ambitious and less exhilarating than Leggatt's, which is full of perceptive touches, such as his comments on Jonathan Miller's medical background being a drawback as well as a strength in his directing of Hordern, or on Olivier's use of his sense of irony to show Lear deferring reality right to the end. Personal recollection and judicious quotation from reviews supplement the more objectively descriptive sections of the book. [P. D.]

3. Criticism

(a) General

The most substantial biographical item this year comes from Sam Schoenbaum, whose revision of his *Shakespeare's Lives* (OUP) supplements the original to include material published after 1970, neatly contextualizing studies of the Lancastrian connection by Hamer and Honigmann, and drawing attention to Jane Cox's discussion of the will signatures. Other book length items are more nugatory, including an exhaustive study of Shakespeare's extended family (David Honneyman's *Closer to Shakespeare*) and a protracted peregrination through Shakespearean sites and myths in Irving Matus's *Shakespeare: The Living Record*. Amongst the articles, A. D. Harvey argues that Shakespeare's retirement to Stratford reflects neither the self-satisfied comfort of a newly enriched player-writer, nor a diminishment in creative powers, but rather the urge to create some now lost masterpiece (*ContempR*). After such *ignis fatuii* it is a pleasure to turn to the solid research of Mary Edmond, who shows the 1623 frontispiece engraving more likely to be the work of Martin Droeshout Senior, perhaps from a painting by Marcus Gheeraerts II (' "It was for Gentle Shakespeare Cut" ', *SQ* 42.339–44).

Essay collections have acquired a certain vogue this year, probably in part because they serve to pad out responses for the research selectivity farce, but also because they do perform the useful function of encompassing the diversity of approaches to Shakespeare criticism in the early 1990s. The more radical collections explore not only the various critical approaches open in today's critical practices but also the institutional structures that shape reading techniques and protocols, or the various culturally formed permutations of the works, the biography or the image over the centuries. Most forthright amongst these is *Shakespeare in the Changing Curriculum* (ed. L. Aers and N. Wheale), a collection that transcends the binary divide between school and university teaching and whose essays are a tribute to the constructive, imaginative and self-critical teaching skills of two beleaguered professions. Essays by Aers, Allen, Inglis and Wheale ponder the impact of the National Curriculum and the various newer approaches to teaching Shakespeare, whilst other essays explore the significance of methods that highlight race, gender and sexuality. Pride of place goes, however, to Simon Shepherd's inventive essay ('Acting Against Bardom: Some Utopian Thoughts on Workshops'), which considers the uses of workshop teaching to expose the assumptions of current criticism, a chapter so full of ideas that I shall not hesitate to pillage it for my own teaching. Although several contributions to the Aers and Wheale collection articulate worthy if perhaps slightly dated sentiments, and some rehearse familiar arguments (notably Hobby on sexuality in *As You Like It*), this pales in comparison to the wholesale repetition found in *Staging the Renaissance* (ed. D. S. Kastan and P. Stallybrass), where only five out of twenty-four chapters are new material. Most cover writers other than Shakespeare, but Randall McLeod (*Random Cloud*) supplies a stimulating essay on the critical implications of speech headings (on *All's Well*). Although the continual reprinting and repackaging of the same essays by the same small group of scholars like bindweed threatens to choke the publishing industry, many of the pieces reprinted here are outstanding and the collection would be useful for most undergraduates. On the conservative slate *The Arts of Performance in Elizabethan and Early Stuart Drama* (essays in honour of G. K. Hunter) provides some interesting moments, especially in Stanley Wells on spectres in Shakespeare, which contains an excellent discussion of the ghost in *Hamlet*, and a subtle and nuanced discussion of the Sonnets by Philip Edwards, although there are also essays on Middleton (Inga-Stina Ewbank) and Marlowe (Ernst Honigmann) as well as some gestures towards performance criticism.

An equally disparate and qualitatively variable collection, *Literature and Nationalism* (ed. V. Newey and A. Thompson), provides surveys of war (J. Barish, 'War, Civil War and *Bruderkrieg* in Shakespeare'), and Welsh figures, and a detailed study of Imogen. Ivo Kamps edits *Shakespeare Left and Right*, a collection that consciously attempts to contain both left and right, represented by Gayle Greene and Richard Levin, respectively. The book's present occasions rest in a heated MLA session on ideology plus the aftermath of Levin's *PMLA* article 'Feminist Thematics and Shakespearean Tragedy' and the opprobrium it attracted. Without this background the first half of the book, with its comments, responses, counter-comments and comments on the backs of lesser comments, remains opaque at best and infuriating at worst. In this recension Levin restates (marginally more temperately) his objections to 'feminist thematics' and to his opponents' ideological approach (although the actual grasp of current conceptualizations of 'ideology' and even the 'author' is seriously flawed). Greene responds with an honest assessment of the state of feminist criticism and women in the academy, contradicting Levin's chimera of non-ideological criticism. Indeed, the problem of ideology draws the wittiest essay in the collection from Edward Pechter ('Against "Ideology" '), while others respond to various aspects of Levin and Greene's cross-critique of each other. Apart from annoyance at the incestuous nature of the discussion and horror at some of the examples cited in Linda Woodbridge's afterword, *Shakespeare Left and Right* just depressed this reader. A more sterile, pedantic, uninspired and uninspiring example of academic squabbling I have not read for a long time. This is more the pity since some of the essays in the second half, notably Maus on *Love's Labour's Lost* and Kastan on the history plays, are fine pieces of criticism, and since the issues addressed are of profound importance, both practically in the kind of academia we wish to create, and the opportunities it should afford to all, irrespective of class, gender, race or sexuality, and also intellectually, in what and how we study and teach.

The best two collections again illustrate the current pluralism of Shakespearean criticism. First, *The Matter of Difference: Materialist Feminist Criticism of Shakespeare* edited by Valerie Wayne provides several significant feminist essays, notably by Christina Malcolmson (' "What You Will": Social Mobility and Gender in *Twelfth Night*') and Valerie Traub ('Desire and the Differences it Makes') and contains an outsanding essay by Peter Stallybrass. More historicist agendas dominate the second significant volume on *The Appropriation of Shakespeare: Post-Renaissance Reconstructions of the Works and the Myth*. Edited by Jean Marsden these diverse essays consider the re-readings of text, biography and cultural icon, with three excellent essays on the Restoration (Dobson, Maguire and Marsden) and interesting contributions from De Grazia and Grady. The most enjoyable chapter came from D. Callaghan who discussed the director Buzz Goodbody, conveying some of the radicalism and enthusiasm of her work, and reminding us how much we lost at her death.

Several essays in *Shakespeare Quarterly* 42 develop the historicist agenda, notably Bruce Smith whose 'Reading Lists of Plays, Early Modern, Modernist and Postmodern' (*SQ* 42.127–44) uses a series of lists to illustrate the dangers of categories we impose upon a radically plural period, especially when its interests differ from ours. Smith uses this as the starting point for an argument that connects plays and ballads, both as commodities and as narrative structures, but along the way illuminates the various competing discourses which enmesh Renaissance theatre. In contrast Leah Marcus rehearses her own work on textual indeterminacy and local reading, and pleads for a 'levelling' Shakespeare criticism that seeks to turn the world upside down ('Levelling Shakespeare: Local Customs and Local Texts', *SQ* 42.168–78). Some of the historical errors that Marcus and other historicists are prone to are scrutinized in D. Cressy's timely and salutary 'Foucault, Stone, Shakespeare and Social History' (*ELR* 21.121–33). Perhaps the best general essay however comes from *Representations* where Katherine Maus articulates an important critique of recent subjectivist criticism, using the problems posed by interiority and 'ocular proof' in *Othello* as the starting point for an important study with wide ramifications ('Proof and Consequences: Inwardness and Its Exposure in the English Renaissance', *Rep* 29–52).

Individual essays on specific subjects include Yonglin Yang on 'How to Talk to the Supernatural in Shakespeare' (*LSoc* 20.247–61) which comments on the use of the familiar 'thou' towards spectres. Jonas Barish appears in *TD* 13 (101–21) with 'Shakespearean Violence: A Preliminary Survey' which emphasizes the 'gentle' Shakespeare in contrast to his more macabre contemporaries, and which tendentiously underplays the brutality in the plays. Several reprint volumes should be noticed, notably a paperback edition of *The Moral Universe of Shakespeare's Problem Plays* by Vivian Thomas (*YWES* 68) and a dismal revised casebook on *The Tempest* edited by D. J. Palmer. The addition of essays by Griffiths and Barker and Hulme does nothing to resurrect this volume which manages to omit most of the interesting *Tempest* criticism of the last thirty years.

(b) Comedies and Later Plays

Several general articles treat groups of comedies. Thomas Mosian explores the way in which marginal exchanges between masters and servants articulate strains in the class system, while their marginal position in the plays is used to suggest that Shakespeare sought to marginalize these issues (' "Knock me here soundly": Comic Misprison and Class Consciousness in Shakespeare', *SQ* 42.276–90). In *HLQ* 54, Grudin proposes that Rudolf II should be seen as a model for both Escalus and Prospero, but despite some attempt to provide contextual support this essay staggers one with its dated view of intellectual history and the interconnections of literary and historical scholarship. Overall the early comedies are less considered this year, with many such as *The Comedy of Errors* only considered in brief notes, in this case arguing for the retention of some controversial owls (at II.2.190) because they actually can be categorized with wicked spirits and so fit the sense of the passage (T. Humby, 'Illusions, Isaiah and "Owles" in The Comedy of Errors', *N&Q* 38.472–3). *The Shrew* receives more substantial commentary in Linda Boose's 'Scolding Brides and Bridling Scolds: Women's Unruly Member' (*SQ* 42.179–213) which argues that V.2 enacts the act of ritual submission required in pre-Reformation marriage services, restaging Petruchio's earlier anti-ceremony. Boose then pursues a detailed discussion of scolds' bridles in the context of the instability of gender relations in early modern England, providing a rich context for the play, mainly aimed at American readers less familiar with such implements of torture from local museums. More conventionally, R. Hillman argues for the influence of a tamed Du Bartas on the play ('La Creation du monde et *The Taming of the Shrew*', *RenR* 249–58). *A Midsummer Night's Dream* is discussed by Stanley Wells ('*A Midsummer Night's Dream* Revisited' *CS* 3.14–29) who critically examines his own Penguin edition (1967) and strengthens his sceptical view of claims that link the play to a specific occasion, such as the Carey wedding. Most usefully he considers the textual evidence for the extension of the role of Egeus and his ambivalent stance towards his daughter's marriage, and revises his view of the play to include the more sinister sexuality that recent productions have powerfully emphasized. David-Everett Blythe (*Expl* 49) argues that 'bottom' explicitly refers to rich land in the valley and provides some evidence to support his thesis.

On *The Merry Wives of Windsor*, notes discuss puns in Brainford references (D. Kehler, 'Shaksepeare's *The Merry Wives of Windsor*', *Expl* 49.76–7) and question the 1597 date (E. Schafer, 'The Date of *The Merry Wives of Windsor*', *N&Q* 38.57–60), but the most substantial criticism arrives in R. S. White's volume for the Harvester New Critical Introductions series which succinctly lays out the major issues for students under four headings ('The Town of Windsor', 'Women', 'Structures' and 'Language') with useful discussions of the texts, critical and stage history and an excursus on operatic adaptations. This structure allows White to eschew the pedestrianism characteristic of many of the volumes in this series, and he provides a sound and subtle introduction to the play, although it is not as racy as the blurb suggests when claiming the book is rooted in recent literary theories. My only real quarrel was White's description of *MWW* as a 'citizen comedy' and his use of *The Shoemaker's Holiday* as a comparison, when this metropolitan emphasis distorts what is essentially a suburban comedy closer to Porter than Dekker. Combined with extracts from Marcus's 'Levelling Shakespeare' (see 3(a)) above), this book would furnish most student needs.

Two essays on *The Merchant of Venice* propose contrasting approaches. Martin Banham ('*The Merchant of Venice* and the Implict Stage Directions', *CS* 3) shows how students might explore the staging possibilities of V.1, and neatly connect the tag game interplay of speeches to Kempe's ludic qualities. In utter contrast, Lawrence Normand presents a dense essay ('Reading the Body in *The Merchant of Venice*', *TexP* 5.55–73) which explores the tension of real bodies and verbal bodies inscribed in rhetoric as a trope for the problematic relation of language and reality. Normand sees a clear pattern in the play, whereby Acts I–IV are constantly disrupted by the physical body until its banishment in Act V, although even there in the final moments it returns to disrupt and problematize. More factually N. Shaheen ('Shylock's "Abram" in *The Merchant of Venice*', *N&Q* 38.56–7) shows that the use of 'Abram' at I.3.72 and I.3.160 is determined by metre rather than arcane biblical differentiation.

As You Like It still attracts most attention, especially the issue of the gender and impact of the boy actors, explored in paired pieces by Jan Kott ('The Gender of Rosalind', *NTQ* 7.113–25) and Lesley Soule ('Subverting Ros: Cocky Ros in the Forest of Arden', *NTQ* 7.126–36). Kott (along lines taken by other critics) argues that the impact of the boy was androgynous, but he distinguishes between the total illusionism required in other transvestite theatres like Kabuki and argues for a fractured illusion in *AYLI*. Kott perceptively argues that modern productions would recover some of the frisson if they used two women. In contrast, Soule argues that the power of the 'cocky Ros' (pun intended) or boy actor dominates the fiction and envisages a double awareness for the audience rooted (she claims) in popular traditions. Russell Fraser ('Shakespeare's Book of Genesis', *CompD* 25.121–8) argues that the play encompasses a serious mood and explores allusions to a version of Genesis.

Much Ado will no doubt benefit from the 1993 Branagh film, although it was already receiving plenty of attention in 1991, both from more traditional critics (G. Edwards, 'Anticipation and Retrospect in *Much Ado About Nothing*', *EIC* 41.277–90) and from more revisionist positions (M. D. Friedman, ' "Hush'd On Purpose to Grace Harmony": Wives and Silence in *Much Ado About Nothing*', *CompD* 25.350–63).

Freidman's more interesting piece argues that editorial decisions, especially over speech-assignation in V.3, have sought to buttress a generic assumption that *Much Ado* belongs with the 'comedies of forgiveness', while Friedman prefers to follow recent stage interpretations and the text and posit a bleaker vision. More pedantically Kieper argues against interpretations of Claudio's derangement as midsummer madness because the reference in I.1.272f to the sixth of July cannot be associated with the summer festival in either the Julian or Gregorian calendars (*N&Q* 38).

Twelfth Night receives a strange treatment from I. Leimberg (' "M.O.A.I." Trying to Share the Joke in *Twelfth Night*', *Connotations* 1.78–93 and 'Maria's Theology and Other Questions', *Connotations* 1.191–6) who argues that 'M.O.A.I' should be read as an anagram of 'I am Alpha and Omega' from *Revelation* and part of Malvolio's self-obssession, a suggestion that J. R. Brown treats with suitable scepticism ('More about Laughing at M.O.A.I.', *Connotations* 1.187–90). John Gouws argues that Malvolio's cross-garters should be seen as indicators of puritanism (*N&Q* 38.478–9), while more substantially, Stephen Dickey explores the 'isomorphic events' of bear-baiting and theatre in relation to Malvolio's treatment in *Twelfth Night* ('Shakespeare's Mastiff Comedy', *SQ* 42.255–75). The article charts the numerous ursine and canine references within the text and makes a good case for the ambivalent reponse to baiting in the period, which saw the sport as entertainment and thus perhaps similarly enjoyed *Twelfth Night*. This is an acute and thought-provoking essay.

The best note this year surfaces on *Measure for Measure* where Roger Holdsworth brilliantly uses Middletonian parallels to argue that 'brakes of ice' should read 'breaks of ice' and imply a sexual meaning ('*Measure for Measure*, Middleton and "Brakes of Ice" ', *N&Q* 38.64–7). Another strong essay which addresses itself to staging comes from the editor of the New Cambridge *Measure*, Brian Gibbons, who accentuates the combined influences of the ceremonial structures of Whetstone's *Promos and Cassandra* and *The Magnificent Entertainment* (1604), and the combination of topographical, topical and specific references with morality play elements (' "Bid them bring the trumpets to the gate": Staging Questions for *Measure for Measure*', *HLQ* 54.31–42). The strongest discussions come when Gibbons tackles the symbolism of clothing in the plays (via *Eastward Ho!*) and also in his insistence that the grandeur of the Duke's return in Act V (a restaging of *The Magnificent Entertainment*) must be emphasized so that Isabella's petition has the greater force. In *RenD*, M. L. Kaplan discusses Lucio as a slanderer of the state and relates his punishment to his exposure of the Duke's own determination to retain the right to criticize the state to himself ('Slander in *Measure for Measure*', *RenD* 21.23–54). In particular, some interesting points are made about Lucio and the Duke as parallel 'fantastics'.

Critical interest in the later plays is clearly marked in the increased number of studies and articles. A full-length study from Cynthia Marshall, *Last Things and Last Plays: Shakespearean Eschatology,* examines the relation between the end-centred last plays and apocalypticism through their fascination with death, and with closure. There are interesting passages on funerary rites in *Cymbeline* and on drama as an alternative site for 'communal eschatology'. Overall, however, the decision to prefer 'eschatology' for the more historical Renaissance term 'apocalypticism', a lack of clarity about the variety of responses that the apocalypse could generate (notably in 'apocalyptic comedy'), and an absence of any discussion of the political reverberations of apocalyptic discourse, rather weakened the study. Of the articles, perhaps the most stimulating was Linda Woodbridge's 'Palisading the Elizabethan Body Politic' (*TSLL* 33.327–54) which used anthropological theory to examine complex attitudes to the body/land analogy and the images of Rome and conquest in the poems and especially in *Cymbeline*. Although the piece is a little confused and some of the anthropology a little undigested, Woodbridge provides an interesting typology of images of Rome, and a fascinating reading of *Cymbeline*, which links the invasion of Imogen's body with the conquest of Britain. She connects a 'hermaphroditic' model of Rome/England as peaceful empire with pre-colonialism in *The Tempest*. With more development and clarity this approach holds much promise.

Three essays on *The Winter's Tale* take different approaches. S. Orgel takes two passages in the Folio text and examines the various emendations and interpretations that have sought to make sense of them, finally reversing the argument to suggest that they are probably deliberately opaque and that the Renaissance applied different (and less demanding) standards of clarity than current culture demands ('The Poetics of Incomprehensibility', *SQ* 42.431–7). Obscurity, impenetrability and the resistance to elucidation, Orgel argues, constituted part of meaning for the period. Michael Bristol pursues the bear in a fearsomely titled article ('In Search of the Bear: Spatiotemporal Form and the Heterogeneity of Economies in *The Winter's Tale*', *SQ* 42.145–67). Bristol relates the temporal distortions to the Renaissance attitudes to time, not only conflicted between lineal and cyclical, but also in the popular models of almanacs, which involved (he argues) a quasi-scientific attitude towards planned and predicted time and events. This he then links to the play's use of calendar feasts, such as Christmas with its complex mixture of excess and penitence, celebration and slaughter, and to the midsummer festivals. *En passant*, he notes the compression of these feasts in the calendar for 1610 and 1611 which reflects the structure of *The Winter's Tale*. Despite the rather toothy jargon ('spatiotemporal') and the generally ursine prose style, this essay repays attention and forms a cogent reading of the play, although I felt the ending rather anti-climactic; and Bristol rather underestimates the bleakness of the play's opening court scenes. Isn't the seasonal festivity of *The Winter's Tale* more deferred and interrupted? In S. M. Kurland's ' "We need no more of your advice": Political Realism in *The Winter's Tale*' (*SEL* 31.365–86) the play is treated as a political text on the failure of royal counsel in the context of the 1610 Great Contract; yet although the points raise interesting issues, the overall thesis seems a little strained.

In her study of *Cymbeline*, Cynthia Lewis emphasizes issues of misperception, arguing that the play creates different kinds of misperception based on incomplete pictures, both for the characters and the audience (' "With Singular Proof Enough": Modes of Misperception in *Cymbeline*', *SEL* 31.343–64). The whole play thus creates new modes of perception for the audience. Misperception of another kind rules when Eric Sams insists on sole Shakespearean authorship of *Pericles* (*N&Q* 38). *The Tempest* merits a whole *Shakespeare Survey* volume, with studies of magic, Restoration appropriations, and a most interesting essay on the style of the play. In 'Reading *The Tempest*' (*ShS* 43.15–28), Russ McDonald illustrates how materialist accounts have flattened the play through their failure to attend to form and particular verse. McDonald traces a 'politics of form', linking the ambiguous, incantatory and fugal qualities of the play (deftly brought out in various citations) and argues that this shifting complexity complicates any simply ideological reading. This essay has much to recommend it, not least its intelligent integration of formal and political issues. Amongst the brief notes, Di Matteo argues for the influence of Schuler's *Metamorphosis* or *Poetic Fables* on the depiction of Ariel as a harpy (' "The figure of this harpy": Shakespeare and the Moralized Ovid', *N&Q* 38.70–3).

(c) Poems

In 'Poems in Sidney and *A Lover's Complaint*' (*RES* 42.157–67), Joan Rees argues for the influence of the Dido/Pamphilus episode of the *New Arcadia* on Lucrece, while Karl Franson argues (unconvincingly) that the dedications to *Venus and Adonis* and *Lucrece* contain numerological references to the Earl of Southampton's age ('Numbers in Shakespeare's Dedications to *Venus and Adonis* and the *Rape of Lucrece*', *N&Q* 38.51–4). More traditionally, A. Kent Hieatt, Charles Hieatt and Anne Prescott use a phenomenally complex computer-aided ascription system to date the core of the Sonnets to 1590–5, with partial revision and additions in the earlier seventeenth century ('When Did Shakespeare Write *Sonnets 1609*?' *SP* 88.69–109). Bryan Crockett in 'Word Boundary and Syntactic Line Segmentation in Shakespeare's *Sonnets*' (*Style* 24.600–10) provides more detail on the quatrain structure and function than you are ever likely to want to know. Problems of ascription are raised by A. D. Inot in 'Shakespeare, the Stanley Epitaphs, and Sir William Dugdale' (*N&Q* 38.499–501). He argues that Dugdale's strong Lancashire connections make the accuracy of his attritubtion of these epitaphs more probable. David Holbrook, in 'Certainly Not by Shakespeare – But Is It a Literary Fake?' (*ContempR* 25–32), contests the authenticity of 'Shall I Die?' on stylistic grounds and argues (with no evidence) that it is a forgery.

(d) Histories

All the book-length studies of the history plays this year are concerned, in various ways, with their dramatizing of contradictions. As the products of intense debate about the nature of history and its ambiguous relationship to fiction, they are postmodernist before their time, argues Phyllis Rackin's *Stages of History: Shakespeare's English Chronicles*. Organizing her material by concept rather than play, Rackin analyses tensions between providential and Machiavellian patterns of causation, the conflicting pulls of anachronism (which stresses the likeness between past and present) and nostalgia (which stresses the distance between them), and the challenges posed by female characters to royal authority. Contradictions are detected, too, in the conditions of theatrical representation, for instance in its capacity to be at once propaganda and subversion, or in its juxtaposition of ideologies and styles. Falstaff, Rackin concludes, is the embodiment of the ability of theatre to undermine official history – and, in his death, the symbol of the risks inextricable from such licence. The range, learning and clarity of the book are impressive: its parallels between sixteenth- and twentieth-century historiography and culture are temperate and illuminating. Barbara Hodgdon, in *The End Crowns All: Closure and Contradiction in Shakespeare's History*, focuses on one aspect of the plays, their endings. Bringing a history play to a conclusion is a more than usually artificial procedure, and in Hodgdon's view Shakespeare uses the convention to legitimize new monarchs within the dramatic action, and outside it to contain potential challenges to royal authority. She thus presents a more conservative playwright than Rackin, while acknowledging his abstention from dogmatism and the fresh perspectives opened up in performances, of which she documents a large number. Actually, this is a source of fuzziness in the book, which hovers uneasily between literary and performance criticism without bringing them into fruitful relationship. The examination of 'strategies of closure' wears perilously thin by the end: Hodgdon writes an awkward prose and didn't convince me that the subject warranted such elaborate treatment.

Few recent periodical articles have taken the opportunity for a broad consideration of Shakespeare's thinking about history, perhaps because of an uneasy awareness that professional historians are witnessing radical revisionism in their own field. Deferential use of the work of Lawrence Stone by literary critics, formerly a safe bet, now has its perils, warns David Cressy in 'Foucault, Stone, Shakespeare, and Social History' (*ELR* 21.121–33); a less apocalyptic view of the seventeenth century now prevails, and Stone's account of the history of the family is heavily contested. Perhaps more conceptual certainty can be derived from the plays themselves. Sherman Hawkins's examination of 'Structural Pattern in Shakespeare's Histories' (*SP* 88:16–45) proposes that the two tetralogies are related like a diptych, the first negatively exploring opposing falsehoods, the second positively approving of competing truths, and in political terms surveying a range of options from despotic tyranny to benevolent imperialism. Shakespeare, Hawkins believes, amalgamated hints from miracle plays, Marlovian drama and the rhetorical trope of *comparatio*, as well as classical sources, specifically Lucan's *Pharsalia* for the first tetralogy and Xenophon's *Cyropaedia* for the second, fusing them into a pattern of loss and restoration informed by the Christian mythos of history. The essay is over-speculative but on this challenging subject boldness may be preferable to myopia.

Two writers trace the influence of civic ceremonial in the *Henry VI* trilogy. Randall Martin's intelligent 'Elizabethan Civic Pageantry in *Henry VI*' (*UTQ* 60.244–64) sees a dual purpose in such debts: to prompt the audience's awareness of certain symbolic stereotypes, but also to embody the unpredictable and contingent in history. He studies in detail the relationship between the actor/presenter and the audience and moments of triumphal pageantry in selected episodes, and speculates that the Cade rebellion draws on the pageant of an actual rising in 1591 by supporters of the messianic claims of William Hacket. He finds the use of the traditional Triumph of Death in *1 Henry VI* more powerful than that of the Triumph of Fortune in the other two parts. Ronald Knowles narrows the focus a little in 'The Farce of History: Miracle, Combat, and Rebellion in *2 Henry VI*' (*YES* 21.168–86), seeing in that play's burlesque moments anticipations of *Henry IV*– an unexceptionable but now familiar line. I must not move on without supporting R. J. C. Watt's welcome, elsewhere in this chapter, for Michael Hattaway's fine NCS *2 Henry VI*: his critical introduction affords real intellectual excitement in its discussion of the meaning of calling this a political play, and he has read the social historians.

Gillian M. Day's ' "Determined to prove a villain": Theatricality in *Richard III*' (*CS* 3.149–56) argues with moderation and clarity that Richard's is a 'determination' in the legal sense, born of a desire to hijack forms of legal argument to his own subversive purposes, and that his attempt fails in one sense (because a higher justice wins) while succeeding in another (because he offers ample proof of his villainy).

Some of the essays on the second tetralogy are outstanding this year, again in part because of a willingness to think in large terms. I shall work my way up to them. Christopher Highley documents some historical background in 'Wales, Ireland and *1 Henry IV*' (*RenD* 21.91–114), setting the play in the context of a critical turning-point in Elizabeth's Irish campaign, when the Earl of Tyrone was bidding for Welsh support by claiming descent from Owen Glendower, whose namesake in the play, Highley argues, is intended to invoke the figure of Tyrone. Highley's grasp of logic is fragile; he asks us, for instance, to accept a connection between Burgh's description of Tyrone as an Amazon, and Shakespeare's depiction of his female characters. Similar in spirit, but even less plausible, is Richard Hillman's ' "Not Amurath an Amurath Succeeds": Playing Doubles in Shakespeare's *Henriad*' (*ELR* 21.161–89), which, while denying a reference to any particular Turkish emperor, sees the depiction of such tyranny (also alluded to in *Othello*) as an opaque comment on the unacceptable face of the English monarchy, and includes, somewhat disconcertingly, a discussion of fifteenth-century conflicts between Turkey and Albania. Jonathan Crewe provides a fairly standard account of the change-and-reformation theme in 'Reforming Prince Hal: The Sovereign Inheritor in *2 Henry IV*' (*RenD* 21.225–42). One of his best points is that the changes from *1* to *2 Henry IV* and from that play to *Henry V* – Shakespeare's 're-formations' of his own material – correspond in formal terms to the thematic undermining of smoothly legitimate successions: if Shakespeare couldn't preserve continuity, what hope for Hal? However, eventually the piece, like Henry IV himself, goes wild into its grave with Oedipal extravagances about the Crown-as-Woman.

A little more respectable is Jonathan Hart on 'Temporality and Theatricality in Shakespeare's Lancastrian Tetralogy' (*SN* 63.69–88), which plays off theatrical against actual experience of time, scrutinizing the handling of plot-time, and characters' attitudes towards time, in the plays, and concluding that, both as readers and spectators, we experience time in a postlapsarian world. Paul Yachnin attempts to lay a restless critical ghost in 'History, Theatricality, and the "Structural Problem" in the *Henry IV* Plays' (*PQ* 70.163–79), dismissing the 'problem' (classically expounded by Harold Jenkins) as a chimera begotten of an anachronistic misapplication of an ideal of organic unity. The plays insist, in his view, not on structure but on sequence – a question-begging distinction, I feel – and embody irreconcilable outlooks (there is, as he says, no evidence that they were ever performed consecutively). They strike a balance between scepticism and cynicism in their search for a meaning in history, which emerges as neither linear nor cyclical. Yachnin may well be felt to redefine the problem rather than to banish it. That the histories are self-consciously about the processes of historical interpretation – including literary history in their relationship to Shakespeare's earlier exercises in the genre – is a point also made by David M. Bergeron ('Shakespeare Makes History: *2 Henry IV*', *SEL* 31.231–45). Like Phyllis Rackin, Bergeron sees Falstaff as a culmination of Shakespeare's twin interests in narrative history and narrative fiction. 'Recorded history', he neatly concludes, 'must always be subject to correction by the history that lives in our lives.' Complementary to this piece is Barbara Everett's British Academy lecture 'The Fatness of Falstaff: Shakespeare and Character' (*PBA* 76.109–28), an abbreviated version of which was reviewed in *YWES* 71. There are some brilliant passages which were omitted in that earlier printing, notably on the need for Hal to be presented not as a distant royal icon but as one real man among many – 'conventions are shaken free into a glitter of relativities' – and on Part 2's relentless weighing down of Falstaff, who deteriorates from a man with balletic intellectual grace to a seamy cadger. Everett's central contention remains gloriously unfashionable and desperately important: that we need the concept of character, not for 'biographical' fantasizing but as a necessary way of grasping the realities the plays explore. Amen to that, say I.

The aptness of the subtitle of *Henry VIII* is demonstrated by two articles with opposed conclusions. Camille Wells Slights' 'The Politics of Conscience in *All is True* (or *Henry VIII*)' (*ShS* 43.59–68) offers a protestant reading, in which Henry's dilemma of conscience is central. She has to indulge in some extremely special pleading, as in her reply to the criticism that we don't see Henry resolving his doubts: this, she explains, shows the 'essentially private nature' of such struggles! However, according to Peter L. Rudnytsky a few pages earlier in the same journal ('*Henry VIII* and the Deconstruction of History', *ShS* 43.43–57), Shakespeare leaned towards a Catholic interpretation of the issues, attributing Henry's motivation to lust. Rudnytsky's certainty about this does not follow from the earlier, stronger part of his essay, which reads *Henry VIII* as a final history-play rather than a romance and detects in it a sceptical relativism about the possibility of attaining 'truth'.

(e) Tragedies

The tragedies were the subject of a special number (2) of *CS* this year which contained essays valuably combining scholarship with accessibility (the journal is aimed at a sixth-form/undergraduate readership). Most relate to individual plays and will be discussed in their place. Of those that range more widely, Jonathan Bate's 'Shakespeare's Tragedies as Working Scripts' (118–27) distils revisionist arguments about the texts of *Hamlet*, *Othello*, *Lear* and *Macbeth* with exemplary lucidity. He presents the existence of textual pluralism as a cause for celebration, a catalyst of more vital debate about the plays than was previously undertaken. Complementary to this, Paul Dean, in 'Shakespeare's True Tragedies' (128–33), argues that the tragedies elude attempts to generalize about them, and are less the embodiments of absolute moral truths than the vehicles of a heuristic exploration of the concept of truth itself. Colin Wilcockson considers *Hamlet* and *Lear* among other plays in 'Father-Directors, Daughter-Performers in Shakespeare' (134–41), showing that Shakespeare altered his sources to emphasize his support for daughters against their fathers' bullying about their potential husbands; the desires of the heart are exalted above the imperatives of the marriage market. Despite its title, Tim Gooderham's 'Shakespeare and "Tragedy" in *The Waste Land*' (178–85) finds Eliot principally indebted to *The Tempest*.

Despite the optimism of Professor Bate, the craving for explanatory books which will iron out the difficulties of the tragedies continues to be catered for. *A Preface to Shakespeare's Tragedies* by Michael Mangan is in fact a preface only to *Hamlet*, *Othello*, *King Lear* and *Macbeth* – and to other things whose immediate relevance is hard to see, such as the English language in Shakespeare's day, the processes of printing his plays (arguably important for all the chosen plays, but Mangan sticks to the Arden for citations, a decision which Bate's essay shows to be irresponsible), and the seating and pricing arrangements in his theatres. Intermingled with this is useful material on the medieval antecedents of tragedy, Elizabethan critical theory of the genre, and the interplay between the texts and their theatrical auspices – none of it particularly new, and rehearsed with excessive leisureliness. The chapters on the four plays themselves create the same somewhat exasperating impression; much is said which is sensible, accurate and moderately interesting, but the discussions are not going anywhere. Coverage of issues is comprehensive to the point of blandness. As so often with introductory books, one is left wondering about the level of readership being targeted, and about the ultimate point of the whole exercise.

Thomas McAlindon's *Shakespeare's Tragic Cosmos*, by contrast, has a point of view: that the universe of Shakespeare's tragedies is predicated upon contrariety and stands in a tradition deriving from Chaucer's *Knight's Tale*. McAlindon takes issue with poststructuralists who deny the possibility of ultimate order in a relativistic tragic world: for him the conflicts which the plays explore are ontological (a matter of feelings) rather than phenomenological (a matter of ideas), and they envisage time as a dark process which may nonetheless bring renewal, rather than as a black hole into which meaning entropically collapses. McAlindon – courageously in the present climate – commits himself to the belief that 'Shakespeare's tragic art is radically informed by essentialist notions of a transhistorical human nature and of unchanging laws encoded in universal nature.' While this will put his book out of court for many readers, his discussions of individual plays cannot be easily dismissed. His fondness for dualistic oppositions verges at times on the schematic but is vindicated by the subtle chapter on *Antony and Cleopatra*, which he finds coloured by Ovidian metamorphosis (independently cited as an influence by Paul Dean in '*Antony and Cleopatra*: An Ovidian Tragedy?', *CahiersE* 40.73–7) and by Plutarch's attempt to mediate between Greek and Egyptian philosophy in his essay 'Of Isis and Osiris'. Contemplating such contentious figures as Antony, Othello and Macbeth, McAlindon feels able to affirm the co-existence in Shakespeare's tragic world of baseness and nobility. The complexities he is drawn to are demonstrably contained in the plays themselves, rather than in his own intellectualizing about them. I admire the independence of this book hugely.

An essay of relevance to a number of the tragedies comes from Carol Thomas Neely. ' "Documents in Madness": Reading Madness and Gender in Shakespeare's Tragedies and Early Modern Culture' (*SQ* 42.315–38) examines the treatment of insanity in Renaissance thought which sees the theatrical depiction of madness as accelerating the recognition that it was no divine visitation but a 'secular, medical, and gendered condition'. The third adjective seems odd, but it is useful to have documentation, for instance from medical records and Bedlam censuses, for the other two.

Cedric Watts's HNCIS volume on *Romeo and Juliet* deliberately underplays the romantic–lyrical elements in its subject, examining instead such things as the substructure of ironies and 'mutually-enhancing contrasts' and the sexual–political implications of the treatment of love. As always, Watts turns in a crisp and energetic performance, but his touch falters occasionally (as in the quotation of a silly passage from David Lodge's *Nice Work* which does nothing to illuminate Shakespeare), and he does not manage to keep a sense of proportion between specific discussion of *Romeo* and references to other plays in the canon (there are some good but, in context, redundant remarks on *Troilus and Cressida*). Like McAlindon, he sees Shakespeare's tragic world as built around contraries, but his evocation of these has less clarity than McAlindon's. Elsewhere on *Romeo* there are two inferior articles, a conventional source-study by Joan Ozark Holmer, ' "Myself Condemned and Myself Excus'd": Tragic Effects in *Romeo and Juliet*' (*SP* 88.345–62) on the heightening of the Tybalt/Mercutio episodes, and a strained sociological piece by Nathaniel Wallace, 'Cultural Tropology in *Romeo and Juliet*' (*SP* 88.329–44), who is reduced to citing the jokes about coal-mining in I.i as reflections of the rapid growth of the Elizabethan coal industry! The concept of the lovers as star-crossed is no longer acceptable, it seems: instead they are victims of conflicting 'cultural representations', which I'm quite prepared to believe are more lethal. Michael J. Collins muses in unbuttoned fashion on 'Teaching *Romeo and Juliet*: "The change of fourteen years" ' (*CS* 3.186–93), an essay more autobiography than criticism which, no doubt, will be interesting to all who know the author.

HSt has again been beyond my reach, and I was especially sorry not to see Harold Jenkins's ' "To be, or not to be": Hamlet's Dilemma' (8–24). Elsewhere there is R. W. Hamilton's 'The Instability of *Hamlet*' (*CS* 3.170–77). Hamilton acknowledges that there are some irresoluble plot-cruces in *Hamlet*, but briskly disposes of two which he considers red herrings: Gertrude's remarriage to Claudius is sinful, the Ghost is from purgatory, hence Catholic. He pleads for a more straightforward *Hamlet* than we are usually allowed, a revenge tragedy in which Hamlet succeeds in saving his country at the cost of his own life in the few minutes during which he is actually its king. Hamilton is not as simplistic as this might suggest, however, observing for instance that what begins as a son's obligation to revenge his father turns into the ruler's obligation to punish the killer of the previous (legitimate) ruler. Robert N.

Watson's 'Giving up the Ghost in a World of Decay: *Hamlet*, Revenge, and Denial' (*RenD* 21.199–223) is an unusually personal essay. Unable himself to believe in an afterlife, Watson suggests that Shakespeare endorses a similar dogmatism about the question, providing Hamlet with something to live by rather than anything to live for, as his revenge mission takes on a life and momentum of its own. Most of us, while respecting Watson's honesty, will prefer to see *Hamlet* as a fruitful and troubled exploration of the issues he regards as cut and dried.

Nicholas Potter's '*Othello* and "The Reading Public" ' (*CS* 3.142–8) quotes F. R. Leavis in its title: Othello's Venice, in Potter's view, like England in Leavis's, lacks an intelligent consensus about central moral issues; this is why the Venetians, like Bradley and his followers, could endorse an excessively admiring view of Othello. Potter is broadly in sympathy with Leavis's strictures on the play, but urges that Othello's motivation for killing Desdemona is clearer than (although as little explored as) Leavis thinks, and that Othello does achieve a glimpse, before his death, of his own moral shortcomings. This essay belongs to a world of academic discussion which now seems astonishingly remote, but is it necessarily outmoded? I can't feel that it is, when the alternatives are represented by volumes such as that edited by Virginia Mason Vaughan and Kent Cartwright, *Othello: New Perspectives*, a collection originating from the Shakespeare Association of America convention in 1988. Such gatherings need to defer to all the latest 'isms', as we can see from the heterogeneity of the twelve essays. They embrace among other things textual study (Thomas L. Berger on Q2's possible preservation of moments from the play in performance), discourse analysis (Joseph A. Porter on Iago's 'speech acts' – a wretched piece of jargon imported from linguistic philosophy, where it is not clear either), feminism (Evelyn Gajowski claiming that 'women in Othello are […] what men make them') and pedagogy. The last-named, represented by Martha Tuck Rozett's account of her students' responses to a first reading of the play, is, however, unusually instructive in showing how much has to be learned by new readers; many of the students were shocked at the idea that human beings might have so little control over their feelings, and some admired Iago's go-getting spirit. (Of course, to suggest that such responses distort the play – might actually be wrong – is to risk charges of elitism and dogmatism.) Probably the most worthwhile contribution is James Hirsch's on '*Othello* and Perception' (Othello's of Desdemona, ours of him), which catches the multifacetedness of the play without turning it into anything-goes relativism. Mediocre though the volume is, it looks gripping by comparison with other items such as Fumio Yoshioka's 'Wrecked in Unknown Fate – Othello's Loss and Recovery of Self' (*SELit* 66.3–22), which posits a 'noble but simple' Moor who finally achieves 'insight into the meaning of life', or Adrian Poole's barren documentation of the play's influence on Henry James's fiction and autobiography ('Henry James, War and Witchcraft', *EIC* 41.291–307). More substantial – and supporting arguments recently advanced by François Laroque (*YWES* 68.248–9, 69.244) – is Michael D. Bristol's 'Charivari and the Comedy of Abjection in *Othello*' (*RenD* 21.3–21). Bristol detects beneath Othello and Desdemona the carnival figures of the clown and his transvestite wife (both mirthlessly demythologized by Iago), and urges recognition of a strain of comic violence in the play. In itself this is unexceptionable, but the game is given away by Bristol's statement that to accept his interpretation we must divest ourselves of the belief that the characters are 'individual subjects endowed with personalities and with some mode of autonomous interiorized life' – in other words, that we must disregard what makes *Othello Othello* and not a charivari.

The domestic context of another tragedy forms the starting-point for '*Macbeth* and the Barren Sceptre' by Sarah Wintle and Rene Weis (*EIC* 41.128–46). They see the play as 'a kind of dialectic between Macbeth manned and unmanned' – an antithesis both counterbalanced and exemplified by the Macbeths' marriage – and set it in the context of references to children and dynastic succession on the one hand, and to barrenness on the other. Macbeth at the end is 'the childless infanticide now facing the father of his victims'. If the article sometimes seems to play with paradoxes, it can point to warrant for this in *Macbeth* itself. After a number of years in which it was fashionable to see the play as vertiginously ambiguous, commentators are again cautiously advocating (surely rightly) its ultimate endorsement of a moral framework to human experience; it isn't true that Macbeth can't distinguish right from wrong, he acknowledges the order he violates, and moral awareness is possessed by most of the other characters. David-Everett Blythe's 'Banquo's Candles' (*ELH* 58.773–8) fusses over 'There's husbandry in Heaven:/Their candles are all out', taking 'out' to mean 'shining' rather than 'extinguished' and therefore stressing Banquo's function as Macbeth's opposite in the moral design of the play. Barbara Riebling, in 'Virtue's Sacrifice: A Machiavellian Reading of *Macbeth*' (*SEL* 31.273–86), explores that design on a wider scale, seeing Malcolm's political sophistication as a norm against which both Duncan's naivety and Macbeth's wickedness are measured and found wanting. She finds the conversation between Malcolm and Macduff in IV.iii particularly reflective of Machiavellianism. Macbeth's inability to dissimulate is a weakness by that criterion, as is his inadequate acceptance of the consequences of his own ambitions. Machiavelli would have predicted his downfall, without ascribing it to Providence. Like all 'readings', this article sees what it wants to see: unlike many, it persuades us that it is seeing something that may really be in the text.

Kenneth J. E. Graham's ' "Without the form of justice": Plainness and the Performance of Love in *King Lear*' (*SQ* 42.438–61) enquires somewhat lumberingly whether the play vindicates the common Renaissance association between stylistic plainness and moral integrity, and decides that on the whole it does, most obviously in Kent, but also in the simplicity of Lear's final utterances. Bruce Thomas Boehrer, in '*King Lear* and the Royal Progress: Social Display in Shakespearean Tragedy' (*RenD* 21.243–61), locates the tragic heart of the play in Lear's separation of the Progress as a social custom from the courtiers' willingness to be made to entertain him. Boehrer believes this had topical relevance; he documents various Progresses of Elizabeth and James as marking a shift towards greater privacy and exclusiveness, and hence a laceration in the bond between sovereign and subject. James, like Lear, plumped for 'the Club Med principle of royal retirement', albeit with more success.

The classical tragedies are scantly represented. The best essay comes from Maurice Hunt: ' "Violent'st" Complementarity: The Double Warriors of *Coriolanus*' (*SEL* 31.309–325). This presents Coriolanus and Aufidius as virtual alter egos, like Othello and Iago, 'alternate versions of a single self', and examines the process whereby Aufidius becomes the kind of person Coriolanus had been at the outset, before doing to the current Coriolanus what the previous Coriolanus would have done – killing him. A less subtle study comes from Christina Luckyj in 'Volumnia's Silences' (*SEL* 31.327–42), who argues that Shakespeare diminishes Volumnia's culpability for her son's death by presenting her as the advocate of the preservation of natural bonds as a greater good than the preservation of self-esteem (this seems dubious) and by showing Aufidius as the immediate agent of Coriolanus' destruction (but Aufidius finds Volumnia a useful scapegoat with which to goad his rival into his final frenzy). Soliloquy, notoriously rare in this tragedy, is replaced by structural repetition, Luckyj suggests, as a way of suggesting Volumnia's changing motives (e.g.

the two supplication scenes in Acts III and IV). While temperately argued, the piece relies on arguments from silence in more than one sense.

Shakespeare's concern with bonds in another play is the subject of Michael Chorost's 'Biological Finance in Shakespeare's *Timon of Athens*' (*ELR* 21.349–70), which dissects Timon's efforts to buy love and the resulting debate over the quasi-biological properties of money, which metaphorically 'breeds' through usury. This trope is documented with reference to contemporary tracts against usury, and traced to its source in Aristotle's *Politics*. Timon thus inverts both human and economic bonds. Michael E. Mooney makes heavy weather of an obvious point in ' "Passion, I see, is catching": The Rhetoric of *Julius Caesar*' (*JEGP* 90.31–50), stressing the conflict between the rhetoric in the play and that of the play.

The Casebook on *Antony and Cleopatra*, edited by John Russell Brown, has been reissued with five new mediocre items, including Michael Long on the Dionysiac element and Kay Stockholder fantasizing psychosexual dramas out of the last two acts. Perhaps an extract from McAlindon's book can be added in the next reprinting. There should be no place for an excerpt from H. W. Fawkner's *Shakespeare's Hyperontology: 'Antony and Cleopatra'*, the sequel to his book on *Macbeth* (*YWES* 71) and just as unreadable. The images and processes of 'leaving' and 'following' (for example, the connections of those words with renunciation, loyalty and death) become the launch-pad for metaphysical speculations so versatile that they can turn every concept into its opposite and make the play affirm simultaneously absolutely everything and absolutely nothing. Towards the end the author declares that 'hyperontologically speaking, then, leaving is no longer leaving. On the contrary, it is staying.' At this point I made my excuses and left – or was it stayed?

Books Reviewed

Aers, L., and N. Wheale, eds. *Shakespeare in the Changing Curriculum*. Routledge. pp. 232. £30.00. ISBN 0 415 05392 7.

Astington, John H., ed. *The Development of Shakespeare's Theater*. AMS. $34.50. ISBN 0 404 62294 1.

Bawcutt, N.W., ed. *Measure for Measure,* by William Shakespeare. OS. OUP. pp. 255. hb £32.50, pb £4.50. ISBN 0 19 812908 4, 0 19 281446 X.

Bertram, Paul, and Bernice W. Kliman, eds. *The Three-Text Hamlet: Parallel Texts of the First and Second Quartos and First Folio.* AMS Studies in the Renaissance 30. AMS. pp. 272. $64.00. ISBN 0 404 62330 1.

Biggs, Murray, ed. *The Arts of Performance in Elizabethan and Early Stuart Drama.* EdinUP. pp. 248. £39.50. ISBN 0 748 60266 6.

Bradley, David. *From Text to Performance in the Elizabethan Theatre: Preparing the Play for the Stage.* CUP. pp. 250. £37.50. ISBN 0 521 39466 X.

Buchman, Lorne M. *Still in Movement: Shakespeare on Screen.* OUP. pp. 171. £22.50. ISBN 0 195 06541 7.

Cartelli, Thomas. *Marlowe, Shakespeare and the Economy of Theatrical Experience.* UPennP. pp. 256. £27.50. ISBN 0 812 23102 3.

Cartwright, Kent. *Shakespearean Tragedy and Its Double: The Rythms of Audience Response.* PSUP. pp. 240. $27.50. ISBN 0 271 00738 9.

Cox, Murray. *Shakespeare Comes to Broadmoor: The Actors Are Come Hither – The Performance of Tragedy in a Secure Psychiatric Hospital.* Kingsley. pp. 240. hb £25, pb £12.95. ISBN 0 853 02135 0, 1 853 02121 0.

Fleissner, Robert F. *Shakespeare and the Matter of the Crux: Textual, Topical, Onomastic, Authorial, and Other Puzzlements.* Mellen. pp. 294. £39.95. ISBN 0 7734 9622 X.

Franklin, Colin. *Shakespeare Domesticated: The Eighteenth-Century Editions.* Scolar. pp. 246. £35.00. ISBN 0 85967 834 2.

Gibbons, Brian, ed. *Measure for Measure,* by William Shakespeare. NCaS. CUP. pp. 213. hb £22.50, pb £4.25. ISBN 0 521 22227 3, 0 521 29401 0.

Grazia, Margreta de. *Shakespeare Verbatim: The Reproduction of Authenticity and the 1790 Apparatus.* Clarendon. pp. 244. £30.00. ISBN 0 19 811778 7.

Hattaway, Michael, ed. *The Second Part of King Henry VI*, by William Shakespeare. NCaS. CUP. pp. 248. hb £22.50, pb £4.75. ISBN 0 521 37330 1, 0 521 37704 8.

Hodgson, Barbara. *The End Crowns All: Closure and Contradiction in Shakespeare's History.* PrincetonUP. pp. 323. $37.50. ISBN 0 691 06833 X.

Holding, Peter. *Romeo and Juliet.* T&P. Macmillan. pp. 80. pb £7.99. ISBN 0333 51912 4.

Honneyman, D. *Closer to Shakespeare.* Merlin (1990). pp. 214. pb £9.95. ISBN 0 86303 482 9.

Ioppolo, Grace. *Revising Shakespeare.* HarvardUP. pp. 247. £23.95. ISBN 0 674 76696 2.

Kamps, I., ed. *Shakespeare Left and Right.* Routledge. pp. 335. pb £12.99. ISBN 0 415 90376 9.

Kastan, D. S., and P. Stallybrass, eds. *Staging the Renaissance: Reinterpretations of Elizabethan and Jacobean Drama.* Routledge. pp. 293. pb £10.99. ISBN 0 415 90166 9.

Leggatt, Alexander, ed. *King Lear.* SiP. HW. pp. 144. hb £37.50, pb £10.95. ISBN 0 710 81111 X, 0 710 80919 0.

Lusardi, James P., and June Schlueter. *Reading Shakespeare in Performance: 'King Lear'.* FDUP. £32. ISBN 0 838 63394 3.

McAlindon, Thomas. *Shakespeare's Tragic Cosmos.* CUP. pp. 280. £35. ISBN 0 521 39041 9.

Mangan, Michael. *A Preface to Shakespeare's Tragedies.* Longman. pp. 244. hb £25, pb £9.99. ISBN 0 582 35501 X, 0 582 35503 6.

Marsden, J. I., ed. *The Appropriation of Shakespeare: Post-Renaissance Reconstructions of the Works and the Myth.* HW. pp. 222. pb £12.99. ISBN 0 7450 0926 3.

Marshall, C. *Last Things and Last Plays: Shakespearean Eschatology.* SIUP. pp. 143. $24.50. ISBN 0 8093 1689 7.

Mason, Pamela. *Much Ado About Nothing.* T&P. Macmillan. pp. 80. pb £7.99. ISBN 0 333 40594 3.

Matus, I. L. *Shakespeare: The Living Record.* Macmillan. pp. 174. £35.00. ISBN 0 333 519817.

Newey, V., and A. Thompson, eds. *Literature and Nationalism.* LiverUP. pp. 296. £27.50. ISBN 0 953 23057 9.

Palmer, D. J., ed. *Shakespeare: The Tempest.* Macmillan. pp. 215. pb £8.99. ISBN 0 333 533623.

Rackin, Phyllis. *Stages of History: Shakespeare's English Chronicles.* Routledge. pp. 264. hb £35, pb £10.99. ISBN 0 415 05838 4, 0 415 05839 2.

Schoenbaum, Sam. *Shakespeare's Lives.* OUP. pp. 612. £25.00. ISBN 0 19 818618 5.

Small, Ian, and Marcus Walsh, eds. *The Theory and Practice of Text-Editing: Essays in Honour of James T. Boulton.* CUP. pp. 221. £30.00. ISBN 0 521 40146 1.

Thomas, V. *The Moral Universe of Shakespeare's Problem Plays*. Routledge. pp. 236. pb £9.99. ISBN 0 415 04226 7.

Thomson, Peter. *Shakespeare's Theatre*. Revised edn. Routledge. pp. 216. hb £35, pb £10.99. ISBN 0 415 07311 1, 0 415 05148 7.

Vaughan, Virginia Mason, and Kent Cartwright, eds. *Othello: New Perspectives*. FDUP. £29.95. ISBN 0 838 63398 6.

Watts, Cedric. *Romeo and Juliet*. HNCIS. HW. pp. 160. hb £40, pb £10.95. ISBN 0 745 00700 7, 0 745 00701 5.

Wayne, Valerie, ed. *The Matter of Difference: Materialist Feminist Criticism of Shakespeare*. HW. pp. 288. hb £45, pb £12.95. ISBN 0 745 00777 5, 0 745 00827 5.

White, R. S. *The Merry Wives of Windsor*. HW. pp. 93. pb £8.99. ISBN 0 7450 0692 2.

Willis, Susan. *The BBC Shakespeare Plays: Making the Televised Canon*. UNCP. pp. 326. $29.95. ISBN 0 807 81963 8.

VIII

Renaissance Drama: Excluding Shakespeare

MICHAEL JARDINE, CAROL RUTTER and SANDRA CLARK

This chapter has three sections: 1. Editions and Textual Scholarship; 2. Theatre History; 3. Criticism. Sections 1 and 3(c) are by Michael Jardine, 2 and 3(b) are by Carol Rutter, 3(a) and 3(d) are by Sandra Clark.

1. Editions and Textual Scholarship

Most of the editorial activity this year appears in the attractively presented Revels series: John Marston's *Antonio and Mellida*, edited by W. Reavley Gair in a separate edition; John Lyly's *Campaspe* and *Sappho and Phao* in a combined edition, edited by George K. Hunter and David Bevington respectively, and the anonymous *Sir John Oldcastle* and *The Famous Victories of Henry V* forming part of a group of texts brought together by Peter Corbin and Douglas Sedge in the RevelsCL series under the title *The Oldcastle Controversy*. Faced with this welcome addition to our library of plays it is worth making some general points about this prestigious series. First, its editorial scholarship remains at a uniformly high standard; second, its focus on performance usefully balances common editorial neglect; third, its general layout and textual apparatus are particularly user-friendly; and fourth, its introductions are trapped in a time warp produced by the conservative bibliographical consensus that editors should pretend they know nothing about developments in English studies during the past twenty years. As a result, editorial commentary is dominated by a tired combination of old historicism and old New Criticism. Thus, Reavely Gair neglects the politics and sexuality of Marston's play and claims too easy access to the author's intentions (how does he know, for example, that 'more often than not these words are used quite seriously'?), while providing a useful sense of the historical moment of children's theatre and Marston's crucial role in its development. His editorial approach is similarly conservative, but with less harmful effects, as he eschews the cavalier emendatory freedom of his precursors and seeks the authority, not of primary authorial intent, but of a hypothetical original performance, an elusive text indeed. Of particular interest is his early (1599) dating of the first performance of the play and the identification of this experimental play as both a possible trigger for the Poets' War and for the success of the relaunch of children's theatre as a parodying threat to the rival adult companies.

Lyly, like Marston, has suffered relative neglect, and it is to be hoped that the new editions of *Campaspe* and *Sappho and Phao*, the first surviving plays in roman type, will help propel him back into critical favour. As the copy text for both plays is particularly dependable, the textual labour is relatively light, producing little more than 'a few new readings', but these will doubtless be the standard editions for a long time to come. G. K. Hunter's edition of *Campaspe* is characteristically thorough. He is most interesting in provision of context, particularly Lyly's sensitivity to the political currents in the court and his skill in negotiating the narrow divide between independence and servility. As with Marston, there is no consensus as to what sort of drama Lyly wrote. Hunter concludes that this is a 'play of commentary', static representation rather than narrative, written in a 'deliberately restricted verbal style'. David Bevington's edition of *Sappho and Phao* is a particularly welcome appearance, being the first critical edition of this play since 1902. He disagrees with W. W. Greg in identifying the 1584 quarto as the first edition and in finding no authority in the earlier copy text, now relegated to Q2 status. Also controversial is his identification of Lyly as author of the songs which appear for the first time in the 1632 edition. As in Hunter's edition of *Campaspe*, a good deal of attention is paid by Bevington both to Lyly's sources and to the tradition in which he was working, as the editor tries to identify the play's elusive generic markings. Like Hunter also, he is concerned to place the author as the product of court pressure, identifying Sappho as a compliment to Elizabeth I, although in dating the play at 1584 rather than the usual 1582 he rejects the linking of the plot of the play with the story of the Duke of Alençon's courtship of the Queen. He argues for a link between Lyly's comedy and the later city comedy and for his initiating a romance tradition based on a love plot in the face of demands for native farce. Both Bevington and Hunter strive to make Lyly palatable to an audience for whom euphuism is dead. In a shared volume comparisons are bound to be made and my preference is for Bevington's edition, where critical analysis is sharper and more receptive to recent developments. He has a harder job than Hunter to sell his play's artistic excellence but does enough to persuade that its 'day is yet to come'.

The Oldcastle Controversy is a hybrid collection of related texts, not all of them dramatic, which are linked by their interest in the controversial figure of Sir John Oldcastle. It will clearly be of particular interest to Shakespeareans because of the Falstaff connection, but Corbin and Sedge succeed in rendering the texts interesting in their own right, as part of 'an issue of literary history which continues to stimulate critical debate'. The editorial work is lighter than is usual in Revels editions, as the main value is in juxtaposition and convenient gathering of related matter. *The Famous Victories*, despite being stigmatized as a 'bad' quarto, is defended persuasively as a lively play, and its reputation will doubtless be enhanced by its inclusion here. *Sir John Oldcastle*, by Drayton, Hathaway, Munday and Wilson, has appeared in nineteen previous editions because of its status as part of the Shakespeare apocrypha, but this is the first to look for alternative points of interest. The collection as a whole is a valuable contribution to literary history and an imaginative and innovative assemblage of disparate materials. The final play to be published this year is the Malone Society reprint of *Tom a Lincoln*, prepared by G. R. Proudfoot. This play, based on a prose romance by Richard Johnson, is hitherto unpublished and untitled. The manuscript copy has only been available for ten years. Proudfoot argues that the play was written between 1607 and 1616 for presentation at Gray's Inn, claiming identification of contemporary figures. This scrupulous edition makes certain valuable observations: that the shift of audience from female romance reader to Gray's Inn gentleman explains a shift in tone to one of parody (although, as with Marston's play discussed above, this is hard to detect); that attribution of the play to Thomas Heywood is plausible but not persuasive; and that there is a good case to be made for professional involvement in a work which has the hallmarks of 'amateur' entertainment for students.

Marie Axton has produced a lively and thought-provoking piece of textual scholarship in an essay called '*Ane Satyre of the Thrie Estaitis*: The First Edition and its Reception' in *A Day Estivall: Essays on the Music, Poetry, and History of Scotland and England and Poems Previously Unpublished*, edited by Alisoun Gardner-Medwin and J. Hadley Williams. Focusing on an annotated copy of the 1604 quarto of Sir David Lyndsay's play, Axton draws suggestive conclusions about the relationship between the physical state of the book and the particular social and political context in London after King James's accession. She concludes that the publication of this radically Protestant play at this time was sponsored by James, who wished to reassure his new subjects that he eschewed his mother's Catholicism. The roman typeface and ornaments and the use of Scottish paper, each discussed in some detail, argue for a courtly connection and royal sponsorship, and the contemporary annotations offer a fascinating insight into the effort made by a learned English reader to come to terms with the striking differences between the English and Scottish cultures at this time of transition.

Several articles this year concern themselves with Ben Jonson's preparation of his work for publication. In 'Jonson's Revision of the Stage Directions for the 1616 Folio *Workes*', (*MRDE* 5.256–86), Peter M. Wright seeks to establish the 'remarkable' nature of this publication, with its 'meticulous concern for design' and the way in which the detail of graphic presentation relates to key critical issues. Wright's principal observation concerns the tension between the popular and public nature of the plays as performed and the private elitism of purchasers of the 1616 Folio. It is here that analysis of the stage directions as amended by Jonson between Quarto and Folio editions is particularly revealing. In the Folio text it is clearly assumed that the intelligent reader can supply the directions, and many are left out or relegated to the margins. Wright concludes that Jonson's aim of combining classical reading with theatrical experience fails because of an irresistible incompatibility, and that this traps Jonson into inconsistency. After exhaustive analysis of the stage-direction changes in the Folio, Wright is able to show that they represent a crucial element in Jonson's efforts to recast the low status plays as high status poems, but that the pull of the material towards performance, their dramatic traces, led him into inconsistency, revealing himself as a schizophrenic poet-playwright.

Jonson's role in raising the status of drama is also noted in John Jowett's 'Jonson's Authorization of Type in *Sejanus* and Other Early Quartos', (*SB* 44.254–65). Jowett argues that we need to take more account of the physical layout of *Sejanus*, making the same point as Peter Wright about the erasure of signs of a performance dimension, with the result that 'In the Folio ... the most distinctive features of the Quarto are weakened, abandoned, or dispersed.' He demonstrates conclusively that meaning resides in the physical appearance of a book, making Jonson a particularly significant author for bibliographers as he was the first dramatist to become aware of the potential of print for conveying meanings not available in the theatre. Jowett, like Wright also, prefers the quartos for their closeness to the staged play and rejects W. W. Greg's thesis of the superiority of an eclectic version. It is difficult to separate the literary critical from the textual interests in the collection of essays edited by Jennifer Brady and W. H. Herendeen, *Ben Jonson's 1616 Folio*, which has a central interest in the materiality of this text. However, Kevin J. Donovan's 'Jonson's Texts in the First

Folio' belongs here as a contribution to bibliographical scholarship. Donovan argues that an over-reliance on the 'outdated' Oxford edition of Percy and Evelyn Simpson and C. H. Herford has led to a general neglect of the Folio and an unquestioning preference for Folio over quarto editions. He pleads for greater flexibility in assigning copybook status, and in reviewing bibliographical work completed on the Folio suggests areas where more work needs to be done. The Folio emerges as a text that could figure as the mark of the final triumph of modern bibliography over Greg's generation. This is a valuable survey for the general reader, though containing less of interest for the specialist.

Another article to focus on the printing of stage directions is Antony Hammond's 'Encounters of the Third Kind in Stage-Directions in Elizabethan and Jacobean Drama' (*SB* 44.71–99), a side product of his forthcoming edition of John Webster's *Works* for Cambridge. He sets out to challenge two basic assumptions; first, that we know what a stage-direction is, and, second, that a stage-direction in a prompt book is a more reliable source than one from foul papers. He argues that current textual theory has not done justice to this area and that regrettably even the most cautious editors feel free to emend stage directions at will. However, he also opposes a slavish following of copy-text, by appealing to 'theatrical sense' above copy-text authority. The binary division he uses in order to register this hierarchy is printed text as 'poem', staged text as 'play'. The bulk of this detailed article is an examination of six types of stage-direction, based on the starting point that the whole of a play could be interpreted as a stage-direction of sorts. The value for editors in this work is that it clarifies the thorny issue of freedom of intervention in play editing. In the light of the above work on Jonson, it appears that Hammond may have been making too easy an assumption that directions put in by an author were close to actual staging practice rather than additions for readers. The printed direction represents a seepage of power from the actor to the author, resulting in Hammond's lament that ninety per cent of what actors did is lost to us. He enters a plea that editors should not be put off by the excesses of such as John Dover Wilson, but should be prepared to seek to recover staging practice, provocatively asserting that 'the implication conveyed by most editions that the text is complete is an obvious falsehood.' In seeking to provide a theoretical basis for editorial intervention in this area, in the face of what has clearly been casual practice in the past, Hammond's work is to be warmly welcomed, although one may have reservations about the humanistic bias which favours stage over page. By contrast, Eric Rasmussen finds a case to be made for actors' improvisations surviving into print. His 'Setting Down what the Clown Spoke: Improvisation, Hand B, and *The Book of Sir Thomas More*' (*Library* 13.126–36) speculates that this manuscript contains passages which are arguably more explicable as clownish interpolations than as scripted lines. To account for this oddity he notes that the play was revived after extempore clowning was no longer a valued art, and hence gaps in the text had to be filled by someone who recollected what earlier clowns had improvised. In this way, Rasmussen makes a lively contribution to the long-running debate over the integrity of Elizabethan play texts, offering a plausible explanation of puzzling features in the text.

The most interesting and thorough of several source-mongering pieces is Julia Gasper's 'The Sources of *The Virgin Martyr*' (*RES* 42.17–31). Because of the uniformity of detail in possible sources for this narrative play by Dekker and Massinger the breadth and rigour of her approach is an absolute necessity. She painstakingly tests out the rival claims and, in so doing, sheds considerable light on religious debate at the time, since both Protestant and Catholic versions of the narratives co-existed, leaving us in considerable difficulty when seeking to determine which religion is endorsed by the play. Two of this year's textual scholars seek the aid of computers to unravel some of the problems left by early English drama. M. W. A. Smith has published two pieces, the more detailed being 'The Authorship of *The Raigne of King Edward the Third*' (*L&LC* 6.166–75). Seeking to distinguish his work from authorship studies which depend on no more than 'strong subjective impression' he makes large claims for 'the independence and objectivity of the stylometric argument' in arriving at the conclusion that the anonymous *Edward III* is by Shakespeare. His method is based on the tracing of 'discriminatory words' across a number of plays and authors to demonstrate 'which disputed work is more akin to one author than to any of the others'. Drawbacks in the system lie in problems over criteria for selection of plays, over determining what is a meaningful difference in the words chosen and over use of modernized spelling. This article is unlikely on its own to lead to an expansion of the canon, but it helps push in that direction. Smith's other article 'The Authorship of *The Revenger's Tragedy*' (*N&Q* 38.8–13) takes a series of common words from four plays by Middleton and applies a method called 'principal component analysis' to determine authorship. He reaches the same conclusion as he did five years ago, which is that Middleton is 'more likely to be the author … than Tourneur'. This conclusion is shared by Macdonald P. Jackson in 'George Wilkins and the First Two Acts of *Pericles*: New Evidence from Function Words' (*L&LC* 6.155–63). Jackson, deploying the chi-square computer-aided method developed by Smith, concludes that the first two Acts of *Pericles* are by George Wilkins. His research is much more thorough than similar work by Smith, as he uses ten 'function words' with a sample of 1000 for each word on which to base his findings.

This year saw the appearance of three notes concerning Marlowe's *Dr Faustus*. (See also section 3(b).) The most substantial is Michael Brennan's 'Christopher Marlowe's *Dr Faustus* and Urbanus Rhegius's *An Homelye ... of Good and Evill Angels*' (*N&Q* 38.466–9). Brennan argues that it is feasible that Marlowe would have read Rhegius at Cambridge, and finds 'a striking level of compatibility' between the two authors' definitions of good and evil. John Henry Jones in ' "Invirond Round with Ayrie Mountaine Tops": Marlowe's Source for *Doctor Faustus*' (*N&Q* 38.469–70) links source-hunting to the dating controversy. He argues for an early dating on the grounds that Marlowe used Braun and Hohenberg's *Civitatis Orbis Terrarum* for his description of a city which is in Trent, not Triers as printed in the 1592 edition of Marlowe's main source, the English Faust Book, which thus must be seen as a *terminus ad quem* not a *terminus a quo*. In ' "Come Away" or "Fetch Them In"? A Note on Marlowe's *Doctor Faustus*' (*N&Q* 38.470–1), Colin Wilcockson questions W. W. Greg's contention that the B-Text is more reliable than the A-Text by demonstrating that Greg has misread as senseless the words 'come away' in the former, when contemporary usage shows that they can mean 'fetch them in', the preferred reading in B-Text.

Finally, three other notes to appear are Duncan Salkeld's 'Ariosto's *Orlando Furioso* and *The Spanish Tragedy*' (*N&Q* 38.28–9), which argues for a 1591–2 dating based on signs of Kyd having read Ariosto in translation; Gary Monitto's ' "Vnsauorie Worde": *The Pilgrimage to Parnassus* (1588–9)' (*N&Q* 38.49) which offers the gloss 'arse' on this 'worde'; and Joost Daalder's 'John Fletcher's *The Pilgrim* I.i.122: A Proposed Emendation' (*N&Q* 38.519) which proposes to replace 'It' with 'That' to produce the more sensible 'Girle / That may be proud' at I.i.122–3.

2. Theatre History

Theatre history, like other histories, is in the process of being renovated. The new theatre historicism is as much about ideology as about bricks and mortar; the maps it draws are as much political as architectural and geographical. Two of this year's contributions stake out the territory. R. A. Foakes is concerned with physical structures. 'The Discovery of The Rose Theatre: Some Implications' (*ShS* 43.141–9) sets out, in his characteristically lucid, economical style, the physical facts the excavations of the Rose site have laid bare and uses what has been discovered in those foundations to reconsider the documents that have heretofore shaped our theoretical model of the Elizabethan playhouse: de Witt's Swan drawing, Visscher's, Norden's and Hollar's views, the *Roxana* and *Messallina* vignettes, Philip Henslowe's building accounts. Foakes considers the size and shape of the Rose, the position of the *frons scenae*, the shape of the stage and its location, and the size of the auditorium (this last in respect of Henslowe's costly rebuilding programme in 1592 which, Foakes concludes, can hardly have been motivated by a desire to increase audience capacity). This is probably the most important article on the Rose excavations to date. Paul Yachnin is concerned with ideological structures. In 'The Powerless Theatre' (*ELR* 21.49–74) he interrogates the New Historicist claim, popularized by Dollimore, Greenblatt, Mullaney et al., that the theatre was subversive, interventionist, powerful in shaping Elizabethan politics and society. Yachnin argues for a closer reading of history: the polemical play in the reign of Henry VIII may have had power to influence its audience in profound ways; the commercialized (and censored) play of Elizabeth's or James's reign did not. In successfully establishing themselves as viable commercial ventures 'the dramatic companies won from the government precisely what the government was most willing to give: a privileged, profitable, and powerless marginality'. Indeed, the players themselves promulgated the idea of the disinterestedness of art so that, even as the stage represented the issues of the moment, 'these representations were seen to subsist in a field of discourse isolated from the real world' and so were 'incapable of intervening in the political arena'.

Taking the theatre as structure first, no book length studies were published this year, but several interesting articles appeared. Franklin J. Hildy reviewed 'The Fifth World Shakespeare Congress, the Tokyo Globe, and the Reconstructing of Shakespeare's Theatre' (*ShakB* 9:iv.5–7). Partly a plea for the excavations of the Globe to proceed apace (it being for him one of the great absurdities 'that the Globe playhouse should have disappeared, leaving hardly a trace, while its contemporary, the Teatro Olimpico, still stands as one of the greatest theatrical failures of all time'), partly a review of the Rose excavations and papers presented on this topic at the World Congress, Hildy's article also considers the 'Panasonic Globe' (with its 650 powder-blue seats, its pink exterior, and its high-tech lighting system) as a laboratory for reconstructing the playing conditions of Shakespeare's plays. John H. Astington investigates 'The Origins of the *Roxana* and *Messallina* Illustrations' (*ShS* 43.149–69) and argues persuasively that these vignettes, depicting small, polygonal, railed stages, with hangings at the rear and spectators above, which historians have assumed to be pictures of indoor playhouses, are nothing of the sort. Their history is literary, not theatrical. They turn out to be derived from earlier engravings, etchings and woodcuts and present a 'confection of iconographic conventions'. Astington gives us eleven illustrations to compare. He's absolutely right. But oh the pity of it! John Orrell also produces illustrations and asks us to compare them in 'Spanish *Corrales* and English Theaters', the opening piece in *Parallel Lives: Spanish and English*

National Drama 1580–1680, edited by Louise and Peter Fothergill-Payne. The open-air playhouses in London and Madrid shared several important structural features, but Orrell urges caution in using what is known definitely about one playhouse to supply gaps in our information about the other. The Spanish playhouse grew organically; the English by deliberate design. And Orrell recycles bits of his *The Human Stage* (*YWES* 69.253–4) to make his points, one of which is clearly under dispute until the Globe is more fully excavated. Orrell argues here that the Globe was 100' in diameter, while Hildy, quoting a site investigator, thinks it may have measured only about 80'. The discrepancy makes for a more or less intimate 'wooden O'. Following on from Orrell, John E. Varey makes far too much of neo-Vitruvian and Hermetic theories in 'Memory Theaters and *Corrales de Comedias*' before admitting their irrelevance; two pages from the end he begins making useful observations about economics, audience–play relationships and stage design, but having chased his wild goose he's shot his bolt when the real hunt is up. A much more informative piece is John J. Allen's 'The Disposition of the Stage in the English and Spanish Theaters'. Allen, a historian of the Spanish theatre, works in reverse direction from Orrell to describe the *corrales* and then to outline eight areas in which a comparative study of the two theatrical traditions helps to resolve doubts about other aspects of design and staging. These essays – along with sixteen others that write the 'parallel life' of English and Spanish drama – were selected from papers presented at an international conference; nothing in them makes me sorry I missed it. Yet another illustration comes with John H. Astington's 'A Drawing of the Great Chamber at Whitehall in 1601' (*REEDN* 16:i.6–11) but this time, the picture is the whole point. It is preserved in a book known as *Vincent's Presidents* in the College of Arms and was unknown to Leslie Hotson when he used an eighteenth-century copyist's transcription of the 1601 Christmas festivities at Whitehall to imagine *The First Night of Twelfth Night* (*YWES* 35). The drawing gives a plan of the Great Chamber as set up for dinner: the 'Quenes state', 'A cupbord of … plate', and the path from the door to the table where the guests will be served are all marked. It provides unique first-hand testimony of the layout of the room in the seventeenth century, and it proves even more of Hotson's claims to have been merely fanciful. So it was a shrewd editorial move to publish Robert J. Alexander's 'A Record of Twelfth Night Celebrations' (*REEDN* 16:i.13–19) as a companion to Astington's piece. Alexander makes a scrupulous re-transcription of the Alnwick document Hotson employed with such *parti pris* all those years ago, even rearranging it to suit his narrative. In notes, Alexander describes the document, discusses its origin and provenance, and points out aspects of the manuscript that raise questions which may lead to further study.

Broadening out from the playhouse as structure to the material practices that determined their performances, this year's contributions considered everything from stage fighting to censorship, plots to properties, bear-baiting to theatrical entrepreneurship. David Bradley, with unflagging enthusiasm for his subject, uses *The Battle of Alcazar* – a unique multiple text that survives both as play script and as theatrical plot – to chart the steps *From Text to Performance in the Elizabethan Theatre: Preparing the Play for the Stage.* Bradley wants to know how a playbook previewed to the players in a company read-through (such as is recorded on occasions in Henslowe's *Diary*) was translated into a rehearsal script; what the relationship was between the cast list (such as Peter Quince has in hand or in mind in *A Midsummer Night's Dream*), the prompt book (such as the King of Portugal arranges on his lap to watch Hieronimo's production of *Soliman and Perseda* in *The Spanish Tragedy*), and the stage plot, only seven of which survive. The plot was 'a skeleton sketch of the action'. It scored the successive entrances and exits that structured the Elizabethan play; it instructed the player through the maze of the narrative and kept straight his multiple doubles; it itemized the stuff of his performance ('3 violls of blood and a sheeps gather'); but first and foremost it managed the cast, fitting the roles called for by the text to the available actors. Bradley has only *Alcazar* to go on: I could wish for *Lear* or *Winter's Tale*. But his meticulous detective work reconstructing the plotter's fit-up shows this theatrical *factotum* 'no mere flunkey' but a powerful coadjutor who 'clearly had ideas of his own about how a scene should go' and who interpreted the 'authorised text' from the outset: a playwright might call magisterially for 'Spare Kings'; it was the business of the plotter to embody that aspiration. Or to erase it. Following the plotter's tracks so attentively, we feel we are very close to the day-to-day life of Shakespeare's theatre. It's an emotion I expected to experience reading Francis Teague's *Shakespeare's Speaking Properties*, the book I most looked forward to among this year's selections. What a disappointment! Instead of speaking, this book is dumb. It could teach students how to read theatrical signifiers; it could historicize and analyse the objects that realize ideas on Shakespeare's stage. But it doesn't. It is formalistic and enumerative, theatrically illiterate, and never gets much beyond the 'discovery' – conspicuously self-evident – that 'properties reify genre'. Teague's characteristic observation runs like this one on Yorick et al.: 'The skull's initial function is to remind the audience visually that the scene's setting is a graveyard.' Teague does supply an appendix that lists properties play by play, but while it is mainly accurate as far as it goes, its self-declared subjectivity is not confidence-inspiring: 'what I ignore as a costume cue might seem an obvious token of identity to a different analyst.' Quite. Perdita's 'unusual weeds' that 'prank' her up 'most goddess-like' at the sheep-shearing – a complex system of theatrical signification – aren't included in Teague's list; neither is Antony's armour which Eros must 'pluck off, pluck off' in IV.xiv (although armour is included elsewhere; which makes me wonder about gender discrimination: is what a man wears his 'prop' but what a woman wears just clothes?). Even worse, Teague misreads the swords in that scene and so loses sight of the ironies the properties visually construct: Antony dies not on Eros' sword (as Teague seems to think) but on his own, Phillipan, the sword Caesar will instantly recognize (and historicize) when Decertas presents it to him. Teague wins my 'lost opportunity of the year' award.

From props on the stage to business on the stage: Charles Edelman is another who wants to know what swords meant. His *Brawl Ridiculous: Swordfighting in Shakespeare's Plays* tries to recuperate not just a technical sense of how fights were choreographed and accomplished and a dramatic sense of how they served Shakespeare's poetic significance, but a performative sense of what they meant to the audience watching them. I would have appreciated more concentration on the latter (and less recourse to 'when I was fight director at Oregon …'): Edelman has chapters on the actors' arms and armour, on the neo-medievalism of Elizabethan culture (as well as on combat in individual play texts from the *Henry VI* trilogy to *King Lear*), but he doesn't give me enough of a sense of how the audience would have interpreted the fight sequences. Were they 'brawl ridiculous'? Or 'royal occupation'? How did spectators interpret Shakespeare's visual superimpositions and deliberate anachronisms, his putting Elizabethan armour on warriors at Agincourt who then interrogate a king's prerogative to send them to their death or to cashier them without further consideration, a pair of policies their own Queen was pursuing vigorously in the campaigns of the moment? I appreciate a theatrical sophistication in Edelman that seems totally lacking in Teague, and a commitment to asking questions of theatre history that inform performance criticism, but I kept muttering as I read, 'Historicize, historicize!'

I claim Roslyn Knutson's *The Repertory of Shakespeare's Company, 1594–1613* under my section heading, not for anything it argues about the Chamberlain's/King's Men *per se* but for the demystifying view it gives of the whole enterprise – hardnosed, entrepreneurial, commerical – that was the London theatre of these decades. The repertory system, the management practices of Shakespeare's company, formed after the plague closures and general reorganizations of 1592–4, were no different than those of rival companies, and to consider this repertory as primarily responsive to box office receipts is to go some way toward repairing the high art/grubby opportunism split that has traditionally privileged the 'band of brothers' management at the Globe over Philip 'Shylock' Henslowe's at the Rose. Knutson covers some of the same ground in 'The Commercial Significance of the Payments for Playtexts in *Henslowe's Diary*, 1597–1603' (*MRDE* 5.195–210). She wants to investigate the system of partial payments towards scripts that is the norm in Henslowe's *Diary*, and she begins by recalling the Victorian prejudice against Henslowe: they found the commerical world of the *Diary* embarrassing, so they constructed that world as antithetical to the democratic world of Shakespeare's playhouse, and they moralized the tale of two houses by watching the defeat of capitalist exploitation at the Rose as the Globe partnership flourished. But Knutson is not one who assumes 'that Henslowe's records show why the Admiral's men failed and the Chamberlain's men triumphed in the "real war" between the theaters'; she thinks the partial payments show the Admiral's Men 'making a potentially lucrative commercial response to a sudden expansion in their playhouse business world'. While I'm on the subject of Henslowe's *Diary*: Winifred Frazer suggests that 'Henslowe's "Ne" ' (*N&Q* 38.34–5) means not, as R. A. Foakes believes, a 'new' play, but a 'Newington Butts' play. Ingenious. But she doesn't account for the consistently high receipts recorded for 'ne' plays throughout the *Diary* as against the dismal receipts recorded for all the plays performed when the Admiral's Men were definitely at Newington and so, by her interpretation, playing 'ne' plays every day. Maybe this is the place, too, to notice S. P. Cerasano's inquiry into another of Henslowe's ventures: 'The Master of the Bears in Art and Enterprise' (*MRDE* 5.195–209). Henslowe and Alleyn did not invest in the Bear Garden as another theatre venture; they pursued the Mastership of Bears because they were interested in baiting as entertainment and because achieving that mastership would place them at the top of the hierarchy of Jacobean entertainment providers. Cerasano describes the sport, names the famous bears ('Black Ned', 'Harey' of Warwick), inventories a menagerie that included two white bears, a leash of greyhounds and a young lion. She understands the bear pit as a play ground. Indeed, baiting at Paris Garden included country dancing, fireworks, a scramble for white bread thrown among the dancers and for apples shed from the exploding firework rose overhead. The 'Game', for Cerasano, 'becomes a choreographed "theatrical event" … more circus-like than desperate' where 'fantasy set off the seriousness of the blood sport'. The Victorian Henslowe-Shylock is metamorphosed Henslowe-Barnum-Bailey.

Several of this year's contributions investigated the players and their profession. Anyone (including libraries) who owns a copy of Chambers's *Elizabethan Stage* or Nungezer's *Dictionary of Actors* will want to pull out Mark Eccles's 'Elizabethan Actors I: A–D' (*N&Q* 38.38–48) and 'Elizabethan Actors II: E–J' (*N&Q* 38.454–66) and bind them as supplements to those earlier records. Eccles is mainly factual but offers some commentary and makes comparative study possible by exhaustive footnotes. Scott McMillin discovers that 'there may be a story to tell about Sussex's men after all': the company 'may have briefly included some of the most important figures of the Elizabethan theatre'. He tells that story in 'Sussex's Men in 1594: The Evidence of *Titus Andronicus* and *The Jew of Malta*' (*ThS* 32.214–23), using the migration of those scripts to argue persuasively what E. K. Chambers suggested (years ago) tentatively: that the turmoil the players were thrown into by plague closures, company collapses, aborted tours and failed amalgamations in 1593 may have produced one extraordinary brief collaboration, the coming together, as 'Sussex's Men' of Burbage, Kempe, Alleyn, and Shakespeare at Henslowe's Rose in April 1594. Shen Lin's 'How Old Were the Children of Paul's?' (*TN* 45.121–31) attaches 45 footnotes to an eight page article that doesn't answer the question. Collating the scant documentary evidence recorded – the ages of only three choristers out of 21 can be ascertained during the period of the second Children of Paul's – Shin draws an open (useless?) conclusion: 'that the playwrights would have been free to decide either to highlight the juvenility of the boy actors for stylistic effects or to strengthen the realism of their plays with the maturity of the superannuated choristers'. This brings us no closer to understanding the spectatorly pleasures of watching children perform Marston's satires. David Farley-Hills produces a much more satisfactory answer to the question he proposes: 'How Often Did the Eyases Fly?' (*N&Q* 38.461–6). If, as Harbage argued, the boys played only once a week, it's improbable that they would have offered a serious commerical threat to the adult companies, so how can we explain that the Admiral's Men and the Chamberlain's Men *did* perceive them as commercially threatening? Farley-Hills (via *Hamlet* and Marston's *Histriomastix*) concludes that the boys played the same schedule as the adults, six performances a week. Two very different articles are much more suggestive in politicizing the profession of boy player on the public stage. Jan Kott mischievously asks 'what gender is gender?' to locate androgyny on the cultural map of Elizabethan England in 'The Gender of Rosalind' (*NTQ* 7.113–25). Kott sometimes plays fast and loose with facts and makes sweeping generalizations ('the roles of ... even mature women were played by fourteen- or fifteen-year-old boys, always of course before their voices broke'; 'Cleopatra ... has no sooner ordered her maid to undo her bodice than she becomes for a moment a squeaking boy: "the quick comedians Extemporally will stage us." '). Such basic ignorance of theatre history and inattention to the sequence of events, scene and speech I find astonishing, but maybe Kott sees himself as Wilson Knight reportedly did in a story I was told as an undergraduate, when he rounded on some unfortunate who had pointed out a factual error: 'Sir, I am not a scholar but a prophet.' So I'll stop quibbling about mere facts and revel in Kott's poetic critical imagination, the way he brings botany, New York's gay Halloween parade, and Botticelli's Flora together to produce observations like one on the Orlando/Ganymede 'marriage' which he calls a 'fake-ritual that takes place on the fragile boundary between carnival and blasphemy'. Lesley Anne Soule writes a companion piece to Kott's, 'Subverting Rosalind: Cocky Ros in the Forest of Arden' (*NTQ* 7.126–36) that begins by re-historicizing the role: Shakespeare's text requires a performance in which the controlling presence is not a female performer but a male adolescent (a figure whose theatrical antecedents she explores). Her 'Cocky Ros' is the player, the 'Roscius', who takes on 'Ros', the role, 'Rosalind', first representing then subverting the feminine fiction of Rosalind, thus 'providing a paradigm of character-actor interplay'. If we give authority to such subversive, gender-free performers as she suggests, 'we can challenge the power wielded by theatrical illusion over our ideas of identity, gender, and love.' For anyone who saw the Cheek by Jowl production – all male – of *As You Like It* this year, all of this makes perfect sense.

Rosalind's impromptus in Arden may have had real-life counterparts. David Dymond has located 'Three Entertainers from Tudor Suffolk' (*REEDN* 16.2–5): a surgeon whose will left 'dysgysings for players'; a weaver who moonlighted as a barber and who, although illiterate, owned four chests crammed with books (whose total value, two shillings four pence, indicates they must have been ballads or chapbooks); and a clothworker who left to his cousin 'all his maskinge geare' from drum and pipes to 'visers' and 'all his new dauncinge crestes'.

If the players had actual counterparts in real life, they had imagined ones in fiction too: Shakespeare and Jonson invented audiences to watch their plays; they also invented players to perform them. And John Marston invented an entire *company* in *Histriomastix*. David Mann asks whether Marston's satire was fancy or documentary: were 'Sir Oliver Owlet's Men; Fact or Fiction?' (*HLQ* 54.301–11). If Marston's meagrely talented but pretentiously ruffling playwright, Posthaste, is a lampoon of Antony Munday, perhaps Owlet's Men are a send-up of the company Munday 'served': Oxford's Men led by the Dutton brothers. This article is valuable as much for its plausible identification as for the discussion of metatheatrical satire that precedes it. This last is partly the subject of James P. Bednarz's 'Representing Jonson: *Histriomastix* and the Origins of the Poet's War' (*HLQ* 54.1–30). Primarily an account of what Bednarz argues was the attack on, not the celebration of, Jonson – Marston's portrait of the arrogant, audience-denouncing playwright Chrisoganus, whom even the negligible Owlet's Men reject in favour of his rival Posthaste, was ingenious and devastating – this article is also concerned to unpack the 'deceptively simple fable of poets and players' contained in the subplot: 'Chrisoganus is a philosopher surrounded by a coterie audience that admires his intellectual gifts, while his opposite Posthaste is a buffoon who advocates naive improvisation and organizes a group of wayward tradesmen into a company of incompetent actors ...' The company performs the 'barren trash' Posthaste produces, as a result of which they fold and find themselves, masterless and now vagabonds, impressed to foreign service in the wars. In throwing light upon this 'fable', Bednarz reminds us that the most informative documents on some aspects of theatre history remain the playtexts themselves.

Audience reaction to plays is certainly more amply documented on the stage itself from the point of view of fictional audiences than in the auditorium of the playhouse with spectators recording impressions, but T. H. Howard-Hill has transcribed and annotated a letter from John Holles to the Earl of Somerset that he says is 'The Unique Eye-Witness Report of Middleton's *Game at Chess*' (*RES* 42.168–78). The play, as Holles reports it, is a 'vulgar pasquin', and although he seems amused at the lampoon on Gondomar in his specially designed sedan chair 'for y[e] ease of y[t] fistulated part', he is likewise indignant at the players' impertinence and alert to the dangers they courted when they dared 'to charge thus Princes actions, and ministers'. We are fortunate this letter survives to record what one spectator saw.

Censoring what audiences saw was the job of the Master of the Revels. Last year Janet Clare's study of dramatic censorship saw *Art Made Tongue-Tied by Authority* (*YWES* 71). Now Richard Dutton suggests a different nature and function of censorship, and a different hegemony, in *Mastering the Revels: The Regulation and Censorship of English Renaissance Drama*. Dutton expands earlier work on individual holders of the mastership: he is writing a history – which is clearly influenced by a historicism Paul Yachnin (above) would recognize – of the office itself through the men appointed to it. Indeed, he sees it as a central riddle of the office and its relationship to the players that the Mastership could have been offered to Ben Jonson, a poacher turned gamekeeper if ever there was one. Dutton's conclusion to this admirable study can conclude my section: 'The position of the Master of the Revels, jealously protecting court privileges as much as he sought to suppress "dangerous matter", made him as much a friend of the actors as their overlord. The stability that his office gave to an exchange of meaning in the early modern theatrical market-place clearly played a part in fostering the unique vitality of the drama of the period. His "allowance" made for a range and complexity of expression on the social, political and even religious issues of the day that was remarkable ... .' This really does take us back to reconsider the question of the powerful, or powerless, theatre. And it points us forward to the challenging recuperation of Elizabethan audiences, their spectatorly power and authoritarian strategies for controlling it argued in Thomas Cartelli's *Marlowe, Shakespeare and the Economy of Theatrical Experience* (reviewed in the Marlowe section).

3. Criticism

(a) General

Undoubtedly the most important work in this category is Richard Dutton' s *Mastering the Revels: The Regulation and Censorship of English Renaissance Drama*, which aims ambitiously to provide 'an intelligible account' of the relations between government and the theatre in this period, and in doing so challenges the views of those like Wickham and Dollimore who regard censorship as as an instrument of hegemonic cultural control. Dutton's focus is much wider than that of Janet Clare's recent *Art Made Tongue-tied by Authority: Elizabethan and Jacobean Censorship* (*YWES* 71); he concentrates not on the evidence for censorship in individual texts, but on the political structures and processes which resulted in inconsistent applications of censorship and enabled many risky plays, which did cause trouble nonetheless, to be staged. This is not to say that Dutton generalizes about textual detail; he gives some rigorously detailed accounts of the actual process of censoring a text, for example, in his discussion of the manuscript of *Sir John Van Olden Barnavelt*, where George Buc's claim to be a Master of the Revels with a good working understanding of actors and playwrights is amply vindicated. More closely than any other critic or historian so far, he examines the different attitudes and practices of a succession of Masters of the Revels from Tilney to Herbert, revealing as he does so many ways in which these officials contributed to and enhanced, rather than suppressed, the vitality of the drama. In this wide-ranging, but scrupulously conducted study Dutton engages with many currently controversial issues, both general, such as the social constitution of theatre audiences and the possibility of changing attitudes to government control between the reigns of Elizabeth and James, and more specific, like the numerous notorious topical references in the drama, and has something illuminating to say on all of them.

None of the other general books on the drama, each of which is by a younger, less established scholar than Dutton, constitutes a major contribution to the scholarship of the period in this way. Martin Wiggins in *Journeymen in Murder: The Assassin in English Renaissance Drama* takes a subject of much potential fascination and begins very promisingly with meticulously detailed chapters relating the changing deployment of the assassin figure in the later sixteenth century to contemporary social issues involving interactions between power and morality. The discussion of problems of tyranny and absolutism in such plays as Greene's *James IV*, *Gismond of Salerne*, or *Richard III* is backed by considerable learning, lightly worn. But the later sections of the book, when Wiggins's attention is more specifically on the plays themselves and their dramatic qualities, are disappointing, with some pedestrian accounts of well-known plays by Webster and Middleton in terms of character-psychology, and there is an air of perfunctoriness about the concluding chapters. The full potential of this subject, particularly in the light of current explorations of cultural change in the early modern period, remains to be realized. Molly Smith's *The Darker World Within: Evil in the Tragedies of Shakespeare and his Successors*, though much more superficial in its scholarship than Wiggins's book, has nonetheless a methodological openness which could have enlivened his cautious approach. Her belief that the intense dramatic fascination with evil in seventeenth-century drama is a direct function of what she calls the 'socio-political atmosphere' which was brewing up for the Civil War is a crude one, crudely expressed. This is one of those books where every play can be read to exemplify some fashionable theory: in *Hamlet*, *Macbeth*, and *The Changeling* weak father-figures symbolically represent the impotence of patriarchy; *'Tis Pity She's a Whore* depicts the Bahktinian grotesque body and in this play consequently 'incest verges on celebration'. There are many wild assertions, about the power of women in the Stuart period, for example, which is held responsible for the 'darker tone' of Stuart tragedy, and about the way drama 'creates a sense of crisis' which then activates the scapegoat mechanism in society, enabling the execution of the king. All in all, this is a book best kept away from undergraduates. Joan Lord Hall's *The Dynamics of Role-Playing in Jacobean Tragedy* is an altogether more temperate work, which identifies itself at the outset with a modified liberal-humanist stance towards its subject; the plays discussed are those in which insights into role-playing are derived from an accentuation of the mimetic dimension of the *dramatis personae*. This results in a predictably canonical selection of texts but also some valuable accounts of their theatrical dimensions. The possiblities for playing Vittoria in *The White Devil* as a 'morally sensitive, even naturally timid woman' are initially startling but also theatrically exciting. Lord writes intelligent analyses of the contrasting uses of role-play in *Women Beware Women* and *The Changeling*, and Middleton's demystification of social convention is interestingly explored. Sometimes the focus appears too limited, as in the discussion of *King Lear*, which is largely confined to arguing for Edgar as a recognizably unified character whose diverse roles can be psychologically reconciled. The narrowness is also reflected in the fact that *The Roman Actor*, a seminal text, one might have thought, in which a play consciously reflects on its own processes, is referred to only in a few sentences in the conclusion.

Feminist approaches dominate in three articles, two from the feminist collection *In Another Country: Feminist Perspectives on Renaissance Drama* (edited by D. Kehler and S. Baker). Coppélia Kahn writes stimulatingly on 'Whores and Wives in Jacobean Drama', exploring the problems presented to men by women's sexuality in plays centring on cuckoldry and virginity. She deals especially well with the plays of Middleton in which opposed sexual categories for women – virgin or wife, and whore – become confused, while male characters struggle to control and define sexual difference. Margaret Lael Mikesell contributes a less substantial piece on 'The Formative Power of Marriage in Stuart Tragedy'; like Kahn, she identifies certain changes taking place in the concept and practice of marriage in this period, and distinguishes between the handling of them in comedy and tragedy. In comedy, women can safely be permitted to challenge handbook models of marital behaviour based on chastity and obedience, whereas in tragedy, defiance of convention is always fatal. Betty S. Travitsky covers related ground in 'Husband-Murder and Petty Treason in English Renaissance Drama' (*RenD* 21.171–98), illustrating women's challenges to the institution of marriage in real life and drama; her heavy reliance on modern cultural theorists rather than Renaissance sources for her notions of the legal status of women in the period vitiates this article, and her accounts of Elizabeth Cary's *Mariam* and *The Life, Reign, and Death of Edward II*, which is central to it, repeat her earlier work on this writer (*YWES* 71).

Materialist feminism combines with New Historicism in two articles by Sophie Tomlinson and Walter Cohen from the collection *The Politics of Tragicomedy: Shakespeare and After*, which contains an introduction by the editors, Gordon McMullan and Jonathan Hope, summarizing and commenting on various aspects of the politics of this currently reviving genre from 1610 to 1650. Tomlinson's ' "She That Plays the King": Henrietta Maria and the Threat of the Actress in Caroline Culture' makes large claims for the Queen's influence in setting in motion a cult of woman culminating in women's propagandist activities during the Civil War and the years immediately preceding it. Her readings of texts by Shirley, Ford and Cartwright reveal different ways in which anxieties aroused by the idea of the woman actor might be contained. This useful piece could well be read in conjunction with Kim Walker's article on Shirley (section (c) below). Cohen is also concerned with gender in his 'Prerevolutionary Drama'. His argument for the 'irreducibly political' character of gender relations in the drama of the period is conducted on very broad and sweeping lines from a 'hindsight' methodology, by which, as he acknowledges, 'political commitment determines critical position'. The seductiveness of many of his readings vanishes on closer inspection. The late Margot Heinemann also has a political agenda in her article for the same collection, ' "God Help the Poor: the Rich Can Shift": the World Upside-Down and the Popular Tradition in the Theatre', which is to discover evidence for popular dissent and protest in tragicomedy; Rowley's *When You See Me, You Know Me* and Dekker's *If it be Not a Good Play, the Devil is in it* duly yield it. The account of Rowley's play is valuable in exposing the attractively 'popular' qualities accorded Henry VIII, but not entirely convincing in suggesting that it offers a message for James I about the control of the church by a far from fallible monarch. In fact, the assumption made in all the articles from Hope and McMullan's collection and also Molly Smith's book, that theatre of this period might be taken seriously as a contribution to the subversion of the status quo, eventuating in the Civil War, is directly challenged by Paul Yachnin's full and provocative article 'The Powerless Theatre' (*ELR* 21.49–71), which draws on a range of material over the Tudor and Stuart periods suggesting that beliefs in the power and efficacy of the theatre, as opposed to non-poetic and non-literary forms of writing, varied considerably. While Nashe and Stubbes saw it as an important influence this ceased to be the case after 1600, when the 'innovative compliance' between theatrical practitioners and Masters of the Revels effectively rendered it harmless; like Dutton, with whose arguments this has some common ground, and Howard-Hill (see section (c) below) Yachnin discusses the case of *A Game at Chesse* as a play which was *not* regarded as a mouthpiece for attitudes of radical dissent. His argument that potentially political meanings in plays are 'depoliticized' by being contained within aesthetic forms and made the product of the audience's reception of the text is, however, pressed too far. But Yachnin's sceptical attitude to the current rage for political readings is refreshing, particularly in relation to an article such as Charlotte Spivack's 'Woman on the Jacobean Stage: Type and Antitype', from *Traditions and Innovations: Essays on British Literature of the Middle Ages and the Renaissance* (edited by B. Allen and R. White). She considers that 'alternative models' for women in Jacobean drama, sympathetically handled, such as prostitutes, witches, and the semi-transvestite Moll of *The Roaring Girl*, constitute direct evidence of theatre acting as the agent of social change. Much more intellectually rigorous is Kathleen McLuskie in 'The Poets' Royal Exchange: Patronage and Commerce in Early Modern Drama' from a special issue of *YES* (21) devoted to 'Politics, Patronage, and Literature in England, 1558–1658' (53–62). She traces confusion about the relationship between patronage and commerce in early modern commentaries on the theatre, and focuses on the contributions of Jonson and Dekker to the War of the Theatres to demonstrate their achievement in bringing about a 'vital cultural accommodation' to the new economic and social system. This closely argued piece probably belongs to the realm of theatre history, as does Paul Whitfield White's 'Patronage, Protestantism, and Stage Propaganda in Early Elizabethan England' from the same journal (49–52), in which he argues cogently for the continuance of stage propaganda well into the 1570s, despite Elizabeth I's proclamation of 1559 against it.

The remaining articles are miscellaneous. One that is, unusually, both useful and enjoyable is D. A. Beecher's 'Antiochus and Stratonice: the Heritage of a Medico-Literary Motif in the Theatre of the English Renaissance' (*SCen* 5.113–32), which traces the motif of the lover sick with desire for a woman who rightly belongs to another man, whose cure can only be obtained through the woman being enabled to respond to his love. The popularity of the motif, the first surviving version of which Beecher finds in Valerius Maximus, stems both from the appealing ironies of the 'therapeutic coitus' situation and its suitability for the development of subtle oppositions between honour and desire. But it appears not only in literary versions such as the Renaissance novellas of Bandello, Belleforest, Painter and the plays they influenced, but also in medical treatises; the solution to the plight of the Jailor's daughter in *The Two Noble Kinsmen* is to be found in Avicenna. Beecher's wryly humourous tone is ideal for the documentation of this 'rapprochement between literature and medicine' which illuminates so much of the Renaissance discourse of sexuality. A. J. Hoenslaars in 'Broken Images of Englishmen and Foreigners in English Renaissance Drama' (*GRM* 72.157–73) discusses stereotypes of European nationals in England and the presentation of English nationals abroad; the subject is a promising, and at this moment, also a timely one, but Hoenslaars's selection of texts is curiously random, and his account of some of the plots (for example, Fletcher's *The Wild-Goose Chase*) is inaccurate. Noemi Messora also deals with relations between England and Continental Europe, through comparison between texts from England and Italy in 'Parallels between Italian and English Courtly Plays in the Sixteenth Century: Carlo Turco and John Lyly', from *Theatre of the English and Italian Renaissance* (edited by J. R. Mulryne). She focuses on Carlo Turco's play *Agnella*, written for the court of Henry II of France, as an intermediate stage in the development of courtly drama between interludes such as *Fulgens and Lucrece* and Lyly's work, and its particular parallels in terms of thematic structures based on dialogue and debate with *Campaspe* and *Endymion*. In the general sense of illuminating the complex origins of Lylyian debate drama this article performs a useful function, but it does not supplant the view of Lyly by Hunter, Orr, and more recently Berry as rooted in the court culture of his own country. Muriel Bradbrook touches briefly on Lyly in 'Castiglione, Lyly, and *The Two Gentlemen of Verona*' from the same collection, as a transitional figure in the assimilation of Italianate courtly ideals into English drama soon to be overtaken by the more sophisticated dramaturgy of Shakespeare's early comedies. Leo Salingar, in 'Elizabethan Dramatists and Italy: A Postscript', the concluding article in this volume, fruitfully stresses tensions between Italian dramatic theory and English practice as well as differences in social organization in the two countries relevant to theatre: he cites the relationship of Marston's *The Malcontent* to

Guarini's *Il Pastor Fido*, from which it borrows, to epitomize some of these points.

Finally, Susan Baker and Lorena L. Stookey in 'Renaissance Drama: A Bibliography for Feminists' from *In Another Country: Feminist Perspectives on Renaissance Drama* provide a full but discriminatingly selected list, excluding a large mass of books and articles that simply discuss plays with prominent female characters without a specific feminist interest.

(b) Marlowe

Scanning Marlowe's books this year I felt much more like Wagner than Dr Faustus. The book I most wanted to review – James Shapiro's *Rival Playwrights: Marlowe, Jonson, Shakespeare* – still hasn't materialized, either in my office or in the university library, despite numerous conjurations; I shall try the publisher's name 'forward and backward anagrammatized': that should produce results which will be reported next year. I was happy to replace Shapiro with Charles Nicholl's darkly brilliant *The Reckoning* at the top of my list until I discovered it bears next year's publication date and so is barred from consideration this year. (Meanwhile, in Stratford-upon-Avon, the Royal Shakespeare Company's production of *The School of Night*, replaying the events leading up to Deptford in May 1593, and no doubt conjuring audiences into the theatre in 1993, has opened, but I can not talk about that here either!) What am I left with? Roger Sales's *Christopher Marlowe*, filling up a place in Macmillan's 'English Dramatists' series, which purports to be aimed at 'students, theatre-goers and general readers who want an up-to-date view of the plays and dramatists, with emphasis on drama as theatre and on stage, social and political history'. This book sounded to me as though it had been written by Wagner – except that Wagner uses more complicated syntax – for transmission down a FAX machine: strings of one-liners culled, it seems, apprentice-like from masters (mostly unacknowledged except in the bibliography) whose complex New Historicist, feminist, psychoanalytic arguments are redacted in the manner of Wagner reproducing the occult. The first part of the book offers 'a reconstruction of the dramatised nature of Elizabethan society' that I found progressively irritating because of Sales's obsession with forcing every observation into a theatrical metaphor as if he were Jonson's Mammon turning every footling andiron or frying pan into pure gold. In the second part, Sales considers the canon play by play. Here is a sample: 'Barabas was played on the Elizabethan stage in a deliberately confrontational manner. Edward Alleyn wore a long gabardine coat and a red wig. He also put on an outrageous hooked nose. Barabas's caricature appearance confirms the propagandist's categories of the central and the marginal, the classical and the grotesque.' There are no notes to any of this. I was not impressed.

I *was* impressed – if not set on fire – by Thomas Dabbs's *Reforming Marlowe: the Nineteenth-Century Canonization of a Renaissance Dramatist*. Dabbs shows how it was that Marlowe, virtually unknown by the eighteenth century, came to be investigated, nay, invented, by the nineteenth, whose practices split the writing of poetry from the writing of criticism and whose legacy to the twentieth century was not just a Marlowe biography but an authorized view of his artistic motives. So the Marlowe Dabbs historicizes is the one who belonged to the Victorians, not to the Elizabethans: he shows how the growth of the book trade and the interest in old texts prompted 'covert interest' in Marlowe and in his 'assumed works' in literary clubs in the eighteenth century, but argues that Marlowe 'could not emerge as a major figure until a form of critical inquiry was developed that allowed an appreciation for [his] verse without calling too much attention either to his life or to the overall themes of his works'. Charles Lamb was Mephistopheles to this project. And Charles Kean played more than a bit part too. By this route, Dabbs takes us from the 'discovery' of Marlowe to the foundation of Marlowe scholarship (on Collier's shifting sands), to the institutionalizing and romanticizing – long after the romantic period was over – of a sensationalized, extravagant Marlowe, and finally to the aestheticizing of one Kit into a thousand long-haired poets: Hart Crane evidently ran down the streets of New York's Little Italy shouting, 'I am Christopher Marlowe'. He wasn't the last. Ultimately, this look at the past tells us about the present: there is, Dabbs claims, 'abundant evidence that twentieth-century studies have suffered as the result of a type of intellectual annexation from [the] specifically nineteenth-century discursive field' he so engrossingly maps.

I wish more writers on Marlowe felt about him as Crane did; it shouldn't be permitted to make him sound dull. I forgive those assiduous writers of notes whose business with Marlowe is pedantic: six of them among this year's contributions. Mishtooni Bose finds in Faustus's farewell to 'being and not-being' an allusion to Peter Ramus's dialectic. In 'On Kai Me On: A Tension in the Ramist Manuals?' (*N&Q* 38.29–31), Bose sees the phrase as significant in highlighting the tensions in Ramist thought between fiction and 'reality', tensions which would have consequences for the status of poetry: at once granted a moral authority by its use in exemplifying logical precepts but likewise threatened by its ambivalent location among the degrees of reality. Michael G. Brennan finds a source for Marlowe's dramatization of the angels in 'Christopher Marlowe's *Dr Faustus* and Urbanus Rhegius's *An Homelye ... of Good and Evill Angels*' (*N&Q* 38.466–9). Rhegius, a Lutheran theologian first published in 1538 and Englished in 1583, was frank in stating the sheer malevolence of the evil angels toward mankind and also in declaring God's permission that he should be so tested, but was equally clear that only man's complicity, his voluntary entrance into a 'league' or 'truce' with evil gives Satan power over him. Marlowe, it seems, read Rhegius. Unfortunately, Faustus did not. John Henry Jones consults *Civitates orbis terrarum* in ' "Inviron'd Round With Ayrie Mountaine Tops": Marlowe's Source for *Doctor Faustus*' (*N&Q* 38.469–70) to show that Marlowe's copy of the *English Faust Book* contained 'Trent' not 'Trier' as the first stop on Faustus's world tour; establishing that copy allows him to assert 1592 as a *terminus ad quem* for dating the play. Colin Wilcockson defends Marlowe from the critics' charges of clumsiness or ineptitude in ' "Come Away" or "Fetch Them In"? A Note on Marlowe's *Doctor Faustus*' (*N&Q* 38.470–1), by pointing out that 'come away' does not mean 'let us depart' but 'come here at once': Lucifer's command is to the Seven Deadly Sins to enter, not to Faustus to exit. David Womersley finds 'An Early Response to *Tamburlaine*?' (*N&Q* 38.471–2), perhaps, in a prefatory letter to Edward Dering's *Works* (1590) in which 'I. F.' refers to 'Tamerlan', his 'blacke tentes', and suppliants 'with Laurell in our hands becladde in white garmentes' as metaphors for God's vengeance and mankind's futile appeals for mercy should the work of the Reformation remain uncomplete. In 'The Politics of Anti-Semitism: *The Jew of Malta* and *The Merchant of Venice*' (*N&Q* 38.35–8), Margaret Hotine reads the performance records of Henslowe's *Diary* against the calendar of the Lopez trial to argue that the 1594 revival of *The Jew of Malta* was used to incite anti-Semitic prejudice. I find this account of the chronology, of the players' practices, and of the relationship between the theatre and the government dubious, and I grow more sceptical when Hotine imagines a scenario in which Essex and the 'young bloods' who followed him (and who followed plays, too, 'their seats in the galleries or even on the stage' making them 'well placed to contribute to the action') stand in some sort of relationship to the 'brash young men in *The Merchant of Venice*'. Shakespeare's 'rounded portrayal of Shylock' makes that play 'appear a counterblast to recent anti-Semitism': in such assertions I feel I'm hearing an echo of those prejudices (at least three generations old) that scorn one repertory (that is, whatever was produced by whichever company was playing under the entrepreneurial auspices of Henslowe at the Rose) while privileging the other repertory (that is, whatever was produced – especially a play by Shakespeare – by the Chamberlain's Men in their benevolent fraternity at the Globe). Such prejudices, and the imaginative spin they put on interpreting the facts of theatre history, are being challenged, and demolished, by Roslyn Knutson, for one (see section 2 above). Hotine could learn from another article reviewed in that section: Scott McMillin's 'Sussex's Men in 1594: The Evidence of *Titus Andronicus* and *The Jew of Malta*' (*ThS* 32.214–22). McMillin is primarily concerned to identify the acting personnel of Sussex's Men, but in using *The Jew of Malta* to make his case he gives an account of the transmission of that playtext (from Strange's Men to Sussex's Men to the Admiral/Chamberlain's association at Newington Butts to the Admiral's Men at the Rose) that links its history to Edward Alleyn (who certainly owned several scripts as personal stock). McMillin may speculate, but never (Hotine, take note) wildly.

I am less forgiving of those whose business with Marlowe is to give us access to some aspect of his high astounding art but who fail to find a critical language that is commensurate with his achievement. That's my complaint against Ruth Lunney's 'Transforming the Emblematic: The Dramatic Emblem in the Plays of Marlowe' (*EiT* 9.141–58). Lunney outlines three categories of emblem: the simple, essentially narrative (Tamburlaine removing his shepherd's weeds to reveal himself as heroic warrior); the complex (Tamburlaine's 'sights of power' scene or Barabas's counting house, which 'combine a multiplicity of visual detail with formal structure and staging' and which subordinate the conventional message to complex rhetorical and narrative work); and the inverted (the bond signing in *Dr Faustus* (where Marlowe 'exploits the allegorical function of dramatic emblems to accomplish a shift of emphasis from concept to individual experience'). She applies her scheme to a close analysis of the 'sights of power' and bond-signing scenes to show how the new emblematic forms have refashioned an old technique. But her failure to align herself imaginatively with Marlowe, to discover a vocabulary imitative of the emotional, theatrical or spectatorly experience those emblems realize, is signified in her repeated references to 'Edward's death by poker'.

Three articles on *Tamburlaine* did satisfy my 'imitative vocabulary' criterion. Mark Thornton Burnett applies Bakhtin's theories of the 'grotesque' and 'classic' bodies – one body that is open and unfinished, the other, closed and complete – in '*Tamburlaine* and the Body' (*Criticism* 33.31–47). He argues that 'classical' and 'grotesque' notions of the body are thematized in *Tamburlaine*, where the body is both the physical material upon which dominance is inscribed and a site where that dominance is contested, and where class aspiration takes the form of Tamburlaine's modelling himself on the 'classical' body even as he humiliates his enemies into 'grotesques'. Poor Tamburlaine. 'Part One charts [his] rise to the "classical", but Part Two dramatizes the "grotesque" claiming him once more', betrayed by his orifices. Burnett expands his analysis to suggest that the metaphor of the body functioned ideologically not just in terms of social, economic and political practices but historically as well: 'as a metaphor which was enlisted to promote notions of harmony, the body was coming under stress in the early modern period, and its political uses were being increasingly scrutinized.' In 'Death, Power, and Representation in *Tamburlaine the Great*' (*CahiersE* 40.1–10) Rick Bowers sees Tamburlaine – who constantly 'demands more/*mors*' – replacing the allegorical figure of Death, familiar on the medieval stage, with his own devastating 'action' of death. Tamburlaine, in short, becomes death; death is the name given to the power he exerts, and death is the object of his primitive, totalizing representations: the king-drawn chariot, the caged Bajazeth, the slaughtered virgins. Witty, ironic, vivid, Bowers's criticism works on the nerve endings the way the production photographs illustrating Brian Singleton's 'The Beauty of the Resistible Tyrant: *Tamerlan* at the Théâtre de l'Epée de Bois' (*ThR* 16.38–108) work on the retina: the faces are bold, fascistic, mistakeable for masks, the costumes and stances Oriental, evocative perhaps of certain postures of tyranny. Singleton is writing a review, but also a profile of the company's working practices, history and ideology: to mention Mnouchkine as model and inspiration is enough to locate the Theatre de l'Epée de Bois on the cultural map of European theatre. This article is particularly useful in analysing how Marlowe's performance text communicates with an audience in a production alert to space, gesture, theatrical signifiers, and committed – as I believe Marlowe's theatre was – to non-realistic externalization of character 'psychology'.

To read about this company's strenuous efforts to discover and release Marlowe's theatricality in *Tamburlaine* and then to turn to Debra Belt's 'Anti-Theatricalism and Rhetoric in Marlowe's *Edward II*' (*ELR* 21.134–60) is to experience an ironic shock. It is not just that Belt identifies Marlowe's strategy in *Edward II* to be the same as Gosson's in his *Play of Plays* (a dramatized version of *Plays Confuted*): indeed, that's the kind of joke Marlowe would relish, the poacher hijacking the game keeper, appropriating the motifs and slogans of the anti-theatre campaign and its complaints about playwrights and actors, and reinventing their moral opprobrium as a tactical challenge. Neither is it Belt's claim that *Edward II* 'is best seen as a study in the ways of moving' (that is, rhetorical suggestion and perception) or that Edward himself should be viewed primarily as an audience to performances devised to delude him. It is rather that her assertion – 'at bottom the work is … a play about rhetoric and its effect on audiences' – while intellectually satisfying and formally credible utterly contradicts the visceral experience of the play in the theatre where it is the seductive body of a young man, a puddle of channel water, and a phallus refashioned in heated iron that 'persuade'. David H. Thurn, invoking Freud, fetishism, Medusa, specular disruption, anamorphosis (and more) in 'Sovereignty, Disorder, and Fetishism in Marlowe's *Edward II*' (*RenD* 21.114–41) comes much closer to taking the emotional temperature of this play. Gaveston is the site where all these ideas converge: 'the protean figure of Gaveston introduces, in effect, an anamorphic blur that works to expose the artifice of sovereign power' by disturbing its spectacles, unmaking its sexual, political, and linguistic proprieties, and unmaking the king as well. Where Tamburlaine, Faustus and Barabas assert themselves in totalizing acts of narcissistic desire, Edward never achieves that moment of self-mastery, of stable self-possession, and Gaveston's association with the fluid, the amorphic, presents the imagery that will eventually claim Edward, humiliatingly emasculated when his beard is shaved off over a mud puddle, horrifically murdered where he stands 'up to the knees' in 'the mire and puddle' of the dungeon. This and Rick Bower's were the most challenging articles on Marlowe I read this year. Three co-responsive articles that I haven't yet seen but want to give notice of appear in the inaugural issue of *Connotations*, a new periodical: Paul Budra's '*Doctor Faustus*: Death of a Bibliophile'; Mark Thornton Burnett's '*Doctor Faustus* and Intertextuality'; and Paul Yachnin's '*Doctor Faustus* and the Literary System' (1.1–11, 173–80, 74–77).

Finally, just when I was feeling terminally grumpy about this year's book-length studies of Marlowe, there appeared, as if by magic, Thomas Cartelli's *Marlowe, Shakespeare, and the Economy of Theatrical Experience*. Reading it, I rediscovered that lost continent 'delight', that is promised in 'a world of profit and delight', to 'the studious'. Cartelli's project is to recover the Elizabethan experience of watching a play, to develop a theatrical model of that experience (the 'economy' of the title) that can then be applied to readings of a group of plays (Marlowe's include *Tamburlaine*, *Doctor Faustus* and *The Jew of Malta*). He wants to recuperate a Marlowe-who-is-not-Shakespeare, and a Shakespeare-who-is-not-Marlowe; but even more challengingly, a Shakespeare-before-he-became-'SHAKESPEARE' and a Marlowe-who-was-Marlowe (before Dabbs's Victorians got their hands on him): what was it like to see a play by an *unknown* playwright called Marlowe or Shakespeare? Cartelli's model is Freudian, but also informed by reappraisals of anti-theatrical invective: the pleasure principle of playgoing is linked to the heterodox material the play contains. This acutely historicized audience-oriented theory underpins the arguments Cartelli then advances about Elizabethan theatrical transactions: 'their encouragement of audience engagement with transgressive fantasy material; their capacity to demystify established structures of belief and behaviour; and their operation as correctives to readerly defined habits of taste and judgement.' A *theatricalized* as well as a historicized Marlowe: I loved it!

(c) Jonson

In a relatively lean year for Jonson studies, what catches the eye is *Ben Jonson's 1616 Folio*, edited by Jennifer Brady and W. H. Herendeen, which has claims to be the best collection of essays on Jonson currently available. As the title suggests, the book proposes to unite around the publication and the text of the extraordinary 1616 Folio of Jonson's *Workes*, although some contributions have only a tenuous link to this topic. Its principal value lies in its resistance to the generic fragmentation that typifies Jonson studies, which it achieves by insisting on the integrity of the *oeuvre*, an objective of which Jonson himself would have approved. Thus, not all contributions have a central focus on the plays. In his introduction, Wyman Herendeen heralds both this book and the Folio itself as successful 'pluralistic' enterprises and claims that the volume offers a radical redefinition of the two basic tenets of Jonson studies, classicism and stability. Although he acknowledges the destabilizing influence of theory, however, one disappointing feature of the book is its marked lack of interest in more recent developments in critical practice, perhaps because the design and character of the collection is delimited by its subject, but also reflecting a more general conservatism in Jonson criticism.

There is plenty here to admire, however, with one of the outstanding contributions being Jennifer Brady's ' "Noe Fault, but Life": Jonson's Folio as Monument and Barrier', which illustrates the rich rewards which can accrue from a historical approach combined with textual awareness and a comprehensive overview of Jonson's works. The persuasive argument here is that in creating a monument in 1616 Jonson, unlike Shakespeare, summed himself up long before his own death. As Brady puts it, 'tomes have an uncanny way of mortifying their authors', or of becoming tombs. Herendeen's 'A New Way to Pay Old Debts: Pretexts to the 1616 Folio' offers an unusual but productive perspective on Jonson's works, via their dedications, showing how these texts raise the same issues as are raised in the rest of his art, to which they can serve as a critical introduction. In face of the current New Historicist orthodoxy, he argues that this sort of material is 'as much generic and textual as it is social and political'. Jonson emerges as proudly independent, eschewing old style patronage by using dedications to repay debts rather than angling for favours. The other particularly noteworthy piece is Joseph Loewenstein's 'Printing and "The Multitudinous Presse": The Contentious Texts of Jonson's Masques', which focuses on a series of tensions in Jonson's life and work; between performance and print, between status of court poet and the stigma of publication, and between Jonson and Samuel Daniel, an analysis which represents a significant contribution to literary history. Less persuasive is Katharine Maus's 'Facts of the Matter: Satiric and Ideal Economies in the Jonsonian Imagination', which argues that because Jonson was not a Marxist therefore Marxist critical theory can have no bearing on his work. In arguing thus, Maus produces a Jonson whose best hope for the future is a vague wish that the power-holders might become more virtuous. Sara Van den Berg's 'Ben Jonson and the Ideology of Authorship', following Foucault, effectively explores Jonson's innovatory exploitation of what is seen as a new humanist concept of the author. It is typical of the strengths of this volume that the argument has wider application than the immediate focus on poetry, and it is also revealing of its limitations that it is the critic of the poetry who is most prepared to make use of modern critical theory. Finally, William Blisset's 'Roman Ben Jonson' discusses *Poetaster*, *Sejanus* and *Catiline*, providing local insights (such as the latter being a failure because Jonson 'required his audience to think themselves back into republican Rome') and written with infectious enthusiasm but with no unifying thesis. As with most other contributions to the Brady and Herendeen volume, it has the interests of the general reader in mind.

Blisset's piece, however, paradoxically offers less insight into Jonson's Latinity than the more specialist article by Robert C. Evans, 'Jonson's Copy of Seneca', (*CompD* 25.257–93), which is based on a reading of Jonson's marginal markings discovered in a 1599 edition of Seneca's philosophical writings. Evans works through these markings chronologically, thus running the risk of tedium and haphazard listing. The other major drawback is that interpretation of why Jonson marked as he did is awkwardly speculative, as when Evans concludes that a mark next to one of Seneca's conservative comments necessarily indicates Jonson's approval. It is also the case that there is little direct linkage between the markings and the plays themselves, but, nonetheless, this reader came from the article feeling that what is offered here is a genuine insight into the working of Jonson's mind, which indeed gives us, as Evans claims, 'rich new insights into his reaction to the Stoicism that was such an important influence on his thinking'. An exception to the rule noted above that Jonson criticism is generally hostile to critical theory, is Howard Marchitell, whose 'Desire and Domination in *Volpone*' (*SEL* 31.287–308) shares Van den Berg's interest in authority and is indebted to the current debate over New Historicism. Marchitell argues persuasively in this fine article that the market economy of Jacobean theatre eludes court control, just as desire for Celia disrupts male exclusivity as represented by Volpone. The struggle for power or domination emerges as being less straightforward than New Historicism maintains and is shown to be a central concern in Jonson.

Another group of useful articles to appear this year approaches Jonson by way of other dramatists, the most substantial of these being James Bednarz's 'Representing Jonson: *Histriomastix* and the Origin of the Poets' War' (*HLQ* 54.1–30), which sets out to pin down the responsibility for the celebrated 'Poetamachia' by re-reading John Marston's portrayal of Jonson (as Chrisoganus) in his *Histriomastix* as neither pure satire nor encomium but a calculated critique which embraced major debates on the theory of literary production and the reforming potential of an artist in a corrupt society on which he is dependent. Marchitell argues that it is over the reformist claims of art that Marston and Jonson fall out, taking us to the heart of the current debate over the extent to which Jonson himself had to compromise his lofty ideals in order to pursue his court career. Bednarz effectively demonstrates that the Poets' War was more than a simple clash of personalities. Douglas Bruster's 'David Mamet and Ben Jonson: City Comedy Past and Present' (*MD* (1990) 33.333–47) oddly juxtaposes Jonson with a modern American playwright, demonstrating the former's continuing relevance, resulting, it is argued, from his acute anticipation of developments in capitalism. Bruster concludes that the claimed distinguishing characteristics of postmodernism are to be found in Jacobean city comedy, although he discerns, in my view unconvincingly, that Jonson is more positive than his modern successor. The case made for Jonson's endings being straightforwardly optimistic is as strained here as it is in much Shakespeare criticism. It is interesting to note that Mamet is condemned as Jonson has been, for lack of 'insight into hearts and heads', that is, for not being like the Bard. Shakespeare and Jonson are brought together in William Slights's thoughtfully argued 'Bodies of Text and Textualized Bodies in *Sejanus* and *Coriolanus*' (*MRDE* 5.181–94), which explores the power of textuality to promote or to destroy, the body on stage being a particularly potent text in both plays. To be textualized in Slights's usage is to be incorporated into a narrative and hence manipulated. Jonson is shown to be highly sensitive to this fate in the extreme caution which he showed in trying to control the meanings of his own texts by such means as prefaces, inductions, epilogues and marginalia. As Jonson's chequered career shows, however, he did not always maintain control over the power of text, though the importance of the struggle is clearly delineated in this article.

The relationship between the play in performance and the play in print is a common interest in this year's publications, and provides the focus of Michael Warren's 'The Theatricalization of Text: Beckett, Jonson, Shakespeare' (*LCUT* 20.38–59), reflecting Jonson's own preoccupation with the implications of the transition from stage to page. Warren argues that an antitheatrical prejudice in Jonson has 'obscured the theatrical reality', with the effect that Jonson has exercised a sort of tyranny over successive editors, who continue to present an 'ideal text format' cleansed of theatrical associations. He is critical of the casualness of stage directions which effectively impose 'particular potential actions that become embedded in the text'. In order to return from the ideal to the material he proposes to develop what he calls an 'electronic book', which would make available versions of plays in 'a relatively unmediated form'. This sounds a little far-fetched, but it makes for a lively end to a lively article. Also concerned with Jonson in the theatre is Lawrence Raw's 'William Poel's Staging of *The Alchemist*' (*TN* 45.74–80), a valuable contribution to Jonsonian theatre history. Raw reconstructs Poel's 1899 revival of *The Alchemist* using prompt-books and reviews, and demonstrates the positive impact this had on Jonson's reputation in the face of Victorian hostility. Raw's impeccable research sheds light on a much neglected area of Jonson studies, draws attention to aspects of Jonson's craft which make him a success in the theatre and reveals something of the cultural standards of the time and Poel's influence in shaping them.

The most significant of the remainder of this year's crop is D. H. Craig's 'Plural Pronouns in Roman Plays by Shakespeare and Jonson' (*L&LC* 6.180–6), a computer-based statistical survey which seeks to place the thorny issue of genre identification onto an objective basis by noting the recurrence in certain plays of strong generic markers, such as plural pronouns. Arguably, Craig achieves this aim but his conclusion appears to be what most readers would arrive at without the aid of a computer, which is that Roman plays, here exemplified by *Catiline* and *Coriolanus*, are more concerned with the functioning of groups than of individuals. The final piece to link Jonson to his contemporaries is Hans Werner's 'A Caricature and a Self-Portrait of the Beaumont and Fletcher Partnership in Jonson's *Bartholomew Fair* and Fletcher's *The Chances*' (*N&Q* 38.514–16). Werner argues that the Damon and Pythias episode in *Bartholomew Fair* is a mildly satirical version of the relationship between Beaumont and Fletcher, who are said by Aubrey to have shared both a house and a woman. Margaret Hotine also seeks identification of a character in Jonson in her 'Ben Jonson, Volpone and Charterhouse' (*N&Q* 38.79–81), returning to the oft cited link between Volpone and Thomas Sutton, the founder of Charterhouse, now reinforced by newly-found references to one 'Johnson' in Sutton's papers. To complete the picture, there is further interest in *Volpone* in a chapter in Joan Lord Hall's *The Dynamics of Role-Playing in Jacobean Tragedy*, a fine example of the conservatism of Jonson criticism, as she pieces together insights into Volpone's true nature, noting the ambivalence of Jonson's attitude towards his protagonist, which other critics spotted many moons ago. In contrast, two reviews of the English Shakespeare Company's 1990 production of *Volpone* directed by Tim Luscombe, one by P. J. Smith (*CahiersE* 39.75–7), the other by Murray Biggs (*ShakB* 9.13–14) celebrate Luscombe's innovative, anarchic interpretation of the play, while noting that this modernized version has trouble coping with the sub-plot and with the more tragic elements of Jonson's vision. One final note is Gilian West's 'Bartholomew Cokes' (*N&Q* 38.514), which draws attention to the inevitability of Cokes's painful career in the fair, given the nature of the parallel life of the saint whose name he shares.

(d) Other Playwrights and Plays

If there is increasing evidence this year of a backlash against New Historicist and cultural materialist approaches to the drama of the period, (see, for example, articles by Yachnin, section (a) above, and Howard-Hills below), feminism, perhaps because it is able to accommodate a wide range of critical perspectives, continues to provide illumination. Carolyn Whitney Brown's challenging article from the feminist collection edited by D. Kehler and S. Baker, *In Another Country: Feminist Perspectives on Renaissance Drama*, ' "A Farre more Worthy Wombe": Reproductive Anxiety in Peele's *David and Bethsabe*' uses a textual fragment as a starting-point to develop a complex reading in terms of 'male self-replication'; the play's focus on the centrality of the David–Absalom relationship constructs female sexuality as a source of anxiety in a patriarchal society where the monarchy is dependent on a 'worthy womb' for its continuation. Whitney Brown supports her reading with reference to contemporary theories of reproduction, and suggests that the David–Absalom situation reproduces the relationship between Elizabeth I and Mary Queen of Scots. Even if one cannot accept all aspects of this article, its ambitiously wide scope is worthy of admiration. *Arden of Faversham*, another play of much interest to feminists, is discussed by David Attwell in 'Property, Status, and the Subject in a Middle-Class Tragedy: *Arden of Faversham*' (*ELR* 21.328–48). This, too, is a full and complex piece; it offers an intelligent critique of Belsey's influential reading of the play in *The Subject of Tragedy* (*YWES* 66.249), arguing that Alice's adulterous behaviour and her fate represent not so much a stage in the process from 'feudal' marriage (with Arden) to 'liberal marriage' (with Mosbie) as changing attitudes to the social value of landed property in conferring power. According to this view the play is more concerned with property relations than with resistance to the tyranny of a patriarchalist marriage.

Apart from this, domestic tragedy hasn't attracted much attention this year. The other article, Michael Wentworth's 'Thomas Heywood's *A Woman Killed with Kindness* as Domestic Morality' (in *Traditions and Innovations: Essays on British Literature of the Middle Ages and the Renaissance*, edited by D. Allen and R. White) rehearses a familiar view of the play as a paradigm of the Fall and the Redemption, with Anne as sinner and Frankford as Christlike redeemer, a very conventional reading by the standards of Belsey or Attwell.

Marston's work is featured in two contrasting articles. Susan Baker's 'Sex and Marriage in *The Dutch Courtesan*', from *In Another Country: Feminist Perspectives on Renaissance Drama*, examines the representation of marriage within a rather narrow conceptual framework which opposes the 'humanist' view of marriage (exemplified in Beatrice and Freevill) to the Puritan view (in Crispinella and Tysefew). She argues that the play's sexual anxieties are pervasive and not purely centred on Malheureux, and that to naturalize the Puritan or companiate marriage, as twentieth-century ideology does, is one way of addressing them. Rather outside the general trend of critical approaches this year is the other article on Marston, Brownell Salomon's 'The "Doubleness" of *The Malcontent* and Fairytale Form' (*Connotations* 1.150–63); this doubleness consists of the combination of a 'culturally serious' plot with an offhand satirical manner. The account of the play's 'witty histrionism' is more enlightening than its dissection of the plot-elements à la Propp in terms of the folktale paradigm of the Returning Hero.

There are two articles on Dekker, of which Julia Gasper's learned and detailed account of 'The Sources of *The Virgin Martyr*' (*ES* 72.17–31) makes an important contribution not only to Dekker studies but to our knowledge of the period more generally. She shows how Dekker and Massinger combined the legends of Saints Agnes and Dorothea, taking material from four Catholic martyrologies, but in particular William and Edward Kinsman's *Flos Sanctorum, The Lives of Saints* (1609). The evidence for widespread use by Protestants of Catholic source-material is fascinating in itself. Jeanne MacIntyre's 'Shore's Wife and *The Shoemakers' Holiday*' (*CahiersE* 39.17–28) is source-study of a different kind, in its account of the relationship of Hammon and Jane as a reworking of the story of Edward IV and Jane Shaw; the connections are feasible, but even so it seems heavy-handed to call this a 'disturbing and subversive' treatment of class relationships. The other contribution to Massinger studies this year is the latest volume in the Critical Heritage series, edited and with an introduction by Martin Garrett, a timely production in view of the attention recently accorded his work in the political reassessment of Jacobean and Caroline drama.

In line with the trend of recent years the focus on Webster's work is narrow – concentration on the two tragedies from a feminist angle. The one refreshing exception is Roy Booth's 'John Webster's Heart of Glass' (*English* 40.97–113), which illuminates the curious quality of Webster's imagination in a study of his references to glass-blowing. Otherwise, Laura Baker, again in *In Another Country: Feminist Perspectives on Renaissance Drama*, labours over 'The Rhetoric of Feminine Identity in *The White Devil*' to reveal the play as a feminist project in which Webster explores 'what it means to be a woman'. Christy Desmet, to better effect in ' "Neither Maid, Widow, nor Wife": The Rhetoric of Woman Controversy in *Measure for Measure* and *The Duchess of Malfi*', from the same collection, claims that Isabella and the Duchess are women whose moral lives confuse the boundaries between virtue and vice. She examines the rhetorical techniques in these plays to show they function in excluding women from the realm of moral agency; the arts of language operate as the property of men. Sara Jane Steen in 'The Crime of Marriage: Arbella Stuart and *The Duchess of Malfi*' (*SCJ* 22.61–76) provides much useful documentation of contemporary reactions to the Arbella Stuart affair, proving that there was sympathy as well as censure for her behaviour, and that some commentators on the affair set a high valuation on romantic love; but her assumption that we can therefore reasonably 'posit similar responses' to Webster's character is too bland and easy without a closer scrutiny of the representation of romantic love in Webster's text.

The continuing rise in Middleton's status is reflected in the large number of articles devoted to his work this year. Two of these are by T. H. Howard-Hill and deal with *A Game at Chesse*. In 'Political Interpretations of Middleton's *A Game at Chesse*' (*YES* 21.274–85), he argues against the theory that the play must have had an influential sponsor in order to get put on at all, refuting the now widely-held understanding of it as an 'instrument of state policy'. This is also the view of the play taken by Dutton and Yachnin (see section (a) above). In 'The Unique Eyewitness Report of Middleton's *A Game at Chesse*' (*RES* 42.168–78) he annotates a letter from John Holles to the Earl of Somerset, usefully elucidating some points of the play's staging in the process. James L. Helm, in 'Thomas Middleton and Renaissance Gerontology' (*CahiersE* 39.41–6), writes a learned and compressed piece on that interesting but rarely discussed play, *The Old Law*, relating it to Cicero's apology for old age, *Cato Maior*, and thus seeing it as a play which challenges the normal drive in comedy for youth to rout and defeat old age. Ingrid Holz-Davies in '*A Chaste Maid in Cheapside* and *Women Beware Women*: Feminism, Antifeminism, and the Limitations of Satire' (*CahiersE* 39.29–39) traces a misogynist subtext in both plays, sensibly suggesting that in *Women Beware Women* Isabella's willingness to marry the Ward after all constitutes an evasion of the feminist position on forced marriage sometimes deduced from her speeches; she is less convincing in her view that the difference between the plays may reveal a maturation in Middleton's attitude to women. Fumiko Takase's more conventionally handled article 'Thomas Middleton's Antifeminist Sentiment in *A Mad World, My Masters*' (in Brink and Horowitz's *Playing with Gender. A Renaissance Pursuit*) defines the play's viewpoint as totally masculinist in its identification between 'lust for women and lust for money', its twin themes. Edward Jones on 'The Confined world of *The Changeling*' (*CahiersE* 39.47–55) rehearses familiar notions of the pervasiveness of the concept of imprisonment in the play. Various notes on aspects of Middleton's work are produced by the following: Paul Mulholland, in 'A Source for the Painter Analogue in the Epilogue of *The Roaring Girl*' (*MLR* 86.817–20), which turns out ultimately to be Pliny; M. W. A. Smith, in 'The Authorship of *The Revenger's Tragedy*' (*N&Q* 38.508–13), who tests the play by computer-aided stylistic techniques against texts by Marston and *The Atheist's Tragedy*, confirming Middleton as a more likely author than Tourneur; and finally R.V. Holdsworth in an interesting discussion of 'The Date of *Hengist, King of Kent*' (*N&Q* 38.516–19), who finds echoes of other plays including *The Duchess of Malfi* and Fletcher's *The Wild-Goose Chase*, and plumps for *c.*1620–2.

Plays from the Beaumont and Fletcher canon have been the subject of some good work this year. Stephan Kukowski provides a provocative discussion of a little-read play in 'The Hand of John Fletcher in *The Double Falsehood*' (*ShS* 43.81–9); the stylistic evidence he reveals for Fletcher's contribution to this text convincingly refutes the accepted view of it as a forgery in Shakespeare's style by Theobald, and thus opens up many new approaches to the play in its own right. Richard Hillman's article on the best-known Shakespeare–Fletcher collaboration, 'Shakespeare's Romantic Innocents and the Misappropriation of the Romance Past: The Case of *The Two Noble Kinsmen*' (*ShS* 43.69–79) finds a way of reading the 'tensions and inconsistencies' of the collaborate text functionally, as productive of radical discontinuities in the treatment of romance that take the play well beyond its Chaucerian source. Laurie E. Osborne's account of 'Female Audiences and Female Authority in *The Knight of the Burning Pestle*' (*Exemplaria* 3.491–517) demonstrates brilliantly how illuminating a feminist reading can sometimes be. Her examination of Nell's role as internal audience reveals not only how the audience's perspective is deliberately masculinized but also how her reactions expose and compromise the patriarchal conventions operating within the internal plays. The article also provides valuable support for the notion that women were regarded as a significant constituent of theatre audiences. Hans Werner argues chancily in a short article, 'A Caricature and Self-portrait of the Beaumont and Fletcher Partnership in Jonson's *Bartholomew Fair* and Fletcher's *The Chances*' (*N&Q* 38.516–19) that Damon and Pythias in Jonson's play and Don John and Don Frederic in Fletcher's represent versions of the 'great pair of authors'; but this is to suppose that posthumous evaluations of the relationship held good in the playwrights' own times, which there is no reason to assume.

Reid Barbour in his overview of 'Recent Studies in John Ford, 1977–89' (*ELR* 21.102–17) traces a movement away from concentration on moral dilemmas in Ford's plays to one on their 'occasions and contexts'. This is not, however, entirely borne out by the two articles on Ford this year. William D. Dyer in 'Holding/Witholding Environments: A Psychoanalytical Approach to Ford's *The Broken Heart*' (*ELR* 21.401–24) explores the idea of split characters and self-division in the play in relation to psychoanalytic theory; he does bring out the 'code of inner suppression', and the disastrous consequences for the characters who uphold it, but this is not new. Nathaniel Strout's 'The Tragedy of Annabella in *'Tis Pity She's a Whore*' (in *Traditions and Innovations: Essays on British Literature of the Middle Ages and the Renaissance*) makes a determined effort to see the play as an Aristotelian tragedy centred on Annabella, who is victimised both in spite and because of her extreme deference to masculine authority; the attention to gender questions in the play is welcome even if the moral perspective is conventional.

To conclude are two further articles of specifically feminist interest. Nancy A. Gutierrez turns her attention to that increasingly popular play, Elizabeth Cary's *Mariam*, in 'Valuing *Mariam*: Genre Study and Feminist Analysis' (*TSWL* 10.233–57). She is not entirely persuasive in claiming the play as 'a highly sophisticated literary exercise' as well as a political statement; and though she makes some effective points about the status of closet drama as participating in both political and sexual discourse, her actual discussion of the text is too generalized entirely to sustain her reading. Kim Walker in 'New Prison: Representing the Female Actor in Shirley's *The Bird in a Cage* (1633)' (*ELR* 21.385–400) locates the play in a context of concern with the female actor and argues cogently that Shirley's 'uneasy' treatment of her, though attempting to confer authority on her, in fact 'recuperates her for patriarchy'.

Books Reviewed

Allen, D. G., and R. A. White, eds. *Traditions and Innovations: Essays on British Literature of the Middle Ages and the Renaissance*. UDelP. £32.50. ISBN 0 874 13355 6.

Bradley, David. *From Text to Performance in the Elizabethan Theatre: Preparing the Play for the Stage*. CUP. pp. 272. £35.00. ISBN 0 521 39466X.

Brady, Jennifer, and W. H. Herendeen, eds. *Ben Jonson's 1616 Folio*. UDelP. pp. 221. £26.50. ISBN 0 87413 384 X.

Brink, Jean R., and Maryanne C. Horowitz, eds. *Playing with Gender. A Renaissance Pursuit*. UIllP. pp. 200. $24.95. ISBN 0 252 01764 1.

Cartelli, Thomas. *Marlowe, Shakespeare and the Economy of Theatrical Experience*. UPennP. pp. 241. £35.00. ISBN 0 8122 3102 3.

Corbin, Peter, and Douglas Sedge, eds. *The Oldcastle Controversy: Sir John Oldcastle, Part I/The Famous Victories of Henry V*. RevelsCL Series. ManUP. pp. 253. £35.00. ISBN 0 7190 2693 8.

Dabbs, Thomas. *Reforming Marlowe: The Nineteenth Century Canonization of a Renaissance Dramatist*. AUP. pp. 170. £22.00. ISBN 0 8387 5192.

Dutton, Richard. *Mastering the Revels: The Regulation and Censorship of English Renaissance Drama*. Macmillan. pp. 305. £45.00. ISBN 0 333 45371 9.

Edelman, Charles. *Brawl Ridiculous: Swordfighting in Shakespeare's Plays*. ManUp. pp 218. £35.00 ISBN 0 7190 3507 4.

Fothergill-Payne, Louise, and Peter Fothergill-Payne, eds. *Parallel Lives: Spanish and English National Drama 1580–1680*. AUP. pp. 329. £35.00. ISBN 0 8387 5194 6.

Gair, W. Reavely, ed. *'Antonio and Mellida' by John Marston*. RevelsCL Series. ManUP. pp. 170. £35.00. ISBN 0 7190 1547 2.

Gardner-Medwin, Alisoun, and Janet Hadley Williams, eds. *A Day Estivall: Essays on the Music, Poetry and History of Scotland and England & Poems Previously Unpublished in Honour of Helena Mennie Shire*. AberdeenUP (1990). pp. 184. £29.95. ISBN 0 08 040914 8.

Garret, Martin, ed. *Massinger*. Routledge. pp. 288. £65. ISBN 0 415 03340 3.

Hall, Joan Lord. *The Dynamics of Role-Playing in Jacobean Tragedy*. Macmillan. pp. 241. £40.00. ISBN 0 333 49975 1.

Hunter, George K., and David Bevington, eds. *'Campaspe'/'Sappho and Phao' by John Lyly*. RevelsCL Series. ManUP. pp. 307. £40.00. ISBN 0 7190 1550 2.

Kehler, D., and S. Baker, eds. *In Another Country: Feminist Perspectives in Renaissance Drama*. Scarecrow. pp. 345. £37.50. ISBN 0 810 824183.

Knutson, Roslyn Lander. *The Repertory of Shakespeare's Company 1594–1613*. UArkP. pp. 252. $32.00. ISBN 1 55728 191 2.

McMullan, Gordon, and Jonathan Hope, eds. *The Politics of Tragicomedy: Shakespeare and After*. Routledge. pp. 240. £35. ISBN 0 415 06403 1.

Mulryne, J. R., ed. *Theatre of the English and Italian Renaissance*. Macmillan. pp. 250. £47.50. ISBN 0 333 48588 2.

Proudfoot, G. R., ed. *Tom a Lincoln*. Malone. OUP. pp. 96. £17.50. ISBN 0 19 729030 2.

Sales, Roger. *Christopher Marlowe*. English Dramatists Series. Macmillan. pp. 177. hb £30. pb £9.50. ISBN 0 333 4535 1.

Smith, Molly. *The Darker World Within: Evil in the Tragedies of Shakespeare and his Successors*. UDelP. £35. ISBN 0 874 13400 5.

Teague, Francis. *Shakespeare's Speaking Properties*. AUP. pp. 222. £28.50. ISBN 0 8387 5208 X.

Wells, Stanley, ed. *Shakespeare Survey 43*. CUP. pp. 281. £35.00. ISBN 0 521 39529 1.

Wiggins, Martin. *Journeymen in Murder: The Assassin in English Renaissance Drama*. OUP. pp. 248. £32.50. ISBN 0 198 11228 9.

IX

The Earlier Seventeenth Century: Excluding Drama

MELANIE HANSEN

This chapter has three sections: 1. General; 2. Poetry; 3. Prose.

1. General

There have been a number of general studies published this year. The first is John M. Steadman's *Redefining a Period Style: 'Renaissance', 'Mannerist' and 'Baroque' in Literature.* This is a densely written study that seeks to challenge 'current assumptions concerning the interrelationships between our concepts of historical periods and the criteria we commonly employ to define and differentiate varieties of literary style'. Steadman identifies a disparity between modern and Renaissance perceptions of 'style', and particularly in the slide between verbal and visual arts, and he argues for a re-examination of the central terms of 'Renaissance', 'Mannerist' and 'Baroque' in order to reveal more clearly their Renaissance critical formulations. The more general analysis of style and sensibility in the classification of historical periods is explored in the first part of the book, while the second concentrates on the baroque and the metaphysical in Renaissance poetry. Also with definitions of cultural criteria very much in mind is Patricia Fumerton's thought-provoking and engaging *Cultural Aesthetics: Renaissance Literature and the Practice of Social Ornament.* Fumerton offers a postmodernist critique of Renaissance aristocratic subjectivity, a critique that examines 'the life of subjectivity caught in the trival intersection between the historical and the aesthetic'. She argues that there is a relationship between the 'trivial' (that is the 'fragmentary, peripheral, and ornamental' constituted by the aesthetic artifacts of gifts and miniature painting, banquets and 'child-giving', masques and sonnets) and the simultaneous construction and fragmentation of aristocratic self-hood. Interweaved in this examination of subjectivity is a continual engagement with contemporary critical and cultural studies; in particular, Fumerton takes issue with attacks on the New Historicist method of employing 'paradigms' as a form of analysis by arguing that 'the moment of fragmentary history I seek to elucidate saturates cultural and literary history even in its quietest and smallest events'. Tessa Watt's *Cheap Print and Popular Piety, 1550–1640* is a fascinating survey and analysis of the production and dissemination of broadside ballads and pictures during the Renaissance. It is divided into three sections. The first examines the broadside ballad as song, the second explores the broadside ballad as a picture for decoration of domestic walls, and the third considers the development of cheap print for popular consumption. Watts situates her survey with reference to critical debates surrounding the assessment of literacy and the development of Protestantism as it affected literacy rates, together with analysis of the cultural implications of the 'popular'. Also included in this study are a range of illustrations and detailed bibliographic references.

Praise Disjoined: Changing Patterns of Salvation in Seventeenth-Century English Literature is a collection of essays edited by William P. Shaw and is part of the Seventeenth-Century Texts and Studies Series. The project of this series is to employ a variety of critical and historical methods in focusing primarily on poetry and prose, a project that defines the scope of this collection of essays. These essays examine a wide range of texts, from Hobbes's *Leviathan* to the poetry of Jonson, Donne and Herbert, to childbearing sermons and the language of herbalism and medical botany. The method of these essays is interdisciplinary, concerned with the 'historical, social, philosophical, religious, and literary activity of the period', and the focus is that of a revisionist examination of the nature of salvation and damnation in a variety of seventeenth-century texts. The essays illustrate the way in which 'individuals and groups ... felt the need to renegotiate their relationship with God and with the principles and practices of the established church and state'.

Also wide ranging is Margaret L. King's *Women of the Renaissance*, which charts the condition of Western European women from 1350–1650, although these dates are only loosely imposed. King displays an impressive range of information, using materials derived from literary texts, parish records, and letters, women's autobiographies and journals. This formidable accumulation of research material is organized under three main headings: women and the family, the church, and high culture. In this way, King is able to negotiate with women from very different religious, political and class backgrounds. In Geoffrey G. Hiller's ' "Where thou doost Live, There let all Graces be": Images of the Renaissance Woman Patron in her House and Rural Domain' (*CE* 40.37–51), however, it is aristocratic women who provide the central area of concern. Hiller explores the representation of women patrons, focusing particularly on Mary Sidney and Lucy, Countess of Bedford. Through examining a range of dedicatory material, Hiller attempts to identify both the construction of the patroness as a fictional ideal and the definitions of patronage as conceptualized by dedicatees. Continuing the examination of women's lives, W. R. Prest's 'Law and Women's Rights in Early Modern England' (*SC* 6.169–87) investigates the relationship between women and the common law. This is a welcome investigation that seeks to question the prevalent critical concern with the distinction between idealized and prescriptive statements about women's legal position and what effect those idealizations had on everyday lives. Prest attempts to gauge the possibilities of women's potential exploitation of the law during this period, noting that between 1613 and 1714, approximately a quarter of all Chancery suits involved women as principal plaintiffs. Exploring the legal situation in England from a different perspective, Richard Helgerson's 'Writing against Writing: Humanism and the Form of Coke's *Institutes*' (*MLQ* 51.224–48), situates Coke's contribution to Elizabethan and Jacobean writing of English law within the vigorous Renaissance formal and linguistic debate on Roman and common law. Helgerson argues that Coke's *Institutes*, far from being the product of intense insularity, were instead a 'self presentational strategy', produced by a 'constant sense of legal and national difference, a persistent awareness of a rival system of law against which English law had to define itself.' Consequently, Helgerson suggests that the writing of law which Coke's *Institutes* represent was both determined by the formal qualities of Roman law and emerged from a nationalist need for an English law.

Andrew Mousley's thought-provoking article, 'Self, State, and Seventeenth Century News' (*SC* 6.149–68) explores the production of 'news' as a problematic form of knowledge during this period. Focusing on the newsletters and books of John Pory, Walter Yonge and John Rous, Mousley questions the production and consumption of news in relation to identity and social position, individual and state, locality and nationality. Mousley's detailed reading of these texts suggests that, for him, seventeenth-century news should not be viewed as a ' "system" of information abstracted from the lives of individuals' but rather, as a 'practice pressing upon individuals these questions of their allegiance and location, within the changing social relationships of the period.' In 'Wizards and Magicians in the King James Old Testament' (*SC* 6.1–10), David H. Darst and Steven L. Jeffers engage with the problem that the translators of the King James Bible faced with the translation and classification of Hebrew occult terminology. That the translators employed entirely new terms, 'wizards' and 'magicians', in place of the occult terminology of previous versions, illustrates for Darst and Jeffers the translators' scientific approach to the original Hebrew texts, their attempt to 'rationalize and formalise the Old Testament text and the beliefs presented there' with the ultimate aim of denouncing natural magic.

There are two articles concentrating on the use of emblems this year. Lyndy Abraham's ' "The Lovers and the Tomb": Alchemical Emblems in Shakespeare, Donne and Marvell' (*Embl* 5.301–20), examines a number of emblems of 'the lovers and the tomb' which refer to the Renaissance alchemical process of 'opus', the dissolution of the old into the new and pure, and identifies in Shakespeare's *Romeo and Juliet*, Donne's *Songs and Sonnets* and Marvell's 'To His Coy Mistress' references to this interweaving of emblem and alchemical process. In 'The English Civil War Flags: Emblematic Devices and Propaganda' (*Embl* 5.341–56), Alan R. Young illustrates the way in which the emblematic devices of tournaments were appropriated in the civil war period by each of the warring factions. These emblematic flags played a significant part in the ideological battlefield articulated by a whole variety of texts, pamphlets, petitions, sermons, speeches and ballads.

2. Poetry

Cleanth Brooks's *Historical Evidence and the Reading of Seventeenth-Century Poetry* is a series of studies of individual poems designed to show 'the bearing of historical fact on aesthetic judgement'. These amount to 'close readings', some previously published, of a number of short or shortish works by minor poets of the seventeenth century: Henry King, Richard Corbett, James Shirley, Aurelian Townshend, Richard Fanshawe, Lord Herbert of Cherbury, Richard Lovelace, and – the one figure currently enjoying more than minor status – Marvell. These readings are linked to the more abstract questions Brooks is interested in: how biographical knowlege might affect evaluative assessment, or what significance should be attached to 'reader response'. This combination of purposes creates something of a problem: the close readings do shed light on some important and interesting poems, without getting bogged down in minutiae (some essays even manage without footnotes); but on the general questions Brooks has nothing to add to previous debates except more examples. For the specialist, then, this is a volume to browse in for information, rather than to be pondered as an argument. As for the non-specialist reader of Shirley, Townshend, et al. such a figure now belongs strictly to the realms of nostalgia.

A. J. Smith's densely written study, *Metaphysical Wit*, follows on from his earlier discussions of 'metaphysical sentience' in Renaissance poetry in *Literary Love* (1983) and *The Metaphysics of Love* (1985). Focusing on the significance of wit for the metaphysical poets, Smith explores formal theories prevalent during the European Renaissance, theories which were to have such a profound effect on poets like Donne and Marvell. He concludes his study with an investigation of the demise of metaphysical wit during the 1660s, suggesting that this demise coincided with the emergence of empirical science. In *The Catholic Religious Poets from Southwell to Crashaw: A Critical Study*, Anthony D. Cousins argues for a critical re-evaluation of Catholic poets as a distinct political as well as a religious group. Cousins suggests that these poets should be situated much more precisely within Reformation and Counter-Reformation devotional literary traditions, and his first chapter delineates theories of plain style, the emblem and meditation as they relate to the Catholic poets. The largest part of this book is taken up with close analysis of individual poets (Robert Southwell, Henry Constable, William Alabaster, Sir John Beaumont, William Habington) and a final chapter is devoted to the most well-known figure, Richard Crashaw.

Soliciting Interpretation: Literary Theory and Seventeenth-Century English Poetry, edited by Elizabeth D. Harvey and Katharine Eisaman Maus, is a pivotal collection of essays for Renaissance studies, one that seeks to draw out the relationship between literature and history. Whilst these essays might be broadly considered as 'New Historicist', the collection does not present a homogenous group of approaches but rather seeks to question and 'disturb' the way in which we read Renaissance texts. It is divided into three sections: the first questions 'the ways in which a literary text can be "political" ' in the writings of Jonson, Donne, Milton and Marvell; the second considers seventeenth-century textual production and reception through Shakespeare, Milton and more generally, Jacobean poetry; and the third discusses 'the particular forms of anxiety that result when seventeenth-century poets modify the traditional rhetoric of sexual desire to serve what seem to be new erotic or religious purposes.' This final section focuses on Donne, Herbert and Mary Wroth. This is a radical collection which will, undoubtedly, become required reading for any student of this period.

The increasing availability of the extensive writing of Mary Wroth has attracted welcome critical attention in a collection of essays edited by Naomi J. Miller and Gary Waller, *Reading Mary Wroth: Representing Alternatives in Early Modern England*. The essays draw upon a range of critical approaches, feminist, New Historicist and psychoanalytic, and the collection is divided into four sections. The first considers the personal and the family constraints against Wroth as a writer; the second situates the huge variety of Wroth's work – poetry, prose, drama – within its literary and cultural contexts; the third considers her work in relation to other writers, Veronica Franco and Shakespeare; and the final section 'examines definitions of female subjectivity, scrutinizing the relation between reading, writing, and gender in Wroth's inscription of her own discourse of sexual difference.' This is a far-reaching and challenging collection of essays, much needed by researchers and students. Admirable work on Renaissance women writers continues with Wendy Wall's 'Isabella Whitney and the Female Legacy' (*ELH* 58.35–62); Wall argues that Whitney's poetry counters class and gender restrictions against publishing and extends the boundaries of the complaint genre by referring to the rhetoric of will-making. This rhetoric, which created a powerful subject position from which to speak, was to provide an important empowering technique for seventeenth-century writers of mothers' advice books. Responding to the increasing need for a variorum edition of Katherine Philips, Claudia A. Limbert's 'The Poetry of Katherine Philips: Holographs, Manuscripts, and Early Printed Texts' (*PQ* 70.ii.181–98) examines the reliability of the holographs, manuscripts and early printed texts. Limbert outlines a list in order of reliability of the six primary sources of Philips's work (one holograph, three manuscript, two printed), adding to this an examination of four smaller collections (two holograph and two manuscript) and sixteen other manuscript sources.

On Jonson this year, James A. Riddell in 'A Previously Unnoticed Source for a Poem by Ben Jonson' (*JDJ* 7.123–4) points out the similarities and discrepancies between Jonson's 'On Groyne' and Martial's XII.16, noting that the discrepancy lies in the former's transformation of a homosexual to a heterosexual subject. And in 'Jonson's "To Penshurst": The Country House as Church' (*JDJ* 7.73– 89), Richard Harp takes issue with economic readings of 'To Penshurst' to claim that the poem celebrates the divine source of 'a "magical" nature' in which Penshurst as a church is situated. Drawing on Renaissance scriptural exegesis, Harp argues that the poem 'embodies a moving contemplative vision' that glances back to Jonson's Catholicism and forward to his enthusiastic Anglicanism.

Herbert studies have been much enhanced this year with Michael C. Schoenfeldt's *Prayer and Power: George Herbert and Renaissance Courtship*. This is a searching and wide-ranging study that examines Herbert's poetry and prose, letters and speeches with reference to courtesy literature and particularly to the preoccupation manifested in conduct material with notions of class and which critics such as Frank Whigham have identified. Through his incisive analysis, Schoenfeldt argues succinctly that Herbert's writing reveals an explicit engagement with formulations of proper conduct and with the concepts of selfhood, authority and discourses of power that such formulations expressed. As a result, Schoenfeldt demonstrates the way in which, rather than understanding Herbert's writing as directly influenced by courtesy literature, instead, 'courtesy literature textualizes the social conduct that Herbert's poems bend to God.' More general in focus is Douglas Thorpe's *A New Earth: The Labor of Language in 'Pearl', Herbert's 'The Temple' and Blake's 'Jerusalem'*. This study concentrates on two main issues: the first is the use of metaphor as a means of articulating the relationship between body and spirit and the second explores the preoccupation with concepts of labour as expressed by each of these poets.

In addressing the vexed question of meditation and mysticism in Herbert's poetry, William R. Miller's 'Herbert's Approach to God in "The Bag" ' (*ELR* 21.38–44) argues that 'The Bag' 'stands as a strange yet challenging record of Herbert's individual "via" and the emphasis he placed upon the poem as a means of religious quest'. Sidney Gottlieb considers Herbert's influence on mid- and late-seventeenth-century Royalist panegyrics and apologists in 'A Royalist Rewriting of George Herbert: *His Majesties Complaint to his Subjects* (1647)' (*MP* 89.211–24) and in order to illustrate this influence, Gottlieb reprints the anonymous poem, *His Majesties Complaint*. He argues convincingly that the poem can demonstrate how Herbert's use of non-topical imagery and dramatic refrain patterns could be deployed to create sympathy for King Charles, suggesting further that in its use of this imagery and refrain pattern, the poem draws on Herbert's 'The Sacrifice' and 'The Thanksgiving'. Comparisons continue in 'Donne and Herbert: Vehement Grief and Silent Tears' (*JDJ* 7.21–34), where Louis L. Martz, commenting on a range of poems by Donne and Herbert, addresses the difference in approach in their otherwise common thematic use of sighs and tears.

Yet another edition of Donne's poetry directed towards a student audience is *John Donne: Selected Poems*, edited by Richard Gill. It is divided essentially into three parts: the first contains the *Songs and Sonnets* and a selection of elegies and religious poems; the second, detailed notes on each poem, and the third, an approach to the poetry which situates it within literary and historical contexts. Mary Ann Radzinowicz in 'The Politics of John Donne's Silences' (*JDJ* 7.1–19) confronts the problem of reading Donne's poetry politically, focusing on four forms of political silence, 'Donne's silence about England's colonization of America, about her pacification of Ireland, about the sociopolitical role of exceptional women, and in English about other poets'. Radzinowicz negotiates with these silences through the interpretative models of coterie, censorship and 'the literary heritage'.

Three individual studies have appeared this year: Helen B. Brooks in ' "Soules Language": Reading Donne's "The Extasie" ' (*JDJ* 7.47–63) gives a detailed and incisive analysis of 'The Extasie', identifying 'significant parallels between the poem's epistemology of love and Aristotle's theory of cognition' as described in the *Metaphysica* and *De Anima*, and employing Wolfgang Iser's conception of the dynamics of reading in order to negotiate with the way in which Donne challenges expressions of love. Dennis Flynn's ' "Awry and Squint": the Dating of Donne's Holy Sonnets' (*JDJ* 7.35–46) addresses the persistent and vexed question of dating these poems. Challenging Helen Gardner's theory by suggesting that it is determined by stereotypical biography and a paucity of evidence, Flynn argues that 'several possible scenarios for their composition ought to be entertained', including the possibility of the 1590s as the date of composition. Distancing her analysis of Donne's poetry from biographical criticism, Sallye Sheppeard in 'Eden and Agony in "Twicknam Garden"' (*JDJ* 7.65–72) offers a thought-provoking reading of the poem which suggests that, far from expressing bitterness, 'Donne's speaker emerges as no ordinary loser in the game of courtly love but as a self-professed self deceiver who suffers self-inflicted misery.'

Critical responses to Thomas Docherty's analysis of Donne's poetry also continue with Bernard Richards's acerbic note in 'Donne's "Air and Angels": A Gross Misreading' (*JDJ* 7.i.119–24) that Docherty's reading of this poem fails to 'elucidate, make sense of or throw light on "Air and Angels" – it is nothing more than an impertinent critical excrescence.' Richards suggests that if there is a pun on pinnace/penis as contended by Docherty, then 'pinnace' is most likely to refer to a prostitute. Finally, John T. Shawcross' 'On Some Early References to John Donne' (*JDJ* 7.i.115–17) identifies six further references which can be added to A. J. Smith's *Critical Heritage of John Donne* (1975); and Mary Arshagouni's 'The Latin "Stationes" in John Donne's *Devotions upon Emergent Occasions*' (*MP* 89.ii.196–210) examines the relationship between the Latin head notes and the *Devotions*, questioning their status in explicating the text as a whole.

A. B. Chambers's *Andrew Marvell and Edmund Waller: Seventeenth-Century Praise and Restoration Satire*, is the first new treatment of the latter poet to appear for quite some time, and might thus have been expected to attempt a major rehabilitation of Waller. The discussions of the two Waller poems Chambers is interested in are expository rather than critical, however, though he does attempt to refocus our sights away from Waller the 'polisher of platitudes' – a figure he has as little time for as most of us. Instead, Chambers turns to Waller the political poet-satirist, giving very detailed attention to the Restoration works *On St James's Park* and *Instructions to a Painter*. Chambers's expositions of these poems, and of Marvell's *Last Instructions to a Painter*, are *tours de force* of ingenuity and erudition, but do not in themselves change one's estimate of either poet, and tend at times to be self-indulgent. There are also accounts of the other 'Advice to a Painter' poems which immediately followed Waller's; a chapter-long discussion of the hoary textual crux 'dew/glew/hue' in *To His Coy Mistress*; and a conclusion vaguely linking Waller's and Marvell's satires on Charles II to Dryden's.

The huge generic and subject range of the 1,130 poems of Robert Herrick's *Hesperides* receive extensive critical examination in *GHJ* 14.i and ii. This welcome collection of essays, introduced by Ann Baynes Coiro, whose *Robert Herrick's 'Hesperides' and the Epigram Book Tradition* (*YWES* 70.323) threw critical light on this poet, acknowledges Herrick as the 'poet of anxiety', the 'great major minor Poet of the seventeenth century', the poet who is both the 'most classical of English Renaissance poets' and yet the 'most eerily modern'. It is this complexity of Herrick's work and our critical response to it that provides the starting point for each of the essays in this issue. Jonathan F. S. Post begins the debate in 'Robert Herrick: A Minority Report' (*GHJ* 14.1–22) by maintaining that Herrick's social standing as goldsmith and parson meant that he 'found it difficult to be anything but revering of English custom and tradition; traditions which Herrick evoked and interlaced with classicism in his lyrics'. More thought-provoking, however, is Mary Thomas Crane's 'Herrick's Cultural Materialism' (*GHJ* 14.21–50) which problematizes Herrick's occupations of goldsmith and educated parson, occupations that enabled the poet to experience different cultural contexts and which subsequently produced a certain ambivalence in his poetry. Engaging with critical debate that interprets Herrick's work as mere Royalist propaganda and taking issue with theories of history that erase individual agency, Crane offers an incisive analysis that identifies Herrick's obsession with transitions and the grotesque. Also arguing against Herrick as monolithic Royalist, Katharine Wallingford's ' "Corinna", Carlomaria, the Book of Sports and the Death of Epithalamium on the Field of Genre' (*GHJ* 14.97–112) suggests that 'Corrina's going a Maying' counters the myth of the ideal marriage between Charles and Henrietta Maria and in doing so, destabilizes the epithalamium as a genre, as the ideals that genre articulated evaporated through increasing political turmoil. Continuing this engagement with revisionist readings, Michael C. Schoenfeldt's 'The Art of Disgust: Civility and the Social Body in *Hesperides*' (*GHJ* 14.128–54) offers a fascinating analysis which confronts the paradoxical status of the *Hesperides* as simultaneously obsessed with 'microphilia' while being contained within a 'messy and sprawling book'. Schoenfeldt focuses on Herrick's preoccupation with bodily functions as they conflict with notions of class, arguing convincingly that like conduct manuals, the obsession with grotesque forms and functions in the *Hesperides* reveals 'the implicit violence on which the very criterion of elegance depends'. Less convincing is William Kerrigan's 'Kiss Fancies in Robert Herrick' (*GHJ* 14.155–71); although Kerrigan engages with the problematic formulations of eroticism in Herrick's poetry, focusing on the epigrams which reveal 'how civilization shapes, and is shaped by, erotic fantasy', the complex interplay of desire and sexuality is never fully confronted.

Concentrating on Herrick's New Year poems, five appearing in the *Noble Numbers* and three in the *Hesperides*, Janie Caves McCauley's detailed readings in 'On the "Childhood of the Yeare": Herrick's *Hesperides* New Year Poems' (*GHJ* 14.72–96), suggests that these personal gift poems offer spiritual solace to social and political conflict. Claude J. Summers's 'Tears for Herrick's Church' (*GHJ* 14.51–71) concentrates on the *Noble Numbers* as an 'important contribution to the literature of Anglican survivalism' and as an expression of Herrick's concern with the persecution of the Established Church by the Parliamentarians. Through his detailed analysis of 'The Widdows teares', Summers illustrates how the poem is a culmination of a 'lamentation for the demise of the British Church as Herrick had known it'. Crys Armbrust's 'Robert Herrick and Nineteenth Century Periodical Publication: *The Gentleman's Magazine* and *The National: A Library for the People*' (*GHJ* 14.133–26) argues that scant critical attention has been paid to the recovery of Herrick's work in the nineteenth century, a recovery that appropriated the poet in terms of antiquarian and gentry class concerns in *The Gentleman's Magazine* and as romantic lyricist in *The National*. The collection of essays concludes with Leah S. Marcus's 'Afterword: Herrick and Historicism' (*GHJ* 14.172–7). Reflecting on the emergence of New Historicism which enabled the reclaiming and resituating of Herrick's work within its political context, noting how current critical debate reveals 'the ways in which *Hesperides* undermines its own apparent Laudian and Caroline "line" ', Marcus points towards a new range of questions that such reconceptualization of Herrick has facilitated.

In ' "Wee, of th'adult'rate mixture not complaine": Thomas Carew and Poetic Hybridity' (*JDJ* 7.91–113), Reid Barbour explores what he perceives as three related constituents of Carew's poetry. Referring to a range of poetic material, Barbour argues that Carew's aesthetic derives from his engagement with the lyric, that 'Carew's elegies and lyrics provide a site at which Caroline culture can display, yet also revaluate its reliance on ornamental surfaces' and finally, that Carew pursued and refashioned the hybrid genre.

Intended to 'combine a topical review of research with a reasonably complete bibliography', John R. Roberts's 'Recent Studies on Richard Crashaw (1977–1989)' (*ELR* 21.425–45) has compiled a comprehensive review of recent criticism which includes a section on the current state of the critical debate.

This year has seen a number of studies on a variety of poets. Glyn Pursglove's *Henry Reynolds: Tasso's 'Aminta' And Other Poems* brings to light the biography and poetry of a little known poet, friend of Drayton, Chapman and Henry King. Providing an introduction that outlines the bibliographic and manuscript evidence available, Pursglove also gives a detailed commentary on individual texts. David Norbrook's 'Levelling Poetry: George Wither and the English Revolution, 1642–1649' (*ELR* 21.217–56) offers a sophisticated reading of Wither's poetry that takes issue with interpretations of this poet as essentially conservative, producing orthodox Royalist propaganda. Instead, Norbrook argues convincingly that Wither 'played a significant part in the radicalization of politics in the 1640s, systematically reworking courtly models of poetic and political representation', a radical position that furthermore influenced John Lilburn and the Levellers.

Thomas Healy's 'Sound Physic: Phineas Fletcher's *The Purple Island* and the Poetry of Purgation' (*RS* 5.341–52) engages with the way in which Fletcher deploys medical discourses of anatomy, arguing firstly that in *The Purple Island* these discourses are used to affirm the priority of poetry to science, and secondly that, like the *Faerie Queene*, Fletcher's poem offers a critique of nationalist politics so that the 'scientific elucidation of the poem offers a medical prescription for reform through a distinctly militant Protestant purgation.' Stephen Clucas's 'Poetic Atomism in Seventeenth-Century England: Henry More, Thomas Traherne and "Scientific Imagination" ' (*RS* 5.327–40) explores the use of metaphors of the atom by both supporters and detractors of atomism. Through his somewhat schematic analysis of a range of texts by Donne, Greville, Browne, Dryden, Milton and Traherne, Clucas suggests that the 'radical instability of matter … its potential for disintegration and consolidation … were focal themes of pro- and anti-atomic discourses in the seventeenth century.'

Two final articles remain for this section: in 'Richard Corbett's "Against the opposing of the Duke in Parliament, 1628" and the anonymous rejoinder, "An Answere to the same, Lyne for Lyne": The Earliest Dated Manuscript copies' (*RES* 165.32–9) V. L. Pearl and M. L. Pearl reprint the two poems and date the composition of Corbett's 'Against the Opposing' between 17 March and 26 June 1628. Albert H. Tricomi's '*A Dialogue betweene Pollicy and Piety* by Robert Davenport' (*ELR* 21.190–216) reprints Davenport's 191 line dialogue adding a description of the date of composition (between 16 May 1634 and 1641, although he favours 1634/5) and a detailed analysis of the poem. Tricomi suggests that the dialogue might 'be called a religious-political dialogue since it treats allusively England's newly initiated policy of religious conversion and economic renewal in the Ireland of the 1630s'.

3. Prose

There are three book-length studies of individual authors, providing a valuable addition to our knowledge of Lancelot Andrewes, Richard Burton, and John Bunyan respectively. Bunyan has long been a figure of historical and literary interest, a fascinating individual who produced a huge variety of material and who is perceived by many as a primary figure in the development of a non-conformist counter-culture in England. The collection of essays edited by Anne Laurence, W. R. Owens and Stuart Sim, *John Bunyan and his England 1628–88*, responds to this complex figure by offering interdisciplinary readings of Bunyan's writings. The collection provides a formidable and challenging range of essays which consider Bunyan as soldier, dissenter and millenarian and his writings with reference to theology, selfhood and attitudes to women. E. Patricia Vicari's *The View from Minerva's Tower: Learning and Imagination in 'The Anatomy of Melancholy'* is a consummately written study of this most eclectic of seventeenth-century writers. Vicari examines the way in which Burton's *Anatomy* negotiates with different forms of knowledge, God, man and nature and she interweaves with this account a thought-provoking reading of its rhetorical strategies. Vicari argues lucidly that the *Anatomy*, in its expression of both personal and educated responses to melancholy, draws upon Baconian, homiletic and humanist modes of rhetoric, so that although the *Anatomy* 'never drops its guises of a manual of hygiene and a personal record of cure by recreation, it becomes more and more concerned with cure by conversion'. *Lancelot Andrewes the Preacher (1555–1626)* by Nicholas Lossky (translated by Andrew Louth) is a welcome investigation of this important Anglican preacher and theologian often neglected in favour of Richard Hookers. Lossky attempts to resituate Andrewes as a major Anglican figure by concentrating on the sermons given at court between 1605 and 1624. Lossky approaches these sermons by outlining the biography of Andrewes, and in subsequent chapters, examining them, through close critical reading, in relation to liturgical times of the year. Wider in focus is Anne Drury Hall's *Ceremony and Civility in English Renaissance Prose*, which explores four prose works, Thomas More's *History of King Richard III*, Philip Sidney's *Defense of Poetry*, Richard Hooker's *The Laws of Ecclesiastical Polity* and Thomas Browne's *Religio Medici*. Hall situates her study in terms of the recent debates surrounding the relationship between history and literature and, in particular, readings which prioritize either 'literary value' or post-Enlightenment values of the individual. She attempts to counter this by offering a model of reading that regards these prose writers as using 'tradition to bolster authority *and* that their version of tradition and authority deserve a hearing beyond the by-now standard attacks on their racism ... and colonialist repression.'

Two invaluable texts for students and teachers alike have appeared this year. The first is *An Anthology of Seventeenth-Century Prose Fiction* edited and introduced by Paul Salzman which reprints a 'representative sampling' of complete prose fiction texts by Mary Wroth, Percy Herbert, Margaret Cavendish, Thomas Dangerfield, John Bunyan, William Congreve and Aphra Behn. The introduction contextualizes this fiction with reference to theories of the novel and to seventeenth-century prose fiction, and gives a brief note on each text together with a select bibliography; explanatory notes are kept to a minimum. The second is D. J. H. Clifford's *The Diaries of Lady Anne Clifford*. While this text is primarily directed towards a more general audience (particularly the prologue), Clifford specifies the four manuscript sources for the diary of this increasingly well-known figure, and he appends a genealogy of the Clifford family, a transcript of 'The Knole Catelogue' and a select bibliography. The diary, which runs from 1603 to 1676, is an immensely important historical and literary record, not only for the remarkable Lady Anne Clifford herself but also as a key text for seventeenth-century study.

Continuing the trend for (re)printing primary material (also reflected in a number of articles published this year) is N. H. Keeble's and Geoffrey F. Nuttall's *Calendar of the Correspondence of Richard Baxter*, volume 1, 1638–1660. The letters contained in this volume not only reveal Baxter as an 'indefatigable correspondent' but also, they illustrate that the largest single group of Baxter's correspondents were men who 'having held benefices in the 1650s, became nonconformists after 1662'. The letters to Presbyterians, Independents and, less frequently, to Quakers and Baptists show 'first hand evidence of the intellectual and emotional demands made by the aftermath of the Civil War and by the uncertainties and ecclesiastical experiments of the Commonwealth and Protectorate'. Including a 'Note on Procedures' and a lucid introduction, this volume might be read profitably in conjunction with Ruth Spalding's *Contemporaries of Bulstrode Whitelocke 1605–1675: Biographies, Illustrated by Letters and Other Documents* (*YWES* 71).

Andrew Bradstock's 'Sowing in Hope: The Relevance of Theology to Gerrard Winstanley's Political Programme' (*SC* 6.189–204) takes issue with critical readings that situate Winstanley only in terms of his acceptance or rejection of Christian doctrine, arguing instead that Winstanley's theology permeated and shaped the Diggers' political outlook. 'Opera and Obedience: Thomas Hobbes and *A Proposition of Advancement of Moralitie* by Sir William Davenant' (*SC* 6.205–50) by James R. Jacob and Timothy Raylor is a detailed and finely researched article which includes a reprint of Davenant's *Proposition* (1653/4) and synopsis, a tract promoting the technical and educative elements of the masque to the public stage. The article situates this text in relation to Davenant's aesthetic theories in *The Preface to Gondibert* (1650), the motivations behind his own theatrical productions during the Civil War period, and the relationship between Davenant's *Proposition* and the educative and aesthetic theories propounded by Hobbes and the Cavendish circle.

A. Rupert Hall's *Henry More: Magic, Religion and Experiment* gives a detailed account of the scientific work of this esoteric figure, a figure who is well-known by scholars but often little understood. Hall's clear exposition of More's involvement with the Cambridge Platonists, his philosophy, science and support of atomism provides useful reading for a more comprehensive understanding of the scientific developments during this period and the role of More within those developments. In 'Samuel Hartlib's *Ephemerides*, 1635–59, and the pursuit of scientific and philosophical manuscripts: the religious ethos of an intelligencer' (*SC* 6:i.33–55), Stephen Clucas investigates the collection of scientific, philosophical, theological and technological notes and memoranda which constitute the *Ephemerides* and uncovers important information concerning the situation and collection of scientific manuscripts and the activities of manuscript collectors during this period. Through his careful analysis of this material, Clucas identifies the religious impulses – 'evangelical fervour' – which motivated scientific development before and through the Commonwealth period. Two essays of related interest appear in *Utopian Vision: Technological Innovation and Poetic Imagination* edited by Klaus L. Berghahn and Reinhold Grimm. The first essay by Klaus Reichert considers the writing of Bacon with regard to the relationship between scientific progress and utopian visions while the second, by Salvatore Calomino, explores the effect on early seventeenth-century formulations of science of Tommaso Campanella's *La citta del sole*.

Books Reviewed

Berghahn, Klaus, and Reinhold Grimm. eds. *Utopian Vision: Technological Innovation and Poetic Imagination*. Winter. (1990). pp 130. pb DM28. ISBN 3 533 04198 0.

Brooks, Cleanth. *Historical Evidence and the Reading of Seventeenth-Century Poetry*. UMP. pp 169. £17.95. ISBN 0 8262 0775 8.

Chambers, A. B. *Andrew Marvell and Edmund Waller: Seventeenth-Century Praise and Restoration Satire*. PSUP. pp. 208. $27.50. ISBN 0 271 00703 6.

Clifford, D. J. H. ed. *The Diaries of Lady Anne Clifford*. Alan Sutton Publishing. (1990). pp. 296. £16.95. ISBN 0 86299 560 4.

Cousins, Anthony D. *The Catholic Religious Poets from Southwell to Crashaw: A Critical Study*. Sheed and Ward. pp. 204. £19.95. ISBN 0 7220 1570 4.

Fumerton, Patricia. *Cultural Aesthetics: Renaissance Literature and the Practice of Social Ornament*. UChicP. pp. 256. £27.25. ISBN 0226 26952 3.

Gill, Richard, ed. *John Donne: Selected Poems*. Oxford Student Texts. Series ed. Victor Lee. OUP. (1990). pp. 169. £4.95. ISBN 0 19 831950 9.

Hall, A. Rupert. *Henry More: Magic, Religion and Experiment*. Blackwell. pp. 304. £35. ISBN 0631 17295 5.

Hall, Anne Drury. *Ceremony and Civility in English Renaissance Prose*. UPennP. pp. 207. £22.95. ISBN 027 100770 2.

Harvey, Elizabeth D., and Katharine Eisaman Maus. eds. *Soliciting Interpretation: Literary Theory and Seventeenth Century Poetry*. UChicP. (1990). pp. 351. ISBN O 226 31876 1.

Keeble, N. H., and Geoffrey F. Nuttall, eds. *Calendar of the Correspondence of Richard Baxter*. Vol. 1. 1638–1660. OUP. pp. 433. £55.00. ISBN 0 19 818568 5.

King, Margaret L. *Women of the Renaissance*. UChicP. pp. 333. pb £16.95. ISBN 0 226 43618 7.

Laurence, Anne, W. R. Owens, and Stuart Sim, eds. *John Bunyan and His England 1628–88*. Hambledon (1990). pp. 181. £28.00. ISBN 1 85285 027 2.

Lossky, Nicholas. *Lancelot Andrewes the Preacher (1555–1626): The Origin of the Mystical Theology of the Church of England*. Trans by Andrew Louth, foreword by Michael Ramsey. Clarendon. pp. 377. £45.00. ISBN 0 19 826185 3.

Miller, Naomi J., and Gary Waller, eds. *Reading Mary Wroth: Representing*

Alternatives in Early Modern England. UTennP. pp. 256. $39.50. ISBN 0 870 49709 X.

Pursglove, Glyn. ed. *Henry Reynolds: Tasso's 'Aminta' And Other Poems*. Mellen. pp. 227. ISBN 3 7052 0060 6.

Salzman, Paul, ed. *An Anthology of Seventeenth-Century Prose Fiction*. OUP. pp. 562. pb £6.99. ISBN 0 19 282619 0.

Shaw, William P., ed. *Praise Disjoined: Changing Patterns of Salvation in Seventeenth-Century English Literature*. Seventeenth Century Texts and Studies. Lang. pp 306. £30.00. ISBN 0 8204 1460 3.

Shoenfeldt, Michael C. *Prayer and Power: George Herbert and Renaissance Courtship*. UChicP. pp. 345. $49.95. ISBN 0226 740021.

Smith, A. J. *Metaphysical Wit*. CUP. pp. 270. £35.00. ISBN 0 521 34027.

Stedman, John H. *Redefining a Period Style: 'Renaissance', 'Mannerist' and 'Baroque' in Literature*. Duquesne. pp. 240. $48.50. ISBN 0 820 70221 8.

Thorpe, Douglas. *A New Earth: The Labor of Language in 'Pearl', Herbert's 'The Temple' and Blake's 'Jerusalem'*. CUAP. pp. 219. £35.95. ISBN 0 813 20728 2.

Vicari, E. Patricia. *The View from Minerva's Tower: Learning and Imagination in 'The Anatomy of Melancholy'*. UTorP. (1990). pp. 250. £31.00. ISBN 0 8020 2685 0.

Watt, Tessa. *Cheap Print and Popular Piety, 1550–1640*. CUP. pp. 385. £40. ISBN 0 521 38255 6.

X

Milton

THOMAS N. CORNS

A new teaching edition of Milton joins Gordon Campbell's 1990 Everyman second edition as a contender for a lucrative place on undergraduate reading lists, Stephen Orgel and Jonathan Goldberg's addition to the Oxford Authors series. Like Campbell's, it is in modern spelling (unlike Roy C. Flannagan's original-spelling version, which is to be published soon). It has some distinct merits. It retains most of the Latin and Greek poems (unlike Campbell's), and it very conveniently prints them in tandem with translations, like a Loeb edition. It makes a sensible choice of the prose, and includes complete texts of *The Doctrine and Discipline of Divorce* (interestingly and usefully transcribed from the first edition, which is almost irrecoverable in the *Complete Prose Works*, swathed in the accretions of the second edition and poorly distinguished typographically), *The Tenure of Kings and Magistrates*, and *The Readie and Easie Way* (quite properly, the second edition), as well as the inevitable *Areopagitica* and *Of Education* (both of which Campbell prints). There are extracts from three other polemical texts and from the *Familiar Letters* and *Christian Doctrine*. Annotation throughout is modest, mostly and uncontentiously confined to glossing hard words and briefly explaining allusions. The introduction, especially in its discussion of recent criticism, strikes me as partial but too brief to give real offence. I do not think many undergraduates will find it helpful, though the edition as a whole has much to recommend it.

Rather surprisingly in view of its publisher and its price, *The Poetic Birth: Milton's Poems of 1645* by C. W. R. D. Moseley is also aimed primarily at an undergraduate readership (though I notice it is reissued in 1992 by Penguin). It is a somewhat uneven achievement. Moseley's primary objective seems to be to interest relatively inexperienced readers in perceiving the poems as a volume, with the appropriate attention to the circumstances of publication and the ordering within the collection that that requires; a sensible idea, though one which perhaps requires a rather richer contextualizing of Milton's work in the Caroline literary tradition at its most critical phase. Moseley plainly rejects most of the critical perspectives which have developed over the last three decades, proferring a jeremiad about 'the disastrous decades of the 1960s and 1970s, when barbarism, not needing to invade, was welcomed in by those who should have known better'. The informing idea, however, is sound.

Better as a critical introduction for undergraduates is Stevie Davies's lively contribution to the Harvester New Readings series. Her brief presumably ran quite counter to Moseley's in that this is a series which is consciously and explicitly 'responsive to new bearings which have recently emerged in literary analysis'. Davies's primary theoretical and methodological focus is on gender politics: 'Sexuality is a major theme of the present book because it is an intense emotional and political preoccupation of Milton's poetry. My feminist approach is based on a perception that Milton at once identified himself with and vehemently disowned something female which was experienced as part of the self.' She is brightest when she sticks closest to this thesis. Her comments on *Paradise Lost* reopen the feminist debate it has occasioned in interesting ways, which perceive in the poem a complex of precise tensions:

> The Miltonic male at once idealises and looks down on the female ... but the power-structure he imposes as fortification to his ego is overturned in the love-relation ... Sexuality violates autonomy and therefore threatens the sense of safety.

I think undergraduates will find much in this to ponder. Her perspective proves particulary rich in her discussion of *Samson Agonistes*, which 'plays out a familiar paradox': 'the male is enervated by his triumph; he is colloquially said to "die", his vigour "spent"; predator becomes prey ... male sexuality opens him to effeminacy.' Some may disagree with this as an account of the narrative of events in *Samson*, but it is a bold and committed reading which should stimulate some of Davies's intended undergraduate readership to debate.

Though she is an astute and sensitive close reader, Davies's larger comments on aspects of Milton's language do not conform to what is known about his linguistic preferences and their place in contemporary practice. Again, while she wishes to relate the major poems to the political crises of the mid-seventeenth century, she is sometimes vague and occasionally inaccurate. The phrase 'propertyless Levelling squatter' confuses two distinct radical movements. Similarly, it is misleading to say Milton 'belonged to the class which persecuted, imprisoned and on occasions tortured the Levellers and Diggers'. He belonged to the same class as many of the Leveller leaders; neither group was subject to torture in the usual sense of that word; and the Diggers were persecuted and imprisoned by the land-owning gentry (and their rural dependents). Nevertheless, this is an excellent book to recommend to undergraduates as an introduction, comparing very favourably with Catherine Belsey's equally lively (and idiosyncratic) *John Milton: language, gender, power* (Blackwell, 1988).

Edward Le Comte's *Milton Re-viewed* is a collection of his essays published for the most part between 1978 and 1987. Its justification is that 'A number of them may be unfamiliar even to a somewhat diligent researcher insofar as they appeared in places that are not the usual ones', though the collection does include pieces from mainstream journals, too. It is a genial volume, which ranges from the war in heaven to the vices and virtues of the index to the Columbia edition, and includes a rehearsal of themes familiar elsewhere from Le Comte's work.

Certainly the largest book of Milton studies this year is *Milton in Italy: Contexts Images Contradictions*, edited by Mario A. Di Cesare. This volume brings together thirty-two papers from the Third International Milton Symposium held in Vallombrosa and Florence in June 1988. That was a large and rather diverse conference of more than a hundred papers – Roy Flannagan has summarized them elsewhere (*MiltonQ* 22.69–108). (Flannagan summarizes the papers of the Fourth International Milton Symposium, Vancouver, 1991, in *MiltonQ* 25.152–72.) Di

Cesare has printed only papers which touch on the central theme. The result is a collection which will probably surprise those who attended the conference by its clarity of focus and its coherence.

The role of Italy in Milton's self-fashioning or self-crowning is felt in my own paper, 'John Milton: Italianate Humanist, Northern European Protestant, Englishman' or in Dustin Griffin's astute 'Milton in Italy: The Making of a Man of Letters?' In my favourite essay from the collection, 'The Escape from Rome: Milton's *Second Defense* and a Renaissance Genre', Diana Trevino Benet ingeniously links such notions to a putative 'genre', of Protestant escapes from Rome, arguing that the account Milton gives in his *Second Defense* rehearses a formula which recurs in other accounts, and she shrewdly concludes, 'To consider Milton's Italian story as mere autobiographical sketch is to scant its subtle artistry and its brilliance as a polemical rejoinder.' Susanne Woods, in ' "That Freedom of Discussion Which I Loved": Italy and Milton's Cultural Self Definition', confronts the same issues a little differently, opposing Milton's hostile references to Rome with those to Florence.

Other contributions are more straightforwardly concerned with the facts of Milton's tour of Italy. Whether he actually visited Vallombrosa is impressively challenged by Edward Chaney in 'The Visit to Vallombrosa: A Literary Tradition': 'Milton nowhere claims to have visited Vallombrosa ... the burden of proof lies not with the sceptics, but with those who subscribe to what is merely an eighteenth-century tradition'. Neil Harris, in 'The Vallombrosa Simile and the Image of the Poet in *Paradise Lost*', besides meditating on the larger literary resonance of the image, concedes that Milton wasn't in Tuscany in the autumn and so 'Milton's Vallombrosa is artificial in at least its imagining of the season, and ... these Italian landscapes are not genuine memories of the scenes of his Continental tour.' Charles A. Huttar, in 'Vallombrosa Revisited', also addresses the issue of the literary and cultural resonance, not only of Vallombrosa but of Etruria generally, and the latter similarly exercises John R. Mulder in 'Shades and Substance'. Not Vallombrosa but Milton's visit to Galileo provides the starting point for Judith Scherer Herz (' "For whom this glorious sight?": Dante, Milton, and the Galileo Question') and for a sensitive essay by Donald Friedman ('Galileo and the Art of Seeing').

William Shullenberger, in ' "Imprimatur": The Fate of Davanzati' ingeniously teases open the larger implications of Milton's decision in *Areopagitica* to cite Davanzati's *Scisma d'Inghilterra* as an example of an officially sanctioned text.

A number of generally informative essays define the cultural experience Milton may have enjoyed in the various locations of his Italian sojourn. Thus, A. M. Cinquemani, in 'Through Milan and the Pennine Alps', describes the culture of Milan which Milton could have encountered. Three essays, by M. N. K. Mander ('The Music of *L'Allegro* and *Il Penseroso*'), by P. G. Stanwood ('Milton's *Lycidas* and Earlier Seventeenth-Century Opera'), and by Margaret Byard (' "Adventurous Song": Milton and the Music of Rome'), relate Milton's work to a range of musical experience to which he was or may have been exposed during his Italian travels. Two others make connections between the poetry and the visual arts of Italy. (The collection has thirty monochrome illustrations.) Thus, Diane McColley, in 'Edenic Icongraphy: *Paradise Lost* and the Mosaics of San Marco', sees possible analogies, not least in a certain aesthetic community: 'But the mosaicist in his exuberance shares with Milton an ability to call forth a pleasure in living things that is durably fresh, to evoke love of innocence, and to stir up hope for the renewal of blessedness.' Mindele Anne Treip, in ' "Celestial Patronage": Allegorical Ceiling Cycles of the 1630s and the Iconography of Milton's Muse', offers a wide-ranging assessment of Milton's relationship with some of the more amibitious manifestations of contemporary art. I find more persuasive, however, Michael O'Connell's quite fiercely argued essay, 'Milton and the Art of Italy: A Revisionist View', which focuses sharply on cultural politics. He notes, shrewdly, that 'Milton's subsequent silence about the painters and sculptors who occupied central positions in the culture of Italy seem … telling' and that 'They became for him not figures in their own right, like Galileo or Ariosto and Tasso, but rather the anonymous "noblest Architects" and "fam'd Artificers" of Satan's guided tour of Rome.' He proposes the question, 'What would Milton have made of this widespread glorification of the image [in the sacred art and ecclesiastical architecture he would have seen]?', and he suggests that 'it manifests itself in a deep suspicion of understanding gained through the image.'

The collection concludes with essays engaging the larger Italianate intertext of Milton's work. Some address its relationship to Italian narrative poetry. Charles Ross ('False Fame in *Paradise Regained*: The Siege of Albraca') ponders the complex relationship between *Paradise Regained* III.337–43 and Boiardo's *Orlando Inamorata*, offering the bold surmise that 'Orlando's omission from the simile of the siege … mocks Satan's illusion that he engages Christ as an equal'. Roy Eriksen ('God Enthroned: Expansion and Continuity in Ariosto, Tasso, and Milton') considers 'the topos of God enthroned' in *Paradise Lost* III.55–79, *Orlando Furioso*, and *La Gerusalemme liberata*. David Reid ('Tasso and Milton on How One Sees Oneself') concludes that Milton 'displays a much more inward understanding of how people work' and that 'Milton's representation of choice has much more to do with a world in which other selves have part than does Tasso's.' Italian works in other genres also find a place as points of comparison with Milton. Robert L. Entzminger ('The Politics of Love in Tasso's *Aminta* and Milton's *Comus*') links Milton's masque with Italian pastoral drama. Michael R. G. Spillar (' "*Per Chiamare e Per Destare*": Apostrophe in Milton's Sonnets') argues that Milton as sonneteer is among British writers uniquely predisposed towards apostrophic openings, a trait which he associates with Italian Cinquecento writers, and particularly Tasso. Anna K. Nardo ('Milton and the Academic Sonnet') argues quite plausibly that Milton's extension of the range of reference of the English sonnet owes something to the social role of the sonnet in contemporary Italian academies. Stella P. Revard ('Milton and Chiabrera') sees the influence of this 'new Pindar' on some of the later poems in Milton's 1645 collection. Wyman H. Herendeen ('Milton and Machiavelli: The Historical Revolution and Protestant Poetics') revisits the interesting question of Milton's relationship to Italian humanistic historiography.

Estelle Haan (' "Written encomiums": Milton's Latin Poetry in Its Italian Context') relates his Latin verse (and particularly the poems that date from during or after the tour) to contemporary Italian practice: 'He echoes Renaissance Latin poems composed by Italians; he replies to Latin tributes which he had received from Italian friends … and he seems to recall in a general, and sometimes more specific, sense Italian poems in praise of, or composed by, his addressees'. John K. Hale ('The Multilingual Milton and the Italian Journey') postulates and engages an interesting paradox: 'In Italy Milton received acclaim for his poems in several languages, yet came back resolved to write in English for the English. Why should his enjoyment of Italy change a polyglot poet into a monoglot?' 'Milton and Holstenius Reconsidered: An Exercise in Scholarly Practice', a characteristically meticulous piece from the late Leo Miller (to whom the collection is dedicated), concludes the volume. He considers Milton's Latinity in the light of alterations to letters to his Italian friends.

Three essays stand rather outside the Renaissance and seventeenth-century focus.

Cedric C. Brown ('Horatian Signatures: Milton and Civilized Community') traces 'Horatian formulations about audience' through Milton's work. Hiroko Sano ('The Lily and the Rose: Milton's *Carpe diem* Sonnet 20') considers another Horatian intertext. Neil Forsyth's 'Of Man's First Dis' has some sharp observations on echoes of Virgil and Ovid.

Milton's prose has been the subject of two books this year, one an account of a relatively unexplored text, the other a new edition. The former is Nicholas von Maltzahn's study of the *History of Britain*. The book offers a patient and untendentious account of numerous aspects of Milton's work. Von Maltzahn carefully considers the evidence relating to the date of its authorship and the circumstances of its publication, and the relationship between the *History* and Milton's critical assessment of the Long Parliament, which was published as *Mr John Miltons Character of the Long Parliament and Assembly of Divines* in 1681 and which offered Restoration England a sort of Tory Milton to oppose the Milton of his Whig admirers and apologists. Chapters consider in detail Milton's place in English historiographical tradition and compare his treatment of the ancient Britons and Saxons in the *History*, both with his comments elsewhere (some discontinuities are particularly revealing) and with the prevailing views of his contemporaries. The sections which deal with Milton's shifting perspectives on the Arthurian tradition are particularly fascinating; von Maltzahn concludes, 'Milton's impatience with the patriotic [Arthurian] myths signals his emergence as a reformer dedicated also to the truer understanding of English history, with a historical perspective enhanced by an open-eyed view of his compatriots, ancient and modern.'

Milton: Political Writings is edited by Martin Dzelzainis for the series Cambridge Texts in the History of Political Thought. The series aims to provide students with useful editions of texts which are presented, primarily, as documents in intellectual history. Milton, whose works are so deeply embedded in the intricate and sometimes rather petty skirmishing of Civil War polemic, perhaps lends himself less well to such a series than Hooker or Hobbes or even Filmer, who already figure in it. Dzelzainis offers just two texts, *The Tenure of Kings and Magistrates* and *A Defence of the People of England*, both of which he presents unabridged, as the series generally prefers. His introduction is lucid and intelligent, though the manifest exigencies of space – he has a mere sixteen pages – mean that arguments of some subtlety appear somewhat truncated. The annotation is light and sensible, though quite how deeply and closely Milton engages his adversaries and matters of immediate and local political concern is perhaps not always apparent. *The Tenure* appears in a new original-spelling transcription, the *Defence* in a new translation by Claire Gruzelier.

Charles Hatten, in 'The Politics of Marital Reform and the Rationalization of Romance in *The Doctrine and Discipline of Divorce*' (*MiltonS* 26.95–113), engages an interesting paradox that 'while [the tract] proposes the progressive reform of easing the restrictions on divorce, its rhetoric employs a sexism of remarkably archaic and stringent type'; his resolution in terms of the intended audience and the polemical moment is close to the mark, I feel. Olga Lucia Valbuena's solutions in 'Milton's "Divorsive" Interpretation and the Gendered Reader' (*MiltonS* 26.115–37) sees the issues in terms of the crises of masculine consciousness: 'Divorce means freedom from the tyranny of enslavement to any woman, monarch, or way of thought that would constrict masculine self-determination', though of course the title pages to both early editions do speak of divorce being 'restored to the good of both sexes.'

A substantial essay by M. L. Donnelly, 'Francis Bacon's Early Reputation in England and the Question of John Milton's alleged "Baconianism" ' (*PSt* 14.1–20), thoroughly scrutinizes (and eventually dismisses) 'the casual claim that Milton was a Baconian at Cambridge'. The essay ranges over the status and currency of Bacon as philosopher of science (as opposed to social and political essayist) in the decades after his death, and it engages with some rigour the supposed echoes of Bacon in Milton's *Prolusions*.

In 'Originality and Plagiarism in *Areopagitica* and *Eikonoklastes*' (*ELR* 21.87–101), Elisabeth M. Magnus argues that Milton's perspectives on literary theft and literary control carry a larger significance. In *Areopagitica* the repressive legislation he attacks engenders a dependence on an easy, indolent orthodoxy and a discouragement of original thought and expression. In *Eikonoklastes* the theft of the Pamela prayer is indicative of and symbolic of a larger failure of Charles I's stewardship.

A number of essays engage the minor poems. In a wide-ranging and judicious account, 'Milton's Self-Presentation in *Poems ... 1645*' (*MiltonQ* 24–5.37–48), John K. Hale queries some received notions of Milton's purposes and emphasizes what is really distinctive about the collection: 'volumes of verse, assembled for a book by the poet, were still rare in the England of 1645; a bilingual one was unique.' Perhaps his most telling point relates to the ideological contradictions which others have noted within the volume: its 'multilingualism entails a kind of pluralism ... One is changed by changes of tongue'. He has some shrewd comments on the ordering of the poems (especially those not in English) within the volume. R. Paul Yoder's 'Milton's *The Passion*' (*MiltonS* 26.3–21) revalues 'Milton's only published fragment', finding in it a new significance: 'he kept the poem because it served as a grim reminder of what could happen to him but for the grace of God, which is finally the point of Christ's Passion ... he published it because, in the myth of himself that Milton was creating, it constitutes a distinctly humanizing moment, and that is also the point of Christ's Passion.' The argument is advanced with an appropriate diffidence, but at the least Yoder has done something to stimulate debate. His views contrast favourably with Moseley's grimmer orthodoxy: 'There is little good one can say about the poem.'

M. N. K. Mander, in 'Music in Milton's *Hymn*' (*RenS* 5.412–26), examines the many musical allusions of the Nativity Ode, relating them to both patristic and Renaissance assumptions about the nature and power of music.

Caroline Moore's 'Milton's St. Michael and Holy Ambidexterity' (*MiltonS* 26.37–57) ponders again the two-handed engine and the 'superbly dark' prophecy of *Lycidas*. Richard Hooker's '*Lycidas* and the Ecphrasis of Poetry' (*MiltonS* 26.59–77), though intermittently opaque, concludes with a familiar finality, 'The work, timeless but obsolete at its conclusion, is abandoned, walked away from, and ultimately replaced in the ongoing process of experience.' Thomas H. Blackburn's '*Lycidas*: Eternity as Artifice' (*MiltonS* 26.79–93), also focuses on the coda, concluding, reassuringly, 'The "artifice of eternity" into which Lycidas is gathered is accepted as a necessary construction, but both poet and reader remain aware of the equally necessary resistance of life and language to the silence that true closure brings with it.'

Of decidedly more significance is ' "Trembling ears": the historical moment of *Lycidas*' (*JMRS* 21.59–81) by John Leonard. This is emphatically the most politically serious reading the poem has received. Adjacent to the death of Edward King, the immediate subject of the poem, Leonard identifies a complex series of allusions to the mutilation of Bastwick, Burton and Prynne in 1637 and their incarceration after dangerous journeys by water, two of them in the Channel Islands (which makes good sense of Milton's puzzling allusion to 'Bellerus' – l. 160 – since *Bellerium* was the

Latin name for Land's End, which both of them would have passed and which is a long way from the site of King's drowning). Leonard's reading offers *Lycidas* as a decidedly and even dangerously anti-Laudian poem at the time of its composition and first publication. He suggests that Milton may have fudged, rather than confirmed, the precise allusions to the martyrdom, especially of Prynne, when he reissued the poem in 1645 with its headnote about 'our corrupted Clergy then in their height' because he and Prynne had become mutually hostile in the early 1640s.

Another substantial essay, '*Lycidas* and the Grammar of Revelation' by Victoria Silver (*ELH* 58.779–808), returns to the mature debate about the coherence of the poem. She argues, a little laboriously at times, but with some ingenuity, that the incoherence others have noted relates to a strategy for the retention and disclosure of truth: 'This coordination in Milton's arguments between formal incongruity and an emergent truth is nothing if not chiliastic.'

An old and interesting problem relates to the identity in Sonnet 12 of those who mean licence 'when they cry liberty'. Stephen R. Honeygosky ('Licence Reconsidered: Ecclesial Nuances', *MiltonQ* 24–5.59–66), working quite deftly from a wide account of what he terms Milton's 'verbal renovation' of some key terms of seventeenth-century religious dispute, concludes, somewhat unusually, that '*licence* refers to the pattern of ecclesiastical self-will, doctrinal stubbornness, compromising hypocrisy, and unchecked use of force to support positions of power. For the radical Milton … *licence* actually refers to all that stands opposed to internal and mystical ecclesial liberty.' Another problem of identification exercises Leo Miller in 'John Milton's "Lost" Sonnet to Mary Powell' (*MiltonQ* 24–5.102–7), where he argues that the most plausible 'real life' context for sonnet 9 is that of the courtship between Milton and Mary Powell, 'a courting sonnet by a great poet who was a great lover even while he was a militant rebel against tyranny in church and state'.

A pugnacious article by John Leonard, 'Saying "No" to Freud: Milton's *A Mask* and Sexual Assault' (*MiltonQ* 24–5.129–40), takes issue with the view most fully developed by William Kerrigan that the Lady's rejection of Comus is in various ways compromised, a notion not infrequently advanced by others. Leonard concludes: 'Kerrigan has read *A Mask* with false preconceptions. The Lady does not suffer from sexual dysfunction: *Comus does* [Leonard's emphasis]. Kerrigan's readiness to dismantle the Lady's psyche, while leaving Comus's intact, is sad testimony to the prejudices which lie at the heart of Freudian theory … It is time we banished suspicions about Milton's Lady and banished them with some moral urgency.'

Several pieces engage *Paradise Lost*. A full and lucid discussion by Claudia M. Champagne, 'Adam and His "Other Self": A Lacanian Study in Psychic Development' (*MiltonQ* 24–5.48–59), radically reappraises the familiar question of Adam's fall and its ethical status: 'The description of male desire offered by French psychoanalyst Jacques Lacan, whose ideas concerning psychic development will form the theoretical basis of this essay, clearly characterizes Adam's desire for Eve: "when one is a man, one sees in one's partner what can serve, narcissistically, to act as one's own support" '. Whatever the merits of the interpretation, Champagne is to be congratulated on the patient and reader-friendly exposition of Lacanian discourse.

In 'A Problem of Knowing Paradise in *Paradise Lost*' (*MiltonS* 26.183–207), Ira Clark engages some of those interesting questions about how and what the prelapsarian Adam and Eve know which John Leonard recently so fruitfully considered in *Naming in Paradise: Milton and the Language of Adam and Eve* (1990). Another subtle issue is the subject of Vincent P. Di Benedetto's 'Scripture's Constraint and Adam's Self-Authoring Freedom: A Reading of the Fall in *Paradise Lost*'

(*MiltonQ* 24–5.1–14). Di Benedetto works to demonstrate the complexities of Milton's procedures in reconciling the exigencies of the Genesis account with his larger aesthetic and philosophical perspectives on Adam's choices.

A felicitous essay by Anna K. Nardo, 'Academic Interludes in *Paradise Lost*' (*MiltonS* 26.209–41), in a mode which would accord well with the Milton in Italy collection, relates the devils' activities after Satan leaves hell and Raphael's visit to Eden to Milton's knowledge of the ideals and the realities of the academies of Italy. The connection yields some amusing points of association: 'As astute as any Machiavellian Medici prince, Satan channels the active elements among his ranks into service to his political goals and removes the intellectuals from the sphere of public influence.' The relationship of bad angels to Western culture recurs in 'Ciceronian *Inventio* and *Dispositio* in Belial's Speech During the Debate in Hell' by Todd H. Sammons (*MiltonQ* 24–5.14–22), which examines Belial's speech in the light of a sixteenth-century English handbook of Ciceronian rhetoric. He concludes, '[Belial] is the ectype of the political counselor who puts private desires above the public good. Belial's Ciceronianism – millenia before Cicero's birth – sharpens this discrepancy, for Cicero, the great republican, always ranked the public good over the merely private. Already Belial is a degenerate Ciceronian orator.'

David Reid ('Spirits Odorous', *MiltonQ* 24–5.140–3) raises a question about the good angels, enquiring whether 'the notion that [they] make good smells has some backing in the angelological traditions he might have drawn on'. Another issue in angelology is addressed by Edward E. Ericson, Jnr, in 'The Sons of God in *Paradise Lost* and *Paradise Regained*' (*MiltonQ* 24–5.79–89). He considers the way in which exegetical tradition offers two alternative interpretations of the passage in Genesis 6:1–4 in which 'the Sons of God' are said to have copulated with the daughters of men. One tradition suggests that the males were fallen angels; another sees them as pious male descendants of Seth. Ericson argues that Milton follows the former tradition in *Paradise Regained* 2.178–81, and the latter in *Paradise Lost* 11.573–92, and he explains the apparent contradiction with the hypothesis that Milton, recognizing the validity of each, chose to represent both.

In ' "Light out of Darkness": The Interlocking Pattern of Visual and Spatial Imagery in *Paradise Lost*' (*MiltonQ* 24–5.89–101), Kirstin P. McColgan discharges the task the title implies. In 'Rewriting the Protestant Ethic: Discipline and Love in *Paradise Lost*' (*ELH* 58.545–59), Laura Lunger Knoppers relates the poem to a version of seventeenth-century social and economic history that owes much to Foucault, though the case perhaps requires rather fuller exposition. She concludes, '*Paradise Lost* evinces not a universal and autonomous spiritual freedom but the marks of seventeenth-century economic conditions. While Milton resists external authorities in favor of inner discipline, his model of paradise is subject nonetheless to broader economic forces. Striving to provide spiritual guidance, Milton in fact shapes subjects subject to domination and deployment from without.' Another account of how Milton's work relates to the larger material and ideological formation is offered in Peter Lindenbaum's 'John Milton and the Republican Mode of Literary Production' (*YES* 21.121–36). He argues that, though *A Masque* appeared in the 1645 collected poems prefaced by references to the patronage of the Bridgewater family, in the edition of 1673 these elements are suppressed. Most significantly, *Paradise Lost* is published without any analogous assembly of prefatory material. This may constitute a movement away from the dependence on others towards the independence and active self-sufficiency which Lindenbaum associates with Milton's republican ideology.

There are two essays on the brief epic. In 'The Son's Presumed Contempt for Learning in *Paradise Regained*: a Biblical and Patristic Resolution' (*MiltonS* 26.243–61), Donald Swanson and John Mulryan return to the familiar anxiety about Milton's Jesus's rejection of the cultural values which most critics believe they share with Milton, and they conclude, to my mind without carrying conviction, that 'the Son's contemptuous dismissal of the temptation to learning and positive hostility to ancient Greek and Roman learning are acts of duplicity [on the part of the Son] supported by biblical, patristic, and Miltonic authority', a sort of deep joke which the reader is to share at Satan's expense.

A substantial article by Gregory W. Bredbeck, 'Milton's Ganymede: Negotiations of Homoerotic Tradition in *Paradise Regained*' (*PMLA* 106.262–76), addresses that section of the short epic where the Son is tempted by 'Tall stripling youths rich clad, of fairer hue / Than Ganymede or Hylas' (2.352–3), which he relates to 'the tradition of sodomy that informs both the pastoral and exegetical histories' behind the poem.

Henry McDonald's 'A Long Day's Dying: Tragic Ambiguity in *Samson Agonistes*' (*MiltonS* 26.263–83) takes an unusual tack in arguing that Milton's Samson follows closely the depiction available in the Book of Judges. In '*Samson Agonistes* and the "Pioneers of Aphasia" ' (*MiltonQ* 24–5.143–8), Anthony Low makes a rather severe response to Noam Flinker's 1990 *Milton Quarterly* article, which, on Low's account, had, in a way paradigmatic of unacceptable current practices, largely ignored much germane earlier criticism in founding a reading on Joseph Wittreich's *Interpreting 'Samson Agonistes'* (1986). Flinker responds tersely but equally testily to what he terms Low's 'patronising insults' ('A Response to Anthony Low', *MiltonQ* 24–5.148–9), defending critical pluralism while indicting Low for 'his blanket dismissal of all literary theory without even a single bibliographical reference'.

John K. Hale's 'Milton's Euripides Marginalia: Their Significance for Milton Studies' (*MiltonS* 26.23–35) is a delicate and meticulous account which teases out their implications for our understanding of some aspects of Milton's classicism. Noam Flinker's 'Miltonic Voices in Haydn's *Creation*' (*MiltonS* 26.139–64) considers 'the echoes of Miltonic voices' in the libretto of the oratorio.

May Ann Radzinowicz's account of the Trinity Manuscript plots for depictions of Abraham, Samson and Joshua, ' "In Those Days There Was No King in Israel": Milton's Politics and Biblical Narrative' (*YES* 21.242–52), shows how adjustments to the Biblical material reflect Miltonic values and perspectives.

Donald L. Guss in 'Enlightenment as Process: Milton and Habermas' (*PMLA* 106.1156–69) offers as an almost painfully earnest polemic a reading of Milton and Habermas as a first instalment of 'a book intended to confront modern theory with a reconstructed enlightenment': 'Through Milton I mean to give Habermasian enlightenment not only a genealogy but also an aggressive, practical tone … to stress that it is active, political, material, pragmatic.'

Two essays from *Language and Style in English Literature: Essays in Honour of Michio Masui* are of some interest to Miltonists. In ' "His Example Whom I Now Acknowledge My Redeemer Ever Blest": The Imitation of the Son in *Paradise Lost*', Hideyuki Shitaka argues that the apostolic imperative of imitating the Son is a recurrent concern of the epic. In 'Logical Equivocation in *Paradise Lost*', Masahiko Agari considers the role of equivocation in Satan's temptation of Eve. Volume 12 of *MCJ News* from The Milton Center of Japan reports on recent symposia and colloquia, with extracts and abstracts of papers read.

Books Reviewed

Davies, Stevie. *Milton*. Harvester New Reading. HW. pp. 223. hb £42.50, pb £10.50. ISBN 0 7108 1355 4, 0 7450 1045 8.

Di Cesare, Mario A., ed. *Milton in Italy: Contexts, Images, Contradictions*. Medieval and Renaissance Texts and Studies. Binghampton. pp. 592. $40.00. ISBN 0 86698 103 9.

Dzelzainis, Martin, ed. *Milton: Political Writings*. Cambridge Texts in the History of Political Thought. CUP. pp. 279. hb £30.00, pb £10.95. ISBN 0 521 34394 1, 0 521 34866.

Le Comte, Edward, ed. *Milton Re-viewed: Ten Essays*. Garland. pp. 147. $23.00. ISBN 0 8153 0306 8.

Moseley, C. W. R. D. *The Poetic Birth: Milton's Poems of 1645*. Scolar. pp. 249. £35.00. ISBN 0 85967 868 7.

Orgel, Stephen, and Jonathan Goldberg, eds. *John Milton*. The Oxford Authors. OUP. pp. 966. hb £30.00, pb £12.95. ISBN 0 19 254188 9, 0 19 281379 X.

von Maltzahn, Nicholas. *Milton's History of Britain: Republican Historiography in the English Revolution*. Clarendon Press. pp. 244. £32.50. ISBN 0 19 812897 5.

XI

The Later Seventeenth Century

STUART GILLESPIE, EDWARD BURNS, ROGER POOLEY
and JAMES OGDEN

This chapter has three sections: 1. General; 2. Dryden; 3. Other Authors. Sections 1(b) and 3(b) are by Edward Burns; sections 1(c) and 3(c) are by Roger Pooley; section 2(b) is by James Ogden; and the rest is by Stuart Gillespie.

1. General

'From fairest creatures we desire increase'; commentators on the later seventeenth century this year leave us no choice in the matter. So numerous has their progeny been that a longer than usual chapter is required to accommodate it. Bibliographical listings of the material were included as ever in *Restoration* (volume 15), compiled by Candy B.K. Schille (41–55) and Richard Hillyer (111–37). These *Restoration* checklists continue to be the swiftest bibliographical aids to appear for our area; their accuracy is also good. *Scriblerian* and *SCN* kept up their usual quotients of reviews, while Paula Backscheider was *SEL*'s 1991 reviewer of 'Recent Studies in the Restoration and Eighteenth Century' (31.569–606). She concentrated on the latter part of her brief, which she felt was 'where the action is'. But given the number of studies reviewed below, one would scarcely hasten to accuse Restoration scholars of inactivity.

Paul Hammond, whose own industry alone ought to have made Backscheider think again, was responsible for three items in the period this year. The first, an essay on 'The King's Two Bodies: Representations of Charles II', appeared in Black and Gregory's *Culture, Politics and Society in Britain, 1600–1800*. It is mainly a survey of Stuart iconography and mythology as disseminated by the Court and as mocked by verse satirists in the 1670s and 1680s, or, in Hammond's words, of 'the language of kingship during the reign of Charles II in the light of the trauma and embarrassment which … afflicted the traditional theory of "the king's two bodies" '. Like the satirists, Hammond is very selective in his treatment of Charles's anatomy and overlooks, for example, numismatic evidence in asserting that 'few of his subjects had any idea … of his physical appearance'; but on its own terms this is a knowledgeable and engaging discussion.

The year would not seem complete, either, without at least a couple of contributions from Anne Barbeau Gardiner. One was her discussion of 'Islam as Antichrist in the Writings of Abraham Woodhead, Spokesman for Restoration Catholics' (*Restoration* 15.89–98). This article has more to do with recusant history than with literature, except that Woodhead was probably read by Dryden (but then, almost everybody was) and that, as we are told, 'Islam in Eastern Europe becomes a trope for English politics in the Restoration' in, for example, satirical verse. Gardiner focuses, though, on the obscure Woodhead's own writings and their context. The same area also happened to attract N. I. Matar, who wrote more generally on 'Islam in Interregnum and Restoration England' (*SCen* 6.57–71). This account does not mention Woodhead, nor Dryden's plays, but the views of a great many other writers, including poets such as Marvell and Traherne, are tracked down and assembled. Why we should be interested is another question, but if we are then this is the article for us. Matar is on less solid ground in another paper this year, 'Peter Sterry and the Puritan Defense of Ovid in Restoration England' (*SP* 88.110–21). Here, he tries to show that the 'Christianized', allegorized Ovid was still popular in the late seventeenth century, and it is an argument that relies on making a little evidence go a very long way. Peter Sterry, the Puritan on whose papers at Emmanuel, Cambridge, Matar has reported in the past, seems interested in such a reading of Ovid. On the other hand, Sterry's statements are vague and general, and even if he does mean what Matar claims, this need not imply any widespread taste of this kind in the Restoration period.

Finally here, Raymond A. Anselment offered a more general study, '*The Confinement*: The Plight of the Imprisoned English Debtor in the Seventeenth Century' (*Restoration* 15.1–16). Anselment has found no good poems about imprisonment for debt in our period, though he quotes several poor ones, but if anyone needs to know about the social and legal position of debtors then the basic information is here. Perhaps, in years to come, this will be seen as a pioneering article in a new field for the study of underprivileged minorities, especially as academics develop a closer first-hand acquaintance with the area.

(a) Poetry

The only publication to come my way on poetry generally was Alastair Fowler's *New Oxford Book of Seventeenth-Century Verse*, an anthology which has found its previous reviewers hard to please. In Fowler's partial defence may be pointed out the admittedly odd editorial principle by which he has 'aimed at alternative' selections from authors anthologized in the old *Oxford Book* of 1934 (*YWES* 15.228): this helps to explain some of the apparent anomalies. Even allowing for this, however, the selection seems indecisive in some cases: the 1934 Dryden is in fact still here with excerpts from *Religio Laici* and *The Hind and the Panther*, while Fowler branches out to reflect newer (or older) tastes by including two complete stories, where his predecessors offered only sixty lines, from the *Fables*. Marvell has more representation than Dryden, which seems peculiar; Fowler has promoted Cowley (fifteen pages) but despaired of Butler (six). Rochester at twelve pages gets more space than in 1934, which was inevitable; but Oldham has only a third of his allocation, which was not. (Also inevitable, I suppose, was my disagreement with Fowler's selections from all these poets.) There is a sprinkling, or perhaps it is more of a shower, of women writers. Generally there are too many single-poem authors, included less for their quality than for representativeness; on the other hand, it is amongst these items that the more widely-read will have the pleasure of finding something they do not already know.

(b) Drama

Curtain Calls; British and American Women and the Theater 1670–1820 (edited by Mary Anne Schofield and Cecilia Macheski) contains a number of general essays, as well as those on individual writers dealt with in the relevant section. Edward A. Langhans chronicles a range of 'Tough Actresses to Follow', comparing examples of different kinds of career and differing degrees of success to construct a pithy account of women's routes through seventeenth- and eighteenth-century theatre. Kendall, in a piece that revises and extends her own previous work, assesses the case for labelling the Queen Anne drama of passionate friendship between women as 'the birthplace of lesbian theater – among white people'. Taking the stance that 'we need new language to talk about old sex', Kendall offers a lively reinterpretation of female sexuality not only in the theatre but in Anne's court. Two articles in the collection offer a useful view: William J. Burling's ' "Their Empire Disjoyn'd": Serious Plays by Women on the London Stage, 1660–1737', fills the gap created by a tendency to focus attention on the comedies of manners in these playwrights' output, and Judith Philips Stanton's ' "This New-Found Path Attempting": Women Dramatists in England, 1660–1800' is impressive in its marshalling of comprehensive statistical and bibliographical information. All in all, this is a valuable collection of essays – though it does perhaps draw attention a little too clearly to the importance of the colon as punctuator of academic titles. Finally, in this context, a welcome anthology, Paddy Lyons's and Fidelis Morgan's *Female Playwrights of the Restoration: Five Comedies*, the comedies being Behn's *The Feigned Courtesans*, Ariadne's *She Ventures and He Wins*, Pix's *The Beau Defeated*, and Centlivre's *The Basset Table* and *The Busy Body*. The plays are newly edited, attractively presented and supported by helpful and unobtrusive notes.

Jon Lance Bacon, in 'Wives, Widows and Writings in Restoration Comedy' (*SEL* 31:iii.227–43) explores 'the common motif of Restoration comedy: the motif of woman as text'. Particularly relevant to the main focus, the Widow Blackacre in Wycherley's *The Plain-Dealer*, are the ideas of legality and power encoded in the motif, especially the fear of women's legal autonomy. Bacon seeks to exonerate the widow from slighting critics, ending with alignment of her to Behn; if I felt I wanted more on other aspects of this idea in relation to *The Way of the World*, for example, or as compared to earlier uses of the motif, this reflects the potential of Bacon's article, obviously an extract from a longer piece.

A chapter by George Parfitt on 'The Exotic in Restoration Drama' in *English Literature and the Wider World, Volume 1, 1660–1780: All Before Them* (ed. John McVeagh) marshals disappointingly familiar examples and generalizations before coming to the more interesting point that the use of the exotic 'contributes to a drama of universals ... Such a use of the exotic works against that awareness of difference that is offered by exploration and cultural exchange'. But, on the whole, the chapter is a potentially suggestive survey, rather than a developed argument. Finally, Judith Milhous's and Robert D. Hume's 'New Light on English Acting Companies in 1646, 1648, and 1660' (*RES* 42.168) uses evidence from contemporary lawsuits to illuminate the make-up and history of acting troupes, evidence that is particularly valuable in establishing the continuity and comparative autonomy of Killigrew's company from before to after the Commonwealth.

(c) Prose

There were two major contributions to the study of prose writing and the history of ideas in the period. Richard W. F. Kroll's *The Material Word: Literate Culture in the Restoration and Early Eighteenth Century* is a wide-ranging study of neo-classical discourse, epitomized by its concern with 'method'. Kroll's great strength is his grasp of new perspectives on the history of ideas, combined with perceptive readings of familiar texts (Dryden and Wilkins particularly) as well as the less well known (his analysis of Walter Charleton's Epicurean writing constitutes a major revaluation). His neo-classical, self-aware reader is at times a little too like a postmodern, but Kroll is persuasive in relating this self-awareness to the empiricism which, he argues, over-dominates older accounts of Restoration thought. His scepticism about the Jones/Adolph account of modernity in science and prose should be taken note of, though more attention to the language for description of phenomena, as well as the language of method, will be needed before this paradigm can be convincingly toppled. Not easy reading, but consistently thoughtful and worth arguing with.

Isabel Rivers's *Reason, Grace, and Sentiment: A Study of the Language of Religion and Ethics in England, 1660–1780, Volume I: Whichcote to Wesley* is the first of a two-volume study on the history of ideas – in this volume, the vocabulary of Restoration Anglicanism and Dissent. It is a self-effacing, traditional treatment, starting with the Whichcote–Tuckney letters on the relative priority of faith, works and reason. The strength is in the comparisons, alternating Anglicans and Dissenters chapter by chapter, with a particularly illuminating comparison of Baxter and Bunyan. The concluding chapter shows Wesley attempting a synthesis of Reformation doctrines (minus Calvin) with subsequent developments in the religion of the heart. The organizing thesis is a bit underplayed, but it is a valuable reconstitution of Restoration religious discourse. The aggressive review by Geoffrey Hill (*TLS* no. 4630, 27 December 1991) should be read, not least for its incidental, remarkable close readings of Restoration prose.

Most New Historicist readings of Renaissance literature, with their stated indebtedness to anthropological method, have succeeded best with texts concerned with the West's encounter with the tropics, potential empire – in other words, the material of classic anthropology in our own time. The achievement of John Stachniewski's *The Persecutory Imagination* is to establish a similar strangeness for Calvinism, a set of doctrines long made accessible and familiar for students of the period by Perry Miller, William Haller and others. The first half of the book, with its emphasis on the high incidence of religious despair engendered by the doctrine of election, and its readings of *Grace Abounding* and *The Pilgrim's Progress*, is particularly relevant to this period; the second half deals with earlier writers, Burton, Donne and Marlowe.

Paul Salzman has edited *An Anthology of Seventeenth-Century Fiction*. From our period, the texts are Margaret Cavendish, *The Blazing World*, a kind of feminist, scientific Utopia; Thomas Dangerfield, *Don Tomazo*, a picaresque tale linked to the Popish Plot; a skilfully abridged *Mr Badman*; Congreve's *Incognita*, and Behn's *The Unfortunate Happy Lady*. The texts are modernized, lightly annotated, with a helpful bibliography. The importance of having this material cheaply, readily and reliably available should not be underestimated; the revival of attention to seventeenth-century narrative, and of course the contribution of women writers, can now be translated into syllabuses, even (if s/he's still there) the ambit of the common reader.

A 1989 *festschrift* for the Opies' work, *Children and their Books* (edited by Gillian Avery and Julia Briggs), contains two articles on the emergence of children's books in Puritan culture. Nigel Smith writes about the child prophet Martha Hatfield, and Gillian Avery more generally about the impact of the Puritans, both on children in books as well as on books for children. She is particularly illuminating on Janeway's *A Token for Children* (1671–2) and its subsequent influence; there are some parallels with Stachniewski's emphases. Margaret J. M. Ezell writes about 'The *Gentleman's Journal* and the Commercialization of Restoration Coterie Literary Practices' in *MP* (89:iii.323–40). The relationship between authorship and readership in the thirty-three issues from 1692 to 1694 are analysed in terms of involving the readers in writing and responding. This is a useful footnote to the development of literary audiences.

2. Dryden

Paul Hammond's *John Dryden: A Literary Life* is not to be compared with James Winn's currently standard biography (*YWES* 68.325): it is, indeed, not a biography in the usual sense at all. It is much closer in conception and structure to David Hopkins's recent *John Dryden* (*YWES* 67.305), offering brief discussions of Dryden's works arranged roughly chronologically. Hammond's tastes tend to be more catholic than Hopkins's, which makes for more extensive treatment of the early works, the satires, and the religious poems; anyway, he prefers to contextualize and expound, where Hopkins concentrated on critical argument and assessment. Hopkins writes with considerably more warmth; Hammond can be more informative. Both have their merits as introductions, but Hammond is far too brief on the translations and here Hopkins's much fuller treatment must be preferred. This year's other full-length book on Dryden was by David Bywaters. In *Dryden in Revolutionary England* he offers 'close political analysis of Dryden's late works', in particular *The Hind and the Panther*, *Don Sebastian*, *Amphitryon*, *King Arthur* and *Cleomenes*. Very specific political points and allusions are found in all of them: in *Don Sebastian* Muley-Moloch 'is' in some ways William III; the Moors 'represent the English Protestants', and even Benducar 'suggests Prince George of Denmark'. This becomes a little far-fetched at times, notably on *King Arthur* and *Cleomenes*, but Bywaters does alert us to political undertones and overtones which have previously gone unremarked. The trouble is that this is much too narrow and reductive to be the comprehensive account of the late Dryden it claims to be – as though Dryden's sole object as a poet and playwright from the late 1680s onwards was to devise rhetorical strategies which would allow him suitable opportunities for political comment.

Three shorter items make up the rest of this section. Alan Roper's 'Dryden, Sunderland, and the Metamorphosis of a Trimmer' (*HLQ* 54.43–72) investigates Dryden's descriptions of Trimmers, and covert allusions to Sunderland as one, in various minor works of the 1680s. There is also an extensive but inconsequential discussion of Sunderland's plate in the *Works of Virgil*. Roper's readings are of varying persuasiveness, very well informed, but unlikely to be of much interest to anyone except future editors. David Haley's 'John Dryden: Protestant in Masquerade?' (*Cithara* 30:ii.10–17) is another politico-historical discussion. Haley locates the motive for the Rose Alley incident in Dryden's 'Prologue to *The Loyal General*'. Dryden, he thinks, was alluding to the Exclusion Bill and insulting the Whigs; the result was that 'some outraged citizen in the audience learned who the author of the prologue was and had him beaten.' This notion is supported by very few hard facts. Finally, David Hopkins notes in his 'Reply' (*N&Q* 38.521) to a previous note of his own (*YWES* 65.324) the source of the anonymous epitaph on Dryden he printed in *N&Q* in 1984.

(a) Poetry

A substantial contribution this year was Geoffrey Hill's *The Enemy's Country: Words, Contexture, and Other Circumstances of Language*, a book in which Dryden is 'at the centre' (to quote the blurb), while more orbital roles are performed by Hobbes, Izaac Walton, Marvell, and others outside our period altogether. The volume is largely a text of the 1986 Clark Lectures. There can be few critics whose dust-jackets would advertise their 'biting erudition', and I am unsure what the expression was intended to denote: there is erudition and there is a certain gruff truculence of tone, but Hill does not see his main business as savaging other critics. The two chapters principally on Dryden range widely, both exploring Dryden's attitudes to his work and to his public. Dryden's prose is often cited, but the second chapter in particular, 'Dryden's Prize-Song', is centrally concerned with his poetry (the song is *To the Memory of Mr Oldham*). The Dryden presented is a deeply serious, deeply troubled man and poet; but Hill is not attempting a complete portrait, and these aspects of Dryden's personality and position probably do require more attention than they sometimes receive.

The other broader study of some of Dryden's poetry this year was Richard W. F. Kroll's *The Material Word: Literate Culture in the Restoration and Early Eighteenth Century*. This is also noticed in section 3(c), but within its wide compass is to be found detailed comment on two Dryden works. It opens with a reading of the epistle to Dr Charleton as a 'great early poem' which documents 'the establishment of what we should properly call neoclassical culture' in England. Kroll sees it as reflecting a range of linguistic, political, and epistemological forces at play immediately following the Restoration, but does not say what makes it a great poem. Dryden also concludes Kroll's volume, in a chapter on 'The Nod of God in *Absalom and Achitophel*' which deals with the satire's ending. Kroll argues that this asserts the 'palpable terms' on which 'cultural knowledge' must be enacted, as against 'David's early desire to force language, against its nature, to his desires'. On the whole I found other parts of the book more inviting, and felt that in these two chapters the Dryden works tended to be made pegs on which Kroll could hang his very ambitious historical arguments.

Other items, on individual poems, are reviewed in chronological sequence. We begin at the very beginning with a note on *Astrea Redux* and *Heroique Stanzas*. Sherry Lavasseur tries in 'John Dryden's Views of Charles I, Cromwell, and Charles II' (*N&Q* 38.173–5) to reconcile the praise of Charles II in the former with the way Dryden 'explicitly criticizes' Charles I in the latter. But it is untrue that there is any explicit criticism – Lavasseur is reduced to quoting Dryden's lines on 'rash *Monarchs*' and citing evidence to show that Charles I's behaviour was often 'precipitate' – and anyway the obvious reasons for the differing attitudes to the monarchy hardly needed this note to point them out. This year's articles on *Absalom and Achitophel* were no more captivating. A. E. Wallace Maurer debated 'The Form of Dryden's *Absalom and Achitophel*, Once More' (*PLL* 27.320–37). He refers to many of the 'well over a hundred' predecessors who have argued for everything from satire to painting as Dryden's base, then to those who have discovered the poem to have no single form. Needless to say, neither party satisfies Maurer: for him, 'the form impelled and represented ... is a continuous, kaleidoscopic multidimensionality that is purposefully adapted, defying further identification.' As it happens, Lawrence K. Dessomes's article 'A Progress from John Dryden to Alexander Pope' (*Cithara* 30:ii.18–25) begins with a sentence that would displease Maurer: '*Absalom and Achitophel* by Dryden and *The Dunciad* by Pope not only share the same form of satiric-allegory but also have much the same content.' The latter extraordinary claim is supported by narrow or impossible Christian readings, or perhaps rather (since there is hardly an accurate quotation in the essay) skimmings of each poem. Dessomes's interests seem actually to lie in promoting censorship, a disconcerting response to *The Dunciad*. Lastly on *Absalom and Achitophel*, Kathryn Walls finds in it a phrase (that of her title) which may be echoed from Spenser's *Mutabilitie Cantos*, VI.23, in 'To "prosecute the Plot": A Spenser Allusion in *Absalom and Achitophel*' (*ANQ* 4.122–4). The argument for direct influence is impossible to substantiate firmly. These three articles may be said to reflect the vitality of most contemporary criticism on *Absalom and Achitophel*.

A comparatively neglected part of the Dryden canon received some attention this year when Carol Virginia Pohli discussed 'Formal and Informal Space in Dryden's Ode, "To the Pious Memory of . . . Anne Killigrew" ' (*Restoration* 15.27–40). But such neglect more taketh me than all the adulteries of this essay. Pohli's main points have to do with the 'space between proposition and its ironic contrary' in the poem. The irony, and questions of gender, are overplayed, the latter seriously so; but this is less important than the grave factual errors and misconceptions that have crept in. Pohli says that 'Dryden writes this poem in 1685, only a few years prior to his conversion to Catholicism': Dryden was openly attending mass by January 1686. She imagines that 'Killigrew's family was Catholic': her father was Anglican chaplain to the Duke of York. And so it continues. Thankfully there is no reason to question the scholarship of the one further contribution on Dryden's poems of the 1680s. Paul Hammond's 'The Printing of the Dryden–Tonson *Miscellany Poems* (1684) and *Sylvae* (1685)' (*PBSA* 84.405–12) is a carefully researched reconstruction, based on their bibliographical idiosyncrasies, of the way these two Tonson editions must have been compiled. It corroborates Stuart Gillespie's recent researches on the early Dryden–Tonson volumes (*YWES* 69.319) in tending to show what Hammond calls 'a combination of careful planning and improvisation' in their construction. Hammond should also have referred to William J. Cameron's informative bibliographical Ph.D. thesis, 'Miscellany Poems 1684–1716' (University of Reading, 1957).

Two items on Dryden's Virgil complete this section. In *Dryden's 'Aeneid': The English Virgil*, Taylor Corse undertakes to attempt a full-scale reassessment of Dryden's translation. After some scrappy treatment of its indebtedness to Spenser and Milton he concentrates on the verbal artistry of the poem, in comparison with the Latin original and with various modern translations. Reasonable as this may sound in principle, the result is a series of exercises in practical criticism, treating only brief selections from the text, which bring out few qualities other than those created by sonic and onomatopoeic effects in Dryden's work and hence are scarcely likely to prompt the radical turnaround in the translation's fortunes which Corse, whose heart at least is in the right place, hopes for. H. A. Mason's 'Milbourne *Redux*?' (*CQ* 20.223–57), on the other hand, on Dryden's *First Georgic*, invokes such wide perspectives that we seem at times to have to move through the whole course of Western literature to see what Dryden achieves. What Dryden achieves, Mason holds, is no less than an indispensable guide to Virgil's poem, and especially to the nature of Virgil's celebration of the divine.

(b) Plays

This year's principal contribution was David Crane's edition of *Marriage à-la-Mode* for the New Mermaids. The text is based on Q1, with the spelling, punctuation, and capitalization modernized as usual in this series. Much trouble has been taken over the italicization of French and frenchified words in Melantha's speeches, though *good graces* is italicized at II.i.45 but not at 180. The introduction maintains that the play 'makes more energetic use ... of the total acting capacity of the Restoration theatre, players and audience alike, than a simple comedy would', and that it can imply 'the radically idealistic possibility that neither the courts of kings nor the lovers need any social context of other human envy and frustration to give them life'. There is relatively little reference to recent scholarship and criticism, perhaps no great loss, but as so much is made of satire on the play in Buckingham's *Rehearsal* I thought something should have been said of similar satire in Arrowsmith's *Reformation* (*YWES* 67.311). In general, this edition is just what was wanted to bring *Marriage à-la-Mode* back to the attention of the theatre and its students.

Two essays in the learned journals undoubtedly made contributions to knowledge. Anne Barbeau Gardiner's 'Dating Dryden's *Amboyna*' (*RECTR* 5.18–27) discerns previously unnoticed allusions to the political situation of 1672–3, and concludes that Dryden wrote this play in March 1673, in response to the anti-war mood stimulated by Peter du Moulin's *England's Appeal*. Robert W. McHenry Jnr's 'Betrayal and Love in *All for Love* and *Bérénice*' (*SEL* 31.445–61) shows that Racine's play was a major source for Dryden's. *All for Love* 'follows *Bérénice* in representing the destructive fear of betrayal finally succumbing to the power of love'; hence the character who most resembles Bérénice herself is not Cleopatra but Antony.

Other essays contributed rather to interpretation, or speculation. Max Harries's 'Aztec Maidens in Satin Gowns: Alterity and Disguise in Dryden's *The Indian Emperor* and Hogarth's *The Conquest of Mexico*' (*Restoration* 15.59–70) applies Tzvetan Todorov and Mikhail Bakhtin to Dryden and Hogarth, with mildly interesting results. Dryden showed more understanding of the alterity of the Aztecs and the dialogic possibilities of drama than Todorov and Bakhtin would have expected; the colonialist perspective is in a measure criticized. Political interpretations were also put forward in three essays about *The Tempest* and its Restoration versions. Matthew H. Wikander's ' "The Duke My Father's Wrack": The Innocence of the Restoration *Tempest*' (*ShS* 43.91–8) maintains that the demotion of Alonzo from King to Duke hardly makes the Dryden–Davenant version innocent of all political meaning. Various possible interpretations are considered, and the conclusion is reached that the play 'both is and is not about the limitations of Stuart ideology'. Eckhard Auberleben's '*The Tempest* and the Concerns of the Restoration Court: A Study of *The Enchanted Island* and the Operatic *Tempest*' (*Restoration* 15.71–88) sees the Dryden–Davenant version (*The Enchanted Island*) more straightforwardly as a 'propaganda piece', showing that constitutional experiments must fail, and that sexual licence must be curbed in the interests of political stability. Michael Dobson's ' "Remember / First to Possess his Books": The Appropriation of *The Tempest*, 1700–1800' (*ShS* 43.99–107) discusses the decline of the Restoration versions into pantomime, and the rise of the Shakespearean original to a new political significance. 'From sustaining Stuart patriarchy', *The Tempest* came 'to certify the enchantedness of Stratford and the cultural superiority of the English bourgeoisie'. These three essays were generally learned, in parts lively, and in other parts overlapping. Gayle Edward Wilson's ' "New Matter for our Wonder and his Praise": Almanzor in *The Conquest of Granada*' (*RECTR* 6.30–8) analyses 'how Dryden combined several features of the commonplace concept of Fortune with conventional epidiectic [*sic*] *topoi* to develop Almanzor as the major figure' in the play. This essay seemed to me to have nothing to do with theatre research, and not much with drama criticism; there was very little 'new matter' in it. Finally, Scott Cutler Shershow's ' "Higlety, Piglety, Right or Wrong": Providence and Poetic Justice in Rymer, Dryden and Tate' (*Restoration* 15.17–26) briefly considers *All for Love*, and decides that 'in Antony and Cleopatra's death, "poetry" and "justice", the moral and aesthetic aspects of poetic justice, are somehow both satisfied.' Yes, somehow.

A valuable article was omitted last year. Andrew Pinnock's 'Play into Opera: Purcell's *The Indian Queen*' (*EMu* 18.3–21) politely disputes Curtis Price's suggestion, in *Henry Purcell and the London Stage* (*YWES* 65.320–1), that Dryden may have done the revision of *The Indian Queen* himself, as it is 'so expertly made'. By Dryden's own criteria, stated in the preface to *Don Sebastian*, the cuts in the operatic version mistakenly emphasize 'the most poetical parts' and obscure 'the connection of the story'. Hence, the success of the opera depended heavily on the skills of the designers, the actors, the musicians, and of course the composer; but the surviving manuscript needs rearrangement if the effects at which Purcell aimed are to be realized.

(c) Prose

E. E. Duncan-Jones identifies in 'Dryden, Benserade, and Marvell' (*HLQ* 54.73–8) the source of some French lines in *An Essay of Dramatic Poetry* which have vexed Dryden's editors. They are from one of Isaac de Benserade's *ballets de cour*, familiar works in the circles to which Buckhurst, Dryden's dedicatee in the essay, belonged. A very short note by Maureen E. Mulvihill, 'Dryden's Allusion to St Teresa' (*Restoration* 15.140), is the only other item here; Mulvihill speculates about the possible background to an allusion in an early Dryden letter.

3. Other Authors

(a) Poets

One item, Annabel Patterson's *Fables of Power: Aesopian Writing and Political History*, deals with two poets as well as other writers of our period such as Locke and L'Estrange. Ogilby and Dryden receive surprisingly full treatment in a volume of 177 pages dealing with some four centuries of literary history. The 'elegant and complex lyric structures' of Ogilby's *Fables of Aesop Paraphras'd* (1651), Patterson believes, 'significantly altered the status of the fable', making it 'a vehicle of protest and solidarity for the Royalist nobility and gentry who seemed to have lost the war'. Dryden in *The Hind and the Panther* and *The Cock and the Fox* stands in this tradition, she says; Patterson's accounts of these poems thus stand in the tradition of Drydenian exegesis in which the interpreter's task consists in the discovery of topical political allusions. She does this quite subtly for *The Hind*.

Claudia A. Limbert published no fewer than three articles on Katherine Philips. They were: 'The Poetry of Katherine Philips: Holographs, Manuscripts, and Early Printed Texts' (*PQ* 70.181–98); ' "The Unison of Well-Tun'd Hearts": Katherine Philips' Friendships with Male Writers' (*ELN* 29.25–37); and 'Katherine Philips: Controlling a Life and Reputation' (*SoAR* 56:ii.27–42). The first requires little comment since it had been largely superseded even before it was published, by Patrick Thomas's full edition of Philips's *Poems* (*YWES* 71). Limbert has herself reviewed this edition favourably, so presumably must agree that the article (conceived as a contribution to the establishment of a 'reliable text containing all of her poems') is largely superfluous. The two biographical articles contain useful material. The first provides notes on friends and acquaintances of Philips's, including some more or less tenuous but intriguing personal links to Milton, Cowley and Marvell. The second does much to discount recent rumours about lesbianism in Philips's poems and, more in sorrow than anger, recognizes the degree of conformity she found herself prepared to practise as a writer and as a woman.

Not to be outdone by the Philips record, Aphra Behn scholars also provide three items to note. One, however, is here only because it was omitted last year (the journal it appeared in is a new one): Mary Ann O'Donnell's 'A Verse Miscellany of Aphra Behn' (*EMS* 2.189–227). O'Donnell here supplements her own, still standard, *Aphra Behn: An Annotated Bibliography* (*YWES* 67.312). This new article is a thorough study of an extensive Bodleian manuscript which proposes an identification of Behn as either compiler (making it a commonplace book) or copyist (making her a paid scribe) of a 117-page segment, mainly of verse on events and personalities of the later 1680s. No previously unknown poems are found in these pages, but the interest of the manuscript to Behn's biographers would nevertheless be considerable if her connection with it could be demonstrated. O'Donnell does a very good job on technical and other aspects of the attribution and I suspect her findings will be generally accepted. Janet Todd and Virginia Crompton's 'Rebellions Antidote: A New Attribution to Aphra Behn' (*N&Q* 38.175–7) is a decidedly less convincing attribution of an ephemeral broadside to Behn: their reasoning is hard to follow. Bernard Duyfhuizen was responsible for a different kind of study altogether in ' "That which I dare not name": Aphra Behn's "The Willing Mistress" ' (*ELH* 58.63–82). Meticulous attention to the textual history of one of Behn's best-known lyrics is here combined with all sorts of speculation on patriarchal structures, lesbianism, and similar fashionable themes.

Alan Bradford's edition of Thomas Traherne's *Selected Poems and Prose* (Carcanet) was not received, but Stephen Clucas offered some thoughts on 'Poetic Atomism in Seventeenth-Century England: Henry More, Thomas Traherne and "scientific imagination" ' (*RenS* 5.327–40). Clucas sees the Traherne of *Commentaries of Heaven*, especially the poem on the Atom, as making atomism a 'metaphorically acceptable proposition' at a time when orthodoxy was hostile to the idea and its associations with chaos, atheism, and Lucretius. This is doubtless broadly right, but it is surprising that Clucas does not take the time to refer to contemporary translations of Lucretius other than Lucy Hutchinson's, or to standard treatments of Lucretius' influence on English writers such as W. B. Fleischmann's (*YWES* 45.252). He is also over-hasty in brief references to Dryden and Cowley. Julia J. Smith dealt with a figure associated with Traherne: 'Susannah Hopton: A Biographical Account' (*N&Q* 38.165–72) is one of those extremely useful and well-researched factual studies which help justify *N&Q*'s existence. It does, as Smith hopes it will, 'increase our knowledge of a woman who was a very interesting person in her own right [and] contribute to elucidating her connection with the Traherne family, and with Traherne's manuscripts'.

Cowley received the attentions of two commentators. Timothy Dykstal considers the *Davideis* in 'The Epic Reticence of Abraham Cowley' (*SEL* 31.95–115), seeking to explain Cowley's difficulties with the poem as the result of 'a hesitancy to assert classical (and pagan) ideals against the values of his often-conflicting Christian rationalism'. Dykstal adduces appropriate evidence from the poem, but tends to imply that any epic of the Enlightenment will succeed or otherwise according to its author's ability to 'solve problems'. Thomas Osborne Calhoun writes on 'Cowley's Verse Satire, 1642–43, and the Beginnings of Party Politics' (*YES* 21.197–206). This mostly factual article briefly contextualizes Cowley's *The Puritans Lecture* and *The Puritan and the Papist*, with reference to the contemporary rise of political satire and perceptions of its purpose and generic possibilities.

Two more satirists were the subject of Raman Selden's posthumously published 'Rochester and Oldham: "High Rants in Profaneness" ' (*SCen* 6.89–103). Selden finds the Oldham poems associated with Rochester to represent not an immature stage in Oldham's career but a 'signifying practice' belonging to a 'definite phase in English poetry', one which exploits the instability of baroque rhetoric in order to release, through constructed personae, 'the forbidden voices of anger and desire'. Nicholas Fisher's 'Miss Price to Artemisia: Rochester's Debt to Ovid and Horace in his Verse Epistles' (*CML* 11.337–53) is an account of all four of Rochester's verse epistles. Rochester's indebtedness to these two exemplars is seen as a result of what he 'had absorbed during the course of his education' in the classics. The evidence does not necessarily imply influence in this first-hand way, the general diffusion of Ovidian and Horatian epistolary models in the Restoration being what it is, but this background for the poems is worth calling attention to. Robert Holton offers another pairing with Rochester in 'Sexuality and Sexual Hierarchy in Sidney and Rochester' (*Mosaic* 24:i.47–65). But nothing very new emerges: it does not take us far to be told for example that 'there is, in Rochester, a general assault on the standards of courtly decorum that had been evolving for centuries', nor even that Sidney exemplifies this decorum. Holton is not ill-informed, but has little new to say.

This leaves two miscellaneous and specialized articles. It is but a short step from Rochester and sexuality to 'Frascatoro's *Syphilis*', the title of an article by Raymond A. Anselment (*BJRL* 73.105–18) on Nahum Tate's translation of the neo-Latin poem. This useful and scholarly discussion is divided into treatments of the medical and poetic aspects of the work, the latter showing reasons why Tate's poem may be thought of as managing to capture the qualities of the original successfully. Finally, the world of bibliography discovered 'An Early Manuscript Fragment of Sir William Temple's Poetry' (*SStud* 6.119–22) in the Brotherton Collection. Oliver S. Pickering has identified in it fragments of two short works first published in the rare *Poems by Sir W. T.*, offering a few variants against later editions.

(b) Dramatists

The most notable feature of this year's output is that work on the women dramatists of the period, a growing concern over the last five years or so, has now come to dominate the field. *Curtain Calls; British and American Women and the Theater 1670–1820*, edited by Mary Anne Schofield and Cecilia Macheski, surveys its subject in a chronological sequence of essays in different hands. Linda R. Payne's thoughtful and sympathetic account of Margaret Cavendish assesses both the gains and losses of her retreat into eccentricity and into the 'Dramatic Dreamscape' of Payne's title. This is probably the best introduction to Cavendish's work. Katherine Philips stands opposite to this isolationist position, 'A Feminist Link in the Old Boys' Network', according to Maureen E. Mulvihill, whose title continues as 'The Cosseting of Katherine Philips'. This is a well-researched and detailed piece whose 'case-study in supportive partnership between literary men and women' is a useful modification to too polarized a view of textual/sexual relationships in this period. 'Dressing to Deceive' is a short and breezy piece by Edna L. Stevens on the 'daredevilishness' of cross-dressing in the comedies of Mary Pix. A much more substantial piece in another collection, Juliet McLaren's 'Presumptuous Poetess, Pen-Feathered Muse: The Comedies of Mary Pix' (in *Gender at Work*, ed. Ann Messenger), offers an account of Pix's career in its theatrical context, with a detailed account of the plays. McLaren's argument presents Pix as a feminist writer, unfashionably so for the time, and a threat by virtue of her limited though real success. Constance Clark unearths an anonymous female critic in 'Critical Remarks on the Four Taking Plays of This Season By Corinna, a Country Parson's Wife', considering the evidence that Corinna was a pseudonym for Eliza Heywood to be inconclusive, and holding that 'Corinna was a feminist certainly, but not as we now understand it ... She echoes her predecessor Aphra Behn.' Douglas R. Butler places Susanna Centlivre ('Plot and Politics in Susanna Centlivre's *A Bold Stoke for a Wife*') as a 'Whiggish writer who believed that society should guarantee ... a citizen's life, liberty and property', and who 'is always aware that her audiences seem to demand ... that virtuous characters find reward and vicious characters punishment'. This for Butler is the main end of Centlivre's virtuoso plotting; his piece is well-argued, but leaves one with the sense that the case for Centlivre is still to be made.

The same case cannot be said of Aphra Behn, who dominates the collection, and elicits some of the sharpest and most ambitious writing in it. Rose Zimbardo gives a typically stimulating conspectus of Behn's career and of critical attitudes to it, pinpointing an important but neglected aspect of Behn's literary personality, her Ovidianism. But as her title suggests – 'Aphra Behn: A Dramatist in Search of the Novel' – Behn is interesting to her as one who 'caught the direction that poetic mimesis had to take in order to be faithful to conceptions of Nature that were born in the Enlightenment'. So Zimbardo's Behn is 'among the best playwrights of her day' but also the writer of, in *Oroonoko*, 'the first genuine novel in English'. Deborah C. Payne, in ' "And Poets shall by Patron-Princes Live": Aphra Behn and Patronage', and Frances M. Kavenik, in 'Aphra Behn: The Playwright as "Breeches Part" ' both locate Behn in the politics of the profession. Payne challengingly draws our attention back to 'the ease – the very eagerness – with which she embraces royalist ideology', thus marking out, in an open-minded and carefully researched piece, the contradictions and conscious ironies in Behn that make her such a compelling and awkward focus for an historicized feminist critique. Kavenik finds in Behn's plays a carnivalesque playing out of the sexual assumptions of her time, but her conclusion, that 'had these comedies come to us unsigned, they would, I suspect, be seen as no more or less feminist than *The Country Wife*, a play that has a good deal to say about the condition of women' seems reductively apiece with her general position that the plays 'respond – much as today's television programmes do – rather than assert.' Jessica Munns, in ' "I by a Double Right Thy Bounties Claim": Aphra Behn and Sexual Space', sees Behn's refusal to work 'on the margins' as necessitating and triumphantly validating an androgynous writerly role, a position which Nancy Cotton qualifies (in 'Aphra Behn and the Pattern Hero') by comparing Behn's notion of the hero to that of her male contemporaries; Behn's perspective here seems, in its very lack of 'the masculine doubts' that lead the men to a nervously pre-emptive undercutting of their heroes, to be identifiably female.

For Behn on the contemporary stage one must turn from this collection. John Barton's adaptation of Behn's *The Rover*, a production whose RSC provenance justifies Nancy Copeland's contention that in it the play 'achieved canonical status', is assessed by Copeland in an analysis of programme, reviews and prompt-book; she does not seem to have seen the production, and the heavyweight analysis, combining reception theory and the cultural materialism of Sinfield and Belsey, seems disproportionate to the ephemera on which she thus necessarily expends it. 'Re-Producing *The Rover*: John Barton's *Rover* at the Swan' comes to the unsurprising conclusion that the adaptation 'is a product of the contemporary horizon of expectations'. (*EiT* 9.45–59)

The publication of the Oxford *Works of Thomas Southerne*, and the apparent anomaly of such an edition of works so little known and still less performed, prompts Robert D. Hume, in 'The Importance of Thomas Southerne', to reassess his work in relation to other dramatists of the period (*MP* 87.273–90). He writes trenchantly of individual plays (pointing out, for example, of *The Wives' Excuse*, 'just how radically *disengaged* a play it is') using as a 'model' of previous comedy that proposed in Rothstein and Kavenik's *The Designs of Carolean Comedy* (*YWES* 71), 'a major breakthrough' for Hume, and finding Southerne more complex and less audience-pleasing than Carolean Comedy as they describe it. Hume sets out the issues clearly, but is not without precedent, as he seems to imagine: chapters in Peter Holland's *The Ornament of Action* (1979) and my own *Restoration Comedy: Crises of Desire and Identity* (1987) discuss Southerne's plays in terms not wholly remote from those Hume outlines. Indeed, his survey is notable in mentioning no British criticism whatsoever which, like the puffing of Rothstein and Kavenik, points to the closed circuit on which the Humean approach, still obviously powerful in the States, would seem to operate. Robert Jordan, one of the editors of the Oxford text, offers just such an assessment, well-supported in close reading of the play, in 'Inversion and Ambiguity in *The Maid's Last Prayer*' (*Restoration* 15.99–110). He suggests we see this and *The Wives' Excuse* as a kind of diptych, one showing men preying on women, the other women preying on men. Thus, what can be seen as an inconclusiveness or sourness in the play is perhaps equally well-described as its achieved statement – a statement of the male characters' inability to control 'the incompatibility of the social and the moral'. Susan Staves (in an article held over from last year; 'The Secrets of Genteel Identity in *The Man of Mode*: Comedy of Manners v. The Courtesy Book', *SECC* 21.117–28) wittily examines the idea of the comedy of manners, as a form taken to be trivial by virtue of having lost its moorings in the Courtesy Book and the Christian morality on which that form can be seen to be based, and in terms of the fear of the Courtesy Book evinced in Etherege's play; a fear of its more pragmatic value, as an exposé of the secret that gentility is made, not inborn.

Sue Owen tackles the question of Lee's political stance in ' "Partial Tyrants" and "Freeborn People" in *Lucius Junius Brutus*' (*SEL* 31.463–82), by exploring audience response to specific figures, in terms of the 'tragic' and the 'affecting'. Her approach gains through sensitive close reading and makes a committed argument for the power of the play. Richard Kroll interrogates 'Emblem and Empiricism in Davenant's *Macbeth*' (*ELH* 58.835–64) in a challenging piece that uses Davenant's adaptation of Shakespeare to chart not only changes in political ideology, but also in modes of representation, seen in terms of a shifting epistemological model. He thus opens up a more intriguing sense of the Restoration Shakespeare than critical condescension normally allows. Nancy Klein Maguire again charts the political life of texts, this time against the life of the amateur dramatist, the Earl of Orrery ('Regicide and Reparation: The Autobiographical Drama of Roger Boyle' in *ELR* 21.2). Maguire's detailed historical argument presents Orrery's plays as where he 'worked out the act of regicide, as in exorcism, in ritualistic reparation'.

The problematic nature of the male who 'puts himself on display' is discussed by Kristina Straub in 'Colley Cibber's Butt: Class, Race, Gender and the construction of Sexual Identity' (*Genre* 23.2–3). Cibber turns up rather late in what is a crowded presentation, both in historical and theoretical terms, of the association of the male performer with ideas of difference, and his consequent place in the construction of the homosexual-as-other. Cibber, for Straub, inhabits an 'empowering' ambiguity, while attention to his context presents examples of the modes of 'negation' by which white male heterosexual culture defends itself.

(c) *Prose Writers*

Aphra Behn as a writer of fiction continues to attract careful and enthusiastic readers, and Jacqueline Pearson has produced the best critical account yet in 'Gender and Narrative in the Fiction of Aphra Behn' (*RES* 42.40–56, 179–90). By concentrating on the narrator figures in the works, she demonstrates the subtlety of Behn's sometimes ironic, sometimes authoritative voices. *Love Letters* and 'The Unfortunate Happy Lady' get particularly discerning treatment. I regret I have been unable to see the beginning of Janet Todd's new edition of the complete works; Behn's release from the unreliability of Summer's text is as important to her reviving reputation as her release from uncritically autobiographical readers.

Bunyan Studies contains an interesting illustrated article on the impact of *The Pilgrim's Progress*, 'Pilgrims and Strangers: The Role of *The Pilgrim's Progress* and *The Imitation of Christ* in shaping the Piety of Vincent van Gogh' by Kathleen Powers Erickson (4.7–36). Though the only hard evidence of the link with Bunyan is from van Gogh's one extant sermon, of 1876, the Kempis material is considerable. Stuart Sim's book on Bunyan and Defoe, *Negotiations with Paradox*, is particularly noteworthy for its resolute investigation of the paradoxes produced by Calvinist predestination in Bunyan's narratives. The method is especially useful for getting to grips with the successes and shortcomings of *Mr Badman*, and there are useful chapters on *The Pilgrim's Progress* and *The Holy War* as well. The treatment of Calvinism is more focused on logic and the question of authority, less on psychology than Stachniewski's; between them they constitute the most substantial critical discussion of the impact of Bunyan's Calvinism on his writing, undisguised in their hostility to that Calvinism. In 'John Bunyan's "Celestial City" and Oliver Cromwell's "Ideal Society" ', Wendell P. MacIntyre compares Bunyan's dreams for a new society in *The Pilgrim's Progress* with Cromwell's application of Puritanism to the rule of the state (*RevAli* 3.77–88). At times it adds up to no more than the fact that Cromwell and Bunyan were both Puritans; and its slim, over-generalized thesis is further weakened by lack of reference to Hill or any of the post-tercentenary studies which tackle Bunyan's social views.

Kristiaan P. Aercke, 'Congreve's *Incognita*: Romance, Novel, Drama?'(*ECF* 2.293–308), is a lively and successful attempt to rescue the book from its twin imprisonments of being part of the 'origins' of the novel, and having a preface that is quoted more often than the text. In identifying the gap between the grouchy narrator of the tale and the confident tone of the preface, she makes a distinction between neoclassical and baroque notions of verisimilitude which illuminates many of the peculiarities of Congreve's scenic construction.

Books reviewed

Avery, Gillian, and Julia Briggs, eds. *Children and their Books, A Celebration of the Work of Iona and Peter Opie*. Clarendon (1989). pp. 424. £25. ISBN 0 19 812991 2.

Black, Jeremy, and Jeremy Gregory. *Culture, Politics and Society in Britain, 1600–1800*. ManUP. pp. 208. £29.95. ISBN 0 7190 3435 3.

Bywaters, David. *Dryden in Revolutionary England*. UCalP. pp. 208. $25.00. ISBN 0 520 07061 5.

Corse, Taylor. *Dryden's 'Aeneid': The English Virgil*. AUP. pp. 151. £22.00. ISBN 0 87413 385 8.

Crane, David, ed. *Marriage A-la-Mode*, by John Dryden. New Mermaids. Black/Norton. pp.118. pb £4.50. ISBN 0 7136 3412 X, 0 393 90064 9.

Fowler, Alastair, ed. *The New Oxford Book of Seventeenth-Century Verse*. OUP. pp. 831. £25.00. ISBN 0 19 214164 3.

Hammond, Paul. *John Dryden: A Literary Life*. Macmillan. pp. 184. hb £35.00, pb £10.99. ISBN 0 333 45379 4, 0 333 45380 8.

Hill, Geoffrey. *The Enemy's Country: Words, Contexture, and Other Circumstances of Language*. Clarendon. pp. 153. £19.95. ISBN 0 19 81126 5.

Kroll, Richard W. F. *The Material Word: Literate Culture in the Restoration and Early Eighteenth Century*. JHUP. pp. 420. £30.00. ISBN 0 8018 4002 3.

Lyons, Paddy, and Fidelis Morgan, eds. *Female Playwrights of the Restoration: Five Comedies*. Dent. pp. 363. £5.99. ISBN 0 4608 7080 7.

McVeagh, John, ed. *English Literature and the Wider World, Volume 1, 1660–1780: All Before Them*. AshfieldP. £38.50. ISBN 0 94866 008 2.

Messenger, Ann, ed. *Gender at Work*. WSUP. pp. 165. $29.95. ISBN 0 81432 147 X.

Patterson, Annabel. *Fables of Power: Aesopian Writing and Political History*. DukeUP. pp. 177. hb £28.45, pb £9.95. ISBN 0 8223 1106 2, 0 8223 1118 6.

Rivers, Isabel. *Reason, Grace, and Sentiment: A Study of the Language of Religion and Ethics in England, 1660–1780, Volume I: Whichcote to Wesley*. CUP. pp. 277. £35.00. ISBN 0 521 38340 4.

Salzman, Paul, ed. *An Anthology of Seventeenth-Century Fiction*. WC. OUP. pp. 562. pb £6.99. ISBN 0 19282 619 0.

Schofield, Mary Anne, and Cecilia Macheski, eds. *Curtain Calls: British and American Women and the Theater 1670–1820*. OhioUP. pp. 375. £33.20. ISBN 08214 0957 3.

Stachniewski, John. *The Persecutory Imagination: English Puritanism and the Literature of Religious Despair*. Clarendon. pp. 400. hb £45.00. ISBN 0 19 811781 7.

XII

The Eighteenth Century

STEPHEN COPLEY and ALAN BOWER

This chapter has three sections: 1. General; 2. Poetry; 3. The Novel. Section 1 is by Stephen Copley; Sections 2 and 3 are by Alan Bower. Because of an editorial error, Nigel Wood's Prose and Drama section will appear in volume 73.

1. General

ECCB n.s. 12 for 1986, edited by Jim Springer Borck, has now appeared. *SEL* 31 and *Scriblerian* 23/24 offer their usual helpful listings. In *The Present State of Scholarship in Historical and Contemporary Rhetoric*, edited by Winifred Bryan Horner (UMissP, 1990), which I have not seen, the editor and Kerri Morris Barton apparently cover 'The Eighteenth Century' by revising 1983 bibliographies of the area. In *DQR* (21.71–81), Peter J. De Voogd surveys 'Recent Trends in Eighteenth-Century Studies'. *The Bowyer Ledgers*, edited by Keith Maslen and John Lancaster for the Bibliographical Society and the Bibliographical Society of America, contains an introductory volume and seventy microfiches. It provides enormously detailed information on the printing business of William Bowyer and his son of the same name, and will undoubtedly prove to be an exceptionally valuable research resource in the area.

ECent (32:iii) is a special issue entitled 'What's Left of the Left?', which aims to represent the state of radical American work on the eighteenth century. James Thompson introduces the issue with a response to the title question (195–202). The later contents are varied: John Richetti considers the relation between novelists and magistrates in the period under the title 'Class Struggle Without Class' (203–18); Kristina Straub writes about Cibber and Pope in 'Men from Boys' (219–39); Lennard J. Davis differentiates 'The Fact of Events and the Event of Facts' (240–55); Carole Fabricant offers 'The Battle of the Ancients and (Post) Moderns' (256–73) as a view of Swift from a modern perspective; and William H. Epstein surveys Gray's Correspondence under the title 'Assumed Identities' (274–88). In 'Vicesimus Knox and the Canon of Eighteenth-Century Literature' (*AJ* 4.345–63), Robert W. Uphaus argues persuasively for the importance of Knox's influence on the formation of the canon, suggesting that it is second only to that of Dr Johnson. David B. Paxman surveys eighteenth-century attempts to define 'The Genius of English' in the poetic discourse of the period, and discusses the importance of these attempts in the development of contemporary aesthetics, (*PQ* 70.27–46). Meanwhile, in 'Spears and Petticoats' (*JEGP* 90.327–41), Mary M. Van Tassel considers debates about truth, reality and the instability of language as they appear particularly in *The Tatler*; and in *ECS* (25.31–56), Adam Potkay provides an interesting discussion of 'Classical Eloquence and Polite Style in the Age of Hume', in which he focuses in particular on Hume's essay 'Of Eloquence'.

Joseph M. Levine's *The Battle of the Books: History and Literature in the Augustan Age* offers to retell the story of a celebrated conflict which does not lead to a clear-cut victory, but in which a series of compromises tends to leave the advocates of the moderns dominant in the sciences and the supporters of the ancients influential in the arts, before 'the arguments ... were finally transformed in such a way that the old quarrel disappeared'. In the first part Levine provides a detailed and meticulous narrative account of the course of the controversy and outlines the contributions to it of the major participants, from William Temple and Swift, to Pope and Richard Bentley. In the second part he covers less well-known ground, arguing that debates about the nature of history 'reflected and deepened the issues that were a stake in the quarrel', and documenting the rival claims of ancient rhetoric and eloquence and modern scientific learning in the field, as they are represented in the writings of figures such as William Wotton.

In *Arguments of Augustan Wit*, John Sitter suggests that 'the arguments of wit' do not involve 'a desire to extricate true judgement ... from the materiality of language', but that they instead 'embrace language as the means rather than barrier to truth'. He discusses several aspects of 'wit' in the period, charting the subversion of Locke's ideas on the subject by Addison and Prior, and suggesting that Pope defines the term as 'forceful writing that gives pleasure', before investigating the treatment of a range of related topics: laughter, the body, 'gravity', and 'dullness', as they are treated by a number of Augustan writers. Sitter sets out to celebrate the intellectual demands made by the Augustans' appeals to common sense, refusing to write off their attacks on the modern world as nostalgic spiritualism; and he insists on the need for a grasp of 'historical intentionality' in reading the satire of the period. In a somewhat tangential opening chapter, he differentiates the period phenomenon of the character progress both from the static Theophrastan character and from the representations of character that emerge in the novel. His attempts to put Augustan literature and late twentieth-century criticism into fuller dialogue are not entirely convincing, but the study offers an interesting historical account of its topic. John Snyder's *Prospects of Power: Tragedy, Satire, the Essay and the Theory of Genre* is a wide-ranging volume in which the author offers to map his theory of literary genre 'into discursive configurations of power', using the work of Foucault and Michel Serres. The section on satire (which is considered as an unstable 'semigenre', alway shifting towards or merging with other genres) contains passing discussion of Swift: the chapter on the essay bypasses the eighteenth-century English essayists. In *ECLife* (15.iii.76–92), Richard Terry surveys 'The Circumstances of Eighteenth-Century Parody' in an attempt to 'place parody in a complex of material conditions and tendencies'.

Ian Bell's *Literature and Crime in Augustan England* is presented as 'an exercise in literary criticism at the service of wider cultural history', in which the author deploys the critical techniques of close reading across a variety of written and pictorial, literary and non-literary, texts, in order to comment on the contending representations of criminal and legal activities in the first half of the eighteenth century. He begins with a useful discussion of the ways in which it is possible 'to misappropriate and misuse Augustan literature in a process of historical analysis', illustrating his case with a reading of Hogarth's *Industry and Idleness* prints, before surveying in turn representations of the criminal in works such as *The Beggar's*

Opera; the 'double standards' involved in eighteenth-century attitudes to the legal position of women; and satiric representations of criminality and punishment. Bell draws tellingly on a wide range of source materials: fittingly, he concludes with a chapter on the writer whose output most clearly straddles the bounds of literature and the law – Henry Fielding. The book offers an intelligent, useful, and very readable contribution to discussion of a fascinating topic. In 'Charity Sermons and the Poor' (*AJ* 4.171–217) Rita Goldberg provides an interesting analysis of the power of the 'rhetoric of compassion' deployed in such sermons throughout the century.

In *The Sociable Humanist: The Life and Works of James Harris 1709–1780*, Clive T. Probyn attempts to redeem Harris's reputation from the neglect that has flowed in part from Johnson's dismissal of him as 'a prig, and a bad prig'. He suggests that Harris's 'modesty has concealed his own originality', and that his career 'touched almost every aspect of Augustan culture, and successfully bridged its provincial and metropolitan contexts'. Probyn makes use of previously unpublished and inaccessible materials to document the course of Harris's friendships, trace his involvements in a wide variety of projects, and survey the evidence of his views, which he suggests were in some ways inimical to the fashions of his age. He comments on Harris's main publications on aesthetics, language and music, and in a series of appendices documents and reprints some of his shorter pieces. The volume makes a persuasive case for an unjustly neglected figure.

The Theory and Practice of Text Editing, edited by Ian Small and Marcus Walsh, collects interesting and useful pieces on a wide range of literary editing projects, involving texts from Shakespeare to D. H. Lawrence. Essays focus on the ways in which editorial procedures throw 'into sharp relief some of the crucial issues recently isolated by literary theorists … the questions of authorial intention, authority, and the relationship between "literary" and non-literary works'. Eighteenth-century topics considered include a discussion by Anne McDermott and Marcus Walsh of the problems involved in editing a text such such as Johnson's *Dictionary*, which is usually seen as being marginal to the literary canon; and another discussion by Walsh of the controversy over non-objective editing surrounding Richard Bentley's 1732 edition of *Paradise Lost*.

Irish Writing: Exile and Subversion, edited by Paul Hyland and Neil Sammells, includes essays on historical and philosophical as well as literary writings from the eighteenth to the twentieth centuries. Eighteenth-century pieces include essays by Stephen H. Daniel on John Toland; Robert Phiddian on the conflicts between the English and Irish aspects of Swift; Paul Hyland, on the anonymous and pseudonymous publication strategies of Swift and Steele; Bryan Coleborne on Anglo-Irish verse; and Alan Booth on the background to Irish writing, revolution, and exile in the 1790s. Other essays cover fairly predictable topics in relation to writers such as Joyce and Beckett. An anthology of *Black Writers in Britain 1760–1890*, edited by Paul Edwards and David Dabydeen, forms a good introduction to a welcome new series of 'Early Black Writers' from Edinburgh University Press. The editors of the volume include a fair amount of eighteenth-century material, in the form of substantial extracts from recorded speeches and private and published letters, as well as from popular published works such as Olaudah Equiano's *Narrative* of his own life.

The editors of *The 'Other' Eighteenth Century*, Robert W. Uphaus and Gretchen M. Foster, present their anthology of eighteenth-century writing by women as an attempt 'to reclaim the tradition of women's writing in England' and restore it to its 'rightful place in the present-day canon of eighteenth-century literature'. Their account of the lost centrality of women's writing is over-ambitious in some of its claims, but the selection of complete texts and substantial extracts, running from pieces by Margaret Fell in the seventeenth century to ones by Maria Edgeworth in the nineteenth, is intelligent and will be useful in teaching the period. Under the title 'Desperate Measures' (*ELH* 58.841–66), Erin Mackie compares the fictional and autobiographical 'Lives' of Mrs Charlotte Chark, refusing the twin temptations of homogenization of the accounts and imposition of a fixed standard of feminist expectation in her reading, while in *AJ* (4.137–69) Claudia Thomas surveys Elizabeth Carter's readings of Pope, Johnson and Epictetus, and their influence on her own writings, under the title ' "Th'Instructive Moral, and Important Thought"'. Also in *AJ* (4.313–43), Betty Rizzo makes the short life of the 'natural poet' Molly Leapor the focus of a more general discussion of the position of 'all those natural poets so much in vogue in her time', under the title 'Molly Leapor: An Anxiety for Influence'. Katherine M. Rogers surveys 'Anna Barbauld's Criticism of Fiction' in *SECC* (21.27–42). In *HLQ* (54.327–51), Carol Barash documents 'The Political Origins of Anne Finch's Poetry' and insists on the importance of politics in her work. In 'The Other Reasons' (*YJC* 5.129–50), Orrin N. C. Wang writes interestingly about 'Female Alterity and Enlightenment Discourse' in the work of Mary Wollstonecraft.

The Blackwell Companion to the Enlightenment, edited by John Yolton et al., takes the (appropriate) form of an encyclopaedia, with entries on topics, concepts and movements as well as individuals, mainly from the period 1720–80. The *Companion* draws on the expertise of an impressive array of contributors, and is attractively presented and illustrated. In his introduction, Lester G. Crocker insists that attempted definitions of the Enlightenment itself 'all fail because the complexities and inconsistencies of historical reality overflow the rationally convenient reduction to a definition, which is, by definition, a limit'. Nonetheless, he surveys the movement's historical development, suggesting, for instance, that the question of 'whether England had an Enlightenment' in the eighteenth century is 'otiose', as this was already a fact in the legacy of the seventeenth century. This question is further addressed in entries such as those on England and Scotland – but it is not pursued in entries on English writers such as Dr Johnson, which might have been developed as test cases, but which remain strictly biographical.

Three volumes by G. S. Rousseau, entitled *Enlightenment Borders*, *Enlightenment Crossings*, and *Perilous Enlightenment*, collect his previously published essays under broad headings, as they cover matters anthropological, sexual, historical, scientific and medical. Rousseau supplies headnotes in an attempt to weld the volumes together, and to link the essays in terms of his own intellectual development. With characteristic modesty he confesses to having traversed the interdisciplinary ground of, and tackled pretty well all the major problems raised by, structuralism and poststructuralism well before those movements got off the ground. It is possible to feel that a little Rousseau in this vein goes a long way, and that a lot runs the danger of becoming very irritating. In fact, the strengths (and limitations) of his work derive more obviously from traditional history of ideas than from the new approaches whose vocabularies he adopts, but whose implications he does not always seem to have fully absorbed. The method of anthologized re-publication adopted in the volumes brings mixed results: some of the essays remain individually impressive as contributions to debates in intellectual history, the history of science or gender politics, but their impact is often weakened by the repetition of arguments in other essays throughout the volumes. Margaret C. Jacob's *Living the Enlightenment* is a survey of the impact of Freemasonry in eighteenth-century Europe. Drawing on newly available archival material, Jacob traces the origins and discusses the status of the movement in Britain, before examining its subsequent spread, and its very different reputation, in Continental Europe. She suggests that its characteristic institutional procedures of democratic election and endorsement of freedom of discussion within a select company were not seen as aspects of a subversive 'counter culture' in the context of contemporary British constitutionalism, but that they posed an immediate threat in an absolutist state such as France. In both contexts, she argues convincingly for the centrality of Freemasonry to the development of Enlightenment thought, and of eighteenth-century civil society.

A special double issue of *ECLife* (15.i and ii) is edited by John Dwyer and Richard B. Sher, and entitled 'Sociability and Society in Eighteenth-Century Scotland'. It includes useful pieces on various aspects of sociability, the importance accorded to it, and its consequences in the Scottish Enlightenment. Among the general essays in the issue, Dwyer considers the complex relation between the models of 'Enlightened Spectators and Classical Moralists' in Scottish thought (96–118); James G. Basker discusses 'Scotticisms and the Problem of Cultural Identity in Britain' (81–95); and Ned C. Landsman considers the importance of Scottish Presbyterianism (194–209). Susan M. Purviance discusses Hutcheson's treatment of 'Intersubjectivity and Social Relations' (23–38); Jeffrey R. Smitten considers 'Hume's *Dialogues Concerning Natural Religion* as Social Discourse' (39–56); and Peter J. Diamond considers the place of 'Rhetoric and Philosophy in the Social Thought of Thomas Reid' (57–80). Deidre Dawson asks 'Is Sympathy So Surprising?' in Adam Smith's work (147–62); Barbara M. Benedict writes on William Creech the bookseller, under the title ' "Service to the Public" ' (119–46); David Daiches (167–80) and R. B. Sher (181–93) explore the American connections of the Scottish Enlightenment; and Kenneth Simpson (210–24), and John Ashmead and John Davison (225–42) write on Burns. In 'A Dance in the Mind' (*SECC* 21.89–100), Kathleen Holcomb surveys the growth and importance of the provincial Scottish philosophical societies. *JHI* 52 contains useful articles by Thomas M. Olshewsky on 'The Classical Roots of Hume's Skepticism' (269–86), and by J. B. Schneewind on 'Natural Law, Skepticism and Methods of Ethics' (289–308), which covers material from Shaftesbury to Kant. In *Language International* (3.i.13–16) Geoffrey Kingscott celebrates 'The Bicentenary of [Alexander Fraser] Tytler's *Principles of Translation*': in the same journal (3.ii.16–19) he offers biographical information on Tytler under the title 'The Quest for Alexander Fraser Tytler'.

In *The Invention of Scotland: The Stuart Myth and the Scottish Identity, 1638 to the Present*, Murray G. H. Pittock charts what he describes as the 'unique fascination' of the Stuarts, their 'legendary' status, and the 'continuing power' of 'the Stuart myth' in Scotland. He insists that 'the roots of the Stuart myth lie in the history of the dynasty, not in the later accretions of sentiment', and in support provides a rather cursory survey of the political events of the seventeenth and eighteenth centuries in which they were involved. His discussion of the development of the myth in the eighteenth and early-nineteenth centuries includes useful comments on Jacobite ballads, and less rewarding short sections on Macpherson, Burns, Scott, and Hogg. In these latter cases there is a tendency on Pittock's part to apply the mantle of Jacobite allegiance rather undiscriminatingly, without the finer distinctions which more detailed examination would have allowed. In this respect, his book sometimes echoes the strained attempts of some recent revisionist historians to discover lurking Jacobitism in every corner of eighteenth-century English political and cultural life – although his argument about the Scottish context is, at least in outline, inherently more plausible.

I have not seen Annette C. Baier's *A Progress of Sentiments: Reflections on*

Hume's 'Treatise' (HarvardUP), or *Liberty in Hume's 'History of England'*, edited by Nicholas Capaldi and Donald W. Livingstone (Kluwer Academic Publishers, Dordrecht, Netherlands, 1990), but the latter contains what looks like an interesting selection of essays, including pieces by by Peter Jones, John Danford, Eugene F. Miller, Craig Walton, and the editors themselves. In *ClioI* (20.169–83), Laura B. Kennelly assesses the influence of Hume's History on Goldsmith's *History of England*, under the title 'Tory History Incognito'. In 'Shelley's "Spirit of the Age" Antedated in Hume' (*N&Q* 38.297–8), Claudia M. Schmidt comments on the significance of the phrase for each writer. Charles Griswold contributes an article to *P&P* (24.iii. 213–37) entitled 'Rhetoric and Ethics: Adam Smith on Theorization about the Moral Sentiments', and Lucinda Cole writes a wide-ranging piece in *ELH* (58.107–40) under the title '(Anti)Feminist Sympathies: The Politics of Relationships in Smith, Wollstonecraft, and More'. At first sight, it is good to find that the new Everyman series includes Adam Smith's *Wealth of Nations* alongside its literary titles. Sadly, the book has been clumsily truncated in order to appear as one volume. The excision of Book V does not simply prune some material of limited interest on revenue and taxation, as D. D. Raphael suggests in his introduction, but removes much of the substantial critique of the cultural effects of the operation of the market which is an essential element in the work – even if this critique is one that was conveniently ignored by the Adam Smith Institute in the 1980s.

Interpretation and Cultural History, edited by Joan H. Pittock and Andrew Wear, contains papers from a conference held at Aberdeen in 1987. Contributors discuss their own approaches to writing cultural history and provide illustrative case histories drawn mainly from the eighteenth century. Among the essays in an interesting collection Roy Porter discusses hierarchic divisions between bodies and minds; G. S. Rousseau examines the 'semiotics of the nerve'; Ludmilla Jordanova argues that 'there is no *thing* that representations of the family depict, only sets of ideas'; Martin Kemp illustrates his discussion of the difficulty of 'placing' artefacts with a consideration of artists' optical devices; Lawrence Lipking outlines the place of the 'common reader' in Johnson's definition of the literary canon; Peter Hulme surveys representations of the Caribbean; and Jonathan Barry comments on provincial town culture in the eighteenth century. Two minor irritants mar the book: the time lapse between the conference and publication means that some of the material included has already become familiar in other forms elsewhere; and the editors include their own synopses of and comments on each essay in headnotes – a reductive practice which is becoming increasingly common in collections, but is no less annoying for that. Stephen Bann's *The Inventions of History: Essays on the Representation of the Past* reprints ten extremely interesting essays on historiography and cultural and art history. One in particular, on 'Views of the Past', draws on eighteenth-century material in its discussion of how history might be viewed in various contexts.

Paul Langford has followed up his extremely impressive *A Polite and Commercial People* (OUP, 1989) with *Public Life and the Propertied Englishman 1689–1798*. The volume surveys the effects of the centrality of property in the political, social and intellectual life of the period. As Langford suggests at the start of the book, 'A world without property was almost inconceivable to eighteenth-century Englishmen': assumptions about it were pervasive in discussions of social institutions, political rights and cultural life. However, as he demonstrates, the complex realities of property ownership, accumulation and transfer confound the simple polarities of land and money which structure many eighteenth-century polemics, and the period is marked as much by 'change and competition within propertied society' as it is by straightforward conflict between a propertied elite and a propertyless majority. Characteristically, Langford is both fluent and eclectic in his survey of these complexities. Ellis Archer Wasson takes up some of the same concerns in his survey of 'The House of Commons 1660–1945' in *EHR* (106.635–51).

Richard Brown surveys eighteenth-century history in two substantial student volumes, *Society and Economy in Modern Britain 1700–1850* and *Church and State in Modern Britain 1700–1850*. Both include useful introductory discussions of the nature of historical study. The former is helpful in its insistence on the multifariousness of the economic and industrial developments commonly treated under the general heading of the Industrial Revolution, and in its separate consideration of Scotland, Wales and Ireland. The latter is especially welcome for the due weight that it gives to religious affairs. *British Politics and Society from Walpole to Pitt 1742–1789*, edited by Jeremy Black, contains a useful selection of introductory survey essays by historians on a period that is often neglected by students in favour of the periods immediately before and afterwards. The Cambridge Texts in the History of Political Thought series now includes volumes of *Richard Price: Political Writings*, edited by D.O. Thomas, and *Tom Paine: Political Writings*, edited by Bruce Kuklick.

Culture, Politics and Society in Britain, 1660–1800, edited by Jeremy Black and Jeremy Gregory, contains a collection of sometimes rather stolid papers from a colloquium on 'Culture and Politics' held in Newcastle in 1989. These cover a wide range of topics in the history of ideas. Shearer West comments on the status of eighteenth-century portraits as manifestations and symbols of patronage and power; Colin Kidd considers 'The Ideological Significance of Scottish Jacobite Latinity'; Roy Porter discusses 'Civilization and Disease'; Black examines the xenophobia evident in eighteenth-century prints and hack histories; and Gregory writes on 'Anglicanism and the Arts'. I have not received a copy of E. P. Thompson's latest volume, entitled *Customs in Common* (MerlinP). Peter Linebaugh's massively documented *The London Hanged* fills out a case first made by him in an essay in *Albion's Fatal Tree* (ed. Douglas Hay, 1975). He suggests in the introduction to the new volume that 'this book explores the relationship between the organized death of living labour (capital punishment) and the oppression of the living by dead labour (the punishment of capital)', and supports his claim that 'Tyburn was the centre of urban class contention' with a wealth of evidence from the period 1690 to 1800, setting individual cases as incidents of a drama of social conflict. Linebaugh's underlying thesis has been repeatedly questioned by other historians: whether or not it is entirely persuasive, his determination to pursue his argument on a broad political and cultural front, and organization of a great range of fascinating eighteenth-century material in support of it is impressive. *Executions and the British Experience from the Seventeenth to the Twentieth Century*, edited by William B. Thesing (McFarland, 1990), apparently contains an essay by John J. Burke, entitled 'Crime and Punishment in 1777', in which the author considers the execution of Dr William Dodd. In *ECLife* (15.iii.58–75), Barbara Brandon Schnorrenberg offers a biography of a medical quack under the title 'A True Relation of the Life and Career of James Graham, 1745–1794'. In *BJECS* (14.159–70), Jeremy Black surveys 'The Development of the Provincial Newspaper Press in the Eighteenth Century', and in *SECC* (21.245–66), John L. Bullion considers 'The Origins and Significance of Gossip about Princess Augusta and Lord Bute'. In 'Gilbert White's *Natural History* and History' (*ClioI* 20/21.iii.271–81), Clarence Wolfshohl compares the two forms of history.

In the introduction to *A Passion for Government: The Life of Sarah Duchess of Marlborough*, Frances Harris admits that the life of the redoutable duchess has been written many times, but suggests that the focus of earlier biographers on her tempestuous personal relationships has been at the expense of consideration of her major preoccupations: politics and the fortunes of her family. This failing is admirably rectified in Dr Harris's biography, which offers both a fluent narrative of the life of the duchess and an adroit analysis of the enormous influence that she wielded in late seventeenth- and early eighteenth-century public affairs, despite the constraints of her gender and her own sometimes near-disastrous behaviour towards her royal patrons and her supposed political allies.

In *Reason, Grace and Sentiment*, Isabel Rivers offers to provide a broad survey of the 'changes in the way in which the relationship between religion and ethics was perceived' between 1660 and 1780, by a wide range of religious groups and individual writers. She describes her approach to her material as being that of a literary historian of ideas, and concentrates on the language of religious and moral prose in the period, defining language to include 'terms and phrases, style, and rhetoric'. The first volume, now published, is subtitled 'Whichcote to Wesley', and deals with 'Anglican moral religion and the reaction against it of movements which ... attempted ... to continue or return to the Reformation protestant tradition in response to what was seen to be its betrayal by the Church of England.' The promised second volume will trace the relation between Anglican moral religion and various forms of naturalism, scepticism, and sentimental ethics. The volume is lucidly written, interesting and informative, even if some will feel that a stronger engagement with the issues raised in recent theoretical work on language would have allowed the author to push her case further.

Janet Louth's edition of *Selected Writings by William Law* offers a useful short introductory selection from Law's major works. In *BJECS* (14.13–30), William H. Trapnell outlines 'What Thomas Woolston Wrote' about allegory and the truth of Scripture, as an example of 'the difference between what a writer wants to say and what others try to make him say'. Paul Turnbull's 'Gibbon's Exchange with Joseph Priestley' (*BJECS* 14.139–58) attempts to do justice to the complexity of Gibbon's thinking about religion by surveying his exchange with Priestley about chapters fifteen and sixteen of *Decline and Fall* 'within the broader historical context of British religion and politics in early 1783'. In *BJRL* (73.ii.159–280), Clive D. Field provides a very full revised bibliography of 'Anti-Methodist Publications in the Eighteenth Century'.

The Blackwell History of Music in Britain: The Eighteenth Century, edited by H. Diack Johnstone and Roger Fiske, sets a high standard for the series, which began life in 1981 as the *Athlone History* with a volume on the Romantic period, but which has not yet seen the appearance of any other volumes. Surveys of 'Music and Society', concert, theatre, church and domestic music, and music literature, by Rosamond McGuinness, Richard Platt, Robert Hoskins, Stanley Sadie, Nicholas Temperley, Thomas McGeary and the editors, are both scholarly and readable. The essays are particularly successful in setting the music of the period in its broader cultural, literary, and political context, offering succinct but informative commentary on matters such as the development of theatre music, changes in musical taste and the terms of polite aesthetic debate about the subject, which will be of immediate interest to students of the literature and cultural history of the period. Of related interest, the first volume of Alvaro Ribeiro's projected four-volume edition of *The Letters of Dr Charles Burney*, covers the years 1751 to 1784. The volume charts Burney's rise to public recognition as a musical 'man of letters', opening with his earliest surviving corespondence, and closing with letters from the year of the Handel Commemoration and the death of Johnson. Ribeiro points out that 154 of the 191 letters in the volume have never been published before, and that others have often appeared previously in unreliable or abridged texts. The volume is generously annotated. Together with Slava Klima's recent reconstructed edition of Burney's *Memoirs* (for which see *YWES* 69.369), it provides invaluable information on, and insight into, the professional musical life of Britain in the mid-eighteenth century. In *BJECS* (14.61–74), Rosamond McGuinness considers 'The *British Apollo* as a Source of Musical Information'.

Sidney K. Robinson's *Inquiry into the Picturesque* is an elegant, often stimulating, and sometimes irritating volume. Taking his cue from the apparent refusal of fixity and centrality which characterizes the picturesque aesthetic itself, Robinson offers his volume as a 'freely composed' series of sceptical essays 'exploring' the notoriously ill-defined boundaries of the category, rather than a sustained attempt at prescriptive definition of them. As he writes: 'The Picturesque is … elusive as a compositional achievement. Inquiring whether one is in its presence or not continuously re-enacts it.' The essays are variably successful: interesting discussions of the place of 'mixture', 'variation', and 'connection' in picturesque aesthetic design are not quite matched by less well focused considerations of the economic context of the movement, pastoral, and what Robinson calls Charles James Fox's 'picturesquely unplanned' political behaviour. Nonetheless, this is a valuable addition to the literature on the subject. In 'Architectural Taste and the Grand Tour' (*JAIS* 1:74–91) Edward Chaney comments on George Berkeley's reactions to Italian architecture, while in *ECent* (32.i.39–57) Robert Miles offers a 'genealogy' of Gothic under the title 'The Gothic Aesthetic'.

BSEAA 33 contains a number of articles (in French) on Hogarth. Frédéric Ogée offers a bibliography of 'Image et société' in his graphic works (35–49); Félix Paknadel offers 'Quelques réflexions sur image et société' in the same works; and Claude Fierobe discusses his relation to the theatre under the title 'Monde du théâtre, théâtre du monde'. Hans-Peter Wagner's 'Eroticism in Graphic Art' (*SECC* 21.53–74) offers a commentary on Hogarth's 'decidedly moral if ironic pictorial discourse' of the erotic, while in *W&I* (7.329–47), Peter Wagner seeks the sources of some of the artist's images in popular literature, under the title 'Hogarth's Graphic Palimpsests'. Also in *W&I* (7.275–99), James Heffernan writes on Joshua Reynolds and J. M. W. Turner, under the title 'Painting against Poetry'. In *RES* (42.425–8), George Watson discusses the relation between Reynolds and Jonathan Richardson, under the title 'Joshua Reynold's Copy of Richardson'. Finally, in *The Paintings of Thomas Gainsborough*, Malcolm Cormack provides an attractively illustrated introduction to the artist for the general reader. His refusal to have anything to do with the interesting approaches to reading the painting of this period that have emerged in the last couple of decades is a shame, and his commentaries on the seventy-five paintings reproduced tend towards the anecdotal rather than the analytical.

2. Poetry

I hope to review eighteenth-century poetry as represented in *The Dictionary of Literary Biography* (Gale), next year, when I have seen it. If only in scope and modernity, this should have more to commend it than the first of the two 'general' books on which I can report. In *The Offensive Art: The Liberation of Poetic Imagination in Augustan Satire*, C. J. Purvis gathers his forces for a long redundant counter-offensive against those who would deny imaginative freedom in Dryden and Pope. The 'book is largely based on research undertaken … during … 1973–76' and the most recent secondary sources cited by Purvis are James Sutherland and Cleanth Brooks, so it seems reasonable to suppose that this is a long-delayed vanity publication left high and dry by the tide of time. Werner Brönnmann Egger certainly proves himself *au fait* with more recent works in *The Friendly Reader: Modes of Cooperation between Eighteenth-Century English Poets and their Audiences* (Wolfgang Iser and Paul Grice in particular) and he has some interesting detailed comment on Gray and Collins, but this comes too often as relief from ponderously mechanical dissection. The cause of the broadly-based monograph is thus well-served only by Betsy Bowden's *Eighteenth-Century Modernizations from 'The Canterbury Tales'*, an invigoratingly animated collection which reproduces a selection from those modernizations not revived during the last two centuries; thirty-two Tales, Tale links and adaptations in all. Bowden's introduction ranges busily over reception aesthetics and reader-response issues and charitably, but unequivocally, dismisses the notion (proposed most notably by Caroline Spurgeon) of Darwinian progress through the centuries of Chaucer 'translation'. Though excluded in its own right, Dryden's practice and theory is everywhere influential, as in the anonymous 1791 version of the *Miller's Tale* (published only four years before William Lipscomb's better known version of a dozen others) with its remarkably cogent defence against 'grossness'. The same anonymous apologist also helps prove Bowden's point about endless intertextuality in his/her use of Dryden's paraphrase theory, promptly witnessed in the modernization itself and a line written by someone who knew Pope well, 'Nods, she to some, to all, would smiles dispense'.

More ancient 'translations' are the subject of a good essay by Kurt Heinzelman, 'Roman Georgic in the Georgian Age: A Theory of Romantic Genre' (*TSLL* 33.182–214), as he ranges from Virgil to Wordsworth to explain how 'the georgic vanished precisely *in spite of* its previous cultural centrality, its absence paradoxically confirming the genre's most powerful aesthetic claim to be first and foremost a genre of history', but one so broadened to accommodate Georgian aspirations that it was no longer generically available to Wordsworth, though its 'entailments' were everywhere apparent. David Paxman's 'The Genius of English: Eighteenth-Century Language Study and English Poetry' (*PQ* 70.27–46) is even more impressive. This dense and fascinating essay traces attempts to define the genius of the language by such theorists as James Burnett, Lord Monboddo and Lord Kames and in the language of middle and late eighteenth-century poetry: for the first time students of language 'were attempting to ground their literary aesthetics in a clear understanding of the workings of their own language … [which] accounted … for the rhythms and harmony of verse … [and] to join their ideas of language structure with those of associational psychology'. Bill Overton reports qualified success in 'Teaching Eighteenth-Century English Poetry: An Experiment' (*English* 40.137–44) made possible by Lonsdale's two recent anthologies. His attempt to broaden the student canon was frustrated by a gender-based drift – the males to Stephen Duck, the females to Mary Collyer – and thus, perhaps, also an unwitting validation of Donna Landry's contention in her review essay ('The Traffic in Women Poets', *ECent* 32.180–92) that Lonsdale's second anthology is 'exemplary in many ways, and even benevolently "feminist" in some respects, but it nevertheless participates in … certain commodification of the very women's writings we hope to recover, revitalize, and restore to possible reading publics'.

Anne Finch, one of the few female poets of the early decades given token attention even before Lonsdale, is politically re-aligned by Carol Barash ('The Political Origins of Anne Finch's Poetry', *HLQ* 54.327–51) as one in the 'community of heroic women' who championed the Stuart cause before transferring their allegiance to Queen Anne as 'guiding mother' of the Church of England. This intriguing essay finally settles into claims about the solitary poetic voice which associate Finch more closely with Wordsworth – whom Barash blames, at the outset, for misreading Finch – than with the 'archetypal Augustan woman poet' she claims her subject to be. Two male Augustans figure in a matching pair of shorter pieces: Marybeth Gugler ('Mercury and the "Pains of Love" in Jonathan Swift's "A Beautiful Young Nymph Going to Bed" ', (*ELN* 77.31–6) claims a rationale for Swift in the historical and medical realities of every whore's fate rather than the author's pathology, and Thomas J. Regan (' "Allum Flower" in Swift's *The Lady's Dressing Room*' (*Scriblerian* 23.292)) seems somewhat embarrassed by his own pedantry but soldiers on to prove Celia equally practical by reference to a Mary Evelyn satire of 1690 on the use of alum powder as an anti-perspirant. In 'Versions of "Female Nature" in John Gay's *Fan*' (*SECC* 21.43–51), Jacob Fuchs prioritizes the 1714 text with its coquettish, free Corinna over the soberly married lady of 1720, though his arguments are more convincing as a concession to recent feminist enlightenment of our times than as a literary assessment of Gay's Enlightenment 'myth of the passive woman, fulfilled only by marriage and a lifetime of subservience'. Dianne Dugaw's 'Folklore and John Gay's Satire' (*SEL* 31.515–33) is most persuasive when she investigates 'Traditional Structures as Templates', for example, ballads as the ultimate source for *The Ravens, The Sexton and the Earth Worm* which 'spirals down the social system, undoing all forms of carrion-feasting and power-parsing'. Two other journal contributions briefly draw attention to obscure versifiers: Alun David, in ' "A Tragick Sense of Endless Woe": Daniel Barker's *History of Job*' (*CS* 3.208–14) puts together a modest biography and sensible evaluation of the one significant poem; Chester Chapin, in 'The Poems of Abel Evans, 1679–1737' questions the attribution to Evans of 'Pre-Existence' (a turgid and uncharacteristically solemn poem) as he argues for its replacement by 'On Blenheim House', an altogether more combative political poem more plausibly ascribed to one of the Tory Wit's like-minded friends. Even Defoe's poetry is treated to a couple of mentions this year: 'Defoe's Quotations' by W. S Watt (*N&Q* 38.349–50) identifies Rutilius Claudius Namatianus as 'the old poet' Defoe remembered when phrasing one of his own couplets; and Daniel Scott makes passing reference to *The True-Born Englishman* as 'that political satire in indifferent verse' which nevertheless set the pattern for a lifetime's campaign in favour of immigration on economic grounds ('Daniel Defoe and Immigration', *ECS* 24–25.293–313).

In his introduction to the thirteen essays which make up *Pope*: *New Contexts*, David Fairer declares the intention to mediate between transcendental assumptions encoded in *The Enduring Legacy* – that other tercentenary collection, which beat this one into print – and the destabilizing partisanship of cultural materialism typified by *The New Eighteenth Century*. It may sound like a *post hoc* rationalization: it turns out to be a not unjustified summary of the parts in a volume which maintains an unusually even quality across a variety of approaches to a few broad subject matrices. For example, the first three contributors write on Pope's politics: J. A. Downie starts the ball rolling, with engagingly disingenuous scepticism, when he fails to find a 'Rhetoric of Jacobitism'; then, with the careful attention to process which is appropriate to an older style of historicism, Christine Gerrard distinguishes Pope from Cobham's anti-Walpole Patriots as a wit marching to the beat of his individual, ethical drum; and Thomas Woodman identifies an ideological conservatism in the last poet who aspired to the great Renaissance ideal of a national laureate. Four others go their different ways on Pope's representation of gender: Carolyn D. Williams takes an instructive step backwards to explore Pope's 'improvement' on tensions in the classics; Steve

Clark embraces the agenda of Laura Brown and Felicity Nussbaum but then questions the relevance of 'gender terms' to Pope's rhetoric; Susan Matthews usefully contrasts 'a series of twentieth-century feminist responses to Pope's discourse of femininity' against those of female novelists of the century following his period; and Stephen Bygrave writes a caveat against the appropriation of *Eloisa* as a proto-feminist text. Rebecca Ferguson would open out the issue from gender *per se* to the 'links between Pope's metaphoric formulation of the body as writing and writing as the body', and the remaining essays are, in one way or another, concerned with the contextualizing mentioned in the collection's title. John C. Whale, unsurprisingly, finds Romantic hostility grounded in Pope's successors' awareness of subversive power in his poetry, Nicholas Roe gets down to specifics and Wordworth's debt to Pope in *The Prelude*, and David Fairer – in one of the best essays printed here – reads Heraclitus, Pope and Blake concurrently to draw parallels between their employment of dynamic opposition (which also 'expresses an interdependence of principle'), then joins with Stephen Copley for a brief but valuable piece on disruption of the generic concordat expected of the essayist *on Man* and its 'polite reader'. Finally, and provocatively, Brean S. Hammond writes on the professional poet's collusion in bourgeois economic activity for all his expressed loathing of 'literary commodification' in the (profitable) *Dunciad*.

ESC prints a couple of essays on Pope this year and both start with the early verse: Raymond Stephanson, in 'The Love Song of Young Alexander Pope: Allusion and Sexual Displacement in the Pastorals' (17.21–35), admits that his psycho-social questions are no more than 'plausible' but he does construct from them an equally plausible case for a Pope who intuited a necessary if 'uneasy, tense intimacy between his sexual self and his poetry'; and Richard Bevis, in 'From Windsor Forest to Bartholomew Fair: The Education of an Imperialist' (17.151–61), argues vigorously that the narrow imperialist so excoriated by Laura Brown outgrows his (and her) straitjacket to anatomize a more threatening empire of Dulness. Predictably enough, Deborah Payne, who writes the one substantial journal essay on *The Rape* this year, muscularly reasserts materialist feminist values against the sceptics in 'Pope and the War Against Coquettes: Or, Feminism and *The Rape of The Lock* Reconsidered – Yet Again' (*ECent* 32.3–24). She finds Clarissa a pliant co-operator with the patriarch: Richard Crider defends the *logic* of Clarrissa's advice on matrimony but avoids any contentious further extension (*Expl* 49.80–2). I have not seen *Pope's Dunciad of 1728: A History and Facsimile*, edited by David L. Vander Meulen for UPVirginia, and can notice only this year's modest crop of shorter pieces. Among these, Frederick M. Keener's 'Pope, *The Dunciad*, Virgil, and the New Historicism of Le Bossu' (*ECLife* 15.35–57) is the most scholarly, and Kristina Sraub's 'Men From Boys: Cibber, Pope and the Schoolboy' (*ECent* 32.219–39) the most ingenious. Keener literally harks back to older concerns as he pays generous tribute to, then modifies, Aubrey Williams on Le Bossu as a mediator between the *Aeneid* and Pope's mock-heroic; Straub works cleverly with that nexus of gender issues which have dominated so much writing on Pope in recent years, here centred on the schoolboy trope in which 'masculinity as contingent and relational … helps to disclose a process by which literary authority is constructed in relation to gender and sexual identity.' Elsewhere, the annotators are at work. In 'Otho: Emperor or Artefact' (*Scriblerian* 23–24.293–4), Carolyn D. Williams adds further levels of condemnation to Pope's Annius, the disreputable dealer in antiques, as she pursues Emperor Otho's association with 'unnatural' femininity; and Taylor Corse, ' "Another Yet the Same": Joseph Hall and *The Dunciad*' (*N&Q* 38.183–4), tentatively suggests replacing Settle by Cibber as the target in Book III by reference to Hall's *Mundus Alter et Idem*. Christopher Fox also pursues origins. His 'Pope, Perhaps, and Sextus: Skeptical Modes in *Moral Essay I*' (*ELN* 77.37–48) is a careful explication of a long recognized but, as Fox believes, also an underestimated debt to Sextus Empiricus by way of Montaigne; and Adam Piette offers a similarly familiar but sprightly reading of Pope's translation of Donne's *Fourth Satire* – here the classical smoothing-iron is judged to be entirely appropriate – as the key to his general refutation of Thomas M. Green's claim that it was all downhill for the art of imitation after Ben Jonson. But the most intriguing single essay on Pope's 'imitation' this year comes in F. E. Salmon's 'Alexander Pope and Circe's Second Dome' (*RES* 42.523–31). Extending Maynard Mack's suggestion that during his translation of the *Odyssey* Pope gave his friends types from the Greek epic, Salmon identifies Henrietta Howard as Circe by reference to evidence which includes a sketch reminiscent of her Marble Hill house. (This is fascinating, circumstantial stuff.) Carolyn Williams, in her third piece on Pope this year, is more cautious as she reworks some biographical details for 'Pope and Granville: Fictions of Friendship' (*N&Q* 38.184–6). Finally, Margaret M. Smith has the tangible evidence of a recently discovered manuscript, which she reproduces, to back up her portrait of Spence as a scrupulously honest 'editor' of material sent for the projected 'Lives of the Poets' in 'Alexander Pope's Notes in *William Wycherley*' (*YULG* 66.26–32).

The appearance of *James Thomson (1700–1748): A Life* is a signal event. James Sambrook is the undisputed authority on his subject and this splendid biography is surely set to remain *the* 'Life' for at least the span commensurate with that which has passed since Douglas Grant's *James Thomson* was published in 1951. Sambrook commands such broad and detailed knowledge, not only about Thomson but also his times, that his reader is drawn into a pellucid network of events, associations, influences and influencers. One could dip into any chapter and find something to enjoy. For example, in the account of Thomson's cat-and-mouse game with the stage censors over *Edward and Elenora* – at best of secondary interest to those who come to the *Life* through the poetry – Sambrook constructs a lucid narrative out of the complex manoeuvering, Thomson's handsome profit, and the death of his friend Richard Savage, which draws together literary politics and personal matters without a hint of special pleading or speculation beyond the evidence. The only other significant mention of Thomson this year comes in William C. Crisman's 'Blake's "The Crystal Cabinet" as a Reworking of Thomson's *Castle of Indolence*' (*ELN* 77.52–9) and a parallel treated to relentless deconstruction which is as blinkered as Sambrook's comparisons are judicious. Thomson knew Edward Young, had no high opinion of his poetry, but kept his counsel. So does Cheryl Wanko in 'The Making of a Minor Poet: Edward Young and Literary Taxonomy' (*ES* 72.355–67) where she studiously avoids the question of whether Young was ever worthy of his fame as she traces his decline to near invisibility between the grinding wheels of 'Augustan' and 'Pre-Romantic'.

Two cheers for *The Poet Without a Name: Gray's 'Elegy' and the Problem of History* by Henry Weinfield. This is an extraordinary, against-the-grain book, as the author recognizes when he acknowledges the publisher who 'had the courage to believe in a project that some might have regarded as eccentric': so *three* cheers for Southern Illinois University Press. In his own words again, Winfield proposes that 'the thematic constellation of poverty, alienation, and unfulfilled potential – or what I refer to as "the problem of history" … is directly confronted in the *Elegy*, and in a way that not only has a profound impact on subsequent poets but also obliges us to reinterpret certain aspects of the previous tradition through the terms that the *Elegy* itself establishes'. He then clears the theoretical ground by reviewing previous criticism (Dr Johnson to Bernard Bronson) before an epic phenomenological reading of the poem – stanza by stanza, with long interpolated sections, 106 pages in all – which progresses to elaboration of his claim for the *Elegy* as a poetic watershed in its 'symbolic dissolution of the pastoral', and concludes with 'one important way in which the terrain encompassed by the *Elegy* opens out on Romantic and even Modernist poetics'. Beyond that description, it would be impossible to do even-handed justice to Weinfield in the scope *YWES* allows. Suffice it to say that anyone with an interest in Gray must find here much to stimulate and irritate them, probably in equal measure. At least Weinfield accuses those critics who were writing during the 1940s and 1950s of no more than attributing the poem's irritating popularity – irksome because they had labelled its author as a minor talent – 'to extrapoetic factors and to the lack of discernment of ordinary readers'. In 'Assumed Identities: Gray's Correspondence and the "Intelligence Communities" of Eighteenth-Century Studies' (*ECent* 32.274–88), William H. Epstein continues his investigative work into the motives of scholars who, though not all covert counter-intelligence agents, 'acted as if they were participating in the reciprocal interpenetration of the academic and intelligence communities' to sustain the fabric of Cold War ideology. Of course, there is no such thing as an ideologically-innocent response, and Chomsky is persuasive, so perhaps we should reserve our position until the Oliver Stone movie appears. It does, though, seem pusillanimous to turn from such matters to welcome S. H. Clarke's bi-partite essay on Gray in two issues of *ECS* (24 and 25), particularly the first ' "Pendet Homo Incertus": Gray's response to Locke. Part One: "Dull in a New Way" ' (273–91). Nevertheless, this is a sinewy essay, which takes the 'Eton College' ode as its focal text to foreground Gray's toughness as he 'scrupulously adheres to the conditions and consequences of *being* a Lockean self ... [and] memory is pushed to the point where the very mechanics of reason, retention and judgement, become imbued with crisis and torment'. In Part Two (484–503), Clarke moves to the prose, *De Principiis Cogitandi*, and Gray facing up to Locke's curtailment of understanding with a rigour for which he 'deserves to be regarded not as a poignant casualty of the Augustan Age but as its supreme practitioner'. William Levine argues an analogous case in 'From the Ridiculous to the Sublime: Gray's Transvaluation of Pope's Poetics' (*PQ* 70.289–309), though here Gray is seen as a clear-sighted fellow-poet responding to Pope's satiric deflation of 'inspiration' in his own pindarics.

It has thus been a good year for those poets who used to occupy the canon's second division, and it is all the better for the editing of Betty Rizzo and Robert Mahoney in *The Annotated Letters of Christopher Smart*. Everything known is here. Not much, to be sure; and what there is shows often that 'compactness [which] sometimes approached implosion', akin to Smart's earlier, gnomic poetry. The sensitivity and learning of the editors in their voluminous annotation and commentary is thus plainly necessary, and we must be grateful for their stamina too. Three substantial essays on Burns confirm the trend towards diversification into less well-trodden fields. Carol McGuirk, 'Burns, Bakhtin, and the Opposition of Poetic and Novelistic Discourse: A Response to David Morris' (*ECent* 32.58–72) praises the critical seriousness of her fellow enthusiast's 'Burns and Heteroglossia', but challenges the rigidity of his categories and argues powerfully that Burns has suffered enough from whisky-and-haggis adulation to be labelled 'singular' by his academic analysts. Kenneth Simpson is a staunch supporter of McGuirk, as he happily admits in 'Burns and Scottish History' (*ECLife* 15.210–24) which, despite Simpson's penchant for Byronic parallels and explosions of rhetorical questioning, is well worth reading on the linguistic, dramatic and conceptual dualities which spring from Burns's 'acute sense of displacement, both in his native Ayrshire and in fashionable Edinburgh'. I reserve for last what seems to me the best piece on Burns – John Ashmead and John Davison, 'Words, Music and Emotion in the Love Songs of Robert Burns', (*ECLife* 15.225–42). That qualification expresses more than formulaic modesty, since I was quite lost by passages such as 'the digression on the modal scales and the Scottish double tonic.' Nevertheless, I was also persuaded by the care with which the co-writers argued that the best songs rank with the finest in Europe and their reaffirmation of the commonsense – also witnessed in Kinsley's pioneering but still standard Oxford edition – that 'as far as possible, criticism of the songs ... should always include music and words.'

3. The Novel

J. Paul Hunter and Peter Sabor tread softly but wield big sticks when they take on the disruptive theorists of earlier decades: Sabor's 'Harold Bloom on Eighteenth-Century Fiction' (*ECF* 4.153–63) is at once measured and remorseless in its dissection of the book-making deficiencies in the Chelsea House collections edited by Bloom (or as frequently ghosted for him); Hunter's 'Novels and History and Northrop Frye' (*ECS* 24.225–41) is just as determined to detail the ahistorical short measure given to the novel in Frye's work on the 'Age of Sensibility' over a quarter of a century ago, but not without some gracious compliments to the Canadian sage. Frye returns the conference decorums but remains serenely unrepentant during his instant reply in the same issue of *ECS* (24:243–9). There is a similar tactical balance but with a more strategic intent in William Beatty Warner's 'Social Power and the Eighteenth-Century Novel: Foucault and Transparent Literary History' (*ECF* 4.185–203) which mixes praise for perceptiveness with condemnation of what he argues is the ultimately disturbing and simplifying concern with power alone as 'the magnetic north for critical enquiry and historical research' in the work of scholars such as Nancy Armstrong, John Bender, Leo Damrosch and Michael McKeon. This is a meaty review essay, if one that seems unlikely to deflect the New Historicist energy of such as Lennard J. Davis who this year reads, in accounts of the first contacts between Europeans and Amerindians in the Caribbean Basin, the creation of 'Discovery' and 'The New World' as quasi-fictional constructs which 'constituted a set of discursive practices that would eventually be normalized in the eighteenth-century novel', ('The Facts of Events and the Event of Facts: New World Explorers and the Early Novel', *ECent* 32.240–55). More concerned with the textual practices of those novels, in 'Marks, Stamps and Representations: Character in Eighteenth-Century Fiction' (*SNNTS* 23.295–311), David Oakleaf continues his pursuit of 'tensions between ... private and social' representations, derived from Johnson's definition of character but mediated through Bakhtin and Terry Castle, on this occasion with some shrewd discriminations between the reconciliations in Defoe and Richardson. Advertisements suggest that Terry Castle herself is represented, but more directly, in *The Country Myth: Motifs in the British Novel from Defoe to Smollett*, edited by H. George Hahn (Britannia Texts), a selection of previously published criticism chosen to illustrate the editor's thesis that claims for the bourgeois novel should be moderated by recognition of the regularity with which major 'Georgian' exempla end happily in country house retirement, but I have not seen the volume to check either promise.

Two very different but equally estimable books tackle the relationship between women's lives and fiction head on. Elizabeth Bergen Brophy, in *Women's Lives and the Eighteenth-Century English Novel*, attempts to negotiate the historical and theoretical minefield between experience and representation by reproducing the comments of over 250 women from journals and letters long buried in Britain's Public Record Office. Her declared aims are to answer the question 'What was it like to be an *average* eighteenth-century woman … [derived from] as representative a group as it is possible to find', then 'to examine the novels in terms of their depiction of these women and of their possible influence on them'. But to declare an exclusive focus on direct comparison rather than modern textual criticism or feminist scholarship is not to answer the other obvious questions about, for example, the complex iteration between lives and the entire range of textual representation, particularly when the experience which provides her template seems anything but 'average' and is ordered under roles (daughter, wife, widow) with little attention to dates. That said, Brophy's readings of Richardson, the Fieldings, Charlotte Lennox, Sarah Scott, Clara Reeve and Frances Burney are never less than absorbing if only because so firmly grounded in the immediacy of the primary material which is the great value of her work. By contrast, Katherine Sobba Green is acutely aware of process and comfortably engaged with the theoretical disputes which swirl around her subject, *The Courtship Novel, 1740–1820: A Feminized Genre*. She argues persuasively that the evolution from marriage as arranged transfer of human property, to its widespread acceptance as 'affective individuation and companionate' partnership was not only important to the nascent feminist agenda but was also interrogated most comprehensively in the 'subgenre [which] … treated the time between a young woman's coming out and her marriage as the most important period in her life'. Here it is precisely the problematic relationship between experience and text which is most revealing, and Green's Bakhtinian tolerance sensibly resists closure. Richardson is given his due, as are the more familiar female novelists such as Frances Burney, Charlotte Lennox and Maria Edgworth; but readers of *YWES* will probably find more to engage them in lively explorations such as those which trace feminizing linguistic awareness in Mary Collyer's *Felicia to Charlotte* (published literally between the first *Pamela* and *Clarissa*) or Jane West's *The Advantages of Education, or, the History of Maria Williams*, 'obviously calculated for readers following the skirmishes of the Feminist Controversy, [which] appeared the year after Mary Wollstonecraft rushed *A Vindication* … into print'. Catherine A. Craft, 'Reworking Male Modules: Aphra Behn's *Fair Vow-Breaker*, Eliza Haywood's *Fantomina* and Charlotte Lennox's *Female Quixote*' (*MLR* 86.821–38) also finds subversion within the limitations allowed by patriarchal discourse, but without adding much to the work of Mary Poovey, Jane Spencer – or Katherine Sobba Green – and two other journal pieces neatly demonstrate the basic uncertainties with which all wrestle. Christine Blouch, 'Eliza Haywood and the Romance of Obscurity' (*SEL* 31.535–52) assembles and speculates on scraps of information about the woman who tried to suppress biographical truth, not least to counter Pope's attack; but, instantly, Gabrielle M. Firmager, 'Eliza Haywood: Some Further Light on her Background' (*N&Q* 38.181–3) covers some of the same ground as she glosses two newly discovered letters only to propose alternative 'facts'. Relevant here might have been Madeleine Kahn's *Narrative Transvestism: Rhetoric and Gender in the Eighteenth-Century English Novel* (Corn UP) but I have not seen it.

Two books with *Robinson Crusoe* as their focus could not be more different. Martin Green takes *The Robinson Crusoe Story* as one of the seven genres within adventure fiction – on which he promises another book – and launches into a cultural historical survey of successive 'folktales of white empire' (along with the anti-imperialist variant). Not unlike Defoe's Crusoe, sifting through the wreckage of his ship, Green's pragmatic interest in the original is in how it may be disassembled into seven useful motifs – the island, survival, prosperity, colonial encounter, and so on – as tools with which to explore a dozen subsequent 'Crusoe stories', from Rousseau's *Emile* in 1762 to Tournier's *Vendredi: ou Les Limbes du Pacifique* in 1967, by way of *Masterman Ready*, *Peter Pan* and *Lord of the Flies*. Of course, that exploration is driven by accretive broadening contextualization. Not so Manuel Schonhorn in his revisionist concentration on *Defoe's Politics: Parliament, Power, Kingship, and 'Robinson Crusoe'*. If Green writes for the generalist with an interest in the broad vistas of literary sociology, Schonhorn takes on those specialists who, he believes, have misrepresented Defoe as a Lockean, Whiggish liberal. Insisting on the seamless political drive of all Defoe's writings, Schonhorn reads Robinson Crusoe as a type of the covenanted 'charismatic warrior-king', akin to the hero whom God ordained to be elected by the people at the Glorious Revolution and after whose death England subsided into rudderless, corrupt parliamentary bureaucracy. This is a densely-argued book which will provoke strong reactions. It is intended to do so, for despite Schonhorn's expertly disposed and supple analysis of, for example, Defoe's problems with the issue of monarchical succession – 'His political tendency, like his fictional, is to be inclusive, compendious, equivocal, and seemingly contradictory' – the argument becomes stubbornly singular when we reach *Robinson Crusoe*. Such is the way of polemic which has the courage of its convictions. Schonhorn declares that his thesis is complementary to the received wisdoms of modern Defoe scholarship: contradictory would be a better description. The consequence is a stimulating and important book. J. F. Burrows is more defensive about his stylometric work in ' "I Lisp'd in Numbers": Fielding, Richardson and the Appraisal of Statistical Evidence' (*Scriblerian* 23–24.234–41) and he is given more grounds for that caution by 'Dangerous Relations' (*Scriblerian* 23–24.242–4) as P. N. Furbank and W. R. Owens (who join the debate 'as scholars who got interested in the subject as a possible aid to Defoe attribution') reject it as dangerous for statistically naïve critics who are therefore prone to discovery of predetermined 'proofs'. Back on firmer, non-statistical ground, two essayists take their cue from John Richetti's detection of a deserted psycho-social space at the core of Defoe's female criminals. John Reitz, in 'Criminal Biography' (*SNNTS* 23.183–95), works assiduously through a couple of earlier comparators and concludes that those proprieties which demanded oxymoronic pressure in the very notion of 'female' conjoined with 'criminal' show that 'Moll Flanders may be an even more realistic portrait ... than we have recognised'. Mark Troy is more adventurous but less lucid as he extends 'the metaphor of the private or uncharted ... non-appropriated area' to Crusoe's island and thence to modernist fiction of our own century ('The Blank Page of Daniel Defoe', *OL* 46.1–12). Gary Hentzi's 'Holes in the Heart: *Moll Flanders*, Roxana, and "Agreeable Crime" ' (*Boundary* 16.174–200) is not only more eloquent but more informative, as it ranges over the Defoe battlefield and finds value in the work of such critics as Novak or Starr, though itself more persuaded by Marxist, Historicist and Freudian contributions to the 'contradictions and ambiguities ... in all their unsettling disharmony' which energize the narratives. For impoverished students who wish to engage with the less readily available originals there is a reissue of James T. Boulton's World's Classics *Memoirs of a Cavalier* introduced by John Mullan.

Most of the combatants on Fielding and Johnson seem to be pausing for breath. Certainly I could find only three journal pieces on Richardson and four on Fielding.

Nevertheless, two of those who write on *Pamela* offer thoughtful and briskly-argued contributions to the feminist debate. Tassie Gwilliam, in '*Pamela* and the Duplicitous Body' (*Rep* 34.104–33) is particularly good on metaphors for the female body in attempts to cope with ideologically-inscribed 'duplicity' and the novel's 'cross-gender identifications' as devices by which Pamela is vindicated from those suspicions of hypocrisy which, however, 'continue to circulate in the novel, irrepressible and apparently unkillable elements of the eighteenth-century ideology of femininity'. Betty A. Schellenberg is no less incisively confident that such Bakhtinian readings offer illusory comfort because literally incomplete: 'Enclosing the Immovable: Structuring Social Authority in *Pamela* Part II' (*ECF* 4.27–42) argues that 'the focus, in Part I, upon the defence of besieged virtue in precarious social limbo becomes, in the sequel, a careful placing of female behaviour within the boundaries describing its acceptable manifestations.' Douglas Murray chooses a less immediate but related scholarly subject for 'Classical Myth in Richardson's *Clarissa*: Ovid Revised' (*ECF* 3.113–24) as he urges myth-tracers to see the novelist 'not as a transcriber but rather as an adapter – even a questioner' in a fiction which reworks myths of mortals raped by Gods to foreground the issue of the struggle to resist capitulation to the rapist's power and discourse.

Joseph F. Bartolomeo's 'Interpolated Tales as Allegories of Reading: *Joseph Andrews*' (*SNNTS* 23.405–15) also proposes re-thinking of a literary device. Here in a packed, occasionally gnomic reading, the three interpolated stories 'serve a paradigmatic function within a text that purports to define, in both theory and practice, a new genre', and Cheryl Wanko busily pursues a similar Iserian line on the process by which *Amelia* teaches us to suspect every character encountered, by forcing us to reverse the novel's overt lesson that we should mimic its paragon of virtue by trusting everyone ('Characterization and the Reader's Quandary in Fielding's *Amelia*', *JEGP* 90.505–23). Astrid Masetti's 'Up and Down Stairways: Escher, Bakhtin, and *Joseph Andrews*' (*SEL* 31.553–68) is much more cleverly idiosyncratic as it relates 'reciprocal doubling' to Escher's visual games and carnivalesque, even if it is finally more satisfying on means than ends. Both of those are very much at issue in the most noteworthy shorter pieces on Fielding this year which focus on the tensions of class war in all that Fielding did and wrote. The first, by Arlene Wilner, pays homage to its origin in a seminar by John Richetti who, in turn, compliments the pioneering investigations of E. P. Thompson and John Barrell to introduce his own 'equal, wide survey': the apprentice's essay, 'The Mythology of History, the Truth of Fiction: Henry Fielding and the Cases of Bosavern Penlez and Elizabeth Canning' (*JNT* 21.185–201), reconciles the apparent contradictions between the persona of the kindly omniscient novelist and the apparently schizophrenic magistrate/pamphleteer (savage and understanding by turns), by reference to Fielding's battles to contain a mobile, displaced proletariat; the sorcerer himself writes one of the year's best essays on the same complex matrix, 'Class Struggle Without Class: Novelists and Magistrates' (*ECent* 32.203–18), drawing in Defoe and Smollett before concentrating on the work of Fielding, particularly *Tom Jones*, as 'a deliberate mis-representation of contemporary life as he himself experiences and renders it passionately'.

'It seems a sign of our times that an issue of *Eighteenth-Century Fiction* devoted to Frances Burney [indeed, to *Evelina* alone] should have arisen spontaneously – that is, not as a result of editorial long-term planning, but as an effect of the essays submitted', notes Margaret Anne Doody as she begins her 'Beyond *Evelina*: The Individual Novel and the Community of Literature' which concludes the July issue of *ECF*. That is palpably true. But there is more in this endpiece to justify turning things on their head by noting Doody's essay before mention of those which precede it. Not only does she review the prior essays so shrewdly that it would be otiose to add much here, she also writes by far the best of the essays in a delightfully discursive, occasionally sardonic style which is an appropriate vehicle both for the amused pride she takes in the other contributors' reflexive use of her own earlier work and for her insistence on the comic vivacity of Burney which is obscured in correct solemnity elsewhere. Of course, the other essayists do have useful things to say, as Doody is the first to admit; Julia Epstein who contextualizes the 'rediscovery' of Burney's novel in 'Burney Criticism: Family Romance, Psychobiography, and Social History'; then Amy J. Pawl (' "And What Other Name May I Claim?": Names and Their Owners in ... *Evelina')*, Gina Campbell ('Bringing Belmont to Justice; Burney's Quest for Paternal Recognition'), and David Oakleaf ('The Name of the Father: Social Identity and the Ambition of *Evelina*') who all explore different aspects of the same core issue; but Susan C. Greenfield's essay ' "Oh Dear Resemblance of Thy Murdered Mother": Female Authorship in *Evelina*' is clearly the runner-up to Doody as it weaves together the novel's deference to patriarchy with its strong matrilineal counter-thrust. Doody herself is judiciously at work again in her introduction to *The Wanderer* (which she also co-edits with Robert L. Mack and Peter Sabor) contrasting this darker 'Romantic' later novel against the 'Georgian' optimism of *Evelina*. Joanne Cutting-Gray, in *Woman as 'Nobody' and the Novels of Fanny Burney*, pursues another kind of contextualization. Indeed, despite the choice of that dismissive form of the author's forename (which will grate on many of her feminist colleagues), Burney is here of interest primarily as a pioneer of woman's position as 'Other', as articulated by Kristeva, Irigary and others, so there is little which will be new to those readers who have followed the spate of monographs on Burney over recent years. For example, those passages of physical and mental torment, long dismissed as mere female weakness but in fact used to explore female identity and voice, have been more intensely (if harrowingly) investigated by Julia Epstein in *The Iron Pen* (*YWES* 70.393).

As in the previous two annual issues of *The Shandean*, Kenneth Monkman writes the scholarly centrepiece for this year's collection, in 'Sterne's Farewell to Politics', which concludes his survey of Sterne's 'long and largely unrewarded apprenticeship in journalism'; and, as usual, it is a delight to follow Monkman's learning and energy as he sifts evidence before the sudden sweep of assertion ('here surely is Sterne') whether here or in his later piece on 'A Letter by (and a Poem to ?) Lydia, and a Letter by Elizabeth'. Three other contributors report on work in alternative seams of the bibliographical mine: Judith Hawley's ' "Hints and Documents" I: A Bibliography for *Tristram Shandy*' opens proceedings with what she herself describes as a 'pseudo-bibliography', ascribing a plausible edition to each of the books mentioned in the novel (and promising an analysis of these in 1992); Anne Bandry's 'The Publication of the Spurious Volumes of *Tristram Shandy*' lists 'the most direct responses to Sterne's constant game with the reader, as well as the most direct attempts to capitalize on his success'; and Diana Patterson's 'Tristram's Marblings and Marblers' is a bibliophile's treasure-house on the first printed run of volume three with its 8000 unique 'wordless jokes on the reader, and even more provoking jokes on the critic'. In support, Peter de Voogd writes his annual piece of ancillary detection, this time on 'Henry William Bunbury, Illustrator of Tristram Shandy', while Madeleine Descargues describes a copy of 'Ignatio Sancho's *Letters*' to illustrate their heavy indebtedness to Sterne's typographical mannerisms. Her distinction between comic Sterne and 'cynic' Swift thus appears after both Michael J. O'Shea's explanation of the playfulness in 'Laurence Sterne's Display of Heraldry' and Melvyn New's own elaborate joke, deliberately confusing Sterne with Swift in a piece of ironically bogus scholarship, to launch his 'Swift as Ogre, Richardson as Dolt: Rescuing Sterne from the Eighteenth Century', an eloquent broadside against the adulation of Sterne by critics determined to denigrate his literary contemporaries while removing him from their orbit: 'Swift is left behind as a mass of psychoses, and Richardson is easily outdone because of his naivete and inability to create real scenes or real people; only Sterne remains in our world and he is "one of us" '. One wonders if New had prior intelligence of the Symposium on 'Laurence Sterne in Modernism and Post-Modernism' advertized in the same issue of *The Shandean* for April 1993 at the University of York. Jacques Berthoud, Professor of English there, must have been in the know, but discreetly busies himself about 'The Beggar in *A Sentimental Journey*' and the anatomy of sentiment subtly dramatized in Yorick's commerce with mendicants – particularly Father Lorenzo – which is inseparable from his erotic attachments. Others have reacted differently to that link between the secular and the religious, as various hands combine with Kenneth Monkman to show in '*A Sentimental Journey* and the *Index Librorum Prohibitorum*', a note on the book's belated proscription in 1819, after an Italian translation. Elsewhere, Paula Loscocco, (' "Can't Live Without 'Em": Walter Sandy and the Woman Within', *ECent* 32.166–79), adds her earnest voice to the debate about Sterne's mysogyny by citing in evidence the patriarchal discourse of the same novel which Melvyn New, 'Job's Wife and Sterne's Other Women' (in *Out of Bounds: Male Writers and Gender[ed] Criticisms*, Laura Claridge and Elizabeth Langland, eds) defends energetically by reading dialogues to counter Ruth Perry's attack on phallocentric language with the argument that Sterne is 'translating a language of opposition … into one that promises … the creative harmony that accepts difference'. Displaced rather than oppositional (or even complementary) discourse is Robert L. Chibka's subject in 'The Hobby-Horse's Epitaph: *Tristram Shandy*, *Hamlet*, and the Vehicles of Memory' (*ECF* 4.125–51), a sinuous reading of *Hamlet* woven into the texture of all Sterne's writing as 'an unlikely sort of *memento mori*'. An altogether different order of source – in a French pun – persuades Frédéric Ogée into some pleasurably uneven speculations on the invisible presence in Sterne's blank page ('Pli ou face? Autour d'un page de *Tristram Shandy*', *EA* 44.257–71); and J. B. Shipley, in 'Tristram's Dearly Beloved: Or, His Jenny's An ***' (*ELN* 77.45–51) adds little to speculation about the origin of Jenny's name let alone her ***; so it is the ubiquitous Melvyn New who is left to increase the store of Sterneana, in issues of *Scriblerian* 23 and 24. His first contribution analyses 'A Manuscript of the Le Fever Episode in *Tristram Shandy*' (165–74), and bewails the implication that there may be over one hundred buried misreadings in the first edition, the others report 'Scholia to the Florida *Tristram Shandy* Annotations' (105–6 and 296–7).

Goldsmith's solitary novel is the subject of uneven attention this year. George H. Haggerty wrestles to some purpose with the old polarities of 'Satire and Sentiment in *The Vicar of Wakefield*' (*ECent* 32.25–38), but Stephen Derry does little more in 'Jane Austen's Use of *The Vicar of Wakefield* in *Pride and Prejudice*' (*ELN* 77.25–7) than enumerate parallels which persuade him 'it may be possible to consider *Pride and Prejudice* as a recollection … and re-presentation … of some of the classic novel material'. Quite so. I have not seen *The Expedition of Humphrey Clinker* edited by Thomas R. Preston and O. M. Brack Jnr for UGeoP and therefore can report only the appearance of two notes by Robert Spector on Smollett's work in the *Briton* (*EA* 44.176–8), another, also by Spector (*ANQ* 4.73–5), on the origin of hot-tempered Scot's antipathy to Pitt in an imagined slight, and 'A Note on Smollett's *Atom*' by Olga

Costopoulos-Almon (*N&Q* 38.191–2) explaining an oxymoronic pun on anodyne and purgative oils which defeated the editors of the Georgia edition. Just as scholarly but more substantial in every sense is John Dwyer's 'Enlightened Spectators and Classical Moralists: Sympathetic Relations in Eighteenth-Century Scotland' (*ECLife* 15.96–118) which includes several annotated illustrations to support his revisionist claim 'that sentimental discourse had more in common with the classical language of virtue than with the rise of affective individualism or the evolution of the modern self', whether used by Sterne, Henry Mackenzie or even James MacPherson. An even more circumscribed protocol of 'virtue' (and a very neo-classical response to restraints on female writers) is the subject of Sarah Zimmerman's entirely persuasive essay on 'Charlotte Smith's Letters and the Practice of Self-Preservation' (*PULC* 53.50–77): this too combines analysis of texts with illustrative matter to demonstrate that in letters, poetry and novels Smith 'depicts herself as a woman wronged by a profligate husband and by a society that excuses his financial abandonment and his emotional and physical abuse' with good cause but also with sensible determination to milk the vogue for sentiment in the entire range of modes, genres, styles and semiotics of writing and publication.

Books Reviewed

Bann, Stephen. *The Inventions of History: Essays on the Representation of the Past.* ManUP (1990). pp. 246. £35. ISBN 0 7190 32970.

Bell, Ian A. *Literature and Crime in Augustan England.* Routledge. pp. 256. £35. ISBN 0 415 02231 2.

Black, Jeremy, ed. *British Politics and Society from Walpole to Pitt 1742–1789.* Macmillan (1990). pp. 274. hb £35, pb £10.99. ISBN 0 333 45488X, 0 333 454898.

Black, Jeremy, and Jeremy Gregory, eds. *Culture, Politics and Society in Britain, 1660–1800.* ManUP. pp. 216. £29.95. ISBN 0 7190 3435 3.

Boulton, James, ed. *Daniel Defoe; Memoirs of a Cavalier.* Intro by John Mullan. OUP. pp. 318. pb £4.99. ISBN 0 19 282710 3.

Bowden, Betsy. *Eighteenth-Century Modernizations From 'The Canterbury Tales'.* Chaucer Studies XVI. Boydell. pp. 263. £45. ISBN 0 85991 309 0.

Brönnimann-Egger, Werner. *The Friendly Reader: Modes of Cooperation between Eighteenth-Century English Poets and their Audience.* Stauffenberg. pp. 120. pb DM 38. ISBN 3 923721 21 8.

Brophy, Elizabeth Bergen. *Women's Lives and the Eighteenth-Century English Novel.* USFlorP. pp. 312. £29.95. ISBN 0 8130 1036 5.

Brown, Richard. *Church and State in Modern Britain 1700–1850.* Routledge. pp. 571. hb £40, pb £12.99. ISBN 0 41501122 1, 0 415 01123 X.

Brown, Richard. *Society and Economy in Modern Britain 1700–1850.* Routledge. pp. 473. hb £40, pb £12.99. ISBN 0 415 01120 5, 0 415 01121 3.

Claridge, Laura, and Elizabeth Langland, eds. *Out of Bounds: Male Writers and Gender(ed) Criticisms.* UMassP. pp. 360. £33.95. ISBN 0 87023 734 9.

Cormack. Malcolm. *The Paintings of Thomas Gainsborough.* CUP. pp. 200 + 75 ill. £19.95. ISBN 0 521 38241 6.

Cutting-Gray, Joanne. *Woman as 'Nobody' and the Novels of Fanny Burney.* UFlorP. pp. 169. £24.95. ISBN 0 8130 1106 X.

Doody, Margaret Anne, Robert L. Mack, and Peter Sabor, eds. *Frances Burney: The*

Wanderer. OUP. pp. 957. pb £8.95. ISBN 0 19 282133 4.

Edwards, Paul, and David Dabydeen, eds. *Black Writers in Britain 1760–1890*. Early Black Writers Series. EdinUP. pp. 239. hb £35, pb £14.95. ISBN 0 7486 0267 4, 0 7486 0327 1.

Fairer, David, ed. *Pope: New Contexts*. HW. pp. 251. £45. ISBN 0 7450 0791 0.

Green, Katherine Sobba. *The Courtship Novel, 1740–1820: A Feminized Genre*. UPKen. pp. 184. £23. ISBN 0 8131 1736 4.

Green, Martin. *The Robinson Crusoe Story*. UPennP. pp. 221. £19.95. ISBN 0 271 00705 2.

Harris, Frances. *A Passion for Government: The Life of Sarah Duchess of Marlborough*. Clarendon. pp. 421. £25. ISBN 0 19 820224 5.

Hyland, Paul, and Neil Sammuells, eds. *Irish Writing: Exile and Subversion*. Macmillan. pp. 256. hb £40, pb £14.99. ISBN 0 333 52541 8, 0 333 52542 6.

Jacob, Margaret C. *Living the Enlightenment: Freemasonry and Politics in Eighteenth-Century Europe*. OUP. pp. 304. £40. ISBN 0 19 506992 7.

Johnstone, H. Diack, and Roger Fiske, eds. *The Blackwell History of Music in Britain: The Eighteenth Century*. Blackwell Reference (1990). pp. 534. £70. ISBN 0 631 16519 3.

Langford, Paul. *Public Life and the Propertied Englishman 1689–1798*. Clarendon. pp. 608. £48. ISBN 0 19 820149 4.

Levine, Joseph M. *The Battle of the Books: History and Literature in the Augustan Age*. CornUP. pp. 428. $29.95. ISBN 0 8014 2537 9.

Linebaugh, Peter. *The London Hanged: Crime and Civil Society in the Eighteenth Century*. Lane. pp. 484. £25. ISBN 0 713 990 457.

Louth, Janet, ed. *Selected Writings by William Law*. Carcanet (1990). pp. 116. pb £6.95. ISBN 0 85635 862 2.

Maslen, Keith, and John Lancaster, eds. *The Bowyer Ledgers*. Bibliographical Society/Bibliographical Society of America. pp. 616 + 70 microfiches. £150. ISBN 0 914 93013 3.

Pittock, Joan H., and Andrew Wear, eds. *Interpretation and Cultural History*. Macmillan. pp. 296. £45. ISBN 0 333 52494 2.

Pittock, Murray G. H. *The Invention of Scotland: The Stuart Myth and the Scottish Identity, 1638 to the Present*. Routledge. pp. 198. £30. ISBN 0 415 05586 5.

Probyn, Clive T. *The Sociable Humanist: The Life and Works of James Harris 1709–1780*. Clarendon. pp. 371. £40. ISBN 0 19 818563 4.

Purvis, C .J. *The Offensive Art: The Liberation of Poetic Imagination in Augustan Satire*. Brynmill. pp. 235. £24. ISBN 0 907839 34 7.

Ribeiro, Alvaro, ed. *The Letters of Dr Charles Burney, Vol. 1, 1751–1784*. Clarendon. pp. 501. £60. ISBN 0 19 812687 5.

Rivers, Isabel. *Reason, Grace and Sentiment: A Study of the Language of Religion and Ethics in England, 1660–1780. Volume I: Whichcote to Wesley*. CUP. pp. 277. £35. ISBN 0 521 38340.

Rizzo, Betty, and Robert Mahony, eds. *The Annotated Letters of Christopher Smart*. SIUP. pp. 184. £24.50. ISBN 0 8093 1609 9.

Robinson, Sidney K. *Inquiry into the Picturesque*. UChicP. pp. 180. $19.95. ISBN 0 226 72251 1.

Rousseau, G. S. *Enlightenment Borders: Pre- and Post-Modern Discourses: Scientific, Medical*. ManUP. pp. 359. £50. ISBN 0 7190 3506 6.

Rousseau G. S. *Enlightenment Crossings: Pre- and Post-Modern Discourses: Anthropological*. ManUP. pp. 259. £45. ISBN 0 7190 3072 2.

Rousseau, G. S. *Perilous Enlightenment: Pre- and Post-Modern Discourses: Sexual, Historical*. ManUP. pp. 336. £50. ISBN 0 7190 3301 2.

Sambrook, James. *James Thomson (1700–1748): A Life*. Clarendon. pp. 332. £40. ISBN 0 19 811788 4.

Schonhorn, Manuel. *Defoe's Politics: Parliament, Power, Kingship, and 'Robinson Crusoe'*. CUP. pp. 174. £32.50. ISBN 0 521 38452 4.

Sitter, John. *Arguments of Augustan Wit*. CUP. pp. 188. £27.95. ISBN 0 521 41120 3.

Small, Ian, and Marcus Walsh, eds. *The Theory and Practice of Text Editing: Essays in Honour of James T. Boulton*. CUP. pp. 221. £30. ISBN 0 521 40146 1.

Smith, Adam. *The Wealth of Nations*. Intro. by D. D. Raphael. Everyman/Random Century. pp. 441 + 181. pb £9.99. ISBN 1 85715 011 2.

Snyder, John. *Prospects of Power: Tragedy, Satire, the Essay and the Theory of Genre*. UPKen. pp. 238. $29. ISBN 0 8131 1724 0.

Uphaus, Robert W., and Gretchen M. Foster, eds. *The 'Other' Eighteenth Century: English Women of Letters 1660–1800*. Colleagues. pp. 465. hb £29.50. ISBN 0 937191 39 6, 0 937191 40 X.

Weinfield, Henry. *The Poet Without a Name: Gray's 'Elegy' and the Problem of History*. SIUP. pp. 236. £32.50. ISBN 0 8093 1652 8.

Yolton, John W., Roy Porter, Pat Rogers, and Barbara Maria Stafford, eds. *The Blackwell Companion to the Enlightenment.* Blackwell. pp. 581. £60. ISBN 0 631 15403 5.

XIII

The Nineteenth Century: Romantic Period

PETER J. KITSON and JOHN C. WHALE

This chapter has two sections: 1. Poetry and Drama; 2. Non-fictional Prose. Section 1 is by Peter J. Kitson; section 2 is by John C. Whale

1. Poetry and Drama

This section has two categories: (a) General Studies; (b) Works on Individual Poets. A number of books and articles were not available to me for review this year and where this is the case they have been mentioned without evaluative comment. The annual review essay in *SEL* 31 of recent studies in the nineteenth century is provided by Herbert F. Tucker (793–42). The primary journals relevant to Romantic poetry and drama are: *Blake* 24/25; *ByronJ* 19; *ChLB*; *ERR* 1; *KSJ*40; *NCC* 15; *NCL* 45/46; the fall issue of *SEL* 31; *SIR* 30; *WC* 22. The first issue of the *BARS Bulletin and Review* (British Association for Romantic Studies) appeared this year. This is published twice yearly (February and October) and is essential reading for Romanticists, providing notices and reviews of conferences and events, brief articles, and reviews of new books in the field. It is edited by Stephen Copley of the University of Wales, Cardiff.

(a) General Studies

This year was marked by the sad news of the death of one of the most influential Romanticists of the twentieth century, Northrop Frye. Among the many works of his substantial output, Professor Frye will probably be best remembered by Romanticists for his seminal work on Blake, *Fearful Symmetry* which, as many of the works reviewed here demonstrate, still influences Blake scholarship, as well as his more generally applicable studies, *An Anatomy of Criticism, A Study of English Romanticism,* and *Romanticism Re-considered.*

1991 has been an important year in Romantic studies and the wealth of material produced during this period is quite staggering. As well as major new editions of Blake's *Songs of Innocence and of Experience* and *Jerusalem*, Mark L. Reed's magisterial edition of *The Thirteen-Book Prelude* in The Cornell Wordsworth series, and several facsimile reprints of Romantic texts in the Revolution and Romanticism 1789–1834 series (Woodstock), there has appeared a plethora of studies of Romantic subjects. The Revolution and Romanticism series has been substantially enlarged by a further number of texts, including canonical works by Blake, Bowles, Burns, Coleridge, Keats, Shelley, and Wordsworth, as well as by less familiar editions of Campbell, Clare, Canning and Frere, Erasmus Darwin, Felicia Hemans, Holcroft, Richard Mant, and Southey. The value of these facsimiles in giving an impression of the actual literary community in which the Romantics lived and wrote is clearly apparent. Jonathan Wordsworth's *Ancestral Voices: Fifty books from the Romantic period* is a collection of the author's prefaces written for the first fifty facsimile reprints in this series, revised and enlarged, presenting a chronological survey of the works reprinted. Wordsworth's book is useful in its restoration of less well-known writers and hitherto peripheral volumes to the period; for instance, the case of Helen Maria Williams, whose influential reporting of the Revolution in France affected the writings of Wordsworth and others. Additionally the discussion of works of contemporary aesthetics, philosophy, political economy alongside the established Romantic texts extends our understanding of the values and interests of the varying literary communities we have lumped together under the portmanteau term 'Romantic'. What is also recovered is the sense of the dialogue between Romantic texts. It is easy to forget that Wordsworth's 'Tintern Abbey' was a response to Coleridge's already published version of 'Frost at Midnight'. More problematic, for some, will be Jonathan Wordsworth's belief that there is something we can call the 'authentic voice of Romanticism', which, in many ways, this collection volume serves to undermine.

The series Revolution and Romanticism includes several examples of the metrical romances, such as Campbell's *Gertrude of Wyoming*, Scott's *Lay of the Last Minstrel*, Southey's *Thalaba*, which are the subject of Hermann Fischer's *Romantic Verse Narrative: The History of a Genre*. This is a translation (by Sue Bollans) of a work submitted by Fischer as a postdoctoral thesis at Munich and first published in Germany in 1964. Fischer's argument in essence derives from Hugo Kuhn's *Gattungsprobleme der mittlehoch Deutschen* (1956) and his enquiry is divided into three aspects: the question of type; the sociological context; and the question of entelechy (the historical purpose of the genre). Fischer's emphasis is partially formal, but basically historical in being concerned with the wider context in which the work is produced and received. Fischer argues that the romantic verse narrative attempted to displace the epic, although it had more in common with the mediaeval or courtly romance. This type of poetry stresses excitement, emotion; it consists of a loose framework and is flexible in its employment of metre. Despite early precursors, such as Landor and Southey, it was Scott who effectively originated the form which was variously exploited or imitated by others. The verse narrative appears to decline in popularity around 1812, only to be re-invigorated by Byron. Fischer covers a very wide range of texts and poets, including less-familiar names, such as Samuel Rogers, James Montgomery, and Barry Cornwall. Fischer is, however, most impressive in his discussion of the production and reception of these texts, especially in his use of period critical comment. The methodology of this study is somewhat unfashionable, as Fischer insists on the importance of the ways in which genre dominates subsequent writing. Only the great artist can transcend such genre limitations and enhance the form as Wordsworth, Keats, Shelley, and Byron (female poets are mentioned fleetingly). The Romantic verse narrative grows out of the tension between the unpopularity of élitist Augustan aesthetics and the need to exploit the new literary marketplace which is middle class, middle brow, and sparingly educated. *Romantic Verse Narrative* is most impressive and scholarly when dealing with the reception of the texts, but less enlightening when discussing the characteristic uses made by the major Romantic poets of the form: Wordsworth adds depth of thought; Byron adds psychological insight and an air of Rousseauistic self-revelation; Keats and Shelley increase the subjective and lyrical elements of their poetry creating archetypal (in Frye's terminology) works of mythopoesis. Rather startling at times is the surety of Fischer's judgements. We are, for instance, encouraged to adjudicate between two opposing views of Wordsworth's 'The White Doe of Rylstone' (from *Blackwoods' Magazine* and the *Edinburgh Review*) and decide 'which of the two positions we consider to be the correct one', and we are perhaps comforted to know that in the case of the standing of this poem, René Wellek is 'perfectly correct'. Fischer is also not shy of ascribing and denying greatness to the texts he discusses. Most surprisingly, Fischer's work contains no extended account of Byron's *Don Juan* which is excluded on genre terms, yet which surely must rate as one of the most important contributions to this kind of writing?

A number of general studies about Romanticism have appeared this year, many concerned with problematizing our notions of canonicity and periodization. David G. Riede, *Oracles and Hierophants: Constructions of Romantic Authority* seeks to deconstruct the processes by which Romantic poets were constituted as oracles. Riede's book is attractively written and highly interesting. It contains substantial discussions of Wordsworth, Coleridge, and Blake which are informed and challenging. Riede's tendency is towards New Historicist criticism, as his frequent citations of Jon P. Klancher and Jerome J. McGann demonstrate, yet he writes with some sympathy for the Romantic poets who wished to destabilize previous authority while, at the same time, establishing their own. This attempt to achieve authority was then revised by Victorian artists and critics, notably Rossetti, Swinburne, Carlyle, and Arnold in the form of a literary church, most obviously demonstrated in the case of Coleridge's idea of the clerisy. Riede is perhaps most convincing on Blake who attacks prophetic certainty in *The Marriage of Heaven and Hell*, before himself trying to re-establish his own prophetic authority in *Milton*, an authority which is ironically divorced from social and political reality by his later aesthetic admirers (Swinburne and Rossetti). Riede has much that is interesting to write about Wordsworthian problems with authority, and that poet's creation of the authoritative 'Wanderer' in *The Prelude, The Borders*, and *The Ruined Cottage*. In both his discussion of Wordsworth and Coleridge the construction of an authoritative self is highlighted. Riede also describes more briefly the ways in which the second generation Romantics, Byron, Hazlitt, Keats, and Shelley responded ambiguously to the authority of their predecessors. Most rewarding is Riede's close reading of Romantic texts, especially in the Blake and Wordsworth chapters, although many of the contextual points made by the book are fairly familiar. Riede relies far too heavily on secondary works, such as Marilyn Butler's *Romantics, Rebels and Reactionaries* (1981), for the historical background to the Romantic age. This is the case especially in the discussion of Coleridge's radicalism which is a more complex and deeply thought out response to a tradition of ideas than Riede suggests. In many ways Riede's book, while carefully citing recent critical deconstructions of Romanticism, remains a very canonical and traditional piece of work itself, combining many of the virtues of traditional scholarship with the informed ironies of New Historicism; a book that perhaps evinces an almost Keatsian yearning for the demystified project that was Romanticism, while carefully demonstrating how the mystificatory process of Romantic authority has proceeded. Paul Michael Privateer's *Romantic Voices; Identity and Ideology in British Poetry 1789–1850* is similarly indebted to Jerome McGann, but departs from McGann's depiction of 'Romantic ideology' as false consciousness in expanding the notion of ideology so it 'becomes a larger crucible in which the romantic ideology is ultimately created'. Like Riede, Privateer is also concerned with the Romantic valorization of self and identity, but his work is more theoretically dense and less accessible. More problematic is Privateer's assumption in his discussion of 'Kubla Khan' that Coleridge's ideas about the self as outlined in *Biographia Literaria* can be read back into poems written, as Riede convincingly shows, when their author did not possess the Romantic notion of a transcendent and unitary self (which he never did anyway). Privateer provides a poststructuralist discussion of the semiotics of the self and combines this with difficult readings of Blake's *Milton*, Wordsworth's *Prelude*, Coleridge's *Kubla Khan,* and Shelley's *Alastor*. Privateer's book is an ingenious account of Romantic attempts to validate the autonomy of the individual self, but many readers will no doubt prefer Riede's more balanced and accessible discussion of similar subjects. An almost polar opposite methodology to that of Privateer is demonstrated by John Powell Ward's rather unoriginal attempt to describe an 'English Line' of verse from Wordsworth to Larkin, a line which is linguistically simple, lyrical, broadly tolerant, and characteristically melancholic and introverted. Ward's attempt to construct such a line from diverse precursors strikes one as impressionistic and, at times, arbitrary and the magnification of Larkin's status results in much bathos. In many ways Ward appears as a traditional critic, almost embarrassed by his own method; hence the frequent, and not altogether helpful, allusions to celebrated poststructuralist criticism which is cited only to be glossed over and not engaged with. Ward's readings of Wordsworth, Coleridge, and Clare will not add much to our understanding of the poetry. Jack Stillinger's *Multiple Authorship and the Myth of Solitary Genius* makes a strong case for biographical criticism as a means of further enriching literary study. Stillinger's wry introduction show how the notion of 'authorship' first became established and then later was destabilized by poststructuralist criticism. He takes the example of Keats's 'Sonnet to Sleep' to show how the biographical context and knowledge of the context and production history of the poem can enhance our study of literary texts: 'like the New Critics earlier, the author-banishing theorists are deceiving themselves if they really believe that one can dispense with authors while still retaining an idea of the literary.' Stillinger, however, goes further in problematizing this return of the author as he shows how the composition of literary texts does involve a plurality of authors. This is shown in his chapter concerning Keats's *Isabella* and the extent to which others aided in the composition of the tale. Stillinger establishes the detailed history of the transmission of the text and demonstrates how precarious the final version actually is, having been worked up by Richard Woodhouse from his shorthand notebook. Keats also employed his friends Brown and Woodhouse to transcribe his poetry for the publishers and generally disregarded his own fair copies. Stillinger shows how Woodhouse worked to curb Keats's extravagance and make the poem more palatable for its audience. This was not necessarily what Keats wanted. Stillinger also analyses changes made to *Endymion* and *The Eve of St Agnes* showing how the printed version of the latter is a much milder composite poem than Keats had intended. Stillinger concludes this chapter with a criticism of Jerome McGann's conclusions about the textual status of *La Belle dame Sans Merci* which he finds to be 'shaky in nearly every detail'. Stillinger also investigates Wordsworth's *Prelude* as the work of a 'multiple author', this time of the poet collaborating with his several past and present selves. Stillinger is particularly critical of *The Cornell Wordsworth*'s preference for the 'earliest complete state' of a text which he argues runs the risk of doing away with all later Wordsworth. Clearly Stillinger has a point in his concern over the inadvertent standardizing of the early texts by the series. Stillinger also discusses Coleridge's 'plagiarisms' as an illustration of multiple authorship. This chapter, an uncomfortable one for Coleridgeans, details the plagiarism debate and exposes some of the unconvincing stratagems that have been used by Coleridgeans, before and after Fruman's *Coleridge the Damaged Archangel,* to defend the integrity of Coleridge's philosophy. Although Stillinger does have as much a professional interest in reopening this issue (it makes for a good chapter in his book) as some Coleridgeans have in wishing to see it closed, there remains the sense that, now textual scholarship has revealed the extent of the borrowing and numerous critics have addressed its implications, we have got beyond this rather reductive and limiting notion of plagiarism. Stillinger's book also contains chapters on Mill's *Autobiography*, the collaboration of Pound and Eliot in *The Waste Land*, and the production processes of novelists and film-makers. Stillinger's book is an attempt at replacing the unsupportable notion of solitary author with the idea of the multiple author; an idea that does not threaten the continuing myth of single authorship. In terms of editing technique, this means producing multiple versions of texts, each with its own authority.

James Holt McGavran Jnr has edited a fine collection of essays on the subject of *Romanticism and Children's Literature in Nineteenth-Century England.* McGavran's introduction focuses on the Romantic re-evaluation of childhood and traces the influence of Romantic views of childhood into the Victorian period. Three essays deal with Wordsworthian subjects. Alan Richardson's scholarly and informed 'Wordsworth's Fairy Tales, and the Politics of Children's Reading' discusses the politics of late eighteenth-century children's literature and questions traditional dichotomies of reason (Locke, Barbauld, etc.) and fantasy (the Romantics), situating Wordsworth's patronage of the fairy tale in Book V of the *Prelude*, in a conservative tradition of reading oral literature. Given the context of the 1790s, Richardson argues that the fairy tale represented a pacifying alternative to radical narratives. James Holt McGavran Jnr argues in 'Catechist and Visionary' that Wordsworth's *Lyrical Ballads* employ a catechetical strategy adapted from Isaac Watts. McGavran takes 'We Are Seven' and 'Anecdote for Fathers' as exemplary models which cast adult narrators in the role of priests catechizing children and ministering to the reader, only to ironically reverse the reader's expectations. McGavran's depiction of context is interesting, although it does not really transform available readings of the poem. Ross Woodman argues in 'The Idiot Boy as Healer' that Wordsworth's political trauma is healed by the living icon of the child, and he takes the depiction of this process in 'The Idiot Boy' to be exemplary. Woodman's reading claims perhaps too much for this poem. Jeanne Moskal discusses ' "The Raven: A Christmas Poem": Coleridge and the Fairy Tale Controversy', arguing that Coleridge's poem is a riposte to the 'Barbauld Crew' of moralistic rationalizers. Moskal's essay is informed, although this poem is a lot darker than she suggests. Mitzi Myers provides a timely reappraisal of Maria Edgeworth in 'Romancing the Moral Tale' in line with the strictures of Richardson's essay. Patricia Demurs discusses 'Mrs Sherwood and Hesba Stretton: The Letter and the Spirit of Evangelical Writing of and for Children' and rather unconvincingly tries to fit them into the Romantic canon. And finally, for those interested in Romantic subjects, Roderick McGillis, in 'Childhood and Growth' sums up George MacDonald's debt to Wordsworth in his children's fiction. This is a useful collection which reaffirms traditional ideas of Romantic attitudes to the child as well as providing (chiefly in Richardson's excellent piece) a sceptical reappraisal of such notions.

Many studies of the concept of 'Romanticism' as a genre or period and its implications for the teaching profession appeared this year. Harriet Kramer Linkin discusses the results of a survey of US University courses on British Romanticism in

'The Current Canon in British Romantics Studies' (*CE* 53.548–70). Linkin's survey contains few surprises. The canonical six Romantic poets are taught with some courses bringing in female writers: Hemans, Mary Shelley, Dorothy Wordsworth, and Mary Wollstonecraft and so on, reflecting what Linkin calls the 'slow infiltration of women writers into our standard teaching canon'. The addition of Mary Shelley to the traditional canon also seems to be a *fait accompli*.

Frances Ferguson in 'On the Numbers of Romanticisms' (*ELH* 58.471–98) surveys the conflicting definitions of Romanticism from A. O. Lovejoy to the recent formulations accepting the return to Kant's aesthetics of the sublime, and she notes an 'unexpected convergence between de Manian deconstruction and contemporary Marxist materialism'. Ferguson's approach is painstaking and ingenious in demonstrating this congruence and simultaneously defending the return to Kant's aesthetics: 'yet far from being escapist or unreal, romantic formal idealism remains as real as it gets.' This is a suggestive essay, which confirms areas of interest current in other Romantic criticism, the ideas of which will remain current for some time. I have not seen Donald G. Marshall's essay on a similar theme, 'Kant and the English Nature Poetry' (*IowaR* 21.78–83), nor Mark Jones's 'Recuperating Arnold: Romanticism and Modern Projects of Disinterestedness' (*Boundary* 18.65–103). Sandra M. Gilbert and Susan Gubar in ' "But oh! that deep Romantic chasm": The Engendering of Periodization' (*KR* 13.74–81) discuss the problems of literary periodization for women writers, excluded because they are in 'the wrong place at the wrong time'. Gilbert and Gubar claim that the various ideologies and aesthetic assumptions associated with Romanticism can be said to have opened a chasm in culture not unlike the 'deep romantic chasm, in Coleridge's "Kubla Khan" '. The valorizing of feminine spontaneity in male poets as irrationality has, however, according to our authors, left little place for the actual women writers of the period. The piece repeats the somewhat hackneyed notion that men are essentially uncreative usurpers and masculinizers of feminine creativity, which has been thankfully abandoned in some recent feminist criticism. More positively Gilbert and Gubar point out the important influences on the 'Big Six' Romantic poets; Joanna Baillie, Anne Radcliffe, Charlotte Smith, Mary Wollstonecraft, and Felicia Hemans. If anything Gilbert and Gubar are perhaps too canonical in their own female tradition, seemingly dependent on the research of Stuart Curran.

Two articles have appeared by Theresa M. Kelley on Romantic notions of allegory. ' "Fantastic Shapes": From Classical Rhetoric to Romantic Allegory' (*TSLL* 33.351–82) is a reply to de Man's elaboration of the literary and historical forces at work in Romantic conceptions of allegory, suggesting that the Romantics were themselves aware of the metafigural character of the trope. Kelley discusses the development of theories about allegory from classic to Romantic times in a highly knowledgeable and interesting way. Superseding many more schematic accounts of this kind of writing she demonstrates the fundamental ambivalence of Romantic writers to allegorical representation. Discussing, in particular, Coleridge's distinction between fancy and imagination and Wordsworth's presentation of 'allegoric shapes' in Book VII of *The Prelude*, Kelley shows how both writers distinguish their work from allegory and yet are, at the same time, deeply conscious of the return of this repressed term in their writing. Kelley is especially interesting when dealing with Wordsworth's attempt to resist allegory in his depiction of the blind beggar. In 'J. M. W. Turner, Napoleonic Caricature, and Romantic Allegory' (*ELH* 58.35–82), Kelley describes the British fascination with gigantic and miniature representations of Napoleon in caricature and poetry, arguing that Napoleon's peculiar fascination for

British radicals (especially Hazlitt) consisted in his meritocratic rise: as such he served as a 'lightning rod for the aspirations of the unrepresented'. Jon Whitman contributes a much slighter discussion of Romantic notions of allegory in his 'From the Textual to the Temporal: Early Christian "Allegory" and Early Romantic "Symbol" ' (*NLH* 22–23.161–76) which contrasts the Pauline use of allegory with Coleridge's distinction between allegory and symbol in *The Statesman's Manual*, arguing that 'whereas for Paul the act of interpreting Scripture anew helps to emancipate individuals from an old Law, for Coleridge it endows them with newly compelling social and cosmic powers'.

David Perkins's 'How the Romantics Recited Poetry' concerns the ways the Romantics recited poetry, explaining that they appear to have preferred a method of chanting to the more rhythmical Augustan practice. Perkins concludes that however various this emphasis on the chanting of poetry was, it certainly marks out their delivery from that of natural speech and moves it closer to a musical experience. Perkins provides many interesting insights into this subject, especially in the ways that the Romantics distinguished blank verse from rhythmic prose in recitation: Wordsworth apparently observed the tradition of observing the end of each line. Style of recitation, according to Perkins, was certainly in a state of transition during the Romantic period. Behind Perkins's essay is a sense that we may have lost something with the acceptance of modernist and New Critical assumptions about poetry (*SEL* 31.655–71).

Charles Larmore in 'Romanticism and Modernity' (*Inquiry* 34.77–89), provides an extended review of Karl Heinz Bohrer's critique of Habermas's notions of modernity, recalling Romantic notions of disunity to characterize the modern age. Bohrer sees the German Romantic interest in *irony* and *fantasy*, detailed in Kelley's account earlier, as proleptic of modernity. Philip W. Martin's 'Romanticism, history, historicism' in Kelvin Everest (ed.), *Revolution in writing: British literary responses to the French Revolution* surveys the writings of the New Historicist critics of Romantic subjects, in particular, Marjorie Levinson. Martin's account is a subtle and penetrating outline of the New Historicist project (as far as this is possible) which unveils many of the paradoxes and difficulties involved in such critics' questioning of the present-minded construction of the past. Gene Ruoff's 'Romanticism with a Difference: The Recent Criticism of Karl Kroeber', (*Boundary* 18.226–37), provides an interesting overview of Kroeber's criticism, especially his recent *Romantic Fantasy and Science Fiction* (1988). Finally, Andrew Roberts's 'Omnipotence and the Romantic Imagination' is a discussion of the Romantic Imagination in the texts of Wordsworth and Coleridge in the light of the psychoanalytical theories of D. W. Winnicott which attempts to explain the contrasting emotions of joy in creativity and sadness with failure. (*English* 40.1–19). I have not seen the following: Jean Hall, *A Mind that Feeds upon Infinity* (FDUP); Diane Long Hoeveler, *Romantic Androgyny: The Woman Within* (PSUP); Mara Kalnis, *Some Noble Theme: Essays on Aspects of Romanticism* (Bristol Press); Jeffrey C. Robinson, *The Current of Romantic Passion* (UWiscP); G. A. Rosso and Daniel P. Watkins, *Spirits of Fire: English Romantic Writers and Contemporary Historical Methods* (FDUP, 1990).

(b) Individual Poets

This year has been a good one for Blake studies with two new editions of the illuminated books, a new biography, an edition of Blake's commercial book engravings, and several monographs appearing. For details of, and astute and informed commentary on, recent publications Blake scholars will need to consult Detlef. W. Dorrbecker's meticulous and exhaustive checklist in *Blake* (25.4–54): the knowledge and expertise demonstrated by Dorrbecker makes this a fascinating and invaluable read for anyone interested in Blake. The market for Blake's works and details of its activity over the last two years are given by Robert N. Essick's 'Blake in the Market Place 1990' also in *Blake* (25.116–41). Essick notes with unease the disturbing trend towards secrecy in some of the major purchasers, despite his 'carefully assembled gang of spies and informers' he was unable to discover the identity of the new owners of *Songs of Innocence and of Experience*, copy D and *The Book of Thel*, copy A. Still on matters bibliographical, G. E. Bentley Jnr and Keiko Aoyama have produced *Blake Studies in Japan: A Bibliography of Works on William Blake Published in Japan 1911–1990* (published privately) which was not available for review. Also unavailable was *Vision of A Collector: The Lessing J. Rosenwald Collection in the Library of Congress, Rare Book And Special Collections Division* (Library of Congress), which is a collection of brief essays describing important items in the Rosenwald collection by leading Blake scholars.

The Blake Trust in collaboration with Tate Gallery Publications has issued the first two volumes of a new series of Blake facsimiles which are intended to make the works of Blake more accessible in high quality reproductions. These are the first volumes of a projected five volume Collected Edition to be produced under the editorship of David Bindman. Both the early volumes contain a new transcription of Blake's text and plate-by-plate commentary. The first volume is a stunning facsimile of Blake's *Jerusalem* edited by Morton D. Paley, perhaps the most complex and difficult of the illuminated books. Copy E of *Jerusalem* is the obvious copy text used, as that is the only one 'finished' in Blake's eyes. Paley's detailed transcription of Blake's text attempts to get as close to the original as possible but does not serve as a variorum edition, as only the most important variants from the other four-and-a-half copies are included. This transcription is painstakingly produced and grapples convincingly with the problems posed by Blake's problematic calligraphy and punctuation. Paley's introduction clearly sets out the circumstances surrounding the production of *Jerusalem* and leaves questions of interpretation for the plate-by-plate commentary on the poem. Clearly this volume is welcome in that it constitutes the only facsimile edition with critical apparatus and edited text by one of the greatest of Blake scholars. The second volume is an equally handsome edition by Andrew Lincoln of Blake's *Songs of Innocence and of Experience*, the best known and most accessible of the illuminated books. Lincoln obviously had a more difficult choice of copy text than Paley as some twenty-four copies of the combined *Songs* have survived. He reproduces the King's College Copy of *Songs* which is certainly one of the more delicately coloured and lavishly produced editions. The Trianon Press edition of *Songs* reproduced in Geoffrey Keynes's OUP edition was from the Lessing J. Rosenwald Collection in the Library of Congress, Washington, D. C. The King's College Copy of *Songs* is certainly a lighter, clearer and more finished edition with greater clarity of illustration, especially in terms of facial expression, costume, trees and branches, although the colours in Keynes's edition are stronger and more vivid. Lincoln's edition is thus to be preferred over Keynes's in that the stronger colouring of the latter often obscures the detail of Blake's line engraving. The King's College Copy also shows a striking use of gold colouring (and is less blue), but its most distinctive feature is its elaborate use of decorative borders to the plates. Although it has been claimed that Blake's wife Catherine was responsible for these, Lincoln prefers justifiably to accept that they are integral to Blake's conception and unlikely to have been added after the rest of the plate was coloured. Undergraduates will obviously prefer Keynes's cheaper Oxford edition of *Songs* to the more costly new edition, but the availability of both makes it much easier to show the differences between individual copies. As both editions are late, the ordering of the plates is identical in both and the variations in colour rarely effect interpretation, except in one or two cases: the childrens' heads against a blue sky and the nurse's against cloud (Lincoln) as opposed to one child's head against blue sky and the nurse and second child against cloud (Keynes) in 'The Fly' may indicate a changed perception of the relative states of minds of the figures. Lincoln helpfully provides a brief number of plates from other editions of the *Songs* for comparison, as well as full and intelligent commentary. Both volumes in the collected works are extremely beautiful editions of Blake's illuminated works and will hopefully reach the wider audience for the work that Blake always desired, but never achieved. Everyman have re-issued their selection of Blake's verse, *William Blake: Selected Poems* edited by P. H. Butter. This selection has a long and complex textual history but the main change between this and previous editions is the addition of *The Song of Los* and 'a few short poems and prose extracts'. Also reissued by Everyman is *William Blake: Poems and Prophecies* with a new introduction by Kathleen Raine.

Robert N. Essick's *William Blake's Commercial Book Illustrations* is a catalogue and study of the plates engraved by Blake (something he found frustrating) from the designs of other artists. This aspect of Blake's work has received comparatively little attention and Essick's catalogue provides an important scholarly tool for those interested in Blake's artistry. Plates designed by Blake and executed by others are not included here but are described in David Bindman's *The Complete Graphic Works of William Blake* (T&H, 1978). The emphasis of Essick's new catalogue is on what Blake produced and with minimum bibliographical information on the publications containing his work. Hence the catalogue is best used in conjunction with G. E. Bentley's *Blake Books* (Clarendon, 1977). Essick provides a careful and detailed account of Blake's career as engraver, as well as suggesting the importance of the commercial engraving for Blake's other productions, both verbal and visual. Most importantly Essick's book raises important questions about the relationship between art and commerce in the Romantic period. Reproductive book engraving was certainly the major area of contact for Blake with the worlds of commerce and with the literary and artistic life of England, especially in the case of his work for the publisher Joseph Johnson and the subsequent acquaintance with the Johnson circle. Essick is also surely right to claim that this context and its possible influence upon Blake's original productions needs much more discussion. The volumes which Blake illustrated for Johnson probably represent his most likely initial point of contact with a much wider circle of influence, extending more variously to Johnson's publications. More specifically, Essick suggests that Blake's denunciations of 'Female Space' and independent 'Female Will' in the later poetry was conditioned by his replacement by Caroline Watson with her softer, more feminine style, on two of Hayley's projects. The illustrations are often at odds with the tenor of Blake's philosophy. For instance, Blake engraves an illustration of David Hartley for Johnson's edition of his *Observations on Man*, the empiricist philosophy of which was quintessentially everything that Blake despised, and it also contains an engraving for Salzmann's *Elements of Morality* with the title 'How happy it is that there are rich men in the world' (although the characters in the engraving look none too happy). This volume certainly is an essential research tool for Blake scholars.

James King's biography of Blake is an attractively written and useful work which will be very helpful for undergraduate readers and those new to Blake studies, but will probably disappoint serious Blake scholars. It will no doubt become the standard undergraduate reading, displacing previous biographies: Mona Wilson, Jack Lindsay, and Michael Davis. King is less reverential towards his subject than earlier biographies and he presents a more sympathetic account of Cromek's dealings with Blake. King is occasionally harsh towards Blake: 'the tendency to blame others for his own failings was the most damaged part of Blake's personality'. Drawing upon popular Freudian psychology King depicts Blake as riven by Oedipal jealousies and suspicions of his father. King's biography is ordered chronologically with chapters covering usually around ten years of the poet's life. Discussion and interpretation of the poetry tends to be fairly perfunctory and often biographical. King does give quite detailed and balanced accounts of the Blake circle: Flaxman, Stothard, Hayley, Cumberland, Trusler, Butts, and so on, and he is also good on the tensions in Blake between his desire for public acceptance as an artist and his refusal to compromise artistically, much to the exasperation of patrons such as Cromek. This biography is concise and accessible, giving the reader some impression of the scope and character of Blake's life and work, and King does manage to weave an interesting narrative from out of Bentley's more indigestible *Blake Records* (Clarendon 1969; supplemented in 1988). This biography lacks detailed critical apparatus. Two further substantial studies of matters relating to Blake's life have appeared this year. In *SIR* 30, G. E. Bentley's ' "They take great libertys": Blake Reconfigured by Cromek and Modern Critics – The Arguments from Silence' discusses the commercial relationship between Blake and Cromek. After a careful sifting of the evidence relating to Cromek's commissioning of Blake's designs for Blair's *The Grave* and the controversy over the Canterbury Pilgrims design and engraving, Bentley concludes that Cromek appears as a 'man whose promises and words are not to be trusted': a view of matters which differs somewhat from King's more sympathetic treatment of Cromek. Secondly Robert N. Essick discusses Blake's relationships with actual women in 'William Blake, So-Called Female-Will and its Biographical Context' (*SEL* 31.615–30). Essick rehearses the arguments for and against Blake's alleged patriarchal sexism, leaving the matter open but noting that Blake was 'deeply ambivalent about female sexuality' and that his writings contain both feminist and anti-feminist arguments. Essick provides a careful and interesting account of Blake's relations with his wife, Mary Wollstonecraft, Elizabeth Butts, and Caroline Watson and indicates the resonances these relationships may have had on texts like *Visions of the Daughters of Albion* and *Jerusalem*. Essick describes the gender distinctions in the Blake household between male conception and female execution, and he speculates that Blake's poem 'The Phoenix' may indicate that some incident involving Elizabeth Butts may have altered Blake's earlier feminism, leading to the development of his aggressive/passive paradigm of the feminine. Just as important aesthetically was Blake's dislike of Caroline Watson's engraving techniques which privileged colour over line. This dislike was intensified by Hayley's preference for Watson's engravings over his own in the *Life of George Romney*. This preference for Watson's soft, indefinite, impressionistic style, over Blake's masculine linearism 'could only have been both a professional and personal blow'. Such events coupled with Blake's own subordination to his feminized patron, Hayley, must have increased Blake's doubts about his own masculinity. Certainly Essick's claim for the importance of Caroline Watson and what she represented professionally and aesthetically is valid. *Blake* (24/25.7–14) also contains 'William Blake and John Marsh' by Essick concerning the manuscript autobiography of Hayley's friend John Marsh and its references to Blake. These include an account of Blake's trial for sedition at Chichester Quarter Sessions

(January 1804) and the mention of the gift of a kitten to Blake. Also in *Blake* (24–25.91–4), Bruce E. Graver's 'New Voice on Blake' draws our attention to an unpublished review (attributed by Graver to Barron Field) of a book of modernized versions of Chaucer's poetry *Chaucer Modernized* (1904). The review praises Blake's picture of *The Canterbury Pilgrims* over that of Stothard and sets up Blake as a true interpreter of Chaucer.

Four important monographs on aspects of Blake's work and one collection of essays have come to my attention for this year. The most substantial is Vincent Arthur De Luca's excellent study *Words of Eternity: Blake and the Poetics of the Sublime*. Thomas Wieskel had seen Blake as aberrant and perverse in his notions of sublimity and De Luca's book poses as a response to those who argue that Blake has no distinct concept of the sublime as a separate category of aesthetic experience. In fact, according to De Luca, Blake has a very distinct notion of the sublime that corresponds to elements of Burke's famous explication, but departs from Burke's empiricism and his praise for obscurity. In line with Payne Knight, Lowth, and others, Blake is convinced of the role of clarity in giving the impression of the sublime. Blake is more singular in attempting to replace the Wordsworthian or Kantian sublime of the natural object with that of the text. Although as De Luca points out, Blake often finds difficulty in trying to depict his actors in anything other than the sublime mode that he is at pains to transcend: 'Blake treats the Burkean style of the sublime as Los might treat his spectrous brother; it is appropriated, assimilated, hated, and perhaps secretly loved, but ultimately made present as negation, the better to reveal the outlines of a new emergent style.' De Luca's observations and arguments are detailed and ingenious, although sometimes unconvincing, perhaps in the case of Blake's eroticized masculinist aesthetics. He deals with Blake's stylistic sublime effects, discussing the bardic and iconic styles, structural organization, and Blake's settings. De Luca's book has many interesting areas of discussion, in particular the treatment of Blake and catastrophist theory (especially the influence of Thomas Burnet) and Blake's relationship to the Kabbalah. De Luca's treatment of Blake's revisionary interest in the sublime and his use of sublime modes is assured and rewarding; ultimately De Luca argues that 'For Blake, as for Derrida, there may be nothing outside of the text – but for the poet, this text is not a Spectral vision out of the Burkean sublime, an abyss of receding origins, but rather the ground of our being, the place of true beginnings, where … we are most ourselves.' De Luca's suggestion that Blake was influenced by Thomas Burnet's theories of the formation of the earth is taken up by Morton D. Paley in 'Blake and Thomas Burnet's *Sacred Theory of the Earth*' (*Blake* 25.75–8). Paley, with his great interest in the Apocalyptic Sublime, takes this suggestion further to cover the third and fourth books of Burnet's work concerning the Conflagration and the New Heaven and New Earth and also to include discussion of the illustrations to some of the early editions of the *Sacred Theory* that Blake might have seen. These illustrations, he argues, have a particular relevance for illustrations to Blake's *Song of Los* and *Jerusalem*. Paley points out that both Burnet and Blake upheld the tradition which accepted the actual physical and concrete regeneration of the Earth as a site for the millennium. Burnet's influence on Blake must, however, remain merely speculative, despite the strong similarities between their ideas that Paley and De Luca posit.

Lorraine Clark's *Blake, Kierkegaard and the Spectre of Dialectic* discusses Blake's later 'prophecies', *The Four Zoas, Milton,* and *Jerusalem* in terms of a revised dialectical struggle which Clarke sees as closer to Kierkegaard than Hegel. Kierkegaard's dialectic is one of 'either/or' whereas Hegel's is one of mediation or 'both/and'. This, argues Clark, is closer to Blake's dramatization of the struggle between Los and the Spectre of Urthona in the later work which marks a turning away from the more Hegelian struggle between Orc and Urizen of the earlier work. Blake's dialectic of Los is thus one of exclusion not inclusion, analogous to Kierkegaard's obsession with, but ultimate repudiation of, Schlegel's Romantic Irony. Clark posits that Blake's turn from a Hegelian dialectic of becoming to an anti-Hegelian dialectic of being in fact discloses a rejection of 'negation' that was present all along: 'This Hegelian anti-Hegelianism is the very structure of Kierkegaard's 'either/or'. Crucially, for Clark, in both writers there exists the centrality of choice. The focus of Clark's study is quite narrow as she herself admits, being mainly concerned with the Spectre in Blake's later poetry, yet discussing Blake's struggle with the contraries in Kierkegaardian terms does pay off. The real problem with Clark's study is that it denies the historic specificity of the two writers. At times the reader feels that Blake and Kierkegaard exist in a kind of hermeneutic vacuum, instead of being a part of an inner-light Protestant tradition. More problematically in regarding Blake as in some sense an anti-Hegelian, engaged in the same project as Kierkegaard, Clark displaces Blake's real opposition to Newton, Locke, and Milton onto a philosopher that he had of course not read. This apart, Clark's study is a lucid and intelligent discussion of this aspect of Blake's work which does benefit from the analogy made with Kierkegaard, especially in terms of irony, perspective and choice.

Peter Otto's *Constructive Vision and Visionary Deconstruction* is an extended discussion of *Milton* and *Jerusalem* which takes as its departure point a reassessment of the Blakean notion of Imagination. For Otto most of contemporary Blake scholarship has accepted that the poetry relates to a system which is outside the text and which is to be translated by the reader. Otto, however, insists that the experience of the reading of the poems undermines the reader's preconceptions revealing the inadequacy of prior knowledge, thus creating a kind of 'visionary deconstruction' which resembles that of Derrida's sceptical philosophy but which additionally offers the possibility of the reader's regeneration through 'constructive vision'. Central to Otto's argument is Blake's play upon ideas of time and eternity which are exploited to effect in this kind of 'visionary deconstruction'. For Otto traditional interpretations of the Blakean Imagination have stressed the creative aspects of the individual. Otto sees this construction of the self and the self's ability to form and control the world it creates as dangerously close to Lockeian epistemology. This translation of difference into the sameness of the self is not what Blake has in mind, rather the imagination functions not as a call from within but from without. Otto's work is erudite and intelligent and his reading of the poems detailed and stimulating (especially in the case of the 'Bard's Song' from *Milton*). Like De Luca, however, he attempts to read Blake on the poet's own terms and is somewhat insensitive to the historical context and Blake's place within it. Otto also discusses the figuring of the birth of Los in *The Four Zoas* (*SEL* 31.631–53). Otto presents a detailed discussion of the multiple births of this figure, showing how truth is mediated by interpretation. It is only in the 'embrace' of these multiple voices that truth in the fallen world can be envisioned: 'an embrace draws self and other into proximity; rather than assimilating the other to the perspectives of the self'. Regrettably I have not seen Kathleen Raine's *Golgonooza: Last Studies in William Blake* (Golgonooza Press), nor Douglas Thorpe's *A New Earth: The Labor of Language in Pearl, Herbert's Temple, and Blake's Jerusalem (CUAP)*.

Hazard Adams has edited a volume of essays on Blake for G. K. Hall's series Critical Essays on British Literature. The collection has two parts, the first being a series of extracts from Deborah Dorfman's *Blake in the Nineteenth Century* (1969) which gives accounts of Blake from his own time, including Robert Hunt's dismissive review of Blake's exhibition in 1809. Part two is a selection which attempts to give an account of the development of Blake criticism as well as covering the significant areas and issues of the work. Adams's collection contains, as one would expect, many familiar and influential accounts of Blake, including representative extracts from Northrop Frye, David V. Erdman, Jean Hagstrum, Morton D. Paley, Thomas R. Frosch, Alicia Ostriker, Susan Fox, Robert N. Essick as well as Steven Shaviro's poststructuralist discussion of Blake, most of which will be familiar to Blakeans. The volume, however, will be useful to students reasonably new to Blake in introducing them to a representative range of Blake scholarship from over the last forty years.

Of an introductory nature is Michael Ferber's *The Poetry of William Blake* in the PCS series. Ferber deals with Blake's poetry and prose between 1789 and 1794 and provides a helpful introduction to *Songs of Innocence and of Experience, America,* and *The Marriage of Heaven and Hell.* Ferber does summarize some of the more difficult interpretations of Blake but generally he prefers traditional readings of poems, such as *London* and *The Tyger*, in which narrators are stable and unironized. Ferber argues that what new readers of Blake need is a 'life-jacket' to aid them when travelling the stormy seas of Blake criticism. Ferber's little study will certainly function as a good starting-place for those encountering Blake for the first time.

A number of studies historicizing Blake's works have appeared this year coincidentally with Dover Press's welcome reprint of David V. Erdman's ground-breaking and still very relevant *Blake: Prophet against Empire*, which remains one of the great works of Blake scholarship which all students of Blake must engage with at some time or another. One of the best such studies, by Robert N. Essick, pays homage to Erdman's book but also expresses the opinion that Erdman's scholarship has deterred others from taking up the historical challenge. Essick, however, goes over a familiar territory in his intriguing piece "Blake, Paine, and Biblical Revolution" in *SIR* (30.189–212). Essick deftly places the similarities between the radical thought of Blake, the Joseph Johnson circle, and Paine before the reader. Not surprisingly, Essick finds the strongest similarities between Paine and Blake in their texts *The Marriage of Heaven and Hell* and *The Age of Reason*. Yet Essick is also careful to point out the differences between the ideas of Blake and those of Paine and the other Enlightenment thinkers of the Johnson school, especially with regard to their differing valorizations of poetry and prophecy: 'Paine's aestheticizing of the Bible is converted by Blake into the spiritualizing of the aesthetic.' Essick is surely right to see Blake's *Book of Urizen* as a parodic adaptation of Paine's historical myth that 'saps the foundation of his politics'. More complex is Essick's discussion of radical and conservative exploitations of the category of the sublime and of the ways Blake destabilizes liberal notions in *Urizen*. Certainly Essick gives us a fascinating, if necessarily speculative, account of Blake's engagement with the discourses of the Johnson literary circle. Essick is convincing when he argues that Blake's 'struggle with the voices of secular liberalism led him to something worse than self-contradiction – isolation'. Essick's is a timely and interesting piece, although the restriction of the discussion to Blake, Paine and the Johnson circle is a limitation. This limitation is shown in greater relief by Jon Mee's placing of Blake's *The Marriage of Heaven and Hell* in the context of the wider prophetic discourse which existed in the 1790s (*BJECS* 14.51–60). Mee takes seriously the popular or 'vulgar' radical millenarianism of Richard Brothers and others in an attempt to understand Blake's own millenarian tendencies. Rather than accepting that Blake's true contemporaries were the prophets Isaiah and Ezekiel, Mee wishes to flesh out this picture by putting back some of Blake's actual contemporary prophets. This project was already begun to some extent by Morton D. Paley in his essay 'William Blake, the Prince of the Hebrews and the Woman clothed with the Sun' (in *William Blake: Essays in Honour of Sir Geoffrey Keynes*, ed. M. D. Paley and Michael Phillips. Clarendon (1973)). However Paley did not go much beyond comparing Blake's prophecies with those of Richard Brothers and Joanna Southcott and Paley did not take these plebeian prophets as seriously as Mee is inclined to. Mee follows previous scholars in locating the *Marriage* in the anti-Swedenborgian movement evident in Joseph Johnson's literary circle (especially in Priestley's dispute with Robert Hindmarsh), but points out that there was also an alternative 'broad and diverse culture of popular enthusiasm active throughout the eighteenth century' which was antithetical to the cool rationalism of Priestley and the Joseph Johnson circle. Mee is also critical of those who wish to identify Blake's enthusiasm with a Swedenborgian source: 'Swedenborg's antagonism to received religious institutions, his use of visions and prodigies, and the millenarian tendencies in his work were commonplaces' in popular radical culture. Radical millenarianism of the sort developed by Richard Brothers provides some interesting parallells with Blake's prophecies. More significantly Mee finds strong resemblances between the visions of Brothers and the 'Memorable Fancies' of *The Marriage* where the author is transported across the spiritual universe: 'such visionary experiences were common in the literature of enthusiasm'. Mee is less forthcoming than he could be about the actual radicalism of Richard Brothers, who after all was a retired naval lieutenant on half pay. Brothers's early prophecies also clearly show a great deal of respect for authoritarian figures: it is only after they rejected his prophetic ministry that Brothers became antagonistic. More important for Mee is the trajectory of ex-Swedenborgians who moved from religious enthusiasm to political radicalism, notably John Wright and William Bryan. Mee finds substantial similarities between Blake's *Marriage* and Wright's *A Revealed Knowledge of Some Things that will Speedily be Fulfilled in the World* (London, 1795). Mee is right to see Blake's *Marriage* as related to the commonplaces of contemporary radical enthusiasm, although it must be admitted that such commonplaces are themselves commonplaces in a larger historical millenarian tradition, as is shown by Morton D. Paley's discussion of Blake and Thomas Burnet reviewed above. Blake, Brothers, Wright, Burnet, Priestley (and Coleridge for that matter) all held the long-established belief in the earthly manifestation of the millennium. A related theme in Mee's article is that of Antinomianism which is present in Blake as well as the popular culture around him. Although again antinomian beliefs like millenarian beliefs could be held by radicals and conservatives alike (and Mee acknowledges Wright's piety). Mee shows how the third part of Wright's pamphlet bears strong similarities with Blake's 'Proverbs of Hell', arguing convincingly that the latter are closer to Wright's maxims than to the traditionally ascribed source: Lavater's aphorisms. Both Essick's and Mee's quite excellent articles demonstrate one thing perhaps; that there is an enormous overlap between the competing discursive circles of rational religious dissent, Paine-ite radicalism, and popular enthusiasm, and that Blake is perhaps somewhat like Christopher Hill's notion of Milton: a figure placed within the overlapping areas of these discourses. Still concerning Blake's work in its political context are two more essays. First, Glen E. Brewster's interesting ' "Out of Nature": Blake and the French Revolution Debate' (*South Atlantic Review* 56.7–22) which outlines the ways in which the debate about the French Revolution shaped Blake's early work. Brewster looks at some of the main tropes employed in the debate by Price, Burke, and Paine and shows how these were re-worked in Blake's *The French Revolution*. Second, Colin Pedley's 'Blake's

"Tyger" and Contemporary Journalism' (*BJECS* 14.45–9) provides a short but interesting discussion on the discourse of tigers in 1790s political writing and contemporary journalism, including Thomas Spence's *Pig's Meat; or, Lessons for the Swinish Multitude* (1793–94). Although such a context has already been demonstrated by Stuart Crehan's 'Blake's "Tyger" and the "Tygerish Multitude" ' (*L&H* (1980).150–60) and Ronald Paulson's *Representations of Revolution* (YaleUP, 1983), Pedley supplements this scholarship by further revealing the political and cultural complexities of such discourses, and finding the closest analogy to Blake's poem in Robespierre's Address to the National Convention of 5 December 1793.

A few more general articles on Blake matters have appeared. Wayne Glausser speculates interestingly on the similarity between Blake's conceptions of Spectre and Emanation and postmodernist formulations of the simulacra, such as those of Baudrillard, in his 'Atomistic Simulacra in the Enlightenment and in Blake's Post-Enlightenment' in *ECent* (32.73–88). G. J. Finch's 'Blake and Civilization' (*English* 40.193–203) is a not very illuminating account of the lyrical impulse in Blake's shorter poems which takes Blake writings unproblematically on their own terms. G. E. Bentley's 'Blake and Napoleon Rediivivus' (*N&Q* 38.293–4) speculates that Blake may have known the Grub Street author William Thomson because both embraced the 'curious hypothesis' of a substitute Bonaparte. Whether or not Blake agreed with Thomson that this Napoleon Rediivivus was the Scottish Jacobin John Oswald is not known. Also in *N&Q* (38.294–6), Bentley discusses Blake's friendship with George Cumberland in 'Mainaduc, Magic, and Madness' and speculates on what occult notions he may have picked up from this source. Bentley assesses Cumberland's informed but sceptical understanding of the occult underworld and counsels that we should be cautious of such hypothetical linkings until we have solid evidence for them. Bentley's notion of solid evidence, however, is somewhat restrictive and limiting and surely a case can be made for Blake's knowledge of such matters without requiring the purely factual, biographical detail. Bentley would probably turn a sceptical eye to Jon Mee's discussion of *The Marriage* reviewed above.

A number of articles have appeared this year on individual works of Blake. William C. [*sic*] Crisman discusses 'Blake's "The Crystal Cabinet" as a Reworking of Thompson's *The Castle of Indolence*' in which, he maintains, Blake takes a wry look at Thomson's poem (*ELN* 28/29.2–9). Crisman develops a close reading of both poems and argues that Blake's own poem is not so much a demonic reading of Thomson's but more an awareness of the ironies already present in *The Castle of Indolence*. J. E. Swearingen's 'Time and History in Blake's *Europe*' (*ClioI* 20/21.109–21) is an important discussion of history and time in Blake's *Europe* which overlaps with areas dealt with in Otto's book. Swearingen distinguishes between linear and cyclical time by gendering the former as masculine and the latter as feminine. This leads Swearingen to argue that Orc is in fact embedded in masculine linear time, whereas Enitharmon is in some sense with time. This is an interesting and valuable discussion of the subject with important implications. I have not seen Patrick Bizarro's 'The Symbol of the Androgyne in Blake's *Four Zoas* and Shelley's *Prometheus Unbound*: Marital Status among the Romantic Poets' in Joanna Stephens Mink and Janet Doubler Ward, eds. *Joinings and Disjoinings: The Significance of Marital Status in Literature* (BGUP). In addition to Jon Mee's article on *The Marriage of Heaven and Hell,* discussed above, is David Steenburg's 'Chaos at the Marriage of Heaven and Hell' (*HTR* 84), a less satisfying application of Chaos Theory to the *Marriage*. Steenburg argues that Chaos Theory avoids the old Newtonian binaries of fact and value, humanism and reductionism etc., and allows for the interplay between art and science; after all, he comments, 'Today Blake himself might be a computer programmer specializing in fractal graphics'[!] More interesting for Blake scholars is Manfred Engel's 'Neu Mythologie in der deutschen und englisch Fruhromantik: William Blake's *The Marriage of Heaven and Hell* and Novalis' Klingsroman-Märchen' (*Arcadia* 26.225–45) in which he compares Blake's *Marriage* with a tale from *Heinrich von Ofterdingen* in an attempt to provide a working methodology within which to historically define European Romanticism. This is a sensible and open attempt at a comparative reading of Romantic myth-making. Still with the *Marriage*, in *N&Q* 38, Philip Cox's 'Blake, Marvell and Milton: A Possible Source for A Proverb of Hell' notes Marvell's 'On Mr Milton's "Paradise Lost" ' as a potential source for Blake's Proverb of Hell: 'Bring out number weight & measure in a year of dearth'. Cox suggests that such an attribution could suggest the fettered nature of *Paradise Lost*, a visionary epic brought out in the limiting times of the Restoration.

Not a great deal of writing on Blake's *Jerusalem* has come to my attention this year. Apart from the discussions of the poem in De Luca and Otto, there is a relatively tangential study, 'Benediction of Metaphor at Colonus: William Blake and the Vision of the Ancients' by Margaret J. Downes which finds a striking resemblance between Blake's *Jerusalem* and that Sophocles' last play (*CLQ* 27.175–83). Neither has much substantial appeared on the *Songs of Innocence and of Experience* this year. The fullest piece is Michael Phillips's, 'Printing Blake's "Songs" ' (*Library* 13.205–37) which describes in detail Blake's invention of Illuminated Printing and how the *Songs* were produced by this process from the issue of *Songs of Innocence* in 1789 to the combined *Songs of Innocence and of Experience* in 1794. Phillips attempts to order the printings of the *Songs* into four distinct groupings. This account is a technical one which it is difficult to fault without a similar expert knowledge. Certainly this article will be useful for those studying the process of texts and transmission during the Romantic period. Walter S. Minot's 'Blake's "Infant Joy": An Explanation of Age' is a brief piece suggesting that the poem contains an ironic Blakean view of the Christian religion (*Blake* 24/25.78), and Norma Greco's 'The Problematic Vision of Blake's Innocence: A View from "Night" ', argues that the text of Blake's 'Night' questions the speaker's apparently innocent viewpoint (*DR* 70.40–51). Donald M. Smith discusses Blake's *Songs* in terms of eighteenth-century children's verse, comparing the *Songs* to the major exponents of this genre, Bunyan, Watts, Wright, Foxton, Doddridge, Wesley, Smart, Barbauld etc. Although not profoundly original, Smith's essay is an attractive and concise introductory discussion (*EAS* 20.1–16). Three discussions of 'The Tyger' have come my way. Inder Nath Kher rehearses some of the more familiar critical viewpoints on the poem, before presenting a rather straightforward reading (*LHY* 32.72–89). I have not seen Stuart Peterfreundt's 'Power Tropes: "The Tyger" as Enacted Criticism of Newtonian Metonymic Logic and Natural Theology', (*NOR* 18.27–35) and Colin Pedley's contextualization is discussed above. I have not seen Ludmilla K. Kostova's 'William Blake and the Poetry of "Faithful Love": A Reading of Two "Elizabethan" Songs' (*Publications du centre Universitaire de Luxembourg: English Studies* 3.179–92); nor Claire Lamont's 'Blake, Lamb, and the Chimney-Sweeper' (*ChLB* 79.109–23). One article has come my way on *The Book of Thel*. A. G. Den Otter's 'The Question and *The Book of Thel*' reverses some of the more traditional interpretations of the poem by placing its reading in the context of Thel's 'quest for existential knowledge' a quest which is reduced by the Rousseauistic responses of Thel's educators, the Lilly, the Cloud, and the Clod of Clay (*SIR* 30.633–55). Den Otter argues that the forms of the question structure the meaning of the poem. Blake is thus trying to teach us something about the 'minutely appropriate execution' of questions. Den Otter's article opens the text with its understanding of the 'many variant possibilities' of the motto and the poem as a whole. Certainly Thel herself is not to be regarded as a failure and Den Otter comments that her shriek is rather a 'sound that pierces the constraints of her mundane shell' preceding her return to the Vales of Har 'presumably equipped with a new "Poetic or Prophetic" character'. Den Otter, however, does not really consider gender as a factor in the poem and some may consider this to be necessary in the current critical climate. *Visions of the Daughters of Albion* is the subject of James A. W. Heffernan's 'Blake, Oothoon, the Dilemmas of Marginality' (*SIR* 30.3–18). Heffernan's essay presents a careful and detailed reading of Oothoon's language which shows the ambiguity of her position. Heffernan makes a convincing case for the impossibility of placing Oothoon within conventional structures of power and submission, as her language will not allow the reader to categorize within the dichotomy of possession and submission: 'She neither wins nor loses.'

Several studies of Blake's illustrations have appeared this year. Nancy Bailer in *Sotheby's Preview* (April–May:16–17) describes the discovery of previously unrecorded copies of 'The Chaining of Orc', 'The Man Sweeping the interpreter's parlour', and a print of Blake's illustrations for Virgil's first *Eclogue*. Blake's literary illustrations of the works of other poets have received some attention. Three writers have commented on Blake's illustrations to Young's *Night Thoughts*. Irene H. Chayes's 'Picture and Page, Reader and Viewer in Blake's *Night Thoughts* Illustrations' applies reader-response theories to the illustrations (*SIR* 30.439–71). Chayes discusses chiefly the figurations of Time and Death in Blake's illustrations and how they relate to the perceptions of a reader encountering both Young's texts and Blake's images. Analysing just five illustrations, Chayes concludes that the impelling movement in them is away from Young's texts and to Blake's drawings. Chayes's analysis and her conclusions are subtle and penetrating; however, her postulation of a reader-viewer for the drawings is somewhat unproblematic. In 'Words in Pictures. Testing the Boundary: Inscriptions by William Blake' (*W&I* 7.85–97), Chayes discusses the relation between words and images in *Urizen*, *Milton*, and *Jerusalem*. Chayes is concerned with words that are subordinated to Blake's pictorial designs including reversed writing, inscriptions, mottoes and so on. For Chayes such arrangements attempt to cross the verbal-visual boundary. Christopher Heppner in 'The Good (In Spite of What You May Have Heard) Samaritan', (*Blake* 25.64–9) counsels against the too easy assumption that Blake's illustrations to literary texts are always antithetical critiques of those texts. To develop his point Heppner takes Blake's illustration of the Good Samaritan from the *Night Thoughts*. Focusing on the ambiguities of the image of the serpent on the Samaritan's chalice and the look of dismay on the face of the victim, Heppner deftly demonstrates how the illustration is faithful to the biblical story if not supportive of Young's economy of love. Also in *Blake*, Morton D. Paley's 'Blake Headgear: The Seventh Head of the Beast in *Night Thoughts*' justifies his identification of the headgear of the sixth head of the Beast in *Night Thoughts* 345 as a Bishop's mitre, against John E. Grant's rather eccentric counter preference for a Turkish antecedent (24.142–4). Jeanne Moskal's 'Blake, Dante, and Whatever Book is for Vengeance' discusses the illustrations to Dante, arguing that Blake was concerned to refute the intellectual error of Dante, his capacity for vengeance, by juxtaposing this with the forgiveness of God (*PQ* 70:311–37). Robert N. Essick's 'The Printings of Blake's Dante Drawings' (*Blake* 24.80–90) describes in meticulous detail the printing history of the same engravings.

A few comparative treatments of Blake with other writers have appeared. David Groves presents a very strong case for the identification of 'W—m B—e, a Great Original' from James Hogg's novel *Confessions of a Justified Sinner* (1824) as a version of Blake. Groves demonstrates that Hogg knew Cromek and was very likely aware of Blake's designs for Blair's poem *The Grave* (*ScLJ* 18.27–45). John A. Lamb's 'William Blake and William Wordsworth: A Study in the Role of the Imagination in the Unitive Principle' (*ACM* 4.139–56) argues, somewhat unconvincingly that Blake and Wordsworth essentially shared the same world view, despite Blake's familiar criticism of the 'Natural Man' in Wordsworth. I have not seen J. M. Q. Davies's 'Iconography and Construal in Some of Blake's Designs to Milton's Poems', (*AUMLA* 75.65–81); C. Bigwood, 'Seeing Blake's Illuminated texts', (*JAAC* 49.307–15); A Depaz, 'The Language of Mythical Vision in William Blake's Pictorial Poetics', (*LeS* 26.365–91); G. I. James, 'The Holy and the Heterodox: William Blake's Transformational Use of Religious Language', (*SMy* 14.31–44); D. Vergnon, 'William Blake and his Friends' (*Oeil: Revue d'Art* 434.83); Thomas B. O'Grady, 'Little Chandler's Song of Experience' (*JJQ* 28.399–405); J. Glendening, 'Ezra Pound and Blake: Method in Madness, Madness in Method', (*Paideuma* 20.95–106).

A substantial body of writing has appeared on Wordsworth this year as last, although we should beware of accepting *de facto* that Wordsworth is becoming metonymic for Romanticism. Central to this way of looking at Romanticism is the project of The Cornell Wordsworth which seeks to present full and accurate texts of the poems with all their variant readings. Already the series includes Stephen Parrish's edition of the two-part *The Prelude, 1798–1799* and W. J. B. Owen's *The Fourteen-Book Prelude*. Now we have Mark L. Reed's superb edition of *The Thirteen-Book Prelude*. It would be difficult to do full justice to such an edition without a substantial and detailed essay on the process of composition of the thirteen-book *Prelude*, but some comment can be made. Reed's principal texts are a reading text of the poem as fair-copied in 1805–6 (known as the A–B stage) and a reading text of the probable form of the poem as Wordsworth left it after a renewed period of revision 1818–20 (known as the C stage). These texts are supplemented by reports, in full transcription and apparatus, of the content of the manuscripts that constitute the textual record of the development of the poem from the two-part version of 1798–1799 through its history as a thirteen-book poem. Photographs of the manuscripts are contained in volume one and transcriptions in volume two. It is possible thus to lay the two volumes side-by-side and compare the photographs of the MS (over 900 pages) with the editor's transcription of it (over 800 pages complete with revisions and excisions of the MSS and enormous numbers of fragments connected with the poem). Reed's edition makes available manuscripts only previously accessible after lengthy stays at the library of Dove Cottage, including MS. WW which was not known to Ernest de Selincourt and which contains first versions of many of the best-known passages in Books III–VIII and XIII of the poem, including the ascent of Snowdon. The influence of Mark Reed's version of the poem will probably be to tip the critical balance even more towards the 1805 version. The chief reading text of the volume is the conflation of two copies of the 1805–6 period of composition known as the AB text. Volume two contains the C text of 1818–20 which Reed has extracted and disentangled from revisions to the A text (a virtuoso performance). Reed's recension of the 1805–6 text is only slightly variant from the previous editions of de Selincourt, J. C. Maxwell, and Jonathan Wordsworth. Yet the C text is a version of the *Prelude* presented for the first time. Fascinatingly, this version of 1818–20 contains many revisions and additions which were then abandoned when Wordsworth returned to the poem in 1830 (producing what is known as the 1850 version). In fact the C version is much more orthodox, pessimistic, and artificial than the later version of the poem, thus problematizing the conventional notion that Wordsworth moved straightforwardly towards conservatism in politics and religion in revising the poem of 1806–7. Much of the poetry of this C version has never been published. As well as bringing forward a new version of the *Prelude*, Reed also convincingly argues that the contentious notion of the 'Five-Part Prelude' (championed by Jonathan Wordsworth) is too difficult and problematic to establish. Clearly the appearance of Reed's edition makes it easier to appreciate the complexity of the composition of the poem as we track Wordsworth's starts and false starts in producing what has perhaps become the quintessential Romantic poem. We should also, however, note the reservations which Jack Stillinger has made with regard to The Cornell Wordsworth's preference for the 'earliest complete text' in his *Multiple Authorship and the Myth of Solitary Genius* reviewed in the above section on books of general interest. Duncan Wu in 'Editing Intentions' (*EIC* 41.1–10) reaches a similar conclusion to Stillinger regarding editions of the *Prelude*. He argues that because of the problems inherent in defining what an author's intention may have been we must accept, on a theoretical level at least, that numerous editorial constructions are possible. Coincidentally with the publication of the thirteen-book *Prelude*, Woodstock Books have also issued their facsimile of *The Excursion* (1814) this year. Jonathan Wordsworth's introduction indicates that this work belongs largely to the years 1810–12, although his statement that the *Prelude* belongs to the years 1798–1805 does not ring as truly as it might have done before Reed's edition of the thirteen-book poem. The availability of this facsimile is bound to increase the critical interest in this less than popular Wordsworth long poem. I have not seen Jared Curtis's edition of Wordsworth's *The Fenwick Notes* (Bristol Press). Routledge have also re-issued R. L. Brett and A. R. Jones's fine version of *Lyrical Ballads*. This volume has been a worthy edition of the ballads since it was published in 1963. Brett and Jones provide a scrupulous and conscientious text of the 1798 and 1800 edition of the ballads with variants from the 1802 and 1805 editions. The 1963 introduction is a sound and interesting discussion from an intellectual historical perspective and serves to introduce students to the biographical and intellectual context of the poems. Some of the comment does, however, look a little dated and some of the suggestions for secondary and further reading are a little thin and disappointing. Perhaps most controversially the editors repeat their acceptance of Arthur Beatty's strong claims (made in 1927) for the influence of David Hartley on the thought of the ballads and of their generally anti-Godwinian tone. Although this reviewer is certainly in sympathy with the Brett/Jones reading, there needs some fuller discussion of this point (including reference to the work of Mark Rader and Newton P. Stallknecht who find traces of Hartleian influence to be slight, and James Averill who argues for the influence of Erasmus Darwin's *Zoonomia*). Overall this remains a fine and reasonably priced edition, although many may prefer the more expensive edition of Michael Mason (Longman, 1992) which will be reviewed next year. Finally Murray have produced a highly attractive volume, *William Wordsworth: A Lakeland Anthology* with a foreword by John Mortimer but selected and illustrated by the artist Piers Browne. This is a beautifully produced and illustrated volume which celebrates Wordsworth primarily as a nature poet. Browne's illustrations are rich and evocative, especially so his recreation of the stolen boat episode from the *Prelude*. Russell Noyes's 1971 study of Wordsworth for *TEAS* has been updated by John O. Hayden. This study is a very accessible and attractively written overview of Wordsworth's life and work which is useful to readers new to the poet. Hayden has chiefly altered

Noyes's discussions of *The Borderers* and the preface to *Lyrical Ballads* and has provided a good select bibliography. Even still this revamped study appears a little dated and does take Wordsworth very much on his own terms, cheering on Wordsworth's abandonment of 'political chimeras' and very much accepting the wisdom of Wordsworth's political and moral philosophy. The strongest parts of this book remain Noyes's discussion of the *Prelude* and *The Excursion*. Jonathan Bate's *Romantic Ecology: Wordsworth and the Environmental Tradition* is an attempt to get beyond notions of left and right which have been applied to the politics of nature and to situate criticism within a 'green' perspective. This actually is more ambitious than it at first appears and Bate's book is full of strong and intelligent comment on both Wordsworth's poetry and recent criticism of it. Bate is excellent when outlining some of the pitfalls of New Historicist criticism, mainly that of Alan Liu and Jerome McGann, and also in demonstrating how the supposedly conservative writings of the later Wordsworth can be viewed in a genuinely radical way. Surely this is an instructive track to take as much recent criticism has explained away, or simply ignored, the genuine contribution made to radical thought by the so-called Tory Radicals who challenged the nineteenth-century Benthamite-Utilitarian consensus. Crucial to Bate's argument is the role of John Ruskin, a figure whom Bate is keen to foreground as the inheritor of Wordsworth's ecological concerns. This encourages Bate to privilege *The Excursion* as the central ecological text in Wordsworth's *oeuvre* and one that is as important as the *Prelude* and as a text which may well speak to the 1990s in a more relevant way than the latter. Certainly this is a provocative and intriguing book which makes strong claims for Wordsworth's consistently radical edge. Ultimately Bate's claim that this book may be described as 'a preliminary sketch towards a literary ecocriticism' is a large and unconvincing one. Clearly ecological concerns are very much in mind (as for instance in Richard Holmes's portrait of a rather green Coleridge in his recent biography), yet a green criticism, as yet, lacks that intellectual depth which would allow it to take root and prosper. An article on a related subject is J. Carter's 'Wordsworth as Environmentalist' in *Alternatives* (17.24–6). Robin Jarvis's *Wordsworth, Milton and the Theory of Poetic Relations* is the first full-length study of its subject since Herbert Grierson's *Milton and Wordsworth: Poets and Prophets* of over fifty years ago. As one would expect, Jarvis problematizes the very notion of influence that Grierson took for granted, approaching this concept through an allusive theory of intertextuality which deftly interweaves various strands of post-structuralist thought, particularly engaging, in a sophisticated and incisive way, with the theories of Harold Bloom. Jarvis's book is divided into two parts. Part one develops a wide-ranging and thoughtful discussion of that slippery concept 'intertextuality' and part two attempts a detailed engagement with textual allusions to and echoes of *Paradise Lost* in *The Prelude*. Although standing on its own right as an elegant critique of theories of influence and intertextuality, the first part of this study attempts to explicate, or, at any rate, clear the ground for a theory of intertextuality that is regrounded in the activity of the reader, and which will be exploited in exploring the allusions of part two, where allusions are constituted by the act of reading in a relational manner. Particularly impressive is Jarvis's critique of Bloom. Accepting Bloom's agonistic notion of influence with its 'mind-bending reflexivities' in preference to what he characterizes as 'the genial complacencies of the Oxford School of Influence', Jarvis focuses on Bloom's revisionary ratio of *daemonization*, its repressive function and its relationship with the Sublime. This he accents in an alternative, reader-constructed way, harnessing Freud's evolving model of primary and secondary processes to a conflictual, open and inventive mode of reading. Part two of Jarvis's study deals with areas of intertextuality in Milton and Wordsworth of varying degrees of visibility. The proviso that 'poetic relations should be posited as a product of interpretation, not as an objective and indelible feature of the text or as something verifiable by historical or biographical means' determines that some allusions will be less visible than others and some, of course, actually invisible to certain readers. Jarvis's very subtle and persuasive commentary increases the visibility of most of the areas of intertextuality he identifies and he does theoretically allow for the possibility of the 'specious attribution' (182n, although it is not clear to me how speciousness would be constituted in his theory). This is a thoughtful, rewarding and original study and one which negotiates the notoriously rarefied and dizzying heights of intertextuality with confidence and intelligence.

Patrick Campbell's *Wordsworth and Coleridge Lyrical Ballads: Critical Perspectives* provides a very readable overview of the critical reception of the first edition of the *Lyrical Ballads* from the date of their first publication (1798) to the modern period. Campbell demonstrates how the *Lyrical Ballads* were not regarded as a central document of the Romantic movement until relatively recent times. Rather oddly, however, this study is only concerned with the first edition of *Lyrical Ballads* and thus important poems from the second edition, such as 'Michael' are not mentioned at all, although the 1800 'Preface' is discussed at some length. Also unusual in a book such as this is a chapter of Campbell's 'Personal Perspectives' on the less-familiar poems in the collection, when there does exist a body of criticism on these poems as well which does need comment. Campbell's own stance is that of 'a pluralist not a purist' critic who confesses to have learnt much from the 'current free-market economy' of criticism that prevails, although he is not adverse to dispensing the odd slap to recent New Historicist and poststructuralist critics. The major critics are presented in Campbell's account and their work will be familiar enough to most Romanticists. Certainly several good essays and books are not mentioned and the discussion of criticism of Coleridge's *Ancient Mariner* is rather limited: no mention is made of important work by Kathleen Wheeler, David Miall or Raimonda Modiano, nor is Kelvin Everest's excellent discussion of Coleridge's 'Nightingale' in *Coleridge's Secret Ministry* (Harvester, 1979) mentioned. Containing no criticism after 1988, this book already looks dated, given the appearance of important studies of Wordsworth by writers such as Theresa Kelley, Alan Liu, and Alan Bewell. Nevertheless it will be useful for undergraduate readers of the poems to consult, introducing them to the often bewildering variety of critical viewpoints without concomitant bewilderment. A number of shorter pieces have appeared on the poems in *Lyrical Ballads*. I have not yet seen David Simpson's 'Public Virtues, Private Vices: Reading Between the Lines of Wordsworth's "Anecdote for Fathers" ' in David Simpson (ed.), *Subject to History* (*CornUP*). Ross Woodman's 'The Idiot Boy as Healer' in James Holt McGavran Jnr (ed.), *Romanticism and Children's Literature* is reviewed above. Paul D. Sheats's ' "Tis Three Feet Long, and Two Feet Wide": Wordsworth's "Thorn" and the Politics of Bathos' (*WC* 22.92–100) makes a strong case for the political importance of 'The Thorn' in demonstrating how the literary strategies of the poem suggest that Wordsworth had not abandoned the humanitarianism of his radical years by 1798. Sheats present us with a close and detailed reading of the poem which highlights Wordsworth's exploitation of low registers, especially in the notorious lines, 'I've measured it from side to side …'. Regrettably I have not yet seen David Bromwich's 'The French Revolution and Tintern Abbey' (*Raritan* 10.1–23) nor Bruce E. Graver's 'Wordsworth's Georgic Pastoral: Otium and *Labor* in "Michael" ' (*ERR* 1.119–34). The 'Multiple Voices in "Nutting": The Urbane

Wordsworth' are discussed by Bruce Bigley's close but seldom revealing analysis of the poem in *PQ* (70.433–52) and James Mulvihill glosses lines 1–21 of 'The Old Cumberland Beggar' (*Expl* 49–50.iv.213–14). J. Douglas Kneale's 'Romantic Aversions: Apostrophe Reconsidered' subjects 'There Was a Boy' to close reading in an attempt to criticize recent critical embarrassment with the figure of the apostrophe, arguing that apostrophe should not be associated with voice, but with the movement of voice, thus distinguishing between apostrophe and address (*ELH* 58.141–65). Two studies of 'We Are Seven' have come to my notice. The first 'Catechist and Visionary' by James Holt McGavran Jr. in his collection of essays on *Romanticism and Children's Literature* is reviewed above, and the second is Margaret Russett's 'Wordsworth's Gothic Interpreter: De Quincey Personifies "We Are Seven" ' (*SIR* 30.345–65), which is an account of how De Quincey's admiration for the poem darkly interprets Wordsworthian notions of restoration by constructing an identity which always appears textual.

Two extended essays on the *Prelude* have appeared this year. Stephen Gill's introduction to the poem for CUP's Landmarks of World Literature is an excellent discussion of the poem for the first-time reader. Gill clearly and accessibly sets out the complexities of the poem's composition, its verse, and large themes in a concise and attractive way. Gill's account of the poem is traditional and scholarly and supports the notion that there is a recognizable Romantic aesthetic of which the *Prelude* is the most important English exemplar. Gill is particularly good on the characteristics of Wordsworth's verse and on the poem's relationship to Coleridge's changing consciousness during the period of composition. With a sensible and shrewd list of further reading, this book is the best short introduction to the *Prelude* which I know of. Ronald Gaskell's *Wordsworth's Poem on the Human Mind* does not work as satisfactorily as Gill's study as an introduction to the poem. Gaskell's approach is rather more impressionistic as he discusses some of the broad themes of the poem; those of nature, imagination, and the human mind. Much of the discussion is familiar and, at times, pedestrian, but Gaskell does grapple with the difficulties involved in interpreting such slippery concerns as Wordsworth's religion, his conception of the imagination and so forth. Gaskell is also good when showing the genesis and development of some of the key passages in the *Prelude*. Overall Gaskell's approach is traditional and aesthetic and many new readers of the poem will no doubt find this approach helpful and sympathetic. However Gaskell's willingness to take Wordsworth almost entirely on his own terms and his reluctance to engage more closely with some of the recent writing about the less-familiar passages of the *Prelude* are undoubtedly weaknesses.

The Prelude has also been the subject of several articles. J. Robert Barth SJ's 'The Temporal Imagination in Wordsworth's *Prelude*: Time and the Timeless' discusses notions of temporality in the poem (*Thought* 261.139–50) and Laurence Lerner's 'Wordsworth's Refusal of Politics' argues that the poem is pulled between politics and autobiography and that it represents a refusal and not an evasion of such issues (*SEL* 31.673–91). David Ferris's dense deconstruction of the Simplon Pass passage from Book VI of the *Prelude*, 'Where Three Paths Meet: History, Wordsworth, and the Simplon Pass' explores the moment as a key site for Romanticism and Romanticists (*SIR* 30.391–438). More approachable is John A. Hodgson's informative discussion of Wordsworth's opening question 'Was it for this?' from the 'Two Part *Prelude*' which argues for the classicism of this rhetorical technique ('Was it for this?: Wordsworth's Virgilian Questioning', *TSLL* 33.125–36). W. J. B. Owen in 'Understanding *The Prelude*' offers a series of difficulties raised by parts of the *Prelude* and shows great erudition and wit in demonstrating his own approach to such difficulties

(*WC* 22.100–9). Eugene L. Stelzig's ' "The Shield of Human Nature": Wordsworth's Reflections on the Revolution in France' tackles the subject of Wordsworth's use of the word 'nature' in relation to his responses to the French Revolution (*NCL* 45–46.415–31). Stelzig's argument, which has Wordsworth torn between the two poles of Hobbes's and Rousseau's natural philosophy is not particularly original, but the point is attractively and interestingly developed. Regrettably I have not seen Stelzig's other piece, 'Rousseau, Goethe, Wordsworth and the Classic Moment of Romantic Autobiography' (*Neoh* 18:249–71). Finally with regard to the *Prelude*, Duncan Wu and Nicola Trott provide some interesting information about three possible sources for the cave simile in Book VIII (*N&Q* 38.298–9).

Anne L. Rylestone's *Prophetic Memory in Wordsworth's Ecclesiastical Sonnets* argues, less than convincingly, for the inclusion of Wordsworth's late sonnet sequence in the critical canon. Certainly the sonnets are deserving of a much wider attention than has been given them so far, but Rylestone supplies only a disappointing apologia for their uneven quality and no indication of their wider importance outside of a few references to celebrated moments from the *Prelude*. Rylestone is keen to argue that the sonnets form an important part of the Wordsworthian *oeuvre*; a minor, but significant, part of the gothic cathedral, an image which Wordsworth used to describe his entire work. This minimizes the strong differences between the 1805 *Prelude* and the more obviously orthodox ecclesiastical sonnets: 'the series is indeed a history of the Church, but it is a personalized Wordsworthian history in which the Church is a manifestation of the natural world.' The problematics of this naturalization of Church history are not explored and Wordsworth's equation of ecclesiastical history with the origin and course of a river is accepted on its own terms and seen as at one with the exploitation of river imagery in the *Prelude*. Basically Rylestone has written a fair enough explication of the sequence but gives us little else. Surprisingly there is no discussion of previous sonnet sequences and the most obvious literary model, John Milton (despite appearing in Sonnet III.4 from the sequence itself) is not mentioned at all! The relevance of this sequence to the ideas of *The Excursion* is not explored either and Coleridge also receives no mention despite the relevance of his *On the Constitution of Church and State* to the debate about Catholic Emancipation: a debate to which the *Ecclesiastical Sonnets* are clearly addressed. We do need a reappraisal of this sonnet sequence but sadly Rylestone's book does not give us this. David Pym's rather dry account 'The Ideas of Church and State in the Thought of the Three Principal Lake Poets, Coleridge, Southey and Wordsworth' suffers from the opposite problem; while being very clear about the ecclesiastical background of Wordsworth's ideas it shows no knowledge of how these ideas were expressed poetically (*DUJ* 53.i.19–26). I have not seen Brian G. Caraher's *Wordsworth's 'Slumber' and the Problematics of Reading* (PennUP), which will be reviewed next year.

A large number of articles have appeared on Wordsworthian subjects. Marilyn Gaull's 'Romantic Numeracy: The "Tuneless Numbers" and "Shadows Numberless" ' (*WC* 22.124–31) provides an interesting discussion of mathematics and Romantic poetry, noting that 'the development of mathematics as a creative art, started during the Romantic period in English literature and reflected many similar experiences'. Gaull demonstrates how Wordsworth's allusions to mathematics in his poetry make sense in terms of the changing public perceptions of Newton and Euclid in the nineteenth century and challenges those critics, such as Mary Jacobus, who have used Wordsworth's references to Newton to argue for, among other things, a suppression of guilt concerning the slave trade. Alan G. Hill's 'Wordsworth and Italy' discusses Wordsworth's relationship to Italy and his use of Italian sources in *JAIS*

(1.111–25). Alan Richardson's excellent 'Wordsworth, Fairy Tales, and the Politics of Children's Literature' in James Holt McGavran Jnr (ed.), *Romanticism and Children's Literature* is reviewed above. Marlon B. Ross discusses Wordsworth's notions of nationalism in 'Romancing the Nation-State' in Jonathan Arac and Harriet Ritvo (eds.), *Macropolitics of Nineteenth-Century Literature: Nationalism, Exoticism, Imperialism*. In Ross's account Wordsworth, even in the 'Letter to the Bishop of Llandaff' and the 'Salisbury Plain' poems, was always really a Burkean who wore his Jacobin clothes rather thinly. This view seems no longer tenable given Nicholas Roe's researches into Wordsworth's radicalism. Ross is too quick to associate, *pace* Marilyn Butler, espousal of property rights with Burkean conservatism. Only the extreme wing of British radicalism desired the abolition of property (John Thelwall certainly did not) and the notion of the independent property owner had a long and distinguished history in British radical thought. Wordsworth's interest in the small independent freeholder is more Harringtonian than Burkean. More productively, Ross compares the conflicting nationalist strategies adopted by Wordsworth's *The White Doe of Rylstone* and Scott's *Rokeby* in the historical context of Napoleonic Europe. Ross's analysis of *Rokeby* as a transferred anti-Bonapartist pro-nationalist fable is illuminating and valuable, and his relating of *The White Doe* to the ideas displayed in the nationalistic *The Convention of Cintra* is enlightening and provoking. A very different view of *The White Doe* is expressed by Evan Radcliffe's 'Wordsworth and the Problem of Action' (*NCL* 45–46.157–80) where Wordsworth's ambivalence over action in the outside world is examined in terms of his interest in Quakerism (especially of his friend Thomas Clarkson), Stoicism and Quietism. Radcliffe's case is that the Christian tradition invoked by the poem provides a justification for inaction, enabling the poet to 'present sympathetically and almost without qualification a heroine who withdraws completely from action'. This is a sensitive and scholarly essay.

Albert Cook's 'The Transformation of "Point": Amplitude in Wordsworth, Whitman, and Rimbaud' (*SIR* 30.169–88) discusses the rhetorical strategy of amplitude in these poets, arguing that the neo-classical notion of point or concision is being superseded in their work by a profoundly different approach to closure, 'an access to an amplitude which redefines the relation between the poetic speaker and the presumed audience'. Bryan Crockett's 'Negotiating the Shade: Wordsworth's Debt to Ovid' discusses Wordsworth's sources in Ovid's *Metamorphoses* (*CML* 11/12.109–18). Mark Jones's 'Interpretation in Wordsworth and the Provocation of Romantic Literature' (*SIR* 30.565–604) is a full and articulate attempt to recover Wordsworth's interpretations as dramatic and provocative. Interpretation *in* Wordsworth is thus designed to invoke interpretations *of* Wordsworth which address the question of whether the Romantic text is invocative or whether we, self-servingly, impose this function upon it'. Jones points out how the Keatsian binary of poetry versus philosophy has become ingrained in modern(ist) readings of Wordsworth and shows how the 'anti-interpretive, anti-philosophical prejudice' discriminates against Wordsworth's revisions and later texts. Surveying a number of Wordsworth's poems and critical responses to them, Jones contributes an eloquent apologia for interpretation in its various modes. Also in *SIR* 30 is William A Kumier's 'A "New Quickening": Haydn's *The Creation*, Wordsworth, and Pictorialist Imagination' which compares the pictorialism of Haydn's aria *Creation* with the ascent of Snowdon from Wordsworth's *Prelude* (535–64).

Peter J. Manning in 'Cleansing the Images: Wordsworth, Rome, and the Rise of Historicism' (*TSLL* 33.271–336) compares Wordsworth's treatment of the Roman Empire in the later poetry with that of Macaulay in a very full and wide-ranging piece of scholarship. Anne McWhir's 'Purity and Disgust: The Limits of Wordsworth's Primitivism' discusses Wordsworth's primitivism, his treatment of purity and the language of rustics in *Mosaic* (24.43–68). *Genre* 24 contains J. O'Rourke's 'Intertextuality, Progress and Literary History; Wordsworth, Shelley, and Arnold' (117–36). Gordon K. Thomas's 'Wordsworth and the Mystery of Things' surveys Wordsworth's concern with the mystery of language and 'things' in his poetry (*WC* 22.118–24). J. Robert Barth's 'The Role of Humankind in the Poetry of Wordsworth and Coleridge' compares Wordsworth's poetic treatment of humanity with Coleridge's, arguing that for Coleridge the 'other' is more vital to the poem's mediation than in the work of the more self-possessed Wordsworth. Coleridge's conversation poems typically surround the poet with loved ones, whereas Wordsworth's figures are almost totally merged with the landscape. Barth suggests that this differing perspective stems from a contrasting notion of God (*WC* 22.160–5). Also in *WC* 22, Jonathan Wordsworth reassesses the vexed issue of 'Wordsworthian Comedy', drawing upon 'The Idiot Boy' and *Peter Bell* to argue that comedy is for Wordsworth 'a voyaging of the mind, an adventure of the imagination, in which the poet permits himself to dispense with the rootedness that Coleridge unkindly calls his "clinging to the palpable" '(141–50). This is a very useful and illuminating article which treats seriously the 'eccentric and powerful vision' of *Peter Bell.*

Moving on to criticism of individual works and poems. In *DVLG* 65, Gerhard Stilz's '*Robbers, Borderers, Millers, and Men*: Englishe Räuberstucke zwischen Revolutionstragödie und melodramatischer Restauration' is a discussion of the outlaw in Schiller's *Die Räuber* and Isaac Pocock's *The Miller and his Men* which are seen as sources for Wordsworth's *The Borderers* (117–31). Three studies of *The Excursion* have appeared. Dan Kenneth Crosby's 'Wordsworth's *Excursion*: An Annotated Bibliography of Criticism' is an annotated bibliography of criticism of the poem from 1814 to 1990 (*BB* 48.33–49); Salick Roydon discusses '*The Excursion* as Epic' (*LHY* 32.86–110), and Sharon M. Setzer's excellent 'Excursions into the Wilderness: Wordsworth's Visionary Kingdoms and the Typography of Miltonic Revision' discusses the heavenly city passages of *The Excursion* seeing them as densely allusive refigurings of both Milton's *Paradise Lost* and Coleridge's *Religious Musings* (*SIR* 30.367–89). Anthony J. Harding's scholarly and detailed 'Forgetfulness and the Poetic Self in *Home at Grasmere*' (*WC* 22.109–18) suggests that the poem struggles with two contradictory ways of seeing nature, arguing that Wordsworth is hesitating between two tropes and two traditions, classical and Christian. 'Laodamia' is the subject of Judith W. Page's sensible and careful essay ' "Judge Her Gently: Passion and Rebellion in Wordsworth's "Laodamia" ' (*TSLL* 33.24–39), which suggests that the text is informed by Wordsworth's own ambivalence about the consequences of his own passion and rebellious nature.

AUMLA 74/75 contains H. Vandeveire's ironic reading of Wordsworth's 'Ode to Duty' (82–96). Wordsworth's translations of classical poets have received some notice this year. Bruce E. Graver's 'Wordsworth's Georgic Beginnings' is a scholarly account of the juvenile Wordsworth's translations and paraphrases of Virgil's *Georgics* which he argues contributed to the georgic vision of 'Michael' and *The Excursion* with its emphasis on hard work, rural economy and human failure (*TSLL* 33.137–59). Graver's discussion of the translation of 'Orpheus and Eurydice' from *Georgic* IV is particularly enlightening, as is his comment on what Virgil's blank verse meant in forming Wordsworth's technique. Duncan Wu contributes four single-authored pieces to *N&Q* 38; the first, 'Wordsworth's *Orpheus and Eurydice*: The Unpublished Final Line', somewhat redundantly, given Graver's transcription of the translation, restoring the final line to Wordsworth's 'Orpheus and Eurydice' (301–2); the second, 'Wordsworth's Translation of Callistratus: A Possible Redating', suggesting that Wordsworth may have been aware of a translation of a Greek lyric by Callistratus by John Baynes when undertaking his own version thus tentatively dating the Wordsworth version to 1778–80 (303); the third, 'Wordsworth's Copy of Smart's Horace' containing details of some recondite domestic material inscribed in Wordsworth's copy of Smart's edition of Horace (303–5); and the fourth, '*The Ancient Mariner*: A Wordsworthian Source', providing a tenuous source for the wind's blowing through the bones of Death in Coleridge's *The Ancient Mariner* in Wordsworth's juvenile *The Vale of Esthwaite* (301). I have not seen Wu's 'William Wordsworth and the Farish Brothers' (*BLR* 14.99–101).

'Resolution and Independence' is the subject of comparison with Goethe's 'Trilogie der Leidenschaft' made by Eugene L. Stelzig's 'Memory, Imagination, and Self-Healing in the Romantic Crisis Lyric' (*JEGP* 90.524–41). Stelzig argues that both poets attempt to counter the momentum of anxiety and depression through a creative and therapeutic use of memory. Karen Swann's 'Suffering and Sensation in *The Ruined Cottage*' discusses the poem in terms of its complex relationship to sensationalist literature and the literary marketplace, ingeniously arguing that Wordsworth's narrative technique allows him to deploy sensationalist incident (abandoned woman) while distancing his own poetry from Gothic excess (*PMLA* 106.83–95). John Rieder's 'Civic Virtue and Social Class at the Scene of Execution' deftly examines the revisions of Wordsworth's Salisbury Plain poems, demonstrating how the poems turn toward a literary audience and away from explicitly addressing themselves to political action and the contemplation of the victims of political, social, and legal oppression (*SIR* 30.325–43). Andrea Henderson's 'A Tale Told to be Forgotten: Enlightenment, Revolution and the Poet in "Salisbury Plain" ' (*SIR* 30.71–84) presents a more problematic text which demonstrates the workings of Wordsworth's strategies for the management of fragmentation and disruption. Henderson's probing analysis of the fracturing in the poem is interesting and original, although some of the conclusions she draws are not always obvious. I have not yet seen the one discussion of 'The Solitary Reaper' this year: Nancy A. Jones's 'The Rape of the Rural Muse: Wordsworth's Solitary Reaper as a Version of Pastourelle' in Lynn A. Higgins and Brenda A. Silver (eds.), *Rape and Representation* (ColUP). Finally Duncan Wu presents a rather fanciful comparison of Wordsworthian notions of language and art with those of William Burroughs in 'Wordsworth in Space' (*WC* 22.150–60). Little has appeared specifically on Dorothy Wordsworth this year. Pamela Woof has produced an attractive and scholarly edition of *The Grasmere Journals* of 1800–1803 and provides a fascinating and detailed account of some of Dorothy's concerns expressed in the Journals and Travel Accounts in 'Dorothy Wordsworth and the Pleasures of Recognition' (*WC* 22.150–60).

The major publishing event in Coleridge studies this year was the appearance of *Table Talk* edited by Carl Woodring, the fourteenth volume of the Bollingen *Collected Works*. Unfortunately this was not made available for me to review. Two of Coleridge's texts have been reprinted in the Woodstock series Revolution and Romanticism. Coleridge and Southey's *The Fall of Robespierre* (1794) is given a welcome reprint and Jonathan Wordsworth's introduction is judicious and shrewd, finding the drama 'surprisingly effective'. Also welcome is the facsimile of *Christabel* (1816) which Coleridge printed with 'Kubla Khan' and 'The Pains of Sleep'. Only one monograph on Coleridge has come to my attention, the excellent *Coleridge's Figurative Language* by Tim Fulford. Fulford is mainly interested in Coleridge as a theorizer of language and he demonstrates how Coleridge's discourse is fashioned from conceits, allusions, and puns as well as metaphor and simile. Fulford discusses Coleridge's early political writings as engaged in constructing a spiritual politics, a venture which continues in different ways throughout his career. This book contains especially valuable discussion of Coleridge's interest in the Hebrew tradition and his relationship to the Kabbalah, and much ground-breaking work on the private codes used by Coleridge in his *Notebooks*, codes which Coleridge used to describe his emotional life with Sara Hutchinson and the Wordsworth circle. This concern with a sympathetic audience constructed through language informs much of Coleridge's poetry and Fulford provides exemplary discussion of the poetry; his treatment of 'Frost at Midnight' is one of the best I have come across. Fulford's knowledge of Coleridge's work is full and assured, based on a close acquaintance with published and unpublished material. His book will fascinate and intrigue Coleridgeans and those interested in Coleridge more generally.

Three collections of essays have appeared this year on Coleridge's works. The first is *Coleridge and the Armoury of the Human Mind: Essays on His Prose Writings* edited by Peter J. Kitson and Thomas N. Corns. Included in the collection are the following pieces: a fine discussion of 'Coleridge, Kabbalah and the Book of Daniel' by Tim Fulford; an erudite and scholarly overview of 'Coleridge as Critic' by John Beer; a detailed discussion of the transformation of celebrated passages from *Notebook* entries to published versions, demonstrating Coleridge's awareness of audience in Kathleen Wheeler's 'Coleridge's Notebook Scribblings'; a fascinating account of De Quincey's dark interpretation of Coleridge's *Biographia Literaria* in the *Confessions of an English Opium Eater*, in Nigel Leask's 'Murdering One's Double'; William Ruddick's 'Coleridge against Romantic Autobiography' which discusses contrasting Romantic notions of autobiography in Coleridge, Hazlitt, and Lamb; and a discussion of the political ideas of Coleridge's highly allusive radical pamphlet *The Plot Discovered*, ' "The electric fluid of truth": The Ideology of the Commonwealthsman in Coleridge's *The Plot Discovered*' by Peter J. Kitson. This collection was first published as the journal *PSt* 13:iii (1990). The second collection of essays is Richard E. Matlak's *Approaches to Teaching Coleridge's Poetry and Prose* in the MLA series Approaches to Teaching World Literature. Matlak provides an interesting indication of the ways in which Coleridge's work is taught by leading Romanticists in the USA with sections describing approaches to teaching both the poetry and the prose, the conversation poems, and the supernatural poems. This collection of approaches is evidence of the richness and variety of Coleridge's work and the wide-ranging strategies adopted by the contributors provide refreshing new ways of looking at Coleridge's work. This is a useful and intriguing collection. Finally the Winter edition of *WC* 22 contains a selection of papers from the Coleridge Summer Conference of 1990. Of especial value are Paul Magnuson's dialogic account of 'The Politics of "Frost at Midnight" '; Kathleen Wheeler's ' "Kubla Khan" and Eighteenth Century Aesthetic Theories'; Susan Luther's illuminating discussion of 'The Garden of Boccaccio' in 'The Lost Garden of Coleridge'; Denise Degrois's 'Making the Absent Present: Self-Portraits and Portraits of the Artist in Coleridge's Work'; David Miall's account of 'Coleridge on Emotion: Experience into Theory'; Marilyn Gaull's discussion of Coleridge and contemporary scientific theories, 'Coleridge and the Kingdoms of the World'; A. C. Goodson's analysis of Coleridge and Burke in 'Burke's Orpheus and Coleridge's Contrary Understanding'; William Galperin's post-structuralist attack on the closures of New Historicism, especially with regard to McGann's reading of *The Ancient Mariner* in his 'Coleridge and Critical Intervention'; John Beer's humanistic comparison of 'Coleridge and Havel'; Mary Anne Perkins's account of 'S. T. Coleridge: Logos and Logosophia'; and finally Tim Fulford's excellent discussion of 'Coleridge and the Wisdom Tradition' in Judaeo-Christian thought. David Miall adds a postscript to this number describing 'The Campaign to Acquire Coleridge Cottage' in Nether Stowey for the nation.

There have been a number of articles on Coleridge subjects. Jerome Christensen's '*Ecce Homo*: Biographical Acknowledgement, the End of the French Revolution, and the Romantic Reinvention of English Verse', in William H. Epstein, ed., *Contesting the Subject* is concerned with Coleridge's participation in the cultural moment that marked the emergence of the literary biography. Christensen's argument is difficult and unusual and, at times, rather tenuous (especially the discussion of the phallic symbolism of 'Fears in Solitude'), nevertheless it contains much insight in its attempt to locate the emergent notion of a literary autobiography in a biographical paradigm beyond revolutionary and counter-revolutionary stereotyping. Mark Parker's 'The Institution of a Burkean-Coleridgean Literary Culture' in *SEL* (30.693–713), shows how Coleridge adapted and modified Burkean notions of tradition and government and how such notions were 'institutionalized' by John Scott, the editor of the *London Magazine*. Parker's article is a good piece of literary-historical research, although he does claim too much for the relevance of his contribution to the debate about Romanticism. Lee Rust Brown's 'Coleridge and the Prospect of the Whole' discusses Coleridge's ideas about fragmentation and wholeness. In a careful and scholarly account of Coleridge's notion of wholeness, Brown criticizes Paul de Man for complaining that the Coleridgean notion of symbol is outside temporality: 'instead of representing the referent as prior to the sign (allegory), symbol represents the sign as *prospective* in regard to its referent' (*SIR* 30.235–53). James Finn Cotter's 'Golden Codger Coleridge' *HudR* (43/44.i.1–25) is an extended and laudatory review of Richard Holmes's recent biography of Coleridge. E. Douka Kabitoglu's 'The Cambridge Platonists: A Reading from Coleridge' is an interesting piece of intellectual history which reappraises Coleridge's understanding of the Cambridge Platonists, but does not add anything especially new to the subject (*SCen* 6.11–31). Coleridge's fascination with and criticism of the Gothic novel is the subject of ' "Excited by trick": Coleridge and the Gothic Imagination' by Bradford K. Mudge in *WC* (22.179–84). Mudge's notion that Coleridge, although critical of the Gothic mode which he believes to be a dangerous genre, is fond of ornamenting his own work with Gothic trappings is one that needs further discussion. I have not seen R. J. Schork's 'The Classics, Coleridge, and Thomas Wolfe' (*CML* 11/12.367–84). Anya Taylor's 'Coleridge and Alcohol' discusses Coleridge's alcohol problem in *TSLL* 33, arguing that this has been somewhat overshadowed by the opium addiction. Taylor's essay is sympathetic, amusing, poignant, and suggestive, never more so than when outlining Coleridge's attempting his own theory of desynonymization in an effort to rescue his inebriate son from the charge of sottishness. Also by Anya Taylor in *SIR* 30.37–56 is a 'A Father's Tale: Coleridge Foretells the Life of Hartley Coleridge', a perceptive and interesting study of Coleridge's relationship with his son Hartley and the ways in which the father depicted the son in his various writings. I have not seen Taylor's 'Coleridge on Persons and Things' (*ERR* 1.163–80). Steven E. Cole takes issue with the current critical assumption that the Romantics believed in a unitary transcendental self in 'The Logic of Personhood: Coleridge and the Social Production of Agency' (*SIR* 30.85–111). For Cole, 'Coleridge's construal of reason and personal identity, far from being reducible to the "romantic ideology" of the transcendent self, is in fact a complexly argued defense of agency as a shared construal of identity.' Key to Cole's argument is his recognition that for Coleridge will is made up of motivation which is originary, but that this motivation is itself constituted in the will's decision to pursue the ends of reason. Cole's complex and careful tracking of Coleridge's ideas about identity avoids the easy opposition of centrality and marginality upon which deconstruction thrives. I have not seen R. A. Foakes, 'Coleridge, Napoleon, and Nationalism' in Vincent Newey and Ann Thompson (eds) *Literature and Nationalism* nor N. Meihuizen's 'Coleridge, Polarity, Circles, Spirals and the Quest for Being' (*EAS* 20.13–20). *HeyJ* 32 contains Mary Anne Perkins's substantial three-part essay 'Logic and Logos: The Search for Unity in Hegel and Coleridge' (1–25, 192–215, 340–5). Perkins presents a scholarly intellectual history of the concept of Logos in both Hegel and Coleridge arguing that this principle is the nucleus of their philosophical systems (1–25), that there are fundamental differences in their understanding of the Logos (192–215), and thirdly that these differences have far-reaching consequences for their understanding of Christianity (340–5). David Pym's 'The Idea of Church and State in the Thought of the Three Principal Lake Poets' (*DUJ* 53.19–26) is a cumbersome discussion of Coleridge, Wordsworth, and Southey's later notions of the Church in an age of crisis. I have not seen Richard Tomlinson's 'The Primary Imagination' (*ChLB* 73.52–61) nor W. Stevenson's 'The Eagle and the Dove': a comparison of Coleridge and Byron in *ByronJ* (19.114–27). Ina Lipkowitz's excellent 'Inspiration and the Poetic Imagination: Samuel Taylor Coleridge' concerns Coleridge's notions of symbol and imagination (*SIR* 30.605–32). Lipkowitz examines Coleridge's life-long interest in scriptural poetics and suggestively makes the case that he humanized the prophets and poets of Scripture by locating the source of their sublimity in the imagination, correspondingly enhancing the status of modern poets, like Wordsworth, who shared in this imaginative vision. This is a superb and very valuable addition to Coleridge scholarship. Scholars of Coleridge should also consult Jack Stillinger's 'Creative Plagiarism: The Case of Coleridge' in his *Multiple Authorship and the Myth of Solitary Genius* discussed in the above general section.

Moving on to criticism of individual works. A. G. Den Otter's 'Literary Criticism as Receptive Data Rather than Interpretive Truth: A Case-Study of *Christabel* Criticism' is an exceptionally reductive piece (*Poetics* 20.363–90). Morton D. Paley's 'Coleridge's "Preternatural Agencies" ' carefully and astutely discusses Coleridge's supernatural machinery and its implications in such poems as *The Destiny of Nations* for *ERR* (1.135–46). I have not seen Michael Grevis's 'Notes on the Place of Composition of "Kubla Khan" by S. T. Coleridge' (*ChLB* 12–19). M. W. Rowe's ' "Kubla Khan" and the Structure of the Psyche' attempts to place 'Kubla Khan' in the context of Freud's *The Ego and the Id* in a rather straightforward and old-fashioned piece of psychoanalytical criticism (*English* 40:145–54). Peter J. Kitson suggests James Burgh's *Political Disquisitions* as a source for Coleridge's 'Recantation' in 'Coleridge, James Burgh and the Mad Ox' (*N&Q* 38.299–301). 'Religious Musings' is the subject of David Collings's deconstructive 'Coleridge Beginning a Career: Desultory Authorship in "Religious Musings" ' (*ELH* 58.167–93). Collings's suggestive discussion repays close attention and his conclusion that Coleridge 'images the possibility of a personality without identity, an oeuvre without a career, authorship without authority, and writings without genres, all of which define his life of writing over the next several decades' is ingenious but perhaps too heavy a deduction to make from such an early work as 'Religious Musings'. Surprisingly little has appeared on 'The Rime of the Ancient Mariner'. William Galperin's 'Coleridge and Critical Intervention' criticizes the totalizing readings of the poem made by New Historicists like Jerome McGann and Marjorie Levinson and prefers an application of the

Derridean shoe which opens the poem in a series of supplementations (*WC* 22.58–64). McGann's article, which Galperin attacks, is reprinted in G. A. Rosso and Daniel P. Watkins (eds.), *Spirits of Fire: English Romantic Writers and Contemporary Historical Methods*. I have not seen Sarah Webster Goodwin's 'Domesticity and Uncanny Kitsch in "The Rime of the Ancient Mariner" and "Frankenstein" ' (*TSWL* 10.93–108). John Ower's 'The Death-Fires, the Fire-Flags and the Corposant in the "Rime of the Ancient Mariner" ' (*PQ* 70.199–218), is a rather literal discussion, arguing that the 'death-fires' of line 128 of the poem could not be St Elmo's fire or the corposant as this only appears in stormy conditions and is generally regarded as a good omen: the weather is, however, still and hot at this point in the poem and the mariner is at a spiritual nadir. The 'death-fires' are literally the *ignis fatuus* described by Joseph Priestley. Finally, Duncan Wu's '*The Ancient Mariner*: A Wordsworthian Source' suggests a possible source for the action of the wind's whistling through the bones of Death in lines from Wordsworth's *The Vale of Esthwaite* (*N&Q* 38.301).

Three editions of Byron's works appeared this year, none of which were made available for review. These are; the sixth volume of Byron's *The Complete Poetical Works* edited by Jerome J. McGann and Barry Weller; *The Complete Miscellaneous Prose* edited by Andrew Nicholson (both Clarendon); *Childe Harold's Pilgrimage; a critical, composite edition, presenting photographic evidence of the author's revisions, rearrangements, and replacements, stanza by stanza, and canto by canto* edited by David V. Erdman and David Worrall (Garland). Only one full-length study of the poet has come my way, Robinson Blann's *Throwing the Scabbard Away: Byron's Battle Against the Censors of Don Juan*, which is an attempt to examine how 'the complicated nexus of censorship affected the composition of *Don Juan*'. Blann constructs an interesting and detailed narrative out of Byron's relationship with publishers, friends, and the reviewers of his poem and he is most rewarding when discussing the cancelled stanzas of the poem. This is an attractive account of an aspect of Byron's career. Blann also gives an account of Byron's creative processes, censorship and the origin of *Don Juan* in *CLAJ* (33/34.72–92). I have not seen D. L. MacDonald's *Poor Polidori: A Critical Biography of the Author of the Vampyre* which no doubt has much material on Byron and which will be reviewed next year.

Three collections of essays on Byron's life and works have come to my attention. Robert F. Gleckner has edited a collection of critical essays for Hall's series Critical Essays on British Literature which intends to be a history of Byron criticism from 1960 onwards. Gleckner contributes a useful introduction outlining the development of Byron criticism and the major landmarks. The essays contained are judiciously selected and show a preference for *Don Juan* as the major Byron text. As Gleckner himself admits, more essays on the drama would be welcome, but as a collection running to nearly three-hundred pages this volume will be of great value to university libraries and their undergraduate readers. More specialized is Wolf Z. Hirst's collection of eight essays from the Twelfth International Byron Seminar (Haifa, 1985), *Byron, the Bible, and Religion*. The collection aims to show that Byron's use of Scripture and his engagement with religious thought is more complex and intricate than has hitherto been understood. Certainly the notion of Byron as a radical atheistic iconoclast, if ever seriously held, is disputed by these essays. None of the essays depicts Byron as impious, or even blasphemous. Sceptical and nonconformist Byron clearly was, but not atheistic: 'nothing I deny'. Two essays deal with *Cain*, Harold Fisch's 'Byron's Cain as Sacred Executioner' argues that Byron substitutes Cain for Adam in a serious exegesis of the biblical myth of origins and Richard J. Quinones's 'Byron's Cain: Between History and Theology' discusses the revisionary role that

Byron played in the regeneration of the figure of Cain. Quinones has some interesting things to say about the doubling of Cain and Abel and later literary perceptions of the Double. Peter L. Thorslev Jnr's 'Byron and Bayle: Biblical Skepticism and Romantic Irony' discusses the relationship between Pierre Bayle's scepticism and Byron's, arguing that there is a close parallel in ironic method between the two writers. Hirst's own contribution, 'Byron's Revisionary Struggle with the Bible' deals with the restraints imposed upon the poet in his use of scriptural materials in biblical and non-biblical stories. Gordon K. Thomas's 'Eros and Christianity: Byron in the Underground Resistance-Movement' discusses Byron's criticism of the Christian establishment and its denial of Eros. Ray Stevens's 'Scripture and the Literary Imagination: Biblical Allusions in Byron's *Heaven and Earth*' explores the influence of the poet's Presbyterian upbringing in *Heaven and Earth*, which is also discussed in Warren Stevenson's 'Hebraism and Hellenism in the Poetry of Byron' which deals with the equally powerful contrasting forces of Hebraism and Hellenism in Byron's work. Finally, Leonard Goldberg's 'Byron and the Place of Religion' discusses the notion of religion in the large transcendental sense, in arguing that Byron invests the profane with sacred properties in *Manfred, Childe Harold* and *Don Juan*. Frederick W. Shilstone has edited the MLA *Approaches to Teaching Byron's Poetry* which does justice to the pedagogic paradox that Byron is probably the most accessible of the Romantic poets to undergraduate readers yet also one of the most difficult to teach and to place. Shilstone provides an admirably thorough guide through the huge body of Byron criticism and is uniformly helpful on materials, editions, and criticism. The volume provides a truly rich and comprehensive selection of views about the teaching of Byron, which unsurprisingly foregrounds *Don Juan* as the key Byron work. Especially helpful are Louis Crompton on Byron's bisexuality, Susan Wolfson on cross-dressing in *Don Juan*, and Scott Simpkins on *The Giaour*.

ByronJ 19 this year contains the following articles. Katrina Bachinger's 'The Sombre Madness of Sex: Byron's First and Last Gift to Poe' discusses Byron's treatment of power, sexuality, and perversion and relates this to his influence on Edgar Allan Poe (128–40); Drummond Bone, 'First Look at Exile: Byron's Art in 1816' analyses Byron's poetic technique in his works of 1816 (69–79); Jean-Paul Forster's '1814–1819: Shift of Focalization in Byron's Narrative Poems' treats the shifts in Byron's portrayal of the Romantic hero 1814–19 (80–9); Terence Allan Hoagwood's 'Historicity and Scepticism in the Lake Geneva Summer' provides an account of scepticism and historicity in the Byron circle in 1816 (90–100); Warren Stevenson compares Byron and Coleridge, 'The Eagle and the Dove' (114–27); M. B. Raizis's 'Byron's Promethean Rebellion in 1816' discusses the fictionality and self-projection of Byron's poetry in 'Prometheus' (41–52); Paul M. Curtis's 'Rhetoric as Hero: A Most Voiceless Thought' provides a treatment of the self-reflexivity of the third canto of *Childe Harold's Pilgrimage* (104–13); and finally Peter Cochran identifies Byron's sources for the shipwreck in the second canto of *Don Juan* (141–5).

Jane Soderholm discusses Byron's relationship to one of his more celebrated mistresses in 'Caroline Lamb: Byron Miniature Writ Large' (*KSJ* 40.24–46). James Buzard's 'The Uses of Romanticism: Byron and the Continental Victorian Tour' is an intriguing piece describing Byron's influence on tourism in the Victorian period in *VS* (34/35.29–49). Michael Williams's 'Byron's "Napoleon" Poems: "Some Yet Imperial Hope" ' casts new light on the relationship of the Napoleon poems to French nationalism in *JDECU* (29.13–33). *TSLL* 33 contains a fairly substantial article by Katrina Bachinger, 'Together (or Not Together) Against Tyranny: Poe, Byron, and Napoleon', which makes a Bakhtinian case for the presence of Byron and Napoleon in Edgar Allan Poe's grotesque tale 'Hop-Frog' (373–402). More traditional in its notion of influence is W. Carpenter's identification of a Byronic source for Stephen Daedalus's villanelle ('Joyce and Byron: Yet Another Source for the Villanelle') in *Portrait of the Artist* (*JJQ* 28.682–5). R. Lansdown reopens the question of Byron's involvement with the Italian secret society the Carbonari in 'Byron and the Carbonari' (*HT* 41.18–25). Regrettably, I have not seen Bernard Beatty's 'Byron and the Paradoxes of Nationalism' in Vincent Newey and Ann Thompson (eds) *Literature and Nationalism*.

Moving on to criticism of individual poems in separate journals. *Cain* is discussed by William D. Brewer's 'The Diabolical Discourse of Byron and Shelley' (*PQ* 70.47–65). Brewer locates the drama in the 'diabolical discourse' which existed between the poets Byron and Shelley. Brewer presents a scholarly and interesting discussion of the intertext of *Cain*, with Shelley's *Queen Mab* and *Prometheus Unbound* which contains much incisive and revealing comment. A few treatments of *Childe Harold* have appeared. Michael O'Neill's ' "A Being More Intense": Byron and Romantic Self-Consciousness' is an interesting analysis of self-consciousness in *Childe Harold* and *Don Juan* which is related to the smoother and more prominent Wordsworthian and Coleridgean varieties (*WC* 22.165–72). *CL* 43 contains J. Macleod's 'Misreading Writing' on the presence of Rousseau in *Childe Harold* (260–79). *Don Juan* is the subject of three more articles. Paul Elledge's 'Breaking Up Is Hard to Do' deals with Juan's farewell to Julia in *SoAR* (56.43–57); Asha Varadharajan's 'The Problem of Textual (Ir)Relevance in Byron's *Don Juan*' is a comment on editorial practice for editions of the poem in *PBSC* (29.23–36); and Carol Shiner Wilson's 'Stuffing the Verdant Goose' approaches the subject of food and drink in *Don Juan* (*Mosaic* 24.33–52).

Byron's *The Gaiour* is receiving more critical attention of late, largely due to its Oriental subject matter which is a current concern of contemporary recent Romantic studies. This very aspect of the poem is discussed by Eric Meyer in a substantial piece, ' "I Know Thee Not/ I Loathe Thy Race": Romantic Orientalism/the Eye of the Other' (*ELH* 58.657–99). Meyer's lengthy treatment of the poem situates its fragmentary nature in the context of recent theories of nationalism. This is an important, if dense, discussion of this poem. Gordon K. Thomas's 'The Forging of an Enthusiasm' discusses the treatment of Judaism in *Hebrew Melodies* and relates this to Zionist thought in *Neophil* (75.626–36). A few further pieces on *Manfred* have appeared. Peter Cochran's 'John Murray, William Gifford, and the Third Act of *Manfred*' (*N&Q* 38.308–10) provides interesting detail about the role of Gifford in the rewriting of *Manfred*'s third act. Barry Edwards's 'Byron and Aristotle: Is *Manfred* a Tragedy?' discusses the play as an Aristotelian tragedy in *UMSE* (9.55–62). *KSJ* 40 has two brief pieces on the drama; Alan Richardson's '*Astarte*: Byron's *Manfred* and Montesquieu's *Lettres Persanes*' compares the two dramatists' treatment of sibling love (19–22); and Keith White and James L. Beazel discuss the 'Manfred Anagram' (18–19). Also in *KSJ* 40 is a more substantial treatment of the nationalist elements of a Byron drama, 'Fantasy Elements in Byron's *Sardanapalus*' by Richard Lansdown (47–72). Finally Susan J. Wolfson's ' "A Problem Few Dare Imitate": Byron's *Sardanapalus* and the "Effeminate Character" ' is a major discussion of Byron's drama *Sardanapalus* (*ELH* 58.867–902). Wolfson develops a fascinating account of the relationship of Byron's effeminate hero to his own divided persona: the man of action, the Regency dandy, and the bisexual lover. Wolfson expertly sets this textual and personal scene against the context of gender politics and Italian nationalism. Wolfson does full justice to the paradoxes and difficulties created by the complicated challenge of Sardanapalus's effeminacy in one of the best articles of the year.

This has not been a particularly good year for Keats studies. To my knowledge only one new edition of Keats's work has appeared: the Woodstock facsimile of *Endymion* (1818) (complete with erratum slip) from the series Revolution and Romanticism. Again this is a welcome reprint with a useful introduction that concentrates on the reception of the text. Three monographs on Keats's poetry have been published. Greg Kucich's *Keats, Shelley and Romantic Spenserianism* and Hermione De Almeida's *Romantic Medicine and John Keats* have not been made available for review. A work which will be of great interest and even more use is Beth Lau's very scholarly *Keats's Reading of the Romantic Poets*. Lau provides essays dealing with Keats's knowledge of the works of Wordsworth, Coleridge, Byron, and Shelley which are broken down into three parts: what actually were the works that Keats read; when did he read them; and a table of the direct references, echoes, and allusions in Keats's work to those of his contemporaries. Lau's essays are cogent and thorough discussions of the relationship between Keats and his contemporaries. In particular Lau is very good indeed on the Keats circle of friendships (Benjamin Bailey, Leigh Hunt, John Hamilton Reynolds, B. R. Haydon) and the access that Keats would have had to their own knowledge and libraries. Nevertheless, Lau does indulge in some tentative speculation about Keats's reading: 'Keats probably at least flipped through Bailey's copies of [Coleridge's] *The Statesman's Manual* and *A Lay Sermon*'. This will be a very good reference book for Keats scholars. The checklist itself offers a welcome shortcut to looking up which influences major critics of Keats have suggested in the works. There has been one collection of essays on Keats, the third in the MLA series Approaches to Teaching World Literature to be concerned with a Romantic subject. Walter H. Evert and Jack W. Rhodes's contribution on *Keats's Poetry* may well be the most useful of the series, given the popularity of Keats among undergraduate readers. Evert and Rhodes provide a useful overview of editions of Keats and critical comment as well as helpful suggestions for teachers in introducing their students to Keats. Included in this volume, but not others reviewed above, is a very welcome indication of some of the assignment titles set by instructors for their students. Again, as with the other two volumes in the series reviewed this year, the accounts of the teaching strategies adopted are interesting and informative, although I am somewhat relieved not to be in the classes of at least one of the contributors.

On a biographical note, Gillian Iles's 'New Information on Keats's Friend' discusses Keats's relationship with Charles Armitage Brown and his family in *KSJ* (40.146–66). Andrew Cooper's excellent and highly informative 'The Apian Way: Virgil's Bees and Keats's Honeyed Verse' is a wide-ranging discussion of the metaphor of the bee and its political implications from Virgil to the Romantics (*TSLL* 33.160–81). Cooper eruditely shows how the Romantic use of the honey-bee represented a Miltonic recovery of 'Virgilian doubt from the eighteenth century's schematic, optimistic view of bee society as exemplary in its monarchism and hierarchical order'. Cooper, however, is more concerned with the implications of consumerism and the transference of the honey-making metaphor to the audience (the transformation of objects into something sweeter) which he finds to be a consistent Romantic concern. Cooper's speculation that Keats devours the flowers of rhetoric of other poets to feed his own honeyed verse is certainly intriguing. Lynda Mugglestone convincingly re-evaluates 'The Fallacy of the "Cockney Rhyme" ' (*RES* 42.57–66) pointing out that the absence of realization of the *r* in its final and post-vocalic position (enabling many of Keats's more unconvincing rhymes) was certainly a distinguishing mark of incorrect speech in the early nineteenth-century. Mugglestone provides much fascinating information about correct pronunciations in Keats's time and how they indicated social class. However, she argues that critics such as Croker or Lockhart, in censuring Keats's failings in linguistic usage, merely reflect the sensibilities of their age rather than accurately assessing dialectal deviation. Keats was closer to the usage of his contemporary poets from 1770 onwards than his singling out suggests; nor were such 'Cockney Rhymes' confined to the Metropolis.

Moving on to treatments of specific poems. *Expl* 49/50 has two pieces on Keats's poetry: Grant F. Scott discusses the treatment of warmth and cold in 'The Eve of St Agnes' (49.146–9); and Michele Leavitt's 'O Thou whose face hath felt the Winter' (49.83–4) deals with plant imagery and its relationship to creativity. *Isabella or the Pot of Basil* is discussed by Jack Stillinger in his chapter 'Keats and His Helpers' from *Multiple Authorship and the Myth of Solitary Genius* reviewed in the above section on general books. Two substantial articles have appeared on the 'Ode on a Grecian Urn'; A. W. Phinney in 'Keats in the Museum: Between Aesthetics and History' (*JEGP* 90.208–9) argues that Keats's poem is not only concerned with the tensions between art and life, but also that it dramatizes the conflicting claims of aesthetic criticism (e.g. Cleanth Brooks) and historical critique (e.g. Jerome J. McGann, Marjorie Levinson), concluding that neither is satisfactory on its own. Phinney's article is a model of clearness and intelligence which demonstrates that while we can locate the poem in its historical context this does not in any way close down the poem, turning it into a site of historically determined and determinate assertions. It is to be hoped that this essay will find its way into subsequent anthologies of Keats criticism, it is one of the best articles of this year and many others. I have not seen the other substantial piece on this poem, Marjorie Garson's 'Bodily Harm: Keats's Figures on the "Ode on a Grecian Urn" ' (*ESC* 17.37–51). *RES* 42 has a note by John B. Gleason, 'A Greek Echo in Keats's "Ode on a Grecian Urn" ', noticing a close parallel between a passage from the Ode and an epigram by Heraclitus, 'Unapparent harmony is better than apparent harmony'. M. Padma's 'Keats's "Satyam, Sivam, Sundaram' is a short piece on Keats's treatment of beauty and its relationship to Hinduism (*LHY* 32.111–17). Two articles have appeared on the 'Ode to Psyche'; R. Kaftan provides a contextual reading of the poem in *ELN* (28/29.49–57); and Maneck H. Daruwala discusses the Ode's metaphors of love, art, and creation (*VIJ* 19.141–88). A. J. Bennett discusses the agrarian politics of the 'Ode to Autumn' in 'Agrarian Politics and the Economics of Writing' (*Criticism* 33.333–52), and finally *WHR* contains Jennifer Wagner's 'Working Against the End' which is a discussion of Keats's use of the sonnet form (45.230–52).

As with Keats, this has not been a vintage year for Shelley studies, but nevertheless a substantial body of criticism has appeared, some of it outstanding. Woodstock Facsimiles of three of Shelley's works have appeared: *The Cenci* (1819); *Posthumous Poems* (1824); and, with Mary Shelley, *History of a six weeks' tour* (1817). The latter includes two of Shelley's letters to Peacock describing the tour as well as the first publication of 'Mont Blanc'. Two volumes have appeared in the Bodleian Shelley Manuscript series published by Garland: *The 'Prometheus unbound' notebooks; a facsimile of Bodleian MSS. Shelley e.1, e.2, and e.3: including fair copies of 'Prometheus unbound', 'Ode to Heaven', 'Misery' – a fragment, and a draft translation of Plato's Ion, together with fragments and prose writings*, edited by Neil Fraistat; and *The 'Charles the First' draft notebook; a facsimile of Bodleian MS. Shelley adds. e. 17*, edited by Nora Crook. Neither has been made available for review. A new selection of Shelley's poetry and prose by Alasdair D. F. Macrae has been produced for the series Routledge English Texts. Macrae's selection is judicious and shows the varying facets of Shelley's style from lyric and 'hectic strain' to plain and satirical. Although in many ways Timothy Webb's cheaper and fuller collection of the poetry for Dent is better for the poetry alone, Macrae's selection has the virtue of containing the 'The Defence of Poetry' and sections from 'A Philosophical View of Reform'. Macrae's annotations are full and informative and he provides the reader with several succinct essays on the historical and intellectual context, and on aspects of Shelley's style, thought, etc., which will be of great help to new readers grappling with the difficulties of Shelley's ideas. Macrae has produced an admirable volume which is extremely useful for teaching purposes.

One monograph and one collection of essays have appeared on Shelley's work: Alan M. Weinberg, *Shelley's Italian Experience* and G. Kim Blank (ed.), *The New Shelley: Later Twentieth-Century Views*. Both are published by Macmillan and neither was made available for review.

Not many articles have appeared on Shelley in contrast to Blake, Wordsworth, and Coleridge. B. C. Barker-Benfield's 'Hogg-Shelley Papers of 1810–12' discusses the relationship between Shelley and John Hogg (*BLR* 14.14–29). W. D. Brewer's 'The Diabolical Discourse of Byron and Shelley' (*PQ* 70.47–65) has been reviewed above in my section on Byron criticism. I. J. Parker's 'Shelley's Descriptive Landscape Imagery' discusses Shelley's landscape imagery and cosmic harmony (*ELN* 28/29.23–41). Claudia M. Schmidt's 'Shelley's "Spirit of the Age" Antedated in Hume' notices that the phrase 'the Spirit of the Age' credited by the *OED* to Shelley has an earlier antecedent in Hume's *Political Discourses* (*N&Q* 38.297–8).

Concerning treatments of individual poetic works. Two discussions of 'Epipsychidion' have come to my attention: E. Douka Kabitoglou in 'Shelley's "Epipsychidion": The Poetics of Prostitution' discusses the poem's treatment of femininity (*RLMC* 44.131–47); and Thomas Pfau's 'Tropes of Desire: Figuring the Insufficient Void' approaches the notion of self-consciousness in the poem (*KSJ* 40.99–126). Sharon Spangler's 'Demon, Ghost, and Heaven' outlines some of the New Testament sources for the 'Hymn to Intellectual Beauty' (*MOR* 5.19–25). William Keach's 'Shelley and the Social Text of Virgil's Tenth *Eclogue*' presents an interesting discussion of 'Julian and Maddalo' in terms of its relationship to the rhetoric and homosociality of Virgil's Tenth *Eclogue* (*TSLL* 33.261–70). 'The Masque of Anarchy' is the subject of Morton D. Paley's excellent 'Apocapolitics: Allusion and Structure in Shelley's "Mask of Anarchy" ' which discusses Shelley's use of apocalypticism or 'apocapolitics' in his political satire (*HLQ* 54.91–109). Paley argues that the poem's shifting registers and the dislocation between its two parts represent the unsettled nature of the relationship between apocalypse and millennium. Tracey Ware suggests another source for the 'destroyer and preserver' of the 'Ode to the West Wind' in the *Boke of Common Praier* (*KSJ* 40.22–3). Robert Young compares 'Ozymandias' to Coleridge's 'Kubla Khan' as 'poems that read themselves' in *Tropismes* (5.233–61). Donna Richardson's 'Witnessing Figures' discusses the dialectics of the self in 'The Revolt of Islam' (*KSJ* 40.73–98). Two pieces have appeared on 'The Triumph of Life'. Orrin N. C. Wang's 'Disfiguring Monuments' identifies a dialectical engagement between Paul de Man's 'Shelley Disfigured' and 'The Triumph of Life' and argues that de Man recovers from Shelley's poem its radical, epistemological scepticism, but he also elides the reason for that scepticism; as a deconstructive critique of history and revolutionary transformation. This is an intelligent critique of de Man's reading of Shelley. Secondly, Peter Vassallo's 'From Petrarch to Dante: The Discourse of Disenchantment in Shelley's "The Triumph of Life" ' discusses the sources of the poem in Petrarch and Dante (*JAIS* 1.102–10).

Moving on to Shelley's dramatic works. Michael Rossington's 'Shelley, *The Cenci* and the French Revolution' provides an interesting and revealing discussion of *The Cenci* in the context of Shelley's revolutionary hopes in Kelvin Everest (ed.), *Revolution in Writing: British Literary Responses to the French Revolution*. Rossington persuasively argues that Shelley here separates public and private morality and that Beatrice cannot be seen as the sole agent of the perpetuation of tyranny, as this is to underestimate the strength of institutional power in the drama. Mark Kipperman's 'History and Ideality: The Politics of Shelley's *Hellas*' (*SIR* 30.147–68) is an outstanding essay replying to McGann's criticism of Shelley's idealizing tendencies. Kipperman, via Adorno and Althusser, demonstrates how, for Shelley, idealization is not ideological mystification if it presents a clarified choice, 'an intensification of the present seen against a progressive future'. Kipperman shows how phil-Hellenism in 1821 was in fact a radical movement and not, *pace* McGann, a mystificatory replacement of Ottoman dominance with liberal British hegemony. Kipperman's excellent essay is reprinted unrevised in Jonathan Arac and Harriet Ritvo (eds), *Macropolitics of Nineteenth-Century Literature: Nationalism, Exoticism, Imperialism* under the title 'Macropolitics of Utopia: Shelley's *Hellas* in Context'. William A. Ulmer's ' "Hellas" and the Historical Uncanny' is also critical of McGann's view of *Hellas* but he argues, deconstructively, that *Hellas* is so overdetermined that 'it cannot sanction critical readings which, reversing the trajectories of displacement, restore the text to history as its determining but occluded truth' (*ELH* 58.611–32). Rather Ulmer claims, following Hayden White, that *Hellas* is an attempt to rethink the problem of historical knowledge in terms of metaphor. 'Prometheus Unbound' is the subject of Christian La Cassagnere's 'Shelley and the Hidden God' (*EA* 44.33–47) and a series of essays edited by La Cassagnere, *Shelley: Lectures du Prométhée, Centre du Romantisme Anglais* 35, (University of Clermont Ferrand) which I have not seen.

A number of editions and works of criticism have appeared concerning the non-canonical Romantic poets and writers. While this is very welcome it in no way compares with the amount of criticism on the fabled Big Six Romantic poets, suggesting that our notions of canonicity in this period are very deeply ingrained in scholarly practice if not theoretical approach. Woodstock Facsimiles have published William Lisle Bowles's *Fourteen Sonnets* (1789) which were so important to the young Coleridge. Burns scholarship is sadly rather limited at present but Angus Calder and William Donnelly have edited an excellent selection of the poetry of Robert Burns for the *Penguin Poetry Library*. This edition has a useful introduction and sensible and unfussy annotation which will be of great value to new readers of Burns and, no doubt, will become the standard teaching edition. Woodstock Facsimiles have issued what could be regarded as the first text of British Romanticism, Burns's *Poems chiefly in the Scottish dialect* (1786). Alan Bold's *A Burns Companion* (*Macmillan*) has not been made available for review. Carol McGuirk's 'Burns, Bakhtin, and the Opposition of Poetic and Novelistic Discourse' is a judicious summing up of recent, perhaps misplaced, attempts to apply Bakhtinian methods to Burns's poetry (*ECent* 32.58–72). This is a welcome attempt to lift Burns scholarship from the antiquarian. McGuirk points out the danger that such a postmodern concern with linguistic diversity threatens merely to recreate the old error of setting Burns apart because of his dialect: Bakhtin can be used by recent critics to describe as 'dialogic' the same mixed poetic diction that traditional criticism describes as vigorous but uncouth. *ECLife* 15 contains two further article on Burns; K. Simpson's 'Burns and Scottish Society' (210–24) and J. Dwyer's 'Social Converse in Scotland from Hutcheson to Burns' (1–22). Very welcome are the Woodstock Facsimile reprints of Thomas

Campbell's *Gertrude of Wyoming* (1809) a popular and influential vision of pastoral America during the War of Independence and George Canning and John Hookham Frere's *Poetry of the Anti-jacobin* (1799).

Disappointingly little has appeared on the poetry of John Clare. Woodstock Facsimiles have reprinted the important collection *The Shepherd's Calendar* (1827). *JCSJ* 10 has a number of noteworthy pieces on Clare: Mark Storey discusses Clare's letters in 'The Poet Overheard' (5–16); Eric Robinson's 'John Clare: Passing the Time of Day' concerns Clare's notions of temporality (17–26); Tom Bates discusses Clare's 'Maying or Love & Flowers' (43–6); and Gregg Crossan looks at some Clare sources in 'Clare's Debt to the Poets in his Library' (41). Crossnan also prints the hitherto unpublished, and probably final, letter that Clare ever wrote ('John Clare's Last Letter', *N&Q* 38.319). It makes for rather poignant reading. Clare's 'mad poem' 'Child Harold' is the subject of a feminist treatment by Lynne Pearce, 'John Clare's *Child Harold*: The Road Not Taken' in Susan Sellers (ed.), *Feminist Criticism: Theory and Practice* which I have not seen. Joseph Cottle's epic poem *Alfred* is discussed by Duncan Wu for its relationship to Coleridge and Wordsworth's ideas and poetry in 'Cottle's *Alfred*: Another Coleridge-Inspired Epic' (*ChLB* 73.19–22). Disappointingly little has come to my attention on the poetry of George Crabbe, perhaps reflecting the feeling that Crabbe does belong with the Romantics but that his poetry is squeezed out by his more distinguished contemporaries. This is very much the point made by Gavin Edwards in his *George Crabbe: Selected Poems* for Penguin Classics/Selected English Poets. Edwards is uncomfortable about the decision to represent Crabbe as the writer of verse tales rather than as the author of 'The Parish Register' and *The Borough* but reasons that, in the Penguin format, it was not possible to do both. This is an excellent scholarly selection of Crabbe's verse. Woodstock Facsimiles are the only texts appearing this year of a number of other poets of the Romantic period. Erasmus Darwin's *The Loves of the Plants* (1789) which was published as *Botanic Garden, Part II* is reprinted. This is a particularly useful facsimile for students of Wordsworth, Coleridge, and Blake to possess. Also important is the facsimile reprint of Felicia Hemans's *Records of Woman* (1828). Hemans was certainly one of the strongest of the female poets writing in the period and this edition will be most useful given the expanding interest in women poets at this time. Hemans is certainly important; she was a prolific and fine poet who outsold all her male counterparts, excepting, of course, Byron. Also in Woodstock Facsimile is Richard Mant's parody of Wordsworthian simplicity *The Simpliciad* (1808) which amply demonstrates the reaction of the average well-educated reader to Wordsworth's new style. Volume six of *The Journal of Thomas Moore* edited by Wilfred S. Dowden has appeared this year. This is the final volume in the series and covers the years from 1843 though to 1847. This volume, like its predecessors, will be of great value to those interested in Moore himself, as well as the literary and political circles within which Moore mixed. Much of this volume is taken up with the index to the complete series. Most welcome of all in the Woodstock Facsimile series this year is that of the much underrated and highly influential romance, Robert Southey's *Thalaba the Destroyer* (1801). This is important in determining Gothic tastes (containing the first published literary vampire) as much for its fashionable orientalism (only Landor's *The Gebir* pre-empts Southey here). Given the importance of Southey and the lack of good editions of his work, this volume (and the other texts by Southey already available or to be published) will be very welcome to those teaching courses on Romanticism. Little else has appeared on Southey. David Pym provides a sound if dry and pedestrian account of Southey's Anglicanism in 'The Ideas of Church and State in the Thought of the Three Principal Lake-Poets' (*DUJ* 53.19–26). Peter Cochran's 'Gifford, Southey and the Closing of the Ranks over the *Vision of Judgement*' is an interesting note concerning William Gifford's unease at being caught up in the worsening literary relations between Byron and Southey (*N&Q* 38.310–13). *Mariner's Mirror* contains the article 'Patriotism Personified: Robert Southey's *Life of Nelson* Reconsidered' by D. Eastwood, which I have not seen (77.143–9). *N&Q* 38 contains David Grove's 'James Hogg's *New Year's Gift*: New Information, and a Correction' which provides information concerning a children's book by Hogg which was printed but not published (313). Finally for the poets, only one piece on Sir Walter Scott's poetry has come to my attention, B. J. McMullin's description of 'Volume XI of Scott's *Poetical Works* in Octavo, 1830' in *Library* (13.351–5).

Little has appeared which is specifically about Romantic drama. Woodstock Facsimiles have printed Thomas Holcroft's drama *The Road to Ruin* (1792). Known mainly for his radicalism and his friendship with Godwin, Holcroft was also the author of this non-political and enormously successful comedy. The one monograph I have identified this year on the subject of Romantic drama, Robert Osborn's *The Main Attempt: The Theatrical Challenge of English Romantic Drama* (Bristol Press) has not been made available for review.

2. Prose

This year's output is dominated by two books which present the work of prose writers in a complex and impressively discursive context: John Barrell's *The Infection of Thomas De Quincey: A Psychopathology of Imperialism* and Jane Aaron's *A Double Singleness: Gender and the Writings of Charles and Mary Lamb*. Barrell's exciting study treats De Quincey's work as a complex Freudian case study. This psycho-analytical structure enables him to produce a linked system from De Quincey's multifarious writings and thereby construct a compelling narrative. With unerring intelligence Barrell focuses on what he calls De Quincey's 'myth of childhood' and centres his ingenious analysis on that primal scene which involves the death of De Quincey's sister Elizabeth from hydrocephalus and the consequent dissection of her skull. From this strange vantage-point, Barrell exposes the connections between De Quincey's domesticity and his virulent orientalism: what Barrell refers to as 'the wound in De Quincey's head'. This is a very disturbing tale not just for its extreme Victorian racism, but for what it uncovers about the incapacity of narrative. De Quincey's compulsive returns to the same haunted spot, so cleverly constructed and reconstructed by Barrell, all end in failure. For all his vexed and vengeful repetitions, desperate surrogates and substitutions there can be, according to Barrell, no redemptive or reparative narrative. This is an impressive piece of scholarship and, at the same time, a virtuoso performance of the literary critic as sleuth.

Jane Aaron's book, if less compulsive than Barrell's, shares the concern to define through its detailed case study the connections between psychic and social structures. She finds in the Lambs an unusual and an alternative configuration of gendered self-hood to that which usually concerns critics in the Romantic period. She significantly improves on recent descriptions of Charles Lamb's femininity, locating his 'habit of mind' in 'a consistently anti-masculine sensibility' and identifying in the Elia essays a 'sanity of play' which refuses the self-aggrandizing projections of ego common in other male Romantic writers. In the complex interaction of this brother and sister, indicated in the 'double-singleness' of her title, Aaron sees an example of peculiarly flexible subject identity which was 'not dependent upon the artificial segregation of rigidly polarized masculine and feminine roles' which, she argues, took place at the end of the eighteenth century. Aaron's book straddles recent French feminist theory and well-researched social documentation. She focuses in detail on social class, structures of labour, domestic economy, constructions of madness and the actual writings of the Lambs in order to produce her complex and valuable double portrait of gendered identity.

Joel Black's *The Aesthetics of Murder: A Study in Romantic Literature and Contemporary Culture* contains this year's other extensive contribution on De Quincey. Black argues that De Quincey's various essays 'On Murder' constitute a 'sustained satiric critique' of a Kantian philosophical tradition which assumes an unproblematic link between ethics and aesthetics. There are some very interesting and contentious commentaries here on De Quincey's relationship to both the Burkean and Kantian sublimes, on the various kinds of Romantic identification with the criminal act and the criminal identity, and on De Quincey's characteristic focus on the terrified by-stander instead of the murderer or the victim. Black's separation of De Quincey's interest in the aesthetics of murder from that evident in detective fiction is, perhaps, one of the most useful and suggestive definitions in the whole book. Although De Quincey is made to service a more ambitious cultural history of murder and representation, Black is careful to preserve De Quincey's historical specificity; his problematization of motive is not to be confused with a postmodern erasure of motive. For all the articulacy and cleverness of Black's study, however, one is left wanting a more materialist and gender-based analysis of the 'aesthetics of murder'.

Margaret Russett's 'Wordsworth's Gothic Interpreter: De Quincey Personifies "We Are Seven" ' (*SIR* 30.345–65) deals with the more familiar and well-trodden territory of De Quincey and identity. Russett explores the elusive and ambivalent nature of De Quincey's construction of a self through intertextual relations by concentrating on his complex involvement with a single Wordsworth poem. According to Russett's intense and sophisticated analysis, this tortuous literary interaction involves both an active and a passive, a masochistic and a sadistic, aspect to De Quincey's transference, and this leads her to the interesting, if unsurprising, conclusion that: 'De Quincey is never more himself than when he inhabits another's text.' In contrast, the neglected area of the explicit political affiliations of De Quincey's prose are dealt with in John Coates's 'Aspects of De Quincey's "High Tory" Prose in Theory and Practice' (*DUJ* 53.175–85). Coates explores De Quincey's attitude to language and, in particular, the political implications of his ideas on the connectedness of style – its 'sequaciousness'. He pays detailed attention to 'Rhetoric,' 'Style,' and 'Language' and analyses De Quincey's response to various classical prose writers and to Dr Samuel Parr. This is an interesting subject which deserves more space as well as a more finely-tuned and more explicit illustration of the connection with Tory politics.

There are a healthy number of contributions this year to our understanding of the nature of political writing in the 1790s and its complex relationship to contemporary 'literary' texts. Kelvin Everest's collection *Revolution in Writing: British Literary Responses to the French Revolution* contains four substantial contributions on prose writers. In 'Hannah More's Counter-Revolutionary Feminism', Kathryn Sutherland argues with forcible clarity and impressive historical knowledge for a reassessment of Hannah More. She urges feminist critics to uncover 'a subtler and more unstable historical dimension to their work' and to avoid a prescriptive leftist historiography of the kind which has tended, in this period, to mythologize Wollstonecraft and largely ignore More. For it is the latter, according to Sutherland, who is the more likely candidate for being called the 'founding mother' of a 'nineteenth-century women's literary tradition' and who 'allows us to constitute women's history as a more complex and more internally divided ... legitimation of women's negotiations with experience'. The essay illustrates how 'More's essentialism is itself a contingent strategy' and analyses in good contextual detail More's 'practical politics of domestic reformation'. Tom Furniss's 'Gender in Revolution: Edmund Burke and Mary Wollstonecraft' is a well-argued and sophisticated contribution to our understanding of the complex configuration of discourses of gender, aesthetics and politics in the writing of the 1790s. Furniss illuminates the complex interaction between the two writers by providing sustained analyses of Burke's *Enquiry* and *Reflections* and of Wollstonecraft's response in her two 'vindications'. According to Furniss, Burke's texts 'paradoxically empower Wollstonecraft's thought even as she seeks to displace them'. The essay concludes with an interesting account of the connection between these two writers' representations of Marie Antoinette and the consequent 'unease' this generates in Wollstonecraft's texts. In comparison, Harriet Devine Jump's essay ' "The cool eye of observation": Mary Wollstonecraft and the French Revolution' makes a much simpler and less sustained contribution in its brief descriptions of the motives, aims, and publishing context of Wollstonecraft's *An Historical and Moral View of the Progress of the French Revolution*. In 'The Limits of Paine's Revolutionary Literalism', John C. Whale focuses with some intensity on 'Paine's deep-seated suspicion of the imaginative faculty' in order to reveal how he 'short-circuits the problem of representation'. By analysing a wide range of Paine's texts which illustrate some of the contradictions in his ideas of the body politic and its connection with a radical individualism, Whale shows that Paine's 'extreme literalism rests on some disturbingly "natural" and metaphysical grounds' and suggests that this makes him as susceptible to appropriation from the born-again Right as from the 'rationalist Left'.

Robert N. Essick's 'William Blake, Thomas Paine, and Biblical Revolution' (*SIR* 30.189–212) investigates the 'inherently unstable compound' of radical political and apocalyptic Christianity in the 1790s through a comparison between Blake's *The Marriage* and Paine's *The Age of Reason*. Essick finds 'the strongest mutualities' between the two works and his detailed and well-informed attention to the texts reveals 'something in Paine's sense of finite space and its mechanism [which] deeply troubled Blake'. In 'Burke's Orpheus and Coleridge's Contrary Understanding' (*WC* 22.52–8), A. C. Goodson attempts to redress what he considers to be the false assumption (operating from Hazlitt to New Historicism) which has linked Coleridge with Burke's 'conservatism'. In a rather brisk and aggressive survey, Goodson claims that reinstating Coleridge's Burke 'is one way of asserting Coleridge's critical difference from Wordsworth, and his enduring importance for the cultural politics of the 1790s'. Peter J. Kitson's ' "Sages and patriots that being dead do yet speak to us": Readings of the English Revolution in the Late Eighteenth Century' (*PSt* 14.iii.205–30) begins from the claim that: 'New Historical writing, whether about the Renaissance or Romantic periods, has tended to neuter the radicalism of figures traditionally regarded as oppositional' and proceeds to detail the different ways in which radical writers of the 1790s use accounts of the English revolution in order to construct their response to the upheavals in France and their repercussions in Britain. Kitson gives careful and well-documented consideration to James Burgh, Richard Price, Joseph Priestley and John Thelwall in their various and often indiscriminate invocation of the Commonwealthsmen, before concentrating his attention on Coleridge.

A more straightforward historical approach to political prose, this time beyond the 1790's, is taken by Karl Schweizer in 'William Cobbett and Sir Francis Burdett' (*DUJ* 53.155–63). Schweizer's brief factual narrative compares the different responses of the two figures to electoral reform and the war with France. He locates a shift in Cobbett's political identity from the rise of Napoleon and the Honiton elections in 1806 and speculates on the way in which Cobbett may have learned from Burdett's example how to become a popular leader of the people and, more particularly, how he may have learnt to 'combine the essential elements of conservatism with the tools of radicalism'.

There are two welcome additions to recent work on the ideological impact of periodical literature and its implication for audiences. In 'William Hazlitt and the "Impressions" of Print Culture' (*KSJ* 40.127–45), James Mulvihill argues that Hazlitt was 'as much as his words, the product of ... a romantic print culture' and that for him 'books seem to take their place alongside nature on the epistemological continuum posited by Wordsworth in "Tintern Abbey" '. Mulvihill focuses on the frequent analogy in Hazlitt's writing between the mind and the printed text and makes some helpful comparisons with Coleridge and Wordsworth in order to claim that 'Hazlitt's thinking is even more radically nominalistic, anticipating the production-based epistemology of twentieth-century media theorists.' In 'Ideology and Editing: The Political Context of the Elia Essays' (*SIR* 30.473–94), Mark Parker argues that we must 'rethink the critical tradition of the Elia essays'. He makes his case by focusing on Scott's editorship of the *London Magazine* in which the subtle placing of articles, he claims, produces a 'subliminal persuasion' on behalf of a 'Burkean-Coleridgean culture'. According to Parker, Scott's versions of Lamb's essays are 'a reflex of their historical moment and their complicated play of nostalgia and reminiscence a cogent resolution of social and political contradiction'.

ChLB and *WC* this year contain relatively few items of significance for the study of prose, but Claire Lamont's 'Blake, Lamb, and the Chimney-Sweeper' (*ChLB* 76.109–23) is a well-researched and interestingly contextualized essay in which she argues that 'Lamb's essay gathers the oral tales and literary motifs connected with the child chimney-sweeper', and presents them 'in the eighteenth-century tradition of the spectator of the urban scene' instead of connecting with 'the protest tradition of Blake's poems'. David Fairer's 'Baby Language and Revolution: The Early Poetry of Charles Lloyd and Charles Lamb' (*ChLB* 74.33–52) gives welcome and careful attention to Lamb's poetry. Fairer exposes the ambivalence of 'baby language' as an instrument of revolution and, in the connections he suggests between simplicity and organic selfhood, he provides us with an interestingly different version of the familiar 1790's story of retreat from social optimism. Pamela Woof's 'Dorothy Wordsworth and the Pleasures of Recognition: An Approach to the Travel Journals' (*WC* 22.iii.150–65) explores 'the mingled yarn' of the Journals and makes some illuminating points on the 'community of observation' in which they are situated. She highlights Dorothy's deployment of 'homely likenesses' and the strong sense of ritual and pilgrimage which haunts these texts. She also offers a tantalizingly brief comparison with William Coxe's *Sketches of Switzerland* (1779).

Books Reviewed

Aaron, Jane. *A Double Singleness: Gender and the Writings of Charles and Mary Lamb*. Clarendon. pp. 220. £27.50. ISBN 0 19 812 890 8.

Adams, Hazard, ed. *Critical Essays on William Blake*. Critical Essays on British Literature. Hall. pp. 214. $40. ISBN 0 8161 8857 2.

Arac, Jonathan, and Harriet Ritvo, eds. *Macropolitics of Nineteenth-Century Literature: Nationalism, Exoticism, Imperialism*. New Cultural Studies. UPennP. pp. 309. £34.95. ISBN 0 8122 8208 6.

Barrell, John. *The Infection of Thomas De Quincey: A Psychopathology of Imperialism*. YaleUP. pp. 235. £25. ISBN 0 300 04932 3.

Bate, Jonathan. *Romantic Ecology: Wordsworth and the Environmental Tradition*. Routledge. pp. 144. hb £30, pb. £8.99. ISBN 0 415 06115 6, 0 415 06116 4.

Black, Joel. *The Aesthetics of Murder: A Study in Romantic Literature and Contemporary Culture*. JHUP. pp. 276. hb A$42.50, pb A$14.95. ISBN 0 8018 4180 1, 0 8018 4181 X.

Blake, William. *Jerusalem The Emanation of the Giant Albion* (1827). ed., intro., and notes by Morton D. Paley. Blake's Illuminated Books. Vol 1. Blake Trust/Tate Gallery Publications. pp. 302. £48. ISBN 1 85437 066 9.

———. *Songs of Innocence and of Experience* (1789). ed., intro., and notes by Andrew Lincoln. Blake's Illuminated Books. Vol 2. Blake's Trust/Tate Gallery Publications. pp. 209. £35. ISBN 1 85437 068 5.

Blann, Robinson. *Throwing the Scabbard Away: Byron's Battle Against the Censors of 'Don Juan'*. American University Studies. Lang. pp. 175. $38.95. ISBN 0 8204 1437 9.

Bowles, William Lisle. *Fourteen Sonnets* (1789). intro. by Jonathan Wordsworth. Revolution and Romanticism. Woodstock Facsimiles. pp. 30. £22.50. ISBN 1 85477 059 4.

Brett, R. L., and A. R. Jones, eds. *Wordsworth & Coleridge Lyrical Ballads*. 2nd ed. Routledge. pp. 346. pb £8.99. ISBN 0 415 06388 4.

Browne, Piers. *William Wordsworth: A Lakeland Anthology Selected and Illustrated by Piers Browne*. Foreword by John Mortimer. Murray/The Shorthorn Press. pp. 98. £20. ISBN 0 7195 5003 3.

Burns, Robert. *Poems chiefly in the Scottish dialect* (1786). intro. by Jonathan Wordsworth. Revolution and Romanticism. Woodstock Facsimiles. pp. 252. £30. ISBN 1 85477 060 8

Butter P. H., ed. *William Blake: Selected Poems*. Everyman's Library. Dent. pp. 304. pb £4.50. ISBN 0 460 87068 8.

Calder, Angus, and William Donnelly. *Robert Burns: Selected Poetry*. Penguin Poetry Library. Penguin. pp. 440. pb. £5.99. ISBN 0 14 058562 1.

Campbell, Patrick. *Wordsworth and Coleridge Lyrical Ballads: Critical Perspectives*. Macmillan. pp. 176. £11.25. ISBN 0 333 52258 3.

Campbell, Thomas. *Gertrude of Wyoming* (1809). intro. by Jonathan Wordsworth. Revolution and Romanticism. Woodstock Facsimiles. pp. 146. £35. ISBN 1 85477 061 6.

Canning, George, and John Hookham Frere. *Poetry of the Anti-Jacobin* (1799). intro. by Jonathan Wordsworth. Revolution and Romanticism. Woodstock Facsimiles. pp. 260. £25. ISBN 1 85477 067 5.

Clare, John. *The Shepherd's Calendar* (1827). Revolution and Romanticism. Woodstock Facsimiles. pp. 258. £25. ISBN 1 85477 062 4.

Clark, Lorraine. *Blake, Kierkegaard, and the Spectre of dialectic*. CUP. pp. 238. £30. ISBN 0 521 39509 7.

Coleridge, Samuel Taylor. *Christabel* (1816). intro. by Jonathan Wordsworth. Revolution and Romanticism. Woodstock Facsimiles. pp. 82. £18. ISBN 1 85477 063 2.

Coleridge, Samuel Taylor, and Robert Southey. *The Fall of Robespierre* (1794). Intro. by Jonathan Wordsworth. Revolution and Romanticism. Woodstock Facsimiles. pp. 48. £18. ISBN 1 85477 064 0.

Darwin, Erasmus. *The Loves of the Plants* (1789). Revolution and Romanticism. Woodstock Facsimiles. pp. 214. £48. ISBN 1 85477 065 9.

De Luca, Vincent Arthur. *Words of Eternity: Blake and the Poetics of the Sublime*. PrincetonUP. pp. 238. $32.50. ISBN 0 69106 8757.

Dowden, Wilfred S. *The Journal of Thomas Moore*. Vol 6. UDelP. pp. 496. £49.95. ISBN 0 87413 2584.

Edwards, Gavin. *George Crabbe: Selected Poems*. Penguin Classics. Penguin. pp. 508. pb £7.99. ISBN 0 14 042365 6.

Epstein, William H., ed. *Contesting the Subject: Essays in the Postmodern Theory and Practice of Biography and Criticism*. PurdueUP. pp. 251. $30.50. ISBN 1 55753 018 1.

Erdman, David. *Blake: Prophet Against Empire*. 3rd edn. pp. 582. Dover. pb $14.95 ISBN 0 48626 7199.

Essick, Robert N. *William Blake's Commercial Book Illustrations: A Catalogue and Study of the Plates Engraved by Blake after Designs by Other Artists*. OUP. pp. 138. £60. ISBN 0 198 17390 3.

Everest, Kelvin, ed. *Revolution in writing: British Literary Responses to the French Revolution*. OpenUP. pp. 176. pb £11.99. ISBN 0 335 09756 1.

Evert, Walter H., and Jack W. Rhodes, eds. *Approaches to Keats's Poetry*. Approaches to Teaching World Literature. MLA. pp. 161. hb $34, pb $19.50. ISBN 0 87352 543 4, 0 87352 544 2.

Ferber, Michael. *The Poetry of William Blake*. Penguin. pp. 120. pb £4.99. ISBN 0 14 077250 2.

Fischer, Hermann. *Romantic Verse Narrative: The History of a Genre*. trans. by Sue Bollans. CUP. pp. 289. £37.50, $49.50. ISBN 0 521 30964 6.

Fulford, Tim. *Coleridge's Figurative Language*. Macmillan. pp. 256. £37.50. ISBN 0 333 51930 2.

Gaskell, Ronald. *Wordsworth's Poem of the Mind: An Essay on the Prelude*. EdinUP. pp. 118. pb £9.95. ISBN 0 748 60263 1.

Gill, Stephen. *William Wordsworth 'The Prelude'*. Landmarks of World Literature. CUP. pp. 110. hb £20, pb £6.95. ISBN 0 521 36218 0, 0 521 36988 6.

Gleckner, Robert F. *Critical Essays on Lord Byron*. Critical Essays on British Literature. Hall. pp. 289. £42. ISBN 0 8161 8859 9.

Hemans, Felicia. *Records of Woman* (1828). intro. by Jonathan Wordsworth. Revolution and Romanticism. Woodstock Facsimiles. pp. 344. £30. ISBN 1 85477 071 3.

Higgins, Lynn A., and Brenda A. Silver, eds. *Rape and Representation*. ColUP. pp. 338. pb £10.50. ISBN 0 231 07267 8.

Hirst, Wolf Z., ed. *Byron, the Bible, and Religion: Essays from the Twelfth International Byron Seminar*. UDelP. pp. 196. £22. ISBN 0 874134 4013.

Holcroft, Thomas. *The Road to Ruin* (1792). Revolution and Romanticism. Woodstock Facsimiles. pp. 112. £21. ISBN 1 85477 072 1.

Jarvis, Robin. *Wordsworth, Milton and the Theory of Poetic Relations*. Macmillan. pp. 208. £35. ISBN 0 333 49888 7.

Keats, John. *Endymion* (1818). intro. by Jonathan Wordsworth. Revolution and Romanticism. Woodstock Facsimiles. pp. 230. £25. ISBN 1 85477 073 X.

King, James. *William Blake: His Life*. W&N. pp. 263. pb £7.99. ISBN 0 297 81246 7.

Kitson, Peter J., and Thomas N. Corns, eds. *Coleridge and the Armoury of the Human Mind: Essays on His Prose Writings*. Cass. pp. 128. £22.50. ISBN 0 7146 3426 3.

Lau, Beth. *Keats's Reading of the Romantic Poets*. UMichP. pp. 198. $32.50. ISBN 0 472 09437 8.

Macrae, Alisdair D. F. *Percy Bysshe Shelley: Selected Poetry and Prose*. Routledge English Texts. Routledge. pp. 301. pb £6.99. ISBN 0 415 01607 X.

Mant, Richard. *The Simpliciad* (1808). intro. by Jonathan Wordsworth. Revolution and Romanticism. Woodstock Facsimiles. pp. 62. £18. ISBN 1 85477 076 4.

Matlak, Richard E., ed. *Approaches to Teaching Coleridge's Poetry and Prose*. Approaches to Teaching World Literature. MLA. pp. 185. hb $34, pb $19.50. ISBN 0 87352 549 3, 0 87352 700 3.

McGavran Jnr, James Holt, ed. *Romanticism and Children's Literature in Nineteenth-Century England*. UGeoP. pp. 265. $35, £27.95. ISBN 0 8203 1289.

Noyes, Russell. *William Wordsworth*. Updated by John O. Hayden. TEAS. Twayne. pp.161. $19.95. ISBN 0 8057 7002 X.

Otto, Peter. *Constructive Vision and Visionary Deconstruction: Los, Eternity, and the Productions of Time in the Later Poetry of William Blake*. Clarendon. pp. 244. £32.50. ISBN 0 19 811751 5.

Privateer, Paul Michael. *Romantic Voices: Identity and Ideology in British Poetry, 1789–1850*. UGeoP. pp. 272. £31.95. ISBN 0 8203 1251 7.

Raine, Kathleen, ed. *William Blake: Poems and Prophecies*. Everyman's Library. Dent. pp. 440. pb £9.99. ISBN 1 85715 0341.

Reed, Mark L., ed. *The Thirteen-Book Prelude by William Wordsworth*. The Cornell Wordsworth. 2 vols. CornU. Vol 1: pp. 1276, Vol 2: pp. 1078. $291.50. ISBN 0 8014 2184 5.

Riede, David G. *Oracles and Hierophants: Constructions of Romantic Authority*. CornUP. pp. 283. $39.95. ISBN 0 8014 2626 X.

Rosso, G. A., and Daniel P. Watkins, eds. *Spirits of Fire: English Romantic Writers and Contemporary Historical Methods*. FDUP. £38. ISBN 0 838 63376 5.

Rylestone, Anne L. *Prophetic Memory in Wordsworth's Ecclesiastical Sonnets*. SIUP. pp. 139. A$19.95. ISBN 0 809 31643 9.

Shelley, Mary, and P. B. Shelley. *History of a Six Weeks' Tour* (1817). intro. by Jonathan Wordsworth. Revolution and Romanticism. Woodstock Facsimiles. pp. 202. £25. ISBN 1 85477 107 8.

Shelley, Percy Bysshe. *The Cenci* (1819). intro. by Jonathan Wordsworth. Revolution and Romanticism. Woodstock Facsimiles. pp. 130. £30. ISBN 1 85477 078 0.

———. *Posthumous Poems* (1824). intro. by Jonathan Wordsworth. Revolution and Romanticism. Woodstock Facsimiles. pp. 438. £42. ISBN 1 85477 079 0.

Shilstone, Frederick W. *Approaches to Teaching Byron's Poetry*. Approaches to Teaching World Literature. MLA. pp. 198. hb £34, pb $19.50. ISBN 0 87352 545 0, 0 87352 546 9.

Southey, Robert. *Thalaba the destroyer* (1801). intro. by Jonathan Wordsworth. Revolution and Romanticism. Woodstock Facsimiles. pp. 238. £22.50. ISBN 1 85477 080 2.

Stillinger, Jack, ed. *Multiple Authorship and the Myth of Solitary Genius*. OUP. pp. 259. £25. ISBN 0 19 506861 0.

Ward, John Powell. *The English Line: Poetry of the Unpoetic from Wordsworth to Larkin*. Macmillan. pp. 200. hb £35, pb £9.99. ISBN 0 333 47168 7, 0 333 47169 5.

Woodring, Carl, ed. *Table Talk*. by S. T. Coleridge. *Collected Works* Vol. 14.

Bollingen/Routledge. pp. 868. £85. ISBN 0 415 02614 8.

Woof, Pamela, ed. *Dorothy Wordsworth: The Grasmere Journals 1800–1803*. OUP. pp. 273. pb £6.99. ISBN 0 19 283130 5.

Wordsworth, Jonathan. *Ancestral Voices: Fifty books from the Romantic period*. Revolution and Romanticism. Woodstock Facsimiles. pp. 234. £30. ISBN 1 85477 084 5.

Wordsworth, William. *The Excursion* (1814). intro. by Jonathan Wordsworth. Revolution and Romanticsm. Woodstock Facsimiles. pp. 480. £65. ISBN 1 85477 083 7.

———. *A Description of the Lakes* (1822). intro by Jonathan Wordsworth. Revolution and Romanticism. Woodstock Facsimiles. pp. 170. £25. ISBN 1 85477 082 9.

XIV

The Nineteenth Century: Victorian Period

LINDA WILLIAMS, DONALD HAWES and LAUREL BRAKE

This chapter has three sections: 1. Poetry; 2. The Novel; 3. Pater, and Periodicals and Publishing History. Section 1 is by Linda Williams; section 2 is by Donald Hawes; and section 3 is by Laurel Brake.

1. Poetry

Whilst 1991 was characterized by a familiar sense of critical diversity and prolific production in scholarship on Victorian verse, three issues dominated work in this area this year: the impact of theory, in particular the extraordinary exponential growth of feminist readings, and new possibilities for interdisciplinary analysis. This was also the year in which Margaret Reynolds's distinguished new edition of Elizabeth Barrett Browning's *Aurora Leigh* appeared, as well as the first two volumes of the Longman Annotated Poets edition of *The Poems of Robert Browning*, Volume Four of the Clarendon Press' own Browning edition, as well as the ninth volume of *The Brownings' Correspondence*. The year's main curiosity was that everyone seemed to choose now to write on Hardy's 1912–13 poems, whilst even though it was the year *before* the Tennyson centenary, a large crop of pieces nevertheless appeared on that poet also. However, it is across work on a range of writers (not simply the Brownings and Rossettis, who have long been thoroughly 'theorized') that literary theory is now clearly making a real difference. Unlike many other periods and genres, scholars of Victorian verse have shown a strong reluctance to embrace new perspectives and reading possibilities, so this shot of energy has lent certain texts reviewed below a tone of excitement, rediscovery and the sense that the poems are really beginning to come alive again, and one quite concrete result is the new direction which the journal *Victorian Poetry* (the traditional backbone of this section of *YWES*) has taken. Hayden Ward's impact as *VP*'s new editor may make this annual review a rather more exciting and forward-looking task in future years, as he promises to extend its canonical range and 'recognise more fully than before the interdisciplinary and pluralistic interests that currently inform our field'. One of his first jobs was initiating the Winter 1991 issue (itself edited by Thais Morgan), which takes an explicitly contemporary view of the subject (individual essays from the 1991 issues will be dealt with in this review in the context of other writings on each poet, except for the Winter Issue, which will be reviewed in *YWES* 73). Two other marked aspects of this year's work are connected to this breath of critical fresh air. Firstly, 1991 was the year in which many writers developed a number of innovative interdisciplinary approaches, but particularly in drawing the verbal and the visual together. Pre-Raphaelitism has always been a strong interdisciplinary resource, but work this year has also included analysis of Tennyson, of William Morris as an intrinsically interdisciplinary figure, and of Browning's musicality. Feminist readings have formed the vanguard of these approaches, continuing to extend the canon, using a range of theoretical possibilities in a way which really opens up the subject, and looking at texts in their connection with other contemporary cultural forms. Lynn Pearce's brilliant feminist reading of the intersection of Pre-Raphaelite painting and Victorian poetry is a good example of this. In *Woman Image Text: Readings in Pre-Raphaelite Art and Literature*, Pearce both analyses Victorian ways of seeing and offers a key feminist interdisciplinary account of women and vision. Through a dynamic reading of Pre-Raphaelite painting and poetry, their politics and continuous appeal, this book engages in a forceful discussion of the intertextuality and re-reading involved in the translation of text to image. The women who figure at the crux of eight poem-painting combinations including Tennyson's Mariana (painted by Millais) and The Lady of Shalott (painted so often that a whole exhibition recently took place only of paintings of her), Tennyson and Morris's Guinevere, Keats's Isabella (painted again by Millais), Swinburne's Venus (painted by Burne-Jones) – are read for their contemporary significance, and as case histories in an interrogation of modern feminist strategies, as they hover between the debate of male poet with male painter. Pearce is primarily concerned with the politics which situated these female representations so centrally in Victorian discourse on femininity, but her analysis of the ambivalences of the poems themselves is finely-worked and passionately argued, particularly the discussion of the play of surfaces in *Mariana* ('it is through lilting refrains and tactile fabrics that both texts effectively smother the cries of their heart-broken maiden'), and of the slippery *Lady of Shalott* as sexual myth or the symptom of the need for myth ('the poem lays itself open to radical deconstruction; the ideological traps, gaps and inconsistencies showing both us, and her, the door'). One of the most dynamic and original of this year's essays was Susan Zlotnick's ' "A Thousand Times I'd be a Factory Girl": Dialect, Domesticity, and Working-Class Women's Poetry in Victorian Britain' (*VS* 35:i.7–27), a path-breaking study of the writing of Fanny Forrester, Ellen Johnston and 'Marie', a Chorley factory worker who wrote militantly outside of 'the Victorian cult of domesticity'. Zlotnick traces the struggle of each as a working writer trying to establish her positions against 'the controlling irony of the dialect tradition: it is a class-based literature that consistently denies working women their class identity by refusing to recognize them as laborers', and the silencing effect dialect conventions have had upon women. The essay offers a fine introductory survey of the womens' relationship to domesticity, Romanticism and morality: Johnson in particular 'relishes her status as a fallen woman', and, 'Casting herself as Romantic rebel, ... engages in Miltonic inversions, transforming the heaven of working-class domesticity into a heel and, in turn, Blake's "dark, Satanic mills' into a personal paradise'. The legacy of Romanticism also forms part of the discussion of the sole piece on Emily Brontë's poetry to appear this year, ('Evading "Earth's Dungeon's Tomb": Emily Brontë, A. G. A., and the Fatally Feminine', (*VP* 29:i.1–15), in which Teddi Lynn Chichester discusses Brontë's Gondal poems as a 'feminine' expression of multiple identity (Cixous's 'concert of personalizations called I') which paradoxically allows Brontë to 'be' many things, even masculine identities. For Chichester, the Gondal poems fluctuate 'between a positive and creatively fluid sense of identity and ... an extreme anxiety about death', and need to be read as more than a prefiguration of *Wuthering Heights*.

The year 1991 saw the publication of several new Browning editions, the pity being that they all enter the market in some sort of competition with each other, especially the Clarendon and Longman versions. Our seriously underfunded libraries will certainly have to choose between these expensive editions, even though scholars would inevitably benefit from the varying advantages of the two. Volume IV of the Clarendon Press' distinguished *Poetical Works of Robert Browning* (*Bells and Pomegranates* VII–VIII and *Christmas Eve and Easter Day*) appeared, covering the period 1841 to 1850, but as the editors Ian Jack, Rowena Fowler and Margaret Smith point out, Browning's work ran to many editions, which poses specific problems of intention and definition. Their textual introduction argues for the well-judged path the editors have negotiated between manuscript and those published editions which were also subject to Browning's own exhaustive scrutiny and amendation, in order to produce a text which is very closely Browning's own, taking the 1888–9 edition as copy-text, and conforming as far as is possible to his corrections and intentions. This is a stunningly full volume, including introductions to each group of works, and comprehensive annotation.

In the introduction to volume one of the new Longman complete edition of Browning these questions are again raised, and the piece serves also as a general discussion of problems of intentionality and authority which are foregrounded in particular when producing an edition of such a prolific and 'hands-on' writer as Browning (*The Poems of Browning*, Volume One [1826–1840] and Volume Two [1841–1846], edited by John Woolford and Daniel Karlin). Arguing for their choice of the first published edition of each poem collected here as their copy-text, Woolford and Karlin state that 'There can be ... no "best text", since each text, as the representative of a different intention, possesses a differing rather than a cumulative value.' Recent challenges to the idea of the overriding 'authority of authors' final intentions', and the possibility that for historical reasons 'an author's earlier editions may have as great a claim on a modern reader's attentions as his final ones', support the stated aim of the Longman series generally, to present works in the chronological order of composition. Foot-of-the-page annotation makes referral easier and infinitely more pleasurable, and reinforces the sense that these are an uncluttered pair of volumes: apart from Woolford and Karlin's open textual introduction, volumes one and two simply present the poems in a clear manner which offers the maximum amount of information and apparatus in as unintimidating a form as possible. The price will no doubt seriously deter students from purchasing these texts, but they will continue to be invaluable library volumes for many years to come.

The new Routledge *Selected Poetry and Prose*, available in paperback is pitched at a somewhat different audience. Again it uses the 1888–9 edition of Browning's works, the last edition supervised by the poet, which, it could be argued, is therefore the edition which represents Browning's latest 'authority'. The editor Aidan Day does not choose to dwell upon this in his introduction, however, instead situating the poetry in a wider discussion of Romantic aesthetics and the Romantic anxiety of absence and desire to which, he argues, Browning's work – in all its modernity – keeps returning. This is a high-powered introductory essay, which demonstrates admirably the possibilities for reading Browning with some theoretical input from psychoanalysis and New Historicism, weaving textual analysis with a skeletal biography, in a manner which is both accessible and a fresh contribution to Browning studies. The selection (limited to choices from *Dramatic Lyrics*, *Dramatic Romances and Lyrics*, *Men and Women* and *Dramatic Personae*) is also framed by a short collage of prose pieces from

Browning's letters and essays, and a substantial critical commentary by Day on the texts included.

Alongside Day's discussion of Browning and Romanticism one might also place John Woolford's 'Browning's *Flight of the Duchess* and Coleridge' (*BSNotes* 21.5–14), which discusses intertextuality and the influence of Coleridge, casting a suspicious eye over Browning's comment to his wife, 'Heaven knows that I could not get up enthusiasm enough to cross the room if at the other end all Wordsworth, Coleridge and Southey were condensed into the little China bottle yonder.' This, as several writers this year have shown, is hardly the case in Browning's *texts.* In the same issue, Paul Kenny traces the marriage of Utilitarianism and Romantic, Godwinist principles in 'an extraordinary ideological melt-down' ('*Pauline*: Browning and Romantic Utilitarianism', *BSNotes* 21.23–31), whilst Richard Smith-Bingham analyses 'Browning's Subjective Mode' (*BSNotes* 21.40–55) 'as a critique of the discourse of Romanticism, a displacement of the "I" of writing onto an unreliable narrator ... Browning shows his characters ... to be interested within discourses that are beyond their control'.

Two pieces exploring Browning's musicality appeared: firstly, Nachum Schoffman's full-length study, *There is No Truer Truth: The Musical Aspect of Browning's Poetry* is 'a musicologist's view', which takes the often flaccid literary critical eulogy to Browning's musicality seriously, arguing for its demonstrability in the poet's work itself. One particularly interesting discussion, made with reference to those moments in the letters when notes and bars replace nouns and sentences, explores musical notation in Browning as a kind of code or alternative vocabulary, but as with much of this book, it is grounded in a rather simple biographical discussion of Browning's own musical education and his understanding of contemporary and earlier composers. Whilst the case for Browning's musical uniqueness amongst Victorian poets is made passionately, ultimately this is an unsophisticated reading even if it offers a promising interdisciplinary cross-over. Deborah Vlock-Keyes tackles the same issue with more sophisticated results in 'Music and Dramatic Voice in Robert Browning and Robert Schumann' (*VP* 29:iii.227–39). This is another of the year's strong interdisciplinary essays, reading Browning's musicality in the context of Schumann's 'literariness'. Vlock-Keyes's argument about the relationship of influence between these figures rests on Browning's reading of Schumann's belief in music as 'truth', and on Browning's 'carnivalisation' of poetic form.

In 'Digging Among the Ruins' (*VP* 29:i.33–45), Ann Farkas explores the ways in which Browning plays with contemporary ideas and images of the ancient ruined city in 'Love Among the Ruins', constructing out of the ruins an 'emblem for *Men and Women'*, within which his 'knowledge of and pleasure in emblematic imagery are exemplified in the city that is real and not real, the thought-provoking motto, the honey-coated didacticism'. The relationship between this poem and the rest of *Men and Women* is also addressed in Thomas P. Walsh's 'The Frames of Browning's *Men and Women*' (*BSNotes* 21.32–9).

This year saw the publication of the definitive *Aurora Leigh*, superbly edited by Margaret Reynolds, and containing plenty of rich annotation and apparatus of general and specialist interest. Her fine editorial introduction discusses the genesis of the novel-poem, its extraordinary and frenetic progress (as it grows and grows and begins to take on a life of its own), its commercial history, the relationship between each of the manuscripts and editions which exist, and an account of Reynolds's choices in her treatment and selection of her copy-text (the revised 1859 edition, although in the case of this text it seems that there *is* no finally 'intended' version which Barrett Browning preferred). The text itself is fully and clearly annotated, and Reynolds's excellent critical introduction offers an account of Barrett Browning which both uses intelligently and questions the use of biographical data in criticism of women poets – Reynolds's introductory warning could productively challenge many a feminist reading: 'if the mythical Elizabeth, the "hothouse flower," bears little resemblance to the poet Elizabeth Barrett Browning, that real woman and poet is but distantly related to the fictional woman and poet whose story is told in the narrative called *Aurora Leigh.*' Reading this piece, I feel that finally feminism has reached the next generation of writing on Victorian women's poetry; starting later than feminist writings on the novel, much recent work on poetry has been stuck at a 'consciousness raising' phase of authenticizing celebration. This, however, is refreshingly anti-essentialist. Cutting against the now-familiar eulogy to primary female poetic experience, recoined ('dangerously') by the recent 'feminist folk-poetics' which reads women's poetry as 'naturally' feminine, Reynolds argues that this is the very feminist humanism which the poem itself argues against. Whilst her reading does the poem full justice as a 'woman's text', this is only part of a substantial essay which also looks at the poem's own analysis of Romanticism, socialism, its formal innovation, its debt to a wide range of literary sources, and the participatory role of the reader. Going beyond simply repeating the 'unrecognized acceptance of the Victorian alliance between poetry and authentic feeling', Barrett Browning is established through the poem as a key Victorian literary theorist and one constantly engaged in questioning the integrity of the political self.

The other important work which appeared this year was volume 9 of the all-embracing, ongoing edition of *The Brownings' Correspondence*, which still sees the pair as-yet unconnected, whilst taking the series right to the moment before the two begin to correspond (January 1845). Edited by Philip Kelley and Scott Lewis, this volume covers June-December 1844 (Letters 1618–1798), and again Barrett Browning's contributions vastly outweigh her future husband's, whose terse letters are even overshadowed by those of his future wife's correspondents who are included – Harriet Martineau, John Kenyon, and even Wordsworth. Key events covered are the publication of Barrett Browning's *Poems* ('Here are your vols!' responds Martineau on 22 August: 'I have looked into them; I repent with shame of my promise to find fault'), individual publications by Barrett and Browning in various magazines, and an event apparently as stirring to the former as the appearance of her *Poems*, the kidnapping of her dog Flush ('Poor Flushie had fallen again into the hands of his enemies … I am so *flushified*, I can write of nothing else'). Like the other volumes in this series (and there are still thirty to come), this is astonishingly full, containing contemporary reviews of the Browning's works, the address books of each (the more worldly Browning's is twice as long as Barrett's, even though his letter-writing prowess hardly matches hers), and solid biographical background to the principal correspondents. One can only eagerly await the next volume's blossoming epistolary romance!

Finally, to complement Reynolds's new edition comes Alison Case's account of the 'recalcitrant discomforts of *Aurora Leigh*' in 'Gender and Narration in *Aurora Leigh*' (*VP* 29:i.17–32), in which Case intricately sets up Barrett Browning's usage and transgression of novelistic narrative conventions against the standard of the retrospective narrative represented by *David Copperfield*. For Case, the novel-poem's two intertwining plots, those of the *Künstlerroman* and the love story, whilst apparently incompatible, allowed Barrett Browning to 'create a kind of double teleology for the novel'.

This was not a good year for work on Arnold or Clough. However, two articles by

R. A. Forsythe on the latter appeared in *DUJ*, one of which analyses his work in the context of that of Arnold. In a dense theological discussion ('Trudging Service – Secularization and the "Devotional Pseudo-Religion" of Arthur Hugh Clough', 53.27–38, Forsythe analyses Clough's position in the 'infinite jumble and mess and dislocation' of the contemporary religious scene, whilst in the July issue he discusses the poet's 'inmost I' in its close relationship to Arnold's 'buried life' ('The "Inmost I" Clough's response to culture and "Mental Anarchy" ', 53.259–268). Arnold's 'debilitating self-consciousness' is contrasted with Clough's notion of a core of selfhood which 'lies deep within the soil of history but is not imprisoned by it'.

Hardy, on the other hand, was evidently one of the year's favourites. The year's major publication was Trevor Johnson's *A Critical Introduction to the Poems of Thomas Hardy*, an introductory text aimed at those unfamiliar with Hardy's poetry. This is a well-organized if uncritical study, beginning with a short literary-biography of Hardy, peppered with personally-telling quotation from the poems, a technique and issue which is later extended in the section analysing biographical poems. As a whole the fact that this text is organized thematically (with sections on people, seasons, places and things, Emma etc.) has crucial drawbacks: it fails to give any sense of the sweep or historical development of Hardy's writing, or of the relationship between the poems and the novels. As a secondary teaching text it does, however, offer information clearly, with a good guided bibliography, but the moments at which it descends into a list of poems (paragraphs begin, for instance, 'There are several good poems about Hardy's immediate family' or, 'There are three fine poems about Jemima') are rather embarrassing. When Johnson stands back and thinks about the aims of poetry *per se*, before plunging into a closer analysis of a few key texts, short practical criticisms which specifically illustrate the points made in the general thematic survey, this emerges as a book of real worth to the student, if not one which will be substantially useful to an advanced Hardy scholar.

Johnson also contributed to the large range of essays on Hardy's poetry which appeared in 1991, publishing ' "Ancestral Voices": Hardy and the English Poetic Tradition' in *VP* (29.i.47–62), an essay which unfortunately meanders through a reverential discussion of what Hardy knew and read, and how his twentieth-century admirers responded to his legacy, to produce an account of Hardy's relationship to tradition read as *baraka*, or holy power. However, 1991 was an excellent year for essays on Hardy's elegies – if Hardy himself had doubts about the ethics of using Emma's death to fuel his work, the situation is magnified in a healthy crop of readings of the 1912–13 poems, all concerned with various aspects of Hardy's 'safeguarding of the dead' (to quote Hillis Miller). Jahan Ramazani's 'Hardy and the Poetics of Melancholia: *Poems of 1912–13* and other elegies for Emma' (*ELH* 58.957–77) is both a lucid introduction to the problematic nature of these works, and a fine contribution to the debate surrounding them, arguing for a self-deceptive substitution of 'the guilt-ridden present with an idealized past' which turns the dead Emma from her live, unpredictable self into both ideal middle-class housewife and ideal audience, 'lacking the power' to speak to him or 'answer' his words, but 'Only listen thereto!'. Ramazani also published 'Hardy's Elegies for an Era: "By the Century's Deathbed" ' in *VP* (29.131–43), which traces Hardy's various responses to death, animal, vegetable and historic, particularly the death of the century. 'The Darkling Thrush' is called 'an elegy for an era and an elegy for the elegiac art of the era', in which Hardy identifies himself as elegist with the century's corpse. This 'poetics of melancholic criticism and self-criticism' evidently carries through into the Emma poems, and a number of essays are concerned with the later Hardy's incessant need to keep the elegy alive. Philip V. Allingham looks even more closely at 'The Darkling Thrush' in 'The Significance of "*Darkling*" in "The Darkling Thrush" ' (*THJ* 7:i.45–6), focusing on the ambiguities and history of the word. What Ramazani calls the 'economic problem of poetic mourning – the production of poems from ... loss' highlights one aspect of Emma's posthumous involvement in Hardy's work. In ' "Undervoicings of loss" in Hardy's Elegies to His Wife' (*VP* 29.193–208), David Gewanter finds another Emma in the text, the (sometimes plagiarized) voice of Emma, pillaged from her diaries, or a mimicked youthful Emma-voice kept alive against the truth of her death and her ageing. Through an intricate reading of the poems this builds toward a bigger account of psychological projection and posthumous ventriloquism; Gewanter's point is that Hardy miraculously makes the dead speak, but the selection of one (young) Emma against another (older) Emma which emerges from Gewanter's reading of Hardy's one-sided conversations is perhaps nearer to 'sheer (poetic) hallucination' than Emma's notorious 'What I think of my husband' notebook.

Reading the poems as a body rather than thematically, M. L. Rosenthal argues for the 1912–13 poems as the 'first true modern lyric sequence', using extremely liberal quotation (several whole poems) and lots of enthusiastic imperative (See 'Hardy's *Satires*: Hard Knowledge, Ghostly Presence, Sexual Loss', *SoR* 27). In 'Phantoms of His Own Figuring: The Movement Toward Recovery in Hardy's "Poems of 1912–13" ' (*VP* 29:iii.209–26), Melanie Sexton also reads the poems as a sequence, unified as a body not primarily by chronology or by their elegiac identity, but by the movement toward acceptance which they enact. Tim Armstrong, on the other hand, supplements Donald Davie's seminal Virgilian reading of Hardy's poetry with a Dantean image of the 1912–13 poems as an encounter with the 'inferno' of absolute loss; this is a dynamic, if short, reading of the colours of the poem as betraying only a terrain of error, betrayal and unrecouperable grief (see 'Hardy's Dantean Purples', *THJ* 7:ii.47–54).

After the plethora of publications celebrating Hopkins's centenary in 1989, there is only a handful of articles to report on this year. The double issue of *HQ* (18:1&2) is largely taken up by Lesley Higgins's 'New Catalogue of the Hopkins Collection at Campion Hall, Oxford', which attempts to redress the lack of a definitive catalogue of Hopkins's works worldwide by offering a survey of what is kept at one of the four main places which hold his work. In *HQ* 18:iii., Joseph J. Feeney gives a full if belated account of 'Hopkins Worldwide: The Centenary Celebrations of 1989', and Gerald Roberts presents a collage of literary and psychological positions on melancholy and depression in connection with a range of Hopkins's work, not simply the sonnets of desolation; melancholy was, by Hopkins's own definition, a condition 'I Have all my life been subject to' (' "I know the sadness, but the cause know not": Reflections on Hopkins's Melancholy', *HQ* 18:iii.97–109). In the Spring edition of *R&L* (23:i.37–50), Maria R. Lichmann explores the notion of Christ as the essential 'inscape' of the natural and human world in a reverential analysis of 'The Incarnational Aesthetic of Gerard Manley Hopkins'. Lichmann's basic premise rests on Hopkins's miraculous poetic success, the unity of word, flesh and God – 'his poems embody the meaning of incarnation'. Whilst this is an intelligent account of Hopkins's religious-poetic theory, Lichmann does not mark a difference between Hopkins's position and her own: Hopkins is both poet *and* priest in this account, and the poem, 'is Eucharist in the sense of bearing the motionless, lifeless Real Presence of Christ, of acting with sacramental, transforming instress on the reader as Hopkins has himself been instressed by nature', (see also Sharon Smulders's essay on Hopkins and Christina Rossetti, discussed below).

Along with Hopkins, both Rudyard Kipling and A. E. Housman have been somewhat neglected this year. A fey, lavishly water-colour illustrated version of Housman's *A Shropshire Lad* was published by Walker Books, accompanied by images by Robin Bell Corfield which make no attempt to evoke the Lad's anguish, only his idealized Shropshire. The text does, however, include a pertinent but brief introduction by Anne Carter, but this is not a text for serious scholars, although it is good to see that Housman is still considered popular reading enough to merit such a volume. The one significant Kipling publication was a reprint of *Something of Myself and other Autobiographical Writings* with a fine introduction by editor Thomas Pinney, which highlights the problems of accuracy which surround these texts: Kipling's factual gaps (or as Pinney tactfully puts it his 'extravagant reduction and concealment of things'). That the interest of these essays lies in the way in which Kipling is economical with the truth of himself highlights one question at the heart of autobiographical writing: are we reading for a reliable 'truth', or for a sense of a voice actively demonstrating the literary fabrication of itself? Pinney quotes one early reviewer who said that the main text included here was not '*Something of Myself* but *Hardly Anything of Myself* '. Reading the main body of this text in conjunction with Pinney's splendidly full and informative notes, which are never afraid to take Kipling's words to task, produces an intriguing, half-revealed and half-concealed 'truth' lying somewhere between the lines.

This was, however, a year which saw the publication of a number of articles on William Morris, as well as several full-length studies. Whilst only three of the books reviewed here are primarily concerned with Morris's writing, the general interest in him as a designer and interdisciplinary cultural figure continues to grow. However, it is the literary critics who are building the bridges from poetry across to vision, and who are taking Morris seriously as a figure interested in the relationship between the visual and the verbal. Amongst the wide range of books on Morris as designer there is little of interest to students of his writing; only Helen Dore's lavishly-illustrated *William Morris*, which is almost exclusively concerned with design, offers a chapter on the Kelmscott Press which, though basic and brief, is well-presented and establishes some relevant biographical co-ordinates. Meanwhile, in 'The Style of Evasion: William Morris' *The Defence of Guenevere, and Other Poems*' (*VP* 29.99–114), Constance W. Haste offers another of the year's fine pieces which forge critical connections between poetry and the visual arts. Morris's peculiar fetishization of body-parts, the relationship between the twisted bodies and the twisted language of his poetry (what Hassett calls 'its attention to the somatic and the nonsemantic'), and his playing with scale in acts of poetic magnification or cruelty, is read in relation to a Pre-Raphaelite 'visual mass of angled limbs, cramped bodies, and jutting chins' which are substituted for conventional forms of composition. These are fragments which also crowd Morris's poetry, signifying what Hassett calls 'Morris's skewed sense of sulphide'.

Three full-length texts on Morris as writer will be of particular interest to scholars of his poetry: Paul Thompson has produced a new edition of his 1967 text *The Work of William Morris*, which claims to take account of recent feminist scholarship and political and environmental developments, but which actually casts an even more reverential eye on the great man's works. The chapter on poetry acts as a good introduction to Morris's work, however, even though it is basically a celebration of Morris's prolific production, and offers a fairly uncritical lance across his poetic career. More substantial is Frederick Kirchhof's *William Morris: The Construction of a Male Self, 1856–1872*, a psychoanalytic study of Morris's life and writings which takes its tools from post-Freudian object-relations theory (which is used particularly well in an account of writing as a working-through of personal fantasy, and of the role of the father in Morris's text and psyche), and claims Eve Sedgwick's pathbreaking *Between Men* as one of its prime influences. This said, the book promises more than it delivers, failing not only to act on the most significant of Sedgwick's cues, but also never addressing the burgeoning body of work on masculinity which has grown up in the last few years. In many ways a distinguished book, it is more of an original form of biography (despite its intricate readings of the poems), finally arguing for Morris's status as a prototype 'new man' whose relations with women, and particularly his marriage, were nevertheless primarily significant only for his connection in the male networks which he inhabited. Morris becomes a male feminist by default: obsessed with his own sexual failure and adopting a curious passive fatalism toward women, the fact that 'he did not use a vocabulary of male sexual dominance to demarcate his relationships with other men' situates him, for Kirchhof, outside of active patriarchy.

David and Sheila Latham's *An Annotated Critical Bibliography of William Morris* does the job of several such books in one. It lists books by and about Morris from 1854–1900, giving critical works chronologically in a series of sections organized by subject-matter, each with a short descriptive annotation. Its comprehensive indexes make the work of cross-referencing straightforward. This is a practical, clearly very useful text, which rightly gives more space to modern texts which students and scholars are likely to access, and, though expensive, is an indispensable text for all libraries. A much shorter study is Jack Lindsay's pamphlet on Morris's political biography, *William Morris, Dreamer of Dreams*, which is basically a celebration of Morris's involvement with left-wing groups, whilst Charles Harvey and Jon Press's *William Morris: Design and Enterprise in Victorian Britain* offers a full biography of Morris's life in business, read in the context of his socialist aesthetics. Finally, two short articles on Morris: Shelley O'Reilly does little more in her article 'Identifying William Morris' "The Gilliflower of Gold" ' (*VP* 29:ii.) than just that, arriving via a circuitous scholarly route, at the point that the obscure blossom is in fact a wallflower, whilst Karen Herbert produces a fresh and engaging analysis of Morris's problematic poetic drama 'Love is Enough' by reading it as an example of Brecht's alienation effect in 'No "Forth Wall": The Experience of Drama in William Morris's *Love is Enough*' (*ESC* 17.301–17).

Christina Rossetti once more proves to be one of the most popular Victorian poets, attracting scholarly attention with a new biography, a popular edition of children's poems, and a large crop of essays. Kathleen Jones's *Learning not to be first: The Life of Christina Rossetti* is a popular text pitched uneasily between one form of writing on the poet and another. There is a vast gulf between those highly theoretically-informed and sophisticated essays which appeared in various journals this year and the surprising number of simplistic, unquestioning accounts which have appeared over the years, following a tradition of reverence established at the point of Rossetti's death, when she quickly became canonized as Saint Christina. Jones's book is a perfectly readable text which contains some lively anecdotes and some genuinely illuminating critical readings of Rossetti as poet, but finally it is pitched uneasily between the two approaches without ever reaching a happy compromise. Furthermore, her criticisms of hagiography fail to convince, as Jones too often adopts an incongruously intimate, personal tone to bring her subject – one of the most impersonal, prickly poets she could have chosen – back to biographical life. Whilst there is much in this substantial book which could persuade non-specialist readers to turn to Rossetti, the clash of tone and subject (the former chummy, knowing and on first-name terms, the latter – even by Jones's account – cold, formal and somewhat unknowable) is at times irritating. Having said that, Jones is a good practical critic, and her sketch of Rossetti's relationship and connections with her contemporaries is valuable. Serious Rossetti scholars will be more interested in the Bryn Mawr Library volume *Christina Rossetti in the Maser Collection* (edited by Mary Louise Jarden Maser and Frederick Maser), which contains forty-five letters written by Rossetti between 1865 and 1886, each followed by an illuminating explanatory comment focusing on the identity of the recipient. Less interesting is Frederick E. Maser's own account of 'Collecting Christina' (Maser is surely a prime candidate for A. S. Betty's next satire on American academic collecting), although in many ways Mary Maser's chapter-length biographical sketch is better than a number of full-length studies. The laudatory gloss on the poet is mercifully contained by the fact that the main purpose of the volume is finally to highlight exactly what is collected at Bryn Mawr.

Isabel Armstrong once wrote that 'Goblin Market' is a poem so outrageous that it could only be read by children. The feminist growth-industry of scholarship on the poem suggests that it is now only read by academics, and 1991 was also the year in which a new, lavishly-illustrated collection of Rossetti's poems for children was published, from which that most outrageous of all 'children's poems' was singularly absent (*Fly Away, Fly Away Over the Sea and Other Poems for Children*, by Christina Rossetti). Nevertheless, this is a collection which inspired at least *this* jaded critic to imagine that the current Rossetti renaissance is touching more than simply the higher reaches of academia. A good crop of essays did appear on the poem itself, as usual. Elizabeth K. Helsinger's 'Consumer Power and the Utopia of Desire: Christina Rossetti's "Goblin Market" ' (*ELH* 58.903–33) is a tightly-worked analysis of patterns of consumption and exchange in 'Goblin Market', read in relation to Rossetti's biographical concern with woman as commodity, and the wider Marxist-feminist point that woman (figured as the Jenny/Jeanie whore-character who haunts the work of both Rossettis) only signifies within a network of male exchange. For Helsinger, 'Goblin Market' 'sets out to undo the double consumption or erasure of woman, textual and sexual or economic'. In 'The Potential of Sisterhood: Christina Rossetti's "Goblin Market" ' (*VP* 29.63–78), however, Janet Galligani Casey argues that Rossetti deploys male and female roles and actions in a non-gender-specific way: women can as easily act the masculine part of Redeemer as men, and in 'Goblin Market' women play the roles usually ascribed to women *and* to men. Moreover, not only does Christ-like Lizzie redeem Laura, but Laura, in setting off a chain of events which inspires Lizzie to act, is Lizzie's redeemer too. This is all argued through in the context of a discussion of women's groups, networks and ideas of sisterhood – particularly Florence Nightingale's nursing 'sisters' – which were contemporary with the writing of the poem, and its famous near-conclusive line, 'There is no friend like a sister'. The final essay looks at Rossetti in a more orthodox religious context and in terms of theories of writing, comparing her to Hopkins: in ' "A Form That Differences": Vocational Metaphors in the Poetry of Christina Rossetti and Gerard Manley Hopkins' (*VP* 29.161–73), Sharon Smulders sets up Hopkins's model of difference between feminine and masculine poetic 'genius' as a frame within which to discuss Rossetti's influence on Hopkins's work, and her own analysis of female poetic vocation, in terms of the devotional priorities of each as a religious poet.

Work on Dante Gabriel Rossetti has not been quite so forthcoming, however. Evelyn Waugh's 1928 text *Rossetti: His Life and Works* (Methuen) was republished in its original form in 1991, and an excellent selection of Rossetti's *Selected Poems and Translations*, edited by Clive Wilmer, appeared courtesy of Carcanet. This is a reasonably-priced collection for the student or general reader, which emphasizes by far the most interesting aspect of Rossetti's work, his lyric poetry and his sonnets, containing liberal selections from *The House of Life*. Wilmer's introduction establishes a fresh image of Rossetti, situating him squarely in an alignment with French symbolism and early modernism rather than as primarily a classic Victorian figure, demonstrating the imagistic quality of his lyrics. I can also only review one solitary work on Swinburne this year. In ' "Erotion," "Anactoria," and the Sapphic Passion', Robert A. Greenberg engages in some classic textual detective-work against the grain of the elusive suggestibility of these poems, tracing the identity of 'erotion' in Swinburne's work, and the influence of Sappho in his life (*VP* 29.79–87).

The year 1991 did however see a reasonable variety of readings of Tennyson, as well as two useful new editions. The most substantial publication was Donald S. Hair's full-length study of *Tennyson's Language*. This is a fine contribution both to Tennyson scholarship, and to an understanding of the various linguistic theories which were current or battling for priority during the period. Hair accessibly negotiates, with constant contextualizing reference back to the poems themselves, the path Tennyson took in forging his own poetics out of contemporary philological developments, particularly the debate with the 'new philology' of Coleridge which takes place across Tennyson's work. An example is the illuminating discussion of Tennyson's use of 'thing' in *In Memoriam*, which is used in various ways as Tennyson thinks through eighteenth- and early-nineteenth-century theories of etymology, and the relationship between word and thing or word and sensation. The first chapter, 'Matter-moulded forms of speech', rests elegantly on the ambiguity inherent in that one line, which could argue for a Lockeian perspective on language ('the phrase suggests that all words, however general or abstract, may be traced back to sense-data') or for a Coleridgean idealist view ('the phrase also suggests the shaping power of the mind and the pattern or forms by which it makes experience intelligible'). As a whole the book traces the movement of Tennyson's theory of language from an early empiricism to (as Hair sees it) the socio-political linguistic theory of *Idylls of the King*; in that an empirical model of the origin of language keeps recurring, this is as much a book about Tennyson's poetic interpretations of the senses as it is a history of early linguistic theories. In this context, there are interesting discussions of the connection between poetry and vision, and of aurality as a factor in Tennyson's use of language – both in the sense of his apprehension of the role of the voice in poetry, and in the influence of onomatopoeic theories of the origin of language on his work. The chapter on vision tends to talk philosophically around the question of Tennyson as 'a painter in poetry', rather than focusing on his visual fixation in the poems themselves, but generally this is a text marked by its clear evocation of a history of ideas married to a meticulous set of close readings.

Two other works which touch on very different aspects of Hair's work are Roger Platizky's short piece 'The Diachronic Frame of Tennyson's "Morte d'Arthur" ' (*VN* 79.41–3), and Lynne Pearce's aforementioned *Woman/Image/Text*, which extends existent analyses of Tennyson's visibility and his poetic discourse on women and looking. Platizky touches on the poet's linguistic theory in the midst of a brief analysis of the complex relationship between the frame and the inset of this poem. Tennyson's deployment not only of pre-Medieval and Malorian Arthurian narratives, but (in keeping with his contemporaries' interests in etymology) of earlier poetic style and language, means that the poem is situated at a point at which two dialogues intersect, between the historical past and present, and between the poetic past and present, and for Platizky this constitutes a double diachronicity. The framing of strategies of *The*

Princess are discussed in connection with William Morris's *The Earthly Paradise* in Isolde Karen Herbert's ' "A Strange Diagonal': Ideology and Enclosure in the Framing Sections of *The Princess* and *The Earthly Paradise*' (*VP* 29.145–59), which argues that the revolutionary subject of Tennyson's poem is enclosed by a more rigid frame and a single regulative consciousness, set against *The Earthly Paradise*, for which the framing devices offer 'a perceptual entrance to a Brechtian chorus of interchangeable tellers and listeners'. Tennyson's poem is thus one of tension between narrative democracy and the narrator's 'inclination to retain his authoritarian voice'.

Lynne Pearce's question of vision and images in Tennyson and Pre-Raphaelitism is also discussed in Andrew Leng's essay, 'The Ideology of 'eternal truth': William Holman Hunt and *The Lady of Shalott* 1850–1905', which tackles the rich relationship between Holman Hunt's various images of the Lady of Shalott and, again, Tennyson's poem (*W&I* 7.314–28). Drawing together an analysis of religious and 'fallen woman' iconography into an ambitious interdisciplinary account which takes on Holman Hunt's ideal of 'true' Pre-Raphaelitism as well as his reading and use of Tennyson and Ruskin, this covers a lot of ground, but for me its most interesting point was its discussion of the relative positions of Holman Hunt's implied spectator and Tennyson's heroine: 'If … Hunt's convex mirror is the counterpart of Tennyson's "magic" one, then the spectator is being placed in an even more privileged position than the Lady, being thus enabled to see her weaker side without suffering her fate.' This is a rich essay which defies brief précis, and although it focuses more clearly on Hunt, readers of Tennyson will be interested in Leng's account of the Hunt-Tennyson debate over Hunt's painted translations (or, as he saw them, 'the definitive verbal-visual representation of "eternal truth" ') as an area within which the limits of both painting and poetry are discussed.

Tennyson also figures centrally in E. Warwick Slinn's *The Discourse of the Self in Victorian Poetry*. After a lucid, two-chapter discussion of developments in continental philosophy from the Hegelian emphasis on consciousness to a Derridean privileging of the text, Slinn engages in a series of close readings of long poems by Tennyson, Browning and Clough which contribute to an argument positing that the philosophical development from consciousness to text is precisely acted out in those poems themselves: 'The movement from Hegel to Derrida is the movement from a totalising process to a process without totality. This is precisely the movement that occurs within Victorian monologues and Victorian long poems.' This is a brave study, taking Isobel Armstrong's important 1982 text, *Language as Living Form in Nineteenth Century Poetry* as its philosophical cue, opening up the complexity and importance of Hegel's *Phenomenology* for Victorian readers and poets in a fresh and unintimidating way. The argument for Romantic irony in Victorian texts as a way of thinking through self-division, and as an active anticipation of deconstruction, is important, but it is the chapter on loss, absence and desire in Tennyson's *Maud* which will interest readers most here. An old theme reworked in a fresh way, this account of how 'loss continually forges the link between absence and desire' in the poem moves toward a feminist deconstruction which has a strong relationship with Pearce's work, especially in the discussion of the figure of Maud herself as central to the speaker's flawed masculine subjectivity: 'unable to possess the woman as object (the speaker) is nevertheless able to possess the woman as sign. Thereby he restores, not lost honour, but the representation of lost honour.' It is the sense of breakdown in linguistic coherence (the poem's emphasis on 'irrational language, on confused, mostly absent referents') which paradoxically promotes the overriding sense that subjectivity in the poem is a public affair. The startling suggestion – coming as it does in the midst of a close reading of confusion and lack – that the insaner moments of *Maud* 'may emerge as the more accurate representation in the poem of human meaning', and that the fragmented subject has no recourse to a private or unspoken language, constitutes Slinn's most significant work for Tennyson scholars. Slinn also offers two fine chapters on Browning's *The Ring and the Book*, as well as a reading of 'Fact and Factitiousness in *Amours de Voyage'*.

Quite different aspects of Tennyson's corpus were explored in a range of rich articles published in 1991. Joseph Bristow also discusses *Maud* in 'Nation, Class and Gender: Tennyson's *Maud* and War' (*Genders* 9.93–111), in which the poem is read as a point of collision between a 'feminine' poetics identified as irrational, uncontrollably emotive (erupting most clearly in the 'Spasmodic' school) and a more classically masculine voice of intellectual strength, with the figure of Maud functioning as both masculine and feminine – a woman who is also positioned by the poem on the side of masculine battle. Sexuality as a politically significant gap is discussed in the context of an analysis of Tennyson as epic poet and constructor of national myth in Herbert F. Tucker's 'The Epic Plight of Troth in Idylls of the King (*ELH* 58:iii.). Here Tucker concentrates on the significance of the adulterous liaison between Guinevere and Lancelot in the poem – its role as narrative lynch-pin and its glaring absence as represented event, an absence which testifies to the power of the epic 'tradition of national legend and received belief' which needs no actual demonstration of guilt, only a consensus tenuously mapped onto fact: 'the power of a national story to hold its people together inheres in the power of a people to hold their story true'.

In 'Tennyson's Analysis of Christianity in "Lucretius" ' (*VP* 29.115–30), John Lammers discusses Tennyson's exploration of Puritan attitudes to sexuality and women, with Lucretius emerging from the text not as a primarily classical figure but as a contemporary sexual symptom, a figure of repression whose struggle is primarily that of Tennyson's moment. Two brief articles on *In Memoriam* also appeared in the Spring edition of *VP* (29:i): James Krasner develops work on Biblical influence by reading *In Memoriam* 6, 7 and 8 in connection with themes of absence in *Song of Solomon* 3, 4 and 5; and Jack Kolb traces a complex network of Keatsian influence and connection in his account of Hallam's 1925 sonnet to his sister. *In Memoriam* is also read by Jeff Nunokawa in '*In Memoriam* and the Extinction of the Homosexual' (*ELH* 58.427–38) as a text across which homoerotic desire is repressed or transformed into something else, a poetic funeral which never quite manages to kill off 'The wish too strong for words to name' (Tennyson's version of a love that dare not speak its name). This is a fine reading which manages to do a number of things in a very short space: it interprets the homoerotic passages persuasively and powerfully; it engages with the problems highlighted by critics dismissive of this interpretation of Tennyson's love for Hallam; and it situates the poem itself in terms of a wider cultural image of tragic gay love: '*In Memoriam* has its after life in the glamourous rumour of pre-ordained doom that bathes the image of live-fast-die-young gay boys … The youthful fatality of homosexual desire, the youthful fatality which *is* homosexual desire in Tennyson's poem' prepares the way for a myth of fatal homoeroticism which never quite dies.

Two significant new editions of Tennyson's work appeared in 1991. Firstly, the excellent Penguin *Selected Poems* edited by Aidan Day contains a full collection representative of the sweep of Tennyson's career, and is particularly useful for the general reader and as a teaching text, as it is priced within the range of the student pocket and contains enough scholarly annotation to be informed but uncluttered. Woodstock Books have produced a reprint of *Poems, Chiefly Lyrical* in their 'Revolution and Romanticism, 1789–1834' series of facsimile reprints. In his introduction, Jonathan Wordsworth emphasizes the links and connected aims between this volume and *Lyrical Ballads*, weaving the biographical relationship between the two pairs of men responsible for these publications, Tennyson and Hallam and Wordsworth and Coleridge respectively, together with a comparative reading of the texts themselves, emphasizing how *Poems* is a text of transition, with 'Romanticism merging into the later period'. Tennyson scholars may also find Joseph Magoon's privately published and bound *Bibliography of Writings about Alfred Lord Tennyson for 1970 to 1989* useful. Whilst the photocopied edition of this text which I read in the British Library is rather roughly produced and graphically inelegant, there is much useful information here; in particular, its subject index cross-references articles and papers with a number of other indexes, including a section which lists readings of individual poems. Finally, in *TRB* (5.230–40), Ann C. Cowley offers various accounts of 'Emily Tennyson's Death Bed' scene in an analysis of its function in Hallam's *Memoir*, which in establishing Emily as exemplary angel in the house, can only be a 'fiction of (her) womanhood rather than the narrative of her individuality'.

To conclude this year's survey, after the excellent whole edition of *VP* dedicated to the 1890s reviewed in *YWES* 71, this year I can offer only one essay, on 'Dowson's Pastoral' (*NCL* 46.376–95). Here Joseph H. Gardner explores the tensions inherent in the pastoral form itself ('Pastoral is an urban poetry, invented by urban poets for the examination of urban dilemmas'), and in its deployment by perhaps the exemplary decadent poet. For Gardner, Dowson is a poet who, through the pastoral form, can only arrive 'at "decadent" conclusions, or rather irresolutions, his work finally attesting to the failure of the pastoral to resolve the conflicts lying beneath the surface of his polished, pristine, and accomplished verse'.

2. The Novel

(a) General

As usual, Dickens, the Brontës, George Eliot, and Hardy predominate among the novelists discussed by critics this year. Thackeray, Trollope, Wilkie Collins, Meredith, and Gissing come close behind, and I have come across articles on Le Fanu, Margaret Oliphant, Bram Stoker, Stevenson, and Rider Haggard. But few critics seem ready to accept the challenge implied by John Sutherland in his *Longman Companion to Victorian Fiction* (*YWES* 69.434–5), where he estimates that there were about 7000 Victorian novelists. Most of our critical explorers like the waters to have been thoroughly charted in advance. Nevertheless, the book I start with covers a wide range of the fiction of the period.

It is heartening to begin this survey with Richard D. Altick's *The Presence of the Present*, an outstanding work of scholarship that is both fascinating and illuminating. Altick points out that Victorian novelists 'sought to make the most of the present'. They used everyday materials and experiences as well as 'a sprinkling of large events' in order to 'satisfy their readers' insatiable interest in the contemporary scene and at the same time authenticate a novel's characters and settings'. He therefore describes in detail the ways in which such things as events and movements, consumer goods, popular entertainments, money, and language are depicted and integrated into the texture of the fiction. His illustrative material comes not only from the major novelists but also from Mary Elizabeth Braddon, Bulwer Lytton, Emily Eden, John Galt, Dinah Mulock, James Payn, Charles Reade, R. S. Surtees, Samuel Warren, Mrs Henry

Wood, and Charlotte Yonge. Annotation of Victorian novels is essential, as we know, for a full understanding. In a sense, this is what Altick has wonderfully proved here, in a comprehensive and appreciative way.

Whereas Altick sees the city ('the great metropolis' of London, in his case) as basically a realistic component in realistic novels, Carol L. Bernstein, in *The Celebration of Scandal*, thinks of cities as collecting themselves 'into veiled entities that are both challenging and elusive'. In prose clouded with the familiar abstract terminology of these days, she first examines the ambiguous presentation of squalid urban scenes in Dickens and Gissing, contrasted with the romantic portrayal of fashionable life in the work of such novelists as Disraeli and Catherine Gore. She then considers the 'sublime', which often represses 'scandal', uncertainties, and fears. Throughout she has in mind her argument that 'the problematic' [i.e. the problem] 'of urban representation must be played out within the labyrinthine vicissitudes of narrative'.

Three books deal in various ways with relationships between literature and history. Christina Crosby's feminist contention in *The Ends of History* is that nineteenth-century 'history' is 'man's truth, the truth of a necessarily historical Humanity, which in turn requires that "women" be outside history, above, below, or beyond properly historical and political life'. The principal novels she discusses to support her thesis are *Daniel Deronda*, *Henry Esmond*, *Little Dorrit*, and *Villette*. There are some thoughtful, acute commentaries here, as in her analyses of George Eliot's treatment in 'masculine' and 'feminine' terms of the roles played by Gwendolen Harleth and the Jews in *Daniel Deronda* and of Thackeray's novel as 'feminized history'. In *The Centre of Things*, Christopher Harvie analyses political fiction in Britain from Disraeli to the present, as the subtitle says. He sees the genre in the nineteenth century as a fusion of 'entertainment' and ideology that produced 'a useful political discourse for a traditional society intent on social and economic change'. He therefore discusses the relevant novels by Disraeli, Elizabeth Gaskell, Trollope, George Eliot, Meredith, and others in terms of this cross-fertilization of literature and society. This is a vigorous, polemical study that has the additional value of placing Victorian political novels (after all, Harvie thinks of those written in mid-century as forming a 'golden age') in a perspective of one hundred and fifty years. The 1991 volume of the English Association's Essays and Studies is *History and the Novel*, edited by Angus Easson. In addition to essays on Scott, Joyce, Virginia Woolf, and Balzac, three deal with Victorian novelists. Most of Leonee Ormond's 'Painting and the Past' describes the ways in which paintings are used for purposes of emphasis, symbolism, and contrast, for example, in the fiction of Dickens, Thackeray, George Eliot, and Hardy, among others. In 'Time and History in *Little Dorrit*', Angus Easson meticulously teases out its intertwined threads of past and present, since the novel is 'a constant unfolding of the ordinary'. Terence Wright's 'Space, Time, and Paradox: The Sense of History in Hardy's Last Novels' discusses questions of what he calls 'spatial confrontation' in *Tess of the d'Urbervilles* and *Jude the Obscure*: this occurs when people in those novels meet their past and 'reveals devastatingly that history is as much "now" as "then" '.

Another collection offers a contrast to this emphasis on 'fact': *The Victorian Fantasists*, edited by Kath Filmer, contains essays by fifteen contributors on fantastic, imaginative, and supernatural writing by Dickens, Morris, MacDonald, Bram Stoker and others. It is impossible to summarize the variety of material presented here but it is worth noting that MacDonald appears in three of the essays, that Alice Mills makes an unexpected comparison between 'Happy Endings in *Hard Times* and *Granny's Wonderful Chair* [by Frances Brown]', and that the editor suggests in her introduction that the genre of fantasy 'was born of pain and disillusionment'.

After 'fantasy', we can turn appropriately to Anne Humpherys's article on 'Generic Strands and Urban Twists: The Victorian Novel' (*VS* 34.455–72), which is a comprehensive account of that particular kind of fiction. Humpherys claims that it is a 'bridge' between the 'Newgate' and the 'sensational' novel and that it is best exemplified by Sue's *Les Mystères de Paris*, G. W. M. Reynolds's *The Mysteries of London*, and Dickens's *Bleak House*. She describes such conventions and themes as the desire for money and sex, the use of the 'haunted house', the 'urbanization of the gothic', coincidences in the plots, and the presence of melodrama. She emphasizes the importance of the urban settings, although she points out that 'in the end the modern city and its institutions as represented in the mysteries fail to fulfil either desires or needs'. Town life as represented in Victorian fiction seems to have been a popular subject this year. Deborah Epstein Nord deals with it from a feminist and socio-historical viewpoint in 'The Urban Peripatetic: Spectator, Streetwalker, Woman Writer' (*NCL* 46.351–75). She considers ways in which women in the streets of nineteenth-century cities are seen by various writers of the period, including Dickens, Flora Tristan, and Elizabeth Gaskell. In comparing and contrasting such depictions by male and female writers (as in *Oliver Twist*, *Dombey and Son* and *North and South*, for instance), Nord argues that 'in the male discourse of urban description ... public woman is fallen woman', whereas female writing exemplifies contradictions, since a woman must 'either confront her own sexuality as it is constructed by men or hide her sexuality by dressing as a man'.

Two critics compare the depiction of female characters in Dickens and women writers. In '*Villette* and *Bleak House*: Authorizing Women' (*NCL* 46.54–81), Robert Newsom notes likenesses between Lucy Snowe and Esther Summerson in their struggles for identity and also in their resistance to the institutions of the Roman Catholic church and Chancery respectively. Furthermore, he sees both novels as explorations of 'the complications of gender roles' and as means of 'promoting gender equality in that both sometimes subvert conventional ideas of masculine and feminine characterization and behaviour'. Although Newsom adopts the fashionable approach that finds ambiguity and complexity everywhere, this is a well-argued and cool-headed essay. Nancy Cervetti's awkwardly titled 'Dickens and Eliot in dialogue: Empty space, Angels and Maggie Tulliver' (*VN* 80.18–23) is a comparison and contrast between Florence Dombey in *Dombey and Son* and Maggie Tulliver in *The Mill on the Floss*. She looks specifically at three episodes in each novel: Florence and Good Mrs Brown, Maggie and the gipsies; both heroines dancing; and the occasions when each is 'struck' physically or emotionally by men (Mr Dombey's hitting Florence and Tom's anger with Maggie). Cervetti maintains that in every case George Eliot presents Maggie more fully and convincingly than Dickens presents Florence, whom he conventionally idealizes.

Another exercise in comparison is Arlene Young's 'The Monster Within: The Alien Self in *Jane Eyre* and *Frankenstein*' (*SNNTS* 23.325–8), in which she attempts to show that Jane Eyre's wanderings after she has left Thornfield can be compared to the monster's. For example, at the end of the respective journeys, 'the monster peers through the chink and watches the De Laceys in the cottage, just as Jane, stooping outside the window of Moor House, watches the Rivers family within'. Mary Shelley's novel, Young maintains, provides necessary 'symbolic undertones', so that the meaning of Jane Eyre's ordeal becomes clear 'when her experiences are viewed in relation to those of the monster'.

(b) Individual Novelists

Captain Marryat's *The Children of the New Forest* is a welcome addition to the WC series. In his appreciative and informative introduction, Dennis Butts points out that Marryat 'laid down almost single-handedly the foundations of the nineteenth-century adventure story for children'. The text is a reprint of the first British edition, with minor amendments, and there are explanatory notes.

Angus Easson's *Elizabeth Gaskell*, in the Critical Heritage series, is a significant contribution to studies of the novelist. It includes no fewer than 135 contemporary or near-contemporary estimates of her work, ranging in time from her own preface (1848) to *Mary Barton* to a centenary tribute written by A. W. Ward (1910). In addition, Easson provides a substantial introduction, in which he gives full details of the publication of all her work and writes an extended commentary on its reception during the period covered by his book. The introduction in itself will prove to be an indispensable source of information and opinion. It is most regrettable that the inordinately high price of this volume will put it out of reach of most students of the Victorian novel. Easson has also written a brief article on 'Elizabeth Gaskell, J. M. Ludlow, and W. R. Greg' (*N&Q* 38.315–17), in which he shows conclusively that the novelist refers to William Rathbone Greg in a letter of 18 March 1851 and disputes the claim that he was the model for Thornton in *North and South*. Anna Unsworth contributes a further small item of biographical information in 'Swinburne on Mrs Gaskell' (*N&Q* 38.323–4). She points out that Elizabeth Gaskell and Lord Houghton were close friends, thus confirming a reference made by Swinburne in a letter of 28 September 1908. Sally Stonehouse reproduces 'A Letter from Mrs Gaskell' (*BST* 20.217–22). The novelist wrote this on 15 March 1856 to her friend Harriet Carr, and alluded to the difficulties she was encountering in writing the *Life of Charlotte Brontë*: 'you see I have to be accurate and keep to facts; a most difficult thing for a writer of fiction'.

Marjorie Stone's 'Bakhtinian Polyphony in *Mary Barton*: Class, Gender, and the Textual Voice' (*DSA* 20.175–200) usefully analyses the 'heteroglossia' of the novel and therefore seeks to combat the view that it is flawed by formal inconsistencies. Stone convincingly shows the complexity of voices and discourses that can be found: 'working-class and middle-class, vernacular and literary, historical and fictional, regional and professional'. She argues, in addition, that the narrative voice is sometimes female and sometimes male and that the identities of the 'inscribed readers' constantly shift. In 'Faith of our Mothers: Elizabeth Gaskell's "Lizzie Leigh" ' (*VN* 78.22–6), Joanne Thompson sensitively demonstrates the way in which Gaskell radically departs from the conventional treatment of the 'fallen woman', in that she emphasizes Lizzie's suffering, her love for her child, and the forgiveness and support she receives from her mother. Furthermore, 'the feminization of the story … projects, though it does not actually articulate, an image of God as mother.'

Rather more interest in Thackeray was evident this year. But Patrick Hickey's 'Thackeray and the Censorship of Neglect' (*ThN* 33.2–5) indicates how little Thackeray is studied today compared to Dickens and suggests that many readers (like some Victorian readers) dislike what they consider to be moral ambiguity in his characterization. He asserts that 'Readers of Thackeray and Dickens should wrestle with this issue that was raised by thoughtful readers of the last century.' Robert P. Fletcher's 'The Dandy and the Fogy: Thackeray and the Aesthetics/Ethics of the Literary Pragmatist' (*ELH* 58.383–404) is an analysis, in philosophical terms, of Thackeray's fusion of what has conventionally been termed his cynicism and sentimentality. 'His irony, which undercuts every performance (even his own), and his sentiment, which treasures the human urge to perform, are both elements of a temperament which [Fletcher designates, after Rorty], as that belonging to the protopragmatist.' It is a careful examination of Thackeray's aesthetics, ethics, and narrative technique but once the fashionable terminology is removed, it says little new. I wonder what Thackeray would have thought!

In 'The "Vanity Fair" of Nineteenth-Century England: Commerce, Women, and the East in the Ladies' Bazaar' (*NCL* 46.196–222), Gary R. Dyer analyses the popularity of 'charity bazaars', showing their association with ideas of Orientalism and their seeming to make 'available' the women who kept stalls in them. Focusing on Becky Sharp's appearance as a stall-keeper at the end of *Vanity Fair* and using John Sutherland's perception that Thackeray forms a complex image in the novel of 'Vanity Fair, the old May fair and metropolitan Mayfair', he demonstrates, with additional reference to Joyce's 'Araby', the way in which 'the bazaar topos encapsulates bourgeois antipathy towards commercialism and the East, as well as an ambivalent and ultimately fearful and hostile understanding of women'. Sheldon Goldfarb compares two works in 'Yawning in Spirit or Trembling at the Portals? *Cox's Diary* and the Boredom of Becky Sharp' (*DUJ* 83.39–43). In *Cox's Diary* (1840), the hero, a barber, unexpectedly enters high society but is finally compelled to return to his original status, which he accepts. In *Vanity Fair*, although Becky Sharp expresses boredom with high society and is eventually cast out from it, she is equally bored by middle-class respectability and Bohemia and longs to return to 'Vanity Fair'. Goldfarb concludes that 'there is no escaping Vanity Fair because, in truth, neither Becky nor Thackeray (at least in this novel) wants to escape it.' Once again, then, the familiar ground of Thackeray's ambiguities and inconclusiveness is explored.

The Thackeray Edition Project continues with the publication of *Pendennis*, edited by Peter L. Shillingsburg, with a commentary by Nicholas Pickwoad on the illustrations. In accordance with the principles of the project (see *YWES* 70.455), the copy-text is 'the earliest known impression of the London edition'. Shillingsburg gives us the definitive account of the complicated processes of writing, revising, and publishing this particular novel, accompanied by a comprehensive textual apparatus. *Henry Esmond* has been edited by Donald Hawes for the WC series. He supplies an introduction that considers the historical and psychological elements in the novel, an historical introduction that gives a factual background to its events, and explanatory notes. The text is a reproduction of the 1908 Oxford Thackeray text, with a few modifications.

R. D. McMaster's *Thackeray's Cultural Frame of Reference* describes and discusses in detail the cultural, social and historical allusions in *The Newcomes*, which in Gordon Ray's words, quoted by McMaster, is 'in some respects the richest, not only of Thackeray's books but of all Victorian fictions'. As a preliminary, McMaster notes that in the novel 'the major intertext, of course, is Ecclesiastes, along with its appendages, *The Pilgrim's Progress* and Thackeray's own *Vanity Fair*'. Let us hope that this study draws readers again to the novel that contemporary readers rated so highly.

Not surprisingly, Dickens has produced an enormous, varied amount of comment and criticism. As its title makes clear, Alan S. Watts's *The Life and Times of Charles Dickens* is a straightforward biographical and historical study. It is a handsome, illustrated book that clearly presents the necessary information and also contains helpful summaries of the novels. Two books show the application of recent theory to examinations of Dickens's technique and message. In *Vanishing Points*, Audrey Jaffe considers his use of omniscience, which 'can be located ... not in presence or absence, but in the tension between the two'. Although her introductory discussion and definitions are often abstract and elusive, she searchingly analyses the functions of various voices in particular novels: *The Old Curiosity Shop*, *Dombey and Son*, *David Copperfield*, *Bleak House* and *Our Mutual Friend*. To take just one specific example: she argues that Esther Summerson's occasional 'detachment from and denial of knowledge ... reproduces the structure of detachment and denial exemplified in the novel's double narration'. Using Bakhtin's 'analysis of the novel as an inherently dialogic form', Pam Morris, in *Dickens's Class Consciousness*, considers internal and external tensions in the novels. She makes the point that characters 'on the margin of the text', usually unrealistically drawn, contrast with the main characters, 'whose presentation usually conforms to realist conventions, in keeping with their function within the ideological "solutions" put forward by the causal moral plot'. Externally, Dickens's texts engage in dialogue, as it were, with the powerful contemporary 'voices' of Utilitarianism and Evangelicalism, heard in such periodicals as the *Westminster Review* and the *Christian Observer*. Doris Alexander's *Creating Characters with Charles Dickens* takes a more traditional approach, with the emphasis on psychological investigation. She suggests that many of Dickens's characters were based on contemporary people (for example, Mr Dombey is a version of Sir Robert Peel and Rosa Dartle owes much to Jane Welsh Carlyle). Some of the identifications are controversial, but there is much patient and interesting character-study here of fictional and factual men and women with occasional insights into Dickens's creative processes.

Some articles have supplied a few additional biographical and historical details. In 'Dickens's Return from America: A Ghost at the Feast?' (*Dickensian* 87.147–52), Michael N. Stanton corrects the accepted accounts of the dinner given to Dickens on his return from America in 1842 and attempts to identify one of the five unidentified guests, a clergyman named Wilde. Paul Graham's 'Dickens, Spiers, and Pond. From the Birth of Anglo-Australian Cricket to the Death of the Missis of Mugby Junction' (*Dickensian* 87.111–20) charts the careers of Felix William Spiers and Christopher Pond, who arranged the first visit to Australia by an English cricket team, tried unsuccessfully to persuade Dickens to undertake a reading tour there, and later established railway catering concerns in England (which Dickens would have welcomed). Carol Mcleod's 'Dickens's Maladies Re-evaluated' (*Dickensian* 87.77–80) is an account of the diagnoses of Dickens's 'many maladies' made by a Canadian medical researcher, Dr E. Carl Abbott, who thinks that the novelist may have suffered from Addison's Disease and hypertension; his death 'was almost certainly due to a thrombosis ... of the middle cerebral artery'. Katherine M. Longley makes some fascinating speculations in 'Ellen Ternan: Muse of the Readings?' (*Dickensian* 87.67–75), suggesting, in a fully documented article, that Mrs Ternan and her daughter, Ellen, may have helped Dickens in his technique in his public readings. In 'Mr Pickwick Lucky to Find a Cab?' (*Dickensian* 87.167–70), William P. Long points out some anachronistic references to hackney-cabs in Dickens's work. He gives detailed evidence concerning invention and legislation but realizes that Dickens would have been amused by such a serious examination of his historical errors. Susan Shoenbauer Thurin surveys references in fiction and non-fiction to 'China in Dickens' (*DQu* 8.99–111), indicating that these are often stereotypes but at the same time 'typically serve as vehicles for satirizing British subjects [presumably, topics]'. In *David Copperfield*, for example, Dora's 'chinese house for Jip' represents 'something foolishly impractical or comically absurd'! Michael Hollington's 'Dickens and Australia' (*CVE* 33.15–32) is a full and interesting critical account of the part played in the novels by emigration to Australia, notably in *Dombey and Son*, *David Copperfield*, and *Great Expectations*. Hollington emphasizes the theme of redemption that is present in these episodes, to varying degrees.

Malcolm Andrews's 'Dullborough – "The Birthplace of his Fancy" ' (*Dickensian* 87.37–49) is a subtle analysis of 'Dullborough Town' in *The Uncommercial Traveller*. Andrews argues that in his depiction of the fictional counterpart of Chatham, Dickens 'undertakes a kind of sentimental archaeology'. There is a relationship among 'three dualities: the past and the present, childhood and maturity, fancy and reality'. Although Dickens asserts the importance of the imagination in overcoming Utilitarianism, he recognizes the dangers of allowing the imagination to 'reconstitute the familiar material world' irresponsibly. This is therefore an essay that illuminates fundamental issues in Dickens's novels. Jay Clayton grapples with the topic of 'Dickens and the Genealogy of Postmodernism' (*NCL* 46.181–95). Studies of Dickens, he says, play no part in postmodernist criticism, but some features of his work can be related to postmodernism, such as his 'narrative impulse and eccentric characters', the use of carnival and parody, and 'the totalizing plots of the late novels'. He thinks that 'by ignoring Victorian precursors the discourse of postmodernism excludes a range of historical questions that would seem to challenge its own highly distinctive mode of historical reference.' His paradoxical conclusion is that a clear recognition of the historical context of Dickens's writing is essential. Lynn M. Alexander's 'Following the Thread: Dickens and the Seamstress' (*VN* 80.1–7) takes an historical and critical approach. The 'thread' is the different ways in which Dickens presents seamstresses in his fiction and non-fiction, from *Sketches by Boz* to *The Uncommercial Traveller*. Alexander's account is clear and competent, although a more precise distinction should have been made between Dickens's imaginative portrayals and such articles as 'The Iron Seamstress' in *Household Words*. As it is, I thought that Alexander could not always follow her opening advice that 'by studying Dickens's fiction as fiction we can gain historical, social, and literary insights'. Patricia Marks, in ' "On Tuesday Last at St George's ...": The Dandaical [sic] Wedding in Dickens' (*VN* 78.9–14) puts forward the interesting proposition that the weddings Dickens describes in detail in novels ranging from *Nicholas Nickleby* to *Our Mutual Friend* represent his version of Carlyle's attacks on dandyism. Such a 'wedding with its finery and ritual is a compound of masquerade and exclusiveness, a dandified exercise whose elaborateness is in inverse ratio to its meaning'. In contrast, he briefly reports weddings based on true love and understanding.

Two critics consider visual realizations of Dickens. Elizabeth Cayzer's 'Dickens and his Late Illustrators: A Change in Style. Two Unknown Artists' (*Dickensian* 87.3–16) is a forthright, critical account of the illustrations made by Marcus Stone and Luke Fildes for *Our Mutual Friend* and *Edwin Drood* respectively, with the former artist seen as far inferior to the latter. Cayzer also discusses the question of Dickens's break with Phiz, whose approach to illustration was unsuited to the 'sterner and less exuberant' imagination shown in the novelist's last works. Robert Giddings is concerned with a more modern medium in 'Great Misrepresentations: Dickens and Film' (*CS* 3.305–12), indicating the basic difficulties a film-maker faces, including the lack of contemporary photographic evidence, the precise period of the action, the elaborate plots, and the authorial voice. To support his argument, he details the shortcomings of the 1946 and 1975 film versions of *Great Expectations*.

In 'Narrative Experience and Specificity: Reading Dickens's "Boarding-House" ' (*DQu* 8.57–67), Michael Schiefelbein suggests that a basic feature of a Dickens narrative is specificity and that readers engage with this feature on three levels, 'two of which are rational – involving memory and intellect – and one of which is emotional'. The first of these 'levels' is typified by our experience of the plot, the second by our organizing thematic elements, and the third by our construction of images. Applying this theory, Schiefelbein analyses "The Boarding House", one of the tales in *Sketches by Boz*, finally stressing the reader's active participation. Paul Schlicke throws new light on Dickens's first novel in 'The Showman of *The Pickwick Papers*' (*DSA* 20.1–15) by examining 'two closely related traditions which demonstrably fed Dickens's imagination': John Richardson's fairground theatrical shows and various popular adaptations of Shakespeare. The latter, for instance, showed him 'that popularity need not mean hackneyed frivolousness'. Stephen Bernstein's '*Oliver* Twisted: Narrative and Doubling in Dickens's Second Novel' (*VN* 79.27–34) is an exercise in tortuous ingenuity, in which he relates 'the story of Conkey Chickweed' (chapter 31) to different frustrated searches made by Oliver. Such a relationship implies that Oliver is as guilty as Chickweed, which can be explained by a 'more surreal psychological reading' that sees Oliver and Monks as two halves of a spirit psyche – Bernstein suggests comparisons with David Copperfield/Steerforth and Pip/Orlick, but at least he concludes that 'Dickens's intention in this matter must remain a moot point'! Gail Turley Houston, in 'Broadsides at the Board: Collations of *Pickwick Papers* and *Oliver Twist*' (*SEL* 31.735–55), sets side-by-side the conspicuous consumption of food in *Pickwick Papers* with starvation in *Oliver Twist*, noting that 'a comparison of the overlapping chapters [of these two near-contemporary novels] reveals that the starvation of *Oliver [Twist]* retroactively tells on the aggressive satiation that is the undercurrent of jovial Pickwickian gusto'. After a detailed analysis, in which she considers Dickens's ambiguous attitudes towards greed and the lack of food, Houston concludes that 'Pickwickian gluttony merges with and resists Twistian [sic] starvation'. I don't know, by the way, what is meant by 'Broadsides at the Board'.

In 'Little Nell and the Marchioness: Some Functions of Fairy Tale in *The Old Curiosity Shop*' (*DQu* 8.68–75), Ella Westland gives a thoughtful political interpretation. On the one hand, Little Nell can be seen as a victim of capitalism, personified by Quilp; furthermore, she 'stands for the country rather than the city, and dies because the countryside is dying'. On the other, 'the Marchioness's story gives the urban poor some hope of escape from the trap of economic exploitation', although this story is counterpointed by Dick Swiveller's ambiguous fate. Elizabeth A. Gitter's 'Laura Bridgman and Little Nell' (*DQu* 8.75–9) traces some likenesses between Nell and Samuel Gridley Howe's description of Laura Bridgman, a blind, deaf and dumb girl, used by Dickens in *American Notes*. But Gitter admits that it is impossible to know whether Howe was influenced by Dickens and speculates whether Dickens retrospectively recognized aspects of *The Old Curiosity Shop* in his own experience at Perkins Institute for the Blind. Despite its strained, punning title, Patrick J. McCarthy's 'The Curious Road to Death's Nell' (*DSA* 20.17–33), is a useful examination of some of Dickens's narrative methods and linguistic effects in the novel and of his treatment of the theme of death.

In 'Charles Dickens: A Method in his Madness?' (*Dickensian* 87.81–4), Valerie L. Gager suggests that Chapter 24 of *Nicholas Nickleby* 'Containing some Romantic Passages between Mrs Nickleby and the Gentleman in the Small-clothes Next Door', is a Shakespearian burlesque, with *Hamlet* as its model. *DQu* 8 celebrated the 150th anniversary of the publication of *Barnaby Rudge* with a number of articles, with an informative preface by David Paroissen, its editor, giving an account of the gestation, writing and publication of the novel (*DQu* 8.3–6). In 'Monstrous Faces: Physiognomy in *Barnaby Rudge*' (*DQu* 8.6–14), Michael Hollington broadly interprets 'physiognomy' to include all kinds of 'false and deceptive surfaces' and the problems encountered by other characters and even 'the reader himself' in understanding these. As a consequence of this comprehensive notion, the article moves from one to another without a clear focus, so that by its end Hollington is considering the issues of responsible and perverted authority Dickens is dealing with. He finally suggests, however, that through Varden Dickens is putting forward the idea of 'an ordered and unambiguous universe'. Barbara L. Stuart's 'The Centaur in *Barnaby Rudge*' (*DQu* 8.29–37) is a detailed examination of Dickens's portrayal of Hugh, whose 'animality reflects the social injustice at the heart of the novel'. The article is well supported by references to the text and is clearly written, although one wonders how Hugh could have 'literally put himself together' after leaving the Maypole! Iain Crawford explores possible relationships between two 'simple' characters in ' "Nature … Drenched in Blood": *Barnaby Rudge* and Wordsworth's "The Idiot Boy" ' (*DQu* 8.38–47), looking at such features as the depiction of the characters' identification with Nature, their imaginative life, and their inadequacies of speech. Crawford also notes that Dickens portrays 'two idiot boys' in that 'Hugh is, in many senses, a dark version of Barnaby'. But he surely overstretches his argument in concluding that Wordsworth's poem is used by Dickens not only 'to define his evolution beyond the simple, idealized child-protagonists of the earlier novels' but also 'to indicate his emerging depiction of a vision of Britain more complex and problematic than that found in the rural landscape of *Lyrical Ballads*'. In ' "Secrets Inside … To Stroke to Your Heart": New Readings from Dickens's Manuscript of *Barnaby Rudge*, Chapter 75' (*DQu* 8.15–28), Joel J. Brattin supplies a transcription, including the passages cut from the proofs and notes on the deleted passages.

Looking at characters in *Martin Chuzzlewit*, Doris Alexander, in ' "Seven Hundred Thousand Imprecations" by Charles Dickens' (*Dickensian* 87.95–101), identifies the original of Pecksniff as Richard Bentley, the publisher and bookseller, using biographical and pictorial evidence to substantiate her claim. She also says that Montague Trigg was modelled on Edward Raleigh Moran, Bentley's friend, and Mr Spottletoe on Andrew Spottiswoode, a Tory printer and publisher. In 'Good Mrs Brown's Connections: Sexuality and Story-Telling in *Dealings with the Firm of Dombey and Son*' (*ELH* 58.405–26), Joss Lutz Marsh examines issues of sexuality in the novel, including a possible likeness between *Fanny Hill* and the Florence/Mrs Brown/Walter plot and connections between Dickens's interest in Urania Cottage for fallen women and his presentation of female narratives. He unsurprisingly concludes that *Dombey and Son* is characterized by 'reticence and frankness' and an 'interbreeding' of fantasy and reality.

Graham Storey's *David Copperfield* is an excellent study that perceptively, clearly and enjoyably places the novel in its historical and literary context and gives a critical reading, including considerations of structure (such as 'the child's-eye vision') and theme (for example, marriage, parents, children, and orphans). Stanley Tick's 'Dickens, Dickens, Micawber … and Bakhtin' (*VN* 79.34–7) is a concise and thoughtful essay, despite its off-putting title. He contends that whereas Dickens's autobiographical fragment was 'monologic' *David Copperfield* has Micawber as 'a participant in the narrative' modifying and enriching the account he gives of his hardships. Tick further suggests that Dickens created Mr and Mrs Micawber because he wanted to forgive his parents in the novel, 'his second autobiography'. David Kellogg presents a subtle analysis in ' "My Most Unwilling Hand": The Mixed Motivations of *David Copperfield*' (*DSA* 20.57–73). He considers the fusions of psychological and social issues as developed in the text itself, concluding that the novel 'seems a highly self-aware literary hall of mirrors, with on the one side happiness and on the other side utility, confession and fiction in infinite regress'. Malcolm J. Woodfield's case in 'The Endless Memorial: Dickens and Memory/Writing/History' (*DSA* 20.75–102) is that Dickens uses Mr Dick in *David Copperfield* as an authorial persona, 'to dramatize or simulate matters of which he can neither speak directly nor write without dissimulation'. These 'matters' include difficulties about generalizing about human nature and writing narrative itself.

R. Bland Lawson conducts a careful comparison in 'The "Condition of England Question": Past and Present and *Bleak House*' (*VN* 79.24–6). Similarities of phraseology, images, and subject-matter provide, as he says, 'a strong case for the congeniality of the authors' sensibilities'. One of the notable points he makes is that Carlyle makes significant references to the Court of Chancery in the same vein as Dickens's presentation of it. In 'William Edmonstoune Aytoun and Another Case of Spontaneous Combustion' (*Dickensian* 87.85–92), William F. Long surveys Aytoun's negative criticisms of Dickens's work made in *Blackwood's* and elsewhere, and summarizes his short story, 'How we got up the Glenmutchkin Railway, and how we got out of it' (*Blackwood's* October 1845), in which a case of 'spontaneous combustion' occurs. Though there is no need to suppose that Dickens was influenced by this, Aytoun, unlike other writers who used this macabre phenomenon, gave it a symbolic significance. David L. Cowles's 'Methods of Inquiry, Modes of Evidence: Perception, Self-Deception, and Truth in *Bleak House*' (*Dickensian* 87.153–63) is an examination of the ways in which Dickens 'examines and evaluates alternative ways of perceiving and interpreting' throughout the novel. Cowles looks first at erroneous interpretations made by the fictional characters and then at Dickens's providing his readers with 'false, misleading, or undependable evidence'. Ironically, therefore, 'Dickens makes his points about the nature of self-deceiving misinterpretation all the more effectively (though unintentionally) by illustrating them so clearly in his own authorial voice'. Douglas Thorpe considers Dickens's handling of a familiar motif in ' "I Never Knew My Lady Swoon Before": Lady Dedlock and the Revival of the Victorian Fainting Woman' (*DSA* 20.103–25), maintaining that his use of this device indicates its 'instability' and ambivalence. The novelist, Thorpe thinks, 'clearly wants us to brood on the question of why Lady Dedlock faints'. Gilian West's 'Some Inconsistencies in *Bleak House*' (*Dickensian* 87.164–5) briefly notes five of these.

In 'Theme, Form and the Naming of Names in *Hard Times for These Times*' (*Dickensian* 87.17–31), Philip V. Allingham deals with possible origins and connotations of the names Dickens gives his fictional characters. Part of Allingham's aim is to show that the novel is not simply the 'moral fable' of Leavis's definition; the names have subtleties that prevent us from accepting such a limited description. Shifra Hochberg argues in 'Mrs Sparsit's Coriolanian Eyebrows and Dickensian Approach to Topicality' (*Dickensian* 87.32–6) that the adjective 'Coriolanian', may be intended to suggest issues of class conflict as shown in Shakespeare's Roman play and in Charlotte Brontë's *Shirley*, though Hochberg thinks it unlikely that Dickens had read the latter. David L. Cowles, in 'Having it Both Ways: Gender and Paradox in *Hard Times*' (*DQu* 8.79–84), analyses Dickens's contradictory attitudes, as he sees them, to Louisa. For example, Dickens condemns 'Tom's selfish wishes regarding Louisa while simultaneously approving Louisa's desire to gratify them'. Cowles finds that his 'treatment of disempowered [sic] workers' parallels this attitude.

Sylvia Manning, in an awkwardly-written essay, considers 'Social Criticism and Textual Subversion in *Little Dorrit* (*DSA* 20.127–47), indicating 'deflections …

confusions, doublings and disruptions' in the narrative and ideology of the novel and showing that some contemporary reviewers were disturbed by these. In ' "As if she had done him a wrong": Hidden Rage and Object Protection in Dickens's Amy Dorrit' (*ES* 72.368–76), Richard A. Currie daringly argues that Amy Dorrit, when analysed in the light of psychoanalytical theories of narcissism, can be seen to direct anger against herself. This characteristic is exhibited 'in her behaviour and choice of dress', and she 'employs love in order to protect and shield her father from her rage'. Although Currie supports his assertions with numerous textual references, the latter seem to me to have the melancholy and gentle tone conventionally associated with the heroine. But it is a provocative piece, worth thinking about. Wilfred P. Dvorak focuses on a less prominent personage in 'The Misunderstood Pancks; Money and the Rhetoric of Disguise in *Little Dorrit*' (*SNNTS* 23.339–47). But he takes Pancks to be a key figure, who despite appearances 'turns out to be a true poet in disguise, and an important object lesson to us'. Pancks's eventual clear sense of human suffering shows that Dickens, like George Eliot, 'makes understanding, not feeling, the foundation of human benevolence'. In comparing 'Dickens and Hawthorne: *Little Dorrit* and *The House of the Seven Gables*' (*ES* 72.414–20), L. R. Leavis sees Dickens as apparently 'reacting against Hawthorne's emphases, while following his own creative occupations'. He juxtaposes Hawthorne's description of 'the Sabbath morning' (ch. 11) with Dickens's famous description (Bk. 1, ch. 3), suggesting that 'Dickens has consciously turned against the Hawthorne delineation'. Similarly, Leavis compares Phoebe with Little Dorrit and Holgrave with Gowan. For once, I felt that expansion was needed, since some of Leavis's comments are over-concise. Two articles supply background information. Trey Philpotts describes in detail 'The Real Marshalsea' (*Dickensian* 87.133–45), noting that Dickens's 'rendering of it in *Little Dorrit*' is remarkably perceptive and, except for the important omission of the licentiousness, accurate'. In 'Benevolent Sage or Blundering Booby?' (*DQu* 8.120–7), Doris Alexander maintains that Dickens's model for Casby in *Little Dorrit* was James Spedding, who had a physiognomy similar to that Dickens gives his fictional character. But because Dickens had discovered that Spedding had written a negative review of *American Notes* in the *Edinburgh Review* he transformed his benevolent character into that of 'a crafty impostor'.

Franklin E. Court covers much ground in '*A Tale of Two Cities*: Dickens, Revolution and other "Other" C– D–' (*VN* 80.14–18), First, he discusses the recurrent images of footsteps – which he calls 'major synecdochic paradigms'! Then he moves to Charles Darnay, who is responsible for 'retailing the framework' [sic] of culture. But the absence of clear social direction at the end of *A Tale of Two Cities* is compensated for in the ending of *Great Expectations*, showing that Pip is an 'extension … of the character of Charles Darnay'. Court's third contention is that Darnay is a surrogate for Dickens. The article would obviously have benefited from reshaping and refocusing.

Questions of morality are raised by Brian Cheadle in 'Sentiment and Resentment in *Great Expectations*' (*DSA* 20.149–74), in which he examines the tensions between these feelings, especially in Pip, 'a troubled and troubling individual whose experience mirrors the deepest repressions and compulsions of his society, and who is accordingly subject to insidious forms of displaced resentment'. Joseph F. Bartolomeo suggests, in 'Charlotte to Charles: *The Old Manor House* as a Source for *Great Expectations*' (*DQu* 8.112–20), that Charlotte Smith's novel of 1793 could have influenced Dickens's novel, since they have features in common: neglected houses, their proud and manipulative owners, and the use of 'expectations' in their plots.

Some of the comparisons seem unremarkable, but this is one of those cases that cannot be conclusively proved or disproved. Like Robert Giddings, whose article was reviewed above, Barry Tharaud considers '*Great Expectations* as Literature and Film' (*Dickensian* 87.102–10). He attacks David Lean's version, which 'subverts the original radical theme of the novel and replaces it with an anodyne or sugar-coated pill'. In 'Charles Dickens's *Great Expectations* (1860–1) and the Probable Source of the Expression "Brought Up By Hand" ', (*N&Q* 38.315), C. J. P. Beatty notes that the phrase could have had its origin in the subtitle of Michael Underwood's *Treatise on the Diseases of Children* (1784), which 'was apparently available and much read, well into Charles Dickens's own lifetime'.

In 'Mutuality in *Our Mutual Friend*' (*DQu* 8.127–34), Michael Greenstein gives a detailed examination of images, objects and activities that convey the idea of 'mutuality' in the novel. Commerce and education, for example, are both forms of exchange that are prominent features in the book. Charles Forsyte continues his investigations into Dickens's last novel in 'Dickens and Dick Datchery' (*Dickensian* 87.50–7). By careful analysis of Chapters 11 and 20 of *Edwin Drood*, he convincingly makes the case that Datchery is Buzzard in disguise.

We have recently had two splendid biographies of Trollope by R. H. Super (*YWES* 69.443) and Richard Mullen (*YWES* 71). We now have a third, N. John Hall's *Trollope*. This, too, is an outstanding book, combining biographical detail and critical assessment in a clear, fluent and enjoyable style and making comprehensive use of Trollope's own words from his fiction, non-fiction and letters. Although Hall disclaims any particular 'slant or angle', he tells us in his introduction that he thinks Trollope 'was more of an intellect than is usually recognized', that he was essentially a comic writer, and that 'he was a writer of care and judgement'. Ruth Rendell has introduced and annotated an edition of *Dr Thorne* for the Penguin Classics series. No information is given about the copy-text used. Trollope's strengths include, in her opinion, his 'scenes', his dialogue (which Hall also praises), and his individuality of characterization that makes his people 'vibrant with life, charged with their creator's own formidable energy'. Three volumes of Trollope's short stories, edited by Betty Breyer, complete the handsome five-volume William Pickering edition of these comparatively neglected works: *Tourists and Colonials*, *Courtship and Marriage*, and *The Journey to Panama and Other Stories*. Each volume has an introduction by the editor and a foreword by Joanna Trollope. James Means provides 'Identification of Literary, Historical and Other References in Trollope's *The Macdermots of Ballycloran* (1847), *The Three Clerks* (1858), *Rachel Ray* (1863), *The Vicar of Bullhampton* (1870), *Ralph the Heir* (1871), and *The American Senator* (1877)' (*VN* 78. 32–38).

Bettina L. Knapp's *The Brontës* traverses familiar ground, beginning with a description of 'The Worlds of Branwell, Anne, Emily, and Charlotte Brontë' and continuing with accounts of the work of each of them. Knapp has no notable reinterpretations to offer, but she writes eloquently and enthusiastically. Bob Duckett offers a new glimpse into Brontë biography in 'A New Eyewitness' (*BST* 20.222–4). He quotes from Joyce Eaglestone's *The Story Tellers* (published by the Bradford Public Library), in which she reproduces a family reminiscence concerning the Reverend Patrick Brontë, his wife and family and their move from Thornton to Haworth. More family reminiscences are used by Jean K. Birkett in 'Sarah Garrs Newsome: An Odyssey from Haworth to the Hawkeye State' (*BST* 20.213–16), which pieces together information about a servant in the Brontë household who settled in Iowa but who maintained a correspondence with Charlotte Brontë.

In 'Art and Artists in Charlotte Brontë's Juvenilia' (*BST* 20.177–204), Christine Alexander gives an account of her references to art and of the ways in which artistic influences 'helped mould her conception of Glass Town and Angria'. John Martin's 'vast apocalyptic canvases', for example, may have influenced her melodramatic conceptions of characters. In short, 'she learnt to shape her experience visually'. Annette Federico's ' "A cool observer of her own sex like me": Girl-Watching in *Jane Eyre*', (*VN* 80.29–33) is a sensitive analysis of the heroine's physical characteristics and dress, and of her observations not only of her own appearance but also that of other women in the novel. Charlotte Brontë is honest in her appraisal of Jane's looks and attitudes, dispensing with such conventional images as 'the tomboy heroine who blossoms into womanhood, with the beauty who is punished for vanity and coquetry, with the less attractive woman whose sweet virtue endears her to all'. Bette London's 'The Pleasures of Submission: *Jane Eyre* and the Production of the Text' (*ELH* 58.195–213) puts forward a complex argument, made obscure by jargon (for example, a letter from Charlotte Brontë to G. H. Lewis is 'couched in the gendered tropes of modesty'). London concludes that rather than expressing revolt the novel enacts the conventions of 'domestic culture'; 'its danger [to Victorian readers] might be, in fact, that it brought to the surface the hidden pleasures of the submissive state.' She therefore adjures the 'modern, feminist reader' to question this possible meaning. Another complex analysis is Joan D. Peters's 'Finding a Voice: Towards a Woman's Discourse of Dialogue in the Narration of *Jane Eyre*' (*SNNTS* 23.217–36). Partly stimulated by – and taking issue with – the opinions of Rosemarie Bodenheimer and Janet Freeman, Peters discerns in the novel an 'evolution of the narrative from parody to inner-speech to dialogue'. She sees this evolution as producing 'a "social voice" that is far more expansive [than the voice of a personally and socially aware narrator], a dialogic voice of gender and of genre, one that ends in a state of potentiality, not in its own beginnings'. Richard Moore contends in '*Jane Eyre*: Love and the Symbolism of Art' (*CS* 3.44–52) that Jane's water-colours foreshadow significant happenings (for instance, her third picture, 'showing a colossal head (but no heart), presumably suggests St John's massive intellect'). He says in a footnote that he thinks the 'technique of foreshadowing by art is ... a new development in the novel'. He makes some interesting suggestions, but I am not sure that the paintings can bear all the symbolic interpretations he gives them.

Charlotte Brontë's attitude towards industrialization, history in general, and feminism is the topic of Susan Zlotnick's 'Luddism, Medievalism and Women's History in *Shirley*: Charlotte Brontë's Revisionist Tactics' (*Novel* 24.282–95). Zlotnick argues that the novelist's view of history includes the rejection of a romanticized medieval past and of the Luddites and a belief that the Industrial Revolution 'works to the benefit of women, often at the expense of men'. Nevertheless, Charlotte Brontë realizes that despite changes 'the old patriarchal order remains largely intact' with the result that *Shirley* gives us reality, with all its inherent disappointments and disillusionments'. Two articles are psychological explorations of Lucy Snowe's character. Mary Ann Kelly's 'Paralysis and the Circular Nature of Memory in *Villette*' (*JEGP* 90.342–60) sees the heroine's repressions and frustrations as based in childhood experiences. Lucy's 'self-knowledge is minimal and her fear of growth is paralysing; she is an individual for whom a permanent state of anomie is a necessity and a torture'. This article deepens our appreciation of Charlotte Brontë's remarkable characterization of the heroine. In 'Epiphany and Subjectivity in *Villette* (in Shaw and Stockwell, eds, *Subjectivity and Literature from the Romantics to the Present Day*), Susan Watkins detects two selves in Lucy's character: 'the first a calm, independent, isolated one, and the second the emotional sexual self'. But the 'narrating voice', ignoring 'environmental' influences on character, artificially forces apart these two selves. At certain 'epiphanies', however, the division is seen to be inadequate and they therefore destabilize 'the conservative construction of subjectivity'.

In 'The Moorlands: The Timeless Contemporary (Part 2)' (*BST* 20.205–12), Hilda Marsden has written another well-researched, factually-based article (see *YWES* 71). While not denying the cosmic and symbolic elements in *Wuthering Heights*, Marsden shows that the novel contains specific references to local buildings and places, indicating that High Sunderland Hall, Northowram, could be the principal model for Wuthering Heights. Lori A. Paige takes issue with Winifred Gérin in 'Helen's Diary Freshly Considered' (*BST* 20.225–7). In opposition to Gérin's opinion that Anne Brontë's device of using Helen's diary in the second part of *The Tenant of Wildfell Hall* is faulty, Paige argues that its 'fidelity to details' validates the novelist's declared intention to 'tell the truth'.

As the summary below of work on Wilkie Collins will show, critics seem to be turning more and more to considering 'sensation' fiction. Helen Stoddart, in ' "The Precautions of Nervous People are Infectious": Sheridan Le Fanu's Symptomatic Gothic' (*MLR* 86.19–34), examines the structure and content of 'Carmilla' and 'Green Tea' in terms of their prefiguration of Freudian psychoanalysis and their exemplification of literary representation as 'a form of policing and control'. She thoroughly analyses and discusses Le Fanu's complex fusion of psychoanalytical approaches and literary convention.

George Eliot studies have flourished this year. A little more material can now be added to George Eliot's biography in the form of letters. Rosemary Ashton, in 'New George Eliot Letters at the Huntington' (*HLQ* 54.111–26), gives the background to six letters from Marian Evans to John Chapman written between 1852 and 1847 and to a note from Lewes to one Schlesinger; all are reproduced in full. William Baker reprints, with annotation, 'An Unpublished George Eliot Letter' (*GEGHL* 18/19.63–4), to Theodore Martin. In 'A Note on George Eliot's "Escapade" to Germany with George Henry Lewes' (*GEGHL* 18/19.66–9), Roland F. Anderson differs from other scholars in thinking that the two went with no definite plans in mind for a liaison. Combining biography, history, and criticism, Graham Handley's *George Eliot's Midlands* sympathetically demonstrates the extent to which 'much of George Eliot's art derives from the personal and intellectual affiliations of her Midland years'. Using extensive quotations, which almost form an anthology, and biographical and historical information, Handley examines her treatment of a wide range of subject matter: politics, education, class and leisure, 'the spoken word', and so on. Perhaps his conclusion that she always wrote 'with the one region she knew predominant in her imagination' has always been recognized, but the knowledge and warm appreciation he brings to his study make it an essential book for 'academic' and 'common' readers. Handley's account of her use of dialect can be supplemented by Maria F. Garcia-Bermejo Giner's 'Phonetic Key to the Non-standard Orthography in the Novels of George Eliot' (*GEFR* 22.50–5), in which she uses the first four novels as her sources.

K. M. Newton has edited and introduced *George Eliot*, a collection of thirteen critical pieces taken from previously published sources. His introduction is an admirable survey of recent critical approaches, including deconstruction, feminism and psychoanalysis. With such contributors as Sandra M. Gilbert and Susan Gubar, J. Hillis Miller, Terry Eagleton, and David Lodge, Newton fulfils his declared aims: 'to show the centrality of George Eliot to contemporary literary theory and critical debate' and 'to provide critical coverage of the whole range of her fiction'. In 'George

Eliot and the Power of Evil-Speaking' (*DSA* 20.201–26), Rosemarie Bodenheimer discusses the novelist's relationship to gossip in her life and in her fiction. She puts forward the proposition that the talk about her pseudonym and the Liggins imposture affected *The Mill on the Floss*, with the result that 'gossip burst into the text … like a flood of violence that only flood can overcome.' But George Eliot treats the subject more calmly and comprehensively later in *Middlemarch*, which is 'a virtual anatomy of all the different ways people can talk about each other'. And by the time she wrote *Theophrastus Such* she was relaxed enough to turn the subject into 'confessional comedy'.

Brenda Ayres-Ricker argues that the 'Dogs in George Eliot's *Adam Bede*' (*GEGHL* 18/19.22–30) are important because they exhibit passion when humans can't. She adduces much textual evidence for her case, but unfortunately expresses it in a markedly awkward manner. Coincidentally, James Eli Adams considers 'Gyp's Tale: On Sympathy, Silence and Realism in *Adam Bede*' (*DSA* 20.227–42). For him, the dog symbolizes 'comprehensive and radical skepticism concerning the authority of language', which is shown in the novel by references made by different characters to the inadequacies of speech to convey emotion. The attention paid recently to 'The Lifted Veil' is presumably due to current critical interest in the macabre and supernatural in nineteenth-century fiction. Millie M. Kidd's 'In Defense of Latimer: A Study of Narrative Technique in George Eliot's "The Lifted Veil" ' (*VN* 79.37–41) makes a strong case for a sympathetic response to the narrator of the story. She says, for example, that we find him 'human and comprehensible when he lays bare his selfishness and egotism' and that the absence of an omniscient narrator 'lends greater impact to his appeal for our compassion'. On the other hand, Mary Carroll's 'The Painful Challenge of George Eliot's Epigraph' (*GEFR* 22.57–60) analyses the sadistic and masochistic elements in Latimer's character. Anne D. Wallace, in ' "Vague Capricious Memories": *The Lifted Veil*'s Challenge to Wordsworthian Poetics' (*GEGHL* 18/19.31–45) sees Latimer as one who contradicts the poet's celebration of the positive powers of memory. Building on the work of previous critics, Marcia M. Taylor, in 'Born Again: Reviving Bertha Grant' (*GEGHL* 18/19.46–7), patiently explores the character of Latimer's wife: 'however we choose to read [her] … George Eliot … leaves Bertha Grant admired by friends in her own neighbourhood, wealthy, and free.'

Sally Shuttleworth has edited an excellent edition of *The Mill on the Floss*. Her introduction places the novel in its social and cultural context, with due attention paid to the work of Comte, Spencer, and Lewes. Her critical commentary discusses questions of realism, narrative structure (including the controversial ending), and the 'social construction of gender identity'. She uses the third edition (December 1862) as her copy-text and provides a bibliography and explanatory notes. In 'The Chains of Semiosis: Semiotics, Marxism, and the Female Stereotypes in *The Mill on the Floss*' (*PLL* 27.32–50), José Angel Garcia Landa takes as his unexceptionable premise the fact that a writer is shaped by literary and social pressures. George Eliot's complex depiction of Maggie Tulliver arises from her experiences of mid-nineteenth-century stereotypes. He maintains that the result of this experience is that *The Mill on the Floss* 'is a direct attack on the subject positions [sic] available to nineteenth-century women'; it is therefore a 'liberating' fiction.

Judith Wilt's 'Felix Holt, The Killer: A Reconstruction' (*VS* 35.51–69) is a well-argued but over-ingenious article. She suggests that Felix Holt's conversion while a student in Glasgow can be related to later events, since 'George Eliot dramatizes origins here, as she often does, in aftermaths, and by the accumulation of parallel stories in other characters' lives which glancingly reflect upon the origin she keeps hidden'. The violent climactic scene of the novel reveals 'the hidden Felix Holt, misanthropic debauchee of the Glasgow streets, Byronic gentleman adventurer' trying again, perhaps, 'by force of egoistic will to make all his desires rush in one current, and failing'. In 'George Eliot, Dante, and Moral Choice in *Felix Holt, the Radical*' (*MLR* 86.553–66), Andrew Thompson seeks to demonstrate the affinities between the two writers. He points out that George Eliot, like Dante, believed in moral responsibility and in literature 'as a force for truth or lies, good or evil'. Thompson goes on to suggest that George Eliot may be 'recasting her own experience' in *Felix Holt*, in that she, like Esther, was faced with testing choices, which ended in a 'difficult blessedness'.

Karen Chase's *George Eliot: Middlemarch* begins with a chronology of the novelist's life and times and a summary of the plot of the novel. Her commentary follows the same lines as Shuttleworth's commentaries on *The Mill on the Floss* – that is, she places the novel in its contexts (including the political context of the 1830s) and also considers its narrative method (its use of realism and plot, for example), its moral significance, and issues of 'gender and generation'. Chase's final chapter surveys its later reputation, taking into account its devaluation as a result of 'the modernizing postures of James, Shaw, Ford, Bennett, Forster and T. S. Eliot'. We have just seen Dante adduced as an influence on George Eliot. Marianne Novy bases her '*Middlemarch* and George Eliot's Female (Re)Vision of Shakespeare' (*JEGP* 90.61–78) on her belief that 'Shakespeare as model [for women writers] suggests possibilities for appropriation more than for confrontation.' In the light of this surely unremarkable contention, Novy traces affinities between his work (particularly *As You Like It* and the sonnets) and the plots, characters and 'the social relations of the sexes' in *Middlemarch*. In 'Technology and Development: Opposition to the Railway in *Middlemarch*' (*GEFR* 22.21–3), Paul H. Lorenz gives a brief but useful account of different class reactions to industrialization, as displayed in Chapter 56 of the novel, where the labourers confront the railway surveyors. John L. Tucker's 'George Eliot's Reflexive Text: Three Tonalities in the Narrative Voice of *Middlemarch*' (*SEL* 31.773–91) is yet another examination of George Eliot's narrative technique. Tucker considers the tone of the novel, which no-one will be surprised to learn is 'varied and complex'. He relates this 'mixed tone' to ways in which George Eliot employs the discourses of 'comedy, history, and science'. Changing his emphasis at the end of the article, Tucker raises the question of the Victorian reader's uncertainty in responding to the novelist's judgements on the fictional world he or she has created. In conformity with an influential theory, he concludes that the reader's 'own consciousness is creative, not merely mimetic'.

Jeanette Shumaker takes a feminist approach in her comparative study of two characters in *Daniel Deronda*: 'The Alcharisi and Gwendolen: Confessing Rebellion' (*GEGHL* 18/19.55–62). Her conclusion, after a concise but detailed analysis, is that 'neither woman can forget the patriarch whose dominance she once fought: both remain enslaved by their memories, haunted by the men they hated'. In '*Daniel Deronda* and George Eliot's Ministers' (*VIJ* 19.89–110), Katherine Sorensen convincingly shows that a character based on a model of a typical eighteenth-century Methodist minister is present in nearly all of George Eliot's fiction. Sorensen draws parallels between 'Janet's Repentance' and *Daniel Deronda*. In George Eliot's fiction, suffering is necessary for conversion, she argues, but 'another person is required who, like Tryan [in 'Janet's Repentance'], acts as an agent of grace'. Like a Methodist minister, therefore, 'Daniel ministers to Gwendolen'. His 'fictional parentage' can accordingly be seen to lie in 'those biographical accounts and journals of early Methodist ministers known so well to George Eliot'.

Another notable biography this year is Catherine Peters's *The King of Inventors: A Life of Wilkie Collins*, which is comprehensive, lucid, and continuously interesting. Peters shows how the novels relate to Collins's own experiences and activities, exploring, for example, elements of characterization that possibly derive from people he knew. Nicholas Rance's *Wilkie Collins and Other Sensation Novelists* is an ambitious and wide-ranging study that attempts to demonstrate that the 'best sensation novels ..... derive their effects from subverting a diversity of early and mid-Victorian ideologies', including the belief in middle-class morality and self-help. But Rance moves so quickly from one idea or interpretation to another and cites so many theorists that it is difficult to grasp the thread of his arguments. In 'Wilkie Collins and the Origins of the Sensation Novel' (*DSA* 20.243–58), John Sutherland relates *The Woman in White* to contemporary legislation that established various forms of amateur and professional detective and to the 1856 trial of William Palmer, who was convicted of poisoning; he also considers the narrative mode of the novel, which he compares to 'a succession of witnesses' who line up 'to address the reader'. Christopher Kent discusses 'Probability, Reality and Sensation in the Novels of Wilkie Collins' (*DSA* 20.259–80), placing these concepts in the context of contemporary science, religion, and spiritualism and looking at his use of 'documentary provenance' and newspaper reports to impart a sense of realism to his fiction. Lewis Horne argues that 'Magdalen's Peril' in *No Name* (*DSA* 20.281–94) is presented in two interwoven modes: the tragic and the melodramatic. These modes, he concludes, lead to responses of fear and admiration respectively, resulting in a feeling of 'complexity and power'. Some biographical information (also incorporated in her biography of Collins) is provided by Catherine Peters in ' "Invite No Dangerous Publicity": Some Independent Women and Their Effect on Wilkie Collins's Life and Writing' (*DSA* 20.295–312). Peters has examined a manuscript written by Harriet Collins, the novelist's mother, and shows how he drew on it for *No Name*. She also considers the effects on his life and work of Frances Dickinson, a close friend, and Caroline Graves, his 'mistress and companion for many years'.

Two critics discuss contemporary religious and political issues respectively as reflected in Meredith's fiction. The subject of the first part of Joss Lutz Marsh's ' "Bibliolatry" and "Bible-Smashing": G.W. Foote, George Meredith, and the Heretic Trope of the Book' (*VS* 34.315–35) is Foote, the prominent secularist journalist who was a friend of the novelist's. Marsh then charts what he calls 'Meredith's anti-Bibliolatry' in *The Ordeal of Richard Feverel*, *Rhoda Fleming*, *The Egoist*, and *Diana of the Crossways*, arguing, for example, that the 'Book of Egoism' in the third of these novels is a 'parodic construction' of the Bible. He suggests that Meredith thereby exemplifies the shift in the second half of the nineteenth century from the authority of the Bible 'to the newly professionalized "author" '. Gayla S. McGlamery's ' "The Malady Afflicting England": *One of Our Conquerors* as Cautionary Tale' (*NCL* 46.327–50) is a scholarly, detailed article, with some repetitiveness. Surveying the political content of the novel, she finds it 'replete with overt commentary about such key issues for England in the late 1880s and early 1890s as the rise of foreign competition, the state of the military, poverty and restiveness among working people, rampant materialism, and the new style of political campaigning'. She successfully relates these concerns to Meredith's techniques, as, for instance, in his presentation of Victor's mental confusion at the outset of the novel. This is an appreciative and illuminating essay.

Appreciation and information about Victorian religious concerns also mark Joseph O'Mealy's 'Scenes of Professional Life: Mrs Oliphant and the New Victorian Clergyman' (*SNNTS* 23.245–61), in which he describes Margaret Oliphant's presentation of clergymen faced with important mid-century issues, including the autonomy of the English church and new perceptions of the role of the priesthood (that is, the need to be 'the committed pastor of the spiritual flock'). O'Mealy sees her concern with the latter problem as something that distinguishes her from Trollope, who excludes the 'spiritual life' from his novels on similar topics. *Lewis Carroll: Looking-Glass Letters*, selected and introduced by Thomas Hinde, uses the texts from Morton Norton Cohen and Roger Lancelyn Green's 1979 edition. Hinde puts his selection in a biographical framework and the book is prolifically and handsomely illustrated.

Marjorie Garson has written a penetrating study of six of the 'canonical' Hardy novels in *Hardy's Fables of Integrity*, demonstrating 'how concern about integrity and wholeness – both psychic and bodily – inform and distort Hardy's fictional material' and thereby helping to account for its strange and grotesque elements. Her treatment of this thesis is detailed and convincing. To take one small example: she notes how bodily disintegration is 'literalized' in *The Woodlanders* in the 'rape of Marty South's locks', Fitzpiers's desire to get hold of people's heads; the dismemberment of John South's tree, and the 'disembodied set of teeth' at the end of the novel. Annette Federico, in a comparative analysis, looks at *Masculine Identity in Hardy and Gissing*. Using four novels by Hardy and six by Gissing, she examines depictions of masculinity at a time when men were, she argues, troubled by self-consciousness and a 'need to keep up with changing expectations of masculinity'. She uses four stereotypes for this purpose: the virile, the chaste, the idealist, and the realist. She therefore interestingly interprets the novels as 'imaginative expressions of an ideological crisis'.

Penelope Pether's 'Hardy and the Law' (*THJ* 7.28–41) is not as clearly focused as her title implies, since she considers various social pressures at work in three of Hardy's short stories, although she pays some attention to his 'literary usage of legal language'. John H. Schwarz points out a possible personal involvement on Hardy's part in 'Hardy and Kipling's "They" ' (*ELT* 34.7–16), suggesting that Kipling's short story about ghostly, 'lost' children may have reminded him of his own regretted childlessness.

A Shakespearean connection is proposed by Paul McClure in 'A Note on the Cliff Scene in Hardy's *A Pair of Blue Eyes*' (*DUJ* 53.53). He thinks that this cliff scene, in which Elfride rescues Knight (chs. 21 and 22), may owe something to Gloucester's 'leap' in *King Lear* (IV.vi.). Simon Tresize considers 'Ways of Learning in *The Return of the Native*' (*THJ* 7.56–64). These 'ways of learning', as embodied in Clym Yeobright's 'career as a thinker, reader and would-be teacher', are contrasted with other ways, including rustic literacy and illiteracy, the interpretation of natural phenomena (especially Egdon Heath), and Susan Nonsuch's superstitions. Hardy leaves his readers with a question: 'will the meek, assisted by the power of what Clym calls a "new" and "true" education, inherit the earth?' Jonathan C. Glance attempts to solve 'The Problem of the Man-Trap in Hardy's *The Woodlanders*' (*VN* 78.26–9) with the answer that the object symbolizes sexual relations, in line with a number of previous incidents. Viewed in that way, the man-trap is part of a pervasive theme and a 'fulfilment of the novel's pessimistic and deterministic tone'. In '*A Group of Noble Dames*: "Statuesque Dynasties of Delightful Wessex" ' (*THJ* 7.24–45), George Wing shows that in some of the short stories in that collection Hardy deals with problems of passion and ambition, among other moral issues, but that any idea of 'moral harmony' is absent. In other words, what Wing oddly calls 'the familiar increments' of Hardy's fiction are present. But Wing's last sentence disarmingly indicates that 'over-analysis ... can poison appreciation'.

Dale Kramer's *Thomas Hardy: Tess of the d'Urbervilles* is a clear and thorough guide that provides information on its 'agricultural' context, suggests literary influences (including Elizabeth Gaskell, Meredith, Zola, and Pater), discusses characterization, plot and 'tragedy', and its own influence on later fiction. Five articles in *THJ* 7 commemorate the centenary of the publication of *Tess of the d'Urbervilles*. All readers and would-be readers of the novel would find James Gibson's '*Tess of the d'Urbervilles* 1891–1991' (*THJ* 7.35–47), which is based on a lecture he gave at the British Library on 4 July 1991, helpful and stimulating, since this is 'traditional' history and criticism at its best. In another article based on a lecture (given at Sturminster Newton on 21 April 1990), Charles P. C. Pettit takes up a frequently aired controversy: 'Hardy's Concept of Purity in *Tess of the d'Urbervilles*' (*THJ* 7.49–56). Crucial to Hardy's thinking is the distinction he makes in the novel between 'a true appreciation of an individual's worth and the superficial world's view'. Purity was important to him, Pettit maintains, as the means of stimulating humanistic values in a godless world. Simon Gatrell's 'Angel Clare's Story' (*THJ* 7.58–83) is a lively exercise in textual, psychological, and moral analysis, indicating how Hardy thought carefully about choosing the right words to describe Angel's feelings. D. G. Mason's 'Hardy and Zola: A Comparative Study of *Tess* and *Abbé Mouret*' (*THJ* 7.89–102) considers specific scenes, symbolic landscape, likenesses between the principal characters (Albine and Tess; Serge and Angel), and 'a whole framework of natural images of regeneration and decay'. He concludes that 'there is a good case for a wholesale revaluation of the question of Zola's influence on the later novels of Thomas Hardy'. In 'The Lure of Pedigree in *Tess of the d'Urbervilles*' (*THJ* 7.103–15), William Greenslade first discusses Hardy's doubts whether a relationship exists between 'nature and social existence'. Hardy thought that the ideas of Spencer, Galton, and Huxley were inadequate for his fictional purposes. Nevertheless, in revising his novel from 1889 onwards, Hardy increasingly objectified Tess, 'by a discourse of hereditary determinism through which her character and actions could be more acceptably assimilated'.

R. P. Draper has brought out a revised edition of his Casebook on *Thomas Hardy: The Tragic Novels*, incorporating some recent critical essays and noting in his introduction that deconstructionist critics 'find ample material to work on' in the contradictions and subversions they detect in the novels. Kathryn R. King's edition of *Wessex Tales*, like all the Hardy volumes in the WC series, is noteworthy for its scrupulous textual editing; it has an informative introduction and explanatory notes.

Bram Stoker's celebrated fictional character is placed in the context of his period (the late nineteenth century) in Jules Zanger's 'A Sympathetic Vibration: Dracula and the Jews' (*ELT* 34.33–44). Zanger links Dracula with Du Maurier's Svengali (in *Trilby*) and with Jewish stereotypes, which were much in people's minds because of Jewish immigration into England between 1881 and 1890. He concludes that 'it was these [archetypal] associations which gave [Stoker's] novel so much of its energy and appeal.' In 'Adolescent Pornography and Imperialism in Haggard's *King Solomon's Mines*' (*ELT* 34.19–30), an article informed by solemn political correctness, William J. Scheick argues that 'at the core of the novel is a joke that yokes male adolescent pornographic fantasies with the misogynist and imperialistic impulses of Haggard's imagined audience of "big and little boys" '. Although some of Scheick's interpretations are far-fetched, he successfully highlights the possible sexual implications of this aggressively 'male' narrative. The sexual tensions and ambivalences of Haggard's

She are explored by Daniel Karlin in his stimulating introduction to his WC edition of the novel; his comments on Holly are especially notable. His copy-text is the first edition, since he thinks that its 'roughness' is preferable to 'its more genteel successors'.

A useful and convenient contribution to Stevenson studies is Peter Stoneley's one-volume edition of *Robert Louis Stevenson: The Collected Shorter Fiction*. Its twenty items 'collect all the fiction of under fifty thousand words written solely by [Stevenson] and published in his lifetime'. Although Stoneley says he has found it impossible to provide 'a full scholarly edition', he supplies bibliographical information about each work. His introduction is a sound evaluation, indicating, for example, Stevenson's differentiating his 'style' from 'aesthetic' practice by means of its 'connotations of independence and self-improvement'. Alan Sandison's 'Robert Louis Stevenson: A Modernist in the South Seas' (*DUJ* 53.45–51) is a convincing account of *The Ebb-Tide* as a modernist text in its use of a 'collective anti-hero', its mostly 'subtle exploration of moral delinquency and self-betrayal' and its 'preoccupation with the fictional nature of fiction'. Sandison relates these qualities to Stevenson's own theories of fiction and to Malcolm Bradbury's definitions of modernism. He also notes the likeness between this work of Stevenson's and Conrad's fiction, especially in the use of myth and symbol.

Contributors to the *Gissing Journal* have supplied us with further informative articles and notes. David Grylls indicates 'A Neglected Resource in Gissing Scholarship: The Pforzheimer MS "Scrapbook" ' (*GJ* 27.i.1–13). He describes the notes, in the New York Public Library, as 'a purposeful collection – of facts, phrases, outlines, booklists, news reports, anecdotes, observations – designed for strategic deployment in fiction'. John Sloan considers a personal and literary relationship in 'In Company with Teufelsdrockh: Gissing's Friendship with John Davidson' (*GJ* 27:ii.1–9). Both shared a 'distaste for mediocrity and for literature as a trade', derived from their own experiences and from their reading of Carlyle. Sloan says that in Davidson Gissing 'must have found an embodiment of the true Teufelsdrockhian spirit', though this comparison seems to ignore the satirical name of Carlyle's fictional 'editor'. In 'A Chicago Pretzel and a Gissing Feast' (*GJ* 27:ii.13–25), Robert L. Selig reports on 'a feast of Gissing stories' he found in the Chicago *Daily News*. In 'Gissing and the *London Figaro*' (*GJ* 27:iv.1–15), Pierre Coustillas describes and reprints reviews of Gissing's novels in the weekly penny newspaper, together with the paper's articles on Morley Roberts and Algernon Gissing, George's brother. Finally, we must note the continuing progress of a project of major importance, with the publication of the second volume (for the years 1881–5) of *The Collected Letters of George Gissing*, edited by Paul F. Mathiesen, Arthur C. Young, and Pierre Coustillas.

3. Pater; Periodicals and Publishing History

(a) *Pater*

Two books on Pater have appeared this year and his work figures significantly in a third, but I have found only two articles in the journals.

Six letters of Pater's which do not appear in Lawrence Evans's edition are published and thoroughly annotated by B. A. Inman in 'Pater's Letters at the Pierpont Morgan Library' (*ELT* 34.407–17). The identities of two unknown recipients, 'Boulton' and 'Mr. Squire' are explored, and letters to George Moore, A. J. Symons, and John Lane are knowledgeably interrogated, and tentatively dated from the late (?) 1870s to 1894.

Jay Fellows's *Tombs Despoiled and Haunted* is on no account to be missed. It is an intriguing and readable narrative which combines criticism of consciousness (i.e. an interest in the author, autobiography, psychology) with deconstruction (its primacy of interest in linguistic models, in textuality, and in close reading). Composed of fragments, the book frequently has the pithiness of aphorism: 'Alienated intimacy is the shaping dynamic of Pater's writing' and 'His portrait is his "refusal" .' There are beginning and concluding framing sections, a 'Narratologist's Pre-Face' and four chapters: one on origins, originality and after-thoughts; a second on the presence of inhabitable language; a third on the relation between the centrifugal and the centripetal (oppositions) in Pater, and the fourth on tombs and death, 'Pater's Oneiric Withdrawing Ground'. The merits of Fellows's textuality are explored in an introduction by J. Hillis Miller which, in its expository mode, does not entirely prepare the reader for the imaginative prose – Paterian and Derridean at once – that follows.

Bernard Richards looks at Gothic buildings (not tombs) in 'Pater and Architecture' in a collection of fifteen essays, *Pater in the 1990s*, edited by Laurel Brake and Ian Small. It is one of Richards's achievements that, in this architectural trawl of Pater's work, he reveals a persistent and detailed attention to architecture, far more than the few dedicated essays such as 'Amiens' and 'Vezelay' might suggest. Pater's phrase 'literary architecture' suggests a link between architecture and style, and this is probed. Given Richards's topic, his comparison of Pater's ideas with Ruskin's is unsurprising, but his conclusions that Pater is 'more concerned with the function of buildings in everyday life' and 'more responsive to lighting effects' are unexpected and provocative.

In an interesting foreword to Brake and Small, Linda Dowling deftly maps the field of Pater studies; noting that half the volume's essays remain formalist, she transforms the meanings generated by traditional scholarship by viewing B. A. Inman's biographical discoveries in light of the New Historicism, and indicates other future directions Pater studies may pursue, such as the cultures and discourses of homosexuality. Inman's 'Estrangement and Connection: Walter Pater, Benjamin Jowett, and William M. Hardinge' offers a closely argued explanation of what, until now, has remained a blurred and crucial series of events in Pater's psychic and professional life, which at the very least empowered Jowett to dissuade Pater from pursuing an academic career. Printing portions of newly discovered letters between undergraduates at Balliol at the time, Inman shows that in 1874 one of Jowett's undergraduates at Balliol, Hardinge, was found to be the recipient of love letters from Pater, and that Hardinge, well known for his licentious life, was sent down for a limited time. Two intriguing scenarios of how the letters came to Jowett, one involving W. H. Mallock, and one 'Miss Pater', are mooted, and a fresh notion of a recalcitrant if scarred Pater aired.

Gerald Monsman and Ian Small address problems emerging from their experience of editing Paterian texts: in 'Editing Pater's *Gaston de Latour*: The Unfinished Work as "A Fragment of Perfect Expression" ', Monsman contrasts the high 'finish' given to the unfinished *Gaston* by C. L. Shadwell, Pater's literary executor, who published it for the first time as a book, after Pater's death, and his own decision, as the editor of the *Gaston* volume of the *Collected Works*, to publish fragments of *Gaston* which exist in manuscript and to work with the periodical text as copy text. To show the process of Shadwell's editorial practice and its implications, Monsman juxtaposes a passage from a holograph manuscript, the periodical version, and the book text as edited by Shadwell. Ian Small, as an editor of *Marius*, combines theorizing with practice in 'Editing and Annotating Pater'. In a genuinely explorative piece, he sets out and compares competing theories on annotation and on choice of copy text in relation to Pater, where one is often choosing between various published texts of the same work. In 'The Discourses of Journalism: "Arnold and Pater" Again – and Wilde' Laurel Brake argues that comparison of the publishing history of individual authors – their publishers, the magazines in which they publish, and the books they compile from their periodical essays – can offer perspectives on authorship, discourse and readership. If Arnold and Pater contentiously addressed and readdressed each other in articles, they shared the same respectable publisher in contrast with Wilde, whose alliance with Pater's ideas is subverted by his publishing policies, the publishers to which he was forced to resort, and the modernists' denial after 1895 of his place on the map.

Several other essays in Brake and Small pertain to Pater in relation to other writers – Pascal, Wordsworth, Hopkins, and Joyce. In ' "The Last Thing Walter Wrote": Pater's Pascal', Hayden Ward effectively uses the position of the essay in Pater's career as a mechanism to look backward at earlier references in Pater's writing to Pascal and related themes, and to assess Pater's own late religious views in relation to Montaigne, Arnold, and Newman, and Pascal, the 'diaphanous man in defeat and despair'. There are two essays relating to these matters, Anne Varty's on 'The Crystal Man: A Study of "Diaphaneite" ' and Jane Spirit's 'Nineteenth-Century Responses to Montaigne and Bruno: A Context for Pater', and two more, by Paul Tucker and Richard Dellamora, on issues raised by Hayden Ward and Spirit.

Varty cleverly uses 'Diaphaneite' (1864), the earliest extant essay by Pater, as the occasion to trace the occurrence of the crystal metaphor and its relatedness to metaphors of sculpture in 'Diaphaneite', 'Winckelmann', and 'Duke Carl of Rosenmold', and in other writers such as Hegel, Carlyle and G. H. Lewes whose usages are echoed in Pater's. And while Hayden Ward's argument regarding Pater's late disillusion with Pascal implies Pater's preference for the alternative of Montaigne, the emphasis of Jane Spirit's essay is on Pater's doubts in *Gaston de Latour* about the moral and aesthetic consequences of Montaigne and Giordano Bruno's philosophies of indifference. Beginning with a catalogue of changing opinions on Montaigne and Bruno, Spirit cites the influence of anti-Catholic feeling in 1889 when several articles about Bruno appeared, Pater's among them. Using manuscript material, Spirit argues that Pater's article, unlike the others', registers disapprovingly a decadence associated with Montaigne and Bruno's philosophies of indifference, an 'indifference' which, in the midst of anti-Catholicism, appeared to Pater's contemporary authors as temperate and 'scientific', meriting approval. Hayden Ward's and Spirit's differing accounts of Pater's degree of commitment to religion in his later years continues a longstanding debate among Paterians.

Paul Tucker, intent on showing the fissures in the construction of 'Pater as a "Moralist" ', identifies and distinguishes two 'ethical directives' in Pater's early work (sympathy and passion/'higher morality'), notes the co-existence of metaphysical elements ('observation'), and examines the place of art in Pater's early aestheticism, all with a view to arguing that the ethical crisis of the 1880s was not caused by extrinisic factors, but lay in Pater's positions in the 1860s and 1870s. In this philosophical essay, Tucker attempts to rescue Pater from those who see him as subjectivist, and detects in the final paragraphs of the 'Conclusion' a 'persistent impulse to an objective knowledge of reality'.

In 'Critical Impressionism as Anti-Phallogocentric Strategy', Richard Dellamora makes a case for a subjectivist Pater whose position is characterized by sexual difference. The aim of this revelatory article is to extricate Pater from the desexualized readings of his work which have been circulated by deconstructionists, such as J. Hillis Miller and Daniel O'Hara. As exemplars of an alternative mode of reading, which shows Pater to be a *critic* of hegemonic masculinity, Dellamora offers readings of passages in *Marius* and 'Denys l'Auxerrois'.

M. F. Morgan also looks at 'Denys l'Auxerrois' along with 'Apollo in Picardy' and 'A Study of Dionysius' in 'Pater's Mythic Fiction: Gods in a Gilded Age'. This is an assured exploration of Pater's mythography, and the ways it and its transformations show the development of 'a modern spirit resistant to the syntheses which classical myths offer' and Pater's notion of a 'modern[ist] consciousness divided against itself'. Moran also argues that the form and narrative strategies of these tales subvert the notion of stable, fixed meanings as an 'outcome' of reading and substitute rather 'a process of provisional negotiation'.

In addition to the essay on Wordsworth which Pater recycled throughout his career, J. P. Ward notes a 'slight but real subtext of Wordsworth' running invisibly through the start of *The Renaissance*, *Marius* and 'Style'. For Ward, in 'An Anxiety of No Influence: Walter Pater on William Wordsworth', Pater never confronts 'the deep disturbance' in Wordsworth's poetry.

Lesley Higgins assesses Pater's impact on Hopkins, his tutee in 1866, in 'Essaying "W. H. Pater esq.": New Perspectives on the Tutor/Student Relationship Between Pater and Hopkins'. Higgins' method is to examine Hopkins's tutorial essays for Pater, on moral philosophy, and aesthetics, and to comment on their constant interplay with Paterian ideas and texts. In concluding this original piece, she suggests that the paradigm of intertextuality found in Hopkins's work at this time is 'answering' (Pater), often antithetically.

F. C. McGrath sets out to fathom Pater's style by looking at Joyce's stylistic experiments in the second half of *Ulysses*, particularly at 'Oxen of the Sun' in which Joyce parodies Pater. In 'Pater Speaking Bloom Speaking Joyce', McGrath suggests that both Pater and Joyce understand style as an instrument of perception which determines or constitutes what we see, rather than mirroring it: that 'different styles ... do not perceive the same things' is McGrath's explanation of the repetitions of the 'Oxen' episode, which he illustrates by comparison of Pater speaking Bloom with Bloom speaking Bloom.

In 'The Pater of Joyce and Eliot' (in Tudeau-Clayton and Warner, eds, *Addressing Frank Kermode*), Richard Poirer is primarily concerned with establishing continuities between Pater and Joyce, and secondarily with gainsaying T. S. Eliot's disingenuous location of Pater in contradistinction to modernism. The principles of Eliot's selection from Joyce's account of Pater in *Portrait* and *Ulysses*, and Eliot's unacknowledged appropriations of Pater's notions of the detachment of the artist are revealed with relation to the 'Conclusion', 'The Child in the House' (here misdated), 'Postscript', *Marius*, 'Style', and 'Sebastian Van Storck'. This is an absorbing critique of a nexus of intertextualities.

Jonathan Freedman devotes one of his five chapters to Pater and James and another to aestheticism in *Professions of Taste*, but Pater remains in view throughout this closely-argued assessment of how aestheticism was addressed, adapted, commodified, and professionalized by James, and how it was appropriated by modernism. Freedman views Pater's 'immanent critique' as an alternative to social criticism, with Pater shifting 'critical attention from the production to the consumption of cultural artifacts'. He has a very interesting account of the linked reputations of Pater and Wilde in the US (as Pater grew acceptable Wilde was demonized), and an important reading of James's ambivalence to the Paterian aestheticism pervasive in

James's fiction of the 1870s and early 1880s, including *The Portrait of a Lady*. This always intelligent book is not narrowly about a single author, but genuinely embraces the phenomena of aestheticism and commodity culture in relation to British and American writing and culture in the late nineteenth century.

Two essays in Brake and Small take up the questions pertaining to Pater and history: J. B. Bullen's 'The Historiography of *Studies in the History of the Renaissance*' usefully locates the texts of Pater's articulated resistance to historical fact, and of his conviction of the supremacy of self-expression and fine art, the precedence of the signifiers, which point to the present as well as the past, over the signified. Bullen contends that an intimate connection exists between Pater's 'personal mode of historical discourse' and his choice of Renaissance as subject, with the historical Renaissance paralleled by 'a personal renaissance' in relation to historiography. This he terms a shift from metaphor to metonymy which took place after the essay on William Morris was written, in 1868. With its emphasis on the Paterian self in conjunction with modernity, this interesting essay draws on the structures of Gerald Monsman's *Walter Pater's Art of Autobiography*.

In 'Walter Pater and the Art of Misrepresentation' (*ASch* 7.165–9), John Conlon continues the defence against the commonplace charge (Christopher Ricks having launched a well-known attack) that Pater falsifies his sources by a number of means. 'Not so,' claims Conlon, who, building on the position of Monsman, attempts anew to make a virtue of these practices: Pater's attempt to make 'artful misrepresentations' is part of 'a high art of misrepresentation ... which extends to ... self-misrepresentation'. Conlon considers various essays from *The Renaissance*, *Appreciations* (including 'Style' and 'Romanticism'), and *Plato and Platonism* in this stylish and suggestive essay.

(b) Periodicals and Publishing History

The nineteenth-century press is well-served bibliographically: both *VPR* 4 and *JNPH* 1 contain annual bibliographies: *VPR*'s by Cheryl Cassidy et al. covers 1990, *JPNH*'s 1988. *VPR* (34–6) also carries a detailed report by Mimosa Stephenson and Alexandra Norton of papers given at the 1990 RSVP conference. Both of these periodicals review new books on the press and related topics.

Issue 12 of the newsletter of the Book Trade History Group (*BTHGNewsl*) contains 'Publishers and Printers' Financial Archives 1830–1939: A Preliminary Listing' (21–56) by Alexis Weedon, and 'A Supplementary Listing' (2–8) appears in Issue 13. These lists indicate the date of the records, the location, and the source of the reference. Issue 13 also includes a 'List of Provincial Book-Trade Sources' from Peter Isaac (11–15) who is compiling a database of such sources for England which will amount to 20,000 entries, some of which are overlapping. Bound into Issue 14 of *BTHGNewsl* is the June issue of *In Ocatavo*, an international bulletin (in French) of information on the history of the book and publishing.

'Book-Publishing 1835–1900: The Anglo-American Connection' by James L. W. West III appears in *PBSA* (84.357–75). This modest piece focuses on the efforts by American and British publishers of the period to establish branches across the water, and limns the entrepreneurial history of two American firms, Putnam and Harper & Bros., neither of which succeeded for long, and one British firm, Macmillan, the only germ which flourished.

JPNH 2 is the first to appear under the imprint of a new and American publisher, Greenwood. It is entirely allocated to *Punch*, which celebrated its 150th year with an appropriately interdisciplinary symposium. Of the six lectures, one treats the first decade of the magazine, and another its depiction of the Irish; two single out famous writer contributors, and two treat the visual contents. '*Punch's* First Ten Years: The Ingredients of Success' (5–16) by Richard Altick provides a compendious overview which compares *Punch* with earlier and contemporary publications, and eyes critically the organization, politics and bigotry of the magazine, whose virulent anti-Catholicism, for example, caused Richard Doyle to resign in 1850. Altick's critical perspective is echoed in the succeeding (on the whole descriptive and adulatory) essays only by Roy Foster's impressive 'Paddy and Mr. Punch' (33–47) which examines the allegation that one of the chief carriers of the 'racialist virus' is *Punch*. The conclusion of this carefully argued case is that Punch did bestialize the Irish, and that it moved in the 1850s from 'the Thackerayan sympathy for a wide range of Irish types and Irish issues and the recognition of specific Irish qualities and legitimate Irish causes' to 'a reflexive Victorian clubman's view of the Irish as hopeless cases'. Amanda-Jane Doran's explanation of 'The Development of the Full-Page Wood Engraving in *Punch*' (48–63), the weekly's cover and 'large cut', is one of the best of its kind – clear, well-written expository prose, full of vivid detail which brings home to the reader the conditions of production. The numerous illustrations back up Doran's discussion of successive covers and 'cartoons', a word coined in Punch in July 1843, to mean a topical, satirical drawing. Frankie Morris's 'Tenniel's Cartoons: "The Pride of Mr. Punch" ' (64–72), though on a more modest scale, is comparative and adroitly contextualizes Tenniel's style and creations, touching on their links with the theatre, high art, news, national symbols and bestiaries.

While it is clear from Andrew Sanders's 'Thackeray and *Punch*, 1842–1857' (17–24) that Thackeray's journalism is viewed teleologically, largely as a prelude to, and separate from, his future 'authorship', it is left for Doran to tell us that Thackeray had been unwilling to contribute to the early numbers of *Punch* and only committed himself after the 'phenomenal success' of the first *Punch Almanack* in December 1841. Sanders takes us through Thackeray's successive contributions, looking particularly at Thackeray's 'ventriloquism', and with a sharp eye to the developed form of some of these ideas in the novels to come. Sanders's intitial questions 'Did *Punch* make Thackeray? Or did Thackeray make *Punch*?' are only rhetorical; the magazine is hardly visible in this lively account of a single contributor's writing. In 'Douglas Jerrold: *Punch*'s First Star Writer' (25–32), Michael Slater positions Jerrold as Thackeray's successful rival during the early years of the magazine, and believes that Jerrold's *Q* papers virtually established the collective persona of the magazine in its first five years. Slater demonstrates through telling quotation and contextualization of Jerrold's contributions the radical cast, 'savage irony', and wit of these pieces, and looks astutely at the interaction of John Leech, Thackeray, and Jerrold on *Punch* in the mid 1840s. While this article foregrounds commentary on Jerrold's most renowned series including the Caudle lectures, it values journalism as a legitimate form of writing, noting that Jerrold's 'most effective and original work' is to be found in his regular contributions of 'dozens of small articles, squibs, and satirical paragraphs prompted by news items of the day'.

Disclaiming that the New Woman of the late-nineteenth century was new, Susan C. Shapiro (*RES* 42.510–22) uses *Punch*, whose ridicule of progressive women bridged the whole of the period 1850–1900, as the anchor of an historical (and witty) exploration of 'The Mannish New Woman. *Punch* and its Precursors'. While the ingenuity and variety of the attacks reveal the compulsion behind their persistence and ubiquity, readers of *YWES* might note that the most common ground for *Punch*'s sniping is the quest for equality of education which peaked at the opening of higher education for women at Oxbridge.

More of a welcome is accorded the educated New Woman by an 1880s monthly magazine: in 'Gendered Space: *The Woman's World*' (*Women* 2.149–62), Laurel Brake examines the negotiation of gender and class by Oscar Wilde and his contributors in this upmarket women's magazine, the discourses of which included for a brief period those of the new woman and gay men. Another article pertains to the nineteenth century in this special issue of *Women* (2) on Journalism Past and Present. Margaret Beetham's ' "Natural but Firm": The Corset Correspondence in *The Englishwoman's Domestic Magazine*' (163–7) rethinks this controversy of the late 1860s as symptomatic of the development of the women's magazine in the last century. In this pithy and illuminating short piece, Beetham reads the corset (both a symbol of the respectable, non-sexual woman and the erotic) and the developing magazine (a mechanism of social control of women) as analogous cultural texts. I have not seen Ballaster, R., M. Beetham, E. Frazer and S. Hebron's *Women's Worlds: Ideology, Femininity and the Women's Magazine* (Macmillan).

In 'Feminism, Femininity and Ethnographic Authority' (*Women* 2.238–54), Lynette Turner draws crucially on periodical reviews of the 1890s (in *The Dial*, *The Athenaeum*, and *The Young Woman*) to probe our construction of Mary Kingsley's books on North Africa as travel writing rather than ethnography as several Victorian critics did. The work of this article is theorizing gender in relation to anthropology but its conclusion reminds us of the opacity and non-transparency of writing: 'any analysis of authority as an anthropological category mirrors or even mimics the manner in which disciplinary/ethnographic authority is formulated'.

The dust cover of Rosemary Ashton's *G. H. Lewes* foregrounds a sketch of the head of Lewes shadowed by a looming head of George Eliot; though it may sell books, this seems less than just to an author and scientist in his own right and antithetical to the spirit of this biography which attempts to focus on Lewes himself. Ashton allocates three of her thirteen chapters to Lewes's journalism in *The Leader*, the *Westminster* circle, and the *Fortnightly Review*, a proportion which acknowledges that as a reviewer, contributor, and editor, Lewes was a professional and working journalist all his adult life. The chapters themselves are well-leavened, mixing thoroughly this biographer's interest in Lewes's disparate skills as a critic, biographer, scientist, editor and man of letters with the ways the private life is inscribed in the writing and activity. This is sprightly, readable biography which integrates the ubiquitous journalism into Lewes's daily life; if it supplies less than a systematic scrutiny of this part of Lewes's work and career, it goes some way towards providing a framework upon which such a reading in the future might be based. There is a good deal that students can learn from Ashton – for example, about Lewes's role as adviser to George Smith for Cornhill.

Some of the detail excluded from the biography appears in Ashton's 'New George Eliot Letters at the Huntington' (*HLQ* 54.111–26) in which is published for the first time six letters addressed to John Chapman that pertain primarily to the *Westminster Review* 1852–1857. The pithy and newsy letters give a detailed account of selection procedures and editorial practice and control, and span the period from Marian Evans's co-editing of the *Westminster* to her authorial identity as George Eliot.

The anonymous contributions of a single Victorian critic to a single serial (the *Pall Mall Gazette*) from 1885–1888 are anthologized, edited and sensibly introduced by Brian Tyson in *Bernard Shaw's Book Reviews*. This is a very readable volume and affords the reader a look at the quotidian fare of minor titles, fiction and non-fiction, published in these years, and of the young Shaw writing for bread for a journal which he abandoned in 1888, impatient with their refusal to give him better books for review. Tyson identifies a numer of little-known authors and his annotation is tactful as well as full; he reprints these texts for the first time and as they appeared in the *PMG*.

Victorian Criticism of American Writers by Arnella K. Turner is not an anthology of essays in Victorian periodicals on American literature, but a digest of these articles, journal by journal. The author has selected the periodicals which appear in *The Wellesley Index* plus four weeklies, *The Athenaeum*, *Chamber's Edinburgh Magazine*, *The Literary Chronicle and Weekly Review*, and *Ward's Miscellany*. Each periodical entry begins with a potted history, perfunctory presumably because of the way the volume shadows *Wellesley*. The succession of abstracts is confined to deadpan restatements of argument of named articles which are listed chronologically under each periodical in the back of the volume. This mini-subject index might be seen and utilized as a welcome adjunct to *Wellesley*, whose finances precluded the full-scale subject index its volumes require. Turner's book itself has an index of authors and article titles, and it is this path which readers who wish to know how some British periodicals reviewed Cleemans or Emerson might profitably take, but students can already refer to several extant books on British attitudes towards nineteenth-century American literature. The new work this book offers pertains to the attitudes of the individual periodicals, but the 'essays' about the contents of each periodical seem redolent with lost opportunities. Unshaped, uncritical, and without any culmination or conclusion, they are unrewarding to read as essays and venture no estimate of the attitudes towards American literature in any of the periodicals covered.

In '*The Spectator* in Alien Hands' (*VPR* 24.187–96) which blends political and periodical history in a cliffhanger narrative, Richard Fulton has a splendid article on a periodical which Turner does not include. It links covert American ownership of a British weekly between December 1858 and January 1861 with the defence of American tolerance of slavery. Using the published diary of Benjamin Moran, Assistant Secretary to the American ambassador to Britain, the diary of the ambassador, George Dallas, and the issues of *The Spectator* edited by Moran's friend Thornton Hunt, Fulton shows sudden changes of editorial policy *vis à vis* the US when Hunt arrives and departs from the weekly. Also in *VPR* (24.170–2), James J. Sack offers a brief footnote to periodical and political history by finally attributing to John Miller the 1830 *Quarterly Review* article 'Internal Policy' which named the Tories 'the Conservative Party' ('The *Quarterly Review* and the Baptism of the "Conservative Party" – a Conundrum Resolved').

Another piece on the treatment of foreign affairs, 'The Indian Mutiny in the Mid-Victorian Press', by E. M. Palmegiano appears in *JPNH* (7.3–11). The focus of this article is the terms in which the event is analysed in the press, and the positions and politics of individual papers are obscured and disregarded. After the introduction, the names of journalists and the titles of magazines are relegated to the footnotes.

Leslie Howsam's *Cheap Bibles: Ninteenth-Century Publishing and the British and Foreign Bible Society* is part of the series Cambridge Studies in Publishing and Printing History, and Howsam's definition of the subject, with chapters on the relations of BFBS with English printers (chapter 3), with London bookbinders (chapter 4) and bookselling (chapter 5), illustrates how the existence of such a series validates and circulates this kind of scholarly research. It is hardly possible to overstate the resonance of this book for scholars of the early and mid-nineteenth century; Howsam's breadth of interest – in evangelicism, readership, translation, individual lives, and social organization and networks, as well as publishing and printing history, and her capacity to write well make her book absorbing as well as extraordinarily informative.

Issue 14 of *BTHGNewsl* largely consists of Rosemary Scott's 'Checklist of Victorian Religious Periodicals Publishing Verse, 1850–75' (5–32); each entry provides dates, publisher, frequency of publication, price, length, denomination, and a location for each periodical title as well as indicating regularity of the publication of poetry and some named poets. Of the two remaining articles on the religious press, 'Anonymity and Editorial Responsibility in Religious Journalism' (*VPR* 24.180–6) by Josef Altholz is commendably broad in scope, drawing in a large number of titles which adopt some position other than complete anonymity which is the general rule in this category of journalism. Altholz is able to show that anonymity in a sphere where doctrine rules has its own hazards; his profile of various uncomfortable accommodations made by individual journals and of myriad sacked editors is informative about the implications of anonymity and its effects on the press in general. Jerry Coats's piece 'John Henry Newman's "Tamworth Reading Room": Adjusting Rhetorical Approaches for the Periodical Press' (*VPR* 24.172–9) treats seven letters to the editor of *The Times* in February 1841, from Newman but anonymous or signed 'Catholicus'. Coats's argument is that Newman changed his rhetorical tack for the last four letters, in response to the terms of the controversy about Puseyites in the press which was stirred by his intitial *ad hominem* attack on Peel and Brougham, alongside his wholesale attack on the secularism he detected in the opening of a free reading room accessible to the public.

Three of the four numbers of *VPR* are special issues, with no. 3, edited by Josef Altholz and Robert A. Colby, on the *Wellesley Index*. This comprises introductions to three periodicals excluded from the index for a variety of reasons, addenda and corrigenda to the existing published volumes, and a review essay on an analogue to *Wellesley*. It results in a useful if bitty number of *VPR*. Written in the *Wellesley* format, the three introductory essays pertain to '*The British Critic*, 1824–43' (111–18), '*The Foreign Review*, 1828–30' (119–36), and '*The Erratic Review*' (143–5) by, respectively, Esther Houghton and Josef Altholz, Eileen M. Curran, and L. J. Neander. Curran's article also includes a full and detailed issue by issue account of *The Foreign Review*. The fourth article by Jonathan Cutmore, 'The *Quarterly Review* under Gifford: Some New Attributions' (137–42), offers, as well as further attributions, a review essay of the methodology in H. and H. Shine's *Quarterly Review* under Gifford (1949) in comparison with that of the *Index*. The 'Addenda and Corrigenda' (146–50) cover ten periodicals as well as the list of contributors. Notwithstanding the long distilled research in this number of *VPR*, it makes for a work of reference rather than a good read.

Ian Fletcher's *Rediscovering Herbert Horne* is a welcome attempt to bring Horne and his projects in visual art, typography and book design (as well as his poetry and architecture) to the notice of scholars. As founder and editor of the *Century Guild Hobby Horse* (1884–94), 'the first of the art-oriented literary magazines of the 1880s and 1890s', Horne's working commitment to 'total design' resulted in a periodical which aspired to be a work of art, with paper, type, margins, and illustrations alike as important as the letterpress which itself showed a decided bias toward book production and the antiquarian. Beside Horne, those in the *Hobby Horse* circle included Selwyn Image, Arthur Galton, A. H. Mackmurdo, and Lionel Johnson whose contributions along with Horne's, are treated here in some detail. In this handsomely produced and generously illustrated book, Fletcher's erudition, critical acumen and sharp eye saturate the chapters on the magazine and 'The Typographer and Book Design'.

The remaining two special numbers of *VPR* (nos 1 and 2), edited by Julie F. Codell, pertain to Victorian Art and the Press. The editor's introductory essay, 'The Aura of Mechanical Reproduction: Victorian Art and the Press' (4–10) brings together existing materialist and theoretical work, and cleverly transfers this synthesis from the discourses of art history to those of publishing history. Both technique and technology help muster her demonstration that 'Victorian reproduction of art placed art in an entirely new context, the page, not the gallery wall'. Alicia Faxon's 'The Medium is NOT the Message: Problems in the Reproductions of Rossetti's Art' (63–70) is a brief piece comparing D. G. Rossetti's drawings for illustrations in the mid 1850s, including those for the Moxon Tennyson, with the resultant woodcut illustrations. Faxon ends her account of Rossetti's dissatisfaction, with the suggestion that accurate colour photographic reproduction or lithography might have changed Rossetti's career, had they been available to him.

In a fascinating article in *VPR* (24.56–63), Joanne Lukitsh examines four periodical reviews to assess the relation of an artist's photographic portraits in 1863 to comercial portraits for *cartes de visite*. 'Reminders of Titian and Van Dyke: *The Reader* Reviews the Portrait Photographs of David Wilkie Wynfield, 1864' does not accurately describe the essay in which articles in *Once a Week* and *The Photographic News* feature as prominently as articles in *The Reader*. The artist's photographer's use of defamiliarizing fancy dress, close-ups, allusions to old master painting, and blurred backgrounds recommend themselves to the critic in *The Reader* whose disdain for the vulgar 'democracy' of commercial *cartes* is clear. It is left to *The Photographic News* to note the commercial appeal of Wynfield's photographs to the affluent, but in the event the business remained with the ordinary *cartes* exhibited on the street in shop windows rather than with Wynfield's means of distributing his series on the page.

The Graphic (1869 onwards) figures in three articles which all address its visual content. Lee Edwards's 'From Pop to Glitz: Hubert von Herkomer at *The Graphic* and the Royal Academy' in *VPR* (24.70–7) treats the traffic between the low art of magazine illustration and the high art of oil painting, in particular Herkomer's contribution in 1871, 'Sunday in Chelsea Hospital', which was the germ of 'The Last Muster' showed to 'rhapsodic' approval in the summer exhibition of 1875.

Ruskin's slighting allusion to this show in his 1875 Academy Notes as 'The Splendidist May Number of the *Graphic*' (*VPR* 24.22–33) fuels Kristine Garrigan's canny piece on Ruskin's pamphlet in which he denounces contemporary British art as allied with periodical illustration, the mechanical, the industrial, and the scientific. Ruskin's intemperate 'guide', which is organized by topic rather than by order of hanging, is contrasted with a contemporaneous pamphlet by Henry Blackburn which, offering itself as a *substitute* for the show which it illustrates through crude sketches, went on to become an annual publication. It represents Ruskin's nightmare compounded.

In 'From Eden to Empire: John Everett Millais's *Cherry Ripe*' (*VS* 34.179–203), Laurel Bradley looks at an image commissioned for the cover of its Christmas annual of 1880. Her iconographical study ranges widely from Millais's Georgian adaptation of which this image is one, to discourses of childhood, Englishness, and empire. A significant portion of this fine article is allotted to the technology and weekly illustrated press (including the *Illustrated London News*) which, effecting a shift from art to commerce, circulated this image and its descendants in engravings and advertisements.

The first five volumes of *The Art-Union* (1839–43) and its projects, before it extended its brief to Arts Decorative and Ornamental, is one of Debra Mancoff's topics in 'Samuel Carter Hall: Publisher as Promoter of the High Arts' (*VPR* 24.11–21). This informative article is balanced precariously between the discourses of biography (Hall as art activist) and publishing history (the contents, form, voice, etc. of the magazine), and leaves the impression that *Hall's* voice is alone that of the periodical. It describes the active role of *The Art-Union* in determining the interior decoration of the new Houses of Parliament, and the concommitant serial publication by Hall of *The Book of British Ballads* (1842) which was 'intended to address the more challenging issues of the national project – British artists working in ensemble, in a specific medium, to interpret national subject matter – in microcosm'.

The Bodley Head is at the heart of Margaret Stetz's 'Sex, Lies and Printed Cloth: Bookselling at the Bodley Head in the Eighteen-Nineties' (*VS* 34.71–86). This well-informed essay, which includes a welcome proportion of technical information, explores some fresh propositions, such as the contention that the true defining feature of the firm's books is the advertisements bound into each volume. Stetz's interest in how the firm commodified its products leads her to conclude that the model for the advertising campaign at the Bodley Head was largely the marketing of fabric in the Liberty catalogues. Content analysis of advertisements and House series such as Keynotes are deployed to good effect in this focused and astute piece.

John Turner's subject in 'Title-Pages Produced by the Walter Scott Publishing Co. Ltd.' (*SB* 44.323–31) does not pertain to the normal pages of this Newcastle-upon-Tyne publisher and printer (1882–1910), but to those tailor-made title-pages which carried the imprint of the customer (e.g. J. M. Dent or Mudies) rather than that of the firm. Turner shows that the firm of Walter Scott inherited this practice from its predecessor (Tyne Publishing Co.), and that the titles were all taken from Scott's current list and remained in print at the same time.

In 'Edward Garnett, Publisher's Reader, and Samuel Rutherford Crockett, Writer of Books' (*PubH* 29/30.89–121), Dorothy W. Collin recounts the history of the interaction between the publishing houses Fisher Unwin, Garnett their reader, and Crockett, a kailyard writer. Using various readers' reports and correspondence, Collin follows the endeavours of Crockett to publish with Unwin and others, and assesses the effect on Crockett's position of his representation by A. P. Watt, a literary agent. Noting that the suggestions of Garnett (a leisured Southerner) deflected Crockett from any real leap forward in Scottish literature, Collin registers the symbiosis of the 'play of commercial enterprise and literary aspiration' in the history of publishing.

In 'Arnold's Publisher: A Neglected Source' (*NCP* 18/19.35–40), William Bell views George Smith's autobiography, now in NLS, as a 'source' for the study of Arnold's life. Bell reproduces the passage on the author with 'a certain grand air', and lightly annotates and briefly introduces it. Pamela Wiens's focus is also authorial. On the strength of good reviews of William Morris's socialist play *The Tables Turned: or Nuppkins Awakened* in the *Pall Mall Gazette*, the *Commonweal*, and the *Saturday Review*, Wiens takes a fresh look at it. If the force of her case for the play stems in part from the stature of these periodicals, it also resides in the fame of the play's critics – G. B. Shaw, Walter Crane, and Yeats, and of its actors who included Morris and his daughter, May.

If John Kijinski's ambitious essay in cultural/publishing history, 'John Morley's "English Men of Letters" Series and the Politics of Reading' (*VS* 34.205–25) alarmingly averts its gaze in places to present a neat overview, this foray into the history of reading repays attention. It begins with an account of reading programmes created in the face of burgeoning literacy and 'popular' literature and how Morley's series of biographies (1878–92) relates to them, and goes on to consider, reductively, the literary values in ten EML biographies of novelists, which gives him an opportunity to comment on the uncertain status of fiction in these years.

Laurel Brake has a theoretical piece in *VPR* (24.163–9) which addresses 'Production of Meaning in Periodical Studies: Versions of the *English Review*'. She attempts to show how different meanings may be generated by different discourses (here the overlapping of 'English Literature' and periodical studies) in connection with the early years (1908–10) of an Edwardian little magazine edited by Ford Madox Hueffer.

Books Reviewed

Alexander, Doris. *Creating Characters with Charles Dickens*. UPennP. pp 218. £16.95. ISBN 0 271 00725 7.

Altick, Richard D. *The Presence of the Present: Topics of the Day in the Victorian Novel*. OSUP. pp. 854. $45. ISBN 0 8142 0518 6.

Ashton, Rosemary. *G. H. Lewes. A Life*. OUP. pp. 369. £25. ISBN 0 198 12827 4.

Bernstein, Carol L. *The Celebration of Scandal: Toward the Sublime in Victorian Fiction*. UPennP. pp. 214. £18.95. ISBN 0 271 00718 4.

Brake, Laurel, and Ian Small, eds. with a foreword by Linda Dowling. *Pater in the 1990s*. ELTP. pp. 282. $30.00. ISBN 0 9443 1805 3.

Breyer, Betty, ed. *Anthony Trollope: The Complete Short Stories*. Vol. 3: *Tourists and Colonials*. William Pickering. pp 260, £13.95. ISBN 1 85196 702 8. Vol. 4: *Courtship and Marriage*. William Pickering. pp. 282. £13.95. ISBN 1 85196 703 6. Vol. 5: *The Journey to Panama and Other Stories*. William Pickering. pp. 219. £13.95. ISBN 1 85196 704 4.

Brown, Joanna Cullen. *Hardy's People: Figures in a Wessex Landscape*. Allison & Busby (1987). pp. 352. pb £16.95. ISBN 0 850 31373 2.

———. *A Journey into Thomas Hardy's Poetry*. Allison & Busby (1989). pp. 135. £14.95. ISBN 0 850 31883 1.

———. *Let me Enjoy the Earth: Thomas Hardy and Nature*. Allison & Busby (1990). pp. 288. £14.99. ISBN 0 850 31875 0.

Butts, Dennis. ed. *The Children of the New Forest* by Captain Marryat. WC OUP. pp. 324. pb £4.99. ISBN 0 19 282725 1.

Chase, Karen. *George Eliot: Middlemarch*. CUP. pp. 99. hb £20, pb £6.95. ISBN 0 521 35021 2, 0 521 35915 5.

Crosby, Christina. *The Ends of History: Victorians and 'The Woman Question'*. Routledge. pp. 186. hb £30, pb £9.99. ISBN 0 415 00935 9, 0 415 00936 7.

Day, Aidan, ed. *Selected Poems by Tennyson*. Penguin. pp. 400. pb £5.99. ISBN 0 140 44545 5.

———, ed. *Selected Poetry and Prose. Robert Browning*. Routledge. pp. 192. £6.99. ISBN 0 415 00952 9.

Dore, Helen. *William Morris*. Book Sales Inc (1990). $14.98. ISBN 1555 21605 6.

Draper, R. P., ed. *Thomas Hardy: The Tragic Novels*, Revised edition. Casebook Series. Macmillan. pp. 259. hb £35, pb £9.99. ISBN 0 333 53363 1, 0 333 53364 X.

Easson, Angus, ed. *Elizabeth Gaskell: The Critical Heritage*. Routledge. pp. 595. £10. ISBN 0 415 03289 X.

———. *History and the Novel*. Essays and Studies. Brewer. pp. 105. £12.95. ISBN 0 85991 322 8.

Federico, Annette. *Masculine Identity in Hardy and Gissing*. AUP. pp. 148. £22.95. ISBN 0 8386 3423 0.

Fellows, Jay. with a foreword by J. Hillis Miller. *Tombs, Despoiled and Haunted*. StanfordUP. pp. 188. $32.50. ISBN 0 8497 1578 5.

Filmer, Kath, ed. *The Victorian Fantasists: Essays on Culture, Society and Belief in the Mythopoetic Fiction of the Victorian Age*. Macmillan. pp. 221. £35. ISBN 0 333 53410 7.

Fletcher, Ian. *Rediscovering Herbert Horne*. ELTP (1990). pp. 188. $25. ISBN 0 944 31802 9.

Freedman, Jonathan. *Professions of Taste. Henry James, British Aestheticism, and Commodity Culture*. StanfordUP. (1990). pp. 305. $29.50. ISBN 0 8047 1784 2.

Garson, Marjorie. *Hardy's Fables of Integrity: Woman, Body, Text*. Clarendon. pp. 198. £27.50. ISBN 0 19 812223 3.

Hair, Donald S. *Tennyson's Language*, UTorP (1991). pp. 198. £35. ISBN 0 802 05905 8.

Hall, N. John. *Trollope: A Biography*. Clarendon. pp. 581. £25. ISBN 0 19 812627 1.

Handley, Graham. *George Eliot's Midlands: Passion in Exile*. A&B. pp. 252. £16.99. ISBN 0 85031 997 8.

Harvey, Charles. *William Morris: Design and Enterprise in Victorian Britain*. ManUP. pp. 300. hb £45, pb £12.99. ISBN 0 719 02418 8, 0 719 02419 6.

Harvie, Christopher. *The Centre of Things: Political Fiction in Britain from Disraeli to the Present*. Unwin Hyman. pp. 245, hb £28, pb £11.95. ISBN 0 04 445593 3, 0 04 445592 5.

Hawes, Donald, ed. *The History of Henry Esmond Esq.* by William Makepeace Thackeray. WC. OUP. pp. 493. pb £4.99. ISBN 0 19 282727 8.

Hinde, Thomas, ed. *Lewis Carroll: Looking-Glass Letters*. Collins & Brown. pp. 160, £14.99. ISBN 85585 038 9.

Housman, A. E. *A Shropshire Lad*, illus. by Robin Bell Corfield, intro. by Anne Carter. Walker Books. pp. 128. £14.95. ISBN 0 744 51117 8.

Howsam, Leslie. *Cheap Bibles. Nineteenth-Century Publishing and the British and Foreign Bible Society*. CUP. pp. 245. £35. ISBN 0 521 39339 6.

Humphreys, Anne. *Browning Institute Studies: An Annual of Victorian Literary and Cultural History*. Vol. 17. Browning Institute Inc. (1989).

Jack, Ian, Rowena Fowler, and Margaret Smith, eds. *Poetical Works of Robert Browning*. Vol. 4. (*Bells and Pomegranates* VII–VIII and *Christmas Eve and Easter Day*). Clarendon. pp. 454. £65. ISBN 0 198 12789 8.

Jaffe, Audrey. *Vanishing Points: Dickens, Narrative and the Subject of Omniscience*. UCalP. pp. 180. $32.50. ISBN 0 520 06918 8.

Johnson, Trevor. *A Critical Introduction to the Poems of Thomas Hardy*. Macmillan. p. 272. hb £35, pb £9.99. ISBN 0 333 49577 2, 0 333 49578 0.

Jones, Kathleen. *Learning not to be first: The Life of Christina Rossetti*. Windrush Press. pp. 256. £16.99. ISBN 0 900 07571 6.

Karlin, Daniel, ed. *She* by Rider Haggard. WC, OUP. pp. 322, pb £3.99. ISBN 0 19 282767 7.

Kelley, Philip, and Scott Lewis, eds. *The Brownings' Correspondence*. Vol. 9. June–December 1844 (Letters 1618–1798). Athlone. pp. 448. £60. ISBN 0485 30027 3.

King, Kathryn, ed. *Wessex Tales* by Thomas Hardy. WC, OUP. pp. 248. pb £2.99. ISBN 0 19 28720 0.

Kirchof, Frederick. *William Morris: The Construction of a Male Self 1856–1872*. OhioUP (1990). pp. 275. $28.45. ISBN 0 821 40954 9.

Knapp, Bettina L. *The Brontës: Branwell, Anne, Emily, Charlotte*. Continuum. pp 204. $18.95. ISBN 0 8264 0514 2.

Kramer, Dale. *Thomas Hardy: Tess of the d'Urbervilles*. CUP. pp. 109. hb £20, pb £6.95. ISBN 0 521 34627 4, 0 521 34695 9.

Latham, David and Sheila Latham. *An Annotated Critical Bibliography of William Morris*. HW. pp. 256. £65. ISBN 0 7108 11535.

McMaster, R. D. *Thackeray's Cultural Frame of Reference: Allusion in The Newcomes*. Macmillan. pp. 194, £35. ISBN 0 333 53958 3.

Magoon, Joseph, ed. *Bibliography of Writings about Alfred Lord Tennyson for 1970–1989*. Privately published.

Maser, Mary Louise Jarden, and Frederick Maser. *Christina Rossetti in the Maser Collection*. Bryn Mawr Library.

Mattheisen, Paul F., Arthur C. Young, and Pierre Coustillas, eds. *The Collected Letters of George Gissing, Volume Two, 1881–1885*. OhioUP. pp. 397. £52.25. ISBN 0 8214 0984 0.

Morris, Pam. *Dickens's Class Consciousness: A Marginal View*. Macmillan. pp. 194, £35. ISBN 0 333 53958 3.

Newton, K. M. *George Eliot*. Longman. pp. 260. £35. ISBN 0 582 04064 7.

Pearce, Lynn. *Woman, Image, Text: Readings in Pre-Raphaelite Art and Literature*. HW. pp. 236. hb £45, pb £11.95. ISBN 0 745 00631 0, 0 745 00632 9.

Peters, Catherine. *The King of Inventors: A Life of Wilkie Collins*. S&W. pp. 498. £20. ISBN 0 436 36712 2.

Pinney, Thomas, ed. *Something of Myself and Other Autobiographical Writings: Rudyard Kipling*. CUP. pp. 256. £27.95. ISBN 0 521 35515 X.

Rance, Nicholas. *Wilkie Collins and Other Sensation Novelists*. Macmillan. pp 199. £40. ISBN 0 333 53745 9.

Rendell, Ruth, ed. *Dr Thorne* by Anthony Trollope. Penguin. pp. 557. pb £4.99. ISBN 0 14 043326 0.

Reynolds, Margaret, ed. *Aurora Leigh* by Elizabeth Barrett Browning. UOhioP. pp. 600. £45. ISBN 0 8214 0956 5.

Rossetti, Christina. *Fly Away, Fly Away Over the Sea and Other Poems for Children*. North and South Books. pp. 32. £8.95. ISBN 1 558 58101 4.

Rossetti, Dante Gabriel. *Selected Poems & Translations*. ed. Clive Wilmer. Carcanet. £5.95. ISBN 0 856 35915 7.

Schoffman, Nachum. *There is no Truer Truth: The Musical Aspect of Browning's Poetry*. Greenwood. pp. 200. £35.95. ISBN 0 313 27401 0.

Shaw, Philip, and Peter Stockwell, eds. *Subjectivity and Literature from the Romantics to the Present Day: Creating the Self*. Pinter. pp. 175. £35. ISBN 0 86187 180 4.

Shillingsburg, Peter L., ed., with commentary by Nicholas Pickwoad. *The History of Pendennis* by William Makepeace Thackeray. Garland. pp. 499. $10. ISBN 0 8240 5098 3.

Shuttleworth, Sally, ed. *The Mill on the Floss* by George Eliot. Routledge English Texts. Routledge. pp. 540. pb £5.99. ISBN 0 415 01316 X.

Slinn, E. Warwick. *The Discourse of the Self in Victorian Poetry*. Macmillan. pp. 290. £14.00. ISBN 0333 47412 0.

Small, Ian. *Conditions for Criticism: Authority, Knowledge and Literature in the Late Nineteenth Century*. Clarendon. pp. 155. £22.50. ISBN 0 198 12241 0.

Stoneley, Peter, ed. *Robert Louis Stevenson: The Shorter Fiction*. Robinson. pp. 664. £19.95. ISBN 1 85487 076 9.

Storey, Graham, *David Copperfield: Interweaving Truth and Fiction*. TMS, Twayne. pp. 111. hb $20.95, pb $9.95. ISBN 0 8057 9415 8, 0 8057 8142 0.

Tennyson, Alfred. *Poems, Chiefly Lyrical (1830)*. intro. by Jonathan Wordsworth. Woodstock. pp. 170. £25. ISBN 1 854 77081 0.

Thompson, Paul. *The Work of William Morris*. OUP. pp. 318. pb £10.95. ISBN 0 192 83149 6.

Timko, Michael, Fred Kaplan, and Edward Giuliano, eds. *Dickens Studies Annual: Essays on Victorian Fiction*, Vol. 20. AMS. pp. 388. $45. ISBN 0 404 18540 1.

Tudeau-Clayton, Margaret and Martin Warner, eds. *Addressing Frank Kermode*. Macmillan. pp. 232. £35.00. ISBN 0 333 53137.

Turner, Arnella K. *Victorian Criticism of American Writers*. Borgo. pp. 456. hb $49.95, pb $39.95. ISBN hb 0 89370 816 X, pb 0 89370 916 6.

Tyson, Brian, ed. *Bernard Shaw's Book Reviews*. UPennP. pp. 511. $50.00. ISBN 0 271 00721 4.

Watts, Alan S. *The Life and Times of Charles Dickens*. Studio. pp. 144. £12.95. ISBN 1 85170 637 2.

Woolford, John, and Daniel Karlin, eds. *The Poems of Browning*. Vol. 1 [1826–1840] and Vol. 2 [1841–1846]. Longman Annotated English Poets. pp. 798, 518. £90, £70. ISBN 0582 481 007, 0582 06399 X.

XV

The Twentieth Century

ADRIAN PAGE, JULIAN COWLEY, MACDONALD DALY, SUE VICE, SUSAN WATKINS, LYNDA MORGAN, STUART SILLARS, JEM POSTER, TREVOR GRIFFITHS and ANNA MCMULLAN

This chapter has the following sections: 1. Fiction; 2. Poetry; 3. Drama. Section 1(a) is by Adrian Page and Julian Cowley; section 1(b) is by Macdonald Daly, Sue Vice and Sue Watkins; section 1(c) is by Lynda Morgan; section 2(a) is by Stuart Sillars; section 2(b) is by Jem Poster; and section 3 is by Trevor Griffiths, with the Beckett material in 3(c) by Anna McMullan.

1. Fiction

(a) General Studies

The fifth edition of *Contemporary Novelists* edited by Lesley Henderson is an immensely valuable compendium of information and opinions on twentieth-century writers of fiction which is undoubtedly indispensable in any good library. As an aid to research it provides a very interesting way of comparing attitudes towards fiction since 1972, when the first edition was published. At that time Walter Allen felt that it was more difficult for contemporary novelists to write convincing realism, as developments in technology and scientific knowledge made the nature of reality inaccessible to the novelist. Nowadays, Jereome Klinkowitz suggests that the novel has regained its vivacity by returning to the world rather than struggling with abstract metafictional issues. The large group of *literati* who have selected the writers included here have done justice to the vast range of novelists throughout the English-speaking world. Writers from Asia, for example, are well represented alongside the acknowledged literary figures we would all expect from England and America. Each entry gives brief biographical details, a list of publications, and a short critical essay which introduces the author's work. Some entrants have also specified critical writings on their work, although others apparently prefer not to do this. Malcolm Bradbury has cited several critics but supplements this with a fairly long essay of his own in which he asserts that 'Liberalism to me is what the novel is about.' This remark may help to characterize the novelists included here and their literary concerns. Unlike some reference works, this largely excludes popular novelists who do not attempt to explore issues of social relevance. Only the likes of Frederick Forsyth are admitted and then their literary failings are drawn to our attention.

It is always pleasing to find good critical ideas on more recent fiction, and *The British and Irish Novel Since 1960*, a collection of essays edited by James Acheson, provides some very competent work on all the major novelists who have emerged in this period. There is a balance between the classic texts of recent fiction, such as William Golding and Iris Murdoch, and the writers who still have to achieve this status, such as John McGahern and Buchi Emecheta. Readers who are searching for a brief introduction to the contemporary novel will find this a valuable starting point. The difficulty inherent in a collection of this kind, however, is that it vacillates between offering a reader's guide to the contemporary novel and some remarkably succinct essays which find thematic coherence in the writers' work. David Punter, for example, summarizes the work of Angela Carter and Russell Hoban with great skill, yet one trend in recent fiction which becomes evident is that, as Peter Conradi is quoted as commenting on John Fowles, each novel can be read as 'braving a new kind of logic'. With such novelists increasingly aiming at a diversity of styles, the constraints of space imposed by the traditional format of the collection of essays seem to gloss over many highly promising issues in the attempt to sustain a comprehensive coverage.

Gregory Currie's *The Nature of Fiction* is a philosophical approach to the problem of distinguishing fiction from other forms of discourse. There have been previous attempts to provide theories of fiction, notably with the pretense theory of John Searle, but Currie dismisses all versions of this theory on the grounds that cases of parody and imitation fulfil Searle's criteria for fiction. Currie argues instead that fiction-making is an act of communication and that the circumstances in which any act achieves this status can be specified using Grice's theory of meaning. According to Grice's theory, a linguistic act has meaning when the speaker's purpose is understood by the listener and the listener believes that an utterance was made with this intention in mind. Thus we need to recognize that we are meant to entertain the fictional ideas seriously, yet in the knowledge that they are ultimately not to be given our wholehearted assent. This is a promising new approach to the task of defining fiction, since it restores the idea of the author as a figure actively engaged in social practices with others rather than a remote aesthetic concept.

Robert Hodge gives a fairly comprehensive account of the notion of literature as 'social semiotic' in *Literature as Discourse: Textual Strategies in Literature and History*. Despite the title, the work is mainly concerned with the application of the terms 'syntagm' and 'paradigm' to various genres of literature in order to demonstrate the social significance of the authors' stylistic choices. It is clearly demonstrated that if these two concepts are applied to literary studies then the concept of the social category from which each significant choice is taken, and its combination with other such chosen items, does reveal a great deal about the underlying structures of fiction. Hodge's theory, however, is so heavily weighted towards the social determinants of meaning that he appears to belong to the now rather dated structuralist theory which overlooks the author. Although this is at times an exciting way of codifying textual differences, Hodge often resorts to unsupported critical observations rather than justifying each assumption through his own methodology. Is it fair to argue that Virginia Woolf cannot distinguish herself from her created characters in *The Waves* and that this is therefore a symptom of schizophrenia? Clearly the author's role needs to be seen in the kind of social contexts which Hodge so ingeniously brings to light.

Several studies this year make efforts to situate fiction in its historical context in rather more conventional ways. One such example is William J. Scheick's *Fictional Structure and Ethics: The Turn-of the Century English Novel*. Scheick's project is twofold: rescue from neglect of those writers grouped by Woolf as Materialists, and promotion of a theoretical position correlating fictional structure and ethical concerns. Structure is conceived largely in architectural and geometric terms, while ethics is more or less restricted to the distinction of Christian–humanist and Schopenhauerian compassion. Circumventing definitional problems, and adopting a stance primarily derived from reader-response criticism, Scheick argues for positive reappraisal of the artistry of fiction that gives priority to structure in its dialectical relation to characterization. The surprise inclusion of Nabokov, as a contemporary writer indebted to Stevenson, Wells, and Chesterton, follows the contention that our anxieties and crises in ethics parallel those of a century ago, and implies that the ethical concerns latent in the practice of some current writers invite development of criticism responsive to issues of communal value.

Josephine M. Guy's *The British Avant-Garde: The Theory and Politics of Tradition* seeks to establish avant-garde credentials for three nineteenth-century writers (Walter Pater, William Morris and Oscar Wilde), linking contemporary accusations of obscurity to their calculated use of tradition as means to progressive ends. A preliminary discussion of avant-gardism, assessing the formalist definition offered by Renato Poggioli and Peter Bürger's political definition, prepares for examination of specific intellectual conditions for avant-garde activity which, Guy insists, should not be regarded as transcultural or transhistorical. The book implicitly raises important issues relating to the development of the concept in the twentieth century, including the vexed question of the usefulness of the very term 'avant-garde'.

Some difficulties of the historical approach are evident in Frank Field's *British and French Writers of the First World War: Comparative Studies in Cultural History*. Field presents these studies as a contribution to interdisciplinary liaison between historians and literary historians. In fact, they are attempts to locate 'literary personalities' within the matrix of political history, introductions neither to new material, nor to unfamiliar methods. The British writers – Brooke, Wells, Shaw, Kipling, Lawrence, Rosenberg, and Owen – are considered from a biographical point of view, rather than through sustained analysis of their work. When Field enters the literary critical arena, it is to contest (unwisely) Paul Fussell's evaluation of *Gravity's Rainbow*. The comparative element of the work scarcely proceeds beyond obvious circumstantial differences. The summaries here may be a useful resource for historians, and to that extent Field may have advanced toward his objective.

Orwell and Huxley's anti-utopias are set in a literary and political context by John Hoyles in *The Literary Underground: Writers and the Totalitarian Experience 1900–1950*. Rousseau is regarded as a precursor of the anti-utopian genre in that he first articulated a political position which can be manipulated towards libertarian or totalitarian politics. The submergence of the individual in an allegiance to the general will may either liberate or subjugate, and it is argued that the dystopian concentration on rebellious individuals explores this crucial political tension. Zamyatin's *We*, however, is preferred to the anti-utopias of Orwell and Huxley, since Zamyatin is able to enlist surrealism in defence of individual freedom. Orwell believed that Huxley had learned from Zamyatin the 'intuitive grasp of the irrational side of totalitarianism' although Zamyatin was clearly the superior writer in his development of this aspect. The result of this broadly European approach to the literature of totalitarianism is that Orwell's contribution is rather easily dismissed, yet this is an exciting and very contemporary account of literature and politics.

The view that modernist writers may have been heavily influenced by their attitudes towards late nineteenth- and early twentieth-century psychology is a relatively new and very helpful way of distinguishing between varieties of modernism. Judith Ryan, in *The Vanishing Subject: Early Psychology and Literary Modernism*, takes a by now familiar phenomenon but accounts for the dissolution of the self in a lucid and persuasive way. The book arranges the study of a wide selection of European writers into four categories: those who adopted the view that the self is no more than a collection of sense-experiences; those who identified consciousness with a particular perceptual field; those who strove to discover 'new ways of consolidating the self'; and those who attempted to establish a new kind of mysticism on the basis of observable facts alone. James Joyce is located in the third category and Stephen Dedalus is argued to place great emphasis on the moral vision which focuses the sense of self in an epiphany. Joyce's responses to the loss of self were varied, whereas Virginia Woolf reflected the 'damned egotistical self' he proclaimed. Woolf is thought to blend empiricism, impressionism and psychoanalysis to alternate between the unbounded world of empiricism and the narrower definitions of personal psychology. Whether the characters in *The Waves* are different or all manifestations of one consciousness is seen as a problem with which Woolf was deliberately engaging. Judith Ryan's book is a very substantial account of a neglected element of modernism.

If it has become something of a critical cliché to speak of modernism in terms of a rapprochement between internal and external through novel literary forms, Michael Levenson produces a rather more sophisticated account of the phenomenon in *Modernism and the Fate of Individuality: Character and Novelistic Form from Conrad to Woolf.* In his discussion of *Heart of Darkness*, for example, the author coins the expression 'the beyond within' to describe the situation where the character of Kurtz is discovered not by introspection, but by his journey to the very periphery of social reality. Here his anthropological discoveries say far more about himself than about the people he encounters and observes. We are accustomed to hearing about the disintegration of the modernist self, but this work approaches the topic in a highly original manner and argues that although the self and society are inextricably involved, there is the opportunity in the fractured and schismatic reality of the modernist self to achieve a small degree of autonomy. Novels such as *Howards End* may literally show the final triumph of history and society over the individual, yet the characters strive to occupy a remote location where their values may survive and flourish. This is an extremely perceptive approach to the central issues of modernism which also succeeds in challenging critical opinion on Conrad, Forster, Wyndham Lewis, Lawrence, Joyce and Woolf whilst elaborating its original position.

In a more contemporary vein, the biographical information on the cover of Robert Giddings's *The Author, the Book and the Reader* informs us that he is one of the increasing number of academics who are involved in teaching literature and media studies nowadays. Giddings is, however, a harsh critic of media studies on the grounds that it has failed to appreciate the historical developments which have meant that what is said in literary contexts depends very much on the technological means available to say it. The book spends a considerable amount of time describing the earlier history of this relationship and culminates in a chapter on Le Carré as an insight into the twentieth century. Here, the author rightly insists that the dominance of sociological media studies has tended to mean that the focus of attention is on establishing the rather deterministic links between society, the media and culture. With respect to Le Carré, Giddings tries to show how a skilful use of the techniques of the cinema enables the writer to achieve new literary effects.

In *Contingent Meanings: Postmodern Fiction, Mimesis, and the Reader,* Jerry Varsava argues that postmodern fiction has been misrepresented, by both its champions and its detractors, as literature separated from life. In his attempt to redress such misrepresentation, the terms for classification of such fiction are left vague, while his overview of its critical reception is highly selective and stylized in service of his polemic. From a broadly phenomenological theoretical basis, 'case studies' are presented to advance claims for a 'significant' mimetic practice of real world referentiality in contemporary writing. Authors primarily addressed are Walter Abish, Robert Coover, Gilbert Sorrentino and Peter Handke. No British fiction is used.

Two studies this year take a rather broader approach to the history of literature by dealing with visual arts as well. George H. Gilpin's *The Art of Contemporary English Culture* eschews the approach of the cultural historian and opts instead to examine a number of 'landmarks' in postwar culture which the author believes will 'delineate the postwar culture as it has been conceived creatively'. The highly eclectic approach ranges over all the arts including sculpture, architecture and painting, yet does not appear to offer any ultimate picture of contemporary art or its representations. Despite the disavowal, historical generalizations abound, and it is very difficult to see how any strongly-inspired personal perceptions sustain a narrative impetus. There is much exposition of the plot of some rather dated fiction from Orwell, Graham Greene and Robert Graves, and some tantalizing remarks, such as the reference to 'ontological insecurity' as a theme for postwar fiction are, unfortunately, not developed. Perhaps the most original contribution here is contained in the two chapters which link Doris Lessing and John Fowles with the epic tradition, yet the severely restricted choice of *The Golden Notebook* and *Daniel Martin* does little to justify the claim to cast an entirely new light on contemporary culture.

British Romantic Art and the Second World War by Stuart Sillars is mainly concerned with the continuity between the high Romanticism of painters such as Turner and artists of the war period, but it also draws on contemporary fiction to substantiate this thesis. The Romantic realism of painting is argued to be a way of confronting the cruel realities of wartime by asserting the primacy of individual experience. There are brief references to writers such as H. E. Bates and editors of Penguin New Writing, which argue that they too show the same kind of psychological involvement with the experience of individuals as can be found in the more socially-conscious Romantic poets. Graham Greene's *The Ministry of Fear* is considered at greater length and its origins in Wordsworthian thought are clearly shown. The book as a whole brings an impressively broad range of cultural allusions into play and ultimately argues convincingly that the success of Romantic art forms in this period lay in fashioning ideals and keeping them alive.

The importance of historical context is also evident in some new studies of literature and colonialism. Paul Hyland and Neil Sammells have edited a broad range of work on Irish literature from the eighteenth century to today in *Irish Writing: Exile and Subversion.* There are three essays of relevance to twentieth-century fiction: Bonnie Kime Scott's 'James Joyce: a Subversive Geography of Gender', Keith Williams's 'Joyce's Chinese Alphabet: *Ulysses* and the Proletarians', and David Seed's 'Parables of Estrangement: the fiction of S. P. Donleavy'.

Scott's article observes the significance for both male and female characters of the journeys depicted in *Dubliners* and argues that the delicate balance of Stephen Dedalus's soul can be seen in terms of his own travelling. Keith Williams defends Joyce against the stern Socialist Realists who maintained that his modernist texts estranged him from the struggles of workers, and shows how some proletarian writers assimilated Joyce's techniques. David Seed gives a polished account of Donleavy's fiction, taking particular care to show how alienation is a recurrent feature of his central characters and contributing to the editors' claim that for the Irish, exile had been what captivity was for the Jews.

Orwell is praised in Joseph Bristow's *Empire Boys: Adventures in a Man's World* for recognizing that the notion of what it meant to be a man was derived from imperialist and supremacist ideologies which had arisen in the nineteenth century. Although this study is largely concerned with the nineteenth century's representations of men and homoerotic desire in popular fiction, the argument does lead to the conclusion that *Heart of Darkness* also shows that, for Marlow, to understand Kurtz is 'to know what manhood means'. The value of this work lies particularly in the way it is able to demonstrate where the foundations were laid for many contemporary attitudes in popular fiction.

D. C. R. A Goonetilleke also writes on 'Joseph Conrad and Imperialism in Africa' in Robert Giddings's collection, *Literature and Imperialism.* This is a very even-handed treatment of *Heart of Darkness* in which the author reminds us that Conrad regarded imperialism as 'the vilest scramble for loot'. Goonetilleke questions some of the more casual attempts to identify Conrad with his narrator, and argues that 'an idealization of imperialism is an attempt to justify an element of inhumanity common to both civilised and primitive societies.'

It should be noted, however, that James Snead is commemorated in *Critical Quarterly,* and the edition includes one of his most provocative essays, 'Racist Traces in Postmodernist Theory and Literature' (*CritQ* 33:i.31–9). The essay condemns the neglect of issues of race in the famous theorists such as Barthes and Derrida and suggests that their theories lead to a reintroduction of racist categories and binary oppositions such as primitive/civilized.

Seamus Deane's introduction to three essays by Terry Eagleton, Fredric Jameson and Edward Said, *Nationalism, Colonialism and Literature,* makes it clear that to the Field Day Theatre Company the political crisis in Northern Ireland is, above all, a colonial crisis. These three essays have all been published previously as pamphlets, but together they provide a powerful insight into the literary ramifications of colonialism. Eagleton's essay, 'Nationalism, Irony and Commitment', exposes some of the theoretical dilemmas created by nationalist feeling and relates them to Joyce's *Ulysses.* Just as women may want to transcend the categories of gender and become fulfilled human beings, yet can only identify their oppression by speaking of themselves as women, so, too, nationalists must work with the very cultural identities they seek to throw off. Eagleton therefore argues that irony becomes a necessary condition of discourse resistant to colonialism. Jameson discusses both Joyce and E. M. Forster in his essay, 'Modernism and Imperialism'. The modernist aesthetic is related to the problem of acquiring knowledge of a vast colonial empire from a relatively enclosed society such as Ireland: 'The form of *Ulysses* is indeed in one sense an aesthetic resolution of historical contradictions.'

In *Border Traffic: Strategies of Contemporary Women Writers,* Maggie Humm discusses the work of women writers as an act of transgression which deliberately breaks through, exceeds and disrupts the existing boundaries of fictional genres in order to find a voice on the margins of recognized forms. Thus, Jean Rhys in *The Wide Sargasso Sea,* for example, resists the classic structure of the colonial romance, whereby the white male both conquers a country and a woman, by refusing to operate within conventional geography and linear time. It is by such tactics that women writers achieve a literary style which subverts the essentialist notions of the feminine which seem to be intrinsic to classical genres. In her work on Jean Rhys, Adrienne Rich, Margaret Atwood, Zora Neale Hurston and feminist detective fiction, Maggie Humm also draws on the cultural implications of the stances taken by women writers and is especially acute on the precise relationship between literary form and ideology in their writing. This is a superb complement to other work on women writers, such as Avril Horner and Sue Zlosnik's *Landscapes of Desire: Metaphors in Modern Women's Fiction* (1990) although the word 'contemporary' in the title is not perhaps as accurate as it might be.

In contrast, Bridget Fowler's *The Alienated Reader: Women and Popular Romantic Literature in the Twentieth Century* defends the escapist tendencies of the romance genre by carefully determining the ideological function of popular literature in contemporary women's lives. Her sociological analysis of popular women's fiction deals with its production, content and reception in a highly readable style which neatly summarizes contemporary sociological theory. Rather than arguing that women readers are capable of reading such texts against the grain, Fowler uses Ernst Bloch's *The Principle of Hope* to defend the literary escapism of the genre as a means of envisioning the social alternatives represented by utopian thinking.

In her account of *First Love: The Affections of Modern Fiction,* Maria DiBattista defends the idealizing tendency of first love. In fiction it often discloses to the lover the 'image of his own longing'. The male pronoun is significant here, since DiBattista chooses to write only about male authors: Joyce, Lawrence, Hardy and Beckett in the main. Her reason for doing so is that these writers exhibit the tendency to narcissism inherent in this concept of first love as self-projection, yet she does not engage with the issues raised by this phenomenon.

Although Laurie Langbauer's *Women and Romance: The Consolations of Gender in the English Novel* dwells mainly on the pre-twentieth-century novel, with only occasional references to authors such as Arnold Bennett, the theoretical approach it advances suggests further implications for the study of the novel as such. The thesis is that romance is the 'other' of the novel proper and is therefore offered as a consolation to women in particular, yet the dominant novel form frequently resorts to the genre from which it attempts to distinguish itself. Langbauer sees this feature as a clear weakness in the male-dominated system of literary categories, yet one which masquerades as a strength.

Lynne Hanley's *Writing War: Fiction, Gender and Memory* sets out to describe some of the ways in which men have reconstructed rather glamorous images of warfare in their writing and women writers have adopted approaches which counteract this tendency. After a rather facile attack on the limitations of Paul Fussell's *The Great War and Modern Memory,* the author contrasts the male view of the battlefield with women's views as expressed by Virginia Woolf, Jean Rhys, Doris Lessing and Joan Didion. The emphasis, however, is on issues such as the struggles of women at Oxbridge colleges, although there is comment on the changing relationships between men and women as war drives out passion. On the whole, the remarks gathered here suffer from a lack of historical perspective which would enable the reader to identify a women's counter-tradition in war writing.

In her article 'Feminist Fiction and the Uses of Memory' (*Signs* 12.290–322), Gayle Green discusses the feminist writings of the seventies and highlights the importance of memory as 'a means of connecting past and present and constructing a self and versions of experience we can live with'. The author deals particularly with the process by which feminist metafiction in writers such as Toni Morrison, Margaret Atwood, Doris Lessing and Margaret Drabble may interrogate the processes of memory (during this decade), but has largely lapsed in recent times into a less radical stance.

Detective fiction seems to hold a permanent fascination for all literary writers, partly, perhaps, because the source of its appeal can be very difficult to determine. Marion Shaw and Sabine Vanacker have written an extremely concise and acute explanation of one kind of detective story in *Reflecting on Miss Marple.* The authors set out to account for the enormous popularity of Agatha Christie's detective when she is a representative of the world of humble domesticity. The reason given is that, in addition to the usual satisfaction of detective fiction in which a world of clear moral certainties is re-established, Miss Marple acts as a foil to the absurdities practised by men. In their discussion of the novels, the authors reveal how threatening the female detective can be and how she reveals the intelligence which might otherwise easily be ignored in such a woman. The influence of this tradition on contemporary women detective fiction writers is also traced.

According to Alistair Fowler, the W. P. Ker lecture which Frank Kermode gave in 1972 is a starting-point for the study of detective fiction. Fowler could be accused of over-stating his indebtedness to Kermode on this occasion, but this essay is included in a collection edited by Margaret Tudeau-Clayton and Martin Warner entitled *Addressing Frank Kermode: Essays in Criticism and Interpretation.* Fowler's essay 'Sherlock Holmes and *The Adventure of the Dancing Men and Women*', is included in the second half of the book where various critics illustrate their admiration for Kermode by pursuing lines of enquiry his work has suggested to them. This piece of work, although very competent, argues only that the reader's hermeneutic task parallels that of the detective work in the story, yet Conan Doyle's story is not as closed as the work of Poe on which he relies.

Richard Poirier elaborates on Kermode's equation of Joyce's epiphany with Pater's 'vision' in *Romantic Image.* Pater's role as a precursor of literary modernism is convincingly made to seem much more influential than is generally thought. In particular, the point is well made that infantile experience is also mediated by language and that the adult artist merely recognizes that this is the case and repeats the process. On the whole, these are stimulating essays, although there is a certain uneasiness about the tone to adopt when criticizing a literary academic of Kermode's reputation.

David Trottor proposes a welcome new perspective on the detective story in 'Theory and Detective Fiction' (*CritQ* 33:ii.66–77). He argues against prevailing notions that the detective story is concerned with the unmasking of desire through the interpretation of signs, and shows instead that many detective fictions can be read in terms of Julia Kristeva's concept of abjection, or the violent rejection of that which disgusts us.

In the same journal, John Sutherland details the deceitful and sometimes exploitative use of sexual imagery by publishers in his study of 'Fiction and the Erotic Cover' (*CritQ* 33:ii.3–18). The commercial pressures which brought about this practice are clearly exposed.

A sense of outrage at the rather homophobic tone of many so-called scholarly studies of writing by lesbians and gay men was the inspiration for *Lesbian and Gay Writing* edited by Mark Lilly. The editor's aim is to promote a series of studies of this body of writing which, for once, reflect the gay views of the community itself. There are essays on Ivy Compton-Burnett, Maureen Duffy, Ann Bannon and fifties writing by lesbians, erotic material for gay men, and Ronald Firbank. The collection convincingly asserts the value of these writers and gives a very informative account of the problems of writing as a gay man or lesbian. The place of writing in the process of developing and asserting an independent gender identity is also revealed. On the whole, the collection justifies the editor's assertion that lesbian and gay critics can highlight issues which might otherwise be ignored.

(b) Individual Authors: 1900–45

Work on G. K. Chesterton appears only sporadically these days, so a new introductory book is worthy of note. But Ian Crowther's *Thinkers of Our Time: G. K. Chesterton* has far too little detachment from the frame of mind of his subject to be a book which will encourage readers to turn to Chesterton's texts themselves. Unrepentantly (though not fashionably) conservative, Crowther spends a hundred pages reproducing and assenting to Chestertonian doctrine, probably shedding readers all the way (one section makes a serious case for Catholicism as the one true religion, for instance). There is no preparedness to engage with Chesterton or to contest even some of his arguments. Such proselytism is unlikely to be successful. After an introduction like this, would anyone actually want to meet G. K.?

There has in much of the work on Joseph Conrad been a perceptible turn against Samuel Hynes's belief that 'a half-page of note paper would contain all the ideas he had'. Richard Ambrosini notes and counters this judgement at length in his *Conrad's Fiction as Critical Discourse*. Ambrosini does all critics a service in pointing out how they value the explicit critical frameworks established by authors themselves in both fictional and conceptual texts rather differently from author to author, this usually depending on mere fashion or personal preference: if one compares the credibility given by many critics to, say, Lawrence's utterances on his own writing, with the widespread neglect of what Conrad has to say about his, it is clear that Ambrosini has a point. His excellent book is an attempt to read Conrad's work as a 'critical discourse' in and about itself.

According to Otto Bohlmann, in *Conrad's Existentialism*, 'It certainly does not require a radical new reading of the novels to find them replete with ideas, attitudes and even phrases redolent of existential texts, which centre on the view that every individual must bear ultimate responsibility for his free actions amid an indifferent world into which chance has thrown him without any guide to absolute conduct.' Adopting a self-confessedly liberal humanist stance, Bohlmann goes on to read Conrad for his 'affinities' with German existentialists and with Kierkegaard, avoiding 'neologistic jargon and "critspeak" as far as possible'. But Bohlmann cannot avoid existential terminology and it is mainly this which, in an otherwise engrossing volume, will cause difficulty for readers. No matter how careful Bohlmann's exposition, Sartrean, Buberian and Heideggerian vocabularies are simply too jagged to sit them comfortably on a waterbed of liberal humanist lit. crit. discourse.

Another attempt to read Conrad as a novelist of ideas is Daphna Erdinast-Vulcan's *Joseph Conrad and the Modern Temper*, which undertakes to 'deconstruct' Conrad, not by means of deconstruction itself, but in the light of Bakhtinian centripetal/centrifugal vectors and their related aesthetic discontinuities. The refusal of deconstruction is apparently made on account of Conrad's own didacticism, prosecuted even in the face of his own self-undermining tendencies. This rationale is not convincing, nor is the more particular thesis that Conrad's general project can be characterized as an attempt to reinstate a Ptolemaic system in a Copernican universe (we forget, perhaps, that Conrad's writing life ended in what might be called the Heisenbergian/Einsteinian era). An even more puzzling feature of this monograph is that, as a result of its welcome emphasis on the fissures and cracks in Conrad's texts, it does not deal with *The Secret Agent* at all because 'these fault lines are not evident

… precisely because it is so technically flawless'. It is not Bakhtinian or deconstructive voices that could speak thus. This aside, Erdinast-Vulcan has produced a thoughtful as well as readable survey of a wide range of Conrad texts.

On the article front, M. C. Benassis asks, 'Where is Costaguana?' (*Conradiana* 23.203–15). Christopher GoGwilt's 'The Charm of Empire: Joseph Conrad's "Karain: A Memory"' (*Mosaic* 24.77–91) looks at Conrad's short story and concludes that it helps us to understand how 'the crisis of modernity is not only a crisis of Western culture. It is a crisis that produces, in reaction, the *idea* of Western culture.' Darrell Mansell's 'Trying to Bring Literature Back Alive: The Ivory in Joseph Conrad's *Heart of Darkness*' (*Criticism* 33.205–15) is a quirky and enjoyable semiotic investigation into the meaning of ivory in the novel (e.g. 'the whiteness of bones and ivory is the potentiality of literature – the whiteness of the blank page'). *Heart of Darkness* is seen as a text which Conrad 'could not get out of the mental jungle'. The political ambiguities of *Heart of Darkness* and *Nostromo* and their relationship to Nietzsche are probed by Graham Bradshaw in 'Mythos, Ethos, and the Heart of Conrad Darkness' (*ES* 72.160–72).

Less impressively, Zohreh T. Sullivan offers a couple of pages explaining how she has taught *Heart of Darkness* to undergraduates in 'Theory for the Untheoretical: Rereading and Reteaching Austen, Brontë, and Conrad' (*CE* 53.571–9). Are students actually so 'untheoretical' anyway, one is tempted to ask? We are told that students' early problems of resistance to and incomprehension of Conrad's text lead them in Sullivan's class 'to an initial discussion of perception, representation and constructions of reality, to a digression on impressionism, on Conrad's declared problems with epistemology, on the implications of Conrad's use of impressionism' and more. Here, a high degree of tutor-directedness is concealed: the students are led, seemingly not by the tutor, but apparently by their own problems as readers, to a series of 'digressions' that look paradoxically tutor-designed. Like many assured accounts of active pedagogy, this one is too smooth to be convincing and too general to be of any real practical use to other teachers. It is less unwittingly daft, however, than L. R. Leavis's 'Joseph Conrad and Creative Integrity' (*ES* 72.28–37), which roundly attacks 'modernising' readings and the process whereby 'the endless shifting of the academic sands of our day' have silted over the real Conrad. And what is the real Conrad? He is an author whose 'highly-civilised understanding of pathos and his natural strength of integrity never allow human reality to be undermined. In Conrad's great art the dramatic poetry of the substantiality of the human condition shines out with the unmistakable power of genius.' There is no explanation as to what all of this rebarbative jargon ('human reality'?; 'dramatic poetry of the substantiality of the human condition'?) means.

Returning to books, the decidedly mixed bag of 'new readings' that appears every year is enlarged by Ruth Nadelhaft's *Joseph Conrad*. It is not the 'obviously' feminist reading one might expect (that is, from the start, it does not present itself as an ideological critique of Conrad). Rather, Nadelhaft wants to run against the grain of the kind of feminist criticism 'which generally does not allow for much critical approval of male authors as they choose to portray female characters' and cannot account, except in rather questionable terms, for the experience of female readers who take pleasure in such authors. This is ambitious, but the problem resides in Nadelhaft's decision to try to account for too much of Conrad's work in too little scope. To scrutiny of *Nostromo*, for instance, only half a dozen pages are really devoted, and one suspects that a wider or deeper analysis could not have produced such a relatively anodyne picture of the function of female characters in that novel. The same might be said of

Nadelhaft's dealings with *The Secret Agent*, which are even more bitty. On the whole, this is a book which suggests new lines of thought on Conrad rather than pursuing them.

Despite its shortcomings, Jeffrey Meyers would have done well to read Nadelhaft's book before going to press with his *Joseph Conrad: A Biography*. His foreword gives an immediate air of protesting too much. Aware that 'Conrad's life and works have been intensively examined', he feels the need to provide a summary list of those matters about which 'my own research and the use of unpublished material has revealed new information'. The items on the list are almost all minor and prompt one to wonder if a volume of more than four hundred pages was really required for their presentation. Why not simply a detailed journal article on Meyers's biographical discoveries, such as the chunk of the book he reproduces in 'Conrad's Examinations for the British Merchant Service' (*Conradiana* 23.123–32), or like M. J. Mclendon's 'Conrad and Calomel: An Explanation of Conrad's Mercurial Nature' (*Conradiana* 23.151–6)? The solution to the puzzle emerges on reading further, for this is essentially a trade biography masquerading as an academic one. Meyers is only too willing to magnify his original research using unpublished material because he has conducted very little. He frequently quotes second-handedly and, more frustratingly, when he does quote what seems to be fresh material he often fails to reference it adequately or at all. The bibliography from which a great deal of this life is largely rehashed is itself a distressingly thin one of only twenty-seven items, and the whole is hardly redeemed by Meyers's blundering style (he spends eleven pages paraphrasing the narrative of *Victory*, for example) and, on occasion, sheer nastiness. As an instance of the latter, take his totally hostile attitude towards Conrad's wife, Jessie. Meyers evidently believes that a biographer's own prejudices with regard to human morphology ought to be stated, hence his appalled description of her as 'grotesquely obese'. The fact that an immobilizing disability exacerbated Jessie's weight problem is grudgingly acknowledged, but does not prevent Meyers from repeating this misogynous slight. The worst thing about this kind of contempt is the consequent lack of real interest in Jessie which it betrays, and Meyers thus fails wholly to illuminate what remains a deeply enigmatic marriage. By contrast, he is positively electrified by thoughts of the 'strikingly handsome' Jane Anderson, the American journalist with whom (Meyers claims) Conrad had an affair in 1916. Indeed, his textual treatment of her is almost obsessive. Not only is an entire chapter given her name, but one lengthy appendix records details of her life after her relationship with Conrad ceased, another relates Meyers's own 'Quest for Jane Anderson' or, more accurately, for information about her, and, to cap it all, a separate bibliography is devoted to her which has nearly four times as many items as that listing Meyers's reading on Conrad himself! (Those seeking a more balanced treatment of Anderson should consult Halverson and Watt's 'Notes on Jane Anderson' in *Conradiana* 23.59–87.) As all of this suggests, Meyers is largely interested in producing a book about Conrad that is sufficiently differentiated from other biographies to ensure a sale. The fact that a great deal of what differentiates it has nothing to do with Conrad does not seem to have deterred him.

Jeffrey Meyers's dealings with Conrad (see above) largely repeat the vices of his lamentable handling of D. H. Lawrence in a biography published in 1990, and it is a relief to note the antidote to this kind of performance in John Worthen's *D. H. Lawrence: The Early Years: 1885–1912*. This is the first of a unique three-volume project, the forthcoming instalments being authored separately by David Ellis and Mark Kinkead-Weekes. The need for a new biography, written in the light of the emerging Cambridge edition of Lawrence's texts and especially his letters, has been clear for some time, although one wishes that the supply for this demand were being offered by a publisher other than CUP, whose interest in Lawrence is increasingly coming to look like the strategy of a corporate monopoly. While there are some issues (for example, Lawrence's relations with the Hopkins, and the political organization of Lawrence's community) with which he could have dealt more adequately, the general excellence of Worthen's particular contribution can hardly be in doubt. He has cast his net much more widely than previous biographers, especially in his investigation of Lawrence's antecedents. He constantly explodes key myths, often produced by Lawrence himself (his mother, we are shown, was working class; his clandestine trip to Europe with Frieda Weekley in 1912 was hardly an elopement). Worthen is careful about his use of fiction as a source for biography, particularly with regard to that trap for the unwary, *Sons and Lovers*. He demonstrates cautiously how Paul Morel may be said to be an autobiographical *representation*, which is quite different from seeing him as a fictional Lawrence. What also comes across strongly – this is perhaps Worthen's real achievement – is the besetting sense of pain, sadness and struggle in Lawrence's early years, and the ways in which his developing sexuality and his complex class situation are seen not as separate but as related matters. If the remaining two volumes of the Cambridge Biography attain this standard, the whole is likely to form the standard reference for Lawrence's life.

The Cambridge edition of the letters itself proceeds with *The Letters of D. H. Lawrence: Volume VI: March 1927–November 1928*, the penultimate volume of letters proper in the series (not received). Some indication of the influence of the editorial conventions of the edition can be gained by pointing to their adoption by Michael Squires in his editorship of *D. H. Lawrence's Manuscripts: The Correspondence of Frieda Lawrence, Jake Zeitlin and Others*. Compared to the Cambridge *Letters*, this is a curious publication, somewhat lacking in resonance: *Hamlet* without the Prince of Denmark. It reproduces over three hundred items of correspondence between Frieda Lawrence and various (but not all) parties interested in Lawrence's manuscripts subsequent to his death, and between those parties themselves. If these letters will be of great moment to a narrow group of bibliophiles, they have also various kinds of interest of which the editor seems unaware. The idea that Frieda von Richthofen-Weekley-Lawrence-Ravagli is herself of any intellectual significance, apart from her connection with Lawrence, is an illusion which far too many Lawrence scholars have been willing to entertain. A more sceptical commentator than Squires might register the irony of Lawrence's manuscripts making much more for Frieda than his writing did for himself, and of how a notably work-shy widow was thereby able to sustain herself and a new spouse in employmentless comfort for over twenty years. Whether or not one is prepared to be so disrespectful, there is plenty in this volume to show how Frieda was a major player in a shrewd game in which Lawrence became a mere commodity, entrammelled in the wheels of exchange in a fashion whose implications the contemporary Lawrence industry is only too eager to ignore. After all, Squires's own edition is an example of how Lawrence's name has become a marketing imprimatur, endorsing even those textual products from which his writing itself is completely absent. We perhaps ought not to mention that the title is, to be accurate, a misnomer. These letters do not tell the story of the distribution of Lawrence's manuscripts, but only that of some of them. One finds little more than a line or two here, for example, on the growth of substantial public and private collections in the United Kingdom.

Nigel Kelsey's *D. H. Lawrence: Sexual Crisis* has, regrettably, all the shortcomings – it is underpunctuated, overitalicized, misspells proper names, and is frequently plain confused – of a doctoral thesis hastily adapted for book publication. Fundamentally, Kelsey's choice of Lawrence as the practical object of a theoretical exercise is baffling, for he seems to be uninterested in most of his work, offers no bibliography to indicate wider reading beyond cited texts, and appears entirely ignorant of recent textual scholarship. The approach itself uses a combination of structuralisms (feminist, Foucauldian, Bakhtinian, Barthesian), Kelsey stressing the need for 'dialogue' between theories which are broadly in alliance. This is well said, but it is difficult to concede authority to the particularly breathless, strident and often ungrammatical prose in which it is (or fails to be) explained. Concerns about the general direction of this study are not allayed by a subsequent chapter in which four Lawrence critics, chosen seemingly at random, are scrutinized in order that the limitations of theoretical enclosure be exposed. One is therefore seventy pages into a fairly slim volume before one encounters comment on a Lawrence text, and the shock then is to find that only the three 'big' novels are discussed. 'It could be argued that *Sons and Lovers* is a horror novel' is, nonetheless, an attention-grabbing way to open a criticism of that text. It is, however, a pity that the following analysis (the best in the volume) has absolutely nothing to do with reading *Sons and Lovers* as 'horror'. This is somewhat typical of the whole enterprise.

In the same series, but at the other end of the theoretical tunnel, is Michael Black's *D. H. Lawrence: The Early Philosophical Works: A Commentary*. The difficulty with this study is again quite fundamental, in that it accords the status of philosophy to a group of Lawrencean textual oddities (such as *Study of Thomas Hardy, The Crown,* and *Twilight in Italy*) in a manner that no philosopher would countenance. (The same might be said, incidentally, of Pamela A. Rooks, who in 'D. H. Lawrence's "Individual" and Michael Polanyi's "Personal": Fruitful Redefinitions of Subjectivity and Objectivity' (*DHLR* 23.21–9) designates herself as a 'scholar who considers Lawrence a serious and provocative thinker'.) Black is under the impression that, if one acknowledges the large scale 'idiosyncrasies' of these works, one is permitted to go ahead and commit this basic category error. One might reply that Hegel, say, is extremely idiosyncratic, but is nonetheless a philosopher. Lawrence had neither the training nor the intellectual habits to merit such an appellation: Middleton Murry specifically and rightly lamented his 'cursed hybrid intellectualism' of 1915–16. The result is that Black treats these texts far too ponderously, at excessive length, and without sufficient emphasis on their gross unreadability. Unsurprisingly, he also fails to embrace the term which many critics would now wish to use to describe the notion of a set of ideas which inform or determine creative work – not 'philosophy' or 'metaphysic', but *ideology*. Why the book should almost sink itself from the outset with an inappropriately Leavisite cargo is, on the other hand, a puzzle.

Peter Fjågesund, in *The Apocalyptic World of D. H. Lawrence*, is much less complicit with the author whose texts he is examining, and as a consequence produces an objective and stimulating study of the web of apocalyptic lore in which Lawrence entangled himself. He not only tracks this influence on Lawrence's thinking throughout his career, but persuasively accounts for it as a general social trend in which religious and secular elements are never easy to differentiate. If there is a weakness, it is that few Lawrence texts are given the prolonged attention that would *conclusively* demonstrate their indebtedness to this strand within modernism. But there are convincing compensations, largely stemming from the scholarliness of Fjågesund's approach. He is learned, for instance, about much European literature, and sensitive to its influence on Lawrence. He has carefully investigated much of Lawrence's known reading. Consequently, he has produced a study which will be of considerable value to those interested in the intellectual, political and historical dimensions of modernism generally, as well as those who have a more specialized concern with Lawrence.

Carol Sklenicka's *D. H. Lawrence and the Child* 'proposes that Lawrence made a significant, pivotal, and unrecognized contribution to literature's notion of what a child means and what it means to be a child', and does so with a great deal of critical acumen. Her main aim is to demonstrate that Lawrence offers a non-Freudian representation of childhood, to the extent that even *Sons and Lovers*, although predominantly Freudian, contains non-Freudian subtexts which are elaborated in later work. The main texts considered are *The Rainbow* and *Women in Love*, although Sklenicka does not answer the still powerful attack on the latter's dealings with reproduction launched by Raymond Williams in his *Modern Tragedy* (1966), which she does not seem to have read. Inevitably, Lawrence's 'psychoanalytic' works get more prominence than they deserve, but for some inexplicable reason (its embarrassingly fulsome recommendation of childbeating, perhaps?) *Education of the People*, although written in the same period, doesn't get a look in. On the whole, however, Sklenicka's book is treading relatively new ground, and ought to be welcomed.

Maria DiBattista devotes two chapters to Lawrence in her *First Love: The Affections of Modern Fiction*. This book analyses 'narratives of First Love', mainly in Hardy, Lawrence, Joyce and Beckett. Is the notion of such narratives any more than yet one more invented pseudo-genre with which to lasso together a bundle of really rather disparate essays? DiBattista would have us believe that they encapsulate a universal human experience: 'Everyone,' her book begins, '... remembers his or her first love'. Do they? If everybody does so, it's not quite clear why the fictional investigations of four male modern writers should command so much attention here. That seems an unnecessary limitation on the scrutiny of this psychological phenomenon. The main thesis is the dubious one that irony is not, as is often supposed, the dominant tone of modernist writing. DiBattista is herself frequently enthralled by the mythology of First Love whose construction she elsewhere dispassionately charts. There are numerous invocations to fashionable theorists – Foucault, Bakhtin, Lacan, Jameson – which would be fine if these figures actually agreed with DiBattista's assumptions. But they don't (and the praise of Barthes is especially ironic, given that its terms actually run counter to his aims). The Lawrence chapters concern *The Rainbow* and *Women in Love*, which DiBattista characterizes as 'beleaguered epics of modern life'.

Notwithstanding the weaknesses of these, they are a good deal more interesting than those in Keith Cushman and Dennis Jackson's edited anthology, *D. H. Lawrence's Literary Inheritors*, which contains essays on Lawrence's putative influence on Tennessee Williams, Peter Shaffer, Sherwood Anderson, Lawrence Durrell, Melvyn Bragg, Henry Miller, Norman Mailer, Eudora Welty, Margaret Drabble, Raymond Carver, Joyce Carol Oates, William Carlos Williams, W. H. Auden, Ted Hughes, and the Black Mountain poets. Like Jeffrey Meyers's edited collection, *The Legacy of D. H. Lawrence* (1987), of which it is an all-too similar echo, this anthology has been put together with no reference to any elaborated theory of 'literary influence' or, perhaps more surprisingly, any consideration of the relative importance of those authors (and half the world is claimed) whom Lawrence is said to have influenced. The fact that Lawrence's respective influences on W. H. Auden and Melvyn Bragg are seen as comparably significant is enough to illustrate the latter point. What emerges is little more than another rag bag of miscellaneous essays, all American in origin, whatever the anthology's claims to Anglo-American coverage, and of dubious quality.

Lawrence's verse remains so comparatively neglected that one looks with favour on virtually any work that has the potential to raise its currency. R. P. Draper's 'Ways of Speaking: The Poetry of D. H. Lawrence' (*JDHLS* (1991).7–15) is not going to do that, however. We need more than commonplaces about Lawrence's poetic range demonstrating his 'highly variegated mind' and an analytic technique of such banality that it can issue statements such as 'the voluptuously sinuous syntax [expresses] the poet's empathy with the snake'. Thérèse Vichy assumes that Lawrence's poetry can sustain more profound and prolonged attention than this, and her 'Lawrence's "Fish" ' (*JDHLS* (1991).17–26) is a salutary attempt to demonstrate that this is so: she notes and explores in particular the relation between the Lawrence poem and Rupert Brooke's 'The Fish'.

A. R. Atkins offers a careful reading of Lawrence's neglected second novel and his sense of his developing 'writerly' identity at the time of its composition in 'Recognising the "Stranger" in D. H. Lawrence's *The Trespasser*' (*CQ* 20.1–20). Earl G. Ingersoll in 'The Theme of Friendship and the Genesis of D. H. Lawrence's *Mr Noon*' (*DUJ* 83.69–74) is similarly concerned to explore the relations between the life and the work, in this respect illuminating both Lawrence's friendship with George Henry Neville and its textual manifestations in the recently published unfinished novel. Jack F. Stewart makes a fascinating 'interart comparison' of representations of miners in 'Primordial Affinities: Lawrence, Van Gogh and the Miners' (*Mosaic* 24.93–113). By comparison, it may be that somewhat formalist readings of isolated 'big' novels simply require more these days in the way of novelty value to excite me, but the same author's 'Dialectics of Knowing in *Women in Love*' (*TCL* 37.59–75), jargon-ridden in both critical and Lawrencean terms, is quite routine. Although Eric P. Levy's 'Lawrence's Psychology of Void and Centre in *Women in Love*' (*DHLR* 23.5–19) is much more readable, one cannot recommend it more strongly.

On a more sociological footing, Lawrence's varying fortunes in China are the subject of three striking and related articles published together: Xianzhi Liu, 'The Reception of D. H. Lawrence in China' (*DHLR* 23.37–42); Ming Dong Gu, 'D. H. Lawrence and the Chinese Reader' (*DHLR* 23.43–7); and Youcheng Jin, 'D. H. Lawrence Studies in China: A Checklist of Works By and About Him' (*DHLR* 23.47–50). These serve to remind us that the Lawrence industry is a global one, and that the assured authority of certain western readings can look very shaky under different cultural conditions. They also raise, although they do not explore, quite crucial questions as to who 'possesses' Lawrence. These are issues which one wishes to see opened up much more often. One of the merits of the *DHLR* is that it has been one of the few journals regularly prepared to do so.

This year has produced a handful of interesting articles on George Orwell. Peter Goodall makes a brief panoramic excursion across Orwell's *oeuvre* to map the treatment of 'Common Decency and the Common People in the Writing of George Orwell' (*DUJ* 83.75–83). Peter Davison, in 'George Orwell: Dates and Origins' (*Library* 13.137–50) illuminates matters such as Orwell's indebtedness to Villon, the dating of 'How the Poor Die' and 'Such, Such Were the Joys', Orwell's meeting with Joseph Czapski, and others which have arisen during the editing of Orwell's *Complete Works*. John Rodden, in 'Reputation, Canon-Formation, Pedagogy: George Orwell in the Classroom' (*CE* 53.503–30), extends theoretical debates regarding canon formation by attempting to chart the canonization of Orwell in a range of institutions, showing convincingly how such a process was a result of multiple and combined professional, educational and political choices made mainly in the fifties. He explains Orwell's curious status as a pillar of the 'low canon' (as opposed to the 'high canon', from which he is absent).

Valerie Meyers's *George Orwell*, by contrast, is a plod through each of his novels, and seems to issue from the assumption that Orwell is 'low canon' because most of his novels aren't much good. Certainly a book whose first sentence expresses the opinion that 'Orwell was primarily a journalist and essayist' is hardly likely to be inspiring about his fiction. The Orwell trajectory is seen in deeply traditional terms. 'Orwell's early novels are limited by their imitative forms and autobiographical bias', we are told, but once he discovered how to 'express political ideas in fiction' he was able to write 'two of the most powerful works of the century'. The possibility that Orwell's early novels are also full of political ideas does not seem to occur to Meyers, who seriously undervalues them. And why is it that 'historical background' must be trotted out to explicate *Animal Farm* but is not seen as having any potential for an understanding of, say, *Burmese Days*? The book ends with a fairly meaningless miscellaneous catalogue, almost a list, of Orwell's posthumous influences. As potted criticism, the book will perhaps pass. But that any undergraduate should prefer it to Raymond Williams's shorter, cheaper and vastly superior *Orwell*, reprinted in a new edition this year, is unimaginable. [M.D.]

This is the year Joyce's work went out of copyright, and there have been various paperback reprintings of his novels and other works by publishers such as Penguin and Minerva. The issue was discussed in the new periodical *James Joyce Annual* in the editor's introduction by Thomas F. Staley (2–6): he pointed out that 1991 was a year in which two issues unfamiliar to most Joyceans were prominent: the 1984 Gabler edition of *Ulysses* and textual editing, and copyright matters. Staley observes that the copyright status of that novel remains unclear.

Sydney Bolt's 1981 *A Preface to James Joyce* has also been reprinted in updated form; the sections on *Finnegans Wake* and Joyce's views on femininity have been expanded. What the latter addition does not mean is that much account has been taken of recent feminist criticism (the reader looks in vain in the index for Bonnie Kime Scott, Suzette Henke or Shari Benstock, and 'feminism' appears as 'feminism and fluidity'). Rather, Bolt comments sharply that the female characters in *Dubliners* are oppressed not as women, but as citizens of Dublin, and that Joyce's view of women being constitutionally unfit for philosophizing is clearly shown in 'Penelope'.

Kimberley J. Devlin's contribution to Joyce studies this year has been notable and compelling. Her *Wandering and Return in Finnegans Wake* uses Freud's notion of the uncanny as a way of analysing Joyce's construction of the *Wake* from his own earlier fictions. She has also written two inspiring essays on gender construction in Joyce's work: the first is 'Castration and its Discontents: A Lacanian Approach to *Ulysses*' (*JJQ* 27.117–44), a wide-ranging and engaging discussion of Lacan's rereading of Joan Riviere's influential essay on femininity as a costume, which Devlin extends to refer also to masculinity. This argument is backed up with scrupulous and lively use of detail from *Ulysses*.

Devlin's essay 'Pretending in "Penelope": Masquerade, Mimicry and Molly Bloom' (*Novel* 25.72–89) takes the issues raised above further in a discussion of Molly's persona in terms of acting: as a career and as a persona. Devlin suggests Molly foregrounds theatrically in order to undo the various roles which constitute femininity, many of which she tries on during the course of 'Penelope'. In this she practices mimicry, which ironizes, rather than masquerade, which acts out. In reply to those who suggest that Molly is trapped in Joyce's limited male imagination, Devlin claims that she is instead his 'self-conscious anatomy of feminine as well as masculine roles'.

Cheryl Herr briefly mentions Joycean attitudes to femininity in 'The Erotics of Irishness' (*CritI* 17.1–34). She raises the relation between Irish mind and Irish body, and says that Joyce became ever more acute in his writing on the 'social systematising of repression, compensatorily troped as immobility': from the paralysis of *Dubliners*, he moves back to Ireland as body, site of both birth and death, in *Finnegans Wake*. Ailbhe Smyth similarly uses Joyce as a touchstone in a more general piece (*FSt* 17.7–28), 'The Floozie in the Jacuzzi', on the statue of ALP erected in Dublin in 1987, 'a figure for the proliferating constructions of Irish womanhood'. Smyth, in an article mainly notable for its rather precious form of 'creative intertextual musing', links Irishness and womanhood, saying that both are constructed under 'overdetermined, subordinating negative signs'.

Daniel Mark Fogel, in *Covert Relations: James Joyce, Virginia Woolf and Henry James*, promisingly raises gender as a determinant in anxieties of literary influence, following 'that other Bloom, the notorious Harold's' infamously patriarchal theory, but then abandons this interest in sexual difference. He discusses the differing ways in which Woolf and Joyce reacted to an earlier writer who profoundly affected both: Woolf self-avowedly so (after reading *The Wings of the Dove* she noted, 'I felt ill for sometime afterwards'), Joyce barely mentioning his precursor except with irony (he referred to James' work as 'tea-slops'). It seems clear that such a difference must be at least partly due to gender, particularly as the anxiety of influence must necessarily affect a woman writer on more levels than a male one; but Fogel's final word is that an apolitical androgyny is the best approach, 'a recognition of the fluidity of sexual identity and therefore of the shifting ground men and women have in common'.

John Burton puts forward an alternative reading of 'Oxen of the Sun' in his article 'Obeying the Boss in "Oxen of the Sun" ' (*ELH* 58.442–68), suggesting that despite critical consensus otherwise, this episode of *Ulysses* is 'consistently endogenous': that is, changes in event determine changes in style. He notes that this episode is the hardest case in *Ulysses* to justify for those, like himself, who consider the text 'representational throughout'.

In his 'Demystifying the Power of the Given: The "Telemachus" Episode of *Ulysses*' (*TCL* 37.38–53), Trevor L. Williams describes how Joyce constructs Stephen's political status thematically, through conversation, and formally, through the structural representation of character and use of internal monologue. Also in *TCL* 37, Mark Ostreen turns his attention to *Dubliners* in his 'Serving Two Masters: Economics and Figures of Power in Joyce's "Grace" ' (76–92), an interesting exploration of the intersection of personal, political and religious economics in 'Grace'. Use is made of economic and geometric tropes to expose the collusion of British rule and Catholicism; Home Rule is Rome Rule with the British in power, Ostreen claims, and general grace, either financial (referring to the period of grace offered to debtors) or spiritual, is impossible in the situation of the story.

James Fairhall's chapter, '*Ulysses*, the Great War, and the Easter 1916 Uprising', in *Literature and War*, edited by David Bevan, interestingly traces echoes of the First World War and the Troubles which resound through *Ulysses*. Such echoes have a proleptic function, referring to events of 1914–22 on a day in 1904; but, as Fairhall points out, Joyce was composing the novel during the turbulent period ten years after it was set, and several chapters thus possess a double time-frame of then and now.

Fairhall also historicizes the story 'After the Race' from *Dubliners* (*JJQ* 29.387–98) in his article 'Big-Power Politics and Colonial Economics: The Gordon Bennett Cup Race and "After the Race" ', which he reads as Joyce's riposte to supporters of the race, including the *Irish Times*. The story suggests that Ireland is the (not unwilling) victim, not only of the British, but of the international community in general, with whom Ireland can hardly compete.

Volumes of Harvester's 'Critical Studies of Key Texts' have been published on

A Portrait of the Artist as a Young Man (David Seed) and *Ulysses* (David Fuller). Both works are useful and concise, offering summaries of critical trends and relatively up-to-date analyses of the text concerned. Seed's book on *Portrait* is rather more adventurous, using Bakhtinian and feminist critical practice to discuss the text; Fuller, while declaring a preference for Bakhtin over Colin MacCabe, spends most of the section on 'Penelope' detailing whether or not it is likely that Molly has been adulterous previous to her encounter with Blazes Boylan. In the Macmillan 'Language of Literature' series is Katie Wales's *The Language of James Joyce*, an oddly old-fashioned, though quite readable, discussion of this main protagonist of Joyce's works, which takes account of recent Bakhtinian, feminist and stylistic work. In the section on 'Penelope', however, Wales uses as a structuring device a refutation of the arguments of linguist Otto Jespersen, writing in the 1920s about women's inferior use of language construction: a case which surely hardly needs to be made.

Vincent J. Cheng and Timothy Martin's edited volume *Joyce in Context* (the proceedings of the 1989 Joyce Symposium) is a fine collection, including contributions from Denis Donoghue ('Is There a Case Against *Ulysses?*') arguing against Fredric Jameson's and Leo Bersani's objections to that novel; Bonnie Kime Scott ('Joyce and Michelet: Why Watch Molly Menstruate?'), who uses a reference to Jules Michelet in *Ulysses* as a way into discussion of Joyce's construction of femininity, and a Michelet-inspired theorizing of how the reader views Molly; and Dan Schiff ('James Joyce and Cartoons'), a professional cartoonist, who sets the record straight about Mutt and Jeff, Popeye and Olive Oyl, and Joyce's use of them.

Bernard Benstock's *Narrative Con/Texts in 'Ulysses'* is a collection of seven unconnected essays, written over a period of ten years, on the subject of how narrative functions in *Ulysses* in relation to its own changing internal context. Some of Benstock's individual readings are illuminating: in the introduction, he traces the non-linear 'retrospective rearrangements' of a phrase shared and remembered between Tom Kernan and Bloom as a model of how the novel as a whole works; and in his final essay, he discusses the thorny issue of Molly's origins, suggesting that she misreads 'Spanish' as 'Jewish', and that maternity for her is as much a fiction, though not a legal one, as paternity is for Stephen. Benstock's style can be at times rather opaque, despite – or because – of the fact that the blurb declares him to be 'jargon-free'; an interesting concept is buried in the following centrally explanatory sentence, which itself requires a certain amount of explanation: ' "Context" as a narrative device usually serves as an agenda for the events of a novel, a programme of action against which the reader tests the accuracy and authenticity of the responses of the characters to those events, and validates thematic determinants from such responses.'

Lacanian perspectives on Joyce abounded in article form this year: Garry Leonard is responsible for several of them, one on 'The Dead', 'Joyce and Lacan: "The Woman" as a Symptom of "Masculinity" in "The Dead" ' (*JJQ* 29.451–72), in which he offers a Lacanian plot summary of that story: Gabriel Conroy attempts to confirm the fictive unity of his masculinity through three different women (Lily, Molly Ivors and his wife Gretta), but is unable to do so. In another article, 'Wondering Where All the Dust Comes From: *Jouissance* in "Evelina" ' (*JJQ* 26.23–42), Leonard again tells the story in Lacanian mode: it is about the expectation that Evelina sacrifice her own sexual desire to veil the illusion of patriarchal power. In *MFS* 37, Leonard Lacanizes the narrator of 'The Sisters' from *Dubliners* ('The Free Man's Journal: The Making of His[S]tory in Joyce's "The Sisters" ', (455–82)), who imagines himself most a 'creature of certainty' at the end of the story when he is in fact most uncertain. Leonard provides a useful introductory account of other critical views of the story, to which he says he is indebted in his own reading. And, on a slightly different tack, in 'Women on the Market: Commodity Culture, "Femininity" and "Those Lovely Seaside Girls" in Joyce's *Ulysses*' (*JJA* 1.70–82), Leonard likens the capitalist division between haves and have-nots, the latter comprising people who go window-shopping, to the way women are encouraged to present themselves as commodities who may be looked at but not touched, as they do in various ways in *Ulysses*.

In his article 'Joyce Between Genders: Lacanian Views', Sheldon Brivic, as guest editor for the Lacanian issue of *JJQ* (27), gives a useful and accessible account of the overlap between Lacan and Joyce (13–22). Among other useful points, he notes that Lacan may himself have been influenced by Joyce, whom Lacan says he met at seventeen, and thereafter carried around 'a mass' of Joyce books; in 1975, Lacan gave the inaugural address at the Fifth International Joyce Conference at the Sorbonne. A list of Lacan's works which mention Joyce is given by Brivic, available only in (unreliable) translation on tape: surely there is an essential publishing project here?

An article which might have benefited from an injection of psychoanalysis is Sidney Monas's 'Literature, Medicine and the Celebration of the Body in Rabelais, Tolstoi and Joyce', in an interesting collection called *The Body and the Text*, edited by Bruce Clarke and Wendell Aycock. Having noted Stephen's unease with corporeality and the medicinal Mulligan in *Ulysses*, Monas concludes simply by summarizing, rather unilluminatingly, 'Penelope'. Do we really need to be told again that 'Molly is a talented singer but not a good reader', or that 'Fidelity and infidelity strangely coexist' in her chapter?

Peter Myers's *The Sound of Finnegans Wake* is both impressive and eccentric. Its thesis, that the sound of words is as important as their meaning, flies in the face of contemporary critical practice from Saussure (as Myers acknowledges) to Derrida (which he does not); and he does not mention Derek Attridge's recent, important work on the fallacy of onomatopoeia as a form somehow transcending the linguistic by reuniting signifier and signified. However, the text is a lively and learned one, with two extended close readings of short passages from the *Wake* to demonstrate its methodology.

In a special issue of *JJQ* (29) on *Finnegans Wake*, various aspects of that work are discussed, including freemasonry (Laura Peterson, 'The Bygmester, His Geamatron, and the Triumphs of the Craftygild: *Finnegans Wake* and the Art of Freemasonry', 777–92), contraception (Mary Lowe-Evans, ' "The Commonest of All Cases": Birth Control on Trial in the *Wake*', 803–14), nineteenth-century circus proprietors (R. J. Schork, 'Barnum at the *Wake*', 759–66), and the significance of the title of the novel with its lack of an apostrophe (Scott Simpkins, 'The Agency of the Title: *Finnegans Wake*', 735–44).

John Harty III's edited volume *James Joyce's 'Finnegans Wake': A Casebook* is a useful collection, including sections on assessments of the work, discussions of Joyce's textual self-referentiality, and on performance (the *Wake* as film, drama and music). Among a wide range of provoking pieces (for instance, John Gordon's 'The Convertshems of the Tchoose: Judaism and Jewishness in *Finnegans Wake*', and Sheldon Brivic's 'The Femasculine Obsubject: A Lacanian Reading of *FW* 606–607'), Kimberley J. Devlin's 'The Female Word' stands out. It discusses masculine curiosity and anxiety about women who write and who may possess a secret shared language; Devlin concludes that in his images of men who strain to hear but can't understand women's words, Joyce 'inscribes the potential limits to his own auditory forays into that terrain'.

Two new reference works have been added to the Joyce library: Morris Beja's

James Joyce: A Literary Life, which is an efficient and useful synthesis of recent material, intended for students and the general reader interested in Joyce's 'triumphant and ... sad' life; and Janet Egleson Dunleavy's edited volume, *Re-Viewing Classics of Joyce Criticism*. This is an interesting project, involving current Joyce scholars (such as Shari Benstock and Bonnie Kime Scott) assessing the importance then and now of earlier scholars (such as Richard M. Kain and Adeline Glasheen). For instance, Patrick A. McCarthy points out that Stuart Gilbert's *James Joyce's 'Ulysses': A Study* may have seemed pedantic and both buoyed up and weighed down by its attention to rigour and logic, but was deliberately scholarly as an act of 'critical propaganda' to make sure that this daringly experimental piece of writing was taken seriously. Suzette Henke gives a lively account of the curious anthology of critical writings published in 1929 on *Finnegans Wake, Our Exagmination Round His Factification for Incamination of Work in Progress*, a review of work which was not itself published for another ten years. While Samuel Beckett's essay is the best known of the twelve, the collection's importance lies partly in the fact that Joyce parodied it and incorporated bits of it into the work it was supposed to be reviewing. Dunleavy's collection is useful as a work of metacriticism and for filling in the background of some of the early Joyceans (James Atherton never left his native Wigan; Harry Levin, as Renaissance scholar, was recommended to New Directions Press by Joyce himself to be the author of a study of his work); its other function, to pay homage to the great and the good, makes for monotonous reading, as everyone's shortcomings and outdatedness are explained away breezily and, on occasion, eulogistically. This gives a rather uncritical air to an interesting critical work.

In the collection *Utopian Vision, Technological Innovation and Poetic Imagination*, edited by Klaus L. Berghahn and Reinhold Grimm, Karl S. Guthke poses the question, 'Are We Alone? The Idea of Extraterrestrial Intelligence in Philosophy and Literature from Copernicus to H. G. Wells', pointing out that modern science fiction actually draws on a long, centuries-old line of speculation about such matters. While the initial question cannot be answered, facts can nonetheless be deduced about 'human nature and human history', Guthke concludes. J. R. Hammond's *H. G. Wells and the Short Story* traces in the stories the clash in Wells between the classical and the romantic, and his assessment of what is distinctive about Wells's contribution to the genre is supported by an appendix including the texts of two short stories now reprinted for the first time since their original publication.

The proceedings of the 1986 International H. G. Wells Symposium have been edited by Patrick Parrinder and Christopher Rolfe as *H. G. Wells Under Revision*. The first section of the volume continues the debate over Wells's identity as one of artist or prophet; the second concerns Wells as novelist; the third, Wells and science; the last, Wells as 'Educationalist, Utopian and Visionary'. Among the essays here are Kirpal Singh's 'Genius Misunderstood: Toward an Asian Understanding of H. G. Wells', Bonnie Kime Scott's 'Uncle Wells on Women: A Revisionary Reading of the Social Romances', and Krishan Kumar's 'Wells and "the So-Called Science of Sociology" '.

Denis Lane has edited a collection on John Cowper Powys, *In the Spirit of Powys: New Essays*, although the presence of a 1985 essay by G. Wilson Knight, and the fact that only one out of twelve contributors is female, might give the reader cause to wonder at the exact nature of this novelty for a moment. The subjects covered here range from Knight's essay on John Cowper in the context of his brothers Theodore and Llewellyn Powys ('Ultimate Questions: Powysian Answers'), to Michael Ballin's essay on Powys's 'Welsh' novel ('*Porius* and the Cauldron of Rebirth'), in which he suggests that Powys's conception of history was more akin to Spengler's or Massingham's than to Darwin's or Freud's. The vogue is for Bakhtinian readings, and Ben Jones has produced an interesting one here in his essay 'The "mysterious word Esplumeoir" and the Polyphonic Structure in *A Glastonbury Romance*'. In contrast to critics who have read Powys monologically, thereby even casting him as a 'crank', Jones suggests that the 'motif of Esplumeoir, read polyphonically, explains the series of transformations and disappearances, and it provides the narratorial repetition that gives the novel its monumental cohesiveness'. [S.V.]

Criticism and biography of Virginia Woolf has continued to discuss the nature of Woolf's relationship with her social and political context. John Mepham's biography *Virginia Woolf: A Literary Life* in Macmillan's Literary Lives series emphasizes 'the material and psychological obstacles and rewards of her life as a writer'. In an exemplary account of Woolf's life and work, he chooses to stress the variety of her literary production, relating this to the differing versions of subjectivity, femininity, power, and literary form that she encountered. This illuminates her position in both feminist and modernist canons, which Mepham sees as tangential and complex. Interestingly, he is unwilling to interpret 'Modern Fiction' and 'Mr Bennet and Mrs Brown' as exclusive, or even particularly useful, outlines of a literary manifesto, finding Woolf's writing on Dostoevsky more relevant in understanding her literary method.

Two books this year have dealt with the issue of Virginia Woolf's writing about the war. Lynne Hanley's *Writing War: Fiction, Gender and Memory* also looks at the work of Joan Didion and Doris Lessing. Hanley fascinatingly discusses the way in which war literature and critical writing about war create a selective view of warfare and exclude 'war in the Middle East, Africa, and Ireland ... war as it is experienced by women and civilians and the modern, high-tech army'. She explicitly responds to and deconstructs Paul Fussell's *The Great War and Modern Memory*, which she sees as instrumental in determining the ways in which war and its literature have been treated. One of her purposes is to break down categories, which she does by intersecting her critical writing with her own short stories dealing with different, and traditionally excluded, perspectives on war. The chapter on Virginia Woolf's war writing emphasizes that her most important strategy is to establish the mutual implication of previously disconnected ways of thinking about war. She traces the development of Woolf's views from *A Room of One's Own* to *Three Guineas*, noting her increasing willingness to link the oppression of women and the drift to war.

Virginia Woolf and War: Fiction, Reality, and Myth, edited by Mark Hussey is, like many collections of conference papers, uneven. An early chapter by Nancy Topping Bazin and Jane Hamovit Lauter on 'Virginia Woolf's Keen Sensitivity to War: Its Roots and Its Impact on Her Novels' is a rather dull overview of Virginia Woolf's treatment of war and its development as a theme or issue in her work. This is somewhat simplistically related to her personal life, and some of the authors' critical comments are similarly bland: 'In *Three Guineas*, Woolf argues that the tyrannies of the patriarchal family become the tyrannies of the fascist state'. There is a problem in some of the chapters with definition and level. Helen Wussow, in 'War and Conflict in *The Voyage Out*' argues that this pre-war novel 'displays Woolf's interest in a topic that was to dominate her later novels'. Wussow argues that this interest is expressed in the way in which the heroine, Rachel Vinrace, becomes the focus for feelings of sexual violence. Although this book reiterates the valuable connection Virginia Woolf made between women's oppression and war, it is the nature, rather than the existence, of this connection that critics, following Woolf's own example, should be trying to uncover.

Some of the collection's best articles suggest that war appears in more than merely the content of Woolf's work. Roger Poole's ' "We all put up with you Virginia": Irreceivable Wisdom about War', William Handley's 'War and the Politics of Narration in *Jacob's Room*', and Judith Lee's ' "This hideous shaping and moulding": War and *The Waves*' all address in different ways the impact of war on formal and aesthetic issues in Virginia Woolf's writing, and the inter-connectedness of form and content.

This issue is also crucial to Pamela L. Caughie's *Virginia Woolf and Post-modernism: Literature in Quest and Question of Itself.* Caughie takes issue with most readings of Woolf that place her within a defining tradition, for example modernism or feminism. She argues for a change of focus, preferring function over form, or use over value. The problem is that her argument is not taken far enough. Her analyses of the use which critics have made of Woolf are interesting, although her criticism of feminist 'appropriations' of Woolf's work does not give sufficient weight to the strategic and political value which it has had for some feminists. When she considers Woolf's writing, she seems to reach an impasse. She asks us to rephrase our questions about Woolf's texts 'from What is the text about? (to what does it refer or correspond) to How does the text come about? or What does the text bring about? (what are its functions and effects?)'. However, her answers are usually confined to the idea that a text is 'about' the processes of narration, characterization or whatever. This excludes consideration of what Virginia Woolf's work actually implies when it talks 'about' narrative or character; for example, what does the narrator's distance from Jacob in *Jacob's Room* suggest about Woolf's concern with narrative? The most enjoyable chapter in the book is '*Flush* and the Literary Canon: The Value of Literary Appeal', which deconstructs the position of *Flush* in the canon in terms of waste or excess, thereby addressing the question of how we determine literary value.

A number of the year's articles on Woolf have considered her relationship with other writers and literary figures. Cheryl Mares, in a chapter on 'Woolf's Reading of Proust' in *Reading Proust Now*, illuminates Woolf's contradictory feelings about this writer. She shows that Woolf was unable to read Proust when working on her own writing because she perceived his work to be too overwhelming. As a result, Woolf was a selective and sporadic reader of Proust. Mares analyses this reaction in terms of obsessional 'approach-avoidance' behaviour, and considers how reading Proust affected Woolf's modernist aesthetics and her attitudes to gender. This chapter cries out for a more explicitly feminist and psychoanalytic interpretation. Woolf seems to occupy an almost Oedipal position in her anxiety about Proust's influence, but this is interestingly complicated by her admiration of his 'androgynous' style.

An article that theorizes similar issues is Beth C. Schwartz's 'Thinking Back Through Our Mothers: Virginia Woolf Reads Shakespeare' (*ELH* 58.721–46). Schwartz argues that, by virtue of his androgynous and anonymous writing, Shake-speare 'seems to play the part of a maternal muse in Woolf's creative process', and suggests that Woolf restores him to the pre-Oedipal world. This discussion of motherhood and the importance of the pre-Oedipal or semiotic phase relies implicitly on the work of Julia Kristeva. Kristeva's privileging of the disruptive appearance of the semiotic in literature has been criticized for the implication that writing by men can express the semiotic more effectively than writing by women. This article could similarly be accused of avoiding some of the issues concerning the reasons why women writers and theorists might want to appropriate male figures as role models.

Sabine Hotho-Jackson's 'Virginia Woolf on History: Between Tradition and Modernity' (*FMLS* 27.293–313) analyses Virginia Woolf's attitudes to history in the context of changing views about the function and role of historical scholarship among her contemporary historians. Woolf might be supposed to fit easily into the 'modern' camp of historians who are coming to accept that an individual's perspective will affect writing about the past, but Hotho-Jackson points out that in some ways Woolf still subscribed to a more traditional view of history as an accurate depiction of the past with a moral and educative function.

Articles on specific texts include Beth Rigel Daugherty's ' "There she sat": The Power of the Feminist Imagination in *To the Lighthouse*' (*TCL* 37.289–308), M. Keith Booker's 'Tradition, Authority and Subjectivity: Narrative Constitution of the Self in *The Waves*' (*CS* 3.290–6), and Kate Flint's 'Revising *Jacob's Room*: Virginia Woolf, Women and Language' (*RES* 62.361–79). Daugherty's article is an analysis of the moment when Lily Briscoe sees the vision of Mrs Ramsay at the end of *To the Lighthouse*. This is rather simplistically seen as an authentically feminist re-visioning of Mrs Ramsay's previously problematic (in Daugherty's terms) character. Booker's article discusses the way in which the disruptive narrative method of *The Waves*, which uses different narrators but the same style for each, suggests relational rather than conflictual forms of subjectivity. Kate Flint's article is an interesting account of the revisions Woolf made to *Jacob's Room*. Flint shows how most of the alterations work to emphasize the public and social, rather than the intimate and physical aspects of women's lives. She connects these changes with Woolf's growing awareness of how women's physical differences from men were being used to justify contemporary chauvinist attitudes. The subtext of this article seems to be an attack on French feminist writers for what are perceived as essentialist ways of theorizing the female body. In contrast, the article valuably re-situates our understanding of the female body in social terms.

Three articles about Rebecca West this year all deal in different ways with her position in the canon. Gloria Fromm's 'Rebecca West: The Fiction of Fact and the Facts of Fiction' (*NewC* 5.44–53) comments that 'the verdict of literary history has yet to be reached on the sprawling body of work full of unexpected twists and turns.' Her article traces the difficult relationship between Rebecca West and her son Anthony, and the effect this had on the fiction of both. It then moves on to discuss the split between Rebecca West's fictional and non-fictional styles of writing. Fromm sees this in terms of West's gendering of the implied readers of her work: 'she wrote fiction as a woman addressing women and non-fiction as a man speaking to men; and men were patently more important in her eyes than women'. She also rather unproblematically maps a split between high and low culture onto this gender division; in other words, Rebecca West wrote popular romantic fiction for women, and serious critical non-fiction for men. Apart from asserting that West had a split literary personality, the implications of this are not taken far enough. We learn that 'Rebecca West herself aspired intellectually to the one [high art] ... and gravitated emotionally to the other [popular culture]', which implies a degree of failure, rather than an attempt (whether misguided or not) to write for a specific audience.

Bonnie Kime Scott's 'Refiguring the Binary, Breaking the Cycle: Rebecca West as Feminist Modernist' (*TCL* 37.169–91) attempts to re-situate two of West's novels, *The Judge* and *Harriet Hume*, as modernist in their deconstruction of binary oppositions. Although part of a valuable debate about the relationship of women writers with modernism, the analysis of the texts does not seem to bear out Scott's points. Ann Norton's article 'Rebecca West's Ironic Heroine: Beauty as Tragedy in *The Judge*' (*ELT* 34.295–308) makes more persuasive reading. Expanding on earlier critics' suggestions that *The Judge* is best understood as a gothic novel, Norton shows how the novel emphasizes and criticizes the function of feminine beauty in gothic fiction by trapping the heroines in male controlled narratives of the downfall of beautiful women.

Janice Rossen's article on Dorothy L. Sayers, 'Oxford *in loco parentis*: The College as Mother in Dorothy Sayers' *Gaudy Night*', appears in *University Fiction*, edited by David Bevan. This may seem an unusual context in which to approach Sayers's work, but Rossen's concern is not primarily with *Gaudy Night*'s position in either detective or campus genre. She provides a psychoanalytic reading of Harriet Vane's relationship with Shrewsbury College and Lord Peter Wimsey as 'respective parent figures', while pointing out how Sayers also satirizes a Freudian reading of the case Harriet and Peter investigate. Rossen also analyses how the novel raises issues concerning women's ability to both work and deal with emotional attachments at the same time.

Jane Emery's biography of Rose Macaulay, *Rose Macaulay: A Writer's Life*, relates Macaulay's life explicitly to her fiction. This would not be a problem if Emery did not feel the need to keep apologizing for doing so. One of many similar comments is the following: 'of course, biographical criticism as a method of reading fiction has severe limitations; it offers little insight into artifice and fails to explain why we are not all novelists.' She also remarks that 'Rose deliberately attempted to avoid writing the transparent autobiography of most apprentice novelists'. Rather than periodically raising this issue, it would have been better dealt with all at once. No-one would deny that biographical interpretation of writers' work is one among many valid ways of looking at a text, and Macaulay's life is interesting in itself. Emery writes well on her childhood, her time at Somerville, her affair, and her relationship with Bloomsbury and other women writers, like Virginia Woolf and Ivy Compton Burnett. However, there is a sense that the narrative is governed by Macaulay's presumed progress to autonomy and self-determination. Emery comments: 'Her advance to control and freedom was intermittent.' This is a more traditional study than John Mepham's biography of Virginia Woolf.

Work on Forster this year has varied in its approach. Stephen K. Land's *Challenge and Conventionality in the Fiction of E. M. Forster* puts forward a rather schematic, structural way of interpreting plot and character in Forster's novels. He argues that the main character types of Forster's fiction are the believer in conventional attitudes and the challenger of those attitudes. The hero is caught between both, but makes a movement towards the challenger's values. A fourth figure, who Land terms 'the rebel woman', also moves towards the challenger, although her connection, unlike the hero's, is false. Any argument of this kind comes up against problems; the most important of these is the place of gender in Land's model. In a footnote to the introduction, he explains that he will use the term 'hero' for protagonists of either sex, implying that gender has little or no effect on this character type and function. However, the rebel woman's femininity is obviously much more crucial to her role. Gender's impact on Land's schema is thus only selectively considered. Land also has problems dealing with *Maurice*, arguing that the absence of the rebel woman flaws the novel, and explains why it is 'inferior'.

Two of the year's articles, both by Tariq Rahman, concern themselves with homosexuality in Forster's work. 'The Double-Plot in E. M. Forster's *A Room with a View*' (*CVE* 33.43–62) argues that the covert plot of the novel is homosexual. Rahman differs from other critics in seeing this in the language used to describe George and Lucy's relationship, rather than in Mr Beebe's possible interest in George. His 'The Under-Plot in E. M. Forster's *The Longest Journey*' (*DUJ* 83.59–67) similarly relates the homosexual under-plot to ideas of alienation in this novel.

There has been an increasing interest this year in *A Passage to India* in the context of the literature of empire. Gerald Docherty's 'White Circles/Black Holes: Worlds of Difference in *A Passage to India*' (*OL* 46.105–22) is a fairly basic deconstruction of the 'oppositional chains – infinite/finite, presence/absence, form/formless, innocence/guilt' that structure the text. Simon Featherstone's 'Passages to India' (*LIT* 3.i.33–55) is a thought-provoking comparison of the novel, David Lean's film, and other films about the India of the British Raj. He argues for the novel's superiority on the grounds that it is actually *about* how we represent or find language for imperial culture. This argument is more convincing in some places than others. In an excellent article, 'The Unspeakable Limits of Rape: Colonial Violence and Counter-Insurgency' (*Genders* 10.25–46), Jenny Sharpe relates the issue of rape in the novel to the way in which the image of black men raping white women has been used to justify colonialism; for example, in accounts of the Indian Mutiny. 'The Prisonhouse of Orientalism' (*TexP* 5.195–218), by Zakia Pathak, Saswati Sengupta and Sharmila Purkayastha, engages somewhat critically with Edward Said's *Orientalism* by examining different critical readings of a variety of texts (among them *A Passage to India*) in the context of their pedagogical practice as teachers in a women's college in Delhi University. Their account of their difficulties in trying to encourage students to rethink their perceptions of England provides a valuable criticism of Said's work. In 'Possibilities of Completion: The Endings of *A Passage to India* and *Women in Love*' (*ELT* 34.261–80), Margaret Proctor considers the impact on *A Passage to India* of the ending of D. H. Lawrence's *Women in Love*, which Forster copied onto his manuscript as he struggled with the ending. She shows how Forster incorporated the device of using dialogue with little authorial commentary to conclude the novel. [S.W.]

(c) Individual Authors: Post-1945

It becomes increasingly difficult to write this section without reference to American literature, Commonwealth literature, and writing in English from Africa and the Caribbean. This reflects the growing critical acknowledgement of work from other cultures, and a trend towards cross-cultural critical approaches. Equally, it is difficult to find a great deal on single, named British writers. There is, instead, emphasis on theoretical issues with passing reference to a range of writers: a focus on ways of looking at texts, rather than on texts themselves. Some names, however, recur. Graham Greene is still a popular choice, along with Angela Carter and John Fowles. Contemporary writers receiving some attention include Graham Swift, David Lodge, and Brian Moore, and there has been a considerable emphasis on women writers. There is also serious attention being paid to the popular forms of detective fiction and spy fiction. However, although some of this work is interesting and provocative, much of it is dull and predictable, and I am left feeling that the most exciting work is being done in other areas.

(i) Women's Writing Melinda G. Fowl's essay 'Angela Carter's *The Bloody Chamber* revisited' (*CS* 1.71–9) concentrates on the short story in three ways: as part of the overall structure of the collection; as part of the fairy tale tradition; and as part of the tradition of other fantasy modes. Fowl is concerned with the way in which the mixing of these three elements is related to the development of characters where a relationship to someone strange or foreign dominates the story. She is also interested in the creation of multiple meanings through binary oppositions in the narrative. In a detailed analysis of 'The Tiger's Bride', she explores the significance of clothes and

masks, suggesting that clothes and appearance can be imprisoning. Beauty is metamorphosized by her relationship with the strange Beast into something new, her imprisoning appearance removed and a tiger-beast revealed. The discussion of 'The Lady of the House of Love' focuses on the transformation of the Countess from a vampire queen into a human being, the change into one whose blood flows out rather than one who sucks blood in, and Fowl disagrees with Patricia Duncker's 1984 review which linked the flowing of blood with the pornographic cliché of sex and death. More far-reaching is Phil Powrie's 'Angela Carter/Chantal Chawaf: Revisiting the Domestic' (*NewComp* 11.127–36). Powrie proposes a new reading of Carter focusing on the incorporation, celebration and subversion of female domestic labour. He challenges the typical view that Carter's novels are fundamentally mimetic, and uses Adam Mars-Jones's 'From Wonders to Prodigies' in the *TLS* as a focus for his disagreement. In the discussion of a passage from *Nights at the Circus*, Powrie suggests that it conveys more than is required for a realist narrative, and that the baboushka is symbolic of Russia and oppressed women, and through the witch-like image, is suggestive of brewing revolution. Thus, domestic oppression leads to the beginnings of revolt. He further suggests that the text delights in the materiality of the word, conveying 'the indissociability of language and the body, in the context of traditional female labour'. This materiality he sees as having little to do with realism. Powrie develops this into an interesting comparison with the work of Chantal Chawaf, suggesting that Chawaf too uses traditional female labour as a metaphor of oppression, and combines it with revolt against oppression. The essay suggests that there is celebration of the traditional female arenas as well as subversion in the works of both writers. Using a short story by Carter, 'The Kitchen Child', Powrie goes on to suggest in a complex argument that the absence of the Father is signified through the absence of the letter X in the kitchen alphabet, so that the Father has no place in this women's kitchen-world. Chapter 2 of Olga Kenyon's *Writing Women: Contemporary Women Novelists* is devoted to Carter, the title of the chapter describing her as 'Fantasist and Feminist', but unfortunately it adds little to an understanding of Carter's work. The chapter begins with an overview of the way in which Carter breaks down the academic and the masculine divisions between élite and popular culture, and treats popular forms seriously. Kenyon suggests that Carter sees fantasy as destructive and desire as self-absorbing, and she refers to the way in which Carter brings in bawdy jokes, slapstick, and sexual innuendo to evade male academic discourse and look at women's subcultures. This is followed by a section on Carter's early life and work. There are obvious points about the way in which Carter takes images from a range of sources such as medieval allegory and film, and about Carter's fascination with the ways in which we construct ideas of ourselves through pressures of socialization. Equally obvious points follow about Carter's desire to entertain and to instruct, and about the way the fiction focuses on 'subterranean areas behind everyday experience'. Comments on the significance of mirrors lead into a section on *The Magic Toyshop*. There is a brief discussion of the stereotypical images of women to which the young Melanie aspires, and the shocking contrast of life with Uncle Philip, without mirrors to confirm the stereotypical identity she has been constructing. Carter is then linked with the Gothic tradition, with references to *The Mysteries of Udolpho*, *Frankenstein*, *Jane Eyre* and *Wuthering Heights*, and to the way in which female repression is highlighted and the ways female authors of these novels show women acting boldly. In a section on Carter's middle period, Kenyon makes clear that her subject's responsiveness to contemporary theory finds expression in the novels, as does her awareness of popular culture. There is brief discussion of *Love and The Infernal Desire Machines of Doctor*

Hoffman. A section on *The Passion of New Eve* follows. This is seen as a feminist novel, but again Kenyon makes obvious points: 'Carter emphasizes here ... that cultural interpretations of sexuality can and do change.' There are further sections on the short stories, on *The New Woman*, and on *Black Venus*. Relating the stories of the novels takes up a certain amount of space in this chapter, and the summaries of themes and approaches are brief and fairly predictable. The division of the chapter into short sections makes it fragmentary and unsatisfying. This kind of overview in one chapter cannot be very far-reaching or provocative, and the issues raised about feminist theory in the first chapter of the book are not related specifically enough to the discussion of Carter. There are brief but insightful references to Carter in Maggie Humm's excellent book, *Border Traffic: Strategies of Contemporary Women Writers*. This is discussed in more detail later in this section.

Thomas Dukes puts Elizabeth Bowen and Penelope Lively into the context of war fiction and of Paul Fussell's cultural analysis of World War II, *Wartime*. Dukes's essay, 'Desire Satisfied: War and Love in *The Heat of the Day* and *Moon Tiger*' (*War, Literature and the Arts* 1.75–98) begins with quotations from Fussell's book. Fussell's point is that novels about World War II have failed to be anything more than 'engaging narratives', and Dukes sees this as an indication of a tradition of fiction about World War II. Fussell refers to the tendency to recognize that the war couldn't be confined in one volume, and the consequent production of several war trilogies. Dukes, in looking at two single novels, suggests that they have in common with the trilogies cited by Fussell a cynical representation of the war: the society of the Allies is shown to be corrupt, even though the Allied cause is the one that is supported in these novels. He doesn't think, however, that Bowen romanticizes war in the way that Fussell suggests is typical. Romantic love is juxtaposed with war, but is seen as an essential antidote to the boredom and depression central to war. Dukes also suggests that the moral defectiveness of the three central characters makes an important contribution to the lack of romanticization. Lively's novel, he suggests, has more in common with what he sees as Fussell's preferred model of war-writing: memoirs and other non-fiction texts. The memoir is Lively's central narrative device, and Dukes suggests this creates greater narrative distance than in Bowen's novel although the point of this suggestion is not made clear since he is not ultimately comparing Bowen unfavourably with Lively. He maintains that the particular use of love and desire as an escape from war, and as part of a determination to find meaning in life when war seems to make meaning impossible, makes these novels quite different from the fictional accounts that Fussell regards as sentimental. One of Dukes's main intentions is to challenge Fussell's statement that World War II was too big to get into one book, by suggesting that there are many different 'real' wars, and that all individuals only perceive war as it impacts on them. Thus, he suggests that in portraying an individual perspective, each of these novels achieves a depiction of the real war: inevitably a partial experience. However, in maintaining that these two novels bring 'honesty, complexity, and ambiguity' to their portrayals of war, Dukes seems to me to be writing from a theoretically simplistic point of view. In spite of having referred early in his essay to a 'tradition of fiction about World War II', he seems to find no place for in-depth discussion of textual strategies and 'naturalized' forms of representation. To write about 'honesty' strikes at the very heart of contemporary concern with constructed discourses, but Dukes does not engage with this. Fussell's ideas about typical depictions of World War II are used to little effect, and the notion of naturalized constructions is not pursued. Indeed, one is left wondering what real purpose the references to Fussell's ideas serve, since there seems to be little more to Dukes's responses than the conclusion that novels about the war do not have to be trilogies and that the juxtaposition of love and war is not necessarily sentimental. This is also an essay that suffers from the tedious relating of the stories of the novels he is concerned with. Equally dull is June Campbell's ' "Both a Joke and a Victory": Humor as Narrative Strategy in Margaret Drabble's Fiction' (*ConL* 32.75–99). The points about humour assuaging horror are hardly new, and the examples of different kinds of jokes in Drabble's fiction become dull and tell us nothing that we couldn't identify easily for ourselves. Similarly tedious is the relating of the stories, and I am puzzled as to why a number of critics I have encountered this year seem to find this necessary. Slightly more interesting is the section on the narrator in *The Realms of Gold* who makes jokes about the form of fiction. This section looks at the way in which humour is part of Drabble's particular postmodern challenge to the conventions of realism, but overall the essay contributes little to an understanding of Drabble's work. In '*The Anna* (Aspern) *Papers*' (*NConL* 1.2), Linda Wagner-Martin suggests that Ellen Gilchrist's 1988 novel is a feminist revisioning of James's *The Aspern Papers*. In the same issue, Robert A. Martin writes on Sylvia Plath in 'Esther's Dilemma in *The Bell Jar*' (6–8), but the commentary on Esther's desire to escape from herself and forge a new persona, and on the notion of her adopting certain people as her doubles, is hardly ground-breaking. The brevity of these papers makes it difficult for them to develop anything of subtlety and complexity, and they are essentially repetitions of pretty obvious points.

Olga Kenyon's *Writing Women: Contemporary Women Novelists* has a chapter on Jewish women writing in Britain, with a section on Bernice Rubens and the mainstream Jewish novel. It is good to see this work receiving attention, and there are occasional illuminating points; for example, the suggestion that the structuring in *Sunday Best* recalls Hitchcock. However, as with the chapter on Angela Carter, the overview technique and the relating of the stories makes for a disappointing approach. The purpose of the book is not clear. In the first chapter Kenyon states that the women writers she is looking at cannot easily be categorized and are vastly different. Why these particular writers have been gathered together in this book, then, is not clear. Since they are 'vastly different', Kenyon does not establish links between them, and, thus, the book ends up as a series of separate, overview (and therefore inevitably superficial) discussions. Some of the points are so much a part of accepted narrative understanding as not to need stating; for example, 'Feinstein has learnt from Proust that the novelist cannot be omniscient'. There is not enough reliance on the reader's perspicacity; points are over-explained, such as 'Feinstein's intertextuality, her use of other writings'. Other chapters in the book cover 'Black Women Novelists', 'Alice Walker', 'Toni Morrison', 'Caribbean Women Writers', and 'Buchi Emecheta and Black Immigrant Experience in Britain'. A listing of the chapters demonstrates the book's scope and, therein, its limitations. Discussion of women's writing, including writing from other cultures, has developed far enough now for us not to gain much from a necessarily superficial overview of this kind. The reader is constantly wanting a more far-reaching discussion and a clearer rationale for the choice and juxtaposition of these particular writers. Although it is beyond the remit of this section, it is worth mentioning that anyone wanting a good introduction to writing from other cultures should consult Robert L. Ross's *International Literature in English*, which, although a survey volume, contains insightful essays, is organized into helpful thematic sections, and suggests links between a range of works affected in some way or another by decolonization. It is a valuable starting point, and a useful reference volume for any academic library.

Finally, Maggie Humm's *Border Traffic: Strategies of Contemporary Women Writers* considers women with long histories of crossing the borders between received languages and undervalued ways of speaking. The introduction, 'Mapping the Territory: Bakhtin, Douglas, Bernstein, Cixous', is a useful, appealing and approachable discussion of postmodernism and of the central focus of the book: the poetics of displacement. The first chapter is general in its coverage, but has useful references to Margaret Drabble, Nell Dunn, Fay Weldon, and Angela Carter among others in the post-1945 era. The way in which Drabble, Dunn and Weldon focus on motherhood, locating it outside the bounds of conventional marriage, is put in the context of the sentimentalized views of Michael Young and Peter Willmott in *Family and Kinship in East London* (1957) and Richard Hoggart in *The Uses of Literacy* (1958). The discussion of Carter sees marginality as generating new kinds of subject matter, and there is an excellent discussion of *Nights at the Circus* which Humm sees as incorporating a number of feminist themes, notably Laura Mulvey's account of the male gaze. Other chapters covering Jean Rhys, Zora Neale Hurston and La Malincha, Margaret Atwood, and Adrienne Rich, are outside the scope of this section, but are illuminating and are highly recommended.

(ii) Popular Fiction For this I return to Maggie Humm's *Border Traffic: Strategies of Contemporary Women Writers*, and her chapter on Anglo-American feminist detective fiction. This reflects contemporary interest in popular fiction and recognition of its engagement with serious issues and its ability to enter into important cultural debates. Humm focuses on Gillian Slovo, Barbara Wilson, Mary Wings, Sara Paretsky and Rebecca O'Rourke, and sees them as challenging the gender norms of detective writing. She suggests that the feminist detective understands that moral justice depends on collective responsibility rather than forms of personal authority, and notes the challenges to the traditional detective plot and linear chronology, with focus on the progression of character development and relationships rather than the progress to the solution of the crime. Humm usefully puts the notion of what the detective sees into the context of Laura Mulvey's film theory, with the notion that seeing is masculine. She locates the feminist detective 'at the impact point of this strong system of interpretation', and makes a striking comment: 'The feminist detective is not a private eye'. Another book that deals with popular fiction is *Spy Fiction, Spy Films and Real Intelligence*, edited by Wesley K. Wark. The introduction, written by Wark, locates the spy novel in the 'literary family' of the detective novel, anarchist novel, terrorist novel, and American dime novel, and establishes it as emerging in the years before World War I. Wark suggests that its attraction lies in its use of the artifice of apparent realism, and suggests that analysis should avoid formalist criticism with its emphasis on internal textual structure, and a reductive historical approach which turns the texts simply into archives of popular thought. Wark takes inspiration from Dominick La Capra's *History and Criticism* (1985) and *History, Politics and the Novel* (*YWES* 68.52) which suggest combining the best features of literary and historical criticism, new ways of assessing the sociological context of literature, and new ways of understanding history through the 'counter discourses' of the past. Then follows a detailed discussion of the evolution of spy fiction's own version of history. Relevant to the novel post-1945 is Wark's discussion of Len Deighton and John le Carré, and their rejection of the fantasy of history as a game in Fleming's Bond novels. He suggests that in le Carré, history is shaped by ideological clashes, and by conspiracy, deception and corruption. Thus, the spy novel is seen as carrying out the task of constructing different versions of history at different

times, and playing an important role in the general cultural construction of versions of reality. Wark goes on to suggest that feminist spy fiction will be significant in the future. This introduction includes a detailed discussion of Orwell's *1984* which suggests that Orwell created a world in which spying was a guarantee of power and escape was futile. Philip Jenkins's essay 'Spy Fiction and Terrorism' does not focus in detail on any one writer, but makes a series of references to a number of contemporary writers of spy fiction. Denis Smyth's essay '*Our Man in Havanna*, Their Man in Madrid: Literary Invention in Espionage Fact and Fiction' considers the relationship between fiction and reality evident in Graham Greene's work, but as an historian, Smyth is more concerned with the insights Greene's fiction can provide into some aspects of secret intelligence than with questions of textuality. As far as this section is concerned, it is Wark's introduction that is of most use, but other useful essays cover spy fiction before 1945.

(iii) Greene, Golding and Isherwood Elliott Malamet's excellent essay 'Graham Greene and the Hounds of *Brighton Rock*' (*MFS* 4.689–703) continues the spy theme by focusing on *Brighton Rock* as a novel full of the metaphoric terminology of detection, containment and capture. He suggests that the characters constantly try to pin one another down, but that some characters, and particularly Pinkie, defy interpretation, and therefore, in the language of spying, 'foil any surveillance' of their inner being. Thus, Malamet suggests a 'tension in the novel between detection and evasion'. While Pinkie remains indecipherable, a number of the other characters become 'hounds' chasing him. The obvious referencing of Conan Doyle and popular detective fiction is an index of the contemporary acknowledgement of the importance of popular fiction, and of its influence on other forms of writing. Malamet likens this novel to Chandler's *The Big Sleep*, and the modern thriller in general, where evil grows and spreads, and the initial act ceases to be of central importance, giving way to the following acts of evil that overlap and move the thriller in new directions. He relates this to an important loss of origins that Pinkie feels. The past is a dark hole. To detect innocence you must go right back to birth. He also points to the irony of Hale whose job is to leave clues, but who ends without trace. He suggests that Hale is an outer edge of thread that keeps unravelling, taking us to the core of the novel: Rose confronting the horror of Pinkie's recording. Malamet identifies Rose as a kind of detective, and thus a danger to Pinkie. This is not new, but the tracing through of the metaphor of detection is interesting and detailed and makes explicit links with popular fiction. Also, Malamet sees Rose as more complex than some critics have done. She is not just a detective, but like Pinkie is undetectable, and this intersects with other recent work on detective fiction which has suggested a close identification between the detective and the criminal. In discussing the idea of Rose crossing over to the other side, Malamet again implicitly signals the thriller/spy novel, which Greene himself signals explicitly in the description of Rose quoted by Malamet: 'she watched them in their dark clothes like a spy.' Indeed, Greene makes explicit the metaphor of detection himself, and Malamet quotes a number of the phrases which demonstrate this. He sees the novel as both presenting undetectable characters and using images of aggression that show the impulse towards detection. He suggests that it is a novel of cages, of windows as barriers, of the determination of something outside to get in and the determination of what is inside to remain unsurveyed. He then develops this into a discussion of the idea of God as a kind of super-detective. He refers to Greene's essay on François Mauriac, where Greene suggests that people are made visible, given form through the surveillance of God, and he relates this to the image of an old man

in Greene's novel. The essay ends with the suggestion that in leaving clues to establish an alibi, Pinkie is manipulating the use of signs in an attempt to control. Malamet says that the final recording is the corruption of a sign, and we are left without resolution or solution, unlike the traditional detective story.

Unfortunately Robert Hoskins's *Graham Greene: A Character Index and Guide* is not of this quality. It is a guide to both the fiction and the drama, and includes all the novels and entertainments, the *Collected Stories*, the *Collected Plays* and *The Last Word*, and an additional short story 'The Bear Fell Free' that doesn't appear in the *Collected Stories*. The novels are presented in chronological order, and under each title there are, covered alphabetically, characters, historical and literary allusions, place names, and foreign phrases likely to be of special interest. There is also a general index: an alphabetized list of all entries in the guide. The introductory chapter is a general introduction to the course of Greene's career with brief comments on the central elements in the novels such as the influence of journalism, the psychology of the characters, Catholicism, and comedy. This is followed by paragraphs on some of the major characteristics of Greene's work, with selected works used to demonstrate them. There is nothing here that is new, but then the purpose of this book is not to offer ground-breaking theories, but to provide an index. The introductory chapter would be of interest only to those who know absolutely nothing about Greene's writing, and the index really gains nothing from its inclusion, except that Hoskins's admiration for Greene is established, and thus his reason for producing such a work. It is difficult to see who might benefit from the index: undergraduates trying to write essays without reading or rereading the books? The mechanical entries under each title obliterate the atmosphere and complexities of the novels, and the descriptions of characters read like clichéd romantic novels: 'Tony and Kate grow apart and lose their ability to feel each other's pain' (entry under *England Made Me*); 'Her deep love for her husband and son make possible a genuine happiness in the alien environment of English suburban life' (entry under *The Human Factor*); 'the strength of his love for Clara earns the respect of Plarr, who realizes that love makes Charley the winner after all' (entry under *The Honorary Consul*). Such entries obliterate the depth of psychology of the characterization claimed for Greene in the introductory chapter.

In *Christopher Isherwood,* Stephen Wade considers the influence of Vedanta on Isherwood's post-1945 fiction, and ultimately suggests that he has more in common with American writing than with English, locating him in the tradition of journey and self-discovery novels, and comparing him, in particular, with Jack Kerouac. There are two very brief contributions on Golding in *NConL*. Lea Tanzman's 'The Mulberry in William Golding's Fiction: Emblematic Connotations' (21.7–8) makes obvious points about the mulberry (a mulberry-coloured birthmark in *Lord of the Flies*, a mulberry-coloured scar on Matty Windrove in *Darkness Visible*, and a rotting berry in *The Spire*) being used to mark out a sacrificial victim. Usha Bande's 'Jocelin's Glorified Self: A Horneyan Interpretation of Golding's *The Spire*' (21.9–10) suggests that the novel can be analysed in terms of Horneyan tenets as a commentary on the tragedy of man betrayed by his inner insufficiency: a tragedy of conflict between man's basic drives and his glorified self-image.

(iv) Fowles and Other Contemporary Writers Fowles continues to receive substantial critical attention, and both M. Keith Booker's essay 'What We Have Instead of God: Sexuality, Textuality and Infinity in *The French Lieutenant's Woman*' (*Novel* 2.178–98) and Frederick M. Holmes's essay 'History, Fiction and the Dialogic Imagination: John Fowles's *A Maggot*' (*ConL* 32.229–43) are excellent. Booker puts

his essay into the context of the framework established by French thinkers, Barthes, Foucault, Lacan, Kristeva and Derrida, and suggests that *The French Lieutenant's Woman* openly and directly explores links between sexuality and language. He sees sexuality and textuality as leading to a confrontation with infinity since 'neither concept can be circumscribed within a univocal structure of totalized meaning.' He links this with the disappearance of God from the world: previously, infinity was contained within the comforting notion of God, but this is no longer so. He maintains that Fowles employs sexuality and textuality as the twin figures of infinity, and that this raises the issues of framing and boundaries that are fundamental to the character of postmodern art in general. Indeed, he suggests that the transgression of boundaries might be the most important characteristic of modern literature and of the novel in particular, and relates this to Fowles. He calls upon Foucault's notion that having lost God we must seek another area in which to construct boundaries, and sexuality has been adopted as this area in the twentieth century. He uses Lacan's notion of *jouissance* and its links with feminine sexuality to suggest that the feminine has a potential for a special transgressive force. He does acknowledge that this might return us to the older idea of the mysteries of the feminine, and be a projection of male fantasy. In a footnote, he points to two opposing views of Sarah in the debate about whether this is a feminist work of fiction or not, and sides with the view of Magali Cornier Michael, that the figure of Sarah can never transcend the boundaries of male fantasy, so the book fails as a feminist statement. In another footnote, he establishes that the word 'Victorian' as it applies to this novel refers to the way in which the twentieth century constructs the nineteenth century, rather than suggesting that the novel gives a realistic picture of that era. He then goes on to look at the Victorian fascination with taxonomy and classification: a desire to contain the secularized sublime, and, in particular, a desire to suppress feminine sexuality. He suggests that the transgression of taxonomies and hierarchies in general is to do with unleashing feminine sexuality and makes interesting links with Newton, gravity and deterministic science, showing that Sarah does not continue to fall as Charles had been sure she would. Thus, he shows Fowles challenging the assumptions on which Victorian science and society were constructed. The essay also considers the way in which the novel parodies the typical Victorian novel. Charles views his own actions in narrative terms, and Sarah is a challenge to his compartmentalized narrative. It is suggested, however, that Sarah is highly influenced by literary convention: constructed by what she has read. The essay then moves to a consideration of Fowles's overt reference to *Madame Bovary*, and in a footnote Booker acknowledges Tony Tanner's point that adultery is employed as a symbol of transgression in nineteenth-century literature, and that the novel itself is a transgressive form. The link with Flaubert is taken further, as Booker puts the notion of the disappointment in the realities of sexual experience into the context of *Bouvard and Pécuchet*, and comments on the reader's disappointment in the realities of the seduction of Sarah after nearly 300 pages of what he calls 'textual foreplay'. This brings us to the central point: that climax is anti-climax; that sexuality cannot be contained within sex; that infinity cannot be contained. Booker then moves to a consideration of Barthes, and suggests that Charles's premature ejaculation, which is a closure of his desire to master Sarah, is analogous to the reader's attempt to master a text and finalize its meaning: 'in both cases closure is achieved at the expense of most of the action.' This is then developed into the idea of Charles as a reader of Sarah's narrative, and is linked with the idea that this text, and most others, posit a male reader. Booker acknowledges that the reader identifies with Charles in his attempt at sexual mastery of Sarah. What Booker is suggesting here is that Barthes is 'one of the many intertexts that plays constantly in the margins of *The French Lieutenant's Woman*', since he sees Sarah as both the figure of the author telling tales and manipulating events, and the figure of feminine sexuality constituted by the literature she has read, by the fantasies of Charles, and by the fantasies of Fowles's narrator and of the reader. Intertextuality is established as an infinite concept, and Booker says that this novel problematizes the frame around the fictional text with its explicit metafictional devices. He reminds us that Fowles's narrator steps outside the frame of the narrator to remind us that we construct our own lives according to the conventions of narrative, and this leads to the conclusion that 'the "real" world is itself a fictional text.' This essay is a bravura performance in its exciting and inventive use of a range of contemporary theoretical ideas. Holmes likens *A Maggot* to *The French Lieutenant's Woman* in that both examine history as a constructed discourse rather than an objective truth. Both are also 'intensely self-reflexive'. These are by now familiar ideas, but they are extremely well-expressed here, and Holmes then goes on to emphasize *A Maggot* as foregrounding the textual nature of history, the novel itself being what he calls a 'medley of texts'. Using Bakhtin's terminology the novel is described as dialogic or polyphonic, and Holmes relates this to the novel's treatment of history, suggesting that it offers a range of perspectives on how the past should be interpreted. Holmes sees Fowles as preoccupied with individual freedom and self-transformation, and far more in sympathy with the romantic individualist approach to truth represented by Lee than with the rational, neo-classical approach represented by Ayscough. The significance of detective fiction as a genre is again made apparent in this essay when Holmes refers to the novel as 'a kind of detective story, the whole point of which is to unearth a truth which stays obstinately buried'. As with Booker's essay, what is really arresting here is the constant location of the novel in the context of critical theory, and this illustrates the point with which I opened this section: the most provocative and interesting work this year is that which foregrounds theory and considers the general workings of literary texts as well as focusing on specifics. Equally, the influence of the popular form of detective fiction is recognized here, and Todorov's comments about this are used to good effect. What this essay demonstrates specifically is continuing interest in the whole question of linear narratives, in challenges to linearity, in notions of resolution and subversion of resolution, in the illusion that readers are constantly involved in an objective *fabula* that has to be reconstructed from the *sjuzet*. These issues remain of significance, intersecting as they do with contemporary interest in history as discourse, literature as discourse, and indeed the whole of human experience as discourse. The popularity of the traditional detective novel is at least partly explained by its suggestion of safe completion, when our current notion of history as discourse challenges such safety, as does Fowles's fiction. Ultimately, Holmes sees *A Maggot* as challenging monologic discourse, and as drawing attention to the distance between the eighteenth and the twentieth centuries: acknowledging the 'otherness' of history rather than eliminating it. Jim Webster's brief piece on D. M. Thomas's '*The White Hotel*: Freud, Medusa, and the Missing Goddess' (*NConL* 21.10–12) suggests that the limitations of psychoanalysis as a process for understanding the psyche is an important theme in the novel, because Freud's explanation of the Medusa is not relevant to Lisa. He sees Freud as misreading the nature of the Medusa, and of his patient's illness. He suggests that the strongest psychic health is achieved by looking closely at the image of the Medusa rather than avoiding it. This essay might usefully be considered alongside Cixous's ideas about the Medusa.

Jo O'Donoghue's *Brian Moore: A Critical Study* is a book in which the often useful material can become tedious through repetition, and the reader can feel patronized by critical terms being explained several times. I am also uncomfortable with O'Donoghue's view that Moore is that rare male who can pass on to us what it feels like to be a woman. This is not only a naïve belief in a simplistic relationship between text and real life, but worrying in the light of the fact that she sees Moore as depicting women as ready to give up everything for love, unlike men who are depicted as more intellectual. However, there is good discussion of crisis of faith as a theme in the novels, and a useful identification of three phases in Moore's creative career.

Hilary Spurling's *Paul Scott: A Life of the Author of 'The Raj Quartet'* is the sort of skilful biography we have come to expect from this writer, with perceptive psychological insight. Spurling doesn't, however, attempt to put Scott's work into the context of now-familiar postcolonial debates, and thus we end up with something that perpetuates the ideology that underpins Scott's work. Graham Swift receives attention in David Leon Higdon's essay 'Double Closures in Postmodern British Fiction: The Example of Graham Swift' (*CS* 1.88–95). The focus is on the problematic nature of endings now that the traditional terminology of closure is no longer appropriate or adequate to contemporary British fiction. There are references to Drabble, Lodge, Murdoch, Fowles, Barnes, and Byatt, and then a focus on Swift, with detailed discussion of *Waterland* which, Higdon suggests, has at least six moments of closure, and overtly searches for meanings without being a novel with multiple endings. He suggests that apparently closed endings go on to generate later action, and apparently open endings are in fact closed, and he goes on to show the duplication of this pattern in Swift's three other novels: *The Sweet-Shop Owner*, *Shuttlecock*, *Out of this World*. In 'The Three Small Worlds of David Lodge' (*CS* 3.324–30), Stuart Laing considers the changes that are made in the transformation of the novel *Small World* into a television drama serial. This reflects increasing cross-disciplinary approaches, and interest in narrative forms other than the written. The essay goes on to discuss a Channel 4 documentary *Big Words: Small World* on the subject of a literature and linguistics conference held at Strathclyde in 1986, the documentary being another transformation of Lodge's original novel.

The Review of Contemporary Fiction 1 was devoted to Alexander Theroux and Paul West. David W. Madden's 'Paul West: An Introduction' (141–53) provides a brief coverage of West's writing career, and some brief but useful comments on the novels. It is a very readable survey introducing the main preoccupations of West's fiction. Robert Lima's 'Words of Power: Openings to the Universe of Paul West' (212–18) is a brisk and elegant overview of West with a focus on his verbal virtuosity and ironic humour. In 'Paul West's *Alley Jaggers*: Escaping the Trap of British Proletarian Fiction' (219–26), Ivor S. Irwin puts West in the tradition of the picaro, the nihilist, the existentialist, and Joyce's Bloom and Beckett's Watt. Christopher S. Schreiner in 'Of Involutes, a Rat, and Hugh's Guitar' (231–9) suggests a tradition of 'involutive writing' which, he maintains, links De Quincey, Malcolm Lowry and Paul West. Joseph Pestino's 'Macrocosm and Microcosm Relations Rethought: Paul West's *Out of My Depths*' (252–61) is a complex response to a complex text. Pestino looks at it as an introduction to West's conception of cosmic relations, and suggests that the reader is invited to enter the book without fixed conceptions about that relationship. William Mooney in 'Those Pearls His Eyes: Paul West's Blind Monologuists and Deaf Auditors' (267–79) contrasts Beckett, who pursues silence, with West, who pursues utterance. David Bosworth makes a comparison between writing and painting in 'Being and Becoming: The Canvas of Paul West's Work'

(280–8), questioning what kind of fictional progress West seeks in the essentially abstract nature of literature, and exploring the portrayal of timelessness in a time-bound medium, focusing on plot and textual strategies in *The Place in Flowers Where Pollen Rests*. Alphonso Lingis also focuses on *The Place in Flowers Where Pollen Rests*, in 'From Under Dismembered Bodies' (289–97), asking what that place is, and querying whether it is memory. In 'The Man Who Breaks Typewriters' (298–302), Charles Mann provides a preliminary list of West's manuscripts in Pennsylvania State University Libraries, and there is also in this edition a list of West's published editions (304–7).

(v) Current literary surveys In *ES* 72, J. M. Blom and L. R. Leavis provide an overview of recent fiction ('Current Literature 1990. New Writing: Novels and Short Stories', 454–69), reaching the lighthearted conclusion that 'fiction based on multi-narrative layers of different voices is obligatory – on this our two reviewers' voices sound as one'. There are also some useful entries in the following: Graham Bradshaw's 'Current Literature 1989. II. Biography, Literary Theory and Criticism' (530–44); Paul Dean's 'Current Literature 1990. II. Literary Theory, History and Criticism' (545–61); Graham Bradshaw's 'Current Literature 1988. II. Literary Theory and Criticism' (38–54).

2. Poetry

(a) Poetry – pre-1945

'The Strange Ride: A Lecture for the Kipling Society, in 1986' (*KJ* (1991).11–25) is the first publication of a lecture written by Angus Wilson and read for him at Rockford College, Illinois. In a tolerant and valuable approach to the writer, it discusses the claustrophobia of England; the range of Kipling's idea of 'law'; and the burden of 'frontier-keeping'. Brad Leithauser's 'A Footnote for Housman' (*NewC* 9.109–16) refers to the poet's note in 'The Name and Nature of Poetry', a lecture delivered in Cambridge in 1933, which the writer uses as a way of exploring the nature of the poet's metrical range. Caroline Zilboorg (*PQ* 70.67–91) looks at a 'Joint Venture: Richard Aldington, H. D. and the Poet's Translation Series'. This is a valuable study not only of the series – described as 'never political and always romantic' – but also of the idea of Hellenism shared by H. D. and Aldington: it is a significant addition to our awareness of one aspect of the pre-war literary scene.

Writers of the First World War were the subject of several articles this year, and also a special number of *CS* (2) from 1990 which was not available for review last year. Some earlier thematic volumes of this journal have been valuable in following through its aim of accessibility and precision: yet this one, with some important exceptions, has less to offer. Robert Jeffcoate (*CS* 2:ii.151– 9) writes on 'Teaching Poetry of the First World War in the Secondary School'. He assesses various anthologies, suggests a visit to the Imperial War Museum, but generally says little that would be of help to any but the most ill-prepared secondary teacher. His conclusion, a complaint about the 'misuse, even abuse' of the poetry 'for the purpose of preaching pacifism', seems to show a fairly ingenious misunderstanding of what the poems themselves say: but then, anyone who mentions the difficulty of teaching *In Parenthesis* with the aside 'assuming one is convinced of its merits' does not reveal an outstanding literary percipience. Long may Mr Jeffcoate enjoy his retirement. Only slightly less insubstantial is Matt Simpson's 'Only a living thing – some notes towards a reading of Isaac Rosenberg's "Break of Day in the Trenches" ' (*CS* 2:ii.128–36). This is a straight, practical criticism exercise (yes, they do still exist): those who feel tempted to read it should instead read the poem and think. Jennifer Breen's 'Representations of the "feminine" in First World War Poetry' (*CS* 2:ii.169–75) has the important aim of seeing whether the poetry 'attempts to subvert accepted mythologies about women'; yet the attempt to do this with regard to David Jones, Rosenberg and Edward Thomas in half a dozen pages is an aim which is inevitably not fulfilled. Thomas seems to come out of it least badly; I would have valued more on the way Jones uses bawdy slang as a generative impulse – he is, at times, vaginocentric in this regard – but perhaps this is only another accepted mythology. Other essays from the volume are discussed in the context of the writers they address. One other general study appeared, Hilda D. Spear and Sonya A. Summersgill's 'Poison Gas and the Poetry of War' (*EIC* 41.308–23). This is a harrowing survey of mentions of gas in poems, along with accounts of the various kinds of gas in use and their effects. Thus summarized, the article appears questionable at the very least, but it is necessary, since to understand the poems we must know of the technological obscenities in full clinical detail.

The outstanding article on Wilfred Owen this year is Douglas Kerr's 'Wilfred Owen and the Social Question' (*ELT* 34.183–95). This charts the poet's involvement with social issues through the church before the war and tellingly notes the congruent roles of priest and army officer which often seem to elide in the poet's letters. Owen's sympathies for the working classes are explicit in 'Miners', but also underlie the images of vulnerable 'lads' in poems such as 'Exposure' and 'Arms and the Boy': the troops have become a new proletariat. Owen is angry at the church's blindness to inequality, yet himself can offer only 'passivity': Kerr's conclusion is that Owen's achievement was to 'rewrite the language of the war' in terms of greater accessibility. It is a further important stage in the critical shift from Owen as war poet to Owen as poet. Michael Williams (*CS* 2:ii.194–202) writes on 'Wilfred Owen: A Poet Re-institutionalised'. This sensitive and provoking essay is mainly concerned with the work of Jessie Pope, whose war poems for children were one source of Owen's anger in 'Dulce et decorum est'. Pope sees England as a 'Motherland': Owen's 'patria' is feminine, but includes the patriarchal structures implicit within the poem, so that the text's achievement is in rejecting both kinds of 'patriotism'. Paul Norgate (*CS* 2:ii.208–15) examines 'Soldiers' Dreams: Popular Rhetoric and the War Poetry of Wilfred Owen'. He sees dream as a significant trope or 'rhetorical strategy' of the war's writing and explores the imagery of sleep and dream in Owen's work within a context of popular writing. Among other insights is the comment that 'Dulce et decorum est' was inscribed above the door of the chapel at the Royal Military College, Sandhurst in 1913.

Three poets whose work is often overlooked or neglected for a range of reasons are considered in the *CS* special number. Jon Stallworthy asks 'Who was Rupert Brooke?' (*CS* 2:ii.185–93), looking at accounts of Brooke by his friends and at the pre-war poems to conclude that he is not a 'War Poet' but 'a poet of peace, a celebrant of friendship, love and laughter'. Doubtless this is true, but it seems unlikely that it is the whole truth. P. Joy King writes on ' "Honour", "Heroics" and "Bullshit": Ivor Gurney's Private Vision' (*CS* 2:ii.144–50). Gurney exposes what language would seek to avoid in the war – its horrors and loss of individuality rather than its 'images of generalised and universal suffering', a claim supported by some valid specific analysis. More satisfying is Nicholas Potter's 'The War Verse of Edmund Blunden' (*CS* 2:ii.176–84). This discusses the concentration of language in poems such as

'Thiepval Wood', and claims persuasively that the poet's realization of defeat and change go 'beyond natural orderliness'. Blunden's poetry is 'remarkably modern' in this: the article is a valuable, if brief, reassessment.

Andrew Motion's study of *The Poetry of Edward Thomas* is very fine indeed. It makes a thoroughly convincing case for Thomas to be given greater importance as a significant twentieth-century voice, in writing which develops tough sinews of thought in a supple and controlled way. The book is arranged around key ideas and stances in Thomas's work, beginning with his disturbing concept of 'the other' and moving on to 'the sense of sound' and his exploration of the rhythms of colloquial speech. The approach to the war poems is particularly perceptive, showing how the war conditions almost all his poetry, as does his very particular brand of patriotism, far removed from popular jingoism. Motion discusses many poems in great detail, quoting them at length and not being afraid to quote the same passage repeatedly. He also reveals the significance of Thomas's prose – even the reviews he so despised – in the growth of the poet's mature voice. The book is written with sensitivity and insight, and adds a great deal to the body of criticism on Thomas.

Stephen McKenzie's ' "Only an avenue, dark, nameless, without end": Edward Thomas's Road to France' (*CS* 2:ii.160–8) asks, Why did the poet fight? After looking at some poems he concludes that it was not to assume the 'positive identity' of a soldier, but to avoid the burden of responsibility for any identity at all, and thus suspend 'the necessarily unresolved enquiries into the state of humanity'. It's a suggestive thought, but the article lacks the breadth and tolerance of Motion's approach to the same subject, ignoring amongst other things the way Thomas saw himself within a long historical context of soldiers who fought for their notions of England.

John Lucas's new D. H. Lawrence anthology *D. H. Lawrence: Selected Poetry and Non-fictional Prose* places contemporary reviews of the poems alongside passages of Lawrence's prose and selections from the poems. This makes available some material otherwise hard to locate – it is good, for example, to have Lawrence's enthusiastic review of *Georgian Poetry*, and Edward Thomas on *Love Poems and Others*. The introduction briefly explores the nature of Lawrence's achievement, and there is a commentary which offers biographical as well as brief critical comments. This will be of much value for the undergraduate or A-level readers at whom the series of which it is part is aimed, and who lack the resources or drive to look further afield for some of the items included. Patricia L. Hagen writes on 'Astrology, Schema Theory, and Lawrence's Poetic Method' (*DHLR* 22.23–37). This is a lengthy account of the workings of metaphor through schema theory in 'Invocation to the Moon' as part of the transformation of consciousness the reader undergoes in a 'process of suspending one's ordinary conceptual structure'. Richard Hoffpauir's *The Art of Restraint* has a laudable aim: the revaluation of poets 'undervalued or misvalued' through their restraint at a time of concern with modernist values. Yet he is concerned as much with attacking poets of the modernist canon as promoting those whose values he finds more sympathetic, often through moral and political stances that are at best ill-defined. There is a lot of assertion here and those who share the writer's stance will find the book supportive, but those who are looking for a balanced explication of an alternative tradition will not, I think, find it much help.

In *Yeats and English Renaissance Literature*, Wayne K. Chapman explores the poet's absorption of earlier models through adaptation and imitation, two terms carefully defined in an opening chapter. Spenser is shown to be as important as Shelley as a model in the earlier poems, both in direct imitation and in contributing to the growth of Yeats's poetic philosophy and recurrent motifs such as the quest. This is followed by a detailed exploration of the influence of Jonson in both the plays and the poems, and a study of the polarity of forces in Donne as they are adapted to Yeats's purposes. A concluding chapter explores the 'Rapprochement with Milton and Spenser' in the later verse. This is a closely-written and meticulous book which interweaves biography, study of manuscripts and analysis of poetry and philosophy in a way which sheds much new light on the nature of Yeats's compositional procedures, language and philosophy. Chapman's article 'Milton and Yeats's "News" for the Oracle: Two Additional Sources' (*ELN* 77.60–4) explores echoes of Milton in 'News for the Delphic Oracle', from marked passages of Yeats's copy of Milton in the Richard Ellman Collection. 'W. B. Yeats: Poet as Reader' by Kinereth Meyer (in Spolsky, *The Uses of Adversity*) is a very fine essay which brings together the poet's concern for tradition, Bloom's ideas of 'the anxiety of response' and notions of the act of creativity in both writer and reader through a balanced study of 'Leda and the Swan' and 'Solomon and the Witch'. It is both effortless and elegant.

YeA 8 contains three previously unpublished texts by the poet. The 'Four Lectures by W. B.Yeats, 1902–4', which Richard Londraville edits, discuss the Irish dramatic movement and were given in Yeats's tour of the United States. To them are added ' "The Irish National Theatre": An Uncollected Address by W. B.Yeats' edited by David R. Clark, a talk given in Rome in 1934 which stresses the political and religious significance of the theatre in Ireland as a parallel to the inner struggle for intellectual perfection. Clark also edits ' "The Poet as Actress": An Unpublished Dialogue by W. B. Yeats'; the text dates from 1916 and explores again the struggle for artistic perfection, in which 'the pain [is] side by side with the ecstasy'. Two articles discuss technical aspects. Helen Vendler's 'Metrical variation in the Earlier Poems of Yeats' looks at overlapping stanza forms, variations of length in rhyme words and other elements which contribute to his later 'incantatory power of reduplicative language': Richard Taylor's 'Metrical variation in Yeats's verse' looks at key poems to suggest the need for full study to place Yeats technically in the context of modernist and more traditional writing. 'The Miltonic Crux of "The Phases of the Moon" ' by Wayne K. Chapman studies the text's origins in relation to the edition of Milton with Samuel Palmer's illustration which Yeats owned. Tim Armstrong's ' "Giving Birth to Oneself": Yeats's late sexuality' shows the poet's discovery of poetic energy along with sexuality in his later years, in an article of considerable subtlety and insight. Neil Mann explores *'A Vision:* Ideas of God and Man' to reveal its symbolism which allows a grasp of the 'aesthetic value' and 'tragic joy' of life. Art is thus not a retreat from life, but a way of making sense of it. Shorter notes include William H. O'Donnell's 'Checklist of Portraits of W. B.Yeats', Wayne K. Chapman on the Yeats library, and Wayne McKenna on 'W. B. Yeats, W. J. Turner and Edmund Dulac: The *Broadsides* and Poetry Broadcasts'. The usual reviews and lists of publications received complete this volume which maintains the high standards of the series.

Michael North's *The Political Aesthetic of Yeats, Eliot and Pound* is a study resting firmly on the theory of Paul de Man and other contemporary aestheticians. It chronicles Yeats's progress from the early Morris-inspired socialism through cultural nationalism, to 'militant aristocratic conservatism' and the final flirtation with fascism. *The Tower* is seen as a key text in which the contradictions of liberalism articulate an essentially Irish condition; yet, North concludes, the poet finally preferred to 'refer the whole problem to another, higher level' where human difficulties become sacred in their insolubility. The account of Eliot includes lucid disentangling of threads in the criticism, especially the conflict in Eliot's ideas of tradition and the individual, which is seen as part of a larger quest to reconcile individual and society – or to explore the difficulties inherent in such a quest – in *The Waste Land*, which moves on to a 'rosy' view of traditional societies in the *Quartets*. Eliot's 'displacement' is shown as the typical conservative sense of separation from the historical state the philosophy idealizes; the apparent reconciliation of apocalyptic opposites in 'Little Gidding' is ultimately unconvincing, and the poems as a whole are seen as a 'gamble'. This is a provocative and necessary study, not least in the more general opening and concluding chapters.

Tony Sharpe's *T. S. Eliot: A Literary Life* has nothing new to offer, but this is not the purpose of the series of which it is a part. Indeed, there is much to be said for the way that it rehearses the main elements of the poet's life and writings and summarizes the more recent ideas and controversies surrounding them. Doubtless it will be of value to undergraduates unwilling to pursue the material in more depth; but, for those who are, it is a pity that the references are so limited, the bibliography so short, and the style at times infelicitous. Less familiar, and more intriguing, biographical ground is trodden by Anthony E. Fathman in 'Viv and Tom: The Eliots as Ether Addict and Co-dependent' (*YER* 11.33–6). This explores the evidence that Vivien was an ether addict and then looks at three features of 'co-dependency' in Eliot – 'frozen feelings', perfectionism, and dishonesty – as forces from which his poetry and his spiritual quest were a form of release. Paul Horgan's 'To Meet Mr Eliot: Three Glimpses' (*ASch* 407–13) records three meetings with the poet, including an illuminating account of Eliot's reading 'Little Gidding' against a Dallas hailstorm. Two essays on Eliot and women begin Ronald Bush's anthology *T. S. Eliot: The Modernist in History*. Lyndall Gordon's 'Eliot and Women' briefly chronicles the relationships with the four key women in Eliot's life, making suggestions about their place in his work in a manner familiar from her two biographical studies. Carol Christ's 'Gender, Voice and Figuration in Eliot's Early Poetry' is much tougher, exploring the links between nineteenth-century female portrait poetry and Eliot's early verse, where 'looking at a woman … decomposes his voice', and the shift in the *Quartets* to an avoidance of both body and gender.

Eliot's poetry is, as usual, the subject of a wide diversity of articles. Several address the poet's kinship with other figures, contemporary and earlier. Nancy K. Gish's 'Eliot and Marianne Moore: Modernism and Difference' (*YER* 11.40–3) stresses the value of reading Eliot 'in parallel, contrast, tension with other voices', revealing how, when their works are read together, Moore and Eliot 'complement and correct' each other. A different sort of relationship is suggested in J. C. Mahanti's 'Dryden and Eliot: A Sense of Kinship' (*YER* 11.1–6). Mahanti finds a major parallel in the two figures' timidity and compound anxieties, which he sees as causing a 'personal inner-world of nightmare' leading them to borrow extensively from others in their writings. Eliot's praise for Dryden perhaps reveals his awareness of the similarity. Jewel Spears Brooker looks elsewhere in 'From Epithalamium to Rhapsody: Mind and World in Wordsworth and Eliot' (*YER* 11.37–9). To the former poet, the relationship is a holy moving; to the latter, prostitution. Memory destroys for Eliot, rather than healing: it is this which, despite the many links, ultimately severs him from the Romantic tradition. A suggestive thought. Yet another pairing is examined by Shyamal Bagchee in 'Subtle Souls and Dry Bones: Hopkins and Eliot' (*YER* 11.48–55). Hopkins 'vivifies his suffering' in discussing sin and redemption, Eliot 'objectifies and intellectualizes', the difference accounting for Eliot's strongly worded antipathy to Hopkins in *After Strange Gods*. As well as defining the differences, Bagchee finds some echoes, but concludes that 'Hopkins' language is not Eliot's language yet a dialogue of sorts has taken place.' A useful article, given the circumstances that led Eliot to have Hopkins as a 'long-dead contemporary'.

A. Walton Litz's study 'The Allusive Poet: Eliot and his Sources' (in Bush's *T. S. Eliot: The Modernist in History*) is a brilliant exploration of the nature of the poet's conscious and instinctual intertextuality, full of fine insights such as the fact that Pound's deletion of the final couplet from the typist's seduction scene in *The Waste Land* leaves the section as a Shakespearean sonnet, the form of which we unconsciously discover as we read; and the significances of the frequent recurrence of the Arnaut Daniel passage of *Purgatorio* XXVI. By contrast. Jibesh Bhattacharyya's 'T. S. Eliot: A Twentieth-Century Metaphysical' (*LHY* 31.26–36) is more basic, but it does offer some straightforward parallels between Eliot and the earlier poets for new entrants to the maze of intertextuality.

Others have been concerned with specific influences on, or confluences in, the poetry. Jeremy Macklin's 'Eliot's use of *The White Devil* in *The Waste Land*' (*ESA* 34.1–11) is a helpful addition to our grasp of intertextuality. It offers felicities such as the common concern with the corpse as a sprouting bulb, the threat of both women and wolves, and the shared themes of lust and insanity, yet concludes that there is a hint of hope in Eliot's text which Webster's lacks. 'T. S. Eliot and A. E. Housman: A Borrowing' (*N&Q* 38.341–2) by K. Narayana Chandran notes the use of 'Be still, my soul' from *A Shropshire Lad* XLVIII in *East Coker* III, and relates this to Eliot's awareness of the 'littleness' of his own poem in offering any Christian faith or hope. Chandran also finds the origin of Eliot's 'Cousin Nancy' in the 'Little Nancy Ellicoat' of a nursery jingle called 'A Cradle', in 'T. S. Eliot's "Cousin Nancy" and a Nursery Riddle' (*N&Q* 38.341). William Atkinson's 'Africa: A Common Topos in Lawrence and Eliot' (*TCL* 37.22–37) is a multi-layered exploration of Africa as discursive opposition to Europe and self-knowledge. Much is concerned with *The Rainbow* and *Women in Love*, but the article also claims Eliot's references to Conrad's river as a liberating use of memory. It is a dense and suggestive article; though is it too simplistic to ask why no mention is made of the contemporary cult of 'primitivism' in European art as a balance to post-Victorian colonialism?

The Waste Land, in its genesis and all its facets, continues to fascinate. James Longenbach's '*Ara vos prec*: Eliot's negation of Satire and Suffering' (in Bush) discusses the complexities of voice, pain and viewpoint from the early private poems to the ambiguity of 'openness and closed authority' of *The Waste Land*. Chris Ackerley's 'T. S. Eliot's superfetation of ...' (*N&Q* 38.41–2) is a macaronic meditation on Eliot's use of the Greek *tohen* as 'contemplation of the generative powers of the neuter word' as 'a figure of the logos'. John T. Mayer looks at '*The Waste Land* and Eliot's Poetry Notebook' (in Bush), examining the earlier city poems and, more important, an unpublished work called 'The Descent from the Cross' to see the finished poem as a serious parody of the descent and harrowing of hell, enriched by anxieties and tensions of the psyche in true modern manner, which involves us, the 'semblable' or protagonist's double, in sharing his vision. Robin Schulze, in 'The Trope of the Police Force in T. S. Eliot's Cambridge Prologue' (*YER* 11.19–23) discusses the deleted passage chronicling the bar–music hall–brothel crawl as a parallel statement of themes of memory, desire, authority and release stated in the published text of *The Waste Land*. 'Forms of Simultaneity in *The Waste Land* and *Burnt Norton*', Alan Williamson's contribution to the Bush collection, finds the spatial form of the quartet anticipated in the 'mythic time' of the earlier text, where different kinds and levels of myth overlap to form 'a single story'. The Bush volume also includes Lawrence Rainey's 'The Price of Modernism: Publishing *The Waste Land*' which appeared in *CritQ* in 1989 (*YWES* 70.547).

'The Integrity of Eliot' (*EIC* 41.222–39) by A. V. C. Schmidt argues that Eliot realized the close relation, or homology, between poetic and religious solitude, seeing *Ash Wednesday* as central to the move towards this realization in the poetry of the thirties; hence Eliot's integrity. In 'Eliot, Lukács, and the Politics of Modernism' (in Bush), Michael North suggestively contrasts the approaches of *Theory of the Novel* and *The Waste Land* to the problem of postulating a return to a tradition or a way beyond it in a modernist convention of fragmentation and negativity. Ronald Bush concludes his collection with his own essay 'T. S. Eliot at the Present Time: A Provocation'. This includes valuable quotations from letters by Edmund Wilson giving a very early response to *The Waste Land*, and concludes that we must see Eliot as a 'toiler' and 'maker' who fashioned tradition for himself knowing that others must re-make it, rather than an élitist staving off barbarity by reinforcing a privileged culture. Russell Elliott Murphy, in 'Demeaning Eliot: The Future of Literary Studies' (*YER* 11.46–7) claims that the poet's anti-Semitism cannot be genuine because 'he was a poet who never ceased to suspect that words chosen without care were words better not used at all.' The doubt that he was anti-Semitic proves that he wasn't. If Murphy thinks that this ghost can be so simply laid, I fear he is mistaken.

In *The English Eliot*, Steve Ellis explores what he sees as a move to a classicizing astringency in several dimensions of the work of the thirties. Instead of the polyphony of *The Waste Land* there is the 'classic exclusion of voices' of the *Quartets*, which are sited in a dehumanized, classic southern landscape familiar from the paintings of Paul Nash. The tone of his poetry, too, moves towards asceticism and negation of self. The study concludes with a comparison between Auden and Eliot, to suggest links often overlooked as well as carefully defined nuances of differences. This is a suggestive book which opens an important new field of discussion, but one that does not wholly convince: can we really agree that Eliot rejects Romanticism when his treatment of landscape depends so surely on the inner–outer equation of the picturesque, even if it is used to wholly different ends? It seems to me that this, and Ellis's rejection of thirties Romanticism and rather limited treatment of Nash and the visual arts, constricts the argument somewhat. Paul Murray's *T. S. Eliot and Mysticism* also explores Eliot's self-negation, but in the context of a full-scale study of the mystical and religious sources of the *Quartets*. Each of the poems is discussed in turn in relation to the mysticism of Henri Bergson, St Augustine, Buddhism, and Kierkegaard, and the link with mythic patterns in Shakespeare and Dante is also explored. This is far more than a catalogue of echoes, though; it is a mature and reasoned exploration of the poet's method which adds much to our grasp of the movement of the *Quartets*.

Rob Jackaman's *The Course of English Surrealist Poetry Since the 1930s* sets itself an ambitious aim – to show the centrality of the Surrealist stance to English poetry in the succeeding years of the century. There are clear summaries of surrealist theory in the thirties, usefully outlining its growth in periodicals such as *Experiment* and Gascoyne's *Short Survey*, and the movement is shown developing from 'psychic automatism' to its more sophisticated form where the unselective subconscious is used metaphorically, not literally. From accounts of the poetry of David Gascoyne and others, Jackaman moves to consider surrealist elements in Lawrence, Dylan Thomas, and the poets of the New Apocalypse, the Movement and the Group, with a section on Mavericks and poetry of the last two decades. There are revealing suggestions about Ted Hughes, whose 'Cadenza' is claimed to be 'virtually one and the same' as Gascoyne's 'The Diabolical Principle', and work by Adrian Henri and Seamus Heaney. It is a valuable introduction to the thirties writers, and makes suggestive points about later material which may develop their use of catachresis and elision, aided by Jackaman's awareness of one origin of English surrealism in the equation between inner and outer reality found in Coleridge and other Romantics.

John Ackerman's *A Dylan Thomas Companion* provides surveys of the life, poetry, prose and film and broadcast work. It is an excellent introduction, making sensible use of the work of Ackerman and other Thomas scholars, and its full bibliography, reproductions of drafts of poems, and the texts of captions to some *Lilliput* photographs by Bill Brandt thought to be by Thomas make this an essential reference tool for undergraduates and others. Stephen Boyd's 'Secular Mysticism: Dylan Thomas' "Fern Hill" ' (*FMLS* 27.177–88) is a wide and thoughtful account which ranges through Traherne, Blake, Wordsworth, Hopkins, Lacan, and others in its exploration of Thomas's childhood imaginings, to conclude that only words in poetry can take us out of time – 'They are what is mystical', as Wittgenstein says. The 'Echoes of *The Waste Land* in Dylan Thomas's "And death shall have no dominion" ' which K. Narayana Chandran finds (*N&Q* 38.346–7) are from 'Death by Water', and are used by Thomas in elegiac rather than ambivalent tone.

Thomas Dilworth's 'The Spatial Imagination of David Jones' (*TCL* 37.240–52) approaches a key notion of modern poetics, the form of the long poem as either temporal or spatial. Dilworth's opening assertions are hopeful: but, though his analysis of *Anathemata* shows well its form as a series of unfolding elements, he fails to follow through the full implications of this in terms of the synchronic perception of a visual text, and hence of *Anathemata* and the results on text and reader. Greg Hill's 'Alun Lewis – the War, Darkness and the Search for Poetic Truth' (*CS* 2.216–22) sees the images of darkness and death in Lewis's poetry as an attempt to 'confront the destructive darkness' caused by war, which 'suffuses the poems at a deeper level than surface reference'. Erica Riggs discusses 'W. H. Auden as a Seriocomic Critic' (*TCL* 37.207–24). The article is a series of explorations of Auden's stress on 'the benefits of attempting resolution through dialectic' in criticism and poetry that is both morally serious and self-deprecating, informed increasingly by a sense of Christian humility and a 'skeptical consideration' to show the mutual correctiveness of diverse critical positions. It is a valid and persuasive approach.

(b) Poetry – post 1945

Chapman devotes much of its Spring/Summer issue to Edwin Morgan. Robert Watson contributes 'An Island in the City: Edwin Morgan's Urban Poetry' (*Chapman* 64.12–22), an examination of the role of the city in Morgan's work. Watson's initial suggestion that Morgan's is a more celebratory vision than that of many of his precursors seems to be partially undermined by the essay's development, which rapidly leads us back to the familiar territory of urban alienation and despair; but this, like Robert Crawford's probing of his subject's literary nationalism in 'Morgan's Critical Position' (*Chapman* 64.32–6), offers interesting insights into the man and his art.

James A. Davies's *Leslie Norris* emphasizes his subject's ambiguous relationship to his native Wales, highlighting the 'exile' in England and the United States and the quarrel with what the poet himself identifies as a prevailing parochialism in Welsh literature; but Davies argues that these 'distancing gestures' are indicative not of simple rejection, but of Norris's 'complex sense of his own poetic identity'. The study traces, largely through detailed analysis of individual poems, the development of his poetry from its awkward beginnings to the publication of the impressive 1989 collection *A Sea in the Desert*.

Larkin, as usual, features prominently in the year's work. The penultimate chapter of John Powell Ward's *The English Line* places him within a tradition which includes Wordsworth, Tennyson, Hardy, and Edward Thomas – poets who have found sustenance in a vision of the English landscape. Larkin's work is, however, as Ward notes, 'a paradox', its landscapes central yet indicative of rootlessness rather than nurture. Larkin may indeed express a sense of the ending of a long and fruitful relationship with nature, but Ward seems too uncritically ready to endorse such a view. The study's conclusion speaks of 'the gap the English line is leaving'; others might be more ready than Ward to acknowledge the ways in which the 'line' (not in any case the best term for the complex web of relationships involved) continues to develop.

Richard Hoffpauir explores similar territory in *The Art of Restraint: English Poetry from Hardy to Larkin*. This is a re-evalution generated by the author's avowed disappointment with the twentieth-century canon as popularly and critically defined; but the approach is disconcertingly crude. Hoffpauir's dubious strategies predictably elevate Hardy at the expense of Yeats and lead inexorably, via Betjeman, to an uninspired account of Larkin's verse. 'I do not presume,' says Hoffpauir, 'to be uncovering hidden depths or saying anything startlingly new about Larkin.' The observation is at once disarming and accurate.

In 'Larkin, Nature and Romanticism' (*CS* 3.53–60), G. J. Finch argues that, notwithstanding Larkin's suggestions of his own distance from Romanticism, his poetry has crucial affinities with that of Wordsworth. The essay itself tends towards appropriately Larkinesque equivocation: the poet's attitude is 'clearly not Romantic' nor 'anti-Romantic', but 'peppered by a consciousness that seems drawn towards Romanticism'. In the same issue, Peter Snowdon's 'Larkin's Conceit' (*CS* 3.61–70) asks important questions about Larkin's literary reputation, suggesting that the poet, obsessed by patterns of limitation, may have denied himself and his readers the wider transcendental possibilities implicit in great poetry. Snowdon is himself guilty of trivializing his subject and his tone is sometimes patronizing; but the essay functions as a useful counterweight to some of the arguably excessive praise of Larkin from other quarters.

John Bayley compares Larkin with Housman in 'Housman and Larkin: Romantic into Parnassian?' (*EIC* 41.147–59). Besides the obvious biographical and ideological similarities, Bayley notes similarities of tone in the poetry: a recurrent self-deprecation, an intimacy, a studied elegance. Like Finch, he also notes links with Romanticism, implicit, he suggests, in the concern of both poets with absences apparently more potent for them than any presence.

Eckhard Auberleben's 'The Theme of Death in the Poetry of Philip Larkin and Charles Tomlinson' (*ArAA* 16.175–203) takes as its starting point Tomlinson's criticism of the Movement Poets' resistance to 'the mystery ... in the created universe' and goes on to compare Tomlinson's poetic treatment of death with Larkin's. Auberleben's pedestrian analysis gives prominence to Tomlinson, whose poetry, he suggests, has a greater range than that of Larkin.

Tomlinson comes under scrutiny again in Hearne Pardee's 'A Distant Vision: Charles Tomlinson and American Art' (*PoetryR* 81.442–53). Pardee makes out a plausible case for using a British painter/poet as a means of access to his wider subject, though much of what he has to say actually centres on Tomlinson's difference from his American counterparts. Portraying Tomlinson as coolly resistant to the post-Romantic urge for fusion with the object of contemplation, Pardee depicts an artist directly relevant to the American quest for 'a new equilibrium'.

Geoffrey Hill's 'The Mystery of the Charity of Charles Pequy' is the subject of Jeffrey Donaldson's 'Must Men Stand by What They Write?' (*PoetryR* 81.548–54), an appropriately complex examination of the question of the writer's moral responsibility as it emerges from, or is embodied in, Hill's poem. The difficulty of Hill's language is brought sharply into focus here as Donaldson, following Hill himself, suggests that one of the writer's responsibilities is to create forms which 'resisting the reader's unburdened passage through the poem', function both as constraint and as a pressure or invitation to transcend that constraint.

Neil Astley's introduction to *Tony Harrison*, a critical anthology from Bloodaxe, is a plea for recognition of Harrison's own claim that 'poetry is all I write'. We cannot, Astley suggests, arrive at an adequate understanding of the poetry unless we acknowledge the seamless integrity of the oeuvre, giving as much weight to the work for theatre, opera-house and television as to the contents of the *Selected Poems*. And this is indeed a wide-ranging anthology: among its offerings are Douglas Dunn's brief but perceptive discussion of Harrison's defiance of the 'proprietorial language' of the literary establishment, Terry Eagleton's Bakhtinian account of 'v' as 'a multiplicity of contending voices', Peter Symes's observations on film-making with Harrison and Peter Levi's laudatory survey of the verse dramas. Poetry and prose by Harrison himself are also included in this substantial and important volume.

Seamus Heaney's *Selected Poems 1966–1987* is the subject of Sidney Burris's 'An Empire of Poetry' (*SoR* 27.558–74). The selection, argues Burris, 'represents one of [Heaney's] most sustained acts of criticism to date'; and he goes on to highlight the poet's continuing engagement with the social implications of his art and his unfailing respect for that local detail which gestures outward to wider and deeper truths.

In 'Creative Tensions in the Poetry of Seamus Heaney' (*CS* 3.80–7), J. R. Atfield examines those conflicts of which the poet himself is so intelligently aware: between his Irishness and the lure of the English language; between actual experience and the art to which that experience gives rise. Atfield's conclusion emphasizes Heaney's own recognition of the artist's power and right to move beyond the limiting oppositions to a new and expansive level of consciousness.

Karen M. Moloney's 'Heaney's Love to Ireland' (*TCL* 37.273–88) explains the rape depicted in Heaney's *Ocean's Love to Ireland* as suggestive of Ireland's resilience, as well as of her humiliation. The concept of 'repossession', arguably ambiguous within the poem itself, is here interpreted as implying a reassertion of personal and national identity.

Repossession, again in an Irish context, is also the theme of 'We Were Never on the Scene of the Crime: Eavan Boland's Repossession of History' (*TCL* 37.442–53). The authors, Patricia L. Hagen and Thomas W. Zelman, link the poets's quest for contact with a Gaelic heritage with that for 'reconnection with a female heritage suppressed by centuries of male domination'. Boland, they argue, cannot simply accept the images, so appealing to her male counterparts, of Ireland as 'triumphant woman', but must reconstruct, rejecting the merely ornamental in favour of harder and more intimate truths; her reconstructions gesture towards 'a new ethic for Irish poetry'.

Derek Mahon comes under scrutiny in the Summer issue of *Poetry Review*. Edna Longley's review of the *Selected Poems*, 'Where a Thought Might Grow' (*PoetryR* 81.ii.7–8), highlights Mahon's 'attraction to the derelict and marginal' and praises the poet while regretting his tendency to revise earlier work. And Mahon speaks for himself in an interview with Wiliam Scammell (*PoetryR* 81.ii.4–6), reinforcing some of Longley's points by referring to himself as having been 'born odd'. Bill Tinley's illuminating essay 'International Perspectives in the Poetry of Derek Mahon' (*IUR* 21.106–17), offers a more complex picture. Citing Mahon's own view that Irish writers 'should be judged by London, New York standards', Tinley depicts a poet eager to transcend his local sources without betraying them. The essay focuses on Mahon's recurrent references to European art, but points out that his approach to that art seeks to redefine it in relation to his own personal and cultural background. Tinley identifies his subject's creative dilemma as that of a poet whose natural impulse towards enlargement is tempered by a perceived need for narrower forms of definition; the conflict, he suggests, gives rise both to despair and affirmation.

Contemporary Poetry Meets Modern Theory (edited by Easthope and Thompson), a collection of essays actually biased towards postmodern theory, offers another essay on Harrison. In 'Tony Harrison's Languages', Rick Rylance examines Harrison's poetic techniques in relation to those of poststructuralist criticism, noting his self-conscious acknowledgement of earlier literature and his use of word-play. Other relevant contributions deal with J. H. Prynne (an interesting essay by Geoffrey Ward, emphasizing the challenge posed by Prynne's multiple meanings and 'outrageously perverse use of words') and Tom Raworth, whose 1984 collection, *Tottering State*, is the focus of Peter Brooker's 'Postmodern Postpoetry', an essay which seeks to locate its subject within a postmodernist framework. And Seamus Heaney is here, too, subjected to a rather heavy-handed analysis by Thomas Docherty in 'Ana-; or Postmodernism, Landscape, Seamus Heaney', an essay which, focusing primarily on *The Grauballe Man*, interprets Heaney's work in postmodernist terms as fluid 'event' rather than fixed 'text'.

Contemporary Poets, now updated in a fifth edition, is a substantial reference work edited by Tracy Chevalier offering detailed information on a wide range of living poets writing in English. Entries provide outline biographies, bibliographies, critical discussion and, in many cases, a relevant personal statement by the poet in question.

3. Drama

This section has three categories: (a) General Studies; (b) Editions of plays (plays are only included if they contain introductions or some kind of critical commentary or have some other claim to be included, such as being based on a previously existing literary work or exciting particular controversy); (c) Individual Authors, in alphabetical order. Coverage of film and television is confined to works by writers with a substantial theatrical reputation. *MD* (34) should be consulted for the annual bibliography by Charles Carpenter, and *London Theatre Record* for reprints of reviews of current London productions. The section on Beckett is by Anna McMullan.

(a) General Studies

The most significant general studies concentrated on Irish theatre and on Women's Theatre. Essays on individual writers in *The Crows Behind the Plough: History and Violence in Anglo-Irish Poetry and Drama*, edited by Geert Lernout, and in an issue of *CLQ* devoted to aspects of Irish theatre, are considered below in alphabetical sequence. In *The Crows Behind the Plough*, Gerald Fitzgibbon explores 'Historical Obsessions in Recent Irish Drama', drawing useful and informative comparisons between the approaches to historical material of Brian Friel, Tom Leonard, Frank McGuinness, and Tom Murphy. In the same volume, Ulrich Schneider tackles similar themes in a more detailed examination of Friel and McGuinness ('Staging History in Contemporary Anglo-Irish Drama: Brian Friel and Frank McGuinness'). In *CLQ*,

Eileen Kearney presents a largely expository account of 'Current Women's Voices in the Irish Theatre: New Dramatic Visions' (27.225–32), which serves the important function of placing names on record to act as a starting point for future research. Steve Wilmer's 'Women's Theatre in Ireland' (*NTQ* 7.353–60) performs a similar function with an account of women's contributions to Irish theatre in the early twentieth century and recently. In *Behind the Scenes*, Adrian Frazier offers an account of the battles for control of the Abbey between Annie Horniman, W. B. Yeats and Augusta Lady Gregory which successfully teases out some of the tangled web of political and psychological alliances which determined the shifting course of the theatre in its early days. This is a good example of some of the very theoretically sophisticated work being done on the Abbey today, but I do look forward to more work on Horniman and Gregory in terms of questions of gender to add another dimension to the debate.

Documentation of women's work in the theatre continues to be a significant element with work covering both the very early twentieth century and the contemporary period. Claire Hirschfield's 'The Suffrage Play in England 1907–1913' (*CVE* 33.73–85) is a straightforward introduction to the work of the Actresses' Franchise League with some account of some of the plays it presented. At the other end of the period, in *Sheer Bloody Magic*, Carole Woddis interviews sixteen British actresses on many aspects of their work. This is an important collection of insights into contemporary theatre, film, and television practice, although the interview format necessarily precludes lengthy consideration of any single issue. Lizbeth Goodman continues her useful documentation of contemporary women's theatre in an interview with Yvonne Brewster, the Artistic Director of Talawa Theatre Company, under the title 'Drawing the Black and White Line: Defining Black Women's Theatre' (*NTQ* 7.361–8).

Eve Lewis's *Ficky Stingers* attracts critical attention in two comparative essays: David Ian Rabey examines the dramatic strategies used by Pinter and Lewis in his consideration of 'Violation and Implication: *One for the Road* and *Ficky Stingers*' (*TD* 13.261–7), while Sue-Ellen Case also looks at the play in her synoptic consideration of 'The Power of Sex: English Plays by Women, 1958–1988' (*NTQ* 7.238–45). Case also offers brief readings of *A Taste of Honey, The Knack, The Love of the Nightingale, Masterpieces, Dusa, Fish, Stas and Vi, Cloud Nine, Rug of Identity, Double Vision, Chiaroscuro*, and *A Mouthful of Birds*. Her conclusion is not unexpected: 'All of these plays have carefully, for the critique and therefore aid of women, precisely sketched the workings of oppressive uses of sexuality. Some have also hinted at the other possibility – the transgressive, revolutionary role of pleasure and of women's reclaiming of their own desire.' Beate Neumeier's 'Past Lives in Present Drama: Feminist Theater and Intertextuality' (in Thérèse Fischer-Seidel's collection) examines Caryl Churchill's *Top Girls*, Pam Gems's *Queen Christina*, Liz Lochhead's *Blood and Ice*, and Michelene Wandor's *Aurora Leigh* in terms of their modes of dramatizing 'the lives of outstanding women of the past, thereby involving directly or implicitly notions of biography and autobiography, and thus questions of intertextuality and identity'.

Other interesting studies covered a wide range with no obvious pattern. David Birch's *The Language of Drama* is a polemical attempt to address its topic in terms of the discursive practices involved in many kinds of dramatic production, including rehearsal and dramatic criticism as well as the creation of dramatic texts. It is lively and provocative, with many examples from contemporary dramatic practice, but falls short of answering many of the questions it sets itself.

Tragicomedy and Contemporary Culture by John Orr is an impressive account of both twentieth-century tragicomedy in general and the dramatic strategies of Samuel

Beckett, Harold Pinter and Sam Shepard in particular. Orr draws effectively on a wide range of sources to construct a compelling theoretical account of twentieth-century drama in relation to modernism and also deploys his insights powerfully on individual works.

Jacqueline Martin's *Voice in Modern Theatre* is an important and innovative full-length study of one of the major factors in theatrical production which places due emphasis on theories of vocal delivery from Stanislavski to Peter Brook.

'Bums on Seats: Parties, Art, and Politics in London's East End' (*TDR* 35.43–65) provides a useful and informative account of cultural politics in the late 1980s in the form of a report by Douglas Anderson, a response from Karen Fricker and a reply to her from Anderson himself. The theatres covered include the Hackney Empire, Stratford East, the Albany, and the Half Moon.

In a special issue of *TJ* devoted to Radio Drama, Richard Imison contributes a self-explanatory account of 'Radio and the Theater: A British Perspective' (43.289–92).

(b) Editions of plays

This year's significant volumes continue the Irish and Women's Theatre themes of section (a). *Modern Irish Drama*, edited by John P. Harrington is a very useful and low priced anthology of plays by W. B. Yeats, Augusta Lady Gregory, J. M. Synge, George Bernard Shaw, Sean O'Casey, Brendan Behan, Samuel Beckett, and Brian Friel. As well as notes on the individual plays, the editor also includes a well-chosen and illuminating selection of relevant secondary material, ranging from programme notes and polemical essays by the dramatists themselves to reviews and academic criticism.

Gabrielle Griffin and Elaine Aston's *Herstory* prints plays first performed by the Women's Theatre Group (*Lear's Daughters*, attributed to the Women's Theatre Group and Elaine Feinstein, *Pinchdice & Co* by Julie Wilkinson, and Bryony Lavery's *Witchcraze* in the first volume; Elisabeth Bond's *Love and Dissent*, *Dear Girl* by Tierl Thompson and Libby Mason, and Joyce Holliday's *Anywhere to Anywhere* in the second), together with a brief account of the group and a theoretically sophisticated introduction to each play. The plays fall into two groups with those in the first volume dating from the later eighties and dealing with mythologized females and those in the second volume dating from the early eighties and dealing with historical women, although the editors rightly point out that this does not reflect a single move from a realist base to a mythological one so much as a concern to 'portray women both within and across time, taking note of audience tastes and changes on the cultural and theatrical scene in general'.

Whereas *Herstory* is edited by academics, *Monstrous Regiment: A Collective Celebration* is edited by Gillian Hanna, one of the founders of the company, so the volume includes more first hand material. As well as an excellent critical and historical introduction which conveys very well the issues and debates that concerned the company, the volume also includes the texts of four plays staged by them: *Scum* by Claire Luckham and Chris Bond, *My Sister in this House* by Wendy Kesselman, Jenny McLeod's *Island Life*, and Clare Venables's adaptation of Stina Katchadourian's translation of *Love Story of the Century* by Marta Tikkanen.

(c) Individual Authors

Gunter Kloss's discussion of *The Last Supper* and *The Bite of the Night* in 'Howard

Barker: Paradigm of Postmodernism' (*NTQ* 7.20–6) argues that Barker 'cuts the umbilical cord to the aesthetic womb that has given consistency and meaning to the drama throughout the centuries of modernity' by developing metadramatic, associative, and disruptive intertextual strategies into a 'new kind of signification' that generates in audiences a sense of 'an unbearable gap between textualization and experience, between the fictionalization of life and life itself'. What such analyses always seem to ignore is that sometimes Barker's strategies work and sometimes they do not.

In 'Peter Barnes and the Problem of Goodness' (in Brater and Cohn, *Around the Absurd*), Bernard F. Dukore continues his long-standing engagement with Barnes's work in a sensitive reading of the ways in which Barnes dramatizes the problem of goodness and its relationship with power.

Christopher Murray considers a young Irish dramatist in ' "Such a Sense of Home": The Poetic Drama of Sebastian Barry' (*CLQ* 27.242–8), finding in his two plays 'a simplicity which encapsulates a world startling, strange, and prophetic' but also admitting that, as he outlines it, one of the plays 'probably seems naive to an absurd degree'. Without having either seen or read any of Barry's work, I reserve judgement.

One of the major new directions emerging in Beckett criticism is the location of Beckett's work in a specifically Irish context. In *The Irish Beckett*, John P. Harrington argues that the reclaiming of Beckett as an Irish writer is related to a 'major reassessment in Ireland of its own cultural identity ... particularly as formulated by its writers'. Through his rejection of the 'narrow chronological and topical bounds of the Irish Literary Revival', Beckett can be placed within a tradition of writers, including Joyce, who resisted the isolationism of the emerging nation state, and sought to combine specific Irish references with wider European cultural influences and traditions. While most of Harrington's attention is directed towards Beckett's fictional writing, chapter five addresses the major dramatic works. This section stresses that the Irish dramatic tradition which can be traced in Beckett's plays is a European tradition 'most antithetical to a local dramatic realism'. Much of the section, however, deals with Beckett's negotiation of themes and issues such as 'the dialectic of self and place and the antinomies of home and abroad', which Harrington sees as characteristic of the Irish writer exploring the 'predicament' of 'the Irish situation'. Such an abstract focus means that some of the material is not entirely convincing, but Harrington gives a useful introduction to Beckett's work in relation to recent debates within Irish Studies.

Perspectives of Irish Drama and Theatre, edited by Jacqueline Genet and Richard Allen Cave, Number 33 in the Colin Smythe Irish Literary Studies Series, includes two articles on Beckett's drama, each ranging across drama for stage, television and radio. Maggie Rose's 'The Actor as Marionnette: Yeats and Beckett as directors of their own plays' provides a concise introduction to Beckett's strategies as director, drawing on currently available material and debates, and points towards the possible influence on Beckett of Jack B. Yeats's puppet theatre, though it does not engage with wider issues around Beckett's place in Irish literature. Katherine Worth's article, 'Beckett's Irish Theatre' describes Beckett as an 'Irish European', and addresses the question of how the Irishness shows through in the plays. The article focuses on Beckett's allusions to Irish places, while removing local signposts; his use of Irish turns of phrase and rhythm; his preoccupation with talk and storytellers, although Worth argues that Beckett breaks new ground by internalizing the process which his Irish predecessors showed from without; his fondness for gallows humour and farce;

and finally the dimension of unworldliness and mystical evocation in his plays. Clearly structured and accessible, this article provides useful signposts for further exploration.

John Orr's study of Beckett in *Tragicomedy and Contemporary Culture: Play and Performance from Beckett to Shepard* continues the debate about Beckett's Irishness. Orr focuses on 'the double exile of culture and language which Beckett found in Paris', but also on the exile of 'the bourgeois Protestant child born on the outskirts of an intensely Catholic city ... The city, one senses, was never his. Nor was the language.' On the one hand, Orr argues, Beckett transforms the local 'into a numb and featureless no-man's land', but on the other, he suggests that this Irish amnesia is 'a forgetting firmly rooted in a remembered tradition, that of Irish theatre without which it would never have been possible'. Orr therefore sees Beckett's drama as 'both an extension and a rejection of his Protestant Irish predecessors'. Orr places Beckett in relation to Synge and Yeats, suggesting that Beckett substitutes a myth of Christian redemption for the myth of a glorious ancient Ireland. The essay then debates Beckett's relation to this Christian myth and to the crisis of value in European culture manifested in existentialism, and includes detailed analyses of *Waiting for Godot* and *Endgame*. Orr writes well, and deals with essential issues in both plays, particularly the use of tragicomedy in *Endgame*, but the absence of any sustained discussion of contemporary debates in performance studies means that his discussion does not take account of some of the most challenging critical work written on Beckett's drama in recent years.

Approaches to Teaching Beckett's 'Waiting for Godot', edited by June Schlueter and Enoch Brater, is an extremely useful book for teachers and students alike. The collection does take account of the variety of new approaches to Beckett's drama informed by aspects of critical and performance theory, while giving a useful representation of seminal essays by established scholars. The book is geared towards undergraduate teaching, and is in two parts: the first deals with materials, including editions and productions, comments on required and recommended readings, and audiovisual materials; the second includes twenty essays in five categories. These sections are grouped as follows: introductory essays, including contributions by Ruby Cohn and Linda Ben-Zvi; influences and backgrounds, which features Martin Esslin on the concept of the absurd, Lance St John Butler on philosophy, Fred Muller Robinson on the music hall, and Claudia Cassius on *Godot* and the Chaplinesque; course contexts outline how specific approaches may be most suited to particular courses, whether a course on tragedy (Mary Scott Simpson), French drama (Dina Scherzer) or Beckett (Charles Lyons); a critical approaches section discusses critical theory (Kevin J. H. Dettmar and Stephen Barker), semiotics and comparative approaches; and finally, a performance section has contributions from Stanton B. Garner Jnr, Toby Silverman Zinman, Sidney Homan and S. E. Gontarski. As these essays are quite short, I will not isolate some in preference to others, but would recommend the collection, which can be used to outline and suggest a range of approaches and contexts for the play.

The World of Samuel Beckett, edited by Joseph Smith as volume 12 in the Psychiatry and the Humanities series, is not the most accessible of collections, though many of the articles are thought-provoking. The psychiatric approach of some of the contributions can be frustrating for the drama specialist. In the introduction, Joseph Smith suggests that 'the "oddities" of Beckettian characters always also portray the particular embodiment of universal issues ... Beckettian characters can't help but remind therapists of their clients and often enough evoke thoughts of cure, not only of the Beckettian characters but of their author'. Joseph Smith's 'Notes on *Krapp*, *Endgame*, and Applied Psychoanalysis' is concerned with healing, and follows the progression from depression to mourning, seeing both Krapp and Beckett the man as 'fair game' for the psychoanalyst to ponder. Robert Winer's 'The Whole Story' sees the heart of the psychoanalytic process as 'the unfolding of narrative ... the ways in which we fracture, fictionalize, plagiarize, and disassemble our stories'. He argues that, in both the content and the form of his writing, Beckett points us towards help, in that the 'opening up of desire and the acceptance of mourning are the remedies that heal fractured narrative'. Winer also tends to personalize the work with references to Beckett's own history, interpreting *Eh Joe* as a reworking of the crisis over Peggy Sinclair, and giving a reading of *Ohio Impromptu* as an analysis, referring to Beckett's analysis with Bion. He does recognize however, that this approach 'is purely speculative'. The article is interesting in relation to narrative, but it doesn't take us very far in understanding how the drama functions as drama. For the drama scholar, the most useful contributions are probably those which combine psychoanalytic, critical and dramatic discourses. In his highly personal voice, which combines subjective and theoretical reflection, Herbert Blau examines the 'double sentence' – of grammar and of punishment – in Beckett's work. The article, entitled 'Qua Qua Qua: The Babel of Beckett', explores connections between theatre, language and the look, in relation to structures of power and domination. John H. Lutterbie deals with the fragmented subject, a recurring concern of the collection, in 'Tender Mercies: Subjectivity and Subjection in Samuel Beckett's *Not I*'. The article is particularly illuminating in its analysis of the relation of subject to body: 'I am always and only the body, and in the final analysis there is nothing else. And yet the play continues to insist it is "not I" '. Lutterbie discusses the social marginalization of the old woman in *Not I*, but this discussion becomes entangled in a rather rigid interpretation of gender roles which sees all male spectators as privileged, while female spectators like the old woman in *Not I* are denied any possibility of agency.

In a dense but rewarding article, 'Post Apocalpyse With Out Figures: The Trauma of Theatre in Samuel Beckett', A. Kubiak discusses mind as *mise-en-scène*, and relates personal trauma and concepts of history: 'the alienation of thought in the unlocatable is precisely what hurts and "what hurts" is what Fredric Jameson calls history'. He argues that for Krapp, in *Krapp's Last Tape*, both memory and history are radically unknowable. Kubiak concludes that the corpus of Western drama seems obsessively trapped in the grinding cycle of history as pain, failure and hopelessness. Bennett Simon's 'The Fragmented Self: The Reproduction of Self and Reproduction in Beckett and in the Theatre of the Absurd', is a provocative and accessible article which discusses a set of modernist concerns with conception and contraception, involving the quest for and possibility of reproduction by technological means. Simon sees a link between the problematic self and the denigration of birth (and intercourse), leading to attacks on and dread of female sexuality. Jon Erickson's 'Self-Objectification and Preservation in Beckett's *Krapp's Last Tape*' reads *Krapp's Last Tape* as a continual recycling and consumption of self leading to a repetitive reification of personality. He refers to Foucault in the 'internalizing of formerly external processes of surveillance and control by the authorities', and suggests that postmodern theatre is a spectacular total theatre which challenges theatre's traditional locus in the human.

The most rewarding essay on the drama is in a book by Michael Vanden Heuvel, *Performing Drama/Dramatizing Performance: Alternative Theatre and the Dramatic Text*. This is a book which evaluates the significance for theatre of recent debates in literary and cultural theory, and provides a valuable assessment of the last 40 years of avant-garde theatre. His second chapter is devoted to Beckett: 'The Sad Tale a Last Time Told: Closing Performance and liberating the text in the plays of Samuel Beckett'. Vanden Heuvel argues that 'it is in Beckett's search for a paradoxical "authorial impotence" that we first find in the theatre a consistent, theorized desire to displace authorial control through performance'. More significantly, Beckett's willingness to accede to his eventual failure in this quest, and to confess to both the failure to write textuality completely out of his plays and to his own profound and contradictory desires for textual order and control in his own work, eventually makes it possible for him to move beyond nominating either power and powerlessness, text or performance, as the single privileged form of expression. The author suggests that Beckett continued to expose new boundaries by enacting in his late plays what lies beyond the poststructuralist horizon in contemporary theatre: 'We are only beginning to uncover what is truly radical in the work and authorial agenda of this most radical of playwrights.' This is an extremely sophisticated but accessible discussion of the relation between power and powerlessness, authorial control and the openness of performance structures in Beckett's work.

Around the Absurd: Essays on Modern and Postmodern Drama, edited by E. Brater and Ruby Cohn, also contains two lengthy, excellent essays on Beckett's drama, one by H. Porter and one by Charles Lyons, as well as a provocative essay by H. Blau. The aim of the book is to carry forward Martin Esslin's Theatre of the Absurd by 'surveying the theatre terrain both before and after that time'. The book posits the key role of the absurd in the transformation from a modern to a postmodern repertory. Herbert Blau's essay is entitled 'The Oversight of Ceaseless Eyes', and it continues his preoccupation with theatre and specularity in a commodified culture of spectacle. Charles Lyons's essay is entitled 'Beckett, Shakespeare and the Making of Theory'. This is a most useful essay which emphasizes how the critical climate and current trends affect the reception and reading of particular authors. He uses Shakespeare as a touchstone for measuring how critical theory has evolved. So, he argues that *Waiting for Godot* 'entered the public world at a time when its interpretative problems could best be explained within the terminology of existentialism'. Lyons argues that 'Beckett's texts enact the assumptions that dominate literary and aesthetic theory in the last two decades.' He poses the challenge of the New Criticism and subsequent critical discourses for dramatic criticism in the 'attempt to deal with the text as it is voiced in the theatre at the moment of performance ... Beckett's later works in particular use the stage to perform what we call the crisis of the subject in critical discourse'. H. Porter Abbott's article is entitled 'Late Modernism: Samuel Beckett and the Art of the Oeuvre'. Engaging with the 'Victorian trope of onwardness ... bound up with the dead metaphor of progress', Porter Abbott discusses the ways in which Beckett parodies this trope – Pozzo and Lucky are seen as 'an outrageous caricature of the westward course of empire' – but is also concerned with avoiding the familiarity and habit attendant on his strategies of repetition and recollection. Indeed, much of Porter Abbott's essay argues that Beckett's 'most significant refinement of modernist oppositional practice' is his strategy of recollection by distortion. Hence, Beckett is able to transform 'the emergent familiarity of his own work and ... make of it – through the method of distorted self-recollection – occasions of renewed surprise'. This is an interesting and incisive essay, broad in scope yet detailed in its argument.

Porter Abbott also has a thoughtful and accessible article in *MD* (34:i.5–22) entitled 'Reading as Theatre: Understanding Defamiliarization in Beckett's Art'.

Porter Abbott focuses on a reading of *Ohio Impromptu*, and on Beckett's defamiliarization techniques, first through the juxtaposition of reading and theatre, and second through the juxtaposition of scholarship, with its associations of pedantry and abstraction, with the extreme grief of the story. The scholarship associations emerge through Porter Abbott's reading of the two figures as 'two dusty scholars poring over an ancient text'. He also refers to the context of composition and audience – the symposium at Ohio State University. Reflecting on modernist poetics, Porter Abbott develops his theory of autographic writing, linking this also to defamiliarization techniques and emphasizing Beckett's strategies of 'syntactic de-rangement'.

Ohio Impromptu is also dealt with in an article by Elizabeth Klaver, '*Ohio Impromptu*, *Quad* and *What Where*: How it is in the Matrix of the Text and Television' (*ConL* 32.366–82). Klaver discusses the late plays for stage and television, and argues that 'the self in *Ohio Impromptu* is thoroughly inhabited by writing processes'. The argument is dense and thoroughly inhabited by postmodern terminology, which at times can be daunting, but it is a thorough investigation of Beckett's playing on textuality and 'generative structures' in the late plays. I found the sections on *Quad* and *What Where* particularly interesting in their discussion of television space and technology and in their comparisons with computer technology: 'lodged in a semiotic universe, the mind as an artifice or as an artificial intelligence is always shown in fragments of textual assemblage ... as if placed within the quotation marks of a computer programme or other image-processing machine in which the same textualized memory revolves with slight distortions through its code'.

Two articles focus on their authors' experience of either producing or acting in Beckett's drama. In *ThR* (16:i.39–54) 'The Dying of the Light: An Actor Investigates *Krapp's Last Tape*', Amiel Schotz explores *Krapp's Last Tape* from an actor's perspective. Schotz underlines the ways in which this perspective differs from that of a critic: 'an actor must make choices, has to justify each distinct action and build these actions on firm foundations of specific images.' Indeed, his approach to the play, which involves a search for psychological or emotional authenticity, including psychological contradictions, emphasizes the way in which the earlier plays, however stylized, are rooted in a view of character not too removed from naturalism. While it would be difficult to apply such an approach to some of the later plays, the article aptly demonstrates the mix of the human, the comic and the abstract in *Krapp's Last Tape*. In *TJ* (43:iii.361–76), Everett C. Frost's 'Fundamental Sounds: Recording Samuel Beckett's Radio Plays' traces Beckett's involvement with the medium of radio since *All That Fall* was commissioned by the BBC in 1955. Frost argues that 'each of the radio plays is a landmark in pioneering the development of acoustic art.' The experiments in radio also exerted a continuing influence on Beckett's writing for other media, making them a significant, not incidental part of his work. The article is a record of the production of Beckett's radio plays for broadcast in America, originated by Martha Fehsenfeld, and directed by Everett C. Frost. In general, the radio plays have received less attention than the stage plays so this is a useful evaluation, and includes detailed discussions of *All That Fall*, and *Words and Music*. The article returns to Irish preoccupations in conclusion, with a discussion of the influence of Ireland on the aural landscape of the radio drama. [A. McM.]

Edward Bond continues not to excite much attention, but 'Answering to the Dead: Edward Bond's "Jackets", 1989–90' (*NTQ* 7.171–83), by Ian Stuart, presents a useful exposition of Bond's idea of 'Theatre Events' in the context of early stagings of the two plays which 'broke new grounds in Bond's theory of acting'.

Another major dramatist who receives relatively little attention is Howard Brenton. Unfortunately, I have not seen Richard Boon's *Brenton the Dramatist* (Methuen), so the only piece that came my way was Patricia M. Troxel's discussion of 'Haunting Ourselves: History and Utopia in Howard Brenton's *Bloody Poetry* and *Greenland*' (in Hartigan's *Text and Presentation*), an interesting but unstartling exposition of some of the ways in which Brenton tackles Utopian themes.

Paul B. Cohen's 'Peter Brook and the "Two Worlds" of Theatre' (*NTQ* 7.147–59) usefully traces Brook's view of 'the true theatrical experience as an interaction between the two modes of reality – those of the "imagination" and the mundane'.

Anthony Burgess is not usually thought of as a dramatist, but ' "What's It Going To Be Then, Eh?": The Stage Odyssey of Anthony Burgess's *A Clockwork Orange*' (*MD* 34.35–48), by William Hutchings, carefully considers different adaptations of Burgess's novel, including Stanley Kubrick's film, and its script, John Godber's unpublished version, and Burgess's own two versions.

Caryl Churchill attracted little individual attention, though her work figures in some of the more general discussions mentioned above. Rolf Eichler offers a general synoptic account of her work in 'Caryl Churchills Theater: Das Unbehagen an des Geschlecterdifferenz' (in Fischer-Seidel).

Continued interest in Brian Friel reflects the general interest in Irish drama and his claims to pre-eminent status. Richard Pine's 'Brian Friel and Contemporary Irish Drama' (*CLQ* 27.190–201), for example, announces that it will advance claims that Friel is the father of contemporary Irish drama, occupies a central position in modern drama, and has 'a crucial relationship to the development of modern criticism'. However the essay, while informative enough, does little to substantiate its claims. In some ways, Brian Arkins's more modest 'The Role of Greek and Latin in Friel's *Translations*' (*CLQ* 27.202–9) is more satisfying as a result of concentrating on a tightly delineated area, although I doubt that theatre audiences would be in a position to make all the fine discriminations between the roots of everyday words which underlie some of his arguments. Similarly, Robert M. Smith examines Friel's debts to George Steiner's *After Babel* in some detail in 'The Hermeneutic Motion in Brian Friel's *Translations*' (*MD* 34.392–409). Rudiger Imhof offers an informative reading of *Volunteers* as 'a case in point for the notion that Irish history consists of an almost Nietzchean never-ending process of eternal recurrence' in 'Re-Writing History: A Fresh Look at Brian Friel's *Volunteers*' (*CJIS* 27.86–92). In similar vein, Christopher Murray examines 'Brian Friel's *Making History* and the Problem of Historical Accuracy' (in Lernout, *The Crows Behind the Plough*), showing how Friel has deliberately conflated actual historical events, changed their chronological order, and omitted some significant events, as part of a process of deconstructing history 'to make an image of possibility' and to demonstrate the uncertainty that lies at the heart of accepted views of historical events. Helen Lojek shows effectively in her discussion of 'Stage Irish-Americans in the Plays of Brian Friel' (*CJIS* 27.78–85) that, where they occur, they are important contrastive elements in the presentation of Ireland. Richard Bonaccorso makes a reasonable claim for the 'considerable intrinsic value' of the short stories in 'Back to "Foundry House": Brian Friel and the Short Story' (*CJIS* 27.72–7).

In *Christopher Fry* Glenda Leeming concentrates on a straightforward and reasonably insightful account of the original stage plays, but I would have welcomed more consideration of the contexts within which they were staged and their critical reception, as well as analysis of the adaptations and screenplays. Without these elements, the study seems curiously incomplete.

The gap between John Galsworthy's contemporary reputation and his current status provides the starting point of Art Borecca's interesting 'Galsworthy's Realism: A Revaluation' (*MD* 34.483–93), a detailed examination of his dramaturgy, with particular reference to *Justice*.

Neil Astley's *Tony Harrison* is an excellent critical anthology blending ephemeral pieces by the writer himself with comments from theatre workers and critics on his contribution to the theatre. It forms an essential introduction to a very challenging and original theatrical voice.

Thomas Murphy continues to attract attention. Nicholas Grene in 'Murphy's Ireland: *Bailegangaire*' (in Giddings, *Literature and Imperialism*) makes a case for Murphy's play as the most extraordinary Irish play of the last twenty-five years, through a detailed synopsis and close textual reading which places it in the context of the Irish peasant play tradition. Grene's 'Talking, Singing, Storytelling: Tom Murphy's *After Tragedy*' (*CLQ* 27.210–24) reworks some of the *Bailegangaire* material in its discussion of *Conversations on a Homecoming*, and *The Gigli Concert*, which together make up the collection printed as *After Tragedy*. Although the approach is largely based on exposition and brief analysis, Grene makes pertinent points about Murphy's impulse to both 'tell it like it is' and develop non-realistic forms, as well as considering briefly Murphy's dramatic strategies in presenting women in his drama. Rudiger Imhof also investigates Murphy's dramaturgy in '*The Gigli Concert* Revisited' (in *The Crows Behind the Plough*), a useful essay grounded in a thorough knowledge of previous attempts to understand this 'challenging ... daunting and dazzling' play.

Joe Orton's debt to Ibsen is examined by Russell McDonald in 'The Naming of Rance: Orton's Allusions to Henrik Ibsen in *What the Butler Saw*' (in Hartigan, *Text and Presentation*). The general point is well taken, but some of the detailed evidence seems rather forced.

As with other essays in the *CLQ* Irish issue, Claudia W. Harris's 'From Pastness to Wholeness: Stewart Parker's Reinventing Theatre' (27.233–41) is largely expository, but it offers an interesting account of an inventive and undervalued writer which introduces a number of useful points without breaking significant new ground.

Brian Richardson's illuminating discussion of 'Pinter's *Landscape* and the Boundaries of Narrative' (*ELWIU* (1991).37–45) suggests that Pinter's disturbing and transgressive dramatic strategies can be approached profitably in terms of contemporary narratology. Contrasting theories which stress temporal succession with those that emphasize causal connection, he suggests that the experience of *Landscape* shows that 'causality is ... a necessary condition of narrativity.' Sheila Rabillard explores similar issues with complex theoretical reference to *Old Times* in 'Destabilizing Plot, Displacing the Status of Narrative: Local Order in the Plays of Pinter and Shepard' (*TJ* 43.41–58), showing that the 'pattern of the drama as a whole becomes the satisfying and exhaustive exploration of dialogic positions'. In 'Camera Language: Picturing Pinter's *The Homecoming*' (in Hartigan, *Text and Presentation*), Jennifer M. Green has the interesting idea of discussing the play in the light of 'the ways in which his words assume the fetishistic power of photographs, authoritative tokens of semantic currency'. The essay is at its best in its insights into the 'conflation and dismemberment' of the female body. Benedict Nightingale offers a useful guide to Pinter's political positions in relation to both his early and later work in 'Pinter/Politics' (in *Around the Absurd*), as does Marc Silverstein in his critically sophisticated '*One for the Road, Mountain Language* and the *Impasse of Politics*' (*MD* 34.422–40).

Peter Shaffer is the subject of one of Garland's useful Casebooks, edited by C. J. Gianakaris, with a mixture of new and reprinted pieces. Although Gianakaris offers to address the discrepancy between audiences' generally favourable responses and critics' more sceptical reactions, his own essay is an inherently laudatory exposition which takes no account of criticisms of Shaffer's dramaturgy, while his disjointed and anecdotal interview with Shaffer will do little to convince those who doubt Shaffer's intellectual credentials. Of the other essays, Charles R. Lyons's 'Peter Shaffer's *Five Finger Exercise* and the Conventions of Realism' is valuable as much as a crisply illuminating study of issues in realism as of Shaffer's play and Michael Hinden's ' "Where All the Ladders Start": The Autobiographical Impulse in Shaffer's Recent Work' manages to discuss questions of twinning and duality with sensitivity and a due sense of both irony and decorum. Essays by Gene A. Plunka, Barbara Lounsberry, James R. Stacy, Felicia Hardison Londre and Dennis A. Klein also make interesting points, covering most of Shaffer's plays up to and including *Lettice and Lovage*.

As ever Shaw continues to attract critical attention. *ShawR* 11 concentrates on 'Shaw and Politics', with an interesting mixture of writers attesting to the variety and longevity of Shaw's political interests and to his continued appeal outside the academy. Among the essayists we find a professor of politics, Bernard Crick, trenchantly taking students of political history to task for their neglect of Shaw's contribution to British political life ('Shaw as Political Thinker, or the Dogs that did not Bark', 21–36), and two parliamentarians from opposing parties considering 'Shaw and Parliamentary Democracy' (Norman Buchan, 65–78) and 'Shaw and the Irish Question' (Peter Archer, 119–30). The problematic aspects of Shaw's political vision are also well presented in David Nathan's 'Failure of an Elderly Gentleman: Shaw and the Jews' (219–38) and in H. J. Fyrth's 'In the Devil's Decade: *Geneva* and International Politics' (239–55). The editor, T. F. Evans, provides a useful introduction to 'The Political Shaw' (1–19), and other essays deal variously with aspects of Shaw's relations with Oxbridge, his views on the Boer Wars, on imperialism, on local government, and on pacifism. Together with the usual batch of reprinted occasional pieces, reviews of books on Shaw (many of them not available to me for review) and John R. Pfeiffer's ever exemplary 'Continuing Checklist of Shaviana' (287–305), this all adds up to a fascinating and important contribution to Shavian scholarship. Ellen Gainer's 'Lesbian Sexuality and Violence in the Plays of G. B. Shaw' (*TD* 13.177–89) makes some important points about Shaw's dramaturgy in terms of the absence of close female friendships, and the presence of female physical violence. Perhaps the case is put too forcibly at times: I am not convinced that a 'motif of violent lesbian sexuality … runs throughout Shaw's work', but the suggestion in the same sentence that Shaw has 'a dark and problematic view of female sexuality and the potential for positive female interaction' is more than plausible. In *CVE* Michel W. Pharand considers 'Shaw's Life Force and Bergson's *Élan Vital*: A Question of Influence' (33.88–101), concluding that they were kindred spirits who owed a debt to Lamarck, rather than influences on each other, and Jean-Claude Amalric's 'Shaw's *Man and Superman* and the Myth of Don Juan: Intertextuality and Irony' (33.103–14) is adequately summarized by its title.

Three of Tom Stoppard's plays are usefully considered in Robert Gordon's T&P volume '*Rosencrantz and Guildenstern are Dead*', '*Jumpers*', and '*The Real Thing*'. The discussions are generally informative and incisive, although inevitably in such a short volume, which not only covers each play from the twin vantage points of 'Text' and 'Performance' but also refers *en passant* to much of Stoppard's other work, there are some gaps, particularly a failure to follow up the question of *The Real Thing* as

Stoppard's most autobiographical play in relation to his 'alleged inability to create convincing female characters'. Both Hersh Zeifman and Toby Silverman address the issue of doubling in *Hapgood*. Zeifman, in 'A Trick of the Light: Tom Stoppard's *Hapgood* and Postabsurdist Theater' (in *Around the Absurd*) sees *Jumpers* as a 'reluctant parting of the ways from the all encompassing absurdism of Beckett's vision' and *Hapgood* as a fine example of Stoppard's unique brand of postmodernist theatre in which 'In the last analysis, Stoppard's eschatology is ameliorist'. Silverman's 'Blizintsky/Dvojniki Twins/Doubles Hapgood/Hapgood' (*MD* 34.312–21) uses the existence of a real Elizabeth Hapgood (1850–1928), an American polyglot translator and unidentical twin, as the basis for her free-wheeling and illuminating consideration of puns, doubling, and language games in the play. Geoff Pywell's examination of 'The Idea of Place in the *Contractor*' (*JDTC* 5.69–79) suggests that Storey's strategy is to offer a piece that masquerades as 'the most commonplace naturalism' whilst 'providing a scenic reality which, by virtue of its very concreteness, distances us'. The incongruousness of the real tent in the playing space questions traditional assumptions since the actual event of erecting the tent and 'the fictional event' are 'identical in space and time but divorced perceptually for the audience in the collision between the place of each'. This is subtle and persuasive essay, which sometimes loses its way in its own rhetorical strategies.

Ann Wilson's '*Our Country's Good*: Theatre, Colony and Nation in Wertenbaker's Adaptation of *The Playmaker*' (*MD* 34.23–34) offers an interesting close reading of the differences between Wertenbaker's play and Thomas Kenneally's novel, which treats the play mainly as a textual variant on the novel, missing some of the ways in which the theatrical dimension informs and determines interpretations of what she sees as lacunae in the script.

Books Reviewed

Acheson, James, ed. *The British and Irish Novel Since 1960*. Macmillan. pp. 217. £35. ISBN 333 49019 3.

Ackerman, John. *A Dylan Thomas Companion*. Macmillan. pp. 176. £35. ISBN 0 333 29445 9.

Ambrosini, Richard. *Conrad's Fiction as Critical Discourse*. CUP. pp. 253. £35.00. ISBN 0 521 40349 9.

Atley, Neil, ed. *Tony Harrison*. Bloodaxe. pp. 512. hb £25, pb £10.95. ISBN 1 852 24079 2, 1 852 24080 6.

Beja, Morris. *James Joyce: A Literary Life*. Macmillan. pp. 150. pb £10.99, hb £35. ISBN 0 333 48737 0, 0 333 487362.

Benstock, Bernard. *Narrative Con/Texts in 'Ulysses'*. UIllP. pp. 234. $39.95. ISBN 0 252 01773 0.

Berghahn, Klaus L., and Reinhold Grimm, eds. *Utopian Vision, Technological Innovation and Poetic Imagination*. CWU. pp. 130. pb DM 28.00, hb DM 40.00. ISBN 3 533 04198 0.

Bevan, David. *University Fiction*. Rodopi Perspectives on Modern Literature 5. Rodopi (1990). pp. 168. pb £15.85. ISBN 90 5183 234 6.

Bevan, David, ed. *Literature and War*. Rodopi. pp. 210. pb £19. ISBN 90 5183 162 5.

Birch, David. *The Language of Drama*. Macmillan. pp. 175. hb £30, pb £8.99. ISBN 0 333 51637 0, 0 333 51638 9.

Black, Michael. *D. H. Lawrence: The Early Philosophical Works: A Commentary*. Macmillan Studies in Twentieth Century Literature. pp. 476. £52.50. ISBN 0 333 46144 4.

Bohlmann, Otto. *Conrad's Existentialism*. Macmillan. pp. 234. £35. ISBN 0 333 43619 9.

Bolt, Sydney. *A Preface to James Joyce*. Second edn. Longman. pp. 226. pb £10.99. ISBN 0 582 08663 9.

Brater, Enoch, and Ruby Cohn, eds. *Around the Absurd: Essays on Modern and Postmodern Drama*. UMichP. pp. 316. £27.50. ISBN 0472 10205 2.

Bristow, Joseph. *Empire Boys: Adventures in a Man's World*. Harper Collins. pp. 228. pb £10.99. ISBN 0 04 445631 X.

Bush, Ronald, ed. *T. S. Eliot: The Modernist in History*. CUP. pp. 213. £25.00. ISBN 0 524 39074 5.

Caughie, Pamela L. *Virginia Woolf and Postmodernism: Literature in Quest and Question of Itself*. UIllP. pp. 236. $15.95. ISBN 0 252 06158 6.

Caws, Mary Ann, and Eugene Nicole. *Reading Proust Now*. Reading Plus 8. Lang. (1990). pp. 312. $45. ISBN 0 8204 1239 2.

Chapman, Wayne K. *Yeats and English Renaissance Literature*. Macmillan. pp. 290. £45.00. ISBN 0 333 521773.

Cheng, Vincent J., and Timothy Martin, eds. *Joyce in Context*. CUP. pp. 292. £45. ISBN 0 521 41358 3.

Chevalier, Tracy, ed. *Contemporary Poets*. St James. pp. 1179. £60. ISBN 1 558 62035 4.

Clarke, Bruce, and Wendell Aycock, eds. *The Body and the Text. Comparative Essays in Literature and Medicine*. TTUP. pp. 222. $24.95. ISBN 0 89672 225 2.

Crowther, Ian. *Thinkers of Our Time: G. K. Chesterton*. Claridge. pp. 101. pb £5.95. ISBN 1 870626 86 9.

Currie, Gregory. *The Nature of Fiction*. CUP (1990). pp. 222. £27.95. ISBN 0 521 381274.

Cushman, Keith, and Dennis Jackson, eds. *D. H. Lawrence's Literary Inheritors*. Macmillan. pp. 287. £40. ISBN 0 333 54951 1.

Davies, James A. *Leslie Norris*. UWalesP. pp. 103. pb £3.50. ISBN 0 708 31117 2.

Devlin, Kimberley J. *Wandering and Return in 'Finnegans Wake': An Integrative Approach to Joyce's Fictions*. PrincetonUP. pp. 224. $29.95. ISBN 0 691 06886 0.

DiBattista, Maria. *First Love: The Affections of Modern Fiction*. UChicP. pp. 277. $24.50. ISBN 0 226 14498 4.

Dunleavy, Janet Egleson, ed. *Re-Viewing Classics of Joyce Criticism*. UIllP. pp. 230. pb $14.95, hb $39.95. ISBN 0 252 06166 7, 0 252 01774 9.

Eagleton, Terry, Frederic Jameson, and Edward Said. *Nationalism, Colonialism and Literature*. UMinnP. pp. 103. pb £7.50. ISBN 08166 1863 1.

Easthope, Anthony, and John O. Thompson, eds. *Contemporary Poetry Meets Modern Theory*. HW. pp. 213. hb £40, pb £10.95. ISBN 0 745 00670 1, 0 745 00671 X.

Ellis, Steve. *The English Eliot: Design, Language and Landscape in 'Four Quartets'*. Routledge. pp. 188. £35. ISBN 0 415 06688 3.

Emery, Jane. *Rose Macaulay: A Writer's Life*. Murray. pp. 381. £25. ISBN 0 7195 4768 7.

Erdinast-Vulcan, Daphna. *Joseph Conrad and the Modern Temper*. English Monographs. OUP. pp. 218. £32.50. ISBN 0 19 811785 X.

Field, Frank. *British and French Writers of the First World War*. CUP. pp. 280. £29.95. ISBN 0 521 39277 2.

Fischer-Seidel, Thérèse. *Frauen und Frauendarstellung in der englischen und amerikanischen Literatur*. Narr. pp. 335. ISBN 3 878 08768 3.
Fjågesund, Peter. *The Apocalyptic World of D. H. Lawrence*. NorUP. pp. 198. £25. ISBN 82 00 21386 2.
Fogel, Daniel Mark. *Covert Relations: James Joyce, Virginia Woolf and Henry James*. UPVirginia. pp. 210. $39.95. ISBN 0 8139 1280 6.
Fowler, Bridget. *The Alienated Reader: Women and Popular Romantic Literature in the Twentieth Century*. Harvester. pp. 232. pb £11.95. ISBN 0 7450 02498.
Frazier, Adrian. *Behind the Scenes: Yeats, Horniman and the Struggle for the Abbey Theatre*. UCalP. pp. 258. $25. ISBN 0 520 06549 2.
Fuller, David. *James Joyce's 'Ulysses'*. Harvester. pp. 124. £7.95. ISBN 0 7450 0574 8.
Genet, Jacqueline, and Richard Allen Cave, eds. *Perspectives on Irish Drama and Theatre*. Irish Literary Studies Series 33. Smythe. pp. 184. £17.50. ISBN 0 861 40309 6.
Gianakaris, C. J., ed. *Peter Shaffer: A Casebook*. Garland. pp. 179. $27. ISBN 0 824 06889 0.
Giddings, Robert. *The Author, the Book and The Reader*. Greenwich Exchange. pp. 220. pb £9.99. ISBN 1 871551 013.
Giddings, Robert, ed. *Literature and Imperialism*. Macmillan. pp. 228. pb £14.95. ISBN 0333 475 25 9.
Gilpin, George H. *The Art of Contemporary English Culture*. Macmillan. pp. 222. £40. ISBN 0 333 519310.
Gordon, Robert. *'Rosencrantz and Guildenstern Are Dead', 'Jumpers', and 'The Real Thing'*. T&P. Macmillan. pp. 110. pb £6.99. ISBN 0 333 43777 2.
Griffin, Gabriele, and Elaine Aston, eds. *Herstory: Plays by Women for Women*. 2 vols. ShAP. pp. 211, 207. pb £8.95. ISBN 1 850 75708 9.
Guy, Josephine M. *The British Avant-Garde: The Theory and Politics of Tradition*. Harvester. pp. 176. £35. ISBN 07450 0776 7.
Hammond, J. R. *H. G. Wells and the Short Story*. St Martin's. pp. 176. £35.00. ISBN 0 312 07582 0.
Hanley, Lynne. *Writing War: Fiction, Gender, and Memory*. UMassP. pp. 151. hb £19.95, pb £9.95. ISBN 0 870 237381, 0 870 23748 9.
Hanna, Gillian, ed. *Monstrous Regiment: A Collective Celebration*. Hern. pp. 270. pb £11.99. ISBN 1 854 59115 0.
Harrington, John P. *The Irish Beckett*. SyracuseUP. pp. 352. £21.95. ISBN 0 815 625286.
Harrington, John P., ed. *Modern Irish Drama*. Norton. pp. 577. pb £6.95. ISBN 0 393 96063 3.
Hartigan, Karelisa, ed. *Text and Presentation*. UPA (1990). pp. 122. £34.90. ISBN 0 819 17784 9.
Harty III, John, ed. *Finnegans Wake: A Casebook*. Garland. pp. 212. $40. ISBN 0 8240 1211 9.
Henderson, Lesley, ed. *Contemporary Novelists*. Fifth edition. St James. pp. 1053. £75. ISBN 1 55862 036 2.
Hodge, Robert. *Literature as Discourse*. Polity (1990). pp. 255. £29.50. ISBN 07456 0479 X.
Hoffpaiur, Richard. *The Art of Restraint: English Poetry from Hardy to Larkin*. AUP. pp. 332. £32.50. ISBN 0 87413 378.
Hoskins, Robert. *Graham Greene. A Character Index and Guide*. Garland. pp. 512. £62. ISBN 0 8240 4111 9.

Hoyles, John. *The Literary Underground: Writers and the Totalitarian Experience 1900–1950*. HW. pp. 294. £40. ISBN 0 7450 0911 5.

Humm, Maggie. *Border Traffic: Strategies of Contemporary Women Writers*. ManUP. pp. 228. pb £9.95. ISBN 07190 27047.

Hussey, Mark, ed. *Virginia Woolf and War: Fiction, Reality and Myth*. Syracuse Studies on Peace and Conflict Resolution. SyracuseUP. pp. 273. $29.95. ISBN 0 8156 2584 7.

Hyland, Paul, and Neil Sammells. *Irish Writing: Exile and Subversion*. Macmillan. pp. 256. pb £14.95. ISBN 0 333 52542 6.

Jackaman, Rob. *The Course of English Surrealist Poetry Since the 1930s*. Mellen. pp. 326. $69.95. ISBN 0 88946 932 6.

Kelsey, Nigel. *D. H. Lawrence: Sexual Crisis*. Macmillan Studies in Twentieth Century Literature. pp. 197. £37.50. ISBN 0 333 52184 6.

Kenyon, Olga. *Writing Women. Contemporary Women Novelists*. Pluto. pp. 150. £16.50. ISBN 0 7453 0307 2.

Land, Stephen K. *Challenge and Conventionality in the Fiction of E. M. Forster*. Studies in Modern Literature 19. AMS (1990). pp. 253. $34.50. ISBN 0 404 61589 9.

Lane, Denis, ed. *In the Spirit of Powys: New Essays*. AUP. pp. 268. £31.50. ISBN 0 8387 5173 3.

Langbauer, Laurie. *Women and Romance: The Consolations of Gender in the English Novel*. CornUP (1990). pp. 271. $12. ISBN 09014 9692 6.

Leeming, Glenda. *Christopher Fry*. Twayne (1990). pp. 171. £15.95. ISBN 0 805 76998 6.

Lernout, Geert, ed. *The Crows Behind the Plough: History and Violence in Anglo-Irish Poetry and Drama*. Rodopi. pp. 173. pb £15.90. ISBN 9 051 83237 0.

Levenson, Michael. *Modernism and the Fate of Individuality: Character and Novelistic Form From Conrad to Woolf*. CUP. pp. 231. £32.50. ISBN 0 521 39491 0.

Lilly, Mark, ed. *Lesbian and Gay Writing*. Macmillan (1990). pp. 218. pb £9.99. ISBN 0 333 47501 1.

Lucas, John, ed. *D. H. Lawrence: Selected Poetry and Non-fictional Prose*. Routledge English Texts. pp. 258. pb £6.99 ISBN 0 415 01429 8.

Martin, Jacqueline. *Voice in Modern Theatre*. Routledge. pp. 229. hb £35, pb £9.99. ISBN 0 415 01256 2, 0 415 04894 X.

Mepham, John. *Virginia Woolf: A Literary Life*. Macmillan Literary Lives. Macmillan. pp. 222. hb £40, pb £10.99. ISBN 0 333 46470 2, 0 333 46471 0.

Meyers, Valerie. *George Orwell*. Macmillan Modern Novelists. pp. 158. hb £35, pb £9.50. ISBN 0 333 40750 4, 0 333 40751 2.

Motion, Andrew. *The Poetry of Edward Thomas*. Hogarth. pp. 194. pb £7.99. ISBN 0 7012 0895 3.

Murray, Paul. *T. S. Eliot and Mysticism: The Secret History of 'Four Quartets'*. Macmillan. pp. 336. £45. ISBN 0 333 47585 2.

Myers, Peter. *The Sound of Finnegans Wake*. Macmillan. pp. 196. £35. ISBN 0 333 55339 X.

Nadelhaft, Ruth L. *Joseph Conrad*. Harvester Feminist Readings. HW. pp. 147. pb. £10.50. ISBN 0 7108 1342 2.

North, Michael. *The Political Aesthetic of Yeats, Eliot and Pound*. CUP (1992). pp. 288. £35. ISBN 0 521 41432 6.

Newey, Vincent, and Ann Thompson, eds. *Literature and Nationalism*. LiverUP. pp. 286. £27.50. ISBN 0 853 23057 9.

O'Donoghue, Joe. *Brian Moore: A Critical Study*. McG–QUP. £30. ISBN 0 717 11713 8.

Orr, John. *Tragicomedy and Contemporary Culture: Play and Performance from Beckett to Shepard*. Macmillan. pp. 208. hb £35, pb £14.99. ISBN 0 333 44879 0, 0 333 53697 5.

Parrinder, Patrick, and Christopher Rolfe, eds. *H. G. Wells under Revision: Proceedings of the International H. G. Wells Symposium London, July 1986*. AUP. pp. 264. £29.95. ISBN 0 945636.

Ryan, Judith. *The Vanishing Subject: Early Psychology and Literary Modernism*. UChicP. pp 207. £23.95. ISBN 0226 73226 6.

Scheick, William J. *Fictional Structure and Ethics: The Turn-of-the Century English Novel*. UGeoP. pp. 183. £26.95. ISBN 0 8203 1242 8.

Schlueter, June, and Enoch Brater, eds. *Approaches to Teaching Beckett's 'Waiting for Godot'*. MLA. pp. 184. $27.20. ISBN 0 873 52541 8.

Seed, David. *James Joyce's 'A Portrait of the Artist as a Young Man'*. HW. pp. 196. £7.95. ISBN 0 7450 0679 5.

Sharpe, Tony. *T. S. Eliot: A Literary Life*. Macmillan. pp. 208. hb £37.50, pb £11.99. ISBN 0 333 45277 1, 0 333 45278 X.

Shaw, Marion and Sabine Vanacker. *Reflecting on Miss Marple*. Routledge. pp. 109. pb £6.99. ISBN 0415 01794 7.

Sillars, Stuart. *British Romantic Art and the Second World War*. Macmillan. pp. 240. £35. ISBN 0 333 4555 92.

Sklenicka, Carol. *D. H. Lawrence and the Child*. UMissP. pp. 191. $27.50. ISBN 0 8262 0778 2.

Smith, Joseph H. *The World of Samuel Beckett*. JHUP. pp. 226. hb £35, pb £21.50. ISBN 0 801 84079 1, 0 801 84135 6.

Spolsky, Ellen. *The Uses of Adversity: Failure and Accommodation in Reader Response*. AUP. pp. 216. £25.50. ISBN 0 8387 5112 1.

Spurling, Hilary. *Paul Scott: A Life of the Author of 'The Raj Quartet'*. Norton. pp. 438. pb £9. ISBN 0 712 65032 6.

Squires, Michael, ed. *D. H. Lawrence's Manuscripts: The Correspondence of Frieda Lawrence, Jake Zeitlin and Others*. Macmillan. pp. 319. £50. ISBN 0 333 53382 8.

Tudeau-Clayton, Margaret, and Martin Warner, eds. *Addressing Frank Kermode: Essays in Criticism and Interpretation*. Macmillan. pp. 218. £40. ISBN 0 333 53137 X.

Vanden Heuvel, Wolfgang. *Performing Drama / Dramatizing Performance: Alternative Theatre and the Dramatic Text*. UMichP. pp. 264. £24.95. ISBN 0 472 10240 0.

Varsava, Jerry. *Contingent Meanings: Postmodernism, Mimesis and the Reader*. UFlorP. pp. 233. £19.95. ISBN 08130 1004 7.

Waddis, Carole, ed. *'Sheer Bloody Magic': Conversations with Actresses*. Virago. pp. 241. pb £6.99. ISBN 1 853 81194 7.

Wade, Stephen. *Christopher Isherwood*. Macmillan. pp. 126. £30. ISBN 0 333 51708 3.

Wales, Katie. *The Language of James Joyce*. Language of Literature Series. Macmillan. pp. 182. pb £9.99. ISBN 0 333 48055 4.

Ward, John Powell. *The English Poetry of the Unpoetic from Wordsworth to Larkin*. Macmillan. pp. 200. hb £35, pb £9.99. ISBN 0 333 47168 7, 0 333 47169 5.

Wark, Wesley K., ed. *Spy Fiction, Spy Films and Real Intelligence*. Cass. pp. 225. £18. ISBN 0 7146 3411 5.

Williams, Raymond. *Orwell*. Fontana Modern Masters. 3rd edn. pp. 128. pb. £4.99. ISBN 0 00 686227 6.
Worthen, John. *D. H. Lawrence: The Early Years: 1885–1912*. CUP. pp. 626. pb. £12.95. ISBN 0 521 43772 5.

XVI

American Literature to 1900

HENRY CLARIDGE and JANET GOODWYN

This chapter has the following sections: 1. General; 2. Early and Eighteenth-Century Literature; 3. Nineteenth-Century Prose and Poetry. Sections 1 and 2 are by Henry Claridge, Section 3 is by Janet Goodwyn.

1. General

Current bibliographical listings for the field and period continue to be available quarterly in *AL* and annually in *MLAIB*. *AmLS* for 1989 offers its customary reliability and thoroughness under its new editor David J. Nordloh who will be replaced next year (1990) by Louis Owens. There are, however, some changes from earlier volumes: there is no chapter on 'Fiction: 1900 to the 1930s' and that on 'Black Literature', again, is omitted as a result of 'the failure of the assigned contributor to complete the work'; but, as Professor Nordloh also points out, 'the amount of publications dealing with black writers is becoming so great that a single chapter assembled by a single contributor is becoming impossible' and 'it's simply inappropriate to treat black writers in a separate chapter while discussing other "groups" – minorities, Native Americans, ethnics – in the regular genre-period chapters.' I think most readers will understandably sympathize with the difficulties caused by the great, frequently insurmountable, obstacles that face any editor of a narrative bibliography.

Three years ago (*YWES* 69.550–1) I reviewed Emory Elliott's *Columbia Literary History of the United States*; this year sees his equally compendious (905 pages) edition, *The Columbia History of the American Novel: New Views*, the list of contributors to which includes some names which will be very familiar to those who keep abreast of American literary scholarship: Cathy N. Davidson, Terence Martin, Robert S. Levine, Robert Shulman, and Valerie Smith, to cite only a few. It is, in some ways, something of a surprise to see a volume like this so quickly assembled after the publication of the general history; one wonders if the ink in the earlier volume has had time to dry. I say this beacuse *The Columbia Literary History of the United States* was, in itself, extremely thorough and comprehensive and didn't shirk at all on coverage of the novel, and so, inevitably, there is a good deal of overlap between the two volumes. The sub-title (I call it such though it only appears on the dust-jacket), *New Views*, will give the reader some idea of how this history differs from those older (and reasonably plentiful) histories of the American novel. In his general introduction

Elliott problematizes the very notion of the novel and the writing of its history, though within three pages a definition is offered which is loose enough ('a text usually of substantial length that is normally written in prose and presents a narrative of events involving experiences of characters who are representative of human agents') to be more or less unproblematic. His subsequent comments, however, on the inherent difficulties of distinguishing ' "good" or even "great" novels from "poor" ones' reveal again the distressing reluctance of contemporary critics to enter into evaluative debates, though I am willing to concede to Elliott his central point here that the critical vocabulary (he might wish to call it 'ideology') which attaches to qualities such as greatness is elusive and, to some extent, socially constructed. Predictably, the strength of the volume as a literary history lies in its treatment of the contemporary and the very recent, though, paradoxically, this is precisely the area where it will most quickly start to age. One wonders whether novelists such as Larry McMurty, Joanna Russ, and Wallace Stegner (all covered here) will survive with anything more than the historical interest that will naturally attach to them. Inevitably, most readers will detect omissions, though I was a little surprised to find, in a volume which affords a good deal of importance to contemporary women's writing, no mention of popular 'feminist' novelists such as Lisa Alther, Marilyn French, and Erica Jong; perhaps they suffer too much from being widely read. The volume concludes with brief, but useful, biographies of selected individual authors and a comprehensive, but selective, bibliography of critical works. The volume as a whole will be a valuable addition to any respectable library of criticism of the American novel.

Like *The Columbia History of the American Novel,* the strengths of the jointly authored *From Puritanism to Postmodernism: A History of American Literature* by Malcolm Bradbury and Richard Ruland, lie in their discussion of twentieth-century American literature, particularly that which has appeared since 1945, and, like many of the contemporary critics of the subject who are reviewed in these pages, they are markedly alert to the elasticity (some might say 'indeterminacy') of critical methodologies and critical language. They refer in their preface to their work as 'no less a fiction than any other' and to the 'breadth of methods and interpretations, a mix of critical attitudes and a dialogic way of writing' that they bring to their history. Such a way about writing (of whatever kind) as a 'fictive' act is neatly co-extensive with the imaginative writings of postmodernists such as John Barth, William Gaddis, William H. Gass, and Thomas Pynchon (on whom they write well), but it seems a barrier in some ways to intelligent consideration of figures such as James Fenimore Cooper and Henry James for whom the massive weight of the received resources bequeathed by the nineteenth-century novel is a very palpable presence. This is not to say that Cooper and James are 'unproblematic', but to suggest that their work isn't easily assimilated within the vocabularies of postmodernism and to try to read them as postmodernists is to miss the moral authority that frequently attaches to their visions. In some ways the chief weakness of this book is that it sees the whole history of American literature – though not merely that of American literature – as a remorseless advance towards the avant-garde, which not only privileges the avant-garde but necessarily writes the history backwards and thus makes this whole history peculiarly ahistorical. The best chapters, as I implied earlier, are the later ones, notably those on American modernism ('The second flowering') and postwar poetry and prose ('Strange realities, adequate fictions').

American Literature and the Destruction of Knowledge: Innovative Writing in the Age of Epistemology by Ronald E. Martin is again a work that considers the history of American literature (here in a somewhat narrower time-scale that goes back only to Emerson) in the light of essentially contemporary preoccupations with the destruction of paradigms, whether literary, linguistic, or intellectual. Martin argues that the destruction of these paradigms was a necessary pre-condition for what he calls the 'liberation' of American literature and he is particularly interesting when considering those writers on whom science had a powerful, if not always desirable impact, notably Whitman, Melville, and, to a lesser extent, Emily Dickinson. Later chapters explore what might be called the epistemological and hermeneutical inheritance of the nineteenth-century in figures such as Conrad Aiken, Stephen Crane, Robert Frost, Ernest Hemingway, William James, John Dos Passos, Ezra Pound, Wallace Stevens, and William Carlos Williams. This book has important things to say, I think, but it makes for somewhat uneasy reading chiefly because of the all too frequently tortured expression.

American Studies: Essays in Honour of Marcus Cunliffe edited by Brian Holden Reid and John White, and with a foreword by Arthur M. Schlesinger, Jnr, brings together a series of diverse essays in honour of one of Great Britain's most distinguished scholars of the United States. The essays reflect the considerable range of Cunliffe's interests: for example, Robert Lawson-Peebles writes on Mason Weems's *The Life of Washington*, a book for which Cunliffe wrote a notable introduction, and Bruce Collins explores the Southern military tradition between 1812 and 1861, again reflecting some of Cunliffe's early interests in American (and, indeed, British) military history. The essays of a more narrowly literary nature include Malcolm Bradbury on anti-Utopian irony in American culture, largely concentrating on the Transcendentalists and Hawthorne's *The Blithedale Romance*, Mick Gidley on the treatment, artistic, historical, and literary, of the Indian, and Arnold Goldman on F. Scott Fitzgerald. Amongst other essays, John White discusses the growth of a distinctive black jazz in Kansas City in the 1920s and 1930s relating it to organized crime and political corruption, and Rupert Wilkinson analyses the formulation of those various accounts of the American character one finds in the writings of Margaret Mead, David Potter, and David Riesman. Whilst the interests of this collection are by no means preponderantly literary, the student of American literature, and American culture more generally, will find much of value here. This is a judicious and well-balanced collection of essays, though at £40 it is forbiddingly priced. Also in what one might call the American Studies 'vein' is Henry F. May's *The Divided Heart: Essays on Protestantism and the Enlightenment in America*, a collection of pieces, all written since 1981, on various aspects of American intellectual history. Those who know May's earlier writings, particularly his *The Enlightenment in America*, will be aware of his gift for lucid and frequently trenchant commentary. Two essays merit particular note: his partly autobiographical essay on Henry Nash Smith's *Virgin Land* and his reprinting of his introduction to the 1966 John Harvard Library edition of Harriet Beecher Stowe's *Oldtown Folks*, which is as good a study of Stowe's religiosity and, indeed, the novel itself, as one will ever come across.

Peter Carafiol's *The American Ideal: Literary History as a Wordly Activity* is probably best seen as a companion to William Spengemann's *A Mirror for Americanists* which I reviewed last year (*YWES* 71), though this is not to say that they have similar methodologies or conclusions. But, like Spengemann, Carafiol is interested in the problematic nature of American Literature, and more particularly, American literary scholarship because, primarily, he is interested in the problematic nature of 'America' itself. The burden of his book is the attempt to show that, as he says, 'American Literary Scholarship and the foundationalist version of theory that, until recently, dominated American critical discourse were mirror images of each other.' This is an extremely abstract proposition and my first reaction on encountering it was to wonder quite how it could be illustrated and, perhaps more pertinently, through whom one would illustrate it. Theoretical approaches to American literature seem to have reached a point of exhaustion (no bad thing) and the only book completely along these lines is *Theorizing American Literature: Hegel, the Sign, and History* edited by Bainard Cowan and Joseph G. Kronick which conspires to pack into its sub-title three words that suggest the remorseless pursuit of the theoretical to which this collection of essays is devoted. Hegel looms very large here, for while the opening sentence of Cowan's introduction paradoxically talks of the 'double forgetting' of Hegel in American culture, it turns out that the volume has uncovered 'consistent traces of Hegel in American writing and cultural activity' and, indeed, it seems that 'Hegelian thought was already present in Puritan America before it was present in Hegel's own person', a quite remarkable feat of incarnation for the German philosopher. The essays, eight in all in addition to the introductory essay, are either on very broad topics, for example, Gregory S. Jay on 'Hegel and the Dialectics of American Literary Historiography: From Parrington to Trilling and Beyond' which seeks to argue a correspondence between Hegel's philosophy of history and American literary history, or fairly narrow, as is the case with John Carlos Rowe's 'Romancing the Stone: Melville's Critique of Ideology in *Pierre*', where he argues that the novel is 'Melville's farewell to the romance', a 'deconstructive "failure" ' that leaves literature behind and anticipates 'the cultural criticism of our present moment'. In Rowe's essay, Hegel's role is to point to the family as the 'unconscious' of the state in a way which suggests that we read Melville's dismal novel as a 'criticism of American capitalism', though anyone who has ever succeeded in finishing *Pierre* will be surprised by such a critical formulation of its concerns. More interesting, and to some extent more persuasive, are the essays by Katheryne V. Lindberg on Whitman and Judith Butler on Wallace Stevens. The reader should be warned that this collection is mercilessly theoretical, presupposes some familiarity with Hegel's writings, and is more concerned with the writers discussed as an arena for critical theory than with the intrinsic value of their works.

A very different kind of scholarship surfaces in *Writing the American Classics*, edited by James Barbour and Tom Quirk, a collection of essays devoted, as the dust-jacket blurb says, to telling the ' "stories of stories" of ten classic American works', Franklin's *Autobiography*, *Moby-Dick*, *Walden*, *Huckleberry Finn*, *The Professor's House*, *The Sun Also Rises*, *The Sound and the Fury*, *Tender is the Night*, *Native Son*, and *East of Eden*. These are all essays in genetic, and, occasionally, textual criticism and they achieve an admirable level of interest and scholarly exactitude. Few of the essays say anything particularly new or striking but they consistently remind us of the complexity of those factors that go into the composition of a major work of art, and the intended audience, the student and the general reader, is one far too frequently ignored by the academic critic.

The classic literature of the nineteenth century is the concern of one of the most important books to appear this year, Joel Porte's *In Respect to Egotism: Studies in American Romantic Writing*. Those who know their Thoreau will be aware that Porte's title comes from the first page of *Walden* and will immediately realize that the burden of his study lies with the place of the first-person, here largely in terms of self-development and self-articulation, in American literature. This is, of course, familiar territory and, at times, Porte struggles to say anything new about it. His book is a series of essays which, fortuitously, has found a common theme, that of the 'modalities of self-display or self-concealment – ways of figuring and disfiguring the self – discernible among American authors' in the period which we loosely call the 'American renaissance'. The best essays, those, I think, on Thoreau, Whitman, and Dickinson (the 'interchapter' entitled 'Walt and Emily', that links the last two is particularly valuable for its insights into the ways in which they both resisted 'that "sickness ... of verbal melody" and the banality of sentiment') contain a great deal of attentive, close criticism, and even if the controlling thesis of *In Respect to Egotism* reformulates much that we already know it has a great deal to commend it.

What might be construed as an interesting article-length footnote to Porte's book, were it not a valuable essay in its own right, is Louis P. Masur's ' "Age of the First Person Singular": the Vocabulary of the Self in New England, 1780–1850' (*JAmS* 25.189–211) where Masur argues that the period between the Revolution and the Civil War 'marked an explosion and transformation in discussions of selfhood and identity' and supports his proposition with perceptive readings of Abigail Adams, William Ellery Channing, and Emerson. David Leverenz's *Manhood and the American Renaissance* first appeared in 1989 and somehow eluded our coverage for that year; its republication in paperback this year thus gives us the opportunity to consider a book that looks at the literature of the mid-nineteenth century from a less familiar angle. Leverenz argues that the pressures of gender and class conflict were as real and palpable for male writers as they were for female writers and that for many of the great writers of the period, notably Emerson, Hawthorne, Melville, Thoreau, and Whitman, the 'prevailing norms of manly behaviour' were norms of both literary and psychosexual discomfort. Leverenz sees these norms in the ideologies of possessive and competitive individualism and, in doing so, he reminds us of the sense many American writers had that their literary careers were somehow effete and dilettante, at odds with the prevailing ethos of the age (something expressed most eloquently in Hawthorne's 'The Custom-House'). His own 'most basic thesis', as he puts it, is that 'any intensified ideology of manhood is a compensatory response to fears of humiliation' and at the heart of his book is a reading of four texts, *The House of the Seven Gables*, 'Benito Cereno', Thoreau's essay on John Brown ('A Plea for Captain John Brown'), and Whitman's 'There Was a Child Went Forth', which he sees as all sharing in a 'drama of humiliation'; it is this relatively brief chapter which sets the terms for much of the discussion that follows, and particularly recommended among the later readings is that of Frederick Douglass's *Narrative*. The writing throughout Leverenz's book is consistently lively and intellectually engaging, though I could have done with a little less of the indulgence in anecdote, whether about family or academic life.

Sister's Choice: Tradition and Change in American Women's Writing is Elaine Showalter's 1989 Clarendon Lectures and brings to a consideration of American women's writings, particularly those of Louisa May Alcott, Kate Chopin, and Edith Wharton, many of the critical preoccupations that were at work in her earlier study of British women novelists, *A Literature of Their Own*. In her book Showalter asks, to use her own words, 'some "American" questions about the history, traditions, and contradictions of American women's writing', but her approach resists the theoretical in favour of what she calls the 'gynocritical' (which she glosses as 'the study of women's writing'). Her first two chapters are largely historical and contextual but the later chapters offer detailed readings of *Little Women*, *The Awakening*, and *The House of Mirth*. The concluding chapter I found something of an oddity, for it is essentially an extended essay on the history of quilt-making (illustrations are dotted about the chapter) which rather ponderously invokes an image of 'threading' to give figurative unity to the various themes and issues she explores in the book.

Criticism of American literature is so remorselessly preoccupied with the novel nowadays that it is a pleasure to come across a book that devotes itself, in part, to American poetry. Stanley J. Scott's *Frontiers of Consciousness: Interdisciplinary Studies in American Philosophy and Poetry* examines 'the way the problem of consciousness is treated by American philosophers and poets of the late nineteenth and early twentieth centuries.' Scott's own philosophical method is 'radical empiricism' characterized by the premise that 'no thinking takes place apart from an experiential context, and radical in its insistence on getting to the roots of experience.' Naturally, such a premise invites some consideration of the American pragmatists, and chapters on Josiah Royce, Charles Pierce, William James, and John Dewey establish a framework for extended discussion of T. S. Eliot, Wallace Stevens, and William Carlos Williams. The balance of the book is more towards the philosophic than the poetic which is a pity since I find Scott's dealings with American poetry consistently trenchant and perceptive. The omission of any account of Robert Frost comes as something of a surprise since much recent work on Frost, notably that of Richard Poirier, has been very insistent on Frost's intellectual kinship with the American tradition of philosophical pragmatism.

Scholarship devoted to American autobiography, of which we have had a superfluity in recent years, seems rather thin on the ground this year and the only important study to come our way is J. Bill Berry's *Located Lives: Place and Idea in Southern Autobiography*, a collection of essays that explores the question as to whether the South has a distinctive autobiographical tradition (distinctive, that is, in relation to other American autobiographical traditions). Berry thinks that it has as a consequence of what he calls, in his introduction, the 'tension between American ideas and an overlapping, sometimes reinforcing, but often conflicting set of southern values and loyalties.' Thus 'selfhood', he argues, without which autobiography is inconceivable, is problematic in the Southern context, since ' "self" has been contingent on the idea of America and the massive, immutable (however fiercely resisted) fact of being an American. Yet it has been equally contingent on being southern.' This, I think, is to ignore that very similar difficulties have been apparent in the writings of ethnic American autobiographers (particularly those of native Americans and Asian-Americans in the last two decades), but it remains an interesting proposition. Berry himself offers a concluding essay on his own migration to the North (he is from Arkansas) for his studies at Princeton, alongside other 'personal' essays by James M. Cox, George Garrett, and Pat C. Hoy, II, but I found such extended anecdote misconceived here, coming, as it does, after more purely academic essays on writers such as Mark Twain, Eudora Welty, and Ellen Glasgow. Other essays follow rather broader topics: William Howarth writes on 'voice and place' in Southern autobiography; Elizabeth Fox-Genovese on the autobiographies of Southern women, particularly those of Harriet Jacobs, Katherine DuPre Lumpkin (her little-known *The Making of a Southerner* published in 1946 sounds a most interesting work), and Maya Angelou; and George Core asks why autobiography appealed so little to those writers we call the 'Vanderbilt Fugitives', answering his question with the intriguing proposition that 'the more minor the southern writer … the more inclined he has been in the past to write autobiography.' James Olney, who is renowned for his work on autobiography, contributes a rather disappointing short piece that compares Welty's *One Writer's Beginnings* with Richard Wright's *Black Boy*, and Sally Wolff's essay, devoted entirely to Welty, which follows it is considerably better. Roy Reed's essay on 'Autobiography in Southern Journalism' is, again, brief and rather disappointing given what seems to be a potentially interesting area of enquiry. The whole collection is distinctly uneven, but something of value, no doubt, will be found by those with interests either in Southern writing or the autobiographical mode in America more generally.

Removals: Nineteenth-Century American Literature and the Politics of Indian Affairs by Lucy Maddox is a study that is very clearly explained by its subtitle. Maddox is eager to 'resituate' some familiar nineteenth-century American texts 'within the context of public debates about the place of American Indians in the civil and cultural institutions of the new American nation', and her first chapter offers a readable and informed survey of the general debate about the 'incorporation of Indians into American public discourse' in the first half of the century. Later chapters, largely historicist in character, look at literary figures such as Melville, Hawthorne, Fuller, Thoreau, and Parkman, though some of her more interesting readings are of minor figures such as Lydia Maria Child and Catherine Sedgwick; James Fenimore Cooper is, oddly enough, treated rather cursorily though this is explained by her desire to locate the debate in the more unexpected contexts. Her book has much that will be of value to those with interests in Indian-white relations in American literature, particularly her consideration of 'family myth' as a means by which 'white America' sought a 'comfortable and justifiable position *vis-à-vis* the Indians.'

A study from 1986 which eluded earlier volumes of *YWES* has just come our way: Nicolaus Mills' *The Crowd in American Literature* is a brisk and lively account of 'the way the crowd has been portrayed in American literature', the word 'literature' being taken here to encompass non-fictional as well as fictional writing. Indeed, Mills is rather more interesting on the non-fictional: his first chapter, 'The Revolutionary Crowd', is a perceptive reading of the responses of eighteenth-century writers (notably John Adams and Thomas Jefferson, though Abigail Adams is also frequently cited) to political events such as the Boston Tea Party and Shays's Rebellion, and the appendix offers an excellent discussion of the depiction of the crowd in American painting. Other chapters look at the presentation of the crowd in writers such as Hawthorne, Melville, Mark Twain, Howells, and Dreiser. His book inclines rather too much towards the descriptive, though behind it lies a counter-thesis to the theory of the 'American romance' articulated in the writings of Lionel Trilling and Richard Chase, although it seems to me that the material with which he is dealing isn't strong enough to sustain his view that 'the politics of the crowd and an obsession with the transcendent were both responses to widespread doubts about the virtues of conventional society.'

Albert Gelpi's *The Tenth Muse: The Psyche of the American Poet* (*YWES* 57.385) – the title, of course, comes from Anne Bradstreet – has been reissued this year in paperback and comes with a preface to the new edition in which he addresses 'certain theoretical perspectives' of race, class, and gender which are largely ignored in the book, but he is right, I think, to propose that *The Tenth Muse* can stand as it was originally conceived. This is an excellent book; the essay on Edward Taylor alone is well worth the price of purchase. Also reissued this year in paperback is *Long Black Song: Essays in Black American Literature and Culture* by Houston A. Baker, Jnr, which first saw publication in 1972. Baker, however, has added only a short note for this new edition simply pointing out that the 'bibliography for the original edition of *Long Black Song* must now be substantially augmented by any student of the field.'

The year has seen the appearance of a number of articles on the theoretical problems involved in the criticism of American literature, some, it has to be admitted, a good deal more cogent than others. The predictable discussions of gender, race, and class surface frequently, but a lively *riposte* to the consequences of these 'obsessions' is mounted by Bruce Bawer in 'Columbia's Assault on the American Novel' (*NewC*

9.20–31), a review of Emory Elliott's *The Columbia History of the American Novel* which I have dealt with above. Problems with the 'canon' are addressed in Phillipa Kafka's 'Another Round of Canon Fire: Feminist and Multi-Ethnic Theory in the American Literature Survey', an article from the journal *Melus* ((1990) 16.31–49) which is rapidly becoming an important forum for the discussion of ethnic American literature and the related issues of multiculturalism. Of particular note in this respect is the December issue of *JAmS*, a special number (25) devoted almost entirely to 'Ethnicity in America'. Wai-Chee Dimock in 'Feminism, New Historicism, and the Reader' (*AL* 63.601–22) takes up a train of thought prompted by Steven Marcus's essay 'Reading the Illegible' and seeks a 'symbiosis of gender and history' in an age that is characterized as one of 'deregulated interpretation'; this may make Dimock's essay seem a little rebarbative but it offers a lively, if finally unconvincing, case. Further discussion of the New Historicism is put forward by Philip F. Gura, again in *AL*, but as his argument turns on early American literature I shall consider his views in the next section. Finally, an extremely useful and lucid overview of the state of critical and scholarly discussion of American realism is offered by John C. Hirsh in 'Realism Renewed' (*JAmS* 25.235–43) where he shows how 'psychology and feminism, together with biographical, and certain critical and historical methodologies are now beginning to influence our understanding of the Realist concept of authorship, and to clarify the effects of capitalism, materialism and mass culture on the authors and texts concerned.'

2. Early and Eighteenth-Century Literature

Stephen Greenblatt's *Marvelous Possessions: The Wonder of the New World* is clearly prompted by the quincentenary in 1992 of Columbus's discovery of the New World, though the origins of his book lie in the Clarendon and Carpenter lectures he delivered at the Universities of Oxford and Chicago, respectively, in 1988. His book is about the various ways in which Europeans took 'possession' of the New World, 'possession' being construed here not in the sense of military mastery but rather the cultural, intellectual, linguistic, and symbolic means by which the Old World appropriated the New. In a sense, *Marvelous Possessions* is a series of fairly discrete essays held together by a common theme and while it is not of direct relevance to those interested in early American literature (most of the writings discussed are the products of Europeans) it is an important contribution to the cultural history of the New World.

The American Dream of Captain John Smith by J.A. Leo Lemay is the first full-length study of Smith to appear for many years and, in many ways, supplants Philip L. Barbour's *The Three Worlds of Captain John Smith* which appeared in 1964. Lemay stresses the secular elements in Smith's vision of America, contrasting it with the more religious vision of the Puritans, and he argues that 'Smith's secular American Dream became the dominant political philosophy', though I feel that is to confuse an economic outlook with a political one. The book, attractively illustrated throughout, is a very valuable addition to our understanding both of Smith and his times. Kevin J. Hayes's *Captain John Smith: A Reference Guide* has yet to be received for review and will, hopefully, be dealt with next year.

Before I come to the article-length literature that pertains to the period it is appropriate to mention yet another work of historical scholarship which has considerable value for those with interests in early American writing. William J. Gilmore's *Reading Becomes a Necessity of Life: Material and Cultural Life in Rural New*

England, 1780–1835, which appeared in 1989, is an immensely detailed study of reading habits and what Gilmore calls 'participation in print culture' in the Upper Connecticut River Valley of Vermont and New Hampshire between 1780 and 1835. His methodology involves the identification of five 'cultural habitats' in rural New England with differing wealth and occupational structures, and drawing on contemporary records he constructs an astonishingly specific analysis of reading patterns, access to printed matter, and what we might, more generally, call the dissemination of knowledge and information. While, as I have said, this is essentially a work of historical scholarship its value to those who are interested in the relationships between reading, literacy, and the 'consumption' of literature in rural America in the early years of the Republic is immeasurable. I am not properly qualified to judge its historical importance but it does seem to me to be a major study. Literacy among women in colonial New England is considered in an article by Joel Perlmann and Dennis Shirley in 'When Did New England Women Acquire Literacy' (*WMQ* 48.50–67). The whole issue of *WMQ* (January 1991), it might be noted, is devoted to gender questions, and the related issues associated with the status of women, in colonial America. Also in *WMQ* 48, 'Forum' in the April issue offers a series of responses to David Hackett Fischer's *Albion's Seed* (*YWES* 70.585) from Jack P. Greene and Barry Levy, among others, who address, particularly, Fischer's insistence on the primacy of the British inheritance in the cultural life of colonial America; a long 'reply' from Fischer to his critics is included here.

Among seventeenth-century writers it is, predictably, Anne Bradstreet and Edward Taylor who receive the most coverage, predominantly in articles (I still await copies of Raymond F. Dolle's *Anne Bradstreet: A Reference Guide*, published last year, and John Gatta's *Gracious Laughter: The Meditative Wit of Edward Taylor*, from 1989, for review). The most substantial article on Bradstreet is that of Jane D. Eberwein, 'Civil War and Bradstreet's "Monarchies" ' (*EAL* 26.119–44) which argues that in 'The Foure Monarchies', the centre-piece of *The Tenth Muse Lately Sprung Up in America ... By a Gentlewoman in Those Parts* (published in 1650) 'Bradstreet's profound concern about monarchy in a period of extreme political agitation motivated her to undertake this staggering historical project in a search for a perspective on current events.' 'Staggering' seems somewhat hyperbolic here particularly as Eberwein convincingly shows how Bradstreet failed to improve the poem to her satisfaction; the reading is valuable, however, for its insistence on 'The Foure Monarchies' as a 'veiled commentary on contemporary political upheaval'. Two further articles on Bradstreet, Raymond A. Craig's 'Singing with Grace: Allusive Strategies in Anne Bradstreet's "New Psalms" ' and Kathryn Zabelle Derounian-Stodola's ' "The Excellency of the Inferior Sex": The Commendatory Writings on Anne Bradstreet' both appear in the rather ponderously titled *Studies in Puritan American Spirituality* (*SPAS* 1–2) and have yet to be seen. Several essays on Edward Taylor appear in the same journal and all, hopefully, will be dealt with next year.

Percy G. Adams writes on 'Edward Taylor's Love Affair with Sounding Language' in *Order in Variety: Essays and Poems in Honor of Donald E. Stanford* edited by R. W. Crump, a collection of essays dedicated to the noted Taylor scholar. Adams's essay is a detailed, technical exegesis of the musical and phonic qualities of Taylor's verse in which he cleverly shows how often Taylor 'let his ear collaborate with his mind and his emotions'. Other notable articles on seventeenth-century writing include Jesper Rosenmeier's ' "They Shall No Longer Grieve": The *Song of Songs* and Edward Johnson's *Wonder-Working Providence*' (*EAL* 26.1–20) which focuses on Johnson's dependence on the *Song of Songs* and the more general indebtedness to Old Testament sources; D. N. Deluna's 'Cotton Mather Published Abroad' (*EAL* 26.145–72), a valuable account of the publishing history of Mather's works in England; and Tara Fitzpatrick's 'The Figure of Captivity: The Cultural Work of the Puritan Captivity Narrative' (*AmLH* 3.1–26), largely on Mary Rowlandson but interesting for its more general comments on the Puritan captivity narrative.

Scholarship and criticism of eighteenth-century figures is notable, once again, for the relative paucity of material on Franklin; the one full-length study, *Benjamin Franklin: Optimist or Pessimist* by J. A. Leo Lemay, has yet to be received for review and will be dealt with as soon as it arrives. There is, however, some recompense in the writing devoted to Jonathan Edwards, though, again, Mason I. Lowance Jnr's 'Jonathan Edwards and the Platonists: Edwardsean Epistemology and the Influence of Malebranche and Norris' from *SPAS* 1–2 has not been seen for review, although I surmise that Lowance's title is squarely indicative of his lines of inquiry. Janice Knight's 'Learning the Language of God: Jonathan Edwards and the Typology of Nature' (*WMQ* 48.531–51) is an article of considerable importance, one of the best on Edwards I have read in recent years. Employing a typological approach she argues for the 'internal harmony of Edwards's thought' and is perceptively attentive to the metaphorical and imagistic texture of Edwards's prose. In 'The Invention of the Great Awakening' (*EAL* 26.99–118), Joseph Conforti offers a lucid historical overview of the Second Great Awakening over which Edwards 'presided'.

There is just one article on Hugh Henry Brackenridge this year, Caryn Chaden's 'Dress and Undress in Brackenridge's *Modern Chivalry*', which in its preoccupation with the symbolic properties of clothing offers various comparisons and contrasts with the writings of Jonathan Swift, though quite whether they point to the shift from 'neoclassical values to an incipient, unfulfilled Romanticism' is another matter. Jay Fliegelman provides a useful, informed introduction to the new Penguin edition of Charles Brockden Brown's *Wieland* which, as usual, is paired with Brown's *Memoirs of Carwin the Biloquist*. In ' "The Arm Lifted Against Me": Love, Terror and the Construction of Gender in *Wieland*' (*EAL* 26.173–94), Andrew J. Scheiber argues that 'the disturbing paradoxes ... in Clara's character and her narration' (notably that conflict between intellect and superstition that many readers see) are not the results of 'authorial confusion or incompetence. Rather, they inscribe a pattern of conflict which defines Clara's problematical identity ...' So much so that he concludes by suggesting that 'Clara ... embraces the ideology that has been the source of her torment..' Scheiber's reading is heavily psychoanalytical, but even more so is it an example of those 'ironic readings' whereby authorial weaknesses or failings are, as it were, almost magically erased (what weaknesses or failings we find are deliberate), and, I think, in the face of most 'common sense' readings of the novel his account is deeply unpersuasive. Contemporary feminist criticism of the 'sentimental novel', particularly that of Nina Baym, Cathy N. Davidson, and Walter P. Wenska Jnr, is intelligently assessed by Klaus P. Hansen in 'The Sentimental Novel and Its Feminist Critique' (*EAL* 26.39–54) where Hansen adverts to the problems inherent in 'ironic readings' of the sentimental novel and the closely-related folly of 'attempts to find iconoclastic elements' where, palpably, they don't exist.

One essay on Phillis Wheatley is of interest. In 'Phillis Wheatley and the New England Clergy' (*EAL* 26.21–38), James A. Levernier shows how the New England clergy influenced Wheatley's poetry, suggesting that she 'would have learnt more than the catechism' from them, though whether the theological and philosophical thinking she would have acquired amounts to a 'poetics of liberation', as Levernier puts it, is an arguable point.

Finally, I return to the article by Philip F. Gura mentioned above. In 'Turning Our World Upside Down: Reconceiving Early American Literature' (*AL* 63.104–12), he remarks that the study of colonial American literature has been 'largely untouched by the New Historicism' and while historians of the same period have 'sharply challenged each other' he questions 'why hasn't there been a more fruitful commerce between scholars in the two disciplines?' Gura's answer – which I find very convincing – takes in a great deal of recent scholarship and insists upon the importance of knowing one's history before serious literary history can be undertaken. He points, also, to the geographical shift in historical scholarship, away from New England to the Chesapeake, and suggests that literary scholars, in turn, should move beyond 'the shoals of Cape Cod', though I'm sure he would concede that the reason literary scholarship concentrates on Puritan New England is a consequence both of the volume of material it presents for our consideration and, in most respects, its quality. As is the case with much of what Gura writes, this is a valuable and well-informed piece and is required reading for those interested in the general questions that surround literary scholarship of the seventeenth and eighteenth centuries. Timothy K. Conley's 'Retrospects and the Strategies of a Puzzled Discipline' (*EAL* 26.73–80), a 'Round Table' essay for *EAL*, explores related issues, though far less trenchantly than Gura.

3. Nineteenth Century Prose and Poetry

(a) General Books

Elizabeth Ammons, in her book, *Conflicting Stories: American Women Writers at the Turn into the Twentieth Century* takes an overview of the period 1890 to the late 1920s and provides a detailed account of responses, some interconnecting, some at odds, to the political and aesthetic questions exercising women writers during this period. This is a work of immense scholarship; Ammons treats seventeen writers in some detail, always providing a close reading of at least one major text by each author, yet also communicating a sense of their wider achievement and their cultural context. All the expected names are here – Chopin, Gilman, Jewett, Stein, Cather, Glasgow and Wharton – but these writers are forced into comparison with Harper, Dunbar-Nelson, Hopkins, Austin, Far, Humishuma, Fauset, Yerzierska, Kelley and Larsen and indeed, Ammons's thesis is predicated on the integrative possibilities offered by the 'shared focus on issues of power' between these writers, but also, crucially, on the frictions generated by their divergence – on lines of colour – on the nature of oppression. She illustrates this very effectively in a discussion of Gilman's 'The Yellow Wallpaper', foregrounding the 'domestic ideology' against which the issues raised in the text are rehearsed in opposition to the 'rape-lynch mythology' which provides the backdrop for work by Frances Harper, specifically *Iola Leroy, or Shadows Uplifted*, published in 1892. Inevitably, Ammons's book is full of lists but its range of reference is such that they usually provide a new connection or point the reader in a different direction via the informative and wide-ranging notes. This study is capacious, ambitious and inclusive; readings of familiar works are imaginative, bold and obsessive in the best sense.

An essay by Elizabeth Ammons on 'Gender and Fiction' features in 'The Late Nineteenth Century' section of *The Columbia History of The American Novel*, edited and with an introduction by Emory Elliott. The essays included in this literary history are organized on a thematic basis: individual author biographies and a general bibliography form a useful supplement. But the greatest strength of the volume is the clarity of its chapter design and scope. Key connections are made: the relationship between American autobiography, the slave-narrative and the early novel is expounded in one essay, the role of 'The Marketplace' in another. Robert S. Levine contributes a wide-ranging discussion of 'Fiction and Reform' which interrogates the novel as 'the genre most responsive to social debates' in the period between 1825 and 1860, viewing African and white American writers as 'dialogic' rather than irremediably enmeshed in the replication of conflicting ideologies. In 'Fiction and Reform II', Phillip Brian Harper discusses the gradualist nature of American 'reform culture' in the second half of the nineteenth century using *Uncle Tom's Cabin* as both catalytic to, and representative of, the development of the sentimental novel into the reform novel. Amy Kaplan's treatment of 'Nation, Region and Empire' charts the movement outlined in the title from Civil War, through 'local color' to imperialism; these terms, it is ably demonstrated here, represent distinct phases in the nation's actual and desired self-image as reflected in its literature.

Macropolitics of Nineteenth Century Literature: Nationalism, Exoticism, Imperialism, edited by Jonathan Arac and Harriet Ritvo, is a collection of essays with a unified approach to a variety of subjects, amongst them *Moby Dick* and *The History of the Lewis and Clark Expedition*. The editors define 'macropolitics' as a rewriting of New Historicism which emphasizes a perspective which is inclusive of cultural change, the three focal points of the title communicating a sense of the process by which a national culture emerges, defines otherness and converts it to its own uses. Bruce Greenfield's essay on the 'four modes of rhetoric' in *The History* – modes invoking national authority, the scientific, ethnographic and aesthetic – examines the dominance of the last-named in the process of the annexation of the West by the American traveller. In 'Ahab's Manifest Destiny', Wai-chee Dimock explores Ahab's kinship with the American Indian, both products of what she calls 'negative individualism', both, according to the rhetoric of their recorders, 'victim and culprit' and thus agents of their own destruction. This capable and capacious essay 'conflates' as the editors note, 'text, self and nation as loci of empire, freedom and doom'.

Workings of the Spirit: The Poetics of Afro-American Women's Writing by Houston A. Baker Jnr seeks to illuminate the work of modern writers, particularly Zora Neale Hurston, Toni Morrison and Ntozake Shange, by placing them in a whole cultural and theoretical context which is crucially concerned with nineteenth- and turn-of-the-century black women writers and their efforts to mediate the Southern experience to the Northern audience. He develops a 'topos' entitled 'The Daughter's Departure' which draws a parallel between those writers – Harriet Jacobs, Pauline Hopkins and Frances Harper – who could find no audience for their slave stories of 'concubinage and childbearing out of wedlock' in the North, and the contemporary resistance to the development of critical theory in Afro-American studies. Baker constructs a poetics of Afro-American women's writing, not seeking to minimize the good reasons for the resistance of both artists and critics to the theoretical configurations that might deny them 'subjecthood', but instead focusing attention on the potential of the autobiographical, what he describes as a 'personal negotiation of metalevels – one that foregrounds nuances and resonances of an-other's story'. His argument is complex but compelling and he writes in a rigorous but lyrical prose that is at once highly personal and theoretically dense.

Dana Brand's study, *The Spectator and the City in Nineteenth Century American Literature*, locates an English language epistemology for the figure of the *flâneur*, beginning in sixteenth-century England. Brand discusses the contingencies of the social and historical development of the *flâneur* and its publicists, notably Addison,

Steele and Dickens, and proceeds to assess the influence of such English manifestations of the phenomenon in the United States in order, specifically, to correct the overstatement of the anti-urban nature of American culture in the nineteenth century. The existence of the milieu of the *flâneur*, the city, the crowd, the exhibition, is authenticated through discussion of writing in New York periodicals, particularly *Knickerbocker* – published in the 1830s and 1840s – thoroughly urban in its concerns and influential, Brand argues, in the development of ideas of 'modernity' in the city-centred writings of Poe, Hawthorne and Whitman. This book exploits the potential for dialogue with, and dissent from, the formulation of the *flâneur* attributable to Baudelaire and Benjamin in its choice of subjects, notably Poe and particularly the detective stories, although it is the tale, 'The Man of the Crowd' to which Brand returns most often in his reading of Poe's 'new kind of urban observer'. Throughout his study and particularly in his conclusion Brand laments the American failure to develop an adequate response to urbanism and links 'the moral and epistemological prejudices against urban spectatorship that made Hawthorne so diffident about representing cities', with the cultural resistance to the modernity that – ironically enough – was a quintessentially American phenomenon.

Clive Bush's book, *Halfway to Revolution: Investigation and Crisis in the Work of Henry Adams, William James and Gertrude Stein* takes its named subjects as representative practitioners of history, psychology and literature between the years 1865 and 1945, representative in that they all, in their writing, bear witness to 'the breakdown of conventional discourse'. The larger context for Bush's work comes from the cultural shifts of the turn into the twentieth century, the rise of the specialist – whether in science, history or manufacturing – and the resulting dilution of democracy and the democratic process. The book is divided into three parts, each dealing with one author, although Bush's cross-referencing, allusive and inclusive style means that nothing is taken in isolation. Gertrude Stein is critically relocated in her age, examined less as the precursor of postmodernism than as a reactionary, as a 'small-town Jeffersonian individualist, pragmatic, even rural'. This is not to say that Bush does not engage with the considerable difficulties of reading Stein and indeed the portion of the book devoted to her work, and particularly to *The Making of Americans*, is the most persuasive and illuminating part of this study, not least because of the enhanced relationship with Adams and James into which Stein is here compelled.

Haunting the House of Fiction: Feminist Perspectives on Ghost Stories by American Women edited by Lynette Carpenter and Wendy K. Kolmar contains essays on Sarah Orne Jewett, Mary Wilkins Freeman, Charlotte Perkins Gilman and a variety of twentieth-century women writers up to and including Toni Morrison. The editors' introduction is a useful guide to the genre, its origins and development, its relationship with local colour realism and consolation literature and the characteristics it inherited from the female Gothic. Carpenter and Kolmar additionally give a coherent sense of scholarship conducted in the field and all the essays in the collection have useful bibliographies. Priscilla Leder's treatment of Jewett's *The Country of the Pointed Firs* compares Captain Littlepage's narration of an arctic expedition with Poe's *The Narrative of Arthur Gordon Pym of Nantucket*, in order to demonstrate Jewett's appropriation and rehabilitation of 'the linear progress of traditional "masculine" history into the circle of natural "feminine" history'. In 'The "Faces of Children That Had Never Been": Ghost Stories by Mary Wilkins Freeman', Beth Wynne Fisken gives an account of stories written by Freeman between 1900 and 1903. Fisken sees these ghost stories as the 'means of addressing some particularly problematic subject matter', specifically Freeman's 'refusal' of motherhood and the resultant conflict of emotions. E. Suzanne Owens in 'The Ghostly Double Behind the Wallpaper in Charlotte Perkins Gilman's "The Yellow Wallpaper" ' also makes a comparison with Poe, but here the informing text is 'William Wilson', which is, in conjunction with *Jane Eyre*, used as the foundation of an argument which has treatment of the 'splitting psyche' at the heart of Gilman's concerns in the story.

From Harlem to Paris: Black American Writers in France, 1840–1980, by Michael Fabre, is a detailed account of the work of black artists, chiefly Americans, who were able to entertain, play, write, sing, paint, speak or otherwise practice their art in a land distinguished by its liberal racial attitudes. Fabre details what he terms 'The New Orleans Connection' as an international phenomenon, with free Creoles of colour from Louisiana mobile between France and America in a manner unique to their topography in the pre-Civil War world. William Wells Brown, escaped slave, speaker in the cause of emancipation, playwright and novelist, went to Paris as a part of the Massachusetts delegation to the 1849 Peace Congress and found himself welcome in the house of Alexis de Toqueville, the minister for foreign affairs. Fabre offers the Parisian experiences of Brown and later Frederick Douglass as versions of the Grand Tour, the black traveller finally becoming fully American in Paris, by laying claim to one of the sites of common cultural heritage for both black and white and often proceeding from there to Africa.

'The Escape: or, A Leap for Freedom' (1858) by William Wells Brown, features in the collection *The Roots of African American Drama*, an anthology of early plays edited by Leo Hamalian and James V. Hatch. Also in the anthology, from the nineteenth century, is 'Peculiar Sam, or The Underground Railroad' (1879) by Pauline Elizabeth Hopkins. A short biography and select bibliography accompanies each play in the volume.

Susan K. Harris builds on her work in *Nineteenth Century American Women's Novels: Interpretive Strategies* (1990) in ' "But is it any good?": Evaluating Nineteenth Century American Women's Fiction' (*AL* 63.43–61). Here, she gives us a working definition of 'process analysis', placing her discussion of *St. Elmo, Ruth Hall, Iola Leroy and The Minister's Wooing* 'within the shifting currents of nineteenth-century American ideologies' in order to evaluate as well as investigate their contextual and rhetorical effectiveness.

In *Labor into Art: The Theme of Work in Nineteenth Century American Literature*, David Sprague Herreshoff looks at accounts of manual work as rendered by Thoreau, Melville, Dickinson, Douglass and Whitman. The writer most near to his purpose here is Thoreau who fortunately sets his own agenda for any discussion of labour which might include him. Herreshoff is a plain speaker and asserts that 'There is a dialectical interdependence between character and fate, personality and occupation' in the writing of his five chosen authors. His narrow definition of the theme of work, however, has a reductive effect upon those under discussion and this is most evident in treatment of Frederick Douglass, in whose writings Herreshoff's ideas could most explosively have come to life. He gives an account of Douglass's work when a slave without the crucial accompaniment of his work as a free man, as orator, writer and diplomat in the cause of freedom. The last word here can usefully be left to Thoreau: 'In the long run men hit only what they aim at.'

Stuart Hutchinson's book of essays on nineteenth-century American literature, *The American Scene*, explores familiar territory. The critical redrawing of the map of the nineteenth-century American literary scene which has taken place over the past few decades is not acknowledged here as Hutchinson devotes a chapter each to Cooper,

Poe, Hawthorne, Melville, Whitman, Dickinson, Twain and James and makes passing comparisons between their work and that of eminent European writers from Chaucer through to Joyce and Kafka. His own models and influences are acknowledged at the outset as Chase, Fiedler, Feidelson, Matthiessen, Poirier and Winters but neither the fiction writers nor the critics are enumerated in celebration, and the book has a subtly denigrating air, especially in its treatment of Cooper. Hutchinson overstates Cooper's 'authorial security' in his landscape and his subject and overdoes the 'tediousness' of the prose and the 'untroubled' nature of Cooper's vision, judgements which do not make convincing or compelling reading. Others fare better than Cooper, but even *Moby Dick* when held up for scrutiny is found wanting in terms of its lack of a 'human drama'.

The American Gentleman: Social Prestige and the Modern Literary Mind by David Castronovo is a witty and erudite account of social class as manifested in ideas of the American gentleman – from the Gilded Age to the present day – in literature. His interest lies in those writers 'who avoid denials about the nature of gentility', beginning his study with a comparison between Young Goodman Brown and George Bush and their respective refusals to say out loud where they have been and with whom they have been consorting, whether in the dark woods or at the Skull and Bones. Castronovo articulates the dissonance at the heart of the American idea of class and privilege: that which refuses to tolerate title and legally enshrined distinction yet conducts an enduring 'romance with discriminations and gentility', which simultaneously sees Thomas Jefferson campaigning against imported laws of entail and primogeniture in the State of Virginia and George Washington considering adoption of the title 'High Mightiness'. In his chapter 'The Gentleman in New England', Castronovo takes in self-presentation in *The Education of Henry Adams* as well as fiction by Henry Ward Beecher and Henry James, to demonstrate the specialized alienation cultivated by the patrician class, that which unfits them for useful work and elevates them as totems. He surveys the Hollywood gentleman in all his versions as toff, academic, stuffed shirt or patrician, the gentleman in the west, as portrayed by Owen Wister, the New York merchant-professional class, born out of Edith Wharton to F. Scott Fitzgerald, and provides a particularly compelling account of the South in the mid-nineteenth century as the 'cultural and historical matrix out of which the gentleman in modern literature emerges', especially as found in the work of Peter Taylor. This book is itself coy about its class and distinction; it would pass unnoticed in the coffee-table set but its pedigree and education qualifies it for the library.

The Theory of the American Romance: An Ideology in American Literary History (1989) by William Ellis reads romance theory as conspiracy theory, declaring at the outset his intention to 'help prevent revival by examining the theory's demerits in detail', whilst reawakening in his readers a proper sense of the centrality of the issues first raised by romance theorists. Ellis's argument, in surveying a vast range of literary critics and cultural commentators, makes a coherent case for the homogeneity of the European and American nineteenth-century novel, both being 'socially concerned, critical and often utopian in aspiration, in which social and cultural tensions, revealed largely through manners, play the key role.' The case for American exceptionalism is thus, in his construction, a result of an ideological over-valuation of American literature or those parts of it dignified with the title 'classic'. A massive re-evaluation of the terms and conditions under which American literary history is predicated is thus undertaken by Ellis in an entirely measured, eminently scholarly manner, his argument leading him to the point where he identifies satire as the most successful and appropriate American mode: Melville and Hawthorne failing to produce great works when they 'take their eye off society' as they do in *Pierre* and *The House of the Seven Gables*, and James and Wharton succeeding brilliantly because their satire is uninhibited by the need to talk up democracy. Stowe, freed in *Uncle Tom's Cabin* by the subject of slavery, did not have to show fidelity to democracy, so Ellis, in drawing attention to the American Romance as 'a vehicle of critical false consciousness', is liberated from the double bind of national and critical 'ideological chains'.

Joel Porte's *In Respect to Egotism: Studies in American Romantic Writing* focusses sharply upon the contingencies of writing, as American, in Emerson's 'age of the the first person singular'. Porte's introduction is witty, erudite and compelling and ranges widely through configurations of American and European Romanticism, claiming as the paradigmatic American Romantic period 1820 to the Civil War, a period which witnessed the 'startling confrontation of the agonized Puritan conscience with both the real and imaginative possibilities of the American sublime'. The range of authors featured here is familiar, but familiar interrogations are counterpointed by original questionings, familiar texts illuminated by the lesser-known; Brown, Irving, Cooper, Poe – these writers are forced to the point of self-predication in the actual American world, reconciling the conflicting discourses invoked by an American rendition of Romanticism. Porte is cogent in discussion of Emerson, particularly on the ecstatic in his writing and speaking, and takes note of Emerson as enabling principle in the development of Whitman's own brand of Romantic self-assertion – his claim for the sublimity of the unconventional in revelation of the American poet. *The Scarlet Letter* is rendered as 'a partial Lexicon of the Letter', *Walden* in terms of renewal – the 'perpetually resurrecting self'; Porte's reading of the inversions of the tropes and narrative forms of Judaeo-Christianity in the work of Frederick Douglass is taken in comparison with *Uncle Tom's Cabin* and this densely packed and provocative study ends with Emily Dickinson as child of Emerson but 'squeezed' rather than enlarged by 'the antinomies of existence'.

Sporting with the Gods: The Rhetoric of Play and Game in American Culture by Michael Oriard draws attention to the absence of the opposition between work and play from the familiar line-up of structural dichotomies in American culture – nature and civilization, individual and society, self and other, etc. In this study, he redresses the balance and also argues convincingly for examination of the trope of game and play as a central indicator of the nation's changing cultural bias. *The Virginian* (1902), as representative of the *Zeitgeist*, opens discussion of ' "The Game and the Nation" ', with the 1890s marked as a period of transition, the closing of the frontier signalling the movement of new, more domesticated mythic figures than Cooper's Leatherstocking – cavalier sportsmen in the South and hunter-sportsmen in the North – into the national consciousness. Oriard does not neglect the games that women were deemed fit to play, ensuring that the terms of his discourse, with their implications for both racial- and gender-based exclusions, dissect the hegemony of the white male. In discussion of the West he moves from Cooper, through the Southwestern humorists, Irving, Caroline Kirkland, the dime novel, up to Bret Harte, and moves on geographically to implicate the idea of the game in the development of nothing less than Southern honour – via hospitality, sport and the duel. Oriard centres his argument in 'Gender and the Game' on *The Bostonians*, the war of words between North and South, the status quo and feminism, business and leisure succumbing to the rhetoric of play in a complex and abrasive contest which allows of no simple versions of political, social and economic certainty for the players. An extensive survey of nineteenth-century women writers concerned with 'the love game', especially as featured in the story papers, culminates in consideration of Wharton's *The House of*

Mirth and Chopin's *The Awakening* for their use of games as the 'marker of the masculine world', and Henry James for his deployment of women as 'stake or plaything' rather than 'contestant'.

Elaine Showalter's 1989 Clarendon Lectures find their way into published form in *Sister's Choice: Tradition and Change in American Women's Writing*. Showalter poses a number of what she calls 'American questions about the history, traditions and contradictions of American women's writing', which take her from Margaret Fuller to Alice Walker in rapid, culminatory style. The discussion of Fuller is predicated as 'Miranda's Story', the woman writer irrefutably 'the product of a rigorous patriarchal education'. The work of another writer dominated by patriarchal transcendentalism, Louisa May Alcott, is considered both in terms of its intimate relationship with the circumstances and events of Alcott's own life and its effect on subsequent generations of women readers. This piece will be familiar to readers of Showalter's 1989 introduction to the Penguin Classic *Little Women*. In the chapter, 'American Female Gothic', Showalter pays tribute to the work of Ellen Moers and goes on to outline a particularly American Gothic via a reading of Gilman's 'The Yellow Wallpaper'. *En route* to the twentieth century, Showalter takes in *The Awakening*, now firmly – and somewhat familiarly – established as a transitional text, rehearsing the story of contemporary critical reaction to the novel and current critical opinion, ending her commentary on Chopin with a glance at the 'rereadings, rewriting, and reinhabiting of women's texts' that form the somewhat bemusingly upbeat tone of this study.

(b) *Individual Authors*

Bert Bender, in 'The Teeth of Desire The Awakening and The Descent of Man' (*AL* 63.459–73) begins a discussion of the influence of Darwin on Chopin with a brief discussion of her early novel *At Fault*. He traces Chopin's use of and divergence from Darwin's 'logic of sexual selection' through her courtship plots and up to *The Awakening*, using her interrogations and interpretations of his theory to chart the movement from 'ambivalence' to 'despair' in her work. Katherine Kearns's essay, 'The Nullification of Edna Pontellier' (*AL* 63.62–88) describes the emergent self of *The Awakening* as in thrall to 'the damning imperatives of a sensuality' which negates any concomitant 'intellectual, spiritual, and artistic growth'. Emily Toth gives an account of two published interviews with Kate Chopin from the *St. Louis Post-Dispatch* in 'Kate Chopin on Divine Love and Suicide: Two Rediscovered Articles' (*AL* 63.115–22). In one of these interviews Chopin gives her thoughts on suicide and in the other she responds to the question: 'Is Love Divine?'

'The Guardian of the Law': Authority and Identity in James Fenimore Cooper by Charles Hansford Adams establishes at the outset the primary significance of legal language and procedure in the formation and sustenance of social relations in Cooper's version of nineteenth-century America. Adams is not the first to locate the natural/civil law dialectic at the heart of Cooper's concerns but he extends and clarifies the ambivalences of writer, fiction and nation on the role of the law as 'parental authority'. He conducts a detailed discussion of a limited number of texts which nevertheless has widespread reverberations for Cooper's work as a whole. Adams uses *The Spy* and *Lionel Lincoln* to examine representations of law in the context of the American Revolution, and *The Pioneers* to place the 'distinction between the law's assumptions and human motivation, between legal form and human identity' in the context of the struggle for a coherent sense of the relationship between public and private in the developing nation. Adams concludes his study with *The Ways*

of the Hour as illustrative of Cooper's abandonment of both aesthetic and intellectual uses of the law in his last years, the 'impasse' which was always inherent in the opposition of ideal law and the reality in both Cooper's life and art. 'Cooper's *Spy* and The Theatre of Honour' (*AL* 63.405–19) by T. Hugh Crawford considers emergent discourses of honour and their manifestation in *The Spy*, focusing specifically on their opposition to representations of an 'eighteenth century theater of honor'.

Geoffrey Rans, in *Cooper's Leather-Stocking Novels: A Secular Reading*, chooses his texts with a dual purpose: to build on the work of those critics who have restored to literary studies the 'respectability of the didactic' and to bring Cooper into the mainstream of any discussion which seeks to historicize our readings of nineteenth-century American literature. As the enabling principle in this endeavour, Rans considers the novels in order of composition, refusing to follow Cooper's injunction in the 1850 prefaces to *The Deerslayer* and *The Leather-Stocking Tales* to read the series in 'the regular course of their incidents'. His methodology allows Rans to be entirely specific on the rebuttal of any reading of Natty Bumppo which sees him as identical with an idealized 'American spirit' for he convincingly demonstrates that the 'radical *meaning* of Natty's life', his merits and ideals, are betrayed at every turn by the prevailing spirit of the developing nation. The series which has as its last authored book *The Deerslayer* (1841) is seen to portray any ideal as *only* ideal, representing 'with an irresistible force what civilization wills not to be.' The introduction to this study includes 'Cooper among the Critics' which both surveys the state of the art and provides a firm context for Rans's own work which, he fulsomely acknowledges, follows and draws on Jane Tompkins's *Sensational Designs* (1985).

In 'Vanishing Americans: Gender, Empire, and New Historicism', (*AL* 63.385–404) Lora Romero conducts an investigation of Cooper's *The Last of the Mohicans* via an interrogation of Foucauldian analysis as practised by New Historicists specifically in discussion of gender and race politics.

Meaning by Metaphor: An Exploration of Metaphor with a Metaphoric Reading of Two Short Stories by Stephen Crane by Gunnar Backman announces unashamedly on its second page that 'The choice of Crane is arbitrary.' There follows a detailed exegesis of metaphor in all its forms which is thoroughly referenced and draws on a wide range of linguistic theory and literary critical material. Backman's general survey of the theory and practice of metaphor prepares the way for the application of a method which arises from his research and which he terms 'componential analysis'. This approach is worthy, and, though dull, exhaustive. 'The Bride Comes to Yellow Sky' and 'The Blue Hotel' are probed minutely for their metaphoric strategies, strategies which make explicit for Backman's readers the probable origins of their understanding of the text and even of the aesthetic experience itself.

In *Rebecca Harding Davis and American Realism,* Sharon Harris places Rebecca Harding Davis firmly in the frontline of the advance of American realism, taking on the critics who have variously misattributed, misread or ignored Davis's writings and have thus failed to recognize her work as that of a 'pioneer realist'. The argument here is not confrontational but measured, well-substantiated and persuasive, and Davis emerges from Harris's reassessment of her work as an innovator, essaying a literature of the commonplace which is most clearly evidenced in her best-known work, 'Life in the Iron Mills'. Davis's literary theory of the commonplace was developed, Harris argues, two decades before Howells attempted a similar definitional enterprise; she identifies Davis's writing as precursive to important elements of naturalist style and language as practiced by Crane, Norris, Chopin, Dreiser, Anderson and Sinclair, and 'Life in the Iron Mills', published in 1861, is predicated as both syncretic of existing literary modes and prophetic of later ones. Indeed, Harris argues that 'Life' provides a guide to 'metarealism', as she terms it, a synthesis of romanticism, sentimentalism and regionalism rendered up as 'an art form that represents quotidian experience.' Harris illustrates the creeping conservatism of Davis's later years through her discussion of the changes in her fiction, delineating clearly its weaknesses but also continuing to examine its strengths and, above all else, giving full credit to Davis's power as an innovator.

Lyric Contingencies: Emily Dickinson and Wallace Stevens by Margaret Dickie seeks to extricate the lyric poem from its confinement within the Emersonian tradition in order to emphasize the discontinuous, the improvisational in the work of these writers. Dickie conducts an examination of the speaker of the lyric, its language and audience in a 'contingent' not an 'ideal' world and, in each case, makes the question of gender central to her argument. In her chapter 'Dickinson and the Lyric Self' she frees the poet from 'the necessity' to be 'representative', refusing readings of Dickinson that locate her either in a literary tradition or in theories which are designed to apply to prose. Dickinson's lyric 'I' is, according to Dickie, expressive of 'a sense of identity as particular, discontinuous, limited, private, hidden' and as such refutes all attempts to make it part of a public 'master narrative'. In an interchapter between discussion of Dickinson and Stevens, the two poets are united via 'pragmatism' so as to elucidate the principle of 'contingency' which guides this study.

Emily Dickinson by Joan Kirkby is one of the latest volumes in the Macmillan Women Writers series. Opening with a quickfire biographical introduction which sets the headlong pace of the study as a whole, every point Kirby makes is reinforced with Dickinson's own words, which, whilst demonstrating the impressiveness of her knowledge of the verse and letters, does tend to delimit further response to the poet. An impressive range of verse is covered under thematic headings, including Nature, Gender and Gothic, this latter chapter expressing a particularly coherent argument substantiated, as elsewhere in this study, by close reading. Kirby's range of allusions, placing Dickinson in the context of thought and writing contemporary with her and also in relation to the concerns of current critical opinion, is as extensive as her knowledge of the verse and the final chapter gives a summary of Dickinson criticism. The book as a whole provides a useful introduction to the poet which in its clear assumptions and exegesis may make the business of approaching Dickinson's verse less fraught with difficulty.

Mary Loeffelholz's *Dickinson and the Boundaries of Feminist Theory* conducts a closely engaged discussion of recent Dickinson criticism and particularly focuses on the manifestations and reverberations of psychoanalytic theory, examining where it both dissects and diverges from feminist criticism. She picks up the challenge of unanswered questions, postulations and difficulties in the most productive and positive way, describing her own approach as a 'conjunction of feminism and deconstruction'. Whilst using the work of her predecessors, most notably, Joanne Feit Diehl, Helen McNeil and Margaret Homans, Loeffelholz establishes a mode of interpretative activity which serves her thesis admirably. It is not only theory which informs her close readings of the verse, however, but Dickinson's vexed relationship with Emerson and Wordsworth and, most compellingly, with Barrett Browning, the Brontës and Adrienne Rich. This is a complicated and complicating reading of Dickinson which makes positive use of conflict, both within the poetry itself and within Dickinson studies; as Loeffelholz readily acknowledges: 'Dickinson's language speaks back to all the theories – deconstructive, feminist, materialist, psychoanalytic – that would address it.'

Frederick Douglass, by William S. McFeely, the latest biography of the man who published three different versions of his own life, is a well-rounded and temperate delineation of Douglass's life and times. McFeely renders a business-like account of Douglass's early years in slavery and conveys a cogent sense of the checks and balances in his relationship with his masters, especially with the Auld family, familiar to readers from *The Narrative*. The far from simple topography of racial prejudice in the United States, as characterized and challenged in Douglass's pre- and post-Civil War oratory to Northern audiences, is construed to good effect when placed in the context of Douglass's own complicated attitude to the South and his sense of the demands made upon the black American in the post-reconstruction world. Douglass's reception in even the most advanced abolitionist circles could never be predicted and McFeely skilfully communicates an understanding of the social and professional difficulties which Douglass both experienced and inflicted as a result of his consciousness of his overdetermined status at home in America and when abroad. Douglass's family, his marginalized wife, Anna, his children, and especially his daughter, Rosetta, having no part in Douglass's public life, form a disappointed chorus to his story; they were left behind in physical, intellectual and political terms when Douglass took his message to the world. McFeely, however, does not apportion praise or blame for Douglass's absorption in those who could help him in his great work, indeed his studied and neutral tone even when dealing with the most contentious and scandalous incidents in Douglass's life often has the effect of neutralizing and distancing events in the life of this most passionate and difficult man.

The introduction to *New Essays on Sister Carrie* by its editor, Donald Pizer, provides an account of the publishing history of the novel in relation to Dreiser's life and work. Pizer briefly surveys critical treatment of *Sister Carrie* from early reviews, through Lionel Trilling's condemnation of Dreiser in 'Reality in America' (1950), to contemporary responses. In his essay, 'Carrie's Blues' Thomas P. Riggio draws extensively on the fuller portrait of Carrie herself in the Pennsylvania edition of the novel, published in 1981 using as source the handwritten first draft of the novel, not the published version of 1907. Barbara Hochman examines the 'complexities inherent in the act of representation' coupling the experiences of Dreiser in the process of writing and Carrie in the theatre, whilst Richard Lehan in '*Sister Carrie*: The City, the Self, and the Modes of Narrative Discourse' claims Spencer's *First Principles* as a 'key' to the novel, consolidating a discussion of naturalism and its various critical manifestations in writings on Dreiser with the making of a case for a new composite edition of *Sister Carrie*. Alan Trachtenberg also provides a summary of previous critical positions on *Sister Carrie*, but in preparation for an analysis of the complex role of the narrative voice in reflecting Dreiser's revision of the realist novel, a revision necessary in order to communicate his abandonment of the representation of 'moral dilemma along with the moral universe'.

Martha J. Cutter, in her essay 'Frontiers of Language: Engendering Discourse in "The Revolt of Mother" ' (*AL* 63.279–91), examines the 'distinctly gendered priorities' of the protagonists in the story and the repression of discourse which effectively silences and disempowers Sarah Penn. She discusses the process by which 'home' and 'barn' merge via the invention of 'a system of discourse which slips free from the binary system of sexual difference, of patriarchal or non-patriarchal language, of speaking men or silent women, of barn versus home.'

William W. Stowe, in 'Conventions and Voices in Margaret Fuller's Travel Writing' (*AL* 63.242–62), places Fuller's *Summer on the Lakes* and her letters to the *New York Tribune* in the developmental context of the genre in America, tracing its evolution from Irving, through Sigourney, Allen, Willard and Greeley and their treatments of 'American possibilities in a European setting', and ending with Fuller employing their diverse voices in her own polyvocal body of work.

Columbia University Press have issued *Charlotte Perkins Gilman: A Nonfiction Reader* edited and with an introduction by Larry Ceplair. This edition makes available lectures, speeches, articles and chapters from larger works and draws heavily on the Gilman holdings at Radcliffe College. The whole woman is on display here, including her suggestion of enforced national service as a solution to 'the Negro Problem'; no *Modest Proposals* for Gilman, her new model army would benefit from 'not enslavement, but enlistment'. Ceplair puts Gilman's racism in context, without minimizing it and yet also without overstating its importance in a career distinguished for its ambitious intellectual engagement with all the problems of human culture and for her ability to produce texts of all kinds. Gilman's writings are organized chronologically here; Ceplair introduces each period in her development by examining the literary, historical and personal context for the work and whilst her concerns can be seen to change over the years the dominating themes of gender, freedom within society, evolution and economics are never far from the centre of the argument.

Douglas Anderson, in his essay, 'Jefferson, Hawthorne and "The Custom-House" ', (*NCL* 46.309–26), extends the political implications of 'The Custom-House' and also Hawthorne's preface to the second edition of *The Scarlet Letter* to the 'publically amended status of the *Declaration of Independence*'. He examines verbal echoes between Hawthorne's and Jefferson's texts and the fact that both final versions repress 'the most turbulent emotions behind [their] composition'.

Lauren Berlant's *The Anatomy of National Fantasy: Hawthorne, Utopia and Everyday Life* comes garlanded with praise from eminent American scholars who testify to the brilliance of both book and author. This study of Hawthorne is dense and difficult; the prose is freighted with signification and the complexities of the argument are boundless. In detailed examination of *The Scarlet Letter*, Berlant analyses the process through which 'national culture becomes local', hence explicating the relationship between 'official, juridical definitions of the nation and its circulation in the culture at large'. Berlant begins with 'Alice Doane's Appeal' in order to mediate Hawthorne's counter-attack on the 'National Symbolic' and moves to an exposure of the means by which he disrupts 'The utopian desire for an inclusive national identity' in *The Scarlet Letter*.

Emily Miller Budick, in her essay, 'Hester's Skepticism, Hawthorne's Faith; or what Does a Woman Doubt? Instituting the American Romance Tradition', (*NLH* 22.129–60) puts Pearl at the heart of an enquiry into the 'relationship between issues of birth (whose child is Pearl?) and questions of interpretation (what does the letter mean?).' 'Fideism vs. Allegory in "Rappaccini's Daughter" ' (*NCL* 46.223–44) by John N. Miller examines in detail the contingencies of the conflict between concepts of the title character in Hawthorne's tale. Miller grounds his interpretation in biographical data thereby differentiating himself from other critics working in the 'light of transcendental epistemology'.

The Scarlet Letter, edited by Ross Murfin, has been issued as one of the *Case Studies in Contemporary Criticism* series. The volume includes a general introduction, the text itself, which is a reprinting of the centenary edition of the novel, originally issued by Ohio State University Press, and five critical essays exemplifying different theoretical approaches to Hawthorne's work: psychoanalytic, reader-response, feminist, deconstructive and New Historicist. Murfin introduces each of the representative essays by practitioners with an explanation of the main features of their theoretical perspective and each part of the case study has its own bibliography, or set of bibliographies, which reflect the background to the critical theory as well as to *The Scarlet Letter* itself. Murfin has brought together five outstanding literary theorists – Joanne Feit Diehl, David Leverenz, Shari Benstock, Michael Ragussis and Sacvan Bercovitch – whose essays provide both rich reading and provocative accounts of what the application of theory to the text might generate; it would be hard to think of a better introduction either to critical theory or to Hawthorne than this volume provides.

Contexts for Hawthorne: 'The Marble Faun' and the Politics of Openness and Closure in American Literature by Milton R. Stern is a study of Hawthorne via the insights provided by a single text examined in a variety of 'contexts'. Stern posits Hawthorne as enmeshed in the contradictions of 'the ideological America (the actual culture) and the utopian America', defining utopias via Karl Mannheim and implicating the oppositions of radical and conservative, Romanticism and Classicism in his exegesis of the politics of opennesss and closure. Stern positions Hawthorne in his 'American Context' looking at writers from Irving through to Wharton and Dreiser to examine the various treatments of 'all the permutations of form and all the cross-migrations of rhetoric, two great constellations of national identity – the millennialist Dream and historical experience'. Another chapter puts Hawthorne in 'A Marketplace Context' where the way is prepared for an analysis of *The Marble Faun* which engages with long-standing critical dissatisfactions with the text, not to dissent from them but to show them as symptomatic of Hawthorne caught 'in the terrible actualities of his own context', that is, his re-entry to the American literary marketplace. In a final chapter Stern demonstrates his own intellectual debt to what is gently called 'science' in prefatory remarks but which, by the end, has become the means by which to relate 'Hawthorne's responses' – via Stephen Hawking and quantum mechanics – to 'moments of punctuation' in the 'space-walls of galaxies'.

Nathaniel Hawthorne: Tradition and Revolution by Charles Swann begins with its author – Hawthorne-like – claiming the neglected, the incomplete, as his inspiration: the Riverside edition of Hawthorne's works, accidently acquired, gives Swann access to little discussed material: 'Alice Doane's Appeal', 'Chiefly About War Matters' and the campaign biography of Franklin Pierce are central to the argument developed here. Swann uses the more obscure texts to progress his construction of the conflict inherent in Hawthorne's recognition of both the power of tradition and that of revolutionary transformations. His reading of *The Blithedale Romance* is thus focused sharply on transformation, and, more specifically, on translation; Coverdale and Fauntleroy as translator and forger respectively are the starting point for a reading of the narrative which has it 'sceptical of its own authority and of the terms on which authority is based'. 'Alice Doane's Appeal' – in order to demonstrate its failure to 'work' as a coherent narrative – is placed in the literary historical context which inevitably 'subverts the Gothic elements' and makes the tale untellable. Swann also conducts a painstaking examination of *The American Claimant Manuscripts* as a means of entry to *The Marble Faun*, and, more crucially, to Hawthorne's struggles with his art and its inevitable failure to match the ambitions he harboured for the American subject. Chapter five of Swann's book, '*The House of the Seven Gables*: Hawthorne's modern novel of 1848' also appears in *MLR* (86.1–18).

In his introduction to *New Essays on 'The Rise of Silas Lapham'* the editor, Donald Pease provides an account of *Silas Lapham* as a critical barometer, assessing the reorientations of ideas of American literary realism as they have affected Howells's novel. In focusing on progressivism, modernism, formalism, deconstructivism, feminism and New Historicism Pease is able to approach the dialectic between realism and romance taken as paradigmatic by the practitioners of these approaches and to argue instead for a 'critically enabling confusion of … categories'. All the contributors to the volume take issue in one way or another with previous critics of the novel and, indeed, reflect in varying degrees the critical stances examined by Pease at the outset. The central focus of Wai-Chee Dimock's essay 'The Economy of Pain: Capitalism, Humanitarianism and the Realistic Novel' is the relationship between the moral and the economic and the historicizing of pain into a question of 'resource management'. This is a question which absorbs all the essayists here to some degree as they are concerned, according to Pease, with the transformation of 'problems to be resolved' into 'resources for renewed understandings of a narrative'.

Ian F. A. Bell's *Henry James and the Past* is a detailed study of three novels: *Washington Square, The Bostonians* and *The Europeans*, identified as precipitate texts, on the cusp between American romance and realism, between producer and consumer culture. Bell focuses on James's female characters as barometers of social change, where 'aesthetic issues of representation and character are caught up within the strategies of the marketplace': they are emergent as 'belonging to a world of manufacture, design and alterability'. Bell notes the opening topographical and temporal specificity of *Washington Square* as pivotal in James's account of the forces which are wrangling over the commodified Catherine Sloper and goes on to identify that very specificity as spurious; the absence of relatedness between the Square and the rest of the city, the contradictions contained within the time-scheme of the novel, these point to James's actual 'purposive tactic of historical removal'. *The Bostonians* is firmly declared to be 'about "publicity" '; it is read as a text representative of its era which dissolves and rebuilds ideas of the relationship between self and world in the new consumer culture. Bell integrates a wide range of reference to James's American and European literary predecessors into his argument, which fruitfully complicates the discussion; additionally, his erudition in the field of consumer culture is positioned so as to derive the most from the vexed question of James's sense of history.

Millicent Bell, in her *Meaning in Henry James*, finds herself, as she says in her preface, unable to resist the assertion of 'final meanings' in a 'cumulative' reading of fiction from 'Daisy Miller' to *The Ambassadors*. In such an assertion, however, Bell is not seeking to minimize the actual process or the uncertainties of reading Henry James, rather she shifts our focus toward the capacity of the narratives to 'propose and cancel meanings at successive moments'. This extended and closely-argued study places James in the context of both American and European literary traditions and uses Balzac and Hawthorne to particularly good effect, positioning James in the reverberative centre of the distinct cultural bind which fixed the two – Balzac's France 'the most rounded and registered, most organised and administered' and Hawthorne's America so lacking in the 'items of high civilization'. In delineating James's means of access to these contrasting worlds Bell reinforces her theme of indeterminacy, an indeterminacy which covers plot, narrative strategy and meaning. Bell's approach strikes particular sparks from *The Portrait of a Lady* as we see Isabel Archer in search of a plot – 'nefarious' or otherwise – which is sufficient to demonstrate the aesthetic principle of making ' "being" a mode of "doing" '.

Ellen Brown argues that the New York edition of *The Aspern Papers* is more than simply a revised text in her article 'Revising Henry James: Reading the Spaces of *The Aspern Papers*' (*AL* 63.163–278). She extends 'the Narrative of revision' from the final version of the text back to the original oral tale that James heard and recorded in his notebooks.

The Portrait of a Lady and The Turn of the Screw: Henry James and Melodrama by David Kirby is one of the Critics Debate Series and is a clearly organized and invaluable book. Sensible, wide-ranging and well-written it has clear merits as a student guide to the texts under discussion and also to the varieties of literary criticism. Kirby does not merely provide a survey of available criticism on James's two works but an interesting and original commentary on the texts themselves. The book does not make any grand claims for itself but its wide yet easy range of reference and ability to consider James in contexts both historical and aesthetic make it an invaluable addition to the available range of 'Guide to ...' books. The study is divided into two parts and these in turn are subdivided into 'Survey' and 'Appraisal'; in reading both texts Kirby's approach is determined by their particular relationship with melodrama.

The Jameses: A Family Narrative by R. W. B. Lewis brings together the variously documented lives of 'the most outstanding intellectual family America has ever produced' from William James of Albany's American beginnings to his present-day descendants. This study is capaciously organized, the relations of the family with all their connections, either by marriage or by friendship, are brought skilfully and illuminatingly within the orbit of the narrative. We see how Henry Senior, disinherited by his father but, under the law of the State of New York, restored to his proper share, made the reluctant legacy from William James of Albany his access to a world in which he was 'leisured for life'. Lewis is chiefly concerned with the effect of this leisure on the intellectual development of the most famous generation of Jameses and its manifestation in their work: 'We were never in a single case, I think, for two generations, guilty of a stroke of business', as Henry junior so disingenuously put it. This volume is immensely readable; wearing its scholarship lightly it provides sufficient detail and range of reference for the purposes of research and, with grateful acknowledgement of the work of F. O. Matthiessen, integrates fruitfully the separate lives.

The family is also at the heart of the matter in the chapter on Henry James in *The Daughter's Dilemma: Family Process and the Nineteenth-Century Domestic Novel* by Paula Marantz Cohen. Cohen uses family systems theory, borrowed from the social sciences, to examine the 'ideological dominance of closure in both nineteenth-century domestic novels and nuclear families', for the purposes of which *Clarissa* is her beginning and *The Awkward Age* her end. James is given a revisionary role in Cohen's argument as the first novelist to grapple with a new ideology in constructing a version of the family that 'carries us beyond modernism', the idea of what it means to be a heroine being obscured in James's narrative. The Brookenham family is read as being without closure in terms of the role of the daughter; the discursiveness of the text in its 'quantity of meaning and number of intentions', as James allows in the preface, is endlessly indeterminate. Cohen's conclusion focuses almost exclusively on James and draws *The Golden Bowl* into the argument in order to emphasize the 'stylelessness' of the late James, and this a 'stylelessness' which causes the removal of 'moral and emotional directives'.

Henry James by Adrian Poole features as a new volume in the Harvester New Readings series. Poole's study is plainly organized, lucidly expressed and offers access to some of the most inaccessible of James's novels. He takes as his key to James the writer's handling of the discomforts of civilization – after Freud – particularly examining the control of anger as both subject and technique and James's relationship with the resources, physical and creative, available to him. Among Poole's declared topics for his exploration of James are 'initiation', the inertia of English society, sexual politics, power relations, and in a final chapter devoted to *The Turn of the Screw*, he looks at the contingencies of 'haunting and commemoration, of revenge and reparation'. The last chapter, in breaking with the chronological approach otherwise followed, allows Poole to use *The Turn of the Screw* as evidence of the circularity he sees as the quintessential Jamesian spectacle, his ability, in his art, 'to make the discomforts of culture circulate, endlessly'.

In *The Trial of Curiosity: Henry James, William James and the Challenge of Modernity*, Ross Posnock constructs an erudite argument for a revaluation of the place of *The American Scene*, the New York prefaces and James's autobiographical writings in the Jamesian canon as a 'second major phase (1907–14)'. His declared subject is the relationship between Henry and William James and their respective styles of 'cultural critique' in response to modernity; Posnock scrutinizes the effects of their membership of the family which 'breathed inconsistency and ate and drank contradictions' and their individual handling of the intellectual legacy which caused Alice to self-immolate and enmeshed both her elder brothers in 'the Jamesian dialectic of abasement and renewal'. The easily erected dualisms, sustained by a picture – presented and perpetuated by the Jameses no less than any commentator – of the brothers as rivals, as opposites in both practice and theory is challenged by Posnock who looks beyond accepted versions of the Jamesian self and its relationships. Posnock describes his approach as both 'contextualist' and 'comparative', locating the Jameses amongst their contemporaries: E. L. Godkin, Charles Eliot Norton, Theodore Roosevelt and George Santayana, but also scrutinizing them in conjunction with Walter Benjamin, Theodor Adorno and John Dewey. This is a complex and ambitious book which is clear in its objectives and persuasive in its argument; it is particularly notable for its treatment of *The Ambassadors* and the relocation of Henry James's responses to immigrant New York in *The American Scene* within 'the contours of a pragmatism that places the fact of urban modernity at its center'.

Jeanne Campbell Reesman in *American Designs: The Late Novels of James and Faulkner* also puts *The Ambassadors* at the heart of her argument, here alongside *Absalom, Absalom!*, in order to problematize discussion of narrative structure in the context of an approach which 'addresses craft as joint purpose and form'. The rationale for placing the work of these two writers in contiguity is their common presentation of 'the search for knowledge of the self and of other people … as a metafictive issue of power, authority and freedom'. In her introductory chapter 'Contexts for Dialogue', Reesman sets out her stool between the philosophical approach of Richard Rorty and the theoretical context offered by the work of Mikhail Bakhtin, the methodology thus providing further justification for the yoking together of her two subjects. *The Golden Bowl* is also discussed in detail as a text successful in the integration of knowledge with power: the novel is seen at once to evade and assert design, an internal contradiction made possible by the 'negativity' inherent in what Reesman defines as the 'hermeneutic techniques' of these writers.

The Cosmopolitan World of Henry James: An Intertextual Study by Adeline Tintner is a Cook's Tour of European literature viewed in its relation to Henry James. Tintner's movement of the celebrated international theme into a more fully-rounded cosmopolitanism begins in England, in discussion of Ouida, Henry Harland and Oscar Wilde, retreats back in time in Germany with Goethe and Hoffmann, spends six chapters in France in a variety of genres, lingers over Italy and ends, after several more excursions into other lands, at the opera. The Henry James who emerges from these comparisons is a writer concerned above all to 'correct' the models he used, especially in their over-obsession with 'one experience: sex'; and, Tintner is without reservation in stating: 'The cosmopolitan world to which James aspired belongs to a Platonic order of his creation, an ideal world refined and purged of the grossness of contemporary versions of the "high life".' James as model of decorum and upholder of 'civilized behaviour' thus interacts with leading European artists, alive and dead, processing their material, transmogrifying both style and content into another form altogether. Tintner's book is impressively organized and brings under close scrutiny the work of an interesting range of writers; it is also extensively, if dimly, illustrated, but its abiding image, unfortunately, is that of Max Beerbohm's cartoon: 'Henry James Listening at a Keyhole' (1904) which, seems, in all sorts of ways, to sum up the argument of the book. Adeline Tintner also has an essay in *The Sweetest Impression of Life: The James Family in Italy*, (1990) edited by James W. Tuttleton and Agostino Lombardo, where she is able to demonstrate her detailed knowledge of the role of Italian art in James's fiction through a discussion of 'Rococo Venice, Pietro Longhi and Henry James'. Tuttleton's essay is an account of the James family in Italy, which takes as its starting point the importance of Italian culture in their lives before they began their travels: the art which they possessed, visited at exhibitions, the music they heard, letters they received, Tuttleton considers as preparation for the 'sensuous education' they were to experience once abroad. Henry James is the central subject for the majority of the essayists here, although in addition to Tuttleton's piece on the family there are two considerations of William James and one of Alice James. Denis Donoghue, in '*William Wetmore Story and His Friends*: The Enclosing Fact of Rome', shows how the book transcends its prosaic and reluctant beginnings to become an exercise in remembrance which is 'an elaborate reconsideration and recovery of old experience'. This collection considers the role of Italian culture as an aesthetic model; the 'interpenetration' of art and life which Edith Wharton noted as the salient feature of Italian civilization is discussed in the variety of its manifestations in the lives of the natives of the James family.

Henry James: The Major Novels by Judith Woolf is a new volume in the Cambridge British and Irish Authors: Introductory Critical Studies series. Concerned above all to place James in the context of the development of the English novel Woolf, like Cohen, shows the work of eighteenth- and nineteenth-century novelists as incremental in pushing James toward complexity. Woolf begins with *The Europeans, Washington Square* and *Daisy Miller*, and with the familiar theme of 'the betrayal of innocence' as her subject she provides a lucid, nicely-judged account of these works charting the turning of the comedic mode James inherited from his predecessors in the novel, specifically Richardson and Austen, to the tragic, from the near-farce of misunderstandings in *The Europeans* to the grave of *Daisy Miller*. Woolf gains access to a full reading of *The Portrait of a Lady* via *Daniel Deronda* and in discussion of all the major novels she alludes easily and productively to a range of English texts, including *Alice in Wonderland* as a prelude to *What Maisie Knew*. Most space is allocated to discussion of *The Wings of the Dove* and *The Golden Bowl*, and Woolf is extremely effective in demystifying these texts without simplifying them.

Philip Young, in 'The Machine in Tartarus: Melville's Inferno' (*AL* 63.208–24) takes a brief look at 'The Paradise of Bachelors' and a longer look at 'The Tartarus of Maids', and in particular at sexual and parturient symbolism, acknowledging Melville's debts to Dante's *Inferno* and also to the work of Dr Augustus Kinsley Gardiner in 'Obstetrics and Lunacy'.

In 'Irresistable Impulses: Edgar Allan Poe and the Insanity Defense' (*AL* 63.623–40) John Cleman examines three stories: 'The Tell-Tale Heart' (1843), 'The Black Cat' (1843) and 'The Imp of the Perverse' (1845) in the context of the 'specific jurisprudential issues of his day', that is, the insanity defence controversy and its blurring of the rational and irrational in human behaviour. Jeanne M. Malloy, in 'Apocalyptic Imagery and the Fragmentation of the Psyche: 'The Pit and the Pendulum' (*NCL* 46.82–95), analyses the story in terms of his use of the biblical apocalypse in a 'typically Romantic way' to show the attainment through suffering of both spiritual and psychological redemption.

Uncle Tom's Cabin: Evil, Affliction and Redemptive Love by Josephine Donovan in the Twayne Masterwork Studies series is a well-organized and intelligent study of both writer and text. Donovan illuminates the literary and historical context, locating Stowe as an individual amongst all those Beechers, quoting her father: 'Harriet is a genius. I would give a hundred dollars if she was a boy', and providing the political and religious consanguinity of the novel which Donovan reads as 'creatural realism'. She deals with the critical reception of the novel, its neglect during the first half of the twentieth century, its rehabilitation by the 'New Americanist' critics Jane Tompkins and Philip Fisher amongst others, and conducts a brisk survey of the most recent work on the novel before developing her own reading of its style, structure and themes. Donovan divides the novel into three parts for discussion, working through the text and bringing critically, historically and culturally significant insights to bear; for instance, Little Eva is read 'within the parameters of Edwardsean Calvinism'. Indeed, this study is particularly effective in its exegesis of Stowe's own version of Calvinism and its manifestations in the novel; Donovan is convincing on the integrality of the soteriological in the overall design of the narrative and on the vital feminization of the processes of salvation enumerated by Stowe.

Robert E. Abrams, in 'Image, Object, and Perception in Thoreau's Landscapes: The Development of Anti-Geography' (*AL* 63.245–62), offers Thoreau's version of American space as endlessly sceptical, predicated by Thoreau himself as 'the interval between that which appears, and that which is', in contrast to the visualization of American westward movement and the 'domestication and pacification of the land'.

In 'Sentimental Liberalism and the Problem of Race in *Huckleberry Finn*' (*NCL* 46.96–113), Gregg Camfield considers conflicting responses to the text as they reflect both sentimental realism and Twain's mistrust of sentimentalism, the opposition between these two stances in turn indicating the 'tension between a cynical worldview and a sentimental one'.

The Man Who Was Mark Twain tackles the question of Twain's 'synechdochic relationship to frontier comedy'. Indeed, the whole question of Twain's identification in the public mind with the West or, in its most extreme form, as the embodiment of America, is scrutinized and the trope rewritten by Guy Cardwell. In 'The Critical Background', Cardwell examines the distinctive positions of Van Wyck Brooks and Bernard de Voto in the construction of the framework for debate about Twain in the first half of the twentieth century and subsequently moves on to 'My Mark Twain' as articulated by W. D. Howells – as folk-hero, historian, fabulist, romance and western archetype. Clemens's dealings with his in-laws, the wealthy eastern Langdon family whose money funded many of his wilder schemes, are detailed, as is his personal obsession with the filthy lucre which he so vigorously denounced in his writing. Informed by Freudian interpretative strategies Cardwell examines 'Sexuality and the Clemenses', 'Impotence and Pedophilia', 'Racism and *Huckleberry Finn*', and it is only in this last chapter that Cardwell makes the fiction a central part of his biographical endeavour, here being concerned to correct the critical overstatement of 'the writer's social and moral percipience'. Cardwell does not abandon the idea of Twain as 'Representative American', for in examining the conditions and processes of hagiography he develops an alternative, 'copyrighted' Mark Twain, 'bourgeois materialist and moral masochist' who can still function in that role.

Sherwood Cummings, in 'Mark Twain's Moveable Farm and the Evasion' (*AL* 63.440–58), examines the topography of the model for the Phelps's farm in *Huckleberry Finn*, the Quarles Farm, and outlines the means by which scholarly disagreements over its location arise directly from Twain's own ambivalence about the 'sociology' of the Phelps plantation.

Writing Huck Finn: Mark Twain's Creative Process by Victor A. Doyno is, as the title indicates, a study of a single text. Exhaustive in its analysis of both stylistics and thematics it brings a wide range of information and interpretation to bear on the novel. Doyno's opening assertion, exegeticized in the closing chapter, is that his study ' "solves" or resolves the ending of *Huck*', and so, in a manner of speaking it does, making a cogent and lively case for a reading of the novel in the historical context of its period of composition. The process which leads him to this resolution is one that involves a close study of the manuscript, international copyright law as it affected Twain during the period of writing, Twain's family life and his method of working – including rewriting and revision. Doyno terms his critical methodology as 'genetic, working with sequential close readings of the first, second, and subsequent versions of a passage, drawing upon other corroborative material as needed'. The final chapter first establishes the strength of the critical opinion – Hemingway, Trilling, T. S. Eliot, Marx – marking the Phelps section of the novel out as failure, and then proceeds to build an effective case for its aesthetic coherence as a text using insights gained from investigation into the post-bellum reality of life for emancipated slaves, the convict-lease system and the interpretative vexations attached to any use of the words ' "Free" and "Slave" or "Freed" and "Prisoner" '.

'Transcending the Limits of Experience: Mark Twain's *Life on the Mississippi*' (*AL* 63.420–39) by Lawrence Howe, takes Twain's contention in Part II of *Life* that experience is the ruination of the story teller – the most powerful narrations deriving from the textual not the actual – in order to establish himself as representative American: 'I am the whole human race without a detail lacking', and in spite of having been what Howe calls a 'Civil War deserter'.

Getting to be Mark Twain by Jeffrey Steinbrink covers the years 1868 to 1871 in the life of Samuel Clemens in considerable detail. Cast as the most formative years in the construction of the Mark Twain familiar to modern readers Steinbrink locates Clemens topographically, in the three eastern cities – Elmira, Buffalo and Hartford – which yielded wife, job and home respectively; but he also locates him intellectually and emotionally, as he assumed the new persona he deemed appropriate to his relocations. Twain's relationship with his wife and her family is central to this portrait of personal upheaval, a relationship catalytic rather than coercive in Clemens's change of style; as Steinbrink says, Twain's 'preconceived notions of respectability had more to do than they with the transformation of the ironist to the zealot'. In Olivia Langdon, Clemens sought to embrace all that was solid, fixed and conventional, in marrying her he could perhaps grow up painlessly, becoming respectable and in control – as husband and professional – of his other self. However, the welter of illness and death into which the newly-weds were plunged belied the vision of domestic tranquility which had seemed to be offered by the prospect of joining the Langdon family, and, according to Steinbrink, forced from Twain, most notably in the composition of *Roughing It*, a new sense of his vocation in becoming: 'not simply a retrospective teller but a seasoned, reflective adult, an initiate able to recall his former naivete vividly'.

Mark Bauerlein in *Whitman and the American Idiom* charts the collapse of Whitman's resistance, as poet, to theory. Bauerlein begins with a brief survey of approaches to Whitman – biographical, historical, feminist, psychoanalytical and materialist – before laying out his own methodology which is to exegeticize the gradual incursion of 'a semiotic vocabulary' into the verse. In order to demonstrate the process of change, the three editions of *Leaves of Grass* published in the decade 1850–1860 are compared and examined for their failing commitment to an organic language, a failing that nevertheless leads to a poetry which becomes a 'complex theoretical enterprise in its own right'. Bauerlein's thesis is complicated and densely argued, he sets out his theory in the first chapter and proceeds to carry through the argument of the 'theoretical problematic' which he outlines and which is both a means to read and a judgement on Whitman. Chapters on composition, reading and revision follow and a postscript which has Whitman surrendering to 'the postmodern condition' in his awareness of his fatal complicity with his audience and his precursors in making meaning.

Walt Whitman: The Poem as Private History by Graham Clarke sets out to interrogate Whitman's advertisement of self as the American public bard, seeking to highlight the 'tensions and conflicts' which result from his construction of a public persona distinct from the private. Clarke locates Whitman in the context of his professional and family life in order to illustrate the processes – re-writings, inventions and omissions – of self creation. So, Whitman the printer or the builder, was able to take his experiences as working man and to render them up 'as symbolic aspects of his new identity'; Whitman, the son and brother, touched up the image of his family for purposes of public display. A discussion of 'Whitman's Myth of the Body' gives way to a comparison between 'Song of Myself' and 'The Sleepers' which highlights the radical oppositions expressed in the two texts, with the latter seen as 'upending the familiar Whitman tropes' in its picture of an internal 'anti-world'. Clarke looks at the manner in which the poet used the photographic image as part of the creation of a unified autobiographical 'frame', takes this discussion and uses it as the means by which to illustrate the terms of the usual antithetical approach to Whitman and Dickinson, then adjusting the focus so that we read Whitman via Dickinson and the hesitancies and elisions of her syntax.

In '*Leaves of Grass Junior*: Whitman's Compromise with Discriminating Tastes' (*AL* 63.641–63), Ed Folsom discusses Whitman's ambivalent attitude toward the four volumes of selections from *Leaves* published over the same period that he was constructing the final three editions of the growing volume which was *Leaves of Grass*. These selections, two published in the United States and two in London, none edited by Whitman himself, made the poet more palatable for a general readership but also had the effect of bringing him wider publicity, for which reason Whitman was able to conquer his reservations about the publishing enterprise.

Michael Moon's *Disseminating Whitman: Revision and Corporeality in 'Leaves of Grass'* negotiates new levels of difficulty in its incremental approach to the poetry, moving from edition to edition of *Leaves of Grass* examining the nature and meaning of Whitman's revisionary practice. Moon conducts his enquiry at the 'macro' rather than 'micro' level, considering the differences between editions of the poetry in terms of the whole book rather than the poem or line. The focus of this approach to revision, and, the author emphasizes, it is not revision in any received literary sense of the word, is Whitman's presentation of sexuality and the bodily: 'the ongoing erotic program' of rewriting and re-presenting *Leaves of Grass*. The place of self-censorship in this process is fully treated as is Whitman's engagement in a variety of dialogues about his work as process; the US constitution is predicated as the single most significant 'pre-text' for *Leaves*, its very provisionality having left it open to infinite revision. Moon's close critical analysis is moved by the same agenda as the whole study and can produce extraordinary readings of quite unexpected verse; it can also, however, lose itself quite comprehensively in its own toils.

Books Reviewed

Adams, Charles Hansford. *'The Guardian of the Law': Authority and Identity in James Fenimore Cooper*. UPenn. pp. 110. $25. ISBN 0 271 00708 7.

Ammons, Elizabeth. *Conflicting Stories: American Women Writers at the Turn into the Twentieth Century*. OUP. pp. 256. £25. ISBN 0 19 506030 X.

Arac, Jonathan, and Harriet Ritvo, eds. *Macropolitics of Nineteenth Century Literature: Nationalism, Exoticism, Imperialism*. UPenn. pp. 320. £26.50. ISBN 0 8122 8208 6.

Backman, Gunnar. *Meaning by Metaphor: An Exploration of a Metaphoric Reading of Two Short Stories by Stephen Crane*. Almquist Wiksell Coronet. pp. 203. pb $34. ISBN 9 155 42741 3.

Baker, Houston A., Jnr. *Long Black Song: Essays in Black American Literature and Culture*. UPVirginia (1990). pp 156. pb $8.95. ISBN 0 8139 1301 2.

Baker, Houston A. *Workings of the Spirit: The Poetics of Afro-American Women's Writing*. UChicP. pp. 240. $19.95. ISBN 0 226 03522 0.

Barbour, James, and Tom Quirk, eds. *Writing the American Classics*. UNCP (1990). pp. 287. $37.50. ISBN 0 8078 1896 8.

Bauerlein, Mark. *Whitman and the American Idiom*. LSU. pp. 191. $22.50. ISBN 0 8071 1681 5.

Bell, Ian F. A. *Henry James and the Past: Readings into Time*. Macmillan. pp. 218. £40. ISBN 0 333 39389 9.

Bell, Millicent. *Meaning in Henry James*. HarvardUP. £35.95. ISBN 0 674 55762 X.

Berlant, Lauren. *The Anatomy of National Fantasy: Hawthorne, Utopia and Everyday Life*. UChicP. pp. 248. hb £25.95, pb £11.95. ISBN 0 226 04376 2, 0 226 04377 0.

Berry, J. Bill, ed. *Located Lives: Place and Idea in Southern Autobiography*. UGeoP (1990). pp. 190. pb £10.95. ISBN 0 8203 1225 8.

Blackman, Gunnar. *Meaning By Metaphor*. Uppsala. ISBN 91 554 2741 3.

Brand, Dana. *The Spectator and the City in Nineteenth-Century American Literature*. CUP. pp 242. £30. ISBN 0 521 36207 5.

Bradbury, Malcolm, and Richard Ruland. *From Puritanism to Postmodernism: A History of American Literature*. Routledge. pp. 381. £35. ISBN 0 415 01341 0.

Bush, Clive. *Halfway to Revolution: Investigation and Crisis in the Work of Henry Adams, William James and Gertrude Stein*. YaleUP. pp. 512. £30. ISBN 0 300 04729 0.

Carafiol, Peter. *The American Ideal: Literary History as a Worldly Activity*. OUP. pp. 212. £27.50. ISBN 0 19 506765 7.

Cardwell, Guy. *The Man Who Was Mark Twain: Images and Ideologies*. YaleUP. pp. 272. £18.95. ISBN 0 300 04950 1.

Carpenter, Lynette, and Wendy K. Kolmar, eds. *Haunting the House of Fiction: Feminist Perspectives on Ghost Stories by American Women*. UTennP. pp. 280. $28.50. ISBN 0 870 49688 3.

Castronovo, David. *The American Gentleman: Social Prestige and the Modern Literary Mind*. Continuum. pp. 192. $22.95. ISBN 0 8264 0532 0.

Ceplair, Larry, ed. *Charlotte Perkins Gilman: A Nonfiction Reader*. ColumbiaUP. pp. 320. pb $20.50. ISBN 0 231 07617 7.

Clarke, Graham. *Walt Whitman: The Poem as Private History*. Vision. pp. 176. ISBN 0 312 03744 9.

Cohen, Paula Marantz. *The Daughter's Dilemma: Family Process and the Nine-*

teenth-Century Domestic Novel. UMichP. pp. 208. $32.50. ISBN 0 472 10234 6.
Cowan, Bainard, and Joseph G. Kronick, eds. *Theorizing American Literature: Hegel, the Sign, and History*. LSUP. pp. 294. £28.45. ISBN 0 8071 1628 9.
Crump, R. W., ed. *Order in Variety: Essays and Poems in Honor of Donald E. Stanford*. AUP. pp. 221. £26.95. ISBN 0 87413 420 X.
Dickie, Margaret. *Lyric Contingencies: Emily Dickinson and Wallace Stevens*. UPennP. pp. 192. £22.75. ISBN 0 8122 3077 9.
Donovan, Josephine. *Uncle Tom's Cabin: Evil, Affliction and Redemptive Love*. Boston. Twayne. pp. 144. $9.95. ISBN 0 8057 8140 4.
Doyno, Victor A. *Writing 'Huck Finn': Mark Twain's Creative Process*. UPennP. pp. 272. $29.95. ISBN 0 8122 3087 6.
Elliott, Emory, ed. *The Columbia History of the American Novel: New Views*. ColUP. pp. 905. $69. ISBN 0 231 07360 7.
Ellis, William. *The Theory of the American Romance: An Ideology in American Intellectual History*. UMI Res. (1989). £19.50. ISBN 0 8357 1984 7.
Fabre, Michel. *From Harlem to Paris: Black American Writers in France, 1840–1980*. UIllP. pp. 464. $35.95. ISBN 0 252 01684 X.
Fliegelman, Jay, ed. *Charles Brockden Brown: 'Wieland' and 'Memoirs of Carwin the Biloquist'*. Penguin. pp. 365. pb £6.95. ISBN 0 14 03 9079 0.
Gelpi, Albert. *The Tenth Muse: The Psyche of the American Poet*. CUP. pp. 327. pb £15.95. ISBN 0 521 42401 1.
Gilmore, William J. *Reading Becomes a Necessity: Material and Cultural Life in Rural New England, 1780–1835*. UTennP (1989). pp. 538. $49.95. ISBN 0 87049 586 0.
Greenblatt, Stephen. *Marvelous Possessions: The Wonder of the New World*. Clarendon. pp. 202. £22.50. ISBN 0 19 812382 5.
Hamalian, Leo, and James V. Hatch, eds. *The Roots of American Drama: An Anthology of Early Plays 1858–1938*. WSU. pp. 455. $29.55. ISBN 0 8143 2141 0.
Harris, Sharon M. *Rebecca Harding Davis and American Realism*. UPennP. pp. 360. pb £15.15. ISBN 0 8122 1335 1.
Herreshoff, David Sprague. *Labor into Art: The Theme of Work in Nineteenth Century American Literature*. WSU. $24.95. ISBN 0 8143 2081 3.
Hutchinson, Stuart. *The American Scene: Essays on Nineteenth Century American Literature*. Macmillan. £35. ISBN 0 333 55024 2.
Kirby, David. *Portrait of a Lady and The Turn of the Screw*. Macmillan. pp. 100. pb £6.50. ISBN 0 333 49238 2.
Kirkby, Joan. *Emily Dickinson*. Macmillan. pp. 176. £25. ISBN 0 333 42066 7.
Lemay, J. A. Leo. *The American Dream of Captain John Smith*. UPVirginia. $29.95. ISBN 0 813 91321 7.
Leverenz, David. *Manhood and the American Renaissance*. CornUP (1989). pp. 372. pb $14.95. ISBN 0 8014 9743 4.
Lewis, R. W. B. *The Jameses: A Family Narrative*. Deutsch. pp. 660. £20. ISBN 0 233 987487.
Loeffelholz, Mary. *Dickinson and the Boundaries of Feminist Theory*. UIllP. pp. 208. pb $13.95. ISBN 0 252 06175 6.
Maddox, Lucy. *Removals: Nineteenth-Century American Literature and the Politics of Indian Affairs*. OUP. pp. 202. £24. ISBN 0 19 506931 5.
Martin, Ronald E. *American Literature and the Destruction of Knowledge: Innovative Writing in the Age of Epistemology*. DukeUP. pp. 391. $39.95. ISBN 0 8223 1125 9.

May, Henry F. *The Divided Heart: Essays on Protestantism and the Enlightenment in America*. OUP. pp 219. £22.50. ISBN 0 19 505899 2.

McFeely, William S. *Frederick Douglass*. Norton. £16.50. ISBN 0 393 02823 2.

Mills, Nicolaus. *The Crowd in American Literature*. LSUP (1986). pp. 146. £23.75. ISBN 0 8071 1286 0.

Moon, Michael. *Disseminating Whitman: Revision and Corporeality in 'Leaves of Grass'*. Harvard UP. £25.95. ISBN 0 674 21276 2.

Murfin, Ross, ed. *The Scarlet Letter by Nathaniel Hawthorne*. Macmillan. Case Studies in Contemporary Criticism. pp. 416. pb £6.99. ISBN 0 333 57559 8.

Nordloh, David J. *American Literary Scholarship: An Annual/1989*. DukeUP. pp. 504. £43. ISBN 0 8223 1139 9.

Oriard, Michael. *Sporting With the Gods: The Rhetoric of Play and Game in American Culture*. CUP. pp. 500. £45. ISBN 0 521 39113 X.

Pease, Donald, ed. *New Essays on 'The Rise of Silas Lapham'*. CUP. pp. 144. hb £22.50, pb £7.95. ISBN 0 521 37898 2, 0 521 37898 2.

Pizer, Donald, ed. *New Essays on 'Sister Carrie'*. CUP. hb £22.50, pb £7.95. ISBN 0 521 38714 0.

Poole, Adrian. *Henry James*. HW. New Readings Series. pb £9.95. ISBN 0 7108 1312 0.

Porte, Joel. *In Respect to Egotism: Studies in American Romantic Writing*. CUP. pp. 316. £30. ISBN 0 521 36273 3.

Posnock, Ross. *The Trial of Curiosity: Henry James, William James, and the Challenge of Modernity*. OUP. pp. 396. pb £15.99. ISBN 0 19 506606 5.

Rans, Geoffrey. *Cooper's Leather-Stocking Novels: A Secular Reading*. UNC. £23.92. ISBN 0 807 81975 1.

Reesman, Jeanne Campbell. *American Designs: The Late Novels of James and Faulkner*. UPennP. pp. 229. $26.95. ISBN 0 8122 8253 1.

Reid, Brian Holden, and John White, eds. *American Studies: Essays in Honour of Marcus Cunliffe*. Foreword by Arthur M. Schlesinger Jr. Macmillan. pp. 378. £47.50. ISBN 0 333 46595 4.

Scott, Stanley J. *Frontiers of Consciousness: Interdisciplinary Studies in American Philosophy and Poetry*. FordUP. pp. 156. $40.00. ISBN 0 8232 1302 1.

Showalter, Elaine. *Sister's Choice: Tradition and Change in American Women's Writing*. Clarendon. pp 198. £22.50. ISBN 0 19 812383 3

Steinbrink, Jeffrey. *Getting to be Mark Twain*. UCalP. pp. 250. $22.50. ISBN 0 520 07059 3.

Stern, Milton R. *Contexts for Hawthorne: 'The Marble Faun' and the Politics of Openness and Closure in American Literature*. UIllP. pp. 201. $34.95. ISBN 0 252 01819 2.

Swann, Charles. *Nathaniel Hawthorne: Tradition and Revolution*. CUP. pp. 304. £35.00. ISBN 0 521 36552 X.

Tintner, Adeline R. *The Cosmopolitan World of Henry James: An Intertextual Study*. LSU. pp. 328. pb £15.95. ISBN 0 8071 1692 0.

Tuttleton, James W., and Agostino Lombardo, eds. *The Sweetest Impression of Life: The James Family and Italy*. NYUP. $36. ISBN 0 81478183 7.

Woolf, Judith. *Henry James: The Major Novels*. British and Irish Authors: Introductory Critical Series Studies. CUP. pp. 180. hb £25.00, pb £8.95. ISBN 0 521 30370 2, 0 521 31655 3.

XVII

American Literature: The Twentieth Century

LIONEL KELLY, PAT RIGHELATO and DEBORAH MADSEN

This chapter has two sections: 1. Twentieth-Century American Poetry; 2. Post-1945 Fiction. Section 1 is by Lionel Kelly and Pat Righelato; section 2 is by Deborah Madsen.

1. Twentieth-Century American Poetry

(a) General

The quantity and quality of critical writing on twentieth-century American poetry is now so extensive that no single commentator can be expected to produce an appropriately informative narrative bibliographical review of work in this field: from this year I am joined in my labours by Dr Pat Righelato, and the commentary that follows is our shared production in which we have each dealt with particular areas of work; though we give our names jointly to the whole of this section, we have kept to the use of the first person singular pronoun throughout whenever this usage was felt to be appropriate. Something of the scale of our enterprise is suggested by the reviews of seven new books on Pound, and six new books on Wallace Stevens this year. Our coverage of journal articles can only be indicative, however, for the scale of Anglo-American journal publication alone in this field is now enormous.

Workings of the Spirit: The Poetics of Afro-American Women's Writing by Houston A. Baker Jnr, comes in UChicP's 'Black Literature and Culture' series, of which he is editor, and this volume completes his recent trilogy of studies of black writing. In his introductory essay Baker seeks to negotiate a role for himself as a male advocate of black women's writing in relation to issues of theory, gender, and race, especially as these have been variously confronted by the makers of contemporary Afro-American women's literary criticism. From this Baker offers what he calls a theoretical poetics of space, place and time as constituting his focus on the imagistic fields of writing he addresses, such as Zora Neale Hurston's *Mules and Men*, Toni Morrison's *Sula*, and Ntozake Shange's *Sassafrass, Cypress and Indigo*. Baker's written text is illustrated with a series of previously unpublished photographs of black women from the 1930s and 1940s, a visually stunning record of women at labour and play, though whether these images allow us to do more than replicate the spectatorial gaze is an open issue.

Representing Modernist Texts: Editing as Interpretation reminds us that transmission is currently a word of academic respectability whereas the 'author's final intentions' is now 'barely whispered in dark corners'. Edited by George Bornstein, this book consists of twelve essays by distinguished contributors on the implications of new developments in editorial theory for the study of literature at the present time. The spur to much theoretical activity has been Valerie Eliot's edition of *The Waste Land* and Hans Gabler's 'synoptic' edition of *Ulysses* – editions which emphasize the process of writing itself and, in the case of Gabler, questions the privileging of final intentions. More cautiously here, Ronald Bush argues that editions of Pound's *Cantos* must reflect the poem as temporal process. The modernists were in some cases powerful text managers themselves: Andrew J. Kappel shows that Marianne Moore, in assembling and disassembling poetic sequences, was creating heartache for future editors. All the essays in this collection are of interest: Lawrence Rainey's on the transmission and canonization of H. D. is characteristically brilliant; Eugene Goodheart argues that for Lawrence censorship was a 'necessary and empowering enemy'; Noel Polk describes having to de-edit Faulkner; Richard J. Finneran continues the controversy over a definitive Yeats. In the end, as Polk reminds us, although creators and works change, editors are usually charged to produce a *text*. But editors who claim to have produced a definitive text may well 'spend eternity in a special circle of hell proof-reading *Finnegan's Wake*'. Michael Groden, in concluding the volume, recalls Fredson Bowers's prescription that 'every practising critic … ought to study the transmission of some appropriate text.' After reading this book, we will.

Anthropological Poetics, edited by Ivan Brady, is dedicated to Stanley Diamond, the anthropologist and poet whose work has been the central inspiration to cultural anthropologists in recent years in the development of modes of writing which admit the poetic to the forms of interpretive work in this field. This collection includes an essay by Dan Rose on Stanley Diamond's anthropological poetics, and this is a helpful place to enter the preoccupations reflected at large in this book. Rose's account of Diamond's book of poems *Totems* (1982) makes rather large claims for Diamond's accomplishment of the sublime in his lyric poems, and Rose seems to me on surer ground when he claims that *Totems* effects what he calls 'a post-hierarchical way of experiencing the multicultural world', and celebrates Diamond for the way in which he has moved human cultures into view which had 'escaped the purview of the gatekeepers of elite Western civilization …'. The list of works referred to in this collection is a valuable bibliography of work in this emergent area of American poetry.

The vexed issue of the term cubism and its possible relation to non-pictorial forms is the subject of Jacqueline Vaught Brogan's *Part of the Climate: American Cubist Poetry*, where she quickly acknowledges the impossibility of any simple definition of poetic cubism. In the event, her definition becomes broad enough to admit all kinds that range between analytic and synthetic cubism, where the aesthetic prerequisites include a concern with visual form on the printed page, the distortions of normative stanza, line, and word boundaries, a self-conscious concern with modernist procedures, an intense preoccupation with perception, narrative and temporal disjuctions that employ multiple voices, sections, and textual fragments, and a heightened sense of textuality itself. This suggests an inclusive categorization sufficient to admit many poems we might not have thought of as cubist, as indeed turns out to be the case. However, a more telling feature of Brogan's book is the anthologizing of these cubist poems within the context of their first appearance in the avant-garde journals from the 1910s to the 1940s, and this is very enlightening. This account opens, appropriately enough, with Gertrude Stein's 'Pablo Picasso' from a 1912 issue of *Camera Work*, and runs on through other journals of the 1910s such as *Rogue, 291, Others,* and *Soil*, a pattern followed in accounts of cubist poetry through the twenties, thirties and forties, a procedure which recuperates many works from the abyss of critical neglect in a well-researched enterprise, though whether it does much to formalize the definitions of cubist poetry is another matter.

Joseph M. Conte's *Unending Design: The Forms Of Postmodern Poetry* is likely to become a focal centre in subsequent considerations of mid-twentieth-century American poetry: Conte offers his study as a typology of postmodern poetry in his attempt to define the dominant idioms of poetic form in the successors of modernism, idioms he characterizes as those of serial form and procedural form: in a polemical conclusion, he looks at the claims of Language Poetry, and the New Formalism, and in this wide address confronts much of the most complex and formally demanding work published over the past sixty years. Conte looks to Roland Barthes and later commentators on postmodern aesthetics for his definitions of serial form, described as a combination of elements which do not obey either an imposed mechanistic structure, or an organic structure, but develop out of 'a set of mobile and discontinuous objects' in which 'each new combination produces a new meaning, reorients itself as a new aesthetic object.' In addition, serial works are said to be characterized 'by the discontinuity of their elements and the centrifugal force identified with an "open" aesthetic'. Conversely, procedural works are 'typified by the recurrence of elements and a centripetal force that promises a self-sustaining momentum', in which 'lexical and semantic' recurrence predominates. Refinements on these primary definitions follow as Conte illustrates his thesis through a consideration of serial work by Robert Duncan, Paul Blackburn, Robert Creeley, Jack Spicer, George Oppen, Louis Zukofsky and Lorine Niedecker, and procedural work by John Ashbery, Louis Zukofsky, Weldon Kees, Robert Creeley, Harry Mathews, William Bronk, and John Cage. The strength of this book seems to me revealed in the analytic accounts of his chosen poets, rather than in the somewhat formulaic introduction, overburdened as it is with a customary anxiety about the divisions between modernism and what follows it, and how we should describe these later phenomena. But this is a highly intelligent anatomy, and particularly valuable for Conte's attention to poets often honoured, but much less often debated, such as Oppen and Zukofsky. As an addendum to this entry, readers might like to know of Donald Davie's reply in (*PNR* 18.43–5), where Davie disputes Conte's dismissive use of Davie's earlier discussion of Lorine Niedecker's 'Lake Superior'.

The second series of Richard Ellmann Lectures in Modern Literature at Emory University were given by Denis Donoghue in 1990 and appear in the Emory Studies in Humanities list under the title *Being Modern Together*. With due decorum, Donoghue writes of these lectures as marginalia to Ellmann and Feidelson's *The Modern Tradition* (1965), though they are admirably broad in their frame of reference, and develop in a trenchant trajectory from considerations of the threatening image of the crowd in Wordsworth, Poe, Baudelaire, and the early modernists, to a defence of the interior life of the mind where the spiritual and metaphysical compulsions of the self are ethical and judicial. Here, Donoghue takes his philosophical direction from Emmanuel Levinas, and returns to the poetry of Wallace Stevens for his primary example of 'a comprehensive method of inventing an adversary world, boldly set off against the one apparently held by science, technology, and politics.'

From Harlem to Paris marks Michel Fabre's latest expansive contribution to the literary history of the Black American writer in France, here covering the years from 1840 to 1980. This thorough survey opens in that American outpost of ethnic cosmopolitanism, New Orleans, as Fabre locates a major link between Afro-

Americans and France in the 1840s in what he calls 'the New Orleans elite – free persons of colour', whose cultural orientation was French, and whose literary and artistic productions derived from French Romanticism. Later chapters deal with the various impulses which took black writers to France, from W. E. B. Dubois who was sent to investigate American military treatment of black troops in World War 1, through the French experience of Langston Hughes, Countee Cullen, Claude McKay and others, to the post-Second World War generation of Parisian expatriates, Richard Wright, James Baldwin and Chester Himes, down to James Emanuel, the contemporary Black-American poet. Fabre's attempt to rationalize the sense of hospitality experienced in France by Afro-American writers, conditioned as it is by his own scholarly and humanistic principles, itemizes jazz as one of the essential ingredients of this cultural bonding, and the residual ruralism of French society, which he argues touches the American black writer's feel for a rooted localism, of both urban and rural modes.

Charles Fishman has edited an anthology of American poems on the Holocaust under the title *Blood to Remember*. It gathers poems by some 180 poets, of whom some had direct experience of the Holocaust, and some who became naturalized Americans. The overwhelming virtue of this enterprise makes any criticism seem quite irrelevant, but a more extensive introduction would have been helpful, and none of the poems is dated. Fishman provides two sets of notes to the poems, one commenting on internal references, the other extrapolating excerpts from the poets' correspondence with him in the making of this anthology.

In 'Quoting Poetry' (*CritI* 18.42–63), William Flesch writes on the ways in which poetic form acts as a 'counterpattern' to meaning, especially where the tension between form and meaning centres on quotations in rhymed poetry, where 'quotations' refers to a 'set of words that is considered not originally to belong to the prosodical context in which it is cited'. In this wide-ranging debate, Flesch discusses quotational effects in poems by James Merrill and John Ashbery, amongst others, and arrives at the conclusion that the prosody is not the clothing or organizing of language in verse but 'a movement of memory where memory remembers nothing but the proximity of alterity, and not the presence of content'. In this issue of *CI*, the philosopher John Koethe meditates on the estrangement between poets, critics, and reviewers of contemporary poetry, and the proponents of 'theory' (18.64–75).

Albert Gelpi's *The Tenth Muse* first appeared in 1975 under HarvardUP's imprint and has now been reissued in hardcover and paperback editions by CUP. A companion volume to Gelpi's *A Coherent Splendor* (1987) (*YWES* 68.614–15), this earlier study has become a standard reference for all those engaged with the evolution of American poetry from its Puritan origins through nineteenth-century Romanticism, and its reappearance is most welcome. Gelpi's preface for this edition is an eloquent defence of his humanistic critical practice in these two books.

Roger Gilbert's fascinating *Walks in the World*, formulates a new genre, that of the 'walk poem' to describe a kind of poem common in American writing in this century, though as Gilbert shows, it has long antecedents in scripture, in medieval and Renaissance poetry, the 'local poem' of familiar eighteenth-century practice, and the greater Romantic lyric, as defined by M. H. Abrams, even if its relationship to these antecedents is equivocal. Gilbert's starting point is A. R. Ammons's essay 'A Poem is a Walk' where Ammons writes of an actual walk as an externalization of an 'inward seeking' and proposes the walk poem as an endeavour to erase the difference between walk and text through the coincidence of language and bodily sensation. As Gilbert suggests, such notions are not far removed from Emerson's idea of experience *as* poetry, the poem as immanent in the world, awaiting transcription, and Gilbert traces the lineage of such ideas in Whitman and Thoreau whom he sees as exemplifying two extreme versions of the walk poem, where Whitman offers lyric intensity against Thoreau's experienced particularity. In this view, American poets are faced with the need to combine the modes of Whitman and Thoreau in which the 'primary challenge is to find a way to affirm the immanent poetic value of ordinary life without writing journalism.' Gilbert then offers readings of walk poems which have become the paradigms of this kind: 'the ambulatory plots' of Frost where the occasion of the walk and the occasion of the poem meet in a resolved utterance of wisdom, the walk poem as meditation in Stevens's 'An Ordinary Evening in New Haven', and the walk poem as densely mimetic of the particulars of scene, place, and presence in book two of Williams's *Paterson* and 'The Desert Music', followed by a discussion of poems by Roethke, Bishop, O'Hara, Snyder, Ammons and Ashbery. These are eloquent, informed and persuasive readings.

Jazz Text by Charles O. Hartman attempts a difficult task, a discussion of the effective interrelationships between jazz, popular music, and modern American poetry. Hartman's point of departure is the concept of voice as a metaphor for the accents of authority, especially of feeling, which find a counterpart in the notion of voice as the musician's personalized sound in performance, which he then considers in relation to improvization, perhaps the single most important constitutent of the aesthetic of jazz, and to ideas of composition, originality, disguise, and recognition in music and poetry. Hartman's chapters on Lee Konitz, Ornette Coleman and Joni Mitchell require some technical musical competence in the reader, though, as in the case of Konitz, the discussion of the relationship between improvization and 'instantaneous composition' is accessible, as is much else on what might be called the sociology of jazz and popular music in these chapters. The poets Hartman chooses are Robert Creeley, David Antin, Jackson Mac Low, and Philip Levine, that is to say poets for whom the vocal and performative dimensions of their work is at least as important as the poem as printed text. If I read him accurately, Hartman's argument is that the instantaneity of music and song in performance contains within itself all the artifice of composition and design, just as the poets he cites seek the here-and-now of the speaking voice, an expressive spontaneity held within the formal artifice of textual appearance.

A collection of essays on Vietnam War literature is edited by Philip K. Jason under the title *Fourteen Landing Zones*. In the single essay on poetry by Vietnam War veterans, Lorrie Smith contends that 'poetry occupies a tenuous position in the canon of Vietnam literature', but sees that marginality as a source of strength rather than a limitation, part of the cultural insurrection against the academic centre in American poetry, and aligns it with the similarly marginalized communities of women and ethnic minorities. Not everyone will be convinced by these claims, and the relative poverty of discussion of Vietnam War poetry, in this volume as elsewhere, may have something to do with the kind of poetry that war has produced. Smith's essay provides a brief account of the work of the most celebrated of these poets, W. D. Ehrhart, John Balaban, Bruce Weigl and D. F. Brown.

Two other anthologies gather poems about familiar and important icons of American life: the farm and the baseball game. In her introduction to the farm poems anthology, *Handspan of Red Earth*, Catherine Lewallen Marconi invokes the names of Crevecoeur and Thoreau as the primary celebrators of farm life, the one for his acute sense of the pleasures of literal possession, the other for that imaginary possession of place and experience which only the poet can tell, and the ensuing poems in this collection explore these polarities from twentieth-century perspectives. There are many excellent poems in this collection, including work by Galway Kinnell, Annie Dillard, Donald Hall, William Stafford, Gary Snyder, Gwendolyn Brooks and Wendell Berry, and the text is illustrated with five lithographs by Grant Wood. Imaginative literature about baseball is a familiar feature of twentieth-century American writing, though its most popular expression is in the form of the novel. Don Johnson's anthology of contemporary baseball poems is a welcome addition to this literature, and *Hummers, Knucklers, and Slow Curves* will give much pleasure to devotees of poetry and baseball. Johnson sees the baseball field as a site of initiation, a place of familiar rituals of testing and skill, and a location where we experience loss, and learn to live with it, and thus by implication, a scene where death always lurks.

Liberating Voices by the novelist and poet Gayl Jones is a study of the oral tradition in African American writing, with a section each on poetry, short fiction, and the novel. In the poetry section Jones works through poems from Paul Laurence Dunbar, Langston Hughes, Sterling Brown, Sherley A. Williams, and Michael S. Harper in an endeavour to give a developmental account of how the oral tradition has flourished in Afro-American poetry this century, particularly through its mimesis of the strategies and tonalities of blues music and jazz. Jones's central argument seems simple enough, that a characteristic poem by Dunbar, such as 'When Malindy Sings', though it goes beyond the Plantation Tradition and the conventions of the local colourists, nevertheless remains fixed in a generalized depiction of the Afro-American character, and it is not until the expressive modernism of open forms in Williams and Harper that a real sense of individuality and wholeness is restored to the African American character in poetry. James Sullivan's 'Real Cool Pages: The Broadside Press Broadside Series' (*ConL* 32.552–72) is a valuable investigation of the function served by Dudley Randall's Broadside Press in Detroit in the wider context of the Black Arts Movement of the sixties and seventies: Sullivan's plea is for a closer attention to the agency of cultural dissemination, such as this Broadside Series, so that we may see the poetic artefact within the frame of the political field where it has its true place.

Writing the Woman Artist, edited by Suzanne W. Jones, is a feminist collection of essays on women writers from different ethnic and national backgrounds. Part I, on American writers, consists of three revisionist versions of deconstruction, which trace women artists' repositioning of the poetic voice and their rewriting of literary convention based on such binary opposites as male writer/female muse. Susan Stanford Friedman's complex essay, 'H. D.'s Rescriptions of Joyce, Lawrence, and Pound', analyses the transmutations in *HER* from passivity within 'the male economy of desire' to a 'mutually desirous and creative relationship' in which 'Love is writing', and is a useful record of H. D.'s intertextualizing of her male modernist peers. Lynda K. Bundtzen's essay on Adrienne Rich's *The Dream of a Common Language* makes heavy weather of mountain language in her analysis of Rich's rejection of Wordsworthian heroics of poetic mastery in favour of instreaming (Emersonian paternity is not acknowledged) and female community. Kathleen Brogan's attractively lucid essay 'Lyric Voice and Sexual Difference in Elizabeth Bishop', argues that Bishop deconstructs male/female dichotomies, and that 'The End of March' creates an 'oblique sublime' in a poetry which seeks outsider status and eludes gender confinement. Other essays of interest to Americanists are on Willa Cather, 'Women of Color', and Audre Lorde.

Diverse Voices: Essays on Twentieth-Century Women Writers in English, edited by Harriet Devine Jump, consists of nine essays derived from a women's writing lecture course including five on American women writers which range from the introductory to the ultra theoretical. Clare Brunt's essay is an account of Gertrude Stein's subversion of the patriarchal structuring of language, while Julia Briggs argues that Willa Cather's self construction as an artist involved the suppression of a domestic model for her own life which is thereby uneasily reasserted as a compensatory role model in her fiction. Dianne Chisholm's essay on H. D. is the most jargon-ridden exercise of the collection, tracing H. D.'s move from Imagism, with Pound as '(tor)mentor' to a 'woman's strategy of self-authorisation' with Freud as intertextual midwife. Of refreshing clarity is Helen Kidd's introduction to five Black women poets, June Jordan, Audre Lorde, Ntozake Shange, Maya Angelou and Alice Walker, which gives generous examples of their work. The essay on Eudora Welty by Diane Roberts relentlessly pursues the theme that 'rape inscribes on women's bodies their subordination.' A student might experience this collection as a doleful catalogue of women's struggle to oppose patriarchal inscribings, but the useful table of works given for each author tells a story of steady and impressive achievement.

Richard Kostelanetz advertises himself as one at the cutting edge of the new: 'In poetry as well as other arts, my taste still inclines to the most extreme, the most audacious, the most innovative, the most idiosyncratic, especially when incorporated in formats previously unavailable to poetry.' This is from his book *The New Poetries and Some Old*, a collection of essays, interviews, and reviews, with a title which reverses that of his earlier collection, *The Old Poetries and the New*. It is good to encounter this abrasive iconoclastic voice within a domain still governed by the conventions of courtesy, though I wish Kostelanetz was not quite so full of himself. One of the two longest pieces here is a reprinted interview with John Berryman from 1969, in which Kostelanetz treats us to an insider's view of Berryman's domestic arrangements, his wife, his children, his drink, his food, his habits of recitation, and so on, and concludes with this gratuitious piety: 'I realize how deeply Berryman came to represent in my own mind the kind of poet/person I didn't want to be.' In this, as in the case of his demolition job on Joseph Brodsky, there is too much flourishing of his own superior personality, and not enough of his commentary on Berryman's poems, or why he thinks Brodsky is overrated, a crucial failure to perform the critic's task precisely in the idioms he sets up for himself. Readers will find this collection most useful for what Kostelanetz has to say about the condition of the avant-garde in contemporary American poetry.

Black Mountain College Sprouted Seeds, edited by Marvin Lane, adds a crucial dimension to the existing accounts of Black Mountain by Martin Duberman and Mary Emma Harris, for unlike their books, this is composed by staff and students who taught or studied at the College. It consists of some ninety personal accounts of the Black Mountain experience, and the contributions range from a seven line anecdote by John Cage (from his *Silence*, 1961), to an interview with Josef Albers of March 1965: however, the majority of these rather short pieces were written specifically for this collection, and represent an attempt to reflect upon the long-term effects of this unique American educational programme. Some notable names are missing from this collection, such as Robert Creeley and Ed Dorn, but otherwise, every aspect of the College's engagement with thought and the creative arts finds expression in recollection here. The text is illustrated with six colour plates of paintings by BMC painters, and twenty-six black and white photographs of BMC buildings and activities.

The Poetics of Appalachian Space, edited by Park Lanier, Jnr, gathers sixteen essays by various hands which all seek to 'exemplify the process of eidetic reduction' employed by Gaston Bachelard in *La poétique de l'espace* (1958), drawing their evidence from the works of Appalachian writers. In pursuit of Bachelard's notion that various concrete particulars all point toward one eidos, or Idea, or Essence, and following upon his nomination of the eidetic specificity of domestic spaces, these essays are concerned with four kinds of images of houses and their furniture: that in which the traditional is juxtaposed with the new; the image of the house as a sacred place; as an area of intellectual space, and the notion of space in relation to place in terms of the psychic as well as the geographic idea of place. This is an unusual collection of essays, and in its explicit homage to Bachelard is some evidence of a recoil from the rebarbative abstractions of poststructuralism and the apparent diminution of value within aesthetics. In the opening essay Nancy Carol Joyner briefly itemizes the relation of Bachelard's thought to Jung, and distinguishes him as the celebrant of 'felicitous space' in an account which neatly centres the conjunction of place and spirit that animates most of these essays.

The ambition of Jack Myers and David Wojahn in *A Profile of Twentieth-Century American Poetry* is comprehensive in scale and humanistic in kind, an endeavour to produce a critical history of this subject free of the esoteric jargon of contemporary critical schools: thus,with the exception of the Whitman scholar Ed Folsom, all the contributors to this volume are poets, though some of them such as Michael Heller, Jonathan Holden and Richard Jackson have also written distinguished works of criticism. The editors rightly regard Folsom's revisionist study as a key marker in the way he seeks to locate the many threads which constitute the full weave of the 'vast fabric' of pre-twentieth-century American poetry, including those kinds of utterance commonly excluded from these histories, slave songs, Native American chants, the diaries of pioneer women, and so on, to uncover the web of interrelationships which constitute the unsung sources of 'the true American aesthetic and historical experience'. The following format of this collection gives us essays on each decade from the 1920s through to Holden's account of American poetry from 1970 to 1990, with additional essays on women's poetry and African American poetry. In all these the emphasis is on the historical context, developments in poetics, seminal creative and critical developments, and 'the continuities and disruptions in the lines of aesthetic force and influence'. This parcelling of the field into decades may well serve the historical focus of many of these essays, but of course it runs counter to the personal history of many of the poets briefly considered here: what, for example, is the true decade of Stevens, and is that an intelligible question? Despite this caveat I think there is much to recommend in this collection as a whole.

In Reading and Writing Nature: The Poetry of Robert Frost, Wallace Stevens, Marianne Moore and Elizabeth Bishop, Guy Rotella argues that these poets continue the American tradition of turning to nature in order to pose epistemological and aesthetic questions about how and how much we know. The opening chapter provides a succinct and useful summary of readings of nature from the Puritans to the Transcendentalists which is linked to a survey of the modern critical debate on the topic. Emily Dickinson, precursor of the modern, then shifts the question from the meaning of God to the meaning of meaning; whereas for the modern poets all readings of transcendence are humanly inscribed. This is familiar ground, but Rotella's closely argued study combines conceptual clarity and an ear for nuance which is particularly acute on Moore and Bishop. He identifies, in their playfulness and intertextuality, postmodernist features, at the same time as he charts their puritan sense of exactitude: for example, Bishop, discerning a world littered with fragmentary textual traces, demotes vision to 'looks'. Rotella's analysis of metaphor, simile, and metonymy is particularly subtle: he shows how such figures become, for these writers, a way of testing of their originality and belatedness.

Frontiers of Consciousness by Stanley J. Scott is sub-titled *Interdisciplinary Studies in American Philosophy and Poetry*, and is an attempt to read a creative relationship between American philosophy from about 1880 to 1950 and the poetry of T. S. Eliot, Wallace Stevens and William Carlos Williams. Scott's thesis is that Josiah Royce, Charles Peirce, William James and John Dewey sought to articulate a new generative idea, 'the idea of emergent unitary experience' as an escape from the metaphysical confines of Cartesian dualism and its corollary of radical subjectivism which has dominated philosophical thought since the seventeenth century. For Scott, this philosophical enterprise meets with the endeavours of Eliot and Stevens, in *Four Quartets* and 'Notes Toward A Supreme Fiction' to transcend the limitations of solipsistic subjectivity, to articulate modes of empirical reality within the frame of an experiential standpoint of timeless consciousness (Eliot), and revelatory perceptions of the real (Stevens), where Scott argues for the congruence of Royce's theories of time and consciousness for Eliot, and William James's essay 'The Will to Believe' and his *Essays in Radical Empiricism* for Stevens. In Williams's case, *Paterson* is read as an 'enactment of contextualist principles of the function of consciousness' to substantiate Williams's suggestion that the basic method of the poem has its roots in Dewey's philosophy of experience. There is a great deal of interest in this yoking together of philosophical ideas and some of the late works of high modernism, though I found the essays on Eliot and Stevens too brief to carry the burden of their argument: if these ideas are as important as Scott suggests, they need more expansive analysis than the summary account given here.

Steven Watson's *Strange Bedfellows: The First American Avant-Garde* is a group portrait of the poets and artists who created modernism, and the critics, collectors, editors, salon hostesses who facilitated its expression in the years 1913 to 1917. This is a chatty but informative and closely focused account and the writer has a real gift for visual display: the text is enlivened with diagrams on such topics as 'Pre-War Poetry Coalitions', '*Camera Work* 1903–1917', 'The Little Magazines', 'The Arensberg and Stettheimer Salons' which chart the cultural and aesthetic network of modernism in America. Equally pleasurable are the photographs and drawings: of Stieglitz, for example, there are photographs by Coburn and Steichen, Marias de Zayas dawings, a Man Ray painting, and an Arthur Dove collage. The colour illustrations include several paintings by Feorine Stettheimer of the avant-garde at play, picknicking and partying. If you want to know about the decorations for the Armory Show, Mabel Dodge's Evenings, the menu for Amy Lowell's Imagist Dinner, the rivalries of the Arensberg Salon, what the cover of *Poetry* looked like, or why Wallace Stevens was afraid to venture beyond Fourteenth Street, it is all here. But this is not a trivial book: the chapter on the little magazines, for example, is a deft and succinct synthesis of the key material, and, furthermore, captures the histrionicisms, the epistolary cut and thrust, the hand to mouth financing, 'the glorious haze' of poetry publishing. The personal chemistry of American modernism is registered in this attractive, intelligent and bargain priced book with a verve altogether appropriate to its subject.

Rob Wilson's *American Sublime: The Genealogy of a Poetic Genre* is an endeavour to rewrite the concept of the 'sublime' in American literary culture through an historical scope which ranges from Anne Bradstreet to Bob Perelman: if the core of his argument is in his attempt to dislodge the valorization of the sublime through its expressive validation in Emerson and Whitman, and thus to find in Anne Bradstreet, William Livingston, and William Cullen Bryant empowering tropes of the 'grandeur of nature and country' befitting 'solitary attempts to represent national "elevation" ', his later reach embraces modernist, postmodernist, and ethnic pluralist versions of the sublime in his attempt to subvert the dominance of the Emersonian 'master-narrative of self reliance that presently controls descriptions of this genre.' Other agendas in the contemporary literary discourse are also questioned here, such as Harold Bloom's 'influence and precursor' theory of literary production, and feminism's substitution of a maternal originator for the enabling 'father-figure' of male gendered theories of writing. There is, too, inevitably, a public political agenda encoded in this study, which is that literary, painterly, and other aesthetic impulses are bound by the same compulsions as those of the material world in their technological, military, and economic pursuits of the fulfillment of the American dream of sublimity which become the dream of the superpower: the dismantling of this dream, in poetic and in political terms, is Wilson's resting point in this deeply absorbing book.

(b) Individual Authors

Miriam M. Clark's essay 'The Gene, and Information Processing in A. R. Ammons's (*TCL* 36.1–9) focusses on Ammons's 'Essay in Poetics' in a discussion of his interest in technological processes, specifically in relation to the gene and the computer as a counterpart to his interest in the non-human processes of nature. James S. Hans (*ELWIU* 17.76–93) writes of Ammons's essentially aesthetic vision of 'the tragic joy that life embodies when it is seen aesthetically'. This deeply engaged reading of Ammons is responsive to the problems inherent in his work and persuasive of its virtues.

Sara L. Lundquist's account of John Ashbery's 'French Poems' (*ConL* 31.403–21) seeks to redress the neglect of these poems in commentary on Ashbery. First published in French in *Tel Quel* (27.29–32), Ashbery translated them into English for the collection *The Double Dream of Spring* (1970). Lundquist argues that these poems are preoccupied with issues of difference and sameness in two modes of signification, the languages they employ, and are thus one more example of Ashbery's 'series of renewals of his idiom'. Samuel Hazo writes an abrasive repudiation of Ashbery's poetry in 'The Poetry of Anemia' (*SR* 99.566–83), an essay marked by its tone of exasperated distaste for what he calls Ashbery's 'associative' practice, which, he argues, gives us wide horizons and very little depth!

In *Elizabeth Bishop: Questions of Mastery*, Bonnie Costello takes Bishop's 'rage for order' as concomitant with her realization of the 'dangers and illusions' of mastery as the poet 'forces herself and her reader to encounter the mess of life, at times even to exhilarate in it'. Costello attends to the 'shifting and unstable' balance between Bishop's 'descriptive vitality' and her 'psychological and philosophical wisdom', and addresses the 'unresolved relationship between observation and metaphor', where metaphor carries the primary drive towards an ordering of a poem's descriptive terrain. Costello therefore investigates the ordering role of metaphor in Bishop's poems impelled by the oblique view and broken frame of postmodern visual perception, the displacement of the Romantic sublime with the vertical sublime of 'her own horizontal accent', the function of travel as the major trope of this horizontal condition, the relationship between travel and memory, and the ekphrastic mode which in Bishop becomes a mode of 'commemoration' rather than a perpetuation of the idea of art as a form of immortality, a subtle modification which admits the contingent and unassimilable as equal to the poet's concerns with her creative desire for order. This is an intelligent reading of Bishop, and in its concern with her visual and temporal awareness has much to tell us about Bishop's equivocal sense of mastery.

Pearl K. Bell's memoir of Elizabeth Bishop (*PR* 58.29–52), recounts a version of the poet's life from Bell's first meeting with her at Yaddo in August 1949, through the remainder of Bishop's life. Victoria Harrison challenges Robert von Hallberg's reading of Elizabeth Bishop's late poem 'One Art' in 'The Dailiness of Her Center: Elizabeth Bishop's Late Poetry' (*TCL* 37.253–72), where she argues that Bishop's late poems dispute the notion of a 'centralized culture' such as von Hallberg calls on, and argues for these poems as expressive of notions of culture not necessarily constituted in institutional actions 'but always in human interactions', and reads these late poems as occasions which locate 'history and politics in daily relationships of power, alienation, curiosity, identification, and love.' In 'Stanley Burnshaw and the Body' (*Agenda* 29.35–48), Robert Zaller writes of the humanistic centre of Burnshaw's work, especially evident, in Zaller's view, in the later poetry of Burnshaw.

The Selected Letters of John Ciardi, edited by Edward M. Cifelli, gives 378 letters from 1935 to 1986, the year of Ciardi's death. The author of sixteen books of poems published in his lifetime, an intimate of the Robert Frost circle, a friend of Theodore Roethke and Richard Wilbur, poetry editor of the *Saturday Review* for many years, translator of Dante, director of the Bread Loaf Writers Conference, Ciardi occupies a central role in one of the narratives of American poetry in the middle of this century, in which he made a successful career. At the same time he seems always out of touch with the mainstream of work. Though he had some feeling for the poetry of William Carlos Williams, the index to this volume makes no reference to Bishop, Eliot, Pound, or Stevens, and the one telling reference to Marianne Moore reveals an unnerving occasion when she read back to him, in public, his review of her *Fables of La Fontaine*. On some of his notable contemporaries he is perplexed: of Berryman he writes 'I couldn't even force my way through his Henry pieces and dream songs.' And he goes on, 'Sexton was an out-and-out self-dramatizing fraud. And Lowell's *Life Studies* are rooted with dumb sentimentalism.' These letters show Ciardi in his various roles as poet, editor, teacher and propagandist for literature, busily engaged with the world of letters.

Eileen Gregory's 'Virginity and Erotic Liminality: H. D.'s *Hippolytus Temporizes*' (*ConL* 31.133–60) records the significance for H. D. of her first visit to Greece in 1920, the site of a visionary experience in Corfu which led eventually to her analysis with Freud and another turn in the phases of her work. Here Gregory is engaged with H. D.'s verse play of 1927, *Hippolytus Temporizes*, which she sees as accomplishing something beyond the scope of H. D's other early lyric poems, and the early prose, in its articulation of an Hellenic eroticism in which 'structurally determined oppositions, including sexual distinctions, are dissolved'. H. D.'s response to Greece, and her analysis with Freud also inform Susan Edmunds's article ' "I Read The Writing When He Seized My Throat": Hysteria and Revolution in H. D.'s *Helen in Egypt*' (*ConL* 32.470–95) where she argues that the revolution in Egypt from 1952–3 adds to the historical background of the poem, along with World War II. This complex revisionary account of *Helen in Egypt* sees its dynamics as an 'acute tension between her strongly articulated desire to reform the patriarchal family and her resilient nostalgia for it ...'. In 'Joint Venture: Richard Aldington, H. D. and the Poet's Translation Series' (*PQ* 70.67–98), Caroline Zilboorg provides an instructive commentary on H. D. and Aldington's shared enterprise in the first sequence of the 'Poet's Translation', a pamphlet series published by the Egoist Press in 1915 and 1916, in which they joined with their contemporaries in publishing versions of ancient Greek and Latin poetry. Zilboorg's account nicely contextualizes the occasion of this first series, and argues convincingly for H. D. and Aldington's shared interest in Hellenic poetry.

Christopher Beach's 'Migrating Voices In The Poetry of Edward Dorn' (*ConL* 32.211–28) is a persuasive view of the originality of Dorn's work in his movement away from Pound and Olson, which Beach marks as first apparent in Geography (1965): Beach likens Dorn's polyvocal narrative practice to Roland Barthes's account of vocal pluralism in S/Z, where 'the boundaries between discourses themselves' and their 'origins or enunciating voices' cease to be apparent, and relates this 'slippage' or 'migration' of voice in Dorn's work to his denial of Pound and Olson's hierarchical presentation of values, as Pound's Eurocentric and Olson's East-Coast gaze is replaced by Dorn's preoccupation with the American West.

A collection of essays from a 1988 conference at the California Institute of Technology, edited by Ronald Bush, *T. S. Eliot: The Modernist in History*, breaks new ground in examining old issues. It includes a perceptive study by Carol Christ on 'Gender, Voice and Figuration', which links Eliot's early experiments with voice to his assimilation of the feminine idiom of nineteenth-century poetry: thus the attempt of the masculine speaker of 'Portrait of a Lady' to impose his 'tom-tom' upon her genteel idiom enables Eliot to 'enact and mask issues of poetic influence'. James Longenbach's precise tracing of the writing of *Ara Vos Prec* and Lawrence Rainey's contextual study of the rivalry to publish *The Waste Land*, 'what they had decided to publish was less a specific poem, more a bid for a discursive hegemony', are examples of the painstaking and perceptive work which characterizes this collection. Ronald Bush's own contribution celebrates the moral idealism of modernism in Eliot's passionate struggles to renew form and to draw the past into present power. He quotes Eliot in Emersonian vein: 'life is always turned towards creation' and contrasts the heroic enterprise of modernism with 'the supermarket of postmodernist tolerance'. This gathering of essays is itself strenuous, patient, and searching, a fitting tribute to the poet it honours.

Lois A. Cuddy and David H. Hirsch, editors of *Critical Essays on T. S. Eliot's 'The Waste Land'*, have provided a useful collection of the classic criticism of the poem with the addition of four newly-commissioned essays. Their introduction provides a review of the prevailing ideologies of each decade of Eliot criticism. It must be said that the early reviews and essays set out a critical agenda which has not really been superseded by the later studies in this book: Edmund Wilson's review in *The Dial*, and Cleanth Brooks provided exemplary elucidatory studies; Conrad Aiken sketched out the modernist technique; R. P. Blackmur's essay on sensibility is complemented by Philip Rahv's incisive identification of the religious and cultural issues, 'in the 20th century it is as possible to be a religious poet as it is possible to be a feudal knight.' Indeed, the editors detect a cyclical pattern with the exponents of deconstruction and postmodernism returning to the preoccupations of the early critics asking the same questions about the poem's relationship to elitist, Christian and humanist values – there is a notably abrasive 1987 contribution from John Xiros Cooper employing Stanley Fish's concept of 'interpretive community'. Recent critics find the same themes of despair and emptiness, but they are 'now located not only in the words but in the spaces of the poem'. The conservative nature of this anthology is evident in the scant attention given to recent gender and contextual studies of the poem.

Two books on the *Four Quartets* appeared this year, Steve Ellis's *The English Eliot: Design, Language and Landscape in Four Quartets*, and Paul Murray's *T. S. Eliot and Mysticism*. I found Ellis's book the more instructive because his reading of Eliot's poem seeks a cultural context to rescue it from its isolation as the *summa* of

Eliot's *oeuvre*, in which it is seen as wholly distinct from contemporaneous British poetry: Ellis attempts to place *Four Quartets* in relation to issues of British nationalism through a variety of contemporary comparisons which take in the concept of a national poetic language, through Eliot's reading of Shakespeare, and an astute comparison of Eliot and Auden, to Eliot's role within the idioms of nationalist pictorial representation as these are reflected in high and popular cultural images. These are the contexts for Ellis's view of Eliot's 'Englishness' which is, ultimately, a representation of the necessary sense of nationality in the poet which gives way to Eliot's desire for a language and mode of reference antagonistic to the narrow concerns of nationalism, and thus universalist in ambition. This is, therefore, a revisionary account of Eliot's 'Englishness', which goes far beyond the conventional portraiture of Eliot in the thirties as the embodiment of English conservatism. Paul Murray has a degree in theology and a doctorate in modern English literature and thus looks to be well qualified to write on *Four Quartets*, but it is the theologian who is most in evidence in this account of 'The Secret History' of the poem, as he undertakes to reveal its patterns of religious and literary echoes, and allusions to the writings of mysticism. The result is a work of piety, the affirmation of a religious significance in the poem which Murray claims has hitherto gone unrecognized in particular detail. There is a certain critical naivety throughout this book: Murray opens, for example, with a tortuous defence against charges no one would now make against Eliot, of fraudulent practice in his 'borrowings', and thereafter, Murray's reference to the body of commentary on Eliot does not engage with the most recent criticism, despite a lengthy bibliography of secondary sources. Murray claims that his book is not simply about sources, but about the manifestation of the techniques of mysticism as a constituent feature of Eliot's compositional strategies, yet his brief comments on 'Mysticism and Music', for example, as a way into an understanding of the rhythmic vocalism of the sections of each poem, does not advance our understanding of their vexed relationship to the musical structure they are supposed to imitate. And late in this book, distinguishing between the two forms under which Christian poets 'have been accustomed to conceive Divine Reality', through the 'doctrine of immanence' or through 'Transcendence', Murray can use this latter term as appropriate to Eliot without any reference to Eliot's American origins, or to Emerson, or to Transcendentalism as a religious philosophy of inward knowing which we are customarily led to believe Eliot rejected for the orthodoxies of Anglo-Catholicism.

The idea of Eliot as a belated Romantic is the impetus for dispute in John Paul Riquelme's major study *Harmony of Dissonances: T. S. Eliot, Romanticism, and Imagination* in which he sets out his counter-theory of Eliot as a poet of anti-Romantic persuasion whose verse is mimetic of the 'antielegiac forms typified by revenge tragedy'. Riquelme repudiates the conventional view of Eliot's poetic career in which *The Waste Land* is read as Eliot's completest diagnosis of the fractured self, and *Four Quartets* seen as the final expression of the recovery of self through the affirmations of Christian meditation, and he sees these poems as similarly structured 'counterparts', marked by shifts in writing practice rather than in significant reversals of conviction or vision: for Riquelme, both poems are collections of fragments, 'whose ways, however different, are also the same'. Part of the programme of this difficult book is an endeavour to see Eliot's complicated relationship to Romanticism, especially on the issue of poetic creation, as anticipatory of deconstructive revaluations of Romanticism; thus Riquelme argues for *The Waste Land* as a nondiscursive dissolution of self and voice which takes Eliot 'to the limits of intelligibility': by contrast, *Four Quartets* is said to present writing 'as an interminable dynamic process' whose 'endlessly cross-referential, internally transforming, disseminating structure … points to a differential creative process, a Heraclitean flux, one name for which is *wit*'. In all this, the 'writing process' itself takes precedence over the self and the individual personal voice in recognition of what is suggested as Eliot's skepticism towards the attainment of positive knowledge of history or of mind; and despite Eliot's contingent relations with the Romantics, duly marked in this thorough analysis, the essence of his poetic style is found in a variety of pre-Romantic orientations, Classical, Dantean, and Renaissance. Riquelme gracefully observes that his reading of Eliot goes in pursuit of what he calls an 'obscure process': this study will appeal to those with a similar theoretical interest in the notion of the writing process in proportion as it will alienate those readers of Eliot who hold to a sense of the identity of the poet as crucial to the poems.

William Atkinson (*TCL* 37.22–37) surveys the topos of 'Africa' in work by D. H. Lawrence and T. S. Eliot, with particular reference to Eliot's interest in Kurtz from Conrad's *Heart of Darkness*: Atkinson reads Victorian imperialism as providing a residue of iconic significance in African scenes, names, and cultural artefacts, and shows how these feature in the *Waste Land, The Hollow Men*, and *The Cocktail Party*. Donald J. Childs's 'T. S. Eliot's Rhapsody of Matter and Memory' (*AL* 63.474–88) argues that Eliot's 'Rhapsody on a Windy Night', composed in 1911, is not an anticipation of Eliot's rejection of Bergsonism, as is customarily proposed, but should be read as the culmination of Eliot's short-lived conversion to Bergson.

In 'The Grin of Tiresias: Humor in *The Waste Land*' (*TCL* 36.137–54), Steven Helmling sees not a Laforguian irony but offers the poem as 'a farce of humours' in the way Eliot proposed *The Jew of Malta* not as a tragedy but as 'farce', or a 'tragedy of humours'. Helmling suggests that Eliot read Marlowe's play as a 'gesture of *contemptus mundi*' and that this became an appropriate mode for Eliot's representation of the 'futility and anarchy which is contemporary history' in *The Waste Land*. 'The Integrity of Eliot' (*EIC* 41.222–39) by A. V. C. Schmidt takes Eliot's thought and art during 1925 to 1939 as his focus, and finds Eliot's essential integrity in the poetry rather than in the often admonitory prose: he sees 'The Hollow Men' as a 'peculiarly personal and naked expression of spiritual bankruptcy', and proposes 'Ash Wednesday' as a central work in Eliot's career, a poem he reads not as a form of confessional, but about 'the nature of love and its subtle and difficult differences, and our need to recognize them, if we are not to confuse the "shadow" with the reality'. In an essay which addresses Eliot's view of the moral bases of action in individual lives, it is odd to find virtually no reference to the agony of Eliot's marital circumstances in this crucial period of his life, so that this view of his religious progress to Catholic Christianity is as loftily impersonal as Eliot could wish for.

Essays on Robert Frost in *AL* are reprinted in *On Frost: The Best From American Literature*, edited by Edwin H. Cady and Louis J. Budd. There are sixteen contributions ranging from Robert S. Newdick's 'Robert Frost and the Sound of Sense' of 1937, to Frank Lentricchia's 'The Resentments of Robert Frost' of 1990 (*YWES* 71). This collection gives us some of the best writing on Frost, and is nicely varied in its inclusion of different approaches to Frost from the rhetorical to the conceptual. It is appropriate to note here that Lentricchia's essay is also reprinted in *Out of Bounds: Male Writers and Gender(ed) Criticism* edited by Laura Claridge and Elizabeth Langland.

Mario L. D'Avanzo's *A Cloud of Other Poets: Robert Frost and The Romantics* stands on the shoulders of that tradition of Frost commentary which has explored his relationship with the British Romantic poets and their American transcendentalist contemporaries: from such a position one must now have something very original to say about Frost and his sense of poetic inheritance to justify another commentary of this kind, and I don't find much evidence of originality here. For example, D'Avanzo argues that by grouping the poems around a common theme or controlling symbol 'my key notion is that a typical Frost poem plays against one or more Romantic predecessor poems': this is not an innovatory strategy for reading Frost, nor does D'Avanzo acknowledge his own indebtedness here to Harold Bloom's theories of the anxiety of influence, which surely inform this approach. The best that may be said for this study is that it is a perfectly respectable introduction to Frost's poems, and to the tradition of critical commentary it follows.

Mordecai Marcus in *The Poems of Robert Frost: an explication*, has provided a painstaking 'basic commonsensical explication of all 355 poems' in the Lathem edition of Frost's poetry. It has been a labour of love directed primarily to the beginning student, but useful also to more experienced readers in the attention given to lesser known poems. The book's refusal of an imperialist strategy, and quiet holding to its own clearly defined aim of providing a basis from which readings develop, rather than the substance of them, is impressive. It has a helpful bibliography on individual poems as well as general books on Frost. More contextualization would have been welcome, but it is a solid book which has chosen, first and foremost, to make some comment on all the poems, 200 of which Marcus claims 'have gone virtually undiscussed until now'.

Judith Oster's reader-response study, *Toward Robert Frost: The Reader and the Poet*, begins inauspiciously in applying Frost's phrase 'braving alien entanglements' to the enterprise of reading his poetry. She is of the 'reading as perilous adventure' variety of reader-response critic. But the gist of Oster's argument is a down-to-earth one, that Frost's reading of nature and of relationships is an education in how to read. The discussion of 'Range-Finding' exemplifies her method and it bears out Jeremy Hawthorn's remark about reader-oriented theories that it is texts which create readers and demand certain ways of reading. The strength of this study is in the informed, well-judged and unforced readings of the major poems; it is no mean feat, for example, to be able to provide a model close reading of 'Stopping by Woods on a Snowy Evening'. The epilogue, however, returns to the theme of reader peril and taking its cue too fulsomely from 'Directive' envisages Oster, a Dante to Frost's Virgil, 'having a sort of hell as part of my trial and education'. The main part of this book, mercifully free from these histrionics of reading, is a reliable guide to Frost's poetry.

A reprinting of Randall Jarrell's 'The Knight, Death, and the Devil' (*Agenda* 29.6) is followed by Philip Hoy's enthusiastic analysis of the verbal and metrical dexterity of Jarrell's poem (7–17), inspired by Durer's engraving of the same name: Hoy calls on Robert Lowell's approval of this particular poem in his review of Jarrell's volume *The Seven League Crutches*, where it first appeared, and Hoy argues that as a poem instigated by a visual picture, it is comparable in achievement to Auden's 'Musée des Beaux Arts'.

The third volume of Tim Hunt's edition of *The Collected Poetry of Robinson Jeffers* appeared this year, and as I have noted before, this must be one of the finest editions of any twentieth-century poet's work, handsomely produced and scrupulously edited. This volume covers the years 1939 to 1962, and thus includes *Be Angry At The Sun, The Double Axe, Hungerfield*, and *Last Poems*. Robert Zaller claims that his edition of *Centennial Essays for Robinson Jeffers* is the first critical collection devoted exclusively to Jeffers, though last year I commented on the collection edited by James Karman, *Critical Essays on Robinson Jeffers* in the Hall American Literature Series

(*YWES* 71). Zaller's collection has nine essays commissioned for this volume, and reprints pieces by Horace Gregory (1961), Robert Boyers (1970), William Everson (1983), and his own essay from *Agenda* of 1987. Both the narrative poems and the shorter lyrics find their advocates in this collection, as in R. W. (Herbie) Butterfield's reading of 'The Loving Shepherdess', and Tim Hunt's account of the lyric idiom of *Tamar*, whilst others write of Jeffers's relationship to modernism, his symbolism, and his metrics, and the collection ends with a fascinating contribution from the poet Czeslaw Milosz of a visit to Carmel two years after Jeffers's death, in which he confronts his doubts about Jeffers whilst honouring the scale of his accomplishment.

Carcanet has issued a *Selected Poems* by Kenneth Koch, based on an American edition but with the addition of poems and passages from *On the Edge* (1986), *Ko* (1959), and *Seasons on Earth* (1987). Koch is a difficult poet to place, partly because his wry humour defeats categorization, and his daring comedy can lead to extravagances not easily accommodated, as for example in 'The Art of Love', with its tongue-in-cheek advocacy of forms of bondage and mutilation explored in the universal manuals of love-making. The surrealist ambition of many of these poems works best when Koch's subversive intentions are orchestrated through his clever literary parodies.

Michael Greer's article on ideology, theory and 'The Naming of "Language Poetry" ' (*Boundary 2* 16.335–55) is a clear-sighted exposition of the post-structuralist contexts of Language Poetry in which he proposes that 'writing' rather than 'language' is the central term in this field, in which the endeavour to 'reinvent attention' to the activities and processes of reading and interpretation should be seen as part of a broad historical shift in the human sciences from 'the *object* of interpretation to its *practices*'. In the same issue George Hartley's 'Realism and Reification: The Poetics and Politics of Three Language Poets' (311–34) investigates the positions on realism of Ron Silliman, Steve McCaffery, and Bruce Andrews through a review of the sophisticated models of Marxist ideas on realism in Georg Lukacs, the Frankfurt School, and Louis Althusser.

Allan Johnston's 'Modes of Return: Memory and Remembering in the Poetry of Robert Lowell' (*TCL* 36.73–94) reads through *Life Studies, Notebook 1967–68, History* and *Day by Day*, for those occasions where memory is exploited in Lowell's constant process to repair himself, particularly in regard to his Oedipal anxieties about his unwanted birth: Johnston's persuasive reading suggests Lowell's realization of the artifice of memory, to the point where a kind of quiescent acceptance of the inevitability of his own death lifts him out of his 'denial of life', and leaves him with a kind of mere knowledge of the interchangeability of 'confession', 'art', and memory itself. In a similar vein, Terri Witek's 'Robert Lowell's Tokens of the Self' (*AL* 63.712–26) makes use of some of the 200 pages of autobiographical prose, much of it still unpublished, begun during Lowell's recovery from mental breakdown following the death of his mother in 1954: Witek proposes that these materials not only show the significance of the 'pull of the Mother' in Lowell's search for a unified self, but also reveal Lowell's understanding that he must 'always identify with the less certain and infinitely more mysterious power of the Father, to achieve a "fixed identity" '. Henry Hart's (*TCL* 37.105–29) account of Lowell's interest in notions of poetic and political power, especially through his contradictory identification with and antagonism towards figures such as Alexander, Caligula, Nero, Napoleon, Hitler and Mussolini, is here read as a feature of Lowell's 'fascinated abhorrence of American sublime', which for Lowell give us expressions both of 'tragic grandeur' and 'comic ridiculousness'. Hart's later essay on 'Robert Lowell and the Psychopathology of the Sublime' (*ConL*

32.496–519) investigates Lowell's relationship to the sublime through the devices of his poetics where the play of aesthetic strategies and the urgings of familial confessionalism compose the antithetical elements that mark the parameters of his negotiation with the poetic voice as both personal and public.

Edgar Lee Masters's autobiography *Across Spoon River*, which first appeared in 1936, has been reprinted with an introduction by Ronald Primeau, in which he sets out the evasions and strategies employed by Masters in this partial self-portrait, and makes a very reasonable claim for its value in relation to the increasingly multi-disciplinary study of Midwestern culture. Despite Masters's public life in the world of writing through the enormous success of *Spoon River Anthology*, and his biographical studies of Lincoln, Vachel Lindsay, Mark Twain, Walt Whitman and Emerson, Primeau shows that Masters was, in a crucial sense, terminally isolated by the conditions and circumstances of his mid-Western upbringing, and that in this autobiography 'the circle of imagination' connecting this account of his life to his prairie town origins remains unbroken.

In 'Auden and Merton at the Movies', Allan Jacobs (*ELN* 77.45–56) discusses the impact of Auden and Merton's separate viewing of a Nazi propaganda film, *Sieg im Polen*, in New York in 1939 (Auden) and 1940 (Merton), and relates their reactions to the horrors espoused by this film to Auden's return to the Christian church, and Merton's turn to the monastic life.

The archival holdings of the manuscripts of W. S. Merwin at the University of Illinois at Urbana-Champaign is an unrivalled collection of the work of a living poet, and Edward J. Brunner has now composed an absorbing study of these materials in his book *Poetry as Labor and Privilege: The Writings of W. S. Merwin*. Brunner's introduction cogently discriminates between the critical enterprise in reading Merwin's published volumes from the vantage point of a given theoretical position and the scholar's almost necessarily revisionist enterprise in re-contextualizing the poet's published volumes in the light of evidence provided by manuscript materials such as are available at Illinois. The effect of this study is to open up the debate about Merwin's poetry in ways which could not have been envisaged without access to these materials. As Brunner notes, for example, 'It seems questionable ... to give credence to the claim that through the 1950s Merwin purused a rigorously formal poetry now that we have become aware of *The Ark of Silence*, a sprawling combination of prose and poetry assembled in 1957 and submitted as a fourth volume of poetry (but rejected by the publisher).' Similarly, Brunner argues that the four volumes of free verse published between 1963 and 1973 can less easily be regarded as 'a single unbroken unit expressing a profound pessimism, once the careful arrangements underlying each collection come under scrutiny.' The great strength of this work is in Brunner's detailed attention to these manuscript materials, a patient study of the determining factors which contributed to Merwin's personal and intellectual circumstances as he brought successive volumes to publication. This is a seminal contribution to the study of Merwin, a work of great labour and affection, and one which all readers of Merwin will be indebted to.

Lois Bar-Yaacov writes on Marianne Moore's much-debated war poem, 'In Distrust of Merits' and Ezra Pound's 'Canto LXXXI' (*AL* 63.1–25), where she defends Moore's 'naive but honest self-doubt' as 'more relevant to my own urgent concerns' against the 'medieval mysticism and pseudo-Biblical pontifications' of Pound, especially in 'Canto LXXXI'. David Roessel (*ELN* 77.63–8) argues that we must take a sceptical view of Marianne Moore's dismissive attitude to her own notes to her poems, as proposed in her preface to the *Collected Poems*, and here provides a brief analysis of her notes to 'The Pangolin', with special reference to Robert Hatt's article 'Pangolin' in the December 1934 issue of *Natural History*.

Donald Allen has done a splendid job of selecting something of the best of Frank O'Hara for Carcanet's edition of *The Selected Poems of Frank O'Hara*, a judicious chronological arrangement which offers many of the familiar O'Hara favourites, and opens with the manifesto 'Personism'. Ironic self-consciousness of his own postures was always a virtue in O'Hara, and his engagement with the world in this selection is a reassuring mix of prosaic knowingness and spontaneous registration of those larger effects he was wary of deliberately seeking. This beautifully produced book is a pleasure to use, and should make many more converts to O'Hara's poetry. John Lowney (*ConL* 32.244–64) seeks to counter the prevailing view of O'Hara's work as a poetry of mere surface, which wilfully refuses significance beyond the expression of the instantaneously personal: Lowney offers a sustained reading of 'Memorial Day 1950' and a handful of later poems, in which he investigates O'Hara's work for its processive revelation 'of the historical and ideological forces which inform the "present" at every moment'.

George Oppen's use of deictic pronouns and prepositional phrases is discussed by Paul Kenneth Naylor in 'The Pre-Position "Of": Being, Seeing, and Knowing in George Oppen's Poetry' (*ConL* 32.100–15) where his principal focus is Oppen's *Of Being Numerous*: debating Oppen's proximity to Heidegger's notion of the *a priori* condition of 'Being', Naylor argues that the intentionally equivocal language that characterizes Oppen's poetry and Heidegger's prose reflects the 'enigmatic essence' of what they understand as 'Being', and thus of how its existence or truth may be mediated in language.

Any new book on Sylvia Plath that engages with the Plath estate seems bound to engender controversy and Jacqueline Rose's brilliant study *The Haunting of Sylvia Plath* is no exception. It is easy to see why, for Rose persistently questions the intervention of the estate in the transmission of Plath's literary remains, and repudiates its appeal to 'factual accuracy' and ethical imperatives as issues which should control the procedures of scholarship and criticism. If Rose is principally concerned with the relationship between writing and fantasy, rather than Plath's 'concretely lived reality', she has some abrasive things to say about the editing and presentation of Plath's work by the estate, and it is difficult to dissent from Rose's account of these matters, or her reasoned analysis of the partiality of Anne Stevenson's recent biography of the poet *Bitter Fame* (*YWES* 70.632). Though this is not an issue Rose specifically addresses, if you look at Ted Hughes's notes to the *Collected Poems*, excluding the juvenilia, his commentary seems to be a parody of scholarly annotation, for these notes rely almost exclusively on 'factual' data, or on what Plath said, or proposed saying, about her poems in a BBC interview programme. The argument of this book is too complex for brief summary, but in essence Rose treats Plath's work as the site of familial, sexual, and political conflict which finds its telling voice in the psychology of fantasy, where 'writing' engages with issues of gender, parentalism, self, and history in a powerfully subversive poetics. Rose's account of Plath's most discussed poem, 'Daddy', is quite stunning: impartial, I would say, and scrupulously responsive to the written poem, what is actually on the page, as against the rhetoric of denial this poem often elicits from those who condemn Plath in this poem, as in 'Lady Lazarus', for her self-aggrandizing use of Holocaust imagery.

Timothy Materer's essay on occultism in Sylvia Plath (*TCL* 2:131–47), chosen as this year's winner of the *TCL* prize in literary criticism, makes a good case for a new orientation in Plath studies. Materer's argument is based on a reading of 'Dialogue

Over a Ouija Board', which he calls one of her most important works, though it is not included in the body of *Collected Poems*, but only as a note to the poem 'Ouija': Materer sees Plath's interest in the occult in Yeatsian terms, and argues that occultism provided Plath with a system of symbols and rituals 'that did not demand intellectual assent to a traditional religion'.

'Anyone may be excused for deciding that life is too short for coming to terms with The Cantos: but if we make that decision we thereby disqualify ourselves from having any opinion worth listening to, about the poetry in English of this century.' This characteristically combative statement comes from Donald Davie's 1985 review of books on Pound by Peter Makin, Christine Froula, and Peter Nicholls, reprinted in Davie's *Studies in Ezra Pound*, the fourth volume of his *Collected Works* currently being issued by Carcanet. Davie's primary interest in Pound has always been in the poetry, in what he calls the 'inventions in imagery and cadence', though these concerns have not deflected him from the political and historiographical problems of Pound's work. Indeed, his case against the *Cantos* is not that Pound's enterprise was doomed to failure from the start, as it is fashionable to claim, but that the work crucially falls apart between *Rock-Drill* and *Thrones* 'because of a misunderstanding about historiography'. Davie's prolonged engagement with Pound and his critics and commentators may be studied at leisure in this volume, which reprints the whole of *Poet as Sculptor* of 1964, and essays, reviews and occasional pieces from 1972 to 1990. It is a pity that two of these items are not attributed to their original publication, 'Pound and *The Exile*', and 'More on the Muddle of *Thrones*', though both are dated in the contents page, and the *LRB* review 'Pound's Friends', from which I have quoted, is undated in the text. These are trifling matters in a collection of such riches, but they must be a source of irritation to Davie, who has a scholarly respect for these matters, as his introduction to this volume makes abundantly clear.

Scott Hamilton's *Ezra Pound and the Symbolist Inheritance* is a study in the mode of Harold Bloom's theory of the anxiety of influence: Hamilton rewrites the story of Pound's relationship to symbolism, convinced that the more insistently Pound disavows it – 'imagism is not symbolism' – the more certainly we shall find it. It must be said that Hamilton makes a very good case, disputing the major commentators' acceptance of this Poundian dogma, with the exception of Frank Kermode who long ago saw the Cantos as 'the only kind of long poem the Symbolist aesthetic will admit'. Hamilton retraces Pound's response to nineteenth-century French romantic poetry, especially Gautier and Baudelaire, and shows his reading of them to be very close to James's, and a deliberate misprision in regard to his dismissive parodies of Baudelaire, and his occlusion of Baudelaire's recognition of the romantic and symbolist dimensions of Gautier. As is well known, Pound chose Gautier as an exemplar, because his method provided one model for a modernist poetics seeking a way out of the 'mushy techniques' and slack verbiage of romantic subjectivity, and the fusion of Gautier's verbal clarity and satirical realism, with Pound's later election of Corbiere and Laforgue, is conventionally understood to have contributed to the development of imagism, vorticism, and objectivism. Hamilton does not significantly dispute this history, but shows that as early as *Hugh Selwyn Mauberley*, Pound's recourse to Gautier admits his romantic idealism along with his realism, and that the tension between these 'irreconcilable poetic modes' comes 'to haunt the *Cantos*', especially the *Pisan* and later *Cantos*. This is a convincing revisionary version of Pound's relationship to French poetry, and has much to tell us about the desired fusion of history with vision in the *Cantos*.

Pound's meetings with his patron John Quinn were limited to two occasions in

1910, and some further contacts when Quinn was visiting Paris in 1921 and 1923, and their relationship was substantially maintained through letters. Timothy Materer has now edited *The Selected Letters of Ezra Pound and John Quinn, 1915–1924*, giving sixty-seven of the 230 letters that Pound wrote, including many of the longest, representing in all 'nearly half the words Pound wrote to Quinn.' Materer's important and persuasive introduction to this volume offers a different view of Quinn as patron from that of Quinn's biographer, B. L. Reid, who saw him as an 'artist *manqué*', and from all those who deplored Quinn's willing his art collection to his family with no provision for conserving it after his death. Using Quinn's intellectual hero Henry James to locate the distinction between those who bought the art of the past for prestige and investment, and those like Quinn who were patrons of contemporary art, and who were aware of the moral effects of wealth upon art, Materer presents a brief portrait of Quinn which is sympathetic to Pound's idea of him as a patron of Renaissance proportions in his direct engagement with the artists he bought from, in painting, sculpture and literature, and in his involvement with avant-garde magazines such as the *Little Review*. Pound's letters, which are copiously annotated, once more reveal the familiar story of his intense efforts on behalf of other writers and artists to secure Quinn's patronage, buoyed almost throughout by the sense that he and Quinn were fellow workers in the making of a new Renaissance. This is one of the best of recent editions of Pound's letters, and takes us to the heart of that difficult conjunction between the poet's aesthetic concerns, and his dealings with those such as Quinn who helped to make the contemporary artist's life possible in the early years of modernism.

The idea that there is a deep unifying structure to the *Cantos* has persisted through several decades of commentary on the poem, despite the failure of all its critics to confidently exhibit such a structure: as an idea, it has both a ready appeal, and is resistant to all kinds of contrary evidence. Akiko Miyake now proposes another version of this elusive totalizing structure, and suggests that the poem is centred on a programme derived from the Eleusinian mysteries. In *Ezra Pound And The Mysteries of Love*, Miyake argues that the aim of the poem is 'to clarify the vision of the unity of the physical and spiritual universe' and that Pound observes 'history and even economics by using the "light from Eleusis" as his standard of critical assessment'. Her book is less valuable for its totalizing endeavour than in its particular discoveries and reassessments of familiar material: first, in her contention that Pound found a model of coherence for his poem in Gabriele Rossetti's *Il mistero dell'amor platonico del medio evo*, a five-volume work of 1840, which transmits a version of the relationship between the Provençal troubadours and the Italian poets of *dolce stil nuovo* and the concepts of mystical love taken from the Greek Eleusinian mysteries; and in her chapter on the innate conflict between Ernest Fenollosa's commitment to Esoteric Buddhism and his earlier training in Hegelian rationalism, with his consequent failures of rationalist enquiry which, Miyake argues, had a fatal impact on the *Cantos* : for with Pound's adoption of Fenellosa's ideogrammatic method, the poet 'lost the way to criticize his own judgements', a failure all too abundantly evidenced by his economic and political judgements from the early 1920s.

Lawrence S. Rainey's book on the Malatesta Cantos, *Ezra Pound and the Monument of Culture*, is an exemplary work of scholarship and criticism, one of the best books on Pound of recent years. Rainey shows, more thoroughly than any previous critic, how the making of the Malatesta Cantos was central to the whole project of Pound's epic, and rescued the poem from the conceptual impasse Pound had reached in the early 1920s. This study has three focal points: Pound's 'reading' of the Tempio at Rimini; his researches in the documentary materials of Sigismundo's history; and the uses made of these matters in Pound criticism, and in this latter case, Rainey's argument becomes a sustained and devastating critique of the failures of recent theoretical readings of the *Cantos* to engage with the issue of textual production. In his second chapter, for example, Rainey takes a single line from Canto 9, 'and Polixena, his second wife, died' to investigate the occasion, nature and effect of Pound's transmission of the blandest version of the death of Sigismundo's second wife, an enterprise that takes us through Papal and civic history in Italy from the fifteenth to the nineteenth century and beyond: what is at issue here is Pound's willingness to accept the best cosmetic version of Polissena's (as she was actually named) death, one that would not infringe upon his representation of Sigismundo, his third wife Isotta, and the reconstruction of the Tempio in Rimini. The relationship of these matters to Pound's involvement with Mussolini and the rise of Italian Fascism is another strand in Rainey's complex recovery of the materials out of which Pound made the Malatesta Cantos. This is an absorbing, instructive study, which suggests how much we have yet to learn about the making of the *Cantos*, and how often commentary has replicated Pound's own elisions and evasions in the transmission of his texts.

Tim Redman supports the view of Donald Davie and others that the 'case' of Pound has served to dethrone the poet from his bardic or seer-like eminence in this century: and Redman subscribes to the view, as another writer has put it, that in contemporary America, there is 'no poetics equal to the import of politics in language or life'. Given the parlous state of American international diplomacy at this time, and the rampant malaise of its internal politics and economics, perhaps this divorce of poetry and politics in America, if true, is no bad thing. Redman cites Conor Cruise O'Brien's stoical acknowledgment of the necessarily diminished scale of his responsibilities as a thinker in the political realm, as a consequence of his practical experience of political life, and the present state of affairs in Eastern Europe and elsewhere suggests that a wise and humane politics is a chimera. These reflections are prompted by the opening chapter of Redman's *Ezra Pound and Italian Fascism*, an excellent book in which he traces the growth of Pound's interests in politics and economics from his association with A. R. Orage and the *New Age*, through the economic theories of C. H. Douglas and Silvio Gesell, and his commitment to Mussolini's fascism. Redman is somewhat dismissive of the work of Robert Casillo and Wendy Flory in this field, because their approach is psychoanalytical, as against his own inductive historical approach, but in the last analysis, all those who write on Pound's anti-semitism and fascism must confront the same set of materials. True, Redman has used unpublished archival material in this history of Pound's development as an economic and political thinker, and his chapter on Pound's discovery of Gesell is particularly instructive. However, the last part of this book gives a detailed version of Pound's active labours on behalf of the Italian fascist regime, an account which is as depressing as it is enthralling in its view of a man driven by good intentions to extremes of folly.

Charlotte Ward follows her 1985 deluxe limited edition of Pound's translations of medieval poems, *Ezra Pound, Forked Branches*, with *Pound's Translations of Arnaut Daniel*, a variorum edition with a commentary culled from Pound's unpublished correspondence. Ward's brief introduction recounts the history of two failed endeavours to have an edition of these poems published, first by Charles Granville in 1911, owner of Swift & Company, who absconded with the firm's monies in 1912, and then with Charles C. Bubb's Clerk's Press in Cleveland, in 1917. This latter attempt failed because the American censors appear to have intercepted delivery of the manuscript to Bubb. Ward's edition now gives the original Provençal texts, those translations Pound used in *The Spirit of Romance*, copies intended for the Swift and Clerk's Press editions, and published and unpublished variants of each translation: in addition, there are two bibliographies, one of Pound's other publications relevant to the Daniel versions, in chronological order, and one of secondary studies of these materials. Ward also gives notes to the Provençal texts, and to the translations, in this very welcome edition.

The Spring and Fall issues of *Paideuma* contain Massimo Bacigalupo's annotated translation of Cantos 72 and 73 (20.9–41) with a brief essay which contextualizes the arguments of these cantos and their centrality to the poem as a whole, and in an appendix gives annotated translations of Italian notes and drafts of Cantos 74–75. Alexander Schmitz's essay on 'Ideogram-Audiogram' (43–62) argues a series of parallels between the ideogrammatic verbal structures of the *Cantos* and the dissonances and juxtapositional idioms of various twentieth-century classical musicians, and finds equations between the rhythmic and aural sounds of the poem and jazz and bebop. Matthew Little and Robert Babcock's account of Pound's interest in Avicenna's *De Almahad* in his 'Cavalcanti' essay is another example of that renewed interest in Pound's sources, where they propose that what may have interested Pound most in Avicenna's text is his 'analysis of relations between physical sexuality, personal imaginative experience, and popular religion', and argue that the edition of Avicenna Pound calls on in this context was that by Andreas Alpagus of Belluno, published in Venice in 1546. Robert Spoo, co-author of *Ezra Pound and Margaret Cravens: A Tragic Friendship, 1910–1912* (1988) (*YWES* 69.613), here writes on Margaret Cravens's enthusiasm for the poetry of the Italian Nobel laureate Giosue Carducci, and argues for Cravens's role 'as confidante and consultant during Pound's work on *Sonnets and Ballate of Guido Calvalcanti*' (77–88). A noteworthy feature of this issue of *Paideuma* is the transcript of interviews with Pound by a then trainee psychiatrist, Dr Jerome Kavka, in St Elizabeth's Hospital from 26 December 1945, over the following few months (143–185).

The Winter issue of *Paideuma* has three articles on an hitherto unfashionable topic, Pound's interest in the Swedish theosophist Emanuel Swedenborg, an interest of Pound's ambiguously nourished by W. B. Yeats's preoccupation with the literature of the occult. Demetres Tryphonopoulos (20.7–15) writes on the persistence of Pound's interest in Swedenborg citing two letters in evidence, the first dated 1907, to William Carlos Williams, where Pound argues for an implied contiguity between Swedenborg's notion of 'angelic language' and his own understanding of 'artistic utterance', and the second from St Elizabeth's about 1956, where Pound comments on Gabriele Rossetti's linking of 'speculative Masonry, Swedenborg, and Dante', a conjunction Pound claims to have identified between Swedenborg and Dante some fifty years earlier. Leon Surette's 'Yeats, Pound, and Nietzsche' (18–30) offers some interesting ideas about Yeats's address to Pound in *A Vision*, where his point of reference is to Yeats's anxious yet hopeful view of Pound 'as a prophet of the New Age'. Andrzej Sosnowski (31–8) debates the similarity between Pound's theory of imagism and Swedenborg's 'theory of correspondences', in which he argues that Pound's imagism 'is not only a poetic theory but also, and perhaps primarily, an esoteric doctrine, an epistemology, a belief, a way of life.' Stephen Sicari in 'Poetry and Politics in Pound and Yeats' (39–49) suggests a common motive for Yeats's and Pound's continuing imaginative confrontation with history and politics, read as a form of creative delight in the tragic mire of human circumstance. Finally, the relationship between the instantaneity of the epiphany in Joyce's work, and its more protracted occasion in the *Cantos*, is briefly explored by Vern L. Lindquist (51–9).

Randolph Chilton and Carol Gilbertson write of the evolution of Pound's 'In A Station of the Metro', (*TCL* 36.225–36), calling not only on the early published variants, but also on the unpublished versions of the poem held in the Joseph Regenstein Library at the University of Chicago. The first published version appeared in *Poetry* in 1913, with a colon after the first line: in *Lustra* of 1916, the colon became a semi-colon, perhaps through a proofreader's or printer's error, perhaps through authorial choice, but in either case, Pound did not change it in any subsequent printing. Chilton and Gilbertson read this change as a paradigmatic break with conventional narrative, aesthetic, and metaphorical continuities in poetry, and see it as marking a significant beginning for the fragmented structures of *Hugh Selwyn Mauberley* and the *Cantos*, and therefore read Pound's experiments with 'In a Station of the Metro' as an important part of his emergent modernist poetics. Reed Way Dasenbrock (*ELH* 58.215–32) reflects on Pound's omission of Petrarch from the line of great Italian poets, because of his dislike of the ornamental and decorative features of Petrarch's verse: Dasenbrock argues that the two poets share three important conditions, their activities as scholarly men of letters, whose letters and prose far exceed their verse in quantity, their mutual sense of belatedness, and their practice of imitation in their own poetry. Furthermore, Dasenbrock shows that the only Italian poet after Dante that Pound had any time for, Giacomo Leopardi (1778–1837) worked in an implied nationalist idiom to reinvigorate the native Italian lyric tradition, in which he included Petrarch, and which affirmed the *canzone* as the crucial form in Italian lyricism, rather than the sonnet. This leads Dasenbrock to propose that the *Cantos* should be read not as a failed epic, but as a sequence of lyric *canzone*, arranged into patterns of larger units. Readers of this section are likely to know of Reed Way Dasenbrock's book *Imitating The Italians: Wyatt, Spenser, Synge, Pound, Joyce*, and though I have not received it for review, this record of publications on Pound this year would be seriously incomplete without acknowledging the appearance of this well-received study of the Italian influence on English literary culture in relation to the concept of imitation, so crucial to Pound's poetics.

'Ezra Pound and the Politics of Patronage' by Cary Wolfe (*AL* 63.26–42) uses the 1937 essay 'The State' to investigate Pound's view of the desired social and economic organization which would allow the artist his due place in the social nexus: Wolfe finds Pound's views 'hopelessly naive', because dependent upon a perpetuation of an aristocracy of the capitalist rich whose interventions in the world of art would remain the consequence of personal choice, and would therefore be ethical in essence, rather than the product of necessary structures of economic change. A further dimension of Wolfe's argument invokes parallels between Pound's ideas of patronage and those of Emerson.

There are two welcome entries to record this year on the 'onlie begetter' of the San Francisco Renaissance, Kenneth Rexroth: Lee Bartlett's edition of *Kenneth Rexroth and James Laughlin Selected Letters*, and Linda Hamalian's definitive *A Life of Kenneth Rexroth*. Bartlett's edition gives some 350 letters and postcards written between 1937 and Rexroth's death in 1982, most of them by Rexroth, though there are enough from Laughlin here to give a sense of the mutuality of this relationship. The extraordinary range and passion of Rexroth's engagement with writing is fully expressed in these letters, which frequently remind one of Pound's epistolary style. Like Pound, the energy of his recommendations to Laughlin of writers he admired is equalled only by the vigour of his contempt for those he found wanting, as for example in a letter of 1955 recommending Denise Levertov, where he goes on: 'I honestly think you have been so conditioned by the good ole fort under the Stars & Bars run by Marse

Allen (Tate) & Con'l (J. C.) Ransom and been taken in by imposters like (Robert) Cal Lowell – who would never have been printed if his name warnt spelled el oh doubleyou ee el el – that you surely are inaccessible to poetry by young people.' Bartlett's annotations are genuinely impressive in the way they flesh out the details of references in these letters, and the informative documentation of contributors to Laughlin's annual anthologies of *New Directions in Prose and Poetry*, which began when Laughlin was still a student at Harvard, constitutes a small history of this enterprising venture to bring new and unorthodox writers to attention. This volume is part of the series which opened with Hugh Witemeyer's edition of the William Carlos Williams/Laughlin correspondence (*YWES* 71).

Linda Hamalian's biography of Rexroth is unflinching in its account of the turmoil of Rexroth's life, particularly in regard to his four marriages, and his volatile relationship not only to the American literary establishment as he conceived it, but also to the wide group of writers loosely gathered under his honorary leadership in San Francisco. Hamalian confesses that she set out with a romantic view of Rexroth as an impassioned seer, whose genius was its own justification for his legendary difficulties in human relations, a view she came to modify as she worked on this book, whilst remaining convinced of his capacity for wisdom, and the power of his 'trusting spirit'. Hamalian has thus developed a necessary scepticism in relation to her subject which allows her to document the history of his public and private life with a nice decorum, and the result is an enthralling book. This is a portrait of a fiercely intellectual man whose advocacy of revolt and the unorthodox was in the highest traditions of philosophical and literary heresy, and as with others in this tradition, found only in the physical world of nature the kind of abiding reassurance of permanence and value for which his spirit yearned.

The most publicized event of the year in Anne Sexton studies was the appearance of Diane Wood Middlebrook's *Anne Sexton: A Biography*, with a foreword by Dr Martin T. Orne, Sexton's principal psychiatrist from 1956 to 1964. Middlebrook's use of the audiotape records of Sexton's therapy sessions with Dr. Orne has occasioned much debate about the sanctity of the doctor-patient relationship, and this, along with the overtones of incestuous relations with her eldest daughter Linda, has ensured that this work has been received with a degree of notoriety quite at odds with the scholarly thoroughness of this sympathetic account of Sexton's life and art. One of the particular pleasures of this book is to read the history of Sexton's development as a poet, of her relations with her mentors and her peers, and the surety of her purpose once she had negotiated the realm of her private anxieties as an available source and occasion of many of her poems. This version of Sexton's life is likely to remain definitive for many years to come. Virago has also issued Middlebrook's and Diana Hume George's edition of *The Selected Poems of Anne Sexton*, first published in the USA in 1988: this generous selection includes poems from the posthumously published work, *The Awful Rowing Toward God* (1975), and the unrevised collections *45 Mercy Street* (1976), and *Words for Dr. Y.* (1978).

Tim Dean's *Gary Snyder and the American Unconscious* is a short bold book which adds significantly to the brief list of full-length studies of Snyder, and is to that extent welcome: however, Dean's interest in Snyder comes framed within a very ambitious programme, no less than a new theory of American culture, and one derived from Jacques Lacan's revision of psychoanalysis. Dean's justification for this approach lies in his acceptance of Lacan's writings on transference, and Lacan's emphasis on the 'language-based relationship between analyst and analysand' in which the analysand's relation to language is seen as the proper object of psychoanalytic inquiry: from this Dean argues for the congruity of literary and cultural criticism with Lacan's psychoanalytic practice. Hence, the use of the word 'Unconscious' in the title of this book, which signifies that in American culture which it has had to repress in order to constitute itself: in the simplest terms, what is repressed is the sense of the land itself, and the peoples who inhabited it prior to the establishment of the European settlements of the seventeenth century. From this a good deal of Dean's argument depends upon the forms of representation of American consciousness in which unconsciousness is 'the trace of representation's excess', that is, what it cannot contain yet which lies in support of 'a specifically American consciousness'. The first part of this book thus takes on the massive history of American 'representational paradigms' dwelling specifically on the emergence of American literary nationalism at the start of the nineteenth century, the image of the frontier, the mythification of the figure of the Indian, the West as the site of myth, Hollywood and the cinema as the twentieth-century site of myth's production, and later versions of literary nationalism. In the second part Dean focuses on Snyder, figured as the poet who 'provides a means toward recognizing the different America, the American Other' in which the traces of the repressed culture are lineated in his poetics. The valorization of Snyder in this study is both a rebuke to the many powerful voices in America who persist in ignoring or marginalizing him, and a confident claim for Snyder's true centrality to the issue of American consciousness as defined in this book.

The relationship of lyric poetry to the contingent and interactional sense of the self suggested by pragmatism is the subject of Margaret Dickie's *Lyric Contingencies: Emily Dickinson and Wallace Stevens*. It has to be said that not much is gained from the comparative nature of this study: the examination of topics such as letters is rewarding on Dickinson in linking her with the idea of the letter as 'token of contingency', but is too theoretically portentous on Stevens. Dickie cites as demonstrative of the 'intrinsic nature of the self and the world' for Stevens, a letter to Barbara Church, in which he wrote that, for him, cakes 'ought merely to be looked at', so he had given a cake to his grandson. It seems rather laboured to convert Stevens's joke about his weight and aesthetic propensities into 'willful(sic) repression' and 'metonymic organisation' of experience; this is representative of the way in which the book strives too hard for theoretical endorsement. The concept of lyric contingency as a poetic strategy is more successfully applied to Dickinson: her radical and fragmented sense of self is located in opposition to Emerson's need for representative public certitude; but the concept seems less valid when Dickie applies it to Stevens's longer poems such as 'The Comedian as the Letter C'. This poem is, after all, in the tradition of the narrative odyssey; however much the genre, or the modernist's adaptability to it, is ironized by Stevens, it is invoked. The value of this book is not in its *mélange* of theory, but in the issues of lyric voice and audience which are raised, and in the illustration of the teasing sense of intimacy yet occlusion which these two poets generate.

Alan Filreis in *Wallace Stevens and the Actual World* offers a much needed contextualization for Stevens's poetry primarily in the years 1939 to 1945, a useful complement to the letters of this period. He revalues Stevens's engagement with the war poem business and the cultural politics of its production, but, most significantly, he traces the effect of the *Mesures* connection. Stevens was a subscriber and contributor to the literary magazine run by Henry Church in Paris before the war. The fate of *Mesures* and its contributors became, for Stevens, an index of the survival of European culture. Jean Wahl, a *Mesures* writer and concentration camp survivor who escaped to America, invited Stevens to his Mount Holyoke Conference in 1943. Filreis's meticulous effort of historical recovery is at its finest in this section; he gets to the heart of the occasion and gives us the resonances of the address and the poetry which it inspired. The distinction of this book lies not only in its painstaking research, a veritable web of cross-reference, but also in its well-judged and never over-stated assessment of the degree and range of Stevens's concerns in this period.

Thomas C. Grey's *The Wallace Stevens Case: Law and the Practice of Poetry* aims to show legal scholars and theorists that Stevens as 'poetic *pragmatist* philosopher' acts as a 'therapist for the habitual and institutional rigidities of the binary thought' which characterize legal theory. For the general reader the poetry has something to teach us about our responses to idea-systems, in particular, the attraction of total explanations, the impulse towards absolutisms which William James acknowledged. Grey argues that Stevens's pragmatism is evident in his concern with cultural particularity, so that philosophically he emerges as a 'perspectivist' engaged in a 'luminous flittering' between binary opposites. Whether or not a 'luminous flittering' would be a valuable *modus operandi* for lawyers, Grey is suggestive on the thought processes of a poem like 'Connoisseur of Chaos': he gives us a Stevens whose practice in framing legalities informs the practice of his poetry.

In *Stevens and the Interpersonal*, Mark Halliday undertakes a moral critique of 'the man figured by the poetry' and contends that Stevens fails to deal with human suffering, women and the sheer presence of others. It is a well-intentioned, but self-defeating enterprise, more useful in unwittingly identifying the pitfalls and parameters of moral criticism than as a critique of Stevens. Indeed this is tacitly acknowledged in the extensive comparisons with other poets, which become reduced at times to drawing up lists of morally acceptable poems. Much of the discussion turns on the moral significance of specificity as opposed to generality and abstraction; Halliday has a Leavisite predilection for the 'felt life' of specificity. It is valuable to question the quasi-religious exaltation and abstraction of high modernism, but it requires contextualization, on which Halliday is erratic and simplistic. This is not a consistent book, but it is disarmingly open, stubborn, human and demanding.

James Longenbach's *Wallace Stevens: The Plain Sense of Things* stands with Filreis as a key contextualization, seeking an economic and political provenance for the poems. Longenbach contends that Stevens should not be read through the lens of the 1947 to 1954 period, but via the insecurity of the early years as a journalist and law student with the ephebe attracted both to Santayana, the aesthete of independent means, and to John Jay Chapman, the literary journalist, as possible role models. Stevens's own solution, professional vocation and artistic vacation, was confirmed by the Depression years; he needed to feel in charge of his economic destiny in order to write, but in the political realm he felt that the poet must *resist* contemporary pressures towards ideological certainty. Longenbach's readings of the poems of the 1930s and 1940s are informed by his understanding of how this resistance infiltrates Stevens's aesthetic and shapes his distrust of 'the self's power to grant its own machinations the status of fate'. In politics, as in his own psychic economy, Stevens required checks, balances and deferrals. Longenbach argues that Stevens, in his interrogation of 'major man', deconstructs his own high romantic tendencies in favour of 'medium man'. This emphasis is occasionally over-corrective, immune, for example, to the sheer euphoria of 'Sea Surface Full of Clouds', and too wary of the late poems, and there are some omissions – no mention of Jean Paulhan or Jean Wahl in the 1940s. However, this is a brilliant historicizing of Stevens through the Depression and the two world wars. Filreis and Longenbach, together, have relocated Stevens.

In *Wallace Stevens: 'Harmonium' and 'The Whole of Harmonium'*, Kia Penso seeks to remind us of some of the poems of *Harmonium*, such as 'Sunday Morning' and 'The Comedian as the letter C,' as works of full accomplishment in their own right, and not as anticipations of Stevens's later poems: the essence of her argument is that the questions Stevens posed in these poems are not significantly 'developed' in the later poems, but reiterated, and she therefore argues for *Harmonium* as sufficient evidence in itself of all the important questions Stevens will address throughout his career. She is antagonistic to some of the most celebrated of Stevens's commentators for their 'misrepresentations' of his endeavour, and equally dislikes recent attempts to narrate the poet's life in a way that might further illuminate our reading of his poems, and appears to hold to an extreme formalist view that the poems and the life are entirely separate, and that the one barely informs the other. I do not see why anyone should feel embarrassed to admit that 'Sunday Morning' is a major Stevens poem: to propose that the issue stops there is, however, another matter.

In what ways is it possible to write of Wallace Stevens as a war poet? This question, or variants on it, has come to engage an increasing number of critics in recent years, and Rita Barnard's essay ' "The Bread of Faithful Speech": Wallace Stevens, Ideology, and War' (*ELWIU* 18.69–75) adds eloquently to this body of commentary. Barnard sees Stevens's use of images of food in the war poems as his way of constantly asking to what extent the poet is 'permitted to make reality *palatable*?', and cites 'Dry Loaf' as evidence of Stevens's symbolic advocacy of 'the only nourishment it is decent to offer in a "tragic time" '. Barnard relates this and other food images to the issues of taste and aesthetic satisfaction they raise, and finds Stevens's advice to develop a taste for 'dry description' a valuable 'plain recipe' in these war poems. S. D. Brint contributes 'A Necessary Distance: Wallace Stevens: The Epigram and the Play' (*DUR* 83.85–90). Eleanor Cook (*EIC* 41.240–52) illustrates Stevens's intimacy with the King James Bible, and explores the strategies of biblical allusion in Stevens in general, and particularly in the seventh canto of 'The Auroras of Autumn'. Cook argues that the density of biblical allusion and verbal play in the three 'heavens' held to view through Stevens's questions in this canto reflects a schematic pattern of assimilation, punning repudiation, and a desired retrieval of our inheritance of the past in the turns these questions enact, turns which may also be read as indicative of the ways criticism has dealt with Stevens, from the new critics, through deconstruction, to the present state of critical engagement with Stevens's work and the questions it asks. Stephen Dunn writes on 'Poetry and Music' with reference to Stevens in (*MAR* 11.226–9). In 'Seeing Through the Woman in Wallace Stevens's *Notes Toward a Supreme Fiction*' (*ConL* 31.208–26), Barbara L. Estrin expands upon Frank Lentricchia's argument in *Ariel and the Police* that the 'you' in the first half of the introductory poem to *Notes* is the poet's significant other, a 'she' who becomes fused with the 'I' of the poem in 'a self-sustaining bi-sexual unit'. Estrin argues that the woman in the poem is 'an argumentative critic who reacts to the poet's progress by questioning it and who challenges his artistic chauvinism by sensitizing him to another ethos – hers', thus fulfilling the Ovidian vision of *genus* difference at the end of the poem. Allen Hibbard writes on 'Teaching "Anecdote of a Jar" ' in (*TenEJ* 2.25–7). Maureen T. Kravec's focus on *Bowl, Cat and Broomstick* in 'Sweeping the Stage of Souvenirs' (*TCL* 37.309–21), sees this last attempt at playwriting by Stevens as a sustained critique of his own early poetry and the state of contemporary poetry in the second decade of this century. Kravec shows that if the model for this play was Dryden's *An Essay of Dramatick Poesie*, Stevens's principle concern here was to distance himself from the influence of 1890s decadent aestheticism. George S. Lensing contributes an essay on 'The Early Readers of Wallace Stevens' in *Order in*

Variety: Essays and Poems in Honor of Donald E. Stanford, edited by R. W. Crump, and Albert Montesi has an essay on 'Joyce's "Blue Guitar": Wallace Stevens and *Finnegans Wake*' in *James Joyce's Finnegans Wake: A Casebook*, edited by John Harty, III. Jahan Ramazani has an essay on 'Stevens and the Self-Elegy: Making Alpha of Omega' in (*ELWIU* 18.93–105) which I have not yet seen, and in a signal contribution, Wallace Stevens's 'Letters to Ferdinand Reyher' are edited with an after-note by Holly Stevens (*HudR* 44.381–409): Michael Trammell writes on 'Stevens's "The Planet on the Table" ' in (*Expl* (1991).112–14). This may be an idle note, but I record here that the *WSJour*'s current bibliography lists ten doctoral dissertations on Stevens for the years 1990 and 1991; further evidence, if it were needed, of the interest in Stevens which survives throughout the American academy.

The Spring issue of *WSJour* opens with C. Roland Wagner's argument for the creative and experiential affinity between Stevens and Proust in an essay which ultimately turns on the conflict between aesthetic accomplishment and sexual failure in these writers (15.3–23): the local evidence of their 'shared vision' is traced in Stevens's echo of Proust in the line from 'Notes toward a Supreme Fiction' – 'A bench was his catalepsy', in Wagner's reading, a citing of the notion of catalepsy he sees as crucial to Swann's emotional development in Proust's novel. The exploration of the significance of the cataleptic trance in Proust and Stevens is more persuasive than Wagner's final view that Proust overcame the limitations of his sexual identity through the 'marvelous unanxious vision of perfection' which his novel gives, whilst Stevens remained trapped in the conflict between sexual desire and impoverishment and failed to 'create a lasting ideal self from which all human experience is viewed.' In 'Stevens and the War Elegy' (15.24–36), Jahan Ramazani argues that the 'fictive hero and the fictive mother' are the primary sources of consolation in Stevens's war elegies, figures who have their prototypes in the parents 'who both occasion one's earliest fears of loss and also help defend against such feelings'. By an odd coincidence, Elisabeth A. Frost's 'Revision of Romanticism in "Notes toward a Supreme Fiction" ' (15.37–54) ends by citing the passage from 'Notes' which Roland Wagner takes as his point of departure: Frost's interest here is not the evidence of Proust in the poem, but of Shelley, and Stevens's revisions of the romantic concept of 'inspiration' in this account of the self-sufficiency of the creative fiction for Stevens. In 'Stevens and Byron on Verrocchio's Colleoni', (15.55–66), D. L. Macdonald compares the ambiguous uses made of Verrocchio's equestrian statue by Stevens in 'The Noble Rider and the Sound of Words', and some few poems, and Byron's historical tragedy *Marino Faliero, Doge of Venice*. Finally in this issue, David R. Jarraway uses 'Credences of Summer' and 'The Auroras of Autumn' (15.67–93) to debate the theoretical reformulations of the agency of metaphor in Stevens, especially as these relate to issues of language and belief in Stevens's late work. The Fall issue of *WSJour*, guest-edited by Jacqueline V. Brogan, gives us a clutch of essays under the general heading of 'Stevens And Structures of Sound', which variously investigate 'the purpose of Stevens' prosody, the meaning of his music', as Sebastian D. G. Knowles puts it in the foreword to this issue. This collection is introduced by Eleanor Cook (15.115–25), followed by Diane Wakoski's brief commentary on the impact of Stevens's prosody on her own poetry, an account of the caesura in Stevens by N. M. Hoffman (15.144–64), repetition in Stevens by Mary Doyle Springer (15.191–208), and the 'apparitional' metres of Stevens by Dennis Taylor (15.209–28). Margaret Dickie writes on the relation of nonsense words and sense in Stevens (15.133–43), Alison Rieke on Stevens's use of foreign words and phrases from a variety of linguistic sources other than contemporary American (15.165–77), and Anca Rosu writes of

'Images of Sound' in Stevens (15.178–90) to explore the way Stevens 'discredits' the traditional oppositions between sound and sense, meaning and meaninglessness in order 'to lay bare the alternative domain of reality that otherwise remains perpetually veiled by all logics of representation or systems of signification as such.'

Jean Toomer's Years With Gurdjieff by Rudolph P. Byrd goes a considerable way towards answering the question, what happened to Toomer after the publication of *Cane* in 1923, and why was the promise of this early work never fulfilled in Toomer's later career? The answer appears to be that Toomer found a life-sustaining practical and spiritual consolation in the teachings of the Russian mystic George I. Gurdjieff. Toomer spent three months at Gurdjieff's 'Institute for the Harmonious Development of Man' at the le Prieuré estate near Fontainebleau in 1924, and on his return to the USA, worked for the next twelve years at disseminating Gurdjieff's theories to study groups in New York, Chicago, Wisconsin and Pennsylvania. Indeed, he set up two experiments in communal living on the model of le Prieuré, the first at Witt Cottage near Briggsville, Wisconsin in 1931, and then at Mill House, Doylestown, Pennsylvania, which survived from 1936 to 1940. Though this period was one of intense creative productivity for Toomer in terms of novels, plays, poems and essays written, little of this material was ever published, and the more committed he became to the furthering of Gurdjieff's ideas of harmonious development, the less he seemed to speak to his contemporaries. Byrd's account of this history of a writer's fatal attachment to a universalizing programme of improvement is well researched and ably documented, and gives a broader view of Toomer's life than we have had so far.

'Sumptuousness is much more prominent in Wilbur's work than destitution, but both elements can be seen there': this summary view from Richard Ellmann and Robert O'Clair's account of Wilbur in the 1973 edition of the *Norton Anthology of American Poetry* is the kind of damning with faint praise explicitly engaged with by Bruce Michelson in his *Wilbur's Poetry: Music in a Scattering Time*, the first full-length study of Wilbur for twenty-five years. Almost casually, Michelson observes early on that Wilbur is a 'darker, more complex, passionate, and original poet than reviewers and sum-up essays about postwar poetry usually make him out to be, a serious artist for an anxious century'. The strength of Michelson's argument thus depends on how well he makes the case for this darker side of Wilbur, and there is something about Michelson's relaxed, even tentative, tone of voice which partly militates against the authority of his readings: yet Michelson's prose is stylish, graceful, reflective, and accomplishes the difficult task of taking serious things seriously without claiming too much for them. At the same time, his argument that Wilbur has much to teach us about the relationship between complexity and intensity is ably demonstrated throughout this book which constitutes the most engaged reading of the entirety of Wilbur's work, including the translations, that we have.

Terence Diggory's *William Carlos Williams and the Ethics of Painting* disputes the poststructuralist and deconstructive readings of Williams by J. Hillis Miller and Joseph Riddel primarily through an analysis of Williams's use of Peter Brueghel's painting 'The Adoration of the Kings', though Diggory's reference to Williams's poetry, and to other works of visual art extend well beyond these parameters. This short, difficult book questions the conditions of violence held to be inseparable from writing, in Foucault and Derrida for example, and looks to the art of painting to discover 'a critical practice that successfully resists violence'. Further, Diggory turns to Julia Kristeva's psychoanalytic and linguistic model of an ethical imperative he holds to be close to Williams in his investigation of the structure of relationships explored in 'The Adoration of the Kings', especially that which admits Brueghel as an interpretive figure in the painting. Diggory argues with deconstruction's 'inability to conceive of an intersubjective relation that is not a violent struggle for possession', by turning from questions of epistemology to questions of ethics, especially as that notion of ethics is informed by Kristeva's view that possession in any form is, if not finally erased, 'continually displaced by an opposing force', the dynamics of which she calls love. Finally, Diggory wishes to see Williams's concern with this painting as a way of formulating his ideas about the relations between reader and text, self and other, viewer and object, and therefore, ultimately, about the ethics and conditions of being and otherness, to which the poem, like the painting, is witness.

Anne W. Fisher-Wirth takes a different marriage as her focus in ' "A Rose to the End of Time": William Carlos Williams and Marriage' (*TCL* 36.155–72), that between Williams and his wife Flossie. Fisher-Wirth moves through a variety of occasions on which Williams wrote of his marriage, from the early imagist poem simply called 'Marriage', through 'Love Song', 'Queen-Anne's Lace', and the sustained elegaic tones of 'Asphodel, That Greeey Flower', to 'To Be Recited to Flossie on Her Birthday', in an eloquent account of Williams's love poems to his wife, noting that in a plangent and ultimately moving sense, Williams repeatedly honours her 'less for what she is in herself than for what she enables him to be'.

Of the two articles in the Spring issue of *WCWR*, Zhaoming Qian's account of Williams's interest in Chinese poetry between 1918 and 1921 (17:i.1–19) is of most value. Qian writes of the impact on Williams of the Tang dynasty poet Po Chu-i, traced here through Arthur Waley's *A Hundred and Seventy Chinese Poems and More Translations from the Chinese* published in 1918 and 1919: the crux of Qian's argument is that Williams found a poetic model in Po Chu-i's 'occasional' poems, where the Chinese poet's rendering of mood and momentary instances of perception is achieved through the clarity of his visual images shaped into formal control, and Qian sees Williams's 1921 volume *Sour Grapes* as particularly indebted to the influence of Po Chu-i. The Fall issue of *WCWR* is the last issue under the editorship of Peter Schmidt, who is to be succeeded in 1993 by Brian Bremen of the University of Texas at Austin. To mark his retirement from this office Peter Schmidt reprints Williams's 'Letter to an Australian Editor' of 1946 (17:ii.8–12), with an introductory commentary in which Schmidt argues for this piece as providing the 'gists of just about all of Williams' central ideas about art and society and New World writing ...' (17:ii.4–7). Also in this issue John Palattella writes on the troublesome relationship between gender and writing in *Kora in Hell* and 'Three Professional Studies' (17:ii.13–38), whilst Anne L. Bower anatomizes the quasi-fictional nature of *A Voyage to Pagany* (17:ii.39–51); George Monteiro's brief discussion of 'Old Doc Rivers' (17:ii.52–8) has some interesting points to make about the transition from horses to automobiles in this disputatious reading of Williams's short story which nicely accounts for its abrupt conclusion. This is an appropriate point to register the reissue of Joseph N. Riddel's *The Inverted Bell, Modernism and the Counterpoetics of William Carlos Williams*, originally published in 1974, and now available in paperback with a new postcript by the author.

In my survey of this field last year it was not uncommon to find James Wright singled out as a type of late Romantic solipsist who did not speak adequately to the significant issues of his time. Andrew Elkins would be unperturbed by these charges, for in his book *The Poetry of James Wright*, he sees all Wright's poetry as 'really one epic poem, a continuing quest, like Wordsworth's *Prelude*, for the poet's self, his identity', in which Wright seeks 'that pure self somehow beneath or beyond the taint of the culture's guilt'. Indeed, Elkins argues for Wright's final two books as the best examples in recent American poetry of an 'open-eyed affirmation of self, history, and culture' . Elkins, who won the 1989 Elizabeth Age Prize in American Literature for this book, reads the changes and renewals in Wright's forms as markers of his relationship to his poetic precursors and contemporaries, and as ways of realizing his place in the conflict between the demands of self and those of community in his later work. This is a judiciously balanced commentary, written in a fluent conversational idiom which I found very persuasive.

This year marks the appearance of a handsome edition of Louis Zukofsky's *Complete Short Poetry*, a gathering of all the poems other than '*A*'. It opens with a lyric of 1922, 'I Sent Thee Late', a remarkable performance written when he was 18, announcing a manner which became his characteristic in the short poem, a densely abbreviated utterance where word impacts upon word, and the scale of observation moves from the epic motion of the sea to a particular wave, and requires the title to signal the intervention of the human in which the archaic 'Thee' registers his sense of the lyric tradition of oblique love poetry. This collection, introduced in a foreword by Robert Creeley, includes the version of Catullus done with Celia Zukofsky, and includes *80 Flowers* (*YWES* 71), otherwise only available in a limited edition. It is perhaps a little surprising that this edition comes without any scholarly or critical apparatus.

2. Fiction Since 1945

(a) General

Postmodernism and Contemporary Fiction, edited by Edmund J. Smyth, comprises two parts: the first is concerned with postmodernist fiction in various national contexts and the second addresses general themes and issues. It is in part two, 'The Critical Agenda', that Linda Hutcheon discusses 'Discourse, Power, Ideology: Humanism and Postmodernism'; Hans Bertens considers the issue of postmodernist cultures; John Mepham attempts to discover what is postmodernist about postmodernism; Dina Sherzer considers the relationship between feminism and postmodernism; and Thomas Docherty discusses the fate of characterization in postmodernist fiction. In part one, David Seed offers an incisive account of postmodernist fiction in America, 'In Pursuit of the Receeding Plot: Some American Postmodernists', on Ronald Sukenick, Raymond Federman, Rudolph Wurlitzer, Tom Robbins, John Barth, and Thomas Pynchon. The postmodernist credentials of these writers include a common indebtedness to Beckett, Nabokov and Borges or, within the American tradition, Kerouac; they all started writing during the sixties; they all share a common self-consciousness about the nature of narrative and of plotting in particular; and their work can be described as being, in one way or another, metafictional. This is a lucid and engaging discussion of a contentious subject.

Though Douglas Tallack does not discuss postmodernist fiction in his book *Twentieth-Century America: The Intellectual and Cultural Context*, his discussion of postmodernity as a cultural concept provides a concise and very clear introduction to postmodernism as a central term in contemporary critical discourse and is a valuable background for anyone interested in contextualizing postmodernist fiction.

Fred Hobson investigates the response of contemporary southern writers to trends in recent southern history in *The Southern Writer in the Postmodern World*. As he writes:'The decade of the sixties ... might be seen as pivotal in southern life and letters in much the same way the 1920s was: it was a time of numerous southern crimes against humanity, of notable attention and criticism from without, of great intellectual ferment. … After the 1960s, it appeared that the South had endured its crisis, had triumphed over itself, had in fact come through. … What was the writer of the seventies and eighties to do with a suddenly Superior South, optimistic, forward-looking, more virtuous and now threatening to become more prosperous than the rest of the country? Success would require a new voice – and less reliance on the models of the past'. In the discussions that follow, Hobson looks at how various writers have responded to this challenge. These new voices articulate the experience of a non-agrarian Sun Belt South but they echo certain attitudes, values, and fictional techniques of an earlier body of southern fiction, in Hobson's account. Fred Chappell and Earnest Gaines are seen to be concerned with traditional southern subjects; Richard Ford and Josephine Humphreys are shown to possess a common indebtedness to Walker Percy; and those writers like Bobbie Ann Mason, Barry Hannah and Lee Smith who write about the incursions of popular commercial culture are equally concerned with the traditionally organized community and family-based culture that is threatened by the new. Hobson calls his book a 'preliminary estimate' of these writers, but his study points to fruitful new directions in criticism of this second southern literary Renascence.

Paul Maltby's *Dissident Postmodernists: Barthelme, Coover, Pynchon* is the latest volume in the Penn Studies in Contemporary American Fiction series. *Dissident* postmodernists (though it is difficult to imagine any other kind of postmodernist) are, according to Maltby, those who take what could be called a deconstructive political stance. Where postmodernist fiction is characterized by its self-reflexivity and metafictional concerns, the work of dissident postmodernists uses 'devices which work to fracture the logic of hegemonic codes'. Unfortunately, this book is riddled with phrases such as this which border on the impenetrable and create the impression that the book is trying to say more than it is. Actually, what Maltby has done is to compound the formalistic elements of postmodernism (which have been subject to New Historicist attack) with a definition of the political that rests crucially upon the identification of ideological codes or discourses. So Maltby can analyse the discursive nature of his chosen dissidents and call this analysis political critique. These relationships are set out in two introductory chapters, 'Constructions of Postmodernism' and 'Language and Late Capitalism'. Though he choses to take the long way around to his central point, it is a point well worth making and the readings of his selected dissident texts at times produce useful insights.

The essays gathered in Huck Gutman's collection, *As Others Read Us: International Perspectives on American Literature*, give account of the status of American cultural studies generally in a number of different countries both in the West and in the East. As such, this book provides an insight into the conditions of reception existing for contemporary writing in the world at large and makes interesting contextual reading for critics of recent fiction. Gutman's book draws attention to the Otherness of American writing for readers outside the United States; writing about the ethnic literatures of the United States focuses upon the Other within.

David Murray's *Forked Tongue: Speech, Writing and Representation in North American Indian Texts* includes discussion of some of the best known of recent Native American fiction writers: Leslie Marmon Silko, James Welch, N. Scott Momaday, and D'Arcy McNickle. Murray's primary interest is in the way representations of Native American Indians serve ideological functions in the wider culture. He addresses the question of translation both as a cultural problematic and a linguistic issue, drawing attention to the fact that the necessary activity of translation is often effaced in representations of Indians. By focusing on the idea of mediation, Murray is able to avoid the danger of exaggerating ethnic differences into absolute Otherness. He identifies what he calls two opposed 'mythical moments of encounter': 'the meeting with untouched and unknowable otherness, beyond the reach of language; and the rapport of unproblematic translatability, and of transparency of language'. Together, these mythic moments constitute a 'discourse of Indianness' which Murray seeks to place by investigating their relation to assumptions about language and nature, and the relation of speech to writing. Murray brings to bear the insights of his reading in contemporary critical and cultural theory so the guiding principles of this study emerge from Said and Foucault, White and Bakhtin. It is refreshing and stimulating to see a keen critical intelligence bringing theory to the field of Native American writing, contributing to the scholarly sophistication that is coming increasingly to characterize this area. Laura Coltelli's excellent collection of interviews, *Winged Words: American Indian Writers Speak*, reviewed in *YWES*, has been reissued as a more reasonably priced paperback.

Two books devoted to Chicano writing have appeared in the DukeUP Post-Contemporary Interventions series: *The Dialectics of our America: Genealogy, Cultural Critique, and Literary History* by José David Saldivar and *Criticism in the Borderlands: Studies in Chicano Literature, Culture, and Ideology*, edited by Hector Calderon and Jose David Saldivar. *Criticism in the Borderlands* is divided into four sections: 'Institutional Studies and the Literary Canon'; Representations of the Chicana/o Subject: Race, Class, and Gender'; 'Genre, Ideology, and History'; and 'Aesthetics of the Border'. The volume concludes with an extremely helpful selected and annotated bibliography of contemporary Chicano criticism which serves as a guide for further and more specialized study. Such a guide is needed for, as Rolando Hinojosa points out in his foreword, Chicano literary study has been lagging behind African American, Native American and Asian American writing in terms of institutional support and academic acceptance, though these forms of legitimation have been slow coming to all minority cultural groups. It is still too easy to overlook the substantial and growing field of Chicano literature and criticism. This volume argues for a Chicano perspective upon the literary history of the Southwest, 'a positive, yet also critical, rendering of [Chicano] bilingual and bicultural experience as a resistive measure against Anglo-American economic domination and ideological hegemony', and for a view of Chicano theory as a sophisticated, diverse and challenging body of work. In the first section, Ramon Saldivar discusses narrative forms, ideology and the reconstruction of American literary history; Luis Leal considers the rewriting of American literary history; and Norma Alarcon analyses the construction of subject positions by Anglo-American feminism and the women-of-colour feminisms represented in the 1983 collection *This Bridge Called My Back: Writings by Radical Women of Color* edited by Chicana writers Cherrie Moraga and Gloria Anzaldua. Genaro Padilla treats New Mexico women's autobiography in his contribution to the discussion of representations of the Chicano subject; Elizabeth J. Ordonez discusses Alma Villanueva's *Life Span*; Ana Castillo's *The Mixquiahuala Letters* and the issue of ethnography is the subject of Alvina E. Quintana's essay; and Renato Rosaldo discusses recent short story cycles by Sandra Cisneros, Denise Chavez and Alberto Rios. In the third section, dealing with literary genre and history, Hector Calderon considers the novel and the community of readers; Rosaura Sanchez analyses ideological discourses in Arturo Islas's *The Rain God*; Angie Chabram discusses Chicano critical discourse; and Barbara Harlow writes of immigration, deportation, prison and exile in Chicano experience. The concluding section features José David Saldivar's analysis of Chicano border narratives as a form of cultural critique; Teresa McKenna's discussion of Chicano poetry and the political context; Sonia Saldivar-Hull's consideration of the role of feminism in border politics; and José E. Limon's essay on society, gender and the political unconscious of the Mexican-American South.

The title of José David Saldivar's *The Dialectics of Our America* refers to his perception of the cultural interdependence of the first and third worlds, the southern and northern hemispheres, Latin and Anglo America. In this book he claims to chart 'an array of oppositional critical and creative processes that aim to articulate a new, trans-geographical conception of American culture – one more politically responsive to the hemisphere's geographical ties and political crosscurrents than to narrow national ideologies'. To this end, he contributes a discussion of relatively unknown Cuban, Afro-Caribbean, African American and Chicano texts, incuding those by Jose Marti, Roberto Fernandez Retamar, Gabriel Garcia Marquez, Rolando Hinojosa, Arturo Islas, and Ntozake Shange. This discussion is seen as part of the development of a new line of comparative American studies which builds upon the question: Do the Americas have a common heritage? By redirecting the Eurocentric focus of earlier American literary criticism, Saldivar identifies a distinctive 'postcolonial, pan-American consciousness'.

Rudolpho A. Anaya and Francisco Lomeli have edited a collection of essays, *Aztlan: Essays on the Chicano Homeland*, which begins with an account of the mythical, cultural, and political significance of Aztlan for the Chicano movement of the sixties and for Chicano ethnicity generally, including a transcript of 'El Plan Espiritual de Aztlan'. The volume presents articles published over a twenty-year period, thus bringing together in one place the diverse ideological interpretations that Chicano writers and scholars have given this legendary origin of the Aztecs as a symbol for political action, the focus of nostalgia, or as a pan-American challenge. The primary aim of the book is 'to give shape to the topic of homeland as a viable way to delineate a culture's trajectory and existence'. The essays combine anthropological and historical studies, comparative cultural analyses, and symbolic literary treatments of this mythical symbol. Among those essays of literary interest, Luis Leal discusses Aztlan as symptomatic of the inseparability of Chicano literary symbolism and Chicano cultural background, with Rudolpho Anaya's *Heart of Aztlan* among the representative texts; Genaro M. Padilla considers the role of Chicano writers like Anaya, Rivera, Valdez, and Alurista as 'guardians of their people's culture and singers of its theme'; Alurista offers a discussion of three Chicano novels: *Pilgrims of Aztlan* by Miguel Mendez, *The Revolt of the Cockroach People* by Oscar Z. Acosta, and *Heart of Aztlan* by Rudolpho Anaya; and in conclusion Anaya sets out his thoughts about 'Aztlan: A Homeland with our Borders'.

Houston A. Baker Jnr's *Workings of the Spirit: The Poetics of Afro-American Women's Writing* includes a 'phototext' by Elizabeth Alexander and Patricia Redmond which underlines Baker's central argument for a 'theoretical return' to 'Afro-America's vernacular and characteristically autobiographical expressions'. This photo-essay of black women from the thirties and forties is, as Baker describes it, 'a visualization of Afro-American women's poetics. ... Eyes and events engage the reader/viewer in a solicitous order of discourse that asks: 'Who reads here?' Baker focuses upon black women's writing – Zora Neale Hurston, Toni Morrison and Ntozake Shange – because of his perception that 'Afro-American women's expressivity and the analyses it has prompted during the past two decades represent the most dramatically charged field for the convergence of matters of race, class, and gender today.' He starts from the awareness of resistance to theory within this area that appears to demand theorizing to argue that theory is inescapable, that it is always already with us all. Baker then teases out the specifics of this persistent theory which characterizes Afro-American intellectual history, and which is preoccupied with 'nonmaterial transactions and spiritual workings'. This study completes Baker's critical trilogy, which began with *Modernism and the Harlem Renaissance* and was followed by *Afro-American Poetics: Revisions of Harlem and the Black Aesthetic*, and completes the argument developed there of the inevitability of theory and the 'spirit work' of Afro-American expressive culture by applying these ideas to the work of Afro-American writers and critics.

Richard Kostelanetz's *American Writing Today* is a very substantial volume which represents a comprehensive critical survey of American writing of the past forty years and incorporates a very useful narrative bibliography of titles concerned with the period as a whole, as well as short bibliographies of selected titles and selected criticism for each author. The essays are based on a series of fifty broadcasts that were produced for Voice of America in 1980 and they combine crtitical commentary with discussions by writers of their own work. Among the contemporary writers who talk about themselves are Leslie A. Fiedler and William S. Burroughs, others like Allen Ginsberg contribute definitive transcripts of interviews; Ihab Hassan discusses Saul Bellow, Jerome Klinkowitz discusses John Updike and John Barth, Joseph Slade discusses Thomas Pynchon; there are essays on Malamud, Baldwin, Heller, Kerouac, Nabokov, Ellison, Henry Miller and others; Samuel R. Delaney contributes an essay on science fiction, Bruce-Novoa an essay on Spanish-American writing, Sharon Spencer one on feminist literature and criticism, and Dick Higgins an essay on small presses. Also included are transcripts of symposia moderated by Kostelanetz on topics such as literary translation, short story writing, literary criticism, literature written in America in languages other than English, writing and performance, and book art. This is a valuable survey that will be of assistance to students and scholars alike.

From Puritanism to Postmodernism: A History of American Literature, by Richard Ruland and Malcolm Bradbury, includes a substantial account of postwar American fiction in a narrative history of American writing since the early seventeenth century. Some attempt is made to describe the 'intellectual life' of the period as a context for the writing in comments like: 'The postwar world, the cultural drive toward what has become known as the postmodern, can be viewed as opposed responses to the challenge of heterodoxy.' This is a competent account of postwar writing; all the names one would expect to find are represented here. While we are not told very much about any single author or movement, this is a useful overview for students coming to contemporary writing for the first time. This book will provide a helpful guide and introduction, assisting students to form a mental topography of the writers of the past half-century.

Julius Rowan Raper's study, *Narcissus from the Rubble: Competing Models of Character in Contemporary British and American Fiction*, investigates the influence of phenomenology and psychoanalysis upon the writing of fiction in the latter half of the twentieth century. Most of the writers with whom he deals are American: Bellow, Pynchon, Kosinski, Barth, though he does discuss John Fowles and Lawrence Durrell as well. Raper analyses the part played by each of these models of human behaviour in the creation of contemporary fictional characters, looking at the conditions that prescribe and govern the relationships between characters and material reality. These two models are seen to be fundamentally incompatible, despite efforts to bring them together. Raper shows how this incompatibility has been dramatized by some contemporary novelists. One of Raper's most significant points concerns the ironic contrast between the perceptions of literary theorists who continue to employ critical concepts that are indebted to phenomenological thinking, and novelists who are concerned to show the alienation, fragmentation and compulsiveness that can follow from a phenomenological model of behaviour. Raper's treatment of individual novelists is described below.

Arnold Goldsmith's approach to contemporary fiction in *The Modern American Urban Novel: Nature as 'Interior Structure'* is essentially formalistic, even New Critical. Goldsmith uses the term 'interior structure' to refer to an interweaving of textual elements such as physical description, setting, characterization, symbolism, imagery and theme. This 'well wrought' structure of interweaving produces an interior form or structure that supports the external narrative. According to Goldsmith's analyses of seven modern novels, including *The Dollmaker*, *The Assistant*, *The Pawnbroker*, and *Mr Sammler's Planet*, nature is an integral part of the setting, language, symbolism and characterization of these narratives. Nature is taken in the Emersonian sense to mean 'essences unchanged by man'. The interplay of personality and the natural world, and the creative tension that can be generated between the mechanized, commercial or urban and the natural with its Arcadian echoes can be used for diverse purposes: to inspire a symbolic vocabulary, to express moods and feelings, to reinforce theme, to delineate character, to generate social criticism through satirical contrasts, to bridge urban realities and a world of dreams and fantasies, to provide a mythic substructure, and as a source of humour. Goldsmith is certainly comprehensive in his investigation of the uses served by nature in modern urban fiction and his study draws attention to an important yet neglected area of critical concern.

Larry McCaffery's *Across the Wounded Galaxies: Interviews with Contemporary American Science Fiction Writers* has appeared in paperback. McCaffery has interviewed Gregory Benford, William S. Burroughs, Octavia Butler, Samuel Delaney, Thomas Disch, William Gibson, Ursula Le Guin, Joanna Russ, Bruce Stirling, and Gene Wolfe. The volume as a whole reflects McCaffery's view that science fiction warrants serious critical attention and that the concerns of science fiction writers are central to late twentieth-century culture. His introduction draws our attention to the diverse and eclectic nature of contemporary science fiction, 'a genre that draws its inspiration from Lou Reed and Karl Marx, Dada and Derrida, Wrestlemania and Heisenberg, Pac-Man and punk, as well as Asimov and Heinlein'. Conversely, features of earlier science fiction seem now to have become part of everyday life: space shuttles and gene-splicing, computer viruses and organ harvesting, ozone holes and artificial intelligence – all would seem to threaten the traditional domain of science fiction and to challenge the creative resources of the science fiction writer. Here, science fiction emerges as an exemplar of postmodernism. McCaffery raises these issues with the authors he interviews. His approach to the interviews is to create a context within which writers can talk about their work, their backgrounds, their poetics; common or divergent goals, methods, themes and the genre as a whole are also discussed. The selection of writers was determined partly by personal taste, McCaffery admits, but more importantly by the desire to represent the views of those who have had a decisive impact upon the development of American science fiction during the past twenty-five years. By seeking writers whose innovations in terms of both form and subject have shaped the genre, McCaffery has bypassed more conservative writers and focused upon those whose concerns overlap to some extent with those of their postmodernist contemporaries. Among the most valuable aspects of this volume is McCaffery's introduction which provides one of the best discussions of the nature of contemporary science fiction available.

What is left for a writer to do when the content of representation collapses into a kind of aesthetic black hole? This is the issue confronted by Jerome Klinkowitz in *Structuring the Void: The Struggle for Subject in Contemporary American Fiction*. Like abstract painters and death-of-God theologians, contemporary writers face the absence of their subject. For writers, this dilemma is complicated by the referential nature of the language that is their medium, but from the deconstructive philosophy of language has come a 'comprehension of system rather than substance', of expression rather than representation, that has motivated recent fiction writing as 'a structuring act that becomes its own reality'. In retrospect, Klinkowitz argues, the influential writers of the 1960s like Brautigan, Reed, Sukenick and Vonnegut were not interested in 'prescriptions for new social, political, and behavioral structures but ... acts of nonreferential structurings themselves'. In an introductory chapter Klinkowitz considers the legacy of these writers in the work of Stephen Dixon, Grace Paley, Thomas McGuane, and Walter Abish. The typical metafictionist of the sixties for Klinkowitz is, however, Kurt Vonnegut and it is with an extended consideration of Vonnegut's self-referential structuring techniques as they are applied to autobiography that this study begins. Klinkowitz then goes on to consider writers of the generation following Vonnegut and their deployment of the structuring powers of such self-made systems as the ritual of national history and popular culture (Max Apple); comedy, game and play (Gerald Rosen and Rob Swigart); such determinants as gender (Grace Paley), and war (the Vietnam conflict). Klinkowitz concludes with a discussion of the privileging of space over time and self-invention over representation which is characteristic of this new style of fiction.

Klinkowitz sees the war in Vietnam as a litmus test for the degree of change that has been wrought in American fiction, because that experience is still close to many readers' lives and because it issued a cognitive challenge, 'eclipsing as it did all previous definitions of military conduct and social response'. In a wide-ranging discussion, Klinkowitz shows how contemporary writers have taken the very problematics of this cognitive puzzle as their fictive subject. Philip Beidler in *Re-Writing America: Vietnam Authors in Their Generation* is also engaged in describing how the experience of the Vietnamese conflict has affected subsequent fiction writing. To a whole range of subjects, genres and modes Vietnam authors have brought their experience of the conflict and the work of cultural revision it prompted. Beidler likens the work of Vietnam authors to that of the British writers who survived the Great War of 1914–18 and who created from the experience of war a mythology that became a part of modern culture. The work of the Vietnam generation of writers, Beidler argues, has been 'fashioned out of experience into imaginative art which in turn inscribes itself into the larger discourse of culture, [here] we find a call, a challenge, and even, given the richly generative concept of language they propose, a medium of enactment for a new art that would be a kind of ultimate cultural revision. It is an art that, even as it acknowledges the painful memory of Vietnam, would make possible the imaginative projection of that memory into new dimensions of consciousness, private and public, individual and collective, often providing equally new insights into knowledge, meaning, and value.' Developing the perception that, as a culture, we become our representations these writers enact a self-critique that penetrates to the centre of national consciousness. The range of writers discussed is impressive but necessarily wide to support the weighty claims Beidler makes for their work: Tim O'Brien, Philip Caputo, Robert Olen Butler, James Webb, Winston Groom, Larry Heinemann, Gloria Emerson, Frances Fitzgerald, Robert Stone, Michael Herr, as well as the dramatist David Rabe and a number of poets. This is a very intelligent treatment of the vast body of Vietnam literature and a fitting companion to Beidler's earlier study, *American Literature and the Experience of Vietnam*.

Michael Oriard's study, *Sporting with the Gods: The Rhetoric of Play and Game in American Culture*, offers an exploration of the metaphor of life as a game as it has been employed throughout American history. Oriard does not, therefore, restrict his discussion to the literary genre of sports fiction but considers this trope wherever it may appear and develops the view that this metaphor can be used to chart general cultural shifts from Puritanism to Transcendentalism and, in the twentieth century, from Social Darwinism to the Beats to the New Age spiritualists. The most interesting chapter from the point of view of contemporary American fiction is that concerning the period since the sixties and the 'playful counterculture of the 1960s youth movement'. In addition to the Beats, Oriard also discusses Bellow, Cheever, Barth, Wright Morris, Salinger and others; he considers the relationship between politics and play in the 1960s before moving on to an extended analysis of John Updike's fiction, the New Age and the debate over play in postwar America. Oriard presents a stimulating and very readable account of a motif that was acknowledged as an important element in the black humour fiction of the early sixties but since appears to have been neglected by critics of recent fiction.

Ellen Leiman, in 'Ivory Towers and their Discontents: The Academic Novel in America' (Serge Ricard, ed. *L'Education aux Etats-Unis: mythes et réalités*), discusses the nature of the campus novel in relation to Stringfellow Barr's *Purely Academic* (1958), Bernard Malamud's *A New Life* (1962), May Sarton's 1961 novel *The Small Room*, Nabokov's *Pnin* (1960), and Carolyn Heilbrun's recent feminist detective fictions like *Poetic Justice*, *Death in a Tenured Position* and *A Trap for Fools*. Leiman's approach is primarily descriptive, but she does offer an interesting picture of an evolution within the genre since the late 1950s.

Studies that do not include extended discussions of post-war fiction yet provide stimulating and valuable contextual analyses are Jan Gorak's *The Making of the Modern Canon: Genesis and Crisis of a Literary Idea*; *Theorizing American Literature: Hegel, the Sign, and History* edited by Bainard Cowan and Joseph Kronick; and Jerry Aline Flieger's *The Purloined Punchline: Freud's Comic Theory and the Postmodern Text*.

(b) Individual Authors

The title of Vincent Piket's study, *Louis Auchincloss: The Growth of a Novelist*, is quite self-explanatory. Piket distinguishes his work from the two existing monographs on Auchincloss, Christopher C. Dahl's 1986 study and David B. Parsell's Twayne volume in the US Authors Series (1988), by stressing his concern with the writer's development from his very earliest juvenile writings to his most recent publications.This is reflected in Piket's extremely comprehensive bibliography of Auchlincloss's writings, covering his fiction and non-fiction as well as magazine and newspaper pieces, contributions to books and journals, and the letter and manuscript collections. The bibliography is more than a supplement to Jackson Bryer's 'Bibliographical Record' (1977), though details are given of new editions of works published before 1977. The study is divided into four sections: 'The Formative Years' (1917–46), 'The Early Novels' (1947–59), 'Maturity and Recognition' (1960–67), and 'Weariness and Recuperation' (1968–present). Though in his introduction Piket claims to take account of the socio-historical and biographical origins of Auchincloss's fiction, what emerges is effectively an intellectual biography that treats the fictions as evidence of the evolution of certain attitudes and ideas as Auchincloss's artistic career has developed. So although Piket deliberately eshews the thematic approach to this portrait of the artist, still he identifies recurring patterns of thought and feeling in Auchincloss's life and works. Most imporant among these is the conflict between filial duty and creative autonomy which Piket perceives as a source of anxiety that dominated Auchincloss's early years and was resolved only by his successful pursuit of a dual career: as a writer and Wall Street lawyer. The emphatically upper-middle class WASPish nature of Auchincloss's own life and the reflection of that social context in his writing provides not only another persistent thread that runs through but also the motivation for Piket's study: he seeks to vindicate the novelist from unfair criticism and so places Auchincloss clearly within the tradition of the novelist of manners, with precursors like Henry James and Edith Wharton. Auchincloss's avowed conviction that the writer should deal with known experience produces an emotional contiguity that is perceptible in themes, characters and settings both geographical and historical. In Piket's account, Auchincloss remained true to his convictions throughout his novelistic career. Though the shorter works, stories and occasional pieces are treated only as adjuncts to the novels, this is a valuable and accessible introduction to an author still obscure to many critics of recent fiction.

Maurice Couturier in 'From Displacement to Compactness: John Barth's *The Floating Opera*' (*Critique* 33.3–21) discusses the postmodernity of Barth's novel in relation to its self-reflexivity. This is an analysis that remains close to the text, investigating the critical stance assumed by the writer towards his characters, story, prospective reader and especially the narrator. Couturier demonstrates how Barth's concern to show that texts are about texts rather than any sort of 'reality' produces a 'compactness' in this novel that is also 'an elaborate form of communication between author and reader'. The imperative that a novel should communicate, that a relationship should be developed between a textual sign and its referent, has produced increasingly sophisticated and complex narrative techniques which circumvent even as they characterize the problematics of postmodernism.

John Barth is nominated as the most inventive, creative and influential writer of contemporary fiction by Julius Rowan Raper in his *Narcissus from the Rubble*. Raper views *Chimera* as the text in which the competing models of human identity – the philosophical and the psychological – and the models of behaviour, the protean and the narcissistic, find their fullest contrast. Both the existential and the psychoanalytical models are transcended by the alternatives to Proteus and Narcissus created by Barth. The contrast of character types and investigation of archetypal lives enables the tales of *Chimera* to 'record the process whereby their author exhausted the familiar heroic myth in order to release the energies of other myths waiting at the periphery of Western consciousness'.

Jerome Klinkowitz's new study of Donald Barthelme's fiction, published so soon after Barthelme's death in 1989, provides a timely and insightful retrospective of the writer's work. *Donald Barthelme: An Exhibition* belongs to that style of writing about contemporary American fiction which publicizes the critic's familiarity with the person as well as the work of the writer. Such a work of criticism then takes on the appearance of an authorized account, having explicit authorial approval. Klinkowitz begins his book with an account of dinner with Barthelme and his wife at their home in Greenwich Village. Despite his claims to the contrary, this introduction does little to illustrate the primary themes of the critical study that follows and serves rather to establish the critic's credentials as the writer's friend. Klinkowitz does not need this authorization; the claims he makes are really quite uncontentious and, in any case, are supported by a rigorously close reading of the texts. His main argument is for *The Dead Father* (1975) as the central text of Barthelme's canon. Coming fourteen years after his first published work and fourteen years before his death, this novel has an historical centrality that matches its thematic and technical centrality within the development of Barthelme's fictional style. It is, in particular, Barthelme's reputation as a pioneering postmodernist that Klinkowitz sees as arising from characteristics most clearly displayed by the narrative of *The Dead Father*. Themes of dominance and domination, philosophical speculation, elements of popular culture and, of course, that most characteristic aspect of the fiction, linguistic play, are combined with a stylistic departure from the earlier technique of collage which Klinkowitz describes by analogy with another technique of the visual arts: silkscreening. 'Whereas the basis of collage is the image cut out of one context and repasted in another ... silkscreen expands the catalog of items and permits a photomechanical superimposition of elements so that they can bleed through, yielding images seen through one another rather than in simple juxtaposition.' Klinkowitz's familiarity with contemporary painting and sculpture comes to the fore as he pursues this insight through the evolution of Barthelme's fictional style from his first serious work. This is an important study of a writer whose significance for the history of postmodernist aesthetics is still being uncovered.

Barthelme is among those writers classified by Paul Maltby as one of his *Dissident Postmodernists*. While Maltby omits from his discussion *The Dead Father*, Klinkowitz's key text, still he begins his analysis of Barthelme's postmodernity with Klinkowitz's assertion that for Barthelme textual autonomy has supplanted any referential imperative: the text can and should simply be, rather than being a representation of something outside itself. The focus upon processes of signification is one strategy by which Barthelme expresses his dissent from the prevailing discourses of late capitalism. For a 'neo-formalist' critic such as Klinkowitz, Maltby argues, radical self-reflexivity is indicative of radical epistemological scepticism when in fact this claim to textual autonomy may function both as a critique of the meaninglessness of mass culture and the reduction of language's power, and as a strategy of resistance in the face of a culturally hegemonic discourse that has politicized even the 'dreck' of everyday life. Maltby restricts his analysis, for the most part, to the early story collections, *Come Back, Dr Caligari*, *Unspeakable Practices, Unnatural Acts*, and the early novel *Snow White*. Despite the restricted focus, this is a refreshing and stimulating approach to Barthelme's work.

Saul Bellow has joined the Macmillan Modern Novelists series with the publication of Peter Hyland's study of his *oeuvre*. In seven chapters, Hyland offers a comprehensive account of Bellow's work. He opens with an introduction to Bellow's life and career, which will be of particular interest to those unfamiliar with Bellow as a literary figure, and then proceeds to describe the fiction by devoting a chapter each to the novels of the forties, fifties, the sixties and seventies together, and the eighties, before giving account of Bellow's short stories and, in a concluding chapter, 'Literary Status', speculating about the reasons for Bellow's popularity and his place within a specifically American literary tradition. Bellow's forays into the world of the theatre are mentioned in the introductory account of his career but, as they add little to the understanding of his novels – his most important achievements – they are not subject to lengthy analysis. Though Hyland acknowledges Bellow's resistance to the idea of becoming the subject of a biography and his refusal of all suggestions that he authorize a biographer to gather the necessary information because he perceives that a biography will seal his work at a given historical point and inhibit any additions to the canon of his work, what Hyland has written is the critical equivalent of a biography. He has provided an authoritative account of Bellow's fiction up to the publication in 1989 of *The Theft* and *The Bellarosa Connection*. Hyland sees Bellow's novels as deeply rooted in the historical moment in which they were written and so, taken together, as expressive of 'the flux of ideas and the major political and cultural tensions' experienced in the West since World War II. This consistency within change is found also in the recurrent themes of Bellow's work: the dynamics of contemporary history, the conflict between high idealism and quotidian reality, the diversity of urban experience and the despair experienced by mass man, the difficulty of historical understanding and its necessity for individual self-assertion, all these ideas are found in recurring patterns throughout Bellow's novels. The elucidation of thematic patterns and connections is balanced by Hyland's fine awareness of the distinctiveness and unique character of each of the novels as they relate to the overall unfolding of Bellow's artistic career.

Seize the Day and *Henderson the Rain King* are discussed by Julius Rowan Raper in *Narcissus from the Rubble* as key texts in the fictional dramatization of conflict between phenomenological and psychological models of personality. It is Bellow's concern with subjective resources and the imperative of modern consumerist culture that we look to objects rather than ourselves that is of interest to Raper. He discusses the way in which both novels 'challenge that predeliction of modernism championing abstraction and objectivity rather than empathy and subjectivity'. Arnold Goldsmith in his study of nature in *The Modern American Urban Novel* devotes a chapter to *Mr Sammler's Planet*. He reads the novel as a celebration of the persistent 'green growth rising from the burnt black' of contemporary society and twentieth-century history. Nature is seen as central to the novel's dialectical approach to such conflicts as 'the old versus the new, the real potency of thought versus the alleged potency of sex, the conservative versus the radical, the sane versus the insane, the stable versus the abnormal, and tempered optimism and hope versus bitter pessimism and despair'.

This has been a conspicuous year for William Burroughs with the release of the movie of *Naked Lunch* (after several unsuccessful attempts at translation to the screen), the first British publication of Ted Morgan's 1988 biography *Literary Outlaw: The Life and Times of William S. Burroughs*, and the collection of critical essays edited by Jennie Skerl and Robin Lydenberg, *William S. Burroughs at the Front: Critical Reception, 1959–1989*. Burroughs has himself been involved in all three projects (Morgan's is, in effect, the authorized biography), advising director David Cronenberg and contributing to the volume of essays an assessment of critical responses to his work.

Skerl and Lydenberg have organized the twenty-five essays in this volume chronologically, and the volume itself is divided into four sections, each reflecting one of the decades during which Burroughs has been writing. The essays reflect both extremes of critical reception: the laudatory and the outright hostile. Interestingly, critical comment has developed in a generally linear historical pattern from the early concern with moral issues, through a critical questioning of Burroughs's relation to humanism and the modernist movement, to more recent investigations into Burroughs's experimentation with language and his designation as a literary postmodernist. The controversies that have surrounded Burroughs – the censorship trial, the debates occasioned by his 'cut-up' method of composition, his unconventional lifestyle and drug addiction – permeate these essays despite the variety of critical approaches that are brought to bear upon Burroughs's fiction: new critical, biographical, poststructuralist, reader-response, psychoanalytical, and linguistic. John Ciardi and Alan Ansen, in the 1950s, were concerned to explain the nature of Burroughs' fictional enterprise and to defend it against charges of obscenity. In the following decade, Mary McCarthy found herself compelled to defend her own defense of *The Naked Lunch*, at the 1962 International Writers' Conference in Edinburgh, as one of the first 'stateless' novels that appeared to be supplanting the 'national novel'. Also reprinted in this section is the exchange of letters to the editor of the *TLS* that followed John Willett's denunciation of Burroughs in his review graphically entitled 'UGH …'; Ihab Hassan's account of Burroughs as a poet of apocalypse and nihilistic absence; Marshall McLuhan's 'Notes on Burroughs' and his relation to contemporary technological culture; David Lodge's discussion of the twentieth-century avant-garde and the 'institutionalization of the 'adversary culture' of modernism'; and the consideration of Burroughs's 'addict vision' by Theodore Solotaroff and Frank D. McConnell. During the 1970s, Tony Tanner identifies an interest in methods of 'deconditioning' and 'decontrol'; Alfred Kazin describes Burroughs as 'a great autoeroticist – of writing'; Cary Nelson identifies a deliberate inscription of frustration, directed at those readers who would empathize; Neal Oxenhandler argues that the cut out method is part of Burroughs's characteristic style of revelation through formal concealment; John Tytell considers Burroughs's relation to the Beat movement; Eric Mottram, an early supporter, and Anne Friedberg deal with the significance of Burroughs's use of montage. Nicholas Zurbrugg discusses Burroughs within the context of Beckett and Proust in his 1983 essay; Jennie Skerl analyses the liberating power of fantasy in the novels of the 1970s, from *The Wild Boys* (1971) to *Cities of the Red Night* (1981); the latter novel forms the focus of Steven Shaviro's essay on Burroughs's 'theatre of illusion'; David Glover considers *The Place of Dead Roads* in relation to the western genre; Wayne Pounds identifies three modern predecessors of Burroughs's 'postmodern asshole'; Robin Lydenberg looks at the Burroughs legend in a review of *The Western Lands* (1987); James Grauerholz (Burroughs's secretary) attempts to contextualize the artwork of Burroughs and Brion Gysin in terms of the shifting philosophical currents of the twentieth century; Oliver C. G. Harris considers Burroughs's and Gysin's experiments with collage, postmodernism's surrealist heritage, and the return to narrative. Skerl and Lydenberg provide a useful introduction which helps to draw together this assemblage of diverging opinion and assists in navigating a path through this most comprehensive collection.

If it seems odd that Ted Morgan should close his biography with the subject still living, stranger still is Burroughs's longevity, given the relentless history of self-inflicted physical abuse that Morgan chronicles. He spares us none of the brutality of drug addiction, from the information that by 1980 Burroughs had only two 'good' veins remaining, one in his right hand and one in his foot, to the full medical details of Billy Burroughs's liver transplant following a massive haemorrage of the kind that killed Jack Kerouac. This biography is, in places, sensational in the worst sense, but it is more deeply flawed than that. The sheer length (more than 650 pages) exaggerates weaknesses of style, and there are many. Most annoying of all is the pretence at objectivity which rings false throughout but particularly when, in the concluding chapter where he describes visiting Burroughs in Lawrence, Morgan refuses to use his own name and instead refers to himself exclusively as 'the biographer'. This is annoying because it is only at this point, at the end of the book, that we are informed of Morgan's long-standing friendship with Burroughs and the 'authorized' nature of the biography. Certainly no reader could miss the sympathetic reading given to the narrative of Burroughs's life but it does seem fraudulent to disguise the obvious interests of the biographer. Not only does Morgan obviously like and approve of

Burroughs, he shares many of his subject's views and assumptions. Most troubling of these to me is Burroughs's misogyny. Morgan openly describes Burroughs's misogyny but distances himself from it. Yet the treatment accorded the women in Burroughs' life displays the same kind of contempt.This is especially apparent in the account of Joan Burroughs's physical and mental deterioration through benzedrine addiction in the period before her death; whilst Morgan does not quite blame the victim for her fate, he comes dangerously close to it. We learn nothing of the fate of Julie, Burroughs's step-daughter, after her mother's death, though we do know that the manner of her upbringing had left her (like Billy Jnr) with serious emotional problems. An entire lengthy chapter is devoted to Billy Burroughs's attempts to come to terms with his father; it seems that Julie was not even approached by the biographer. The amount of space given over to Billy's biography is symptomatic of another weakness of Morgan's style: he interpolates numerous life stories into his narrative. Often one has the impression that Burroughs's 'times' are more important than the 'life' Ted Morgan purports to describe. For instance, we learn as much about Allen Ginsberg, one of Morgan's primary sources of information, as we do about Burroughs. If this book were leaner and a little more honest it would make infinitely better reading.

Bakhtin's theory of the dialogic is certainly in fashion as a theoretical context for the reading of modern fiction. This contextualization is given an innovative twist in Miriam Marty Clark's essay, 'Raymond Carver's Monologic Imagination' (*MFS* 37:ii.240–7). Clark uses Bakhtin's comments on heteroglossia in order to show how Raymond Carver's stories are *not* 'many-voiced or multi-languaged'. As she argues, 'Carver reduces polyphony, backgrounds the many voices and the carnival spirit, which are the essence of "modern literature" and novelistic discourse as Bakhtin understands them.' This reduction to a monologic style of writing is fitted to Carver's thematic interest in 'curtailment to the point of solipsism' and 'varying degrees of xenophobia'. This is an essay with interesting things to say about Carver's writing and the nature of modern fiction more generally.

Kirk Nesset studies Raymond Carver's representation of the vicissitudes of love and its absence in ' "This Word Love": Sexual Politics and Silence in Early Raymond Carver' (*AL* 63:i.292–313). Nesset shows how Carver's stories reveal an 'obsession' with the pressure exerted by love, a dark and irresistible force, upon marriages and the identities of the individuals involved, producing a diversity of responses ranging from bewilderment and outrage to isolation, diminishment and entrapment. But, ultimately, 'the politics of sex reflect a kind of larger politics, more tenuous and more ominous even yet: the politics of fortune and fate, which, forever unseen and unheard, dictate the bleak circumstances of their [Carver's characters'] lives, provoking the bafflement and dismay that is for them a daily fact of existence.'

Peter Josyph's piece, 'The John Cheever Story: A Talk with Richard Seltzer' (*TCL* 37.335–42) takes the form of an interview but concentrates upon one moment in Seltzer's life: his meeting with John Cheever in 1980 at the artists' colony Yaddo in upstate New York. Whilst this makes for an interesting anecdote, the story casts little light upon the literary work of either of these two writers.

In *Dissident Postmodernists*, Paul Maltby discusses Robert Coover's *Pricksongs and Descants*, *The Universal Baseball Association* and *The Public Burning* as examples of postmodernist fiction where metafictional style becomes a strategy of ideological resistance. Coover's self-referential fictions have been accepted by most critics as characteristic of contemporary metafiction. Maltby extends that perception into an analysis of the socio-political implications of the questioning of signification:

its power and its limits. By drawing attention to the discursivity of powerful cultural myths, the writer registers his own dissent from accepted cultural myths or valuations and promotes a potentially dissident self-consciousness in the reader as the consumer of those cultural discourses.

John G. Parks's account of *E. L. Doctorow* in the Literature and Life: American Writers series provides a comprehensive introduction to the writer's life, work and critical reception. The book is prefaced by a chronology of Doctorow's career and ends with a very full bibliography of primary sources and secondary critical material. Parks discusses each of Doctorow's seven novels as well as the play, *Drinks Before Dinner* and also *Lives of the Poets: Six Stories and a Novella*. The diverse nature of the Doctorow canon, neither experimental nor conventional, neither postmodernist nor realist, is acknowledged by Parks who shows a fine awareness of Doctorow's interest in the mythical dimension of American history. The mythologization of America, the infusion of ideological values into the texture of American society, Parks sees as one of the abiding characteristics of Doctorow's work, together with a passionate concern for the potential of narratives (and his fiction combines in juxtaposition narratives of all kinds) to shape cultural attitudes. One of the primary themes that Parks follows through the development of Doctorow's work is, then, the possibility of social justice. Parks is careful to distance Doctorow from the murky domain of 'the political novelist': 'As a critic of America's failures to fulfill its dreams and founding convictions, he does not advocate new political systems, but rather provokes the reader to a radical reassessment of the American experience in essentially moral terms.' The liberation of narrative, and hence the human spirit, from the power of institutionalized language is, in Parks's view, the prime political goal of Doctorow's writing. John Parks offers a sensitive, lucid and intelligent contribution to criticism of contemporary fiction generally and E. L. Doctorow's work in particular.

John Parks has also written 'The Politics of Polyphony: The Fiction of E. L. Doctorow' (*TCL* 37.454–63). In this essay he discusses Doctorow's treatment of modern history and interprets *The Book of Daniel*, *Ragtime*, and *Loon Lake* as fictions in which Doctorow 'seeks to disclose and to challenge the hegemony of enshrined or institutionalized discursive practices'. It is the capacity of certain forms of power to establish a 'monological control of culture' that Parks finds challenged, disrupted and dismantled in Doctorow's writing, and which constitutes the political dimension of Doctorow's work.

In 'Cultural Hegemony Goes to the Fair: The Case of E. L. Doctorow's *World's Fair*' (*AmerS* 33.31–44), Michael Robertson employs Doctorow's novel as a case study with which to counter the interpretation of the New York World's Fair of 1939–40 by historians who see the Fair as an exercise in cultural hegemony. Where such historical scholars are interested in the Fair as illustrative of certain models of social control, Robertson views the novel as a fictionalized account of the way in which consumers receive, respond to and reshape their culture. The accuracy of Doctorow's historical description and the proximity of narrative details to his own life which is such as to lead some critics to term the novel autobiography, and Doctorow to call it 'the illusion of a memoir', certainly assist Robertson to make his case. He concludes that the World's Fair offers evidence that, rather than passively consume the cultural products offered them, many visitors to the Fair constructed its meaning for themselves and actively resisted the 'packaged' meanings offered them.

William Gaddis is the subject of Patrick O'Donnell's essay 'His Master's Voice: On William Gaddis's *JR*' (*Postmodern Culture: An Electronic Journal of Interdisciplinary Criticism* 1, 2 January, no pagination). O'Donnell analyses the novel as a parody of American capitalism. The disparate voices that are interwoven to form the narrative texture are described as the analogue to postmodern identity. Voice, through the media of television especially, has been instrumentalized and commodified. Within the context of Gaddis's parody of the McLuhanesque 'global village', O'Donnell argues, the body is represented as a form of resistance to the hierarchical structure of the capitalist marketplace. The postmodernist quality of Gaddis's novel emerges from its refusal of resolution as the resistances it represents are themselves revealed to be forms of desire commodified.

Starclimber: The Literary Adventures and Autobiography of Raymond Z. Gallun is a very readable account of what is was like to be a science-fiction writer during the heyday of the genre magazines of the 1930s and 1940s. Gallun (with Jeffrey M. Elliot) describes his life and work, discussing the origins of some of his best known stories, and repeating anecdotes about some of the famous people he encountered in the course of his travels. The volume includes photographs, a complete bibliography of Gallun's work, and a chronology.

Joseph Heller, Judith Ruderman's second contribution to the Literature and Life: American Writers series, has a slightly wacky quality which is probably appropriate to her subject. She begins with an extended simile 'On Heller and Halvah' – 'Reading a book by Joseph Heller can be compared to eating that sticky, sweet confection called halvah, favored by Jews of Eastern European extraction: a little bit is very rich, surfeits the appetite quickly, and can lead to indigestion. It is also, however, tasty and nourishing' – and goes on to chapters with titles such as 'Angst for the Memories: The Life and Times of Joseph Heller' and 'A Stage in the Career: Joseph Heller as Playwright.' Despite this, Ruderman's is a refreshingly sensible approach to Heller's work. She is well aware of the dangers of writing about an author whose novels are as funny as are Heller's and takes care to avoid destroying the delicate comic texture of the narratives with which she deals. Within the constraints imposed upon her book by the style of the series to which it belongs, Ruderman offers new insights into the nature of Heller's achievements. She provides details of Heller's life and his historical and aesthetic context, and indicates the points at which this biographical context intersects with his writing. Most interesting is Ruderman's perception of Heller as a Jewish-American writer and his work as belonging to the tradition of Yiddish schlemiel humour. In addition to chapters devoted to the fiction, and one chapter concerned with his drama, Ruderman includes two extended discussions of Heller's canon and here she is able to view his work in a comparative manner and to present a view of Heller's importance to contemporary American fiction that does not depend upon claims made for one central text. This is an engaging and instructive addition to Heller criticism.

Shirley Geok-lin Lim has edited *Approaches to Teaching Maxine Hong Kingston's 'The Woman Warrior'* for the MLA series of pedagogical handbooks. This volume is much more than a handbook, though it does contain such useful information as bibliographical details of reference works, background studies, the cultural background to Kingston's novel, biographical information, and critical studies; a list of relevant films, video productions, and recordings; and guidance on courses and contexts. The primary intention of the volume is to extend academic interest from this single novel to Asian-American and ethnic (women's) writing more generally: 'The volume is not so much an end in itself as a part of the process of empowering teachers and students to function in a diverse American society', Lim writes in her preface. The critical essays that comprise part two of the book, which is introduced by a 'personal statement' by Maxine Hong Kingston, seek to place *The Woman Warrior* in a number of different contexts: different literary and cultural traditions, diverse canons and courses, each envisioning different student audiences.

Sau-ling Cynthia Wong discusses Kingston's use of traditional Chinese sources but in doing so treats Kingston as an American writer who uses and creates elements of Chinese and American culture. Patricia Lin places the book within the context of films and studies from the social sciences in order to illuminate the historical, social, linguistic and cultural factors against which *The Woman Warrior* is projected. Kathryn Van Spanckeren enlarges the reception of Kingston's narrative as 'a recasting, if not a recent flowering, of a three-thousand-year-old literary tradition', by analysing the Asian literary background, and Robert G. Lee discusses the competing claims to ethnography and to fiction that have been made for the book, as he considers *The Woman Warrior* as an intervention in Asian American historiography. Vincente F. Gotera presents the responses of students who answered a questionnaire about their experiences of reading Kingston's book and he gives his recommendations about how teachers might assist students to overcome the difficulties they experience. Judith M. Melton describes her experience of teaching *The Woman Warrior* as part of a women's studies course, focusing on the misogynistic culture of feudal China and its legacy in modern America. An interesting inclusion is James R. Aubrey's discussion of teaching the book to students at the Air Force Academy, as a focus for the consideration of the role of women in military combat. Kathleen A. Boardman explains why she has found *The Woman Warrior* such a rich text to use in writing classes, while Paul W. McBride describes *The Woman Warrior* in the history classroom, and Marlyn Peterson and Deirdre Lashgari describe teaching the narrative to high school and community college students. In the section devoted to 'critical contexts' Marilyn Yalom analyses *The Woman Warrior* as representing a form of postmodern autobiography; Joan Lidoff questions the whole issue of autobiography and genre as it involves Kingston's narrative; Colleen Kennedy and Deborah Morse debate the issue of literary canons (men's and women's) and the place of *The Woman Warrior* within these traditions; Victoria Myers uses speech-act theory to analyse the theme of the search for identity in *The Woman Warrior*. Gayle K. Fujita Sato describes her close reading of the text which follows the ghost motif to reveal the text's thematic and dramatic patterns; Kingston's use of mythic elements and mythologizing techniques is discussed by Cheng Lok Chua; and Timothy Dow Adams describes the similarity that is created between the reader of *The Woman Warrior* and Kingston's position as an autobiographer as both struggle to separate history from fiction or fantasy. Shirley Geok-lin Lim has put together a very useful and extremely stimulating collection that will serve critical and pedagogical readers alike.

Those interested in Kingston's two biographical works will appreciate Wendy Larson's *Literary Authority and the Modern Chinese Writer: Ambivalence and Autobiography*. Larson investigates the conflict between tradition and modernity in the work of writers of 'the May Fourth era – a time when ideas of realism, romanticism, feminism, science, democracy, anarchism, liberalism, socialism, liberation, and communism' were current. Kingston is only mentioned in passing by Larson, yet her discussion of the relationship between aesthetic authority and history, in both its cultural and subjective aspects, is of obvious relevance to Kingston's innovative use of the autobiographical form.

Welch D. Everman's *Jerzy Kosinski: The Literature of Violation* treats Kosinski's fiction, rather as a literature of extremes, particularly in view of its moral dimension. The disquieting and difficult aspects of Kosinski's writing, and the unlikely popularity that these novels enjoy, forms one of the questions that Everman seeks to answer.

Everman sets his interest in Kosinski against those biographical and psychoanalytical approaches that have sought to see reflected in the fiction aspects of the writer's sensational life. Everman addresses himself to the texts and a close reading that attends to the artistry of Kosinski's narratives. Thematic coherence derives from the analysis of the idea of violation in these texts where violation – especially of a sexual nature – is a means of self-exploration, a 'crisis situation' where the discovery of other selves becomes possible. The reader of this kind of fiction is placed in the position of the voyeur who still participates in the process of revelation that the fiction enacts: 'The Kosinski novel is an arena in which the reader might come to recognize something of himself through his own will, his own powers, his own unique individuality'.

Julius Rowan Raper, in *Narcissus from the Rubble*, discusses Kosinski as a novelist belonging to the tradition of creative narcissism. Kosinski's fiction, in this view, is so strongly grounded in the individual imagination that the issue of whether his characters represent legitimate social criticism is irrelevant. Raper analyses *Being There* as an 'existential fiction of individual being' where the central character, an exaggeration of the Protean, offers a penetrating satire of Heidegger's concept of *Dasein*. The novel satirizes not only the phenomenological but the Freudian as well, representing a delicate balance between the decentred and the self-centered.

Norman Mailer's attitude towards the idea of America, his ambition to write a great national novel which later in his career became the Whitmanesque desire to embody in his own life the destiny of the nation, is the subject of Joseph Tabbi's essay, 'Mailer's Psychology of Machines' (*PMLA* 106.238–50). Tabbi discusses *Of a Fire on the Moon* 'one of Mailer's most formidable attempts to read history – the flight of Apollo 11 to the moon – as a chapter in an ongoing fiction of his own'. But Tabbi identifies in Mailer's confrontation with the impersonal technology of modern history a challenge to Mailer's egocentric transformations of experience. Mailer fails, in this novel, to surrender the rhetoric of selfhood yet also fails to transform a discourse of the machine through the pressure of his own subjectivity. Tabbi grounds this failure in the American tradition of Henry Adams and others who have faced the difficulty of 'imposing or accommodating the self and its imaginative constructions on or within a universe of impersonal force'.

The dialectics of the sociological and the aesthetic in Mailer's work are under discussion in Steve Shoemaker's 'Norman Mailer's "The White Negro": Historical Myth or Mythical History?' (*TCL* 37.343–60). Shoemaker explores the fate of the Romantic genius in an age where the prophet has been reduced to 'the bourgeois self' by analysing the permutations to which this figure is subject in Mailer's writing. Historical and 'historicist' pressures that have affected the Romantic myth and their manifestation in Mailer's vision of 'the hipster' provide the focus for Shoemaker's discussion.

Jacky Martin's essay, 'Bodily Marks as Factors of Identity and Difference in Toni Morrison's Novels' (in Serge Ricard, ed. *Modèles et contre-Modèles dans la Culture et la Société Nord-Americaines: Identité et Différences*), discusses the incidence of physical marks, disabilities and mutilations among Morrison's fictional characters. These marks are identified by Martin as symbolic markers which, while they are not central to the characterization of a fictional personality, they do obtrude upon and prescribe in certain ways our reception of these characters. These bodily marks inscribe the doubleness of racial Otherness and the politics of domination.

Edward Arnold's series Modern Fiction sees the inclusion of Tony Sharpe's volume on *Vladimir Nabokov*. Sharpe combines fine critical analysis with an awareness of Nabokov's life and career, written in a lucid and readable style. The volume opens with a consideration of Nabokov's memoir, *Speak, Memory*, which leads Sharpe to ask which is the more meaningful description of Nabokov: as a Russian or an English-American writer. In this chapter, Sharpe describes how Nabokov, decontextualized by history, took pains further to decontextualize himself both in literary and nationalistic terms. Sharpe, however, offers a useful discussion of the American, Russian, and Western European backgrounds to Nabokov's fiction. In the chapters that follow this introduction, *Invitation to a Beheading* and *Bend Sinister* are considered as the two novels that most closely approach a political or historical engagement on Nabokov's part; *Pnin* and *The Enchanter* are discussed in view of Nabokov's opinion that 'the good writer is first of all an enchanter'; and an entire central chapter, 'Dreamers and Demons', is devoted to *Lolita*. *Pale Fire* is the subject of the chapter 'Readers and writers' in which Sharpe considers the complex metafictional character of Nabokov's work. This is not a comprehensive critical study of Nabokov's *oeuvre* but it is a concise and lucid introduction to the nature of his achievement.

Pat Macpherson in *Reflecting on 'The Bell Jar'*, part of Routledge's 'Heroines?' series, attempts to elucidate 'the details of post-war American middle-class life that made Sylvia Plath typical of her time and place'. Macpherson seeks to restore Plath and her heroine, Esther Greenwood, to their social context and emerges from her investigations with a view of *The Bell Jar* as the representation of 'the first heroine of our own popularized therapeutic culture'. The image of America in the 'anaesthetized' fifties is analysed in its constituent elements: Cold War paranoia and McCarthyism; the nuclear family and the suburban ideal; 'Momism' and matrophobia. Macpherson forges some interesting links, as between communism and the perception of 'gender maladjustment', and national well being and mental health. These lead Macpherson to an investigation of the Rosenberg trial and connections with the electrotherapy experienced by Plath and her heroine. Connections between the political gaze of surveillance and the formation of female identity also provide insights into the problematic nature of Plath's fictional Other.

The essays gathered in Patrick O'Donnell's collection, *New Essays on 'The Crying of Lot 49'*, seek to place Pynchon's novel in its historical, cultural, scientific and literary contexts. As O'Donnell comments in his introduction, *The Crying of Lot 49* speculates upon the whole idea of 'connection', or the activity of connecting, as *the* characteristic human endeavor, whether it be in writing and reading literary works, or in articulating ourselves – our identities – as historical beings'. The novel's representation of the dangers inherent in the quest for connection and hence meaning is matched by the essays here to the social and political contexts of the 1950s and 1960s in America and to the aesthetic context of postmodernist fiction. Debra A. Castillo discusses Pynchon's novel in the comparative or, more accurately, the intertextual frame offered by Jorge Luis Borges, as the work of a fellow-master of metafictional play. John Johnston discusses the novel as a 'schizo-text': with paranoia the motivating principle behind the semiotic logic of the narrative. In Johnston's reading, the interpretation of signs takes precedence over paranoia as a form of mental aberration to such an extent in Pynchon's work that we as readers are led to neglect paranoia as anything but the generation of significances or a 'regime of signs'. Bernard Duyfhuizen uncovers a central line of questioning in *The Crying of Lot 49*: 'How does a culture or society transmit a heritage – its ideals or its corruptions – and how are these transmissions disrupted? ... What *are* our cultural transmissions? How are cultural patterns valorized by a society formed from precursor social structures? How are these patterns produced to meet local needs for order and control? How do they establish a status quo that strives always to reproduce itself and, thus, to ensure the unencumbered transmission of sociocultural formations to the next generation?' Duyfhuizen's analysis of cultural formation and the construction of privileged representations offers the most original approach to Pynchon's novel of all the essays that appear here. N. Katherine Hayles analyses the techniques of ambiguity that are so often the subject of critical comment by investigating Pynchon's use of metaphor or, as she defines it, his creation of 'meta-metaphors'. Finally, Pierre-Yves Petillon views Pynchon's novel within the context of its 'Americanness', represented by the Beats and by the American literary tradition generally.

Pynchon's *V* is among those works of contemporary fiction identified by Julius Rowan Raper as engaged in a crucial debate between the claims of philosophy and psychology to define authoritatively the nature of human character. In *V*, according to Raper, this debate is enacted as between Sartre and Freud, where Pynchon illustrates Sartre's proposition that we are our consciousness of objects by representing characters who are obsessively focused upon objects and who are progressively becoming more like objects. Raper discusses Profane, Stencil, Majistral and the woman V as representative of 'American freedom that allows us to become something different by a simple shift of attention'.

The last of Paul Maltby's 'dissident postmodernist' writers is, unsurprisingly, Thomas Pynchon. Maltby analyses *V* as an investigation into the processes of colonialism, consumerism and reifying technologies which threaten to transform that cultural product we know as humanity. The possibility of a cultural alternative to late-capitalist America focuses the discussion of *The Crying of Lot 49* but in *Gravity's Rainbow* the emergence of the age of the 'Rocket State' would seem to indicate that the rationalization of western cultures into massive military economies is now complete. Maltby designates as the dissident quality of Pynchon's work his critique of control over the processes of signification.

The readerly role of the heroine in *The Crying of Lot 49* is the subject of Chris Hall's essay, ' "Behind the Hieroglyphic Streets" Pynchon's Oedipa Mass and the Dialectics of Reading' (*Critique* 33.63–77). Hall takes what is, as she admits, an area that has been subject to considerable critical analysis, and provides a searching investigation that sheds new light on the intertextual complexity of Pynchon's novel. Starting with the parodic significances of 'The Courier's Tragedy', she traces a complex network of allusions to and echoes from a whole range of texts and critical methods that permeate the narrative and create an ironic texture in which Oedipa's experience is situated.

J. Kenneth Van Dover's *At Wolfe's Door: The Nero Wolfe Novels of Rex Stout* provides a comprehensive guide to Stout's fiction. For each novel and short story published bewteen 1934 and 1975 is given a synopsis, identification of every principal character, and a comment on noteworthy aspects of the text. The Nero Wolfe titles are dealt with separately and in chronological order. Van Dover discusses characteristics of the Wolfe series, Stout's other detectives and his place within the genre of detective fiction. The book closes with a comparative discussion of Nero Wolfe and Perry Mason. This is an invaluable introduction for the novice approaching Stout's novels and the genre of detective fiction for the first time.

Darkness Visible is a harrowing autobiographical account of William Styron's descent into a near-fatal clinical depression. Though this book has little bearing on Styron's fiction, and so is not a 'critical' study, it does illuminate his thinking about certain philosophical issues, in particular his attitude towards existentialism. We learn a little about the role of music and alcohol in the creative processes that produced Styron's novels. We discover how his enforced abstention from drinking (when suddenly his body rejected alcohol and even a small amount made him violently ill) precipitated his depression and how it was music, penetrating his consciousness at a time when he had become oblivious to all else, that impressed upon him an awareness of his proximity to the abyss and forced him to act by having his wife hospitalize him. The avowed aim of this account is to raise awareness of the significance of clinical depression, to insist that it is an affliction quite different to 'feeling down', and to restore to this medical condition the more weighty term 'melancholia'. Styron brings all of his considerable imaginative power to this task and produces a narrative that impresses upon the reader a terrifying sense of the precariousness of sanity and the fragility of our sense of self. Patrick Badonnel discusses 'le sujet a la solitude existentielle' in 'Le scriptural et le symptomatique dans *Darkness Visible*' (in Serge Ricard, ed. *Modèles et contre-Modèles dans la Culture et la Société Nord-Americaines: Identité et Différences*).

William Styron is interviewed by Victor Strandberg and Balkrishna Buwa ('An Interview with William Styron', *SR* 99.463–77). They begin by discussing Styron's interest in classical music, and go on to consider his time spent with the Marine Corps during the Second World War, the importance of the Bible in Styron's fiction and the historical/biographical contexts of some of Styron's primary characters. Styron makes a clear and important distinction between historical fiction and 'costume melodrama', pointing to the necessity that 'historical fictional narrative [has] meaning for the writer's period of time'. This then leads the interviewers to ask about Styron's reception in Europe, his response to and treatment of the Holocaust, his status as a 'southern' writer, the issue of race in contemporary culture and writing. Styron is also asked about his techniques of composition, his feelings about those who criticize his work, and about the *Vanity Fair* essay (recipient of the National Magazine Award for the best article of 1989) which formed the basis of *Darkness Visible*.

MFS has produced a special issue devoted to John Updike (37.i). Matthew Wilson discusses 'The Rabbit Trilogy: From Solitude to Society to Solitude Again' (5–24) and concludes that this novel sequence is paradigmatic of its kind in its representation of a character who finds through his experience of society, an enrichment of life; Basem L. Ra'ad uses Updike's memoir, *Self-Consciousness* as a starting point for a consideration of 'Updike's New Versions of Myth in America' (25–33); Derek Wright discusses the idea of form and flights from it in *Rabbit, Run* in his essay, 'Mapless Motion: Form and Space in Updike's *Rabbit, Run*' (35–44); Updike's representation of a declining America underpins Stacey Olster's piece, 'Rabbit Rerun: Updike's Replay of Popular Culture in *Rabbit at Rest*' (45–59); Barbara Leckie in ' "The Adulterous Society": John Updike's *Marry Me*' (61–79) considers Updike's treatment of adultery and asks whether adultery, after it has been publicly legitimated, can retain a 'transgressive, liberating and, for Updike, quasi-religious status'; John N. Duvall discusses 'The Pleasure of Textual/Sexual Wrestling: Pornography and Heresy in *Roger's Version*' (81–95); Sanford Pisker treats 'John Updike and the Distractions of Henry Bech, Professional Writer and Amateur American Jew' (97–111); and Malini Schueller attempts to correct the largely apolitical reception and interpretation of Updike's work by reading *The Coup* within the context of colonialist/imperialist ideology in her essay 'Containing the Third World: John Updike's *The Coup*' (113–28). The issue concludes with a selected checklist of critical work on John Updike's writing published between 1974 and 1990, compiled by Jack De Bellis (129–56). This checklist is intended to continue the previous bibliography which appeared in the *Modern Fiction Studies* Updike issue, Spring 1974.

The subversive potential of Alice Walker's *The Color Purple* is discussed by Linda Abbandonato in 'A View from "Elsewhere": Subversive Sexuality and the Rewriting of the Heroine's Story in *The Color Purple*' (*PMLA* 106.1106–15). Abbandonato argues that by telling the story of an 'invisible woman' Walker 'challenges patriarchal constructions of female subjectivity and sexuality and thus makes representation itself a compelling issue for all women, regardless of their ethnicity or sexual orientation'.Walker's novel is contextualized in terms of *Clarissa* – the eighteenth-century paradigm for patriarchal representation – Freud's theory of the Oedipal and Levi-Strauss's kinship theories, to show how Walker exposes the ideological workings of 'compulsory heterosexuality' and so appropriates the woman's narrative for herself.

Peter Schmidt's study of Eudora Welty's short fiction, *The Heart of the Story*, represents a self-conscious departure from the kinds of approach that have characterized criticism of Welty's fiction. Schmidt has employed the insights of feminist and New Historicist criticism to question and supplant the formalist and archetypal or myth-critical assumptions that have guided interpretation of Welty's work. Schmidt treats the complete set of published stories collectively in order to uncover the hidden affinities, connections, foreshadowings and patterns that are not readily perceptible when the stories are read individually. Following Welty's account in *One Writer's Beginnings* of her discovery that the stories in *The Golden Apples*, though conceived independently, were linked in important ways, Schmidt treats all of her short fiction as forming a story cycle. The close reading which this project entails is complemented by Schmidt's interest in Welty's place within the larger context of women's writing and the American literary canon. He demonstrates how these stories 'are able to teach us new ways of reading and different ways of defining an artist's historical context and social engagement. ... Welty's stories impress because of their volatile, decentering energy, not merely for the (unmistakable) perfections of their surface, and her critiques of social stereotyping – particularly as it involves the shaping of women's identities – have never appeared more timely or daring'. Schmidt's book is itself timely, and should signal a new and productive direction in Welty criticism.

Susan V. Donaldson's essay, 'Recovering Otherness in *The Golden Apples*' (*AL* 63.489–506), addresses the related issues of storytelling, authority and power in Welty's representation of the fictive town of Morgana. Drawing upon the theoretical contexts furnished by Foucault and Bakhtin, Donaldson sets out to show how 'Morgana's stories determine who exists inside and outside the community, who has the power to tell stories and who does not, and who constitutes the "proper" sort of audience for all too familiar tales'. Rather than the burden of the past, the voices of Southern history form the literary legacy of Welty's fiction, according to Donaldson's acutely argued essay.

Books Reviewed

Allen, Donald, ed. *The Selected Poems of Frank O'Hara*. Carcanet. pp. 233. £18.95. ISBN 0 85635 939 4.

Anaya, Rudolpho J., and Francisco Lomeli, eds. *Aztlan: Essays on the Chicano Homeland*. UNMP. pp. 248. pb $13.95. ISBN 0 8263 1261 6.

Baker, Houston A., Jnr. *Workings of the Spirit: The Poetics of Afro-American Women's Writing*. UChicP. pp. 239. $24.95. ISBN 0 226 03522 0.

Barlett, Lee, ed. *Kenneth Rexroth and James Laughlin: Selected Letters*. Norton. pp. 292. £18.95. ISBN 0 393 02939 5.
Beidler, Philip D. *Re-Writing America: Vietnam Writers in their Generation*. UGeoP. pp. 333. $35. ISBN 0 8203 1264 9.
Bornstein, George, ed. *Representing Modernist Texts: Editing as Interpretation*. UMichP. pp. 283. pb $16.90. ISBN 0 472 09439 4 .
Brady, Ivan. *Anthropological Poetics*. R&L. pp. 398. hb $55, pb $27.50. ISBN 0 8746 7636 6, 0 8476 7672 2.
Brogan, Jacqueline Vaught. *Part Of The Climate: American Cubist Poetry*. UCalP. pp. 343. $45. ISBN 0 520 066848 3.
Brunner, Edward J. *Poetry as Labor and Privilege: The Writings of W. S. Merwin*. UIllP. pp. 329. $44.95. ISBN 0 252 01775 7.
Bush, Ronald, ed. *T. S. Eliot: The Modernist in History*. CUP. pp. 210. £25. ISBN 0 521 39074 5.
Byrd, Rudolph, P. *Jean Toomer's Years With Gurdjieff: Portrait of an Artist 1923 –1936*. UGeoP. pp. 212. $30. ISBN 0 8203 1248 7.
Cady, Edwin H., and Louis J. Budd, eds. *On Frost: The Best from American Literature* DukeUP. pp. 255. £33.25. ISBN 0 8223 1159 3.
Calderon, Hector, and José Saldivar, eds. *Criticism in the Borderlands: Studies in Chicano Literature, Culture, and Ideology*. DukeUP. pp. 289. pb $18.95. ISBN 0 8223 1143 7.
Cifelli, Edward, M., ed. *The Selected Letters of John Ciardi* UArkP. pp. 475. $30. ISBN 1 55728 171 8.
Claridge, Laura, and Elizabeth Langland, eds. *Out of Bounds: Male Writers and Gender(ed) Criticism*. UMassP. pp. 344. hb $42.50, pb $16.95. ISBN 0 87027 734 9, 0 87023 735 7.
Coltelli, Laura. *Winged Words: Native American Writers Speak*. UNebP. pp. 212. £8.50. ISBN 0 8032 6351 1.
Conte, Joseph M. *Unending Design: The Forms of Postmodern Poetry*. CornUP. pp. 314. hb $42.50, pb $13.95. ISBN 0 8014 2469 0, 0 8014 9914 3.
Costello, Bonnie. *Elizabeth Bishop: Questions of Mastery*. HarvardUP. pp. 265. £23.95. ISBN 0 674 24689 6.
Cowan, Bainard, and Joseph G. Kronick, eds. *Theorizing American Literature: Hegel, the Sign, and History*. LSUP. pp. 294. $29.95. ISBN 0 8071 1628 9.
Crump, R. W., and Albert Montesi, eds. *Order in Variety: Essays and Poems in Honour of Donald E. Stanford*. UDelP. $29.95. ISBN 0 874 13420 X.
Cuddy, Lois, and David H. Hirsch, eds. *Critical Essays on T. S. Eliot's 'The Waste Land'*. Hall. pp. 288. $40. ISBN 0 816 17302 8.
D'Avanzo, Mario L. *A Cloud of Other Poets: Robert Frost and The Romantics*. UPA. pp. 241, pp. 175. hb $38, pb $21.11. ISBN 0 8191 7997 3, 0 8191 71998 1.
Davie, Donald. *Studies in Ezra Pound Chronicles and Polemics*. Carcanet. pp. 388. £25. ISBN 0 85635 880 0.
Dean, Tim. *Gary Snyder and the American Unconscious: New Directions in American Studies*. General editor, Eric Homberger. Macmillan. pp. 240. £40. ISBN 0 333 49294 3.
Dickie, Margaret. *Lyric Contingencies: Emily Dickinson and Wallace Stevens*. UPennP. pp. 196. $24.95. ISBN 0 8122 30779.
Diggory, Terence. *William Carlos Williams and the Ethics of Painting*. PrincetonUP. pp. 162. $27.50. ISBN 0 691 06852 6.
Donoghue, Denis. *Being Modern Together*. ScholarsG. pp. 76. $29.95. ISBN 1 55540

608 4.
Elkins, Andrew. *The Poetry of James Wright*. UAlaP. pp. 288. $33.95. ISBN 0 81733 0496 7.
Ellis, Steve. *The English Eliot: Design, Language and Landscape in 'Four Quartets'*. Routledge. pp. 187. £35. ISBN 0 415 06688 3.
Everman, Welch D. *Jerzy Kosinski: The Literature of Violation*. Borgo. pp. 158. pb $19.95. ISBN 0 89370 276 5.
Fabre, Michel. *Black American Writers in France, 1840–1980: From Harlem to Paris*. UIllP. pp. 358. $35.95. ISBN 0 252 01684 X.
Filreis, Alan. *Wallace Stevens and the Actual World*. PrincetonUP. pp. 362. $35. ISBN 0 691 106864 X.
Fishman, Charles. *Blood to Remember: American Poets on the Holocaust*. TTP. pp. 426. $25. ISBN 0 89672 214 7.
Flieger, Jerry Aline. *The Purloined Punchline: Freud's Comic Theory and the Postmodern Text*. JHUP. pp. 291. £21.50. ISBN 0 8018 4048 1.
Gallun, Raymond Z., with Jeffrey M. Elliot. *Starclimber: The Literary Adventures and Autobiography of Raymond Z. Gallun*. Borgo. pp.168. $14.95. ISBN 0 89370 448 2.
Gelpi, Albert. *The Tenth Muse. The Psyche of the American Poet*. CUP. pp. 327. hb £40, $54.40, pb £14.95, $17.95. ISBN 0 521 41339 7, 0 521 42401 1.
Gilbert, Roger. *Walks In The World: Representation and Experience in Modern American Poetry*. PrincetonUP. pp. 290. $35. ISBN 0 691 06858 5.
Goldsmith, Arnold L. *The Modern American Urban Novel: Nature as 'Interior Structure'*. WSUP. pp. 179. $29.95. ISBN 0 8143 1994 7.
Gorak, Jan. *The Making of the Modern Canon: Genesis and Crisis of a Literary Idea*. Athlone. pp. 309. £35. ISBN 0 485 11388 0.
Grandjeat, Yves Charles, Elyette Andouard Labarthe, Christian Lerat, and Serge Ricard, eds. *Écritures Hispaniques aux États Unis: Memoire et Mutations*. UProvence. pp. 256. 160.00FF. ISBN 2 85399 247 0.
Grey, Thomas C. *The Wallace Stevens Case: Law and the Practice of Poetry*. HarvardUP. pp. 155. £19.95. ISBN 0 674 94577 8.
Group de Recherche et d'Etudes Nord Americaines. *L'Éducation aux États Unis: Mythes et Realités*. UProvence. pp. 214. FF130.00. ISBN 2 85399 282 9.
Gutman, Huck, ed. *As Others Read Us: International Perspectives on American Literature*. UMassP. pp. 254. $29.95. ISBN 0 87023 629 6.
Halliday, Mark. *Stevens and the Interpersonal*. PrincetonUP. pp. 196. $29.95. ISBN 0 691 06548 9.
Hamalian, Linda. *A Life of Kenneth Rexroth*. Norton. pp. 444. £16.95, $30. ISBN 0 393 02944 1.
Hamilton, Scott. *Ezra Pound and the Symbolist Inheritance*. PrincetonUP. pp. 257. $35. ISBN 0 691 06924 7.
Hartman, Charles O. *Jazz Text: Voice And Improvisation in Poetry, Jazz, and Song*. PrincetonUP. pp. 192. $29.95. ISBN 0 691 06817 8.
Hobson, Fred. *The Southern Writer in the Postmodern World*. UGeoP. pp. 114. $17.95. ISBN 0 8203 1275 4.
Hunt, Tim, ed. *The Collected Poetry of Robinson Jeffers, Volume Three 1938–1962*. StanfordUP. pp. 485. $60. ISBN 0 8047 1847 4.
Hyland, Peter. *Saul Bellow*. Macmillan. pp. 140. £9.50. ISBN 0 333 51697 4.
Jason, Philip K. *Fourteen Landing Zones: Approaches to Vietnam War Literature*. UIowaP. pp. 250. hb $32.50, pb $13.95. ISBN 0 87745 314 4, 0 87745 315 2.

Johnson, Don, ed. *Hummers, Knucklers, and Slow Curves, Contemporary Baseball Poems*. UIllP. pp. 130. hb $29.95, pb $12.95. ISBN 0 252 01810 9, 0 252 06183 7.

Jones, Gayl. *Liberating Voices: Oral Tradition in African American Literature*. HarvardUP. pp. 228. $27.95. ISBN 0 674 53204 1.

Jones, Suzanne W., ed. *Writing the Woman Artist: Essays on Poetics, Politics, and Portraiture*. UPennP. pp. 453. £15. ISBN 0 8122 1343 pb.

Jump, Harriet Devine, ed. *Diverse Voices: Essays on Twentieth Century Women Writers in English*. Harvester. pp. 278. hb £45, pb £12.50. ISBN 0 7450 0752 X, 0 7450 0753 8 pb.

Klinkowitz, Jerome. *Donald Barthelme: An Exhibition*. DukeUP. pp.146. £25. ISBN 0 8223 1152 6.

Klinkowitz, Jerome. *Structuring the Void: The Struggle for Subject in Contemporary American Fiction*. DukeUP. pp.181. £25. ISBN 0 8223 1205 0.

Koch, Kenneth. *Selected Poems*. Carcanet. pp. 284. £18.95. ISBN 0 85635 916 5.

Kostelanetz, Richard, ed. *American Writing Today*. Whitston. pp. 605. $55. ISBN 0 87875 379 6.

———. *The New Poetries and Some Old: Crosscurrents, Modern Critiques, Third Series*. SIUP. pp. 279. $24.95. ISBN 0 8093 1656 0.

Lane, Marvin, ed. *Black Mountain College: Sprouted Seeds An Anthology of Personal Accounts*. UTennP. pp. 346. $32.50. ISBN 0 87049 663 8.

Lanier, Park Jnr, ed. *The Poetics of Appalachian Space*. UTennP. pp. 215. $22.95. ISBN 0 87049 692 1.

Larson, Wendy. *Literary Authority and the Modern Chinese Writer: Ambivalence and Authority*. DukeUP. pp. 208. $34.95. ISBN 0 8223 1113 5.

Lim, Shirley Geok-lin, ed. *Approaches to Teaching Maxine Hong Kingston's 'The Woman Warrior'*. MLA. pp. 178. pb $19. ISBN 0 87352 704 6.

Longenbach, James. *Wallace Stevens: The Plain Sense of Things*. OUP. pp. 342. £15. ISBN 0 19 507022 4.

Macpherson, Pat. *Reflecting on 'The Bell Jar'*. Routledge. pp. 101. ISBN 0 415 04393 X.

Maltby, Paul. *Dissident Postmodernists: Bartheleme, Coover, Pynchon*. UPennP. pp. 232. $27.95. ISBN 0 812 23064 7.

Marconi, Catherine Lewallen, ed. *Handspan of Red Earth: An Anthology of Farm Poems*. UIowaP. pp. 181. hb $24.95, pb $10.95. ISBN 0 87745 325 X, 0 87745 326 8.

Marcus, Mordecai. *The Poems of Robert Frost: An Explication*. Hall. pp. 267. $35. ISBN 0 8161 7267 8.

Masters, Edgar Lee. *Across Spoon River, with an introduction by Ronald Primeau*. Prairie State books, UIllP. pp. 426. pb $14.95. ISBN 0 252 006051 2.

Materer, Timothy. *The Selected letters of Ezra Pound and John Quinn, 1915–1924*. DukeUP. pp. 238. £35.65. ISBN 0 8223 1132 1.

McCaffery, Larry, ed. *Across the Wounded Galaxies: Interviews with Contemporary American Science Fiction Writers*. UIllP. pp. 267. $12.95. ISBN 0 252 06140 3.

Michelson, Bruce. *Wilbur's Poetry: Music in a Scattering Time*. UMassP. pp. 258. £26. ISBN 0 87023 741 1.

Middlebrook, Diane Wood. *Anne Sexton: A Biography*. Virago. pp. 488. pb £8.99. ISBN 1 85381 510 1.

———, and Diana Hume George, eds. *The Selected Poems of Anne Sexton*. Virago. pp. 266. pb £7.99. ISBN 1 853 81416 4.

Miyake, Akiko. *Ezra Pound and the Mysteries of Love: A Plan for the Cantos*. DukeUP. pp. 287. $29.95, £28.45. ISBN 0 8223 1105 4.

Morgan, Ted. *Literary Outlaw: The Life and Times of William S. Burroughs*. Bodley. pp. 659. £20. ISBN 0 370 31586 3.

Murray, David. *Forked Tongue: Speech, Writing, and Representation in North American Indian Texts*. Pinter. pp.181. £27.50. ISBN 0 86187 785 3.

Murray, Paul. *T. S. Eliot and Mysticism: The Secret History of 'Four Quartets'*. Macmillan. pp. 326. £40. ISBN 0 333 47585 2.

Myers, Jack, and David Wojahn. *A Profile of Twentieth Century American Poetry*. SIUP. pp. 296. hb $25.95, pb $16.95. ISBN 0 8093 1348 0, 0 8093 1349 9.

O'Donnell, Patrick, ed. *New Essays on 'The Crying of Lot 49'*. CUP. pp. 174. £8.95. ISBN 0 521 38833 3.

Oriard, Michael. *Sporting with the Gods: The Rhetoric of Play and Game in American Culture*. CUP. pp. 579. £45. ISBN 0 521 39113 X.

Oster, Judith. *Toward Robert Frost: The Reader and the Poet*. UGeoP. pp. 336. $45. ISBN 0 82203 1322 X.

Parks, John. *G. E. L. Doctorow*. Continuum. pp.156. $19.95. ISBN 0 8264 0488 X.

Penso, Kia. *Wallace Stevens: 'Harmonium' and 'The Whole of Harmonium'*. Archon. pp. 128. $26.50. ISBN 0 208 02305 4.

Piket, Vincent. *Louis Auchincloss: The Growth of a Novelist*. Macmillan. pp. 258. £35. ISBN 0 333 52611 2.

Rainey, Lawrence S. *Ezra Pound and the Monument of Culture: Text, History, And The Malatesta Cantos*. UChicP. pp. 353. £23.95. ISBN 0 226 70316 9.

Raper, Julius Rowan. *Narcissus from the Rubble: Competing Models of Character in Contemporary British and American Fiction*. LSUP. pp.165. £23.50. ISBN 0 8071 1712 9.

Redman, Tim. *Ezra Pound and Italian Fascism*. CUP, pp. 288. £27.50, $34.50. ISBN 0 521 37305 0.

Ricard, Serge, ed. *Modèles et contre modèles dans la culture et la société Nord Americaines: identité et différences*. UProvence. pp. 180. Ff 110.00. ISBN 2 85399 284 5.

Riquelme, John Paul. *Harmony of Dissonances: T. S. Eliot, Romanticism, and Imagination*. JHUP. pp. 354. £23.50. ISBN 0 8018 4058 9.

Rose, Jacqueline. *The Haunting of Sylvia Plath*. Virago. pp. 288. £15.99. ISBN 1 85381 307 9.

Rotella, Guy. *Reading and Writing Nature: The Poetry of Robert Frost, Wallace Stevens, Marianne Moore and Elizabeth Bishop*. NortheasternU. pp. 253. £38. ISBN 1 55553 0869.

Ruderman, Judith. *Joseph Heller*. Continuum. pp. 216. $19.95. ISBN 0 8264 0516 9.

Ruland, Richard, and Malcolm Bradbury. *From Puritanism to Postmodernism: A History of American Literature*. Routledge. pp. 381. £35. ISBN 0 415 01341 0.

Saldivar, José David. *The Dialectics of Our America: Genealogy, Cultural Critique, and Literary History*. DukeUP. pp. 213. pb $12.95. ISBN 0 8223 1169 0.

Schmidt, Peter. *The Heart of the Story: Eudora Welty's Short Fiction*. UPMissip. pp. 312. $14.95. ISBN 0 87805 501 0.

Scott, Stanley J. *Frontiers of Consciousness: Interdisciplinary Studies in American Philosophy and Poetry*. FordUP. pp. 156. $40. ISBN 0 8232 1302 1.

Sharpe, Tony. *Vladimir Nabokov*. Arnold. pp.116. £5.99. ISBN 0 7131 6575 8.

Skerl, Jennie, and Robin Lydenberg, eds. *William S. Burroughs at the Front: Critical Reception, 1959–1989*. SIUP. pp. 274. $29.95. ISBN 0 8093 1586 6.

Smyth, Edmund J. *Postmodernism and Contemporary Fiction*. Batsford. pp. 206. £9.95. ISBN 0 7134 5776 7.

Styron, William. *Darkness Visible*. Cape. pp. 84. £8.99. ISBN 0 224 03045 0.

Tallack, Douglas. *Twentieth Century America: The Intellectual and Cultural Context*. Longman. pp.432. hb £24, pb £11.99. ISBN 0 582 49454 0, 0 582 49455 9.

Van Dover, J.Kenneth. *At Wolfe's Door: The Nero Wolfe Novels of Rex Stout*. Borgo. pp. 119. hb $22.95, pb $12.95. ISBN 0 893 70189 0, 0 893 70289 7.

Ward, Charlotte. *Pound's Translations of Arnaut Daniel: A Variorum Edition with Commentary from Unpublished Letters*. Garland. pp. 157. $47. ISBN 0 824 0 5468 7.

Watson, Steven. *Strange Bedfellows: The First American Avant Garde*. Abbeville, pp. 439. £19.95. ISBN 0 869 59934 5.

Wilson, R. *American Sublime: The Genealogy of a Poetic Genre*. UWiscP. pp. 337. hb £35.95, pb £16.65. ISBN 0 299 12770 2, 0 299 12774 5.

Zaller, Robert, ed. *Centennial Essays for Robinson Jeffers*. AUP. pp. 282. £27. ISBN 0 87413 414 5.

Zukofsky, Louis. *Complete Short Poetry,* intro. by Robert Creely. JHUP. pp. 365. $34.95. ISBN 0 801 84103 8.

XVIII

New Literatures in English

CORAL ANN HOWELLS, GAY RAINES, PHILLIP LANGRAN,
PAULA BURNETT, JEAN-PIERRE DURIX and CAROLE DURIX

This chapter has five sections: 1. Canada is by Coral Ann Howells; 2. Australia is by Gay Raines; 3. India is by Phillip Langran; 4. The Caribbean is by Paula Burnett; 5. New Zealand and the South Pacific is by Jean-Pierre Durix and Carole Durix.

1. Canada

(a) *General*

It is with great regret that we record the death of Northrop Frye (1912–1991) of whom Margaret Atwood wrote in her memorial tribute, 'He knew that the writer and the intelligent reader – the 'educated imagination' in his terms – were both required for the completion of a work of literature, and he laboured mightily to help readers see what it was that they were reading' (*Brick* 40.3). In *JCP* 6, dedicated to the memory of Frye, M. Atwood, J. Buckley and A. C. Hamilton in 'Northrop Frye Remembered by His Students' (1–7) give personal reminiscences with emphasis on him as charismatic teacher as well as literary critic and theorist, with twenty-seven books to his credit from *Fearful Symmetry* (1947) to *The Double Vision: Language and Meaning in Religion* (1991).

The following annual checklists of Canadian creative and critical writing have reliably appeared: *JCL*'s 'Annual Bibliography of Commonwealth Literature 1990' in the second issue (26.48–86), with the Canadian section introduced by W. H. New and compiled by Moshie Dahms, comprising an introduction which highlights new native and ethnic writing and contextualizes a list of general and serially published bibliographies, research aids, a wide selection of new poetry, drama, fiction and criticism; there is also a list of six new literary journals; *UTQ*'s 'Letters in Canada 1990' (vols. 61–2) with its comprehensive 'Humanities' section of critical reviews (62:i.103–228), plus *JCP*'s comprehensive reviews of forty individual poetry collections and anthologies published 1989. *BJCS* (6) continues to review over two hundred Canadian publications annually, and *BCan* (20) continues its lively journalistic style with its monthly coverage of new creative and critical writing. *IJCS* continues its policy of two thematic issues per year, and vol. 3 on 'The Changing Dimensions of Ethnicity in Canada' contains an excellent bibliography of multicultural writing and criticism as appendix to Enoch Padolsky's 'Cultural Diversity and Canadian Literature: A Pluralistic Approach to Majority and Minority Writing in Canada' (3.111–28). There is no retrospective 'The Year That Was' in *Kunapipi* (13) for 1991.

The most significant area of critical debate has been on the topic of literary canons. *Giving Canada a Literary History: A Memoir by Carl F. Klinck*, edited by Sandra Djwa, is the autobiography of one of Canada's most foremost canon makers, prepared by himself before his death in 1990 with the assistance of Djwa, who has done final revisions and a twenty-three page introduction for this tribute to him. This is a narrative of personal reminiscence and public purpose designed to document the evolution of Canadian literary studies, for as Djwa says, 'His own projects are the history of the development of Canadian literature since 1924.' Best known as the founding editor of the *Literary History of Canada* (1965), Klinck was also a strong supporter of and contributor to the *NCL* series. His lifelong enthusiasm for Canadian Literature was a scholarly enterprise fuelled by a strong nationalist impulse, from his choice of Canadian literary subjects for his MA and PhD at the University of Columbia in the 1920s and 1940s where he proposed to study his own country's literature 'without surrendering to American'. Klinck was convinced that the national soul is expressed through a country's literature, and publication of this memoir pays tribute to the principal architect of Canadian literary scholarship since 1960. The Klinck papers are deposited at the University of Western Ontario.

But is it possible to define a Canadian literary canon? This is a question discussed by Frank Davey in 'Politics and Canonicity in Recent English-Canadian poetry' (*BJCS* 6:i.101–9) and is also the topic of *Canadian Canons: Essays in Literary Value*, edited by Robert Lecker. The deliberately plural emphasis in these twelve essays by anglophone and francophone critics reflects the shifting forms of current canonical debate, symptomatic of a postmodern questioning of the grand narratives of tradition and authority, in a society which is bilingual and multicultural. Several essays argue that canon formation is closely related to cultural nationalism and reflects a conservative unified concept of Canadian identity; Leon Surette's 'Creating the Canadian Canon', Dermot McCarthy's 'Early Canadian Literary Histories and the Function of a Canon' and Stephen Scobie's 'Leonard Cohen, Phyllis Webb and the End(s) of Modernism' are of this opinion; while Carole Gerson's 'The Canon between the Wars: Field-notes of a Feminist Literary Archaeologist' argues for gender bias to be considered in evaluating canon formation. Klinck's *Literary History of Canada* was one important step in the evolutionary process, and a significant attempt at updating by the 1978 Calgary Conference of the Canadian Novel is the subject of two essays: Donna Bennett's 'Conflicted Vision: A Consideration of Canon and Genre in English-Canadian Literature' and Lawrence Mathews's 'Calgary, Canonization and Class'. As a narrative about Canada's literary history the collection is very informative, though conclusions on the possibility, desirability, or even the relevance of a Canadian canon are diverse, and the essays reflect a growing scepticism about centralized authority and about the politics of canon formation.

Literary Genres/Les Genres Littéraires, edited by I. S. MacClaren and C. Potvin, is the fifth volume in the *RICL* series of conference proceedings in English and French, collectively entitled *Towards a History of the Literary Institution in Canada* (see *YWES* 69 and 71). Most of the theoretical essays are in French, while the English essays discuss mixed genres and less easily classifiable texts. D. M. R. Bentley's 'Trees and Forest: Notes on Variety and Unity in Nineteenth-Century Canadian Writing' argues for two distinct literary aesthetics in the period (the miscellany and the work with a single theme), and after analysing mixed texts like Isabella Valancy Crawford's *Malcolm's Katie* and Susanna Moodie's *Roughing it in the Bush*, he warns against the obvious dangers of misreading these texts through the distorting lens of New Critical criteria. Germaine Warkentin offers a fascinating scholarly account of a little-known text by a late seventeenth-century Hudson's Bay Company employee in '"The Boy Henry Kelsey": Generic Disjunction in Henry Kelsey's Verse Journal', while Kenneth Heoppner's 'Responses to Canonical Literature and Paraliterature' is a rather unsatisfactory survey report on the interesting topic of the extent to which genre affects readers' responses to texts. The most distinguished contribution is Mary Lu MacDonald's meticulously researched 'Newspaper Literature in Early Nineteenth-Century Canada' which argues for the importance of literary distribution to general readers of the period, with their lyric poems, fiction instalments and short stories, and consequently for the significant role played by newspaper editors as literary critics. It is accompanied by a useful appendix on 'Sources of Literary Content in Newspapers and Periodicals of Upper and Lower Canada 1817–1850'. *The Canadian Essay*, edited by Gerald Lynch and David Rampton, is an interesting anthology featuring a rather neglected non-fictional genre and comprises twenty essays chronologically arranged, on literature, history, biography, philosophy, science and technology, by Margaret Atwood, Robertson Davies, Robert Fulford, Linda Hutcheon, Stephen Leacock, Hugh MacLennan, Marshall McLuhan, W. L. Morton, and George Woodcock. The critical introduction highlights the important Canadian literary magazines as places of publication, from *Canadian Forum* (established 1920) to *Queen's Quarterly, Tamarack Review* and *Saturday Night*. Among the most interesting essays are those dealing with history and the North, such as W. L. Morton's 'The North in Canadian Historiography' (*Transactions of the Royal Society of Canada*, 1970), Robert Fulford's 'How the West Was Lost' (*Saturday Night*, 1985) and another *Saturday Night* piece, Margaret Atwood's 'True North' (*Saturday Night*, 1987).

The shift towards decentralization apparent in canonical debates is paralleled in discussions about national identity, where the emphasis is clearly away from cultural nationalism and focused on multiculturalism and this is having a marked effect on the way Canadian literary canon is perceived. No longer is it exclusively white anglophone/francophone, but many other voices are now being represented as well. *Out of Place: Stories and Poems*, edited by Ven Begamudre and Judith Krause, is an attractive selection of stories and poems by thirty-seven contributors. Introduced by Alberto Manguel who highlights the twin themes of exile and homecoming, it represents work by ethnic and immigrant and native writers, offering shifting frames of perception. Many writers hark back to lost languages and cultures, while Kristjana Gunnars (Finnish-Canadian) and Nigel Barbarie (Caribbean-Canadian) reflect on the double perception of immigrants. To the editors' credit, they have netted a wide range of often conflicting perceptions on Canadianness and dislocation, opening out at the end with a poem by George Amabile (Italian-Canadian) called 'Horizons'. Lisette Boily's review article (*TSAR* 9:iii.77–87) on 'Other Solitudes: Canadian Multicultural Fictions' (*YWES* 70) explores definitions of multiculturalism, pointing out that Other Solitudes privileges immigrant experience, thereby undervaluing Native Canadian writing, and that within 'multiculturalism' the concepts of 'centre' and 'other' underline possibilities of compartmentalization. She provides a good summary of the complexities of the issue and the need for multicultural ideology to recognize political issues of empowerment coded into cultural discourse. Writing out of her own Polish-Ukrainian background, Janice Kulyk Keefer argues in 'From Mosaic to Kaleidoscope' (*BCan* 6.13–16) for a dynamic reading of cultural diversity and for a change in terminology to describe an ongoing process of shifts and fusion as a change from 'multiculturalism' to 'transculturalism'. In 'Bridges and Chasms: Multiculturalism and Mavis Gallant's "Virus X" ' (*WLWE* 31:ii.10–111), she argues persuasively that by Gallant's exposure of the problematic role played by ethnicity in Canada's social formation, her 1965 story of hyphenated Canadians in Europe offers a critique of what has since become Canada's dominant official ideology. *Writers in Transition: The Proceedings of the First National Conference of Italian-Canadian Writers*, edited by C. Dino Minni and Anna Foschi Ciampolini (1990), contains most of the papers delivered at this 1986 conference, plus a sampling of seminar presentations, all in English (though English, French and Italian were the official languages). The collection is arranged under topics like ethnic viewpoint, literary criticism, poetry, theatre, women's issues, history and the future, with parallels between issues like language and ethnicity between sections. Many papers are short and constitute a dialogue between representatives of the Italian-Canadian literary community on how to find a voice and position as a cultural minority in Canada, though several address wider issues. Francesco Loriggio's 'Italian-Canadian Literature: Basic Critical Issues', besides providing a useful bibliography of Italian-Canadian writing of the 1980s, discusses the importance of images of voyage and dislocation, and this essay gestures towards a 'transcultural future for Italian-Canadian writing'. Pasquale Verdicchio's 'The Failure of Memory in the Language Re-membering of Italian-Canadian Poets' discusses the relation between the mother language and the other language, and Dorina Michelutti's 'Coming to Terms with the Mother Tongue' treats a similar area, for as poet and translator she constructs her voice through criss-crossing languages. Roberta Sciff-Zamaro's round table contributions 'A Different Perspective' and 'What Does It Mean?' discuss immigrant experience from a woman's perspective, with examples from Caterina Edwards's short stories and Mary di Michele's poetry, while C. D. Minni's 'Reflecting Today's Ethnic Reality' speaks from his experience as a critic, anthologist and short story writer to point beyond the thematics of immigrant experience towards a literature of transculturalism. Michael Thorpe's ' "Turned Inside Out": South Asian Writing in Canada' (*ArielE* 22:i.5–20) surveys creative writing by Bharati Mukherjee, Neil Bissoondath, Surjeet Kalsey Siddartha, Uma Paramsswaran, and Arun Mukherjee's cultural critique in *TSAR* 9:iii (founded 1982 by M. G. Vassanji, himself a novelist) noting the shared thematics of expatriation, but also the crucial importance of literature for negotiating new positions in a developing multicultural society. Chelva Kanaganayakam's ' "Broadening the Substrata": An Interview with M. G. Vassanji' (*WLWE* 31:ii.19–35) quotes Vasanji's statement of his position, 'The stories I tell always begin somewhere else. Just like myself' and his discussion of problems within multiculturalism, which are curiously similar to Keefer's discussions on this topic.

Highlighting the problem of Canada's official bilingualism, Barbara Godard's 'Comparative Poetics: Reader-response and Canadian Literature'(*ECW* 44.61–6), a review essay on R. Heidenreich's *The Postwar Novel in Canada* (*YWES* 70) traces the history of comparative studies in English-Canadian and Quebec fiction since 1960, and signals that the promises of such a discipline grounded in a comparative theory of the sociology of literature have not yet been realized, though its potential usefulness as a challenge to conservative paradigms of dominance is increasingly obvious. *BCan* optimistically signals a new attempt at rapprochement and wider coverage of the national literary scene with their symposium 'Quebec: The Writers Speak' (20:ii.12–18), incidentally revealing a lack of consensus by writers about anything, though francophones like Yves Beauchemin and Monique Bosco show a degree of ideological commitment to Quebec, while anglophones like Louis Dudek and Ann Charney feel 'on the edge of cultural dissociation'.

There are two important books on Native writing. *Our Bit of Truth*, edited by Agnes Grant, offers a valuable overview from a historical as well as contemporary perspective. Published by one of the two major Native presses, its primary objective is to educate readers, as its introduction and bibliographies indicate. Arranged in seven sections, it begins with Native oral stories in translation (myths, legends, dream songs) and memoirs, many of which were written in the white man's language, and they are fascinating, often painful, historical and personal documents, stretching back to pre-white settlement. A strong tradition of native storytellers emerges, many of whom lived in two languages, as Eleanor Brass described in her autobiography *I Walk in Two Worlds*. Contemporary Native writing in English is well represented in short stories, poems and extracts from four novels. This anthology is a useful endeavour to explain and to rewrite the conventions for representing the Native in literature. There is, however, no index, which makes it difficult to retrace names of particular writers. Hartmut Lutz's *Contemporary Challenges: Conversations with Canadian Native Authors* consists of interviews with eighteen writers, including Thomson Highway, Jeanette Armstrong, Maria Campbell, Rita Joe and Thomas King, taped and transcribed by Lutz and co-edited with the help of his interviewees. Useful for biographical and cultural information as well as on the political issue of appropriation of voice, it also gives a strong sense of these writers' dilemmas on Native identity questions when faced with white cultural institutions which tend either to marginalize their otherness or to assimilate their discourse in response to the demands of international publishing.

One of the most significant shifts in Canadian studies outside Canada is towards a pan-European, international, and multidisciplinary perspective, and proceedings from several European conferences offer models for this new intiative. The most important is *Canada on the Threshold of the 21st Century: European Reflections upon the Future of Canada*, edited by Cornelius Remie and Jean-Michel Lacroix. These selected papers of the first All-European Canadian Studies conference, held at The Hague in October 1990, represent a collaborative effort by European and Canadian scholars to explore a number of interlocking contemporary issues in the fields of demography, environment, economics, identity, native issues, domestic and foreign policy. The proceedings include the three keynote addresses and fifty-six papers, of which only the papers on anglophone literature will be discussed here. Colin Nicholson's 'The Invention of the Past: Post-Colonial Elements in Recent Canadian Fiction' focuses on the relevance of novelists' preoccupation with history where the divisions within Canada's colonial past pose problems for contemporary reconstructions of Canadian identity; among the novelists he considers are Rudy Wiebe, Graeme Gibson, Timothy Findley, Margaret Laurence and Margaret Atwood. Coral Ann Howell's 'No Transcendental Image: Canadianness in Contemporary Canadian Women's Fiction in English', Marcienne Rocard's 'Canadian Woman's Ultimate Frontier in Aritha van Herk's *Fictional World*', and Anna Jakabfi's 'Anti-Survivalism in Prairie Fiction' constitute a group which presents a gendered perspective on identity. Significantly, the focus of all three papers is on Van Herk's *No Fixed Address* which appears to be a representative text for the defamiliarization that the Canadian female subject experiences towards culture, landscape, and language. The collection as a whole is valuable for its representation of a multiculturalism among European critics, revealing a kaleidoscope of conflicting and sometimes converging interpretations of Canadianness.

Probing Canadian Culture, edited by Peter Easingwood, Konrad Gross and Wolfgang Klooss, brings together eighteen papers given at a 1989 joint literature and cultural history conference at Kiel, Germany. The section on cultural history and canon formation presents a variety of English, German and French perspectives on the same issues debated in Lecker's Canadian Canons, with essays on possible models for a history of Anglo-Canadian literature (Helmut Bonheim), the Canada Council (Maria Tippett), the ideology behind canon formation (Lynette Hunter), Canadian literary standards) Colin Nicholson, and translation (Jean Sourisseau). Historical perspectives are developed through explorers' narratives (Ian D. MacLaren), and popular historiography (Michael Freidrichs), and the pervasiveness of the classical tradition in modern Canadian poetry (Walter Pache). Contemporary Canadian writing is explored through novels and short stories (Andrew Gurr and Coral Ann Howells), drama (Albert-Reiner Glaap), and an anthology of Inuit writing since the 1960s (Karla El-Hassan), while a general perspective on Native writing is presented in Hartwig Iserhagen's 'Multiculturalism, Ethnicity, and Contemporary Anglophone Canadian Indian Literature'. There are also two papers on English Canadian and Quebec film (John O. Thompson and Ian Lockerbie). The collection represents a positive European perception of the cultural diversity of contemporary Canada. *BJCS* 6:i, which contains selected papers from the BACS Annual Conference at the University of Nottingham in 1991, again focuses on perceptions of Canada from outside the country. As the title of Annis May Timpson's introductory essay 'Re-Constituting and Re-Constructing Canada' suggests, questions about Canada's political and cultural identity are again high on the agenda for Canadian studies in Europe. The three literary essays exemplify the view of a decentred Canada: Frank Davey's 'Politics and Canonicity in Recent English-Canadian poetry' discusses patterns of poetry publishing and distribution with their regional tendencies which work against coherent updating of a single poetic canon, exemplified in his examination of eight anthologies published since 1970. Coral Ann Howells's essay is reprinted from the Hague Conference proceedings, and John Thieme's 'A Sanctioned Babel: Myth and Language in Robert Kroetsch's *What the Crow Said*' explores the use of mythemes from classical and Biblical narrative in this postmodern novel, constructing a Canadian world 'of indeterminate mapping and signification' where the male dream of transcendental signification has become impossible in a hybridized culture. Like Davey and Howells, Thieme emphasizes process rather than the concept of an already-achieved national identity.

On comparative Canadian-American criticism, the appearance of *Studies on Canadian Literature: Introductory and Critical Essays*, edited by Arnold Davidson, is significant. A book on Canadian literature published by the MLA in New York would seem, as Davidson suggests, to signal the 'arrival of a national literature on the international stage', or more precisely on the North American stage. These nineteen essays by Canadian and American contributors represent a dialogue with American traditions which have excluded Canadian literature. Addressing questions like 'What is distinctive about Canadian literature?', the essays give overviews and information, complemented by two excellent annotated bibliographical guides to English-Canadian and Quebec literature. The design of the book is itself politically interesting: eight essays on Canadian writing in English, eight on Canadian writing in French, and three on Native writing, teaching Canadian literature outside Canada, and Robert Kroetsch's cleverly deconstructive piece 'Reading Across the Border', all of which function as supplements unsettling some of the traditional positions advanced in the main section. Linda Hutcheon's 'The Canadian Postmodern: Fiction in English since 1960' emphasizes Canada's historically ex-centric position in relation to the United States and to Britain, focusing on distinctively Canadian versions of postmodernism. To put Annette Kolodny's 'Margaret Atwood and the Politics of Narrative' beside this is to witness, by contrast, the Americanization of Atwood's fiction, where it is briskly contextualized in relation to Nathaniel Hawthorne and Hayden White. Other versions of Canadian-American dialogue are Arnold Davidson's 'The Reinvention of the West in Canadian Fiction' and Shirley Neuman's essay on English-Canadian Poetry since 1960 (see section (c)). The double voicedness within the Canadian tradition can be heard clearly in the essays on critical discourse: Barry Cameron's 'English Critical Discourse in/on Canada' and Barbara Godard's more sinuously theoretical 'Critical Discourse in/on Quebec'. Acknowledgement of multicultural ideology comes with Robin McGrath and Penny Petrone's historical account of 'Native Canadian Literature' which establishes a context in which white readers might welcome the current explosion of native creative writing, while Lorna Irvine and Paula Gilbert's 'Altering the Principles of Mapping: Teaching Canadian and Quebec Literature outside Canada' addresses problematic questions about theorizing Canadian literature which are highlighted when that literature is exported. The collection offers a series of signposts and maps to Americans who may be interested in reading writing from North of the border. Peter Dale Scott's 'The Difference Perspective Makes: Literary Studies in Canada and the United States' (*ECW* 44.1–60) written from the perspective of a Canadian temporarily at Berkeley, gives an evaluative comparative study of 'difference' rather than any simple binary analysis, emphasizing the asymmetries involved in such transnational comparisons. Well worth reading and pondering for its controversial insights, the essay is divided into sections on marginality, the 'emergent nation' syndrome, interactive Canadian dialogue, and cultural pessimism versus technological optimism. *Borderlands: Essays in Canadian-American Relations*, for which Robert Lecker was co-ordinating editor, is a collection of fourteen essays dealing with transport, free trade, migration, boundary disputes and cultural identity. There are three substantial literary essays: Sherrill Grace's 'Comparing Mythologies: Ideas of West and North'; Frances W. Kaye's 'Canadian-American Prairie-Plains: Literature in English' and Laurie Ricou's eclectic piece, 'Crossing Borders in the Literature of the Pacific Northwest' which ponders on the complexities of borders and develops his argument through a comparison between Daphne Marlatt's *Steveston* (1974) and John Keeble's *Yellowfish* (1980).

On home territory, there are several interesting regional studies: Gwendolyn Davies's *Studies in Maritime Literary History, 1760–1930* is strongly localized in the best sense. In the thirteen essays, Davies represents the range and distinctive qualities of Maritime writing in English, from eighteenth-century planters' journals to contemporary poetry of black Nova Scotian George Elliott Clark. Like Janice Kulyk Keefer's *Under Eastern Eyes* (*YWES* 68), this is a spirited ideological and practical response to restrictive national literary histories which have neglected Maritime writing. The Maritimes, as home of the Empire Loyalists and later of the Confederation Poets, has a long literary tradition, as individual essays indicate. 'Persona in Planters Journals' looks at the social documentary value of the journals of four of the eight thousand New England planters who took up the lands left by deported Acadians after 1760. 'Penetrating into Scott's Field: The Covenanting Fiction of Thomas McCulloch' which discusses his *Mephisboseth Stepsure Letters* (*YWES* 71) serially published in the *Acadian Recorder* 1821–3, has more in common with Stephen Leacock than with the Planters' conventional narratives. 'The Home Place in Modern Maritime Literature' focuses on contemporary writers' sense of regional identity being focused on the 'home place' as 'symbol of cultural continuity in the face of social fragmentation, outmigration, and a continuing hardscrabble economy'. *Time and Place: The Life and Works of Thomas H. Raddall*, edited by Alan R. Young, is a reassessment of this mid-twentieth-century Maritime novelist and historian of Atlantic Canada, by literary critics, historians and folklorists. This composite approach highlights not only Raddall's better known historical fictions and autobiography, but also his work as preserver of local history records and buildings. Moving from east to west, *Words We Call Home: Celebrating Creative Writing at UBC,* edited by Linda Svendsen, is an anthology of the work of sixty-nine writers who have been graduates and teachers from the Department of Creative Writing at that university. Begun by Earl Birney as a creative writing workshop in the late 1940s, this programme has produced an impressive list of award winners and writing in a variety of genres. The anthology offers an historical perspective on Canadian West Coast writing with its adventurous sampling of poems, stories, screenplays and translations. Perhaps the most striking pieces are Gladys Hindmarsh's 'Ucluelet', Daphne Marlatt's three short astonishing poems, and Morris Panych's postmodern play *Last Call! A Post-Nuclear Cabaret,* Act 2. An earlier West Coast artist is memorialized in *Dear Nan: Letters of Emily Carr, Nan Cheney and Humphrey Toms*, edited by Doreen Walker, in this scrupulously edited collection of more than two hundred letters exchanged between three close friends 1930–45. It constitutes a significant element in Carr's autobiographical record and has genuine narrative interest as a story of friendship between two artists (Carr and Cheney) and between an artist and a young admirer (for Toms was a soldier, teacher, plant pathologist and genealogist). It is also a document of Carr's later painting career and records her fascination with Indian subjects and with landscape ('I am wrestling again with my forests' as she wrote to Cheney in 1932). The book is beautifully illustrated with black and white photographs and some glorious colour reproductions of Carr's paintings.

Rosemary Sullivan's biography *By Heart: Elizabeth Smart. A Life* offers a map of Smart's life, a life which is both intensely personal and also emblematic of the fate of an expatriate colonial woman writer whose life and career were shaped by her colonialism, her gender and her literary passions. Sullivan tells a story of female desire, imitating the model of her subject's best known fiction *By Grand Central Station I Sat Down and Wept*, for Smart herself continually blurred the boundaries between words and life (falling in love with George Barker through his poetry long before she ever met him) and writing romantic scripts for her life which she then read as fate. Sullivan documents the legendary romance and the daily life in what is a 'celebration' of Smart rather than a critical assessment of her literary career as journalist and modern novelist; that still remains to be done.

To end this section with a work that defies classification, Aritha van Herk's *In Visible Ink: Crypto-Frictions* might be described as 'regional writing' in so far as van Herk describes herself as belonging to the West and to the region of Woman. These thirteen recent essays show van Herk mapping the territory of West and North, woman and language, as she crosses borderlines between genres, between fiction, literary criticism and autobiography, between realism and fantasy. Her second essay 'Blurring Genres: Fictioneer as Ficto-Critic' playfully and usefully defines her methodology: 'After reading a text, she would write a parallel text, a story or not a story that was ficto-commentary on the fiction she was supposed to elucidate.' Many of these essays are about reading Western writers: Sinclair Ross, Nellie McClung, Robert Kroetsch, Henry Kreisel, Sheila Watson, and several are strongly feminist. 'Writing the Immigrant Self: Disguise and Damnation' deserves mention as van Herk's first excursion into multiculturalism, as she explores the problems of writing immigrant fiction.

(b) Fiction

ECW's excellent series of reference texts for fiction and poetry, *Canadian Writers and Their Works*, edited by Robert Lecker, Jack David and Ellen Quigley and with general introductions to all twenty volumes by George Woodcock, is now complete. The series presents the best and fullest account of Canada's literary history and should be part of every library's holdings on Canadian literature. The last one to appear in the Fiction series is Volume IV, with critical essays and bibliography of primary and secondary materials on Western writers Martha Ostenso, Frederick Philip Grove, W. O. Mitchell, Sinclair Ross, and Raymond Knister (who is the one non-Westerner). Woodcock's introduction discusses the tradition of Prairie fiction and what he sees as the frequent over-valuation of its significance in Canadian literature. In a sensible, balanced essay he canvasses the appeal of a fiction about the land and outposts of civilization in a regional realist tradition, but he also insists on the Gothic fantasy elements within Gorve's and Ostenso's fiction, which are still apparent in their transformations in Mitchell. W. J. Keith's learned and thoughtful essay on Frederick Philip Grove discusses the biographical oddities of Grove's career as revealed by Douglas Spettigue, and the duplicities of his life in contrast with his literary integrity. Keith looks at all Grove's fiction and non-fiction, noting his two German novels that belong with his pre-Canadian persona, as well as doing a detailed study of his novels about immigrants and pioneers of the Canadian West, from *Settlers of the Marsh* (1925) to *The Master of the Mill* (1944). Morton L. Ross's essay on Sinclair Ross treats all his novels and short stories, though inevitably highlighting *As For Me and My House* as his best novel, and engages vigorously with the debate about Mrs Bentley as narrator, insisting on a critical rebalancing in readings of her and on paying adequate attention to the multiple ironies of the novel's ending.

Dundurn continues with its extremely useful project begun in 1980 of biocritical guides on Canadian writers, *Profiles in Canadian Literature*. Vol. 8, edited by Jeffrey M. Heath, contains essays on eighteen writers – fifteen anglophone and three francophone – mainly novelists, but also one poet (Dennis Lee) and three dramatists (Ken Gass, Rick Salutin, Margaret Hollingsworth) as well as genre evaders like Michael Ondaatje. Their economical format (7–8 pages, double columns) of biocritical essay and chronology, selected authorial and critical comments, and bibliography, offers interesting critical perspectives to students. Elspeth Cameron's essay on Janette Turner Hospital traces the variety of form as well as continuities within her novels and short stories, reading her fiction within the context of Hospital's early fundamentalist Australian background and her itinerant adult life, focusing on her preoccupations with the philosophical and psychological implications of crossing borders, as exemplified in her postmodernist fictions, *Borderline* and *Charades*.

This year saw Carleton University Press's scholarly edition of Julia Catherine Beckwith Hart's *St Ursula's Convent; or, The Nun of Canada*, edited by Douglas G. Lochhead. It follows the established format of lengthy editorial biographical and critical introduction, complete text, explanatory notes, and bibliographical information. Hart's romance novel (1824) is a literary landmark, being the first novel published by a native-born Canadian and published in Canada. (It was published by subscription). Though Lochhead makes an elegant case for its social significance as an exploration of early Canadian manners with their already distinctively multicultural mix of French, British and Canadian protagonists, the novel has less literary significance. It is much indebted to early nineteenth-century English Gothic conventions, merely transposing exotic landscapes from Italy and France to Quebec. Indeed, one contemporary Montreal reviewer described it as 'another of those reviewer's miseries', and Lochhead's scholarly edition is only the second time of the novel's publication. The University of Calgary has produced Number 9 in its Canadian Archival Inventory Series, *The Clark Blaise Papers: First and Second Accession*, compiled by M. Chevrefils. This volume, introduced by Catherine Ross's biocritical essay on Blaise as 'resident alien', documents holdings on Blaise's literary activities since the early 1960s, from his early work at Harvard and Iowa Writers' Workshop (including his first published story 'The Little Orphan' 1961) through his three short story collections, two novels and one travel journal of the 1970s and 1980s. The catalogue also lists essays and correspondence as well as holograph, typescript and computer-generated manuscripts. It is to be noted that Calgary's holdings of the Bharati Mukherjee papers are included in this volume.

ECW continues to publish its user-friendly student series *Canadian Fiction Studies*, and at least one appeared in 1991: Neil Besner's *Introducing Alice Munro's Lives of Girls and Women*, following the typical format that includes a chronology of the author's life, critical reception and close reading of the text, together with a selective bibliography. Ten more in the series are projected for 1992.

As far as genre studies are concerned, again it is the short story which is prominent. *New Women: Short Stories by Canadian Women 1900–1920*, edited by Sandra Campbell and Lorraine McMullen, is an anthology of twenty stories by women who were all well-known as novelists, journalists or contributors to magazines. It offers a fascinating range of feminine/feminist perspectives on issues ranging from women's suffrage and women in the professions, stories of World War I, to wilderness romantic comedy and problem fiction dealing with labour unrest and immigrant and native women. The stories also illustrate the variety of writing styles at the time, from Adeline M. Teskey's moralistic rural story 'A Common Man and his Wife: The Ram Lamb' (1901), to J. Georgina Sime's 'Munitions!' (1919), a well-documented feminist protest against the working conditions of women. Sara Jeannette Duncan's 'The Heir Apparent' (1905) is an ironic handling of multiple perspectives, while Nellie McClung's 'The Live Wire' (1910) is a satire on the vanity of the male political world. Not only does this excellent collection make available women's stories before 1920, but as McMullen says in her annotated introduction, it makes clear the close relation between women's fiction and women's changing social position. *New Directions from Old*, edited by J. R. (Tim) Struthers, is a collection of nine essays and an interview with Rudy Wiebe, all relating to short stories. Dedicating the book to George Woodcock, while aligning himself with John Metcalf's position as critic, Struthers shows his preference for modernist and postmodernist short fiction. Of course Metcalf is here speaking of 'Tradition' and challenging the assumption that realism is the dominant mode or that an authentic literary tradition existed prior to the 1960s. Louis K. MacKendrick's 'Reordering the Real: Metcalf and Rooke's 81: Best Canadian Stories' analyses the principles behind the selection process of that anthology, while offering readings of individual stories by Clark Blaise, Mavis Gallant, Norman Levine and Alice Munro. Stories by several of these writers are the subjects of other essays, the best of which is Simone Vauthier's 'Portrait of the Artist as a (no longer) Young Man: Norman Levine's "We All Begin in a Little Magazine" ', where she considers the questions of fictionalized autobiography, revisions, and the importance to stories of afterwords. Leon Rooke's end piece 'A Coherent Fictional Oeuvre' featuring 'three blithe and creaky short fictions' accompanied by three pieces of criticism, provides a wryly witty comment on the critical enterprise. Coral Ann Howells's 'Canadian Signatures in the Feminine' attempts to construct a multicultural definition of Canadianness from the woman's angle in her examination of seven contemporary short stories by women from Anglo-Saxon backgrounds, ethnic backgrounds, native women and immigrant women. This sampling tends to deconstruct any coherent national self image as it is replaced by the pluralism of regional, gender, ethnic and racial perspectives. Ben-Z. Shek's *French-Canadian and Quebecois Novels* is a short historical and critical survey of fiction available in English translation, from nineteenth-century historical novels to contemporary *écriture feminine*. Accompanied by a bibliography of primary texts and criticism, it is a reliable and uncontentious teaching text, which is doubtless its modest intention.

Early prose writing is much more visible this year, beginning with I. S. MacLaren's 'Samuel Hearne's Acounts of the Massacre at Bloody Fall, 17 July 1771' (*ArielE* 22:i.25–51), which raises the question of the relation between history and fiction. Through an examination of three different versions of Hearne's travel narrative produced over twenty years and citing his field notes, report, draft manuscript and published book, MacLaren shows how the factual report of brutalities has been metamorphosed into Gothic fiction. Michael Hurley's 'Double Entendre: Rebel Angst and Beautiful Losers in John Richardson's *The Monk Knight of St John*' (*CanL* 128.107–18) is an intriguing essay on this bizarre novel of 1850 which reproduces many of Richardson's doppelganger figures and Chinese box plot formulae, arguing that the dream cycle of Richardson's narrative prefigures Cohen's and Davies's perversely saintly figures with their strange combination of the metaphysical, sexuality and violence. Some interesting work is being done on Susanna Moodie, with John Thurston's anthology of fourteen sketches and stories written in addition to *Roughing It in the Bush* and five serialized novels. Many of the stories in *Voyages: Short Narratives of Susanna Moodie* are autobiographical fictions like 'Rachel Wade, or Trials from the Burthen of a Life' (1848) and are concerned with emigration and exile, reworked as romance plots. This material collected for the first time, provides new perspectives on Moodie's characteristic themes and narrative methods. Franz K. Stanzel's 'Innocent Eyes? Canadian Landscape as Seen by Frances Brooke, Susanna Moodie and Others' (*IJCS* 4.97–110) shows that eighteenth- and nineteenth-century settlers' accounts of Canada were predetermined by imported aesthetic ideas of the sublime and the picturesque. In a sometimes amusing study of the history of taste, Stanzel highlights 'the changing aesthetics of tree stumps in a landscape.' James De Mille, the nineteenth-century Maritime writer who is best known for his novel *A Strange Manuscript Found in a Copper Cylinder* gets some attention from Patricia Monk in *The Gilded Beaver: An Introduction to the Life and Work of James De Mille*, though this is not a particularly distinguished biographical or literary critical study. Bruce F. MacDonald's '*Helena's Household*: James De Mille's Heretical Text' (*CanL* 128.120–40) is rather more interesting in opening up new directions for academic criticism of this prolific novelist. He looks at this early novel about Roman Christians which De Mille was forced to alter because of its unorthodox theology. His scholarly investigations of the author's religious beliefs combined with an examination of rhetorical structures in the novel lead him to the conclusion that its challenge to orthodoxy lay in its peculiar combination of faith and doubt, a very Victorian dilemma.

Misao Dean's *A Different Point of View: Sara Jeannette Duncan* offers a reading of Duncan's novels, short stories, and journalism from a feminist post-colonial perspective, focusing on Duncan's late nineteenth-century formulation of a colonial point of view which was shaped by her growing up in Canada, her work as a professional journalist in America and her married life in India. Arguing that Duncan was doubly marginalized by being a woman and a colonial who published in America and England, Dean focuses on her technique of employing a detached ironic (female) narrator who obliquely but consistently criticized dominant ideologies of imperialism and capitalism. The chapters on Duncan's journalism and short story collection *The Simpole Adventures of a Memsahib*, and the last chapter which discusses *The Imperialist* present Duncan's radicalism as ambivalent: 'Duncan could not be a whole-hearted nationalist because she was an imperialist, could not be an unqualified feminist because she finally accepted patriarchally imposed definitions of the female'. Contrary to Dean's assertion, this looks like a typical (not a 'different') late nineteenth-century woman's point of view. Gabriella Ahmansson's *A Life and Its Mirrors: A Feminist Reading of L. M. Montgomery's Fiction*, volume 1, is a scholarly study, the outgrowth of a doctoral dissertation on stories for girls 1900–15, which offers a thorough overview of Montgomery criticism and close readings of *Anne of Green Gables* and *Anne's House of Dreams*, locating a duality between Montgomery's submission to romance conventions and her subversive critique of them.

Fiction by male writers from early- to mid-twentieth-century receives far more attention than usual. R. S. MacDonald's 'Measuring Leacock's Mariposa against Lewis's Gopher Prairie: a Question of Monuments' (*DR* 71:i.84–103) compares *Sunshine Sketches* with Sinclair Lewis's *Main Street* as Canadian and American representations of small town life, arguing that Leacock's irony and humour present a more coherent view of a social and spiritual condition than Lewis's satirical and reductive stereotyping of the small town. David Stouck, editor of *Sinclair Ross's 'As For Me and My House': Five Decades of Criticism*, claims that Ross's novel has been the subject of more critical debate than any other Canadian novel, and his claim would seem to be supported by this collection, which comprises contemporary reviews and seventeen substantial essays produced fittingly to mark the fiftieth anniversary of the novel's publication (in New York). This is a major book on Ross's novel, and the last two essays exemplify current critical trends. Frank Davey's 'The Conflicting Signs of *As For Me and My House*' focuses attention on gaps within the diary form in his exposure of the conflicting structures of sexuality, ideology and economic forces here. Helen M. Buss's 'Who Are You, Mrs Bentley? Feminist Re-vision' considers current theoretical views of women's life writing and Ross's construction of a female subject; a stimulating and powerful essay on the woman artist figure in prairie fiction. John Orange's 'Filling in the Blanks' (*ECW* 44.88–93) is an informative review essay on Claude Bissel's biographical and personal memoir *Ernest Buckler Remembered* (*YWES* 70). It is most valuable for its comments on his three major novels, which were structured as a trilogy, that traced the departure of an artist from the timeless world of childhood, through a descent into alienation, to his return at the end to memory and recreation. Barbara Pell's 'Faith and Fiction: Hugh MacLennan's *The Watch That Ends the Night*' (*CanL* 128.39–50) treats structures of religious belief and their representation in MacLennan's realist novel, arguing that his portrayal of the protagonist's spiritual pilgrimage compromises its fictional form and undermines its narrative resolution. The reading focuses on the final mystical encounter and the epilogue where realism is transposed into metaphysical abstraction. David Creelman's 'Charles Bruce: *The Channel Shore* between Realism and Nostalgia,' (*DR* 70:iv.460–79) is a close study of Bruce's only novel which Creelman reads as maritime historical fiction, arguing for the doubleness of this text where Nova Scotia regionalism is balanced against conservative idealism and a nostalgic vision of a knowable community.

Several very good collections of essays on twentieth-century fiction have appeared, notably W. J. Keith's *An Independent Stance: Essays on English-Canadian Criticism and Fiction*. This retrospective collection which gathers together twenty-one of

Keith's essays published since 1977, is chronologically arranged and divided into two parts: statements on literary-critical matters and discussions of specific authors and texts. It is a record by one of Canada's major critics of his formulation of his functions and responsibilities, and it is also, in characteristically Keith fashion, an evaluative narrative of selected twentieth-century fiction and critical fashions. Beginning with a 1977 review of Carl Klinck's *Literary History of Canada*, and continuing with his 1978 paper at the Calgary Conference, 'The Thematic Approach to Canadian Fiction' and his tribute to Metcalf, 'Criticism in Practice: John Metcalf's Private Part', Keith examines key issues in Canadian criticism, like the importance of evaluation, and while maintaining a sceptical attitude towards canonical fixities or fixations, argues for reliable editions of early Canadian texts. Of the essays on F. P. Grove, Ethel Wilson, Hugh MacLennan, Robertson Davies, Margaret Laurence, Hugh Hood, Rudy Wiebe, Jack Hodgins and Margaret Atwood, two stand out as significant new readings: 'Jack Hodgins and the Sources of Invention' and 'Interpreting and Misinterpreting "Bluebeard's Egg" '. Keith's defence of the critic's art on the last page defines his own position and practice: 'We need to approach literature with a flexible, verbally sensitive critical practice that attempts tentatively, humbly, sometimes painfully, to develop a tradition of close and accurate reading'.

Narrative Strategies in Canadian Literature: Feminism and Postcolonialism, edited by Coral Ann Howells and Lynette Hunter, provides an informative overview of Canadian fiction and a glimpse of the poetry of the last twenty years by ten British critics.These essays focus theory through readings of individual texts or groups of texts by single writers: Margaret Laurence's *A Bird in the House* (Peter Easingwood), Alistair MacLeod's *Short Fiction* (Colin Nicholson), Michael Ondaatje's *Running in the Family* (John Thieme), Neil Bissoondath's *Digging Up the Mountain* and *A Casual Brutality* (David Richards), Daphne Marlatt's *Steveston* (Shirley Chew), Marian Engel's *Bear and The Tattooed Woman* (Coral Ann Howells), Alice Munro's short stories (Rosalie Osmond), Margaret Atwood's *The Handmaid's Tale* (Jill Le Bihan); while Andrew Gurr discusses short fiction and whole-books by Alice Munro, Rudy Wiebe, Katherine Mansfield and V. S. Naipaul. Stephen Regan's excellent essay, 'The Presence of the Past: Modernism and Postmodernism in Canadian Short Fiction' provides a perspective on the preceding essays as it canvasses problems of representation in fictional discourse, and prevailing anxieties within Canadian postcolonial writing, concluding that writers are defined not by geography or national consciousness but by their responses to the distortions of history. There is a useful appendix of biographical sketches and suggestions for further reading compiled by Armando E. Jannetta. David Williams's *Confessional Fictions: A Portrait of the Artist in the Canadian Novel* is highly theorized criticism embracing European decadence, aestheticism and modernism, as it considers forms of fictive autobiography in Canadian novels by F. P. Grove, Robertson Davies, Sinclair Ross, Robert Kroetsch and Timothy Findley. This is a difficult book which offers a valuable perspective on the survival of a humanist tradition within Canadian postmodernism.

Elizabeth Thompson's *The Pioneer Woman: A Canadian Character Type* offers a good introduction to Margaret Laurence's fiction, for this is a literary and historical study of the female pioneer figure from stories of nineteenth-century settlement to more metaphyscial fictions dealing with women's psychological and spiritual quests. In many ways it is a more stimulating introduction to Laurence than Patricia Morley's *Margaret Laurence: The Long Journey Home*, which is a reissue of Morley's earlier study of the 1970s with an additional eighteen-page epilogue 'Her Final Years'. The earlier text has not been revised: it is a sound critical study of Laurence's twelve books of fiction, criticism and autobiography, treated in chronological order. It highlights links between her African and Canadian writings in terms of maturing political awareness of herself as a Third World writer, and also notes the importance of her ten years in England during which much of the Manawaka cycle was written. Paul Comeau's 'Hagar in Hell: Margaret Laurence's Fallen Angel' (*CanL* 128.11–29) pursues a study of literary archetypes in *The Stone Angel* beyond the biblical story of Hagar, to consider the significance of Milton's *Paradise Lost*, arguing almost persuasively that this novel represents Laurence's vision of Hell, with Hagar Shipley mainifesting many of the characteristics of Satan the rebel angel. Elisabeth Potvin's 'A Mystery at the Core of Life: Margaret Laurence and Women's Spirituality' (*CanL* 128.25–38) argues that Laurence's fiction is evolving toward a female identified spirituality receptive to sensuality and natural mystery in its shift away from androcentric orthodox Christianity.

As always, a great deal of critical attention has been paid to Margaret Atwood's fiction, and this year the first book-length study of Atwood in German (also available in English translation) has appeared. Reingard M. Nischik's *A Theory of Mind Style: A Contribution to Stylistics and Narrative Theory*, with examples from Margaret Atwood's fiction develops and theorizes Roger Fowler's concept of 'mind style', which encompasses the features of style relating to the representation of feeling in fiction. For Nischik the concept functions primarily as a means of linguistic character delineation, which she demonstrates in a systematic analysis of speech acts and point of view in Atwood's novels and short stories. This is an innovative approach to narrative analysis, which works particularly well for Atwood, and it should be adaptable as a model for decoding 'mind style' in other fictional texts. An excellent essay by Marilyn Patton, '*Lady Oracle*: The Politics of the Body,' (*ArielE* 22:iv.29–48) begins with a discussion of the White Goddess as the most significant mythic figure for Atwood, and explores the crucial importance of this figure in *Lady Oracle*, citing unpublished manuscript materials to support her argument that the goddess functions here as a generalized sign for myths about women and femaleness. Earl G. Ingersoll's 'Margaret Atwood's *Cat's Eye*' (*ArielE* 22:iv.18–27) argues for this as Atwood's first full-fledged postmodern work in its play with forms of fictional autobiography and self-referentiality, while there are fascinating insights into daughter figures in this novel.

Alice Munro's fiction continues to generate stimulating criticism, with Beverly J. Rasporich's *Dance of the Sexes: Art and Gender in the Fiction of Alice Munro* (1990). This study covers all Munro's fiction, commenting on female romance fantasy, women's quests for independence, and on Munro's version of 'writing the body.' It is a careful close reading, but the overall effect is one of paradigmatic criticism which fails to get anywhere near the subtleties of Munro's stories. In her review essay on Munro's latest collection, *Friend of My Youth*, Ildiko De Papp Carrington's 'Rubble or Remedy?' (*ECW* 44.162–9) astutely points to the continuity of Munro's preoccupation with perception, belief and knowledge, with characters who fictionalize their own lives, and with retrospective narrative techniques, while noting a new explicitly metafictional dimension in Munro's narratives. In an interview with Eleanor Wachtel in *Brick* (40.48–53), Munro speaks about mother–daughter relationships and how she 'figured out' the title story in *Friend of my Youth*, while she also explains how she uses her craft to register the way that beliefs and values keep changing and the way 'we keep losing ourselves and the worlds we used to live in'.

BJCS 2 has two essays on Mavis Gallant: Charlotte Sturgess's 'Mavis Gallant's *In Transit*: Stories from the Border' (313–19) which discusses varieties of border play in the way Gallant's narratives engage with the failures in private and public history. Sturgess offers a detailed analysis of 'April Fish' from *In Transit* to show the way Gallant uses Freudian dream codes to suggest submerged knowledge beneath fractured surfaces. Flora Alexander's 'Quebec Storytellers: Mavis Gallant's Narrators in their Settings' (304–12) looks at the social documentaion of Quebec Anglo-Scots culture of the 1940s and 1950s in the novella *Its Image in the Mirror* and the Linnet Muir stories in *Home Truths*, revealing the ironies and ambiguities in Gallant's representation of an ingrown and repressive society.

Lisa Laframboise's 'Maiden and Monster: The Female Caliban in Canadian *Tempests*' (*WLWE* 31:ii.36–49) offers a feminist reading of five Canadian revisions of 'The Tempest', from Charles G. D. Roberts to Robertson Davies, Margaret Laurence, Sarah Murphy and Suniti Namjoshi, focusing on refigurings of Miranda and a female Caliban, though it is only in Namjoshi's poetic text 'Snapshots of Caliban' that the Miranda and Caliban figures move beyond imperialist patterns towards becoming allies against Prospero's rule. C. A. Howells's 'A Question of Inheritance: Canadian Women's Short Stories' in *Determined Women: Studies in the Construction of the Female Subject*, edited by Jennifer Birkett and Elizabeth Harvey, explores women's problematic relation to tradition within the Canadian postcolonial context, through close analysis of Atwood's 'Bluebeard's Egg', Munro's 'Heirs of the Living Body', and Audrey Thomas's 'Crossing the Rubicon', showing that fictional strategies focus attention on women's revisionism of old stories. Hartmut Lutz explores similar territory in 'Uses of Mythology in Aritha van Herk's *No Fixed Address*' (*IFR* 18.15–20) developing her feminist myth revisions in relation to classical and Indian Spider Woman myths. Sue Gillet's '*Charades*: Searching for Father Time: Memory and the Uncertainty Principle' (*NLitsR* 21.68–81) discusses the combination of discourses of feeling and of science in Janette Turner Hospital's novel as a narrative of memory. Hospital is interviewed by Beryl Langer (*ACS* 9.1 and 2.143–50) where she rather strangely positions herself as an 'ethnic writer' in Canada, drawing her imaginative energy out of an internalized psychic Queensland landscape.

There has been a spate of feminist readings of two male novelists, Robert Kroetsch and Timothy Findley in 1991. Susan Rudy Dorscht's *Women, Reading, Kroetsch: Telling the Difference* brings together Kroetsch and feminist theory, arguing that his fictional representation of decentred subjectivity has much to recommend it to feminist readers. In this heavily theorized study (perhaps the only way to critique Kroetsch?), Dorscht analyses Kroetsch's fiction, poetry, and criticism in an effort not so much to deconstruct as to reverse power relations between feminist readers and Kroetsch the writer; a teasing and valuable study, very consciously poststructuralist. Dorothy Seaton's 'The Postcolonial as Deconstruction: Land and Language in Kroetsch's *Badlands*' (*CanL* 128.77–89) argues that Kroetsch's novel addresses notions of radical strangeness in his discourse about the land, investigating both land and language as archaeological sites in a narrative of male quest for dinosaur bones, adding an interesting feminist dimension in speculations on women and silence as radical alternative possibilities which problematize the concepts of discourse and mythmaking. Kathleen Wall's non-feminist reading, 'What Kroetsch Said: The Problem of Meaning and Language in *What the Crow Said*' (*CanL* 128.90–106) begins from Kroetsch's provocative comment that the novel was his own personal struggle with the temptation of meaning and attempts an interpretation, though coming to the unsatisfactory/necessary conclusion that the playfulness and polyvalency of this text represent Kroetsch's own struggle with his postmodern view. Two important book-length studies of Findley's fiction have appeared. Donna Penee's monograph *Moral Metafiction: Counterdiscourse in the Novels of Timothy Findley* is a detailed analysis of the way Findley's self-conscious fictions pose ethical challenges for his readers. This is a scrupulous study of the techniques deployed in historiographic metafiction, and as a way into understanding the complexities of Findley's fictional methods, it is extremely valuable. Lorraine M. York's *Front Lines: The Fiction of Timothy Findley* is a more ambitious project than Pennee's, arguing that the concept of warfare as male text is central to Findley's *oeuvre* and developing an interesting interplay between war and history as the twin texts through which Findley creates the discursive space for his fictions. Chapter 4, 'The Bomb Beneath our Feet: *Not Wanted on the Voyage* and *The Telling of Lies*', is particularly illuminating in its reading. York's essay 'Songs and Whispers: The Novels of Timothy Findley' (*Brick* 40.60–2) discusses the sexual politics of his fiction, pointing to his anti-patriarchal stance, most explicitly with his use of female first-person voice in *Not Wanted on the Voyage* and *The Telling of Lies* and his stinging indictments of the male military mystique. Michael Foley's 'Noah's Wife's Rebellion: Timothy Findley's Use of the Mystery Plays of Noah in *Not Wanted on the Voyage*' (*ECW* 44.175–82) is concerned with Findley's feminist recreation of Noah's Wife as rebel figure which, he argues, is paralleled in the Noah play of the Wakefield (Towneley) mystery cycle, though the essay remains as a shrewd speculation. Priscilla Walton's ' "This isn't a fairy tale ... It's Mythology": The Colonial Perspective in *Famous Last Words*' (*CE&S* 13:i.9–15) focuses on marginalization and exile as parallel conditions of characters within the text and of Findley as Canadian writer, arguing that this postmodern historical narrative displaces imperial perspectives on history and allows for multiple ex-centric interpretations.

There is one extremely well-researched essay on Hugh Hood, Dave Little's 'On the Trail of Hugh Hood: History and the Holocaust in *Black and White Keys*' (*ECW* 44.142–61) which discusses Hood's semi-documentary technique of storytelling, demonstrating the accuracy of Hood's historical research by his own, though the essay is perhaps rather light on Hood's fictional transformations. Two essays on Leon Rooke's novel *A Good Baby* are remarkable for their opposite interpretations of this text: Michele Kaltemback's 'Leon Rooke's Distinctive Mode of Writing in *A Good Baby*' (CE&S 13:i.41–6) notes the scarcity of referential markers of time and place as a prelude to her elegant structural analysis of the novel, showing its narrative patterns of concentric circles (set up by parallels and echoes) and its mixed genre pattern of Gothic, fairytale and parable. By contrast, Rosemary Sullivan's '*A Good Baby*' (*Brick* 40.54–6) emphasizes the precision of its North Carolina setting, its slice of life reality and its Biblical allusions, reading as an allegory or redemption. Om Juneja, M. F. Salat and Chandra Mohan's 'Looking at our Particular World: An Interview with Rudy Wiebe' (*WLWE* 31:ii.1–18) made in India 1991, allows Wiebe to discuss questions of national identity, history and postmodernism, though Wiebe insistently transfers the emphasis from unitary national identity to ethnic and regional diversity, as he translates his version of postmodernism into rewriting history from multiple points of view; Wiebe also discusses his own position as Mennonite 'outsider' in Canada, where he makes an interesting comment on the necessity of all writers for what he calls 'ancestral stories to sustain us'. Ancestral stories are an important element in Michael Ondaatje's fiction, as several essays show. John Russell's 'Travel Memoir as Nonfiction Novel: Michael Ondaatje's *Running in the Family*' (*ArielE* 22:ii.23–40) is really a structural analysis of this book's complex 'architecture', paying attention to oral tale elements, photographs and history. John Thieme's more sophisticated analysis 'Historical Relations: Modes of Discourse in

Michael Ondaatje's *Running in the Family*' (in Howells and Hunter) focuses on the novel's postmodernist investigations of language as the site for constructing personal and cultural identity, while suggesting that individual and national identities are formed through a series of random, often bizarre, accretions. Fotios Sarris's '*In the Skin of Lion*: Michael Ondaatje's Tenebristic Narrative' (*ECW* 44.83–201) explores formal components of light and dark imagery and their thematic implications for Ondaatje's revisionist history. Interpreting imagery though the late seventeenth-century Italian artistic practice of 'tenebrism' (dark manner), the clue to which lies in the immigrant protagonists name Caravaggio, Sarris's reading continually uses the terminology of that period, its humanism, its iconoclasm, its separate moments of illumination, so producing an elegant critical construction which runs parallel to the novel text. Deborah Bowen's 'The Well-Lit Road and the Darkened Theatre: Photography in Biographies by Michael Ignatieff and Michael Ondaatje' (*WLWE* 31:i.43–9) assesses different uses of photographs in *The Russian Album* and *Running in the Family*, contrasting the documentary use of photographs as authenticating devices in Ignatieff's linear narrative with Ondaatje's highlighting of photographs as moments of theatrical performance. The essay suggests that photographs may not be agents of realism but signs of the problematic relationship between fiction and empirical reality.

(c) Poetry

The emphasis this year is almost entirely on contemporary poetry and on discussions that relate to the poetic canon. The most significant collection of criticism is *ECW*'s thematic issue 43, Recent Canadian Poetry; guest edited by Ken Norris, it focuses on the work of new Canadian poets who have come to prominence during the 1980s. Ken Norris's opening interview with Mary di Michele 'Stealing the Language' (9–13) is a mixture of personal anecdote and critical comment, most interesting on her sense of herself not as excluded immigrant but as inheritor of a polyglot tradition, and about her sense of blurring differences, seeing poetry as being alive not only in 'a limited edition print, that's what a book of poetry is', but also in visual images of film and song. Her 'Notes towards reconstructing Orpheus: The Language of Desire' (14–22) with its tribute to Rilke in the title, speaks of the language of desire as one shared by women and ethnic writers, expressing disenfranchisement and difference; this is a prelude to a discussion of the use of poetic language of the body by writers marginalized because of gender or national origin, Erin Moure and Pier Giorgio di Cicca. Douglas Burnet Smith's 'Hyperbole in Peter van Toorn's *Mountain Tea and Other Poems*' (23–36) discusses this writer's work since 1970 and his preoccupation with literary allusion, outrageous hyperbole and verbal coinages in a postmodern poetry which foregrounds rhetorical and formal construction; it is a good, well-illustrated introduction to van Toorn's poetry. The poet George Amabile argues for serious critical consideration of an Australian-Canadian poet whose work is concerned with articulating individual displacement and the wider postcolonial search for a language of difference in his essay 'From Image to Vision: Self, Place and History in the Poetry of Kevin Roberts' (37–53). Arthur Adamson's ' "Between Two Lives, Breathing": Poetic Identity in George Amabile's *The Presence of Fire*' (108–17) and Patrick Lane's 'George Amabile's Quest for Wholeness in the Elemental Male' (118–32) both consider Amabile's development in his exploration of the themes of mortality and the fragility of the self that runs as an undercurrent to the dazzling imagistic surfaces of his lyric and narrative poems. Lane's essay carries thematic study further into Amabile's confrontation with various archetypal figures in his search of a mystical androgyny. The valuable close textual studies of twenty poems in these two essays make them the most comprehensive criticism of Amabile's work to date. There are two essays on Sharon Thesen's five volumes of poetry, all published since 1980. Bruce Whiteman's ' "We Talk Anyway/Being Human" ' (54–66) discusses her concern with language as a 'separate materiality' in her lyrics and poetic sequences, especially 'Parts of Speech', 'Long Distance: "An Octave" ', and *Confabulations*. John Harris's 'In the Arms of Susan' (83–96) offers a reading of the connections Thesen's poetry makes between personal exploration and its identification with historical and social crises. Susan Gingell's ' "Let Us Revise Mythologies": The Poetry of Lorna Crozier' (67–82) reads Crozier as a woman poet who challenges patriarchal narratives, offering not a single feminized vision but a number of alternative mythologies, always insisting on the multiple and contradictory discourse in which the female subject participates. This lively essay offers detailed analyses of seven of Crozier's poems. Susan Glickman's 'Speaking in Tongues: The Poetry of Erin Moure' (133–43) begins by offering a detailed comparative study of Moure's 'Thrushes' and Gerard Manley Hopkins's 'The Caged Skylark' to illustrate the peculiar combination of subversiveness and traditionalism of both these poets, who share a profoundly religious response to the world. The essay analyses Moure's distinctive combination of mysticism, rage at abuse of political power and frustration with the corruption of language, developing a feminist critique. Paul Denham's ' "My Modern Life": The Poetry of Leona Gom' (144–52) is a careful though rather lack-lustre analysis of Gom's poetry as prairie documentary. Francis Mansbridge's 'The Voyage that Never Ends: The Poetry of Paulette Jiles' (153–63) focuses on Jiles's travelling ladies and her feminist revision of woman as picaresque hero, voyaging through strangely familiar or celestial landscapes without signs of possible homecoming or destination, going beyond thematics and narrative design to a close discussion of Jiles's poetic strategies of language and imagery in *Celestial Navigation*. The volume ends with Lorraine York's brief assessment (164–77) of contemporary feminist poetics and the principles of selection involved in the most significant feminist poetry anthology to date, *SP/ELLES: Poetry by Canadian Women/Poesie des femmes canadiennes*, edited by Judith Fitzgerald (1986).

ECW 44 contains another essay by York, 'Poetic Emergenc(i)es' (133–41) which discusses Mary di Michele's *Luminous Emergencies* and Erin Moure's *WSW (West South West)* in relation to the development of a new feminist poetics heavily theorized in Moure's writing, though increasingly experiential with Michele. Through close analysis, York demonstrates Moure's experiments with syntactic disruptions in her long poems and Michele's recognition of the gaps in language and relationships, exacerbated in her own particular case by severance from her mother tongue, Italian. *Orbis* 80/81 is a special Canadian double issue, edited by Rhona McAdam, designed to introduce Canadian poetry to British readers. It contains a multicultural (but monolingual) selection of short lyrics by thiry-nine contemporary poets, ranging from Irving Layton and Miriam Waddington to younger writers like Erin Moure and Nancy Mattson. The excellently informative poetry index (46–51) has a listing of twenty-eight Canadian periodicals which publish contemporary poetry.

Beyond TISH: New Writing, Interviews, Critical Essays, edited by Douglas Barbour, is a collection compiled thirty years after the first issue of the now-defunct experimental Vancouver poetry newsletter was published. Inevitably, every one of that TISH group has got older and many of them have become eminent as writers, critics and academics: George Bowering, David Bromige, Frank Davey, David Dawson, Gladys Hindmarsh, and Fred Wah. Much of the writing continues to display old delight in experimentalism and panache, particularly Davey's metafictional meditation on literature and death 'Dead in France', which is an eclectic homage to the late B. P. Nichol (11–21) and Jamie Read's poem 'Homage to Lester Young' (22–32). The collection is, as we might expect, constructed as a form of dialogue between essays and interviews which advance a distinctively TISH position in favour of privileging linguistic and formal experiment. There are also several essays by non-TISH critics like Lynette Hunter who writes on Davey in 'War Poetry: Fears of Referentiality' (144–60). This is an important book, or as they would say, a 'Tishstory', documenting the historical significance of this West Coast group and demonstrating the survival of TISH traditions which arguably have contributed a great deal to postmodern Canadian poetry. The contemporary poetry debate is vigorously articulated in essays by Stephen Scobie and Shirley Neuman. Scobie's 'Leonard Cohen, Phyllis Webb and the End(s) of Modernism' in Lecker's *Canadian Canons* situates the influence of these two poets on the evolution of the Canadian poetic canon. Arguing that modernism and postmodernism are the two major tensions, he examines the public images and poetry of two radically different poets, Cohen the popular entertainer and Webb the isolated recluse, offering a brief derogatory summary of criticism of their work, and then his own astute reading of Cohen as 'a modernist in the trappings of postmodernism' and of Webb as 'a postmodernist in the trappings of modernism'. Scobie's somewhat polemical position is that the work of these two offers a possible paradigm for the history of Canadian poetry over the last thirty years in the transition from modernism to postmodernism. On the other hand, Neuman's essay 'After Modernism: English-Canadian Poetry since 1960' in Davidson's *Studies on Canadian Literature* sets out to revise the canon of contemporary Canadian poetry in ways different from Scobie, displacing the current postmodernist master narrative (which Neuman sees as unduly influenced by Black Mountain poetics) by a more flexible model which would accommodate European influences and feminist perspectives in a distinctively Canadian poetics, that would be postcolonial and postpatriarchal as well as postmodernist.

On poetry of the modernist period, Robert K. Martin's 'Sex and Politics in Wartime Canada: The Attack on Patrick Anderson' (*ECW* 44.110–25) is an interesting biographical and critical essay which sets out terms for the re-evaluation of Anderson's poetry and its importance to the gay poetic tradition in Canada. It points to Anderson's attempts to integrate his homosexuality and his Communism in his writing of the 1940s, and his consequent marginalization and continuing neglect in accounts of Canadian modernist poetry. The essay looks closely at a small number of poems which link the sexual and political in a specifically modernist idiom influenced most markedly by Hart Crane. Though Malcolm Lowry is known mainly as a novelist, he also wrote a considerable body of poetry, and *The Collected Poetry of Malcolm Lowry*, edited by Kathleen Dorothy Scherf, has appeared with 490 poems collected for the first time. The notes give detailed textual histories, dating and annotations, plus excellent biographical and critical introductions. Gwendolyn Davies's 'The Song Fishermen: A Regional Poetry Celebration' (in Davies) discusses a forgotten group of Nova Scotia romantic poets writing in the 1920s, neglected in the poetic canon because their traditional ballad and lyric forms do not fit into the master narrative of 1920s poetic modernism. Davies has done some excellent historical work here on the membership and activities of the Song Fishermen, who organized lectures and recitals in Halifax, published poetry broadsheets and kept in touch with maritime writers living outside the region, luring Charles G. D. Roberts, Bliss Carman and Charles Bruce back to the Maritimes on tour. The group dispersed during the Depression of the 1930s.

The literary biography by Dermot McCarthy, *A Poetics of Place: The Poetry of Ralph Gustafson*, is a useful revaluation of Gustafson's poetry and literary criticism which extends from 1935 to the present. It traces the shifts from his early modernist verse to a postmodernist phase since 1960. In that year, he published *Rocky Mountain Poems* which represents a decisive change in poetic vocabulary which has continued to evolve up to *Winter Prophecies* (1987). The strength of this study is its close attention to poetic craftsmanship and its detailed analysis of particular poems, drafts, interviews and letters.

Once again a great deal of attention has been paid to the long documentary poem, a form inherited from the nineteenth century and arguably the site of some of the most significant experimental writing in Canada. Smaro Kamboureli's *On the Edge of Genre: The Contemporary Canadian Long Poem* is a challenging theoretical and critical study which analyses individual works by George Bowering, Dennis Cooley, Frank Davey, Daphne Marlatt and Michael Ondaatje, to argue for the long poem as a mixed form of lyric, epic, discursive narrative, and its generic restlessness in its engagement with disparate genres, only to subvert their functions and ideologies. A useful companion to Kamboureli's study is *The New Long Poem Anthology*, edited by Sharon Thesen, which contains sixteen contemporary book-length and serial poems. Accompanying each is a discussion by its author of subject and poetic methodology, and the appendix includes biographical and bibliographical information on contributors.

(d) Drama

Debates about canonicity are as prominent in drama criticism and scholarship as in fiction and poetry, and here they represent an ongoing process which was signalled last year. The two drama essays in Lecker are very much concerned with theatre history and contemporary criticism in relation to the canon. Denis Salter's 'The Idea of a National Theatre' is a valuable historical study which argues that the agitation for a distinctively national theatre began in the nineteenth century and 'remains unabated even now,' politically motivated by ideas of national destiny 'like the railroad and other government-sponsored initiatives.' Regarding these projects as self defeating, Salter treats the Dominion Drama Festival (founded 1932), the Stratford Shakespeare Festival (founded 1953), and Theatre Canada (1970) as being unrepresentative of a polyvalent conception of nationalism and argues that any such project of canonization can reach no resolution. In a somewhat similar vein, Richard Paul Knowles's 'Voices (off): Deconstructing the Modern English-Canadian Dramatic Canon' (in Lecker), taking as the canon the play choices by editors in Canadian drama anthologies of the 1980s, identifies traditional values of cultural nationalism, which marginalize a variety of politically radical, ethnic, feminist and Native voices. He recommends as an alternative to canon formation a regional decentralizing of play production, the publication of single play texts, and a drama criticism which is more politically self-conscious and geared towards the analysis of diversity. Knowles's essay 'Otherwise Engaged: Towards a Materialist Pedagogy' (*THIC* 12.193–9) offers a demonstration of his final point from the other essay, for here he examines teaching theory and practice in his own university drama department and advocates a curriculum approach which openly acknowledges the teacher's political engagement. Such acknowledgement would make it possible to question historical and cultural assumptions within Canadian drama as an area of study, to challenge notions of canonicity and the concept of nationalism behind its constructions. Recommending a 'materialist' pedagogy, Knowles outlines very precisely how this ideological positioning would influence theatre issues discussed and choice of curriculum, in a move away from constructing unities to teaching differences in a deconstruction of dominant discourse of cultural nationalism. He offers a detailed discussion of a curriculum designed in such a way that literary and theatre history, acting, directing , design, and technical theatre are seen to be interdependent, in a course which privileges, as it deconstructs and reconstructs, Canadian drama. This offers a challenging and eclectic model for drama teaching.

Nigel Hunt's 'The Pre-Text of the Post-Text: Thoughts on Play Publishing by Smaller Canadian Presses' (*THIC* 12.206–12) is an informative survey of recent trends in play publishing, providing a useful list of small publishers and the distinctive characteristics of every presses' list: Coach House (Toronto), Blizzard Publishing (Winnipeg), NeWest (Edmonton), Nu Age and Guernica (Montreal), Fifth House (Saskatoon), Women's Press and Sister Vision (Toronto), Wild East Publishing Co-Operative (Fredericton) and of course Playwrights Canada Press, the publishing imprint of the Playwrights' Union of Canada, who also reproduce members' plays in a computer-printed 'copyscript' format. Hunt also notes the theatre periodicals that regularly publish plays in English: *Theatrum*, *The Canadian Theatre Review*, and *Canadian Drama*, and the innovative attempts in these periodicals to offer photographic documentation and interpretive essays on new plays. This is a valuable assessment of the current theatre publishing scene by a theatre magazine editor, which presents no Canadian canon but instead a decentred patterning based on regional, gender and racial interests which parallels the conclusions in the essays in Lecker. Playwrights Canada Press and Talon Books continue to publish their excellent series of contemporary single play texts, reflecting the diversity (of subject and of quality) in contemporary drama: Sally Clarke's *The Trials of Judith K.*, Don Druick's *Where is Kabuki?*, David Fennario's *Joe Beef*, Norm Foster's *Opening Night*, Rod Langley's *The Dunsmuirs: Alone at the Edge*, Wendy Lil's *Sisters*, Robert Moreos's *Patches*, and Raymond Storey and John Robey's *The Dreamland* and *Girls in the Gang*. Providing a brief author's foreword and production history as a prelude to the text, these are excellent value for teachers, students and producers. A similar format is followed by NeWest with *Rebels in Time: Three Plays*, which contains historical dramas of the 1980s by Ken Mitchell. *'And Do You Have Anything Else?' Audition Pieces from Canadian Plays*, edited by Margaret Bard, Peter Messaline and Miriam Newhouse, is a useful performance text of monologues from Canadian plays of the 80s, with excerpts from Sally Clarke, Thomson Highway, Sharon Pollock and Michel Tremblay, among others; it also includes reference information as to where to obtain the complete play scripts.

There is not much on early theatre history this year, though one essay by Rick Bowers is particularly interesting, 'Le Théâtre de Neptune en la Nouvelle France: Marc Lescarbot and the New World Masque' (*DR* 70:iv.483–501). The first theatrical production in North America for which a script survives, performed at Port Royale, Nova Scotia in 1606, is subjected here to a semiotic reading as celebration of the European cultural myth of the New World at a particular historical moment, which combines exploration and survival narrative with appropriation of Native myths and language by the gods of European classical mythology. Bowers argues for the significance of this early masque as encoding European cultural hegemony and offering a visual lesson in cultural dominance and celebration. There are several biographical studies of theatre performers, such as Mary Janer Warner's 'Anne

Fairbrother Hill: A Chaste and Elegant Dancer' (*THIC* 12.169–91) which documents the career of this Englishwoman (1804–90) who came to North America as a professional dancer from the Drury Lane Theatre, married to the actor manager Charles Hill; before the Civil War she danced in New York, then came to Montreal where she started a ballet school.This informative essay is interesting both as document of the mobility of mid nineteenth-century theatrical lives and also as an alternative image of the female immigrant. Jill Tomasson Goodwin's 'A Career in Progress, Part 2: Donald Davis, Canadian Actor and Director, 1959–1990' (*THIC* 12.56–78) is a well-researched account of Davis, who made his name acting in Beckett's and Albee's plays in New York and returned to Canada as theatre director in the 1980s. J. M. C. Meiklejohn's 'Theatre Education after World War II: A Memoir edited with an Introduction and Notes by Denis W. Johnston' (*THIC* 12.141–68) records his experiences in the time preceding the establishment of the Canada Council (1957), when he was the only federal civil servant involved with encouraging theatrical activities in his role as Theatre Consultant with (oddly) the Physical Fitness Division of the Department of National Health and Welfare. His anecdotal coast-to-coast survey of theatrical activity (including the Dominion Drama Festival, growth of children's theatre, and summer schools for the arts from Banff School of Fine Arts to Nova Scotia Community Service programme) gives support to the idea of a decentred view of Canadian drama. Anton Wagner's 'Herman Voaden and the Group of Seven: Creating a Canadian Imaginative Background in Theatre' (*IJCS* 4.145–64) traces the influence of Lawren Harris on the expressionist playwright and director of the 1930s. Pointing to the complex synthesis of international and Canadian influences on Voaden from theatre and the visual arts, Wagner outlines the multi-media production techniques Voden employed in his symphonic plays *Northern Song* and *Rocks*, for representing spiritual responses to Northern landscape. He argues for a reassessment of Voaden's plays in production as an expression of early Canadian cultural nationalism.

A comprehensive analysis of James Reaney as playwright is provided in George D. Parker's book length study, *How to Play: The Theatre of James Reaney*. Arguing that Reaney's plays present 'a world of heightened, often hyperbolic action' in which characters and narrative are informed by a metaphysic and by social ethics, Parker discusses in detail *The Killdeer, Listen to the Wind*, and the Donnelly trilogy, as well as his dramatic criticism. Parker's approach combines reading of plays as poetic texts and as dazzling theatrical performance, and there is particularly valuable discussion of Reaney's eclecticism and innovative techniques derived from such varied sources as folk drama, Peking National opera, Elizabethan and Jacobean plays, magic lantern shows and circuses. Influenced by Blake, Milton, and Frye's mythopeic criticism, Reaney combines these elements with a minute concern for local history, and sustained experiments in the genre of modern verse drama. There is an excellent ten page bibliography of primary and secondary sources which contextualize Reaney in Canadian theatrical tradition.

Much contemporary drama criticism shows an increasing engagement with theory, as Robert Nunn's essay on David French's 1988 play demonstrates: 'The Subjects of Salt-Water Moon' (*THIC* 12.3–21) closely examines the play as a test case for theories about reader/audience reception, and the importance of gender and the Gaze. This is an argument based on close reading of the published text, though his critical discourse elides the position of reader with that of spectator (explained, I suppose, by extensive reference to reviews of the play in production). Nunn's conclusion is that *Salt-Water Moon*, as text and as performance, is a tissue of contradictions, the site of struggle between a privileged male 'spectator' character and the female protagonist who offers a deconstructive analysis of him, so that her role as object of his gaze is transformed, making this a play divided between the views of a male and a female subject. Gary Boire appropriates postcolonial theory in his 'Tribunalation: George Ryga's Postcolonial Trial "Play" ' (*ArielE* 22:ii.5–20) where he notes the different uses of legalistic discourse in postcolonial writing from European parent texts, and through the lens of Foucault's *Discipline and Punish* he explores Ryga's *The Ecstasy of Rita Joe* as a paradigmatic anti-colonial trial play which theatricalizes and exposes the oppression of indigenous peoples and imposed fictions of legality. Carol Roberts's 'The Perfection of Gesture: Timothy Findley and Canadian Theatre' (*THIC* 12.22–36) is biographical in its orientation, being a dicussion of Findley's non-novelist self as actor, playwright and writer for radio and television. Roberts argues that his theatrical search for the perfection of gesture has continued throughout his writing, and her essay documents in fascinating profile Findley's involvement with radio, film and television, extending from his scripting of CBC's first full-length colour film *The Paper People* (1967) to his recent adaptations of three of his own short stories for radio drama, and ending with reference to the opening scene of a play in progress entitled *Inquest* (*BCan* 1989).

Judith Thompson's unsettling postmodern dramas are given attention in *Brick* 41 in an essay and an interview. Richard Paul Knowles's 'The Plays of Judith Thompson' (33–6) assesses Thompson's plays over the last ten years, including *The Crackwalker* and *Lion in the Streets*, focusing on her uses of fragmented characters and action, where theatrical effect sustains a tension between empathy and disrupted audience engagement. The essay makes the point that this effect is the result of the play's being rooted in realistic convention while refusing to present characters in safely contained actions, for they continue to evade the symbolic order of realism. Eleanor Wachtel's 'An Interview with Judith Thompson' (37–41) focuses on the horrifying moments of confession and revelation in these plays, though Thompson explains that she is interested in representing the dark side of the psyche and in finding theatrical forms to represent metaphysical concepts of good and evil as inner psychological forces.

The final essay in this section calls in question once again notions of canonicity and any centralized concept of cultural nationalism, in a well-researched historical and cultural study of rural theatre activities in North West Alberta, which suggests that in isolated country districts theatre often has a distinct character of its own related directly to local geographical, ethnic and religious conditions. Moira Day's ' "The Country Mouse at Play": Theatre in the Peace River District 1914–1945' (*THIC* 12.115–30) gives a fascinating documentary of local entertainments: an arts festival with drama and folk dancing in 1925 to which spectators came from distances of up to two hundred miles, a gaslit production of *Ben Hur* in 1928, a production of R. C. Sherriff's *Journey's End* in 1930 played only by war veterans, and popular radio talent shows in the 1930s in English, Norwegian, French and Ukrainian, culminating in the 1939 Peace River and Battle Festival which attracted over six hundred entries. In conclusion, Day argues that the myth of culturally dead rural backwaters needs to be revised and that any 'national' narrative of Canadian theatre history is challenged by the history documented in newspapers of decentralized regional and local activities.

2. Australia

(a) General

The *ALS* Bibliography for 1990 (1.56–77), compiled by *ALS* research assistants from the Fryer Memorial Library, UQ, and other sources (e.g. the *Australian National Bibliography*) is by far the strongest of the usual bibliographies this year. It continues, as last year, to list only important newspaper reviews, new works only by writers of first importance, and only *Ariel* (22) and *WLWE* (31) articles from North America. These limitations are necessary because the volume of Australian literary scholarship continues to increase. The bibliography is detailed and dense with material. *JCL*'s 1990 Bibliography, 'Australia (With Papua New Guinea)' (2.13–43), compiled by Van Ikin and Kieran Dolin, is much less forceful. The introductory sketch of the year's creative output is perfunctory and loose. *Overland*'s reviewers give a far more thorough overview in 'After Poetry 8' (122.55–9); 'After Poetry 10' (124.53–7) by Graham Rowlands; 'After Poetry 9' (123.58–64) and 'After Poetry 11' (125.61–7) by Kevin Hart; and 'Australian Fiction' (123.72–7) by Helen Daniel. Moreover, *JCL*'s listings do not separate even slight articles from book-length studies so that one has to dig to find the main items. Its difference from *ALS* has been complementary in the past but this year there is no need to look further than *ALS* which, unlike *JCL* (26), now also covers language studies.

Antipodes' third annual bibliography of 'Australian Literature and Criticism Published in North America', compiled by Nan Bowman Albinski, continues in the same format of author's publication followed by articles and reviews under each author's name. It has now caught up, needing to list only very recent items. This makes it possible to see the main outlines of current American interest: the longest entries are, predictably, for Patrick White, Les Murray and Thea Astley. But, oddly, almost as long is the entry for Germaine Greer, rating more interest than Peter Carey, Janette Turner Hospital, Shirley Hazzard and Mudrooroo Narogin who follow closely, but behind. The range of Australian authors published and reviewed in America remains far wider than in England. Sue Murray's *Bibliography of Australian Poetry: 1935–1955* is the first of a series of Working Papers towards the National Bibliography of Australian Literature project. It is as complete a listing as possible, in alphabetical order, and numbered format. There is a year index and a place index at the end, but no other sectional division to reflect the different kinds of poetry mentioned in the introduction, where Murray claims to show 'the diversity and range' of the material. The scale of the national project probably dictates this basic presentation but the introduction hints at numerous promising lines of research indicated by material in the original database located in the National Library of Australia and Monash University Library.

Debra Adelaide's *Bibliography of Australian Women's Literature: 1795–1990* is the most exhaustive listing of its subject area available and is not constrained by belonging to a larger project. It is neither 'descriptive' nor 'annotated' but includes extra information whenever Adelaide has picked it up. Though presented alphabetically by author, indexes usefully re-list the names in categories of fiction, non-fiction, children's literature, drama and poetry. The twenty seven pages used to re-list the main author list could, however, have been better filled with more annotation. Laura Gallou has edited Serge Liberman's 1987 *A Bibliography of Australian Judaica* omitting year books, periodicals and annual reports and including substantial new listings of books. The profile of achievement is clearer for this. The fourteen sections make the information easy to access from a variety of points of view. Section 3 on 'The

Jew in Australian Literature' invites someone's immediate embarkation on a thesis. Even more fascinating is the poorly printed, clumsily laid out, enormous labour of love, privately published by Ian Nicholson, *Log of Logs: A Catalogue of Logs, Journals, Shipboard Diaries, Letters, and All Forms of Voyage Narratives, 1788 to 1988, for Australia and New Zealand, and Surrounding Oceans*. This labour of twenty years, finally assisted by a contribution to the cost of publication from the Australian Association for Maritime History, commands respect and will be a treasure trove to researchers of many kinds, though they will have to search hard as there are no indexes produced from data-based sorts. The listings of all kinds are run together alphabetically and there is much space-saving abbreviation, filling 630 densely packed pages, which is hard to read. Justin Macgregor's 'Annotated Bibliography of Mudrooroo Narogin (Colin Johnson)' (*WLWE* 31:ii.84–99) runs to two and half pages of primary works and ten and a half pages of articles on their significance, indicating by this imbalance that the aboriginal writer is a phenomenon of interest rather than that his writing is of great stature. There is a useful description of each item.

There has been some miscellaneous discussion of the various activities defining and securing the body of Australian literature. In 'Oh No, Not a Nos!: the Perils of Bibliography' (in *Views From Behind the Lines* ed. Graham Spindler), Kerry White describes her difficulties while compiling *Australian Children's Books 1973–1988: A Bibliography*, clearly and directly to encourage young students into bibliography. Jenna Mead, in '(Re)producing a Text: Caroline Leakey's *The Broad Arrow*' (*Meridian* 1.81–8) tries to produce a 'poetics of editing' by situating her discussion 'at the intersection of a number of discursive practices'. She only makes scholarly editing harder to understand. Judith Rodriguez is much more accessible in 'Behind the Orange Spine' (*AuWBR* 1.16–17), describing the rather different task of editing poetry for Penguin. Other aspects of selection and compilation are discussed by Ross Coleman in 'Collecting Australian Literature: A Sensitive Issue for Librarians' (*AuSA* 15.55–9). The Australian Library and Information Association published the *Conference Proceedings* of it first biennial conference, some 1360 pages in two large volumes. Much of it is about administration and work conditions, but volume I has a few items of interest on collection development and management, and volume II has information on the use of CD-ROM and hypertext in retrieval of information by tertiary library users. It is eye-opening and constructive to become aware of the infrastructure of the services on which scholarship relies.

Hilary Kent has edited the *Index: Volumes 1 to 12 1788–1939* of the *Australian Dictionary of Biography*. The alphabetical listing of names, and reference to volume, is accompanied by indexes giving occupation. Apart from giant lists of politicians and soldiers, 'writer' is one of the largest categories indicating the usefulness of the *ADOB* for literary studies. It is possible to cross reference to another listing and discover places of birth – which writers were born at sea, for example! Peter Spearritt's foreword to Thorpe's *Who's Who of Australian Writers* identifies it as 'a unique map of contemporary literary culture in Australia' listing 5,000 authors over one hundred areas of interest. It is certainly useful in making authors immediately accessible by address and telephone number – I dialled a number and Archie Weller picked up the 'phone – but though it is also the most recent record of authors' publications it can be inaccurate in that respect. It listed one book by Chris Wallace-Crabbe which had only been considered for publication and discarded, and two by Archie Weller which have not yet been written.

Michael Denholm's *Small Press Publishing in Australia: the late 1970s to the mid to late 1980s*. Vol. II is a cross between a history and a reference book. An introductory chapter outlines the development of small publishing in Australia in the chosen period; a second section lists firms alphabetically, giving a short history of each; the third section does likewise for small magazines. The latter section is of great interest but it is a pity that it does not include members of the Australian Small Magazines Association or of the Magazine Arts Group (such as *ALS*, *Hecate*, *Meanjin*, *Overland*, *Westerly* and *Quadrant*). Another disappointing omission this year is OUP's failure to have the new paperback version of *The Oxford Companion to Australian Literature* updated. Apart from corrections, it stands as in 1985 with no cover of the rich developments of the last half of the eighties. Booker Prize-winning novelist Peter Carey is described as a short story writer with two volumes to his credit, while at the other end of the alphabet Archie Weller, Tim Winton and B.Wongar remain unlisted.

Michael Clyne's book *Community Languages: The Australian Experience* demonstrates the unique contribution that study of Australia's language experience will make to linguistics. Apart from the one hundred and fifty Aboriginal languages still in use, one hundred languages other than Australian English are spoken. Newspapers are published in thirty different languages, television broadcasts are made in thirty, and radio in sixty-one languages. In such a society monolingualism and multilingualism exist in uneasy tension. Clyne has begun the study of what happens to community languages (i.e. languages spoken in the Australian community which should not be described as 'foreign') in this context. His work indicates that they persist and thrive but begin to modify structurally in certain ways which will reward further study. A highly technical book, it is nevertheless clearly enough written to be accessible to scholars in neighbouring fields.

This is not always the case in the chapters in *Language in Australia* edited by Suzanne Romaine. Romaine also identifies the wealth of opportunity for language study in Australia and, like Clyne, offers a concluding section on the necessary formulation of public policies to safeguard existing languages. But the balance of the book reflects the numbers of languages rather than the numbers of their users. By far the larger part is given to the study of the very many Aboriginal and Islander languages, pidgins and creoles spoken by only tiny minorities. Essays on transplanted languages other than English examine only the German, Greek, Dutch, Italian and Serbo-Croat languages as spoken in Australia, while there is only a small section on varieties of Australian English. Scholarly as each contribution is, the result is that this book gives more an impression of the fascination of languages, than an awareness of the full experience of 'language in Australia'. Two other books are more interesting in contrasted ways. There is a second revised edition of Barry J. Blake's *Australian Aboriginal Languages : A General Introduction* (1981) which is the best book for the general reader, written by an expert intent on persuading the uninitiate of the sophistication of aboriginal languages. R. M. W. Dixon's *Words of Our Country: Stories, Place Names and Vocabulary in Yidiny, the Aboriginal Language of the Cairns-Yarrabah Region* is hard to read as his information is not embodied in explanatory prose, but it is a fascinating record of a now dead language which he managed to catch from its last four or five elderly speakers. Sigi Curnow's essay, 'Language Poetry and the Academy' (*Meanjin* 50:i.171–7), on a different topic, is even more difficult to read and less forgivable: 'Language's materiality becomes the focus of a problematic that has haunted writing in the Western world, namely the articulation and subsequent loss of presence!'

It is a relief to turn to Nancy Keesing's 'Australian Language' (*Overland* 124.42–4) in which she suggests that the study of 'slang' in Australia will reveal Yiddish, low life and 'buzz word' contents which are an inevitable part of mixed societies world wide. John Blackman's *Don't Come the Raw Prawn* is an informal dictionary of Australian slang which belongs more to folklore than to linguistics. In similarly in-between territory is Frank Povah's *You Kids Count Your Shadows* which, although it is a small collection of Aborigines' tales, was funded by the Folklore Trust in order to provide an urban aboriginal equivalent to the many collections of white Australian folklore, rather than to add to the kind of Aborigine story collections published by anthropologists. Hugh Anderson's *George Loyau: The Man Who Wrote Bush Ballads* contains clear print copies (rather than facsimiles of the poorly printed originals) of *The Queenslander's New Colonial Camp Fire Song Book* (1865) by 'An Old Explorer' which was rediscovered thirty years ago, and *The Sydney Songster*, 'Original local and comic songs, by George Chanson, as sung at the Sydney Concert Rooms' (no date). Anderson's introduction argues that both were written by George Loyau, and that he also used the name 'Remos' in other compositions. Peter Buttress, in 'Did "Remos" Call His House "Emoh Ruo"? The Authorship of Some Early Bush Songs' (*AuFolk* 6.29–31) argues that the Remos songs were written by one Philip Somer.

Anderson, in 'On the track with "Bill Bowyang" ' (*AuFolk* 6.3–27) compiles a first outline of the work of journalist Alex Vindex Vennard who, during the 1930s, initiated the collection of bush songs, recitations and yarns. Butterss, in 'From Punishment to Purification: Ploughing the Fatal Shore' (*Island* 47.69–71), argues that the famous transportation ballad 'Van Dieman's Land' was composed in Britain around 1830 and, like others of its kind, reinforced the morality of the transporters rather than the views of the transported. Unseen, but reviewed 'well worth adding to any collection of Goldfields material', is S. Le Maitre's *Songs of the Goldfields* (Garravembi) edited by Frank Cusack. The best piece of folklore scholarship this year, however, is Graham Seal's *Digger Folksong and Verse of World War One: An Annotated Anthology*. Fifty-nine pieces have been newly-compiled from scattered private and public collections of trench newspapers, reunion songsheets, and so on; from a nation-wide press appeal; and from material discovered by a number of other folklorists. The annotations insert the verses and songs into the historical situation, and let the unselfconscious voice of the ordinary soldier into the history. A paperback edition of Jacqueline Kent's *In the Half Light: Reminiscences of Growing Up in Australia, 1900–1970* (1988) is welcome. The sections are divided into pre-1914, the First World War, the twenties, the depression, the Second World War, the fifties, and so on. In each, a number of named but otherwise ordinary and unknown people record their memories. The effect is of almost anonymous folk history but with all the virtues of specificity. *Australian Childhood: An Anthology*, edited by Gwyn Dow and June Factor, performs a similar composite task, though this is more of a cultural reader than an exercise in folk scholarship. The book is divided into four parts: 1788–1849, 1850–1889, 1890–1929, and 1930–1949. The earlier sections draw mainly on archival material, and the later ones on autobiographical writing. The texts are many and individual, combining to record Australian childhood as it mutated through changing kinds of education, economic conditions, and ideologies of childhood. The range of materials and sources reflects the long and wide scholarship of the editors. Agnes Nieuwenhuizen, in *No Kidding: Top Writers for Young People Talk About Their Work*, presents interviews with a wide range of writers of teenage fiction in Australia, revealing the varying ideologies behind the very best of this writing, as well as the high level of preoccupation with the craft of writing. There has not been much work on children's literature, as such, this year. A second edition of Maurice Saxby's and Gordon Winch's *Give Them Wings: The Experience of Children's Literature* (1987) has brought all bibliographical information up to date and re-ordered the index. It continues to be useful. In 'From *Ulla Dulla Mogo* to *Serene Azure Vault of Heaven*: Literary Style in Australian Children's Books' (*JPC* 3.63–77) John Foster describes the development of the Australian comic book industry from 1940 and some of the national and racial stereotyping it employs.

Considerations of traditional critical concerns are few in the face of expanding discussion of 'Australian Studies', cultural studies, and feminist, post-colonial or migrant literatures. Dieter Riemenschneider's 'Literary Criticism in Australia: A Change of Critical Paradigms' (*ALS* 25:ii.184–202) is a useful review of the development of Australian literary criticism towards today's multiple theoretical approaches, based on a wide-ranging bibliography. Typically various essays in 1991 were: Denis Altman's 'A Closet of One's Own' (*Island* 48.30–2), which argues that homosexual/gay writers need to be accorded social space and recognition so that they can become writers – novelists or poets etc. – instead of political apologists; David Foster's mock-grumpy attack on 'The Reader-Writer Feedback Cycle' (*Island* 46.30–4), in which aspects of the system, from grant awards to the attention of academia, generate too many novelists writing about being novelists; and Marion Halligan's ' "Shall I Shoot her Dead or Just Wound Her?" ' (*Island* 46.9–12), which argues that violence is prerequisite to narrative, while the difficulties of writing of violence only ever remind us of the truth of Chekhov's comment 'When you want to touch the heart write more coldly.' 'Australian Studies' generated more discussion in the journals, however. Stephen Alomes's 'The Nature of Australian Studies' (*JAS* 30.13–28) is a full survey of the development, and a complex argument about the nature, of the beast. It also lists twelve aspects of Australia which should be embraced in any 'studies' programme. Too packed to have an impact as a contribution to theorizing this newish discipline, it nevertheless covers all the ground which should be taken into account. In 'Return to Oz: Populism, the Academy and the Future of Australian Studies' (*Meanjin* 50.19–31), Graeme Turner recalls early attempts to theorize cultural studies in his own work, and discusses ways in which early hopes had failed. In the same issue, Meaghan Morris (32–4) and Chris Wallace-Crabbe (35–6) add to the debate their own replies to Turner's criticism, and their reasons for believing that Australian Studies must be pursued: it is a discipline which has to tie its thinking and system-building to local practices, and generate modes of analysis which are intrinsic to Australia and not merely derivative or weakly international.

Dorothy Green's *Writer, Reader, Critic* is a posthumous collection of her critical essays between 1973 and 1986. 'The Place of Literature', 'Writers as Social Critics', 'The Writer', 'The Reader' and 'The Critic' all use her formidable skills of argument to promote literary studies but also to promote 'literature as a common cultural form'. Her analysis of the defects of popular culture is accompanied by an analysis of the cultural responsibilities of all parties to literary experience. One thinks of Leavis, but her individual voice also seems to be laying the ground for an emerging disipline of cultural studies. Bruce Bennett's *An Australian Compass: Essays on Place and Direction in Australian Literature* collects essays on authors and topics published over a number of years and noted by *YWES* in the relevant place as they came. Some unevenness in the collection is inevitable, but there has been some rewriting to co-ordinate the pieces into a general preoccupation with Australian culture, its digestion of colonial influences and its place in the world. Horst Priessnitz's essay, 'The Bridled Pegaroo, or, Is There a Colonial Poetics of Intertextuality' (*ALS* 15:ii.14–31) argues that Australian writing now reveals an awareness of intertextuality parallel to that in British and American writing, by way of that very process of digestion of colonial influences. The best contribution to cultural studies this year is John Docker's long-awaited follow-up to *Australian Cultural Elites* (1974). After that study of the contrasting cultures of Sydney and Melbourne, Docker has spent many years researching the period which begot them. Nevertheless, *The Nervous Nineties: Australian Cultural Life in the 1890s* is lean and almost colloquially written, rather than packed and pedantic, though it has the authority of being long mulled. The nineties are presented, not as the time of the radical nationalism of the 'bush' realists, Lawson and Furphy, or the converse Australian metropolitanism of Christopher Brennan, but as a time of uncertainty amidst the emergence of a number of 'golden ages': of literary journalism; of first-wave feminism; and of fantasy literature springing from fascination with the Orient. It was, especially, a time when there was much local production of overseas literary modes and much collision of the new Australian *élan* with English cultural imperialism. *Anzac: Meaning, Memory and Myth*, edited by Alan Seymour and Richard Nile, is more specifically focused. It is a collection of eight essays which probe the emergence and content of the Anzac myth via the different disciplines of historians, literary critics and cultural scholars. Particularly useful is Richard Nile's survey 'The Anti-Hero and the Anzac Tradition: Australian Literary Responses to the 1914–1918 War'. While it is heartening to see people commit themselves to a booklength study, instead of presenting yet another collection of essays, Robin Gerster's and Jan Bassett's *Seizures of Youth: 'The Sixties' and Australia* ranges rather too loosely over its material to be completely authoritative. It has the virtue of copious references to fiction writers and dramatists and their contributions to what is projected as 'The Disobedient Age', but the effect is to sketch an outline which is still more satisfyingly filled by Frank Moorhouse's documentation of the latter end of the period in *Days of Wine and Rage* (1980). Brian Matthews's *Oval Dreams: Larrikin Essays on Sport and Low Culture* are about 'sport, literature, memory and vernacular Australia'. If these essays were railway lines, writes Matthews, they would be not quite parallel. The pieces on contemporary criticism (' "Pretty Dulcie" Markham and the St. Kilda realists'), on biography ('Biographical Discourse Under a Gum Tree') and on Patrick White ('Falling Down in Adelaide') are presented as easily-of-a-piece with other humorous cultural analyses such as 'Fractal's Castel: Observations on Cricket and Chaos Theory'. *Post Pop: Popular Culture, Nationalism and Postmodernism*, edited by Stephen Alomes and Dirk den Hartog, collects eight much more serious essays, attempting to move 'From Popular Culture to Cultural Studies – and Beyond'. Of inestimable value is the thirty-page 'Thematic Bibliography of Popular Culture Studies'. Its division into twenty topic sections combines an Australian with an international focus and reveals the variety of national research areas currently 'live' in the field. Such studies are given the stamp of approval by the Australia Council's publication of *Cultural Diversity: Media and the Arts*, a discussion paper from the National Ideas Summit, written up by Paul Totaro. The paper concludes by announcing the need to identify the cultural variety of Australia and ways of retaining it through the media and arts bodies. Essays in the field include Cathy Greenfield's and Peter Williams's 'The Uses of Gossip: Women's Writing, Soaps and Everyday Exchange' (*Hecate* 17:i.124–35), which reviews the range of sociological studies of gossip as a cultural practice powerful in organizing social relations, and notes a number of contemporary novels and plays which display different strategies in its use. Chilla Bulbeck's 'Remembering Ourselves' (*Meanjin* 50.406–14) is about public monuments in Australia, and argues that the story they tell is one of conflicting hierarchical pluralism, noting the way multiple interest groups are given memorial sites as space in which to signal their versions of history. In 'Freud, Fiction and the

Australian Mind' (*Island* 49.8–13), David Tacey develops a review of Brian Castro's *Double-Wolf* (1991) into a discussion of Australian 'psychophobia' or fear of the mind. In a culture which encourages constant outward looking, to look inwards transgresses social taboos. Such taboos, he suggests, underlie the work of critics like Helen Daniel or Andrew Riemer whose value of 'humaneness' in a work invariably equates with an anti-theoretical stance. On the other hand, Don Anderson's 'Conjunctions of the Mind' (*Meanjin* 50.129–42) ponders on the significance of 'mind' in recent Australian fiction in which Ludwig Wittgenstein is the implicit culture hero. He goes on to explore the epistemological circularity of modern prose in the work of writers like David Brooks, Marion Campbell, Beverley Farmer, Mark Henshaw, Barry Hill, Janette Turner Hospital and Drusilla Modjeska. Returning to a more familiar preoccupation, Martin Leer complicates the usual connection between literature and the land in 'Imagined Counterpart: Outlining a Conceptual Literary Geography of Australia' (*ALS* 15:ii.1–13). Thomas Shapcott more practically conducts a survey of Australian 'Poetry and Place' (*Voices* 2.5–23) for the National Library of Australia. He covers the range of styles in the poetry of place, the way colloquialisms can convey place without actual description, the use of place names as invocations, and the way echoes of the ballad tradition salute the vastness of the country. He compares different poets on the same place, the groups of poets from different areas of Australia, and outlines the way aboriginal readings of the country are feeding more into the poetry of the nineties. He concludes that the true test of a vital culture is its ability to keep discovering new ways of seeing the same things. E. R. Hills, in 'The Imaginary Life: Landscape and Culture in Australia' (*JAS*12–27) is also concerned with the way a European version of the Australian land has become reinscribed with Aboriginal meanings, in an essay about the way psychic and cultural consciousness is structured into the depiction of landscape, and how certain narratives and myths then work in the countries of the mind to produce meaning. In 'The Eliza Fraser Story and Constructions of Gender, Race and Class in Australian Culture' (*Hecate* 17:i.136–49), Kay Schaffer, after her earlier work on the nineteenth-century sources of the story, examines the way twentieth-century reconstructions of it, by Patrick White's novel and Sydney Nolan's paintings, act within the culture, removing the reality, for when the figures enter history they become the effects of discourse and the real person can never be known.

Bronwen Levy confronts contemporary constructions of women's writing in 'Mainstreaming Women Writers' (*Hecate* 17:i.110–15). Pinpointing an intellectual area which is at the intersection of women's studies, Australian studies, and literary studies she describes it as in flux. Use of the metaphor 'coming of age' by critics in the area of women's writing implies an attitude that it is 'growing up' from a state of childishness; and that of 'joining the mainstream' implies it is re-merging into the culture from which it had tried to separate. Women's writing in this parlous phase is also being taken over by modern marketing techniques which overlay the creative work of men and women alike. Susan McKernan also scrutinizes what is happening in 'Feminist Literary Theory and Women's Literary History: Contradictory Projects?' (*Hecate* 17:i.150–6). According to John Docker's lengthy review of the fifty years of *Meanjin*, 'The Temperament of Editors and a New Multicultural Orthodoxy' (*Island* 48.50–5), the intellectual biases through which the journal has moved in that time have passed feminist and other phases and emerged with a new doxa for migrant/multicultural studies, spearheaded by the essays of Sneja Gunew.

Alienation and Exile: Writings of Migration, third in the Footprint Australian Writers series edited by Robert Pascoe, contains memoirs from Ukrainian, Greek, and

Italian immigrants to Australia, and an autobiographical section from a Vietnamese Australian's novel. Ludmilla Forsyth's opening essay, 'On the Slippery Margins', is a valuable review of the attitudes of literary historians and theorists to migrant or multicultural writing, from Harry Heseltine in *The Penguin Book of Australian Verse* (1974), through the work of Laurie Hergenhan, Don Castan, John Docker, Jane Munro, Sneja Gunew, Manfred Jurgensen and Robert Adamson. Forsyth's commentary reveals the essentially mobile, even slippery, aspect of the concept of 'the margin' at which so many of them argue migrant or multicultural writing exists. Manfred Jurgensen's 'The Politics of Imagination' (in Goodman et al., *Multicultural Australia: the Challenges of Change*) distinguishes between multicultural literature and migrant literature. The latter is folk art aiming to reinforce ethnicity, while multicultural literature is essentially committed to cultural richness and tolerance. It 'grows beyond ethnic origins to be Australian writing which is responsive to all the cultural impulses in contemporary society'. Understandably, he finds that a truly multicultural imagination is rare but claims it is an essential ingredient of the Australian people's cultural identity. *From Berlin to Burdekin: The German contribution to the development of Australian science, exploration and the arts*, edited by Jurgen Tampke and David Walker, collects papers from a conference at the University of New South Wales. The introduction claims that, after the Aborigines and the British-Irish, Germans were the third most important section of the settler community – although their contribution was depreciated in the anti-German environment after the two World Wars. Part 3, 'Literature and Identity', does not offer extensive material, however. It has pieces on the nineteenth-century German journalist, Hugo Zoller; on Ludwig Leichhardt and the editing of his diaries; and a comparison between Patrick White's *Voss* (1957) and Leichhardt's *Journal of an Overland Expedition* (1847). The most ambitious work in this area this year is Bob Hodge's and Vijay Mishra's *Dark Side of the Dream: Australian literature and the postcolonial mind.* Arguing that the main colonial relation was between the Aborigines and the settling whites, the authors devote, in their new 'history of Australian literature', almost half of their account to Aboriginal matters and materials, attempting by an overbalance to rectify the minimal treatment given in previous histories. They nevertheless create a context which blends perceptions and arguments drawn from multiculturalism, cultural studies, postcolonial theory and aboriginal studies in a fruitful way. Claiming to work like archaeologists – probing depths to recover lost forms – they occasionally over-emphasize some of their comparisons between what is deep or on the surface, authentic or inauthentic, in the texts and commentaries they evaluate.

Aboriginal studies have been extended by a reconstruction and a facsimile reproduction of early settler accounts of native Australians, written while the indigenous community were still relatively undepleted by contact with the invaders. In *Jorgen Jorgensen and the Aborigines of Van Diemen's Land*, N. J. B. Plomley gathers as much as is known of Jorgensen – a Danish sailor, author, spy, convict, explorer and colonial constable – and compiles some of his journalistic writings. In 1837, Jorgensen announced the impending publication of 'A Narrative of the Habits, Manners and Customs of the Aborigines of Van Diemen's Land' but it never appeared. The almost completed manuscript has been discovered in the Mitchell Library, and it is here reconstructed and published for the first time. Jorgensen's style is fluent and often vivid, the observation is close, and the reflection on what he records is sensible and constructive. The 'Narrative' is a fascinating book in its own right. So also are the two documents in the facsimile reproduction of *Kamilaroi and Kurnai* (1880) by Lorimer Fison and A.W. Howitt. Fison's account of 'Kamilaroi Marriage, Descent and

Relationship' reveals the theoretical and generalizing frame of mind of a man of his particular time as it engaged with the first Australians. Howitt's description of 'The Kurnai Tribe: Their Customs in Peace and War' is packed with descriptive detail, and even includes material which Aborigines would later claim as 'secret' and refuse to discuss with white men. Both are very readable and deserve to be considered as much as classics of Australian writing as of anthropology. Ken Gelder's *Private Knowledges and the Public Gaze: Aboriginal Writing as Property in the Late Twentieth Century* argues that Stephen Muecke's and Paddy Roe's *Reading the Country: Introduction to Nomadology* (1984) and Sally Morgan's *My Place* (1987) are part of an on-going but often submerged dispute between informants and transcribers. 'Secret' knowledges are seen as a point of resistance in Aboriginal textuality, which inevitably attracts modernity's preoccupation with 'revelation' and 'universality'. Gelder concludes that nineteenth-century colonial anthropologists, believing everything was available for investigation, began a discourse of acquisition which, in its present phase, is being resisted by the critical writings of Mudrooroo Narogin. Nevertheless, telling their story their way continues to be part of Aboriginal attempts to resist dominant cultural narratives, and two more large collections have been gathered by white scholars: *Hidden Histories: Black Stories from Victoria River Downs, Humbert River and Wave Hill Stations*, by Deborah Bird Rose, which records Aboriginal versions of episodes in history, from the arrival of Cook onwards, as they have been passed down within their communities and are still told today; and *Living Aboriginal History of Victoria: Stories in the Oral Tradition*, recorded and presented by Alick Jackomos and Derek Fowell. These stories include childhood memories which reach back to life on mission stations, but they reveal more of the texture of personal experience in contemporary Aboriginal culture than in that of the past. Each story is printed under the name of the teller, and the whole thing suggests a community speaking. More self-conscious, fully developed autobiographies are *Unna You Fellas* by Glenyse Ward – filling in her childhood before the time of her life as a domestic described in *Wandering Girl* (1988); and *A Boy's Life* by the black poet and playwright Jack Davis – revealing the humorous but shrewd vision of his later work in the making. In 'Writing My Mother's Life' (*Hecate* 17:i.88–94), Jackie Huggins charts the development of oral history in recording Aboriginal life stories and her own difficulties, as a younger generation activist, in achieving co-operation from her mother while writing her mother's story. Margaret Somerville, in 'Life (Hi)story: the Relationship Between Talk and Text' (*Hecate* 17:i.95–109), examines the problems of developing such a collaborative methodology, arguing that both the process and resulting text are potentially deconstructive of conventional autobiography and biography.

Two books focus on aboriginal spirituality this year. *Voices of the First Day – Awakening in the Aboriginal Dreamtime*, by Robert Lawlor, is copiously filled with stories and philosophy, scientific and anthropological information, and many illustrations. It is the work of a polymath rather than an expert. In *Creation Spirituality and the Dreamtime*, Catherine Hammond presents seven papers given at the 1990 Creation Spirituality Workshop (including one by the formidable critic Veronica Brady) which are equally enthusiastic in elucidating the relevance of Aboriginal Creation stories for today's world. Both are works of imaginative identification in spite of their scholarly presentation. More pragmatic, though equally committed, are Judith Wright's essays in *Born of the Conquerors*. Mostly short, 'occasional' and political, two essays, 'Critics, Reviewers and Aboriginal Writers' and 'The Writer as Activist', treat of Aboriginal writing and writing about Aborigines respectively. In 'Aboriginal

Writing as a Reassertion of Cultural Identity' (*Antipodes* 5.101–6), Gay Raines questions whether 'Aboriginal writing' is really possible. In 'Fringe Finds Focus: Developments and Strategies in Aboriginal Writing in English' (*ALS* 15:ii.32–44), Eva Rask Knudsen argues that, whether an Aboriginal writer appropriates European forms, parodies or inverts them, re-employs traditional formulae of his own community in a new context, uses standard English or Aboriginal creole, the work will be Aboriginal as long as the writer identifies himself as such. Any more stringent criterion would mean the exclusion of too much that is vital. Ken Gelder's 'Aboriginal Narrative and Property' (*Meanjin* 50.353–65) outlines the history of Aboriginal studies: first the process of offering 'enlightenment' on the subject was originally underwritten by a discourse of acquisition, of assumed right to Aboriginal cultural property in the pursuit of 'knowledge'; this was then resisted by a discourse which constructed a dichotomy between secret and public stories which enabled the post-colonized to achieve a triumphant return to 'difference'. In Patsy Cohen's and Margaret Somerville's 'Reflections on *Ingelba*' (*Westerly* 36:ii.45–9), however, the Aboriginal author of *Ingelba* and the white facilitator of the work explain how they negotiated the 'difference' between them to co-operate in production: the 'white' had to learn to see from a different centre, and the Aboriginal had to choose her own speaking position, and collaboration without colonization became possible. In 'The Environment: A "Bran Nue Dae" or a Very Ancient One?' (*Westerly* 36:iv.100–6), Veronica Brady argues that the Aboriginal life stories which have recently managed to enter the culture in such ways have directed white readers to a new perception of the environment, not just in terms of physical space, but in terms of psychic space, history, culture and nature. Graham Huggan's 'Maps, Dreams and the Presentation of Ethnographic Narrative: Hugh Brady's Maps and Dreams and Bruce Chatwin's Songlines' (*ArielE* 22:i.57–70) argues that both texts choose the map as the principal spatial paradigm to conduct their argument, but it is an 'alternative' Aboriginal concept of a map as a network of interconnected voices. Ruth Brown argues more sceptically, in '*The Songlines* and the Empire that Never Happened' (*Kunapipi* 13:iii.5–13), that Chatwin is an anti-activist who projects a dream of a return to a nomadic Golden Age in which Aborigines are dying happily while the whites accumulate sacred knowledge. In 'Only When I Laugh: Humor, Gender and the Rewriting of Colonialism in Black Australian Fiction' (*JNT* 21:i.62–71), Bill Perrett recalls Archie Weller's comment that white people cannot 'hear' the humour in Aboriginal texts, and suggests its presence in Mudrooroo's *Doin Wildcat* is not sufficiently perceived. Humour as a narrative device recurs frequently in Mudrooroo's work and it is usually the locus of his unresolved concerns with issues of colonialism and gender relations. Likewise, Geoffrey Milne's ' "Our Side of the Story": Plays from Black Australia' (*Meridian* 10:i.64–9) points out the way in which Aboriginal plays written near to the Bicentenary are full of unresolved rage and hold out little hope for peaceful co-existence of white and black in the future, and yet their most characteristic feature is that they are rich in humour. A slightly quirky article, Edward Watts's 'In Your Head you are not Defeated: the Irish in Aboriginal Literature' (*JCL* 26:i.33–48), takes issue with Mudrooroo's perception – revealed in his criticism – of an Anglo-Celt monolith opposed to Aborigines, citing the way Jack Davis' *Kullark* (1979) and Eric Willmott's *Pemulwuy the Rainbow Warrior* (1987) divide the Irish from the English white men, in the belief that they best demonstrate white potential for non-destructive, spiritual and receptive behaviour. While true of these two texts, there is not much wider validity to this argument. Finally, Patsy Poppenbeek, in 'Black Women in Australian Writing' (*Overland* 124.31–6), reviews the incidence of the figure of

Aborigine woman in Australian writing from the time of Kingsley and Boldrewood onwards. She notes that Aborigines are usually subsumed into a single, male, stereotype, but that latterly, a stereotype of an Aborigine woman being strong for her people is beginning to appear more frequently.

In 'Plotting: Australia's Explorer Narratives as "Spatial History" ' (*YJC* 3:ii.91–107), Paul Carter indicates the size of the body of Australian explorer narratives and argues that they differ from Indian and African counterparts in that the indigenous population have not helped to structure them, and in not being emplotted to end in discoveries. Australian narratives, wanting in discoveries to record, defer conclusions by opening up further hypotheses, and fan out inconclusively until, concludes Carter, they spread wide and resemble the spatial aspect of the country they describe, which is an important part of its history. Few will get access to the numerous obscure items he lists. Bolton, Vose and Jones, however, make more accessible *The Wollaston Journals* first presented to the world by Burton and Henn in 1948 and 1954. Volume One of the planned new edition, *1840–1842*, begins with a biographical note on the Reverend Wollaston's history and the previously unpublished account of his voyage to Australia, thus setting the scene for the ensuing journals more effectively than did Burton and Henn. Footnotes at the bottom of each page give the reader information about the people mentioned in the journals, as their names come up. Every help is needed to become engaged in these dense accounts of the detail of everyday life in the earliest days of Western Australian society, very often in note form and using shorthand versions of frequently used words. The Journals are a mine of information but their present editors comment on the dominantly masculine account given, and the interest Mrs. Wollaston's voice might have added. Fremantle Arts Centre Press supply the lack of a woman's voice from Western Australia of that period with a new edition of *A Faithful Picture: the letters of Eliza and Thomas Brown at York in the Swan River Colony 1841–1852* (1977). Edited by Peter Cowan, their descendant, Eliza's voice is the more engaging and informative of the two. The essentially optimistic energy and view of these early colonists is dramatically counterpointed by the much more vivid account of the alienation of an unsuccessful immigrant. *Out of Work Again: The Autobiographical Narrative of Thomas Dobson 1885 –1891*, edited by Graeme Davison and Shirley Constantine, is an account of the struggle for life and bread in Sydney in the last decades of the nineteenth century. Dobson is a close recorder of some details of daily life, but more striking is the political energy of his writing describing heartless employers, incompetent officials and corrupt politicians, to forewarn any other unwary victims of the Emigration Agents painting so rosy a picture in England as the colony tried to increase its workforce. John Neilson's 'Autobiography', compiled from letters written during 1934, also records an unending search for work and his struggle against the land and starvation. Included in Cliff Hanna's *John Shaw Neilson: Poetry, Autobiography and Correspondence* it is here textually more accurate than Nancy Keesing's 1978 edition, but we are still only offered about two thirds of the five remaining letters (two having been stolen and never recovered). It does two things well, however: presents a good account of the psychological as well as physical stress of poverty, and reveals that, in spite of the image of an impractical dreamer projected by the poet, he was, in fact, a practical and worldly man with strong political, social and literary opinions. David Martin's autobiography, *My Strange Friend*, is complete and aptly titled. Known best as a writer for young people he has also written many novels, books of verse, two plays, and general commentary on society and travel. An Hungarian Jew who moved to Germany and then, in the thirties, to Holland, Palestine, and Spain before settling in Britain, only later to move to India and then finally to settle in Australia, where he has now lived for forty years, his is an authoritative voice in discussions about the making of multicultural Australia, and the book is important for that reason. It is also disturbing, for it reveals a strange temperament with absolute, humourless, honesty. In contrast, Alister Kershaw's *Hey Days: Memories and Glimpses of Melbourne's Bohemia 1937–1947* is so laid back that it is tempting to dismiss its offering. It is a vivacious account of the group of mainly young people – such as Max Harris and Sidney Nolan – who tried to pursue modernism in Australia in the 1930s and 1940s in spite of every one else, and not always succeeding particularly well. The determined light-heartedness seems an explanation in itself for the failure of the *Angry Penguins* group to make more than a passing mark in its own time. It is more interesting in retrospect and this document therefore has its value. Clement Semmler's *Pictures on the Margin: Memoirs* focuses on people he has met, rather than on his own prosaic life as a critic working in academic, broadcasting, literary and entertainment worlds. He has chapters on Patrick White and Frank Hardy, which painstakingly record moments which are of little more than sidelight value, and are fullsome in manner. This text does not make a good case for the kind of autobiography which attempts to direct attention away from the only subject the writer could have written fully about. Playwright Barry Dickins adds to the discussion – how *should* autobiography be written? – in *I Love to Live*, which he describes variously as 'autobiographical fiction examining my forty years' and 'me with all my friends on the road to salvation ... written with baggy-eyed tenderness for Australia'. The novelizing position he takes, which frequently fades into playscript and then reconstitutes, makes the humour and sentiment excusable (after all this is a fiction!). He does not undercut his own authority as Kershaw's throwaway manner undercuts his. Material here does, in its own way, explain the artist, and cast light on the activities of Melbourne's alternative theatre, The Pram Factory. Dickins does joke about his witness, but it is because he is aware of the problem of writing autobiography. Keith Dunstan's *No Brains At All: an Autobiography* is a straightforward, old-fashioned, formally unfolded autobiography, which is given energy by Dunstan's passion for his job as a journalist. When he digresses from his own more prosaic story to record the characters at work with him during his years at the *Sydney Herald*, he is reporting from a front on which he is expert, and it is one which deserves recording, as it throws light on the production of one of Australia's premier newspapers. Dunstan contributes usefully to the developing interest in journalism which last year's report discerned. John Kingsmill's *Australia Street: a boy's-eye view of the 1920s and 1930s* began as articles in the *Sydney Morning Herald*. Expanded into a book-length memoir, it retains the good journalist's commitment to accurate detail, the writing self being channel rather than subject. The result is a time capsule account of Australian suburbia, part of a cultural heritage, which will be reprinted whenever a need is felt to re-examine that part of Australia's past, just as Judith Wallace's account of station life in the years before and after the Second World War, *Memories of a Country Childhood* (1977), has this year been re-issued for the sixth time. The National Library in Canberra holds a collection of oral history recordings, made by Hazel de Berg between 1957 and 1984, chiefly of Australian artists and writers, and a few politicians and scientists, all now dead. *Self Portraits*, selected and introduced by David Foster, presents fifteen of these recordings, indicating the range and value of this archive. Those of David Campbell, Charmian Clift and Stephen Murray-Smith are of particular interest to the literary scholar. Susan Mitchell's *Tall Poppies Too*, a follow-up to her successful *Tall Poppies* (1984), condenses into first person essays interviews with eight living Australian women who have achieved individual distinction in a number of fields. Anne Summers and Colleen McCullough are the writers included. In 'Constructions of the Self' (*Hecate* 17:i.79–87), Joan Newman examines Mollie Skinner's autobiography, *The Fifth Sparrow* (1972), to demonstrate that identity is an historical and cultural formation, and that there are no essential human qualities independent of the social environment in which they are defined; in 'Autobiography: the Limitations of Quest' (*JNT* 21:i.83–97) also, Newman compares Skinner's with Manning Clark's autobiography, *Puzzles of Childhood* (1972), to discuss the triple function of the writer's name in such texts. Writer, narrator and character share the same name sign, but the signification in each case refers to distinctly different textual functions. Moreover, each text incorporates other cultural structures beyond the usual one of autobiography as quest: Clarke's is shaped didactically, like *Pilgrim's Progress*, and Skinner's by the concept of destiny. In 'Writing the Self' (*Island* 48.18–22), Joy Hooton reverses accepted critical opinions of Germaine Greer's *Daddy We Hardly Knew You* (1989) and Dorothy Hewett's *Wild Card* (1990). Both works, she says, present the self as an obsessive, but Greer's obsession constantly transmutes from the private to the public sphere, while Hewett's never emerges from her private hothouse world.

Biographies have also proliferated this year, in both number and kind. There are two on Ada Cambridge. Margaret Bradstock and Louise Wakeling, in *Rattling the Orthodoxies: A Life of Ada Cambridge*, argue that this form of life writing cannot hope to yield a definitive portrait of the elusive self. Neither of the biographies manage to capture a particularly living impression of their subject. Bradstock and Wakeling's serious feminist purpose, and Audrey Tate's *Ada Cambridge: Her Life and Work 1844–1926* – a rather humourless and simplistic patronage of Cambridge – do not do sufficient justice to the flexibility and wit of Cambridge and the stature of some of her output, though both are dedicated to raising her profile. Bradstock and Wakeling have researched more conscientiously beyond Cambridge's own autobiographical statements, and give closer readings of some of her works. Tate gives far the best, and usefully organized, bibliography. Diane Kirkby's *Alice Henry: The Power of Pen and Voice* is a model of careful scholarship, by a social historian with respect for her sources and a warm admiration for her subject, which gives Alice Henry's life without resorting to fictional massage. Henry's life spanned 1857 to 1943. A close friend of novelists Catherine Spence and Miles Franklin, she was a campaigning journalist of formidable achievements in her time, in the fields of the Australian and American labour movements and women's rights. The account of her life is also valuable background in understanding the context of Franklin and Spence. *The Romantic Lives of Louise Mack*, by Nancy Phelan, is another 'fictionalized biography' even though, as her subject's niece, Phelan might have been thought to be too well-informed to need such a resource. The method makes for lively reading, but excuses detailed investigation of Mack's life in London and the reasons she gave up serious writing, although there is a good account of her early life in literary Sydney at the time of Christopher Brennan, Henry Lawson and A. G. Stephens, and of her attempts to be a correspondent during the First World War. There is, however, an irritating degree of poor proofreading surprising in a UQP publication. Colin Roderick's *Henry Lawson: A Life* is three times as long as Phelan's book but brings the reader less close to the spirit of his subject. This is doubtless because Roderick, a Lawson scholar of long standing, deliberately confines himself to the task of compiling all the known evidence about Lawson's life, rather than attempting to penetrate either his psyche or his work. This could be an admirable restraint, but so long a read could do with an inspiring vision to help it along. Lawson scholars will, however, be grateful for this detailed and comprehensive account, fruit of Roderick's forty years work on the subject. As a companion to this, excluding biographical cover from his introduction in deference to Roderick, Geoffrey Dutton edits the Picador *Henry Lawson*. Drawing on autobiography, journalism, letters, poems and stories, Dutton reveals the range of Lawson's interests by dividing the material into sixteen sections such as 'The Family', 'Socialist and Republican', 'Sydney and Poverty', 'Women', 'Immigrants', 'Literature and Art' and 'Dogs'. Dutton has also produced *Kenneth Slessor*, another long, thoroughly researched work which supercedes biographies by Douglas Stewart (1948 and 1977) and Clement Semmler (1966). Dutton undertakes to present not only the subject, but his literary milieu, and does so by exploration of documentary evidence accompanied by discussions with a surprising number of his surviving contemporaries. Chasing details through numerous readings of poems, Dutton seems to present the close seaming of recurring themes, but some reviewers have found the treatment of the poetry less adequate than the account of the life. The biography is accompanied by Dennis Haskell's selection of poetry, essays, war dispatches, war diaries, journalism, autobiographical material and letters for UQP's *Kenneth Slessor*. More biographical material on Slessor appears in the journals: in Haskell's ' "My Rather Tedious Hero" ' (*Westerly* 36:iii.27–36); Frank Palmos's 'A View from Knee-high, 1955–1959' (*Westerly* 36:iii.37–9); Adrian Mitchell's 'On the Personal Element in Kenneth Slessor's Poetry' (*Antipodes* 5.84–9) and Clement Semmler's 'The Masks of Kenneth Slessor' (*Overland* 123.65–9). The only journal article on Slessor's work this year is Dennis Haskell's ' "On water stranger and less clear": Conceptions of time and death in the work of Kenneth Slessor' (*Voices* 1.5–22). *One of the First and One of the Finest: Beatrice Davis, Book Editor*, by Anthony Barker, is miniscule in comparison to Dutton's biography of Slessor. It is more of a tribute than a 'life'. Davis was general editor for Angus and Robertson from 1937 to 1973 and as such had an enormous formative influence on Australian literary output between those years. On friendly terms with most of Australia's leading writers for almost fifty years, her own memoirs would have been fascinating, but professional discretion held them back. Barker's small book sketches the outline of her contacts, and gives evidence of the high regard she acquired amongst them. Julie Lewis's *Olga Masters: A Lot of Living* lacks any self-consciousness about method, and deals with her subject in a conventional and polite way. Everything is thoroughly recorded, speculation is minimal, no obtrusive questions raised. The result is disappointing. The domestic arena and quiet style of Masters's writing is strengthened by a uniqueness of vision which Lewis doesn't manage to touch or explain. She leaves the reader of the biography fearful that Masters's work may be as dull as the woman thus described. This impression outweighs the conscientiousness of the account.

The major biography of the year is, undoubtedly, David Marr's *Patrick White: A Life*. Well over six hundred pages long, its painstaking pace is hard to get into. There is none of Phelan's rhythm in her account of Louise Mack. But the effect here is cumulative and compelling. The detail embraces all known sources, and the author takes on every aspect of his subject's life, writing, and literary milieu. He retains a calm and objective distance from White, and yet seems to penetrate his psyche as completely as one man may another's. Every duty of a biographer is carried out with distinction, and the book is well presented. *God's Fool: The Life and Poetry of Francis Webb*, by Michael Griffith, documents the life and work of this little known Catholic poet, the difficulty of whose writing has been compared with that of Gerard Manley Hopkins. Webb struggled for many years with mental illness, but his output in spite of this is impressive. A&R Modern Poets series presents, concurrently, *Cap and Bells: The Poetry of Francis Webb*, edited by Michael Griffith and James A. McGlade, which reveals a committed craftsman with a predominantly tragic and humourless vision. Finally, Peter Coleman's *The Real Barry Humphries*, though drawing on a thirty year friendship with his subject and beginning from his childhood in Melbourne, remains anecdotal, and records only Humphries's professional progress without making any serious attempt to explain the man or evaluate his work.

In *Entertaining Australia*, edited by Katharine Brisbane, the newspaper-style layout belies the serious value of a book containing a scholarly introduction and conclusion together with a reference text produced by 131 contributors. Ranging from the first professional theatre in Sydney (1832) to the present day, the historical cover is good, but Eric Irving (*ADS* 21.195) lists numerous 'palpable errors'. Leonard Radic's *The State of Play* does not range as widely, covering Australian theatre only from the 1960s onward. Written by a distinguished critic, the text is full and knowledgeable, but it deliberately eschews an academic manner without managing to gain much in passion or dynamism. Seeing too much, and the need to pronounce judiciously, neutralizes his work. It is nevertheless a fairly useful source on the experimental companies such as La Mama, Nimrod and The Pram Factory. Sister Veronica Brady's *Playing Catholic* errs in the opposite direction. Fine critic though she can be, Brady on this occasion discusses plays by Ron Blair, Peter Kenna, John O'Donoghue and John Summons in order to defend the Catholic Church vigorously, rather than to elucidate the quality of the plays. Peter Fitzpatrick's *Stephen Sewell: the Playwright as Revolutionary* is a much more useful book covering Sewell's nine plays thoroughly and clearly and presenting appendices and bibliography of use to the student of his work. In comparison, Luke Simon's *Michael Gow's Plays: A Thematic Approach* is sketchy. He outlines each play, and then goes over them again under themes of 'Going Away' and 'Family'. There is a short postscript on style. It is a useful start on this author, however. Richard Beynon's *Simpson, J. 202*, dramatizing the legend created by C. E. W. Bean about the man in World War I trenches who carried the wounded to aid on his donkeys while under continual fire, is printed for the first time with a useful introduction by Alan Gill. In 'George Crichton Miln: an individualist on the Australian stage' (*ADS* 19.94–1), Eric Irvin gives the first, full account of the career of Miln (1850–1917), a successful Shakespearean actor in Australia, who failed dismally in America and finally became a journalist in London. The account of the early staging of Shakespeare plays in Australia is of interest. Also of interest to historians of more contemporary Australian theatre is Geoffrey Milne's 'Playbox at the Malthouse: a new home for new Australian writing' (*ADS* 19.3–12). Milne outlines the history of Hoopla Productions, which began in 1976, and the first year (1990) of performances in the new Melbourne theatre devoted exclusively to new Australian drama. Joanna Tompkins, in 'Time passed/time past: the empowerment of women and blacks in Australian feminist and Aboriginal drama' (*ADS* 19.13–24), is more theoretical as she claims that 'the manner in which these two locations of colonised existence intersect in drama' has been overlooked. No books on Australian film were received this year, and only one article discovered outside technical journals, 'Australian Film: Into the Nineties' (*AuSA* 15.30–7) by Jack Clancy examines how public policy decisions might effect the future of Australian film.

The process of cultural definition and redefinition by way of reprints and anthologies continues unabated. The Imprint Classics series has short but useful introductions: by Susan Sheridan to Christina Stead's *The Salzburg Tales* (1934); by Patrick Buckridge to Brian Penton's *Landtakers* (1934); and, the best of them, by Fay Zwicky, to Hal Porter's *Selected Stories* (1971). Australian war writing has a high profile. Paul

Fussell gives a shrewd introduction to Frederic Manning's *The Middle Parts of Fortune* (1930) and E.E. (Weary) Dunlop continues to present the Penguin Australian War Classics series with Lawson Glassop's *We Were the Rats* (1944), Eric Feldt's *The Coast Watchers* (1946), Rohan D. Rivett's *Behind the Bamboo* (1946), and Don Charlwood's *No Moon Tonight* (1956). Margaret Trist's *Morning in Queensland* (1958) has been corrected and retitled *Tansy*, and Randolph Stow has updated and added a new preface to *To the Islands* (1958).

The Faber Book of Modern Australian Verse, edited by a distinguished poet, Vincent Buckley, just before his death, has an aura of canonical status about it. But the traditional introduction, and the traditional touchstone ('Does this shape, this music, this deep form have an equivalence with this Saying?'), are entirely unpretentious. The collection is mainly of shorter lyrical poems of time-acknowledged quality, from John Shaw Neilson to Kevin Hart. Two hundred pages longer, drawing on an extra forty poets, representing long poems as well as shorter ones, John Tranter's and Philip Mead's *The Penguin Book of Modern Australian Poetry* pretends to greater representation and to offer a balanced view, but an emphasis on self-reflexive writing suggests that the editors are trying to promote a more biased view than Buckley's. The two collections should be taken together to appreciate the contrasting facets of modern Australian poetry. Les Murray's *The New Oxford Book of Australian Verse* is re-presented in an 'Expanded Edition'. The collection continues to show its generous representation of Aboriginal poetry, and to reach out into folksong and popular rhyme, revealing Murray's own characteristic fondness for rural experience. R. F. Brissenden and Philip Grundy have selected *The Oxford Book of Australian Light Verse*. Not all Australian poets have to be bush realists, and the cultured wit and skill in many of these poems surprises when it should not. It is strange to note that nearly every Australian poet of distinction is represented here when only Henry Lawson, John Shaw Neilson and Dorothea MacKellar are the only known names to appear in Pamela Allardice's anthology of Australian love letters, poetry and prose, *The Language of Love*. As a result of a dearth elsewhere, most of the material here seems to be garnered from colonial archives but it is so poorly organized and documented it is difficult to assess.

Leon Cantrell's edition of short stories, verse and essays, *Writing of the Eighteen Nineties* (1977), has been re-issued with a new preface. Cantrell argues that current concerns with Australia's future, the status of women, the environment and national identity were also the concern of the literature of the 1890s. This reappearance is timely, for the collection is a model of how to use an anthology for the definition and balancing of issues. David Headon's *North of the Ten Commandments: A Collection of Northern Territory Literature* is too copious to make any definitive impact. Though organized into sixteen thought-provoking thematic sections, no distinctive Northern territory voice emerges. Stephanie Dowrick and Jane Parkin's *Speaking with the Sun: New stories by Australian and New Zealand writers* is intended to be the first of a series which will bring writers of the whole Pacific region together for the readers of the region to encounter and compare. Some sense of a differing environment emerges, but not much more at present. The project may well contribute to breaking down the barriers between the Australian and New Zealand communities of writers, which are quite marked. *Memory*, edited by Ivor Indyk and Elizabeth Webby (*Southerly* 3), gathers poems, pictures, stories, essays and excerpts from works in progress of forty authors/artists, all exploring the theme of 'memory'. Likewise, Helen Daniel's *Millenium* invites prominent Australian writers to reflect on the past, the present and the future as the year 2000 approaches. Though each project generates some valuable insights as Australia's writers obediently ponder on the nation's behalf, each also has much which could have been rejected in order to achieve a more definitive impact. The inclusion of weaker material does not add breadth, it makes the collections seem more occasional than weighty. Yet another anthology of women's writing from Dale Spender is called *Heroines*, though it is difficult to see why. The material gathered includes essays, plays, stories, journalism, speculative and experimental fiction, reviews, and a television script. It is linked together by the notion that it reflects the diversity of women's writing in a technological age. Perhaps the writers are heroines for trying to write at all in the midst of such confusing diversity of opportunity. Ranjini Rebera's and Michaela Richards's collection, *Remembering the Future: Australian women's stories, dreams and visions for the twenty-first century*, has a more specific remit and a promising multicultural range, but the editors often include material more for its religious sentiment than for the quality of writing or perception. Much more purposeful and powerful is R.F. Holt's *Neighbours: Multicultural Writing of the 1980s*. Unlike the Spender, and Rebera and Richards collections, there is still a point to be made, a field to be defined, by this anthology. We can do without more collections of women's writing for a while, for the field is now established. We need more presentation of multicultural writing, of the quality in Holt's anthology of short stories, until this corner of the Australian literary scene is securely lodged within critical attention.

As with poetry, there have been two collections of stories aimed at revivifying the traditional canon. Mary Lord's *The Penguin Best Australian Short Stories* has the usual historical introduction, and the usual range of authors, but freshens the account offered by trying to choose stories which have not been previously anthologized. She presents the genre as a vehicle for social criticism which, after the factual stories of the nineteenth century, and the realism of Lawson and his followers, has begun to proliferate in styles and themes in a way which shows no sign of slowing down. Carmel Bird's *Relations: Australian Short Stories* attempts to freshen perception of the tradition by beginning with her most recent writer, George Papaellinas, and moving backwards chronologically to early-nineteenth-century Mary Fortune. Building on the Lawson, Bail and Moorhouse versions of 'The Drover's Wife', and the reflections and relationships between them, Bird developed her collection by expanding to include other stories which would similarly interrelate. This gives the collection a firm identity, and one based on works and issues central in Australian story writing. Of all the new anthologies, this comes nearest to matching Leon Cantrell's account of the 1890s.

(b) Individual Authors: 1789–1920

Not surprisingly, in the present academic climate, studies of individual authors are comparatively few and far between. It may even become necessary to construct a new division of sections for this report. One poet rated two articles. Ken Stewart's 'Henry Kendall and "The Legacy of Guilt" ' (*Southerly* 51:iv.48–62) argues that the incipient Christian existentialism, implicit questing, and confessional quality in Kendall's verse is more serious than dismissive comments on his 'melancholy' allow. Michael Ackland, in ' "Behind the Veil": Metamorphosis and Alienation in the Poetry of Henry Kendall' (*Southerly* 51:iv.105–22), tries to further reappraise Kendall with specific reference to works published between 1866 and 1869. The mythopoeic verse of those years, he argues, generated a menacing vision which carried Australian poetry beyond established credos towards a vortex of colonial and literary disbelief. The only prose writer to gain attention, however, generates the very best of the year's scholarship. Frances Devlin-Glass, Robin Eaden, Lois Hoffmann and G.W.Turner introduce and edit '*The Annotated Such is Life*' by Joseph Furphy. The notes are as elaborate and full as the text itself: scholarly, entertaining and well-judged. A pleasure to read, the notes also constitute the fullest account of the text, its meanings and its background, which surely will not be surpassed. Julian Croft's *The Life and Opinions of Tom Collins: A Study the Works of Joseph Furphy* provides a history of Furphy's reputation; three chapters on *Such Is Life* – the text, approaching the novel, and a reading of the novel; and two chapters covering the rest of Furphy's work. The readings both clarify complex material and allow for the kinds of negotiations between reader, author and text which the current critical climate encourages. Together with John Barnes's *The Order of Things: A Life of Joseph Furphy* (OUP), which is unseen, but is reviewed as 'plainly and carefully presenting a portrait of a Christian socialist who believed in the order of things', these books lay the foundation for all future work on one of the major Australian writers who, to date, had been found too intimidating to tackle. In the journals, Frances Devlin Glass, in 'Furphy and the Land: The Feminine as a Metaphor for Landscape' (*Westerly* 36:iv.39–44), tries to mitigate the sexism in Furphy's work by arguing that explicit misogyny is subverted by irony and finely drawn cameos of female characters. Furphy's attitudes to gender are presented as complex and multi-layered. Lyndy Abraham pinpoints an odd corner of nineteenth-century Australian thought in 'The Australian Crucible: Alchemy in Marcus Clarke's His Natural Life' (*ALS* 15:i.38–55), as does Christopher Lee in 'What Colour are the Dead? Madness and the National Gaze in Henry Lawson's "The Bush Undertaker" ' (*Kunapipi* 13.14–25). Lee has a more interesting essay on 'Strategies of Power in Catherine Martin's *An Australian Girl*' (*Southerly* 51.189–206), while Susan Martin, in 'She Rewrite Mate?' (*AuWBR* 3.12–14), discusses the trials of reprinting nineteenth-century Australian women's novels such as Martin's. In *European Perspectives* (*ALS* 2.140–8), Isabel Carrera-Suarez's essay, 'A Gendered Bush: Mansfield and Australian Drover's Wives', presses discussion of the numerous versions of 'The Drover's Wife' stories in Australia further, on to a comparison with Katherine Mansfield's 'The Woman at the Store', while Delys Bird continues the gender and landscape discussion more usually connected with Kay Schaffer in an article about Eliza Brown's letters and journal, 'Women in the Wilderness' (*Westerly* 36.433–8). Jill Roe continues a long-standing discussion in 'Miles Franklin and Australian Identity' (*Hecate* 17:i.67–73) without successfully re-theorizing the topic, as the special issue of *Hecate* was inviting contributors to do. Graham White has contributed two more essays on the images of landscape in pre-1920 Australian writing, drawing attention to two lesser-known writers, in 'Beyond Windswept Branches: Simpson Newland's Images of Central Australia' (*Westerly* 36:iv.63–9); and 'Louisa Atkinson: Celebrant of the Colonial Landscape' (*Southerly* 51.113–26).

(c) *Individual Authors: Post-1920*

Two collections of essays deserve to head this section. Robert Ross's *International Literature in English: Essays on the Major Writers* is a formidable editorial achievement, comprising fifty-nine essays on the best writers from Africa, Australia, Canada, Hong Kong, India, New Zealand, Pakistan, Samoa, Sri Lanka and the West Indies. Preceded by Ross's own sensible introduction to these literatures, 'The Act and Art of Decolonisation', fifteen of the essays are on Australian authors – four poets, one dramatist, and ten novelists and short story writers. It is good to see Australian writers given so high a profile but, more importantly, it emphasizes the post-colonial dimension of Australia's modern and contemporary writing, removing the tendency to see it as a sequence of faint imitations of British or American art. Another American editor, Ray Willbanks, presents a collection of interviews with sixteen living Australian prose writers. As they talk with an American, these authors are inclined to speak more of their American influences than they might otherwise have done. They also seem more self-conscious about trying to define their national identity. But Willbanks is good at leading them through their own work and, on the whole, eliciting discussion which is useful rather than a promotion performance. The interview with David Malouf produces particularly complex, intelligent and thoughtful answers. Strangely, Malouf is not mentioned in Michael Wilding's idiosyncratic 'narrative of Australian fiction from the sixties through the eighties' which 'begins with rejecting the Australian legend and ends up with American lies'. Wilding's chapter in Bruce King's otherwise unseen *The Commonwealth Novel Since 1960* (Macmillan) moves from Johnston to Carey via Keneally, Don'O Kim, and Janette Turner Hospital, and is notable for emphasizing the whereabouts of postmodern elements, of visible fabrication and refusal to be significant, in Australian fiction. There are also two essays of more general range in the journals. Kateryna Olijnk Arthur, in 'Recasting History: Australian Bicentennial Writing' (*JNT* 21:i.52–61), highlights the number of novels written in 1988 which set out to revise inherited patterns of Australian vision; and Carolyn Bliss, in 'Categorical Infringement: Australian Prose in the eighties' (*JNT* 21:i.43–51), argues that category infringement is a standard tactic in modern art. The example she focuses on is the way books like *A Fortunate Life* (Facey, 1981), *Evil Angels* (Bryson, 1985), *My Place* (Morgan, 1987) and others, privilege orality over literacy, thus denying closure of thought or form. Laurie Hergenhan's 'The "I" of the Beholder: Representations of Tuscany in Some recent Australian Literature' (*Westerly* 36:iv.107–14) naturally turns attention to David Malouf who, together with Patrick White, generated most critical attention this year. Karin Hansson's book, *Sheer Edge: Aspects of Identity in David Malouf 's Writing*, is as careful and wary of brilliance as is her subject himself. She offers no more than a thematic essay with a little biographical information on the way. It will be difficult for students to use, as the works are not treated separately. In chapters on the search for identity through interrelationships, through the definition of time and place, and through the use of language and metaphysics, Hansson draws on her thorough knowledge of all Malouf's work in whatever order or way will serve her argument. A complex knowledge of Malouf's writing is needed to follow her thread, but her carefulness and attention to her subject enables the book to focus on the precise quality of Malouf's perception and message. This is, itself, seen at its best in 'A Personal Multicultural Biography' (*AuS* 5.73–80), in which Malouf takes himself as an example to reveal the many multicultural levels to be identified in any one life by biography. The exercise reveals the multiplicity of his own identity, and blurs the distinction between biography and autobiography. As Malouf says, in Barbara Williams's 'An Interview with David Malouf: "People Get Second Chances" ' (*ANZSC* 5–8.81–94), though he is not an experimental writer, he is constantly driven to keep pushing across borders, both mental and technical, in a process rather like moving back into the great chain of being, in order to discover the identity of both characters and oneself. A number of essays analyse single works, drawing attention to Malouf's use of oppositional modes, in particular those of cultural reference and contrast. Peter Knox-Shaw's 'An Art of Intersection: David Malouf's *Künstlerroman*, *Harland's Half Acre*' (*Antipodes* 5:i.31–46) identifies an effect of dispersal from self containment, a musical unity of separate parts, an haphazard falling into relation of a group of stories, as the unique structural principle of this novel. Philip Neilson's 'The Conflict between Australia and Europe in David Malouf's *Johnno* and *An Imaginary Life*' (*Outrider 91* 8.175–9) argues that among the limited number of oppositions in Malouf's 'mythologies', the most important is that between Australia and Europe, which is used to construct a sense of 'Australianness' for his readers. In 'Malouf's Epic and the Unravelling of a National Stereotype' (*JCL* 26:i.79–100), Peter Knox-Shaw argues that multiplying references to Tolstoy's *War and Peace* in *The Great World* show Malouf about the business of fictionalizing 'the matter of Australia', just as Shakespeare fictionalized 'the matter of England' or Tolstoy 'the matter of Russia'. In the process, Malouf finds it necessary to dismantle prevailing paradigms, such as that of the Digger. Helen Gilbert, in 'The Boomerang Effect: Canonical Counter-discourse and David Malouf's *Blood Relations* as an oppositional reworking of *The Tempest*' (*WLWE* 31:ii.50–64), argues that the apparent congestion of Malouf's only play evaporates when it is perceived as a post-colonial text writing specifically back to the Shakespeare play and questioning its discourse of right to power. Xavier Pons's ' "Savage Paradise": History and Violence and the Family in Recent Australian Fiction' (*European Perspectives ALS* 2 15:ii.72–82) examines examples from the work of Malouf as well as that of Rodney Hall and Thomas Keneally. The latter generated two other articles: Genevieve Laigle's 'The White World and Its Relationship with Aborigines in Keneally's *The Chant of Jimmy Blacksmith*' (*CE&S* 14:i.102–10); and David Kennedy's ' "Poor Simulacra": Images of Hunger, the Politics of Aid and Keneally's *Towards Asmara*' (*Mosaic* 3/4.179–89), which argues that Keneally's novel shows that images of the hunger of the Eritreans are political manipulations of actual suffering, and suggests that failure to eradicate famine is not just a failure of political will, but deliberate. Both critics seem to grant Keneally's work more weight than his prolific output could have permitted. Peter Quartermaine's book, *Thomas Keneally*, might have helped to get this wide-ranging writer into focus, but the space limit in Edward Arnold's Modern Fiction Series only gives him room to deal fairly quickly with half a dozen of the novels. Keneally's own exploration of his roots, *Now and In Time To Be: Ireland and the Irish*, is little more than a travel book. The death of Patrick White was marked by *Patrick White: Life and Writings: Five Essays*, edited by Martin Gray. A memoir by Alan Seymour, the playwright, with whom White fell out, is shrewd and entertaining, but two of the essays, 'Patrick White and Australia as "Terra Nullius" ', by Ruth Brown, and ' "Et in Australia Ego": Framing the Pastoral Experience in Patrick White's *A Fringe of Leaves*', by Sally Dawson, are of the best quality written this year – shrewd, knowledgeable, witty and thorough. The third of the year's best essays (impossible to choose between them) is David Coad's 'Patrick White's Libidinous Eudoxical Lexis in *The Twyborn Affair*' (*CE&S* 14:i.65–9), which is closely argued, penetrating and yet clear. White has been well served by these commentators. Varying responses to David Marr's biography produced a certain amount of debate. David Tacey's view, in 'Patrick White Marred' (*Quadrant* 35:x.7–11), is rebutted by Axel Clark in 'Marr's Patrick White' (*Scripsi* 7–8:iii.37–41), gently backed by Elizabeth Jolley in 'Marr's Patrick White: Some Impressions' (*Scripsi* 7–8:iii.27–36). David Marr, in conversation with Jill Kitson (*Quadrant* 35:ix.21–6), revealing the extent of White's co-operation with the biography, lets slip that White called it 'The Monster of all Time'. Joan Kirkby also takes issue with David Tacey in 'Fetishizing the Father' (*Meridian* 10:i.35–44). Two essays on *Memoirs of Many in One* ask whether this last work was 'Autobiography or Fiction?' (Antonella Reim in *Westerly* 36:iii.95–101), or White's 'Last Flight to Byzantium' (Hena Maes-Jelinek in *European Perspectives*, *ALS*

15:ii.173–83). D. R. Burns's 'The Elitist Case for Equality: Patrick White's Pioneering "Visionary Monster" Novel' (*Overland* 125.68–75) is a lively discussion of *Riders in the Chariot*, and the way in which White's baleful glare at Australian suburban society nevertheless becomes an even-handed account by the end of the novel. Angela Smith compares *Voss* with Ethel Anderson's *At Parramatta* in 'Is Phallocentricity a Sin? or a Pecadillo?' (*European Perspectives*, *ALS* 15:ii.149–61), and Glen Thomas compares White's 'Appropriations of "The Prodigal Son" ' (*ALS* 15:i.81–6 'notes and documents') with those of Murray Bail. Overlooked last year was A. J. Hassall's *Strange Country: A Study of Randolph Stow* (1986), which was re-issued with a revised and updated bibliography and updated chronology. There are two essays on Stow this year: John McLaren's on 'Security and Violation: Randolph Stow's *The Merry-Go-Round in the Sea*' (*Westerly* 36:iv.75–81) and Martin Leer's 'Mal du Pays: Symbolic Geography in the work of Randolph Stow' (*ALS* 15:i.3–25). The last of the books on post-1920 novelists is *Elizabeth Jolley: New Critical Essays* edited by Delys Bird and Brenda Walker. Delys Bird's essay on Jolley's manuscripts is interesting; Martin Gray's on her ironic dissonance is a model of humour and common sense; and Constance Rook is genuinely illuminating on *Mr. Scobie's Riddle*. It is unfortunate that the conscious play with the author's role and the fictive aspect of her texts, which is so frequent in Jolley's novels, leave her vulnerable to commentators who are not able to deal as lightly and skilfully with such matters as Jolley can herself. Consequently, several of the essays are indigestible because they are over-theoretical. However, the bringing together of a number of essays in this way will help to consolidate serious study of Jolley's work. Peter Carey attracts three essays: Kirsten Holst Petersen' s 'Gambling on Reality' (*European Perspectives*, *ALS* 15:ii.107–16) is a reading of *Oscar and Lucinda*, and Sue Ryan examines 'Metafiction in *Illywhacker*: Peter Carey's Renovated Picaresque Novel' (*CE&S* 14.1.33–40); Carolyn Bliss, in 'The Revisionary Lover: Misprision of the Past in Peter Carey' (*ANZSC* 6.45–54), examines both novels and refers back to an early story 'Do You Love Me?' to reveal Carey arguing that it is not Christianity, immigration or entrepreneurship which are wrong for Australia, but the loveless way in which each is promoted. There are three essays, also, on Murray Bail: Xavier Pons examines the attitudes of Bail's tourists in 'Australia Takes on the World: Identity and Representation in Murray Bail's *Homesickness*' (*CE&S* 14.1.1–8), while Wenche Ommundsen argues that the novel's postmodern framing device is paradoxically used to reinforce the relationship of the text to historical contingencies; Robert Dixon's essay is on 'The Great Australian Emptiness Revisited' (*ALS* 15:i.26–37) in Bail's *Holden's Performance*. It is pleasing to see a couple of essays on Gerald Murnane whose self-referential work is – a paradox to my mind – a delight. Stephen Kolsky, in 'Exploring *Inland*' (*Outrider* 8.97–109), actually reviews all Murnane's work, even though finally focusing on the Borgesian influence on *Inland*. Ian Adams tackles the unbeatable problem of writing accessibly about this kind of author in 'The Referentiality of the Deconstructed: Gerald Murnane's *The Plains*' (*Westerly* 36:i.25–9). A number of prose writers from the early part of the post-1920 period benefit from only one essay this year: Thomas E. Tausky, in 'Orpheus in the Underworld: Music in the novels of Robertson Davies and Martin Boyd' (*Antipodes* 5:i.5–30) describes the way music is used to annotate the alienated individual in the Langton Quartet; John Scheckter, in ' "Before It Is Too Late": George Johnston and the Doppler Effect' (*ANZSC* 5.115–30) applies the Big Bang theory of cosmic motion as an analogy for the Meredith trilogy; Gerry Turcotte examines 'Hybrids and Gothic Discourses in Louis Nowra's Novels' (*Westerly* 36:iii.61–72) and Giovanna Capone attempts to define 'The Quintessence of Porterism' (*European Perspectives*, *ALS* 15:ii.162–72) in Hal Porter's *The Tower*. Single essays on later male prose writers are: Ken Gelder's 'David Ireland's Novels: Australia, Community and the "Illegality" of Fiction' (*JNT* 21:i.32–41), which argues that Ireland's changing view of Australia is becoming more conservative; Narelle Shaw's '*Testostero*: David Foster's Comic Novel' (*JCL* 26:i.65–78) which argues that, having used *commedia del l'arte* characters to champion the integrity of his use of the comic genre, Foster has produced a stridently un-Australian book; Veronica Brady's 'An Approach to Vigilance' (*Westerly* 36:i.47–58) discusses the politics of Nicholas Hasluck's imaginary account of Australian behaviour as a colonial power, *The Country Without Music*; Paul Sharrad's 'Pastoral, Romance, Post-colonial Consciousness: Spenser and Koch' (*CE&S* 14:i.111–23) is another examination of contemporary Australian use of the English tradition; Simone Vauthier's 'Reading the Signs of Michael Wilding's "Knock, Knock" ' (*ALS* 15:ii.128–39) is helpful in reviving interest in this not very productive author; Tony Thwaite's 'Two Eleactic Tales: John A. Scott, Seymour Chatman and some Occlusions of Narrative' (*JNT* 1.98–120) did little to attract me to these authors; Michael Sharkey did, however, make me want to read 'David McKee Wright's Roman Novel' (*Southerly* 51.71–87). There is a useful interview with Tim Winton by Jeri Kroll in *Southerly* (51.222–4).

Essays on post-1920 women prose writers are grouped hereafter, for no other reason than to break the material down into more easily memorable units. They are not unduly feminist in slant. In fact, Jennifer Gribble, in 'Christina Stead's *For Love Alone*' (*CR* 31.17–27), argues that the novel has been de-natured by being appropriated for feminist purposes. It is about love as an amoral force, and that does not emerge clearly in feminist readings. Ann Blake's 'Christina Stead's *Miss Herbert (The Suburban Wife)* and the English Middle Class' (*JCL* 26:i.49–64) is more concerned to illuminate Stead's dislike of England and the English, and Maria Teresa Bindella's 'Search Lights and the Search for History in Christina Stead's *Seven Poor Men of Sydney*' (*European Perspectives*, *ALS* 15:ii.95–106) aims to shift attention from the elaborate prose and complex structure of the novel towards a reading of it as Michael's search for his origins, finalized by his death in Sydney Harbour, the place where recent European past meets the natural and Aboriginal past of the ancient continent. Finally, R. G. Geering, as Stead's executor, releases more material in 'From the Personal Papers of Christina Stead: Extracts and Commentaries' in *Southerly* (51:i.5–17). John Clower's 'The Anarchistic Craft of *The Children's Bach*' (*ANZSC* 6.55–75) argues that Helen Garner uses deep-cutting irony to reveal that the home is fatally flawed, and Karen Grundy's 'Serving in the Home Guard: Housekeepers and Homemakers in *The Children's Bach* and *Dancing in the Dark*' argues that Garner, like Joan Barford, indicates only minor rumblings of discontent on the domestic front, as the majority of their women have no desire to see beyond their domestic walls. Nicholas Mansfield sees only 'A pleasant but meaningless discord' in 'Helen Garner's *The Children's Bach*' (*Westerly* 36:ii.17–22). Eden Liddelow, in 'Helen Garner: A Retrospective with Angels' (*Scripsi* 7:iii.106–18), examines Garner's work up to Bach to reveal moments of 'unaccountable blessedness', but sees the new *Cosmo Cosmolino* as a book about the desperation of life without intimacy. K. M. Twidale's 'Discontinuous Narrative and Aspects of Love in Shirley Hazzard's Short Stories' (*JCL* 26:i.101–16) argues that the preoccupations explored in the short stories are those expanded in the novels. Anna Grazia Mattei, on the other hand, describes 'The Novel as "Work in Progress" ' when writing about Hazzard's *Transit of Venus* in *European Perspectives* (*ALS* 15:ii.117–27). Cassandra Pybus has an interview with Glenda Adams, 'Fiddling With Words' (*Island* 47.20–5) accompanied by Adams's own comments, 'Calling Up the

Spirits: some thoughts on the writing process' (*Island* 47.26–9). A number of women attracted only a single essay: Maryanne Dever outlines the political activities of Marjorie Barnard and Flora Eldershaw in ' "No Time is Inopportune for a Protest" ' (*Hecate* 17:ii.9–21); Barbara Garlick examines the dialogic imperative in Jessica Anderson's work in 'Of Rhinos and Caryatids' (*JNT* 21:i.72–82); Roslyn D. Haynes's 'Fatalism and Feminism in the Fiction of Kate Grenville' (*WLWE* 31:i.60–79) reviews all Grenville's work, to show her exploring socio-psychological issues pertinent to the structure of society as a whole, in a variety of kinds of book; in 'Margin? Center? The Polychromagic Realism of *The Frangipani Gardens*' (*Antipodes* 5:i.47–50), Ian Adam discusses Hanrahan's painterly play of colour which facilitates the differing cultural modalities, and innumerable loops of cultural exchange, which are the mark of magic realism; and in 'Scrambled Lives' (*Hecate* 17:i.74–8), Julie Lewis outlines the vision of Olga Masters's 'sly, fussy, garrulous, sensual alertness' which governed her work on Masters's biography. Finally, a number of essays addressed issues of genre: Efi Hatzimanolis's 'Immigrant Writing Come of Age? The Getting of Genre in Angelica Fremd's *Heartland*' (*JNT* 21:i.24–31); Marie Maclean 's 'Do-It-Yourself, B.Y.O. and Australian Science Fiction' (*JNT* 21:i.136–41); Tamsin Donaldson's 'Australian Tales of Mystery and Miscegenation' (*Meanjin* 50.341–52); Alison Littler's 'Marele Day's "Cold Hard Bitch": The Masculine Imperative of the Private-Eye Genre' (*JNT* 21:i.121–35); and Fiona Giles's 'Love, Death and Charging Bulls: Recent Australian Women's Romance' (*AuWBR* 2.13–14).

Although, as usual, poetry fares less well than prose in terms of bulk, in terms of quality it has done well. The *Last Poems* of Vincent Buckley, compiled by Penelope Buckley and Chris Wallace-Crabbe from Buckley's posthumous papers, is a book well worth having, revealing a less rhetorical, more easily direct but equally authoritative last phase in his work. The selection could have been more stringent, but much was included in pursuit of fullness of information given Buckley's death, rather than selection being finely honed, as Buckley himself might have made it. Barbara Petrie's edition *William Hart-Smith: Hand to Hand: A Garnering* is another post-mortem piety. She presents the garnering Hart-Smith had himself made for a final 'Selected', adds as many uncollected poems as could be found, and a near complete bibliography of his work. Critical essays by Douglas Stewart, Arthur Murphy and Gary Catalano round out a first presentation on the work of this Jindyworobak poet who outlived the movement to become a writer respected for his openness to new poetic influences throughout his long life. UQP present the latest definition of Bruce Beaver's achievement in *New and Selected Poems 1960–1990*. Not noticed last year, but of importance, is a slight-seeming 'Occasional Paper' (number 49 from the University of Tasmania), *Poetry and Belief*, by the poet and academic Chris Wallace-Crabbe. In this paper, wearing both his hats, he takes on the century which has laid great stress on the detachment of the creative artist, and argues for the existence of 'belief' of some kind in all creative work. Describing his own self, after Charles Harpur, as a 'humanist with a thin wash of deism', he describes the nature of belief in the work of Judith Wright, Christopher Brennan, Kenneth Slessor, Peter Porter, A. D. Hope, Vincent Buckley, Fay Zwicky and Robert Adamson, and concludes that the artist must say 'I write, therefore I believe'. Bruce Bennett's *Spirit in Exile: Peter Porter and his Poetry* is included here because its biography is mostly derived from discussion of the successive volumes of Porter's work. Including accounts of reviews and criticism, Bennett not only defines the Australian aspect of this expatriate poet, but extensively researches the English context of a great deal of his writing and success. *Spirit in Exile* is a scholarly and thorough treatment such as is rarely hazarded in these days of fast publication, even though one has a niggling suspicion that the subject may not quite deserve such careful and well-judged attention. Shirley Walker's subject, in *Flame and Shadow: A Study of Judith Wright's Poetry*, does deserve such attention. Cautious in all its conclusions, and careful to explore Wright's philosophy beyond merely accounting for her ecological campaigning, Walker writes one of the best overviews of Wright's work in the introduction. The rest of the book shifts uncomfortably between chapters discussing particular collections and others exploring themes from a number of works. But, though overall organization is weak, what is said is worth reading. Also well worth reading is Elizabeth Lawson's *The Poetry of Gwen Harwood*; written for the OUP/SUP 'Studies in Literature Series', it is intended for a student audience, but its sensible placing of the subject against the complexities of current literary theory, and the shrewd commentary on the poems, achieves the balance that all critics should aim for. In the journals, Gerhard Stilz brings the well-worn theme of the landscape up to date in 'Topography and the Self: Coming to Terms with the Australian Landscape in Contemporary Australian Poetry' (*European Perspectives*, *ALS* 15:ii.55–7). Two other conspectus essays are Lyn McCredden's 'Australian Women's Poetry' (*AuWBR* 1.13–15) and Werner Senn's 'Australian Poems on European Paintings' (*European Perspectives*, *ALS* 15:ii.83–94). Peter Anderson, in 'Ern Malley: The Greatest Poet that (N)ever Lived' (*SoRA* 24:i.21–31), reviews the way the 'Ern Malley' poems were constructed, and suggests that it echoes the way current literary theory argues all literary art is essentially produced. Paul Kane, however, in 'An Australian Hoax' (*Raritan* 11:ii.82–98), questions whether 'Ern Malley' alone could account for the failure of modernism in Australia; the hoax, he argues, is more important for its recurring power as an event. In 'Notes and Documents' (*ALS* 15:i.78–80), David Brooks indicates a connection between 'Ern Malley and *Les Déliquescences D'Adore Floupette*'. Dennis Haskell's 'European and Australian *Vision*' (*AuS* 5.1–72) introduces the *Vision* group to an audience outside Australia, while Paul Gillen assesses 'Jack Lindsay's Romantic Communism' in *Westerly* (36:ii.65–77), and Adrian Lawlor refocuses 'Alister Kershaw' in *Overland* (122.6–9). Two essays on A. D. Hope carry the same message: Patrick Deane's 'A. D. Hope, T. S. Eliot and the "Counter- Revolution" in Modern Poetry' (*ANZSC* 5.97–114) argues that Hope's classicism was not a reaction against T. S. Eliot but a continuation of his ideas; and Kevin Hart's ' "To Hear the Siren Sing": A Reading of A. D. Hope' (*Scripsi* 7:iii.43–65) argues that Hope accepts both classic and romantic traditions in his verse, and it is the interplay of them that leads to his originality. Two articles on the controversial John Tranter argue in his defence: Andrew Taylor, in 'Resisting the Mad Professor: Narrative and Metaphor in the Poetry of John Tranter' (*JNT* 21:i.14–23), takes issue with Kate Lilley's accusation that the subject is absent in Tranter's verse (*ALS* 14:i.41–50), and replies that Tranter simply resists closure and his poems work by metaphor and 'mean something else'; Erica Travers replies to Livio Dobrez (in *Parnassus Mad Ward*, 1990) that Michael Dransfield is not the voice of the original thesis of Australian New Poetry – John Tranter is really the centre of the movement. Travers also has 'An Interview with John Tranter' in *Southerly* (51:iv.14–28). Three poets generated one essay: Dorothy Hewett gives a realistic overview of Robert Adamson's work in 'Beyond the Pale' (*Scripsi* 7:i.247–58), revealing the development of a 'light-footed, light-fingered, light-tongued Hermes', whose borrowings nevertheless emerge in something original; Lyn McCredden's 'Between Position and Desire' (*Southerly* 51.35–54) reviews the love poetry of James McAuley; and Susan Ballyn examines 'John Shaw Neilson's Concept of Love' (*CE&S* 14:i.97–101). Peter Kirkpatrick has an interview with Ronald McCuaig, 'Thus Quod

McCuaig' in *Southerly* (51.267–82). *Outrider* has two articles protesting Geoff Page's exclusion of migrant poetry from his account of 'Australian Poetry: the Last Twenty Years' (*Outrider* 8.88–93): Con Castan's 'Migration and the Diversification of Australian Poetry' (119–31) and Gun Gencer's 'Praise the Plumage' (117–18). Together, these articles outline the current multicultural scene. Igor Maver argues the case for 'The Poetry of Slovene Immigrants in Australia' (*Outrider* 8.210–24), Bert Pribac in particular, whose Slovene themes and landscapes blend with Australian landscapes to show the advantage of giving Australian culture its widest possible base. A very helpful essay from Sue Gillet shows the way to approaching a more difficult but exciting writer in 'At the Beginning: Ania Walwicz's Writing' (*Southerly* 51.239–52).

Overall, this has been another very satisfactory year for Australian writing. The 'studies' base continues to widen until it is almost top heavy, and one wonders whether traditional criticism and scholarship might disappear altogether, but while works like the *Annotated 'Such if Life'*, the David Marr biography of Patrick White, and Bruce Bennett's critical biography of Peter Porter, can all arrive in one year, all will continue to be well.

3. India

(a) General and Poetry

Shyamala A. Narayan's entry on India (*JCL* 26:ii.87–111) offers a trenchant survey of recent publications and a useful bibliography, showing a fairly healthy output of fiction, poetry and criticism and a familiar paucity of drama written in English. Her introduction raises the question of categorization, in view of the large number of Indian writers resident abroad. Salman Rushdie continues to be claimed as an Indian writer, partly because *Haroun and the Sea of Stories* shows him 'incapable of getting India out of his consciousness', but more specific questions of verisimilitude are also felt to be important. Hence, Indu K. Mallah's first novel, *Shadows in Dreamtime*, is noted for its authentic depiction of Indian life, whilst another first novel, the expatriate Indira Ganesan's *The Journey*, is severely criticized for its factual inaccuracies.

Salman Rushdie's own views on the placing of himself, and the relative importance of factual accuracy, resurface in *Imaginary Homelands: Essays and Criticism 1981–1991*, a wide-ranging and very welcome collection which includes a number of pieces on the literature and politics of the subcontinent and, notably, *Midnight's Children*. ' "Errata": or Unreliable Narration in *Midnight's Children*' is a stimulating account of the conflict between 'literal and remembered truth' and a justification for employing the latter in Saleem's narrative. Also worth noting is Rushdie's 1983 contribution to the centre/periphery debate, ' "Commonwealth Literature" Does Not Exist', which offers a challenging writer's-eye view of the problems that have beset this area of academic work, not least in the attempts to find a name for the study of what he calls 'we rough beasts'. A sharply contrasting approach to the subject is found in William Walsh's *Indian Literature in English*, which offers a survey of poets, novelists, 'sages and autobiographers', from Roy to Rushdie, concentrating throughout on 'a few truly gifted and creative writers for reasons of particularity and significance'. These include the first 'genuine Indian novelists' writing in English (Rao, Anand and Narayan), a selection of poets from the 1950s onwards, some women novelists such as Desai and Markandaya, and, for their achievements in autobiography, Nirad Chaudhuri and Ved Mehta. Walsh provides some lengthy appreciations of individual works, underpinned by frequent reminders of the debt that their creators owe to 'the expressive and creative capacities of the English language', but he pays scant attention to the developments of the last decade or so, as is evident in his assertion that the Indian novel in English has not been 'much affected by developments in the technique of fiction of the experimental kind'. The final chapter, 'India in English Fiction', is concerned with 'the British writers' response to the experience of India'. It seems that, for Walsh, the centre still holds.

Ronald Warwick's 'Studies of South Asian Literature in Britain: A Personal View' (*Wasafiri* 13.2–4) notes a scarcity of material from the subcontinent held by British libraries and a 'relative lack of interest in South Asian writing' in higher education. There follows an impressively succinct overview of the critical and cultural context, which suggests that the 'obstructions of the learned' are partly responsible for this bleak scenario. Although saddened by the 'kind of criticism which exaggerates the influence of the West, because of understandable ignorance of the East', Warwick believes that a 'partnership between academics, teachers, writers and other agencies' is providing a 'wider framework in which the Anglophone writing of the subcontinent can and ought to be studied'.

Susheila Nasta's *Motherlands: Black Women's Writing from Africa, the Caribbean and South Asia* aims to generate 'a cross-cultural dialogue between critics and writers whether in "First" or "Third" worlds'. This stimulating anthology of essays includes three pieces on Indian fiction (which are reviewed in the following section of this survey), and Ranjana Ash's 'The Search for Freedom in Indian Women's Writing'. Ash looks at five writers (Kamala Das, Anita Desai, Shashi Deshpande, Amrita Pritam and Nayantara Sahgal) who, between them, have produced fiction, autobiography and poetry in English and indigenous languages. Although perhaps over-ambitious in its scope, the essay usefully draws attention to a variety of responses by writers who view women's freedom 'not as a uniform entity but as a plurality shaped and modified by diverse religious, linguistic and historical factors', whilst retaining 'a common commitment in trying to maintain their cultural identity, their relationship to the motherland'.

Questions concerning the individual voice and the claims of the community are raised by Bijay Kamar Das in 'Indian English Poetry by an Expatriate Indian: A Note on G. S. Sharat Chandra's "Heirloom" ' (*LHY* 32:i.34–42). Das finds in Sarat Chandra's poetry a concern with identity and a sense of nostalgia which is evident in the work of other expatriate poets, such as Ramanujan. The conclusion is a rather routine assertion that, expatriates or not, Indian poets writing in English have much in common in terms of 'themes, attitudes, vocabulary, manner of expression [and] thought content'. A more satisfying attempt to locate a poet in a recognizable framework is D. R. Pattanaik's 'Silence as a Mode of Transcendence in the Poetry of Jayanta Mahapatra' (*JCL* 26:i.117–26). Beginning with a discussion of some Western literary and philosophical speculations about language and silence, Pattanaik argues that 'silence' in Mahapatra's work is not merely 'a Beckettian subversion or a self-indulgent narcissism' but 'a positive gesture, an effort to realise spiritual transcendence'. This view is supported by a sensitive reading of the poems and a consideration of Mahapatra's debt to the Oriya poetic tradition, which locate the poet 'in a perspective nearer home'.

(b) Fiction

In her introduction to *Motherlands,* Susheila Nasta suggests that the contributors' choices of texts and writers 'are perhaps indicative of another "canonisation" developing in western audiences and readers'. This is clearly true of Anita Desai, whose work is discussed in all of the essays on Indian fiction. Julie Newman's 'The Untold Story and the Retold Story: Intertextuality in Post-Colonial Women's Writing' points to the 'double marginalisation' of post-colonial women writers, stressing 'the need to question acculturated models and exemplary representations'. The value of intertextual strategies in 'repositioning the text in relation to its point of origin, or offering revisions of canonical texts' is illuminated by an analysis of Ruth Prawer Jhabvala's *Heat and Dust* and, more briefly, Desai's *Baumgartner's Bombay*. The ways in which Jhabvala and Desai 'rewrite' Forster are sensitively delineated in this essay. Shirley Chew's 'Searching Voices: Anita Desai's *Clear Light of Day* and Nayantara Sahgal's *Rich Like Us*' is a lucid and compelling discussion of the task of reconstructing the past in Indian women's writing. A useful consideration of Gayatri Spivak's theories suggests that 'the equivocal basis of woman's "freedom" ' is a consequence of both colonial and Brahminical discourse. The 'textual space' opened up by Spivak has also been explored in the work of Desai and Sahgal, which enacts the 'struggle to reclaim the past' and to retrieve for women 'a voice and a presence within their motherland'. Brahminical discourse and Desai's fiction are also examined in Helen Kanitkar's ' "Heaven Lies beneath her Feet?" Mother Figures in Selected Indo-Anglian Novels', which also considers *That Long Silence* by Deshpande. Both writers move to break the silence imposed by social convention and cultural ideals which, in turn, present 'such a far distant mark to aim at' that Indian women are 'foredoomed to failure'. The constraints of Hindu mythological representations of women, and the writers' consequent demythologizing strategies in their search for self-expression point to a conflict in modern society which in Kanitkar's sombre conclusion, must be resolved before it turns destructive.

Anthony Boxill offers a sympathetic reading of Bharati Mukherjee's collection, *Darkness*, in 'Women and Migration in Some Short Stories of Bharati Mukherjee and Neil Bissoondath' (*LHY* 32:ii.43–50). Many of Mukherjee's expatriate Indian women are the victims of marriage and migration; having 'no say in where they go ... they will never be at home anywhere ... unless they willingly reconcile themselves to their status as prisoners'. A striking contrast to all of the above views is provided by Ragini Ramachandra in 'Bharati Mukherjee's Wife: An Assessment' (*LCrit* 26:iii.56–67). This is an impassioned attack on Mukherjee's 'grotesque distortion of Indian womanhood' in a novel which tries 'to subvert the framework of an entire culture'. It is also a reminder of the depth of feeling that may be aroused by an expatriate writer.

Syd Harrex's informed survey of contemporary fiction ('India', in *The Commonwealth Novel Since 1960*, ed. Bruce King) shows a pleasing awareness of its own limitations. Apart from a brief consideration of Anand's work, the essay is chiefly concerned with Rao, Narayan and Desai. Harrex suggests that 'culturally embedded narrative metaphor' such as one finds in Narayan's novels, is 'more than a technical device' in Indo-Anglian fiction; 'it is virtually a national characteristic'. Hindu archetypes, in particular, provide 'a psychological and dramatic basis for many a modern or contemporary Indian novel'. Whilst much of the essay locates a small selection of novels within their cultural frames of reference, Harrex does summarize some other fruitful areas of writing and research, notably the 'expatriate traditions' and the 'commanding ... contribution of women novelists to the fiction of the recent era'. Finally, he notes the impact of *Midnight's Children*, and suggests that 'experimentation under the post-modernist shadow of Salman Rushdie' is proceeding in a very promising manner in the work of writers such as Amitav Ghosh and Vickram

Seth. Also worth noting in this volume is Mark Williams's 'The Novel as National Epic', which offers a comparative study of fiction by Wilson Harris, Salman Rushdie and Keri Hulme, further endorsing the view of Rushdie as pre-eminently a post-modernist writer whose India is 'teeming … manifold, multitudinously shapeless'.

In 'Shadow Lines: Cross-Cultural Perspectives in the Fiction of Amitav Ghosh' (*CE&S* 14:i.28–32), Louis James and Jan Shepherd usefully employ Bakhtin's notion of heteroglossia to illuminate Ghosh's narrative strategies, arguing that his use of 'languages' such as popular journalism, folk tales and the 'memory patterns of the extended family' enable him to 'deconstruct traditional European novel forms' and explore 'Vedic concepts of Maya'. A cross-cultural, interdisciplinary approach is also evident in K. D. Verma's 'Alienation, Identity and Structure in Arun Joshi's *The Apprentice*' (*ArielE* 22:i.71–90), which offers a detailed, if somewhat tortuous discussion of the progress of Joshi's protagonist-narrator in the context of both Indian and European modes of thought.

M. D. Fletcher's 'Salman Rushdie: An Annotated Bibliography of Scholarly Articles about his Fiction' (*JIWE* 19:i.15–23) gives details of pieces on *Midnight's Children* and *Shame* up to 1990. In terms of critical attention Rushdie now rivals Anand, Rao and Narayan. The latter's work continues to inspire criticism of a widely variable quality. Despite its grand title, T. Srinivas's 'The Dialectics of Inner Transformation: A Study in R. K. Narayan's *A Tiger for Malgudi*' (*JIWE* 19:ii.16–18) is a slight, mainly descriptive piece. In 'Narayan as a Gandhian Novelist' (*JIWE* 19:ii.1–9), Michael Pousse makes a somewhat erratic and over-generalized attempt to label Narayan, asserting that his characters are 'literary incarnations of the Gandhian ideal' and that in his novels 'Gandhi's preaching is echoed on every page'. It is something of a relief to turn to Chitra Sankaran's 'Patterns of Story-telling in R. K. Narayan's *The Guide*' (*JCL* 26:i.127–50). This is a diligent examination of the shaping influence of the *katha* (the ancient Sanskrit tale) on Narayan's narrative. The essay also provides a useful discussion of 'myth-motifs' in *The Guide*, including a consideration of the 'trickster-sage' figure of Hindu mythology. The detailed exposition of indigenous cultural influences on Indian writing is to be welcomed, since elsewhere the more unhelpful aspects of an Anglocentric discourse continue to appear. For example, K. C. Belliappa's 'The Question of Form in Raja Rao's *The Serpent and the Rope*' (*JCL* 26:i.156–68) makes the familiar claim that R. K. Narayan 'finds the comic-ironic mode of Jane Austen suitable to describe his vision of life'. This is an unfortunate generalization, given that Belliappa is at pains to demonstrate that *The Serpent and the Rope* is 'a truly Indian novel', and is prepared to criticize David McCutchion for adopting 'an accepted, traditional [i.e. Western] point of view'. A potentially cogent analysis of the *purana*-like 'encyclopaedic sweep' of the novel is marred by a distracting concern with other critics' generalizations. One takes the point, however, that Rao extends the 'frontiers of the fiction form through an intelligent use of traditional Indian literary modes'.

In 'The Exclusions of Postcolonial Theory and Mulk Raj Anand's *Untouchable*: A Case Study' (*ArielE* 22:iii.27–48), Arun P. Mukherjee argues eloquently against 'the prison hold of binaries' that dominates 'the discourse of post-colonial theory'. The critical attempt to create a 'meta-theory' to interpret all postcolonial writing 'homogenizes and standardizes these diverse literatures'. Mukherjee questions the criteria by which certain texts are canonized; Anand's *Untouchable* is subjected to a 'hermeneutic of suspicion' that reveals important 'repressions and omissions' in which 'the untouchable himself remains mute, the object of bourgeois discourses about what to do about him'. Anand's supposedly 'radical or subversive' text is too readily located in a narrow theoretical framework which, it is argued, not only takes the text at face-value but also 'erases the local and the specific concerns' of disparate literatures; i.e. 'their dialogue ... with their fellow citizens'. In the field of general theoretical approaches it is also worth noting Makarand R. Paranjape's 'The Ideology of Form: Notes on the Third World Novel' (*JCL* 26:i.19–32), which usefully considers the strategic nature of the 'Third World Novel' through a wide-ranging discussion of ideology and culture.

Binary oppositions are explored in Louis R. Barbato's 'The Arrow in the Circle: Time and Reconciliation of Cultures in Kamala Markandaya's *Nectar in a Sieve*' (*ArielE* 22:iv.7–15). Whilst chiefly concerned with different cultural perceptions of time (cyclical and linear, 'Eastern' and 'Western'), Barbato is also careful to note that more localized conflicts such as urban versus rural values are presented in Markandaya's novel. Ultimately, he argues, *Nectar in a Sieve* is about reconciliation: 'Things fall apart in this novel where cultures conflict, but the author puts them back together through her central character's ability to reconcile the potentialities of these cultures and to overcome their restrictions.' No such happy resolution seems possible in P. Geeta's overview of Markandaya's fiction, 'Images and Archetypes in Kamala Markandaya's Novels: A Study in Cultural Ambivalence' (*JCL* 26:i.169–78). This essay sees a 'pattern of unresolved oppositions' as the basis of Markandaya's plots and includes some interesting observations on the subject of tradition, conflict and change.

Finally, Meenakshi Mukherjee continues to occupy critical space that denies facile polarities. In 'Narrating a Nation' (*IndH* 40:iii/iv.19–27), she ably demonstrates how narrative texts themselves 'remind us of the impossibility of ... a segmented view' of binary oppositions, whether 'moderate and extremist' or 'secular and religious'. Her analysis encompasses texts in Bengali, Hindi and English, and ranges from Rabindranath Tagore to Amitav Ghosh, to conclude with a stimulating survey of the ground covered by Indian novelists; recent texts such as *Shadow Lines* 'have moved a long way from the totalizing narratives of territorial nationalism' to a 'more protean' form of story-telling.

4. The Caribbean

(a) General

In 'Voiceprints' (*PoetryR* 80:iv.19), a review of currently available sound recordings of Caribbean literature, chiefly poetry, Stewart Brown reminds us of the importance of orality in the black tradition, and of the way in which often 'the poem-as-text is only a shadow on the page of the poem-as-performance'. That said, he resists the stereotype of 'rant-chant-dance minstrelsy', pointing out the wide range of tones and styles which can benefit from being delivered as sound, and scathingly dismissing the 'banality' of Zephaniah's verse which the oral delivery cannot disguise. It seems therefore appropriate to begin with a round-up of sound and video cassette recordings of Caribbean literature. As well as the poets reading their own work – Agard, Berry, D'Aguiar, Dabydeen, Amryl Johnson, Markham, Nichols, and Zephaniah – there is the delight of Sam Selvon reading 'Brackley and the Bed' and an extract from *Moses Ascending*. Available from the British Library National Sound Archive, these tapes add an important dimension to Caribbean literature, as well as providing an invaluable teaching resource. The Jamaica-produced videotape (Caribbean Images Ltd) of Lorna Goodison introducing and speaking her poetry demonstrates a further potential area for development, rather different from the useful ICA series of video-recorded interviews with international writers in that it foregrounds and contextualizes the work itself. Caribbean writers available on video from the ICA are Fred D'Aguiar interviewed by Caryl Phillips, Pauline Melville also with Phillips, and Janice Shinebourne and Beryl Gilroy in conversation with Susheila Nasta. A Trinidadian production by Stage One Theatre Productions of Derek Walcott's play *Ti-Jean and his Brothers* is also now available on videotape (Banyan, Port of Spain), and should make the play much more accessible to those who do not share the Caribbean language background, for whom the printed text, readily available in Errol Hill's collection of four Caribbean plays, can pose problems as real as Shakespeare's; for both, the visual image of the drama and the sound of the language brings alive the text on the page.

Bibliography for the region, still suffering from the absence of a Caribbean chapter in the annual survey of *JCL*, has no doubt had this lack compensated for by M. J. Fenwick's *Writers of the Caribbean Area: A Bibliography*, of which it has not been possible to inspect a copy. *Kunapipi*'s useful series of annual reviews titled 'The Year That Was' is to include a section on the Caribbean in the second half of its 1991 survey. The *JWIL* did not issue an edition during 1991.

Anthologies of short stories seem deceptively simple, when in fact there is all the difference in the world between good and mediocre examples. Mervyn Morris's excellent selection for Faber, *Contemporary Caribbean Short Stories*, which brought forward new stories from familiar names with some exciting new work by writers no doubt destined to become familiar, included five women among its twenty-four authors, but now a whole collection of short stories by women of the Caribbean has demonstrated the wealth of female talent in the region. Lizabeth Paravisini and Carmen C. Esteves have edited a collection of twenty-eight stories by different authors from all parts of the Caribbean. French, Spanish, and Dutch speaking communities are represented, as well as English speaking ones, although the rather odd title, *Green Cane and Juicy Flotsam* is derived from a poem by Jamaica's Pamela Mordecai. The introduction provides an excellent overview of the collection, but its claim that 'there has been until now no collection of short stories where the student of literature as well as the general reader could experience the richness and variety of the genre as practiced [*sic*] by Caribbean women', is perhaps unfair on Pamela Mordecai's and Betty Wilson's anthology of women's writing, *Her True-True Name*, which does include a number of short stories as well as extracts from longer prose works. It, too, includes writers from the francophone and hispanophone groups, although the editors regret that lack of space forced them to exclude Dutch-speakers. The merits of extracts, however, will always pale before the strengths of entire works. In the complete short stories of *Green Cane and Juicy Flotsam* the welcome translation into English of work bearing well-known names, such as Astrid Roemer or Ana Lydia Vega, as well as some less familiar ones, not only opens up realms of exciting writing which stimulates the appetite for more, but also makes possible some illuminating juxtapositions. The influence of magic realism on Jamaica Kincaid's 'Girl', for instance, is unmistakable when it is seen sandwiched between stories by Martinique's Jeanne Hyvrard and Puerto Rican, Olga Nolla. Nolla's story, in particular, has an imaginative force and originality which would make the volume worthwhile all by itself. Her story, 'No Dust Is Allowed In This House', is narrated by an aging parasol which witnesses a revolution in the life of its owner, as the wider social drama is conveyed through her story of resistance to patriarchy. The brilliant, surreal conclusion shows Nolla to have learned from male writers such as Marquez, but to have created a different, feminist standpoint. Taken together, the stories in this collection provide a resounding affirmation, if any were needed, that a shared artistic project for Caribbean women of all cultural groups exists and thrives. As well as established names such as Jean Rhys (here represented by 'The Day They Burned the Books'), and Phyllis Shand Allfrey (represented by a provocative, previously unpublished story), the volume includes many young and new writers of great promise. Ramabai Espinet's story 'Barred', for example, is a strikingly original narrative which uses a range of language and voices to get to grips with the predicament of being an Indian woman in Trinidad in 1987. Other writers included from the English language group are Hazel Campbell, Michelle Cliff, Opal Palmer Adisa, Velma Pollard and Olive Senior, all contributing fresh and interesting work, much of it published for the first time. With its useful supporting biographies and bibliographies, the volume should prove a valuable teaching text for post-colonial and women's issues, and should help to achieve the greater inter-racial solidarity between Caribbean women to which the editors in their introduction direct their aspiration.

Women's studies in the region also benefit from Susheila Nasta's fine collection *Motherlands*. It offers essays on writers from Africa and South Asia as well as the Caribbean, prefaced by an indicative introduction from Nasta and a memorable multi-voiced poem by Marlene Philip. Grouped under the headings, 'Breaking the Silence: New Stories of Women and Mothers', 'Mothers/Daughters/Sisters?' and 'Absent and Adopted Mother(land)s', it presents a wide range of studies of evenly impressive quality, which inhabit with confidence the continuum between the specific and the general. Thus while there are excellent critiques of individual writers, such as Velma Pollard's identification of the plural language codes woven into a new whole by Olive Senior and Lorna Goodison, there are also more wide-ranging studies such as Carolyn Cooper's consideration of works by Una Marson, Sylvia Wynter, Erna Brodber, Paule Marshall and Toni Morrison, in relation to the trope of spirit possession. The bringing into the canon of a previously 'unknown' play of Una Marson's is particularly welcome. Anne Morris and Margaret Dunn look at the theme of 'Female Identity and the Caribbean Mothers'-land' in works by Kincaid, Rhys, Marshall, and Cliff. But the collection as a whole is stimulating reading for anyone concerned with the way women writers in post-colonial societies are coming to terms with their own identity. In addition, it serves as a welcome reminder of the quality of women's critical writing coming from regions such as the Caribbean.

Robert L. Ross, in his weighty volume geared to library reference shelves, *International Literature in English: Essays on the Major Writers*, finds room for only six Caribbean writers. Unfortunately, such a tome, with its wide margins and emphatic lay-out, inevitably comes to be seen as marking out a new canon, just when the old one was making not only its own obsolescence, but that of the concept, obvious. The whole notion of 'major writers' is no longer simple. A volume of this sort immediately provokes all sorts of unease: does quantity count, or quality, and if so who is to judge, and are those who have been historically significant to be regarded as equally as 'major' as those who have acquired a wider readership and a consolidated literary reputation? The editor signals the difficulty in his preface and comments that while most have been selected on the basis of their international reputation and publication abroad (the meaning of 'abroad' in relation to such writers is not self-evident), some newer writers have been included, mysteriously, on the basis of 'future importance'. But while the inner voice may say it really cannot matter who is in it and who is not, another more cynical voice whispers in the ear that the selection for such apparently authoritative works has in the past been hugely influential on the way writers are perceived, and may well be so again. The volume presents itself as a reference work to what are known elsewhere as the 'new literatures' in English (that is, excluding writers from the USA and Britain), but the terms in which Ross chooses to describe the relationship between the two groups are disturbing in their affirmation of a damaging, neo-imperialist stereotype: hastening to allay fears that these writers might eventually eclipse those of the old centres of cultural power, he asserts that 'the writing from abroad enriches the very literature that, in the first place, provided the language, the traditions, the text for a creative expansion comparable to the Roman Empire's dispersal of Latin'. For a volume such as this to be so rooted in a model of dependency is a betrayal of all the raised consciousness which (it was hoped) post-colonial studies had achieved. Even as he tries to mark the difference of these 'other' literatures, Ross only succeeds in digging himself in deeper: 'the major writers have built and reversed, negated and revised, re-formed and altered *that on which they drew*' [my italics]. There is little sense here of the multiple local traditions which have informed the use of English by creative writers away from the centres of hegemonic power. On the Caribbean front, those chosen to carry the reputation of the region are the predictable quartet of Wilson Harris, V. S. Naipaul, Jean Rhys and Derek Walcott, plus a less predictable pair, George Lamming and Earl Lovelace. Not Edward Kamau Brathwaite, not Sam Selvon ... There are many whose absence can be regretted. In fact, Walcott is something of an exception for the volume, as a poet and a dramatist; Ross acknowledges that in his selection fiction dominates, commenting, not unreasonably, that 'Possibly fiction travels better than poetry or drama'. What is on offer for the six in question is a two and a half thousand word critical essay accompanied by biographical and bibliographical information, the latter of undoubted usefulness, the former of variable quality. Ross's choice of critics varies from apt to inept, and the nature of their tasks is very different: a short survey of Earl Lovelace's work, for instance, ought to be a more manageable proposition than the equivalent for Wilson Harris, but it is Hena Maes-Jelinek who serves Harris admirably. In bemoaning the paucity of critical work to flesh out his bibliography on Lovelace, however, Read Way Dasenbrook makes a pertinent general comment: 'The study of Caribbean literature suffers from an overly restrictive canon in which three or four writers receive the lion's share of critical attention; and Lovelace is not one of those writers.' The need for serious critical attention to be paid to the host of talented writers, particularly the younger or 'newer' ones, who are not listed in rolls of honour such as this, has perhaps never been so great as now, as we witness a plural tradition hardening into a canon.

(b) Fiction

This makes it all the more satisfactory to see an article on Lovelace accompanied by an interview (*WLWE* 31:i.8) in which he makes an important contribution to the Caribbean aesthetic: 'the artist in the Caribbean – not only writers, *but every artist in the Caribbean* – has been subsidizing the idea and the spirit of the Caribbean. The steelbandsmen and the calypsonians – no one gives them a scholarship! They are neglected in the same way writers are ... we've been busy with freedom and we've ignored liberation ... Liberation is the beginning of making your life, liberating yourself, becoming yourself, deciding who you are, what you want to do ... what you are shaping.' Like Walcott, he refuses to see black history as a negative: 'I hold the view that Africans in the Caribbean have not been slaves. To me a slave is someone who gives up responsibility for his life and his future. By every demonstration, every gesture, Africans in the New World struggled to maintain control of their lives. So we haven't been slaves'. Likewise, characters such as Aldrick and Fisheye 'have not surrendered' but make 'their resistance a living expression of themselves, so that their entire life is that struggle'. Challenged on the rise of materialism he answers in terms of the attitude, rooted in rural society, that 'Living is more important than money', which he uses in his fiction: 'In *The Dragon Can't Dance*, people husband poverty like a prized possession.' Money was not relevant to his choice of career, he says: 'I did what I had to do.' But western consumerism is threatening the fabric of Caribbean society, calling for a concerted response: 'There's a strong need for a Caribbean self in which we would be more linked than we are now. It is so important that we have a spiritual self to guide us in our contacts with the rest of the world ...' In his accompanying article, ' "Progress" and Community in the Novels of Earl Lovelace' (*WLWE* 31:i.1), H. Nigel Thomas, the interviewer, considers Lovelace's fiction, particularly *The Wine of Astonishment*, as resistance to the neocolonialist materialism which threatens the sense of community in the Caribbean – and, he says, by extension, all former colonies. In a carefully argued study of the Trinidadian project of imagining the nation, 'Nation Time: Earl Lovelace and Michael Anthony Nationfy Trinidad' (*Commonwealth* 13:ii.31), Steve Harney pairs Lovelace with Anthony to counter Fredric Jameson. Enlisting C. L. R. James's distinction between these two as 'native and national' in a sense that Lamming, Naipaul and Harris are not, Harney takes on the postmodern debate about the postcolonial construction of national cultural identity, finding that Lovelace and Anthony both share and transcend the national discourse they work in, with their insistence that nationalism is not a prerequisite for 'self-fulfilment and achievement of individual identity'. In so doing, he champions the already-formed Trinidadian culture, demonstrable in such phenomena as carnival, through which artists like Minshall lead their community, as providing a model for the Caribbean in its integration and its realized imaginative community. Harney's argument, that through such a culture the 'unfettered individual' acquires a national identity which is also universal, may not altogether persuade, but the range and force of his thesis are stimulating.

Another Trinidadian for whom critical attention is overdue is Sonny Ladoo. Roydon Salick, who says in 'The Bittersweet Comedy of Sonny Ladoo: a Reading of *Yesterdays*' (*ArielE* 22.3) that Ladoo, who died in 1973 having written two novels, would have become 'a major voice', considers *Yesterdays* a bittersweet comedy rooted in the tragedy of *No Pain Like This Body*; it is 'a sort of linguistic version of the three-dimensional erotic sculptures' of Indian sacred art, part of a long tradition of Hindu eroticism. He sees the novel as subverting the stereotype of the Indo-Caribbean peasant as a sexless workaholic by celebrating a 'grand sexual feast'.

Wilson Harris scholarship is not in its infancy; he has long been well served by Hena Maes-Jelinek and Michael Gilkes, whose work leads a distinguished field of intelligent criticism. It might be thought that it would be difficult to follow some of the existing exegesis, but Hena Maes-Jelinek has edited a new collection of essays which is a model of its kind, as a tribute to mark Harris's seventieth birthday. Her *Wilson Harris: The Uncompromising Imagination*, gathers the work of a longish list of contributors, ranging from those well-established in the field to some less familiar names, but all make well-argued and stimulating contributions to their topic. Interestingly, the first thing the volume signals is its quest for a different approach – to respond to Harris's imaginative work with imagination. It opens with a gathering of poems, by poets as various as Kathleen Raine and David Dabydeen, who add luminous dimensions to Harris. Michel Fabre, to his credit, records his reluctance to respond in the conventional way to the invitation to take part ('little did I suspect that something in me would deeply resist glossing and writing an exegesis in the usual "scholarly" fashion', his fear being that 'I might petrify you into the stasis of a philosopher, to the detriment of your gentle and generous human self', when 'What is at stake here may be nothing less than our cultural survival'), and offers instead writings by Harris himself, most of them previously unpublished. The volume also offers the text of two illuminating recent interviews, with Michael Gilkes, and with Kirsten Holst Petersen and Anna Rutherford, in which Harris expounds his own position. He asserts that we live 'in one civilization', and that the text of his fiction 'is alive ... in its own right' and can reveal 'unsuspected links ... that I may not perceive even though it appears I have put them there myself'. He is sceptical of present fashion – 'when one scrapes away the crust of post-modernism, one is left with a pervasive and uniform despair' – for while he does not disguise the horrors of the modern world, he does not accept them as inevitable or final, if people could only learn, through art, to 'approach themselves in a different way', since the language of the imagination has 'deep intuitive roots'.

Those new to Wilson Harris might be well advised to read on with Gareth Griffiths's study, 'Post-Colonial Space and Time: Wilson Harris and Caribbean Criticism', which contextualizes Harris as a post-colonial writer (*vis à vis* in particular Edward Brathwaite's demotic critical position, and in relation to the hieratic founders of modernism), and asserts 'the insights produced in the creative and critical work can ... be seen to be addressing the radical issues in ways which can consolidate his claim to be amongst the most important of contemporary post-colonial writers and critics'. Griffiths goes on to draw attention to an insidious re-enactment of suppression, this time in the field of criticism, and to give an important pointer to a future direction for post-colonial critical practice, in which the polarization between rhetorical opposites would be replaced with a discourse of true pluralism: because of the importance of the debate, he says, 'the time seems to me to be ripe for a more integrative account of post-colonial critical positions in the Caribbean which will acknowledge both the powerful differences and the great similarities of the two main streams of critical thought that I have represented by the work of Brathwaite and Harris. In the face of recent tendencies to write the existence of this body of criticism out of the record in favour of concentration on contemporary academic critics such as Spivak, Bhabha, etc., the international and internecine critical struggles between these positions which characterized the debate of the seventies and eighties seems increasingly futile and self-defeating. Such an account would not oppose the politics of opposition, but would suggest the need for seeing in work like Harris's a model for dismantling the more unsustainable binarisms and developing a genuine sense of textual syncreticity and transformation as in itself the most profoundly radical and oppositional of positions for the post-colonial writer and critic to adopt.' Such clear and original thinking seems the rule in this volume, rather than the exception. It is as if Harris's own genius of imagination presides.

Wilfred Cartey's ambitious study of the Caribbean novel does not quite deliver what it promises. The title, *Whispers from the Caribbean; I Going Away, I Going Home*, is explained in the introduction; the project is 'to design an esthetic paradigm within which to study Caribbean novels written in English, and by extension to locate Caribbean consciousness', a project further defined as 'to note and to signify images that are characteristic not only of the Caribbean area, but that are also related to the African images in *Whispers from a Continent*', Random House's 1968 publication on the literature of black Africa. This is to be achieved by the analysis of some seventy novels, says Cartey, but in the event the scope is more manageable. The seven chapters offer extended commentary on a clutch of novels, mostly four or five per chapter, with enough room, it would seem, to get to grips with the individual texts and put them into a coherent overall frame. The overall, antiphonal structure is clearly described at the outset. Part one, 'I Going Away', is subtitled, 'The Shaping of the Caribbean Personality', part two, 'I Going Home', is 'The Evolution of the Caribbean Presence', but this is immediately glossed in an eccentric way: '*Personality* as used here is a historical term; it evokes the person as affected by the combined forces of colonialism, of economics, of historical imperialism and Great Power rivalry. *Presence* is a cultural or spiritual term; it suggests the person in his own spiritual interiority, [*sic*] his selfhood as bestowed upon him by his own people, their values, their worldview, their mores. Both *personality* and *presence* are in a constant state of tension and interaction.' The quirkiness of this is extended into the arrangement of the material under the chapter headings. The first chapter, for instance, titled 'Rhythm of Man and Landscape: the Mixings', contains a lot of commentary on Edgar Mittelholzer, embracing, and rather swamping, a short section on Jan Carew, and turns out to be less about man and landscape than Chapter Two, which purports to be about 'The Rituals of the Folk: the Crossing of Rhythms'. This chapter has an extended analysis of Naipaul's *A House for Mr. Biswas*, yet, despite its title, no mention of the Hindu rituals which frame Biswas's struggle for self-liberation. The attempt to get away from the chronological approach is stimulating: new relationships are thrown up between texts as, for instance, Mittelholzer, Merle Hodge, Michael Anthony and Garth St.Omer rub shoulders in chapter four, and Lamming, Harris, Thelwell, Lovelace and Paule Marshall meet in chapter seven, but the opportunities for searching juxtapositions are not quite realized. Naipaul, perhaps predictably, gets an unsympathetic interpretation, being described, for instance, as, with Biswas, attempting 'to ascribe a negativity, a sense of nothingness, to his character, to his so anti-heroic character'. Cartey's analysis tends to inspire uneasiness rather than glad recognition of insight, as when Biswas's quest for a home is described as 'radial and totally central to the action of the novel'. One of Cartey's favorite words is 'argumentation', which perhaps sums up the problem of style. This is all a great pity, as it is a big and in some ways valuable book. Much of the commentary is illuminating (as, for instance, the analysis of the role of water in McDonald's *The Humming Bird Tree*), and, although the overall organization is distinctly unhelpful, the index will make it practically useful to students of individual novels. It has to be said, however, that the selection of novels seems dated, and the work as a whole falls short of its intention both to locate a Caribbean sensibility, and to place it within a larger African-American frame of reference as the title suggests. The claim which is centrally placed in the book, that 'the emergence of West Indian writers represents a transformation that hails no less than the creation of a new language, the presentation of a revolutionary way of seeing – and speaking of – things', may be true, but remains unestablished in this book.

Dolly Hassan gives an admirably dispassionate analysis of V. S. Naipaul's attitude to the Caribbean political phenomenon of the messianic leader. In 'The Messianic Leader in V. S. Naipaul's West Indian Works' (*CNIE* 4:ii.55), she relates his statements in interviews and non-fiction both to his fiction and to political events in the region. She strides through the steam generated by Naipaul's pronouncements, to pinpoint the issue dividing the black community and Naipaul as his failure to acknowledge the existence of neo-colonial socio-economic systems. Her perception that his target is often the blinkered and cowardly white liberals who prop up local tyrants, rather than the Caribbean poor, is astute. Her reminder that Naipaul resists the 'myth' of himself, in his words, as 'reactionary, totally out of sympathy with progressive movements, ... hard-hearted and cruel – none of which is true', is consolidated by his statement of his artistic project in terms which perhaps his readers should inscribe on their bookmarks: 'I long to find what is good and hopeful and really do hope that by the most brutal sort of analysis one is possibly opening up the situation to some sort of action, an action which is not based on self-deception.' Salman Rushdie's views on Naipaul must always be of interest. His collection of essays, *Imaginary Homelands*, reprints two short reviews, one of Naipaul's study of the Islamic world, and the other of his most recent fiction, *The Enigma of Arrival*. In 'Naipaul Among the Believers' Rushdie recognizes and enjoys much of the book's detail, but pinpoints also its partiality, unmasking Naipaul's pose of straight reportage: 'The trouble is that it's a highly selective truth, a novelist's truth masquerading as objective reality.' Its silence on the role of military power in Pakistan, for instance, is one of the features which lead Rushdie finally to dismiss the book as superficial. In the other essay, 'V. S. Naipaul', Rushdie recalls Naipaul's wish of a few years earlier, to write a comedy to match *A House for Mr. Biswas*, as the lead-in to his characterization of the recent novel as unrelievedly melancholic. Rushdie's insights are many. The novel is, he says, 'autobiographical in the sense that it offers a portrait of the intellectual landscape of one who has long elevated "the life of the mind" above all other forms of life'. The rebirth in a new landscape is the migrant's experience which Rushdie recognizes as the impulse to art, in which the world has to be 'described into existence': 'The immigrant must invent the earth beneath his feet'. But for all the book's beauties of style Rushdie finds it 'bloodless', and while he regards some of its socio-political attitudes as 'untenable', he finally wearies of its minimalism. The problem as he sees it is not just its lack of life, but its lack of love – so remote from the early books, which though 'cutting and unsentimental' had been 'essentially affectionate'.

Jean Rhys scholarship continues to flourish. Carole Angier's impressive biography-cum-critical study, published in hardback by Deutsch, is to be reissued in paperback by Penguin, for which all financially hard-pressed students (not to mention librarians) should be thankful. Angier offers major critical studies of Rhys's five novels (over forty pages on *Wide Sargasso Sea*, for instance), but not, for reasons of space, the short stories. Her view of Rhys as 'distilling truth out of evasion and art out of pain' is communicated in a magnum opus of great scholarship and imaginative sympathy, which remains, despite its encyclopaedic scope, intensely readable. For once, a dust-jacket eulogy, that this is 'a work of exceptional intimacy, sensitivity and power', is amply confirmed by the seven hundred and fifty pages which follow. There are a few quibbles, one being the opening premise, which seems to be over-determined by Rhys's fiction, of Dominica as an exotic, demonic 'other': Angier writes, for instance, 'All this careless, cannibal life is beautiful, but also sinister … The beauty is mainly on the surface, the violence beneath'. But the joys of the work far outweigh its demerits. Jean Rhys, in all her troubled humanity, emerges from these pages with a clarity which persuades us of its truth. Countless memorable details impress: for instance, a mere footnote about her intended contribution to the historic series of autobiographical essays titled 'Leaving School' which Alan Ross commissioned for *The London Magazine* in 1962, which she reworked on and off for fourteen years, writing 'dozens of versions of each page', and which finally went into *Sleep It Off Lady* as 'Overture and Beginners Please' – a small item in the book, but one which tells so much about Rhys's panic-striken daring in ever becoming a writer at all. Pierrette Frickey takes a firmly anti-biographical stance in her collection of essays, *Critical Perspectives on Jean Rhys*, pointing out that the terms of Rhys's will prohibit biography. She collects a rather motley assortment of writings, most of them already available in print, dividing them into three groups, 'Rhys on Rhys', in which two of the three are others' accounts of encounters with Rhys, 'Perspectives on Jean Rhys', which reprints a V. S. Naipaul review from 1972, and 'The Works of Jean Rhys', which is heavily weighted towards *Wide Sargasso Sea*, to which no less than five articles are devoted. Contributors include Rhys scholars, Helen Nebeker, Louis James, and Thomas Staley, as well as less predictable figures such as John Updike, and Caribbean critics such as Kenneth Ramchand and John Hearne. Frickey's own contribution is a short, practical introduction, which as well as surveying Rhys's life as background to the production of the works, presents the rationale of her selection of essays as to 'examine the form and style of her fiction, her superb craftsmanship'. She clearly regards her role as remedial, correcting a false emphasis: 'Critics on both sides of the Atlantic have elaborated to excess on the theme of alienation and on speculative interpretations of Rhys's fiction as facts at the expense of examining the craftsmanship which places Rhys among the best women contemporary writers'. She recommends Kristien Hemmerechts's structuralist study, although she does not include any of Hemmerechts's work in her collection, but however much the insistence on the texts rather than the life is proper and timely, the collection as a whole does not really meet the stated objective, being patchy rather than convincing. Those looking for existing (and rather dated) scholarship in accessible form will find it useful, however, and it has the benefit of a thorough bibliography.

Coral Ann Howells's book, *Jean Rhys*, is a different matter. With all the coherence possible in a short monograph, Howells presents a new and illuminating reading of Rhys, building on existing scholarship (not including the Angier book which came after Howells's text was complete) but offering fresh insights derived from evaluation of the Rhys archive at Tulsa, some of it, she claims, new to critical attention. A manuscript text which is central to Howells's reading of Rhys is her narrative of an erotic teenage encounter with an elderly Englishman, Mr Howard, written in an exercise book in the late 1930s, which 'pervades Rhys's own narrative of the creative life and her heroines' enslavement to romantic fantasies'. Although the terms in which this is presented early in the book carefully leave open the possibility that the account is a fantasy narrative, it is later referred to unequivocally as 'Rhys's traumatic adolescent sexual encounter with Mr. Howard', which is a very different proposition. In general, however, the book is convincingly scholarly. The grounding of the critique in Rhys's manuscript writings means that a lively sense of informal perspectives on the literature is created – inevitably also dependent on the scholarship of predecessors such as Francis Wyndham and Diana Melly who edited the letters. The first chapter introduces the three critical matrices which Howells applies, 'contemporary feminist theory, theories of colonial and post-colonial discourse, and revisionist studies of modernism which take gender into account', while subsequent chapters proceed concisely and with clarity with readings in historical sequence of the fiction. The unfolding argument reaches its conclusion with the late stories, which respond to the question Howells posited at the beginning – 'In what sense is Rhys's fiction so multiple, so secretive, that it constitutes a kind of blankness on to which critics can project their own ideological interests?' – with the finding that they are 'multivoiced fragmented discourses from the margins', Rhys's final contribution to 'a poetics of female space', which, though a 'Waste Land', is also about 'precarious survival'.

Against the odds, Barbara Ewell manages to produce a useful commodity in 'Otherness and Self-Exile in *Wide Sargasso Sea*' (*CNIE* 4:ii.75) Perhaps because the body of Rhys scholarship is now growing so intricate and extensive, an essay such as this has the merits of offering *multum in parvo*, covering a lot of central issues perceptively in a small compass. In a clear and jargon-free style it proceeds consecutively with its critique of the novel, to Ewell's conclusion that Antoinette resists the patriarchal and racist construction of herself in an act of self-affirmation: 'Tia *is* herself.' The evil, for Jean Rhys, she says, is 'not that profound otherness of the self, that silent, indifferent secret of our sargasso seas, but rather the failure to embrace that mystery, to love it in all its complex danger'.

A contemporary Caribbean woman writer who shares much of Rhys's antipathy to the north, although in a very different vein, is Jamaica Kincaid. In a revealing essay, 'On Seeing England for the First Time' (*Transition* 51.32), she develops elements of *A Small Place*, recounting the myth of England with which she was raised, and which she came to hate, and setting it against her experience of the reality. Her bitter dislike is rooted in the sense of difference, not only from the English but paradoxically from her own community too, where her passionate antipathy is atypical: '... a great feeling of rage and disappointment came over me as I looked at England, my head full of personal opinions that could not have public, my public, approval. The people I come from are powerless to do evil on a grand scale'. As always, it is a provocative and thought-provoking engagement with complex issues, in language as brilliant and naked as a rapier.

It has to be an important occasion when a writer is for the first time the subject of a critical monograph. Following on from Susheila Nasta's anthology of critical work on Sam Selvon, is the first Selvon monograph. Clement Wyke has chosen to foreground Selvon's use of language in his study, *Sam Selvon's Dialectal Style and Fictional Strategy*, but it is not a linguist's book. As a critical introduction to Selvon's work it is readable and stimulating, and welcome in that it raises consciousness of the language question, without which any discussion of Selvon is a non-starter. Wyke divides his study between the early, middle and late periods (sometimes unfortunately writing as if Selvon were no longer alive, and able to change 'late' to 'late middle', perhaps). His thesis is that the 'pure and unpretentious' Trinidad Creole in the early works gradually shifts to a 'waning of the original local patterns' as the influence of Standard English becomes more marked, a thesis which is not in itself new or exceptional. In his evaluation of the 'late' phase, however, he challenges the view of critics such as Mervyn Morris, who sees this change as a sad and classic instance of authenticity giving way to exoticism, arguing that the new hybrid language is, after all, authentic 'in representing the changing language of the characters who people the world of his fiction', although he does concede that it is sometimes 'difficult to decide if Selvon is in full control' of his linguistic code-shifting. Unfortunately, in his analysis of the 'late' work, Wyke himself seems insufficiently attuned to the different language codes being deployed; in his discussion of Brenda's haranguing of Moses for his use of language in *Moses Ascending*, his comments reveal a blind spot about the essential feature of the exchange – that Brenda's claim to 'correctness' is itself pretentious and ill-founded. Wyke's view of Selvon as a 'seriocomic' writer is rooted in a welcome awareness of his depths, which some who label him only as comic skate over, but to fail to comment on the rich comic irony of a passage such as this, in a critique about irony, argues an inattentive reading. Likewise, to criticize as non-naturalistic Selvon's placing of Standard English in a Port of Spain taxi driver's mouth after an altercation in which he uses Creole, seems to miss the whole point. However, while there are details which are disturbing in his book, Wyke does succeed in his main objective, which is to lead the non-linguist into an awareness of Selvon's language use as the vehicle of his fiction. Shrewdly, he identifies at the outset what is likely to be the problem: that his bringing together of 'the two worlds of language and literature' may tend to 'create higher expectations among specialists in both fields than may be fulfilled'. He introduces some linguistic concepts and jargon without perplexing the reader, and in fact offers in his introduction a generally useful survey of the language situation in Trinidad, of interest not only to Selvon fans (although the section on African elements is rather skimped). He quite properly acknowledges his debts to accepted experts, and disclaims the status of linguist for himself; a linguist would probably have written a study impenetrable to the general reader. But there are inaccuracies – obvious even to a non-linguist – which undermine the reader's confidence in his ability to handle his topic, as, for instance, when he mentions Urdu as the 'Muslim equivalent' to Hindi. It is, however, perhaps the price of such an interdisciplinary project that such rough edges should cause friction; the greater truth is that the enterprise was worthwhile, and the results are valuable.

(c) Poetry

In an illuminating interview, Lorna Goodison talks to Wolfgang Binder about her life and work (*Commonwealth* 13:ii.49), including her sense of herself as Jamaican, how she became a poet as well as a visual artist, and the genesis of particular poems and themes. The account of her creative engaging, for example, with the Nanny myth as subject enriches the reading of the poem. Asked about her use of the language continuum, she replies: 'Some things I think of in standard English and some in creole ... I am really not intimidated by the English language. Also, I am not ashamed of the creole. For that reason, I don't make any kind of differentiation when I write'. She describes how her use of the term 'mulatta' was given to her by Latin American usage, as an unpejorative, unproblematic term. The cathartic effect of some of her poems on listeners is something she finds moving, but although there is a special attention to women and to female heroes in her work, she is careful not to exclude men from her concerns. It is a sense of community which she thinks can save the world, a philosophy which results in a characteristic inclusiveness. Asked about her use of European myths, she replies, 'If somebody tells you, take some and leave some, that is his or her problem. I am not going to do that. All of it belongs to me!'

This is also very much Walcott's approach to the artistic project. The chief event in poetry studies for the year has to be Stewart Brown's much needed *The Art of Derek Walcott*. Credit is due to the Welsh publishers, Seren Books of Bridgend, for commissioning this collection of separately authored essays, which provide a chronological survey of Walcott's long and productive career, although it is irritating that proof-reading should have allowed so many misprints to survive. Brown both edits the volume and contributes an informative introduction and the first study, of the little known early work, and in so doing lays a scholarly and thoughtful foundation. What follows is uneven in quality, and sometimes frustratingly light, as some substantial and muscular works are given bantam-weight treatment. There are some editorial decisions which are partly responsible; for instance, Ned Thomas, whose survey of *Sea Grapes* and *The Star-Apple Kingdom* is condensed into some two and a half thousand words, excluding quotation, elects to concentrate on one poem from each volume, 'Sainte Lucie' and 'The Schooner *Flight*', a valid choice given the parameters, but the question remains as to whether two such important collections should have been compressed into one chapter. It is only the later collections which are given a chapter each, and there the results are less reductive, although unsatisfactorily, if inevitably, disjunct. The decision to lump some of the earlier work together was presumably the price of allocating chapters to other aspects of the work – the drama, the essays, and the relationship with painting, here represented by Van Gogh – which might otherwise have been squeezed out from a two hundred page survey; if the choice had to be made, it is probably more important that the presence of the wider work is signalled, but there seems no good reason why the volume could not have been a little longer. It is good to see Mervyn Morris roundly refuting Helen Vendler's sniffy criticism of Walcott's 'ventriloquism' in juxtaposing different tones of voice, in a beautifully precise reading of the language used in *The Fortunate Traveller*, and it is good to have first impressions of *Omeros* from such a redoubtable figure as John Figueroa, but it will come to seem a curiosity, perhaps, that Figueroa considers it 'much more a novel than an epic'. Brown's collection will prove itself most useful as a handbook to Walcott's daunting *oeuvre*, giving basic information, suggesting thought-provoking angles of approach, and adducing useful intertexts. It also brings a substantial bibliography which will be of great benefit to serious students, pointing them to further reading, for this is a real bonus of the volume. Given the scope of the bibliography, it seems strange to suggest that Walcott scholarship is in its infancy, but this is still in a sense true. Robert Hamner's monograph is now long out of date, and apart from Edward Baugh's valuable book on *Another Life*, critical attention has been limited to essays, which take on one topic, or parts of books with a wider scope. While it is good to see critics who are themselves creative writers of the region contributing here – not only Morris and Figueroa but Fred D'Aguiar – there are other scholars in the field who might have been more appropriate choices than some of the others. Lloyd Brown's perceptive Walcott critique, for instance, available most substantially in his survey of Caribbean poetry, is missed in Stewart Brown's volume. In the end, however, it is a useful book, although, for all its merits, *The Art of Derek Walcott* returns us to the need for the kind of in-depth engagement that, for instance, Richard Ellmann offered the reader of Joyce; the Walcott art has become too extensive and too rich for its entirety to be easily addressed in two hundred pages.

(d) Drama

Two of the most stimulating essays in *The Art of Derek Walcott* are the chapters on his drama. Laurence Breiner contextualizes the early plays, from *Henri Christophe* in 1950 to *Dream on Monkey Mountain*, begun, as he recalls, in 1959, performed in 1967, and published in 1970 – the kind of detail which helps to revise perception of how it relates to the black power movement. His readings of the plays are knowledgable and perceptive, making very good use of the limited scope, without sacrificing range or depth. Walcott's choice of subjects reminds the reader that his epic concerns are not confined to his poetry. The later published plays are addressed by Lowel Fiet, who quite properly draws attention to the wealth of unpublished scripts and the ongoing nature of Walcott's productivity, which makes 'later' a misnomer. The affiliation to other language traditions is an important factor identified by Fiet, particularly that of the francophone Caribbean; he places Walcott in a roll-call of international great names, as well as at the heart of a Caribbean theatre aesthetic, although again the small compass restricts analysis to little more than headlines at times. Walcott's plays are also the subject of two interesting articles in *Commonwealth* (13:ii.1, 8). Anthony Boxill gives a sharp and profound reading of *Malcochon* by taking the role of the Conteur as key to the meaning, located in a motif of redemption between St. Lucian myth, history, and intertexts such as Kurosawa's *Rashomon* and Blake's 'Tiger'. Daizal Samad considers *Dream on Monkey Mountain* as an expression of a plural Caribbean identity, a concept of 'home' which we all share: 'the Caribbean lives in a manifestly splintered presence within the oceanic layers of our psyche', an unusual generalization of the play's meaning. He reads the execution of Makak's White Goddess as a necessary stage in the process of securing a healthful, balanced integration of all the fragments of ancestral memory, where none should be allowed to dominate, 'lest the West Indian become – remain – a mimic man'.

Walcott himself in his London lecture 'The Poet in the Theatre', published in *PoetryR* (80.4), champions the reintroduction of poetry to the theatre, and not only poetry, but ecstasy. He comments ironically that 'Exuberance in contemporary theatre is permitted only in certain second-rate shapes, such as musicals', and calls for liberation from limits to feeling and from restrictions on form: 'all sustained metre is now rejected as artifice and not life.' Illustrating his thesis that great poetry can also be vividly colloquial from the likes of Webster, he wonders whether current circumscriptions have denied us a second Elizabethan age in the theatre, and concludes, 'Modern poetry should reinvade the theatre, not hang out in the lobby shabbily like a second cousin.' Walcott is here making a significant step; not only does his art, and that of other post-colonial writers, transcend confining concepts of national or regional status, but his critical pronouncements refuse to stay within the limits which some might wish to impose. As a Caribbean critic, with a particular culture from which to approach art in the world, he here addresses one of the central assumptions of contemporary western aesthetic practice, a case where the pressure of acceptability, of ephemeral taste – always particularly powerful in the theatre with its urgent commercial considerations – is exposed as limiting and dangerously exclusive. It remains to be seen whether Walcott's injunction will result in some different plays making the difficult journey to audiences – in London or anywhere else.

Walcott may have dominated the critical scene in drama, but there is a timely reminder of other possible approaches to an epic theatre from Yvonne Brewster, who regularly takes on London audiences. In an illuminating interview with Lizbeth Goodman, 'Drawing the Black and White Line: Defining Black Women's Theatre' (*NTQ* 7.361), Brewster reminds us that her London-based feminist theatre company, Talawa, is named after a Jamaican word indicating a woman to be reckoned with, as in the saying 'She lickle but she talawa', which Brewster glosses, 'she is small in size, but you best not mess with her'. She sees her own feminism as the product of the West Indian matriarchal society, and finds the northern brand of feminism 'a bit difficult. It's hard to understand what all the fuss is about.' The origins of the company in the days of liberal Greater London Council arts funding seem light years away; to the great credit of the women founders, it is still going strong in the lean years of the 1990s. Brewster only regrets the difficulty of completing the hat trick – of not only having a company run by women, and predominantly female performers, but also staging plays written by women. The scope of Talawa's style is at odds with the way women tend to write, according to Brewster: 'We do epic theatre. We need epic plays. Epic, that is, in the sense that we use big, bold powerful images … Even if it's specific in a domestic sense, my theatre must have a vision which goes beyond the domestic. I know this is contentious, but I'll say it anyway: I think women are better than men at looking at things on the small scale …' While this may raise some hackles, in an account of the collective working up of a play by Yazmin Judd she says disarmingly, 'That's the sort of thing that a company like Talawa can do. We can bring up plays like babies.' And she is not anti-men: 'men can and (in my experience) often do help and encourage women's accomplishments, just as women encourage men and other women.' Her kind of inclusiveness has at least resulted in making things happen. On the concept of black theatre, she makes the race of the director as central a criterion as the race of the performers; she defines herself, as a black West Indian woman directing in Britain, as an outsider, but continues more surprisingly: 'being an outsider can be a good thing: it can be a position of power.' Brewster's pragmatism and humanity are a salutory reminder that received ideas should be continually tested in the real world, both for their power to frighten and for their power to help.

5. New Zealand and the South Pacific

(a) General

The New Zealand section of the *JCL* Annual Bibliography of Commonwealth Literature 1990 (*JCL* 26:ii.112–36), compiled this year by Stuart Murray, provides the usual excellent checklists of bibliography, research aids, poetry, drama, anthologies, criticism and new journals. The introduction by Mark Williams deplores the decline of *The New Zealand Listener* which, since the Second World War, had upheld a very high standard of cultural information for the general public; the appearance of *Metro* in the eighties was not able to fill the void left by the *Listener,* since the latter has abandoned the cultural field in order to entice a wider public – a policy which has however failed, since readership continues to decline. Williams paints a decidedly grim picture of the political and economic state of the country and regrets that there has been little innovatory reaction among writers to accompany the refreshing magic realism of other Commonwealth artists such as Rushdie in *Midnight's Children* or Carey in *Illywhacker.* From the point of view of criticism, Williams welcomes *The Penguin History of New Zealand Literature*, which is the first to appear since E. H. McCormick's *New Zealand Literature: A Survey* (1959) but notes that, while the work is entertaining, challenges the conservatism of the former generation and debunks the idea of 'tradition'; it lacks a bibliography and ignores children's literature and drama altogether.

However, this need has been quickly and exhaustively filled by *The Oxford History of New Zealand Literature in English* edited by Terry Sturm. The enterprise took over six years to complete and was undertaken by a team of respected experts in the various fields. The sheer size and variety of chapters witnesses to the literary activity of the nation over the years; the authority and knowledge of Sturm himself was probably a key factor in the completion of such a monumental task. In his introduction, the editor exposes the problems and discussions that were the preliminary mapping out of the finished volume. Efforts were made to probe back into history – into the arrival of literarity itself on islands which up to the time of colonization had been infused by the oral Maori tradition; nevertheless the Maori tradition had to be put to one side, as it is the subject of similar diversity which the present work could not include. However, Jane McRae's section, entitled 'Maori Literature: A Survey' provides an insight into the resources of archives in Maori writing. By rejecting the canonical approach, the team avoided accusations of sectarian choices – no uncertain advantage in a country where, within literary circles, in-fighting is rife at times.

The very diversity of the genre called 'non-fiction' defies a strict structuring of material, but Peter Gibbon manages to articulate his text around the themes of exploration, the description of indigenous phenomena, the shift from Britain as 'home' to New Zealand as homeland, and the consequent construction of a national identity. He claims that non-fiction has been neglected as a literary form because it supposedly deals with facts rather than style; to counter this argument, he includes autobiography and literary biography which illustrate the complexity of the tenuous divide between non-fiction and its literary expression.

The vast field of the development of the novel as addressed by Lawrence Jones falls into four historical periods: pioneer 1861–89, late colonial 1890–1934, provincial 1935–64 and the post-provincial which runs to the present day. Jones traces the historical and economic changes across this tapestry of history and analyses the contemporary novelists' reactions to the major changes and the various literary strategies they devised to render their environment in fiction. Themes and modes of expression rather than individual authors are discussed. Thus Jones discerns in the pioneering period a didactic naïve realism, while in the late colonial period there was a general move towards quiet realism. The thirties began what proved to be the Golden Age of New Zealand literature; critical essays encouraged novelists to produce by providing a reader's response; Sargeson and Mulgan erected the first milestones of Puritan critical realism which was to dominate the literary scene for several decades. From 1965 onwards, there is the general recognition of the breakdown of the Puritan monoculture. The Maori has produced recognized published writers, thus widening the scope of national expression and, although critical realism and impressionism remain, a new postmodernist metafictional genre has appeared. Simultaneously, New Zealand literature has moved onto the international scene.

For Lydia Wevers, the short story has established an independence *vis-à-vis* the home country, because its essential brevity excludes outside influences; it flourishes in an atmosphere where all needs to be formulated, defined and refined. The conventions of short fiction aim at representing colonial questions of race, culture, identity and nationhood in a new country where recent experiences needed to be placed within a familiar context. Mansfield's early writing endeavours to fit into the colonial mould by evoking 'real life' and 'local colour' while consciously subverting colonial styles in order to question their validity by using a complicated narrative technique. Sargeson is recognized as a yardstick against whose writing younger writers were measured. Frame has come to challenge realism in writing, using language to destroy the apparent in order to question reality itself. Since the 1960s, many contributions to the short story have been made by Maori writers such as Patricia Grace and recent migrants (Batistich, du Fresne) from countries other than the UK. Wevers refers to the 'free' story (Shadbolt, Marshall, Stead) as one of the modes which, in the last thirty years, has responded to social pressures rather than modernism. Precursors in the postmodern story have been Pakeha and male (Haley, Wedde, Else and Morrissey); their texts were concerned with the fictional nature of subjectivity, language and the art of writing as subject matter. The pieces play on language, on silence, and on incompatible historical parallels, so that the pact between author and reader is constantly challenged. Women's stories often reflect the environment and social pressures under which they live; stories are set in confined, walled-in spaces where women struggle to establish self-knowledge.

In his chapter on drama, Howard McNaughton claims that theatre is as much the expression of audience values as authorial statement, and the boundary between colonial imposition and postcolonial identity cannot be clearly defined. In the nineteenth century, theatre was largely British-influenced and there was little reference to the colonized inhabitants. In a new, scarcely populated country, it was difficult to unite a theatre audience and, owing to lack of funds, drama was essentially amateur until the end of the Second World War. From 1945 onwards, local theatre groups began staging productions of a national nature which opened up new social perspectives and explored the possibilities of a new cultural identity where minority groups were also able to express themselves. During this period, McNaughton distinguishes four basic milestones: from 1945 to 1960, established writers began to explore the possibilities of the stage; in the mid-sixties, a new generation of playwrights succeeded the state-subsidized theatres; with the founding of the professional writers' agency, Playmarket, the expansion was confirmed in the seventies and, in a final section, McNaughton follows the more recent developments and draws parallels with the similar dramatic phenomena present in both radio and television plays.

For Mac D. P. Jackson there is a definite New Zealand tradition in poetry because texts have begun to respond to their predecessors. He quotes as a paradigm the famous 'Baxterian' sonnet consisting of fourteen unrhymed, irregular, paired lines. In her survey of poetry from 1945 to 1990, Elizabeth Caffin stresses Allen Curnow's ruling part in sketching out one of the main debates concerning what others have seen as narrow nationalism, a debate which still continues among contemporary poets. In recent years, feminist voices and the articulation of New Zealand's two languages have supplanted the struggle between nationalists and postmodernists.

Betty Gilderdale's chapter on children's literature shows a gradual disappearance of the clear-cut separations between genres like the adventure story, the family story and fantasy. The New Zealand landscape in particular has become the setting for fantastic events which produce effects close to so-called 'magic realism'. For Betty Gilderdale, the dual heritage of the country and its vulnerability in a world threatened by ecological disaster have progressively replaced the stereotypes of previous literature for children.

Terry Sturm breaks new ground in a work of this type by including 'popular fiction', because this mode, represented by Ngaio Marsh and Mary Scott, reaches a wide public, is well-known abroad and deserves more than the usual patronizing acknowledgement of 'minor' works. Sturm excels in showing some of the social stereotypes represented in romance. He shows that, until the 1960s, one of the common plots concerns the emigration of a young English heroine who marries the owner of a sheep station whose prosperity enables her to achieve comfort she would not have been able to obtain had she remained in the British Isles. Such popular books tell much about the ruling founding myths, about race and gender relations.

Dennis McEldowney traces the history of publishing in the country. The state of this vital activity reflects government policies and the ensuing freedom of expression of the individual, of groups and the press.

John Thomson's commented bibliographical chapter is most thorough and complete; it is divided into four sections: bibliographies and other works of reference, literary history and criticism, anthologies and periodicals; there is also a very complete list of individual bibliographies for 144 authors. It is the essential reference tool for any researcher in need of precise bibliographical, biographical or critical information, a source that has been sadly lacking until this publication.

The *JNZL* is now being edited from the University of Otago. Issue seven gives an overview of New Zealand literature in 1988–9. In his article 'Literary Biography in New Zealand' (*JNZL* 7.87–105), John Garaets examines the possible traps of which the biographer who feels that he is writing fact must be aware. He covers the problem of point of view and the fact that the end-product of the subject's life may be used to influence accounts of the earlier experiences. Taking the Fairburn, Baxter and Ashton-Warner biographies as examples, he illustrates the fact that the actual writing of biography can at times create fictions of reality.

After surveying the different novels published in 1988 in 'Continuing Accomplishment: Novels in 1988' (*JNZL* 7.106–30), Lawrence Jones chooses Frame's *The*

Carpathians as the landmark of the year while giving special mention to Colleen Reilly's *Christine.* He concludes that, while only two of the central novelists of the eighties are present (Frame and Wedde), a number of first or second time publications augur well for the immediate future of the New Zealand novel and show a direct move away from the realist tradition.

John Watson's 'From Mansfield to Svensson: The Female Hero in Recent Short Fiction by Women Writers' (*JNZL* 7.44–64) follows the development of Mansfield's female character. Recent fiction moves away from the genteel and sexually restrained figure of earlier times. More active, she no longer questions patriarchy but simply goes it alone. The seeds of feminine independence are present in the works of Mansfield and the challenge has been taken up and amply exploited by such story-writers as Duckworth, Kidman, Reidy, Svensson and Ngahuia Awekotuku to name but a few.

In his perceptive article 'Repetitous Beginnings: New Zealand Literary History in the Late 1980s' (*JNZL* 7.65–86), Mark Williams makes a critical assessment of the genre at the end of the 1980s in which he maintains that, in spite of a voluntary effort to break away from the canons established by Curnow and his contemporaries, in *The Penguin History of New Zealand Literature*, editor Patrick Evans uses these former evaluations to define his position negatively without confronting certain valid ideas put forward in order to progress towards a new form of criticism. Williams also addresses the question of middle-class writers seeking to adapt the oral structures of Maori and working-class people in their creative writing in ' "Would You Like to Be Maori?": Literary Constructions of Oral Culture' (*ANZSC* 4.89–105). In the majority of cases, this results in the undue romanticization of the oral culture and the risk of inauthencity of language. Quoting Subramani, Williams makes the point that the translation of orality into literacy may lead to a reduction of the original vitality of expression. He also underlines that both Frame and Tuwhare, writers from working-class backgrounds, recognize the important role of literature during their childhood and warns that by yielding to the temptation of idealizing orality, bourgeois writers may simply project a compensating image onto their own discontents.

In 'The New Zealand Goldfields in Literature' (*Stout Research Centre Occasional Papers* 1.5–34), Nelson Wattie gives an exhaustive overview of both the history of Goldfield Literature and the place of literature in the world of the gold-diggers; he also includes a chronological bibliography of the various publications on the subject. The second essay 'Frank Sargeson's Encounter with Karl Wolfskehl' (*Stout Research Centre Occasional Papers* 1.35–48) is more concerned with the excellence of Wolfskehl's intellect and his linguistic and literary capacities than with Sargeson himself; the two men met regularly until Sargeson suddenly broke off the friendship; later it proved that it was this German Jew's vast culture which discouraged Sargeson because he felt Wolfskehl's influence might hinder his own aim to create a national image of a New Zealander.

(b) Fiction

Perhaps the most important collection of general critical articles on international authors published this year is *International Literature in English: Essays on the Major Writers* edited by Robert L. Ross. Each entry in the volume is followed by a list of the author's published work and a select bibliography of critical readings. New Zealand writing has earned an honourable place in the selection with five authors. Patrick Morrow's 'Katherine Mansfield: The Idea of the Perfect Story' (in Ross) gives a general picture of this writer's work by examining *The Urewera Journal* and a selected number of short stories chosen for their representive nature. Certain analyses and comparisons however are highly questionable and, while a number of themes are approached, it is regrettable that that these have not been more deeply explored in relation to the exceptional poetics of Katherine Mansfield.

Janet Frame has also become a major literary figure to be included in general anthologies. Nancy Potter gives a general introduction to Frame in 'Janet Frame: The Voyage between Self and Society' (in Ross) noting that writing is a life-saving and life-giving activity for this writer. Frame not only deals with the limits of language and memory but also questions the reliability of her own narrators and the viability of language itself as a means of communicating. In so doing, she extends the traditions of both literature and language. Potter notes that frequently Frame's fiction is more terrifying than her biographical accounts, although the two are closely associated.

In other journals, Janet Frame is the author who has inspired the greatest number of critics this year; their articles range from Riemke Ensing's 'Talking Treasure' (*CE&S.* 14:i.47–57), a biographical introduction to the work of Janet Frame, to Marc Delrez's 'Love in a Post-Cultural Ditch: Janet Frame' (*Kunapipi* 13:iii.108–16).

In 'Autobiographie et Connaissance: Le Cas de Janet Frame ou l'auto-bio-graphie et la co-naissance' (in Gasser, *Connaissance et Communication*), Jacqueline F. Ferry explores the complex relationships between the writing of autobiography and the gradual acquisition of knowledge by the individual. Through her study of Frame's writing, she also highlights the fact that, besides the exotic myth, New Zealand has also been a country of unemployment and misery.

Simon Petch examines in detail Janet Frame's own consciousness of autobiographical existence in his illuminating essay 'Janet Frame and the Languages of Autobiography' (*ANZSC* 5.58–71). He points out that, far from confusing the two genres, Frame is at pains to highlight their separateness and yet is able to successfully integrate her fiction as an essential element of her own existence and identity; in so doing she creates a personal myth by harnessing the power of language to transform experience.

In her article 'A Portrait of the Artist as a Young Woman: Janet Frame's Autobiographies' (*SPAN* 31.85–94) Suzette Henke compares the restricted life led by Frame in New Zealand in the 1950s with that experienced by the fictional Stephen Dedalus in nineteenth-century Catholic Ireland; both take refuge from colonial family life by retreating into an introverted world of verbal imagination. Henke analyses Frame's writing as a double-voiced discourse: that of the writer masking the chaos of the mind and yet the trauma of institutional dehumanization remains ever-present on the borders of her text. Henke also studies the dualities that a post-colonial writer such as Frame integrates into her writing in 'The Postmodern Frame: Metalepsis and Discursive Fragmentation in *The Carpathians*' (*ANZSC* 5.29–38). In her opinion, Frame parodies the post-colonial paradigm by enveloping 'a New Zealand narrative of referential fracture in the context of Euro-American anthropological investigation'. This critic concludes that, while Frame succeeds in demonstrating the breakdown of language in a post-colonial society, she leaves the reader to interpret the complex relationships between this language and the Euro-American context.

The limits of post-colonial fiction are extended to include the role of the artist and the nature of self according to Nicholas Birns in 'Space, Time and Language in *The Carpathians*' (*ANZSC* 5.16–28). He maintains that Frame uses temporal and geographical disjunctiveness to achieve the sense of the multi-faceted universe.

In 'The Narrative Frame: "Unleashing (Im)possiblities" ' (*ANZSC* 5.1–15), Susan Ash perceptively uses Derrida's concept of the *parergon* to bring into play the various narrators of *The Carpathians*. Her arguments are convincing when she discusses what she believes to be mis-readings of the text by certain critics who have tried to codify and simplify Frame's textual strategies. She concludes: 'Even as this novel troubles ontological boundaries with its narrative indeterminacies, even as it subverts notions of "truth", it remains firmly underpinned by a dependence on some inaccessible, but nevertheless existing "hinterland" of essential truth.'

In her rather disjointed article '*The Edge of the Alphabet* – Journey: Destination Death' (*ANZSC* 5.39–57), Gina Mercer studies the theme of death and the antagonistic attitudes of different characters towards life and the inability to communicate. Although Thora Pattern is endowed with the power of narrating, she is indecisive and unable to assume the role of the reliable authority figure. In a final section, the two manuscripts of the novel are compared to illustrate the development of Thora's perception of the battle between the forces of creativity and the forces of death.

The continuing growth and development of non-Pakeha writing on the New Zealand literary scene is reflected in Ross's choice for *International Literature in English*; of the five New Zealanders selected, two are Maori and one is Samoan. All three are included in the section 'Decolonizing History'. Margery Fee in 'Keri Hulme: Inventing New Ancestors for Aotearoa' analyses in some detail *The Bone People* in which Hulme brings together and re-organizes the different characters that live in New Zealand and the various genres (myth, fantasy, realism etc.). She examines the theme of self-fulfilment in the character of Kerewin, violence in Joe and handicap in Simon; these three characters suffer from appearing to be what they are not and exist by their interdependence. The spiral-like progression of the novel enables Hulme to throw different light onto the conflicting ideals and aims of her characters. It could be described as a nation-building novel in its attempt to create a new coherence between the differing strands of New Zealand society.

Nan Bowman Albinski's 'Witi Ihimaera: Glimpses of Childhood' (in Ross) is a comparison of the general situation of the Maori within New Zealand society since the early seventies, when Ihimaera began publishing and the development and treatment of themes within his work, in particular that of the child. The degradation of Maori/Pakeha relations is regularly seen through the eyes of a growing child. *ANZSC* 4 (Fall 9, 106–11) also includes a brief bibliography of Witi Ihimaera.

In ' "Stories That Show Them Who They Are": An Interview with Patricia Grace' (*ANZSC* 6.90–102), Thomas E. Tausky encourages Patricia Grace to describe her family background and how she developed into a writer. Grace acknowledges that her primary interest is in her characters rather than in plot and explains at length the influence of her culture on her life and writing.

Using the philosophy of Kierkegaard as a framework, in ' "Another Foothold": Exile and Return in Patricia Grace's *Mutuwhenua*' (*ANZSC* 6.103–11), William McGaw tries to follow the inner dualities of Ripeka/Linda which govern her reactions, as she attempts to reconcile her biculturalism and yet keep her two worlds separate.

Shadbolt was also interested in the effect of history on contemporary worlds when he was writing his novel *Strangers and Journeys* more than thirty-five years ago. In ' "A Fair Enough Try": *Strangers and Journeys*' (*ANZSC* 5.72–80), Murray Martin reassesses this work in the light of recent events; in his opinion the weaknesses of the novel stem from the fact that Shadbolt was too involved in the later period of history he describes and so lacked the distance necessary to make it convincing. Nevertheless *Strangers and Journeys* remains a landmark in the literary history of New Zealand.

In quite different domains, the silencing of fact or truth is examined in the following two articles. By applying relatively simplistic feminist theory to analyse

Kidman's novel, Elizabeth Rosner's 'Silencing the Ventriloquist: *The Book of Secrets*' (*WLWE* 31.80–6) illustrates how the author subverts the dominant patriarchal voice by renaming and decentring male characters, thereby reducing their power. In her informal essay 'Child's Play' (*NZListener* 9 December 1992, 49–50), Marion McLoed reviews Joy Cowley's latest publication *Bow Down Shadrach* which explores the question of honesty between parent and child.

(c) *Poetry*

Bill Manhire's 'Dirty Silence: Impure Sounds In New Zealand Poetry' (*ANZSC* 4.57–71) attempts to show that, while traditionally poetry is seen to use 'pure' language to express '*envolées*' of feeling, today's poet is more interested in interrogating words for multiple meanings which clash to create new resonances. Purity can also mean uniformity, behind which lurk the authoritarian ideologies of racism. Manhire quotes various New Zealand poets who have broken with Victorian tradition, thus paving the way for present day poetry which, in his particular case, breaks down barriers by incorporating changes of language and code so that in and between lines hovers a range of imprecise meanings.

Manhire, the poet, becomes the subject of comparison for Douglas Barbour when he parallels him with the Canadian poet Sharon Thesen. Each writes on opposing sides of the Pacific Ocean. In 'Writing Through the Margins: Sharon Thesen's and Bill Manhire's Apparently Lyric Poetry' (*ANZSC* 4.72–87), Barbour maintains that both put into question the concept of 'traditional standard' poetry by creating works whose boundaries of form and content are duplicitous. In their respective 'new' countries, they represent a new dynamic attitude to poetry which challenges the Imperial centre of tradition.

In 'Tremendous Forgeries, Confabulations and Graphologies Elliptical: The Lyric/Anti-Lyric Poetry of Sharen Thesen and Elizabeth Smither' (*ANZSC* 6.112–34), Pamela Banting explains that, while both poets show a deep relationship with language and at times sidestep meaning to bring into play new resonances, Thesen is a more theoretical poet while Smither, although familiar with open form poetics, has more confidence in instinct. Her 'lightness' of style conceals things subversive and she tends to write short poems in order to leave them open-ended.

(d) *Theatre*

New Zealand theatre has rarely been the object of such scrutiny as in 1991. As well as McNaughton's fundamental chapter in the *Oxford History, Australasian Drama Studies* 18 was totally devoted to the New Zealand stage. The perspectives and subject matter are wide-ranging and informative.

Peter Harcourt gives an account of the valuable theatre scripts dating back to the nineteenth century that were originally placed in the vaults of the Justice Department in Wellington under the Copyright Act of 1877 and which can now be consulted at the National Archive in the capital in his article ' "There's gold in them thar files": Playscripts deposited for Copyright Registration' (*ADS* 18.7–21).

Karen Sherry's 'Popular Entertainment in Auckland 1870–71' (*ADS* 18.22–9) accounts for entertainment during a time of economic and political depression because of the recent Land Wars. The entertainment ranged from bellringers to strongmen, from minstrels to dioramas.

Murray Edmond discusses the *commedia dell'arte* tradition in New Zealand in 'Lighting Out for Paradise: New Zealand Theatre and the "Other" Tradition' (*ADS*

18.183–206). He illustrates that this form of theatre often counters the establishment as represented by the Arts Council-financed Erudita theatres; the former is intent on forging a national identity, the latter on raising cultural standards. While the one produces classical plays, the other branches out and offers the stage to minority groups with often radical ideas. The duo performance was not alone in finding its place in this genre; feminist and Maori theatre also fitted into this 'other' theatre, using the stage to project an image of the Other.

Roma Potiki in 'A Maori Point of View: The Journey from Anxiety to Confidence' (*ADS* 18.57–63) puts forward a plea for excellence in Maori theatre; admitting that drama is an opportunity to reclaim Maori identity, the author rejects the idea that Maori theatre should be written in Maori, since this would eliminate many Maori spectators and writers. On the other hand, despite the difficulty in establishing a place among Pakeha playwrights, myths about emotional well-being, family support, spiritual communication with nature and the 'noble savage' in Maori society must be debunked, and the use of a *hangi* or *tangi* within the theatre to create a Maori folklore must be avoided. Maori theatre must have the confidence in itself to 'disturb, heal and celebrate' within its own context and because of its innate quality so as to illustrate 'the joy and hell that we [Maori] as survivors of the damage of colonialism have learnt to live with, and live through'.

In 'Women's Theatre and Why' (*ADS* 18.159–82), Judith Dale isolates three theoretical positions in the women's movement which may be applied to theatre: liberal feminism, radical feminism and feminist poststructuralism. She then goes on to present a historical account of feminine and feminist theatre and its attitude to male domination of women, to racism and to things Maori. Finally, she studies how feminists address lesbianism as an alternative to heterosexuality through a brief analysis of Stephanie Johnson's *Accidental Phantasies*, in which women play the role of men and, through this theatrical device, are able to find a feminine voice.

Simon Garrett argues that theatre in New Zealand has a very regional flavour and that performances vary widely according to the town in which they are performed in 'The Plays, Playmakers and Playhouses of Recent New Zealand Theatre: An Overview' (*ADS* 18.30–46). Whereas Dunedin has a very active theatre and is chosen for many of the premières of New Zealand authors, Christchurch, under the direction of Hooper, has produced few locally written plays; Wellington, with two professional theatres and two co-operative theatres, has been very active since 1984 producing both classical drama and New Zealand plays; while Palmerston North is a small centre, Auckland, although it has by far the largest population, has a theatre output that is markedly limited with only one professional theatre, The Mercury. The variety of theatre groups funded by various means must be upheld for each has a contribution to give and the alternative theatres do much to revitalize traditional subsidized theatre.

Helen Watson White, in her exhaustive survey 'New Drama 1988–89: An Expanding Field' (*JNZL* 7.3–43), examines the year's drama events in the widest sense of the term from musicals that have no written script to the more 'literary' forms of theatre. Each performance is commented on and there is an appendix listing the dates of performances of New Zealand plays, television fictional drama and serials, radio play broadcasts and finally a list of plays published in 988–89.

Stuart Hoar's 'A Playwright's Perspective' (*ADS* 18.64–9) is a cry against monetarian theatre and naturalist writing for a performance which sets out to be make-believe and claims that a lively theatre could help to uplift the nation out of its current dreariness.

In '"A Life Long Affair": Renée's Writing for the Theatre Commentary/Interview'

(*ADS* 18.70–90) Lisa Warrington underlines the principal qualities of Renée's characters who have a natural authority and who keep their private griefs under control by throwing themselves into hard work. She also shows that this playwright's writing is economical and essentially theatrical rather than intellectual, based as it is on real-life experience rather than on an academic theoretical approach. The ensuing interview confirms these affirmations throwing light upon Renée who has confidence in the legitimacy of her writing and is able to visualize and hear the effects of her dialogues on stage. She produces an enormous number of drafts before the final version and enjoys working on scripts to modify balance of silence, conversation and action.

Gary Boire considers 'how the law as *text* undergoes a ferocious interrogation during the act of anti-colonial re-presentation' in his article 'Resistance Moves: Mervyn Thompson's *Songs to the Judges*' (*ANZSC* 6.15–26); his study compares and contrasts George Ryga's *The Ecstasy of Rita Joe* and Thompson's play as demonstrations that the colonial encounter is primarily a variation of class struggle. Mervyn Thompson himself presents the final section of his latest play in 'Passing Through' (*ADS* 18.47–56)

'Tragic Power in Vincent O'Sullivan's *Shuriken*' (*ADS* 18.91–4, 147–58) is a truly exceptional analysis in which Phillip Mann brings into sharp relief the techniques used in Sullivan's *Shuriken* to express tragedy on stage and his own capacity to highlight these in performance. The impact of this play on audiences has been exceptional; Mann isolates four dramaturgical events in which playwright and producer combine their talents to achieve emotional release among spectators. The first occurs at the moment of the suicide of the Japanese soldier when Pom decides to tell a dirty joke to the audience – the incongruity of the two divides the onlooker between guilty laughter and horror at death, thereby involving the audience in the predicament. Yet death unites all. In a second direct dialogue, the audience is invited by Tai to participate in the grief of a family who loses a dear one in war; this ends with a sung Maori *waiata* and an uncontrolled sob. Shocking illustrations are alternated with direct emotional appeals in the play. The third epiphany involves Earnie, a simple Christian soul whose outlook on life has been perturbed by confrontation with death as a child. The ensuing confusion of the man leads him to be a character of great introverted violence; but again, the audience is not in a position to either judge or condemn. Finally, the massacre scene has to be conducted with restraint in order for it to strike deep into the emotions of the audience – a freeze frame technique slows down the action allowing all the horror to surface. At the end of the play, when the 'dead' rise to acknowledge the audience, the impact is further deepened by the distancing thus achieved between the event and its *mise-en-scène*.

(e) The South Pacific

In 'Satendra Nandan, *The Wounded Sea*' (*SPAN* 32.79–84), Vijay Mishra traces the history of the Indian migrants in Fiji and underlines the bruised feelings of these people who remain outsiders in a country to which they were exiled over a hundred years ago. He then underscores the various influences at work in Nandan's latest book and in particular that of V. S. Naipaul; he concludes that 'the act of writing can only gesture helplessly towards the precarious unity of word and deed lost during the original banishment' and in this Satendra Nandan's book is a comfort to those Fiji Indians who live with a sense of loss.

'Albert Wendt: The Attempt "To Snare the Void and Give It Word" ' (in Ross) contains a general survey of Wendt's opus to date. Jean-Pierre Durix (ibid.) also puts into relief the complexities of the multi-cultural vision of life that Wendt endeavours to commit to paper; he destroys the stereotypes that the West has imposed on the South Seas and yet recognizes those aspects that colonization brought to improve the standards of living. His writing cannot however be reduced to mere history or anthropology, for it explores the power and the ambiguity of language and uses its multifaceted possibilities to probe the frontiers of the absurdity of everyday situations in order to create islands of meaning.

Books Reviewed

ALIA 1990 : Conference Proceedings. Vols. I & II. ALIA 1990. pp. 675 and 687. pb A$105. ISBN 1 86308 005 8.

Adelaide, Debra. *Bibliography of Australian Women's Literature: 1795–1990*. Thorpe. pp. 270. pb £45. ISBN 0 909532 90 7.

Ahmansson, Gabriella. *A Life and Its Mirrors: A Feminist Reading of L. M. Montgomery's Fiction*. Vol. I. Uppsala. pp. 183. ISBN 91 554 2673 5.

Allardice, Pamela, ed. *The Language of Love: An Anthology of Australian Love Letters, Poetry and Prose*. A&R. pp. 162. A$29.95. ISBN 0 207 16895 4.

Alomes, Stephen, and Dirk den Hartog, eds. *Post Pop: Popular Culture, Nationalism and Postmodernism*. Footprint. pp. 130. pb A$8. ISBN 1 86297 012 2.

Anderson, Hugh. *George Loyau: The Man Who Wrote Bush Ballads*. Rooster. pp. 58. A$37. ISBN 0 908247 24 9.

Angier, Carole. *Jean Rhys*. Deutsch. (1990). pp. 762. hb £17.99, pb £9.99. ISBN 0 233 98597 2, 0 14 015865 0.

Barbour, Douglas, ed. *Beyond TISH: New Writing, Interviews, Critical Essays*. NeWest. pp. 236. pb C$14.95. ISBN 0 920897 94 0.

Bard, Margaret, Peter Messaline, and Miriam Newhouse, eds. *'And Do You Have Anything Else?' Audition Pieces from Canadian Plays*. S&P. pp. 106. pb C$14.95. ISBN 0 88924 217 8.

Barker, Anthony. *One of the First and One of the Finest: Beatrice Davis, Book Editor*. Society of Editors. pp. 47. ISBN 0 646 02058 7.

Beaver, Bruce. *New and Selected Poems 1960–1990*. UQP. pp. 276. pb A$19.95. ISBN 0 7022 2338 7.

Begamudre, Ben, and Judith Krause, eds. *Out of Place: Stories and Poems*. Coteau. pb C$14.95. ISBN 1 55050 019 8.

Bennett, Bruce. *An Australian Compass: Essays on Place and Direction in Australian Literature*. FACP. pp. 271. pb A$24.95. ISBN 0 949206 93 8.

Bennett, Bruce. *Spirit in Exile: Peter Porter and his Poetry*. OUP. pp. 294. £25. ISBN 0 19 554970 8.

Besner, Neil K. *Introducing Alice Munro's Lives of Girls and Women*. ECW. pp. 79. C$18.95. ISBN 1 55022 122 1.

Beynon, Richard. *Simpson, J. 202*. intro. by Alan Gill. Currency. pp. 79. pb £6.99. ISBN 0 86819 306 2.

Bird, Carmel, ed. *Relations: Australian Short Stories*. HoughtonM. pp. 235. A$17. ISBN 0 86770 133 1.

Bird, Delys, and Brenda Walker, eds. *Elizabeth Jolley: New Critical Essays*. A&R. pp. 240. pb £9.50. ISBN 0 207 17060 6.

Birkett, Jennifer, and Elizabeth Harvey, eds. *Determined Women: Studies in the*

Construction of the Female Subject. Macmillan. pp. 213. pb $14.99. ISBN 0 333 448239 1.

Blackman, John. *Don't Come the Raw Prawn! The Aussie Phrase Book.* Pan Macmillan. pp. 140. pb A$14.95. ISBN 07251 0685 9.

Blake, Barry J. *Australian Aboriginal Languages: A General Introduction* (1981) 2nd. edn. UQP. pp. 138. pb A$29.95. ISBN 0 7022 2353 0.

Bolton, Geoffrey, Heather Vose and Genelle Jones, eds. *The Wollaston Journals: Volume I 1840–1842.* UWAP. pp. 284. £29.95. ISBN 1 875560 01 7.

Bradstock, Margaret, and Louise Wakeling. *Rattling the Orthodoxies: A Life of Ada Cambridge.* Penguin. pp. 271. pb A$18.95. ISBN 0 14 012998 7.

Brady, Sister Veronica. *Playing Catholic: Essays on four Catholic plays.* Currency. pp. 61. pb A$6.50. ISBN 0 86819 256 2.

Brisbane, Katharine, ed. *Entertaining Australia: an illustrated history.* Currency. pp. 360. pb A$39.95. ISBN 0 86819 286 4.

Brissenden, R. F., and Philip Grundy, eds. *The Oxford Book of Australian Light Verse.* OUPA. pp. 171. hb A$35. ISBN 0 19 554512 5.

Brown, Stewart, ed. *The Art of Derek Walcott*. Seren Books. Dufour Editions. pp. 231. hb £16.50, pb £7.95. ISBN (UK) 1 85411 021 7, 1 85411 027 6; (US) 0 8023 1290 X.

Buckley, Vincent, ed. *The Faber Book of Modern Australian Verse*. Faber. pp. 275. £14.99. ISBN 0 571 15064 0.

———. *Last Poems.* Compiled by Penelope Buckley and Chris Wallace-Crabbe. McPheeG. pp. 91. pb A$19.95. ISBN 0 86914 240 2.

Campbell, Sandra, and Lorraine McMullen, eds. *New Women: Short Stories by Canadian Women 1900–1920.* UOttawaP. pp. 336. pb C$14.95. ISBN 0 7766 0323 4.

Cantrell, Leon, ed. *Writing of the Eighteen Nineties: Short Stories, Verse and Essays.* (1977) 4th edn. UQP. pp. 290. pb A$18.95. ISBN 0 7022 2019 1.

Capone, Giovanna, Bruce Clunies Ross and Werner Senn, eds. *European Perspectives: Contemporary Essays on Australian Literature.* Special Issue of *Australian Literary Studies.* UQP. pp. 208. pb A$16.95. ISBN 0 7022 2423 5.

Cartey, Wifred. *Whispers from the Caribbean: I Going Away. I Going Home*. Center for Afro-American Studies. UCLA. pp. 503. hb $43, pb $25.95. ISBN 0 934934 35 5, 0 934934 36 3.

Charlwood, Don. *No Moon Tonight* (1956) pres. E. E. (Weary) Dunlop, Australian War Classics. PenguinA. pp. 177. pb A$12.95. ISBN 0 14 015447 7.

Chevrefils, M. compiler. *The Clark Blaise Papers: First and Second Accession.* Canadian Archival Inventory Series 4. UCalgaryP. pp. 585. pb C$33.95. ISBN 0 919813 79 8.

Clarke, Sally. *The Trials of Judith K.* PlaywrightsCan. pp. 120. pb C$9.95. ISBN 0 88754 465 7

Clyne, Michael. *Community Languages: The Australian Experience.* CUP. pp. 294. £35. ISBN 0 521 39330 2.

Coleman, Peter. *The Real Barry Humphries.* H&S. pp. 192. pb £3.99. ISBN 0 340 55907 1.

Cowan, Peter, ed. *A Faithful Picture: the Letters of Eliza and Thomas Brown at York in the Swan River Colony 1841–1852.* FACP. pp. 184. pb A$16.95. ISBN 1 86368 006 3.

Croft, Julian. *The Life and Opinions of Tom Collins: A Study of the Works of Joseph Furphy.* UQP. pp. 364. pb A$29.95. ISBN 0 7022 2364 6.

Daniel, Helen. ed. *Millenium: Time-Pieces by Australian Writers*. PenguinA. pp. 342. pb A$14.95. ISBN 0 14915481 7.

Davidson, Arnold E. *Studies on Canadian Literature: Introductory and Critical Essays*. MLA. pp. 371. ISBN 0 87352 199 4, 0 87352 380 6.

Davies, Gwendolyn. *Studies in Maritime Literary History, 1760–1930*. Acadiensis. pp. 206. pb C$16.95. ISBN 0 919107 34 6.

Davis, Jack. *A Boy's Life*. Magabala. pp. 145. pb A$14.95. ISBN 0 9588101 7 6.

Davison, Graeme and Shirley Constantine, eds. *Out of Work Again: The Autobiographical Narrative of Thomas Dobeson 1885–1891*. Monash Publications in History: 6 (1990). pp. 98. pb A$9.50. ISBN 0 7326 0170 3.

Dean, Misao. *A Different Point of View: Sara Jeannette Duncan*. McG-QUP. pp. 191. $33.20. ISBN 0 7735 0792 2.

Denholm, Michael. *Small Press Publishing in Australia: the Late 1970s to the mid to late 1980s* Volume II. Footprint. pp. 309. pb A$63. ISBN 1 86297 011 4.

Derek Walcott. *Ti Jean and his Brothers*. Port of Spain: Banyan.

Dickins, Barry. *I Love to Live: The Fabulous Life of Barry Dickins*. PenguinA. pp. 270. pb A$14.95. ISBN 014 013350.

Dixon, R. M. W., compiler and ed. *Words of Our Country: Stories Place Names and Vocabulary in Yidiny, the Aboriginal Language of the Cairns-Yarrabah Region*. UQP. pp. 312. pb A$34.95. ISBN 0 7022 2360 3.

Djwa, Sandra, ed. *Giving Canada a Literary History: A Memoir by Carl F.Klinck*. CarletonUP. pp. 228. ISBN 0 88629 162 3.

Docker, John. *The Nervous Nineties: Australian Cultural Life in the 1890s*. OUP. pp. 251. pb £18. ISBN 0 19 553247 3.

Dorscht, Susan Rudy. *Women, Reading, Kroetsch: Telling the Difference*. WLUP. pp. 138. US$24.95. ISBN 0 88920 205 2.

Dow, Gwyn, and June Factor, eds. *Australian Childhood: An Anthology*. McPheeG. pp. 328. pb A$29.95. ISBN 0 86914 159 7.

Dowrick, Stephanie, and Jane Parkin, eds. *Speaking With the Sun: New Stories by Australian and New Zealand Writers*. A&U. pp. 228. pb A$16.95. ISBN 0 04 442296 2.

Druick, Don. *Where Is Kabuki?* PlaywrightsCan. pp. 64. pb C$9.95. ISBN 0 88754 504 1.

Dunstan, Keith. *No Brains At All: An Autobiography*. PenguinA (1990). pp. 274. pb A$16.95. ISBN 0 14 015786 7.

Dutton, Geoffrey, ed. *The Picador Henry Lawson*. Pan Macmillan pp. 552. pb A$25. ISBN 0 330 27176 8.

———. *Kenneth Slessor: A Biography*. PenguinA. pp. 377. pb A$16.95. ISBN 0 14014501.

Easingwood, Peter, Konrad Gross, and Wolfgang Klooss, eds. *Probing Canadian Culture*. AV-Verlag. pp. 234. ISBN 3 925274 40 5.

Feldt, Eric. *The Coast Watchers* (1946). Intro. by E. E. (Weary) Dunlop, Australian War Classics. PenguinA. pp. 424. pb A$14.95. ISBN 0 14 014926 0.

Fennario, David. *Joe Beef*. PlaywrightsCan. pp. 103. pb C$9.95. ISBN 0 88922 291 6.

Fenwick, M. J. *Writers of the Caribbean Area: A Bibliography*. 2 vols. Garland. Vol. 1 pp. 776; Vol. 2 pp. 845. $200. ISBN 0 8240 4010 4.

Fison, Lorimer, and A. W. Howitt. *Kamilaroi and Kurnai* (1880) Facsimile edition. ASP. pp. 372. pb A$19.95. ISBN 0 85575 222 X.

Fitzpatrick, Peter. *Stephen Sewell: The Playwright as Revolutionary*. Currency. pp. 168. pb £9.99. ISBN 0 86819 285 6.

Foster, David, ed. *Self Portraits.* National Library of Australia. pp. 154. pb A$23.95. ISBN 0 642 10513 8.

Foster, Norm. *Opening Night.* PlaywrightsCan. pp. 116. pb C$9.95. ISBN 0 88754 475 4.

Frickey, Pierette. *Critical Perspectives on Jean Rhys.* Three Continents Press (1990). hb $25, pb $15. ISBN 0 894 10 058 0, 0 894 10 059 9.

Furphy, Joseph. *The Annotated Such is Life*, with an introduction and notes by Frances Devlin-Glass, Robin Eaden, Lois Hoffman and G. W. Turner. OUP. pp. 592. pb £15.95. ISBN 0 19 553086 9.

Gallou, Laura, ed. *A Bibliography of Australian Judaica* comp. Serge Liberman. (2nd rev. edn). Mandelbaum Trust & University of Sydney Library. pp. 257. pb A$30 ISBN 0 86758 379 7.

Gasser, B., ed. *Connaissance et Communication.* CORAIL., Université de Nouméa. pp. 306. (Abstracts in English).

Gelder, Ken. *Private Knowledges and the Public Gaze: Aboriginal Writing as Property in the Late Twentieth Century.* Working Papers in Australian Studies No: 64. SRMCAS. pp. 13. pb £2.50. ISBN 1 85507 029 4.

Gerster, Robin, and Jan Bassett. *Seizures of Youth: 'The Sixties' and Australia.* Hyland House. pp. 216. £19.50. ISBN 0 947062 75 0.

Glassop, Lawson. *We Were the Rats* (1944). Intro. by E. E. (Weary) Dunlop, Australian War Classics. PenguinA. pp. 275. pb A$14.95. ISBN 0 14 014924 4.

Goodison, Lorna. *Poems from Jamaica.* Caribbean Images Ltd, P.O. Box 1530, Constant Spring P.O., Kingston 8, Jamaica W.I. ISBN 976 8012 41 2

Goodman, David, D. J. O'Hearn, Chris Wallace-Crabbe, eds. *Multicultural Australia: The Challenges of Change.* Scribe. pp. 236. pb A$19.95. ISBN 0 908011 21 0.

Grant, Agnes, ed. *Our Bit of Truth: An Anthology of Canadian Native Literature.* Pemmican (1990). pp. 380. pb C$19.95. ISBN 0 921827 10 5.

Gray, Martin, ed. *Patrick White: Life and Writings: Five Essays.* Centre for Commonwealth Studies, University of Stirling. pp. 89. pb £5. ISBN 1 85769 000 1.

Green, Dorothy. *Writer, Reader, Critic.* Primavera. pp. 198. pb A$14.95. ISBN 1 875368 01 9.

Griffith, Michael, James A. McGlade, eds. *Cap and Bells: The Poetry of Francis Webb.* Collins/A&R. pp. 251. pb A$16.95. ISBN 0 207 166994.

Griffith, Michael. *God's Fool: The Life and Poetry of Francis Webb.* Collins/A&R. pp. 306. pb A$16.95. ISBN 0 207 17058 4.

Hammond, Catherine, ed. *Creation Spirituality and the Dreamtime.* Millenium. pp. 94. pb £5.95. ISBN 0 85574 364 6.

Hanna, Cliff, ed. *John Shaw Nielson: Poetry, Autobiography and Correspondence.* UQP. pp. 360. pb A$22.95. ISBN 0 7022 23123.

Hansson, Karin. *Sheer Edge: Aspects of Identity in David Malouf's Writing.* Lund U. pp. 170. pb £17.95. ISBN 91 7966 149 1.

Hart-Smith, William. *Hand to Hand: A Garnering. With Uncollected Poems and Essays on His Life and Work.* Ed. Barbara Petrie. Butterfly. pp. 425. pb A$19.95. ISBN 0 947333 35 5.

Haskell, Dennis, ed. *Kenneth Slessor: Poetry, Essays, War Despatches, War Diaries, Journalism, Autobiographical Material and Letters.* UQP. pp. 290. pb A$22.95. ISBN 0 7022 23190.

Hassall, Anthony J. *Strange Country: A Study of Randolph Stow.* UQP (1990). pp. 215. pb A$29.95. ISBN 0 7022 2273 9.

Headon, David, ed. *North of the Ten Commandments: A Collection of Northern Territory Literature*. H&SA. pp. 348. pb A$34.95. ISBN 0 340 52666 1.
Heath, Jeffrey M., ed. *Profiles in Canadian Literature*. Vol.8. Dundurn. pp.155. pb C$17.95. ISBN 1 55002 146 1.
Hodge, Bob, Vijay Mishra. *Dark Side of the Dream: Australian literature and the postcolonial mind*. A&U. pp. 253. pb £9.95. ISBN 0 04 442346 2.
Holt, R. F., ed. *Neighbours: Multicultural Writing of the 1980s*. UQP. pp. 244. pb A$14.95. ISBN 0 7022 2318 2.
Howells, Coral Ann, and Lynette Hunter, eds. *Narrative Strategies in Canadian Literature: Feminism and Postcolonialism*. OpenUP. pp.143. $35. ISBN 0 335 09770 7.
Howells, Coral Ann. *Jean Rhys*. HW. pp. 171. hb £35, pb £11.95. ISBN 0 7108 1220 5, 0 7108 1221 3.
Indyk, Ivor, and Elizabeth Webby, eds. *Memory: Southerly Number Three*. A&R. pp. 256. pb A$14.95. ISBN 0 207 17059 2.
Jackomos, Alice, and Derek Fowell. *Living Aboriginal History of Victoria: Stories in the Oral Tradition*. Museum of Victoria. pp. 203. £25. ISBN 0 521 41409 1.
Kamboureli, Smaro. *On the Edge of Genre: The Contemporary Canadian Long Poem*. UTorP. pp. 244. hb $29, pb $12.95. ISBN 0 8020 5908 2, 0 8020 6848 0.
Keith, W. J. *An Independent Stance: Essays on English-Canadian Criticism and Fiction*. Porcupine's Quill. pp. 311. pb C$16.95. ISBN 0 88984 121 7.
Keneally, Thomas. *Now And In Time To Be: Ireland and the Irish*. Pan Macmillan. pp. 208. A$45. ISBN 07329 0752 7.
Kent, Hilary, ed. *Index: Volumes 1 to 12 (1788–1939): Australian Dictionary of Biography*. Gen. ed. John Ritchie. UMel. pp. 326. A$45. ISBN 0 522 84459 6.
Kent, Jacqueline. *In the Half Light: Reminiscences of Growing up in Australia, 1900–1970*. Doubleday (1988). pp. 265. pb A$19.95. ISBN 0 86824 448 1.
Kershaw, Alister. *Hey Days: Memories and Glimpses of Melbourne's Bohemia 1937–1947*. Collins/A&R. pp. 104. pb A$12.95. ISBN 0 207 16675 7.
King, Bruce, ed. *The Commonwealth Novel since 1960*. Macmillan. pp. 268. £45. ISBN 0 333 48740 0.
Kingsmill, John. *Australia Street: A Boy's-Eye View of the 1920s and 1930s*. H&I. pp. 192. pb A$17.95. ISBN 0 86806 440 8.
Kirkby, Diane. *Alice Henry: The Power of Pen and Voice: The Life of an Australian-American Labor Reformer*. CUP. £32.50. ISBN 0 521 39102 4.
Langley, Rod. *The Dunsmuirs: Alone at the Edge*. Talonbooks. pp. 103. pb C$10.95. ISBN 0 88922 297 5.
Lawlor, Robert. *Voices of the First Day: Awakening in the Aboriginal Dreamtime*. Inner Traditions International. pp. 414. pb A$24.95. ISBN 0 89281 355 5.
Lawson, Elizabeth. *The Poetry of Gwen Harwood*. SydneyUP. pp. 82. pb A$8.95. ISBN 0 424 00175 6.
Lecker, Robert, ed. *Borderlands: Essays in Canadian-American Relations*. ECW. pp. 328. pb C$45. ISBN 1 55022 133 7.
———, ed. *Canadian Canons: Essays in Literary Value*. UTorP. pp. 251. hb $23, pb $11. ISBN hb 0 8020 5826 4; pb 0 8020 6700 x.
Lecker, Robert, Jack David, and Ellen Quigley, eds. *Canadian Writers and Their Works: Fiction Series*. Vol. IV. ECW. pp. 308. C$45. ISBN 1 55022 052 7.
Lewis, Julie. *Olga Masters: A Lot of Living*. UQP. pp. 201. pb A$22.95. ISBN 0 7022 2387 5.
Lill, Wendy. *Sisters*. Talonbooks. pp. 96. pb C$9.95. ISBN 0 88922 289 4.

Lochhead, Douglas G., ed. *'St Ursula's Convent': or, 'The Nun of Canada', by Julia Catherine Beckwith Hart*. CarletonUP. pp. 237. pb C$25. ISBN 0 88629 140 2.

Lord, Mary, ed. *The Penguin Best Australian Short Stories*. PenguinA. pp. 335. pb A$14.95. ISBN 0 14 013916 8.

Lutz, Hartmut. *Contemporary Challenges: Conversations with Canadian Native Authors*. Fifth House. pp. 276. pb C$15.95. ISBN 0 920079 75 X.

Lynch, Gerald, and David Rampton, eds. *The Canadian Essay*. Copp Clark Pitman. pp. 360. pb C$17.95. ISBN 0 7730 4983 5.

MacLaren, Ian S., and C. Potvin, eds. *Literary Genres/Les Genres Litteraires*. RICL. pp. 164. pb Individual C$18, Institution C$27. ISBN 0 921490 06 2.

Maes-Jelinek, Hena, ed. *Wilson Harris: the Uncompromising Imagination*. Dangaroo. ISBN 187 104 9377.

Manning, Frederick. *The Middle Parts of Fortune* (1929). Intro. by Paul Fussell. PenguinA 1990. pp. 248. pb A$12.95. ISBN 0 14 012257 5.

Marr, David. *Patrick White: A Life*. Cape. pp. 727. £20. ISBN 0224 02581 2.

Martin, David. *My Strange Friend*. Pan Macmillan. pp. 330. pb A$18.95. ISBN 0 330 27265 9.

Matthews, Brian. *Oval Dreams: Larrikin Essays on Sport and Low Culture*. McPheeG. pp. 160. pb A$14.95. ISBN 0 86914 243 7.

McCarthy, Dermot. *A Poetics of Place: The Poetry of Ralph Gustafson*. McG-QUP. pp. 323. $37.95. ISBN 0 7735 0815 5.

Minni, C. Dino, and Anna Foschi Ciampolini. eds. *Writers in Transition: The Proceedings of the First National Conference of Italian-Canadian Writers*. Guernica. pp. 236. pb C$15. ISBN 0 920717 26 8.

Mitchell, Ken. *Rebels in Time: Three Plays*. NeWest. pp. 200. pb C$12.95. ISBN 0 929897 05 3.

Mitchell, Susan. *Tall Poppies Too*. PenguinA. pp. 203. pb A$12.95. ISBN 0 14 012204 4.

Monk, Patricia. *The Gilded Beaver: An Introduction to the Life and Work of James De Mille*. ECW. pp. 293. pb C$26. ISBN 1 55022 106 X.

Mordecai, Pamela, and Betty Wilson, eds. *Her True-True Name*. Heinemann. 1989. pb £4.95. ISBN 0435 989 065.

More, Robert. *Patches*. PlaywrightsCan. pp. 56. pb C$9.95. ISBN 0 88754 502 5.

Morley, Patricia. *Margaret Laurence: The Long Journey Home*. Rev. edn. McG-QUP. pp. 195. pb £14.20. ISBN 0 7735 0856 2.

Morris, Mervyn, ed. *Contemporary Caribbean Short Stories*. Faber (1990). pp. 275. pb £5.99. ISBN 0 571 15299 6.

Murray, Les, ed. *The New Oxford Book of Australian Verse*. Expanded Edn. OUPA. pp. 420. pb £15. ISBN 0 19 553362 3.

Murray, Sue. *Bibliography of Australian Poetry: 1935–1955*. D. W. Thorpe in association with the National Centre for Australian Studies. pp. 274. pb £27.00 ISBN 1 875589 00 7.

Nasta, Susheila, ed. *Motherlands. Black Women's Writing from Africa, the Caribbean and South Asia*. WP. pp. 366. pb £8.95. ISBN 0 7043 4269 3.

Nicholson, Ian. *Log of Logs: A Catalogue of Logs, Journals, Shipboard Diaries, Letters, and All Forms of Voyage Narratives, 1788 to 1988, for Australia and New Zealand, and Surrounding Oceans*. Roebuck. pp. 631. pb A$40. ISBN 0 7316 6534 1.

Nieuwenhuizen, Agnes, ed. *No Kidding: Top Writers for Young People Talk About Their Work*. Pan Macmillan. pp. 338. pb A$14.99. ISBN 0 7251 0663 8.

Nischik, Reingard M. *A Theory of Mind Style: A Contribution to Stylistics and Narrative Theory, with Examples from Margaret Atwood's Fiction*. Narr. pp. 299. DM 68. ISBN 3 8233 4115 4.

Paravisini, Lizabeth, and Carmen C. Esteves, eds. *Green Cane and Juicy Flotsam*. RutgersUP. pp. 273. ISBN 0 8135 1737 0, 0 8135 1738 9.

Parker, George D. *How to Play: The Theatre of James Reaney*. ECW. pp. 315. pb C$26. ISBN 1 55022 119 1.

Pascoe, Robert, ed. *Alienation and Exile: Writings of Migration*. Footprint Australian Writers Series No. 3. Footscray Foundation for Australian Studies (1990). pp. 73. pb A$10. ISBN 1 86297 010 6.

Penee, Donna. *Moral Metafiction: Counterdiscourse in the Novels of Timothy Findley*. ECW. pp. 120. pb C$20. ISBN 1 55022 138 8.

Penton, Brian. *Landtakers*. intro. Patrick Buckridge. A&R/HarperCollins (1934). pp. 360. pb A$17.95. ISBN 0 207 16291 3.

Phelan, Nancy. *The Romantic Lives of Louise Mack*. UQP. pp. 268. pb A$19.95. ISBN 0 7022 2361 1.

Plomley, N. J. B. *Jorgen Jorgenson and the Aborigines of Van Diemen's Land*. Blubber Head Press. pp. 165. $A49.95. ISBN 0 908528 22 1.

Porter, Hal. *Selected Stories*. intro. Fay Zwicky. A&R/HarperCollins. pp. 264. pb A$14.95. ISBN 0 207 16158 5.

Povah, Frank. *You Kids Count Your Shadows*. Povah (1990). pp. 28. pb A$10. ISBN 0 646 00 311 9.

Quartermaine, Peter. *Modern Fiction: Thomas Keneally*. Arnold. pp. 111. pb £5.99. ISBN 0 340 51826 X.

Radic, Leonard. *The State of Play: The Revolution in the Australian Theatre since the 1960s*. PenguinA. pp. 259. pb A$24.95. ISBN 0 14 014471 4.

Rasporich, Beverly J. *Dance of the Sexes: Art and Gender in the Fiction of Alice Munro*. UAlbertaP (1990). pp 223. hb C$27.00, pb C$16.95. ISBN 0 88864 207 5, 0 88864 208 3.

Rebera, Ranjini, and Michaela Richards, eds. *Remembering the Future: Australian Women's Stories, dreams and visions for the twenty-first century*. David Lovell. pp. 186. pb A$14.95. ISBN 1 86355 010 0.

Remie, C. H. W., and Jean-Michel Lacroix, eds. *Canada on the Threshold of the 21st Century: European Reflections on the Future of Canada*. Benjamins. pp. 565. ISBN 90 272 2088 3.

Rivett, Rohan D. *Behind Bamboo* (1946). Intro. by E. E. (Weary) Dunlop, Australian War Classics. PenguinA. pp. 400. pb A$14.95. ISBN 0 14 014925 2.

Roderick, Colin. *Henry Lawson: A Life*. A&R. pp. 447. A$39.95. ISBN 0 207 15773 1.

Romaine, Suzanne, ed. *Language in Australia*. CUP. pp. 415. £50. ISBN 0 521 32786 5.

Rose, Deborah Bird. *Hidden Histories: Black Stories from Victoria River Downs, Humbert River and Wave Hill Stations*. ASP. pp. 268. pb A$22.95. ISBN 0 85575 224 6.

Ross, Robert L., ed. *International Literature in English; Essays on the Major Writers*. Garland. pp. 762. £55. ISBN 0 8240 3437 6.

Rushdie, Salman. *Imaginary Homelands: Essays and Criticism 1981–1991*. Granta. pp. 432. £17.99. ISBN 0 14 014224 X.

Saxby, Maurice, and Gordon Winch, eds. *Give Them Wings: The Experience of Children's Literature*. 2nd edn. MacmillanA. pp. 431. pb A$32.95. ISBN 0 7329

0564 8.
Scherf, Kathleen Dorothy, ed. *The Collected Poetry of Malcolm Lowry*. UBCP. pp. 320. £35. ISBN 0 7748 0362 2.
Seal, Graham. *Digger Folksong and Verse of World War One: An Annotated Anthology*. Antipodes. pp. 61. pb A$15. ISBN 1 86342 133 5.
Semmler, Clement. *Pictures on the Margin: Memoirs*. UQP. pp. 399. hb A$39.95. ISBN 0 7022 2411 1.
Seymour, Alan, and Richard Nile, eds. *Anzac: Meaning, Memory and Myth*. SRMCAS. pp. 91. pb £4.50. ISBN 1 85507 031 6.
Shek, Ben-Z. *French-Canadian and Quebecois Novels*. OUP. pp. 151. pb £7.99. ISBN 0 19 540723 7.
Simon, Luke. *Michael Gow's Plays: A Thematic Approach*. Currency. pp. 59. pb £4.99. ISBN 0 86819 280 5.
Spearritt, Peter. *Who's Who of Australian Writers*. D. W. Thorpe in association with the National Centre for Australian Studies. pp. 660. pb £42. ISBN 0 909532 81 8.
Spender, Dale, ed. *Heroines: A Contemporary Anthology of Australian Women Writers*. PenguinA. pp. 478. pb A$16.95. ISBN 0 14 014697 0.
Spindler, Graham, ed. *Views From Behind the Lines*. ALIA. pp. 48. pb A$18. ISBN 0 86804 458 X.
Stead, Christina. *The Salzburg Tales* (1934). Intro. by Susan Sheridan. A&R/HarperCollins. pp. 498. pb A$17.95. ISBN 0 207 16798 2.
Storey, Raymond, and John Robey. *The Dreamland and The Girls in the Gang*. PlaywrightsCan. pp. 250. pb C$14.95. ISBN 0 88754 463 0.
Stouck, David, ed. *Sinclair Ross's 'As For Me and My House': Five Decades of Criticism*. UTorP. pp. 288. hb C$45.00, pb C$16.95. ISBN 0 8020 5897 3, 0 8020 6835 9.
Stow, Randolph. *To the Islands*. Minerva (1958). pp. 126. pb A$13.95. ISBN 0 7493 9191 X.
Struthers, J. R. (Tim). *New Directions from Old*. Red Kite. pp. 261. hb C$27.50, pb C$17.50. ISBN 0 920493 09 2, 0 920493 08 4.
Sturm, Terry, ed. *The Oxford History of New Zealand Literature in English*. OUP, Auckland, pp. 748. pb NZ $69.95. ISBN 0 19 558240 3.
Sullivan, Rosemary. *By Heart: Elizabeth Smart, A Life*. Lime Tree. pp. 416. £17.99. ISBN 0 413 45341 3.
Svendsen, Linda, ed. *Words We Call Home: Celebrating Creative Writing at UBC*. UBCP. pp. 375. pb C$19.95. ISBN 0 7748 0367 3.
Tampke, Jurgen, and David Walker, eds. *From Berlin to the Burdekin: The German contribution to the development of Australian science, exploration and the arts*. NSWUP. pp. 274. A$44.95. ISBN 0 86840 332 6.
Tate, Audrey. *Ada Cambridge: Her Life and Work 1844–1926*. UMel. pp. 319. A$24.95. ISBN 0 522 84410 3.
Thesen, Sharon, ed. *The New Long Poem Anthology*. Coach House. pp. 396. pb C$2.95. ISBN 0 88910 407 7.
Thompson, Elizabeth. *The Pioneer Woman: A Canadian Character Type*. McG-QUP. pp. 199. £33.20. ISBN 0 7735 0832 5.
Thurston, John, ed. *Voyages: Short Narratives of Susanna Moodie*. UOttawaP. pp. 256. pb C$15. ISBN 0 7766 0326 4.
Totaro, Paul. *Cultural Diversity: Media and the Arts*. Discussion paper, Forum II, National Ideas Summit. Australia Council. pp. 31. ISBN 1 86257 092 2.

Tranter, John, and Philip Mead, eds. *The Penguin Book of Modern Australian Poetry*. PenguinA. pp. 474. pb A$19.95 ISBN 0 14 058649 0.
Trist, Margaret. *Tansy (Morning In Queensland* 1958*)*. UQP. pp. 189. pb A$12.95. ISBN 0 7022 2363 8.
Van Herk, Aritha. *In Visible Ink: crypto-frictions*. NeWest. pp. 218. pb C$14.95. ISBN 0 920897 07 X.
Walker, Doreen, ed. *Dear Nan: Letters of Emily Carr, Nan Cheney, and Humphrey Toms*. UBCP (1990). pp. 437. hb C$ 39.95, pb C$24.95. ISBN 0 7748 0376 2, 0 7748 0390 8.
Walker, Shirley. *Flame and Shadow: A Study of Judith Wright's Poetry*. UQP. pp. 230. pb A$29.95. ISBN 0 7022 2352 2.
Wallace, Judith. *Memories of a Country Childhood*. UQP (1977) rep. 138. pb A$10.95. ISBN 0 7022 1626 7.
Wallace-Crabbe, C. *Poetry and Belief*. UTas (1990). Occasional Paper 49. pp. 17. ISBN 0 85901 436 3.
Walsh, William. *Indian Literature in English*. Longman. pp. 219. ISBN 0582 49479 6, 0 582 49480 X.
Ward, Glenyse. *Unna You Fellas*. Magabala. pp. 182. pb A$16.95. ISBN 0 9588101 9 2.
Wattie, Nelson. *Two Essays*. Stout Research Centre Occasional Papers 1. Wellington. pp. 48.
White, Alison, ed. *The Australian Anthology of New Poets 1991*. Elephas (1990). pp. 276. pb A$9.95. ISBN 1 875273 11 5.
Wilde, William H., Joy Hooton, and Barry Andrews, eds. *The Oxford Companion to Australian Literature*. Paperback edition with corrections. OUP (1985). pp. 760. pb £19.50. ISBN 0 14 553273 2.
Willbanks, Ray. *Australian Voices Writers and Their Work*. UTexP. pp. 233. US$40. ISBN 0 292 70429 1.
Williams, David. *Confessional Fictions: A Portrait of the Artist in the Canadian Novel*. UTorP. pp. 291. hb £30, pb £13.50. ISBN 0 8020 588878 7, 0 8020 6807 3.
Wright, Judith. *Born of the Conquerors: Selected essays by Judith Wright*. ASP. pp. 156. pb A$22.95. ISBN 0 85575 217 3.
Wyke, Clement. *Sam Selvon's Dialectal Style and Fictional Strategy*. UBCP. pp. 144. ISBN 0 7748 0364 9
York, Lorraine M. *Front Lines: The Fictions of Timothy Findley*. ECW. pp. 147. pb C$25. ISBN 1 55022 101 9.
Young, Alan R. *Time and Place: The Life and Works of Thomas H. Raddall*. Acadiensis. pp. 200. C$ 16.95. ISBN 0 919107 31 1.

Books Received

Chapter I. Reference, Literary History, and Bibliography

Beal, Peter, comp. *Index of English Literary Manuscripts, II: 1625–1700: Part I: Behn–King*. Mansell (1987). ISBN 0720108985.

Davison, Peter, ed. *The Book Encompassed: Studies in Twentieth-Century Bibliography*. CUP (1992). pp. 360. ISBN 052141878X.

Gollnick, James, ed. *Comparative Studies in Merlin from the Vedas to C. G. Jung*. Mellen (1991). pp. 131. ISBN 0889463964.

Harner, James L. *English Renaissance Prose Fiction, 1500–1600: An Annotated Bibliography of Criticism (1984–1990)* . Hall (1992). pp. 185. ISBN 0816190887.

Jankofsky, Klaus P., ed. *The South English Legendary: A Critical Assessment*. Francke (1992). pp. 189. ISBN 3772018564.

Levenston, E. A. *The Stuff of Literature: Physical Aspects of Texts and Their Relation to Literary Meaning*. SUNY Press (1992). pp. 177. ISBN 0791408892.

Melon, Edda, ed. *L'Effetto Autobiografico: Scritture e Letture del Soggetto nella Letturatura Europea*. Tirrenia (1990). pp. 201. ISBN 8877637676.

Reiss, Timothy, J. *The Meaning of Literature*. CornUP (1992). pp. 395. ISBN 0801426464.

Stainsby, Meg. *Sir Gawain and the Green Knight: An Annotated Bibliography 1978–1989*. Garland (1992). pp. 219. ISBN 0815305044.

Chapter II. English Language

Bettinger, Elfi, and Thomas Meier-Fohrbeck, eds. *Von Shakespeare bis Chomsky: Arbeiten zur Englishchen Philologie an Der Freien Universität Berlin*. Frankfurt University Press (1987). pp. 343. ISBN 3820491511.

Ching, Marvin, Michael C. Hayley, and Ronald F. Lunsford, eds. *Linguistic Perspectives on Literature*. Routledge (1980). pp. 332. ISBN hb 071000382X, pb 0710003838.

Danner, Horace, and Roger Noel. *A Thesaurus of Word Roots of the English Language*. UPA (1992). pp. 788. ISBN 081918666X.

Hyldgaard-Jensen, Karl, and Arne Zettersten, eds. *Symposium on Lexicography V*. Niemeyer (1992). pp. 425.

Subbiondo, Joseph L., ed. *John Wilkins and Seventeenth-Century British Linguistics*. Benjamins (1992). pp. 374. ISBN hb 9027245541, pb 1556193629.

Svensson, Orjan. *Saxon Place Names in East Cornwall*. LundU Press (1987). pp. 191. ISBN 9179660037.

Toolan, Michael, ed. *Language, Text and Context: Essays in Stylistics*. Routledge (1992). pp. 320. ISBN hb 0415056462, pb 0415069955.

Chapter III. Old English Literature

Dumville, David N. *Wessex and England from Alfred to Edgar. Six Essays on Political, Cultural and Ecclesiastical Revival.* Boydell (1992). pp. 234. ISBN 0851153089.

Dumville, David N. *Liturgy and the Ecclesiastical History of Late Anglo-Saxon England. Studies in Anglo-Saxon History V.* Boydell (1992). pp. 193. ISBN 0851153313.

Farrell, Robert and Carol Neuman de Vegvar, eds. *Sutton Hoo: Fifty Years After.* American Early Medieval Studies 2 (1992). pp. 197. ISBN 1879836027.

Filmer-Sankey, William, ed. *Anglo-Saxon Studies in Archaeology and History 5.* Oxford University Committee for Archaeology. pp. 134. ISBN 0947816976.

Ford, Boris, ed. *Early Britain. The Cambridge Cultural History.* 2nd ed. CUP (1992). pp. 289. ISBN 0521428815.

Fulk, R. D. *A History of Old English Meter.* Middle Ages Series. UPennP (1993). pp. 466. ISBN 0812231570.

Gibson, Margaret, T. A. Heslop, and Richard W. Pfaff, eds. *The Eadwine Psalter: Text, Image, and Monastic Culture in Twelfth-Century Canterbury.* PMHRA 14. UPennP (1992). pp. 228. ISBN 0947623469.

Hall, Joan N., Nick Doane, and Dick Ringler, eds. *Old English and New: Studies in Language and Linguistics in Honor of Frederic G. Cassidy.* Garland. pp. 460. ISBN 0815310862.

Hicks, Carola. *England in the Eleventh Century.* Harlaxton Medieval Studies 11. Paul Watkins (1992). pp. 356. ISBN 187161550X.

Hollis, Stephanie, and Michael Wright, with Gwynneth Mills, and Adrienne Pedder. *Old English Prose of Secular Learning.* Annotated Bibliographies of Old and Middle English Literature IV. Boydell (1992). pp. 383. ISBN 0859913430.

Hollis, Stephanie. *Anglo-Saxon Women and the Church.* Boydell (1992). pp. 323. ISBN 0851153178.

Keenan, Hugh T., ed. *Typology and English Medieval Literature.* AMS (1990). pp. 332. ISBN 0404632076.

Kendall, Calvin B., and Peter S. Wells, eds. *Voyage to the Other World. The Legacy of Sutton Hoo.* UMinnP (1992). pp. 222. ISBN 0816620237.

Klinck, Anne L., ed. *The Old English Elegies: A Critical Edition and Genre Study.* McG-QUP (1992). pp. 469. ISBN 0773508368.

Korhammer, Michael, with Karl Reichl, and Hans Sauer. *Words, Texts and Manuscripts: Studies in Anglo-Saxon Culture Presented to Helmut Gneuss on the Occasion of his Sixty-Fifth Birthday.* Brewer (1992). pp. 498. ISBN 0859913635.

Newton, Sam. *The Origins of Beowulf and the Pre-Viking Kingdom of East Anglia.* Brewer (1993). pp. 177. ISBN 0859913619.

Ramsay, Nigel, Margaret Sparks, and Tim Tatton-Brown, eds. *St Dunstan, His Life, Times and Cult.* Boydell (1992). pp. 343. ISBN 0851153011.

Scragg. D. G., ed. *The Vercelli Homilies and Related Texts.* OUP (1992). pp. 478. ISBN 0197223028.

Webber, Teresa. *Scribes and Scholars at Salisbury Cathedral.* Oxford Historical Monographs. Clarendon (1992). pp. 220. ISBN 019820308X.

Chapter IV. Middle English: Excluding Chaucer

Allen, David, G., and Robert A. White, eds. *The Work of Dissimilitude: Essays from the Sixth Citadel Conference on Medieval and Renaissance Literature*. UDelP (1992). pp. 299. ISBN 0874134358.

Atkinson, David William. *The English Ars Moriendi*. Peter Lang (1992). pp. 387. ISBN 0820419036.

Brabant, Margaret, and Jean Bethke Elshtain, eds. *Politics, Gender, and Genre: The Political Thought of Christine de Pizan*. Westview (1992). pp. 240.

Busby, Keith, ed. *Arthurian Yearbook* I. Garland (1991). pp. 220. ISBN 092407209X.

Chappell, Julie, ed. *The Prose Alexander of Robert Thornton: The Middle English Text with a Modern English Translation*. Peter Lang (1992). pp. 291. ISBN 0820415081.

Ciavolella, Massimo, and Amilcare A. Iannucci, eds. *Saturn from Antiquity in the Renaissance*. Dovehouse (1992). pp. 181.

Davidson, Clifford, and Thomas H. Seiler, eds. *The Iconography of Hell*. WMU (1992). pp. 215. ISBN hb 187928801X, pb 1879288028.

Fabiny, Tibor. *The Lion and the Lamb: Figuralism and Fulfillment in the Bible, Art, and Literature*. St Martin's (1992). pp. 164. ISBN 0312075448.

Foley, John Miles, J. Chris Womack, and Whitney A. Womack, eds. *De Gustibus: Essays for Alain Renoir*. Garland (1992). pp. 596. ISBN 0815303955.

Fries, Maureen, and Jeanie Watson, eds. *Approaches to Teaching the Arthurian Tradition*. Modern Language Association of America (1992). pp. 195.

Gildea, Joseph. *Source Book of Self-Discipline: A Synthesis of Moralia in Job by Gregory the Great*. Peter Lang (1991). pp. 373. ISBN 0820416509.

Harwood, Britton J. *Piers Plowman and the Problem of Belief*. UTorP (1992). pp. 237. ISBN 0802057993.

Holloway, Julia Bolton, Constance S. Wright, and Joan Bechtold, eds. *Equally in God's Image: Women in the Middle Ages*. Peter Lang (1990). pp. 336. ISBN 0820415170.

Jankofsky, Klaus P., ed. *The South English Legendary: A Critical Assessment*. Francke (1992). pp. 202. ISBN 3772018564.

Krishna, Valerie. *Five Middle English Arthurian Romances*. Garland (1991). pp. 254. ISBN 0824062477.

Linden, Stanton, J., ed. *The Mirror of Alchimy: Composed by the Thrice-Famous and Learned Fryer, Roger Bachon*. Garland (1992). pp. 144. ISBN 0824083989.

McEntire, Sandra J., ed. *Margery Kempe: A Book of Essays*. Garland (1992). pp. 258.

Marti, Kevin. *Body, Heart, and Text in the Pearl-Poet*. Mellen (1991). pp. 210. ISBN 0773497641.

Mojsisch, Burkhard, and Olaf Pluta, eds. *Historia Philosophiae Medii Aevi: Zur Geschichte der Philosophie des Mittelalters, I & II*. B. R. Gruner (1991). pp. 1163.

Sargent, Michael, ed. *Nicholas Love's Mirror of the Blessed Life of Jesus Christ*. Garland (1992). pp. 342. ISBN 0824058968.

Simons, John, ed. *From Medieval to Medievalism*. St Martin's (1992). pp. 161. ISBN hb 0333532732, pb 0333532740.

Sinnreich-Levi, Deborah, and Gale M. Sigal, eds. *Voices in Translation: The Authority of 'Olde Bookes' in Medieval Literature*. AMS (1992). pp. 242. ISBN 0404614477.

Chapter V. Middle English: Chaucer

Brownlee, Kevin, and Sylvia Huot, eds. *Rethinking the Romance of the Rose: Text, Image, Reception*. UPennP (1992). pp. 386. ISBN 0812213955

Dean, James M., and Christian K. Zacher, eds. *The Idea of Medieval Literature: New Essays on Chaucer and Medieval Culture in Honor of Donald R. Howard*. UDelP (1992). pp. 354. ISBN 0874134404.

Dor, Juliette, ed. *A Wyf Ther Was: Essays in Honour of Paule Mertens-Fonck*. ULiège (1993). pp. 300.

Fisher, John H. *The Importance of Chaucer*. SIUP (1992). pp. 198. ISBN 0809317419.

Hansen, Elaine Tuttle. *Chaucer and the Fictions of Gender*. UCalP (1992). pp. 301. ISBN 0520074998.

Kinney, Clare Regan. *Strategies of Poetic Narrative: Chaucer, Spenser, Milton, Eliot*. CUP (1992). pp. 261. ISBN 0521405423.

Mink, Joanna Stephens,and Janet Doubler Ward, eds. *Joinings and Disjoinings: The Significance of Marital Status in Literature*. BGUP (1991). pp. 173. ISBN hb 0879725230, pb 0879925249.

Oizumi, Akio, and Kunihiro Miki, eds. *A Complete Concordance to the Works of Geoffrey Chaucer, X*. Olms-Weidmann (1991). pp. 718. ISBN 3487094223.

Ruud, Jay. *'Many a Song and Many a Lecherous Lay': Tradition and Individuality in Chaucer's Lyric Poetry*. Garland (1992). pp. 338. ISBN 0815311427.

Chapter VI. The Sixteenth Century: Excluding Drama After 1550

Allen, David G., and Robert A. White, eds. *The Work of Dissimilitude: Essays from the Sixth Citadel Conference on Medieval and Renaissance Literature*. UDelP (1992). pp. 299. ISBN 0874134358.

Bates, Catherine. *The Rhetoric of Courtship in Elizabethan Language and Literature*. CUP (1992). pp. 236. ISBN 0521414806.

Bellamy, Elizabeth J. *Translations of Power: Narcissism and the Unconscious in Epic History*. CornUP (1992). pp. 261. ISBN 0801426987.

Brooks-Davies, Douglas, ed. *Silver Poets of the Sixteenth Century*. Dent (1992), Charles E. Tuttle (1992). pp. 484. ISBN 046087103X.

Cerasano, S. P., and Marion Wynne-Davies, eds. *Gloriana's Face: Women, Public and Private, in the English Renaissance*. Wayne State UP (1992). pp. 24.

Evans, Maurice, ed. *Elizabethan Sonnets*. Dent (1992), Charles E. Tuttle (1992). pp. 238. ISBN 0460871137.

Greenblatt, Stephen J. *Learning to Curse: Essays in Early Modern Culture*. Routledge, Chapman and Hall (1992). pp. 188. ISBN 0415903521.

Healy, Thomas. *New Latitudes: Theory and English Renaissance Literature*. Hodder & Stoughton (1992). pp. 183. ISBN 0340493089.

Helgerson, Richard. *Forms of Nationhood: The Elizabethan Writing of England*. UChicP (1992). pp. 367. ISBN 0226326330.

Kinney, Clare Regan. *Strategies of Poetic Narrative: Chaucer, Spenser, Milton, Eliot*. CUP (1992). pp. 261. ISBN 0521405423.

Krontiris, Tina. *Oppositional Voices: Women as Writers and Translators of Literature in the English Renaissance*. Routledge, Chapman and Hall (1992). pp. 182. ISBN 0415063299.

Lupack, Alan, ed. *Modern Arthurian Literature: An Anthology of English and American Arthuriana from the Renaissance to the Present*. Garland (1992). pp. 494. ISBN hb 0815300557, pb 0815308434.

Rhodes, Neil. *The Power of Eloquence and English Renaissance Literature*. St. Martin's (1992). pp. 244. ISBN 0312084218.

Chapter VII. Shakespeare

Adelman, Janet. *Suffocating Mothers: Fantasies of Maternal Origin in Shakespeare's Plays, Hamlet to the Tempest*. Routledge, Chapman & Hall (1992). pp. 379. ISBN 0415900395.

Astington, John H., ed. *The Development of Shakespeare's Theatre*. AMS (1992). pp. 208. ISBN 0404622941.

Barroll, Leeds. *Politics, Plague, and Shakespeare's Theatre: The Stuart Years*. CornUP (1992). pp. 249. ISBN 0801424798.

Bloom, Harold, ed. *Caliban*. ChelseaH (1992). pp. 262. ISBN 0791009149.

Bradley, David. *From Text to Performance in the Elizabethan Theatre: Preparing the Play for the Stage*. CUP (1992). pp. 273. ISBN 052139466X.

Charney, Maurice. *How to Read Shakespeare*. Peter Lang (1992). pp. 118. ISBN 0820416673.

Copley, Stephen, and John Whale, eds. *Beyond Romanticism: New Approaches to Texts and Contexts, 1780–1832*. SyracuseUP (1991). pp. 261. ISBN 0415052017.

Coursen, H. R. *Shakespearean Performance as Interpretation*. UDelP (1992). ISBN 0874134323.

Donker, Marjorie. *Shakespeare's Proverbial Themes: A Rhetorical Context for the Sententia as Res*. Greenwood (1992). pp. 199. ISBN 0313284105.

Epstein, Norrie. *The Friendly Shakespeare: A Thoroughly Painless Guide to the Best of the Bard*. Viking (1992). pp. 550. ISBN 0670844470.

Fleissner, Robert F. *Shakespeare and the Matter of the Crux: Textual, Topical, Onomastic, Authorial, and Other Puzzlements*. Mellen (1991). pp. 294. ISBN 077349622X.

Fraser, Russell. *Shakespeare, The Later Years*. ColUP (1992). pp. 380. ISBN 0231067666.

Gajowski, Evelyn. *The Art of Loving: Female Subjectivity and Male Discursive Traditions in Shakespeare's Tragedies*. UDelP (1992). pp. 153. ISBN 087413398X.

Hamilton, Donna B. *Shakespeare and the Politics of Protestant England*. UKenP (1992). pp. 253. ISBN 0813115574.

Hawley, William M. *Critical Hermeneutics and Shakespeare's History Plays*. Peter Lang (1992). pp. 227. ISBN 0820416827.

Hoeniger, F. David. *Medicine and Shakespeare in the English Renaissance*. UDelP (1992). ISBN 0874134250.

Holderness, Graham, ed. *Shakespeare's History Plays: Richard II to Henry V*. St. Martin's (1992). pp. 209. ISBN 0312083718.

Hunt, Maurice, ed. *Approaches to Teaching Shakespeare's The Tempest and Other Late Romances*. Modern Language Association of America (1992). pp. 195. ISBN 0873527070.

Jacobus, Lee A. *Shakespeare and the Dialectic of Certainty*. St. Martin's (1992). pp. 203. ISBN 0312080638.

King, T. J. *Casting Shakespeare's Plays: London Actors and Their Roles, 1590–1642*. CUP (1992). pp. 284. ISBN 0521327857.

Lewis, Anthony J. *The Love Story in Shakespearean Comedy*. UPKen. ISBN 0813117860.

McMullan, Gordon, and Jonathan Hope, eds. *The Politics of Tragicomedy: Shakespeare and After*. Routledge (1992). pp. 212. ISBN 0415064031.

Marsden, Jean I. *The Appropriation of Shakespeare: Post-Renaissance Reconstructions of the Works and the Myth*. St. Martin's (1991). pp. 222. ISBN 0312071981.

Pearlman, E., and Arthur F. Kinney, eds. *William Shakespeare: The History Plays*. Twayne (1992). pp. 192. ISBN 0805770208.

Rosenberg, Marvin. *The Masks of Hamlet*. UDelP (1992). pp. 971. ISBN 0874134803.

Ryan, Kiernan, ed. *William Shakespeare: King Lear*. St. Martin's (1992). pp. 189. ISBN 0312085419.

Sherbo, Arthur. *Richard Farmer, Master of Emmanuel College, Cambridge: A Forgotten Shakespearean*. UDelP (1992). pp. 223.

Truax, Elizabeth. *Metamorphosis in Shakespeare's Plays: A Pageant of Heroes, Gods, Maids, and Monsters*. Mellen (1992). pp. 298. ISBN 0773 494340.

Woodbridge, Linda, and Edward Berry, eds. *True Rites and Maimed Rites: Ritual and Anti-Ritual in Shakespeare and His Age*. UIllP (1992). pp. 303. ISBN 0252018974.

Chapter VIII. Renaissance Drama: Excluding Shakespeare

Biggs, Murray, Philip Edwards, Inga-Stina Ewbank, and Eugene M. Waith, eds. *The Arts of Performance in Elizabethan and Early Stuart Drama: Essays for G. K. Hunter*. EdinUP (1991). pp. 227. ISBN 0748602666.

Braunmuller, A. R. *Natural Fictions: George Chapman's Major Tragedies*. UDelP (1992). ISBN 0874134048.

Copley, Stephen, and John Whale, eds. *Beyond Romanticism: New Approaches to Texts and Contexts, 1780–1832*. SyracuseUP (1991). pp. 261. ISBN 0415052017.

Evans, Robert C. *Jonson, Linsius and the Politics of Renaissance Stoicism*. Longwood Academic (1992). ISBN 0893416827.

Fothergill-Payne, Louise, and Peter Fothergill-Payne, eds. *Parallel Lives: Spanish and English National Drama 1580–1680*. BuckUP/AUP (1991). pp. 329.

Hayes, Tom. *The Birth of Popular Culture: Ben Jonson, Maid Marian and Robin Hood*. Duquesne (1992). pp. 207. ISBN 0820702412.

Jankowski, Theodora A. *Women in Power in the Early Modern Drama*. UIllP (1992). pp. 239. ISBN 0252062388.

Kastan, David Scott, and Peter Stallybrass, eds. *Staging the Renaissance: Reinterpretations of Elizabethan and Jacobean Drama*. Routledge (1991). pp. 293. ISBN hb 04159011669, pb 0415901677.

Levin, Carole, and Karen Robertson, eds. *Sexuality and Politics in Renaissance Drama*. Mellen (1991). pp. 288. ISBN 0889460787.

Palmer, Daryl W. *Hospitable Performances: Dramatic Genre and Cultural Practices in Early Modern England*. PurdueUP (1992). pp. 220. ISBN 1557530149.

Chapter IX. The Earlier Seventeenth Century: Excluding Drama

Armstrong, Nancy and Leonard Tennenhouse. *The Imaginary Puritan: Literature, Intellectual Labor, and the Origins of Personal Life*. UCalP (1992). pp. 275. ISBN 0520077563.

Cain, T. G. S., and Ken Robinson, eds. *Into Another Mould: Change and Continuity in English Culture 1625–1700*. Routledge (1992). pp. 196. ISBN hb 0415010837, pb 0415010845.

Chappell, Vere, ed. *Thomas Hobbes*. Garland (1992). pp. 330. ISBN 0815305796.

Clark, Ira. *Professional Playwrights: Massinger, Ford, Shirley and Brome*. UKenP (1992). pp. 232. ISBN 0813117879.

Ferguson, Moira. *Subject to Others: British Women Writers and Colonial Slavery, 1670–1834*. Routledge (1992). pp. 465. ISBN hb 0415904757, pb 0415904765.

Kyne, Mary Theresa, and Samuel J. Hazo. *Country Parsons, Country Poets: George Herbert and Gerard Manley Hopkins as Spiritual Autobiographers*. Eadmer (1992). pp. 250. ISBN 0929914120.

McCanles, Michael. *Jonsonian Discriminations: The Humanist Poet and The Praise of True Nobility*. UTorP (1992). pp. 306. ISBN 0802059554.

McGovern, Barbara. *Anne Finch and Her Poetry: A Critical Biography*. UGeoP (1992). pp. 278. ISBN 0820 314102.

Shaw, William P., ed. *Praise Disjoined: Changing Patterns of Salvation in Seventeenth-Century English Literature*. Peter Lang (1991). pp. 307. ISBN 0820414603.

Stanwood, P. G. *The Sempiternal Season: Studies in Seventeenth-Century Devotional Writing*. Peter Lang (1992). ISBN 0820417785.

Summers, Claude J., and Ted-Larry Pebworth, eds. *On the Celebrated and Neglected Poems of Andrew Marvell*. UMoP (1992). pp. 288. ISBN 0862207952.

Chapter X. Milton

Florén, Celia, ed. *John Milton: A Concordance of Paradise Lost*. Olms-Weidmann (1992). pp. 1171. ISBN 3487094517.

Kinney, Clare Regan. *Strategies of Poetic Narrative: Chaucer, Spenser, Milton, Eliot*. CUP (1992). pp. 200. ISBN 0521405423.

Marjara, Harinder Singh. *Contemplation of Created Things: Science in Paradise Lost*. UTorP (1992). pp. 376. ISBN 0802027504.

Miller, Leo. *John Milton's Writings in the Anglo-Dutch Negotiations, 1651–1654*. Duquesne (1992). pp. 342. ISBN 0521405423.

Chapter XI. The Later Seventeenth Century

Lawrence, Robert G., ed. *Restoration Plays*. New edn. Dent (1992), Tuttle (1992). pp. 678. ISBN 0460870696.

Stanwood, P. G. *The Sempiternal Season: Studies in Seventeenth-Century Devotional Writing*. Peter Lang (1992). ISBN 0820417785.

Weckerman, Hans-Jurgen, ed. *Abraham Cowley: Naufragium Iocularie/William Johnson: Valetudinarium*. Olms (1991). ISBN 3487078708.

Chapter XII. The Eighteenth Century

Adams, Leonard, ed. *William Wake's Gallician Correspondence and Related Documents, 1716–1731* IV. Peter Lang (1991). pp. 415. ISBN 0820410543.

Adickes, Sandra. *The Social Quest: The Expanded Vision of Four Women Travelers in the Era of the French Revolution*. Peter Lang (1991). pp. 158. ISBN 0820406570.

Allan, D. G. C. and Abbot, John L., eds. *The Virtuoso Tribe of Arts and Sciences: Studies in the Eighteenth-Century Work and Membership of the London Society of Arts*. UGeoP (1992).

Armstrong, Nancy and Leonard Tennenhouse. *The Imaginary Puritan: Literature, Intellectual Labor, and the Origins of Personal Life*. UCalP (1992). pp. 275. ISBN 0520077563.

Barker-Benfield, G. J. *The Culture of Sensibility: Sex and Society in Eighteenth-Century Britain*. UChicP (1992). ISBN 0226037134.

Copley, Stephen and John Whale, eds. *Beyond Romanticism: New Approaches to Texts and Contexts, 1780–1832*. Syracuse UP (1991). pp. 261. ISBN 0415052017.

Ferguson, Moira. *Subject to Others: British Women Writers and Colonial Slavery, 1670–1834*. Routledge (1992). pp. 465.

Gournay, Jean-Francois, ed. *L'Erotisme en Angleterre XVIIe–XVIIIe siècles*. Lille UP (1992). pp. 107. ISBN 2865310450.

Keymer, Tom. *Richardson's Clarissa and the Eighteenth-Century*. CUP (1992). pp. 270. ISBN 0521390230.

Kraft, Elizabeth. *Character and Consciousness in Eighteenth-Century Comic Fiction*. UGeoP (1992). pp. 202. ISBN 0820313653.

Kropf, Carl R., ed. *Reader Entrapment in Eighteenth-Century Literature*. AMS Press (1992). pp. 267.

Lonker, Fred, ed. *Die Literarische Ubersetzung als Medium der Fremderfabrung*. Schmidt (1992). pp. 272.

Naglee, David Ingersoll. *From Everlasting to Everlasting: John Wesley on Eternity and Time II*. Peter Lang (1991). ISBN 0820411140.

Quintero, Ruben. *Literate Culture: Pope's Rhetorical Art*. UDelP (1992). ISBN 0874134331.

Straub, Kristina. *Sexual Suspects: Eighteenth-Century Players and Sexual Ideology*. PrincetonUP (1992). pp. 194. ISBN 0691015155.

Thomas, Donald, intro. *Tom Jones*. Dent (1992). Tuttle (1992). pp. 837. ISBN 0460871684.

Todd, Janet M., ed. *Mary: Maria: Matilda*. NYUP (1992). pp. 217. ISBN 0814792529.

Todd, Janet M. *The Sign of Angelica: Women, Writing and Fiction, 1660–1800*. ColUP (1989). pp. 328. ISBN 0231071345.

Chapter XIII. The Nineteenth Century: Romantic Period

Barton, Anne. *Byron: Don Juan. Landmarks of World Literature*. CUP. (1992). pp. 128. ISBN 0521329337.

Barbauld, Ann Laetitia. *Poems (1792)*. Woodstock (1993).

Bialostosky, Don H. *Wordsworth, Dialogics, and the Practice of Criticism*. CUP (1992). pp. 300. ISBN 0521412498.

Birenbaum, Harvey. *Between Blake and Nietzsche: The Reality of Culture*. AUP (1992). pp. 168. ISBN 1854771272.
Blumenberg, Jane. *Byron and the Shelleys: The Story of a Friendship*. Collins & Brown (1992).
Bode, Christopher. *'And Where Were Thou ?': Essay uber Shelley und das Erhabene*. Blaue Eule (1992). pp. 155. ISBN 3892064946.
Bourke, Richard. *Romantic Discourse and Political Modernity: Wordsworth, the Intellectual and Cultural Critique*. Harvester (1993). pp. 384. ISBN 074501318X.
Brinkley, Robert, and Keith Hanley, eds. *Romantic Revisions*. CUP (1992). pp. 384. ISBN 052138074X.
Byron, Lord George Gordon. *Don Juan Cantos I & II (1819)*. Woodstock (1992). pp. 240. ISBN 1954771213.
Caraher, Brian G. *Wordsworth's 'Slumber' and the Problematics of Reading*. PSUP (1991). pp. 228. ISBN 0271 007206.
Chase, Cynthia. *Romanticism*. Longman (1993). pp. 296. ISBN hb 0582047994, pb 0582050006.
Christensen, Jerome. *Lord Byron's Strength: Romantic Writing and Commercial Society*. JHUP (1993). pp. 416. ISBN 08018 43553.
Claridge, Laura. *Romantic Poetry: The Paradox of Desire*. CornUP (1992). ISBN 0801480167.
Coleman, Deidre and Peter Otto, eds. *Imagining Romanticism: Essays on English and Australian Romanticism*. Locust Hill (1992).
Coleridge, Samuel Taylor. *Conciones Ad Populum (1795)*. Woodstock (1992). pp. 80. ISBN 1854771167.
Collins, Philip, ed. *Tennyson: Seven Essays*. St Martin's (1992). pp. 185. ISBN 0333457900.
Cope, Kevin L., ed. *Compendious Conversations: The Method of Dialogue in the Early Enlightenment*. Lang (1992).
Copley, Stephen and John Whale, eds. *Beyond Romanticism: New Approaches to Texts and Contexts 1780–1832*. SyracuseUP (1991). pp. 261. ISBN 0415052017.
Cox, Jeffrey, and Nancy Cox, eds. *Seven Gothic Dramas 1789–1825*. OhioUP (1992). pp. 432. ISBN 0821410156.
Cox, Stephen. *Love and Logic: The Evolution of Blake's Thought*. UMichP (1992). pp. 260. ISBN 0472103040.
Curran, Stewart. *The Cambridge Companion to British Romanticism*. CUP (1993). pp. 250. ISBN hb 0521333555, pb 0521421934.
Curreli, Mario, and Anthony L. Johnson. *Paradise of Exiles: Shelley and Byron in Pisa*. ETS Editrice (1993).
Eilenberg, Susan. *Strange Power of Speech: Wordsworth and Coleridge and Literary Possession*. OUP (1992). pp. 278. ISBN 0195068564.
Ellison, Julie. *Delicate Subjects: Romanticism, Gender, and the Ethics of Understanding*. CornUP (1990). pp. 336. ISBN 08014 23783.
Everest, Kelvin, ed. *Percy Bysshe Shelley: Bicentenary Essays*. Brewer (1992). pp. 134. ISBN 085991352X.
Ferguson, Frances. *Solitude and the Sublime*. Routledge (1992). pp. 256. ISBN hb 0415905486, pb 0415905494.
Ford, Boris, ed. *The Romantic Age in Britain: The Cambridge Cultural History*. CUP (1992). pp. 336. ISBN 0521428866.
Franklin, Caroline. *Byron's Heroines*. Clarendon (1992). pp. 280. ISBN 0198112300.
Frere, James Hookham. *Whistlecraft (1818)*. Woodstock (1992). pp. 134. ISBN 1854771221.

Fulford, Tim, and Morton D. Paley. *Coleridge's Visionary Languages*. Brewer (1993). pp. 242. ISBN 0859913880.

Galperin, William H. *The Return of the Visible in British Romanticism*. JHUP (1993). pp. 352. ISBN 080184505X.

Gelpi, Barbara Charlesworth. *Shelley's Goddess: Maternity Language, Subjectivity*. OUP (1992). pp. 311. ISBN 0195073835.

Greenfield, John R., ed. *British Romantic Prose Writers, 1789–1832: First Series*. Gale (1992).

Hamilton, Paul, ed. *Dorothy Wordsworth: Selections from the Journals*. P&C (1992). pp. 288. ISBN 1851960309.

Handley, Graham. *Jane Austen*. St Martin's (1992). pp. 139. ISBN 0312086024.

Heffernan, James A. W., ed. *Representing the French Revolution: Literature, Historiography, and Art*. UPNE (1992). pp. 416. ISBN hb 0874515653, pb 0874515866.

Hoeveler, Diane Long. *Romantic Androgyny: The Women Within*. Pennsylvania State UP (1990). pp. 272. ISBN 0271007044.

Hudon, Glenda. *Sibling Love and Incest in Jane Austen's Fiction*. St Martin's (1992). pp. 143. ISBN 0333457900.

Hunt, Lynne. *The Family Romance of the French Revolution*. Routledge (1992). pp. 208. ISBN 0415082366.

Ingram, Alison. *The Madhouse of Language: Writing and Reading Madness in the Eighteenth Century*. Routledge (1992). pp. 208. ISBN 0415031907.

Jackson, H. J., and George Whalley, eds. *The Collected Works of Samuel Taylor Coleridge* Vol 12. PrincetonUP (1992). pp. 1300. ISBN 041507648X.

Jackson, J. J. de J. *Romantic Poetry by Women: a Bibliography 1770–1835*. Clarendon (1993). pp. 484. ISBN 0198112394.

Kent, David A., and D. R. Ewen, eds. *Romantic Parodies, 1789–1831*. AUP (1992). ISBN 0 8386 34583.

Kneale, J. Douglas. *The Mind in Creation: Essays on English Romantic Literature in Honour of Ross G. Woodman*. McG-QUP (1992). pp. 192. ISBN 0773508988.

Landor, Walter Savage. *Gebir (1798)*. Woodstock (1993). pp. 92. ISBN 1854771280.

Lansdown, Richard. *Byron's Historical Dramas*. OUP (1992). pp. 259. ISBN 0198112521.

Leask, Nigel. *British Romantic Writers and the East*. CUP (1993). pp. 275. ISBN 0521 1411688.

Low, Donald A. *The Songs of Robert Burns*. Routledge (1993). pp. 800. ISBN 0415034140.

Macdonald, D. L. *Poor Polidori: A Critical Biography of the Author of the Vampyre*. UTorP (1991). ISBN 0802027741.

McFarland, Thomas. *William Wordsworth: The Intensity of Achievement*. Clarendon (1992). pp. 176. ISBN 019811253X.

McGann, Jerome J. *The New Oxford Book of Romantic Period Verse*. OUP (1993). pp. 832. ISBN 0192141589.

McGavran, James Holt, Jnr, ed. *Romanticism and Children's Literature in Nineteenth-Century England*. UGeoP (1991). pp. 265.

McNeice, Gerald. *The Knowledge that Endured: Coleridge, German Philosophy and the Logic of Romantic Thought*. Macmillan (1992). pp. 244. ISBN 0333552415.

Mason, Michael, ed. *Lyrical Ballads*. Longman Annotated Texts. Longman (1992). pp. 236. ISBN hb 0582033020, pb 0582033039.

Maturin, Charles. *Bertram (1816)*. Woodstock (1992). pp. 110. ISBN 1854771205.

Mee, Jon. *Dangerous Enthusiasm: William Blake and the Culture of Radicalism in the 1790s*. Clarendon (1992). pp. 251. ISBN 0198122268.

Minahan, John. *Word Like a Bell: John Keats, Music and the Romantic Poet*. KSUP (1992). pp. 288. ISBN 0873384539.

Murray, E. B., ed. *The Prose Works of Percy Bysshe Shelley* Vol. 1. Clarendon (1993). pp. 592. ISBN 0198127480.

Myerson, George. *The Argumentative Imagination: Wordsworth, Dryden, Religious Dialogues*. MUP (1992). pp. 208. ISBN 0719036763.

Newlyn, Lucy. *Paradise Lost and the Romantic Reader*. Clarendon (1992). pp. 295. ISBN 01981122777.

O'Neill, Michael. *Shelley*. Longman Critical Readers. Longman. pp. 292. ISBN hb 058208668X, pb 0582086671.

Pinion, F.B. *A Keats Chronology*. Macmillan (1992). pp. 160. ISBN 0333552725.

Raimond, Jean, and J. R. Watson. *A Handbook to English Romanticism*. Macmillan (1992). pp. 326. ISBN hb 0333469518, pb 0333607066.

Reeve, William C. *Kleist on Stage 1804–1987*. McG-QUP (1993). pp. 256. ISBN 0773509410.

Reed, James. *Sir Walter Scott: Selected Poems*. Carcanet (1992). pp. 240. ISBN 085635980.

Robinson, Eric, David Powell, and P. M. S. Dawson, eds. *John Clare Cottage Tales*. Carcanet (1993). pp. 216. ISBN 1857540328.

Roe, Nicholas. *William Wordsworth: Selected Poems*. Penguin (1992).

Scott, Walter. *The Lay of the Last Minstrel (1805)*. Woodstock (1992). pp. 334. ISBN 1854771124.

Scrivener, Michael, ed. *Poetry and Reform: Periodical Verse from the English Democratic Press 1792–1824*. WSUP (1992).

Simpson, David, ed. *Subject to History: Ideology, Class, Gender*. CornUP (1991). pp. 256. ISBN 0801497914.

Smith, Charlotte. *Elegiac Sonnets (1789)*. Woodstock (1992). pp. 136. ISBN 1854771116.

Stone, Brian. *The Poetry of Keats*. PCS. Penguin (1992). pp. 160. ISBN 0140772669.

Sutherland, Guilland, ed. *British Art 1740–1820: Essays in Honour of Robert R. Wark*. Huntingdon (1992). pp. 239. ISBN 0873281357.

Tighe, Mary. *Psyche with Other Poems* (1811). Woodstock (1992). pp. 352. ISBN 1854771108.

Vine, Steve. *Blake's Poetry: Spectral Vision*. Macmillan (1992). pp. 192. ISBN 0333531361.

Watson, J. R. *English Poetry of the Romantic Period 1789–1830*. 2nd edition. Longman (1992). pp. 440. ISBN 0582088445.

Williams, John, ed. *Wordsworth: Contemporary Critical Essays*. Macmillan (1993). pp. 192. ISBN 033354904X.

Wilson, Douglas B. *The Romantic Dream: Wordsworth and the Poetics of the Unconscious*. UNebP (1993). pp. 288. ISBN 0803247613.

Winter, Kari J. *Subjects of Slavery, Agents of Change: Women and Power in Gothic Novels and Slave Narratives, 1790–1865*. UGeoP (1992). pp. 172. ISBN 082031420X

Wood, Nigel, ed. *Don Juan*. Theory in Practice. OpenUP (1993). pp. 208. ISBN 0335096255.

Wood, Nigel, ed. *The Prelude*. Theory in Practice. OpenUP (1993). pp. 224. ISBN 0335096263.

Wordsworth, Jonathan. *Visionary Gleam: Forty Books from the Romantic Period*. Woodstock (1993). pp. 256. ISBN 1854771264.

Wordsworth, William. *Lyrical Ballads (1798)*. Woodstock (1993). pp. 236. ISBN 1854771248.

Wordsworth, William. *Peter Bell (1819)*. Woodstock (1992). pp. 108. ISBN 1854771140.

Worrall, David. *Radical Culture: Discourse, Resistance and Surveillance, 1790–1820*. Harvester (1992). pp. 288. ISBN 0333457900.

Yarrington, Alison and Kelvin Everest, eds. *Reflections of Revolution: Images of Romanticism*. Routledge (1992). pp. 208. ISBN 0415077419.

Chapter XIV. The Nineteenth Century: Victorian Period

Auerbach, Nina, and U. C. Knoepflmacher, eds. *Forbidden Journeys: Fairy Tales and Fantasies by Victorian Women Writers*. UChicP (1992). pp. 380. ISBN hb 0226032035, pb 022632043..

Basham, Diana. *The Trial of Woman: Feminism and the Occult Sciences in Victorian Literature and Society*. Macmillan (1992). pp. 264. ISBN 0 333 48202 6.

Block, Ed, Jnr, ed. *Critical Essays on John Henry Newman*. University of Victoria Press (1992). pp. 138. ISBN 0920604625.

Bonaparte, Felicia. *The Gypsy-Bachelor of Manchester: The Life of Mrs Gaskell's Demon*. UPVirginia (1992). pp. 352. ISBN 081391390X.

Bonnecase, Denis. S. T. *Coleridge: poemes de l'experience vive*. Ellug (1992). pp. 230. ISBN 2902709803.

Brooks, Peter. *Reading for the Plot: Design and Intention in Narrative*. HarvardUP (1992). pp. 384. ISBN 0674748921.

Campbell, Ian, foreword. *The Carlyle Society Papers Session 1991–92*. Carlyle Soc (1992). pp. 50.

Cheney, Liana De Girolami, ed. *Pre-Raphaelitism and Medievalism in the Arts*. Mellen (1993). pp. 328. ISBN 077349491X.

Coleman, Deirdre, and Peter Otto, eds. *Imagining Romanticism: Essays on English and Australian Romanticisms*. Locust Hill (1992). pp. 300. ISBN 0933951426.

Forster, Margaret, introd. *Selected Poems of Elizabeth Barrett Browning*. Dent (1992), Tuttle (1992). pp. 330 ISBN 0460871501.

Garrigan, Kristine Ottesen, ed. *Victorian Scandals: Representations of Gender and Class*. Ohio UP (1992). pp. 350. ISBN 0821410199.

Gibson, Mary Ellis, ed. *Critical Essays on Robert Browning*. Hall (1992). pp. 275. ISBN 0816188610.

Haight, Gordon S., and Hugh Witemeyer, eds. *George Eliot's Originals and Contemporaries: Essays in Victorian Literary History and Biography*. UMichP (1992). pp. 239. ISBN 0472102648.

Harrison, Antony H., and Beverly Taylor, eds. *Gender and Discourse in Victorian Literature and Art*. Northern Illinois UP (1992). pp. 286. ISBN 0875801684.

Heineman, Helen K. *Three Victorians in the New World: Interpretations of the New World in the Works of Frances Trollope, Charles Dickens, and Anthony Trollope*. Peter Lang (1992). pp. 297. ISBN 0820409677.

Heller, Tamar. *Dead Secrets: Wilkie Collins and the Female Gothic*. YaleUP (1992). pp. 208. ISBN 0300045743.

McKay, Margaret. *Peacock's Progress: Aspects of Artistic Development in the Novels of Thomas Love Peacock*. AUUp (1992). pp. 170. ISBN 9155429149.

Milbank, Alison. *Daughters of the House: Modes of the Gothic in Victorian Fiction*. Macmillan (1992). pp. 255. ISBN 0333566157.
Miller, J. Hillis. *Ariadne's Thread: Story Lines*. YaleUP (1992). pp. 320. ISBN 0300052162.
Morgan, Nicholas H. *Secret Journeys: Theory and Practice in Reading Dickens*. FDUP (1992). pp. 148. ISBN 0838634478.
Nestor, Pauline. *Charlotte Brontë's Jane Eyre*. HW (1992). pp. 144. ISBN hb 0745008984, pb 0745008992.
Norbelie, Barbro Almqvist. *Oppressive Narrowness: A Study of the Female Community in George Eliot's Early Writings*. AUUp (1992). pp. 163. ISBN 9155429823.
Pathak, Pratul. *The Infinite Passion of Finite Hearts: Robert Browning and Failure in Love*. Peter Lang (1992). pp. 208. ISBN 0820417769.
Prance, Claude A. *The Characters in the Novels of Thomas Love Peacock, 1785–1866, with Biographical Lists*. Mellen (1992). pp. 316. ISBN 077349510X.
Sammons, Jeffrey L., introd. *Thomas Carlyle's Life of Friedrich Schiller (1825)*. Camden House (1992). pp. 288. ISBN 1879751100.
Selig, Robert L., ed. *George Gissing; Lost Stories from America: Five Signed Stories Never Before Reprinted, a Sixth Signed Story and Seven Recent Attributions*. Mellen (1992). pp. 196. ISBN 0773494855.
Shillingsburg, Peter L. *Pegasus in Harness: Victorian Publishing and W. M. Thackeray*. UPVirginia (1992). pp. 320. ISBN 0813913977.
Welsh, Alexander. *Strong Representations: Narrative and Circumstantial Evidence in England*. JHUP (1992). pp. 320. ISBN 0801842719.
Winn, Sharon A., and Lynn M. Alexander, eds. *The Slaughter-House of Mammon: An Anthology of Victorian Social Protest Literature*. Locust Hill (1992). pp. 344. ISBN 0933951418.

Chapter XV. The Twentieth Century

Acheson, James, ed. *The British and Irish Novel since 1960*. St. Martin's (1991). pp. 217. ISBN 0312057784.
Barker, Francis, Peter Hulme, and Margaret Iversen, eds. *Uses of History: Marxism, Postmodernism, and the Renaissance*. ManUP (1991). pp. 192. ISBN 0719035120.
Bayley, John. *Housman's Poems*. OUP (1992). pp. 202. ISBN 0198117639.
Bornstein, George, ed. *Representing Modernist Texts: Editing as Interpretation*. UMichP (1991). ISBN 0472094394.
Bush, Ronald. *T. S. Eliot: The Modernist in History*. CUP (1992). pp. 144. ISBN 0521390745.
Cixous, Hélène. *Readings: Poetics of Blanchot, Joyce, Kafka, Kleist, Lispector and Tsvetayeva*. Transl. V.A. Conley. HW (1992). pp. 272, 178. ISBN hb 0745011497, pb 0745011500.
Cusic, Don. *The Poet as Performer*. UPA (1992). pp. 136. ISBN 0819183962.
Davie, Donald. *Under Briggflatts: A History of Poetry in Great Britain 1960–1980*. Carcanet (1989). pp. 320. ISBN 0856358207.
Erkkila, Betsy. *The Wicked Sisters: Women Poets, Literary History, and Discord*. OUP (1993). pp. 279. ISBN 019507211.
Fjagesund, Peter. *The Apocalyptic World of D. H. Lawrence*. Universitetsforlaget, Oslo (1992). pp. 198. ISBN 8200213862.

Gindi, Hoda, ed. *Images of Egypt in Twentieth-Century Literature*. University of Cairo Press (1991). pp. 437.

Hussey, Mark, and Vara Neverow-Turk, eds. *Virginia Woolf Miscellanies*. UPA (1992). pp. 260. ISBN hb 0944473083, pb 0944473091.

Ingersoll, Earl G. *Representations of Science and Technology in British Literature since 1880*. Peter Lang (1992). pp. 320. ISBN 0820416800.

Innes, Christopher. *Modern British Drama. 1890–1990*. CUP (1992). pp. 584. ISBN hb 0521305365, pb 0521315557.

Jain, Manju. *A Critical Reading of the 'Selected Poems' of T. S. Eliot*. OUP (1992). pp. 258. ISBN 0195625463.

Jones, Gwyn. *Background to Dylan Thomas and Other Explorations*. OUP (1992). pp. 210. ISBN 0198112831.

Kinney, Clare Regan. *Strategies of Poetic Narrative: Chaucer, Spenser, Milton, Eliot*. CUP (1992). pp. 200. ISBN 0521405424.

Loeffelholz, Mary. *Experimental Lives: Women & Literature, 1900–1945*. Twayne (1992). pp. 256. ISBN 0805789766.

Lupack, Alan, ed. *Modern Arthurian Literature: An Anthology of English and American Arthuriana from the Renaissance to the Present*. Garland (1992). pp. 494. ISBN hb 0815300557, pb 0815308434.

Makin, Peter. *Bunting: The Shaping of His Verse*. OUP (1992). pp. 370. ISBN 0198112548.

Marcus, Phillip L. *Yeats and Artistic Power*. Macmillan (1992). pp. 268. ISBN 0333524896.

North, Michael. *The Political Aesthetic of Yeats, Eliot and Pound*. CUP (1992). pp. 288. ISBN 05214143260.

O'Neill, Michael, and Gareth Reeves, eds. *Auden, MacNiece, Spender: The Thirties Poetry*. Macmillan (1992). pp. 264. ISBN hb 0333451171, pb 033345118X.

Onderdelinden, Sjaak, ed. *Interbellum und Exil*. Rodopi (1991). pp. 293.

Sena, Vinod, and Rajiva Verma, *The Fire and the Rose: New Essays on T. S. Eliot*. OUP (1992). pp. 196. ISBN 0195630718.

Sherry, Vincent. *Ezra Pound, Wyndham Lewis, and Radical Modernism*. OUP (1993). pp. 228. ISBN 0195076931.

Sturgess, Philip J. M. *Narrativity: Theory and Practice*. OUP (1992). pp. 322. ISBN 0198119542.

Chapter XVI. American Literature to 1900

Adams, Henry. *Selected Letters*, ed. Ernest Samuels. HarvardUP. ISBN 0674387570.

Albert, Octavia V. Rogers. *The House of Bondage, or Charlotte Brooks and Other Slaves*. OUP (1992). pp. 224. ISBN 0195052633.

Allmendinger, Blake. *The Cowboy: Representations of Labor in an American Work Culture*. OUP (1993). pp. 201. ISBN 019507243X.

Austen, Roger. *Genteel Pagan: The Double Life of Charles Warren Stoddard*. UMassP. ISBN 0870237500.

Bauerlein, Mark. *Whitman and the American Idiom*. LSUP (1992). pp. 191. ISBN 0807116815.

Benfrey, Christopher. *The Double Life of Stephen Crane*. Andre Deutsch. ISBN 0233988203.

Bercovitch, Sacvan. *The Rites of Assent: Transformations in the Symbolic Construction of America*. Routledge. ISBN 041590014X.

Boren, Lynda S., and Sara de Saussure Davis, eds. *Kate Chopin Reconsidered: Beyond the Bayou*. LSUP.

Buell, Lawrence, ed. *Ralph Waldo Emerson: A Collection of Critical Essays*. Prentice-Hall (1993).

Callow, Philip. *Walt Whitman: From Noon to Starry Night*. Allison & Busby (1992). pp. 416. ISBN 0850319080.

Carpenter, Lynette, and Wendy Kolmar, eds. *Haunting the House of Fiction: Feminist Perspectives on Ghost Stories by American Women*. UTennP.

Castronovo, David. *The American Gentleman: Social Prestige and the Modern Literary Mind*. Continuum. ISBN 0826405320.

Cavell, Stanley. *The Senses of Walden: An Expanded Edition*. UChicP (1992). pp. 160. ISBN 0 226 098133.

Cohen, Hennig, and Donald Yannella. *Herman Melville's Malcolm Letter: 'Man's Final Lore'*. Fordham UP (1992). pp. 200. ISBN 0823211843.

Davis, Thomas M. *A Reading of Edward Taylor*. AUP. pp. 233. £28. ISBN 0874134285.

Dawidoff, Robert. *The Genteel Tradition and the Sacred Rage: High Culture vs. Democracy in Adams, James and Santayana*. UNCP.

Doyno, Victor A. *Writing 'Huckleberry Finn': Mark Twain's Creative Process*. UPennP (1991). pp. 256. ISBN 0812230876.

Ellis, William. *The Theory of the American Romance: An Ideology in American Intellectual History*. UMI Research Press. ISBN 0835719847.

Farr, Judith. *The Passion of Emily Dickinson*. Harvard UP. pp 390. ISBN 0674656652.

Fender, Stephen. *Sea Changes: British Emigration and American Literature*. CUP (1992). pp. 300. ISBN 0521411750.

Giles, Paul. *American Catholic Arts and Fictions: Culture Ideology, Aesthetics*. CUP.

Godbeer, Richard. *The Devil's Dominion: Magic and Religion in Early New England*. CUP (1992). pp. 272. ISBN 0521403294.

Goshgarian, G. M. *To Kiss the Chastening Rod: Domestic Fiction and Sexual Ideology in the American Renaissance*. CornUP. ISBN 080142559X.

Hopkins, P. *Contending Forces*. OUP (1992).pp. 402. ISBN 0195067851.

Johnson, R. *Clarence and Corinne, or God's Way*. OUP (1992). pp. 218. ISBN 0195075749.

Johnson, R. *The Hazeley Family*. OUP (1992). pp. 230. ISBN 0195075773.

Kaplan, Fred. *Henry James: The Imagination of Genius: a Biography*. Hodder and Stoughton. ISBN 034055553X.

Kelley, G. *Four Girls at Cottage City*. OUP (1992). pp. 379. ISBN 0195067878.

Kirkby, Joan. *Emily Dickinson*. Macmillan. ISBN 0333420667.

Kopley, Richard, ed. *Poe's Pym: Critical Explorations*. DukeUP (1992). pp. 304. ISBN hb 0822312352, pb 0822312468.

McConachie, Bruce A. *Melodramatic Formations: American Theatre & Society 1820–1870*. UIowaP. ISBN 0877453608.

Maddox, Lucy. *Removals: Nineteenth-Century American Literature and the Politics of Indian Affairs*. OUP. ISBN 0195069315.

Martin, Robert, ed. *The Continuing Presence of Walt Whitman: The Life After the Life*. UIowaP (1992).

Meyers, Jeffrey. *Edgar Allan Poe: His Life and Legacy*. John Murray (1992). pp. 352. ISBN 0719550238.

Miller, Edwin. *Salem is My Dwelling Place: A Life of Nathaniel Hawthorne*. Duckworkth (1991). pp. 606. ISBN 0715624008.

Mobley, Marilyn Sanders. *Folk Roots and Mythic Wings in Sarah Orne Jewett and Toni Morrison: The Cultural Function of Narrative*. LSUP (1991).

Monteiro, George, ed. *The Correspondence of Henry James and Henry Adams, 1877–1914*. LSUP (1992). pp. 128. ISBN 0807117293.

Morey, Ann-Janine. *Religion and Sexuality in American Literature*. CUP (1992). pp. 304. ISBN 0521416760.

Moss, Elizabeth. *Domestic Novelists of the Old South: Defenders of Southern Culture*. LSUP.

Mudimbe, V. Y., ed. *The Surreptitious Speech: 'Presence Africaine' and the Politics of Otherness*. UChicP. ISBN 0226545075.

Munk, Linda. *The Trivial Sublime: Theology and American Poetics*. Macmillan. ISBN 0333539877.

Murfin, Ross, ed. *The Scarlet Letter: Nathaniel Hawthorne*. Macmillan. ISBN 0333575598.

Murphy, Brenda, ed. *A Realist in the American Theatre: Selected Drama Criticism of William Dean Howells*. OhioUP. ISBN 0821410369.

Myerson, Joel, ed. *Studies in the American Renaissance*. UPVirginia (1991). pp 436. ISBN 0813913373A.

Myerson, Joel, ed. *Emerson and Thoreau: The Contemporary Reviews*. CUP (1992). pp. 336. ISBN 0521 383366.

Nelson, Dale. *The Word in Black and White: Writing 'Race' in American Literature, 1638–1867*. OUP. ISBN 0195065921.

Peck, Daniel, ed. *New Essays on the 'Last of the Mohicans'*. CUP (1992). pp. 160. ISBN hb 0521374146, pb 0521377714.

Pfister, Joel. *The Production of Personal Life: Class, Gender & the Psychological in Hawthorne's Fiction*. StanfordUP (1991).

Posnock, Ross. *The Trial of Curiosity: Henry James, William James, and the Challenge of Modernity*. OUP. ISBN 0195066065.

Roman, Margaret. *Sarah Orne Jewett: Reconstructing Gender*. AlabamaUP (1992). pp. 248. ISBN 0817305335.

Scheick, William J. *Design in Puritan American Literature*. UPKen (1992). pp. 167. ISBN 0813117755.

Sealts, Merton. *Emerson on the Scholar*. UMissP (1992). pp. 352. ISBN 0826208312.

Sherman, Joan R., ed. *African-American Poetry of the Nineteenth Century: An Anthology*. UIllP. ISBN 0252062469.

Short, Bryan. *Cast by Means of Figures: Herman Melville's Rhetorical Development*. UMassP (1993). pp. 144. ISBN 0870238124.

Silverman, Kenneth, ed. *New Essays on Poe's Major Tales*. CUP (1993). pp. 144. ISBN hb 0521410185, pb 0521422434.

Sochen, June, ed. *Women's Comic Visions*. Wayne State UP (1991).

Stack, George. *Nietzsche and Emerson: An Elective Affinity*. OhioUP (1993). pp. 400. ISBN 0821410377.

Steele, Jeffrey, ed. *The Essential Margaret Fuller*. RutgersUP.

Sundquist, Eric J. *To Wake the Nations: Race in the Making of American Literature*. Harvard UP. ISBN 0674893301.

Traubel, Horace. *With Walt Whitman in Camden, Volume 7: July 7, 1890–February 10, 1891*. (ed. Jeanne Chapman and Robert MacIssac). Southern Illinois Press (1992).

Walton, P. L. *The Disruption of the Feminine in Henry James*. UTorP. ISBN 0802059872.

Winter, Kari J. *Subjects of Slavery, Agents of Change: Women and Power in Gothic Novels and Slave Narratives, 1790–1865*. UGeoP. ISBN 082031420X.

Wolstenholme, Susan. *Gothic (Re)Visions: Writing Women as Readers*. SUNY Press. ISBN 0791412199.

Wong, Hertha D. *Native American Autobiography: Pre-Contact Traditions and Contemporary Innovations*. OUP. ISBN 0195069129.

Chapter XVII. American Literature: The Twentieth Century

Bassett, John E. *Harlem in Review Critical Reactions to Black American Writers, 1917–1939*. SusquehannaUP (1992). ISBN 0945636288.

Beach, Christopher. *ABC of Influence Ezra Pound and the Remaking of American Poetic Tradition*. UCalP.

Bernstein, Charles. *A Poetics*. HarvardUP (1992). pp. 240. ISBN hb 0674678540, pb 0674678575.

Brooker, Jewel Spears, ed. *The Placing of T. S. Eliot*. UMissP (1991). pp. 216. ISBN 0826207936.

Callan, Ron. *William Carlos Williams and Transcendentalism: Fitting the Crab in a Box*. Macmillan (1992). pp. 176. ISBN 0333542932.

Chisholm, Dianne. *H. D.'s Freudian Poetics: Psychoanalysis in Translation*. CornUP.

Clayton, Jay and Eric Rothstein, eds. *Influence and Intertextuality in Literary History*. WisconsinUP (1992). pp. 360. ISBN hb 0299130304, pb 0299130347.

Dickey, James. *The Whole Motion, Collected Poems, 1948–1992*. WesleyanUP (1992). pp. 448. ISBN 0819522023.

Erickson, Darlene Williams. *Illusion is More Precise than Precision: The Poetry of Marianne Moore*. UAlaP (1992). pp. 272. ISBN 081730570X.

Everson, William. *Naked Heart Talking on Poetry, Mysticism, and the Erotic*. UNMP.

Finnegan, Ruth. *Oral Poetry: Its Nature, Significance and Social Context*. IndianaUP (1992). pp. 328. ISBN hb 0253322006, pb 0253207088.

Gerogiannis, Nicholas, ed. *Ernest Hemingway: Complete Poems*. UNebP.

Gillman, Richard, and Michael Novak, eds. *Poets, Poetics, and Politics: America's Literary Community Viewed from the Letters of Rolfe Humphries, 1910–1969*. UKanP (1993). pp. 300. ISBN 0700605894.

Goldensohn, Lorrie. *Elizabeth Bishop: The Biography of a Poet*. ColUP (1993). pp. 328. ISBN 0231076630.

Greenblatt, Stephen, and Giles Gunn, eds. *Redrawing the Boundaries*. Modern Language Association of America (1992). pp. 595. ISBN hb 0873523954, pb 0873523962.

Heuving, Jeanne. *Gender in the Art of Marianne Moore: Omissions are not Accidents*. WayneStateUP.

Holden, Jonathan. *The Fate of American Poetry*. UGeoP (1992). pp. 176. ISBN hb 0820313645, pb 082031398X.

Hollahan, Eugene. *Crisis-Consciousness and the Novel*. UDelP (1992). pp. 269. ISBN 0874134455.

Hugo, Richard. *Making Certain it Goes on: The Collected Poems of Richard Hugo*. Norton (1992). pp. 478. ISBN 0393307840.

Kaye, Jacqueline, ed. *Ezra Pound and America*. Macmillan (1992). pp. 236. ISBN 0333558057.

Leggett, B. J. *Early Stevens: The Nietzschean Intertext*. DukeUP (1992). pp. 280. ISBN 0822312018.

Limon, Jose E. *Mexican Ballads, Chicano Poems: History and Influence in Mexican–American Social Poetry*. UCalP.

MacGowan, Christopher, ed. *William Carlos Williams Paterson*. Carcanet.

Marsack, Robyn. *Sylvia Plath: Open Guides to Literature*. OpenUP (1992). pp. 120. ISBN 0335093531, 0335093523.

Moramarco, Fred, and Al Zolynas, eds. *Men of Our Time: An Anthology of Male Poetry in Contemporary America*. UGeoP (1992). pp. 472. ISBN hb 0820314048, pb 0820314307.

Murphy, Margueritte S. *A Tradition of Subversion: The Prose Poem in English from Wilde to Ashbery*. UMassP (1992). pp. 192. ISBN 0870237810.

Newcomb, John Timberman. *Wallace Stevens and Literary Canons*. UMissP.

North, Michael. *The Political Aesthetic of Yeats, Eliot and Pound*. CUP (1992). pp. 288. ISBN 0521414326.

Pack, Robert. *The Long View: Essays on the Discipline of Hope and Poetic Craft*. UMassP (1991). pp. 288. ISBN 0870237616.

Pratt, William, and Robert Richardson, eds. *Homage to Imagism*. AMS (1992). ISBN 0404615902.

Reinfeld, Linda. *Language Poetry Writing as Rescue*. LSUP.

Richardson, J.A. *Falling Towers: The Trojan Imagination in the 'Waste Land', the 'Dunciad', and 'Speke Parott'*. AUP.

Scholnick, Robert J., ed. *American Literature and Science*. UKenP.

Schweik, Susan. *A Gulf So Deeply Cut: American Women Poets and the Second World War*. UWiscP (1991). pp. 392. ISBN 0299130401, 0299130444.

Schweizer, Harold, ed. *The Poetry of Irving Feldman: Nine Essays*. AUP.

Sharpe, Tony. *T. S. Eliot: A Literary Life*. Macmillan. pp. 208. ISBN hb 0333452771, pb 033345278X.

Weisberg, Richard. *Poethics: and Other Strategies of Law and Literature*. ColUP (1992). pp. 312. ISBN 0231074549.

Zapf, Hubert. *Kurze Geschichte der Anglo-Amerikanischen Literaturtheorie*. Wilhelm Fink (1991). pp. 263. ISBN 3770527070.

Chapter XVIII. New Literatures in English

Ackland, Joan, ed. *The Whirling Spindle: An Anthology of Poetry by Women*. National Council of Women of Victoria. pp. 173. ISBN 0959930116.

Albinski, Nan Bowman. *Directory of Resources for Australian Studies in North America*. pp. 211. ISBN 0732604354.

Alderman, Belle. *Best Books for Children*. Ashton Scholastic. pp. 120. ISBN 0868968706.

Aldrich, Robert, and Gary Wotherspoon, eds. *Gay Perspectives: Essays in Australian Gay Culture*. SydneyUP. pp. 197. ISBN 0867585633.

Anderson, Don. *Real Opinions: Polemical and Popular Writings*. McPheeG. pp. 239. ISBN 0869142763.

Barry, Elaine. *Fabricating the Self: The Fictions of Jessica Anderson*. UQP. pp. 215. ISBN 0702223999.

Bassett, Marnie. *The Governor's Lady: Mrs Philip Gidley King: An Australian Historical Narrative*. UMelP. pp. 142. ISBN 0522844995.

Bayard, Caroline, ed. *100 Years of Critical Solitudes: Canadian and Quebecois Criticism from the 1880s to the 1980s*. ECW (1992).

Bean, C. E. W. *Making the Legend: The War Writings of C. E. W. Bean*. UQP. pp. 246. ISBN 0702223980.

Beckett, Wendy. *Peggy Glanville-Hicks*. HarperCollins/A&R. pp. 214. ISBN 0207170576.

Bennett, Bruce, and Dennis Haskell, eds. *Myths, Heroes and Anti-Heroes: Essays on the Literature and Culture of the Asia–Pacific Region*. UWAP. pp. 223. ISBN 0864222211.

Bennett, Bruce, and Susan Miller, eds. *Peter Cowan: New Critical Essays*. UWAP (1993). pp. 158. ISBN 1875560106.

Blight, John. *Selected Poems 1939–1990*. UQP. pp. 283. ISBN 0702224251.

Bolton, Ken. *Selected Poems 1975–1990*. Penguin. pp. 192. ISBN 0140586881.

Bottomley, Gillian. *From Another Place: Migration and the Politics of Culture*. CUP (1992). pp. 200. ISBN 0521410142.

Bourke, Lawrence. *A Vivid Steady State: Les Murray and Australian Poetry*. NSWUP. pp. 174. ISBN 0868400459.

Brennan, Christopher. *Poems (1913)*. HarperCollins/A&R. pp. 178. ISBN 0207174504.

Brennan, Frank. *Sharing the Country: The Case for an Agreement between Black and White Australians*. Penguin. pp. 176. ISBN 0140138676.

Broadbent, James, and Joy Hughes, eds. *The Age of Macquarie*. UMelP. pp. 194. ISBN 052284460X.

Broinowski, Alison. *The Yellow Lady: Australian Impressions of Asia*. OUP (Australia). pp. 260. ISBN 0195533828.

Bulbeck, Chilla. *Australian Women in Papua New Guinea: Colonial Passages 1920–1960*. CUP (1992). pp. 360. ISBN 0521412854.

Carroll, John, ed. *Intruders in the Bush: The Australian Quest for Identity*. OUP (1982). pp. 256. ISBN 0195533747.

Carter, Paul. *The Sound in Between: Voice, Space and Performance*. NSWUP and New Endeavour Press. pp. 198. ISBN 0868401099.

Chesaina, C. *Oral Literature of the Kalenjin*. Heinemann (Kenya) (1991). pp. 167. ISBN 9966468919.

Clyde, Anne, and Marjorie Lobban. *Out of the Closet and into the Classroom: Homosexuality in Books for Young People*. D. W. Thorpe (1992). pp. 200. ISBN 1875589023.

Cooley, Dennis, ed. *Inscriptions: A Prairie Poetry Anthology*. Turnstone (1992).

Cranny-Francis, Anne. *Engendered Fictions: Analysing Gender in the Production and Reception of Texts*. NSWUP. pp. 288. ISBN 086840165X.

De Groen, Frances, and Peter Pierce, eds. *Xavier Herbert: Episodes from Capricornia, Poor Fellow my Country and Other Fiction, Nonfiction and Letters*. UQP. pp. 326. ISBN 0702224081.

Docker, John. *Dilemmas of Identity: The Desire for the Other in Colonial and Post-Colonial Cultural History*. SRMCAS. pp. 18. ISBN 1855070375.

Donaldson, Ian, Peter Read, and James Walter, eds. *Shaping Lives: Reflections on Biography*. ANUP. pp. 296. ISBN 073151470X.

Doyle, James. *Stephen Leacock: The Sage of Orillia*. Canadian Biography Series ECW.

Dunton, Chris. *Make Man Talk True: Nigerian Drama in English since 1970*. Hans Zell Publishers (1992). pp. 240. ISBN 0905450876.

Dutton, Geoffrey, ed. *Country Childhoods*. UQP. pp. 227. ISBN 0702224340.

Duwell, Martin, and Laurie Hergenhan, eds. *The Als Guide to Australian Writers*. UQP. pp. 370. ISBN 0702224391.

Emenyonu, Ernest. *Studies on the Nigerian Novel*. Heinemann Educational Publishers (1991).

Fee, Margery. *Silence Made Visible: Howard O'Hagan and Tay John*. ECW (1992).

Ferrier, Carole, ed, *As Good as a Yarn with you: Letters Between Miles Franklin, Katherine Susannah Prichard, Jean Devanny, Marjorie Barnard, Flora Eldershaw and Eleayor Dark*. CUP. pp. 448. ISBN 0521393140.

Ferrier, Carole, ed. *Gender, Politics and Fiction: Twentieth-Century Women's Novels*. 2nd edn. UQP (1985). pp. 316. ISBN 0702223344.

Foott, Bethia. *Ethel and the Governors' General: A Biography of Ethel Anderson (1883–1958) and Brigadier-General A. T. Anderson (1868–1949)*. Rainforest Publishing. pp. 282. ISBN 0947134069.

Fotheringham, Richard. *Sport in Australian Drama*. CUP (1992). pp. 280. ISBN 0521401569.

Fraser, Janet, ed. *Canadian Literature Index 1988: A Guide to Periodicals and Newspapers. Cumulative Index to 1988 Publications*. ECW (1992).

Gallagher, Nancy Elizabeth, ed. *A Story to Tell: The Working Lives of Ten Aboriginal Australians*. CUP (1992). pp. 144. ISBN 0521424321.

Giles, Fiona, ed. *Melanie*. Picador. pp. 314. ISBN 0725106948.

Ginibi, Ruby Langford. *Real Deadly*. A&R (1992). pp. 111. ISBN 0207174210.

Goldsworthy, Peter, and Brian L. Matthews. *Magpie*. Wakefield (1992). pp. 143. ISBN 1862542724.

Gorman, G.E., ed. *Australian Studies: Acquisition and Collection Development for Libraries*. Mansell Cassell. pp. 368. ISBN 0720121345.

Gould, Alan. *Formerlight: Selected Poems*. A&R (1992). pp. 138. ISBN 0207170568.

Grace, Sherrill. *Swinging the Maelstrom: New Perspectives on Malcolm Lowry*. McG-QUP (1992). pp. 296. ISBN 0773508627.

Gunew, Sneja, and Kateryna Longley, eds. *Striking Chords: Multicultural Literary Interpretations*. A&U. pp. 256. ISBN 1863730893.

Gunew, Sneja, Lolo Houbein, Alexandra Karakostas-Seda, and Jan Mahyuddin, comps. *A Bibliography of Australian Multicultural Writers*. Deakin UP. pp. 291. ISBN 0730015033.

Gwynn-Jones, Terry, ed. *By the Seats of their Pants: More Great Australian Air Stories*. UQP. pp. 215. ISBN 0702223654.

Harris, Margaret, and Elizabeth Webby, eds. *Reconnoitres: Essays in Australian Literature in Honour of G. A. Wilkes*. SUP (1993). pp. 252. ISBN 0424001810.

Harris, Michael. *Outsiders & Insiders: Perspectives of Third World Culture in British and Post-Colonial Fiction*. Peter Lang (1992). pp. 203. ISBN 0820416681.

Hart, Kevin. *A. D. Hope*. OUP (1993). pp. 130. ISBN 0195532686.

Heffernan, James A. W., ed. *Representing the French Revolution: Literature, Historiography, and Art*. UPNE (1992). pp. 416. ISBN hb 0874515653, pb 0874514866.

Hergenhan, Laurie, ed. *The Australian Short Story: A Collection: 1890s–1990s*. UQP. pp. 351. ISBN 0702223484.

Hewett, Dorothy. *Collected Plays*. Currency (1992). pp. 274. ISBN 0868191663.

Hope, A.D. *Selected Poems*. A&R. pp. 269. ISBN 0207177597.

Hungerford, T. A. G. *The Ridge and the River (1952)*. Penguin. pp. 220. ISBN 0140175857.

Hutcheon, Linda, ed. *Double-Talking: Essays on Verbal and Visual Ironies in Contemporary Canadian Art and Literature*. ECW (1992).

Ikonne, Chidi, Emelia Oko, and Peter Onwudinjo, eds. *African Literature and African Historical Experience*. Heinemann (1991). pp. 136. ISBN 9781291850.

Johnson, Colin. *Wild Cat Falling*. A&R. pp. 131. ISBN 0207174466.

Johnston, Grahame, Joy W. Hooton and Harry Heseltine. *Annals of Australian Literature* 2nd edition. OUPA (1993). pp. 367. ISBN 0195534751.

Jolley, Elizabeth. *Central Mischief*. Penguin. pp. 207. ISBN 0670843148.

Jones, Eldred, ed. *The Question of Language in African Literature*. African Literature Today 17. Currey (1991). pp. 192. ISBN 085255 5172.

Jones, Eldred, ed. *Orature in African Literature Today*. African Literature Today 18. Currey (1992). pp. 192. ISBN 0852555180.

Jurgensen, Manfred. *Eagle and Emu: German-Australian Writing 1930–1990*. UQP. pp. 438. ISBN 0702223573.

Kershaw, Alister. *Collected Poems*. A&R. pp. 143. ISBN 0207176116.

Kertzer, Jon. *'That House in Manawaka': Margaret Laurence's A Bird in the House*. Canadian Fiction Studies II. ECW (1992).

King, Bruce, ed. *Post-Colonial English Drama: Commonwealth Drama Since 1960*. Macmillan (1992). pp. 284. ISBN 0333534174.

Kirkpatrick, Peter. *The Sea Coast of Bohemia: Literary Life in Sydney's Roaring Twenties*. UQP. pp. 368. ISBN 0702224324.

Knight, Stephen. *Sterling Settlement and Colonial Currency: Post Colonial Patterns in Australian Crime Fiction*. SRMCAS (1993). pp. 13. ISBN 1855070561.

Koval, Ramona. *One to One*. ABC Enterprises. pp. 187. ISBN 073330110X.

Kuester, Martin. *Framing Truths: Parodic Structures in Contemporary English-Canadian Historical Novels*. UTorP (1993). pp. 192. ISBN 0802028187, 0802076904.

Kuwabong, Dannabang, Naa Konga. *A Collection of Dagaaba Folktales*. Woeli Publishing Services (1992). pp. 81. ISBN 9964978073.

Langhelle, Carol. *The Counterfeit and the Real in Jack Hodgins' the Invention of the World*. Nordic Association for Canadian Studies (1992).

Lecker, Robert, Jack David, and Ellen Quigley, eds. *Canadian Writers and their Works: Poetry Series*. Volume VIII. ECW (1992).

Llewellyn, Kate. *Selected Poems*. Hudson Publishing. pp. 128. ISBN 094987339X.

Lucas, Robin, Clare Forster, eds. *Wilder Shores: Women's Travel Stories of Australia and Beyond*. UQP. pp. 229. ISBN 0702224774.

Lyons, Martyn, and Lucy Taksa. *Australian Readers Remember: An Oral History of Reading 1890–1930*. OUPA (1992). pp. 230. ISBN 0195533046.

McCrae, Hugh, ed. *Georgiana's Journal (1934) by Georgiana McCrae*. A&R. pp. 262. ISBN 0207175640.

McCredden, Lyn. *Oxford Australian Writers: James Macauley*. OUPA. pp. 118. ISBN 0195533496.

McCuaig, Ronald. *Selected Poems*. HarperCollins/A&R. pp. 124. ISBN 0207174296.

McFarlane, Brian, and Geoff Mayer. *New Australian Cinema: Sources and Parallels in American and British film*. CUP (1992). pp. 272. ISBN hb 0521383633, pb 052138768X.

Macleod, Jock, and Patrick Buckridge, eds. *Books and Reading in Australian Society*. Griffith University Press. pp. 154. ISBN 0868574619.

Maja-Pearce, Adewale. *A Mask Dancing: Nigerian Novelists of the Eighties*. Hans Zell Publishers (1992). pp. 240. ISBN 0905450922.

Malouf, David. *Poems 1959–89*. UQP. pp. 242. ISBN 0702224103.

Mant, Gilbert, ed. *Soldier Boy: The Letters and Memoirs of Gunner W. J. Duffell 1915–1918*. SPA Books (1992). pp. 168. ISBN 090759039X.

Masters, Chris. *Inside Story*. A&R (1994). pp. 248. ISBN 0207161763.

Monk, Patricia. *Mud and Magic Shows: Robertson Davies's Fifth Business*. Canadian Fiction Studies 13. ECW (1992).

Moore, Susan. *What Should My Child Read?* Albatross. pp. 175. ISBN 0867600411.

Moorhouse, Frank. *The Americans, Baby*. A&R (1989). pp. 258. ISBN 0207159726.

Muecke, Stephen. *Textual Space: Aboriginality and Cultural Studies*. NSWUP. pp. 214. pb ISBN 0868401013.

Muir, Marcie and Kerry White, eds. *Australian Children's Books: A Bibliography*. UMelP (1992). pp. 569. ISBN 0522844561.

Murray, Kevin D. S., ed. *The Judgement of Paris: Recent French Theory in a Local Context*. A&U (1991). pp. 192. ISBN 1863730559.

National Centre for Australian Studies, comp. *International Directory of Australian Studies*. International development program of Australian universities and colleges. pp. 106. ISBN 0732604206.

Nickas, Helen. *Migrant Daughters: The Female Voice in Greek-Australian Prose Fiction*. Owl Publishing. pp. 272. ISBN 0646101307.

Niechoda, Irene. *A Source for Books 1 and 2 of B. P. Nichol's 'The Martyrology'*. ECW (1992).

Nnolim, Charles, ed. *Ken Saro Wiwa's Sozaboy: A Novel in Rotten English*. Saros International Publishers (1992).

Nowra, Louis. *Summer of the Aliens*. Currency (1992). pp. 84. ISBN 0868193259.

Nunukul, Oodgeroo. *Stradbroke Dreamtime*. A&R (1972). pp. 103. ISBN 0207176167.

Ojinmah, Umelo. *Chinua Achebe: New Perspectives*. Spectrum Books (1991). pp. 128. ISBN 9782461164.

Oram, James. *The Last Showman: Larry Dulhunty's Larrikin Life*. PanMacmillan. pp. 245. ISBN 0725107065.

Page, Geoff, ed. *On the Move: Australian Poets in Europe*. Butterfly. pp. 149. ISBN 0947333509.

Panofsky, Ruth. *Adele Wiseman: An Annotated Bibliography*. ECW (1992).

Park, Ruth. *A Fence Around the Cuckoo*. Penguin. pp. 294. ISBN 0670846791.

Park, Ruth. *The Harp in the South (1948)*. Penguin. pp. 230. ISBN 0140146962.

Pearce, Sharyn. *The Shameless Scribbler: Louisa Lawson*. SRMCAS. pp. 32. ISBN 185507043X.

Pershall, Mary K. *A Long Way Home*. PenguinA. pp. 300. ISBN 0140129979.

Prentice, Jeffrey, and Barbara Bennett. *A Guide to Australian Children's Literature*. D. W. Thorpe. pp. 200. ISBN 1875589112.

Reid, Ian. *Narrative Exchanges*. Routledge (1992). pp. 265. ISBN 0415072344.

Richardson, Henry Handel. *The Getting of Wisdom (1910)*. Virago (1981). pp. 256. ISBN 0860681793.

Riddell, Elizabeth. *Selected Poems*. A&R (1992). pp. 132. ISBN 0207173451.

Ripley, Gord and Anne Mercer, ed. *Who's Who in Canadian Literature 1992–93*. Reference (1992).

Roscoe, Adrian A., and Mpalive-Hangson Msiska. *The Quiet Chameleon: Modern Poetry from Central Africa*. Hans Zell (1992). pp. 240. ISBN 0905450523.

Ross, Catherine Sheldrick. *Alice Munro: A Double Life*. Canadian Biography Series. LECW (1992).

Rowlands, Graham. *Selected Poems*. Wakefield Press. pp. 24. ISBN 1862542759.

Rutherford, Anna, ed. *Populous Places: Australian Cities and Towns*. Dangaroo (1993). pp. 295. ISBN 1871049776.

Ryan, Peter. *Fear Drive my Feet (1959)*. UMelP (1960). pp. 230. ISBN 0140172564.

Semmler, Clement, ed. *A. B. 'Banjo' Paterson: Bush Ballads, Poems, Stories and Journalism*. UQP. pp. 317. ISBN 0702223077.

Shiell, Annette, and Peter Spearritt. *The Lie of the Land: Exhibition Catalogue*. Monash University. pp. 64. ISBN 073260298X.

Simpson-Housley, Paul and Gled Norcliffe. *A Few Acres of Snow: Literary and Artistic Images of Canada*. Dundurn (1992).

Smith, Sidonie, and Julia Watson, eds. *De-Colonizing the Subject: The Politics of Gender in Women's Autobiography*. UMinnP (1992). pp. 512. ISBN hb 0816619913, pb 0816619921.

Smythe, Karen E. *Figuring Grief: Gallant, Munro, and the Poetics of Elegy*. McG-QUP (1993). pp. 216. ISBN 0773509399.

Soderlind, Sylvia. *Margin/Alias: Language and Colonization in Canadian and Quebecois Fiction*. UTorP (1991). pp. 264. ISBN hb 0802059031, pb 0802068456.

Sparrow, Fiona. *Into Africa with Margaret Laurence*. ECW (1992).

Stead, Christina. *A Web of Friendship: Selected Letters (1928–1973)*, ed. R. G. Geering. HarperCollins/A&R. pp. 497. ISBN 0207168881.

Stead, Christina. *Talking into the Typewriter: Selected Letters (1973–1983)* ed. R. G. Geering. pp. 402. ISBN 0207170762.

Steele, Peter. *Peter Porter*. OUPA (1993). pp. 120. ISBN 0195532821.

Stevens, Peter. *Dorothy Livesay: Patterns in a Poetic Life*. Canadian Biography Series. ECW (1992).

Stovel, Nora. *Rachel's Children: Margaret Laurence's 'A Jest of God'*. Canadian Fiction Studies 12. ECW (1992).

Strauss, Jennifer. *Boundary Conditions: The Poetry of Gwen Harwood*. UQP. pp. 223. ISBN 070222412X.

Stuart, Lurline. *A Very Busy Smith: An Annotated Checklist of the Works of James Smith, Nineteenth-Century Melbourne Journalist and Critic*. National Centre for Australian Studies. pp. 122. ISBN 0732602971.

Sugars, Cynthia, ed. *The Letters of Conrad Aitken and Malcolm Lowry, 1929–1954*. ECW (1992).

'Sybylla' ed. *Second Degree Tampering: Writing by Women*. Sybylla Feminist Press. pp. 188. ISBN 0908205104.

Veit-Wild, Flora. *Teachers, Preachers, Non-Believers: A Social History of Zimbabwean Literature*. Hans Zell (1992). pp. 320. ISBN 1873836155.

Veit-Wild, Flora. *Dambudzo Marechera: A Source Book on his Life and Work*. Hans Zell (1992). pp. 400. ISBN 0905450973.

Walker, David, Julia Horne, and Martyn Lyons, eds. *Books, Readers, Reading*. Deakin University. pp. 142. ISSN 07828433.

Ward, Peter. *A Singular Act: Twenty Five Years of the State Theatre Company of South Australia*. Wakefield (1992). pp. 157. ISBN 1862542732.

Weller, Archie. *The Day of the Dog* . A&U (1993). pp. 167. ISBN 1863732411.

Whiteman, Bruce, ed. *The Letters of John Sutherland. 1942–1956*. ECW (1992).

Whitlock, Gillian, and David Carter, eds. *Images of Australia*. UQP. pp. 269. ISBN 0702224472.

Who's Who of Australian Children's Writers. D. W. Thorpe (1992). pp. 240. ISBN 0909532990.

Williams, Margaret. *Dorothy Hewett: The Feminine as Subversion*. Currency (1992). pp. 161. ISBN 0868193208.

Index I. Critics

Authors such as Margaret Atwood and Salman Rushdie, who are both authors of criticism and subjects of discussion by critics, are listed in whichever index is appropriate for each reference.

Aaron, Jane 306–7
Aarsleff, Hans 22
Abbandonato, Linda 504
Abbott, Barbara 57
Abbott, H. Porter 411–12
Abels, Richard 91
Abercrombie, David 17, 23, 35
Abraham, Lyndy 211, 550
Abrams, Lesley 114
Abrams, Robert E. 448
Acheson, James 362
Acker, Paul 70
Ackerley, Chris 400
Ackerman, John 402
Ackland, Michael 549
Adam, Ian 555
Adams, Bronte 7
Adams, Charles Hansford 438–9
Adams, Hazard 280
Adams, Ian 553
Adams, James Eli 341
Adams, Jon-K. 64
Adams, Percy G. 430
Adams, Robert 104
Adams, Timothy Dow 499
Adamson, Arthur 526
Adamson, Robert 540
Adegbija, Efurosibina 63
Adelaide, Debra 533
Aercke, Kristiaan 244
Aers, L. 166
Aertsen, H. 135
Agari, Masahiko 229
Ahmansson, Gabriella 521
Aijmer, Karin 16, 56
Aiken, Conrad 465
Aitchison, Jean 19
Akindele, Femi 61
Alarcon, Norma 486
Albinski, Nan Bowman 533, 579
Alexander, Christine 339
Alexander, Doris 332, 335, 337
Alexander, Elizabeth 487
Alexander, Flora 524
Alexander, Lynn M. 333
Alexander, Robert J. 188
Algeo, John 56
Alladina, S. 31
Allan, Keith 55
Allardice, Pamela 548
Allen, Donald 470–1
Allen, John J. 188
Allen, Mark 111, 129
Allen, Rosamund 106, 108
Allingham, Philip V. 320, 336
Alomes, Stephen 537, 538
Alsop, J. D. 151
Alston, Robin C. 9
Altenberg, Bengt 16, 17, 57
Altholz, Josef 354
Altick, Richard D. 327–8, 351
Altman, Denis 537
Alurista 487
Amabile, George 526
Amalric, Jean-Claude 415
Amano, Masachiyo 40
Ambrosini, Richard 369
Ammons, Elizabeth 432–3
Amorós, J. A. Alvarez 64
Amos, Ashley Crandell 57
Anaya, Rudolpho A. 487
Anderson, Don 539
Anderson, Douglas 407, 442
Anderson, Earl R. 56, 82
Anderson, Hugh 536
Anderson, J. J. 119
Anderson, John 52
Anderson, Patricia 9–10
Anderson, Peter 556
Anderson, Roland F. 340
Andersson, Theodore M. 83
Andreas, James 133
Andrew, Malcolm 127
Andrews, Malcolm 333
Angier, Carole 568
Anselment, Raymond A. 232, 241
Anzaldua, Gloria 486
Arac, Jonathan 292, 304, 433
Archer, Peter 415
Archibald, Elizabeth 107, 108, 137
Arkins, Brian 413
Armbrust, Crys 216
Armstrong, Nancy 260
Armstrong, Tim 320, 398
Aronoff, Mark 36
Arshagouni, Mary 214
Arthur, Kateryna Olijnk 551
Arthur, Ross G. 102
Ash, Ranjana 558
Ash, Susan 579
Ashley, Kathleen M. 102
Ashmead, John 250, 260
Ashton, Rosemary 340, 352
Astell, Ann W. 131
Astington, John H. 164, 187, 188
Astley, Neil 404, 414
Aston, Elaine 407
Atfield, J. R. 404
Atherton, James 380
Atkins, A. R. 375
Atkins, B. T. S. 55
Atkinson, William 400, 467

Atoye, Raphael 27
Attwell, David 204
Atwood, Margaret 510, 512
Auberleben, Eckhard 238, 403
Aubrey, James R. 499
Avery, Gillian 234
Axton, Marie 184
Aycock, Wendell 379
Ayres-Ricker, Brenda 341
Baayen, Harald 35, 36
Babcock, Robert 475
Bachinger, Katrina 299, 300
Bacigalupo, Massimo 475
Backman, Gunnar 439
Backschieder, Paula 231
Bacon, Jon Lance 233
Badonnel, Patrick 503
Bagchee, Shyamal 399
Baier, Annette C. 250–1
Bailer, Nancy 285
Bailey, Guy 46
Bailey, Richard 27–8
Baker, C. L. 41, 42
Baker, Denise N. 128
Baker, Houston A. Jnr 428, 433, 454, 487–8
Baker, Laura 205
Baker, Susan 197, 204–5
Baker, William 340
Baker-Smith, Dominic 144
Bakshi, Raj N. 29
Baldrick, Chris 3
Balliet, Gay L. 131
Ballin, Michael 380–1
Ballyn, Susan 556
Bamiro, Edmund 27
Banaji, Mahzarin 63
Bande, Usha 391
Bandry, Anne 264
Banham, Debby 75–6
Banham, Martin 169
Bann, Stephen 251
Banting, Pamela 580
Barash, Carol 249, 255–6
Barbarie, Nigel 512
Barbato, Louis R. 561
Barber, Charles 127
Barber, Nicholas 127
Barbour, Douglas 527–8, 580
Barbour, James 425
Barbour, Reid 207, 216
Bard, Margaret 530
Barish, Jonas 167, 168
Barker, Anthony 546
Barker, Stephen 409
Barker-Benfield, B. C. 72
Barnard, Rita 480
Barr, Helen 104
Barrell, John 306
Barry, John A. 56
Barry, Jonathan 251
Barth, J. Robert 290, 293
Bartlett, Lee 476–7
Bartolomeo, Joseph F. 263, 337
Barua, Dibakar 62
Bar-Yaacov, Lois 470
Bar-Yosef, Hamutal 64
Basker, James G. 250
Bassett, Jan 538
Bate, Jonathan 159, 175, 288
Bately, Janet M. 79, 91, 92–3
Bates, Catherine 151, 158
Bates, Tom 305
Battenburg, John D. 57
Bauerlein, Mark 449
Baugh, Edward 572
Bawcutt, N. W. 154–5
Bawcutt, Priscilla 110
Bawer, Bruce 428–9
Bayley, John 403
Baylor, Jeffrey 131
Baym, Nina 431
Baynard, Donn 26
Bazin, Nancy Topping 381
Beach, Christopher 465
Beadle, Richard 97
Beal, Joan 55, 64
Beale, Paul 3
Beardon, Colin 18
Beatty, C. J. P. 338
Beaugrande, Robert de 18–19
Beazel, James L. 300
Beckett, Samuel 380
Bednarz, James P. 192, 202–3
Beecher, D. A. 196
Beer, John 295–6
Beetham, Margaret 352
Begamudre, Ven 512
Beidler, Peter G. 107, 132
Beidler, Philip 491
Beilin, Elaine V. 145–6
Beja, Morris 379–80
Bell, Alan 32, 33
Bell, Ian 247–8
Bell, Ian F. A. 444
Bell, Millicent 444
Bell, Pearl K. 464
Bell, William 356
Belliappa, K. C. 560
Belsey, Catherine 222
Belt, Debra 148, 200
Benassis, M. C. 370
Bender, Bert 438
Bender, John 260
Benedict, Barbara M. 250
Benet, Diana Trevino 223
Bennett, A. J. 302
Bennett, Bruce 537, 555–6
Bennett, Donna 511
Ben-Porat, Ziva 60
Benskin, Michael 97
Benson, C. David 101–2, 124, 128, 136
Benstock, Bernard 378
Benstock, Shari 380, 443
Bent, Geoffrey 165
Bentley, D. M. R. 511
Bentley, G. E. 278, 283
Benton, Richard 26
Ben-Zvi, Linda 409
Bercovitch, Sacvan 443
van der Berg, Jan 83
Bergan, Bruce 130
Berger, Harry Jnr 149
Berger, Sidney E. 8
Berger, Thomas L. 177
Bergeron, David M. 174
Berghahn, Klaus L. 219, 380
Bergvall, Åke 146
Berlant, Lauren 442
Berlin, Brent 57
Bernac, Martin 5
Bernstein, Carol L. 328
Bernstein, Stephen 334
Beroud, Elizabeth 165
Berry, J. Bill 427
Berthoud, Jacques 265
Bertolet, Craig 108
Bertram, Paul 155
Besner, Neil 519

Besserman, Lawrence 139
Bevan, David 377, 384
Bevington, David 119, 182, 183
Bevis, Richard 257
Bhattacharyya, Jibesh 400
Biber, Douglas 19
Bickerton, Derek 29
Biggs, Frederick M. 94, 104–5
Biggs, Murray 204
Bigley, Bruce 289–90
Biletzki, Anat 21
Bindella, Marai Teresa 554
Binder, Wolfgang 571
Bindman, David 276, 277
Birch, David 61–2, 406
Bird, Carmel 549
Bird, Delys 550, 553
Birkett, Jean K. 338
Birkett, Jennifer 524
Birns, Nicholas 578
Bitel, Lisa M. 75
Björklund, Martina 61
Bjørge, Anne Kari 55
Black, Jeremy 231, 252
Black, Joel 307
Black, Michael 373
Blackburn, Mark 91
Blackburn, Thomas H. 226
Blackman, John 536
Blackmur, R. P. 465
Blake, Ann 554
Blake, Barry J. 535
Blake, N. F. 159
Blanch, Robert J. 101, 103
Blanchfield, Lynne S. 106
Bland, Cynthia Renée 22
Blann, Robinson 298
Blau, Herbert 410, 411
Bliss, Carolyn 551, 553
Blisset, William 202
Bloch, R. Howard 125–6
Blockley, Mary 86
Blom, J. M. 395
Bloom, Harold 463, 468, 472
Blouch, Christine 261
Blythe, David-Everett 169, 178
Blythe, Ronald 7–8
Boardman, Kathleen A. 499
Bodenheimer, Rosemarie 341
Boehrer, Bruce Thomas 178
Boenig, Robert 88–9, 130–1
Boffey, Julia 97, 109, 111, 113
Boguraev, Branimir K. 55
Bohlmann, Otto 369
Boily, Lisette 512
Boire, Gary 532, 582
Boitani, Piero 124
Bolinger, Dwight 23
Bollans, Sue 270
Bolt, Sydney 376
Bolton, Geoffrey 543
Bolton, W. F. 56
Bonaccorso, Richard 413
Bone, Drummond 299
Bonheim, Helmut 515
Booker, M. Keith 126, 383, 391–3
Boon, Richard 413
Boose, Linda 168
Booth, Alan 248
Booth, Roy 205
Borck, Jim Springer 246
Borecca, Art 414
Bornstein, George 455
Borris, Kenneth 148–9
Borroff, Marie 135
Borsley, Robert D. 18
Bose, Mishtooni 198
Boss, J. A. 149
Bosworth, David 394–5
Bould, Geoffrey 7
Bowden, Betsy 255
Bowen, Deborah 526
Bower, Anne L. 483
Bowers, Bege K. 123
Bowers, Rick 199–200, 530
Boxill, Anthony 559, 572
Boyd, Stephen 402
Boyers, Robert 469
Bradbrook, Muriel 196
Bradbury, Jane 58
Bradbury, Malcolm 361, 423, 424, 488
Braden, George 144
Bradley, David 164, 188–9
Bradley, James 76
Bradley, Laurel 355
Bradshaw, Graham 370, 395
Bradstock, Andrew 218
Bradstock, Margaret 545
Brady, Ivan 455
Brady, Jennifer 184, 201
Brady, Veronica 541, 542, 547, 554
Braeger, Peter C. 128, 129, 131, 133, 134, 135
Bragg, Lois 81
Brake, Laurel 8, 347, 348, 350, 352, 357
Brand, Dana 433–4
Braswell-Means, Laura 129
Brater, Enoch 409, 411
Brattin, Joel J. 335
Bredbeck, Gregory W. 229
Breen, Jennifer 396
Breeze, Andrew 56, 59, 86, 87–8, 92–3
Breiner, Laurence 572
Breivik, Leiv 49
Bremmer, Rolf H. Jnr 83
Brenmen, Brian 483
Brennan, Michael G. 186, 198
Brett, R. L. 287
Brewer, William D. 300
Brewster, Glen E. 282
Brewster, Yvonne 573–4
Breyer, Betty 338
Briggs, Julia 460
Brink, Jean R. 143, 150
Brint, S. D. 480
Brinton, Laurel 64
Brisbane, Katharine 547
Brissenden, R. F. 548
Bristol, Michael D. 171, 177
Bristow, Joseph 326, 366
Britton, Derek 112
Brivic, Sheldon 379
Brockbank, Philip 156
Broderick, George 20–1
Brodeur, Arthur Gilchrist 83
Brogan, Jacqueline V. 455, 481
Brogan, Kathleen 459
Brooker, Jewel Spears 399
Brooker, Peter 405
Brookes-Davies, Douglas 151
Brookes-Davies, Mary 151
Brooks, Cleanth 211–12, 255, 465
Brooks, David 556

Brooks, Helen B. 214
Brooks, Nicholas 91
Brooks, Van Wyck 448
Brophy, Elizabeth Bergen 261
Brown, Carolyn Whitney 204
Brown, Cedric C. 225
Brown, Ellen 444
Brown, J. R. 170
Brown, John 117
Brown, Keith 19
Brown, Lee Rust 296
Brown, Lloyd 572
Brown, Peter 113, 129
Brown, Richard 252
Brown, Ruth 542, 552
Brown, Stewart 561, 571
Brown, Vivian 35
Brown, Whitney 204
Browne, Piers 287
Bruccoli, Matthew J. 8
Brunner, Edward J. 470
Brunt, Clare 459–60
Bruster, Douglas 203
Bryant, Pauline 25
Bryson, Bill 2
Buchan, Norman 415
Buchman, Lorne M. 163–4
Buckley, J. 510
Buckley, Penelope 555
Buckley, Vincent 548
Buckridge, Patrick 547
Budd, Louis J. 467
Budick, Emily Miller 442
Budny, Mildred 91
Bulbeck, Chilla 538
Bullen, J. B. 350
Bullion, John L. 252
Bumke, Joachim 100
Bundtzen, Lynda K. 459
Burchfield, Robert 21
Burger, Henry G. 57
Burke, John J. 252
Burke, P. 33
Burling, William J. 233
Burnett, Mark Thornton 141, 199
Burnley, David 106
Burns, D. R. 553
Burridge, Kate 55
Burris, Sidney 404
Burrow, J. A. 104
Burrow, John 126
Burrows, J. F. 262
Burton, John 377
Bush, Clive 434
Bush, Ronald 399, 401, 455, 465
Buss, Helen M. 521
Butler, Douglas R. 242
Butler, Judith 425
Butler, Lance St John 409
Butter, P. H. 277
Butterfield, R. W. 469
Butterss, Peter 536
Butts, Dennis 330
Buwa, Balkrishna 503
Buzard, James 299
Byard, Margaret 223
Bygrave, Stephen 257
Byrd, Rudolph P. 482
Bywaters, David 235
Cable, Thomas 101
Cadogan, Mary 5
Cady, Edwin H. 467
Caffin, Elizabeth 576
Calder, Angus 304
Calderon, Hector 486
Calhoun, Thomas Osborne 240
Callaghan, D. 167
Calomino, Salvatore 219
Camargo, Martin 110, 138
Cameron, Barry 516
Cameron, Elspeth 518
Cameron, Kenneth 58–9
Camfield, Gregg 448
Campbell, A. P. 73
Campbell, George L. 19
Campbell, Gina 264
Campbell, June 388
Campbell, Patrick 289
Campbell, Sandra 519
Candido, Joseph 159
Cannon, Garland 23
Cantrell, Leon 548
Caplan, Rosemary E. 117
Capone, Giovanna 553–4
Carafiol, Peter 424–5
Cardwell, Guy 448–9
Carley, James P. 114
Carlson, David R. 108, 144, 145
Carpenter, Charles 405
Carpenter, Lynette 434
Carpenter, W. 300
Carrera-Suarez, Isabel 550
Carrington, Ildiko De Papp 523
Carroll, Mary 341
Carruthers, Leo M. 115
Carson, David 103
Cartelli, Thomas 163, 193, 201
Carter, Angela 8
Carter, Anne 321
Carter, J. 288
Carter, Paul 543
Cartey, Wilfred 566–7
Cartwright, John 109–10
Cartwright, Kent 163, 177
Case, Alison 318
Case, Sue-Ellen 406
Casey, Janet Galligani 323
Cassidy, Cheryl 350
Cassius, Claudia 409
Castan, Con 540, 557
Castillo, Debra A. 501
Castronovo, David 436
Catalano, Gary 555
Caughie, Pamela L. 382
Cave, Richard Allen 408
Cayzer, Elizabeth 333
Ceplair, Larry 442
Cerasano, S. P. 161, 190
Cervetti, Nancy 329
Chabram, Angie 486
Chaden, Caryn 431
Chambers, A. B. 214
Chambers, J. 29–30
Chambers, J. K. 24
Champagne, Claudia M. 227
Chance, Jane 83, 101, 129, 134, 139
Chandran, K. Narayana 400, 402
Chaney, Edward 223, 254
Chapin, Chester 256
Chapman, Wayne K. 397–8
Chase, Karen 342
Chayes, Irene H. 285
Cheadle, Brian 337–8
Cheng Lok Chua 499
Cheng, Vincent J. 378
Cher-Leng 29
Cheshire, Jenny 20, 24, 26, 30
Chevalier, Tracy 405

Chevrefils, M. 519
Chew, Shirley 522, 559
Chiba, Shuji 44
Chibka, Robert L. 265
Chichester, Teddi Lynn 315–16
Chickering, Howard 123
Childs, Donald J. 467
Chilton, Randolph 476
Chinitz, David 150
Chisholm, Dianne 460
Chorost, Michael 178–9
Christ, Carol 399, 465
Christensen, Jerome 296
Christian, Margaret 148
Ciampolini, Anna Foschi 513
Cifelli, Edward M. 464
Cinquemani, A. M. 223
Clancy, Jack 547
Claridge, Laura 265, 467
Clark, Axel 552
Clark, Constance 242
Clark, David R. 398
Clark, George 83, 95
Clark, Ira 227
Clark, James Andrew 145
Clark, Lorraine 279–80
Clark, Miriam M. 463, 496
Clark, Steve 257
Clarke, Bruce 379
Clarke, Graham 450
Clarke, S. H. 259
Clayton, Jay 333
Cleman, John 447–8
Clifford, D. J. H. 218
Clopper, Lawrence M. 116
Clough, Francis M. 93
Clower, John 554
Clucas, Stephen 216, 219, 240
Clyne, Michael 20, 535
Coad, David 552
Coates, John 307
Coates, Richard 58, 59
Coats, Jerry 354
Coatsworth, Elizabeth 91
Cochran, Peter 299, 300, 306
Codell, Julie F. 8, 355
Cohen, Patsy 542
Cohen, Paul B. 413
Cohen, Paula Marantz 445
Cohen, Walter 195
Cohn, Ruby 409, 411
Coiro, Ann Baynes 215
Colby, Robert A. 354
Cole, Ann 59
Cole, Lucinda 251
Cole, Steven E. 296–7
Coleborne, Bryan 248
Coleman, Peter 547
Coleman, Ross 534
Collier, Wendy E. J. 91
Collin, Dorothy W. 356
Collings, David 297
Collins, Bruce 424
Collins, Michael J. 176
Colman, Fran 48
Coltelli, Laura 486
Comeau, Paul 523
Conforti, Joseph 431
Conlee, John W. 112
Conley, Timothy K. 432
Conlon, John 350
Conradi, Peter 362
Constantine, Shirley 544
Conte, Joseph M. 455
Cook, Albert 292
Cook, Eleanor 480, 481
Cook, Eung-Do 28
Cook, Guy 62
Cooper, Andrew 301
Cooper, Carolyn 563
Cooper, Helen 98, 104
Cooper, John Xiros 465
Coote, John 6
Copeland, Nancy 242
Copeland, Rita 99, 108
Copley, Stephen 257, 269
Corbett, Grenville 18
Corbin, Peter 182, 183
Core, George 427
Cormack, Malcolm 254
Corns, Thomas N. 223, 295
Correale, Robert M. 131
Corse, Taylor 237, 257
Costello, Bonnie 463
Costopoulos-Almon, Olga 265–6
Cotter, James Finn 296
Cotton, Nancy 242
Coulmas, F. 33
Coupland, J. 32
Coupland, N. 32–3
Court, Franklin E. 337
Cousins, A. D. 150–1
Cousins, Anthony D. 212
Coustillas, Pierre 346
Couturier, Maurice 492
Cowan, Bainard 425, 491
Cowan, Peter 543
Cowen, Janet 108–9, 113
Cowgill, Bruce Kent 130–1
Cowles, David L. 336
Cowley, Ann C. 327
Cox, James M. 427
Cox, Jane 166
Cox, Murray 162
Cox, Philip 284
Cox, Robert 90
Craft, Catherine A. 261
Craig, Beth 28
Craig, D. H. 203–4
Crane, David 237–8
Crane, Mary Thomas 215
Crawford, Iain 335
Crawford, T. Hugh 439
Creeley, Robert 484
Creelman, David 521
Cresswell, Julia 58
Cressy, David 173
Crewe, Jonathan 174
Crick, Bernard 415
Crick, Julia 100
Crider, Richard 257
Crisman, William C. 258, 283
Crocker, Lester G. 249
Crocker-Owen, Gale R. 91
Crockett, Bryan 172, 292
Croft, Julian 550
Crompton, Louis 299
Crompton, Virginia 240
Cronan, Dennis 86
Crook, Nora 302
Crosby, Christina 328
Crosby, Dan Kenneth 293
Cross, J. E. 93–4
Cross, Paul 11
Crossan, Gregg 305
Crowley, Tony 17, 33
Crowther, Ian 369
Crump, R. W. 430, 481
Cruz, Isagani R. 29
Crystal, David 3, 19, 55
Cuddy, Lois A. 465
Cullen, Patrick 148
Cummings, Sherwood 449

Cunningham, John 116–17
Curnow, Sigi 535
Curran, Eileen M. 354
Currie, Gregory 362
Currie, Richard A. 337
Curtis, Paul M. 299
Cushman, Keith 374
Cutmore, Jonathan 354
Cutter, Martha J. 441
Cutting-Gray, Joanne 264
Cutts, John P. 116
Cutts, Martin 33
Daalder, Joost 147, 186
Dabb, Thomas 197–8
Dabydeen, David 4, 12, 248
D'Aguiar, Fred 572
Dahms, Moshie 510
Daiches, David 250
Dale, Judith 581
Damroach, Leo 260
Danchev, Andrei 49
Daniel, Helen 533, 539, 548–9
Daniel, Stephen H. 248
Darnell, Regna 24
Darst, David H. 211
Daruwala, Maneck H. 302
Das, Bijay Kamar 558
Dasenbrock, Reed Way 143–4, 476, 564
Daugherty, Beth Rigel 383
D'Avanzo, Mario L. 467–8
Davenport, W. A. 113
Davey, Frank 511, 515, 521
David, Alun 256
David, Jack 518
Davidson, Arnold 515, 516, 528
Davidson, Cathy N. 422, 431
Davidson, Clifford 116, 117
Davie, Donald 456, 472
Davies, Anthony 76
Davies, Gwendolyn 516, 528–9
Davies, James A. 402
Davies, Stevie 221–2
Davis, Adam Brooke 78–9, 104
Davis, Lennard J. 246, 260
Davis, R. H. C. 71–2
Davis, Steven 20, 57, 92
Davison, Graeme 543
Davison, John 250, 260
Davison, Peter 375
Dawson, Dierdre 250
Dawson, Sally 552
Day, Aidan 316, 326–7
Day, Gillian M. 173
Day, John T. 145
Day, Moira 532
Dean, James 108, 112
Dean, Misao 520–1
Dean, Paul 175, 395
Dean, Tim 477–8
Deane, Patrick 556
Deane, Seamus 366
De Bellis, Jack 503
Deegan, Marilyn 91
De Grazia, Margreta 156, 167
Degrois, Denise 295
De Haan, Pieter 46
De Jong, Kenneth 34
Delaney, Frank 6
Delaney, Samuel R. 488
Delasanta, Rodney 124
Dellamora, Richard 348–9
De Looze, Laurence N. 83
Delrez, Marc 578
De Luca, Vincent Arthur 279
Deluna, D. N. 431
Demurs, Patricia 273
Denham, Paul 527
Den Hartog, Dirk 538
Denholm, Michael 534–5
Den Otter, A. G. 284–5, 297
Derrick, Patty S. 161
Derry, Stephen 265
Descargues, Madeleine 264
Desmet, Christy 205
Dessomes, Lawrence K. 236–7
Dettmar, Kevin J. H. 409
Dever, Maryanne 555
Deverson, Tony 26, 58
Devlin, Kimberley J. 376, 379
Devlin-Glass, Frances 550
de Vegvar, Carol Neuman 70–1
De Voogd, Peter J. 246, 264
de Voto, Bernard 448
Diamond, Peter J. 250
DiBattista, Maria 367, 374
Di Benedetto, Vincent P. 227–8
Di Cesare, Mario A. 222–3
Dick, John A. R. 145
Dickey, Stephen 170
Dickie, Margaret 440, 478, 481
Diehl, Joanne Feit 443
Diekstra, F. N. M. 115
Diggory, Terence 483
Diller, Hans-Jürgen 55, 116
Dilnot, Alan 158
Dilworth, Thomas 402
Di Michele, Mary 526
Dimock, Wai-Chee 429, 433, 444
Dinshaw, Carolyn 108, 137
Diverres, Armel 114
Dixon, R. M. W. 25, 45, 58, 535
Dixon, Robert 553
Djwa, Sandra 511
Doane, A. N. 87
Dobson, Michael 161, 167, 238
Docherty, Gerald 385
Docherty, Thomas 405, 484
Docker, John 538, 539, 540
Dodgeson, John McN. 91
Doelman, Jim 147
Doherty, Gerald 64
Dolin, Kieran 533
Donaldson, Jeffrey 403–4
Donaldson, Susan V. 504
Donaldson, Tamsin 555
Donnelly, M. L. 225–6
Donnelly, William 304
Donner, Morton 38, 103
Donoghue, Daniel 82
Donoghue, Denis 378, 447, 456
Donovan, Josephine 448
Donovan, Kevin J. 184–5
Doody, Margaret Anne 263–4
Doran, Amanda-Jane 351
Dore, Helen 321
Dorfman, Deborah 280–1
Dorrbecker, Detlef W. 276
Dorscht, Susan Rudy 524
Dow, Gwyn 536
Dowden, Wilfred S. 305

Dowling, Linda 347
Downes, Margaret J. 284
Downey, Charlotte 21–2
Downie, J. A. 256
Dowrick, Stephanie 548
Doyno, Victor A. 449
Draper, R. P. 345, 375
Dry, Helen Aristar 62–3
Dubey, Vinod 29
Du Boulay, F. R. H. 105
Duckett, Bob 338–9
Dugaw, Dianne 256
Dukes, Thomas 387–8
Dukore, Bernard F. 408
Dumville, D. N. 100
Duncan-Jones, E. E. 239
Duncan-Jones, Katherine 146
Dunleavy, Janet Egleson 380
Dunlop, E. E. 548
Dunn, Douglas 404
Dunn, Margaret 563
Dunn, Stephen 480
Durix, Jean-Pierre 583
Dutton, Geoffrey 546
Dutton, Richard 192–3
Duyfhuizen, Bernard 240, 502
Dvorak, Wilfred P. 337
Dwyer, J. 304
Dwyer, John 250, 266
Dyer, Gary R. 331
Dyer, William D. 207
Dykstal, Timothy 240
Dymond, David 192
Dzelzainis, Martin 225
Eaden, Robin 550
Eades, Diana 25
Eagleson, Robert 33
Eagleton, Terry 340, 366, 404
Earl, James W. 85
Easingwood, Peter 514, 522
Easson, Angus 328, 330
Easting, Robert 109, 111, 112
Eaton, Roger 105–6
Eberwein, Jane D. 430
Eccles, Mark 190
Echard, Sian 108
Eckhardt, Caroline D. 100
Ecsedy, Judith 10
Edelman, Charles 189–90
Edmond, Mary 166
Edmond, Murray 581
Edmunds, Susan 464
Edwards, A. S. G. 108, 132, 134, 139
Edwards, Barry 300
Edwards, G. 169
Edwards, Gavin 305
Edwards, Lee 355
Edwards, Paul 4, 12, 248
Edwards, Philip 167
Edwards, Robert R. 124, 134–5, 136, 138, 139
Edwards, V. 31
Egger, Werner Bronimann 255
Eichler, Rolf 413
Eisikovits, Edina 30
Eldredge, Larry E. 114
El-Hassan, Karla 515
Elkins, Andrew 483–4
Elledge, Paul 300
Elliot, Jeffrey M. 498
Elliott, Emory 422–3, 432
Elliott, Ward 158
Ellis, Deborah S. 134
Ellis, Roger 112
Ellis, Steve 401, 465–6
Ellis, William 436–7
Ellman, Richard 482
Emery, Jane 384
Emmerson, Richard K. 111
Engel, Manfred 284
Engler, Balz 60
Enkvist, Nils Erik 60
Enlund, Nils 10
Enright, D. J. 6, 7
Ensing, Riemke 578
Entzminger, Robert L. 224
Epps, Garrett P. J. 117
Epstein, Julia 264
Epstein, William H. 246, 259, 296
Erdinast-Vulcan, Daphna 369–70
Erdman, David V. 281
Erickson, Jon 410
Erickson, Kathleen Powers 244
Ericson, Edward E. 228
Eriksen, Roy 224
Espinal, Teresa 43
Essick, Robert N. 276, 277, 278–9, 281, 285, 308
Esslin, Martin 409
Esteves, Carmen C. 562
Estrin, Barbara 480
Evans, Lawrence 346
Evans, Marian 352
Evans, Patrick 577
Evans, Robert C. 202
Evans, T. F. 415
Everest, Kelvin 304, 307
Everett, Barbara 174
Everman, Welch D. 499–500
Everson, William 469
Evert, Walter H. 301
Ewbank, Inga-Stina 167
Ewell, Barbara 569–70
Ezell, Margaret J. M. 235
Fabre, Michael 435, 456–7, 565–6
Fabricant, Carole 246
Factor, June 536
Fairer, David 256, 257, 309
Fairhall, James 377
Fanego, Teresa 51
Fanger, Claire 88, 108
Fanning, Steven 56, 71
Farkas, Anne 317
Farley-Hills, David 147, 191
Fathman, Anthony E. 399
Favier, Dale A. 139
Faxon, Alicia 355
Feather, John 9
Featherstone, Simon 385
Federico, Annette 339, 344
Fee, Margery 579
Feeney, Joseph J. 320
Fein, Susanna Greer 128, 129, 130, 133, 134, 136
Feinstein, Sandy 131
Fell, Christine 80
Fellow, Jay 347
Fellows, Jennifer 106
Ferber, Michael 281
Ferguson, Frances 274
Ferguson, Rebecca 257
Ferris, Connor 46–7
Ferris, David 290
Ferry, Jacqueline F. 578
Ferster, Judith 125
Fichte, Joerg O. 98
Field, Clive D. 253
Field, Frank 363

Field, John 59
Field, Rosalind 106
Fierobe, Claude 254
Fiet, Lowel 572
Figueroa, John 572
Filmer, Kath 328–9
Filppula, Markku 21
Filreis, Alan 478–9
Finch, G. J. 283, 403
Finneran, Richard J. 455
Firmager, Gabrielle M. 261
Fisch, Harold 298
Fischer, David Hackett 430
Fischer, Hermann 270–71
Fischer, Olga 50–1
Fischer-Seidel, Thérèse 406
Fisher, Nicholas 241
Fisher, Philip 448
Fisher-Wirth, Anne W. 483
Fishman, Charles 457
Fishman, Joshua 26
Fiske, Roger 253
Fisken, Beth Wynne 434–5
Fison, Lorimer 540–1
Fitzgerald, Judith 527
Fitzgibbon, Gerald 405
Fitzpatrick, Peter 547
Fitzpatrick, Tara 431
Fjågesund, Peter 373–4
Flannagan, Roy 222
Fleissner, Robert F. 156
Fleming, John 3
Flesch, William 457
Fletcher, Alan J. 99, 104, 105, 115, 134
Fletcher, Bradford Y. 113
Fletcher, Ian 354
Fletcher, M. D. 560
Fletcher, Robert P. 330
Flether, Alan J. 135
Fliegelman, Jay 431
Flieger, Aline 491
Fligelstone, Steven 17
Flinker, Noam 229
Flint, Kate 383
Fludernik, Monika 64
Flynn, Denis 214
Foakes, R. A. 187
Fogel, Daniel Mark 377
Foley, John Miles 78
Foley, Michael 525
Folsom, Ed 450, 461
Ford, Boris 2, 13
Forster, Jean-Paul 299
Forsyte, Charles 338
Forsyth, Ludmilla 540
Forsythe, R. A. 319
Foster, David 537, 544
Foster, Donald W. 161–2
Foster, Gretchen M. 248–9
Foster, Roy 351
Fothergill-Payne, Louise 188
Fothergill-Payne, Peter 188
Fowl, Melinda G. 385–6
Fowler, Alastair 5, 232, 368
Fowler, Bridget 367
Fowler, Roger 61
Fowler, Rowena 316
Fox, Christopher 258
Fox, Susan 281
Fox-Genevese, Elizabeth 427
Fradenburg, Louise O. 125
Frank, Hardy Long 135
Frank, Robert Worth Jnr 104
Frank, Roberta 79–80, 91
Frankis, John 55
Franklin, Colin 156
Franson, J. Karl 160, 172
Frantzen, Allen J. 77–8, 79, 84–5, 95, 98
Franzen, Christine 73–4
Fraser, Russell 169
Frayling, Christopher 7
Frazer, Winifred 190
Frazier, Adrian 406
Freedman, Jonathan 349
Freeman, Arthur 11
Freeman, Janet Ing 11
Freidrichs, Michael 515
Frickey, Pierrette 568–9
Friedberg, Anne 495
Friedman, Donald 223
Friedman, John B. 99–100
Friedman, M. D. 170
Friedman, Susan Stanford 459
Friel, Brian 405
Fries, Udo 55
Frisby, Deborah S. 86
Fromm, Gloria 383
Frosch, Thomas R. 281
Frost, Elizabeth A. 481
Frost, Everett C. 412
Froula, Christine 472
Fry, Dennis 35
Frye, Northrop 260, 281
Fuchs, Jacob 256
Fukuchi, Hajime 41
Fukuda, Shohachi 148
Fukui, Naoki 44
Fulford, Tim 294–5, 296
Fulk, R. D. 82–3
Fuller, David 378
Fulton, Richard 353
Fumerton, Patricia 209
Furbank, P. N. 262
Furniss, Tom 308
Fussell, Paul 387, 547–8
Fyfe, Christopher 4
Fyler, John M. 124–5
Fyrth, H. J. 415
Gager, Valerie L. 334
Gainer, Ellen 415
Gair, W. Reavley 182
Gajowski, Evelyn 177
Gallacher, Patrick J. 105
Gallagher, Lowell 142–3
Gallou, Laura 533–4
Galperin, William 295, 297
Ganim, John 126
Garaets, John 576
Garde, Judith N. 81
Gardiner, Anne Barbeau 231–2, 238
Gardner, Joseph H. 327
Gardner-Medwin, A. 184
Garlick, Barbara 555
Garner, Stanton B. Jnr 409
Garrett, George 427
Garrett, Martin 205
Garrett, Simon 581
Garrigan, Kristine O. 2, 13, 355
Garson, Marjorie 344
Garvin, Paul 23
Garza-Cuarón, Beatriz 57
Gascoyne, David 401–2
Gaskell, Ronald 290
Gasper, Julia 185, 205
Gatch, Milton McC. 80
Gatrell, Simon 345
Gaull, Marilyn 291–2, 295
Gaylord, Alan T. 134–5
Geering, R. G. 554
Geeta, P. 561
Gelder, Ken 541, 542, 554
Gelpi, Albert 428, 457
Gencer, Gun 557

Genet, Jacqueline 408
George, Diana Hume 477
George, J. Anne 88
Georgianna, Linda 133–4
Gerrard, Christine 256
Gerrig, Richard 63
Gerson, Carole 511
Gerster, Robin 538
Gewanter, David 320
Gianakaris, C. J. 414–15
Gibbons, Brian 154–5, 170
Gibbons, Peter 4, 574–5
Gibbs, Raymond 63
Gibson, James 345
Giddings, Robert 333–4, 364, 366, 414
Gidley, Mick 424
Gielgud, John 162
Gilbert, Helen 552
Gilbert, Paula 516
Gilbert, Roger 457–8
Gilbert, Sandra M. 274, 340
Gilbertson, Carol 476
Gilderdale, Betty 576
Giles, Fiona 555
Giles, H. 32–3
Gilkes, Michael 565, 566
Gill, Alan 547
Gill, Richard 214
Gill, Stephen 290
Gillen, Paul 556
Gillet, Sue 524, 557
Gilmore, William J. 429–30
Gilpin, George H. 365
Giner, Maria F. Garcia-Bermejo 340
Gingell, Susan 527
Gish, Nancy K. 399
Gitter, Elizabeth A. 334
Glaap, Albert-Reiner 515
Glance, Jonathan C. 344
Glasheen, Adeline 380
Glasser, Marion 150
Glauser, Beat 31
Glausser, Wayne 283
Gleason, John B. 302
Gleckner, Robert F. 298
Glickman, Susan 527
Glicksohn, J. 62
Glover, David 495
Gneuss, Helmut 79
Godard, Barbara 513, 516
Godden, Malcolm 79, 80
Goldberg, Jonathan 221
Goldberg, Leonard 299
Goldberg, Rita 248
Goldfarb, Sheldon 331
Goldman, Arnold 424
Goldsmith, Arnold 489, 494
Goldsmith, Margaret E. 83
Gontarski, S. E. 409
Goodall, Peter 375
Goodblatt, Chanita 62, 64
Gooderham, Tim 175
Goodheart, Eugene 455
Goodman, David 540
Goodman, Lizbeth 406, 573–4
Goodson, A. C. 295–6, 308
Goodwin, Jill Tomasson 531
Goonetilleke, D. C. R. A. 366
Gorak, Jan 491
Gordon, John 379
Gordon, Lyndall 399
Gordon, Robert 415
Görlach, Manfred 18
Gotera, Vincente F. 499
Gottlieb, Sidney 213
Gouws, John 170
Grace, Sherrill 516
Graham, Kenneth J. E. 178
Graham, Paul 332
Graham, Richard H. 145
Graham-Campbell, James 72
Granger, Sylviane 55
Grant, Agnes 514
Grant, Raymond J. S. 89
Grauerholz, James 495
Graver, Bruce E. 279, 289, 293–4
Gray, Martin 552, 553
Greco, Norma 284
Green, Dorothy 537
Green, Gayle 367
Green, Jennifer M. 414
Green, Katherine Sobba 261
Green, Martin 261–2
Green, Richard Firth 111, 132, 134
Greenbaum, Sydney 45
Greenberg, Joseph 23
Greenberg, Robert A. 324
Greenblatt, Stephen 166, 429
Greene, Gayle 167
Greene, Jack P. 430
Greenfield, Bruce 433
Greenfield, Cathy 538
Greenfield, Stanley B. 83
Greenfield, Susan C. 264
Greenhalgh, Anne 62
Greenslade, William 345
Greenstein, Michael 338
Greer, Michael 469
Gregerson, Linda 149–50
Gregory, Eileen 464
Gregory, Horace 469
Gregory, Jeremy 231, 252
Grene, Nicholas 414
Grey, Thomas C. 478–9
Gribble, Jennifer 554
Grice, Paul 255
Griffin, Dustin 223
Griffin, Gabrielle 407
Griffith, M. S. 91
Griffith, Michael 546–7
Griffiths, Bill 76
Griffiths, Gareth 566
Grimal, Pierre 3
Grimm, Reinhold 219, 380
Griswold, Charles 251
Groden, Michael 455
Gross, John 5–6
Gross, Konrad 514–15
Groves, David 286, 306
Grudin, Michaela Paasche 136, 168
Grundy, Karen 554
Grundy, Philip 548
Gruzelier, Claire 225
Grylls, David 346
Gubar, Susan 274, 340
Gugler, Marybeth 256
Guilfoyle, Cherrell 117
Gunew, Sneja 539, 540
Gunnars, Kristjana 512
Gura, Philip F. 432
Gurr, Andrew 141, 515, 522
Guss, Donald L. 229
Guthke, Karl S. 380
Gutierrez, Nancy A. 207
Guy, Gregory 24, 27
Guy, Josephinne M. 363
Gwilliam, Tassie 263
Haan, Estelle 224
Haegeman, Liliane 18
Hagan, Susan K. 132
Hagen, Patricia L. 397, 404

Hager, Alan 146
Haggerty, George H. 265
Hagstrum, Jean 281
Hahn, Thomas 124
Hair, Donald S. 324
Hale, John K. 224, 226, 229
Haley, David 235
Hall, A. Rupert 218–19
Hall, Anne Drury 217–18
Hall, Chris 502
Hall, Joan Lord 194, 204
Hall, N. John 338
Hall, Robert Jnr 24
Hall, Thomas N. 93
Hall, William Keith 151
Halliday, Mark 479
Halligan, Marion 537
Halpern, Richard 141–2
Hamalian, Leo 435
Hamalian, Linda 477
Hamel, Mary 135
Hamerow, H. F. 71
Hamilton, A. C. 147–8, 510
Hamilton, R. W. 176
Hamilton, Scott 472
Hammond, Antony 185
Hammond, Brean S. 257
Hammond, Catherine 541
Hammond, J. R. 380
Hammond, Paul 231, 235, 237
Hampton, Timothy 142
Handley, Graham 340
Handley, William 382
Hanks, D. Thomas Jnr 114
Hanley, Lynne 367, 381
Hanna, Cliff 543
Hanna, Gillian 407
Hannay, Margaret P. 148
Hans, James S. 463
Hansen, Elaine Tuttle 124
Hansen, Klaus P. 431
Hansson, Karen 551
Haouas, Ali 31
Happé, Peter 120
Harcourt, Peter 580
Harding, Anthony J. 293
Hardy, Donald E. 63
Harlow, Barbara 486
Harney, Steve 565
Harp, Richard 213
Harper, Phillip Brian 433
Harrex, Syd 559–60
Harries, Max 238
Harrington, John P. 407, 408
Harris, A. Leslie 113
Harris, Claudia W. 414
Harris, Frances 252–3
Harris, John 527
Harris, Joseph 83
Harris, Michael 11
Harris, Neil 223
Harris, Oliver C. G. 495
Harris, P. R. 11
Harris, Sharon 439–40
Harris, Susan K. 435
Harrison, Victoria 464
Hart, Henry 469–70
Hart, Jonathan 174
Hart, Kevin 556
Hartley, George 469
Hartman, Charles O. 458
Harty, John III 379, 480, 481
Harvey, A. D. 166
Harvey, Charles 322
Harvey, E. D. 144, 212
Harvey, Elizabeth 524
Harvie, Christopher 3, 328
Harwood, Britton J. 98, 101, 105
Haskell, Dennis 546, 556
Hasmann, Franz Josef 57
Hassall, A. J. 553
Hassan, Dolly 567–8
Hassan, Ihab 488, 495
Haste, Constance W. 321
Hatch, James V. 435
Hatt, Robert 472
Hattaway, Michael 155, 173
Hatten, Charles 225
Hatzimanolis, Efi 555
Haugland, Kari 55
Hawes, Donald 331
Hawkins, Sherman 173
Hawley, Judith 264
Hay, Douglas 252
Hayden, John O. 287–8
Hayles, Katherine 502
Haynes, Roslyn D. 555
Hayward, Malcolm 62
Hazo, Samuel 463
Headon, David 548
Healy, Thomas 216
Hearne, John 569
Hearst, Marti 56
Heffernan, James A. W. 254, 285
Heinemann, Margot 195
Heinzelman, Kurt 255
Helgerson, Richard 149, 210–11
Helinga, Lotte 10
Heller, Michael 461
Helm, James L. 206
Helmling, Steven 467
Helsinger, Elizabeth K. 323
Hemmerechts, Kristien 569
Henderson, Andrea 294
Henderson, Lesley 1, 361
Hendrix, Howard V. 143
Heng, Geraldine 103
Heninger, S. K. Jnr 149
Henke, Suzette 380, 578
Henley, Nancy 33
Hentzi, Gary 262
Heoppner, Kenneth 512
Heppner, Christopher 285
Herbert, Isolde Karen 322, 325
Herendeen, Wyman H. 184, 201–2, 224
Hergenhan, Laurie 540, 551
Herman, Peter C. 136
Herman, Vimala 63
Herr, Cheryl 376–7
Herreshoff, David Sprague 435
Herz, Judith Scherer 223
Hess-Lüttich, Ernest 60
Heuvel, Michael Vanden 410–11
Hewett, Dorothy 556
Hewitt-Smith, Kathleen M. 104, 137
Hibbard, Allen 480
Hickey, Patrick 330–1
Hieatt, A. Kent 148, 157, 172
Hieatt, Charles W. 157, 172
Higdon, David Leon 394
Higgins, Dick 488
Higgins, Lesley 320, 349
Highley, Christopher 173
Hildy, Franklin J. 187, 188
Hill, Alan G. 291–2
Hill, Archibald 23
Hill, F. J. 11

Hill, Geoffrey 234, 236
Hill, Greg 402
Hill, Joyce 75, 94
Hill, Thomas D. 105
Hiller, Geoffrey G. 210
Hillman, Richard 168, 173–4, 208
Hills, E. R. 539
Hinde, Thomas 344
Hinden, Michael 415
Hines, John 21
Hinojosa, Rolando 486
Hirsch, David H. 465
Hirsch, James 177
Hirschfield, Claire 406
Hirsh, John C. 429
Hirst, Wolf Z. 298, 299
Hoagwood, Terence Allan 299
Hoar, Stuart 581
Hobson, Fred 484–5
Hochberg, Shifra 336
Hochman, Barbara 441
Hodgdon, Barbara 172
Hodge, Robert 362, 540
Hodges, Laura F. 129
Hodgson, John A. 290
Hoenslaars, A. J. 196
Hoey, Michael 57
Hoffman, Manfred 145
Hoffmann, Lois 550
Hoffpauir, Richard 397, 403
Hogg, James 146
Holbrook, David 172
Holcomb, Kathleen 250
Holden, Jonathan 461
Holding, Peter 162–3
Holdsworth, R. V. 160, 170, 206
Hollington, Michael 332–3, 334–5
Holm, Janis Butler 146
Holmer, Joan Ozark 176
Holmes, David I. 56
Holmes, Frederick M. 391, 393
Holmes, Geoff 18
Holmes, Janet 26
Holt, R. F. 549
Holton, Robert 241
Holz-Davies, Ingrid 206
Homan, Sidney 409
Honda, Satomi 40
Honeygosky, Stephen R. 227
Honigman, Ernst 167
Honneyman, David 166
Honour, Hugh see Fleming, John (3)
Hooke, Delia 71
Hooker, Richard 226
Hooton, Joy 545
Hope, Jonathan 195
Hopkins, David 235
Horgan, Paul 399
Horne, Lewis 343
Horner, Avril 367
Horvath, B. 25, 32
Hoskins, Robert 253, 391
Hotho-Jackson, Sabine 382–3
Hotine, Margaret 198–9, 204
Houghton, Esther 354
Houston, Gail Turley 334
Howard-Hill, Trevor H. 161, 192, 206
Howarth, William 427
Howe, Lawrence 449
Howell, Peter 35
Howells, Coral Ann 514, 515, 519–20, 522, 524, 526, 569
Howells, W. D. 448
Howitt, A. W. 540
Howsam, Leslie 353
Hoy, James 138
Hoy, Pat C. II 427
Hoy, Philip 468
Hoyles, John 363
Hozeski, Bruce W. 123
Huggan, Graham 542
Huggins, Jackie 541
Hughes, Geoffrey 55
Hughes, Joan 58
Hughes, M. E. J. 100
Hulme, Peter 251
Humby, Terry 158, 168
Hume, Robert D. 233, 243
Humm, Maggie 366–7, 387, 389
Humphery, Anne 329
Hunt, Maurice 178
Hunt, Nigel 530
Hunt, Tim 468, 469
Hunter, George K 182, 183
Hunter, J. Paul 260
Hunter, Lynette 515, 522, 526, 528
Hurley, Michael 520
Hussey, Mark 381
Hutcheon, Linda 515
Hutcheson, B. R. 82
Hutchings, William 413
Hutchison, Stuart 435–6
Huttar, Charles A. 223
Hyland, Paul 248, 365
Hyland, Peter 493–4
Hymes, Dell 33
Ike-uchi, Masayuki 42–3
Ikin, Van 533
Iles, Gillian 301
Imhof, Rudiger 413, 414
Imison, Richard 407
Indyk, Ivor 548
Ingersoll, Earl G. 375, 523
Inman, B. A. 346
Inot, A. D. 172
Ioppolo, Grace 155–6, 161
Irace, Kathleen 159
Ireland, Colin A. 89–90
Irvine, Lorna 516
Irvine, Martin 78
Irving, Edward B. Jnr 83
Irving, Eric 547
Irwin, Ivor S. 394
Isaac, Peter 350–1
Iser, Wolfgang 255
Iserhagen, Hartwig 515
Iwakura, Kunihiro 40
Jack, George 51, 100
Jack, Ian 316
Jackaman, Rob 401–2
Jackson, Dennis 374
Jackson, MacDonald P. 157, 160, 186, 576
Jackson, Richard 461
Jackson, Russell 157
Jacob, James R. 218
Jacob, Margaret C. 249–50
Jacobs, Allan 470
Jaffe, Audrey 331
Jager, Eric 87
Jakabfi, Anna 514
Jambeck, Thomas J. 119
James, Louis 560, 569
Jameson, Fredric 366
Jannetta, Armando E. 522
Janssen, Frans 10

Jardine, M. D. 141
Jarraway, David R. 481
Jarvis, Robin 288–9
Jason, Philip K. 458
Jay, Gregory S. 425
Jeffcoate, Robert 395
Jeffers, Steven L. 211
Jeffrey, Sally 2
Jenkins, Harold 157–8
Jenkins, Philip 390
Jennings, Margaret 89
Johansson, Stig 17, 45–6, 56–7
Johnson, David F. 83, 105
Johnson, Don 459
Johnson, Lesley 101
Johnson, Lynn Staley 101, 115
Johnson, Trevor 319
Johnston, Alexandra F. 117, 119
Johnston, Allan 469
Johnston, Denis W. 531
Johnston, Jackie 118
Johnston, John 501
Johnstone, H. Diack 253
Jolley, Elizabeth 552
Jonassen, Frederick B. 113, 128
Jondorf, Gillian 100
Jones, A. R. 287
Jones, Ben 381
Jones, Charles 34
Jones, Edward 206
Jones, Emrys 5
Jones, Gayl 459
Jones, Genelle 543
Jones, John Henry 186, 198
Jones, Kathleen 322–3
Jones, Lawrence 575, 577–8
Jones, Mark 292
Jones, Suzanne W. 459
Jordan, Constance 143
Jordan, Robert 243
Jordanova, Ludmilla 251
Josyph, Peter 496
Jowett, John 184
Joyner, Nancy Carol 461
Jucker, Andreas 49, 50
Jump, Harriet Devine 308, 459
Juneja, Om 525
Jung-Ying Lu 29
Jurgensen, Manfred 540
Justeson, John 56
Kabitoglou, E. Douka 296, 303
Kafka, Phillipa 429
Kaftan, R. 302
Kageyama, Taro 36–7
Kahn, Coppelia 194
Kahn, Victoria 125
Kahri, Stanley J. 119
Kain, Richard M. 380
Kaltemback, Michele 525
Kamboureli, Smaro 529
Kamowski, William 134
Kamps, Ivo 167
Kanaganayakam, Chelva 513
Kane, Paul 556
Kanitkar, Helen 559
Kaplan, Amy 433
Kaplan, M. L. 170
Kappel, Andrew J. 455
Karlin, Daniel 316, 346
Kastan, D. S. 166, 167
Kastovsky, Dieter 49, 50, 52, 53, 54, 55
Katz, Slava 56
Kavenik, Frances M. 242
Kavka, Jerome 475
Kay, Paul 57
Kaye, Frances W. 516
Kazin, Alfred 495
Keach, William 303
Kearney, Eileen 405–6
Kearns, Katherine 438
Keating, Peter 5
Keeble, N. H. 218
Keefer, Janice Kulyk 512–13
Keeling, Denis F. 9
Keener, Frederick M. 257
Keesing, Nancy 535–6
Keesing, Roger 25
Kehler, D. 169, 204
Keiser, George 108
Keith, W. J. 518, 521–2
Kelley, Philip 318
Kelley, Theresa M. 274–5
Kellogg, David 335
Kelly, H. Ansgar 137
Kelly, Mary Ann 339–40
Kelsey, Nigel 372–3
Kemble, J. M. 76
Kemp, Martin 251
Kendall, Calvin B. 83–4
Kennedy, Alan 91
Kennedy, Colleen 499
Kennedy, David 552
Kennedy, Elspeth 114
Kennedy, Graeme 16
Kennelly, Laura B. 251
Kenny, Paul 317
Kent, Christopher 343
Kent, Hilary 534
Kent, Jacqueline 536
Kenyon, Olga 386–7, 388
Kerr, Douglas 396
Kerr, Philip 8
Kerrigan, John 110
Kerrigan, William 215
Kershaw, Alister 544
Keynes, Geoffrey 276–7
Keynes, Simon 91
Khan, Faraht 24–5
Kher, Inder Nath 284
Kidd, Colin 252
Kidd, Helen 460
Kidd, Millie M. 341
Kiernan, Kevin S. 84
Kijinski, John 356
Kimmen, Andrew C. 73
King, Alec Hyatt 11
King, Bruce 559
King, James 277–8
King, John N. 143
King, Kathryn R. 345
King, Margaret L. 210
King, P. Joy 396
Kingscott, Geoffrey 250
Kinney, Clare 147
Kipperman, Mark 304
Kirby, David 445
Kirchhof, Frederick 321–2
Kirkby, Diane 545
Kirkby, Joan 440, 552
Kirkpatrick, B. 2
Kirkpatrick, D. L. 1
Kirkpatrick, Peter 556
Kitagawa, Yshihisa 43
Kitson, Joan 552
Kitson, Peter J. 295, 297, 308
Klaver, Elizabeth 412
Klawitter, George 151
Klein, Dennis A. 415

Klima, Slava 254
Kliman, Bernice W. 155
Klinkowitz, Jerome 361, 488, 490, 492–3
Klooss, Wolfgang 514–15
Kloss, Gunter 407–8
Knapp, Bettina L. 338
Knapp, Peggy 127
Kneale, J. Douglas 290
Kniesza, Veronica 54
Knight, G. Wilson 380
Knight, Janice 431
Knoppers, Laura Lunger 228
Knowles, Richard Paul 529–30, 532
Knowles, Ronald 173
Knowles, Sebastian D. G. 481
Knox, Dilwyn 143
Knox-Shaw, Peter 551, 552
Knudsen, Eva Rask 542
Knutson, Roslyn 190
Kobayashi, Eichi 108
Koerner, Konrad 23
Koethe, John 457
Koktova, Eva 43–4
Kolb, Jack 326
Kolmar, Wendy K. 434
Kolodny, Annette 515–16
Kolsky, Stephen 553
Kondo, Makoto 44
König, Ekkehard 52
Kooper, Erik 76, 105
Korrel, Lia 47
Korshin, Paul 10
Kortlandt, Frederik 37
Kortmann, Bernd 47–8
Koskenniemi, Inna 38, 62
Kostelanetz, Richard 460, 488
Kott, Jan 169, 191
Kramarae, Cheris 33
Kramer, Dale 345
Krasner, James 326
Krause, Judith 512
Kravec, Maureen T. 480
Krochalis, Jean E. 139
Kroetsch, Robert 515
Kroll, Jeri 554
Kroll, Richard W. F. 234, 236, 243
Kronick, Joseph G. 425, 491
Kruger, Steven F. 105
Kubiak, A. 410
Kucinkas, Susan 62–3
Kuklick, Bruce 252
Kukowski, Stephan 158–9, 206–7
Kumar, Krishan 380
Kumier, William A. 292
Kuno, Susumo 44
Kurland, S. M. 171
Labov, William 27, 30
La Capra, Dominick 389
Lacroix, Jean-Michel 514
Ladd, Paddy 31
Laframboise, Lisa 524
Laigle, Genevieve 552
Laing, Stuart 394
Laird, Edgar S. 133
Lamb, Mary Ellen 146–7
Lambo, John A. 286
Lammers, John 326
Lamont, Claire 309
Lancaster, John 246
Land, Stephen K. 384
Landa, José Angel Garcia 341–2
Landman, Fred 20
Landry, Donna 255
Landsdown, Richard 300
Landsman, Ned C. 250
Lane, Dennis 380
Lane, Marvin 460
Lane, Patrick 526–7
Langbauer, Laurie 367
Lange, Deborah 46
Lange, Lorrayne Y. Baird 123
Langer, Beryl 524
Langford, Paul 251–2
Langhans, Edward A. 233
Langland, Elizabeth 265, 467
Lanier, Parks Jnr 460–1
Lanoue, Guy 28
Lansdowne, Richard 300
Lapidge, Michael 74–5, 79, 80, 91
Larmore, Charles 275
Laroque, Francois 177
Larson, Richard 39–40
Larson, Wendy 499
Lascombes, André 116
Lashgari, Deirdre 499
Lasing, Margaret 97
Lass, Roger 37
Latham, David 322
Latham, Sheila 322
Lau, Beth 301
Laurence, Anne 217
Lauter, Jane Hamovit 381
Lavasseur, Sherry 236
Laver, John 17, 35
Lavid, Julia 61
Lawless, Donald S. 151
Lawlor, Andrew 556
Lawlor, Robert 541
Lawlor, Traugott 127
Lawrence, D. H. 397
Lawrence, Veronica 146
Lawson, Elizabeth 556
Lawson, R. Bland 336
Lawson-Peebles, Robert 424
Leal, Luis 486, 487
Leask, Nigel 295
Leavis, L. R. 337, 370, 395
Leavitt, Michele 302
Le Bihan, Jill 522
Lecker, Robert 511, 516, 518, 528, 529
Leckie, Barbara 503
Le Comte, Edward 222
Leder, Priscilla 434
Lee, Christopher 550
Lee, Judith 382
Lee, Robert G. 499
Leech, Geoffrey 16, 17
Leeming, Glenda 413
Leer, Martin 539, 553
Lees, Clare A. 95
Leggatt, Alexander 165
Lehan, Richard 441
Leicester, H. Marshall 125
Leiman, Ellen 491
Leimberg, I. 170
Leithauser, Brad 395
Leitner, Gerhard 21–2
Lemay, J. A. Leo 429
Lendinara, Patrizia 80
Leng, Andrew 325
Lensing, George S. 480
Lentricchia, Frank 467
Leonard, Garry 378–9
Leonard, John 226–7, 227
Lerer, Seth 77, 85, 126
Lerner, Laurence 290
Lernout, Geert 405, 413

Le Saux, Francoise 113
Lester, G. A. 90
Lester, Geoff 117
Levenson, Michael 364
Leverenz, David 426, 443
Levernier, James A. 431
Levi, Peter 404
Levin, Beth 55
Levin, Harry 380
Levin, Richard A. 149, 167
Levine, Joseph M. 247
Levine, Robert S. 422, 433
Levine, William 259
Levinson, Marjorie 297
Levy, Barry 430
Levy, Bronwen 539
Levy, Eric P. 375
Lewis, C. S. 124
Lewis, Cynthia 171
Lewis, Julie 546, 555
Lewis, R. W. B. 445
Lewis, Scott 318
Leyerle, John 83
Lichman, Maria R. 320–1
Liddelow, Eden 554
Lidoff, Joan 499
Lieber, Rochelle 35, 36
Lightfoot, David 50, 51
Lilley, Kate 556
Lilly, Mark 368
Lim, Shirley Geok-lin 498
Lima, Robert 394
Limbert, Claudia A. 213, 239–40
Limon, José E. 487
Lin, Patricia 499
Lin, Shen 191
Lincoln, Andrew 276
Lindberg, Katheryne V. 425
Lindenbaum, Peter 228
Lindquist, Vern L. 475
Lindsay, Jack 322
Linebaugh, Peter 252
Lingis, Alphonso 395
Linkin, Harriet Kramer 273–4
Lipking, Lawrence 251
Lipkowitz, Ina 297
Little, Dave 525
Little, Matthew 475
Littler, Alison 555
Littman, David 63
Litz, A. Walton 400
Livingstone, Carol Rose 9
Locherbie-Cameron, Margaret A. L. 91
Lochhead, Douglas G. 518–19
Lochrie, Karma 98
Lockerbie, Ian 515
Lodge, David 340, 495
Loeffelholz, Mary 440
Loewenstein, Joseph 202
Logan, Harry M. 55
Logan, Marie-Rose 145, 146, 147, 151
Lojek, Helen 413
Lombardo, Agostino 447
Lomeli, Francisco 487
London, Bette 339
Londraville, Richard 398
Londre, Felicia Hardison 415
Long, William P. 332, 336
Longenbach, James 400, 465, 479
Longley, Edna 404
Longley, Katherine M. 332
Longsworth, Robert 103
Lord, Albert B. 92
Lord, John 62
Lord, Mary 549
Lorenz, Paul H. 342
Loriggio, Francesco 513
Loscocco, Paula 265
Lossky, Nicholas 217
Louis, Cameron 111
Lounsberry, Barbara 415
Louth, Janet 253
Lovelace, Earl 564–5
Low, Anthony 229
Lowe-Evans, Mary 379
Lowney, John 471
Luborsky, Ruth Samson 148
Lucas, John 397
Lucas, Michael 64
Lucas, Peter 28, 33
Luckyj, Christina 178
Lukitsh, Joanne 355
Lumsden, David 18
Lumsden, John 29
Lund, Nils 91
Lundquist, Sara L. 463
Lunney, Ruth 199
Lusardi, James P. 165
Luther, Susan 295
Lutterbie, John H. 410
Lutz, Hartmut 514, 524
Lydenberg, Robin 494, 495
Lynch, Gerals 512
Lynch, Kathryn L. 138
Lyons, Charles 409, 411, 415
Lyons, John 17, 19–20
Lyons, Paddy 233
Lyotard, Jean-François 142
McAdam, Rhona 527
McAlindon, Thomas 175–6
Macaulay, Ronald 30
McBride, Paul W. 499
McCaffery, Larry 489
McCarthy, Dermot 529
McCarthy, Patrick A. 380
McCarthy, Patrick J. 334
McCarthy, Terence 113
McCauley, Janie Caves 215
MacClaren, I. S. 511
McClure, Paul 344
McColgan, Kirstin P. 228
McColley, Diane 223
McConnell, Frank D. 495
McCormick, E. H. 574
McCredden, Lyn 556
McCully, Christopher 34
McCutcheon, R. J. 145
McDermott, Anne 248
MacDonald, A. A. 151
MacDonald, Bruce F. 520
Macdonald, D. L. 481
McDonald, Henry 229
MacDonald, Mary Lu 512
MacDonald, R. S. 521
McDonald, Russell 171, 414
McEldowney, Dennis 4, 576
McFeely, William S. 441
McGann, Jerome 60, 295, 297–8
McGavran, James Holt Jnr 273
McGaw, William 579
McGeary, Thomas 253
McGillis, Roderick 273
McGlade, James A. 547
McGlamery, Gayla S. 343–4
McGowan, Joseph 95
McGrath, F. C. 349
McGrath, Robin 516

Macgregor, Justin 534
McGuiness, Ilona M. 144
McGuiness, Rosamond 253, 254
McGuirk, Carol 259, 304–5
Machan, Tim William 98, 111
Macheski, Cecilia 233, 241
Machlin, Jeremy 400
McIntosh, Angus 38, 56, 97
MacIntyre, Jeanne 205
McIntyre, Wendell P. 244
Mack, Robert L. 265
MacKendrick, Louis K. 519
McKenna, Teresa 487
McKenna, Wayne 398
McKenzie, Stephen 397
McKeon, Michael 260
McKernan, Susan 539
Mackie, Erin 249
MacLaren, Ian D. 515, 520
McLaren, John 553
McLaren, Juliet 241
Maclean, Marie 555
Mclendon, M. J. 371
McLeod, Carol 332
Macleod, J. 300
McLeod, Marian 580
McLeod, Randall 166
McLuhan, Marshall 495
McLuskie, Kathleen 195–6
MacMahon, Michael 23, 34
McMaster, R. D. 331
McMillan, Scott 190–91, 199
McMullan, Gordon 195
McMullen, Lorraine 519
McMullin, B. J. 306
McNamee, M. B. 83
McNamer, Sarah 110–11
McNaughton, Howard 575–6, 580
MacPherson, Pat 501
Macrae, Alasdair D. F. 302
McRae, Jane 4, 574
McVeagh, John 233
MacWhinney, Brian 17
McWhir, Anne 293
Madden, David W. 394
Maddox, Donald 114
Maddox, Lucy 428
Maes-Jelinek, Hena 552, 564, 565
Magennis, Hugh 70, 95
Magnus, Elisabeth M. 226
Magnuson, Paul 295
Magoon, Joseph 327
Magoun, Francis P. Jnr 83
Maguire, Nancy Klein 243
Mahanti, J. C. 399
Mahoney, Dhira B. 114
Mahoney, Robert 259
Mair, Christian 46
Makin, Peter 472
Malamet, Elliott 390–1
Malcolm, Karen 27, 61
Malcolmson, Christina 167
Maley, Willy 148
Malloy, Jeanne M. 448
Malmkjaer, Kirsten 19
Malone, Ed 130
Malouf, David 551
Maltby, Paul 485, 493, 496, 502
Mancoff, Deborah 355–6
Mander, M. N. K. 223, 226
Mangan, Michael 175
Manguel, Alberto 512
Manhire, Bill 580
Manley, Lawrence 149
Mann, Charles 395
Mann, David 192
Mann, Jill 124
Mann, Neil 398
Mann, Philip 582
Manning, Peter J. 292–3
Manning, Sylvia 336–7
Mansbridge, Francis 527
Mansell, Darrell 370
Manser, Martin H. 3
Mansfield, Nicholas 554
Marchand, James W. 90
Marchitell, Howard 202–3
Marconi, Catherine Lewallen 458–9
Marcus, Leah S. 161, 168, 169, 216
Marcus, Mordecai 468
Mares, Cheryl 382
Marks, Patricia 333
Marotti, Arthur F. 141, 151
Márquez, Miguel 56
Marr, David 546, 552
Marsden, Hilda 340
Marsden, Jean 167
Marsden, Richard 94
Marsh, Joss Lutz 335, 343
Marshall, Cynthia 170
Marshall, Margaret 29
Martin, Jaqueline 407, 500
Martin, John 339
Martin, Murray 579
Martin, Philip W. 275
Martin, Randall 173
Martin, Robert A. 388
Martin, Robert K. 528
Martin, Ronald E. 423–4
Martin, Susan 550
Martin, Terence 422
Martin, Willy 55
Martin-Jones, Marilyn 32
Martz, Louis L. 144, 213–14
Masciandaro, Franco 100
Maser, Frederick 323
Maser, Mary Louise Jarden 323
Masetti, Astrid 263
Maslen, Keith 246
Mason, D. G. 345
Mason, H. A. 237
Mason, Pamela 163
Masur, Louis P. 426
Matar, N. I. 232
Materer, Timothy 471, 472–3, 474
Matheson, Lister M. 124
Mathews, Lawrence 511
Mathiesen, Paul F. 346
Matlak, Richard E. 295
Mattei, Anna Grazia 554
Matteo, Di 171
Matthews, Brian 538
Matthews, Peter H. 19
Matthews, Susan 257
Matus, Irving 166
Maurer, A. E. Wallace 236
Mauriac, François 390
Maus, Katherine 144, 167, 168, 202, 212
Maver, Igor 557
May, Henry F. 424
May, Stephen W. 150
Mayer, John T. 400
Mbangwana, Paul 27
Mead, Jenna 534
Mead, Philip 548
Meale, Carol M. 97, 106
Means, James 338

Mee, Jon 281–2
Meier, Hans H. 157
Melly, Diana 569
Melton, Judith M. 499
Mepham, John 381, 484
Mercer, Gina 579
Meredith, Peter 97
Merrill, Charles 135
Messaline, Peter 530
Messora, Noemi 196
Metcalf, John 519
Metcalf, Michael 72
Mey, Jacob 63
Meyer, Charles 16
Meyer, Eric 300
Meyer, Kinereth 398
Meyer, Michael 300
Meyer, Russell J. 148
Meyers, Jeffrey 371
Meyers, Valerie 376
Miall, David 295, 296
Michael, Ian 21
Michelson, Bruce 482
Michelutti, Dorina 513
Middlebrook, Diane Wood 477
Mieszkowski, Gretchen 137
Mikesell, Margaret Lael 194
Miles, Robert 254
Milhous, Judith 233
Miller, Anthony 145
Miller, J. Hillis 340, 347
Miller, Jacqueline T. 150
Miller, Jim 19
Miller, John 162
Miller, John N. 442
Miller, Leo 224, 227
Miller, Miriam Youngerman 101
Miller, Naomi J. 212
Miller, Paul Allen 147
Miller, William R. 213
Mills, A. D. 58
Mills, Alice 328
Mills, David 118
Mills, Maldwyn 106
Mills, Nicolaus 428
Millus, Donald J. 145
Milne, Geoffrey 542, 547
Milosz, Czeslaw 469
Milroy, James 19, 33
Milroy, Lesley 19, 33
Ming Dong Gu 375
Minkova, Donka 33–4, 49
Minni, C. Dino 513
Minnis, A. J. 107, 126
Minot, Walter S. 284
Mishra, Vijay 540, 582
Mitchell, Adrian 546
Mitchell, Bruce 51
Mitchell, Susan 544–5
Miyake, Akiko 473
Mohan, Chandra 525
Moloney, Karen M. 404
Monas, Sidney 379
Monitto, Gary 186
Monk, Patricia 520
Monkman, Kenneth 264, 265
Monsman, Gerald 347
Monteiro, George 483
Montelaro, Janet J. 134–5
Montesi, Albert 481
Montgomery, Michael 46
Moon, Michael 450–1
Mooney, Bel 8
Mooney, Linne R. 139
Mooney, Michael E. 179
Mooney, William 394
Moore, Bruce 116, 130
Moore, Caroline 226
Moore, Richard 339
Moorehouse, Frank 538
Moraga, Cherrie 486
Mordecai, Pamela 562–3
Morenberg, Max 18
Morey, James H. 105, 148
Morgan, Fidelis 233
Morgan, Gerald 102
Morgan, Gwendolyn 111
Morgan, M. F. 349
Morgan, Sally 541
Morgan, Ted 494, 495–6
Morgan, Thais 314
Morley, Patricia 522–3
Morris, Anne 563
Morris, Frankie 351
Morris, Meaghan 537
Morris, Mervyn 562, 572
Morris, Pam 332
Morrison, Michael A. 164
Morrow, Patrick 578
Morse, Deborah 499
Morse, Ruth 98–9
Mortimer, John 287
Morton, W. L. 512
Moseley, C. W. R. D. 221–2
Mosher, Harold 64
Mosian, Thomas 168
Moskal, Jeanne 273, 285
Motion, Andrew 397
Mottram, Eric 495
Mount, David B. 206
Mousley, Andrew 211
Mudge, Bradford K. 296
Muecke, Stephen 541
Mueller, Robert J. 149
Mufwene, Salikoko 29
Mugglestone, Lynda 34, 301–2
Muhkin, Anatoli 54
Muhlhausler, Peter 25
Muir, Bernard J. 89
Mukherjee, Arun P. 560–1
Mukherjee, Meenakshi 561
Mulac, Anthony 52–3
Mulder, John R. 223
Mulholland, Paul 206
Mullan, John 262
Mullin, Michael 165
Mullini, Roberta 117
Mulryan, John 229
Mulryne, J. R. 196
Mulvihill, James 290, 309
Mulvihill, Maureen E. 239, 241
Munns, Jessica 242
Munro, Jane 540
Murfin, Ross 442–3
Murphy, Arthur 555
Murphy, Michael 127
Murphy, Russell Elliott 401
Murray, Christopher 408, 413
Murray, David 485–6
Murray, Douglas 263
Murray, Les 548
Murray, Paul 401, 466
Murray, Stephen 23–4
Murray, Stuart 574
Murray, Sue 533
Myers, Jack 461
Myers, Jeffrey Rayner 158
Myers, Mitzi 273
Myers, Peter 379
Myers, Robin 11
Myers, Victoria 499
Nadelhaft, Ruth 370–1

Nakajima, Heizo 36, 44
Nakumara, Masaru 44
Narayan, Shyamala 557
Nardo, Anna K. 224, 228
Nasta, Susheila 558–9, 562, 563
Nathan, David 415
Naylor, Paul Kenneth 471
Neander, L. J. 354
Nebeker, Helen 569
Needham, Paul 10
Neely, Carol Thomas 175
Neilson, Philip 552
Nelson, Cary 495
Nelson, Marie 90
Nerlich, Brigitte 22
Nesset, Kirk 496
Neuman, Shirley 516, 528
Neumeier, Beate 406
Nevalainen, Terttu 51, 54
New, Melvyn 265
New, W. H. 510
Newey, V. 167
Newhouse, Miriam 530
Newman, Joan 545
Newman, Julie 559
Newman, Karen 64
Newsom, Robert 329
Newton, K. M. 340
Nicholls, Alex 56, 94
Nicholls, Peter 472
Nichols, Ann Eljenholm 116, 117–18
Nichols, Stephen G. 128
Nicholson, Colin 514, 515, 522
Nicholson, Lewis E. 93
Nicholson, Peter 107, 131
Nida, Eugene 23
Nieuwenhuizen, Agnes 536
Nightingale, Benedict 414
Nile, Richard 538
Niles, John D. 80
Nischik, Reingard M. 523
Niwa, Satomi 42
Noland, Daniel 53
Norbrook, David 216
Nord, Deborah Epstein 329
Nordloh, David J. 422
Norgate, Paul 396
Norland, Howard B. 116
Normand, Lawrence 169
Norris, Ken 526
North, Michael 398–9, 401
North, Richard 81–2, 92
Norton, Alexandra 350
Norton, Ann 383–4
Novoa, Bruce 488
Novy, Marianne 342
Nunn, Robert 531–2
Nunnally, Thomas 38, 41
Nunokawa, Jeff 326
Nuttall, Geoffrey F. 218
Nyquist, Mary 125
Oakleaf, David 260, 264
O'Brian, Timothy D. 133
O'Brien, Jennifer 63
Ochs, Elinor 33
O'Clair, Robert 482
O'Connell, Michael 224
Odlin, Terence 21, 30–1
O'Donnell, Anne M. 145
O'Donnell, Daniel P. 86
O'Donnell, Mary Ann 240
O'Donnell, Patrick 497–8, 501
O'Donnell, W. 19, 33
O'Donnell, William H. 398
O'Donoghue, Jo 393–4
Ofuani, Ogo 62
Ogée, Frédéric 254, 265
Ogura, Michiko 48–9
Ohlgren, Thomas H. 70, 71
Oizumi, Akio 123
Okasha, Elisabeth 72
O'Keefe, Katherine O'Brien 80, 92
Olney, James 427
Olsen, Karin 87
Olshewsky, Thomas M. 250
Olster, Stacy 503
O'Mealy, Joseph 344
Ommundsen, Wenche 553
O'Neill, Michael 300
O'Neill, Patrick P. 73
Orange, John 521
Ordonez, Elizabeth J. 486
O'Reilly, Shelley 322
Orgel, Stephen 160–1, 171, 221
Oriard, Michael 437–8, 490–1
Ormond, Leonee 328
Orne, Martin T. 477
O'Rourke, J. 293
Orr, John 406–7, 409
Orr, Patricia R. 138
Orrell, John 187–8
Orton, Peter 90
Osakwe, M. I. 63
Osborn, Marijane 72
Osborne, Laurie E. 207
O'Shea, Michael J. 264–5
Osmond, Rosalie 522
Oster, Judith 468
Ostreen, Mark 377
Ostriker, Alicia 281
Otto, Peter 280
Overing, Gillian R. 87
Overon, Bill 255
Owen, Charles A. Jnr 134
Owen, Louis 422
Owen, Peter 7
Owen, Sue 243
Owen, W. J. B. 286, 290–1
Owens, E. Suzanne 435
Owens, W. R. 217, 262
Ower, John 298
Oxenhandler, Neal 495
Paccaud, Josiane 62
Pache, Walter 515
Padilla, Genaro M. 486, 487
Padma, M. 302
Padolsky, Enoch 510–11
Page, Geoff 557
Page, Judith W. 293
Page, Raymond I. 95
Paige, Lori, A. 340
Paknadel, Felix 254
Palattella, John 483
Paley, Morton D. 276, 279, 281, 282, 285, 297, 303
Palmegiano, E. M. 353
Palmer, D. J. 168
Palmer, Jerry 3
Palmos, Frank 546
Pandharipande, Rajeshwari 29
Paranjape, Makarand R. 561
Paravisini, Lizabeth 562
Pardee, Hearne 403
Parfitt, George 233
Parker, George D. 532
Parker, Gerald D. 531
Parker, I. J. 303
Parker, Mark 296, 309
Parker-Benfield, B. C. 303
Parkin, Jane 548
Parkinson, David J. 109

Parks, John G. 497
Paroissen, David 334
Parrinder, Patrick 380
Parrish, Stephen 286
Pascoe, Robert 539–40
Pasternak, Carol Braun 89
Pathak, Zakia 385
Patrick, Peter 29
Pattanaik, D. R. 558
Patterson, Annabel 142, 239
Patterson, Diana 264
Patton, Marilyn 523
Pauwels, Anne 25
Pawl, Amy J. 264
Paxman, David B. 246, 255
Payne, Deborah C. 242, 257
Payne, Linda R. 241
Pearce, Lynn 315, 324–5
Pearl, V. L. 217
Pearl, M. L. 217
Pearsall, Derek 123–4
Pearson, Jacqueline 244
Pease, Donald 443–4
Pechter, Edward 167
Pedley, Colin 283
Pelan, Mark 133, 136–7
Pell, Barbara 521
Pendleton, Thomas A. 161
Pennee, Donna 525
Penso, Kia 479–80
Penzl, Herbert 24
Perkins, David 275
Perkins, Mary Anne 296, 297
Perlman, Joel 430
Perrett, Bill 542
Perry, Ruth 265
Pestino, Joseph 394
Petch, Simon 578
Peters, Catherine 343
Peters, Hans 37–8
Peters, Joan D. 339
Petersen, Kirsten Holst 553, 566
Peterson, Laura 379
Peterson, Marlyn 499
Pether, Penelope 344
Petillon, Pierre-Yves 502
Petrie, Barbara 555
Petrone, Penny 516
Pettit, Charles P. C. 345
Pevsner, Nikolaus 3
Pfau, Thomas 303
Pfeiffer, John R. 415
Pharand, Michel W. 415
Phelan, Nancy 545
Phiddian, Robert 248
Phillips, Caryl 562
Phillips, Michael 282, 284
Phillpots, Bertha 83
Philpotts, Trey 337
Phinney, A. W. 302
Pickwoad, Nicholas 331
Pietropoli, Cecilia 117
Piette, Adam 258
Piket, Vincent 491–2
Pilkington, Adrian 60
Pine, Richard 413
Pinney, Thomas 321
Pinnock, Andrew 239
Pisker, Sanford 503
Pittenger, Elizabeth 161
Pittock, Joan H. 251
Pittock, Murray G. H. 250
Pizer, Donald 441
Platizky, Roger 324–5
Platt, Richard 253
Plomley, N. J. B. 540
Plummer, John 102
Plunka, Gene A. 415
Pohli, Carol Virginia 104, 237
Poirier, Richard 349, 368
Polk, Noel 455
Pollard, A. W. 9
Pollard, Carl 39
Pollard, Velma 563
Pollock, Jean-Yves 42
Pons, Xavier 552, 553
Poole, Adrian 177, 445–6
Poole, Roger 382
Pope, John C. 83
Poplack, Shana 28
Poppenbeek, Patsy 542–3
Porte, Joel 425–6, 437
Porter, Joseph A. 177
Porter, R. 33
Porter, Roy 6, 251, 252
Posnock, Ross 446
Post, Jonathan F. S. 215
Potiki, Roma 581
Potkay, Adam 247
Potter, Nancy 578
Potter, Nicholas 177, 396–7
Potvin, C. 511
Potvin, Elisabeth 523
Pounds, Wayne 495
Pousse, Michael 560
Povah, Frank 536
Powell, Susan 115
Powrie, Phil 386
Prescott, Anne Lake 147, 157, 172
Press, Jon 322
Prest, W. R. 210
Priessnitz, Horst 537–8
Primeau, Ronald 470
Privateer, Paul Michael 271–2
Probyn, Clive T. 248
Proctor, Margaret 385
Proudfoot, G. R. 183
Puhvel, Martin 86
Pulju, Tim 24
Pullum, Geoffrey K. 17–18, 41
Pulsiano, Phillip 73, 75
Punter, David 362
Purdon, L. O. 107
Purkayastha, Sharmila 385
Pursgove, Glyn 216
Purviance, Susan M. 250
Purvis, C. J. 254–5
Pybus, Cassandra 554
Pym, David 291, 297, 305
Pywell, Geoff 416
Quartermaine, Peter 552
Quigley, Ellen 518
Quinones, Richard J. 298–9
Quintana, Alvina E. 486
Quirk, Tom 425
Ra'ad, Basem L. 503
Rabey, David Ian 406
Rabillard, Sheila 414
Rackin, Phyllis 172
Radcliffe, Evan 292
Radic, Leonard 547
Radzinowicz, Mary Ann 214, 229
Rae, Simon 6–7
Ragussis, Michael 443
Rahman, Tariq 29, 384
Rahv, Philip 465
Raine, Kathleen 277
Raines, Gay 541–2
Rainey, Lawrence 400, 455, 465, 473–4
Raizis, M. B. 299
Ramachandra, Ragini 559

Ramazani, Jahan 319–20, 481
Rambuss, Richard 138
Ramchand, Kenneth 569
Ramisch, Heinrich 22
Rampton, Ben 32
Rampton, David 512
Ramsay, Alan 20
Rance, Nicholas 343
Rans, Geoffrey 439
Raper, Julius Rowan 488–9, 492, 494, 500, 502
Raphael, D. D. 251
Rasmussen, Eric 185
Rasporich, Beverley J. 523
Raumolin-Brunberg, Helena 54
Raw, Barbara C. 80
Raw, Lawrence 203
Rawlinson, David 6
Raybin, David 128, 129, 131, 133, 134, 135
Raylor, Timothy 218
Rebera, Ranjini 549
Redgrave, G. R. 9
Redman, Tim 474
Redmond, Patricia 487
Reed, Mark L. 269, 286–7
Reed, Roy 427
Rees, Joan 146, 171–2
Reesman, Jeanne Campbell 446
Regan, Stephen 522
Regan, Thomas J. 256
Reichardt, Paul F. 101
Reichert, Klaus 219
Reichmann, Oskar 57
Reid, Brian Holden 424
Reid, David 224, 228
Reim, Antonella 552
Reitz, John 262
Remie, Cornelius 514
Rendall, Ruth 338
Revard, Stella P. 224
Reynolds, Margaret 314, 317–18
Rhodes, Jack W. 301
Ribeiro, Alvaro 253–4
Ricard, Serge 500, 503
Rice, Anne 7
Richards, Bernard 214, 347
Richards, David 522
Richards, Michaela 549
Richards, Thomas 5
Richardson, Alan 273, 300
Richardson, Anne 145
Richardson, Brian 414
Richardson, Christine 118
Richardson, Donna 303
Richardson, Malcolm 128
Richetti, John 246, 262, 263
Richmond, Colin 97
Richmond, Velma Bourgeois 126
Rickford, John 28
Ricou, Laurie 516
Riddel, Joseph N. 483
Riddell, James A. 213
Riddy, Felicity 97, 110
Rider, Philip R. 9
Riebling, Barbara 178
Riede, David G. 271, 272
Rieder, John 294
Rieke, Alison 481
Riemenschneider, Dieter 537
Riemer, Andrew 539
Riggio, Milla 116
Riggio, Thomas P. 441
Riggs, Erica 402
Rigter, Bob 55
Ringler, Richard N. 83
Riquelme, John Paul 466–7
Rissanen, Matti 51–2
Ritvo, Harriet 292, 304, 433
Rivers, Isabel 234, 253
Rivers, Theodore John 72
Rizzo, Betty 249, 259
Roach, Peter 19
Roberts, Andrew 275
Roberts, Brian K. 59
Roberts, Carol 532
Roberts, Diane 460
Roberts, Gerald 320
Roberts, Jane 109
Roberts, John R. 216
Robertson, Elizabeth 115
Robertson, Michael 497
Robinson, Eric 305
Robinson, Fred C. 76–7, 80, 104
Robinson, Fred Muller 409
Robinson, J. W. 117
Robinson, Jane 5
Robinson, Pamela 139
Robinson, Sidney K. 254
Rocard, Marcienne 514
Roche, Thomas P. Jnr 148
Rodden, John 375
Roderick, Colin 545–6
Rodriguez, Judith 534
Roe, Jill 550
Roe, Nicholas 257
Roe, Paddy 541
Roessel, David 470
Rogers, David 11
Rogers, Gillian 106
Rogers, Katherine M. 249
Rogers, Pat 2
Rolfe, Christopher 380
Romaine, Suzanne 20, 24, 25, 33, 46, 535
Romero, Lora 439
Romm, James 144
Rook, Constance 553
Rooke, Leon 519
Rooks, Pamela A. 373
Roper, Alan 235
Rosaldo, Renato 486
Rosand, David 147
Rose, Dan 455
Rose, Jacqueline 471
Rose, Maggie 408
Rosen, Mike 7
Rosen, Stuart 35
Rosenbaum, Peter 38–9
Rosenmeier, Jesper 430–1
Rosenthal, M. L. 320
Rosier, James L. 73
Rosner, Elizabeth 580
Ross, Catherine 519
Ross, Charles 224
Ross, Marlon B. 292
Ross, Morton L. 518
Ross, Robert L, 388, 550–1, 563–4, 577–8, 583
Rossen, Janice 384
Rossington, Michael 303–4
Rosso, G. A. 298
Rosu, Anca 481
Rotella, Guy 461
Rothwell, W. 56
Rousseau, G. S. 249, 251
Rowe, John Carlos 425
Rowe, M. W. 297
Rowlands, Graham 533
Rozett, Martha Tuck 177
Rubin, Stanley 91
Rudanko, Juhani 41
Rudat, Wolfgang E. H. 133

Ruddick, William 295
Ruderman, Judith 498
Rudnytsky, Peter L. 144–5, 146, 147, 151, 174
Ruffing, John 105
Ruland, Richard 423, 488
Ruoff, Gene 275
Rushdie, Salman 4, 557, 568
Russell, John 525
Russett, Margaret 290, 307
Russom, Geoffrey F. 83
Rutherford, Anna 566
Ruthrof, Horst 62
Ruud, Jay 133
Ryan, Judith 364
Ryan, Sue 553
Rydén, Mats 54
Rylance, Rick 405
Rylestone, Anne L. 291
Sabol, Ruth 64
Sabor, Peter 260, 264
Sack, James J. 353
Sadie, Stanley 253
Sag, Ivan 39
Said, Edward 5, 366
St-Jacques, Raymond 105
Saito, Miki 44
Salat, M. F. 525
Salda, Michael N. 114
Saldivar, José David 486, 487
Saldivar, Ramon 486
Saldivar-Hull, Sonia 487
Sales, Roger 197
Salick, Royden 565
Salinger, Leo 196
Salkeld, Duncan 186
Salmon, F. E. 258
Salmon, Vivian 23
Salomon, Brownell 205
Salter, Denis 529
Salzman, Paul 218, 234
Samad, Daizal 572–3
Sambrook, James 258
Sammells, Neil 365
Sammonds, Todd H. 228
Sammuells, Neil 248
Sams, Eric 159, 171
Samuels, M. L. 97
Sanchez, Rosaura 486
Sand 27–8
Sanders, Andrew 351
Sanders, Robert 22
Sandison, Alan 346
Sandred, Karl 37
Sankaran, Chitra 560
Sankoff, David 25
Sano, Hiroko 225
Sarris, Fotios 526
Sato, Gayle K. Fujita 499
Saukkonen, Pauli 62
Sawada, Harumi 42
Saxby, Maurice 536–7
Scammell, William 404
Scattergood, John 98
Schaar, Claes 60
Schafer, Elizabeth 161, 169
Schaffer, Kay 539
Scheckter, John 553
Scheiber, Andrew J. 431
Scheick, William J. 345, 362–3
Schell, Edgar 119–20
Schellenberg, Betty A. 263
Schellinger, Paul E. 1
Scherf, Kathleen Dorothy 528
Scherzer, Dina 409
Schiefelbein, Michael 333–4
Schiff, Dan 378
Schille, Candy B. K. 231
Schipper, William 93, 115
Schlesinger, Arthur M. Jnr 424
Schless, Howard H. 105, 130
Schlicke, Paul 334
Schlueter, June 165, 409
Schmidt, A. V. C. 400–1, 467
Schmidt, Claudia M. 251, 303
Schmidt, George D. 102
Schmidt, Peter 483, 504
Schmied, Josef 20, 26–7
Schneewind, J. B. 250
Schneider, Ulrich 405
Schnorrenberg, Barbara Brandon 252
Schoenbaum, Sam 166
Schoenfeldt, Michael C. 213, 215
Schoffman, Nachum 317
Schofield, Mary Anne 233, 241
Schonhorn, Manuel 262
Schotz, Amiel 412
Schourup, Lawrence 62
Schrader, Richard J. 84
Schreiner, Christopher S. 394
Schueller, Malini 503
Schulze, Robin 400
Schwartz, Beth C. 382
Schwarz, John H. 344
Schweizer, Karl 309
Sciff-Zamaro, Roberta 513
Scobie, Stephen 528
Scott, Bonnie Kime 365, 378, 380, 383
Scott, Daniel 256
Scott, Grant F. 302
Scott, Kathleen L. 104
Scott, Peter Dale 516
Scott, Rosemary 354
Scott, Stanley J. 427, 462
Scragg, Donald 79, 91–2
Seal, Graham 536
Seaton, Dorothy 524
Sedge, Douglas 182, 183
Seed, David 365–6, 378
Selden, Raman 241
Selig, Robert L. 346
Sell, Roger 61
Semino, Elena 64
Semmler, Clement 544, 546
Sengupta, Saswati 385
Senn, Werner 556
Setzer, Sharon M. 293
Sexton, Melanie 320
Seymour, Alan 538, 552
Seymour, M. C. 132
Shaheen, N. 169
Shapcott, Thomas 539
Shapiro, Susan C. 351
Sharkey, Michael 554
Sharpe, Jenny 385
Sharpe, Tony 399, 500–1
Sharrad, Paul 554
Shaver, Anne 148
Shaviro, Steven 281, 495
Shaw, Marion 368
Shaw, Narelle 554
Shaw, William P. 164–5, 210
Shawcross, John T. 214
Sheats, Paul D. 289

Shek, Ben-Z. 520
Shen, Yeshayahu 63
Shepherd, Jan 560
Shepherd, S. H. A. 106
Shepherd, Simon 166
Sheppeard, Sallye 214
Sher, Richard B. 250
Sheridan, Dorothy 8
Sheridan, Susan 547
Sherry, Karen 580
Shershow, Scott Cutler 238
Sherzer, Dina 484
Shillingsbury, Peter L. 331
Shilstone, Frederick W. 299
Shine, H. 354
Shipley, J. B. 265
Shippey, T. A. 83
S'hiri, Sonia 63
Shirley, Denis 430
Shitaka, Hideyuki 229
Shoaf, R. A. 132
Shoemaker, Steve 500
Shorrocks, Graham 22, 56
Showalter, Elaine 426, 438
Shullenberger, William 223
Shulman, Robert 422
Shumaker, Jeanette 342
Shuttleworth, Sally 341
Sicari, Stephen 475
Sichert, Margit 110
Siewierska, Anna 45
Sillars, Stuart 365
Silver, Victoria 227
Silverman, Toby 416
Silverstein, Marc 414
Silverstein, Michael 24
Sim, Stuart 217
Simmons-O'Neill, Elizabeth 133
Simon, Bennett 410
Simon, Eckehard 118–19
Simon, Luke 547
Simons, John 106
Simpkins, Scott 299, 379
Simpson, James 108
Simpson, Kenneth 250, 259–60, 304
Simpson, Mary Scott 409
Simpson, Matt 395–6
Sinclair, John 56
Singh, Kirpal 380
Singleton, Brian 200
Sitter, John 247
Skerl, Jennie 494, 495
Sklenicka, Carol 374
Slade, Joseph 488
Slater, Andrew 351–2
Slights, Camille Wells 174
Slights, William 203
Slinn, E. Warwick 325–6
Sloan, John 346
Small, Ian 156, 248, 347–8, 350
Smarr, Janet Levarie 133
Smith, A. H. W. 114
Smith, A. J. 212
Smith, Angela 553
Smith, Bruce 167
Smith, Donald M. 284
Smith, Douglas Burnet 526
Smith, Jeremy J. 97
Smith, Joseph 409–10
Smith, Julia J. 240
Smith, Lorrie 458
Smith, M. W. A. 159–60, 186, 206
Smith, Margaret 258, 316
Smith, Molly 194
Smith, Nigel 234
Smith, P. J. 204
Smith, Robert M. 413
Smith, Robin D. 76
Smith, Sidney 24
Smith, Valerie 422
Smith-Bingham, Richard 317
Smitten, Jeffrey R. 250
Smulders, Sharon 320, 323
Smyth, Ailbhe 377
Smyth, Denis 390
Smyth, Edmund J. 484
Snead, James 366
Snowden, Peter 403
Snyder, John 247
Soderholm, Jane 299
Solotaroff, Theodore 495
Somerville, Margaret 541, 542
Sorensen, Katherine 342
Sosnowski, Andrzej 475
Soule, Lesley Anne 169, 191
Sourisseau, Jean 515
Sowell, Madison U. 100
Spalding, Ruth 218
Spangler, Sharon 303
Spear, Hilda D. 396
Spearing, A. C. 107, 137
Spearritt, Peter 534
Spector, Robert 265–6
Spector, Stephen 119, 124, 134–5, 136, 138, 139
Spencer, Andrew 18
Spencer, Sharon 488
Spender, Dale 549
Spillar, Michael R. G. 224
Spindler, Graham 534
Spirit, Jane 348
Spivack, Charlotte 195
Spivak, Gayatri 559
Spolsky, Ellen 398
Spoo, Robert 475
Springer, Mary Doyle 481
Spurling, Hilary 394
Squires, Michael 372
Srinivas, T. 560
Stachniewski, John 234–5
Stacy, James R. 415
Staines, David 118
Staley, Thomas 376, 569
Stallworth, Jon 396
Stallybrass, Peter 166, 167
Stanbury, Sarah 101, 103, 111, 138
Stanley, E. G. 76–7, 90, 113
Stanton, Judith Philips 233
Stanton, Michael N. 332
Stanwood, P. G. 223
Stanzel, Franz K. 520
Staves, Susan 243
Steadman, John M. 209
von Stechow, A. 57
Steen, Gerard 60
Steen, Sara Jane 205–6
Steenburg, David 283–4
Stein, Dieter 52
Stein, Gabriele 57
Steinbrink, Jeffrey 449
Stelzig, Eugene L. 291, 294
Stenström, Anna-Brita 17, 45–6, 56–7
Stephanson, Raymond 257
Stephenson, Mimosa 350
Stern, Milton R. 443
Sternberg, Meir 60, 64
Stetz, Margaret 356
Stevens, Dorothy 150
Stevens, Edna L. 241

Stevens, Holly 481
Stevens, Martin 119, 120
Stevens, Ray 299
Stevenson, Warren 299
Stewart, Douglas 555
Stewart, Jack F. 375
Stewart, Ken 549
Stewart, Stanley 148
Stillinger, Jack 272–3, 302
Stilz, Gerhard 293, 556
Stock, Lorraine Kochanske 102, 105
Stockwell, Robert 49
Stoddart, Helen 340
Stone, Marjorie 330
Stonehouse, Sally 330
Stoneley, Peter 346
Stookey, Lorena L. 197
Storey, Graham 335
Storey, Mark 305
Storm, Melvin 127
Stouck, David 521
Stowe, William W. 441–2
Strandberg, Victor 503
Straub, Kristina 243, 246, 257
Strite, Sheri Ann 103
Stroupe, John H. 116, 117
Strout, Nathaniel 207
Struthers, J. R. 519
Stuart, Barbara L. 335
Stuart, Ian 412
Stump, Donald V. 148
Stump, Gregory 36
Sturges, Robert S. 99
Sturgess, Charlotte 523–4
Sturm, Terry 4, 574, 576
Stuurman, Frits 40, 45
Sullivan, James 459
Sullivan, Margaret M. 143
Sullivan, Rosemary 517, 525
Sullivan, Zohreh T. 370
Summers, Claude J. 215–16
Summersgill, Sonya A. 396
Sundby, Bertil 55
Suppes, Patrick 57
Sure, Kembo 27
Surette, Leon 475, 511
Sutherland, James 255
Sutherland, John 343, 368
Sutherland, Kathryn 91, 307–8
Sutton, Peter 25
Svartvik, Jan 16–17
Svendsen, Linda 517
Swan, Toril 53
Swann, Charles 443
Swann, Karen 294
Swanson, Donald 229
Swanson, R. N. 115, 136
Swearingen, J. E. 283
Swenson, Karen 89
Symes, Peter 404
Taavitsainenen, Irma 115
Tabbi, Joseph 500
Tacey, David 539, 552
Tagliamonte, Sali 28
Takami, Ken-ichi 44
Takase, Fumiko 206
Tallack, Douglas 484
Tampke, Jurgen 540
Tanaka, Hiroaki 44
Tanaka, Tomoyuki 40
Tanner, Ron 120
Tanner, Tony 495
Tanzman, Lea 391
Tate, Audrey 545
Tate, Trudi 7
Tausky, Thomas E. 553, 579
Taylor, Andrew 99, 117, 556
Taylor, Anya 296
Taylor, Barry 142
Taylor, Dennis 481
Taylor, Gary 159–60, 161
Taylor, John R. 35, 57
Taylor, Lita 17
Taylor, Marcia M. 341
Taylor, Paul Beekman 85–6
Taylor, Richard 398
Teague, Francis 189
Temperley, Nicholas 253
Terry, Richard 247
Tharaud, Barry 338
Thesen, Sharon 529
Thesing, William B. 252
Thieme, John 100, 515, 522, 525–6
Thomas, Claudia 249
Thomas, Edward 397
Thomas, George 19
Thomas, Glen 553
Thomas, Gordon K. 293, 299, 300
Thomas, H. Nigel 565
Thomas, Ned 571
Thomas, Vivian 168
Thompson, A. 167
Thompson, Andrew 342
Thompson, Ann 161
Thompson, Anne B. 112
Thompson, Elizabeth 522
Thompson, James 246
Thompson, Joanne 330
Thompson, John 100, 106, 113
Thompson, John O. 515
Thompson, Mervyn 582
Thompson, Paul 321–2
Thompson, Sandra 52–3
Thomson, John 576
Thorne, J. R. 105
Thornton, Ginger 113
Thorpe, Douglas 213, 336
Thorpe, Michael 513
Thorslev, Peter L. Jnr 299
Thurin, Susan Shoenbauer 332
Thurn, David H. 200
Thurston, John 520
Thwaite, Tony 554
Tick, Stanley 335
Tidcombe, Marianne 10
Tieken-Boon van Ostade, Ingrid 55
Tiggs, Wim 55, 90–1, 135
Timpson, Annis May 515
Tindall, Gillian 3
Tinley, Bill 404–5
Tintner, Adeline 446–7
Tippet, Maria 515
Tite, Colin 11–12
Tkacz, Catherine Brown 129
Todd, Janet 3, 240
Todd, L. 19, 33
Tolkien, J. R. R. 83
Tollefson, J. 32
Tomlinson, Sophie 195
Tompkins, Jane 448
Tompkins, Joanna 547
Tonoike, Shigeo 44
Torsello, Carol T. 64
Torti, Anna 108
Totaro, Paul 538
Toth, Emily 438
Tottie, Gunnel 17, 53
Trachtenberg, Alan 441

Trahern, Joseph B. Jnr 80
Trammell, Michael 481
Tranter, John 548
Trapnell, William H. 253
Traub, Valerie 167
Traugott, Elizabeth 52–3
Travers, Erica 556
Travitsky, Betty S. 194–5
Treip, Mindele Anne 223
Tresize, Simon 344
Trevor, William 8
Tricomi, Albert H. 119, 217
Trigg, Stephanie 103–4
Triki, Mounir 64
Trilling, Lionel 441
Trollope, Joanna 338
Trott, Nicola 291
Trottor, Richard 368
Troy, Mark 262
Trudgill, P. 29–30
Tryphonopoulos, Demetres 475
Tsur, Reuven 62
Tucker, Herbert F. 269, 326
Tucker, John L. 342
Tucker, Paul 348
Tudeau-Clayton, Margaret 349, 368
Turcotte, Gerry 553
Turnbull, Paul 253
Turner, Arnella K. 353
Turner, G. W. 550
Turner, Graeme 537
Turner, John 356
Turner, Lynette 352
Turville-Petre, Thorlac 115
Tuttleton, James W. 447
Twidale, K. M. 554
Twomey, Michael W. 101, 105
Twycross-Martin, Henrietta 109
Tyson, Brian 352
Ufomata, Tatilayo 27
Ulmer, William A. 304
Unsworth, Anna 330
Updike, John 569
Uphaus, Robert W. 246, 248–9
Urdang, Laurence 3
Ureland, P. Sture 20
Valbuena, Olga Lucia 225
Valenza, Robert 158
Vanacker, Sabine 368
Vance, Eugene 98, 128
Van den Berg, Sara 202
Vanderveken, Daniel 20
Vandeveire, H. 293
Van Dover, J. Kenneth 502
Van Herk, Aritha 517
Van Peer, Willie 60
VanSpanckeren, Kathryn 499
Van Tassel, Mary M. 246–7
Varadharajan, Asha 300
Varey, John E. 188
Varsava, Jerry 364–5
Varty, Anne 348
Vassallo, Peter 303
Vassanji, M. G. 513
Vaughan, Míceál F. 105
Vaughan, P. see Horvath, B. (32)
Vaughan, Virginia Mason 177
Vauthier, Simone 519, 554
Vendler, Helen 398
Ventola, Eija 60, 61
Verdicchio, Pasquale 513
Verdonk, Peter 60
Verhaar, John 25
Verma, K. D. 560
Vicari, E. Patricia 217
Vickrey, John F. 93
Vidal, Gore 5
Vink, James 150
Virtanen, Tuija 61
Vlock-Keyes, Deborah 317
von Maltzahn, Nicholas 225
Vose, Heather 543
Wachtel, Eleanor 523, 532
Wächtler, Kurt 22
Wack, Mary F. 93
Wade, Stephen 391
Wagner, Anton 531
Wagner, C. Roland 481
Wagner, Hans-Peter 254
Wagner, Jennifer 302
Wagner, Peter 254
Wagner-Martin, Linda 388
Wakelin, Martin 21
Wakeling, Louise 545
Wakoski, Diane 481
Walcott, Derek 573
Waldman, Louis 148
Waldron, Ronald 97
Wales, Katie 378
Walker, Brenda 553
Walker, David 540
Walker, Doreen 517
Walker, Kim 195, 207
Walker, Shirley 556
Walker-Pelkey, Fay 127
Wall, Kathleen 524
Wall, Wendy 151, 212–13
Wallace, Anne D. 341
Wallace, David 101, 128
Wallace, Nathaniel 176
Wallace-Crabbe, Chris 537, 555
Waller, Björn 115
Waller, Gary 212
Wallingford, Katharine 215
Walsh, Marcus 156, 248
Walsh, Thomas P. 317
Walsh, William 557–8
Walton, Alan 21
Walton, Priscilla 525
Wang, Orrin N. C. 249, 303–4
Wanko, Cheryl 258, 263
Ward, Charlotte 474–5
Ward, Geoffrey 405
Ward, Hayden 314, 348
Ward, J. P. 349
Ward, John Powell 272, 402
Wark, Wesley K. 389–90
Warkentin, Germaine 512
Warner, Martin 349, 368
Warner, Mary Janer 530–1
Warner, William Beatty 260
Warren, Michael 203
Warrington, Lisa 581–2
Warwick, Ronald 558
Wasserman, Julian N. 101
Wasson, Ellis Archer 252
Waterhouse, Ruth 82
Watkins, Daniel P. 298
Watkins, Susan 339
Watson, George 254
Watson, John 577
Watson, Robert 402
Watson, Robert N. 176–7
Watson, Steven 462
Watt, Tessa 209–10
Watt, W. S. 256
Wattie, Nelson 577
Watts, Alan S. 331
Watts, Cedric 175

Watts, Edward 542
Watts, Richard 60
Watts, Victor 59
Waugh, Evelyn 323
Wawn, Andrew 22
Wayne, Valerie 167
Wear, Andrew 251
Webby, Elizabeth 548
Webster, Jim 393
Weedon, Alexis 350
Weinfield, Henry 258–9
Weis, Rene 177–8
Weiss, Judith 106
Weiss, Victoria L. 102
Weissman, Hope 128
Wekker, Herman 55
Wells, John 11
Wells, Stanley 157, 161, 166, 168–9
Wenska, Walter 431
Wentworth, Michael 205
Werner, Hans 204, 207
Werner, Martin 72
West, Gillian 204, 336
West, James L. W. III 350
West, Shearer 252
Westland, Ella 334
Wetherbee, Winthrop 107, 125, 126, 130
Wettstein, Howard 20
Wevers, Lydia 575
Whale, John 257, 308
Wheale, N. 166
Wheeler, Kathleen 295
White, Graham 550
White, Helen Watson 581
White, John 424
White, Keith 55, 300
White, Kerry 534
White, Paul Whitfield 196
White, R. S. 169
Whiteman, Bruce 527
Whitman, Jon 275
Whittington, Graeme 59
Whitworth, Charles 156–7
Whobrey, William T. 92
Widgery, David 7
Wiegand, Herbert Ernst 57
Wieman, J. 32–3
Wiens, Pamela 356
Wiggins, Martin 193–4
Wiggins, Peter De Sa 149
Wikander, Matthew H. 238
Wikle 27–8
Wilcockson, Colin 175, 186, 198
Wilcox, Jonathan 92, 93
Wilding, Michael 551
Wilkes, G. A. 58
Wilkinson, Rupert 424
Willbanks, Ray 551
Willett, John 495
Williams, Aubrey 257
Williams, Barbara 551
Williams, Carolyn D. 256–7
Williams, Colin 31
Williams, David 522
Williams, Elizabeth 106–7
Williams, J. Hadley 184
Williams, Keith 365
Williams, Mark 560, 574, 577
Williams, Michael 299–300, 396
Williams, Peter 538
Williams, Trevor L. 377
Williamson, Alan 400
Willis, Susan 164
Wilmer, Clive 323–4
Wilmer, Steve 406
Wilner, Arlene 263
Wilson, Angus 395
Wilson, Ann 416
Wilson, Betty 562–3
Wilson, Carol Shiner 300
Wilson, Edmund 465
Wilson, Gayle Edward 238
Wilson, Geoffrey 59
Wilson, John 63, 90
Wilson, Katharina M. 1
Wilson, Matthew 503
Wilson, Rob 462–3
Wilt, Judith 341
Wimsatt, James I. 134
Winch, Gordon 536–7
Windeatt, Barry 136
Winer, Robert 410
Wing, George 344–5
Winterbottom, Michael 74–5
Wintle, Sarah 177–8
Witek, Terri 469
Woddis, Carole 406
Wogan-Browne, Jocelyn 100
Wojahn, David 461
Wolfe, Cary 476
Wolff, Sally 427
Wolfshohl, Clarence 252
Wolfson, Susan J. 300
Womersley, David 151–2, 198
Wong, Sau-ling Cynthia 499
Wong-Scollon 29
Wood, Chauncey 107, 136
Woodbridge, Linda 167, 170–1
Woodcock, George 518
Woodfield, Malcolm J. 336
Woodman, Ross 273
Woodman, Thomas 3–4, 256
Woods, Susanne 143, 223
Woods, William F. 129
Woof, Pamela 294, 309
Woolf, Judith 447
Woolford, John 316, 317
Wordsworth, Jonathan 270, 287, 293, 294, 327
Wormald, Patrick 79
Worth, Katherine 408–9
Worthen, John 371–2
Wright, Charles D. 93
Wright, Derek 503
Wright, Judith 541
Wright, Peter M. 184
Wright, Stephen K. 116, 119, 120
Wright, Susan 52
Wright, Terence 328
Wu, Duncan 287, 291, 293–4, 298, 305
Wunderlich, D. 57
Wussow, Helen 381
Wyke, Clement 570–1
Wyndham, Francis 5, 569
Xianzhi Liu 375
Yachnin, Paul 174, 187, 195
Yalom, Marilyn 499
Yeager, R. F. 107–8, 126–7, 131–2, 133, 137, 138
Yoder, R. Paul 226
Yolton, John 249
Yonglin, Yang 63, 168
York, Lorraine 525, 527
Yoshioka, Fumio 177
Youcheng Jin 375
Young, Alan R. 211,

516–17
Young, Arlene 329
Young, Arthur C. 346
Young, Philip 447
Young, Robert 303
Youssef, Valerie 28
Yulikova, Natalya 54
Zaefferer, Dietmar 57
Zaller, Robert 464, 468–9
Zanger, Jules 345–6
Zeeman, Nicolette 108
Zeifman, Hersh 415
Zelman, Thomas W. 404
Zernik, Uri 17
Zgusta, Ladislav 57
Zhang, John Z. 129
Zhaoming Qian 483
Zilboorg, Caroline 395, 464
Zimbardo, Rose 242
Zimmerman, Sarah 266
Zinman, Toby Silverman 409
Zitter, Emily Stark 135–6
Zlotnick, Susan 315, 339, 367
Zurbrugg, Nicholas 495
Zwicky, Fay 547

Index II. Authors and Subjects Treated

Authors such as Margaret Atwood and Salman Rushdie, who are both authors of criticism and subjects of discussion by critics, are listed in whichever index is appropriate for each reference; a page number in bold represents the main entry for a particular author. Under each author, subjects are grouped showing the author's relationship first with other authors and second with other subjects; the author's characteristics follow, and finally the works themselves are listed.

Abbey theatre, Dublin 406
Abercrombie, David 35
Abish, Walter 365, 490
abjection, concept of 368
Aborigines: early settler accounts 540–1; and post-colonialism 540; women, in Australian literature 542–3
Aboriginal languages 25, 535; English 20
Aboriginal literature **541–2**; drama 542; poetry 548; tales 536
absolutes: in English language 47–8
absolutism: Renaissance drama 193–4
absurd, theatre of the 411
abverbial change 53–4
academic novel: in America 491
academic press 10
Acosta, Oscar Z.: *Revolt of the Cockroach People* 487
acting companies: Restoration 233
actors and acting: boys 169, 191; Admiral's Men 190; Chamberlain's Men 190, 199; Elizabethan 185, 190–1, 192
Actresses' Franchise League 406
Adams, Abigail 426, 428
Adams, Glenda 554–5
Adams, Henry 500; crisis in 434; *Education of Henry Adams* 436
Adams, John 428
Adamson, Robert 555, 556
addict vision: of Burroughs 495
Addison, Joseph 247; and the flaneur 433–4
Adisa, Opal Palmer 563
adjectives 64; Old English 38; separative 46–7
Admiral's Men 190
Adonmnán 89
Adorno, Theodor: and James 446
adultery: Anglo-Saxon 72; in Updike 503
adverbial shifts 53
adverbs: Middle English 38
advertisements: and Bodley Head 356; poster 62
Ælfric 76, 80; and *Genesis* 94; *Vita S. Aethelwold* 75
Aesop's Fables 142; and Ogilby 239
aestheticism: and modernism 350
aesthetics, cultural 209
Æthelberht of Kent: adultery law 72
Aethicus Ister: *Cosmographia* 92
Africa: English language 20, 24, 26–7; imperialism 366; in Lawrence and Eliot 400, 467
Afro-American literature 487–8; drama 435; oral tradition 459; women writers 433, 487; *see also* black literature
Afro-American vernacular 28
Afro-Americans: in France 456–7
Afro-Caribbean literature 487; *see also* Caribbean literature
Agard, John: sound recording 561
age: and language 32
Agrippina of Nettesheim: *Of the Nobilitie and Excellencie of Womankynde* 143
Aiken, Conrad 424
Alabaster, William 150–1, 212
Alamanni, Luigi 145
Albers, Josef: and Black Mountain College 460
alcohol: and Coleridge 296; and Styron 502
Alcott, Louisa May: *Little Women* 426, 438
Aldington, Richard: and Hellenism 395, 464–5

Alfred 72, 78; and *Cura Pastoralis* 77, 92
alienation: and Donleavy 365–6
allegory 274–5
Allen, Hervey 442
Allen, Walter 361
Alleyn, Edward 191, 197, 199; and Bear Garden 190
Allfrey, Phyllis Shand 563
alliteration: in newspapers 55; in York cycle 117
alliterative poetry: ME 101
allusions: in Chaucer 125
Alpagus, Andreas, of Belluno 475
alternative theatre 410–11
Alther, Lisa 423
Althusser, Louis: and realism 469
Amabile, George **526–7**; 'Horizons' 512; *The Presence of Fire* 526
Amazons: in Sidney 143
America: Australian literature published in 533; literary nationalism 478; possession by Europeans 429
American art: and Tomlinson 403
American dream: and Hawthorne 443; and Captain John Smith 424
American English: syntactic change 46
American Indian *see* Amerindian
American literature: before 1900 **422–51**; 19th C **432–51**; 20th C **454–504**; and Canadian literature 515–16; southern writers 484–5; Victorian criticism 353
American sublime 462–3; and Lowell 469
American West: and Dorn 465; and Twain 448
Amerindian literature: fiction 485–6
Amerindians: language 28; and *Moby Dick* 433; politics 428; treatment of 424
Amis, Kingsley: influence of OE literature 70
Ammons, A. R.: 458, **463**; walk poetry 457; 'Essay in Poetics' 463; 'Poem is a Walk' 457
Anand, Mulk Raj 557, 559; *Untouchable* 560–1
Anaya, Rudolpho: *Heart of Aztlan* 487
Anderson, Ethel: *At Parramatta* 553
Anderson, Jane: and Conrad 371
Anderson, Jessica: 'Of Rhinos and Caryatids' 555
Anderson, Patrick: homosexuality and Communism 528
Anderson, Sherwood 439; and Lawrence 374
André, Bernard: *Hymni Christiani* 145
Andrew legend 88
Andrewes, Lancelot: sermons 217
Andrews, Bruce 469
androgyny: in 16th C 143; in Amabile 526–7; boy actors 169; Elizabethan theatre 191
Angelou, Maya 460; autobiography 427
Anglican church: 18th century 253; Restoration 234
angling vocabulary 56
Anglo-American feminist detective fiction 389
Anglo-French: in English etymology 56
Anglo-Latin literature 74–5
Anglo-Saxon art 70–1
Anglo-Saxon Chronicle 76, 78, 91
Angry Penguins group 544
annotation: and Pater 348
Ansen, Alan: and Burroughs 494
anthologies **5–8**
Anthony, Michael 567; and nationalism 565
anthropological poetics 455
anthropology: Aboriginal tribes 540–1; and gender 352
anti-Catholicism: of *Punch* 351
anti-Semitism: and T. S. Eliot 401; and Marlowe 198; and Pound 474
anti-Utopian irony: in American culture 424
Antin, David: poetry in performance 458
antinomianism: and Blake 282
Anzac myth 538
apocalypticism: in Lawrence 373; in Shakespeare 170
Apollonius of Tyre 95, 107, 108
Appalachian writers: on space 460–1
Apple, Max 490
apprentice literature 141
Aquinas, St Thomas 144
archaeology: and literary study 78
architecture 2, 3; Italian 254; and OE poetry 82; and Pater 347
Arden of Faversham 204
Arensberg Salon 462
Ariadne: *She Ventures and He Wins* 233
Ariosto, Ludovico 149; and Milton 224; *Orlando Furioso* 186
aristocratic subjectivity 209
Aristotle 144; and Byron 300; and Donne 214; and Shakespeare 179; *De Anima* 214; *Metaphysica* 214; *Politics* 179

Armstrong, Jeanette 514
Arnold, Matthew: and Pater 348; and literary authority 271; and publishing 356
Arrowsmith: *Reformation* 238
art: and 19th C commerce 277; American avant-garde 462; Anglo-Saxon, images of women 70–1; and Australian media 538; book 488; Caribbean 564–5; eroticism in 254; Italian, in Henry James 447; in literary magazines 354–5; and ME drama 116, 119; and Milton 223–4; and the press 8, 355; symbolism 339; Victorian 8; *see also* visual arts
art history 251
'Arthur the Rat' 34
Arthurian romances 113, 324–5; and Milton 225
Arthurian verse 98
arts: Augustan age 1–2
Ashbery, John 458, **463**; procedural work 456; quotational effects 457; *Double Dream of Spring* 463; 'French Poems' 463
Ashby, George 109
Ashton-Warner, Sylvia 576
Asian writing: in Canada 513
Asian-American writing: and Kingston 498–9
Asimov, Isaac 489
Askew, Anne: *Dialogue with Authority* 145–6
assassin figure: Renaissance drama 193
Asser: *Life of Alfred* 77
Astley, Thea 533
Atkinson, Louisa 550
atomism 216, 218–19, 240
Atte ston castinges 111
attribution studies: Renaissance 185–6
Atwood, Margaret 366, 389, 512, 514, **523**; Americanization of fiction 515–16; and memory 367; *Bluebeard's Egg* 522, 524; *Cat's Eye* 523; *The Handmaid's Tale* 522; *Lady Oracle* 523; *Surfacing* 61
Auchinloss, Louis **491–2**
auction: rare books 11
Auden, W. H.: and T. S. Eliot 401, 466; and Lawrence 374; reaction to Nazi film 470; as seriocomic critic 402; 'Musée des Beaux Arts' 468
audience: reaction to Renaissance drama 192; reaction to Shakespeare 189
audition pieces: from Canadian plays 530
Augustine, St 401; and Spenser 149–50
Austen, Jane: and Golding 265; and James 447; *Pride and Prejudice* 63, 265
Austin, William 432
Australia: in Dickens 333
Australian language 20, 24, 25; dictionaries 58; English 535
Australian literature 533–57; literary criticism 537; and New Zealand literature 548; Northern Territory 548
authorial control: in drama 411
authorial security: and Cooper 436
authorship: disputed *see* attribution studies; multiple 272–3
autobiography: American 427–8, 433; Australian 543–5; New Mexican women 486; Romantic 295; and subject knowledge 578; and *The Woman Warrior* 499
avant-garde: American 462; and American novel 423; and Burroughs 495; concept of 363
avant-garde theatre: assessment 410–11
Avicenna 196; and Pound 475; *De Almahad* 475
Awekotuku, Ngahuia 577
Ayr, Scotland: dialect 30
Aytoun, William Edmonstoune 336
Aztlan 487
Bachelard, Gaston: *La Poétique de l'espace* 460–1
Bacon, Francis 219; and Milton 225–6
Bail, Murray 549, **553**; and White 553; 'The Drover's Wife' 549; *Holden's Performance* 553; *Homesickness* 553
Bailey, Benjamin 301
Baillie, Joanna 274
Bakhtin, Mikhail 260, 446, 486; and Burns 304–5; and Chaucer 113, 128; and Dryden 238; and Fowles 393; and Joyce 378; and Poe 299–300; and first love 374; theory of the dialogic 332, 496
Balaban, John 458
Baldwin, James 488; in France 457
ballads: 16th C 9; bush 536; Jacobite 250; and plays 167; Renaissance 209–10
Balzac, Honoré de 328; and Henry James 444
Bandello, Matteo 196
Bannon, Anne: and lesbian writing 368

Barbauld, Anna 249, 273
Barker, Daniel: *History of Job* 256
Barker, George 517
Barker, Howard: *The Bite of the Night* 407–8; *The Last Supper* 407–8
Barnard, Marjorie 555
Barnes, Peter 394; and goodness 408
Barnfield, Richard: complete poems 151
baroque genre 209
Barr, Stringfellow: *Purely Academic* 491
Barrie, J. M.: *Peter Pan* 262
Barry, Sebastian: poetic drama 408
Barrymore, John: and Shakespeare 164
Barth, John 423, 488, 491, **492**; and postmodernism 484; *Chimera* 492; *The Floating Opera* 492
Barthelme, Donald **492–3**; and post-modernism 485; *Come Back* 493; *The Dead Father* 493; *Dr Caligari* 493; *Snow White* 493; *Unnatural Acts* 493; *Unspeakable Practices* 493
Barthes, Roland 392–3; neglect of race 366; postmodern aesthetics 456; vocal pluralism 465
Barton, John: and *The Rover* 242
baseball poems 458–9
Basque language 26
Bates, H. E. 365
Batistich, Amelia 575
Battle of Alcazar, The: stage preparation 188–9
Battle of Brunanburh, The 78
Battle of Maldon, The 74, 80, 85, 91
Baudelaire, Charles 434; and Pound 472; and crowd image 456
Baxter, James K. 576
Baxter, Richard 234; correspondence 218
Baxterian sonnet 576
Bayle, Pierre: and Byron 299
Baynes, John 294
bear gardens: Jacobean 190
Beat Movement 490; and Burroughs 495; and Pynchon 502
Beatty, Arthur 287
Beauchemin, Yves 513
Beaumont, Sir Francis: partnership with Fletcher 206–7; (with Fletcher) *Double Falsehood* 206–7; *Knight of the Burning Pestle* 207
Beaumont, Sir John 212
Beaver, Bruce: poetry 555
Beckett, Samuel 61, 367, 374, 394, 407; and Burroughs 495; and Ireland 248; and American postmodernists 484; as director 408; drama **408–12**; Irish context 408, 409; tragicomedy 406–7; *All That Fall* 412; *Eh Joe* 410; *Endgame* 409; *Krapp's Last Tape* 410, 412; *Not I* 410; *Ohio Impromptu* 410, 411–12; *Quad* 412; *Waiting for Godot* 409, 411; *What Where* 412; *Words and Music* 412
Bede 80, 94; 'imperial' vocabulary 71; *Caedmon* 77, 78, 81; *History* 71–2; *Imma* 77; *Nomina locorum* 92
Bedford, Lucy, Countess of: as patron 210
bee: metaphor of 301
Beecher, Henry Ward: and American gentlemen 436
Beerbohm, Max: 'Henry James Listening at a Keyhole' 447
Behan, Brendan 407
Behn, Aphra 218, **242, 244**; and Ovid 242; and patronage 242; attributed manu-script 240; royalist ideology 242; *Fair Vow-Breaker* 261; *Feigned Courtesans* 233; *Love Letters* 244; *Oroonoko* 242; *The Rover* 242; 'The Unfortunate Happy Lady' 234, 244; 'The Willing Mistress' 240
Belleforest, Francois de 196
Bellow, Saul 488, **493–4**; *The Bellarosa Connection* 494; *Henderson the Rain King* 494; *Mr Sammler's Planet* 489, 494; *Seize the Day* 494; *The Theft* 493
Benedictine Reform 75
Benford, Gregory 489
Benjamin, Walter 434; and James 446
Bennett, Arnold 367
Benserade, Isaac de 239
Bentley, Richard 247; and Dickens 335; edition of *Paradise Lost* 248
Beowulf 77, 80, 81, 82, **82–6**, 94; archaeology 78
Bergson, Henri 401; and *élan vital* 415
Bergsonism: T. S. Eliot's rejection of 467
Berkeley, George 254
Berkoff, Steven 61
Bernardus Silvestris 138
Bernard, Jeffrey 7
Berry, James: sound recording 561
Berry, Wendell 459
Berryman, John: and Ciardi 362; private life of 460
Betjeman, John 403
Beynon, Richard: *Simpson, J. 202* 547

Bible: British and Foreign Bible Society 354; and Chaucer 140; King James Bible 211, 480; OE 80; and Stevens 480; and Styron 503; and Tyndale 145
bibliography **8–12**
Bierce, Ambrose: 'Oil of Dog' 63
bilingualism: in Canada 513
biographical criticism: and Macaulay 384; and multiple authorship 272–3
biographical journals 9
biography 1; Australian 545–7; and Malouf 551; and Morley 357; New Zealand literary 576
bird poems 113
Birney, Ed 517
birth-scenes 70–1
Bishop, Elizabeth 62, 458, **463–4**; and nature 461; and sexual difference 459; 'One Art' 464
Bissel, Claude: *Ernest Buckler Remembered* 521
Bissoondath, Neil 513, 559; *A Casual Brutality* 522; *Digging Up the Mountain* 522
Black Arts Movement: and Broadside Press 459
black literature: 18th C 248; American women poets 460; American writers in France 435, 456–7; and culture 428; Indian women writers 558; women writers 388; *see also* black theatre
Black Mountain College 460
Black Mountain poets 528; and Lawrence 374
black theatre 574; women's 406
Blackburn, Henry 355
Blackburn, Paul: serial form 456
Blair, Robert: *The Grave* 278, 286
Blair, Ron 547
Blaise, Clark **519**; 'The Little Orphan' 519
Blake, William 257, **275–86**, 402; and Hogg 286; and Marsh 278–9; and Reaney 531; and Sophocles 284; and Thomson 25, 283; and Wordsworth 286; and authority 271; and chaos theory 283–4; and French Revolution 283; and millenarianism 281–2; and occult 283; purchasers of works 276; biography 277–8; engravings 277; facsimiles 276–7; illuminated books 276–7, 284; illustrations 285; imagination 280; relationship with women 278; *America* 281; *Book of Thel* 284–5; *Book of Urizen* 281; *The Canterbury Pilgrims* (picture) 279; 'Crystal Cabinet' 258, 283; *Descriptive Catalogue* 127; *Europe* 283; *The Four Zoas* 279, 280; 'Infant Joy' 284; *Jerusalem* 60, 213, 276, 278, 279, 280, 284, 285; *London* 281; *Marriage of Heaven and Hell* 271, 281, 282, 283–4, 308; *Milton* 271, 272, 279, 285; 'Night' 284; 'The Phoenix' 278; 'Proverbs of Hell' 282; *Song of Los* 279; *Songs of Innocence and of Experience* 276–7, 281, 284; 'Tyger' 281, 283, 284, 572; *Urizen* 285; *Visions of the Daughters of Albion* 278, 285
Bloch, Ernst: *Principle of Hope* 367
Bloom, Harold 288
Bloomfield, Leonard 23–4
blues music: and oral tradition 459
Blunden, Edmund: 'Thiepval Wood' 396–7
Boccaccio, Giovanni: *Decameron* 133
Bodleian Library 9, 11, 114
the body: and Burnshaw 464; and Charles II 231; in Jonson 203; in Joyce 379; and Marlowe 199; in Shakespeare 203; and Whitman 450
Boethius 109; *De Consolatione Philosophiae* 78, 107, 126, 134, 138
Bogdanov, Michael: and Shakespeare 162–3
Boiardo, Matteo: *Orlando Inamorata* 224
Boland, Eavan: and repossession 404
Bond, Chris: *Scum* 407
Bond, Edward: theory of acting 412
Bond, Elizabeth: *Love and Dissent* 407
The Book of Sir Thomas More 185
bookbinding 10
border narratives 486
borders: and Canadian literature 516; in Gallant 523–4
Borges, Jorge Luis: and Pynchon 501; and American postmodernists 484; influence of OE literature 70
Bosco, Monique 513
boundaries: transgression of 392
Bowen, Elizabeth: *Heat of the Day* 387
Bowering, George 527–8; long poems 529
Bowles, William Lisle 270; *Fourteen Sonnets* 304
Bowyer, William: printing business 246
Boyle, Roger 243

Brackenridge, Hugh Henry: *Modern Chivalry* 431
Braddon, Mary Elizabeth 327
Bradstreet, Anne: **430**; and the sublime 462; 'Foure Monarchies' 430; 'New Psalms' 430; *The Tenth Muse* 430
Brady, Hugh: *Maps and Dreams* 542
Bragg, Melvyn: and Lawrence 374
Brahminical discourse 559
Branagh, Kenneth 169
Brando, Marlon 5
Brandt, Bill 402
Brass, Eleanor: *I Walk in Two Worlds* 514
Brathwaite, Edward 566
Braun and Hohenberg: *Civitatis Orbis Terrarum* 186
Brennan, Christopher 545, 555
Brenton, Howard **412–13**; *Bloody Poetry* 413; *Greenland* 413
Brewster, Yvonne **573–4**; black women's theatre 406
British Library 9, 11, 112
British Museum Library 10–11
British Sign Language 31
Brodber, Erna 563
Brodsky, Joseph 460
Bromige, David 527–8
Bronk, William: procedural form 456
Brontës 338–9; and E. Dickinson 440
Brontë, Anne: *Tenant of Wildfell Hall* 340
Brontë, Charlotte **338–40**; juvenilia 339; *Jane Eyre* 329, 339, 386, 435; *Shirley* 336, 339; *Villette* 328, 329, 339–40
Brontë, Emily: Gondal poems 315–12; *Wuthering Heights* 340, 386
Brook, Peter: and Shakespeare 162, 163, 164–5, 165; and voice 407; modes of reality 413
Brooke, Frances 520
Brooke, Rupert 363; as poet of peace 396; 'The Fish' 375
Brooks, David 539
Brooks, Gwendolyn 459
Brothers, Richard: millenarianism 281–2
Brown, Charles Armitage: and Keats 301
Brown, Charles Brockden: and Romanticism 437; *Memoirs of Carwin the Biloquist* 431; *Wieland* 431
Brown, D. F. 458
Brown, Eliza and Thomas: letters and journals 543, 550
Brown, Frances: *Granny's Wonderful Chair* 328
Brown, Goold 22
Brown, Sterling 459
Brown, William Wells: in France 435; 'The Escape' 435
Brown, Young Goodman 436
Browne, Thomas: and atomism 216; *Religio Medici* 217
Browning, Barrett 317–8
Browning, Elizabeth Barrett: and E. Dickinson 440; letters 314, 318; *Aurora Leigh* 314, **317–19**
Browning, Robert **316–17**; and authority 316; intertextuality 317; letters 314, 318; musicality 315, 317; sense of self 325; *Amours de Voyage* 326; *Flight of the Duchess* 317; 'Love Among the Ruins' 317; *Men and Women* 317; *Ring and the Book* 326
Bruce, Charles 528; *The Channel Shore* 521
Brueghel, Peter: 'Adoration of the King' 482–3
Bruno, Giordano: and Pater 348
Bryan, William 282
Bryant, William Cullen: and the sublime 462
Bryson, John: *Evil Angels* 551
Bubb, Charles C. 474–5
Buc, George 193
Buckingham, George Villiers, 2nd Duke of: *Rehearsal* 238
Buckley, Vincent: *Last Poems* 555
Buddhism: and Eliot 401
Budé, Guillaume 142
Bunbury, Henry William 264
Bunyan, John 217, 218, 234, **244**; and Van Gogh 244; and Calvanism 244; *Grace Abounding* 234; *The Holy War* 244; *Imitation of Christ* 244; *Mr Badman* 234, 244; *Pilgrim's Progress* 234, 244, 331
Burbage,Richard 191
Burdett, Sir Francis: and Cobbett 309
Bürger, Peter 363
Burgess, Anthony: *Clockwork Orange* 413
Burgh, James 308; *Political Disquisitions* 297
Burke, Edmund: and Coleridge 295–6, 308; and gender 308; and sublimity 279; *Enquiry* 308; *Reflections 308;*
Burne-Jones, Sir Edward 315
Burnet, Thomas 279, 282
Burnett, Ivy Compton 384

Burnett, James, Lord Monboddo 255
Burney, Dr Charles: letters 253–4; *Memoirs* 254
Burney, Frances 261, **263–4**; *Evelina* 263–4; *The Wanderer* 264
Burns, Robert 250, **259–60**, 270; and Bakhtin 304–5; love songs 260; *Poems chiefly in the Scottish dialect* 304
Burnshaw, Stanley: and the body 464
Burroughs, William 294, 488, 489, **494–6**; controversies 494; drug addiction 495; family 495–6; *Cities of the Red Night* 495; *Naked Lunch* 495; *Place of Dead Roads* 495; *Western Lands* 495; *Wild Boys* 495
Burton, Richard: and Shakespeare 165
Burton, Robert 234; *Anatomy of Melancholy* 217
Bush, George 436
Butler, Olivia 489
Butler, Robert Owen 490
Butler, Samuel 232
Butts, Elizabeth: and Blake 278
Byatt, A. S. 394
Byron, George Gordon, Lord 7, **298–301**; and Coleridge 299; and Southey 306; and Stevens 481; and authority 271; and religion 299; censorship 298; verse narrative 270, 271; *Cain* 298–9, 300; *Childe Harold* 299, 300; *Don Juan* 271, 299, 300; 'Fare Thee Well!' 60; *Giaour* 299, 300; *Heaven and Earth* 299; *Hebrew Melodies* 300; *Manfred* 299, 300; *Marno Faliero, Doge of Venice* 481; Napoleon poems 299–300; *Sardanapalus* 300
Caesarius of Heisterbach: *Dialogues miraculorum* 116
Cage, John: and Black Mountain College 460; procedural form 456
Callistratus 294
Calvanism: and Bunyan 244; and Beecher Stowe 448
Cambridge Platonists 218, 296
Cambridge, Ada: biographies 545
Campanella, Tommaso: *La Citta del Sole* 219
Campbell, David: recording of 544
Campbell, Hazel 563
Campbell, Maria 514
Campbell, Marion 539
Campbell, Thomas 270; *Gertrude of Wyoming* 270, 304–5
Canadian languages 24, 28
Canadian literature **510–33**; West Coast writing 523
Canadian North 512
Canadian West 518
Canning, George 270; (with Frere) *Poetry of the Anti-Jacobin* 305
canon: Canadian 511, 514–15, 529, 559; and Orwell 375
capitalism: and Gaddis 498
Caputo, Philip 490
Carducci, Giosue 475
Carew, Jan 567
Carew, Thomas: poems 216
Carey, Peter 533, 551, **553**; 'Do You Love Me?' 553; *Illywhacker* 553, 574; *Oscar and Lucinda* 553
Caribbean literature 561–74; women writers 388
Carlyle, Jane Welsh 332
Carlyle, Thomas 336; and Gissing 346; and authority 271
Carman, Bliss 528–9
carols, shepherds' 116
Carr, Emily: letters 517
Carr, Harriet 330
Carroll, Lewis: *Alice in Wonderland* 447; *Looking-Glass* letters 344
Carry On... films 5
Carter, Angela 362, **385–7**; *Black Venus* 387; The *Bloody Chamber* 385; 'The Kitchen Child' 386; 'The Lady of the House of Love' 386; *Love and the Infernal Desire Machines of Dr Hoffman* 386–7; *The Magic Toyshop* 386; *The New Woman* 387; *Nights at the Circus* 386, 389; *The Passion of New Eve* 387; 'The Tiger's Bride' 385–6
Carter, Elizabeth 249
cartoons 351; and Joyce 378; Beerbohm: 'Henry James Listening at a Keyhole' 447
Cartwright, Thomas 195
Carver, Raymond **496**; and Lawrence 374; sexual politics 496
Cary, Elizabeth: *Mariam* 195, 207
Castiglione, Baldassare, Count 142
Castillo, Ana: *The Mixquiahuala Letters* 486
The Castle of Perserverance 116
Castle, Terry 260
Castro, Brian: *Double-Wolf* 539

casuistry: Renaissance 142–3
Cather, Willa 432, 459; and domestic roles 460; *The Professor's House* 425
Catholic church: and Australian drama 547
Catholic novel 3–4
Catholic poets 150–1, 212
causation: in Shakespeare 172
Cavendish, Margaret 218, 241; *Blazing World* 234
Caxton, William: vocabulary 56
censorship: and Byron 298; and Lawrence 455; Renaissance drama 192–3
Centlivre, Susanna: *The Basset Table* 233; *Bold Stroke for a Wife* 242; *The Busy Body* 233
ceremony: in 17th C prose 217–18
Cervantes Saavedra, Miguel de: *Don Quixote* 142
Chamberlain's Men 190, 199
Chandler, Raymond: *Big Sleep* 390
Chandra G. S. Sharat: 'Heirloom' 558
Channel Islands: place names 59
Channing, William Ellery 426
Chanson, George 536
chaos theory: and Blake 283–4
Chapman, George 216
Chapman, John 340; and George Eliot 352
Chapman, John Jay: and Stevens 479
Chappell, Fred 485
character and characterization: American 424; in American postmodern fiction 484; in Beckett 409–10; in contemporary fiction 488; in Thackeray 330–31
charity bazaars, Victorian 331
charivari tradition: and Shakespeare 177
Chark, Charlotte 249
Charles I: and Dryden 236
Charles II: and Dryden 236; Stuart iconography 231
Charleton, Walter 234
Charlwood, Don: *No Moon Tonight* 548
Charney, Ann 513
charters: OE 71
Chase, Richard 428
Chatman, Seymour 554
Chatwin, Bruce 4; *Songlines* 542
Chaucer, Geoffrey **123–40** and Gower 107–8, 126–7, 131–3, 136, 137; and Hoccleve 108–9; and Shakespeare 175; and Spark 126; and American writers 436; ancestry 124; bibliography 123; character of Theseus 127; concordance 123; familiarity with languages 126–7; life 123–4; modernized versions 255, 279; politics 126; sexual politics 124–5; *Anelida and Arcite* 134, 139; *The Book of the Duchess* 124, 138, 148; *The Canterbury Tales* 125, **127–36**; General Prologue 129, 134, 137; Canon's Yeoman's Tale 135; Clerk's Tale 128, **133**; Cook's Tale 132, 126; Franklin's Tale **134**; Friar's Prologue 129; Knight's Tale 109, 127, **129–30**, 175; Man of Law's Tale **131–2**; Manciple's Tale **136–7**, 138; Merchant's Tale 133; Miller's Tale **130–1**; Monk's Tale 135; Pardoner's Tale 113, 134; Parson's Tale 136; Prioress's Tale **135**; Reeve's Tale **130–1**; Second Nun's Tale 136; Shipman's Tale 134; Squire's Tale 126, 134; Summoner's Tale **133–4**; Tale of Sir Thopas 136; Wife of Bath's Tale **132–3**; *The Complaint of Mars* 134; *The Envoy to Bukton* 139; *Equatorie of the Planetis* 123, 139; *The House of Fame* 124, 126, 127, 139; *The Legend of Good Women* 99, 108, 124, 126, 127, 139; *The Parliament of Fowls* 111, 113, 124, 138–9; *Roman de la Rose* 123, 130; *Troilus and Criseyde* 109, 110, 124, 125, 127, 134, **136–8**
Chaudhuri, Nirad 557
Chauliac, Guy de 115
Chavez, Denise 486
Chawaf, Chantal: and Angela Carter 386
Cheever, John 491; and Seltzer 496
Cheney, Nan: letters 517
Chesterton, G. K. 363, **369**
Chestre, Thomas: *Sir Launfal* 107
Chicano literature 486–7
Child, Lydia Maria 428
childhood: Australian 536; and Lawrence 374; New Zealand 579
Children of Paul's 191
children's literature 5; Australian 534, 536–7; and Marryat 330; New Zealand 576; in Puritan culture 234; Rossetti's poems 323; and Romanticism 273
children's theatre: and Marston 182; relaunch of 182
China: in Dickens 333; and Lawrence 375; and *The Woman Warrior* 498–9
Chinese language 29
Chinese poetry: and Williams 483

Chinese writers: conflict between tradition and modernity 499
Chithien, Nguyen 7
Chomsky, Avril Noam 19–20
Chopin, Kate 432, **438**; and games 437–8; *At Fault* 438; *The Awakening* 426, 437–8
Chrétien de Troyes: Arthurian romances 114
Christ I and Christ II 81
Christ III 80, 81, 89
Christianity: in *Beowulf* 83
Church, Barbara 478
Church, Henry 478
Churchill, Caryl 61, 410; *Cloud Nine* 403; (with Lan) *Mouthful of Birds* 406; *Top Girls* 406
Churchill, Sarah, Duchess of Marlborough: biography 253
Ciardi, John 464; and Burroughs 494; letters 464
Cibber, Colley 246, 257, 258; male sexual identity 243
Cicero 128; and Milton 228; *Cato Maior* 206
circus: and *Finnegans Wake* 379
Cisneros, Sandra 486
civility: in 17th C prose 217–18
Clancy, Tom 6
Clare, John 270, **305**; *Shepherd's Calendar* 305
Clark, George Elliott 516
Clark, J. P.: 'Abiku' 63
Clark, Manning: *Puzzles of Childhood* 545
Clarke, Marcus: *His Natural Life* 550
Clarke, Sally: *The Trials of Judith K* 530
Clarkson, Thomas 292
class: American gentlemen 436; and Gaskell 330; and male writers 426
classics: and Dryden 237; Wordsworth's translations 293–4
classification: and Victorians 392
Cliff, Michelle 563
Clifford, Lady Anne: diaries 218
Clift, Charmian: recording of 544
closure: in fiction 394; and Hawthorne 443; and Henry James 445
Clough, Arthur Hugh: and religion 318–19; and the self 325
Cobbett, William: and Burdett 309
Cobden-Sanderson, Thomas 10
Cocteau, Jean 7
Cohen, Leonard 511, 528
Cohen, Matt 520
Coke, Sir Edward: *Institutes* 210–11
Coleman, Ornette 458
Coleridge, Hartley 296
Coleridge, Samuel Taylor 270, **294–8**, 327, 401; and Browning 317; and Burke 295, 308; and Byron 299; and Wordsworth 289, 290; and millenium 282; and Scriptural poetics 297; allegory 274; figurative language 295; literary authority 271; new philology 324; personal identity 297; plagiarism 272–3; *The Ancient Mariner* 289, 294, 295, 297–8; *Biographia Literaria* 272, 295; *Christabel* 294–5, 297; *The Destiny of the Nations* 297; 'Fears in Solitude' 296; 'Frost at Midnight' 270, 295; 'Kubla Khan' 272, 294–5, 297, 303; *Notebooks* 295; *On the Constitution of Church and State* 291; 'Pains of Sleep' 294; *The Plot Discovered* 295; 'The Raven' 273; 'Recantation' 297; 'Religious Musings' 293, 297; *The Statesman's Manual* 275
Colette 7
Coliphizacio 118
collage: and Barthelme 493; and Burroughs 495
Collier, John Payne 9
Collins, Harriet 343
Collins, Wilkie: and sensation novels 343; *No Name* 343; *Woman in White* 343
Collins, William 255
Collyer, Mary 255; *Felicia to Charlotte* 261
colonial America: women's literacy 430
colonial American literature: and new historicism 432
colonialism 365–6; in Aboriginal literature 542; and Forster 385; and Pynchon 502; and Updike 503
comedy 490
comic book industry: Australian 537
commedia dell'arte: in Foster 554; in New Zealand 581
commerce: and art in Romantic period 277
commodity culture 5
commonwealth literature **510–84;** problems 557
communism: and Plath 501
community languages: Australian 535
Compilatio de astrorum scientia 133
complaint genre: Renaissance 212–13

complement constructions 38–40
compound words: in Jacobean tragedy 38, 62
Compton-Burnet, Ivy: and lesbian writing 368
computational linguistics 18
computer corpora 17, 46, 57
computers: 'computerese' 55–6; and Renaissance drama 185–6; and Shakespeare 172
Comte, Auguste 341
Conan Doyle, Sir Arthur 368; and Greene 390
concordances: Chaucer 123
Congreve, William 218; *Incognita* 234, 244
connection: in Pynchon 501
connotation 57
Conrad, Jessie 371
Conrad, Joseph **369–71**; and Stevenson 346; adjectives 64; *Heart of Darkness* 364, 366, 370, 467; 'Karain: A Memory' 370; *Lord Jim* 64; *Nostromo* 370; *The Secret Agent* 369–70, 371; *Under Western Eyes* 62; *Victory* 371
conscience, prisoners of 7
Conservative Party: baptism of 353
The Consolation of Philosophy 99
Constable, Henry 150–1, 212
contemporary English 19, 33
contemporary theory: and OE 70
contraception: and *Finnegans Wake* 379
control theory 39
conventions: ME 98–9
Cooley, Dennis: long poems 529
Cooper, James Fenimore 423, 428, 435–6, **438–9**; and Romanticism 437; *The Deerslayer* 439; *The Last of the Mohicans* 439; *Leather-Stocking Tales* 439; *Lionel Lincoln* 438; *The Pioneers* 438; *The Spy* 438, 439; *The Ways of the Hour* 438–9
Coover, Robert 365, **496**; *Pricksongs and Descants* 496; *Public Burning* 496; *Universal Baseball Association* 496
Copernicus, Nicolas 380
copula deletion 28
Corbett, Richard 211; 'Against the Opposing of the Duke in Parliament, 1628' 217
core grammar 41–2
Corinna: and E. Heywood 242
Cornwall, Barry 270
Cornwall: language 21
corpora *see* computer
corpus linguistics 16–17
corrales, Spanish: compared to English theatres 187–8
corsets: in *Englishwoman's Domestic Magazine* 352
Cosijn, Pieter 83
Cottle, Joseph: *Alfred* 305
Cotton, Sir Robert 11–12
courtesy literature, Renaissance 213
courtier poets: Elizabethan 150
courtiership: in Castiglione and Jonson 142
courtly plays: in England and Italy 196
courtship novels 261
Cowley, Abraham 232; and K. Philips 239; *Davideis* 240; *The Puritan and the Papist* 240; *The Puritans Lecture* 240
Cowley, Joy: *Bow Down Shadrach* 580
Coxe, William: *Sketches of Switzerland* 309
Crabbe, George: 'Parish Register' 305
Crabbe, George **305**; *The Borough* 305; 'Parish Register' 305
Crane, Hart 528; and Marlowe 198
Crane, Stephen 424, **439**; *The Blue Hotel* 439; *The Bride Comes to Yellow Sky* 439
Crane, Walter 356
Crashaw, Richard 212, 216
Cravens, Margaret: and Pound 475
Crawford, Isabella Valency: *Malcolm's Katie* 511–12
Creech, William 250
Creeley, Robert 460; poetry in performance 458; serial and procedural form 456
creole: Australian 535; in Goodison 571; in Selvon 570
creolistics 25, 29
Crèvecoeur, J. Hector St John de: farm poetry 458
crime 1; 18th century 247–8, 252; female criminals in Defoe 262; *see also* detective fiction; murder
critical linguistics 61
Crockett, Samuel Rutherford 356
Cromek, Robert Hartley: and Blake 278; and Hogg 286
Crompton, Richard 151
Cromwell, Oliver 244
cross-cultural critical approaches 385
crowd: in American literature 428; image of 456

Crozier, Lorna: and female subject 527
Crucifixion: green tree motif 93
Cruisinga, Etsko 21
Cuban texts 487
cubist poetry: American 455–6
Cullen, Countee: in France 457
cultural influences: on Indian literature 560
cultural nationalism 514–15; Canadian 512
cultural politics: 20th-century theatre 407; and Milton 224
cultural studies: Australian 537–8; OE 71–2
culture: 18th century 251, 252; aesthetics 209; black American 428; Canadian 514–15; and Pynchon 501; World War I 363
Cumberland, George 283
Cumberland: place names 59
Cunliffe, Marcus: interests 424
Curme, George 21
Curnow, Alan 576
Cursor Mundi 113
Cynewulf 74
Cynewulf and Cyneheard 82
Czapski, Joseph 375
Dabydeen, David 565; sound recording 561
Dadaism 489
D'Aguiar, Fred: sound recording 561; on videotape 562
Dallas, George 353
Dame Sirith 116
damnation: in 17th C 210
dance: and Fairbrother Hill 531
dandyism 333
Dangerfield, Thomas 218; *Don Tomazo* 234
Daniel 77, 88
Daniel, Samuel: and Jonson 202
Daniels, Sarah: *Masterpieces* 406
Dante Alighieri: and George Eliot 342; and T. S. Eliot 401; and Langland 105; and Melville 447; and Ovid 100; and Swedenborg 475; Ciardi as translator 464; Blake as illustrator 285; *Divine Comedy* 100; *Inferno* 447; *Paradiso* 12 129; *Purgatorio* 111; *Vita Nuova* 111
Darwin, Charles: and Kate Chopin 438
Darwin, Erasmus 270; *The Loves of the Plants* 305; *Zoonomia* 287
Das, Kamala 558
Davanzati: *Scisma d'Inghilterra* 223
Davenant, William: and Dryden 238; *Macbeth* 243; *The Preface to Gondibert* 218; *A Proposition of Advancement of Moralitie* 218
Davenport, Robert: *Dialogue betweene Pollicy and Piety* 217
Davey, Frank: long poems 529; war poetry 528; 'Dead in France' 527–8
Davidson, John: and Gissing 346
Davidson, William 4
Davies, Robertson 512, 520, 522; and *The Tempest* 524
Davis, Beatrice: biography 546
Davis, Donald 531
Davis, Jack: *A Boy's Life* 541; *Kullack* 542
Davis, Rebecca Harding 439–40
Dawson, David 527
Day, Marele: 'Cold Hard Bitch' 555
De Antichristo 94
death: in Frame 579
Death and Life 112
The Debate of the Carpenters' Tools 112
debate poetry 112
De Beauvoir, Simone: and Chaucer 138
De Berg, Hazel: oral history recordings 544
debtors: Restoration 232
decentralization: in Canadian literature 512
deconstruction 61–2; and Chaucer 125; and Conrad 369–70; and G. Eliot 341; and feminist women writers 459; and Friel 413; and Renaissance casuistry 142–3
De die iudicii 80
defamiliarisation techniques: of Beckett 411–12
Defoe, Daniel: and Bunyan 244; *Memoirs of a Cavalier* 261–2; *Moll Flanders* 262; *Robinson Crusoe* 262; *Roxana* 262; *True-Born Englishman* 256
Deighton, Len 389
Dekker, Thomas: and patronage 196; Catholic source material 205; *If it be Not a Good Play, The Devil is in it* 195; *The Shoemaker's Holiday* 169, 205;(with Massinger) *The Virgin Martyr* 185, 205
Delaney, Shelagh: *A Taste of Honey* 406
Delany, Samuel 489
Les Déliquescences D'Adore Floupette 556
De Man, Paul 303, 398
De Mille, James **520**; *A Strange Manuscript Found in a Copper Cylinder*

520; *Helena's Household* 520
Deor 90
De Quincey, Thomas 394; and Wordsworth 290; and identity 307; and murder 307; and politics 307; psychoanalysis of 306; *Confessions of an Opium Eater* 295
Dering, Edward 198
Derrida, Jacques 379, 392, 489; and Blake 279, 280; and Frame 579; neglect of race 366
Desai, Anita 557, 558, **559**; *Baumgartner's Bombay* 559; *Clear Light of Day* 559
Descent into Hell 81
De Selincourt, Ernest 286
Deshpande, Shashi 558; *That Long Silence* 559
destruction: in American literature 423–4
detective fiction 368; Australian 555; feminist 366–7, 389, 491; and Fowles 393; and Greene 390; and Stout 502
Deux maris et leur deux femmes, Les 132
Dewey, John 427; and James 446; and poetry 462
De Zayas, Marias 462
diachronic changes 50–1
diachronic lexicology 56
dialect: and George Eliot 340
dialectology **24–33**
dialogue, fictional 60–1
Diamond, Stanley: anthropological poems 455; *Totems* 455
diaries: anthology 7–8
Di Cicca, Pier Giorgio 526
Dickens **330–8**; and the flaneur 433–4; female characters 329; maladies 332; urban settings 328; *American Notes* 334; *Barnaby Rudge* 289, 334; *Bleak House* 329, 329, 332, 336; 'Boarding House' 334; *David Copperfield* 318, 332, 333, 335–6; *Dombey and Son* 329, 332, 333, 335; *Edwin Drood* 333, 338; *Great Expectations* 333, 334, 337–8; *Hard Times* 328, 336; *Little Dorrit* 328, 337; *Martin Chuzzlewit* 335; *Nicholas Nickleby* 333, 334; *Old Curiosity Shop* 332, 334; *Oliver Twist* 329, 334; *Our Mutual Friend* 332, 333, 338; *Pickwick Papers* 334; *Sketches by Boz* 333, 334; *Tale of Two Cities* 337; *Uncommercial Traveller* 333
Dickins, Barry: *I Love to Live* 544
Dickinson, Emily 435–6, **440**; and Whitman 450; and meaning 461; and Romanticism 437; and science 424; and sense of self 478; and work 435
Dickinson, Frances 343
dictionaries 2–3, 57–8
Dictys, Cretensis: *Ephemeris Belli Troiani* 138
Didion, Joan 6, 381; and war 367
Diggers: and Milton 222
Dillard, Annie 459
dime novels: and the West 437
di Michele, Mary 513; interview 526; *Luminous Emergencies* 527
Disch, Thomas 489
discourse analysis 62–3; and pragmatics 62–3; and Shakespeare 177; and stylistics 60–1
disenchantment: in Chaucer 125
disjunct constituents 43
displacement: and women writers 389
Disraeli, Benjamin 328
dissent 7, 234; Restoration 234
divorce: and Milton 225
Dixon, Stephen 490
Dobson, Thomas: autobiography 543
Doctorow, E. L. **497**; *The Book of Daniel* 497; *Drinks Before Dinner* 497; *Lives of the Poets* 497; *Lonn Lake* 497; *Ragtime* 497; *World's Fair* 497
Dodd, Sir William 252
Doddesham, Stephen 108
Dodge, Mabel 462
dogs: in George Eliot 341
Dolce, Lodovico 147
domestic labour: female 386
domestic novels: and Henry James 445
domesticity: and American women writers 432; and Cather 460; and detective fiction 368; and Victorian women 315
Donleavy, S. P.: and alienation 365–6
Donne, John: 'Air and Angels' 214; 'The Extasie' 214; 'Twicknam Garden' 214
Donne, John 210, **214**, 234; and atomism 216; and Aristotle 214; and Herbert 213–14; and Yeats 398; and politics 212, 214; emblems 211; 'Air and Angels' 214; *Devotions upon Emergent Occasions* 214; 'The Extasie' 214; *Fourth Satire* 258; *Holy sonnets* 214; *Songs and Sonnets* 211, 214; 'Twicknam Garden' 214
Dorn, Edward 460, **464–5**; *Geography*

465
Dos Passos, John 424
double object analysis 40
Douglas, C. H. 474
Douglas, Sylvester: *A Treatise on the Provincial Dialect of Scotland* 34
Douglass, Frederick **441**; in France 435; Judaeo-Christianity in 437; and labour 435; *The Narrative* 426, 441
Dove, Arthur 462
Doves Press books 10
Dowson, Ernest: pastoral form 327
Drabble, Margaret 389, 394; and Lawrence 374; and memory 367; humour in 388; *The Realms of Gold* 388
drama: 17th C 233, **241–4**; 19th C 305; 20th C **405–16**; Aboriginal 542; Australian 547; Canadian 515, **529–32**; Caribbean **572–4**; compound words in Jacobean tragedy 38, 62; critical linguistics 61; importance of embarrassment 5; ME 111, **116–20**; New Zealand 575–6, **580–2**; Renaissance 164, **181–206**; teaching 529–30; *see also* Shakespeare
Dransfield, Michael 556
Drayton, Michael 183, 216
Dream of the Rood, The 80, 81, 89
dreams: American dream 429; ME 105; in Wilfred Owen 396
Dreiser, Theodore 439, **441**, 443; depiction of crowds 428; 'The Revolt of Mother' 441; *Sister Carrie* 441
dress: in Brackenridge 431
drink 6–7
Droeshout, Martin Senior: Shakespeare engraving 166
'Drover's Wife, The' 549, 550
Druick, Don: *Where is Kabuki?* 530
Drummond, William of Hawthornden 147
Dryden, John 232, 234, **235–9**; and Chaucer 255; and Davenant 238; and Eliot 399; and Racine 238; and Spenser 237; and Stevens 480; and Tonson 237; and *Aeneid* 237; and atomism 216; and politics 235; later works 235; plays **237–9**; poetic imagination 254; poetry **235–7**; *Absalom and Architophel* 236–7; *All For Love* 238–9; *Amboyna* 238; *Amphitryon* 235; *Astrea Redux* 236; *Cleomenes* 235; *The Cock and the Fox* 239; *Don Sebastian* 235, 239; *The Enchanted Isle* 238; 'Epistle to Dr Charleton' 236; *An Essay of Dramatick Poesie* 480; *Fables* 232; *First Georgic* 237; *Heroique Stanzas* 236; *The Hind and the Panther* 232, 235, 239; *The Indian Emperor* 238; *The Indian Queen* 239; *King Arthur* 235; *Marriage à-la-Mode* 237–8; *Miscellany Poems* 237; *Religio Laici* 232; *Sylvae* 237; *The Tempest* 238; *To the Memory of Mr Oldham* 236; 'To the Pious Memory of...Anne Killigrew' 237; *Works of Virgil* 235
Dubois, W. E. B.: in France 457
Duck, Stephen 255
Duckworth, Marilyn 577
Dudek, Louis 513
Duffy, Maureen: and lesbian writing 368
Dugdale, Sir William 158, 172
Dulac, Edmund 398
Du Maurier, Daphne: *Trilby* 345
Du Moulin, Peter: *England's Appeal* 238
Dunbar, Paul Laurence: 'When Malindy Sings' 459
Dunbar, William: *Goldyn Targe* 110
Duncan, Robert: serial form 456
Duncan, Sara Jeanette **520–1**; 'The Heir Apparent' 519; *The Imperialist* 521; *The Simple Adventures of a Memsahib* 521
Dunn, Nell 389
Dunstan, Keith: *No Brains At All* 544
Dürer, Albrecht: and Jarrell 468
Durham Prologue 116
Durrell, Lawrence 488; and D. H. Lawrence 374
Dyer, Sir Edward 150
Dyirbal languages 25
écriture féminine 521
Eden, Emily 327
Edgeworth, Maria 249, 261, 273
editors and editing: OE works 74; 18th C works 248; Chaucer, punctuation in 123; dictionaries for 2–3; Jonson 203; modernist texts 454–5; OE works 74; and Pater 348; poetics of 534; poetry 534; problem of authority 316; stage directions 185
Edward III, Reign of King 160; authorship study 186
Edwards, Caterina 513
Edwards, Dorothy 7
Edwards, Jonathan: and typology of nature 431

egotism: in American literature 425–6
Ehrhart, W. D. 458
Eldershaw, Flora 555
Elene 81, 87–8
Eleusinian mysteries: and Pound 473
Eliot, George 6, **340–3**; letters 340, 353; Adam Bede 341; *Daniel Deronda* 328, 342, 447; *Felix Holt* 341–2; 'Janet's Repentance' 343; 'Lifted Veil' 341; *Middlemarch* 341, 342; *Mill on the Floss* 329, 341–42; *Theophrastus Such* 341
Eliot, T. S. **398–401**, **465–7**; and A. D. Hope 556; and Pater 349; and Shakespeare 175; and Dylan Thomas 402; and Twain 449; and philosophy 427, 462; 'Englishness' of 465–6; text editing 455; *After Strange Gods* 399; *Ara Vos Prec* 465; *Ash Wednesday* 401, 467; 'Burnt Norton' 400; *The Cocktail Party* 467; 'Descent from the Cross' 400; *Four Quartets* 399, 401, 462, 465–6; 'The Hollow Men' 467; 'Little Gidding' 399; 'Portrait of a Lady' 465; 'Rhapsody on a Windy Night' 467; *Theory of the Novel* 401; *The Waste Land* 175, 273, 398–9, 400, 401, 402, 455, 465, 466, 467
Eliot, V. 399; edition of *The Waste Land* 455
Elizabeth I 150; and Lyly 183; portrait 143
Elliott, Michael: and Shakespeare 165
Ellis, A. J. 22
Ellis, Alice Thomas 4
Ellison, Harlan 488
Elmi, Saida Botan 7
Elyot, Sir Thomas 143
Emanuel, James: in France 457
emblems: 17th C 211; in Golding 391; in Marlowe 199
Emecheta, Buchi 362; immigrant experience 388
Emerson, Gloria 490
Emerson, Ralph Waldo 426, 478; and E. Dickinson 440; and Masters 470; and experience 457; and Romanticism 437; and the sublime 462
empire: and Forster 385
encyclopedia: Enlightenment 249; on Sidney 147–8
encyclopedic dictionaries 58
Engel, Marian: *The Bear and the Tattooed Woman* 522
England's Helicon 144
English language *see* language
English Revolution: and radical writers 308–9
English-Canadian literature 515; fiction 513
Enlightenment: encyclopedia 249; in America 424
entertainers: Jacobean 192
epic plays 573
epic tradition 365
Epicureanism 234
epistles, love 110
epithalamium 215
Equiano, Olaudah: *Narrative* 248
Erasmus, Desiderius 142; language 145; *Encomium Moriae* 144
'Ern Malley' poems 556
eroticism: in graphic art 254; Hindu 565
Erthe Toc of Erthe 111
Espinet, Ramabai: 'Barred' 563
essays 4–5; anthologies 5–6; Canadian 512
Essex, Robert Devereux, second earl of 150, 151, 198
Etherege, Sir George: *The Man of Mode* 243
ethics: 18th century 253; and fictional structure 362–63; Restoration 234
ethnic literature: America 429; Canada 513; Chicano 486; and *The Woman Warrior* 498–9
Euclid 291
euphemism 55
European literature: and James 446–7
Evangelicalism: in Dickens 332
Evans, Abel 256
Evans, Augusta Jane: *St Elmo's* 435
Evelyn, Mary 256
Everyman 116–17, 120
evil: in *Dr Faustus* 198; in ME drama 117; in Jacobean drama 194
exemplarity: in 16th C 142
Exeter Book **89–91**; Riddles 77, 90–1
existentialism: and Beckett 411; and Conrad 369; and Styron 502
Exodus 87–8, 93
exotic: in Restoration drama 233
expatriation: Americans in France 456–7
explorer narratives: Australian 543; Canadian 515
fables 2, 239; Aesopian 142
Facey, A. B.: *A Fortunate Life* 551

facsimile reprints: of Blake 276–7; Romantic period 269–70
Fairburn, Rex 576
fairy tales 8; and Angela Carter 385
falling: in *Canterbury Tales* 129
family systems theory: and Henry James 445
famine 552; ME 104
The Famous Victories of Henry V 182, 183
Fanshawe, Richard 211
fantasy: in Burroughs 495; in A. Carter 386; in Plath 471
farm poems 458–9
Farmer, Beverley 539
fascism: and Pound 474
fate 80; in *Beowulf* 83
The Fates of Men 89
Faulkner, William: editing 455; *Absalom, Absalom!* 446; *The Sound and the Fury* 425
Fauset, Jessie 432
Federman, Raymond: postmodernism 484
Fehsenfeld, Martha 412
Feinstein, Elaine: and Proust 388; *Lear's Daughters* 407
Feldt, Eric: *The Coast Watchers* 548
Fell, Margaret 249
Felton, John: *Sermones dominicales* 99
female body 383
female hero: in women's writing 577
female subject: and saints 100
feminine and femininity: in 18th C 263; and Joyce 376; in war poetry 396
feminism and feminist theory 7; and *Beowulf* 83; and Brewster 573; and A. Carter 387; and Chaucer 124, 133; and Conrad 370–1; and E. Dickinson 440; and G. Eliot 341, 342; and Fowles 392; and ghost stories 434–5; and history 328; and Joyce 376; and Kroetsch 524; and Milton 222; and Hannah More 307–8; OE poetry 87; and Pope 257; Renaissance drama 197, 205, 206, 207–8; and Rossetti 323; and Shakespeare 167, 177; Victorian age 315, 318; and Welty 504; and West 383; and Woolf 381, 382, 383; women of colour 486; *see also* feminine; gender; women
feminist criticism: of sentimental novels 431
feminist detective fiction 366–7, 389, 491
feminist drama 581; and intertextuality 406; Caribbean 573–4
feminist literature 488; American 423, 429, 484; Canadian 519, 522; fiction 367; *see also* women writers
Fennario, David: *Joe Beef* 530
Fenollosa, Ernest: and Pound 473
feudalism 98
fiction: 18th C **260–6**; 20th C **361–95**; American **433–49**, **484–504**; Canadian **518–26**; Caribbean **564–71; exotic covers 368;** Indian 558–9; New Zealand 577–80; structure 363; theories 362;
fictional genres: and women writers 366
Fiedler, Leslie A. 488
Field, Barron 279
Fielding, Henry 248, 261, 262, 263; and class 263; *Amelia* 263; *Joseph Andrews* 263; *Tom Jones* 263
Fife: place names 59
fights: in Shakespeare's plays 189–90
figurative language: of Coleridge 295
Fiji Indians 582
Fildes, Luke 333
films: Canadian 515; and Dickens 333–4; Nazi propaganda 470; and popular culture 5; and Shakespeare 163–4; *Clockwork Orange* 413; *Great Expectations* 334; *Naked Lunch 494; Passage to India* 385;
film techniques: and Le Carré 364
financial archives: of printers and publishers 350
Finch, Anne 249; and Wordsworth 256; and politics 255–6
Findley, Timothy 514, 522, **524–25**; and the media 532; *Famous Last Words* 525; *Not Wanted on the Voyage* 525; *The Paper People* 532; *The Telling of Lies* 525
fine art: and Pater 249
Firbank, Ronald: and homosexual writing 368
Fitzgerald, F. Scott 424; and American gentlemen 436; *The Great Gatsby* 8; *Tender is the Night* 425
Fitzgerald, Frances 490
flaneur: in American literature 433–4
Flaubert, Gustave: *Bouvard et Pécuchet* 392; *Madame Bovary* 392
Fleming, Ian 389
Fleming, J. W.: *Rug of Identity* 406

Fletcher, John: and *Cardenio* 158; *The Chances* 204, 207; *The Pilgrim* 186; (with Shakespeare) *The Two Noble Kinsmen* 196, 206; *The Wild-Goose Chase* 196, 206; *see also* Beaumont
Fletcher, Phineas: *Purple Island* 216
food: in Dickens 334; in Stevens 480
Ford, Ford Madox 5; The Good Soldier 64
Ford, John 195, **207**; *The Broken Heart* 207; *'Tis Pity She's a Whore* 194, 207
Ford, Richard 485
foreign authors 7
foreigners: in Renaissance drama 196
formal poetry 456
Formulae Communes 119
Forrester, Fanny 315
Forster, E. M. 143, 366, **384–5**; *Howards End* 64, 364; *The Longest Journey* 384; *Maurice* 384; *A Passage to India* 385; *A Room with a View* 384
Forsyth, Frederick 361
Fortune, Mary: short stories 549
fortune 99–100; in Chaucer 135
Foster, David: *Testostero* 554
Foster, Norm: *Opening Night* 530
Foucault, Michel 168, 374, 392, 486; and Jonson 202; and Milton 228; and Shakespeare 173; and power 247; *Discipline and Punish* 532
Four Foster Children of desire 149
Fowler, Henry and Frank 21
Fowles, John 362, **391–3**, 394, 488; and epic tradition 365; *Daniel Martin* 365; *The French Lieutenant's Woman* 391–93; *A Maggot* 391, 393
Fox, Charles James 254
Frame, Janet 577, **578–9**; *The Carpathians* 577–8
France: black American writers in 435, 456–7; ME literature 99, 100; World War I writers 363
Franco, Veronica 212
Frankfurt School: and realism 469
Franklin, Benjamin *Autobiography* 425
Franklin, Miles 545, 550
Franks Casket 72
Frascatoro: *Syphilis* 241
free adjuncts 47–8
Freeman, Mary Wilkins: ghost stories 434; *Faces of Children That Had Never Been* 434–5
freemasonry: 18th century 249–50; and *Finnegans Wake* 379
Fremd, Angelica: *Heartland* 555
French, David: *Salt-Water Moon* 531–2
French, Marilyn 423
French-Canadian novels 520
French Revolution: and Blake 282; and Mary Wollstonecraft 308
French Romanticism 457
Frere, John Hookham 270; (with Canning) *Poetry of the Anti-Jacobin* 305
Fresne, Yvonne du 575
Freud, Sigmund 145, 288–9, 297, 502; and H. D. 460, 464; and Australia 538–9; and Medusa 393; notion of the uncanny 376; oedipal theory 504
Friel, Brian 405, 407; and Irish drama 413; short stories 413; 'Foundry House' 413; *Making History* 413; *Translations* 413; *Volunteers* 413
friendship 6
frontier comedy: and Twain 448
Frost, Everett C. 412
Frost, Robert 424, **467–8**; and Ciardi 464; and nature 461; walk poetry 458; 'Stopping by Woods on a Snowy Evening' 468
Froude, J. A. 4
Fry, Christopher **413**
Frye, Northrop 269; and Reaney 531; *Double Vision* 510; *Fearful Symmetry* 510
Fugard, Athol 61
Fulford, Robert 512
Fulgens and Lucrece 196
Fulgentius 138
Fuller, Margaret: 428, **441–2**; travel writing 441–2; 'Miranda's Story' 438
Furphy, Joseph **549–50**; *Such is Life* 549–50
Fussell, Paul 363; *The Great War and Modern Memory* 367, 381; *Wartime* 387
Gabler, Hans: edition of *Ulysses* 455
Gacoyne, David: *Short Survey* 401
Gaddis, William 423, **497–8**
Gaines, Ernest 485
Gainsborough, Thomas: introduction to paintings 254
Galileo: and Milton 223
Gallant, Mavis 519, **523–24**; 'April Fish' 524; *Home Truths* 524; *In Transit* 524; *Its Image in the Mirror* 524; 'Virus X' 513
Gallun, Raymond Z.: autobiography 498

Galsworthy, John 413–14; *Justice* 414
Galt, John 327
Galton, Arthur 354
Gambon, Michael 165
games: in American culture 490; rhetoric of 437–8
Gandhi, Mahatma: and Narayan 560
Ganesan, Indira: *The Journey* 557
Gardiner, Dr Augustus Kinsley: and Melville 447
Gardner, Erle Stanle: *Perry Mason 502*
Garner, Helen **554**; *The Children's Bach* 554; *Cosmo Cosmolino* 554; *Dancing in the Dark* 554
Garnett, Edward 356
Gascoigne, George 142
Gascoyne, David: 'Diabolical Principle' 401
Gaskell, Elizabeth 328, **330**, 345; *Life of Charlotte Bronte* 330; 'Lizzie Leigh' 330; *Mary Barton* 330; *North and South* 329, 330
Gass, Ken 518
Gass, William H. 423
Gautier, Théophile: and Pound 472
Gawain-poet **101–4**; *Cleanness* 101; *Patience* 101–2, 104; *Pearl* 101, 104, 143, 213; *Purity* 101; *Sir Gawain and the Green Knight* **102–4**
Gay, John: *Fan* 256; *The Ravens* 256; *The Sexton and the Earth Worm* 256
gay writing *see* homosexual writers and writing; lesbianism
gaze: male, in Chaucer 128–9; women's 111
Gems, Pam: *Dusa, Fish, Stas and Vi* 406; *Queen Christina* 406
gender 490; androgyny 169; and anthropology 352; and canon formation 511; and E. Dickinson 440; in Elizabethan theatre 191; and Forster 384; and French 531–2; and Furphy 550; in Jacobean drama 195; and Joyce 376, 377; and Charles and Mary Lamb 306–7; language 18, 25; and male writers 426; and Milton 222; in Renaissance 143; and Tennyson 326; in Victorian novels 329; and West 383
generalized binding theory 44
Generides 106
Genesis: OE 86–7, 94; and Milton 228; and Shakespeare 169
genitives 43
genres: in Hulme 579
gentlemen: American 436
Geoffrey of Monmouth: *Historia Regum Britanniae* 100, 114
geolinguistics 31
Germanic legend: in OE poetry 79–80
Germans: in Australia 540
Germany: ME literature 100
gerontology: Renaissance 206; sociolinguistics 32
gerunds 41
Gesell, Silvio 474
Gheeraerts, Marcus II: Shakespeare painting 166
Ghosh, Amitav 559, 561; language 560
ghost stories: feminist perspectives 434–5
Gibbon, Edward: *Decline and Fall* 253
Gibson, Graeme 514
Gibson, William 489
Gielgud, John: and Shakespeare 165
Gifford, William 306; and the *Quarterly Review* 354
Gilchrist, Ellen: *The Anna Papers* 388
Gilman, Charlotte Perkins 432, **442**; ghost stories 434; non-fiction writings 442; *The Yellow Wallpaper* 432, 435, 438
Gilroy, Beryl: on video 562
Ginsberg, Allen 488; and Burroughs 496
Gissing, Algernon 346
Gissing, George **346**; masculine identity 344; scrapbook 346; urban settings 328
Glasgow, Ellen 427, 432
Glassop, Lawson: *We Were the Rats* 548
Glastonbury 114
Globe Theatre 164, 199; excavations 187, 188; management 190
Glossa ordinairia 119
glosses 73–4; scriptural 94
Godber, John: script of *Clockwork Orange* 413
Godkin, E. L.: and James 446
Goethe, Johann Wolfgang von: and James 446; *Trilogie der Leidenschaft* 294
goldfields: New Zealand 577
Golding, Oliver: and Austen 265
Golding, William 362; and mulberry emblem 391; *Darkness Visible* 391; *Lord of the Flies* 262, 391; *The Spire* 391
Goldsmith, Oliver: *History of England* 251; *The Vicar of Wakefield* 265
Gom, Leona 527
Goodbody, Buzz 167

Goodison, Lorna 563; interview 571; on video 561–2
goodness, problem of 408
Googe, Barnabe 151
Gore, Catherine 328
Gorges, Sir Arthur 150
Gospel of Nicodemus 93
gossip 538; and George Eliot 341
Gosson, Stephen: *Play of Plays* 200
Gothic 254; American 438; Canadian 518; and A. Carter 386; and Coleridge 296; and E. Dickinson 440; and R. West 383–4
Gothic buildings: and Pater 347
Gow, Michael: plays 547
Gower, John: and Chaucer 107–8, 126–7, 131–3, 137, 138; *Confessio Amantis* 99, 107, 108, 131; *Tale of Florent* 132
Grace, Patricia 575; interview 579; *Mutuwhenua* 579
Gracian, Baltasar 150
Graham, James 252
grammar 18, 21–2, 44–6; 19th C 22; of *Beowulf* 84; core 41–2; medieval 22; universal 41–2
grammaticalization 52–3
Granville, Charles 474
Granville, George, Lord Lansdowne 258
Granville Barker, Harley: and Shakespeare 162
graphology 62
Graves, Caroline 343
Graves, Robert 365
Gray, Thomas 246, 255; and Locke 259; correspondence 259; *De Principiis Cogitandi* 259; *Elegy* 258–9
Greco, El: and Spenser 150
Greece: and H. D. 464
Greeley, Horace 442
Greene, Graham 365, **390–1**; and Mauriac 390–1; 'Bear Fell Free' 391; *Brighton Rock* 390; *England Made Me* 391; *The Honorary Consul* 391; *The Human Factor* 391; *The Last Word* 391; *Ministry of Fear* 365; *Our Man in Havana* 390
Greene, Samuel 22
Greer, Germaine 533; *Daddy We Hardly Knew You* 545
Greg, William Rathbone 330
Gregory, Augusta, Lady 407; and the Abbey theatre 406
Grenville, Kate: and fatalism 555
Greville, Fulke (Lord Brooke): and atomism 216; *Caelica* 150
Grice, H. P.: theory of meaning 362
Grierson, Herbert 288
Grimm, Jacob 22
Groom, Winston 490
The Group 401
Grove, Frederick Philip **518**, 522; *As For Me and My House* 518; *Master of the Mill* 518; *Settlers of the Marsh* 518
Guarini, Giovanni: *Il Pastor Fido* 197
Gullah language 29
Gurdjieff, George I.: and Toomer 481–2
Gurney, Ivor 396
Gustafson, Ralph **529**; *Rocky Mountain Poems* 529; *Winter Prophecies* 529
Gysin, Brion 495
H. D. 7, **464**; and Greece 395, 464; and self-authorisation 460; canonisation of 455; intertextuality of 459; *Helen in Egypt* 464; *Hippolytus Temporizes* 464
Habermas, Jurgen: and Milton 229; and Romanticism 275
Habington, William 212
Hacket, William 173
Hackney Empire 407
Haggard, Rider: *King Solomon's Mines* 345; She 345–6
hagiography 75, 80
Haiti: language 29
Haley, Russell 575
Half Moon theatre 407
Hall, Donald 459
Hall, Peter: and Shakespeare 162
Hall, Rodney 552
Hall, Samuel Carter: and T*he Art-Union* 356
Hallam, Arthur: and Tennyson 326, 327; *Memoir* 327
Hamilton, Briton 4
Handke, Peter 365
Hands, Terry: and Shakespeare 162–3
Hannah, Barry 485
Hanrahan, Barbara: *The Frangipani Gardens* 555
Hapgood, Elizabeth: and Stoppard 416
Hardinge, William M.: and Pater 347
Hardy, Thomas **319–20**, 344–5, 367, 374, 402; 1912–13 poems 314, 319–20; 'By the Century's Deathbed' 319; 'Darkling Thrush' 319–20; *Jude the Obscure* 328; *A Pair of Blue Eyes* 344; *The Return of the Native* 344; *Tess of the*

d'Urbervilles 328, 345; *Wessex Tales* 345; *The Woodlanders* 344, 345
Hardy, Frank 544
Hardy, Thomas 367, 374
Harington, Sir John: *Ariosto* 150
Harland, Henry: and James 446
Harper, Frances: slave stories 433; *Iola Leroy* 432, 435
Harper, Michael S. 459
Harpur, Charles 555
Harris, James 248
Harris, Lawren: and Voaden 531
Harris, Max 544
Harris, Wilson 560, 564, 565–66, 567; and post-colonialism 566
Harrison, Tony: critical anthology 404, 414; poetic techniques 405
The Harrowing of Hell 116, 117
Hart, Julia Catherine Beckwith: *St Ursula's Convent* 518–19
Hart, Kevin 548
Hart-Smith, William: *Hand to Hand* 555
Harte, Bret 437
Hartley, David: and Wordsworth 287; *Observations on Man* 277
Hartlib, Samuel: *Ephemerides* 218
Harwood, Gwen: poetry 556
Hasluck, Nicholas: *The Country without Music* 554
Hastings, Adrian 3
Hatfield, Martha 234
Hatt, Robert: 'Pangolin' 470
Havel, Vaclav: and Coleridge 296
Havelok 107
Hawking, Stephen 443
Hawthorne, Nathaniel 428, 435–6, **442–3**; and Atwood 515–16; and H. James 444; campaign biography for Franklin Pierce 443; depiction of crowds 428; modernity in 434; 'Alice Doane's Appeal' 442, 443; 'Benito Cereno' 426; *Blithedale Romance* 424, 443; 'Chiefly About War Matters' 443; 'Custom-House' 426, 442; *The House of the Seven Gables* 337, 426, 436–7, 443; *The Marble Faun* 443; 'Rappaccini's Daughter' 442; *The Scarlet Letter* 437, 442–3
Hay, Sir Gilbert: *Alexander* 109
Haydn, Franz Josef: *Creation* 229, 292
Haydon, B. R. 301
Haywood, Eliza: biography 261; *Fantomina* 261
Hazlitt, William 275; and authority 271; and autobiography 295; and print culture 309
Hazzard, Shirley 533; short stories 554; *Transit of Venus* 554
Healy, John 7
Heaney, Seamus 401; and Ireland 404; influence of OE literature 70; *The Grauballe Man* 405; *Ocean's Love to Ireland* 404
Hearne, Samuel: travel narrative 520
Hebrew: occult terminology 211; poetry 60
Hegel, George Wilhelm Friedrich 373, and American literature 425; concept of Logos 297; *Phenomenology* 325
Heibrun, Carolyn: *Poetic Justice* 491
Heidegger, Martin: and Oppen 471; concept of *Dasein* 500
Heilbrun, Carolyn: *Death in a Tenured Position* 491; *A Trap for Fools* 491
Heinemann, Larry 490
Heinlein, Robert 489
Heisenberg, Werner 489
Hellenism: of Aldington and H. D. 395, 464
Heller, Joseph 488, **498**
Hemans, Felicia 270, 274; *Records of Woman* 305
Hemingway, Ernest 424; and Twain 449; 'The Short Happy Life of Francis Macomber' 63; *The Sun Also Rises* 425
Henri, Adrian 401
Henry VIII: and drama 195
Henry, Alice: biography 545
Henryson, Robert: *Orpheus and Eurydice* 109; *The Testament of Cresseid* 109
Henshaw, Mark 539
Henslowe, Philip 199; playhouse structure 187; theatre management 190
Heraclitus 257, 302
Herbert of Cherbury, Edward, Lord 211
Herbert, George 144, 210, 212, **213–14**; and Donne 213; and courtship 213; meditation and mysticism 213; *The Bag* 213; 'The Sacrifice' 213; 'The Thanksgiving' 213; *The Temple* 213
Herbert, Percy 218
Hereford Gospels 70
Herford, C. M. 184–5
hermaphrodites 143
hermeneutics: ME 99
hero: female hero in women's writing 577; heroic values, OE literature 80

Heroides 110
Herr, Michael 490
Herrick, Robert **215–16**; and periodicals 216; cultural materialism 215; royalism 215; social standing 215; *Hesperides* 144, 215–16; *Noble Numbers* 215
Hesse, Hermann 7
Hewett, Dorothy: *Wild Card* 545
Heywood, Eliza: and Corinna 242
Heywood, Thomas: and *Tom a Lincoln* 183–4; *A Woman Killed with Kindness* 204–5
Hiberno-English 21
Hiberno-Latin literature 89–90
Highway, Thomson 514, 530
Hill, Anne Fairbrother: biography 530–1
Hill, Barry 539
Hill, Charles 531
Hill, Geoffrey: influence of OE literature 70; 'Mystery of the Charity of Charles Pequy' 403–4
Himes, Chester: in France 457
Hindmarsh, Gladys 527; *Ucluelet* 517
Hindmarsh, Robert 282
Hinduism: and Keats 302
Hinojosa, Rolando 487
His Majesties Complaint: and Herbert 213
Historia Apollonii 107
historical fiction: and Styron 503
historical scholarship: American, geographical shift 432
historicism: and Wordsworth 292
history: Aboriginal 541; and H. Adams 434; American literary 425; as constructed discourse 393; and Hegel 425; and literature 328; New Zealand literature 574–6, 577; and Woolf 382–3; *see also* historicism, New Historicism
Hitchcock, Alfred 388
hoax: 'Ern Malley' poems 556
Hoban, Russell 362
Hobbes, Thomas 236, 291; and Davenport 218; *Leviathan* 210
Hoccleve, Thomas: and Chaucer 108–9; *The Regement of Princes* 108; *Tale Jereslaus' Wife* 108–9
Hodge, Merle 567
Hodgins, Jack 522
Hoffman, Ernst: and James 446
Hogarth, William: and the erotic 254; graphic art 254; *The Beggar's Opera* 247–8; *The Conquest of Mexico* 238; *Industry and Idleness* 247–8
Hogg, James 250; *Confessions of a Justified Sinner* 286; *New Year's Gift* 306
Hogg, John 303
Hoggart, Richard: *Uses of Literacy* 389
Holcroft, Thomas 270; *The Road to Ruin* 306
Holdern, Michael: and Shakespeare 165
Hollar, Wenceslaus: Elizabethan playhouse 187
Holles, John 192
Holliday, Joyce: *Anywhere to Anywhere* 407
Hollingsworth, Margaret 518
Holocaust: in American poetry 457; in Plath 471; in Styron 503
holographs: reliability 213
Holstenius: and Milton 224
homecoming: Canadian literature 512
homilies 93, 95
homoerotic desires: and Tennyson 326; in popular fiction 366
homoerotic verse 151
homosexual writers and writing 368–9, 537
homosexuality: and Anderson 528; and Forster 384; *see also* lesbianism
honour: and Fenimore Cooper 439
Hood, Hugh 522; *Black and White Keys* 525
hooked tags, Anglo-Saxon 72
Hooker, Richard: *Laws of Ecclesiastical Polity* 142, 216
Hoopla Productions 547
Hope, A. D. 555; and classicism 556
Hopkins, Gerard Manley **320–21**, 402, 432; and Eliot 399; and Lawrence 372; and Moure 527; and Pater 348, 349; and religion 320–21; influence of OE literature 70; 'The Caged Skylark' 527
Hopkins, Pauline Elizabeth: slave stories 433; 'Peculiar Sam' 435
Horace: and Milton 224–5; and Rochester 241; and Wordsworth 294
Horne, Herbert: and *Century Guild Hobby Horse* 354
Horniman, Annie: and the Abbey theatre 406
Hospital, Janette Turner 533, 539, 551; and memory 524; *Borderline* 518; *Charades* 518
Hostiensis, Henricus: *Summa Theologie*

112
Hotson, Leslie 188
Houghton, Richard Monckton Milnes, 1st Baron: and Gaskell 330
Housman, A. E.: and Eliot 400; and Larkin 403; metrical range 395; *A Shropshire Lad* 321, 400
Howard, Henrietta 258
Howe, Samuel Grindley 334
Howell, Jane: and Shakespeare 164
Howells, William Dean **443–4**; depiction of crowds 428; *Silas Lapham* 443–4
Hueffer, Ford Madox 357
Hughes, Langston 459; in France 457
Hughes, Ted: and Lawrence 374; and Plath 471; 'Cadenza' 401
Hugo, Hermann 150
Hulme, Keri 560; *The Bone People* 579
Hume, David 250; and Goldsmith 251; *Of Eloquence* 247; *Political Discourses* 303
humour: in Aboriginal literature 542; in Heller 498; as narrative strategy 388; in *The Waste Land* 467
Humphreys, Josephine 485
Humphries, Barry: biography 547
Hungary: printers 10
Hunt, Leigh 301
Hunt, Robert 281
Hunt, Thornton 353
Hunt, William Holman: and *The Lady of Shalott* 325
Hurston, Zora Neale 366, 389, 433, 487; *Mules and Men* 454
Hutcheon, Linda 512
Hutcheson, Francis 250
Hutchinson, Sara: and Coleridge 295
Huxley, Aldous: anti-Utopia 363
Hynes, Samuel 369
Hyvrard, Jeanne 562
Ibsen, Henrik: and Orton 414
iconography 72; Stuart 231
identity: Canadian 514; Caribbean 573; and Malouf 551;
ideology: and Shakespeare 167
Ignatieff, Michael: *The Russian Album* 526
Ihimaera, Witi 579
illuminated printing: of Blake 284
illustrations: and painting 355; of Blake 285; in Dickens 333
Image, Selwyn 354
imagination: Romantic 275
imagism: H. D.'s move from 460
immigrant experience: in Britain 388
imperialism 366; in American literature 433; and S. J. Duncan 521; and T. S. Eliot 467; *see also* colonialism
improvisations, actors' 185
In Parenthesis 395
India: in English fiction 558; language in North India 24–5
Indian-English 29
Indian literature **557–61**; women writers 558
Indian Mutiny: in Victorian press 353
Industrial Revolution 252
infinitives: early syntax 50–1
Innes, Hammond 6
innocence, betrayal of: in James 447
Innsbruck playbook 120
institutional history **10–11**
interdisciplinary analysis 314; and Victorians 315
interdisciplinary cross-overs: poetry and art 321, 325; poetry and music 317; poetry and painting 315; poetry and philosophy 461–2
international literature 1, 563–4, 577–8; and Australia 550–1; in English 388
international perspectives: on American literature 485
intertextuality: Australian literature 537–8; and Browning 317; and Eliot 400; and Fowles 393; and H. D. 459; Indian literature 559; and James 446–7; and Milton 289; in plays by women 406; and Pynchon 502; and Wordsworth 289
intrasentential anaphora 43–4
Inuit writing 515
Ireland, David: conservatism of 554
Ireland: and Beckett 408, 409; and Heaney 404; and Joyce 376–7; monasticism 75; pilgrimage traditions 89–90; and repossession 404; and Shakespeare 173
Irish: in Aboriginal literature 542; and *Punch* 351
Irish drama: 20th C 405–6, 407; and Friel 413; Irish dramatic movement 398; women in 405–6
Irish language 26; 18th and 19th C grammar 21; Hiberno-English 21; transference into Irish English 30–1
Irish literature: 18th C 248; 20th C 362, 365–6; peasant plays 414; short stories 8
irony 63; in *Beowulf* 83; and Brockden

Brown 431; and colonialism 366; Renaissance 143; and sentimental novels 431; and Sidney 146
Irving, Washington 442, 443; and Romanticism 437
Isherwood, Christopher: and American writing 391
Isidore of Seville: *Etymologiae* 92
Islam: and Restoration 231–2
island language studies 28–9
Islas, Arturo 487; *Rain God* 486
Italian fascism: and Pound 474
Italian poets: and Pound 476
Italian-Canadian writers 513
Italy: architecture 254; courtly plays 196; culture for English writers 143; and James family 447; and Milton 222–4, 228; narrative poetry 224; and Wordsworth 292
Jack Upland 112
Jackson, Kenneth H. 59
Jacob's Well 115
Jacobites: Stuart myth 250
Jacobs, Harriet: autobiography 427; slave stories 433
Jacobus, Mary 291
Jakobson, Roman 24
Jamaica: language 29
James I 154; and Jacobean drama 195; and Lyndsay 184; *The Kingis Quair* 109
James family 445, 446; in Italy 447
James, Alice 446, 447
James, Henry 423, 435–6, **444–7**; and Joyce 377; and Pater 349; and Shakespeare 177; and American gentlemen 436; and games 438; as novelist of manners 492; satire 437; *The Ambassadors* 446; *The American Scene* 446; *The Aspern Papers* 388, 444; *The Awkward Age* 445; *The Bostonians* 437, 444; 'Daisy Miller' 444, 447; *The Europeans* 444, 447; *The Golden Bowl* 445, 446, 447; *Portrait of a Lady* 350, 444, 445, 447; 'The Speech of American Women' 33; *The Turn of the Screw* 62–3, 64, 445, 446; *Washington Square* 444, 447; *What Maisie Knew* 447; *The Wings of the Dove* 377, 447
James, William 424, 427; and crisis 434; and modernity 446; and poetry 462; *Essays in Radical Empiricism* 462; 'Will to Believe' 462
James, William, of Albany 445
Jameson, Fredric 374, 565
Janeway, James: *Token for Children* 234
Japanese language 44
Jarrell, Randall: 'Knight, Death and the Devil' 468; *The Seven League Crutches* 468
jazz: and American poetry 458; black 424; and black Americans in France 457; and oral tradition 459; and Pound 475
Jeffers, Robinson **468–9**; *Be Angry at The Sun* 468; *The Double Axe* 468; *Hungerfield* 468; *Last Poems* 468; 'The Loving Shepherdess' 469; *Tamar* 469
Jefferson, Thomas: response to political events 428; *Declaration of Independence* 442
Jellicoe, A. *The Knack* 406
Jerrold, Douglas: and *Punch* 351
Jespersen, Otto 378
Jewett, Sarah Orne: ghost stories 434; *The Country of the Pointed Firs* 434
Jewish-American: Heller as 498
Jews: and Marlowe and Shakespeare 198–9; and *Finnegans Wake* 379; women writers 388; *see also* anti-Semitism; Hebrew
Jhabvala, Ruth Prawer: *Heat and Dust* 559
Jiles, Paulette **527**; *Celestial Navigation* 527
Johan Johan 116
John of Freiburg: *Summa Confessorum* 112–13
John of Gaunt: and Chaucer 137–8
Johnson, Amryl: sound recording 561
Johnson, Edward: and Old Testament 430–1
Johnson, George: Meredith trilogy 553
Johnson, Joseph: and Blake 277, 282; and Milton 281
Johnson, Lionel 354
Johnson, Richard 21; and *Tom a Lincoln* 183
Johnson, Samuel 249, 251; *Dictionary* 248
Johnson, Stephanie: *Accidental Phantasies* 581
Johnston, Ellen 315
Jolley, Elizabeth **553**; *Mr Scobie's Riddle* 553
Jones, David: and the feminine 396; *Anathemata* 402
Jones, Sir William 23
Jong, Erica 423
Jonson, Ben: 'On Groyne' 213; 'To

Penhurst' 213
Jonson, Ben **201–4**, 210; and Mamet 203; and Marston 192, 202–3; and Martial 213; and Seneca 202; and Shakespeare 203; and Yeats 397–8; and patronage 141, 196, 202; and politics 212; and publication 202, 203; dedications 201–2; drama **184–5**; as Master of Revels 192–3; revisions 184; *The Alchemist* 203; *Bartholomew Fair* 204, 207; *Catiline* 202, 204; 'On Groyne' 213; *Poetaster* 202; *Sejanus* 184, 202, 203; 'To Penhurst' 213; *Volpone* 202, 204; *Workes* 184, 201
Jordan, June 460
Jorgensen, Jorgen: and Aborigines 540
Joseph, St: trade 76
Joshi, Arun: *The Apprentice* 560
journalism: in Australia 544; and autobiography 427; discourse of tigers 283
Jowett, Benjamin: and Pater 347
Joyce, James 328, 367, 374, **376–80**, 408; and H. D. 459; and Pater 349; and Pound 475; and Stevens 480; and American writers 436; and Irish writing 248; editing 454; epiphany 368; sense of self 364; 'After the Race' 377; 'Araby' 331; 'The Dead' 378; *Dubliners* 365, 376, 377; 'Evelina' 378; *Finnegans Wake* 376, 377, 379, 380, 480; 'Grace' 377; 'Oxen of the Sun' 377; 'Penelope' 376, 378, 379; *Portrait of the Artist as a Young Man* 300, 349, 378, 578; 'The Sisters' 378–9; *Ulysses* 349, 366, 376, 377, 378, 379, 380, 455
Judaica: Australian 533–4; *see also* anti-Semitism; Jews
Judd, Yasmin 573
Judgement Day II 80
Judith 82
Julian of Norwich 115
Juliene 100
Jung, Carl Gustav: and Bachelard 461
Junius manuscript 81, **86–8**
Juvenal: and Wyatt 145
Kafka, Franz: and American writers 436
Kames, Henry Home, Lord 255
Kamilaroi tribe 540–1
Kant, Immanuel 250, 274
Kaske, Robert E. 104
Katchadourian, Stina 407
Kavanagh, P. J. 6
Kean, Charles: and Marlowe 198
Keats, John 270, **301–2**; and authority 271; and Cockney rhyme 301–2; and Romantic poets 301; rhymes 34; verse narrative 271; *Endymion* 272, 301; *The Eve of St Agnes* 272, 302; *Isabella* 272, 302; *La Belle Dame Sans Merci* 272; 'Ode on a Grecian Urn' 302; 'Ode to Autumn' 302; 'Ode to Psyche' 302; *Sonnet to Sleep* 272
Keeble, John: *Yellowfish* 516
Kees, Weldon: procedural form 456
Kelmscott Press 321
Kelsey, Henry: verse journal 512
Kempe, Margery 115; and Chaucer 134
Kempe, William 191
Kendall, Henry **549**
Kenna, Peter 547
Kenneally, Thomas 551, **552**; *The Chant of Tommy Blacksmith* 552; *Ireland and the Irish* 552; *The Playmaker* 416; Towards Asmara 552
Kenya: language 27
Kenyon, John 318
Kermode, Frank 349; and detective fiction 368
Kerouac, Jack 488, 495; and Isherwood 391; and American postmodernists 484
Kershaw, Alister 556
Kesselman, Wendy: *My Sister in This House* 407
Kidman, Fiona 577; *The Book of Secrets* 580
Kierkegaard, Søren Aabye: and Blake 279–80; and Conrad 369; and Eliot 401; and P. Grace 579; and Hegel 279–80
Killigrew's company 233
Kincaid, Jamaica 563, **570**; 'Girl' 562; *A Small Place* 570
King, Edward: and *Lycidas* 226–7
King, Henry 211, 216
King's Men 190
Kingsley, Mary 352
Kingsmill, John: *Australia Street* 544
Kingston, Maxine Hong **498–9**; *The Woman Warrior* 498
Kinnell, Galway 459
Kinsman, William and Edward: *Flos Sanctorum* 205
Kipling, Rudyard 4, 363; and Hardy 344; and law 395; *Something of Myself* 321
Kirkland, Caroline 437
Kiswahili 27

Klinck, Carl 511, 522
Knister, Raymond 518
Knox, Vicesimus 246
Koch, Chris 554
Koch, Kenneth **469**; 'Art of Love' 469; *Ko* 469; *On the Edge* 469; *Seasons on Earth* 469
Konitz, Lee: improvisations of 458
Kosinski, Jerzy 488, 499–500; *Being There* 500
Kreisel, Henry 517
Kristeva, Julia 392; and Williams 483; concept of abjection 368; motherhood 382
Kroeber, Karl 275
Kroetsch, Robert 517, 522, **524**; *Badlands* 524; *What the Crow* Said 515, 524
Kubrick, Stanley 413
Kuhn, Hugo: *Gattungsprobleme der mittlehoch Deutschen* 270
Kurnai tribe 540–1
Kurosawa, Akira: *Rashomon* 572
Kyd, Thomas: *The Spanish Tragedy* 186
Kyle, Barry: and Shakespeare 162–3
Lacan, Jacques 374, 392, 402; and Joyce 378, 379; and Spenser 149–50; and femininity 376; male desire 227; transference 477–8
Ladefoged, Peter 35
Ladoo, Sonny: *No Pain Like This Body* 565; *Yesterdays* 565
Lai le Freine 107
La Mama theatre company 547
Lamarck, Jean: and Bernard Shaw 415
Lamb, Caroline 299
Lamb, Charles 309; and Marlowe 198; and autobiography 295; and gender 306–7
Lamb, Mary: and gender 306–7
Lambeth Psalter 73
Lamming, George 564, 567
land: in Kroetsch 524
Landor, Walter Savage 270; *The Gebir* 305
landscape: Australian 539, 550, 556; Canadian 520; Caribbean 567; New Zealand 576
Lane, John: and Pater 346
Langdon, Olivia 449
Langland, William 104–5, 143
Langley, Rod: *The Dunsmuirs* 530
language 3; 18th C poems 255; in Australia 535–6; Canadian bilingualism 513; and Chaucer 136–7; definition 17; in drama 406; and Dreiser 441; English **16–64**; and Frame 578; and Ghosh 560; and Goodison 571; and Kroetsch 524; minority languages 31–2; North Amerindian 485–6; OE studies 77–9; purity in poetry 580; and A. Rich 459; and Selvon 570–1; and sexuality 392–3; study of 98; and Walcott 572; and Whitman 450
language change 19
language contact 20–1
language planning 32
language poetry 456, 469
languages, foreign: access in ME 126–7
Larkin, Philip 272, **402–3**; theme of death 403; 'Talking in Bed' 60
Larsen, Nella 7, 432
Latin: influence in ME 100
Latin American literature 485–6
Laughlin, James: and Rexroth 476; *New Directions in Prose and Poetry* 477
Laurence, Margaret 514, **522–3**; and *The Tempest* 524; *A Bird in the House* 522; *The Stone Angel* 523
Lavater, Johann 282
Lavery, Bryony: *Witchcraze* 407
Lavynham, Richard: *Litil Tretys* 115
Law, William 253
law: 17th century 210–11; and Fenimore Cooper 438; and Stevens 478–9
Lawrence, D. H. 143, 363, 364, 367, 369, **371–5**; and T. S. Eliot 400; and H. D. 459; and censorship 455; antecedents 372; letters 372; poetry 375, 397; reviews 397; surrealism 401; *The Crown* 373; *Education of the People* 374; 'Fish' 375; 'Individual' 373; 'Invocation to the Moon' 397; *Mr Noon* 375; *The Rainbow* 374, 400; *Sons and Lovers* 372, 373, 374; *Study* of Thomas Hardy 373; *The Trespasser* 375; *Twilight in Italy* 373; *Women in Love* 374, 375, 385, 400
Lawson, Henry 545, 548, 549; biography 545–46; 'The Bush Undertaker' 550; 'The Drover's Wife' 549
Laȝamon 106
The Lay Folks' Catechism 115
Layton, Irving 527
Leacock, Stephen 516; essay 512; *Sunshine Sketches* 521
Lean, David 338; and *A Passage to India* 385
Leapor, Molly 249

Leavis, F. R. 177
Le Carré, John 389; and cinema techniques 364
Lee, Nathaniel: *Lucius Junius Brutus* 243
Lee, Dennis 518
Leech, John: and *Punch* 351–52
Le Fanu, Sheridan: 'Carmilla' 340; 'Green Tea' 340
Legend of the Seven Sleepers 95
Legenda Aurea 112
legends: ME 112
Le Guin, Ursula 489
Leichhardt, Ludwig: *Journal of an Overland Expedition* 540
Lennox, Charlotte 261; *Female Quixote* 261
Lentricchia, Frank 480
Leonard, Tom 405
Leopardi, Giacomo: and Pound 476
lesbianism: and feminist theatre 581; and G. B. Shaw 415; Restoration 233
lesbian writing 368–9
Lessing, Doris 381; and epic tradition 365; and memory 367; and war 367; *The Golden Notebook* 365
Letter of Dydoto Eneas 110
letters: anthology 7–8
Levellers 216; and Milton 222
Leverson, Ada 5
Levertov, Denise 476
Lévi-Strauss, Claude: kinship theories 504
Levinas, Emmanuel 456
Levine, Norman: 'We All Begin in a Little Magazine' 519
Levine, Philip: poetry in performance 458
Levinson, Marjorie 275
Lewes, G. H. 341; and C. Brontë 339; and G. Eliot 340; journalism 352–3
Lewes: place name 59
Lewis, Alun: and war 402
Lewis, Eve: *Ficky Stingers* 406
Lewis, Meriwether: *History of the Lewis and Clark Expedition* 433
Lewis, Sinclair: *Main Street* 521
Lewis, Wyndham 364
lexical acquisition 17
lexicography 55–6, **57–8**, 81–2; in *Beowulf* 85–6
lexis 62
libraries: history 9, 10–12
lies 8
Life of Oswald, The 91
Life of St Christopher, The 95
Lil, Wendy: *Sisters* 530
Lilburn, John 216
Lincoln, Abraham 470
Lincolnshire: place names 58–9
Lindsay, Jack 556
Lindsay, Vachel 470
linguistic analysis 16–17
linguistic atlas: ME 97
linguistic theory 18–19
linguistics: history of English **21–4**; in USA 23–4; *see also* language
literacy: in OE literature 77; Restoration literate culture 233–4, 236
literary biography: and Coleridge 296
literary criticism: Australian 537
literary culture: and Lacan 477–8
literary histories **3–8**; Canadian 512
literary scholarship: American 424–25
literary terms 3
literary theory: and 17th C poetry 212
little magazines 462; Edwardian 357
liturgical practices: OE 75
'Liudhard Medalet' 72
Lively, Penelope: *Moon Tiger* 387
Livingstone, William: and the sublime 462
Liyong, Taban Lo: *Another Nigger Dead* 62
Lochhead, Liz: *Blood and Ice* 406
Locke, John 273; and Gray 259; wit 247; 'An essay concerning human understanding' 33
Lodge, David: *Nice Work* 176; *Small World* 394
logs, ships' 534
Lollard debate 134
London: 16th C 149; Cockney rhyme 34
London Library 11
long poems: Canadian 529
Longhi, Pietro 447
Lord Chamberlain's Men 164
Lorde, Audre 459, 460
loss: and Chaucer 125
love: and Carver 496; divine, and K. Chopin 438; first 367, 374; in Australian literature 548; in wartime 387–8
love epistles 110
Love's Labour Won 156
Lovejoy, A. O. 274
Lovelace, Earl 564, 567; and nationalism 565; interview 564–5; *The Dragon Can't Dance* 565; *The Wine of Astonishment* 565
Lovelace, Richard 211

low culture: Australian 538
Lowell, Amy 462
Lowell, Robert **469–70**, 477; and Ciardi 464; *Day by Day* 469; *History* 469; *Life Studies* 464, 469; *Notebook 1967–68* 469
Lowry, Malcolm 394; poetry 528
Loyau, George: bush ballads 536
Lucan: *Pharsalia* 173
Lucian 144
Luckham, Claire: *Scum* 407
Lucretius: and Tennyson 326; influence of 240
Lukács, Georg 401; realism 469
Lumpkin, Katherine DuPre: *The Making of a Southerner* 427
Luscombe, Tim 204
Luther, Martin: and More 145
Lydgate, John: *The Fall of Princes* 108; *The Lyf of Our Lady* 108; *The Siege of Thebes* 108; *Troy Book* 108
Lyly, John 151; courtly plays 196; *Campaspe* 182–3, 196; *Endymion* 196; *Sappho and Phao* 182–3
Lyndsay, Sir David: *Ane Satyre of the Thrie Estaitis* 184
lyrics: ME **110–13**
Lytton, Bulwer 327
Macaulay, Rose: biography 384
Macaulay, Thomas 292
McAuley, James 556
MacCabe, Colin 378
McCaffery, Steve 469
McCarthy, Mary: and Burroughs 495
McClung, Nellie 517; 'The Live Wire' 519
McCuaig, Ronald 556–7
McCulloch, Thomas: *Mephisboseth Stepsure Letters* 516
McCullough, Colleen: interview 545
MacDonald, George 328; children's fiction 273
McDonald, Ian: *The Humming Bird Tree* 567
McGahern, John 362
McGuane, Thomas 490
McGuiness, Frank 405
Machaut, Guillaume de: *Remede de Fortune* 134
Machiavelli, Niccolò 142
Machiavellianism: in Shakespeare 178
Mack, Louise: biography 545
McKay, Claude: in France 457
MacKellar, Dorothea 548
Mackenzie, Henry 266
Mackmurdo, A. H. 354
Maclean, Alistair 6
MacLennan, Hugh 512, 522; *The Watch That Ends the Night* 521
MacLeod, Alistair: *Short Fiction* 522
McLeod, Jenny: *Island Life* 407
MacLow, Jackson: poetry in performance 458
McLuhan, Marshall 512
McMurty, Larry 423
McNickle, Darcy 485
MacNiece, Louis: influence of OE literature 70
Macpherson, James 250, 266
Macrobius, Ambrosius Theodosius 128
madness 6; in Shakespeare 162, 176
magic realism 576
Magnus Herodes 118
Mahapatra, Jayanta: silence in 558
Mahon, Derek **404–5**
'Maiden in the Moor' 99
Mailer, Norman **500**; and Lawrence 374; *Of a Fire on the Moon* 500; *The White Negro* 500
major writers: notion of 563–4
Malamud, Bernard 488; *The Assistant* 489; *A New Life* 491
male gaze: and D. French 531–2
male writers: Canadian 521; gender and class conflict 426
Mallah, Indu K.: *Shadows in Dreamtime* 557
Malone, Edmund: and Shakespeare 156
Malory, Sir Thomas 52, 143; *Morte Darthur* 113–14
Malouf, David **551–2**; *Blood Relations 552; The Great World* 552; *Harland's Half Acre* 551; *An Imaginary Life* 551–2; *Johnno* 551–2
Mamet, David: and Jonson 203
Manhire, Bill: and Thesen 580
Mankind 116, 117, 118, 120
mannerist genre 209
manners: novelists of 492
Mannheim, Karl: utopias 443
Manning, Frederic: *The Middle Parts of Fortune* 548
Mansfield, Katherine 522, 575, 577–8; female hero 577; short stories 578; *The Urewera Journal* 578; 'The Woman at the Shore' 550
Mant, Richard 270; *Simpliciad* 305

manuscript studies: OE 72–4
manuscripts: collectors in 17th century 219; reliability 213
Maori language 26
Maori literature 4, 574
Maori theatre 581
Maoris: place in society 579
maps 542
Marenbon, John: 'English our English' 33
Margaret, St 115
Marie (Victorian poet) 315
Marie de France: lais 107
Maritime writing 516, 528; of Bruce 521
Markandaya, Kamala 557, **561**; *Nectar in a Sieve* 561
marketplace: and Hawthorne 443; role of 433
Markham, E. A.: sound recording 561
Marlatt, Daphne 517; long poems 529; *Steveston* 516, 522
Marlborough, Duchess of see Churchill, Sarah
Marlowe, Christopher 166–7, **197–201**, 234; and T. S. Eliot 467; growth in interest in 197–8; and Shakespeare 163; fetishism 200; rhetoric 200; *Dr Faustus* 186, 198, 199, 201; *Edward II* 200; *Hero and Leander* 144; *The Jew of Malta* 191, 198–9, 201, 467; *Tamburlaine* 198, 199–200, 201
Marquez, Gabriel Garcia 487
marriage 8; in Jacobean drama 194–5; in Renaissance drama 205; and Williams 483
Marryat, Captain *Children of the New Forest* 330; *Masterman Ready* 262
Marsh, John: and Blake 278–9
Marsh, Ngaio 4, 576
Marshall, Owen 575
Marshall, Paule 563, 567
Marson, Una 563
Marston, John: and Jonson 192, 202–3; child performers 191; *Antonio and Mellida* 182; *The Dutch Courtesan* 205; *Histriomastix* 191–2, 202–3; *The Malcontent* 196, 205
Marti, Jose 487
Martial: and Jonson 213
Martianus Capella 99
Martin of Broya 128
Martin, Catherine: *An Australian Girl* 550
Martin, David: *My Strange Friend* 543–4
Martin, Florence 110
Martin, Theodore 340
Martineau, Harriet 318
martyrologies: use by Dekker 205
Marvell, Andrew 211, 232, 236; and K. Philips 239; and Waller 214–15; and politics 212; emblems 211; *Last Instructions to a Painter* 214; 'On Mr Milton's Paradise Lost' 284; *To His Coy Mistress* 211, 215
Marx, Karl 489; on Twain 449
Marxism: and Jonson 202
masculine identity: in Harding and Gissing 344
masculine subjectivity: in Chaucer 128–9
masculinity: and imperialist ideology 366; *see also* male
Mason, Bobbie Ann 485
Mason, Libby: *Dear Girl* 407; *Double Vision* 406
Massinger, Philip: Catholic source material 205; *The Roman Actor* 194; (with Dekker) *The Virgin Martyr* 185, 205;
Masters, Edgar Lee: *Across Spoon River* 470
Masters, Olga 555; biography 546
mastery: and Elizabeth Bishop 463
materialism 363
mathematics: and Romantic poetry 291–2
Mather, Cotton: publishing history 431
Mathews, Harry: procedural form 456
Mattson, Nancy 527
Mauriac, Francois: and Greene 390–1
Mead, Margaret: and American character 424
meaning: in drama 61; and James 444; and poetic form 457; theory of 362
media: and Australian arts 538; and Findley 532; language of 32; *see also* films; newspapers; periodicals; television; video
media studies: and historical developments 364
Medici, Lorenzo de' 100
medico-literary motifs: in Renaissance drama 196
medieval grammar 22
Mehta, Ved 557
Meiklejohn, J. M. C.: theatre education 531
Melanesian pidgin 25
melodrama: and Henry James 445
Melville, Herman 426, 428, 435–6; and labour 435; and science 424; depiction of crowds 428; *Billy Budd* 61; *Moby*

Dick 425, 433; 'Paradise of Bachelors' 447; *Pierre* 425, 436–7; 'Tartarus of Maids' 447
Melville, Pauline: on video 562
Memling, Hans 119
memory 548; and feminist fiction 367
Mendez, Miguel: *Pilgrims of Aztlan* 487
mental illness 6; and Plath 501; and Pynchon 501; and Styron 502–3
Meredith, George 328, **343**, 345; *Diana of the Crossways* 343; *The Egoist* 343; *One of Our Conquerors* 343–4; *The Ordeal of Richard Feverel* 343; *Rhoda Fleming* 343
Meres, Francis 156
Merrill, James: quotational effects 457
Merton, Thomas: reaction to Nazi film 470
Merwin, W. S. **470**; manuscripts 470; *Ark of Silence* 470
messianic leader: in Naipaul 567
metaphor 60, 63–4; and E. Bishop 463; and Crane 439; and Pynchon 501–2; and Stevens 481
Metcalf, John 519, 522
Methodists: anti-methodist publications 253; ministers in G. Eliot 342
Mexican-American literature 486–7
Meynell, Francis 10
Michener, James 6
middle constructions 44
Middle English **97–120**; adverbs 38; alliterative poetry 101; drama **116–20**; infinitive 51; lyrics and verse **110–13**; prose **115–16**; romances **106–7**; *see also* Chaucer
Middle Saxon Shift 71
Middle Scots poetry **109–10**
Middleton, Thomas 143, 166–7, **206**; and Shakespeare 160, 170; and female sexuality 194;and *The Revenger's Tragedy* 186, 206; *The Changeling* 38, 194, 206; *A Chaste Maid in Cheapside* 206; *A Game at Chesse* 192, 195, 206; *Hengist, King of Kent* 206; *Mad World, My Masters* 206; *Michaelmas Term* 206; *The Old Law* 206; *The Roaring Girl* 195, 206; *A Trick to Catch the Old One* 206; *Women Beware Women* 194, 206
Midlands: and George Eliot 340
migration literature 539–40; Australian 555, 556–7
military combat: and *The Woman Warrior* 499
military history: American 424
Mill, John Stuart: *Autobiography* 273
Millais, Sir John Everett: poem-painting combinations 315; *Cherry Ripe* 355
millenarianism: and Blake 281–2
Miller, Henry 488; and Lawrence 374
Miller, John 353
Miller, Jonathan: and Shakespeare 164, 165
Miln, George Crichton: career of 547
Milton, John **221–9**; and Bacon 225–6; and Cicero 228; and Habermas 229; and Haydn 229; and Horace 224–5; and Reaney 531; and Tasso 224; and Wordsworth 289; and Yeats 398; and Arthurian tradition 225; and atomism 216; and cultural politics 224; and Italy 222–4, 228; and Long Parliament 225; and politics 212, 222, 225–6; classicism 229; epics 143; language 222; Latin poetry 224; minor poems 226; prefaces 228; prose 225; sonnets 224; textual production 212; *L' Allegro* 223; *Areopagitica* 221, 223, 226; *Carpe diem* 225; *Christian Doctrine* 221; *Comus* 224, 227; *A Defence of the People of England* 225; *Doctrine and Discipline of Divorce* 221, 225; *Eikonoklastes* 226; *Familiar Letters* 221; *History of Britain* 225; *Hymn* 226; *Lycidas* 223, **226–7**; *Paradise Lost* 144, 222, 223, **227–8**, 229, 284, 288, 293, 523; *Paradise Regained* 224, 228–9; *The Passion* 226; *Il Penseroso* 223; *Prolusions* 226; *Readie and Easie Way* 221; *Samson Agonistes* 222, 229; *Second Defense* 223; Sonnet 12 227; *Tenure of Kings and Magistrates* 221, 225
mimesis 364–5
mind style: in Atwood 523
miners: in Lawrence 375
minority languages 31–2
minstrels: manuscripts 99
miracle plays 116
Mirk, John: *Festial* 115
miscommunication 32–3
Mishima, Yukio 7
mismatches, morphosemantic 36
Mitchell, Joni 458
Mitchell, Ken: plays 530
Mitchell, W. O. 518

Mittelholzer, Edgar 567
modal analysis: of Shakespeare's poems 158
modern writers: influence of OE literature 70
modernism 7; and aestheticism 350; and American avant-garde 462; in American literature 423, 434; and American novel 423; in Australia 544; and Beckett 411; in Canadian literature 522, 528; and drama 406–7; and T. S. Eliot 401, 465; and individuality 364; and Lawrence 373–4; and poets 397; and psychology 363–4; and Romanticism 275; and Sterne 265; and Stevenson 346; and West 383; and Woolf 381
modernist texts: editing 454–5
Modjeska, Drusilla 539
Moers, Ellen 438
Momaday, N. Scott 485
monarchy: and Bradstreet 430
monastic schools 80
monasticism: Irish 75; OE 75; and sign language 75–6
Monboddo *see* Burnett, James
montage: and Burrough 495
Montaigne, Michel Eyquem de: and Pater 237; *Essais* 142
Montesquieu, Charles Louis de Secondat, Baron de : *Lettres Persanes* 300
Montgomery, James 270
Montgomery, L. M. **521**; *Anne of Green Gables* 521; *Anne's House of Dreams* 521
monuments, public: Australian 538
Moodie, Susanna **520**; 'Rachel Wade' 520; *Roughing it in the Bush* 511–12, 520
Moore, Brian **393–4**
Moore, Marianne **470–1**; and Ciardi 464; and Eliot 399; and nature 461; and text editions 455; *Fables of La Fontaine* 464; 'In Distrust of Merits' 470; 'Pangolin' 471
Moore, Thomas: journal 305
Moorhouse, Frank 'The Drover's Wife' 549
Morales, Lucia 7
morality plays 119, **120**
Moran, Benjamin 353
Moran, Edward Raleigh 335
Mordecai, Pamela 562
More, Hannah: and feminism 307–8
More, Henry 251; and atomism 216; and science 218
More, Sir Thomas 54, 143, **144–5**; *Epigrammata* 145; *History of King Richard III* 144–5, 217; *Responsio ad Lutherum* 145; *Utopia* 142, 144
Moreo, Robert: *Patches* 530
Morgan, Edwin: urban poetry 402
Morgan, Sally: *My Place* 551
Morley, John: and history of reading 356–7
morphological theory 18
morphology **35–8**; history 37–8
Morris, May 356
Morris, William **321–22**, 328; avant-gardism 363; as interdisciplinary figure 315; *The Earthly Paradise* 325; *Love is Enough* 322; *The Tables Turned* 356–7
Morris, Wright 491
Morrison, Toni 388, 433, 487, 563; and body marks 500; and memory 367; ghost stories 434; *Sula* 454; *Tar Baby* 63
Morton, W. L. 512
Moshinsky, Elijah: and Shakespeare 164
mothers and motherhood: Anglo-Saxon 76; and women writers 389; and Woolf 382
motifs: woman as 233
Motley design team: and Shakespeare 165
mountain language: in A. Rich 459
Moure, Erin 526; 'Thrushes' 527; WSW (West South West) 527
The Movement Poets 401, 403
Mudrooroo Narogin 533, 541; bibliography 534; *Doin Wildcat* 542
Muirchú 89–90
Mukherjee, Arun 513
Mukherjee, Bharati 513, **559**; papers 519; *Darkness* 559
Mulgan, John 575
Mulock, Dinah 327
multiculturalism: American literature 429; Australia 539–40, 549; Canadian literature 512–13
multilingualism 31
multiple identity: of E. Brontë 315–16
Mulvey, Laura 389
Munday, Anthony 183, 192
Munro, Alice **523**; short stories 522; *Friend of My Youth* 523; 'Heirs of the Living Body' 524; *Lives of Girls and Women* 519
murder: in mystery plays 118; in Renaissance drama 193; in Romantic literature

307; *see also* crime; detective fiction
Murdoch, Iris 362, 394
Murnane, Gerald **553**; *Inland* 553; *The Plains* 553
Murphy, Sarah: and *The Tempest* 524
Murphy, Thomas **414**; *After Tragedy* 414; *Bailegangaire* 414; *Conversations on a Homecoming* 414; *Gigli Concert* 414
Murphy, Tom 405
Murray, Les 533
Murray, Lindley 21, 22
Murray, Middleton: and Lawrence 373
Murray-Smith, Stephen: recording of 544
music: 16th C ballads 9; 18th C 253; and American poetry 458; Australian songs of First World War 536; and M. Boyd 553; and Browning 317; and Burns 260; and Chaucer 130–1; and cultural bonding 457; and R. Davis 553; and T. S. Eliot 466; and Milton 223, 226; in morality plays 120; and oral tradition 459; and Pound 475; Renaissance ballads 209–10; and Stevens 480; and Styron 502
Mussolini, Benito: and Pound 474
mystery plays **116–18**, 119; and Findley 525
mystery tales: Australian 555; writers 1; *see also* crime
mysticism: and T. S. Eliot 401, 466
mythemes: Canadian 515
mythologization: of America 497
mythology: classical 3
myths 2; and Mailer 500
N town cycle 97, 117–18, **119–20**
Nabokov, Vladimir 363, 488, **500–1**; and American postmodernists 484; *Bend Sinister* 501; *The Enchanter* 501; *Invitation to a Beheading* 501; *Lolita* 501; *Pale Fire* 501; *Pnin* 491, 501; *Speak, Memory* 500
Naipaul, V. S. 522, 564, 567–8, 569; *A House for Mr Biswas* 567, 568; *The Enigma of Arrival* 568
names **58–9**; and social classification 63
Namjoshi, Suniti: 'Snapshots of Caliban' 524
Nandan, Satendra: *The Wounded Sea* 582
Napier, Arthur S. 70
Napoleon Bonaparte: and Byron 299–300; influence on radicals 274–5
Narayan, R. K. 557, 559, **560**; *The Guide* 560; *A Tiger for Malgudi* 560
narrative 64; boundaries 414;in Barrett Browning 318–19; in G. Eliot 342; in Fowles 393; in Joyce 378; boundaries 414; linear 393
narrative analysis 64; in Atwood 523
narrative poetry: Italian 224
narrative strategy: humour as 388
Nash, Paul: paintings 401
Nashe, Thomas 143; pornographic poem 151
national identity: in Canadian literature 512
National Trust: book catalogue 9
nationalism 366; American 433, 478; British 467; Caribbean 565; Italian 300; and T. S. Eliot 465–6; and Malouf 551–2
nationality: categorization of writers 557
native writing: Canadian 514, 515, 516
natural language 17, 18
nature: in American poetry 461; and E. Dickinson 440; and urban novel 489
negation 17, 53
Neilson, John Shaw 548, 556; autobiography 543
neo-classicism: and Dryden 236; Restoration 233–4;
neurolinguistics 35
Neville, George Henry: and Lawrence 375
New Apocalypse 401
New Formalism 456
'New Grammar' 45
New Historicism 141, 297; in American literature 432; backlash against 204; and Browning 316–17; and Herrick 216; and Jonson 201–2; and Pater 347; and Pope 257; and Reformation 234; and Romantics 271, 275; and Welty 504; and Wordsworth 288
new literature 563–4
New Mexico: women's autobiography 486
new philology 324
new woman: of 19th C 351
New York World's Fair 497
New Zealand language 26; lexicography 58
New Zealand literature 4, **574–82**; and Australian literature 548
Newland, Simpson 550
Newman, John Henry: and Pater 348; letters to *The Times* 354
news: 17th C 211
newspaper literature: in 19th century Canada 512

newspapers: 18th century 252; alliteration and rhyme usage 55; electronic systems 10
Newton, Isaac 291–2
Nichol, B. P. 528
Nichols, Grace: sound recording 561
Niedecker, Lorine: serial form 456; 'Lake Superior' 456
Nietzsche, Friedrich: and Conrad 370; and Pound 475
Nigerian language 27
Nigerian literature 63
Nightingale, Florence 323
Nimrod drama company 547
Nolan, Sidney 539, 544
Nolla, Olga: 'No Dust is Allowed In This House' 562
Norden, John: Elizabethan playhouse 187
Norfolk: scribes 97
normative grammar 55
Norris, Leslie: and Wales 402
North American Indian writers 485–6; *see also* Amerindians
Norton, Charles Eliot: and James 446
Norwegian language 53
noun phrase 54; Old English 38
nouns, concrete singular: in *Beowulf* 86
Novalis: *Klingsroman-Märchen* 284
novel: 18th C **260–6**; 19th C **327–46**; American, history 422–3; New Zealand 575; *see also* fiction
Nowra, Louis 553
Nunn, Trevor: and Shakespeare 162–3
Oates, Joyce Carol: and Lawrence 374
O'Brien, Conor Cruise 474
O'Brien, Tim 490
O'Casey, Sean 407
occult: and Blake 283; and Plath 471; and Yeats 475
occult terminology: and King James Bible 211
Octavian 106
O'Donoghue, John 547
Ogilby, John: *Fables of Aesop Paraphras'd* 239
O'Hara, Frank: 458, **470–1**; 'Memorial Day 1950' 471; 'Personism' 471
Old English: morphology 37–8; syntax 48–55
Old English literature **70–95**; and modern writers 70
Old English metre: in *Beowulf* 84
'Old Grammar' 45
Oldham, John 232; and Rochester 241
Oliphant, Margaret: clergymen in 344
Olivier, Laurence: and Shakespeare 162, 163, 165
Olson, Charles: and Dorn 464–5
Ondaatje, Michael **525–6**; long poems 529; *Running in the Family* 522, 525–6
onomastics **58–9**
onomatopoeia 379
Oppen, George **471**; serial form 456; *Of Being Numerous* 471
oppression: and A. Carter 386
oracles: and Romantic poets 271
Orage, A. R. 474
oral tradition: Aboriginal 541; in Afro-American writing 459; in Canada 514; Maori 577; OE poetry 78–9; and sound recordings 561
The Order of the World 80
orientalism 385; and charity bazaars 331; in Romantic period 300
Orléans, Charles d' 109
Orne, Martin T.: and Sexton 477
Orosius 92–3
O'Rourke, Rebecca 389
Orrery, Roger Boyle, Earl of 243
orthography **33–5**
Orton, Joe: and Ibsen 414; *What the Butler Saw* 414
Orwell, George 365, **375–6**; 1984 390; and anti-utopianism 363; and imperialism 366; *Animal Farm* 376; *Burmese Days* 376; 'How the Poor Die' 375; 'The Moon Under Water' 7; *Nineteen Eighty Four* 390; 'Such, Such Were the Joys' 375
Ostenso, Martha 518
O'Sullivan, Vincent: *Shuriken* 582
Oswald, John 283
Ouida: and James 446
Ovid 171; and Dante 100; and Milton 225; and Rochester 241; and Shakespeare 175; and Sidney 147; and Restoration 232; *Metamorphoses* 292
Ovide moralisé 99
Owayne Miles 112
Owen, Wilfred 363; and social issues 396; 'Arms and the Boy' 396; 'Dulce et decorum est' 396; 'Exposure' 396; 'Miners' 396
The Owl and the Nightingale 113
owners: of *Canterbury Tales* manuscripts 128

Oxford, Edward de Vere, 17th Earl 150, 158
Oxford's Men 192
Pacific: language 24
paganism: in OE texts 80, 81–2
pageantry: and Shakespeare 173
Paine, Thomas 252; and Blake 281; literalism 308; *The Age of Reason* 281, 308
Painter, William 196
painting: and 18th C poetry 254; American crowd scenes 428; Australian poems on 556; and T. S. Eliot 401; and magazine illustration 355; poem-painting combinations 315; Victorian 2, 8; and Victorian fiction 328; and Walcott 572; and war 365; and P. West 394–5; and Williams 482–3; 254; 325
Paley, Grace 490
Palmer, Samuel 398
Palmer, William 343
Panych, Marris: *Last Call! A Post-Nuclear Carabet, Act Two* 517
Papaellinas, George: short stories 549
Paramsswaran, Uma 513
parasitic gaps 44
Paretsky, Sara 389
Paris Psalter 73, 91
Parker, Stewart **414**
Parkman, Francis 428
The Parliament of Birds 112
The Parliament of the Three Ages 112
Parmigianino: and Spenser 150
parody: 18th C 247
Parr, Dr Samuel 307
The Partridge 90
Pascal, Blaise: and Pater 348
pastoral poetry: and Dowson 327
pastourelles 110
Pater, Walter 345; **346–50**; and architecture 347; avant-gardism 363; vision 368; 'Amiens' 347; 'Apollo in Picardy' 349; *Appreciations* 350; 'Child in the House' 349; 'Conclusion' 349; 'Denys l'Auxerrois' 349; 'Diaphaneite' 348; 'Duke Carl of Rosenmold' 348; *Gaston de Latour* 348; *Marius* 348, 349; *Plato and Platonism* 350; 'Postscript' 349; 'Renaissance' 350; 'Romanticism' 350; 'Sebastian Van Storck' 349; 'Study of Dionysius' 349; 'Style' 349, 350; 'Vezelay' 347; 'Winckelmann' 348
patriarchy: and American women writers 438
patriotism: and Wilfred Owen 396
patronage: 16th C 141; 18th C 252; and Behn 242; and Jacobean drama 196; and Pound 472–3, 476; and Renaissance women 210
Paul of Hungary: *Quoniam circa confessiones* 115
Paulhan, Jean 479
Payn, James 327
Paz, Octavio 7
Peasants' Revolt 126
Peel, Sir Robert 332
Peele, George: *The Battle of Alcazar* 164; *David and Bethsabe* 204
Peirce, Charles 427; and poetry 462
penance 79
Penguin New Writing 365
Penton, Brian: *Landtakers* 547
Peraldus: *Summa de Virtutibus* 128
Perceval, John: *Narrative of the Treatment Received by a Gentleman* 6
Percy, Walker 485
Perelman, Bob: and the sublime 462
performance: compared to print 203
performance history: Renaissance 188–9
performance structures: in Beckett 411
performance theory: and Beckett 409
periodicals 455; and production of meaning 8; biographical journals 9; impact of 309; and production of meaning 8; *American Notes* 337; *Arcadian Recorder* 516; *Art-Union* 356; *Athenaeum* 352, 353; *Blackwoods' Magazine* 271, 336; *Book of British Ballads* 355; *Camera Work* 455, 462; *Canadian Forum* 512; *Century Guild Hobby Horse* 354–5; *Chamber's Edinburgh Magazine* 353; *Christian Observer* 332; *Commonweal* 356; *Dial* 352, 465; *Edinburgh Review* 271, 337; *English Review* 357; *Englishwoman's Domestic Magazine* 352; *Experiment* 401; *Foreign Review* 354; *Fortnightly Review* 352; *Gentleman's Journal* 234–5; *Gentleman's Magazine* 216; *Graphic* 355–6; *Household Words* 333; *Illustrated London News* 356; *Irish Times* 377; *Knickerbocker* 434; *Leader* 352; *Literary Chronicle* 353; *Little Review* 473; *London Figaro* 346; *London Magazine* 296, 309, 568;

Melus 429; *Mesures* 478; *Metro* 574; *National* 216; *Natural History* 470; *New York Tribune* 441–2; *New Zealand Listener* 574; *Once a Week* 355; *Others* 455; *Pall Mall Gazette* 353, 356; *Penny Magazine* 10; *Peterborough Chronicle* 115; *Photographic News* 355; *Poetry* 462; *Punch* 351–52; *Punch Almanack* 351; *Quarterly Review* 354; *Queen's Quarterly* 512; *Reader* 355; *Rogue* 455; *Saturday Night* 512; *Saturday Review* 356–7, 464; *Soil* 455; *Spectator* 353; *Sydney Herald* 544; *Tamarack Review* 512; *The Tatler* 246–7; *Tel Quel* 463; *Times* 354; *TISH* 527–8; *Vanity Fair* 503; *Victorian Poetry* 314; *Ward's Miscellany* 353; *Weekly Review* 353; *Wellesley Index* 353, 354; *Westminster Circle* 352; *Westminster Review* 332, 353; *Woman's World* 352; *Young Woman* 352; *see also* little magazines; newspapers
periphrastic do 51–2
Perlesvaus 114
personality: Caribbean 567
Petrarch 143–4; and Pound 476; and Sidney 147
Petrarchanism 162
phenomenology: influence on fiction 488
Philip, Marlene 563
Philip Sparrow 113
Philips, Katherine **239–40**; and feminism 241; and lesbianism 239; biography 239–40; primary sources 213
Phillipines: language 29
philology, comparative: paganism in OE texts 81–2
philosophical societies: Scottish 250
philosophy: and American poetry 426; and Lawrence 373; and poetry 461–2
Phiz 333
Phoenix 81
Phoenix Theatre 164
phonetics 19, 22–3, **33–5**
phonology 19, 27, **33–5**, 62; 18th and 19th C 34
photographic images: and Whitman 450
photographs: and Pinter 414; American avante-garde 462; portrait 355
photography: in Ondaatje and Ignatieff 526
phototext: of Afro-American women 487
picturesque: concept of 254
pidgin languages 25, 29; Australian 535
Pierce, Franklin 443
Piers of Fulham 113
Piers Plowman 98, **104–6**
Piers the Plowman's Crede 112
Pilgrimage to Parnassus 186
pilgrimage traditions 89–90
Pinter, Harold 61, **414**; and tragicomedy 406; *The Homecoming* 414; *Landscape* 414; *Old Times* 414; *One for the Road* 406
pioneer women: Canadian 522–23
Pisan, Christine de: *Cité des Dames* 143
Pix, Mary: and cross-dressing 241–2; *Beau Defeated* 233
place 3; in Australian poetry 539; in Southern states 427
place names 58–9
plantation tradition: and oral tradition 459
planters' jounals: Canadian 516
Plath, Sylvia **471–2**, **501**; literary remains 471; *The Bell Jar* 388, 501; 'Daddy' 471; *Dialogue Over a Ouija Board* 471; 'Lady Lazarus' 471; 'The Moon and the Yew Tree' 62
Plato 144; and Sidney 147
play: in American culture 490–1; in American literature 437–8
playhouses *see* theatres
plays: and ballads 167; *see also* drama
playscripts 580
Pliny: and Middleton 206
plural pronouns: in Jonson and Shakespeare 203–4
Plutarch: and Shakespeare 175–6
Po Chu-i: and Williams 483
Pocock, Isaac: *The Miller and his Men* 293
Poe, Edgar Allan 435–6; **447–8**; and Byron 299; and crowd image 456; and modernity 434; and Romanticism 437; 'Black Cat' 447–8; 'Imp of the Perverse' 447–8; 'Man of the Crowd' 434; *Narrative of Arthur Gordon Pym of Nantucket* 434; 'The Pit and the Pendulum' 448; 'Tell-Tale Heart' 447–8; 'William Wilson' 435
Poel, Wiiliam: and Jonson 203
Poet's Translation Series 464
poetry: 17th C **211–17**, 232; 18th C **254–60**; 19th C **269–306**, **314–27**; 20th C **395–405**; 20th century American **454–84**; alliterative 101;

American 427; anthologies 5; Australian 539, 548, 555; Canadian 511, 515, **526–9**; Caribbean 571–2; Chicano 486; editing 534; Indian 558; ME **110–13**; Middle Scots **109–10**; OE 54–5, 56, **91–2**; New Zealand 576, **580**; phonology 62; Scriptural 297; and Shakespeare 158; in the theatre 573; in Victorian religious periodicals 354
poets: psyche of American 428
Poets' War 182, 202–3
Poggioli, Renato 363
poison gas 396
Polanyi, Michael: 'Personal' 373
Polidori, John 7
politeness strategies 63
political fiction 3
politics: 16th C 151–2; and 16th C literature 141–2; in 17th C poetry 212; 18th C 252; of 18th C children's literature 273; of Amerindians 428; and Elizabethan drama 187; and Jacobean drama 195; and Marston 182; and Orwell 376; and Pound 474, 475; and Bernard Shaw 415; totalitarianism 363; in Victorian novels 328; and Yeats 398
Pollard, Velma 563
Pollock, Sharon 530
Polynesians 26
polyphony: in Doctorow 497
Pond, Christopher 332
Pontanus 150
Pope, Alexander 246, 247, 255, **256–8**, 259; and feminism 257; and gender 257; and *Odyssey* 258; pastorals 257; poetic imagination 254; politics 256; *The Dunciad* 236–7, 257, 258; *Eloisa* 257; *On Man* 257; *The Rape of the Lock* 158, 257
Pope, Jessie: children's poems 396
popular culture 5; 19th C 9–10; Australian 538; and A. Carter 386
popular entertainment: New Zealand 580
popular fiction 3, 4, 389–90; American feminist 423; homoerotic desire in 366; New Zealand 576; *see also* detective fiction
popular music: and American poetry 458
popular romance 367; Australian 555; New Zealand 576
pornography: in Updike 503
Porter, Hal: *Selected Stories* 547; *The Tower* 554
Porter, Peter: biography 555–6
portrait poetry: and Eliot 399
portraits: 18th C 252
Pory, John 211
post-colonialism: and Anand 560–1; in Australian literature 540; in Canadian literature 514, 522; and Caribbean writers 566; and Frame 578; in Indian literature 559
postmodern fiction 364–5
postmodernism: and American novel 423; and American poetry 456; and Chaucer 124, 126; in Canada 515; in Canadian literature 522, 528; and contemporary American fiction 484–5; and contemporary poets 405; and Dickens 333; and racism 366; role of the absurd 411; and science fiction 489; and Sterne 265; and women writers 389; and Woolf 382
postmodernists: dissident 485
poststructuralism: and women's theatre 581
postwar culture: and visual arts 365
Potter, David: and American character 424
Pound, Ezra 424, **472–7**; and Dorn 464–5, and T. S. Eliot 400; and H. D. 459, 460; and *The Waste Land* 273; editing 455; influence of OE literature 70; letters 472–3; 'Canto LXXXI' 470; *Cantos* 455, 472, 473–4, 475, 476; 'Cavalcanti' 475; *The Exile* 472; *Hugh Selwyn Mauberley* 472, 476; 'In a Station of the Metro' 476; *Lustra* 476; Malatesta Cantos 473–4; *Pisan* 472; *Poet as a Sculptor* 472; *Rock-Drill* 472; *Sonnets and Ballate of Guido Calvalcanti* 475; *The Spirit of Romance* 475; 'The State' 476; *Thrones* 472; *Translations of Arnaut Daniel* 474
Powell, Dawn 5
Powell, Mary: and Milton 227
power: and Beckett 411; and genre 247; and Lowell 469
Powys, John Cowper **380–1**; *Glastonbury Romance* 381; *Porius* 380–1
Powys, Theodore and Llewellyn 380
pragmatics 20, 60, 62–3; 18th C 21
pragmatism: of Stevens 479
prairie fiction 514, 518; in S. Ross 521
Pram Factory theatre company 547
Pre-Raphaelites: and literature 315

prefaces: Romantic authors 270
prepositions 54
preposition stranding 44
Presbyterianism: 18th C 250
prescriptivism, linguistic 33
the present: Victorians' love of 327–8
press: American academic 10; and language 32, 61; and Victorian art 8
presuppositional constructions 62–3
pretense theory 362
Pribac, Bert 557
Price, Richard 308; politics 252
Prick of Conscience 112–13
Priestley, Joseph 282, 298, 308
Prima Pastorum 118–19
printed texts: early, reliability of 213; proliferation of 10
printers and printing: history 9–10; and ME lyrics 112; typographical design 10
prints: Renaissance 209–30
Prior, Matthew 247
Pritam, Amrita 558
private knowledge: Aborigines 541
private library history **11–12**
procedural form 456
Processus Noe 119–20
productivity, morphological 35–6
pronouns of address 63
propaganda: Elizabethan drama 196
property: 18th C 251–2; 19th C 292
prosody, Elizabethan: and phonology 34
Protestantism: in America 424
Proust: and Burroughs 495; and Feinstein 388; and Stevens 481; and Woolf 382
Prynne, J. H.: multiple meanings 405
Prynne, William 226, 227
psalters 73
Pseudo-Seneca 128
psychoanalysis: and Beckett 410; and Browning 316–17; and Chaucer 125; and E. Dickinson 440; and G. Eliot 341; influence on fiction 488; and Lawrence 374; and Le Fanu 340; and literary culture 477–8; and Morris 322; and Romantics 275; and D. M. Thomas 393
psychology: and W. James 434; and modernism 363–4; and realism 429
psychophobia: Australian 539
publication: electronic 10; and Jonson 184
publishers and publishing: 19th C **350–57**; Angus and Robertson 546; Australian reprints 550; Australian small press 534–5; authors' publishing history 348; Blizzard Publishing 530; Bodley Head 356; Broadside Press 459; Canadian poetry 515; Catholicon Press 10; Clerk's Press 474; Coach House 530; correction of factual errors 8; and exotic covers 368; Fifth House 530; Guernica 530; Harper and Bros. 351; history 9–10; Macmillan's 351; and C. Mather 431; NeWest 530; in New Zealand 4, 576; Nu Age 530; Playwrights Canada 530; Putnam 351; Sister Vision 530; small presses 488, 534–5; Swift and Co 474; Talon Books 530; Wild East 530; Women's Press 530
Punch 350–2
punctuation: and Chaucer 123
punishment: 18th C 252
puns: ME 111
Purcell, Henry: and Dryden 239
Puritan captivity narrative 431
Puritanism: and Bunyan 244; and children's literature 234
Puttenham, George 142
Pynchon, Thomas 423, 488, **501–2**; and postmodernism 484, 485; 'The Courier's Tragedy' 502; *The Crying of Lot* 49 501, 502; *Gravity's Rainbow* 363, 502; *V.* 502
Pywell, David: *Contractor* 416
quantifiers 44
Quebec literature 515; fiction 513; novels 520
Queensland Kanaka English 25
quilt-making 426
Quinn, John: and Pound 472–3
Quirk, Randolph 21
quotational effects: in poetry 457
Rabanus Maurus 119–20
Rabe, David 490
Racine, Jean: *Bérénice* 238
racism: and Douglass 441; and Perkins Gilman 442; and postmodernism 366; of *Punch* 351; and Twain 448
Radcliffe, Ann 274; *The Mysteries of Udolpho* 386
Raddall, Thomas H. 516–17
radical writers: and English Revolution 308–9
radio broadcasts: American writers 488
radio plays 407; of Beckett 412
Radway, Janice: *Reading the Romance* 3

Raine, Kathleen 565
Ralegh, Sir Walter 150; *Ocean to Cynthia* 151
Ramanujan, A. K. 558
Randall, Dudley: and Broadside Press 459
Ransom, J. C. 477
Rao, Raja 557, 559; *The Serpent and the Rope* 560
rape: in Heaney 404; in *Passage to India* 385; and Welty 460
rape-lynch mythology: and American women writers 432
Rask, Rasmus 22
Raworth, Tom: *Tottering State* 405
Ray, Man 462
Read, Jamie: 'Homage to Lester Young' 528
Reade, Charles 327
reading: history of 357; *see also* literacy
reading habits: early American 429–30
realism: American 428; and Harding Davis 439–40; and Howells 443–4; and language poets 469
Reaney, James **531**; Donnelly trilogy 531; *The Killdeer* 531; *Listen to the Wind* 531
recitation, poetry: and Romantics 275
Reed, Lou 489, 490
Reeve, Clara 261
reference works **1–3**
reform novel 433
Regius Psalter 73
Reid, Thomas 250
Reilly, Colleen: *Christine* 577
religion: 18th C 253; and Australian drama 547; and Clough 319; and De Mille 520; and T. S. Eliot 466; and Hopkins 320–21, 527; and language 29; and Meredith 343–4; and Moure 527; and Oliphant 344; and Pater 348; Restoration 234; and Beecher Stowe 424; and *The Virgin Martyr* 185, 205; and P. Wheatley 431
religious periodicals: and Victorian verse 354
religious poets 150–1
'Remos' 536
Renée: characters 581–2
repossession: and Ireland 404
Repp, Þorleifur 22
representation: in North Amerindian texts 485–6
Restoration: literature **231–44**
Retamar, Roberto Fernandez 487
Revels series 182
Revels, Master of the: 192–3
'Revertere' 113
revisionary practice: of Whitman 450–1
Rexroth, Kenneth **476–7**; biography 477; letters 476
Reynolds, G. W. M.: *Mysteries of London* 329
Reynolds, Henry 216
Reynolds, John Hamilton 301
Reynolds, Joshua 254
Rhegius, Urbanus: *An Homelye...of Good and Evill Angels* 186, 198
rhetoric 64; in Marlowe 200; ME 98–9
rhyme: Cockney 34; and Keats 301–2; mosaic 62; in newspapers 55
Rhys, Jean 7, 389, 563, 564, **568–70**; and war 367; 'The Day They Burned The Books' 563; 'Overture and Beginners Please' 568; *Sleep It Off Lady* 568; *Wide Sargasso Sea* 366, 568, **569–70**
Rich, Adrienne 366, 389; and E. Dickinson 440; *Dream of a Common Language* 459
Richardson, Charles 22
Richardson, John 334; *The Monk Knight of St John* 520
Richardson, Jonathan 254
Richardson, Samuel 261, 262, 265; and James 447; and A. Walker 504–5; *Clarissa* 263, 445, 504; *Pamela* 263
Riesman, David: and American character 424
Rimbaud, Arthur 292
Rios, Alberto 486
rivalry: in Chaucer 131
Rivett, Rohan D.: *Behind the Bamboo* 548
Riviere, Joan 376
Robbins, Tom: postmodernism 484
Roberts, Charles G. D. 528–9; and *The Tempest* 524
Roberts, Kevin 526
Roberts, Morley 346
Robey, John (with Storey) *The Dreamland* 530; *Girls in the Gang* 530
Rochester, John Wilmot, Earl of 232; and Oldham 241; and Sidney 241; and classics 241; sexuality 241
Roemer, Astrid 562
Roethke, Theodore 458; and Ciardi 464
Rogers, Samuel 270
Roland 99

role play: in Jacobean tragedy 204
Rolle, Richard 115
Roman d'Alexandre 110
Roman de la Rose 129, 134
Roman Georgic: in 18th C 255
Roman plays: of Shakespeare and Jonson 203–4
Romance of Alexander, The 11
romances: ME **106–7**
romantic art: and Second World War 365
romantic genre 367; and Chaucer 136; and Howells 443–4; and Roman Georgic 255
romantic poetry: and Pound 472
Romanticism **269–313**; and American literature 436–7; and T. S. Eliot 401, 466–7; in France 457; and Frost 467–8; and Larkin 403; and Stevens 481
Rooke, Leon 519; *A Good Baby* 525
Roosevelt, Theodore: and James 446
Rorty, Richard 446
Rose Theatre 164, 199; management 190; physical structure 187; Sussex's Men at 191
Rosen, Gerald 490
Rosenberg, Isaac 363; and the feminine 396; 'Break of Day in the Trenches' 395
Ross, Sinclair 517, 518, 522; *As For Me and My House* **521**
Rossetti, Christina 320, 322–3; letters 323; *Goblin Market* 323
Rossetti, Dante Gabriel **323–4**; and authority 271; art production 355; *The House of Life* 324
Rossetti, Gabriele: and Pound 473, 475; *Il mistero dell' amor platonico del medio evo* 473
Rous, John 211
Rousseau, Jean Jacques 291, 300; anti-Utopianism 363; *Emile* 262
Rowe, Nicholas: and Shakespeare 159
Rowlandson, Mary: and Puritan captivity narrative 431
Rowley, William: *When You See Me, You Know Me* 195; *see also* Middleton
Roxana playhouse illustrations 187
royal progress: in Shakespeare 178
Royce, Josiah 427; and poetry 462
Rubens, Bernice: *Sunday Best* 388
Rudolf II 168
The Rune Poem 87–8
runes: Anglo-Saxon 76
rural theatre activities: in Canada 532
Rushdie, Salman 560; *Haroun and the Sea of Stories* 557; *Midnight's Children* 62, 557, 559, 560, 574; *Shame* 560
Ruskin, John 347; and Wordsworth 288; and art 355
Russ, Joanna 423, 489
Ryga, George: *The Ecstacy of Rita Joe* 532, 582;
Sacco, Nicola 7
Sahgal, Nayantara 558; *Rich Like Us* 559
Said, Edward 486; *Orientalism* 385
St Omer, Garth 567
saint plays 119
saints 80; and Dekker and Massinger 205; and the female subject 100; litanies of 75; ME 115–16
Salinger, J. D. 491
Sallust 144
salons: American avant-garde 462
Salutin, Rick 518
salvation: in 17th C 210
Salzmann: *Elements of Morality* 277
Sancho, Ignatio 4; *Letters* 264
Sangüesa sculptures 86
Santayana, George: and James 446; and Stevens 479
Sapir, Edward 24
Sargeson, Frank 575, 577
Sarton, May: *The Small Room* 491
Sartre, Jean-Paul 502
satire: 18th C 247; in American literature 436–7
Saussure, Ferdinand de 379
Savage, Richard 258
Savile, Sir Henry: 'Ende of Nero and Beginning of Galba' 151
Sawles Warde 100
Sayers, Dorothy L.: *Gaudy Night* 384
Scandinavian English 21
Schiller, Johan Christoph Friedrich von: *Die Räuber* 293
schools: monastic 80
Schort, Thomas 22
Schumann, Robert 317
science: 17th C 218–19; impact on writers 424; manuscripts 219; and Victorians 392
science fiction 488, **489**; Australian 555; extraterrestrial intelligence 380; and Gallun 498
Scotland: 18th C 250, 266; accession of

James I 184; dialects 30, 34; philosophical societies 250
Scott, John (19th C) 296
Scott, John A. 554
Scott, Mary 576
Scott, Paul: *The Raj Quartet* 394
Scott, Sarah 261
Scott, Sir Walter 250, 306, 309, 328; verse narrative 270; *The Lay of the Last Minstrel* 270; *Rokeby* 292
sea, tales of 6
The Seafarer 80, 82, 89–90
seamstresses: in Dickens 333
Searle, John 362
Secunda Pastorum 119
Sedgwick, Catherine 428
The Sege of Melayne 106
the self: alien 329–30; in American literature 425–6; and Beckett 410; and European writers 364; and Lowell 469; and lyric poetry 478; in Victorian poetry 325–6; and Whitman 450
Seltzer, Richard: and Cheever 496
Selvon, Sam: sound recordings 561; 'Brackley and the Bed' 561; *Moses Ascending* 561, 570
semantics 20, **56–7**
Seneca: and Jonson 202
Senior, Olive 563
sensation fiction: and Collins 343; and Le Fanu 340
sentimental novel 433; feminist criticism of 431
sentimentalism: and Twain 448
serial form 456
sermons 248
Sernes, Michel 247
Seth, Vickram 559–60
Settle, Elkanah 258
settlement patterns: Anglo-Saxon England 71
'The Seven Sleepers' 82
Sevon, Sam **570–1**
Sewell, Stephen: plays 547
sex and sexuality: Anglo-Saxon attitudes 76; in Fowles 392–3; in Lawrence 372–3; in Marston 182; and medico-literary motif in drama 196; in plays by women 406; and Proust 481; in Bernard Shaw 415; and Stevens 481; in Tennyson 326; and Whitman 450; in A. Walker 503–4; and Yeats 398
Sexton, Anne **477**; and Ciardi 464; biography 477; *The Awful Rowing Toward God* 477; *45 Mercy Street* 477; *Words for Dr Y* 477
Sextus Empiricus 258
sexual difference: and Elizabeth Bishop 459
sexual politics: of Carver 496; in Chaucer 124–5, 128–9
Shadbolt, Maurice *Strangers and Journeys* 579
Shadwell, C. L.: and Pater 347
Shaffer, Peter **414–15**; and Lawrence 374; *Five Finger Exercise* 415; *Lettice and Lovage* 415
Shaftesbury, Anthony Ashley Cooper, 3rd Earl of 250
Shakespeare, William **154–79**; and Aristotle 179; and Beckett 411; and Chaucer 175; and Dickens 334; and G. Eliot 342; and T. S. Eliot 175, 401; and James 177; and Jonson 203; and Machiavelli 178; and Malouf 552; and Marlowe 163; and Middleton 160, 170; and Ovid 175; and Sidney 147; and Sterne 265; and Woolf 382; and Wroth 212; and *Cardenio* 158; and civic pageantry 173; and discourse analysis 177; and *Double Falsehood* 158; and *Edward III* 160, 161, 186; and madness 162, 176; and memory 159; and royal progress 178; and sword-fighting 189–90; teaching 166; attributed works 160, 172; causation 172; comedies **168–70**; emblems 211; evil 194; histories **172–4**; Irish politics in 173; language in history plays 56; later plays 170–2; on screen 163–4, 165; performance history **162–5**; poetry 158, 160; pronouns of address 63; stage properties 189; staging in Australia 547; strategies of closure 172; structure 173, 174; textual production 212; textual revisions **154–62**; tragedies **175–9**; *All's Well that Ends Well* 166; *Antony and Cleopatra* 163, 175–6; *As You Like It* 157, 169, 191; *The Comedy of Errors* 156–7, 158, 164, 168; *Coriolanus* 142, 178, 204, 336; *Cymbeline* 160, 171; *Hamlet* 155, 156, 157–8, 159, 161, 162, 163, 164, 165, 167, 175, 176–7, 194, 334; *1 Henry IV* 173, 174; *2 Henry IV* 161, 174; *Henry*

V 159, 161, 173, 174; *2 Henry V* 156; *Henry VI* trilogy 173; *Henry VIII* 56, 174; *Julius Caesar* 142; *King John* 56, 159; *King Lear* 142, 155, 156, 159, 162, 163, 165, 175, 178, 194, 344; *Love's Labour's Lost* 167, 169; *A Lover's Complaint* 100, 171–2; *Macbeth* 159, 164, 175, 177–8, 194; *Measure for Measure* 64, 154–5, 160, 162, 170, 205; *Merchant of Venice* 169, 198–9; *Merry Wives of Windsor* 161, 169; *Midsummer Night's Dream* 157, 168–9; *Much Ado about Nothing* 156, 158, 163, 169–70; *Othello* 143, 159, 163, 168, 175, 177; *Pericles* 159, 160, 171, 186; *The Rape of Lucrece* 160, 172; *Richard II* 160; *Richard III* 173; *Romeo and Juliet* 162–3, 165, 176, 211; Sonnet 51 157; *Sonnets* 62, 157, 167, 172; *The Taming of the Shrew* 168; *The Tempest* 168, 171, 552; *Timon of Athens* 178–9; *Titus Andronicus* 164, 164–5, 191, 199; *Troilus and Cressida* 164, 165, 176; *Twelfth Night* 164, 170; *Two Gentlemen of Verona* 196; (with Fletcher) *Two Noble Kinsmen* 206; *Venus and Adonis* 160; *The Winter's Tale* 144, 160–1, 171
Shange, Ntozake 433, 460, 487; *Sassafrass, Cypress and Indigo* 454
Sharriff, R. C.: *Journey's End* 532
Shaw, George Bernard 356, 363, 407, 415; and lesbian sexuality 415; and politics 415; contributions to *Pall Mall Gazette* 353; *Man and Superman* 415
Shelley, Mary 274; *Frankenstein* 329, 386; (with Shelley) *History of a six weeks' tour* 302
Shelley, Percy Bysshe 270, **302–4**; and Stevens 481; and Yeats 397; and authority 271; verse narrative 271; *Alastor* 272; *The Cenci* 302; 'Defence of Poetry' 303; 'Epipsychidion' 303; *Hellas* 304; (with Mary Shelley) *History of a six weeks' tour* 302; 'Hymn to Intellectual Beauty' 303; 'Julian and Maddolo' 303; 'Mask of Anarchy' 303; 'Mont Blanc' 302; 'Ode to the West Wind' 303; 'Ozymandias' 303; 'A Philosophical View of Reform' 303; *Posthumous Poems* 302; *Promethus Unbound* 300; *Queen Mab* 300; 'Spirit of the Age' 251; 'Triumph of Life' 303–4
Shepard, Sam: and tragicomedy 406
Sher, Antony 165
Sheridan, Thomas: 'A course of lectures on elocution' 33
Sherwood, Mary Martha 273
Shinebourne, Janice: on video 562
Shirley, James 195, 211; *The Bird in a Cage* 207
Shirley, John 126
short fiction 7
short story: Australian 549; Canadian 519–20, 524; Caribbean women writers 562–3; Irish 8; New Zealand 575; and Trollope 338
Siddartha, Surjeet Kalsey 513
Sidney, Mary: as patron 210
Sidney, Sir Philip 142, **146–7**, 150; and Rochester 241; and Shakespeare 171–2; and Spenser 148, 149; and publishing 141; biography 146; *Arcadia* 143, 146–7, 149; *Astrophel and Stella* 146, 147; *The Defence of Poetry* 146, 217; *A Lover's Complaint* 147
sign language 28, 31; monastic 75–6
Sigourney, Lydia 442
Silko, Leslie Marmon 485
Silliman, Ron 469
Sime, J. Georgina: 'Munitions!' 519
Simpson, Percy and Evelyn 185
Sinclair, Upton Bell 439
Sinclair, Peggy: and Beckett 410
Sir John Oldcastle 182, 183
Sir John Van Olden Barnavelt 193
Sir Landevale 107
Sixties (1960s): in Australia 538
Skeat, W. W. 151
Skelton, John 98, 142, **144**; *The Garland of Laurel* 144; *Phyllyp Sparowe* 144; 'The Recuke against Gaguyne' 144
Skinner, Molly: *The Fifth Sparrow* 545
slang 3; Australian 535–6
slave-narrative 433
slavery: and *The Spectator* 353
Slessor, Kenneth 555; biography 546
Slovene: immigrant poetry 557
Slovo, Gillian 389
small clause complements 40
small magazines: Australian 535
small town life 521
Smart, Christopher: letters 259

Smart, Elizabeth: biography 517; *By Grand Central Station I Sat Down and Wept* 517
Smith, Adam 250; *The Wealth of Nations* 251
Smith, Charlotte 274; letters 266; *The Old Manor House* 337
Smith, George 352, 356
Smith, Henry Nash: *Virgin Land* 424
Smith, Lee 485
Smith, Roswell 22
Smither, Elizabeth 580
Smollett, Tobias: *Atom* 266; *Expedition of Humphrey Clinker* 265–6
Snyder, Gary 458, 459, **477–8**
sociolinguistics 20, **24–33**; and stylistics 61
Socrates 7
solipsism: poetry 462
Solomon and Saturn 92
Solomon Islands: language 29
Somer, Philip 536
Song Fishermen 528–9
song: in morality plays 120
Sophocles: and Blake 284
Sorrentino, Gilbert 365
sound: and Stevens 481
sound of words: importance of 379
sound recordings: of Caribbean literature 561
South African English 34–5
South Asia: language 24
South Asian literature: in Britain 558
South Pacific literature **582–3**
Southampton, Henry Wriothesley, 3nd Earl: Shakespeare dedications 172
Southcott, Joanna 282
Southern states of America: fiction writers 484–5
Southerne, Thomas **242–3**; *The Maid's Last Prayer* 243; *The Wives' Excuse* 243
Southey, Robert 270; *Fall of Robespierre* 294; *Thalaba the Destroyer* 270, 305–6
Southwell, Robert 150–1, 212
Southworth, Richard 128
Soyinka, Wole 61; 'Abiku' 63; *Madmen and Specialists* 63
space: Appalachian 460–1; in Dryden 237; and Thoreau 448
Spain: Sangüesa sculptures 86; theatres 187–8
The Spanish Tragedy 188
Spanish-American writing 488
Spark, Muriel: and Chaucer 126
spatial perception: in OE texts 82
spatial relationships: in Chaucer 129–30
specificity, moral significance of: and Stevens 479
Spedding, James 337
speech: in North Amerindian texts 485–6; study of 17
speech accommodation theory 32
speech acoustics 35
speech acts: in Atwood 523; in Shakespeare 177
speech-act theory 117; and drama 63; and *The Woman Warrior* 499
speech areas 27
speech communities 25
spelling, modern: and *The Canterbury Tales* 128
Spence, Catherine 545
Spence, Joseph 258
Spence, Thomas: *Pig's Meat* 283
Spencer, Herbert 341
Spenser, Edmund: 'Legend of Justice' 143
Spenser, Edmund **147–50**; and Dreiser 441; and Koch 554; and Yeats 397, 398; and publishing 141; encyclopedia 147–8; *Amoretti* 144, 148; *Complaints* 150; *Daphnaida* 148; *Epithalamion* 148, 150; *The Fairie Queene* 143, 144, 148–50; *First Principles* 441; *Mother Hubberd's Tale* 142; *Muiopotmos* 148; *Mutabilitie Cantos* 237; *The Shepheardes Calender* 142, 148
Spicer, Jack: serial form 456
Spiers, Felix William 332
spirituality, women's: and M. Laurence 523
sport: Australian 538
Spottiswoode, Andrew 335
sprituality: Aboriginal 541
spy fiction 389–90
Stacions of Rome 132
Stafford, William 459
stage directions: in Elizabethan and Jacobean drama 185; in Jonson 184
stage properties: Shakespearean 189
staging: of *The Alchemist* 203
Stanislavski: and voice 407
Stanley Epitaphs 158, 172
Stead, C. K. 575
Stead, Christina **554**; *For Love Alone* 554;

Miss Herbert 554; *The Salzburg Tales* 547; *Seven Poor Men of Sydney* 554
Steele, Sir Richard 248; and the flaneur 433–4
Stegner, Walter 423
Steichen, Edward 462
Stein, Gertrude 432, 460; and crisis 434; *The Making of Americans* 434; 'Pablo Picasso' 455
Steinbeck, John: *East of Eden* 425
Steiner, George: *After Babel* 413
Stephens, A. G. 545
stereotypes: foreigners in Renaissance drama 196
Sterne, Laurence **264–5**; and Shakespeare 265; and Swift 264–5; misogyny 265; *Sentimental Journey* 265; *Tristam Shandy* 264, 265
Sterry, Peter: and Ovid 232
Stettheimer Salon 462
Stettheimer, Feorine: paintings 462
Stevens, Wallace 424, 425, **478–82**; and Dickinson 440; and Wahl 478; and the avant-garde 462; and nature 461; and philosophy 427, 462; adversary world of 456; walk poetry 458; as war poet 480; 'Anatomy of a Jar' 480; *Ariel and the Police* 480; 'Auroras of Autumn' 480, 481; 'Comedian as the Letter C' 478, 479; 'Connoisseur of Chaos' 479; 'Credences of Summer' 481; *Harmonium* 479–80; 'Man with the Blue Guitar' 480; 'The Noble Rider and the Sound of Words' 481; 'Notes Toward a Supreme Fiction' 462, 480, 481; 'An Ordinary Evening in New Haven' 458; 'Planet on the Table' 481; 'Sea Surface Full of Clouds' 479; 'Sunday Morning' 480
Stevenson, Robert Louis **346**, 363; *The Ebb-Tide* 346
Stieglitz, Alfred: photographs and drawings 462
Stirling, Bruce 489
Stoker, Bram 328; and Jews 345; *Dracula* 7
Stone, Lawrence 168; and Shakespeare 173
Stone, Marcus 333
Stone, Robert 490
Stoppard, Tom **415–16**; *Hapgood* 416; *Jumpers* 416; *The Real Thing* 415; *Rosencrantz and Guildenstern are Dead* 415
Stopyndon, John 128
Storey, David **416**
Storey, Raymond *see* Robey
story telling: Aboriginal 541; native Canadian 514
Stothard, Thomas 279
Stout, George 22
Stout, Rex 502; *Nero Wolfe* novels 502
Stow, John: *Survey of London* 151
Stow, Randolph **553**; *The Merry-Go-Round in the Shop* 553; *To the Islands* 548
Stowe, Harriet Beecher **448**; *Minister's Wooing* 435; *Oldtown Folks* 424; *Uncle Tom's Cabin* 433, 437, 448
Stowe Psalter 73
Stratford East theatre 407
Stretton, Hesba 273
Strode, Ralph 124
Stuart myth 250
Stuart, Arbella 205–6
style: redefining period 209
stylistics **60–4**; stylistic analysis 63; stylistic theory 61–2
Styron, William **502–3**; *Darkness Visible* 502–3
subject: in contemporary American fiction 489–90
subjectivity: aristocratic 209; and Beckett 410; female 212, 503–4; and A. Walker 503–4
subjunctive complements 44
sublime: in American literature 462–3; and E. Bishop 463; and Blake 279; in Canadian landscape 520; and Lovell 469; and Victorians 328
Sue, Eugène: *Les Mystères de Paris* 329
suffrage plays 406
suicide: Kate Chopin on 438
Sukenick, Thomas 490; postmodernism 484
Summers, Anne: interview 545
Summons, John 547
supernatural: in 19th C fiction 328–9, 341;
surrealist poetry 401–2
Surrey, Henry Howard 150
Surtees, R. S. 327
Sussex's Men 190–1, 199
Sutton, Thomas: and Jonson 204
Sutton Hoo 78
Swan Theatre 164

swearing 55
Swedenborg, Emanuel: and Blake 282; and Pound 475
Sweet, Henry 21, 22–3
Swift, Graham **394**; and closure 394; *Out of this World* 394; *Shuttlecock* 394; *The Sweet-Shop Owner* 394; *Waterland* 394
Swift, Jonathan 247; and Sterne 264–5; and dress 431; and Ireland 248; 'A Beautiful Young Nymph Going to Bed' 256; *The Lady's Dressing Room* 256
Swigart, Rob 490
Swinburne 324, 330
Swinburne, Algernon Charles 324, 330; and literary authority 271
swordfighting: in Shakespeare's plays 189–90
Swynford, Catherine 137–8
symbols and symbolism: in Morrison 500; in Pound 472
Symons, A. J.: and Pater 346
'Syng y wold, butt, alas!' 111
Synge, J. M. 407; and Beckett 409
syntactic change 46
syntactic theory 18
syntax 19, 62; early **48–55**; modern English **38–48**
Tacitus 151
Tagore, Rabindranath 561
Talawa theatre company 573
Tale of Beryn, The 113
Tasso, Torquato 150; and Milton 224; and Spenser 149; *Aminta* 224; *Gerusalemme Liberata* 142, 224
Tate, Allen 476–7
Tate, Nahum: and Frascatoro 241
taxonomy: and Victorians 392
Taylor, Edward: musical verse 430; psyche of 428
Taylor, Peter: and American gentlemen 436
teaching: Shakespeare 166
Teatro Olimpico 187
technological culture: and Burroughs 495
technological processes: and Ammons 463
technology: and Mailer 500
teenage fiction: Australian 536
television: and Beckett 412; and Lodge's *Small World* 394; and Shakespeare 164, 165;
Temple, Sir William 247; poetry manuscript 241
Tenniel, Sir John: and *Punch* 351
Tennyson, Alfred, Lord 314, 315, **324–7**, 403; language 324; 'The Charge of the Light Brigade' 61; *Idylls of the King* 324, 326; *In Memoriam* 324, 326; *The Lady of Shalott* 325; 'Lucretius' 326; *Mariana* 315; *Maud* 325–6; 'Morte d'Arthur' 324–5; *The Princess* 325; *Song of Soloman* 326
Teresa, St: and Dryden 239
Ternan, Ellen 332
Teseida 130
Teskey, Adeline M.: 'A Common Man and his Wife: The Ram Lamb' 519
textual criticism: OE literature 74–5
textual production 454–55
textuality: medieval 78
Thackeray, William Makepeace 330–1; and Punch 351–2; *Cox's Diary* 331; *Henry Esmond* 328; *The Newcomes* 331; *Pendennis* 331; *Vanity Fair* 331
Théâtre de l'Epée de Bois 200
theatre history: Australia 547; Canadian 530–1; Renaissance 187–93
theatres: New Zealand 581
Thelwall, John 308, 567
Theobald, Lewis 206; *Double Falsehood* 158
thesaurus 2–3
Thesen, Sharon **527** and Manhire 580; *Confabulations* 527; 'Long Distance' 527; 'Parts of Speech' 527
Third World novel 561
Thomas, Audrey: 'Crossing the Rubicon' 524
Thomas, D. M.: *White Hotel* 393
Thomas, Dylan: **402**; metaphors 64; surrealism 401; 'And death shall have no dominion' 402; 'Fern Hill' 402; 'The Visitor' 64
Thomas, Edward 403; and the feminine 396; war poems 397
Thomas, J. J. 4
Thompson, Judith **532**; *The Crackwalker* 532; *Lion in the Streets* 532
Thompson, Mervyn: *Songs to the Judges* 582
Thompson, Tierl: *Dear Girl* 407
Thomson, James: and Blake 258; biography 258; *Castle of Indolence* 258; *Castle of Innocence* 283; *Edward and Elenora* 258
Thomson, William 283
Thoreau, Henry David 428, **448**; and J.

Brown 426; and labour 435; farm poetry 458; walk poetry 458; *Walden* 425, 437
three estates theory 115
Tiberius Psalter 73
Tikkanen, Marta: *Love Story of the Century* 407
time: and language 27–8; Renaissance attitudes to 171; and separative adjectives 46–7; in Shakespeare 174
Tippett, Michael 7
Tírechán 89–90
Todorov, Tzvetan 238
Tok Pisin 25
Toland, John 248
Tolstoy, Leo: *War and Peace* 552
Tom a Lincoln 183–4
Tomlinson, Charles: and American art 403; theme of death 403
Toms, Humphrey: letters 517
Tonson, Jacob: and Dryden 237
Tooke, John Horne 22
Toomer, Jean **482**; and Gurdjieff 481–2; *Cane* 481–2
Toqueville, Alexis de 435
totalitarianism: 20th-century writers 363
Tourneur, Cyril: *The Atheist's Tragedy* 206; *The Revenger's Tragedy* 186, 206; *Vendredi* 262
Towneley cycle 117, 120
Townshend, Aurelian 211
Tractarius de Purgatorio Sancti Patricii 112
tragedy: 162; dramatic effects 582; and madness 162
tragicomedy: and contemporary culture 406–7
Traherne, Thomas 232, 402; and atomism 216, 240; *Commentaries of Heaven* 240
transcendence: OE literature 80
Transcendentalism: and T. S. Eliot 466; and poetry 461
Transcendentalists, American 424
transculturalism: Canadian literature 512–13
transgression 98
transience: OE literature 80
translation: and Ælfric 94; King James Bible 211; ME 99; North Amerindian texts 485
transmission: of texts 454–55
transvestism: Renaissance drama 191
Tranter, John: and absent subject 556
travel narrative 520
travel writing: and M. Fuller 441–2
Tremblay, Michael 530
'Tremulous' scribe 73–4
Trench, Richard Chenevix 22
Trevet, Nicholas: *Chronicle* 131
Trilling, Lionel 428; and Twain 449
Trimmers 235
Trinidad: language 28
Trinity College Cambridge 114
Trist, Margaret: *Morning in Queensland* 548
Tristan, Flora 329
Troilus 98
Trollope, Anthony 328, **338**, 344; short stories 338; *The American Senator* 338; *Dr Thorne* 338; *The Macdermots of Ballycloran* 338; *Rachel Ray* 338; *Ralph the Heir* 338; *The* Three Clerks 338; *The Vicar of Bulhampton 338*
Turco, Carlo: Agnella 196
Turner, J. M. W. 254
Turner, Victor 128
Turner, W. J. 398
Tuwhare, Hone 577
Twain, Mark 427, 435–6; **448–9**; and Masters 470; depiction of crowds 428; *The American Claimant* 443; *Huckleberry Finn* 425, 448, 449; *Life on the Mississippi* 449; *Roughing It* 449
Twelfth Night celebrations 188
Tyndale, William 145; biblical translation 145; *Answer unto Sir Thomas More's Dialogue* 145; *The Obedience of a Christian Man* 145; *The Parable of the Wicket Mammon* 145; *A Pathway into the Holy Scripture* 145; 'The Practice of Prelates' 145
typology 49; of nature 431
tyranny: Renaissance drama 193–4
Tytler, Alexander Fraser 250
uncanny, concept of 144–5
unconscious: American 477–8
Underwood, Michael: *Treatise on the Diseases of Children* 338
universal grammar 17, 41–2
Updike, John 488, 491, **503**; *The Coup* 503; *Marry Me* 503; *Rabbit at Rest* 503; *Rabbit, Run* 503; *Roger's Version* 503; *Self-Consciousness* 503
urban novel 488–90

urban poetry: of Morgan 402
urban settings: in Victorian novels 328, 329
urban spectatorship: in American literature 433–4
USA: 19th C grammar 21–2; academic press 10; linguistics 23–4; sociolinguistics 27–8; syntax 46; vowels 35; *see also* America
Usk, Thomas 109
Utilitarianism: in Dickens 332, 333
utopia: and Hawthorne 442, 443; *see also* anti-Utopianism
valency, study of 54
Vallombrosa: and Milton 223
vampires 7
'Vanderbilt Fugitives' 427
'Van Diemen's Land' 536
Van Gogh, Vincent 375; and Bunyan 244; and Walcott 572
Van Herk, Aritha: *Fictional World* 514; *No Fixed Address* 514, 524
Van Toorn, Peter: *Mountain Tea* 526
Vanzetti, Bartolomeo 7
Vassanji, M. G.: and multiculturalism 513
Vaux, Thomas 150
Vega, Ana Lydia 562
Venables, Clare: *Love Story of the Century* 407
Vennard, Alex Vindex 536
Vercelli Book **88–9**, 93
Vere, Edward de, 17th Earl of Oxford 150, 158
Verrocchio, Andrea del 481
verse: 16th C 150–1; ME 110–13
verse narrative: Romantic 270–1
verse texts: OE 76–7
Vespasian Psalter 73
videos: of Caribbean writers 561–2
Vietnam War: poetry 458; writers 490–1
Villanueva, Alma: *Life Span* 486
Vinaver, Eugene 114
Vindicta Salvatoris 93
violation: in Kosinski 499–500
violence: and narrative 537; in G. B. Shaw 415; and writing 482
Virgil 144; and Dryden 237; and Milton 225; and Wordsworth 293; bee metaphor 301; *Eclogue* 285, 303; *Georgics* 293–4
Vision group 556
Vision of William of Stranton 112
Visser's generalization 39–40
visual arts: and Barthelme 493; green tree motif 93; and postwar culture 365; and Victorian poetry 321; *see also* art; painting
Vitellius Psalter 73
Vives, Juan Luis 143; preface to *Instruction of a Christian Woman* 146
Voaden, Herman: influences 531; *Northern Song* 531; *Rocks* 531
vocabulary **55–6**
voice: and Dorn 465; and T. S. Eliot 465; in modern theatre 407; in Southern states 427; in Walcott 572
Vǫlundarkviða 90
Von Herkomer, Hubert 355; 'Last Muster' 355; 'Sunday in Chelsea Hospital' 355
Vonnegut, Kurt 4; autobiography 490
vowels 34–5
Vox and Wolf 113
voyeurism: in Chaucer 137–8
Vulgate cycle 114
Waddington, Miriam 527
Wah, Fred 527
Wahl, Jean: and Stevens 478, 479
Wakefield, John 22
Wakefield cycle 117–18, **119**; and Findley 525
Walcott, Derek 564, **571–3**; drama **572–3**; poetry **571–2**; video recording 562; *Dream on Monkey Mountain* 572–3; *Henri Christophe* 572; *Malcochon* 572; *Omeros* 572; 'Sainte Lucie' 571; 'The Schooner *Flight*' 571; *Sea Grapes* 571; *The Star-Apple Kingdom* 571; *Ti-Jean and his Brothers* 562; *The Unfortunate Traveller* 572
Wales: and Norris 402
Waley, Arthur: *Hundred and Seventy Chinese Poems* 483
walk poetry 457–8
Walker, Alice 388, 438, 460, **504**; *The Colour Purple* 504
Wallace, Judith: *Memories of a Country Childhood* 544
Wallace-Crabbe, Chris 555
Waller, Edmund: and Marvell 214–15; *Instructions to a Painter* 214; *On St James's Park* 214
Walter Scott Publishing Co. 356
Walton, Izaac 236
The Wanderer 81, 89
Wandor, Michelene: *Aurora Leigh* 406
war 7–8; in Findley 525; writing about

367
war fiction: Bowen and Lively compared 387–8
war literature: Australian 547–8; Vietnam 490; and Woolf 381–2; First World War **395–7**
war poetry: of Davey 528; and Stevens 478, 480, 481; Vietnam 458
Ward, Glenyse: *Unna You Fellas* 541; *Wandering Girl* 541
Warren, Samuel 327
Washington, George 436
Watson, Caroline: and Blake 277, 278
Watson, Sheila 517
Watts, G. F. 2
Webb, Francis: biography 546–7
Webb, James 490
Webb, Phyllis 511, 528
Webster, John 143, 185, **205–6**; and Eliot 400; *The Duchess of Malfi* 205–6; *Heart of Glass* 205; *The White Devil* 194, 205, 400
Wedde, Ian 575, 577
weddings: in Dickens 333
Weekley, Frieda: and Lawrence 372
Weems, Mason: *Life of Washington* 424
'We happy Herdsmen here' 116
Weigl, Bruce 458
Welch, James 485
Weldon, Fay 389
Welles, Orson: and Shakespeare 162, 163
Wells, H. G. 363; short stories 380
Welty, Eudora 427, **504**; and Lawrence 374; and rape 460; *The Golden Apples* 504; *The Heart of the Story* 504; *One Writer's Beginnings* 427, 504
Wendt, Albert: multi-cultural vision 582–3
Werden Heptateuch 72
Wertenbaker, Timberlake: *Love of the Nightingale* 406; *The Playmaker* 416
Wesley, John 234
West, Anthony 383
West, Jane: *Advantages of Education* 261
West, Paul **394–5**; *Alley Jaggers* 394; *Out of My Depth* 394; *Place in Flowers Where Pollen Rests* 395
West, Rebecca **383–4**
Wharton, Edith 432, 443; and American gentleman 436; and games 437–8; and Italy 447; as novelist of manners 492; satire 437; *The House of Mirth* 426, 437–8
Wheatley, Phillis: and the clergy 431
Whetstone, George: *Magnificent Entertainment* 170; *Promos and Cassandra* 170
White, Gilbert 252
White, Hayden: and Atwood 515–16
White, Leslie 486
White, Patrick 533, 538, 544, **552–3**; and Eliza Fraser story 539; biography 546; *A Fringe of Leaves* 552; *Riders in the Chariot* 553; *The Twyborn Affair* 552; *Voss* 540, 553
Whitehall: drawing of Great Chamber 188
Whitman, Walt 292, 425, 426, 435–6, **449–51**; and Masters 470; and labour 435; and science 424; and the sublime 462; modernity in 434; walk poetry 458; 'Leaves of Grass' 450; 'Sleepers' 450; 'Song of Myself' 450; 'There was a Child Went Forth' 426
Whitney, Isabella: complaint genre 212–13
Whitney, William 22
Whittinton, Robert: 'Lauri Apud Palladem Expostulatio' 144
Why I Can't Be a Nun 112
Whytford, Richard: *Boke of pacience* 146; *A Looking glace for the religious* 146
Wiebe, Rudy 514, 522; interview 525; short stories 519
Wilbur, Richard **482**; and Ciardi 464
Wilde, Oscar: and Pater 350; and Wilde 446; and *Woman's World* 352; avant-gardism 363; publishing policies 348
Wilding, Michael: 'Knock, Knock' 554
Wilkins, George: and *Pericles* 160, 186
Wilkinson, Julie: *Pinchdice & Co* 407
will-making: and complaint genre 212–13
Willard, Josiah 442
Williams, William Carlos **482–3**; and Ciardi 464; and Lawrence 374; and Pound 475; and Breughal's 'The Adoration of the Kings' 482–3; and Chinese poetry 483; and philosophy 427, 462; walk poetry 458; *Asphodel, That Grey Flower* 483; 'Desert Music' 458; *Kora in Hell* 483; 'Letter to an Australian Editor' 483; 'Love Song' 483; 'Marriage' 483; 'Old Doc Rivers' 483; *Paterson* 458, 462; 'Queen Anne's Lace' 483; 'Rose to the End of Time' 483; *Sour Grapes* 483; 'Three Professional Studies' 483; 'To Be Recited to Flossie on Her Birthday'

483; *Voyage to Pagany* 483
Williams, Helen Maria 270
Williams, Sherley A. 459
Williams, Tennessee: and Lawrence 374
Willmott, Eric: *Pemulwuy the Rainbow Warrior* 542
Willmott, Peter *see* Young
Wilson, Arthur 183
Wilson, Barbara 389
Wilson, Edmund 401
Wilson, Ethel 522
Wilson, John Dover 185
Wings, Mary 389
Winner and Waster 112
Winnicot, D. W. 275
Winstanley, Gerrard: and politics 218
Winton, Tim 554
Wisdom 116
Wister, Owen: *Virginian* 437
wit: Augustan 247; metaphysical 212
Wither, George: and politics 216
Wittgenstein, Ludwig: and Australian literature 539
Wolfe, Gene 489
Wolfskehl, Karl 577
Wollaston Journals 543
Wollstonecraft, Mary 249, 251, 274; and Blake 278; and French Revolution 308; and gender 307; *A Vindication of the Rights of Women* 261
womanhood: Irish 377
women: and 18th C fiction 261; in 19th C cities 329; American, and games 437; American, literacy of 430; in Anglo-Saxon art 70–1; in Australian drama 547; in *The Canterbury Tales* 128; and T. S. Eliot 399; in Jacobean drama 194–5; and ME verse 110–11; in *Punch* 352; in Renaissance 210; and Sidney circle 146–7; women of colour 459
women detectives: fictional 368
women patrons: Renaissance 210
women travellers 5
women writers 1, 3; 18th C 248–9; 20th C 385–9; Afro-American 487–8; American 426, 432, 438; American novelists 435; Australian 533, 539, 549, 554; Australian poets 556; Canadian short story 519–20; contemporary 366–7; crossing borders 389; female characters 329; female hero 577; feminist 459; Jewish 388; and love 437–8; and men 379; Renaissance 151, 212–13; Restoration 232; short fiction 7; and war 8, 367; women of colour 486
women's rights: Early modern England 210
women's theatre: 17th C dramatists 233, 241–2; in 20th C 405–6, 407; contemporary work in 406; feminist 581; Restoration women actors 233; threat to men 195
Women's Theatre Group: first performances of plays 407
Wood, Grant 459
Wood, Mrs Henry 327–8
Woodcock, George 512
Woodhead, Abraham: and Islam 231–2
Woodhouse, Richard: and Keats 272
Woolf, Virginia 328, 363, **381–83**, 384; and Joyce 377; and war 367; sense of self 364; *Flush* 382; *Jacob's Room* 382, 383; 'Modern Fiction' 381; 'Mr Bennet and Mrs Brown' 381; *A Room of One's Own* 381; 'Solid Objects' 64; *Three Guinees* 381; *To the Lighthouse* 64, 383; 'Voyage Out' 381; *Waves* 362, 364, 382
Woolston, Thomas 253
Worcester: OE manuscripts 73–4
Worcestre, William: *Itineraries* 59
word guide 3
word order 48–50
Wordsworth, Dorothy 274; *Grasmere Journals* 294; *Travel Journals* 309
Wordsworth, William 255, 270, 270, **286–94**, 402, 403; and Barrett Browning 318; and Blake 286; and Coleridge 289, 290; and E. Dickinson 440; and T. S. Eliot 399; and Finch 256; and French Revolution 291; and Milton 289; and Italy 291–2; and Ovid 292; and Pater 348, 349; and allegory 274; and crowd image 456; and environmental tradition 288; and nationalism 292; and poetry recitation 275; and verse narrative 271; classical translations 293–4; fairy tales 273; revised editions 286–7; *The Borderers* 271, 288, 293; *Ecclesiastical Sonnets* 291; *The Excursion* 287, 288, 291, 293; *Home at Grasmere* 293; *The Idiot Boy* 273, 289, 293, 335; 'Laodamia' 293; *Lyrical Ballads* 287, 289, 327;

Lyrical Ballads (Preface) 288; *Mosaic* 293; 'Nutting' 290; 'Ode to Duty' 293; 'Old Cumberland Beggar' 290; *Orpheus and Eurydice* 293–4; *Peter Bell* 293; *The Prelude* 257, 271, 272, 272, 274, 286, 287, 288, **290–1**, 292, 483 *The Ruined Cottage* 271, 294; Salisbury Plains poems 294; 'There was a Boy' 290; 'The Thorn' 289; 'Tintern Abbey' 270, 309; *The Vale of Esthwaite* 294; *We Are Seven* 290; *The White Doe of Rylstone* 271, 272
work: in American literature 435
working-class women poets: Victorian 315
World War I: Australian folksong and verse 536; Australian literature 538; British and French writers 363; and *Ulysses* 377; writers **395–7**
World War II: fiction about 387–8; and romantic art 365
Wotton, William 247
Wright, David McKee 554
Wright, James **483–4**; and identity 483–4
Wright, John: *Revealed Knowledge of Some Things* 282
Wright, Judith 555; poetry 556
Wright, Richard: in France 457; *Black Boy* 427
Wright, Thomas: *On the Times* 111
writers: dictionaries for 2
Wroth, Mary 212, 218; *Pamphilia to Amphilanthus* 147
Wulfstan of Winchester 76, 80, 93–4; *The Life of St Æthelwold* 74–5
Wurlitzer, Rudolph: postmodernism 484
Wyatt, Sir Thomas 143–4; 'Myne Owne John Poyntz' 145
Wycherley, William: *The Country Wife* 242; *The Plain-Dealer* 233; *The Way of the World* 233
Wynfield, David Wilkie: portrait photographs 355
Wynter, Sylvia 563
Xenophon: *Cyropaedia* 173
Yaoundé: language 27
Yeats, William Butler 356, **397–8**, 403, 407; and Beckett 409; and Pound 475; and Abbey theatre 406; and Irish dramatic movement 398; and occult 473, 475; as director 408; editing 455; influences 397–8; 'Easter 1916' 61; 'Leda and the Swan' 398; 'News for the Delphic Oracle' 398; 'Phases of the Moon' 398; 'Solomon and the Witch' 398; *The Tower* 398; *A Vision* 398, 475
Yeats, Jack B.: puppet theatre 408
Yerzierska, Anzia 432
Yiddish schlemiel humour: in Heller 498
Yonge, Charlotte 328
Yonge, Walter 211
York cycle 117, 118, 120
York Primer 119
Yoruba: language 27
Young, Edward 258; *Night Thoughts* 285
Young, Michael: (with Wilmott) *Family and kinship in East London* 389
Youth 120
Zaire: version of Chaucer 135
Zambia: language 24
Zamyatin, Evgeny Ivanovich: *We* 363
Zeffirelli, Franco: and Shakespeare 162–3
Zeitlin, Jake 372
Zephanien, Benjamin 561
Zephirus: image in Chaucer 129
Zita, St 115
Zoller, Hugo 540
Zukofsky, Louis **484**; serial and procedural work 456; (with C. Zukofsky) *Catullus* 484; *Eighty Flowers* 484; 'I Sent Thee Late' 484
Zwicky, Fay 555